THE LAW OF CONTRACT
IN SCOTLAND

THE LAW OF CONTRACT IN SCOTLAND

by

WILLIAM W. McBRYDE
LL.B., PH.D.

*Solicitor, Senior Lecturer in Private Law
in the University of Aberdeen*

Published under the auspices of
THE SCOTTISH UNIVERSITIES LAW INSTITUTE

EDINBURGH
W. GREEN & SON LTD.
1987

First Published . . 1987

ISBN   0   414   00793   X

Computerset by Alphabyte Ltd., Cheltenham
Printed in Great Britain by
Eastern Press of London and Reading

PREFACE

THE feeling which the completion of this work induces in the author is humility. It seemed an easier book to write at the beginning of the task than it did at the end. As a result there is an increased respect for Professor W. M. Gloag's *Law of Contract*. It has been stated recently that Gloag's book contains many flaws. An author, however, is not entirely responsible for difficulties and inconsistencies in the exposition of the law. From time to time obscurities are caused by judges and Parliament. The author whose words are a model of clarity may at the same time delight his reader and do him a disservice by over-simplification.

At the beginning the decision was made to write a completely fresh book on the law of contract. Accordingly, the existing textbooks were set aside until the completion of an examination of the authorities from the foundation of the Court of Session until the present. It is hoped that in this way some new light has been shone on the law.

It is probable that the Scots law of contract has suffered from a lack of critical analysis. This may induce a pragmatism in a judge which, while possibly satisfactory for the decision in a particular case, makes it difficult to have a coherent development of the law. The constant problems with terminology are but one example of a lack of understanding of how a particular dispute fits into the general picture. Despite what is sometimes claimed, our predecessors did not always show an appreciation of principle or a concern for the future of the law. Whether our system of contract law will develop as a good, rational and coherent system remains to be seen.

In the course of writing this book, it has been necessary to examine tens of thousands of decisions. Inevitably, sometimes, the author will have failed to appreciate all the subtleties of a case, or will have misunderstood its effect. He apologises, but, in the words of Bob Shaw, who provided encouragement during difficult times, it is hoped that "the book provides, at the least, something for the practitioner to react against." One of the book's aims has been to provide ideas for use by the court pleader and the draftsman.

Thanks are due to those who assisted the preparation of the text. Lord Dunpark, the President of the Scottish Universities Law Institute, read the whole of the text and made a number of useful comments. Professor D. A. O. Edward made valiant efforts to improve some chapters. Alfred Phillips is due a very special thanks for an enormous amount of work on a close reading of an early draft. A number of other persons provided assistance, notably Angus Campbell, Donald Caskie, Peter Duff, Robert Hunter and Colin Reid. Research facilities were provided at Glasgow University and at Aberdeen University.

Christine McLintock, Donna Mckenzie, Roderick Paisley and Craig Scott prepared the tables of statutes and cases, which was a particularly laborious task.

Typing of early drafts was done by Maureen Mercer. Angie Link typed the whole book. Her services and those of a word-processor were provided by Iain Smith & Co., Aberdeen, who took the generous view that this was a contribution which they could make to legal writing.

The law is stated as at December 31, 1985, but it has been possible to add some later authorities. It was anticipated that the Bankruptcy (Scotland) Act 1985 would come into force in 1986.

WILLIAM W. McBRYDE.

Aberdeen.
December 1986.

ABBREVIATIONS

It has not been thought necessary to supply a bibliography, since most of the materials cited are familiar or can be traced readily from other sources. The latest edition, at the time of writing, is wherever possible referred to, unless otherwise stated. Two works which may not be known to Scottish readers are S. Williston, *A Treatise on the Law of Contracts* (3rd ed., 1957, New York) (cited "Williston") and A. L. Corbin, *Corbin on Contracts* (1963, St Paul, Minn.) (cited "Corbin"). The citation "Macphail" refers to the *Research Paper on the Law of Evidence in Scotland*, by Sheriff I. D. Macphail (prepared for, and published by, the Scottish Law Commission, Edinburgh, 1979).

CONTENTS

TABLE OF CASES

TABLE OF STATUTES

CHAPTER 1

INTRODUCTION

PART 1

The Definition of Contract

(a) The promise based approach

–01   In Anglo-American works it has been customary to consider a contract as a promise. Thus Chitty commences with the sentence: "A contract is a promise or set of promises which the law will enforce."[1] Anson says:

> "We may provisionally describe the law of contract as that branch of the law which determines the circumstances in which a promise shall be legally binding on the person making it. We have therefore to analyse the concept of a promise, and to ascertain the circumstances in which the law secures to the promisee the satisfaction of the expectations created by the promise."[2]

–02   The American Law Institute's *Restatement of Contracts* adopts a definition based on promise.[3] A draft of the second *Restatement* states: "A contract is a promise or a set of promises for the breach of which the law gives a remedy, or the performance of which the law in some way recognises as a duty."

–03   There is some controversy about whether a definition based on promise is satisfactory. Part of this arises from an analysis of the nature of promise. There are competing theories of contract based on a benefit principle, a reliance principle or the idea of an obligation imposed by the community.[4] These ideas cannot be analysed here but the concept of promise is discussed in detail later.[5] A further problem is that it can be unrealistic to divide a contract into promises; "promise" is an unnecessary concept which gets in the way of the true issue which is that a contract is the creation of obligations by the agreement of the parties. So

---

[1] Chitty, para. 1, citing *inter alia*, Pollock, *Principles of Contract* (13th ed.), p. 1.
[2] Anson, p. 2.
[3] *Restatement of Contracts*, para. 1.
[4] Two of the more recent works which take opposing views and which in turn refer to other authorities are C. Fried, *Contract as Promise* (1981); P. S. Atiyah, *Promises, Morals and Law* (1981). See also C. J. Goetz and R. E. Scott, "Enforcing Promises: An Examination of the Basis of Contract" (1979) 89 Yale L.J. 1261; C. Fried, (1980) 93 Harv.L.R. 1858; A. T. Kronman, "A New Champion for the Will Theory" (1981) 91 Yale L.J. 404; P. S. Atiyah, (1981) 95 Harv.L.R. 509; J. Raz, "Promises in Morality and Law" (1982) 95 Harv.L.R. 916.
[5] See Chap. 2.

1

the Uniform Commercial Code defines a "contract" to mean "the total legal obligation which results from the parties' agreement as affected by this Act and any other applicable rules of law."[6] The *Corpus Iuris Secundum* says that: "A contract is an agreement which creates an obligation. Its essentials are competent parties, subject matter, a legal consideration, mutuality of agreement, and mutuality of obligation."[7]

1–04　　The concentration in the United States on the idea of an obligation arising from agreement instead of the promise-based definition has been described as viewing the commercial contract in a more realistic context, with words, acts, prior understandings, custom and usage all going together to form a contract. This excludes the need to search for what may be fictional promises.[8] Whether this approach will gain widespread acceptance is a matter for speculation.

(b) Scots law

1–05　　In Scotland the Institutional writers saw contract as a form of obligation. Stair distinguished conventional obligations from other obligations. Conventional obligations were subdivided into "promise, pollicitation or offer, paction and contract."[9] There has been learned discussion about the meaning of pollicitation.[10] For present purposes it is sufficient to note that promise is treated as a separate form of conventional obligation from contract.

1–06　　Erskine[11] and Bell[12] also concentrated on contract as a species of obligation. Erskine defined an obligation as "a legal tie, by which one is bound to pay or perform something to another."[13] Applied to an obligation arising by agreement, this definition is both too narrow and too wide. It is too narrow because a contract may exist which binds a person *not* to do something, as in the case of an obligation in restraint of trade. It is too wide because it does not recognise the unenforceable obligation, which has a legal effect although performance cannot be compelled. Erskine's definition of "contract" does not help further because it appears to suggest that there is a need for consideration.[14]

---

[6] U.C.C., para. 1–201(11). The abandonment of "promise" in the Code is discussed and supported in J. E. Murray, *Contracts* (2nd ed., 1974), para. 2.

[7] *s.v.* "Contracts" para. 1(1).

[8] See Murray, *sup. cit.*

[9] Stair, I.x.3.

[10] G. D. MacCormack, "A Note on Stair's Use of the Term Pollicitatio," 1976 J.R. 121, criticising A. F. Rodger, "Molina, Stair and the *Jus Quaesitum Tertio*," 1969 J.R. 34 at p. 41 and 128 at p. 130; D. N. MacCormick, "*Jus Quaesitum Tertio*; *Stair* v. *Dunedin*," 1970 J.R. 228. D. N. MacCormick acknowledged G. D. MacCormack's correction in *Stair Tercentenary Studies*, Stair Soc. Vol. 33 p. 197n. See also T. B. Smith, "Pollicitatio—Promise and Offer," in *Studies Critical and Comparative* (1962) p. 175.

[11] *Inst.*, III,i,1 *et seq.*

[12] *Comm.*, I,312; *Prin.*, ss.5 *et seq.*

[13] *Inst.*, III,i,2.

[14] *Inst.*, III,i,16.

-07 Bell thought that a unilateral obligation might more strictly deserve the description "obligation" rather than use "obligation" for a mutual obligation, but this semantic difference does not seem to have been thought important.[15] He avoided the criticism of a definition which ignores the contract with a negative effect, but went on to insist on a right to compel performance. He said[16]: "A conventional obligation is an engagement or undertaking to deliver, or to pay, or to do, or to abstain from doing, something; conferring on him to whom the engagement is undertaken, a right to demand performance of it."

(c) The problem of invalidity

-08 One of the great problems for a definition of contract based on obligation is to take account of invalidity in an obligation. The problems of invalidity are considered in detail later.[17] A void contract, for example, might be said to be something other than a contract. The expression is, however, convenient. "To speak of a 'void contract' is rather like speaking of a dead or an unborn 'person'; we may be puzzled, but we are not misled."[18] There are other forms of invalidity, namely, the unenforceable, voidable, or illegal contract. These have a variety of contractual effects. Further, despite Bell's definition, even if there is a valid obligation to perform, specific implement may not be granted.[19]

-09 There are hazards in tying the definition of a conventional obligation to the remedies which the law might or might not use. The law must in some way recognise the statement by a party, or it cannot be a contract. It might be an agreement with, perhaps, some moral force, such as an arrangement to come to dinner or a statement of intention.[20] But to be a contract there must be a legal effect, although we need not be precise about what that effect is.

Whether it is necessary for the parties to intend that their arrangement is binding in law is discussed later.[21]

(d) A definition based on "consent"

-10 Definitions of basic legal concepts can never be accurate. Such a concept is like the elephant which the child does not describe correctly, but which is always recognised when seen. The following definition, however, may be serviceable for most purposes. A contract is created by the consent of the parties to an obligation or obligations intended by the parties to have a legal effect and creating a patrimonial interest which the law recognises. An obligation may be further defined as an under-

---

[15] *Prin., sup. cit.*
[16] *Prin.,* s.7.
[17] See Chap. 26.
[18] S. J. Stoljar, *Mistake and Misrepresentation* (1968), p. 73.
[19] See paras. 21–08 *et seq.*
[20] "Agreement" is, therefore, a wider term than "contract."
[21] paras. 4–38 *et seq.*

taking to do or abstain from doing something. This definition inevitably gives rise to further problems. The difficulties of what is meant by "consent" form a large part of this book. The concept of "patrimonial interest" needs further explanation.[22] If each word is explained fully, the result is a book on contract.

1–11   It is tempting, and probably wise, to add to any definition of contract the words "except marriage." The sole similarity between a contract and marriage is that neither can be entered into without the consent of the parties. Thereafter the differences arise.[23] The law of husband and wife governs the relationship of marriage and much of that law cannot be altered by the agreement of the parties. Termination of marriage does not solely depend, as terminating contract can, on the consent of the parties.

To apply frustration of contract to marriage would produce peculiar and interesting results. Marriage creates a status with effects much more fundamental than does a contract of partnership.

1–12   Even the consent required for the creation of marriage is not treated in the same way as the consent which makes a contract. If a woman fraudulently conceals her pregnancy at the time of marriage, or induces her fiancé to believe that he is the father when he is not, the marriage is valid. The contractual rules on fraud and error are inapplicable.[24] However, if there have been problems in the law of marriage as a result of regarding it as part of the law of contract, the converse is not true. No one is likely to confuse contract law by injecting into it the specialities of the law of husband and wife.

PART 2

The Development of Contract Law

1–13   Increasingly types of contract are being made subject to specialised rules. In recorded history in Scotland there always were relationships which had contractual elements but also many special consequences. The rights of superior and vassal, landlord and tenant or secured creditor and debtor are examples. But now statutory control affects many contracts. Sale, employment, carriage, insurance and other contracts have their own rules. Some of those who talk of the disappearance of classical contract law[25] consider this shows a change in the nature of contract, which renders a study of general principles fruitless. But in reality rules on types of contracts have existed since Roman times or earlier.[26] We developed in Scotland principles of contract law at common law.

---

[22] See para. 4–45.
[23] Fraser, *Husband and Wife* (2nd ed.), pp. 155 *et seq.*
[24] *Lang* v. *Lang*, 1921 S.C. 44; overruling *Stein* v. *Stein*, 1914 S.C. 903.
[25] See paras. 1–26 *et seq.*
[26] The Laws of Hammurabi (ed. G. R. Driver and J. C. Miles, 1952) show concern with specific contracts.

Much of the common law remains of vital importance despite statutory encroachment. The common law is like a canvas on which a picture is being painted. The cloth may be obscured by layers of pigment, but it is ever apt to show through and without it the whole image crumbles. There are those in the Anglo-American world who do not see the general law of contract in this way. For them it is "the law of left-overs, of miscellaneous transactions, the rag-tag and bob-tail which do not get treated elsewhere."[27] Insofar as Scots law is based on principle, this is an approach which Scots law has not yet followed.

The history in Scotland

▶14   The Scots law of contract awaits a historian. Although there have been some essays on the development of the law,[28] there is a lack of thorough and comprehensive analysis. In a book which is concerned mainly with the problems of practitioners it would be out of place to embark on a detailed historical survey except in so far as that illuminates or affects the present law. At appropriate places in the chapters of this book historical development is traced.[29] There are certain trends which are summarised here.

▶15   **(a) Early law.** Little is known about contract law prior to Stair.[30] The fullest compilation of rules and decisions is in Balfour's *Practicks*, the exact date of which is uncertain but which derives from the end of the sixteenth century.[31] But collections of decisions at the time do not provide a theoretical analysis of the law. Stair's main contribution was reasons for the rules. In his time the law showed two features which appear to conflict. One was the concentration in some instances on the form of deeds and the method of proof. The other was the idea that all

---

[27] C. W. Summers, "Collective Agreements and the Law of Contracts" (1969) 78 Yale L.J. 525 at p. 565.

[28] *e.g* A. J. Mackenzie Stuart, "Contract and Quasi Contract" in *An Introduction to Scottish Legal History*, Stair Soc. Vol. 20; P. Stein, "The General Notions of Contract and Property in Eighteenth Century Scottish Thought," 1963 J.R. 1.

[29] The details will be found in several chapters, in particular in the chapters on Error and Public Policy.

[30] Consider, *e.g.* the doubts on the extent to which the *Regiam Majestatem* represented Scots law. In any event the passages on pacts add little to our knowledge. Their origins are discussed in H. G. Richardson, "Roman Law in the *Regiam Majestatem*," 1955 J.R. 155. Most of the available medieval sources have been printed by various history societies. What they reveal is largely concerned with law in the lowlands of Scotland. A history of what was happening throughout Scotland is probably not possible. For a simple guide to sources, see B. Webster, *Scotland from the Eleventh Century to 1603* (1975). A list of some sources is in Stair Soc. Vol. 1.

[31] See intro. in Balfour's *Practicks*, Stair Soc. Vol. 21, p. xxxii. Craig, *Ius Feudale* (1655; 1716; 1732) and Hope, *Major Practicks* (1608–33) are of some assistance as are some printed records, such as A.D.A., A.D.C. and A.D.C. et S. There are also unpublished works such as the *Practicks* of Sinclair, Maitland, Colvil, Haddington and others, which are in the Advocates' Manuscripts in the National Library. See Summary Catalogue of the Advocates' Manuscripts (H.M.S.O.) 1971, pp. 74 *et seq*. The extent to which some of these cases have been reported in Morison's *Dictionary* is discussed in the notes to Tait's *Index to the Decisions* (1823). For lists of authorities see Stair Soc. Vol. 1.

contracts would be enforced. "Every paction produceth action."[32] The first unfortunately survives, the second has been modified.

1–16   The law on constitution and proof of obligation has, if anything, become more involved over the centuries. Acts of the Scottish Parliament on the subscription of deeds are still in force.[33] The landmark case was *Paterson* v. *Paterson*[34] which, in the view of Gow, "makes it almost impossible to state the law in terms of cohering principle."[35] The Scottish Law Commission have produced consultative memoranda which propose simplification of the law.[36]

1–17   **(b) The eighteenth century.** Informalities in execution apart, the dominant pattern at the beginning of the eighteenth century was that contracts were enforced despite their subject-matter. By the end of the century it was more possible to attack a contract on the grounds of public policy. Combinations of workmen were struck at in 1726. The trend of the authorities on the Act anent buying pleas altered in 1774. The attempts to have smuggling contracts held *pacta illicita* failed until 1776. The sale of public offices was attacked by the Court of Session in 1786. Wagers were enforceable until 1787. In a period of about a dozen years from 1774 the law was changed by what was arguably one of the ablest Benches of judges which Scotland has had.[37]

1–18   The reasons for this change are debatable, but an important factor was probably the development of native Scottish attitudes to utilitarian philosophy. Philosophy may be an unpopular subject amongst legal practitioners today, few of whom could name three or four modern philosophers, let alone readily discuss their work. But in the age of the Enlightenment the ideas of Hutcheson, Hume, Adam Smith and others had an impact on intellectual thought in Edinburgh. Utility provided a reason for enforcing a contract, but also gave society a reason for refusing to enforce. Kames in his *Principles of Equity* devoted Book II to a discussion of the principle of utility. He chose for four out of his seven chapters, acts which were contrary to the interests of society.[38] A century after Stair the maxim "every paction produceth action" was receiving a more limited effect.

---

[32] Stair, 1,x,7.

[33] Subscription of Deeds Acts of 1540, 1579 and 1681; Deeds Acts 1696; Blank Bonds and Trusts Acts 1696.

[34] (1897) 25 R. 144.

[35] *Mercantile and Industrial Law*, p. 3. See also W. A. Wilson, "In Modum Probationis," 1968 J.R. 193.

[36] Memoranda Nos. 34–39, *Constitution and Proof of Voluntary Obligations* (1977).

[37] In the early part of 1776 the Bench could have consisted of Lord President Dundas, Lord Justice-Clerk Glenlee and Lords Auchinleck, Kennet, Pitfour, Barjarg, Hailes, Stonefield Covington, Gardenstoun, Kames, Coalston, Elliock and Monboddo. In February Ankerville took his seat on the death of Alemore. In December Coalston was replaced by Braxfield (information derived from Brunton and Haig, *Senators of the College of Justice* (1849)). The details of the case-law are in Chap. 25.

[38] And see the conclusion of Book II, "Justice and Utility compared," pp. 361 *et seq.* (1825 ed).

-19 (c) **English influence.** From the beginning of the nineteenth century the English influence on the law of contract began to dominate. English cases on offer and acceptance were frequently cited in Scotland. The solution to problems on incorporation of terms into contracts relied on English authority. The footnotes of Bell's *Principles*[39] and *Commentaries*[40] cited many English cases. So it is not surprising that when Professor Gloag produced his two editions of *The Law of Contract* in 1914 and 1929, English authority was freely cited on doubtful points.

-20 Sometimes the English rule merely restated the Scottish position. The classic case on measure of damages, *Hadley* v. *Baxendale*,[41] is not an improvement on earlier Scottish authority, but it is likely to be *Hadley* and its successors, mainly English, which will now be cited in a Scottish court.[42] On other occasions the influence from south of the border was not for the good, as the history of the law of error, misrepresentation and fraud demonstrates.[43] There was a realisation that parts of Scots law might be different. We have not had the distinction between common law and equity. We do not have the doctrine of consideration. We do have a wide concept of unilateral promise, a doctrine of *jus quaesitum tertio*, a very different series of rules on contractual incapacity, different methods of execution of documents and proof of obligations, and our own rules on quasi-contract, to list just some of the distinctions from English law. So, for example, English law was rejected in considering the effect of insanity.[44] English authorities were treated, despite a passage in Gloag, with disdain in determining the meaning of "subject to contract."[45] The leading case on restitution following frustration was decided in the House of Lords with an elaborate citation of Roman law and a rejection of English authority,[46] and in the Court of Session, English cases on fundamental breach did not receive a warm reception.[47]

-21 The existence of differences is apparent to an English lawyer who reads a properly drafted Scottish commercial contract. The Scots lawyer writes "assignation" not "assignment," "arbiter" not "arbitrator," "apparent insolvency" not "act of bankruptcy," "delict" not "tort," "heritable and moveable" not "real and personal." More insidious are words which are used in both Scots and English law but which mean different things, such as "minor," "condition," "deed" and "property."

-22 The English lawyer might assume that all that is necessary is an appropriate phrase-book or an interpreter. Equipped with either he may con-

---

[39] 4th ed. by Bell, 1839 (10th ed., edited by Guthrie, 1899).
[40] 5th ed. by Bell, 1826 (7th ed., edited by MacLaren, 1870).
[41] (1854) 9 Exch. 341.
[42] See Chap. 20.
[43] See Chaps. 9 and 10.
[44] *John Loudon & Co.* v. *Elder's C.B.*, 1923 S.L.T. 226.
[45] *Stobo Ltd.* v. *Morrisons (Gowns) Ltd.*, 1949 S.C. 184; *cf.* Gloag, p. 44.
[46] *Cantiere San Rocco* v. *Clyde Shipbuilding and Engineering Co.*, 1923 S.C.(H.L.) 105.
[47] *Alexander Stephen (Forth) Ltd.* v. *J. J. Riley (U.K.) Ltd.*, 1976 S.L.T. 269; *cf. W. L. Tinney & Co. Ltd.* v. *John C. Dougall Ltd.*, 1977 S.L.T.(Notes) 58; *Wolifson* v. *Harrison* 1977 S.C. 384.

verse intelligently on all aspects of the Scots law of contract. It would be a natural assumption because Parliament has sometimes legislated as though translation is all that is needed. An example may be found in the Consumer Credit Act 1974.[48] This Act makes provision for the different usage of "assignation" for "assignment," "expenses" for "costs" and other terms for which substitution of one word for the other is all the Act requires. A moment's thought, however, may indicate at least a doubt whether these are really different names for the same concept. It would, for example, be a bold person who would assert, as the Act appears to, that the Scots law on hiring of goods is the English bailment in different guise.

1–23   Differences in terminology can be a reflection of differences in substance. There have been attempts to point out the dangers of incorporating too much English law into Scotland. Several Scottish judges have been alive to this.[49] Professors Smith and Gow produced works which emphasised the distinctive nature of Scots law.[50] Inevitably not all have agreed with this approach, which has been characterised as the Cooper-Smith account of Scots law.[51] This is more a tribute to the influence of those mentioned than a historically correct indication that they were those responsible for demonstrating Scottish virtues.[52]

1–24   The influence of English law on Scots law is a wide issue but it affects the law of contract which illustrates an intricate pattern of acceptance and rejection of English authority. The truth may be that the real dangers are chauvinism and lack of knowledge. Both Scots and English lawyers are capable of conceit, which is all the more harmful when combined with ignorance.

Future Development

1–25   It is becoming common to observe that Parliamentary intervention in the law of contract has been spasmodic and increasing. Regulation of some contracts has existed for centuries. The historian would point to many Acts of the Scottish Parliament which attempted control of commercial activities. The nineteenth century saw statutes which dealt with, amongst other contracts, sale and carriage. Employment and insurance are favourite subjects for modern legislators, and some of the influence comes from Brussels not from London. Provisions in restraint of trade have been unenforceable for many years, but the modern practitioner has to grapple with a multitude of rules on competition and restrictive trade practices. There has been an increase in concern about standard-

---

[48] s.189.

[49] See Dunedin, *Divergencies and Convergencies of English and Scots Law* (1935).

[50] T. B. Smith, *Short Commentary on the Law of Scotland* (1962); J. J. Gow, *The Mercantile and Industrial Law of Scotland* (1964).

[51] I. D. Willock, "The Scottish Legal Heritage Revisited," in *Independence and Devolution* (ed. J. P. Grant, 1976).

[52] See, *e.g.* J. A. Lovat Fraser, "Some Points of Difference Between English and Scotch Law" (1894) 10 L.Q.R. 340; H. Burn Murdoch, "English Law in Scots Practice" (1908–09) 20 J.R. 346; (1909–10) 21 J.R. 59, 148.

form contracts the terms of which cannot be negotiated, in practice, by one of the contracting parties. One result of this concern has been the Unfair Contract Terms Act 1977.[53] That Act illustrates another development, namely, protection for consumers when they enter into contracts.[54] "Consumer law" has emerged as a subject for articles and books,[55] although its concerns are much broader than the law of contract. The trend is away from enforcement of the strict terms of a contract. So far as can be foreseen this trend will continue, although the extent of future development is a matter for speculation.

–26 Because of a tendency for the law, in effect, to rewrite the terms of a contract, some academics in England and the United States have restated the theory of contract. It has been said: "We are told that contract, like God, is dead. And so it is. Indeed the point is hardly worth arguing anymore."[56] Professors Stuart Macaulay and Lawrence Friedman are two of the main proponents of a change in the nature of contractual theory.[57] Professor Friedman, in his *Contract Law in America*, criticised the teaching of an abstract system of contract law based on appeal court cases. Businessmen were bringing their disputes to court less often because (1) commercial problems are now so complex that a judge's knowledge of them comes only from a partial and vague experience, the value of which decreases with time. A lawyer's experience and some business sense do not bridge a gulf between courts and business life; (2) litigation, particularly for small claims, is expensive; (3) litigation is inconsistent with a continuing business relationship. The result is that courts only see a small proportion of disputes. The matters discussed in classical contract law are either covered by statute or drafted into oblivion by practitioners.

---

[53] See Chap. 12.

[54] See, *e.g.* The Fair Trading Act, 1973, the Consumer Credit Act 1974.

[55] This work is not concerned primarily with the rules which affect specific contracts, and an analysis of consumer law must be sought elsewhere. See, *e.g.* Ross Cranston, *Consumers and the Law* (2nd ed., 1984); B.W. Harvey, *The Law of Consumer Protection and Fair Trading* (2nd ed., 1982); R. Lowe and G. Woodroffe, *Consumer Law and Practice* (2nd ed., 1985). A relatively recent discussion of policy is in the Hamlyn Lectures by Sir Gordon Borrie, *The Development of Consumer Law and Policy—Bold Spirits and Timorous Souls* (1984).

[56] Grant Gilmore, *The Death of Contract*, (1974), p. 3. Despite its title this book is more a description of other people's theories, than an advocacy of the point made in its first three sentences, which are quoted above.

[57] See S. Macaulay, "Non-contractual Relations in Business," 1963 Am.Soc.Rev. 45; L. M. Friedman, *Contract Law in America* (1965); "Symposium on the Relevance of Contract Theory," 1967 Wisc.L.R. 303 *et seq.* See also for an economic approach I. R. Macneil, *The New Social Contract; An Inquiry Into Modern Contractual Relations* (1980). Much of Professor Macneil's work is not readily available in Scotland, but a sample published in the U.K. with a bibliography, is "Economic Analysis of Contractual Relations," in *The Economic Approach to Law*, ed. P. Burrows and C. G. Veljanovski (1981). See also A. Kronman and R. Posner, *The Economics of Contract Law*, (1979), *Readings in the Economics of Law and Regulation*, ed. A. I. Ogus and C. G. Veljanovski (1984), Chap. 4. It has been argued that economic and social changes have been responsible for a transformation in the function and substance of contract—W. Friedman, *Law in a Changing Society* (2nd ed., 1972), Chap. 4.

1–27   What is, perhaps, surprising is that Friedman's approach should have been thought to affect contractual theory. Given that the attitude of businessmen to the courts is as he describes, it does not follow that the rules of contract law should be changed. Disputes in any part of the law are often settled without the application of the strict legal result just for reasons similar to those he mentions. Nor is it clear that much has changed. Was it not always the case that expense and other factors inhibited litigation? That judges had gaps in their knowledge? Nor is there anything dramatic in a modern draftsman trying to avoid disputes. To do it successfully requires an understanding and knowledge of the details of contract law.

1–28   In England, Professor Atiyah has adopted a controversial stand.[58] He is an apostle of the approach that obligations should arise as much from what people do as from what they agree. Agreement is not as important as what parties have done at the time of entering into the contract and subsequently. Indeed it may not matter too much whether there is a contract. If goods or services have been supplied, satisfactorily or otherwise, let us look at that and decide what financial adjustment is reasonable. This has the advantage that a fair solution can be reached. The unplanned event is easily catered for. We can abandon the fiction which ties the solution of contractual disputes to "the intention of the parties." We are not much concerned with error or mistake or consensus, which are topics much overrated by textbooks. We are realists. We look at what has happened and then decide what to do. Precedent may inhibit them, but judges are in fact doing this, even if they have to convert their reasons into the collapsing currency of traditional theory. So the argument goes.

1–29   The disadvantages of this approach are (1) an increased difficulty in defining contractual obligations; (2) the blurring of the distinction between contract and other parts of the law of obligations; (3) the avoidable uncertainty caused by the idea that rights should be enforceable reasonably[59]; and (4) the curious adherence it sometimes produces to the doctrine of consideration.

1–30   Part of the danger of incorporating ideas such as these into Scotland is that we have a quite different history from the American systems which are at their root.

To quote Gilmore, in *The Death of Contract*[60]:

"Speaking descriptively we might say that what is happening is that

---

[58] See *Introduction to the Law of Contract* (3rd ed., 1981); *The Rise and Fall of Freedom of Contract* (1979) contains a full account of the interplay of economic, social and legal doctrines. See, though, a review: C. Fried (1979–80) 93 Harv.L.R. 1858.

[59] See G. H. Treitel's inaugural lecture, "Doctrine and Discretion in the Law of Contract" (1981). Classical contract law has a considerable number of blurred edges. The concept of "material breach" and the measure of damages for breach have scope for judicial flexibility and these areas are central to contract law. But avoidable uncertainty is another matter.

[60] p. 87.

'contract' is being reabsorbed into the mainstream of 'tort.' Until the general theory of contract was hurriedly run up late in the nineteenth century, tort had always been our residual category of civil liability. As the contract rules dissolve, it is becoming so again. It should be pointed out that the theory of tort into which contract is being reabsorbed is itself a much more expansive theory of liability than was the theory of tort from which contract was artificially separated a hundred years ago."

–31 Whether this is accurate history for the United States and England is beside the point. Its beliefs are (a) that a theory of contract did not emerge until the nineteenth century; (b) that tort is the residual category; and (c) that contract is merging once again with tort. But, as Atiyah recognises,[61] Stair, Kames and Hutcheson had theories which did not find their counterpart in England until the nineteenth century. In Scotland we started our law of contract in a different way and we should be cautious about adopting conclusions which are based on premises we would not accept. The relationship between contract and delict is a fascinating problem. In particular, discussion of negligent misrepresentation and recovery of economic loss shows how contract and delict may overlap; but it does not follow that the law of contract is disappearing.[62]

–32 We will continue to have debate on the extent to which judicial discretion should play a part in contract law.[63] The businessman wishes certainty; but he is less likely to find it if his contract is subject to a "fair and reasonable" test under the Unfair Contract Terms Act. The grounds on which the courts refuse to enforce a contract change. Control by invalidity of consent or form can give way to control by construction. The history of exclusion clauses is a classic example.[64] There is also the possibility of challenge of the extortionate bargain,[65] and the use of the concept of inequality in bargaining power to determine whether or not statements are incorporated into contracts.[66] Lord Denning has observed:

"The time is not yet here, but I hope it is coming, when Judges will realise that people who draft statutes, wills or contracts cannot envisage all the things that the future may bring; that words are a most imperfect instrument to express the mind of man, and that the better role of a Judge is to be a master of words, and to mould them to fit the purpose in hand—by way of implication, presumed intention or what you will—so as to do therein 'what to justice shall

---

[61] *Promise, Morals and Law* (1981), pp. 13–15.
[62] See, *e.g.* A. S. Burrows, "Contract, Tort and Restitution—A Satisfactory Division or Not?" (1983) 99 L.Q.R. 217; J. Holyoak, "Tort and Contract after Junior Books" (1983) 99 L.Q.R. 591; A. J. E. Jaffey, "Contract in Tort's Clothing," 1985 *Legal Studies* 77; F. M. B. Reynold, "Tort Actions in Contractual Situations," 1985 N.Z.U.L.R. 215.
[63] See G. H. Trietel, *sup. cit.*
[64] See Chap. 12.
[65] See Chap. 12.
[66] See cases cited at paras. 3–04 to 3–06.

appertain.' Such was the task entrusted by our Sovereign to the Justices on the opening of every Assize. Such is the task which they would do well to undertake today."[67]

1–33   In a commercial community this is a highly controversial approach. Time will show how far it prevails. For the present we attempt to explain the rules—not just what they are—but why they are. If the reasons cease to be valid, *cessante ratione legis, cessat lex ipsa.*

---

[67] *The Discipline of Law* (1979), pp. 56, 57. In *Brikom Investments Ltd.* v. *Carr* [1979] Q.B. 467 at p. 484, Lord Denning said: "I prefer to see that justice is done; and let the conveyancers look after themselves."

CHAPTER 2

PROMISE

WHAT IS A "PROMISE"?

-01 The noun "promise" has several meanings but the one relevant for present purposes is that given in the *Shorter Oxford English Dictionary* as: "A declaration made to another person with respect to the future, stating that one will do, or refrain from, some specified act, or that one will give some specified thing."

-02 Not all declarations of this type are enforceable in law as promises. This may be for one of two reasons. The statement may be unenforceable, or otherwise invalid, on the usual grounds which invalidate contractual obligations, namely incapacity, improper method of obtaining the obligation, improper form, or contravention of public policy. The other reason for refusing to enforce a promissory statement, as a promise, is that the law allocates it to another category. Statements about the future have to be distinguished. They may be promises, declarations of intention, testamentary provisions, donations *mortis causa*, offers or part of a mutual contract. The practitioner drafting a document must be aware of these distinctions if he is to give effect to the intentions of his client. The problem is particularly acute with the unilateral gift, although in theory it can arise in other situations. The layman blunders on regardless of the difficulties in construing such an apparently simple phrase as "I will give my son £100," or "You will get £100 from me on my death." This chapter discusses the distinction of a promise from (a) a declaration of intention, (b) a testamentary provision, (c) a *donatio mortis causa* and (d) an offer. The proof and ascertainment of facts is then considered.

(a) Distinction of Promise from a Declaration of Intention

-03 A promise is different from a declaration of intention.[1]

-04 A debtor may write to his creditor saying: "You have accepted what I sent in full payment of your claim, but I assure you that I will pay the balance whenever I am able to do so." The statement of future intent is within the dictionary definition of "promise," but it is not necessarily enforceable. A similar statement was held to be binding in honour only

---

[1] At least so far as Scots law is concerned. A philosopher may view the matter differently. See P. S. Atiyah, *Promises, Morals and Law* (1981), p. 165.

in *Ritchie* v. *Cowan & Kinghorn*.[2] In that case there was clear evidence from letters that the obligation was not intended to have legal effect. A statement may be considered in the context of all the admissible evidence, but sometimes the only evidence is the document and a construction *contra proferentem* goes against the words being a promise in a case of doubt.[3]

2–05 A person may write to a relative: "I intend to leave you £500 in my will," or "I hope to make provision for your family on my death." These are, without other facts added, declarations of future intention and not binding.[4] A will is revocable and a statement of intention to insert a provision in a will can hardly be less revocable. But the principal reason for non-enforcement is unconnected with the law on testaments. Good resolutions are not, by themselves, enforceable obligations.

2–06 A statement in the form, "I intend to make provision for your family," may only be an expression of resolution and not obligatory as found in *Kincaid* v. *Dickson*,[5] a case relied on by Stair in a passage in which he distinguished three acts of will, namely desire, resolution and engagement.[6] A man may desire an effect or be resolved about a course, but the law allows him the free will to change his mind. It is only at the stage of engagement that legal obligation arises.

2–07 How can it be decided when the state of engagement has been reached? The problem with unilateral promises is no different in theory from that of other contractual situations, although it may be more complicated in practice because the statement need only be unilateral. "I offer £X for the house" and "I am thinking of offering £X for the house" are clearly different in meaning; so are "I will pay you £X" and "I am considering paying you £X." The reason we say that there are differences is that in one situation the utterer intends to be bound. He wants the house. He is prepared to pay the money. In the other situation he is at the stage of contemplation and is, as it were, thinking aloud. Which stage has been reached on particular facts is a matter of objective interpretation of the words used in the context in which they were used. The context is important. To ignore previous correspondence or other background circumstances on a view that the words alone must be interpreted is to take a blinkered approach to evidence of intention. For example, "I think I will offer £X" might often indicate no intention to be bound at that stage. But not always. Those words stated to the auctioneer at an auction sale during bidding may acquire a different connotation by the circumstances of their use. The more so if the speaker is a Highland gentleman who habitually expresses himself less directly than the Lowlander.

---

[2] (1901) 3 F. 1071; see also *Scott* v. *Dawson, infra.*
[3] *Scott* v. *Dawson* (1862) 24 D. 440.
[4] See *Gray* v. *Johnston*, 1928 S.C. 659.
[5] (1673) Mor. 12143.
[6] Stair, I,x,2.

(b) Distinction of Promise from a Testamentary Provision

08 A promise is different from a testamentary provision. The typical problem is a claim against executors that the deceased when alive wrote a letter promising money to the claimant on the deceased's death. If the letter is more than a statement of intention it is enforceable, but categorisation is still important. If the statement is a contractual promise it is a debt due by the deceased and must rank as such on the estate. If the statement is testamentary it is a legacy and must be paid as such. Further an obligation by a promissor may be due to the heirs and successors of a predeceasing promisee. A legatee's representatives do not automatically take on the predecease of the legatee. The promise, once delivered, if delivery is required,[7] may not be unilaterally revoked. The testamentary provision may be.

09 There can be a contractual obligation to pay money, the time of payment being the death of X. As Lord Cringletie put it: "It appears wonderful to me that people ever should have doubted that an obligation on a party's heirs to perform something after his death was good." In the case concerned[8] a lady had delivered to a relation who was a captain in the Aberdeenshire militia, a letter binding her heirs and successors to pay to him an annuity after her death. The promise was gratuitous, but it had been delivered and so was enforceable. It could not be revoked, although revocation had been attempted.

10 The issues were discussed in *Miller* v. *Milne's Trs.*[9] where a lady wrote letters to an adjutant of the famous Aberdeenshire militia. The man was not her husband. She intended to reward him for his kind attentions. The case was decided on the ground that a condition had not been fulfilled. There were dicta on the distinction between promise and legacy. There were differences of opinion about which category applied to the letters. Four of the judges considered the letters an irrevocable obligation; five that there was a legacy; and three that there was *donatio mortis causa*—a third category considered below. Those with an equally perplexing problem before them may sympathise with Lord Ivory's discomfort.

11 "[I]f the vote were to be taken on each point separately, it is very probable that I should in the end find myself in the minority, although, in fact, I arrive at the same general result with the majority,—that this pursuer's claim is not well-founded—a result they have arrived at on a *tota re perspecta* view of the case, rather than on the points of law submitted, as to which I am more puzzled now than I was at first."[10]

---

[7] See Chap. 7.
[8] *Duguid* v. *Caddall's Trs.* (1831) 9 S. 844.
[9] (1859) 21 D. 377.
[10] at p. 393.

2–12   A similar case is *Cairney* v. *Macgregor's Tr.*,[11] where the letter was in the form: "Dear Mr. Cairney,—As desired by you I hereby put in writing my promise to you namely that you are to receive out of my estate, after my decease, the sum of fifteen thousand pounds sterling." This was held to be a binding promise.

2–13   Where the promise is adjected to testamentary statements it is indicative of the promise being testamentary, as in *Trotter* v. *Trotter*[12] where the letter read: "My dear Joanna,—The five hundred pounds I had settled, as a legacy, to my sister, she has given up; so I give it to you, besides the two hundred I had left you before; all from your affectionate aunt."

(c) Distinction of Promise from Donatio Mortis Causa

(i) The introduction of donatio mortis causa

2–14   In a case already referred to, *Duguid* v. *Caddall's Trs.*,[13] Lord Glenlee is reported as saying that: "We have nothing like the Roman doctrine as to their peculiar *donatio mortis causa.*" This, according to Lord Deas in a later case, may not have been what his Lordship said, which is an interesting, if unusual, method of disposing of an authority which is contrary to a favoured proposition. In that later case, *Morris* v. *Riddick*,[14] there were important observations on the nature of the doctrine of *donatio mortis causa* including a definition by Lord President Inglis in these terms:

2–15   "*Donatio mortis causa* in the law of Scotland may, I think, be defined as a conveyance of an immoveable or incorporeal right, or a transference of moveables or money by delivery, so that the property is immediately transferred to the grantee, upon the condition that he shall hold for the granter so long as he lives, subject to his power of revocation, and, failing such revocation, then for the grantee on the death of the granter. It is involved of course in this definition, that if the grantee predeceases the granter the property reverts to the granter, and the qualified right of property which was vested in the grantee is extinguished by his predecease."

2–16   Lord Curriehill agreed. Lord Deas' definition had important differences. The phrase itself, *"donatio mortis causa,"* supports his observation that the gift must be in the prospect of death. However, this must surely be easy to infer when the gift refers to death. The gift must contemplate death or it is not *donatio mortis causa*. More awkward might have been his Lordship's view that the gift took effect only in the event of death occurring from the existing illness. Must there be an illness? Surely the soldier in battle who has the prospect of death can make a *donatio mortis causa* although he is not wounded? Must death be in

---

[11] 1916 1 S.L.T. 357.
[12] (1842) 5 D. 224.
[13] *Sup. cit.*
[14] (1867) 5 M. 1036.

immediate prospect? Some individuals contemplate their decease more frequently than others. May someone who sees doom round every corner donate *mortis causa* when an individual of normal fortitude may not?

Lord President Inglis' approach is preferable because it avoids these dubious issues. It has the support of McLaren on *Wills and Succession*.[15] That there need be no immediate apprehension of death was decided in *Blyth* v. *Curle*.[16]

–17 Until *Morris* v. *Riddick* there were few instances of the doctrine. The case may have drawn attention to the concept. Coincidentally there was the development of the Scottish banking system, with the result that several cases arose involving deposit receipts which were a normal method of making interest-bearing deposits with Scottish banks until the deposit account was introduced in 1928 to attract small deposits.[17] All this provided a fruitful source of litigation when added to a problem which has always been with us—the transfer, or alleged transfer, of property by a person in ailing health to those near to him. Terminal illness is not required for the concept to operate, as explained earlier, but it is its natural breeding-ground. In the extreme case there was the position described by Lord President Dunedin:

–18   "The story of the gradual absorption of old Mr. Brownlee's fortune by his nearest relatives is pathetic enough, and were it adequately described would seem more like the closing scenes of the life of Père Goriot than the history of a middle-class family in Glasgow. . . . As was naively said in the proof by the defender, 'the old man had been ground between two millstones.' "[18]

–19 There were perhaps three other reasons why donation *mortis causa* acquired a popularity, despite its complexities. There is a stronger presumption against donation outright than against donation *mortis causa*, a matter examined below. Thus a pursuer can more readily prove a case of donation *mortis causa*. Secondly when the *jus mariti* existed there could be little point in showing an outright gift from husband to wife[19] and thirdly, there was some doubt, later resolved, about whether outright donation was provable by parole evidence.[20]

(ii) The requirements for donatio mortis causa

–20 According to modern authority there are three requirements. (1) The donor must act in contemplation of his death, in the sense only that the gift receives full effect on his death. That is the "*mortis causa*" element.

---

[15] (3rd ed., 1894), p. 435.
[16] (1885) 12 R. 674; and see *Aiken's Exrs.* v. *Aiken*, 1937 S.C. 678.
[17] W. W. Wood, *Scottish Banking Practice, Banker and Customer* (3rd ed., 1979), p. 48.
[18] *Brownlee's Exrx.* v. *Brownlee*, 1908 S.C. 232 at p. 236.
[19] *Robertson* v. *Taylor* (1868) 6 M. 917.
[20] *Robertson* v. *Taylor, sup. cit.*; *Gibson* v. *Hutchison* (1872) 10 M. 923. Parole proof was allowed in *Wright's Exr.* v. *City of Glasgow Bank* (1880) 7 R. 527 and *Thomson's Exr.* v. *Thomson* (1882) 9 R. 911. See now Walker and Walker, *Evidence*, p. 156.

(2) There must be an intention to make an immediate, and not a future gift. From this the third condition follows. (3) The subject of donation must be delivered or transferred to the donee (but formal delivery is not required).[21] The gift is subject to a double resolutive condition. It is revoked either if the donee predeceases the donor or if, during the joint lives of donor and donee, the donor revokes. Otherwise death of the donor before the donee perfects the gift. The common calamity in which both die together will raise the problem of section 31 of the Succession (Scotland) Act 1964 and *Lamb* v. *Lord Advocate*.[22] If neither can be shown to have survived the other, the probable result is that the donor's representative will be unable to prove the operation of the resolutive condition, predecease of the donee, and so the donation will be effective. The modern authorities explaining the present scope of the doctrine are *Macpherson's Exrx.* v. *Mackay*,[23] *Aiken's Exrx.* v. *Aiken*,[24] *Graham's Trs.* v. *Gillies*[25] and *Gray's Trs.* v. *Murray*.[26]

(iii) Presumption against donatio mortis causa

2–21   It is well established that there is a strong presumption against outright donation.[27] By contrast there is less of a presumption against the revocable gift constituted by *donatio mortis causa*.

2–22   Lord President Normand in *North of Scotland Bank* v. *Cumming*[28] is authority for this, as are Lord Deas in *Sharp* v. *Paton*[29] and the Lord Ordinary in *Dawson* v. *McKenzie*.[30] There is a contrary opinion by Lord President Clyde in *Macpherson's Exrx.* v. *Mackay*.[31] Lord Shand said in one of the leading cases on donation *mortis causa*, *Crosbie's Trs.* v. *Wright*[32]:

> "It is obvious that, in the case of a donation *mortis causa* totally different principles are applicable from the case of donation *inter vivos*. The latter, to be effectual, requires delivery. In the former case the benefit is to result after the donor's death, hence formal delivery is not necessary; but a title of such a kind as occurs in this case, and evidence of purpose to make a donation, will be enough to operate the transfer."

---

[21] On delivery see Chap. 7; *Graham's Trs.* v. *Gillies*, 1956 S.C. 437; *Gray's Trs.* v. *Murray*, 1970 S.C. 1. It may be that the evidence of delivery needed to establish outright donation is stronger than the evidence required to show *donatio mortis causa*.

[22] 1976 S.C. 110.

[23] 1932 S.C. 505.

[24] 1937 S.C. 678.

[25] 1956 S.C. 437.

[26] 1970 S.C. 1.

[27] *Sharp* v. *Paton* (1883) 10 R. 1000 at p. 1006 *per* Lord President Inglis, appd. in *Dawson* v. *McKenzie* (1891) 19 R. 261 at pp. 271 and 274 and in *Brownlee's Ex.* v. *Brownlee*, 1908 S.C. 232 at p. 241; *Penman* v. *White*, 1957 S.C. 338; *Grant's Trs.* v. *McDonald*, 1939 S.C. 448 at p. 453; *Macauley* v. *Milliken*, 1967 S.L.T.(Notes) 30.

[28] 1939 S.L.T. 391 at p. 394.

[29] *Sup. cit.* at p. 1008.

[30] *Sup. cit.* at p. 269.

[31] 1932 S.C. 505 at p. 513.

[32] (1880) 7 R. 823 at p. 834.

There is a requirement that there be delivery, but weak evidence of delivery may be eked out by strong evidence of intention.[33]

–23   The reason for the relaxation of the rules on donation in the case of *mortis causa* gifts has been said to be the

> "clearest reasons of expediency and justice. The gift is made on deathbed, and when the person is in contemplation of death. Materials for writing may not be at hand, even although there were the capacity to use them, which could not in such circumstances be expected. To require, therefore, that the donation should be proved by a writing or by the actual physical delivery of the gifted article would be to require what was not in many cases possible, and would extinguish the law of *donatio mortis causa* altogether."[34]

–24   Lord McLaren did not like this exception to the normal rules, and would have preferred to have seen *Crosbie's Trs.* reconsidered.[35]

–25   Illustrations of how the evidence may show donation *inter vivos* or *mortis causa* include *Lord Advocate* v. *Grierson*[36] and *Lord Advocate* v. *King.*[37] This last case and others on deposit receipts are discussed in a useful article by David G. Antonio.[38] The cases must be looked at with the warning of Lord President Clyde in *Macpherson's Exrx.* that: "It is, indeed, idle to argue from the facts proved in one case what should be the decision in another case on a different set of facts."[39]

(iv) Donatio mortis causa distinguished from promise

–26   A *donatio mortis causa* is very different in theory from a legacy, a promise or a donation (which may be the implementation of a promise). In practice the distinction may not be easy to make.

–27   Take first an example which does not appear to pose much difficulty. The statement, "I promise that you will receive £100 on my death," does not look like a *donatio mortis causa* because there is no immediate donation. Whether it is a legacy or a contractual promise depends on factors discussed earlier. More awkward is a letter delivered to the donee which says: "If you present this to my executors on my death you will receive £100." It was a similar form which provoked dissension amongst the whole court in *Miller* v. *Milne's Trs.*[40] The one factor which may distinguish the promise from the donation *mortis causa* is revocability. A promise is not normally revocable unilaterally, nor can the irrevocable gift be a *donatio mortis causa*. The answer in the end depends

---

[33] *Macpherson's Exrx.* v. *Mackay, sup. cit.* at pp. 514, 515 *per* Lord President Clyde; *Graham's Trs.* v. *Gillies, sup. cit.* at p. 448 *per* Lord President Clyde; *Gray's Trs.* v. *Murray, sup. cit.*

[34] *McSkimming* v. *Stenhouse* (1883) 21 S.L.R. 3 at p. 5 *per* Lord Fraser.

[35] *Macfarlane's Trs.* v. *Miller* (1898) 25 R. 1201 at p. 1212.

[36] (1877) 15 S.L.R. 105.

[37] (1953) T.R. 119.

[38] "*Mortis Causa* or *Inter Vivos* Donation?" 1954 S.L.T.(News) 121, 213.

[39] *Sup. cit.* at p. 515.

[40] *Sup. cit.*

on the intention of the obligor, which is a question of fact. While it is pleasant in court to be able in a case involving a deposit receipt endorsed by a spinster aunt, to refer to a reported case of a deposit receipt endorsed by a bachelor uncle, the limitations of this approach are obvious. The guidance which a textbook writer can give is to indicate the factors which may need to be explored in evidence.[41]

(d) Promise and an Offer

(i) General

2–28   A standard statement is that a contract arises from offer and acceptance. This is a useful analysis, but it is not applicable in all situations.[42] The complicated commercial contract signed by the parties who are seated at a boardroom table may not be capable of dissection into offers and acceptances. The contract is made when the last party signs. There is also the example, more theoretical than practical, of a contract between A and B on terms to be provided by C. The agreement between A and B may be in offer and acceptance form; its important conditions provided by C are not. A promise and an offer are unilateral acts. If either is accepted there is, it is suggested, a contract. That is trite law for an offer, but what of the promise which is accepted?

(ii) The accepted promise

2–29   Acceptance of a promise is not necessary for it to be binding. Does that mean that acceptance has no effect? The question is important because it may affect the method of proof of the obligation. It may affect the ability of the promisee to reject the promise without incurring the penalties for breach of contract.

2–30   X says: "I promise to sell my house so that you can use the proceeds to build a church." "Thank you," say the church authorities, "please do," X sells his house. The authorities change their mind about building the church. Has X no redress for any loss caused by his acting in reliance on the acceptance of his promise? Is he to be in a worse position than the person who made an offer which was accepted by the authorities? Surely not. The acceptance of a promise places the acceptor under an obligation.

(iii) The promise which is not accepted

2–31   Scots law is unusual in that a promise is binding without acceptance. Not that the making of the promise may itself give rise to obligation. It may need to be delivered before it is binding, but that having been done, the promisee need not respond for the promise to be binding.

---

[41] See para. 2–52.
[42] See para. 5–02.

2–32   Stair was definite about this. He distinguished a promise, which did
not require acceptance, from an offer which did.[43] It follows that there
can be a promise to an incapax who cannot accept an offer. Erskine and
Bell followed Stair.[44]

2–33   The promise, after delivery of it, if that is required, is irrevocable by
the promissor. As Professor Walker has put it: "the promissor of a
reward for the return of a lost dog cannot revoke the promise even by
notice, when he sees a good citizen leading the dog back towards his
house."[45] *Campbell* v. *Glasgow Police Commrs.*[46] may illustrate this
idea but there is a possibility in that case that the fact of cashing of the
cheque for the police gratuity could have represented acceptance of the
promise. The relevant problems are not discussed in the report. The
best case is *Duguid* v. *Caddall's Trs.*[47] discussed above, in which there
was an unsuccessful attempt to revoke a promise of an annuity.

2–34   No one is forced to welcome a promise. If it is rejected by the promisee he can no longer enforce it. As Stair said: "It is true, if he in
whose favour they are made, accept not, they become void, not by the
negative non-acceptance, but by the contrary rejection. For as the will
of the promissor constitutes a right in the other, so the other's will, by
renouncing and rejecting that right, voids it, and makes it return."[48]
Bell said likewise[49] and referred to a case[50] which is not authority for the
proposition stated.

(iv) How is a promise distinguished from an offer?

2–35   There are important dicta on what is a promise in *Macfarlane* v. *Johnston.*[51] Lord Justice-Clerk Inglis said[52]:

> "It appears to me that the use of the verb 'agree' is of very little
> consequence; for, when a person agrees to pay a particular sum on
> a particular day, he grants a promissory-note, for the distinction
> between a promise and an obligation of a different kind does not
> consist in the use of the word promise. There is a philosophical and
> practical distinction between a promise and an obligation, which is
> nowhere better stated than by Lord Stair (I,x,3). A promise is a
> pure and simple expression of the will of the party undertaking the
> obligation, requiring no acceptance, and still less requiring mutual
> consent. A promise is distinguished by Lord Stair from a pollici-
> tation or offer which requires acceptance to make it binding, and
> still more from a paction which, in order to be binding, requires the
> mutual consent of two parties."

---

[43] Stair, I,x,3; I,x,4.
[44] Ersk., *Inst.*, III,iii,88; Bell, *Prin.*, s.9.
[45] *Contracts*, para. 2.9.
[46] (1895) 22 R. 621.
[47] *Sup. cit.*
[48] Stair, I,x,4.
[49] *Prin.*, s.8.
[50] *Allan* v. *Colzier* (1664) Mor. 9428.
[51] (1864) 2 M. 1210.
[52] at p. 1213.

2-36   Lord Neaves stated[53]:

> "A promise is something more than the mere constitution of the
> relation of debtor and creditor; it is the delivered expression of the
> serious engagement by the person promising that he will do the
> thing promised. For that purpose there are no particular words
> required. 'I promise' is the most natural form of expressing that
> engagement; but such expressions as 'I engage,' or 'I will do it,' are
> of the nature of promises, being a serious declaration by which the
> person pledges his faith that he will do a certain thing. The word
> 'agree' is ambiguous, and, strictly, ought to be confined to pactions;
> and an agreement, properly speaking, means a paction, a *consen-
> sus*, of a plurality of persons *in idem placitum*. But it is also used
> improperly as a word of unilateral signification; and if it be so used,
> I see no difference between the expressions 'I agree to pay,' and 'I
> promise to pay.' "

2-37   Stair's division of conventional obligations was into three categories,
promises, offers, and contracts.[54] That is a gloss on what Stair said.
There has been learned discussion on the true form and meaning of his
text, concentrating on his use of the word "pollicitation." It is of little
importance for the present discussion whether, as Dr Alan Rodger has
argued, Stair distinguished an offer from pollicitatio[55] or, as Professor
Geoffrey MacCormack says, pollicitatio and offer were treated by Stair
as being similar.[56] Stair's distinction was twice accepted by Lord President Inglis.[57]

(e) The Reluctance to Construe a Statement as a Promise

2-38   The words "I promise" are not essential to create a promise. Unfortunately, neither can it be maintained that their use always means that there
is a promise. The words can be used without the intention to be bound
(see earlier) or in a sense not beneficial to the promisee as, "I promise
that I will sue you." There is also a sense distinguishable from that
involving an intention to be bound and "thinking aloud" in which "I
promise" is merely declaratory. Here the words mean, "I assure you,"
or "I tell you plainly" as in "I promise you, you will not do it."

2-39   Even if the indications are that there is an intention to be unilaterally
bound there may be a further obstacle to construing the phrase as a promise which does not require acceptance. If the promisee to implement
the promise must himself act, as in a sale of heritage, there may be a
judicial reluctance to consider the obligation binding on the granter, but
not on the grantee.[58] A statement in the form "I . . . do hereby sell my
share of the holding" was construed by the Lord Ordinary in *Anderson*

---

[53] at p. 1214.
[54] Stair, I,x,3.
[55] "Molina, Stair and the *Jus Quaesitum Tertio*," 1969 J.R. 34 and 128 at p. 131.
[56] "A Note on Stair's Use of the Term Pollicitation," 1976 J.R. 121.
[57] *Macfarlane* v. *Johnston, sup. cit.*, and *Vallance* v. *Forbes* (1879) 6 R. 1099 at p. 1101.
[58] *Malcolm* v. *Campbell* (1891) 19 R. 278; *Haldane* v. *Watson*, 1972 S.L.T.(Sh.Ct.) 8).
But see cases of a promise to give an option cited in n. 61 below.

v. *Anderson*[59] as an offer, because of the inherent improbability that promise was the intention of the granter. On appeal the document was treated as neither a promise nor an offer but an invalid attempt to effect a sale by a unilateral document. If the deed has mutual obligations, such as a gift of property on the one hand, and an obligation to take over a loan on the other, this suggests that the deed cannot be unilateral.[60] But there can be a unilateral obligation which is subject to a condition and it is this which poses the most difficulty. A unilateral obligation to dispone heritage on payment of a price may need to be distinguishable from a contract of sale.[61] If there is no direct benefit to the obligor that may suggest unilateral gift rather than mutual contract.[62]

-40   Confusion of terminology between offer and promise is shown in *Morton's Tr.* v. *Aged Christian Friend Society of Scotland*.[63] There were offers to subscribe funds to the society, including the provision of pensions. There was mention of promises. Lord Kinnear observed[64]: "What is necessary is that the promisor should intend to bind himself by an enforceable obligation and should express that intention in clear words." He then applied that "doctrine" to the facts which, as he pointed out later, were instances of offer and acceptance. Not only did the donor's letters appear more like offers than promises, because they read as being conditional on acceptance, but the offers were in fact accepted. What may have happened here was a tendency to equate a generous gift, in the form of an offer, with a promise—a tendency which should be resisted. What if the Society had never replied to the letters? In that situation an offer lapses, a promise does not. The distinction is crucial.

-41   The practitioner anxious to avoid reliance on the distinction between promise and offer looks for evidence of acceptance. As has been indicated, if there is express acceptance there should be a contract. Actings may be the equivalent of express acceptance, as when a subsidiary company acts on the promise of funds from its holding company. Unfortunately, the simplicity of the situation is marred by the rules on proof by writ or oath.

Problems of proof

-42   Difficulties arise with *Smith* v. *Oliver*.[65] This was another case of alleged promises to a church. Mrs Oliver was said to have taken a considerable part in the building of a Roman Catholic church at Slateford.

---

[59] 1961 S.C. 59.
[60] *Mowat* v. *Thain*, 1947 S.N. 180.
[61] As in *Malcolm* v. *Campbell*, *sup. cit.*, in which earlier authorities are referred to. There can be a promise to give an option: *Sichi* v. *Biagi*, 1946 S.N. 66; *Stone* v. *MacDonald*, 1979 S.C. 363.
[62] *Smith* v. *Oliver*, 1911 S.C. 103 at p. 111 *per* Lord President Dunedin.
[63] (1899) 2 F. 82.
[64] at p. 85.
[65] 1911 S.C. 103.

She was said to have made various promises about the cost. She
expressed wishes on such details as the tiles to be used on the floor. She
"pressed for having a particular kind of heating apparatus installed in
the church, saying that she would otherwise be debarred from entering
it." She was alleged to have undertaken to provide in her will for the
cost. The promises were verbal. They could not be proved by her writ or
oath. The action against her executor failed.[66] Given that our law has, at
the moment, the strange doctrine that a promise must be proved by writ
or oath[67] there is no complaint so far.

2–43   The difficulty is that the church was built. The pursuers averred that
they, "in reliance upon Mrs Oliver's said obligation, and as her manda-
tories, and acting on her instructions, caused the church to be erected in
accordance with her desires at a cost greatly exceeding that which they
would otherwise have incurred." It could be argued that if there was a
contract it was gratuitous or it was innominate and unusual and therefore there were grounds for restricting the mode of proof. Also, in so far
as there was a contract to bequeath money by testament, parole proof
would have the undesirable result in practice of allowing proof of a testamentary writing by parole.[68]

The court in *Smith* v. *Oliver* rested its decision on other grounds and
these create difficulties. Lord President Dunedin said[69]: "Now it is quite
well settled by a series of cases that a party cannot turn what is, in its
nature, a mere promise into a contract, so as to be allowed to prove it by
parole, by simply averring that on the faith of the promise certain things
were done by him; that is to say he cannot turn a promise into a contract
by *rei interventus*, so to speak."

2–44   Lord President Dunedin's first authority was *Millar* v. *Trema-
mondo*.[70] The master of the Edinburgh Academy was said to have made
promises to an occulist who married his daughter. They were possibly
promises to furnish a house and give a share of moveables, but the
reports are obscure. The court by a narrow majority, and after some difficulty, held that the promises were only provable by writ or oath. Lord
Dunedin interpreted the arguments as based on the view that there were
promises followed by *rei interventus* in the form of marriage. There are
objections to this. It is not clear that the promises came first and the
marriage later. The Lord Justice-Clerk in Hailes' report indicates otherwise. All that is clear is that the promises were in view of the marriage,
but it does not follow that this reveals which came first. Even assuming
that the promises were first it would be necessary, to show *rei interventus*, to demonstrate that the marriage was in reliance on the promises.

---

[66] See the result of proof: 1911 1 S.L.T. 451.
[67] See Walker and Walker, p. 134.
[68] See Walker and Walker, p. 133 and authorities cited, esp. *Edmonston* v. *Edmonston*
(1861) 23 D. 995.
[69] at p. 111.
[70] (1771) Mor. 12395; Hailes' Dec. 409.

-45   "Unequivocally referable to the agreement" were Bell's words in his classic definition of *rei interventus*.[71] Perhaps when marriage for money rather than for love and companionship was more common than now, the occulist could have shown that he took his bride because of a promise of a snuff-box, rings, laces and other items. On the other hand perhaps he would not have proved this. The point is that we do not know. The relevance of the marriage to the arguments may have been to show that the promise was onerous rather than to show *rei interventus*. In any event the case is obscure and does not clearly settle the proposition stated by Lord Dunedin.

-46   His Lordship's other authority was *Edmonston* v. *Edmonston*,[72] but as the Sheriffs Walker have pointed out this was not a case of promise but of bilateral onerous contract.[73] Contrary to Lord Dunedin was Bell, in a passage cited to the court.[74]

-47   There is no reason in principle why a promise cannot be turned into a contract by the actings of the promisee. Indeed some distinguished writers have argued that contracts consist of a series of promises.[75] If *Smith* v. *Oliver* is restricted in its application to its peculiar facts[76] which could by themselves have justified proof by writ or oath, there is no general problem. It would be unfortunate if it affected the normal sphere of commercial contracts by making it dangerous to act in reliance on the verbal promises of businessmen. But the standard view remains that a promise must be proved by writ or oath, with a possible exception if it is ancillary to a contract which may be proved by parole.[77]

Promise with a condition attached

-48   If the promise has attached to it a condition requiring acceptance by the promisee, it is considered that the promise is not a true promise in Stair's sense. It is an offer not binding until acceptance. That is why it has been said[78] that Bell was wrong to refer to *Allan* v. *Colzier*[79] for his statement that "a promise may be discharged . . . by the failure of any annexed conditions."[80] The case involved an offer to be a debtor subject to the condition of acceptance.

-49   If the condition attached to the promise is something other than acceptance it may be another matter. There is no reason why fulfilment of a condition should not be required before implementation of the pro-

---

[71] Bell, *Prin.*, s.26, and see case law referred to in Walker and Walker, p. 312.
[72] (1861) 23 D. 995.
[73] *Op. cit.*, p. 134, n. 14.
[74] *Prin.*, s.8.
[75] See above, paras. 1–01 *et seq.*
[76] But it was followed in *Gray* v. *Johnston*, 1928 S.C. 659; and see *Jackson* v. *Ogilvie*, 1933 S.L.T. 533.
[77] See Gloag, p. 52; Walker and Walker, para. 130.
[78] para. 2–34.
[79] (1664) Mor. 9428.
[80] *Prin.*, s.8.

mise as in: "I will buy you a car if you pass your exam." Similarly there could be a resolutive condition as in: "I will pay you £100 a year unless and until you marry." The condition could also be potestative or casual. The existence of a condition may not only affect when the promise may be performed but may limit the actings of the promisor. If he impedes performance of the condition it may be held purified.[81]

Delivery of the promise

2–50   The situations in which a deed requires to be delivered before being obligatory are discussed in Chapter 7. If a promise is made to A, it cannot be sued on by B,[82] unless there is competent assignation or the creation of a *jus quaesitum tertio*.

Examples of the operation of the law on promises

2–51   Examples of cases involving promises (even if not so called) are as follows: a letter to a brother saying, "I will give you two bonds for £250 each"[83]; a letter binding heirs to pay an annuity[84]; letters guaranteeing payments under bills[85]; an obligation to keep an offer open[86]; a declaration in a letter that a sum was children's money[87]; a decision of a public body to award a gratuity[88]; a promise to leave something in a will[89]; an obligation to subscribe for shares[90]; an obligation in the form "I the undersigned herewith agree to repay the sum of Two hundred pounds, £200, borrowed today 10th August 1744"[91]; a formal deed to pay sums to the Burgh of Dumbarton[92]; an obligation to grant an option to purchase a shop[93]; a promise by letters to pay a sum out of a deceased's estate[94]; a promise to renounce an interest in an estate.[95]

---

[81] *Pirie* v. *Pirie* (1873) 11 M. 941 at p. 949 *per* Lord Justice-Clerk Moncreiff.

[82] *Cambuslang West Church* v. *Bryce* (1897) 25 R. 322.

[83] *McLachlan* v. *McLachlan* (1821) 1 S. 45.

[84] *Duguid* v. *Caddall's Trs.* (1831) 9 S. 844.

[85] *National Bank* v. *Robertson* (1836) 14 S. 402; *Watt* v. *National Bank* (1839) 1 D. 827.

[86] *Littlejohn* v. *Hadwen* (1882) 20 S.L.R. 5 at p. 7 *per* Lord Fraser, *obiter*. Appd. in *A. & G. Paterson* v. *Highland Ry. Co.*, 1927 S.C.(H.L.) 32 at p. 38 *per* Viscount Dunedin; contrast a statement that an offer must be accepted by a certain date which is a condition of acceptance rather than a promise to keep the offer open—*Effold Properties Ltd.* v. *Sprot*, 1979 S.L.T.(Notes) 84.

[87] *Shaw* v. *Muir's Ex.* (1892) 19 R. 997.

[88] *Campbell* v. *Glasgow Police Commrs.* (1895) 22 R. 621.

[89] *Smith* v. *Oliver*, 1911 S.C. 103; *Cairney* v. *Macgregor's Trs.*, 1916 1 S.L.T. 357.

[90] *Beardmore & Co.* v. *Barry*, 1928 S.C. 101; affd. 1928 S.C.(H.L.) 47.

[91] *McTaggart* v. *MacEachern's J.F.*, 1949 S.C. 503—held to be a promissory note requiring stamping. The authorities were reviewed. The separate head of stamp duty on promissory notes was abolished by the Finance Act 1970, Sched. 7. If the note is linked to other chargeable transactions it may in some cases be liable to duty.

[92] *Denny's Trs.* v. *Dumbarton Mags.*, 1945 S.C. 147.

[93] *Sichi* v. *Biagi*, 1946 S.N. 66.

[94] *Dick* v. *Dick*, 1950 S.L.T.(Notes) 44.

[95] *Jackson* v. *Ogilvie*, 1933 S.L.T. 533.

Contents of a precognition

2-52   As so much turns on evidence of the circumstances, investigation of whether a statement was a promise is assisted by precognitions. The reported cases show the factors which may need to be investigated.[96] They are gathered together here. Precognitions should reveal:

(1) The state of health of the alleged grantor. Was he dying? Was there a state of facility which could lead to the operation of the doctrines of facility and circumvention in the law applying both to contracts and to wills? Was he sane?

(2) What was the relationship with the grantee? This question covers more than the technicalities of blood ties or affinity. How long had they known each other? Were the parties staying together and in what circumstances?

(3) Was the grantee the natural recipient of the grantor's benevolence? Were there circumstances indicating that a gift and in particular one of this value was normal, *e.g.* that the grantee was about to be married? Were there contrary indications, *e.g.* a poor man transferring a large part of his estate to a wealthy person?

(4) Is there evidence other than that of the grantee? Are there impartial witnesses? To whom was the grantor's intention communicated and how? If there was no communication to disinterested persons, such as a legal adviser, minister or doctor, why not?

(5) What are the terms of the deposit receipt or other writing? Is there evidence of delivery of the document to anyone?

(6) What happened after an alleged transfer or obligation to transfer? Was the jewellery still worn by the grantor? Did he continue to receive interest on the deposit receipt? Were there actions or writings by the grantee which indicate acceptance of an offer? Was there an attempt to revoke the transfer or obligation to transfer? Have grantor or grantee died, and if so, when?

(7) What was the knowledge of the grantee about the transaction? Was it kept secret from him?

(8) Are the actings of the grantor inconsistent with the terms of other writings, *e.g.* an existing or later will?

(9) What else could the grantor have done to make an effectual transfer? Why was it not done?

(10) In general, are there any elements which indicate whether the transaction was genuine or suspicious?

---

[96] A useful example of the type of evidence needed to establish *donatio mortis causa* is *Union Bank of Scotland* v. *Fulton*, 1929 S.L.T.(Sh.Ct.) 37.

CHAPTER 3

PRE-CONTRACT NEGOTIATIONS

WHAT ARE NEGOTIATIONS?—DIFFERENCE BETWEEN A REPRESENTATION
AND A TERM

3–01   The initial difficulty is to decide what is negotiation and what is part of the contract. The distinction is crucial. Normally an aggrieved party would prefer to sue for breach of contract, rather than hazard his case on part of the law on misrepresentation. If he can show that a statement is part of the contract his case will often be stronger than if the offending statement was merely made during the negotiations leading up to the contract.

3–02   There is not much difficulty in holding that a statement made at or about the completion of the agreement is part of the agreement: for example, assurances on the soundness of a horse made by the seller at the time of sale and made to complete the sale.[1] A conversation in the mind of parties when an order was given has formed part of the transaction.[2] At the other extreme a statement made in a circular many months prior to the contract is not a term of the contract unless the contract refers to it.[3] A warranty about the soundness of a horse made on April 10 and not renewed did not form part of a sale entered into on June 2.[4] The difficult cases lie between those extremes. The problem has been analysed in a series of English cases.

English Case Law

3–03   If a statement is made some days prior to the sale it is not a part of the contract.[5] If the statement is made at the time of the sale, for example when a beast is in the auction ring, the statement is part of the contract.[6]

3–04   A difficult case is *Oscar Chess Ltd.* v. *Williams.*[7] A car was sold to motor dealers. It was without any dishonesty on the part of the seller described as an 1948 model. It was in fact a 1939 model. The statement on the year of the car was held to be an innocent misrepresentation, and not a warranty, because (1) the seller did not know the correct year and

---

[1] *Scott* v. *Steel* (1857) 20 D. 253.
[2] *Crichton & Stevenson* v. *Love*, 1908 S.C. 818.
[3] *Paul* v. *Corp. of Glasgow* (1900) 3 F. 119.
[4] *Malcolm* v. *Cross* (1898) 25 R. 1089.
[5] *Routledge* v. *McKay* [1954] 1 All E.R. 855.
[6] *Couchman* v. *Hill* [1947] K.B. 554; *Harling* v. *Eddy* [1951] 2 K.B. 739.
[7] [1957] 1 All E.R. 325.

(2) the buyers being motor dealers, were the experts who could have checked the true year. Despite this, it is debatable whether the respective knowledge of the parties is a satisfactory test for deciding whether or not a statement is a representation, or part of a contract. It might be possible to view the case as decided on the ground that any statement on age was a matter of opinion and could never be a term of the contract.[8] Given the dramatic effect which age has on price in the sale of second-hand cars, this is an unlikely interpretation. It may be that the dissenting opinion of Morris L.J. was correct. In his view the statement of the age of the car was the foundation of the contract which was made.

–05 *Oscar Chess* was distinguished in *Dick Bentley Productions Ltd.*[9] which involved the sale of a car by a motor dealer. There was an innocent misrepresentation on mileage by the seller. Lord Denning founded on the ability of the seller in that case to ascertain the true facts. The buyer was "completely innocent of any fault." The result was a breach of warranty and an award of damages.

–06 In *Esso Petroleum* v. *Mardon*[10] a statement by an oil company about the potential throughput of a filling station was treated as a warranty because of the knowledge and skill of the party making the statement. It was also treated as a negligent misrepresentation.

–07 Whether this concentration on the knowledge of parties and their fault is relevant to a decision on the content of a contract, remains to be decided in Scotland. There is much to be said for the view that some of the English cases adopted devices to avoid the rule that damages were unobtainable for innocent misrepresentation, a rule now modified, in England, by the Misrepresentation Act 1967, s.2(*a*) and, in Scotland, by the Law Reform (Miscellaneous Provisions) (Scotland) Act 1985, s.10. Another reason for cautious reliance on English authority is the doctrine of collateral warranty. Lord Denning put it this way[11]:

> "Ever since *Heilbut, Symons & Co.* v. *Buckleton* [1913] A.C. 30, we have had to contend with the law as laid down by the House of Lords that an innocent misrepresentation gives no right to damages. In order to escape from that rule, the pleader used to allege—I often did it myself—that the misrepresentation was fraudulent, or alternatively a collateral warranty. At the trial we nearly always succeeded on collateral warranty. We had to reckon, of course, with the dictum of Lord Moulton, at p. 47, that 'such collateral contracts must from their very nature be rare.' But more often than not the court elevated the innocent misrepresentation into a collateral warranty; and thereby did justice—in advance of the Misrepresentation Act 1967. I remember scores of cases of that kind, especially on the sale of a business. A representation as to the profits that had been made in the past was invariably held to be a warranty."

---

[8] See opinion of Hodson L.J.
[9] [1965] 2 All E.R. 65.
[10] [1976] 1 Q.B. 801.
[11] *Esso Petroleum* v. *Mardon, sup. cit.* at p. 817.

3–08   There will be less need in English law to rely on collateral warranty where there is a representation of present or past fact because a remedy in damages may be available under the Misrepresentation Act 1967. Where the assurance is as to the future the Act does not apply and the concept of collateral warranty may be used.[12]

Collateral Statements and Scots Law

3–09   In Scots law the idea of collateral warranty in the English sense does not exist. There can be collateral agreements (and presumably collateral promises) but in practice founding on these can run into the difficulty that an agreement in writing should not be contradicted or added to by oral terms.[13]

Proof of collateral agreements is "very limited indeed."[14] It has been held competent to prove that a writing was executed subject to an oral understanding that it would not take effect until a condition was purified.[15] In *Renison* v. *Bryce*,[16] the defender alleged that there was a verbal agreement on the size of the capital of a company to be formed. There was some ambiguity in the terms of the written agreement and a proof of the verbal agreement was allowed.[17] A letter of application for a job has been held to at least embody a collateral undertaking to a contract of employment.[18] In *McInally* v. *Esso Petroleum Ltd.*[19] the pursuer founded on a verbal agreement prior to a formal contract relating to a petrol filling and service station. He did not attempt to alter or contradict the formal contract. Lord Avonside allowed a proof before answer but was reluctant to use the term "collateral." What is meant by "collateral" in this context has not been decided and remains, in Lord Justice-Clerk Thomson's words, "a nice question."[20]

PRACTICAL PROBLEMS ARISING FROM THE DISTINCTION BETWEEN A REPRESENTATION AND A TERM

3–10   The problem of the content of the contract is in the first instance a problem of fact. What did the parties agree? No general principle is applicable nor are decided cases always helpful. The factors which the courts

---

[12] *J. Evans & Son (Portsmouth) Ltd.* v. *Andrea Merzario Ltd.* [1976] 2 All E.R. 930.

[13] *e.g. Inglis* v. *Buttery & Co.* (1877) 5 R. 58 at p. 69 *per* Lord Gifford, 5 R.(H.L.) 87; *Alexander* v. *Gillon* (1847) 9 D. 524 and *Norval* v. *Abbey*, 1939 S.C. 724; *Perdikou* v. *Pattison*, 1958 S.L.T. 153.

[14] Walker and Walker, p. 25; *Garden* v. *Earl of Aberdeen* (1893) 20 R. 896; *William Masson Ltd.* v. *Scottish Brewers Ltd.*, 1966 S.C. 9.

[15] *Dodds* v. *Walker* (1822) 2 S.81; *Semple* v. *Kyle* (1902) 4 F. 421; *Abrahams & Sons* v. *Robert Miller (Denny) Ltd.*, 1933 S.C. 171.

[16] (1898) 25 R. 521.

[17] *Cf.* Gloag's treatment of this case in *Contract*, pp. 370, 371.

[18] *British Workman's and General Ass. Co.* v. *Wilkinson* (1900) 8 S.L.T. 67.

[19] 1965 S.L.T.(Notes) 13.

[20] *Perdikou* v. *Pattison, sup. cit.* at p. 157. See also Sheriff-Substitute Allan G. Walker at p. 155; Macphail, *Evidence*, para. 15.12.

(mainly in England) have looked at are relevant for the precognoscer who needs to collect the following information:

1. Evidence of all statements and contracts oral and in writing which have been founded on.

2. The period of time between the making of the statement and the formation of the contract.

3. The relative knowledge the parties had, or reasonably could have had, about the accuracy of the statement.[21] What prior dealings were there between the parties? What was the nature of their respective trades?

4. Whether fraud can be proved.[22]

5. Whether the statement can be viewed as an expression of opinion or an advertising "puff."[23]

6. Whether the terms of the contract would be varied or added to by the statement.

3-11 To avoid the difficulties created by the distinction between a representation and a term and by the possible existence of a collateral agreement the draftsman of a contract may make express provision in a form similar to this:

"This is the complete agreement between the parties and supersedes all prior agreements and negotiations."

3-12 The contract may go further and state that the contract is not affected by the statements of an agent or employee.

3-13 These expressions of the intentions of the parties are effective subject to some observations. The authority of an agent is a question of fact and it does not follow that a party has excluded his liability for the misrepresentation of an authorised agent.[24]

3-14 A person cannot exclude his liability for a fraudulent misrepresentation or take advantage of the false and fraudulent (or perhaps merely false) statement of his agent.[25] Problems of modes of proof do not prevent the proof of fraud by parole evidence. "The gates of justice are open wide in the tracing of fraud."[26] If the contract is attacked on the ground that the assent to it was invalid (*e.g.* induced by innocent misrepresentation or fraud and circumvention) that is subject to parole proof, and if proved and if the contract is reduced, the terms of the contract, including the clause quoted, will no longer apply.[27] This result also

---

[21] Depending on the view taken of the application in Scotland of the English cases cited above at paras. 3–03 to 3–06.

[22] On the importance of this, see para. 3–14.

[23] See para. 3–25.

[24] *Laing* v. *Provincial Homes Investment Co.*, 1909 S.C. 812.

[25] *Mair* v. *Rio Grande Rubber Estates Ltd.*, 1913 S.C.(H.L.) 74; *Boyd & Forrest* v. *Glasgow & S.W. Ry. Co.*, 1915 S.C.(H.L.) 20 at pp. 35, 36 *per* Lord Shaw.

[26] *Tennent* v. *Tennent's Trs.* (1868) 6 M. 840 at p. 874 *per* Lord Ardmillan; *Bell Bros.* v. *Aitken*, 1939 S.C. 577 at p. 585 *per* Lord President Normand.

[27] *Napier* v. *Sharp* (1851) 14 D. 313; *British Guarantee Association* v. *Western Bank* (1853) 15 D. 834; *Steuart's Trs.* v. *Hart* (1875) 3 R. 192.

applies to clauses in contracts which attempt to exclude all that was said or done before by a statement that one party has satisfied himself as to the condition of the goods.[28]

Invitations to Treat; Estimates and Tenders

3–15 Some of the statements made during negotiations are not intended to form part of a contract. A distinction can be drawn between an expression of willingness to contract and an offer to contract. Only the offer to contract can be accepted with the result that there is a contract.

3–16   The difference between the various types of statements depends on the objective intention of the parties. Examples can be given of how the courts have approached these problems, but each case must be looked at on its facts.

3–17   The potential seller of goods or services may advertise his products, send out lists of prices on or without request, or display his wares in a shop.

3–18   The following have been held not to be offers:

The circulation of a catalogue or price list[29]; a statement in a telegram as to price[30]; a statement (in response to an inquiry) that a council "may be prepared to sell"[31]; a display of goods in a shop with prices attached[32]; advertisements of products[33] or prizes[34] or an exhibition[35]; the invitation of bids by an auctioneer.[36]

3–19   On the other hand, the following have been held to be offers:

A letter offering linseed for shipment at a stated price and with the words, "I shall be glad to hear if you are buyers"[37]; a form to be filled in by the customer with the words, "we hereby agree to hire on the above conditions"[38]; a display of deck-chairs for hire with conditions stated on a notice[39]; a notice at the entrance to an automatic car park[40]; a promise in an advertisement to pay £100 to any person who used a carbolic smokeball and who then caught influenza.[41]

---

[28] *Bell Bros.* v. *Aitken, sup. cit.*

[29] *Grainger & Son* v. *Gough* [1896] A.C. 325.

[30] *Harvey* v. *Facey* [1893] A.C. 552; *Rapalli* v. *Take Ltd.* [1958] 2 Lloyd's Rep. 469.

[31] *Gibson* v. *Manchester C.C.* [1979] 1 All E.R. 972.

[32] *Fisher* v. *Bell* [1961] 1 Q.B. 394 (effect of decision changed by Restriction of Offensive Weapons Act 1961, s.1).

[33] *Partridge* v. *Crittenden* [1968] 2 All E.R. 421.

[34] *Rooke* v. *Dawson* [1895] 1 Ch. 480.

[35] *McAskill* v. *Scottish Exhibition of National History, Art and Industry, Glasgow* (1912) 28 Sh.Ct.Rep. 176 (a person may travel a long way to the exhibition and incur expense; on the other hand the organisers wish a discretion to refuse entry. The contract is concluded when the entrance fee is accepted).

[36] *British Car Auctions Ltd.* v. *Wright* [1972] 3 All E.R. 462.

[37] *Philp & Co.* v. *Knoblauch*, 1907 S.C. 994.

[38] *Chisholm* v. *Robertson* (1883) 10 R. 760.

[39] *Chapelton* v. *Barry U.D.C.* [1940] 1 K.B. 532.

[40] *Thornton* v. *Shoe Lane Parking Ltd.* [1971] 2 Q.B. 163.

[41] *Carlill* v. *Carbolic Smoke Ball Co. Ltd.* [1893] 1 Q.B. 256.

20   The potential purchaser of goods or services may request tenders. Generally he is inviting offers. The request itself is not an offer. Usually the tender (even if called an estimate) will be an offer.[42] On the other hand preliminary work may be evidence of a contract.[43]

Letters of intent

21   A letter of intent is one of those ambiguous documents used by businessmen when they wish both to have a contract and to be able to get out of the contract. A letter of intent may be no more than an expression of willingness to contract. On the other hand it can be an offer. If, to the knowledge of the parties, work has followed on the letter, there may be a contract, provided that the essentials of a contract have been agreed.[44] If the essentials have not been agreed payment for the work depends on the principles of recompense. There can be a concluded contract followed by a letter of intent.[45]

22   An "understanding" can create similar problems about whether it gives rise to a binding contract or not.[46]

Letters "without prejudice"

23   Letters written "without prejudice" may be part of a binding contract and not merely statements in negotiation. It has been observed in England[47]:

> "What is the meaning of the words 'without prejudice'? I think they mean without prejudice to the position of the writer of the letter if the terms he proposes are not accepted. If the terms proposed in the letter are accepted a complete contract is established and the letter, although written without prejudice, operates to alter the old state of things and to establish a new one."

---

[42] *Manchester Diocesan Council for Education* v. *Commercial and General Investments Ltd.* [1969] 3 All E.R. 1593.

[43] See para. 3–29.

[44] *British Steel Corp* v. *Cleveland Bridge and Engineering Co. Ltd.* [1984] 1 All E.R. 504. An expression of intention by a government or local authority is in a special position because it may be incompetent to fetter future executive action. See *Rederiaktiebolaget Amphitrite* v. *R.* [1921] 3 K.B. 500 and para. 8–66.

[45] *Uniroyal Ltd.* v. *Miller & Co. Ltd.*, 1985 S.L.T. 101; on a contract to be followed by a formal document see para. 4–13.

[46] *Muirhead* v. *Gribben*, 1983 S.L.T.(Sh.Ct.) 102; *Sterling Engineering Co.* v. *Patchett* [1955] A.C. 534. *J. H. Milner & Son* v. *Bilton* [1966] 2 All E.R. 894; *cf. Gore* v. *Van der Laun* [1976] 2 Q.B. 31.

[47] *Walker* v. *Wilsher* (1889) 23 Q.B.D 335 at p. 337 *per* Lindley L.J.; followed in *Tomlin* v. *Standard Telephones and Cables Ltd.* [1969] 3 All E.R. 201. A distinct reservation of rights when making a payment (not merely a protest) may enable the payments to be recovered under the *conditio indebiti*, as when payments were made without prejudice, under objection and reserving all competent rights: *British Railways Board* v. *Glasgow Corp.*, 1976 S.C. 224. There can also be an implied contract between parties in similar circumstances; *Haddon's Exrx.* v. *Scottish Milk Marketing Board*, 1938 S.C. 168; on the possible effect of payment made without reservation of rights, see para. 23–16.

"Ex gratia" offers

3–24   The words *"ex gratia"* do not necessarily or even probably imply that a statement is to be without legal effect. The expression is equivalent to "without admission of liability," and binding settlements of disputes are often made on that basis.[48] The words may mean: "I do not admit any antecedent liability, but I agree to pay."[49]

Opinions and advertising "puffs"

3–25   An expression of opinion or *verba jactantia* is not a representation with the effect of giving the remedies applicable to misrepresentation inducing a contract. Even if part of the contract, the statements may be without legal effect. To say that a mare was "sound" and "good" was treated in the circumstances as *verba volantia*.[50] "It would," said Lord President Inglis, "be absurd to attach any importance to such words." A statement in a newspaper advertisement of the number of animals which could be grazed on a hill farm was treated as an expression of opinion and not as a warranty.[51] A statement that a motor vehicle was in good running order was viewed as an expression of the seller's opinion.[52]

3–26   A prospectus did not contain a misrepresentation but merely "some high colouring or grandiloquence" in a statement which was substantially true.[53] In Lord Ardmillan's words,[54] there was not a misrepresentation:

> "in respect of any mere inaccuracy in the prospectus, or of any mere exaggeration and high colouring in the sanguine and attractive painting of the anticipated advantages and the encouraging prospects of the company. Exaggeration is common, and is indeed to be expected in such a matter, and the language of a prospectus is always received with some qualification. Unless something of the character of fraud or wilful falsehood has been instructed, I do not think that the defender can succeed on this plea."

Other cases

3–27   Whether an agreement or a statement is binding in honour or whether it is a contract is an issue raised in other cases which are discussed elsewhere.[55]

---

[48] *Edwards* v. *Skyways Ltd.* [1964] 1 All E.R. 494.

[49] *Wick Harbour Trs.* v. *Admiralty*, 1921 2 S.L.T. 109 at p. 111 *per* Lord Sands (this opinion gives examples of the difference between an intention to pay and an agreement to pay).

[50] *Robeson* v. *Waugh* (1874) 2 R. 63; See also *Wilson* v. *Turnbull & Co.* (1896) 23 R. 714; *cf. Rose* v. *Johnston* (1878) 5 R. 600.

[51] *Hamilton* v. *Duke of Montrose* (1906) 8 F. 1026.

[52] *Flynn* v. *Scott*, 1949 S.C. 442. See also *Brownlie* v. *Miller* (1880) 7 R.(H.L.) 66; *Sutherland* v. *Bremner's Trs..* (1903) 10 S.L.T. 565; *Romanes* v. *Garman*, 1912 2 S.L.T. 104 at p. 105 *per* Lord President Dunedin; *cf. Carlill* v. *Carbolic Smoke Ball Co.*, *sup. cit.*

[53] *City of Edinburgh Brewery Co.* v. *Gibson's Tr.* (1869) 7 M. 886 at p. 891 *per* Lord President Inglis.

[54] *Ibid.* at pp. 892, 893; on compensation for subscribers misled by a statement in a prospectus, see Companies Act 1985, s.67.

[55] See paras. 4–38 *et seq.*

Cost of pre-contract negotiations and work

28   Negotiations may break down after one party has incurred considerable expense. Surveys may have been carried out, reports prepared,
fabrication work carried out and legal documents drafted. At the last
minute one party refuses to sign. *Quid juris?* There are two possible
answers.

29   (1) **Implied contract** It may be that preliminary work was done on the
instructions of one party who must pay for the work even if the project
does not proceed. There is an implied contract. When printers carried
out work for a catalogue which was eventually not ordered, they were
entitled to remuneration *quantum meruit*.[56] The preliminary drawings of
architects had to be paid for[57] as had the drawings of proposed alterations to premises produced by a joiner.[58] It was not a defence to an
architect's claim for remuneration for preparing plans for a school that
the building of the school had been postponed by war.[59] A surveyor has
been paid for measurements although the building was not built.[60]

30   When parties are engaged on an object of common interest and the
end aimed for is not achieved, one party may have an indemnity for
expenses from the other party. This may be on the basis of an implied
condition of the arrangement[61] or as a consequence of a partnership or
joint venture.[62]

31   If parties have agreed that their arrangements are to be embodied in a
formal written contract there may be *locus poenitentiae* until either the
execution of the document, or the setting up of a contract by *rei interventus*.[63] In the absence of a contract there can neither be a claim for
damages for breach of contract nor a claim for remuneration *quantum
meruit*.[64] The existence of a contract may, on the other hand, bar a claim
in recompense.[65] A person should normally exercise his contractual

---

[56] *Pillans & Wilson* v. *Castlecary Fireclay Co. Ltd.*, 1931 S.L.T. 532. A contract may
also be implied when work is done in breach of contract but nevertheless accepted: *PEC
Barr Printers Ltd.* v. *Forth Print Ltd.*, 1980 S.L.T.(Sh.Ct.) 118.

[57] *Robert Allan & Partners* v. *McKinstray*, 1975 S.L.T. (Sh.Ct.) 63 (which discusses calculation of remuneration). See also para. 6–41.

[58] *Sinclair* v. *Logan*, 1961 S.L.T.(Sh.Ct.) 10.

[59] *Constable* v. *Uphall School Board* (1918) 35 Sh.Ct.Rep. 27.

[60] *Rattray* v. *Yuille* (1878) 2 Guthrie Sh.Ct.Rep. 107.

[61] *Dobie* v. *Lauder's Trs.* (1873) 11 M. 749; see comments on this case in *Microwave
Systems (Scotland) Ltd.* v. *Electro-Physiological Instruments Ltd.*, 1971 S.C. 140.

[62] Partnership Act 1890, s.24(2).

[63] *Van Laun & Co.* v. *Neilson Reid & Co.* (1904) 6 F. 644. There can be an agreement
which is followed by formal writing. Whether or not the existence of writing is suspensive
of obligation is discussed at para. 4–13.

[64] *Van Laun & Co.* v. *Neilson Reid & Co., sup. cit.*

[65] Because another legal remedy is available—*Varney (Scotland) Ltd.* v. *Burgh of
Lanark*, 1976 S.L.T. 46; *Express Coach Finishers* v. *Caulfield*, 1968 S.L.T.(Sh.Ct.) 11.

rights by, for example, claiming against his employer, rather than seeking recompense from those who may have benefited from his services.[66]

3-32 (2) **Recompense** If one party has benefited from the work of another, it might be possible in the absence of a contract, to claim recompense. No one is entitled in bad faith to enrich himself at the expense of another.[67] When parties have acted in good faith, it appears very difficult in this context to have a successful case based on recompense.

3-33 In *Gilchrist* v. *Whyte*[68] there were abortive negotiations for a loan on heritage. Expense had been incurred. An action was raised which claimed alternatively for damages for breach of contract or for recompense. Both grounds of the action were dismissed as irrelevant. The claim based on recompense failed because the statement which induced expense was held to be an expression of opinion and not, as claimed, a representation.

3-34 Lord Ardwall concluded from the authorities[69]:

"I think it may be inferred that an action of damages founded on the ground of recompense for loss caused through the failure to complete or carry out a contract, but where there has been no breach of contract, will only be entertained by the Court in very special circumstances indeed, and for the most part only in cases where (1) loss has been wrongfully caused by one of the parties to the other, excluding, however, loss or expense incurred as part of the abortive negotiations between the parties; (2) where the wrong has been done without any excuse; and (3) where the losing party is in no way to blame for the loss.

"But it need hardly be pointed out how inconvenient and ridiculous it would be if in any case where a person has been put to expense and trouble in the hope or expectation or anticipation of a contract being concluded, and after all no contract is concluded, he should be entitled to ask a court of law to entertain and investigate a claim of damages against the party who withdrew from the negotiations, it being in law the right of everyone to resile from a contract before final consents have been exchanged, or, in the case of heritage, before it has been concluded *habili modo* by writing or otherwise. If such actions were to be allowed it would necessitate an inquiry in every case of the kind into nice and difficult questions as to which of the parties had behaved reasonably or unreasonably in order to determine the question of who was to blame for the contract not being proceeded with. Such actions accordingly will not as a rule be entertained by Courts of law."

3-35 In *Microwave Systems (Scotland) Ltd.* v. *Electro-Physiological Instruments Ltd.*[70] negotiations for a company merger broke down after one party had occupied space in the other party's factory. There was a claim

---

[66] *Thomson, Jackson, Gourlay and Taylor* v. *Lochhead* (1889) 16 R. 373; *Robertson* v. *Beatson McLeod & Co. Ltd.*, 1908 S.C. 921. For an exceptional case see *Fernie* v. *Robertson* (1871) 9 M. 437 and other cases involving *negotiorum gestio*; Gloag, pp. 334, 335.

[67] *Bell* v. *Bell* (1841) 3 D. 1201; *Allan* v. *Gilchrist* (1875) 2 R. 587 at p. 592 *per* Lord Deas.

[68] 1907 S.C. 984.

[69] *Ibid.* at pp. 993, 994.

[70] 1971 S.C. 140.

for the cost of lighting, heating and other facilities. The averments based on recompense and implied contract were held to be irrelevant. The case based on recompense failed because what was supplied was to the benefit not of the defenders but of the company to be created by the merger. Nor were the circumstances such as to imply a condition that in the event of a breakdown in negotiations the defenders should reimburse the pursuers for services rendered primarily to benefit the company to be formed.

36   In *Site Preparations Ltd.* v. *Secretary of State for Scotland*[71] the pursuers sought recompense for the preparation of plans to develop Peterhead Harbour. The plans had been produced in the hope of a contract to do the work. No such contract was made. The pursuers averred that the defender had used the information supplied by the pursuers. The action was dismissed as irrelevant on the grounds that a claim for recompense was excluded when the expenditure was incurred in the expectation of benefit to the spender.

37   The difficulty in recovering loss arising from abortive negotiation is bringing the heads of loss within the conditions for a recompense claim which are: (1) the pursuer must show a loss; (2) the pursuer must not have had the intention of donation; (3) the defender must have gained; (4) the expense must not have been incurred for the pursuer's benefit; (5) according to some authorities, but not others, there must be an error of fact; and (6) reimbursement must in all the circumstances be equitable.[72]

38   In *Mellor* v. *William Beardmore & Co.*[73] an employee was entitled to recompense as a result of his employer's use of his invention.

Acting on an inchoate agreement

39   There may not be a contract, but that might not be the end of the problem. Part of the inchoate agreement may have been implemented. In *Wilson* v. *Marquis of Breadalbane*[74] bullocks were delivered. The parties disagreed on price and restitution of the bullocks was not offered.[75] There was no contract of sale because of the absence of *consensus*, but the defender had to pay the value of the cattle received by him. In *Stuart & Co.* v. *Kennedy*[76] there was no *consensus* on price

---

[71] 1975 S.L.T.(Notes) 41.

[72] *Varney (Scotland) Ltd.* v. *Burgh of Lanark*, 1976 S.L.T. 46; *Lawrence Building Co. Ltd.* v. *Lanark C.C.*, 1978 S.C. 30; *Trade Development Bank* v. *Warriner & Mason*, 1980 S.C. 74. Other legal remedies may bar recompense: *City of Glasgow D.C.* v. *Morrison McChlery & Co.*, 1985 S.L.T. 44; *Cliffplant Ltd.* v. *Kinnaird*, 1981 S.C. 9 at p. 28 *per* Lord Avonside.

[73] 1927 S.C. 597; see now Patents Act 1977, s.40.

[74] (1859) 21 D. 957.

[75] The cattle were delivered in October 1854 and correspondence continued for nearly a year thereafter. The decision in three courts was that a price had been fixed. Only on appeal to the Second Division in 1859 was it held that a contract did not exist. Presumably by then *restitutio in integrum* was impossible.

[76] (1885) 13 R. 221.

because of a misunderstanding about whether stone coping had to be paid for according to lineal feet or superficial feet. A substantial quantity of coping had been delivered. Lord President Inglis observed[77]:

> "If there is no *consensus in idem placitum*, the effect of course is, that there is no contract at all, and that parties are as free as they were before they had had any negotiations. But if something has followed, if the contract is partly or wholly performed, you cannot then undo the contract and hold both parties free. Now, here, coping to the extent of 394 feet, or more than half of the whole, had been delivered and received.[78] That being so, *res non sunt integrae*, the contract cannot be resolved or undone, and therefore we must see that there shall be some kind of performance on the other side. To determine what that is to be, we revert to the rule of *Wilson's* case, and hold that the actual value of the subject delivered, as that is ascertained by the market price, is the measure of the defender's liability."

In *Lennox* v. *Rennie*[79] the principles mentioned were applied to the delivery of horses where there was no agreement on price. In *Glynwed Distribution Ltd.* v. *S. Koronka & Co.*,[80] however, the cases of *Wilson* and *Stuart* were treated as cases where there was a contract of sale but a misunderstanding in relation to the price. In *Glynwed* the parties had sold steel but each party claimed that the sale had been at a different price. The court fixed a reasonable price in terms of the Sale of Goods Act. But it is suggested that *Glynwed* was wrongly decided, because if a price is not agreed, nor is a method of fixing it agreed, there is no sale.

3–40   In England actions following on an agreement have led the courts to imply reasonable terms to give effect to the intention of the parties.[81]

---

[77] at pp. 222, 223.

[78] In the report, (1885) 23 S.L.R. 149 at p. 152, Lord President Inglis referred to a payment to account of the price as evidence of performance of part of the agreement. In this case, as in the report of *Wilson* at (1859) 31 Sc.Jur. 525, there are differences between the Session Case Reports and other reports.

[79] 1951 S.L.T.(Notes) 78.

[80] 1977 S.C. 1: *cf. R. & J. Dempster* v. *Motherwell Bridge and Engineering Co.*, 1964 S.C. 308 at p. 332 *per* Lord Guthrie; *Steel* v. *Bradley Homes*, 1972 S.C. 48 at p. 58 *per* Lord Dunpark; para. 4–03.

[81] See para. 4–33.

CHAPTER 4

THE FORMATION OF A CONTRACT

Is there a contract?

-01   In the mass of verbal communications, letters, telexes and other missives between the parties, there may or may not be a contract. People do not always sign a document headed "Contract" or "Agreement." The components of their bargain have to be searched for. Even if it is decided that agreement has been reached on certain identified points, it does not always follow that there is a contract. There may not be an enforceable contract because: (1) there is failure to agree on all the essentials required by law for the type of contract in question; (2) there remains dispute between the parties on some matter affecting the contract; (3) the agreement, or part of it, is void from uncertainty; (4) the parties did not intend to enter an enforceable contract; or (5) the agreement is void, voidable, unenforceable or illegal because of invalidating factors such as lack of capacity to contract or because it is an agreement contrary to public policy. The last of these is the subject-matter of other chapters. This chapter is concerned with the other four issues.

FAILURE TO AGREE ON ESSENTIALS REQUIRED BY LAW

-02   As Viscount Dunedin put it[1]:

> "To be a good contract there must be a concluded bargain and a concluded contract is one which settles everything that is necessary to be settled and leaves nothing to be settled by agreement between the parties. Of course, it may leave something which still has to be determined, but then that determination must be a determination which does not depend upon the agreement between the parties. In the system of law in which I was brought up, that was expressed by one of those brocards of which perhaps we have been too fond, but which often express very neatly what is wanted: 'Certum est quod certum reddi potest.' Therefore, you may very well agree that a certain part of the contract of sale, such as price, may be settled by someone else. As a matter of the general law of contract all the essentials have to be settled. What are the essentials may vary according to the particular contract under consideration."

-03   So it was that failure to agree on the four cardinal elements of a lease meant that there was no contract. The essential elements for that type of contract are the parties, the subjects, the rent and the duration.[2]

---

[1] *May & Butcher Ltd.* v. *R.* (1929), noted at [1934] 2 K.B. 17, at p. 21.

[2] *Gray* v. *Edinburgh University*, 1962 S.C. 157. On failure to agree on ish see *Hyams* v. *Brechin*, 1979 S.L.T.(Sh.Ct.) 47; *Trade Development Bank Ltd.* v. *W. Haig (Bellshill) Ltd.*, 1983 S.L.T. 510.

A contract of sale requires *inter alia* agreement on price or the method of fixing a price,[3] as may a contract for services.[4] It may be, however, that a reasonable price is implied.[5] On the other hand in *R. & J. Dempster* v. *Motherwell Bridge and Engineering Co.*[6] there was a valid contract to manufacture oil storage tanks although there was no agreement on price. There were special market circumstances. It was observed by Lord Guthrie[7]:

> "The object of our law of contract is to facilitate the transactions of commercial men, and not to create obstacles in the way of solving practical problems arising out of the circumstances confronting them, or to expose them to unnecessary pitfalls. I know of no rule of law which prevents men from entering into special agreements to meet the requirements of special circumstances."

4-04   In Lord President Clyde's words[8]: "the essence of commerce is making bargains, and unenforceable arrangements are the exception and not the rule."

4-05   There is a similar approach in England.[9] Thus latitude has been allowed on the terms of a contract of employment,[10] on a right of pre-emption[11] and on an option.[12]

THE PARTIES REMAIN IN DISPUTE

4-06   Apart from the essentials required by law, there may not be a completed contract because the parties have not agreed on all the issues between them. For example, a failure to agree on servitudes although the subjects sold and the price had been agreed[13]; a dispute on a liability for streets and sewers in a contract of loan secured over heritage[14]; and a failure to agree on furniture in the sale of the leases of a castle, although the items in dispute might not have been of great money value.[15] On the other hand, parties can have a completed contract although there is an item of detail to be settled in the future.[16]

---

[3] *Foley* v. *Classique Coaches Ltd.* [1934] 2 K.B. 1; *May & Butcher Ltd.* v. *R. supra*; *Hillas & Co. Ltd.* v. *Arcos Ltd.* (1932) 147 L.T. 503.

[4] *Courtney & Fairbairn Ltd.* v. *Tolaini Bros. (Hotels) Ltd.* [1975] 1 All E.R. 716.

[5] Sale of Goods Act 1979, s.8; *Glynwed Distribution Ltd.* v. *S. Koronka & Co.*, 1977 S.C. 1. See, however, para. 3–39.

[6] 1964 S.C. 308.

[7] at p. 332.

[8] at p. 328.

[9] *Brown* v. *Gould* [1972] Ch. 53.

[10] *National Coal Board* v. *Galley* [1958] 1 All E.R. 91.

[11] *Smith* v. *Morgan* [1971] 2 All E.R. 1500.

[12] *Brown* v. *Gould, supra.*

[13] *Heiton* v. *Waverley Hydropathic Co.* (1877) 4 R. 830.

[14] *Gilchrist* v. *Whyte*, 1907 S.C. 984.

[15] *Burnley* v. *Alford*, 1919 2 S.L.T. 123—the contract was regarded as indivisible. In other circumstances there could be separate contracts for heritage and moveables. See also para. 4–17.

[16] *Freeman* v. *Maxwell*, 1928 S.C. 682.

07   It can be taken from the cases cited that the parties may themselves determine the scope of their contract, for example, whether a sale includes both heritage and moveables. If there is disagreement on an item of an inchoate contract, there will not be a contract even although a bargain could be made out of what has been agreed.

A contract subject to a suspensive condition

08   There are two types of suspensive condition. A condition may be suspensive of the whole contract. This is our present concern and distinguishable from a condition suspensive of part of a contract, such as a condition suspensive of the passing of property under a contract of sale.[17] But in both cases there may be a contract. Neither party may resile. As Mungo Brown put it[18]:

> "When a sale is made under a suspensive condition the contract is not complete until the accomplishment of the condition. It is not to be supposed from this, however, that the agreement of parties produces no effect whatever in the intermediate period, or that no right whatever arises to either party from the imperfect contract. On the contrary, while the condition is yet pendent, neither party is at liberty to resile, any more than in the case of an unconditional bargain, and if the condition happens to be accomplished the accomplishment of it has a retrospective effect to the date of the contract, so that if either party have died in the interim his rights under contract will pass to his heir."

09   Despite this, if the condition is suspensive of the whole contract, there are two possible theoretical positions. The first is that there is no contract. For example, a man says to a shop assistant: "I will buy the vase, if my wife likes it." "Certainly, sir," is the reply. The approving wife returns with her husband to the shop next day. In the interim the vase has been sold to a third party. If there is a contract, the shopkeeper is in breach. But a reasonable view might be that the parties were still at the stage of negotiating. There may have been one fact preventing a concluded bargain. That fact might be suspensive of agreement.[19] But even if it were purified there would not, it is suggested, automatically be a contract. The fact of purification would need communication to the relevant parties who should assent to a concluded contract.

10   The second view is that there is a contract. This has the consequence (unlike the first view) that purification of the condition would automatically have an effect. *Locus poenitentiae* would not exist. The differences

---

[17] *e.g. Murdoch & Co. Ltd.* v. *Greig* (1889) 16 R. 396. *Aluminium Industrie Vaassen B.V.* v. *Romalpa Aluminium Ltd.* [1976] 2 All E.R. 552. See "Retention of Title," para. 13–67 *et seq.*

[18] Brown on *Sale*, p. 43, quoted with approval *per* Lord President Inglis in *Murdoch & Co. Ltd.* v. *Greig, supra.*

[19] *e.g. Towill & Co.* v. *British Agricultural Assoc.* (1875) 3 R. 117; *Stobo Ltd.* v. *Morrisons (Gowns) Ltd.*, 1949 S.C. 184. Obviously if the suspensive condition is the entering into of a concluded written contract, the purification of the condition produces a contract.

between these views have not received analysis in Scottish courts, yet there is a difference between a condition suspensive of a contract and a contract subject to a suspensive condition. In most cases the difference may be immaterial, particularly if there is no purification of the condition. However, if there is purification, but one party then wishes to resile, the difference is crucial.

4–11   Examples of "suspensive conditions" applying to the whole obligation (without the distinction just referred to being elaborated upon) have been the confirmation or ratification of a board, or party to the contract[20]; a requirement that mines be purchased[21]; an agreement subject to a licence being transferred,[22] or the approval of a curator *ad litem* obtained[23]; the failure to obtain the approval of other creditors to an arrangement to pay debts[24]; the refusal of all the feuars to pay for a servitude[25]; the failure of one son to accept an arrangement on his mother's liferent[26]; the failure of a railway company to make a railway.[27] When a bankrupt failed to implement a compromise, the original agreement revived and the whole debt was due.[28]

4–12   When a contract is subject to a suspensive condition the parties are not necessarily bound indefinitely because the condition cannot be purified. The contract may fix a date for purification of the condition or it may be implied that the condition must be fulfilled within a reasonable time.[29] A suspensive condition which is solely for the benefit of one party may be waived by that party, who can then insist on implement of the contract. But if more than one party has an interest in the condition, even if that interest may arise exceptionally, unilateral waiver is not possible.[30] Waiver must take place before the condition is purified, or not, as the case may be.[31]

An agreement to be followed by writing

4–13   Parties may enter into an agreement which is to be followed by a formal written agreement. This gives rise to various problems about the relationship between the two agreements. Of present concern is a stipu-

---

[20] *Towill & Co. v. British Agricultural Assoc., supra; Abrahams & Sons v. Robert Miller (Denny) Ltd.*, 1933 S.C. 171.

[21] *Consolidated Copper Co. of Canada v. Peddie* (1877) 5 R. 393.

[22] *McArthur's Exrs. v. Guild* 1908 S.C. 743.

[23] *Donaldson's Exr. v. Sharp & Sons*, 1922 S.C. 566.

[24] *Culcreuch Cotton Co. v. Mathie* (1823) 2 S. 513.

[25] *Brown v. Nielson* (1825) 4 S. 271—money already paid had to be returned.

[26] *Paterson v. Paterson* (1849) 11 D. 441.

[27] *Philip v. Edinburgh, Perth & Dundee Ry.* (1857) 19 D. (H.L.) 13.

[28] *Duke of Argyll v. McAlpine's Trs.* (1825) 4 S. 32.

[29] *T. Boland & Co. v. Dundas's Trs.*, 1975 S.L.T.(Notes) 80.

[30] *Ellis & Sons Second Amalgamated Properties Ltd. v. Pringle*, 1974 S.C. 200, discusses *Dewar and Finlay Ltd. v. Blackwood*, 1968 S.L.T. 196; *Gilchrist v. Payton*; 1979 S.C. 380; *Imry Property Holdings Ltd. v. Glasgow Young Men's Christian Assoc.*, 1979 S.L.T. 261.

[31] *Gilchrist v. Payton, supra.*

lation that the first agreement is subject to the preparation of a written document incorporating its terms. This is distinct from (1) a writing ancillary to a verbal contract, *e.g.* a ticket with conditions incorporated into an oral contract; (2) a verbal contract followed by writing, *e.g.* an oral sale later incorporated into printed order forms or followed by a written confirmation[32]; and (3) an informal writing to be followed by a formal deed, *e.g.* missives to be superseded by a disposition. In all these cases the existence of the further writing is not suspensive of obligation. But there are other situations in which it is.

14   As Lord President Cooper put it[33]:

> "It is perfectly possible for the parties to an apparent contract to provide that there shall be *locus poenitentiae* until the terms of their agreement have been reduced to a formal contract; but that the bare fact that the parties to a completed agreement stipulated that it shall be embodied in a formal contract does not necessarily import that they are still in the stage of negotiation. In each instance it is a matter of the construction of the correspondence in the light of the facts, proved or averred, on which side of the border-line the case lies."

In that case the words "subject to contract" were treated as suspensive of agreement. In *Alexander* v. *Montgomery*[34] there was written correspondence on the sale of coal which did not amount to a final agreement because the parties had stipulated that their contract was to be in a formal deed. In *Van Laun & Co.* v. *Neilson Reid & Co.*[35] an arrangement was subject to the parties entering "a proper legal contract."

15   As Lord President Kinross said[36]:

> "This document quite recognises that there is to be a proper legal contract, and that that legal contract is to contain the expression, and the only binding expression, of the agreement, and in the ordinary case where it is arranged that a legal contract in certain terms is to be entered into, an action *ex contractu* will not lie unless and until that legal contract has been entered into."

16   Therefore there can be writing indicating a willingness to sell, but no concluded bargain in the absence of a formal minute.[37] It can be dangerous to pick out isolated parts of correspondence to find agreement, when the whole evidence is that a formal deed was necessary for a bind-

---

[32] *Croudace* v. *Annandale Steamship Co. Ltd.*, 1925 S.L.T. 449.

[33] *Stobo Ltd.* v. *Morrisons (Gowns) Ltd.*, *supra* at p. 192. An example of a formal memorandum not being a prerequisite to a concluded contract (although a formal document was in the mind of the parties) is *Damon Cia Naviera SA* v. *Hapag-Lloyd International SA* [1985] 1 All E.R. 475. On the other hand parties may not be bound until there is a signed agreement: *Okura & Co. Ltd.* v. *Navara Shipping Corp. SA* [1982] 2 Lloyd's Rep. 537. There can be a completed contract although one party has stated that a "letter of intent" will follow: *Uniroyal Ltd.* v. *Miller & Co. Ltd.*, 1985 S.L.T. 101.

[34] (1773) 2 Pat. 300.

[35] (1904) 6 F. 644.

[36] at p. 650.

[37] *Bakers of Edinburgh* v. *Hay* (1868) 6 S.L.R. 144.

ing contract and all else was preliminary. The principle is that there is a rebuttable presumption that parties were waiting for the duly executed instrument before binding themselves.[38]

Future adjustment

4–17   To complete a contract it is not necessary that parties have settled every matter at the time of the contract. There may be a contract although there is a formal deed with fuller clauses to be executed at a later date.[39] In a contract of sale the price may be left to be fixed by a third party.[40] In a contract for services the price may need to be adjusted in the future by the parties.[41] In a very curious and doubtful decision it was held that the contract for the sale of a villa was complete although details of the finishing of the house remained to be settled.[42]

VOID FROM UNCERTAINTY

Terminology

4–18   Gloag said: "In order to create a contractual obligation an agreement must be reasonably definite. Vague general understandings cannot be enforced."[43] He later referred to an agreement as being "void from uncertainty."[44] That phrase may mislead. The word "void" is best reserved for those situations in which consent is invalid or not recognised by the law. In cases of indefiniteness the parties are able to contract and there is not any legal prohibition affecting the subject-matter of the contract. The defect appears on the face of the contract. It may sometimes be cured by extrinsic evidence or the subsequent actings of the parties. The contract is not "void" beyond redemption. However, the phrase "void from uncertainty" is common, and likely to remain so, rather than any alternative that might be suggested such as "unenforceable from uncertainty."

---

[38] *Gordon's Exrs.* v. *Gordon* (H.L.) 1918 1 S.L.T. 407 at p. 411 *per* Viscount Haldane; *Comex Houlder Diving Ltd.* v. *Colne Fishing Co. Ltd.*, 1986 S.L.T. 250.

[39] *e.g. Erskine* v. *Glendinning* (1871) 9 M. 656; *Wight* v. *Newton*, 1911 S.C. 762.

[40] Sale of Goods Act 1979, s.8.

[41] *R. & J. Dempster Ltd.* v. *Motherwell Bridge & Engineering Co. Ltd.*, 1964 S.C. 308.

[42] *Westren* v. *Millar* (1879) 7 R. 173. Gloag appears to have doubted the case: *Contract*, p. 45, n. 1. The case can be supported on the view that there were two contracts, (1) for the sale of the house, and (2) for finishing the house. However, this is unrealistic because the price in (1) would be affected by the cost of (2). Alternatively, there was a contract for sale with the obligation on the seller, as Lord Gifford put it, to finish the house in the usual and ordinary way. But surely there was no usual and ordinary way of completing a new house on an estate in Edinburgh? To hold, as appears to have been done, that the court would, through a man of skill, fix a suitable size for the coal cellar is to assume a judicial role on style, taste and utility which is questionable. When missives had an incomplete term about a bond this was a matter of detail which did not prevent enforcement of the missives: *Freeman* v. *Maxwell*, 1928 S.C. 682.

[43] *Contract*, p. 11.

[44] *Ibid.*

19   Nor is it necessary that the terms of a contract be "certain." Precision of expression is not required. There may be much uncertainty about what is a reasonable price[45] or the effect of "about" or "approximating to."[46] Parties may use words with several meanings or say "from six to eight" weeks.[47] They may defy the rules of grammar or use slang. They may use abbreviated references.[48] Yet it is still possible for a contract to exist. The presumption is that an agreement between parties has a meaning.

20   Language is often impressionistic. That is its nature. "Words, as is well known, are the great foes of reality."[49] There may be a particular problem with English because of the richness of the tongue. We may agree with Max Beerbohm that English is a magnificent vehicle for emotional poetry, "by its very looseness, by its way of evoking rather than defining, suggesting rather than saying."[50] These are not merits in the drafting of commercial contracts. But a court would depart too far from the standards of the common man if it refused to enforce a bargain merely because there was doubt as to its meaning. "The essence of commerce is making bargains, and unenforceable arrangements are the exception and not the rule."[51] However, there comes a point at which even a court intent on a benevolent construction of a contract reaches the conclusion that the words used are too vague to have one meaning, or are incurably incomplete, or have irreconcilable conflicts.

The test of uncertainty

21   The classic test is that of Lord President Inglis in *McArthur* v. *Lawson*.[52] A contract which could not be enforced by specific implement, if implement were a competent remedy, is no contract at all. It should be noted that this was said in the context of an agreement which was lacking essential information. It is not a standard of universal application to all cases which may come under the heading of vagueness. If a word has many meanings it would be possible for the court to choose one meaning and then grant decree of specific implement. If the court refuses to select one meaning or define the application of a word it does so for considerations other than the nature of a possible remedy. There may, for example, be a reluctance to make a contract for the parties. The specific implement test has the germ of the correct approach if it is removed from the technical requirements of remedies. Assume a reasonable bys-

---

[45] Sale of Goods Act 1979, s.8 (2).

[46] *Edwards* v. *Skyways Ltd.* [1964] 1 All E.R. 494.

[47] *Ashforth* v. *Redford* (1873) L.R. 9 C.P. 20.

[48] *Bishop & Baxter Ltd.* v. *Anglo-Eastern Trading and Industrial Co. Ltd.* [1944] K.B. 12 at p. 16.

[49] Joseph Conrad, *Under Western Eyes* (1911), Part 1, prologue.

[50] *And Even Now* (1921), "On Speaking French."

[51] *R. & J. Dempster* v. *Motherwell Bridge & Engineering Co.*, 1964 S.C. 308 at p. 328 *per* Lord President Clyde: see also *Brown* v. *Gould* [1972] Ch. 53.

[52] (1877) 4 R. 1134 at p. 1136.

tander who observes the actions of the parties. Ask him: "What should happen under the contract?" The contract is unenforceable for uncertainty if he replies: "I cannot say, because the parties have not made it clear nor does the law imply an answer."

The leading cases

4–22   Before listing the cases on uncertainty of expression, it may help the pleader in search of useful *dicta* to state that the leading authorities are three decisions of the House of Lords, namely: *May & Butcher Ltd.* v. *The King*[53]; *Hillas & Co. Ltd.* v. *Arcos Ltd.*[54]; and *G. Scammell and Nephew Ltd.* v. *H.C. & J.G. Ouston.*[55] Authorities on the reluctance to hold an instrument "void" for uncertainty were gathered by Megarry J. in *Brown* v. *Gould.*[56] The decisions on the uncertainty of testamentary bequests do not apply to contractual obligations.[57]

The important case on disregarding a meaningless term is *Nicolene Ltd.* v. *Simmonds.*[58] In considering the cases it should be noted that they are only decisions on their particular facts and, moreover, it has been said that few if any topics have given rise to a greater difference of judicial opinion.[59]

The analysis of the cases

4–23   The case law can for the purposes of analysis be divided into three categories: (1) the words are too vague in meaning; (2) the agreement is incurably incomplete; and (3) parts of the agreement are contradictory. The categories are not completely distinct.

Words too vague in meaning

4–24   The following expressions have been held too vague to be enforced: an agreement to pay money if a horse was "lucky"[60]; a right to "patches of arable or improved land, at an adequate rent"[61]; a contract for the sale of an estate which reserved "the necessary land for making a railway"[62]; the meaning of "unnecessary interference" in a lease[63]; to retire

---

[53] (1929) noted at [1934] 2 K.B. 17.
[54] (1932) 147 L.T. 503, dictum of Lord Wright disapproved in *Courtney & Fairbairn* v. *Tolaini Brothers (Hotels)* [1975] 1 All E.R. 716.
[55] [1941] A.C. 251.
[56] [1972] Ch. 53.
[57] *Denny's Trs.* v. *Dumbarton Mags.*, 1945 S.C. 147.
[58] [1953] 1 Q.B. 543.
[59] *Scammell and Nephew Ltd.* v. *H. C. & J. G. Ouston, sup. cit.* at p. 254 *per* Viscount Maugham.
[60] *Guthing* v. *Lynn* (1831) 2 B. & Ad. 232.
[61] *Lord Clinton* v. *Brown* (1874) 1 R. 1137; opinions in (1874) 11 S.L.R. 665.
[62] *Pearce* v. *Watts* (1875) L.R. 20 Eq. 492.
[63] *Mundy* v. *Duke of Rutland* (1883) 23 Ch.D. 81.

from a business "so far as the law allows"[64]; a "due allowance. . . . in a fair and reasonable manner" to a borrower[65]; "to provide for" a relation[66]; the meaning of "develop" in the context of prospecting and mining[67]; "I agree absolutely to deliver 11,000 tons of coal, but I am to be relieved reasonably in certain circumstances" or an agreement subject to a reasonable strike clause[68]; imprecision in the phrasing of an option clause[69]; an order "subject to war clause" when there were many such clauses[70]; a sale of "the ground at present being quarried by our client and the surroundings thereto extending to twelve acres"[71]; "force majeure conditions" when a variety of such conditions were in use[72]; "permanent employment"[73]; "should you be instrumental in introducing a person willing to sign a document capable of becoming a contract to purchase"[74]; "subject to the purchaser obtaining a satisfactory mortgage"[75]; payment of instalments of price for "a proportionate part of" land.[76]

25   While imprecision in the amount of money to be paid may result in an unenforceable provision,[77] there is more latitude when a standard of behaviour is imposed on a party. So the courts have applied these clauses: "in an efficient state"[78]; "all convenient speed"[79]; "regular employment"[80]; "quick despatch"[81]; "as soon thereafter as can conveniently be arranged[82]; "business of similar nature"[83]; "gross misconduct"[84]; "arbitrators and umpire shall be commercial men and not lawyers."[85]

---

[64] *Davies* v. *Davies* (1887) 36 Ch.D. 359.

[65] *Re Vince, ex p. Baxter* [1892] 2 Q.B. 478.

[66] *Richardson* v. *Garnett* (1895) 12 T.L.R. 127.

[67] *Douglas* v. *Baynes* [1908] A.C. 477.

[68] *Love and Stewart Ltd.* v. *S. Instone & Co. Ltd.* (1917) 33 T.L.R. 475 at p. 477 *per* Lord Parker.

[69] *County Hotel and Wine Co. Ltd.* v. *London and North Western Ry. Co.* [1918] 2 K.B. 251.

[70] *Bishop and Baxter Ltd.* v. *Anglo-Eastern Trading and Industrial Co. Ltd.* [1944] K.B. 12, commented on in *Nicolene Ltd.* v. *Simmonds* [1953] 1 Q.B. 543.

[71] *Grant* v. *Peter G. Gauld & Co.*, 1985 S.L.T. 545.

[72] *British Industries* v. *Patley Pressings* [1953] 1 All E.R. 94—*contra* the phrase "subject to force majeure," *ibid.* at p. 97. See comments on this case in *Nicolene Ltd.* v. *Simmonds, sup. cit.*

[73] *Cook* v. *Grubb*, 1963 S.C.1. (O.H.).

[74] *Jaques* v. *Lloyd D. George & Partners Ltd.* [1968] 2 All E.R. 187.

[75] *Lee-Parker* v. *Izzet (No. 2)* [1972] 2 All E.R. 800.

[76] *Bushwall Properties Ltd.* v. *Vortex Properties Ltd.* [1976] 2 All E.R. 283.

[77] But not always: "approximately to" was upheld in *Edwards* v. *Skyways Ltd.* [1964] 1 All E.R. 494.

[78] *Hogarth* v.*Miller, Brother & Co.* (1890) 18 R.(H.L.) 10.

[79] *Thomas Nelson & Sons* v. *Dundee East Coast Shipping Co. Ltd.*, 1907 S.C. 927.

[80] *Lawrie* v. *Brown & Co. Ltd.*, 1908 S.C. 705.

[81] *Crown S.S. Co. Ltd.* v. *Leitch*, 1908 S.C. 506.

[82] *Craig* v. *Craig's Trs.*, 1918 2 S.L.T. 293.

[83] *Randall Ltd.* v. *Summers* 1919 S.C. 396.

[84] *Cook* v. *Grubb*, 1963 S.C. 1.

[85] *Rahcassi Shipping Co. S.A.* v. *Blue Star Line Ltd.* [1969] 1 Q.B. 173—dicta at p. 182 that contract is different from rules on defeasance clauses in wills.

Incomplete expression

4–26   In cases of incomplete expression, which are not always distinguishable from the category above, the meaning of the parties may be clear so far as it goes, but there is an absence of expression on an essential term of their contract. Some cases relate to future bargains of an imprecise nature, others to failure to supply an essential term in an existing arrangement.

4–27   The following have been held unenforceable: an agreement on "the buying of another horse"[86]; to give "a substantial interest" by way of a partnership[87]; an agreement to enter into a new arrangement for carrying on a medical partnership with no definite termination[88]; an option to extend a contract on terms to be agreed[89]; "the balance of purchase price can be had on hire purchase terms over a period of two years"[90]; an option in a lease for a further term "at such rental as may be agreed" and no arbitration clause.[91] In general there cannot be a contract to negotiate or a contract to agree.[92]

4–28   Failure to agree on the four essentials of lease meant that there was no contract.[93] A contract of sale requires *inter alia* agreement on price or a method of fixing price,[94] as may a contract for services.[95]

4–29   An expression could be incomplete because of the insertion of a meaningless jumble of letters such as "the piece will be one round" instead of "the price will be one pound" or "at Peebles" inserted for "at present."[96] However, a blunder by a draftsman is one of the instances in which extrinsic evidence may be allowed in the construction of a contract.[97]

Contradictory agreement

4–30   This problem is likely to arise when parts of different standard forms are used together. As it was put by Fletcher Moulton L.J.[98]:

"The difficulty in the case is due solely to the slovenly way in which

---

[86] *Guthing* v. *Lynn* (1831) 2 B. & Ad. 232.

[87] *McArthur* v.*Lawson* (1877) 4 R. 1134.

[88] *Traill* v. *Dewar* (1881) 8 R. 583.

[89] *Loftus* v. *Roberts* (1902) 18 T.L.R. 532; *British Homophone Co. Ltd.* v. *Kunz and Crystallate Gramophone Record Co.* (1935) 152 L.T. 589.

[90] *Scammell and Nephew Ltd.* v. *H. C. & J. G. Ouston* [1941] A.C. 251.

[91] *King's Motors (Oxford) Ltd.* v. *Lax* [1969] 3 All E.R. 665.

[92] *Courtney and Fairbairn Ltd.* v. *Tolaini Bros. (Hotels) Ltd.* [1975] 1 All E.R. 716.

[93] *Gray* v. *Edinburgh University*, 1962 S.C. 157; see also *Hyams* v. *Brechin*, 1979 S.L.T.(Sh.Ct.) 47.

[94] *Foley* v. *Classique Coaches Ltd.* [1934] 2 K.B. 1; *May & Butcher Ltd.* v. *The King* (1929), noted at [1934] 2 K.B. 17; *Hillas & Co. Ltd.* v. *Arcos Ltd.* (1932) 147 L.T. 503; Sale of Goods Act 1979, s.8; see paras. 4–03 and 3–39.

[95] *Courtney and Fairbairn Ltd.* v. *Tolaini Bros. (Hotels) Ltd.*, *sup. cit.*

[96] *Hunter* v. *Fox*, 1964 S.C.(H.L.) 95 at p. 100, *per* Lord Reid: a case on servitudes to which different principles of construction apply.

[97] See Walker and Walker, para. 258; *Krupp* v. *Menzies*, 1907 S.C. 903; *Anderson* v. *Lambie*, 1954 S.C.(H.L.) 43, and see para. 19–44 *et seq.*

[98] *The Hibernian* [1907] P. 277 at p. 282.

the document constituting the contract of carriage is drawn up. I regret to say that in this respect it resembles many other mercantile documents which by their nature have grown up by a long process of adding new terms and conditions to documents of older date, without any regard to whether they fit in with the provisions of those prior documents. Such documents become well-nigh unintelligible as contractual documents, and so far as my experience goes I have never met with so gross a case as the present one. Again and again I have found myself on the point of coming to the conclusion that it is the duty of the Court to refuse to interpret this document."

31   In the end his Lordship did interpret the document. Lord Denning noted that if there was an acceptance saying:

" 'I desire to have *either* the freehold *or* an extended lease,' then there is no contract, because no one knows which it is. It is too uncertain to be a contract. It is just as if I say: 'I offer to sell you my horse for £100 *or* my cow for £50' and you reply: 'I accept your offer.' There is not a contract: for the simple reason stated by Lord Wright: When the words 'fail to evince any definite meaning on which the court can safely act, the court has no choice but to say that there is no contract.' ">[99]

32   There is no meaningful agreement if there is a clause for arbitration in London and another clause for arbitration in Moscow.[1] The effect may be to preserve the application of the common law. As it has been said of shipping documents, which are prime examples of the possibility of conflict in printed clauses, "an ambiguous document is no protection."[2] Because of the indulgence given to commercial documents rules of construction may avoid the conclusion that there is invalidity from uncertainty.[3]

The difference between executory and non-executory contracts

33   It is possible that a court will be less inclined to hold a contract void from uncertainty when part of the contract has been carried out. In *F. & G. Sykes (Wessex) Ltd.* v. *Fine Fare Ltd.*[4] an agreement was certain in its operation for one year. Then the agreement said: "and thereafter such other figures as may be agreed between the parties hereto." It was

---

[99] *Byrnlea Property Investments Ltd.* v. *Ramsay* [1969] 2 Q.B. 253 at p. 264.

[1] *E. J. R. Lovelock Ltd.* v. *Exportles* [1968] 1 Lloyd's Rep. 163.

[2] *Elderslie Steamship Co. Ltd.* v. *Borthwick* [1905] A.C. 93 at p. 96 *per* Lord Macnaghten: *Adamastos Shipping Co. Ltd.* v. *Anglo-Saxon Petroleum Co. Ltd.* [1959] A.C. 133 at pp. 174 *et seq.*, *per* lord Reid.

[3] On conflict between bills of lading and charterparties, see *The Annefield* [1971] P. 168 and cases there cited; *Astro Valiente SA* v. *Pakistan Min. of Food and Ag. (No. 2)* [1982] 1 All E.R. 823; *Miramar Maritime Corp.* v. *Holburn Oil Trading Ltd.* [1984] A.C. 676.

[4] (1967) 1 Lloyd's Rep. 53. See also *Foley* v. *Classique Coaches Ltd.* [1934] 2 K.B. 1; *British Bank for Foreign Trade* v. *Novinex* [1949] 1 K.B. 623. Actings on an inchoate agreement are considered at para. 3–39 *et seq.*

argued that this was a contract to enter into a contract, and was too indefinite to be binding.

4-34 Lord Denning observed[5]:

> "In a commercial agreement the further the parties have gone on with their contract, the more ready are the Courts to imply any reasonable term so as to give effect to their intentions. When much has been done, the Courts will do their best not to destroy the bargain. When nothing has been done, it is easier to say there is no agreement between the parties because the essential terms have not been agreed. But when an agreement has been acted upon and the parties, as here, have been put to great expense in implementing it, we ought to imply all reasonable terms so as to avoid any uncertainties. In this case there is less difficulty than in others because there is an arbitration clause which, liberally construed, is sufficient to resolve any uncertainties which the parties have left."

Resolution of the problem by extrinsic evidence

4-35 In cases of ambiguity of expression where the meaning of a contract is uncertain from an interpretation of its terms, it is possible in some instances to resolve the problem by looking at extrinsic evidence. Thus, in a contract of supply, proof was allowed of the meaning of "all our requirements"[6] and of "your usual requirements."[7] However, one form of extrinsic evidence is in general not admitted, and that is evidence of direct declarations of intention or understanding. The details of the law should be sought in works on evidence.[8]

Resolution of the problem by subsequent actings of the parties

4-36 The actings of parties subsequent to a contract may explain an ambiguity.[9] The actings may cure the lack of expressed agreement on an essential term of a contract.[10] A full citation of authority will be found in the work cited.[11] Subject to the rules on constitution and proof of obligations, there is nothing wrong in parties leaving their agreement on a term, even an essential term, of a contract to be evidenced by their actings, although other terms are expressed orally or in writing. Nor are parties prevented from substituting one contract for another,[12] a practice which is common in commercial life. As Lord Reid put it in a case on a choice of law clause[13]:

---

[5] at pp. 57–58.

[6] *Von Mehren & Co.* v. *Edinburgh Roperie and Sailcloth Co. Ltd.* (1901) 4 F. 232.

[7] *Blacklock & Macarthur* v. *Kirk*, 1919 S.C. 57.

[8] Walker and Walker, paras. 268–270, 273; Macphail, paras. 15.20–15.23. See also para. 19–13.

[9] *e.g. Hunter* v. *Barron's Trs.* (1886) 13 R. 883; *A. M. Carmichael Ltd.* v. *Lord Advocate*, 1948 S.L.T.(Notes) 88.

[10] *Gray* v. *Edinburgh University*, 1962 S.C. 157 at p. 164, *per* Lord Justice-Clerk Thomson; *McAllister* v. *McGallagley*, 1911 S.C. 112; *Watters* v. *Hunter*, 1927 S.C. 310.

[11] Walker and Walker, paras. 263, 269; and see para. 19–13.

[12] *e.g. Johnston* v. *Greenock Corp.*, 1950 S.L.T.(Notes) 53; *Hawthorns* v. *Whimster*, 1917 2 S.L.T. 63.

[13] *Whitworth Street Estates Ltd.* v. *Miller* [1970] A.C. 583 at p. 603.

"Of course the actings of the parties (including any words which they used) may be sufficient to show that they made a new contract. If they made no agreement originally as to the proper law, such actings may show that they made an agreement about that at a later stage. Or if they did make such an agreement originally such actings may show that they later agreed to alter it."[14]

The consequences of a phrase being "void from uncertainty"

-37   If a phrase in a contract is void from uncertainty it may be possible to ignore the phrase and enforce the remainder of the contract. As in other parts of the law of contract in which separability is in issue, the dividing line can be narrow between giving effect to the intention of parties and remaking their contract. The survival of a contract after the operation of a "blue pencil" rule is illustrated by the English case of *Nicolene Ltd.* v. *Simmonds*.[15] A contract for the sale of steel bars was subject to "the usual conditions of acceptance." There were no such conditions and the meaningless phrase was ignored. The case has been referred to without disapproval in the House of Lords,[16] and applied to the words "subject to contract" in a contract for the sale of property.[17] The principle was used to disregard a contradictory arbitration clause.[18] In Scotland the words "at present" have been treated as inserted by mistake and disregarded.[19] This was in the construction of a burden on land to which stricter principles of construction are applied than to contracts.[20] When missives had an incomplete term about a bond this was held to be a matter of detail which was not of the essence of the contract. The missives were a concluded agreement which could be enforced.[21]

INTENTION TO CREATE LEGAL RELATIONS

-38   In English law there is a doctrine that an agreement is not binding as a contract if it is made without any intention of creating legal relations.[22] It is debatable whether this is part of Scots law. The doctrine is not a necessary part of contract law. The American writer Williston argued[23]:

---

[14] See also at p. 606 *per* Lord Hodson, at p. 611 *per* Viscount Dilhorne, at p. 614 *per* Lord Wilberforce; *Cie. d'Armement Maritime* v. *Cie. Tunisienne de Navigation* [1971] A.C 572 at p. 593 *per* Viscount Dilhorne. See para. 23–22 *et seq.*

[15] [1953] 1 Q.B. 543.

[16] *Adamastos Shipping Co. Ltd.* v. *Anglo-Saxon Petroleum Co. Ltd.* [1959] A.C. 133 at p. 176 *per* Lord Reid.

[17] *Michael Richards Properties Ltd.* v. *St. Saviour's* [1975] 3 All E.R. 416.

[18] *E. J. R. Lovelock Ltd.* v. *Exportles* [1968] 1 Lloyd's Rep. 163.

[19] *Hunter* v. *Fox*, 1964 S.C.(H.L.) 95.

[20] e.g. *Anderson* v. *Dickie*, 1915 S.C.(H.L.) 79; *Ewing's Trs.* v. *Crum Ewing*, 1923 S.C. 569; *Porter* v. *Campbell's Trs.*, 1923 S.C.(H.L.) 94; J. Burns, *Handbook of Conveyancing* (5th ed., 1960), pp. 149, 150.

[21] *Freeman* v. *Maxwell*, 1928 S.C. 682; see also para. 4–17 *supra.*

[22] e.g. Chitty, paras. 117 *et seq.*

[23] Williston, para. 21.

"The common law does not require any positive intention to create a legal obligation as an element of contract. Conversely, though both parties may think they have made a contract, they may not have done so. The views of parties to an agreement as to what are the requirements of a contract, as to what mutual assent means, or consideration, or what contracts are enforceable without a writing, and what are not, are wholly immaterial. They are as immaterial as the views of an individual as to what constitutes a tort. In regard to both torts and contracts, the law, not the parties, fixes the requirements of a legal obligation."

4–39   Corbin argued[24]:

"Agreement consists of mutual expressions; it does not consist of harmonious intentions or states of mind. It may well be that intentions and states of mind are themselves nothing but chemical reactions or electrical discharges in some part of the nervous system. It may be that some day we may be able to observe a state of mind in the same way that we observe chemical processes and electrical discharges. At present, however, what we observe for judical purposes is the conduct of the parties."

4–40   He goes on to state that parties' intentions, while not ignored by the courts, are not conclusive in determining what result has been produced by parties' conduct. In one American case it was observed[25]: "A contract has, strictly speaking, nothing to do with the personal, or individual, intent of the parties. A contract is an obligation attached by the mere force of law to certain acts of the parties, usually words, which ordinarily accompany and represent a known intent."

4–41   For Scots law, Stair said[26]: "In the act of contracting, it must be of purpose to oblige, either really or presumptively, and so must be serious, so that what is expressed in jest or scorn makes no contract." It should be noted that this does not support an idea that there must be an intention to create legal relations apart from the requirement that the parties must seriously consent to their agreement. An agreement between an association of employers and a trade union may be solemnly made, but the further question of enforceability in the courts remains unanswered. Likewise, Bell may have gone no further than to require a contract to have serious consent.[27]

4–42   Scots law does recognise that some agreements, however seriously made, are binding in conscience only. It does this whenever it refuses to give effect to an agreement because it is improperly constituted, for example, a verbal agreement to sell heritage. Kames argued that at an early stage in the development of courts only the most useful agree-

---

[24] Corbin, para. 9.
[25] *Hotchkiss* v. *National City Bank*, 200 F. 287, affd. 231 U.S. 50, 58 L. Ed. 115, quoted Williston, para. 21, n. 8.
[26] I,x,13.
[27] *Prin.*, s.10.

ments were enforced by legal authority.[28] A modern example of an honourable understanding which was not legally binding because it was not constituted in the manner required by statute occurs in a case on marine insurance, *Clyde Marine Insurance Co.* v. *Renwick*.[29] An agreement may not be an enforceable contract.[30]

-43 The parties may expressly state that their agreement is not to be enforced by law. Does this have effect? In principle it is difficult to see why not. Parties may exclude the jurisdiction of the courts by referring their dispute to arbitration. Historically, Scots law has favoured this more than English law. Why should parties not go a stage further and say that they do not want any dispute to be under the jurisdiction of either the courts or arbitration?[31] In *Woods* v. *Co-operative Insurance Society*[32] effect was given to a statement that there was to be no contractual liability. If, however, there have been actings following on the statement, there could be a contract based on those actings.[33] In situations where a body is acting *ultra vires* or its rules are against public policy, a court would not allow a statement of parties to prevent it intervening.[34]

-44 If parties may expressly exclude the jurisdiction of courts and arbitration, it follows that this express term may be implied. It is thought, however, that the inference that a serious agreement was not intended to have legal consequences should be drawn only in exceptional cases, for example, where there could be no patrimonial interest in either party to insist on performance. As Lord Kinnear put it[35]:

> "Nobody has a right which he can enforce at law to compel other people to play a game of football with him. If there be an agreement between them to play a game together, that is not an agreement which the law will enforce. The general rule is that such agreements are personal. Agreements to associate for purposes of recreation, or an agreement to associate for scientific or philanthropical or social or religious purposes, are not agreements which Courts of law can enforce. They are entirely personal. Therefore, in order to establish a civil wrong from the refusal to carry out such an agreement, if it can be inferred that any such agreement was made, it is necessary to see that the pursuer has suffered some practical injury either in his reputation or in his property."

---

[28] *Historical Law Tracts* (4th ed., 1792), pp. 67–70.

[29] 1924 S.C. 113.

[30] See also Trade Union and Labour Relations Act 1974, s.18.; *Commission of The European Communities* v. *United Kingdom* [1984] 1 All E.R. 353; *Gibbons* v. *Assoc. British Ports* [1985] I.R.L.R. 376.

[31] In England the express exclusion of legal rights arising from football pools has been effective: *Jones* v. *Vernon's Pools Ltd.* [1938] 2 All E.R. 626; *Appleson* v. *H. Littlewood Ltd.* [1939] 1 All E.R. 464.

[32] 1924 S.C. 692; see also *Rose & Frank Co.* v. *Crompton* [1925] A.C. 445.

[33] *Shaw* v. *Muir's Exrx.* (1892) 19 R. 997: *Rose & Frank Co.* v. *Crompton, supra.*

[34] *Skerret* v. *Oliver* (1896) 23 R. 468; *St. Johnstone Football Club* v. *Scottish Football Association*, 1965 S.L.T. 171.

[35] *Murdison* v. *Scottish Football Union* (1896) 23 R. 449 at p. 466.

4-45   Thus there are a series of cases on the refusal of the courts to interfere in the resolutions of organisations because of the lack of patrimonial interest in the complainant.[36] It is thought, however, contrary to some English authority, that at common law collective agreements could be enforceable subject to problems of title to sue. This is because there is a patrimonial interest to enforce and normally a serious agreement is enforceable by the courts.[37] The usual position is as Stair put it centuries ago—"every paction produceth action."[38] There is a heavy onus on a person seeking to establish that an agreement, particularly a business agreement, was not intended to created legal relations.[39]

4-46   When the matter comes to be argued fully in Scotland, it may be necessary to consider the English cases.[40] For example, in England it has been held that the inference is against an agreement between spouses creating a legal relationship.[41] In *Esso Petroleum Ltd.* v. *Commissioners of Customs and Excise*[42] the House of Lords considered a petrol sales promotion scheme. Esso supplied garages with tokens called "World Cup Coins." One token was distributed with every purchase of four gallons of petrol. The majority of the Lords were of the opinion that there was no "sale" of the tokens, but differing views were expressed on whether there was any form of contract involved.[43]

---

[36] *Smith* v. *Galbraith* (1843) 5 D. 665; *McMillan* v. *Free Church* (1861) 23 D. 1134—a case with frequently-quoted dicta; *Forbes* v. *Eden* (1867) 5 M.(H.L.) 36; *Wight* v. *Presbytery of Dunkeld* (1870) 8 M. 921; *Cocker* v. *Crombie* (1893) 20 R. 954; *Skerret* v. *Oliver* (1896) 23 R. 468; *Anderson* v. *Manson*, 1909 S.C. 838; *Drennan* v. *Assoc. Ironmoulders of Scotland*, 1921 S.C. 151; *McDonald* v. *Burns*, 1940 S.C. 376; *Marshall* v. *Cardonald Bowling Club*, 1971 S.L.T.(Sh.Ct.) 56; *Bell* v. *The Trustees*, 1975 S.L.T.(Sh.Ct.) 60.

[37] *Contra. Ford Motor Co. Ltd.* v. *Amalgamated Union Of Engineering and Foundry Workers* [1969] 2 Q.B. 303; see now Trade Union and Labour Relations Act 1974, s.18. *Commission of the European Communities* v. *United Kingdom* [1984] 1 All E.R. 353; *Gibbons* v. *Assoc. British Ports* [1985] I.R.L.R. 376. For a view that collective agreements are enforceable in Scotland see R.L.C. Hunter, "Collective Agreement Fair Wages Clauses and the Employment Relationship in Scots Law," 1975 J.R. 47 at pp. 52–53. See this point also discussed in the context of invalidities of consent, para. 26–16.

[38] I,x,7.

[39] *Edwards* v. *Skyways Ltd.* [1964] 1 All E.R. 494.

[40] See Chitty, paras. 123–133.

[41] *Balfour* v. *Balfour* [1919] 2 K.B. 571; *Gould* v. *Gould* [1970] 1 Q.B. 275; *Pettitt* v. *Pettitt* [1970] A.C. 777; *cf. Pyatt* v. *Pyatt*, 1966 S.L.T.(Notes) 73.

[42] [1976] 1 All E.R. 117.

[43] The tokens were also of little monetary value. Contrast the weight given to this by Viscount Dilhorne (at p. 121) and Lord Russell (at pp. 125, 126) on the one hand and Lord Fraser (dissenting) (at p. 124) on the other hand.

CHAPTER 5

OFFER AND ACCEPTANCE

THE IMPORTANCE OF OFFER AND ACCEPTANCE

-01 One of the methods of making a contract is an offer followed by an acceptance. Subject to the rules on constitution and proof of obligations, either offer or acceptance may be in any form. There may be speech, writings, telegrams, telexes or nods of the head.[1] The theoretical discussion has too often assumed that there is writing. In Scotland this may have been because of the rules on constitution of contracts relating to heritage. In England not only is writing required for the sale of land but, until 1954, a contract for the sale of goods over £10 in value, with some exceptions, needed a note or memorandum in writing. The influence which these requirements have had on the development of this part of the law is for the legal historian to explore. For present purposes any satisfactory theory would apply to writings, or communications by satellite, laser beams or methods not yet invented. The businessman may not wait for his legal system to catch up with him.

-02 Analysis in terms of offer and acceptance can become too complicated if the facts are complex. Imagine more than two parties. Let each address the others in the manner of a group of excited businessmen. The timing of an offer and responses and interactions may not correspond to the formula, "A speaks to B who replies to A." Yet a contract may be concluded. So also when a lengthy document, the product of weeks of negotiation is signed. An analysis in terms of offer and acceptance is unrealistic.

Such an analysis is possible. The first party who signs is making an offer to contract on certain conditions to the other parties. The next party signing is both accepting that offer and making an offer to the other parties. This is artificial, however, because the order of signing will normally be accidental. To dissect complicated negotiations or documents into statements belonging to one of two categories is like asking at the end of a boxing match—who hit whom, when? The answer may not much matter provided it is clear what the final result is.[2]

-03 Offer and acceptance is a useful tool in deciding whether or not there is *consensus in idem*.[3] It is a technique for analysis but no more, except in so far as certain rules have developed on communication between the

---

[1] For a contract concluded by telex, see *The Master Stelios* [1983] 1 Lloyd's Rep. 356 (P.C.); *Damon Cia Naviera S.A.* v. *Hapag-Lloyd International S.A.* [1985] 1 All E.R. 475 (on appeal to the House of Lords).

[2] For other examples of the fictions produced by offer and acceptance analysis, see Scottish Law Commission, Memo. No. 36.

[3] *e.g. Harvela Investments Ltd.* v. *Royal Trust Co. of Canada* [1986] 1 A.C. 207.

parties. It should not be regarded as the necessary form of every contract. The strain involved if this is done was shown in a case in the Privy Council on a bill of lading:

> "It is only the precise analysis of this complex of relations into the classical offer and acceptance, with identifiable consideration, that seems to present difficulty, but this same difficulty exists in many situations of daily life, *e.g.* sales at auction; supermarket purchases; boarding an omnibus; purchasing a train ticket; tenders for the supply of goods; offers of rewards; acceptance by post; warranties of authority by agents; manufacturers' guarantees; gratuitous bailments; bankers' commercial credits. These are all examples which show that English law, having committed itself to a rather technical and schematic doctrine of contract, in application takes a practical approach, often at the cost of forcing the facts to fit uneasily into the marked slots of offer, acceptance and consideration."[4]

Terminology

5–04   Confusion can result over the use of the terms "offer" and "acceptance." Unfortunately as our law has developed, with its concentration on the simple transaction, classification of a statement as one or the other may be important. It affects the rules on when the statement takes effect or how it may be recalled. A large part of the controversy over *Countess of Dunmore* v. *Alexander*[5] arises because one of the letters was classified by Gloag as an acceptance when it was more likely to have been an offer.[6]

5–05   The Countess of Dunmore wrote three letters to Lady Agnew. The first was an inquiry about a servant. Lady Agnew replied in terms which indicated a willingness on the part of the servant to be employed. The second of the Countess's letters was an offer of employment. The third letter was a retraction of that offer. The second and third letters reached the servant by the same post.

5–06   On Gloag's view of the case, Lady Agnew's letter was an offer on behalf of the servant which was accepted by the second of the Countess's letters. If this was so, there was a completed bargain when the acceptance was posted.

5–07   A more plausible analysis, however, is that Lady Agnew's letter only indicated a willingness to contract. On any view the classification of that letter is crucial to an understanding of the case.

5–08   A person may say that the "first offer" or the "highest offer" secures an object for sale. Assuming that statement is not merely an invitation to treat, but an offer, or an offer coupled with a promise, the person who replies with the "first offer" or the "highest offer" is not making an

---

[4] *N.Z. Shipping* v. *Satterthwaite* [1975] A.C. 154 at p. 167.
[5] (1830) 9 S. 190.
[6] See Gloag, p. 38; Walker, *Contracts*, para. 7.69. Chitty recognises the mistake (Chitty, para. 74, n. 45), as does Anson, p. 49.

offer, even if he calls it that. In law it is an acceptance. The parties' terminology is not decisive.[7]

The meaning of consensus in idem

–09   The theory is that a contract requires *consensus in idem* amongst the parties. The rules on offer and acceptance show that there can be a contract without the parties ever having been agreed at the one instant. This is the result of practical considerations. *Consensus*, for these purposes, means objective *consensus*, not a meeting of minds.

–10   It is customary to say that the parties to a contract must mutually agree on its terms. Bell put it in this way: "To a perfect obligation (besides the proof requisite), it is necessary that there shall be a deliberate and voluntary consent and purpose to engage; excluding, on the one hand, incapacity by nonage, disease, or imbecility; and, on the other, Error, Force and Fraud."[8]

–11   "Consent" is used in two senses, one subjective and the other objective. The difference is between, "Did he consent?" and "Did he appear to consent?" It is probable that in the early history of the law of contract the subjective sense was dominant, but was replaced in the nineteenth century with an appreciation that in business dealings the objective sense was more realistic. One result of this is that the subjective sense remains in a part of the law largely formed a long time ago, namely incapacity to consent and factors invalidating consent because it was improperly obtained. We ask, "Was he insane?" or "Was he under age?" or "Was he deceived?" rather than whether he appeared to be in those states. The history of the law of error shows a conflict between the two approaches nowhere better illustrated than in the case of *Stewart* v. *Kennedy*.[9]

–12   Leaving aside those situations in which consent is invalidated, *consensus* is tested objectively. This has the consequence that a person's secret intent is not relevant. Intention in the law of contract is not the same as intention in the criminal law.[10] It is misleading in the context of formation of contract to talk of a meeting of minds, because that is not what is required. This was made clear in Scotland by *Thomson* v. *James*[11] which is, by a long way, our most important case on offer and acceptance.

–13   In *Thomson* a seller posted the acceptance of an offer on the same day as the offeror was posting a retraction. One of the arguments was that there was no concurrence of the will of the parties. The offeror could

---

[7] *Harvela Investments Ltd.* v. *Royal Trust Co. of Canada, supra. See also Dickinson* v. *Dodds* (1876) 2 Ch.D. 463—"I hereby agree to sell" was an offer.

[8] *Prin.*, s.10; see also *Comm*, I,313.

[9] (1890) 17 R.(H.L.) 25; see Chap. 9 and S.L.C. Memo. No. 42, *Defective Consent and Consequential Matters* (1978), Vol. 11, para. 3.15.

[10] See Williston, para. 22.

[11] (1855) 18 D. 1.

have changed his mind before the acceptor decided to accept. Lord President McNeill said[12]:

> "In a great many cases the maxim that there must be a concurrence of will at the moment of completion of the contract cannot be rigidly or literally applied. The very opposite may be the fact. Although one cannot, by accepting an offer, bind a dead or insane person, he may bind an unwilling person, one who has altogether changed his mind. Such cases are not infrequent. If an offer bears that it is to be binding for a certain number of days or hours, the offerer may repent before the lapse of the given time, and yet at the end of it may find himself unwillingly bound; or if an offerer changes his mind, but does not take the proper steps to have his change of mind conveyed to the offeree—either writes no letter, or writes a letter which he omits to send, or sends it by mistake to a wrong place, he may find himself unwillingly bound. Other cases may be figured. Mere change of mind, on the part of the offerer, will not prevent an effectual acceptance—not even although that change of mind should be evinced by having been communicated to a third party, or recorded in a formal writing, as for instance in a notarial instrument. In all these cases a binding contract may be made between the parties without that *consensus* or *concursus* which a rigidly literal reading of the maxim or rule would require."

5–14   The result is that there can be a contract although at no point were the parties' minds *ad idem*. *Consensus* is tested objectively. A further illustration of this is that it will not avail a person to say he did not read a document before signing it, or that he did not understand it.[13]

5–15   It is obvious to anyone with some knowledge of the workings of courts that the concept of objective *consensus* might be unpalatable to a judge in certain cases.

5–16   The uneducated person who is imposed upon may have judicial sympathy. There may be insufficient grounds to hold that there has been undue influence or facility and circumvention. A doctrine of extortion which might be the logical solution has not yet been properly developed.[14] The concerned court may be tempted to apply the subjective approach—the man did not know what he was doing, therefore he did not consent. This happened in *Harvey* v. *Smith*.[15] Missives were held not to be binding on an illiterate man because he did not understand the effect of the words "adopted as holograph." The factors mentioned in the opinion of Lord President Kinross are revealing. The defender had not informed his wife or anyone else of his intention on the day to purchase the pursuer's lodging house. There was no adequate reason for the defender assenting to an increase in the price which he had formerly

---

[12] at p. 11.

[13] *Young* v. *Clydesdale Bank Ltd.* (1889) 17 R. 231; *Laing* v. *Provincial Homes Investment Co.*, 1909 S.C. 812; *L'Estrange* v. *F. Graucob Ltd.* [1934] 2 K.B. 394; *The Luna* [1920] P. 22. If there is misrepresentation as to the contents of the deed other issues are raised. Some of the English case law is concerned with the technicalities of the plea of *non est factum*.

[14] See Chap. 12.

[15] (1904) 6 F. 511.

been willing to give. The pursuer had a law agent present; the defender had not. The defender had insufficient funds to purchase the property. There was some evidence that he was under the influence of drink. He was not a person of much education or intelligence. Lord Kinnear explained the difference from the normal case in this way[16]:

> "I do not doubt that a man must be held bound by the plain meaning of words to which he puts his hand, but that is a different thing from holding that he must be assumed to know the legal effect of words to which a very artificial operation is ascribed by a highly technical rule of law, when he knew nothing of the rule beforehand, and when it was not explained to him at the time."

–17 This reasoning is not satisfactory. It introduces a distinction between "plain meaning" and highly technical rules. To apply this distinction generally to contracts would produce undesirable results. For example, many exclusion and indemnity clauses are difficult to understand and an analysis of the reported case law would soon show that the "plain" or "obvious" meaning of these clauses has not always been the meaning applied by judges, nor have judges always agreed on the construction of these clauses. If failure to understand complicated law is a ground for holding that a contract is not binding, businessmen would enter into commercial contracts at their peril. Professor Gloag had difficulty appreciating the exact ground of decision in *Harvey*.[17] He concluded, with some force, that a decision on the ground of failure to understand the effect of "adopted as holograph"

> "seems to involve the violent assumption that [the defender], though unable to appreciate the technical effect of adopting a deed as holograph, was in a condition to appreciate the equally technical rule that a contract relating to heritage is not binding unless entered into by writing probative of both parties."[18]

The case should, perhaps, be regarded as wrongly decided.

–18 The parties' intentions are not the only factor in determining the character of a transaction. A question of law may be involved.

–19 An illustration of the objective approach is *Muirhead & Turnbull* v. *Dickson*.[19] One party thought the contract was one of hire-purchase; the other that it was one of sale. It was held to be sale. Lord President Dunedin said[20]:

---

[16] at p. 522.

[17] *Contract*, p. 96; see also *Maclaine* v. *Murphy*, 1958 S.L.T.(Sh.Ct.) 49. It is tempting to suggest that the basis of the decision in *Harvey* was that the defender did not understand that he was entering into an irrevocable contract. However, the normal rules require evidence of insanity, undue influence, facility and circumvention, or other invalidity of consent before a person is not bound by a deed which is properly executed.

[18] *Contract*, p. 96.

[19] (1905) 7 F. 686. The effect of an agreement is a matter of law—"it is trite law that if on analysis a transaction has in law one character, the fact that the parties either accidentally or deliberately frame the transaction in language appropriate to a transaction of a different character will not deny to it its true character": *Esso Petroleum Ltd.* v. *Commrs. of Customs and Excise* [1976] 1 All E.R. 117 at p. 125 *per* Lord Russell.

[20] at p. 694.

"Now, of course, if the matter really was as to what in their inmost hearts people thought, I think that, taking these people as honest people on both one side and the other, what they thought would lead me to the conclusion at which the Sheriff has arrived, namely, that Grant thought he was selling on the hire-purchase system, and the other person thought he was buying upon some instalment plan. But commercial contracts cannot be arranged by what people think in their inmost minds. Commercial contracts are made according to what people say."

5–20   The legal effect of a contract should be a matter apart from the intention of the parties. If a misunderstanding on the legal effect is induced in one party by the other the problem is in the realm of *Stewart* v. *Kennedy* or of fraud and is discussed elsewhere.[21] If there is error as to the corpus of the document being signed there may be a void contract on the grounds of unilateral essential error. Lord President Dunedin gave the case of a man signing what he thought was a visitors' book but which was really a chequebook.[22]

The problem of the distinction between this and the *Muirhead* type of case is posed by the preservation of a law of unilateral error which is subjective in origin. The result is, to an extent, two irreconcilable trends. Although not a complete answer it may help to distinguish two types of events.

(1) Where a party has no intention to contract—as when he signs a visitors' book. There is no contract.

(2) Where a party is capable of consenting and does intend to contract. His acts will be judged objectively. There may be a contract although he has changed his intention. There may be a different legal effect from what he intended.

Offer distinguished from invitations to treat and other statements

5–21   Elsewhere we consider the difference between an offer and an invitation to treat or an advertising "puff" or a promise or other statement.[23]

General Offers

5–22   An offer[24] is normally made to a particular person but it need not be. An offer may be addressed to everyone in the world, for example, a reward offered for finding a lost child, or it may be addressed to a particular class of people, for example, an offer to pay money to those carrying a certain newspaper and who comply with stated conditions. It is a matter of construction whether the offer may be accepted by more

---

[21] See Chaps. 9 and 10.
[22] *Ellis* v. *Lochgelly Iron and Coal Co.*, 1909 S.C. 1278 at p. 1282; an example of fraudulent misrepresentation as to the nature of a document signed is *Maclachlan* v. *Glasgow*, 1925 S.L.T.(Sh.Ct.) 77.
[23] See Chap. 3, paras. 3–15 and 3–25; Chap. 2, para. 2–28.
[24] On the distinction between an offer and other statements, see note above.

than one person. The first person to find the lost child might accept the offer. If the find is by a group, the reasonable man would understand that the group shares the reward.[25] On the other hand more than one person may carry the issue of a newspaper. That is probably the earnest hope of the proprietor who is making the offer. This offer may be accepted by several persons, each of whom is entitled to be paid the full sum specified in the offer.[26] It may be more correct, however, to regard the "offers" in these cases as being unilateral promises.[27] The similarity between promise and offer in these circumstances has been noted in the Privy Council.[28]

–23   In *Carlill* v. *Carbolic Smoke Ball Co.*[29] an advertisement promised to pay £100 to any person who caught influenza using the defendant's smoke balls. It was an offer capable of being accepted by more than one person. The same applies where a person who collects labels from a manufacturer's product can claim a cooking utensil, poster, or other such item at a reduced price. On the other hand it is possible that only one person may win one of the prizes in a competition for listing the features of a product in order of merit, submitting a slogan or guessing the position of a football on a photograph.

–24   A further problem with competitions arises if a disappointed contender argues that the wrong person won. The point has arisen in Scotland in a series of cases involving bursaries.[30] These cases show that while a court may investigate compliance with the conditions of a bursary award, it will not interfere, in a claim based on contract, in a matter at the discretion of the examiners or appointers.[31] If the discretion is fraudulently exercised there is a delictual remedy.[32] In the case of sporting and other contests there may be a *sponsio ludicra*[33] or a lack of patrimonial interest.[34] The suggestion that there was no contract between bursary promoters and examinees was made in *Martins* and in *McDonald*, but this is doubtful.[35] There may be contracts with all those who take part, not only with the few who win. The formation of a contract

---

[25] *Lockhart* v. *Barnard* (1845) 14 M. & W. 674.

[26] *Williams* v. *Carwardine* (1833) 4 B. & Ad. 621; *Lancaster* v. *Walsh* (1838) 4 M. & W. 16; *Spencer* v. *Harding* (1870) L.R. 5 C.P. 561 at p. 563 *per* Willes J.; *Gibbons* v. *Proctor* (1891) 64 L.T. 594; *cf. Law* v. *Newnes Ltd.* (1894) 21 R. 1027; *Hunter* v. *Hunter* (1904) 7 F. 136.

[27] On the distinction between an "offer" and a "promise," see para. 2–28.

[28] *N.Z. Shipping* v. *Satterthwaite* [1975] A.C. 154 at p. 168.

[29] [1893] 1 Q.B. 256.

[30] *Martins* v. *Macdougall's Trs.* (1885) 13 R. 274; *McDonald* v. *McColl* (1890) 17 R. 951; *McQuaker* v. *Governors of Ballantrae Educational Trust* (1891) 18 R. 521.

[31] See also *Thorne* v. *University of London* [1966] 2 Q.B. 237; *Thomas* v. *University of Bradford* [1985] 2 All E.R. 786.

[32] Negligent exercise of the discretion is not a matter yet explored in Scotland. It involves the ramifications of *Hedley Byrne & Co.* v. *Heller & Partners Ltd.* [1964] A.C. 465. These must be looked for in other works.

[33] See para. 25–15.

[34] See para. 4–45.

[35] On whether there is a contract between a university and a student, see *Casson* v. *University of Aston* [1983] 1 All E.R. 88.

(when an entry is made for an exam or for a race) should not be confused with purification of a condition (on X event £100 will be paid). Nor should the failure by one party to comply with a condition (*e.g.* that he speaks Gaelic or was born in the county of Perth) prevent the formation of a contract. Formation and breach of contract are different concepts. Breach has its consequences, including inability to enforce the contract by the party in breach when the mutuality principle applies, and damages for the loss caused by the breach, but apparent acceptance of conditions is required for a contract to exist, not actual compliance with the conditions.

5–25   In a competition there may be a contract not only with the organisers but also amongst the competitors.[36] The contracts could, depending on the facts, be formed at different times. The organisers enter into the contract when the entry is received; the competitors when they gather to compete. The consequence of the relationship amongst the competitors is that one may have a contractual remedy against another if the rules are broken, as in *The Satanita* when a yacht was sunk.[36]

5–26   Acceptance of general offers and the revocation of offers pose special problems which are discussed below.[37]

5–27   A person should be wary of making a general offer. Take the offer of a reward for the arrest or conviction of a person. This type of offer is illustrated by English nineteenth-century cases, American cases and in Scotland by *Petrie* v. *Earl of Airlie*.[38] The interpretation of these offers has led to difficulties. What type of information must be supplied to secure the reward? What happens if more than one person each supply bits of information which complete a picture? What if the facts are communicated not to the offeror but to someone else, such as a friend, who passes the tip on to a police constable? Is a person acting in the course of public duty entitled to the reward?[39] The unlucky offeror may end up fighting claimants. The newspaper offers will frequently make the selection of the winner a matter for the discretion of the editor. The exercise of this discretion will normally not be interfered with by the courts.[40]

Communication of an Offer

5–28   An offer[41] must be communicated to the offeree before it has legal effect. Thus if a committee resolve on a course of action, but this decision is not communicated, no offer has been made.[42] An offer which

---

[36] *The Satanita* [1895] P. 248, affd. *sub nom. Clarke* v. *Dunraven* [1897] A.C. 59. See also *Meggeson* v. *Burns* [1972] 1 Lloyd's Rep. 223.

[37] at para. 5–30.

[38] (1834) 13 S. 68.

[39] See Corbin, para. 64; Anson, p. 31; Cheshire and Fifoot, p. 48.

[40] See the bursary cases mentioned above.

[41] On the distinction between an offer and other statements, see paras. 3–15 and 3–25; para. 2–28.

[42] *Gilmour* v. *Scottish Miners' Friendly Society*, 1918 1 S.L.T. 39, may have been decided on this basis, but that is not clear. See also *Burr* v. *Commrs. of Bo'ness* (1896) 24 R. 148 and cases on communication of acceptance, paras. 5–97 *et seq*.

is lost in the post would be ineffective. An offer by telegram which was materially distorted in transmission would not, on acceptance, result in a contract.[43] As Lord President McNeill put it: "An offer is nothing until it is communicated to the party to whom it is made, and who is to decide whether he will or will not accept the offer."[44]

–29 The reason behind this rule is that there cannot be objective *consensus in idem* when the acceptor is ignorant of the offer. There could be subjective *consensus*, as where A is willing to sell his house for £10,000 to B, and B is willing to buy the house from A at the same price. Each writes to the other at the same time. A's offer to sell is lost in the post. It cannot be accepted by B's letter sent in ignorance of it. Similarly, if identical offers cross in the post there is no contract.[45]

–30 A special problem is posed by a general offer of reward. More than with any other type of offer the acts constituting acceptance may be performed by a person ignorant of the offer. Is he entitled to the reward? There is no Scottish authority, but in principle there can be no contract. This is the view in most, but not all, jurisdictions in the USA.[46] There may be a remedy under the principle of recompense.

–31 As an offer must be accepted within a reasonable time, or prior to the expiry of an express time limit, it may in some circumstances be important to know exactly when the offer is made. Until it is made, the time limits cannot start to run. Must there be actual communication to the offeree? As Winfield put it[47]:

> "If an offer is posted to you and the postman puts it in your letter box in the ordinary way at about 7.30 a.m., it would be hard upon you if the mere dropping of the letter into the box were held to be a communication of its contents to you. You may be in bed and asleep, or in your bath, or shaving, and, like most business and professional people, you do not open your letters until you reach the breakfast table."

–32 The writer then considers what happens if you are lazy and do not get up until lunchtime, or if the letter is received by your agent, or you are away on holiday when it arrives. These are not problems which have arisen in reported law in exactly this context, but some help may be obtained by analogy from cases of revocation of offers discussed below.

Duration of an Offer

–33 An offer may lapse and can no longer be accepted on the occurrence of certain events. These are (1) rejection by the offeree; (2) lapse of time; (3) revocation by the offeror; (4) material change of circumstances; and (5) death and insanity.

---

[43] *Verdin Bros.* v. *Robertson* (1871) 10 M. 35.
[44] *Thomson* v. *James* (1855) 18 D. 1 at p. 10.
[45] *Tinn* v. *Hoffman & Co.* (1873) 29 L.T. 271.
[46] Williston, para. 33A; Corbin, para. 59.
[47] "Some Aspects of Offer and Acceptance" (1939) 55 L.Q.R. 499 at p. 503.

(1) Rejection by the offeree

5–34   It is reasonable in principle that if the offeree indicates that he does not wish to accept the offer, the offer lapses. The offeree could reject the offer outright or reply with a counter-offer. Either is rejection. In *Hyde* v. *Wrench*[48] an offer to sell a farm for £1000 was met by an offer for £950 which was not accepted. It was not possible then for the £1000 offer to be accepted. It had been revoked by the counter-proposal. In Scotland, calling a summons and continuing with steps in an action have been held to be rejection of an offer in settlement of a claim.[49]

5–35   A reply which commences, 'I accept the offer subject to the following conditions . . . " is not rejection of the offer. It is a normal part of the bargain for the sale of heritage which includes the offer, although at the stage of the reply the bargain is inchoate.[50] Nor is an inquiry about the terms of an offer, or an indication that it is being considered, rejection of it.

5–36   It is obvious that whether the reply by the offeree is to be treated as a rejection or not may be difficult to decide on the facts. As it depends on interpretation of the actings of the offeree, decisions on other circumstances would not be conclusive. The problem is illustrated by the cases noted.[51] Scottish authority sometimes cited[52] does not clearly demonstrate the point. One problem is that rejection can be by actings, rather than by express statement, and these actings can amount to a material change of circumstances or cause a lapse of time, either of which by itself would result in the offer lapsing.

5–37   It is undecided when rejection of an offer by post takes effect. An analogy with acceptance would suggest that rejection is effective at the moment of posting by the offeree. This avoids a result which may be unjust if (1) the offeree posts a rejection and (2) before the rejection reaches the offeror, the offeree posts an acceptance. Applying different rules to the acceptance and the rejection could have the consequence that the offeror is bound by the acceptance, not only when he does not know that he is, but after receiving the rejection. On the other hand if, after posting the rejection, which is then effective, the offeree telegrams acceptance and the telegram arrives before the letter, the offeror thinks he is bound when he is not. This may be more convenient than the converse situation. If the offeror loses because of any misapprehension caused by the actings of the offeree, a delictual remedy would seem

---

[48] (1840) 3 Beav. 334; followed in *Butler Machine Tool Co. Ltd.* v. *Ex-cell-o Corporation (England) Ltd.* [1979] 1 All E.R. 965.

[49] *Lawrence* v. *Knight*, 1972 S.C. 26.

[50] This issue is discussed further at para. 5–87 in relation to *Wolf and Wolf* v. *Forfar Potato Co.*, 1984 S.L.T. 100.

[51] *Tinn* v. *Hoffman & Co.* (1873) 29 L.T. 271 at p. 278; *Stevenson, Jacques & Co.* v. *McLean* (1880) 5 Q.B.D. 346; *Wolf and Wolf* v. *Forfar Potato Co.*, discussed later at para. 5–87.

[52] See Gloag, p. 37; Scottish Law Commission, Memo. No. 36, *Constitution and Proof of Voluntary Obligations, Formation of Contract*, para. 29.

appropriate. If the point comes to be argued in Scotland some help may be gained from English and American sources.[53]

-38 If the offeror has bound himself to keep the offer open for a certain time, rejection within that time will terminate the offer. Corbin argues, however[54]:

> "This effect should not be given to a rejection, if it is contrary to the offeror's own expressed intention and desire. In making an offer, the offeror has control of its terms and the time and mode of acceptance; he can create such a power of acceptance as he pleases. The rule that a rejection terminates power is solely for the protection of the offeror; and there seems to be no sufficient reason for terminating the power of acceptance against his will. Suppose that an offer is made thus: this offer will be left open for acceptance for 30 days, without regard to any rejection, conditional acceptance, or counter offer. After a rejection by the offeree, he would still have power to accept during the unexpired portion of the 30 days. The offeror's own statement would tend to make the offeree less ready to give due deliberation before putting up rejections and counter offers as trial balloons."

-39 While it may be that an offer expressed in the terms suggested by Corbin would receive effect in Scots law, caution must be exercised in using Anglo-American authority on this point. These legal systems do not, speaking generally, have our concept of the unilateral promise binding without consideration. In Scots law a statement to keep an offer open is a promise.[55] A promise ceases to be effective if rejected.[56] A statement that an offer is not accepted must impliedly reject the promise accessory to it.

-40 If, contrary to what we have stated, the offer does not fall, there would need to be a change in the practice of solicitors when they are offering for heritage. A standard phrase is: "This offer unless previously withdrawn, is open for acceptance reaching us here not later than . . . " If, within the time limit, a communication of rejection could be followed by a valid acceptance, not only would the offeror be confused, but his solicitor should have said something like: "unless previously withdrawn or rejected."

(2) Lapse of time

41 **(a) Time specified.** An offer may be expressed as open for acceptance within a specified time. An acceptance outwith this time is too late. Instead of stipulating a fixed time the offer might give the right to extend the time for acceptance as, for example, when an offer for shares stated:

---

[53] *e.g.* Chitty, para. 89; Williston, para. 52; Corbin, para. 94.
[54] para. 94.
[55] *Marshall* v. *Blackwood*, 1747 Elchies, *voce* Sale No. 6 and Notes; *Littlejohn* v. *Hadwen* (1882) 20 S.L.R. 5; *A. & G. Paterson* v. *Highland Railway Co.*, 1927 S.C.(H.L.) 32 at p. 38 *per* Viscount Dunedin.
[56] Stair, I,x,4; Bell, *Prin.*, s.8.

"We reserve the right to extend the time of acceptance until such later date as we notify you in writing."[57]

5–42 The offer which specifies a time without reference to standard units of time may pose difficulties of interpretation. When the offer said, "Please let me know on receipt of this letter," an acceptance over a month later was too late.[58] The decision is obvious enough, but the reference to "receipt of this letter" could have been awkward if the issue had been what was meant by "receipt."[59] When an acceptance of an offer was required "in course of post," a reply six days later was not timeous.[60] Imagine the difficulties which could arise with this phrasing. If the offer is sent first-class post, is a reply by second-class post sufficient? What happens if the offeree knows that there will be delays in the post? What protection has the offeror if the offer is redirected to the offeree's new address with consequent delay? Other hypothetical cases can be figured such as the layman who writes, "Let me know immediately" or who says he wants an answer "by" or "before" or will wait "until" a certain day, which can raise doubt as to whether that day is included or excluded. The moral for the draftsman of an offer is that a reference to the day and the time is best, provided it is clear which of the many of the world's times is being used.

5–43 An acceptance may be effective when posted.[61] The result is that an offer requiring a reply by Monday can be timeously accepted by an acceptance posted on the Monday, but reaching the offeror on Tuesday or even later.[62] For this reason the offeror may, and perhaps should, frame the condition so that the acceptance should reach him (or his agent) before the expiry of the time.

5–44 **(b) Reasonable time.** If the offer fixes no time for acceptance, it must be accepted within a reasonable time. Professor Bell said that an offer could be accepted until it was withdrawn except in cases of mercantile transactions where it must be accepted without delay.[63] This dictum was noted in *Murray* v. *Rennie & Angus*[64] without a decision on its accuracy. In *Hall-Maxwell* v. *Gill*,[65] Lord Stormonth Darling decided that it was wrong. He quoted Stair, who said: "if the acceptance be not adhibited *presently*, or within the time expressed in the offer, in which the other party hath liberty to accept, there ariseth no obligation."[66] There are dicta in *Thomson* v. *James* to the effect that an offer lapses after a

---

[57] *Musson* v. *Howard Glasgow Associates*, 1960 S.C. 371—guidelines can be drawn from the opinions in the case on how to frame the letter extending the time, so as to avoid the type of dispute which led in that instance to a hearing in the Inner House.

[58] *Hall-Maxwell* v. *Gill* (1901) 9 S.L.T. 222.

[59] See above on when an offer is communicated, para. 5–31.

[60] *Farries* v. *Stein* (1800) 4 Pat. 131.

[61] See *infra*.

[62] *Jacobsen, Sons & Co.* v. *Underwood & Son* (1894) 21 R. 654.

[63] *Comm.*, I,343.

[64] (1897) 24 R. 965.

[65] (1901) 9 S.L.T. 222.

[66] *Inst.*, I,iii,9.

reasonable time.[67] Similarly, Lord President Inglis in *Glasgow Steam Shipping Co.* v. *Watson*[68] said: "every offer requires to be timeously accepted."[69]

45 What is a reasonable time is a question of fact. It depends on the circumstances of each case. It is also a problem to be solved by the standard of the reasonable observer, rather than the secret whims of the parties.

An offeror who needs an unusually quick acceptance should specify this in the offer. If he is silent he cannot complain if the acceptor, ignorant of the urgency, acts with the deliberation of the reasonable man.

46 Several factors suggest themselves as worthy of investigation by a person with a problem in this area. (1) Usage of trade may be relevant.[70] (2) The market in which the offer is made. If the market is fluctuating, the time may be short. Five weeks' delay has been held unreasonable in dealing involving iron,[71] as was a delay of over two months in accepting an offer to supply coal.[72] On the Stock Exchange a delay of minutes could be unreasonable. On the other hand nearly two weeks were allowed to accept an offer to execute masonwork.[73] (3) The subject-matter of the offer. If it changes in quality this may be a ground on which the offer lapses.[74] (4) The method of communication between the parties. In the absence of authority some speculation is necessary. According to the standard of the reasonable observer, the shopkeeper's offer to his customer over the counter may need almost immediate acceptance. It is too late for the customer to return next day, even although the goods are not perishable or the price has not altered. The shopkeeper would reasonably have regarded himself as free to sell the goods to someone else after his customer had left his presence. A written offer of sale of the same goods by the same shopkeeper made to the local hospital, may be capable of acceptance by letter after several days. The reasonable offeror expects a quicker acceptance when in instant communication, than when contact with the offeree is more leisured. (5) The actings of the offeror after making the offer. It is possible that he could consent to an extension beyond a "reasonable time." In *Glasgow Steam Shipping Co.* v. *Watson*[75] a continuation of negotiations after receipt of an offer was not, by itself, consent to allowing the offer to be accepted late.

---

[67] Lord President McNeill at p. 10, Lord Curriehill at p. 18, Lord Deas at pp. 23, 24.

[68] (1873) 1 R. 189 at p. 193.

[69] See also *Heron* v. *Caledonian Ry. Co.* (1867) 5 M. 935; *Lawrence* v. *Knight*, 1972 S.C. 26; *Ramsgate Victoria Hotel Co.* v. *Montefiore* (1866) L.R. 1 Ex. 109; Williston, para. 54; Corbin, para. 36.

[70] *Higgins & Sons* v. *Dunlop & Co.* (1848) 6 Bell 195.

[71] *Wylie & Lochhead* v. *McElroy & Sons* (1873) 1 R. 41.

[72] *Glasgow Steam Shipping Co.* v. *Watson, sup. cit.*

[73] *Murray* v. *Rennie & Angus, sup. cit.*

[74] See paras. 5–58 to 5–61.

[75] *Sup. cit.*

5–47   Exceptionally some offers may be open for acceptance for a very long time. A provision in a policy of insurance on surrender of the policy has been held to be a standing offer capable of acceptance by letter.[76] An option to buy shares might be exercised by a director or employee many years later.[77] Similarly the offer of reward could remain open for acceptance until the offer lapsed for other reasons such as recall or change of circumstances.

5–48   The effect of the lapse of a reasonable time on an offer should be distinguished from the same time limit operating on a promise, such as a promise to keep an offer open, or an option which is in the form of a promise. A promise is an obligation; an offer is not. It follows that to hold that a promise lapses after a reasonable time is to introduce a new period of prescription into the law. A promise remains binding until the lapse of the quinquennial prescription from the date when, broadly speaking, the promise is enforceable.[78] The problem was recognised by Lord Keith in *Sichi* v. *Biagi*,[79] whose views are preferable to those of Gloag.[80]

(3) Revocation by the offeror

5–49   A promise may not be revoked by the promissor, but an offer may be revoked by the offeror. In *Smith* v. *Colquhoun's Tr.*[81] an offer to sell shares was validly withdrawn before acceptance. When an offer and withdrawal arrived through the same post they were treated as one document and there was no contract. The case involved, *Countess of Dunmore* v. *Alexander*,[82] has been the subject of controversy.[83] It was distinguished in *Thomson* v. *James*,[84] in which it was held that the revocation of an offer had to reach the offeree to be effective. Lord Deas indicated doubts about the soundness of *Dunmore*. Gloag also had his doubts[85] and Professor Walker says it is no longer authoritative.[86] It is thought that there is no problem if the Countess's second letter (that of November 5) is treated as an offer of employment made after preliminary inquiries. The problem of conflict with other authority only arises if the letter is given the more unlikely construction of an acceptance. Eng-

---

[76] *Ingram-Johnson* v. *Century Insurance Co.*, 1909 S.C. 1032—but query whether this was an offer. Could the insurance company have recalled it? Surely not. If it had been treated as a promise, it would have been enforceable and the problem of acceptance would have disappeared.

[77] *Cf. Reynolds* v. *Atherton* (1922) 127 L.T. 189.

[78] Not the date of the promise. See Prescription and Limitation (Scotland) Act 1973, s.6 and Sched. 1, para. 1(e) and (g), Sched. 2.

[79] 1946 S.N. 66 at p. 68.

[80] *Contract*, p. 25.

[81] (1901) 3 F. 981.

[82] (1830) 9 S. 190.

[83] See para. 5–04.

[84] (1855) 18 D. 1.

[85] *Contract*, p. 38.

[86] *Contracts* (2nd ed.), para. 7–69.

lish authors cited earlier[87] consider the letter an offer. The result is that the case can be properly cited as an authority on revocation of offers.

50   If an offer is retracted by post on the same day as an acceptance is posted, there is a contract.[88] On special facts in *Burnley* v. *Alford*[89] an offer was held recalled when the recall would in the normal course have reached the offeree but did not do so because there was no one at the address. Lord Ormidale observed[90]:

> "It is one thing for the addressee to be absent from his office after business hours so that the delivery of the letter is delayed until his office opens the following day. It is a totally different thing for him to be absent from his office during business hours, with the result that the letter may lie on his desk unopened for a considerable length of time. In the present case the telegrams are said to have been left unopened or unread from the morning of the 12th September to the evening of the 14th. They ought to have been read on receipt . . . "

51   This rule is also illustrated by English authority.[91] It has the advantage of preventing the receiver's evidence of what happened when the mail arrived having an almost conclusive effect. It would be too easy otherwise for him to claim that he had not read an awkward communication. The result is that, in certain circumstances, knowledge is imputed to him.

52   In England it has been held that an offer is revoked although the information on the revocation is not communicated to the offeree by the offeror but by someone else. The case is *Dickinson* v. *Dodds*.[92] The rule has been criticised in England on the ground that it makes it hard for the offeree to know when it is impossible for him to accept the offer.[93] As Cheshire and Fifoot say[94]: "Is the offeree bound by any hint or gossip that he may hear, or must he winnow the truth from the chaff?" Anson points out[95] what might be the grave inconvenience of the businessman. The case has been followed in the USA, but it has also been severely criticised.[96] The case was decided on a subjective view of *consensus* which is not Scots law at least since *Thomson* v. *James*.[97] As Lord President McNeill said[98]: "Mere change of mind, on the part of the offerer, will not prevent an effectual acceptance—not even although that change of mind should be evidenced by having been communicated to a third

---

[87] See para. 5–04.
[88] *Thomson* v. *James*, *sup. cit.*
[89] 1919 2 S.L.T. 123.
[90] at p. 127.
[91] *Eaglehill Ltd.* v. *J. Needham (Builders) Ltd.* [1973] A.C. 992, at p. 1011; *The Brimnes* [1975] Q.B. 929.
[92] (1876) 2 Ch.D. 463.
[93] Chitty, para. 90; Treitel, p. 35.
[94] at p. 51.
[95] at p. 56.
[96] Williston, para. 57; Corbin, para. 40; see also in England *Henthorn* v. *Fraser* [1892] 2 Ch. 27; *Cartwright* v. *Hoogstoel* (1911) 105 L.T. 628.
[97] (1855) 18 D. 1.
[98] at p. 11.

party, or recorded in a formal writing, as for instance in a notarial instrument." *Dickinson* v. *Dodds* should not be followed in Scotland.

5–53   Revocation is not possible if the offeror has promised to keep the offer open for a certain time,[99] contrary to English law in which such a promise may not be binding because of lack of consideration.[1] A promise to keep an offer open should be distinguished from a time limit after which the offer lapses. An offer made on condition that it is accepted within three days may be withdrawn prior to the expiry of the three days.[2]

5–54   Revocation of general offers has special problems. The offer of reward may have been made *urbi et orbe*. How should it be recalled? A commonsense answer is to use the same method as making the offer, but that might not always be practicable. An offer may be made during a television programme and be repeated by the media because it is newsworthy. Its recall is ignored by the media. Must the offeror hire expensive advertising time on television and space in newspapers, to recall the offer?

5–55   The famous case in the USA is *Shuey* v. *United States*.[3] President Andrew Johnson offered a reward of $25,000 for the apprehension of Surratt, who was believed to be an accomplice of Booth in the assassination of President Lincoln. After publication of a revocation a zouave in the military service of the Papal government in Italy, ignorant of the revocation, identified a fellow-zouave as Surratt. The arrest of Surratt followed but he escaped to Egypt before he could be extradited to the USA. The Supreme Court held that the offer of reward could be revoked in the same manner in which it was made.

5–56   There are several problems with this reasoning. (1) As already mentioned it may not be practicable to revoke in the same manner as the offer is made. (2) Is a notice on a board which has been seen by many to be revoked instantly by tacking on a notice of revocation which has not been seen by those to whom it is addressed? (3) Why should the general offer be an exception to the normal rule that revocation requires communication to the offeree?

5–57   The question is, who should lose? The offeror, who has revoked, or the offeree who, in ignorance of the revocation, and perhaps with some trouble, has carried out the task which was to be rewarded.[4] Logic and equity suggest that the offeror should pay for the consequences of his actions known to and relied upon by the offeree. Until the question is decided in this country—(1) Be very wary of making a general offer.

---

[99] See above, para. 5–48.

[1] Chitty, para. 207.

[2] *Heys* v. *Kimball & Morton* (1890) 17 R. 381; *Effold Properties* v. *Sprot*, 1979 S.L.T.(Notes) 84.

[3] 92 U.S. 73, 23 L.Ed. 697 (1875). The facts are more explicitly described in the findings of the court below. With a reproduction of the reward poster they are in J. P. Dawson and W. B. Harvey, *Cases and Comment on Contract* (3rd. ed., 1977), pp. 365–367.

[4] What if an offer of a reward for rowing the Atlantic is recalled when the rowers are half-way across?

There are other problems, discussed above.[5] (2) If a general offer is to be made, put in a time limit for acceptance or specify the method of recall.

(4) Material change of circumstances

58   Apart from the lapse of a reasonable time there may be a material change of circumstances which results in the termination of an offer. Lord President Inglis said in *Macrae* v. *Edinburgh Street Tramways Co.*[6]:

> "It may, in my opinion, as a general rule in the law of offer and acceptance, be stated that, when an offer is made without a limit of time being stated within which it must be accepted, it may become inoperative by reason of any important change of circumstances, without any formal withdrawal of the offer being made. It may have been made in such circumstances as to be a reasonable offer as between both parties, but after it is made circumstances may so alter as to make it utterly unsuitable and absurd, and I do not suppose that it can be disputed that when the change of circumstances is so important the offer would not remain binding."

59   That case involved a tender which could not be accepted after a judicial referee had issued notes of his proposed award. Similarly a tender could not be accepted after the judgment of the judge of first instance[7] or, in a reparation action, after the death of a pursuer.[8] One aspect of *Lawrence* v. *Knight*[9] was the change in circumstances between making an offer in settlement of a claim and its acceptance by the pursuer. After making the offer the defender's advisers alleged that they had learned that the pursuer had left her husband, had not been supported by him, was contemplating divorce proceedings, and was living with another man. These facts made a material alteration to her claim for damages following her husband's death in a road traffic accident. The offer, made in ignorance of these facts, was no longer binding on the defender.

60   On similar principles an offer to buy goods cannot be accepted after the goods have been seriously damaged.[10] An offer of life insurance cannot be accepted after the life to be insured has sustained serious injuries by falling over a cliff[11] or when the insured contracts pneumonia and is dying.[12]

61   To avoid argument about what is "material" there is no reason in principle why the offeror should not provide that the offer will lapse on the occurrence or non-occurrence of an event, *e.g.* that the offer for all

---

[5] paras. 5–22 and 5–30.
[6] (1885) 13 R. 265 at p. 269.
[7] *Bright* v. *Low*, 1940 S.C. 280.
[8] *Sommerville* v. *N.C.B.*, 1963 S.C. 666.
[9] 1972 S.C. 26.
[10] *Financings Ltd.* v. *Stimson* [1962] 3 All E.R. 386.
[11] *Canning* v. *Farquhar* (1885) 16 Q.B.D. 727.
[12] *Looker* v. *Law Union Insurance Co.* [1928] 1 K.B. 554.

the shares of a company will lapse unless X per cent accept within 30 days.[13]

(5) Death and insanity

5-62   Once a contract is made, the effect of death or insanity of the parties is discussed elsewhere.[14] The problems here discussed arise from the death or insanity of the offeror or the offeree. Death or insanity could be a factor in an offer lapsing through material change of circumstances. The death of a pursuer in a reparation action affects a tender to him.[15] If a contract involves *delectus personae* it may be surmised that the death or insanity of the party who was chosen would prevent a binding acceptance. The more general question is the effect of these factors on their own.

5-63   Gloag assumed that death or insanity did prevent acceptance,[16] and there is some support for this in Bell[17] and Stair.[18] Lord President McNeill said in *Thomson* v. *James*[19]:

> "Death or insanity may prevent the completion of the contract as effectually as the most complete revocation, but they are not properly revocations of the offer. They are not acts of the will of the offerer, and their effect does not rest upon a supposed change of purpose. They interrupt the completion of the contract—that is, the making of the contract, because a contract cannot be made directly with a dead man or lunatic. The contract is not made until the offer is accepted: and if the person with whom you merely intend to contract dies or becomes insane before you have contracted with him, you can no longer contract directly with him. You cannot by adhibiting your acceptance to an offer, and addressing it to a dead man or a lunatic, make it binding on him, whether his death or insanity be or be not known to you."

5-64   This is a dictum based on the general ground that capacity to contract ceases. The importance of this is that the reasoning is equally applicable to an offeree. In *Sommerville* v. *N.C.B.*[20] the offeree died. The effect of this was argued but not decided.

5-65   English authority is ambivalent.[21] Particular care should be taken in using English cases on insanity because a completed contract by an insane person is not void, as in Scots law. The English approach to insanity as an invalidating factor is different from ours.[22]

---

[13] See Scottish Law Commission Memorandum No. 36, *Constitution and Proof of Voluntary Obligations: Formation of Contract*, para. 60.
[14] Chap. 24 (death) and para. 8–55 (insanity).
[15] *Sommerville* v. *N.C.B.*, *sup. cit.*
[16] *Contract*, p. 37.
[17] *Prin.*, s.79.
[18] I,x,6.
[19] (1855) 18 D. 1 at p. 10.
[20] *Sup. cit.*
[21] See Chitty, paras. 98 *et seq.*
[22] *Loudon* v. *Elder's C.B.*, 1923 S.L.T. 226.

66   Apart from the lack of authority the source of confusion is the conflict between the subjective and the objective theories.[23] A subjective approach would say that there was no contract if there could be no consent. An objective approach says that there is the outward appearance of a contract while admitting that there are difficulties if (1) the contract involves *delectus personae*, or (2) the death or insanity of the offeror was known to the offeree.

American authority has strongly argued that death or insanity of the offerer do not normally affect the power to accept.[24] So far as Scots law is concerned we, rightly or wrongly, adopt a subjective approach to questions of capacity to contract. When a person lacks capacity to contract it is a contradiction to state that thereafter he has entered into a valid contract. The *incapax* cannot make an offer. If the offer is made by a sane adult who then becomes *incapax*, his incapacity has supervened while negotiations are proceeding. The negotiations are at an end.

Acceptance of Offers

Silence by the offeree

67   Oliver Goldsmith wrote: "Silence gives consent." In some of our early cases there were indications that in dealings between businessmen, silence inferred acceptance. In 1817 Lord President Hope said: "It must be understood that if a man does not answer a letter of business addressed to him he is held to concur in the proposals that may be contained in it. This principle is firmly established in the law and practice in England; and it is important that it should be so established in this country."[25]

68   In a later case, his Lordship observed, apparently with approval: "I know that manufacturers often send goods without any order, merely stating that they are such as may be serviceable to the retail dealer; and the understanding distinctly is, that if they are not immediately rejected, and notice given to that effect, the party to whom they are sent is held to be the purchaser."[26]

69   Other case law indicates that a doctrine of acceptance inferred from silence was emerging.[27]

70   The doctrine expounded by Lord President Hope is no longer the law. The contrary is the correct position. Silence implies dissent from the offered terms,[28] or it may be that the offeree did not receive, read or

---

[23] See para. 5–11.

[24] Corbin, para. 54. But Williston states that it is not the law: Williston, paras. 62, 62A.

[25] *Serruys & Co.* v. *Watt*, Feb. 12, 1817, F.C.

[26] *Sharrat* v. *Turnbull* (1827) 5 S. 361 at p. 364.

[27] *Hunter & Co.* v. *Levy & Co.* (1825) 3 S. 605; *Jaffray* v. *Boag* (1824) 3 S. 266; *Webster* v. *Thomson* (1830) 8 S. 528.

[28] *Higgins* v. *Wilson & Co.* (1847) 9 D. 1407 at p. 1413 *per* Lord Fullerton; on appeal (1848) 6 Bell 195.

understand the offer. In a case involving a qualified acceptance it was observed: "It would have been both more courteous and more safe had they sent a reply declining the new terms proposed. But that their mere silence inferred acceptance is a most unreasonable contention."[29] The classic English case is *Felthouse* v. *Bindley*[30] in which the plaintiff offered to buy a horse from his nephew, adding: "If I hear no more about him, I consider the horse mine at £30.15/–." There was no reply and so no contract, although the nephew had intended his uncle to have the horse at that price. The intention was not communicated nor had there been at the relevant time actings to bind the nephew. The case also illustrates that an offeror cannot impose a contract by waiving the need for acceptance.[31]

5–71   The result is that the offeree does not need to go to the trouble of refusing an offer. He cannot be forced to incur the expense of buying a stamp or making a telephone call. However, silence may not always be the prudent course, because acceptance can be inferred from conduct.[32] For example, intimating rejection of goods sent, but not ordered, may prevent acquiescence being established.[33] To prevent an argument that personal bar has arisen, it may be prudent to intimate rejection of an offer particularly if dealings between the parties are to continue. Rejection of an offer terminates the offer.[34]

5–72   Unsolicited goods were a problem, resulting in the Unsolicited Goods and Services Act 1971.[35] In the circumstances mentioned in the Act a person who receives unsolicited goods may as between himself and the sender, use, deal with or dispose of them as if they were an unconditional gift to him and any right of the sender to the goods is extinguished.[36] To seek payment for goods knowing that they are unsolicited is a criminal offence.[37]

Form of acceptance

5–73   Express acceptance is effective, but as a general rule acceptance need not be by word of mouth, or writing, even if the offer is in one of those forms. There is an exception if the offer specifies a particular form or

---

[29] *Wylie and Lochhead* v. *McElroy & Sons* (1873) 1 R. 41 at p. 44 *per* Lord Neaves. See also *Liquidator of Edinburgh Employers Co.* v. *Griffiths* (1892) 19 R. 550 where silence rebounded on the offerees who wished later to found on an offer to rescind a contract. The result was their liability as contributories of a company.

[30] (1862) 11 C.B.(N.S.) 869. The decision has been criticised on the result on the facts: see Chitty, para. 79; Treitel, p. 26. The doubt turns on what may be required to waive the need for acceptance.

[31] See also Uniform Laws on International Sales Act 1967, Sched. 2, art. 2(2).

[32] See below.

[33] *McLean & Hope* v. *Thomas* (1869) 42 Sc.Jur. 159.

[34] See para. 5–34.

[35] Amended in particular by the Unsolicited Goods and Services (Amendment) Act 1975.

[36] s.1(1).

[37] s.2.

method of acceptance, *e.g.* if it requires an acceptance to reach the offeror.[38] An equivalent mode may suffice and the prescribed method may be waived.[39] Further the rules on constitution and proof of obligations may require writing.

Conduct as acceptance

74   Acceptance may be inferred from conduct. Whether this inference is justified is a matter of fact, and decisions on particular facts do not rule other cases. The parties may act as though there was a completed contract by implementing the offer or starting to implement it.[40] As Lord Craighill put it, in a case of a lease:

> "It is not mere lapse of time that will suffice to make up an equivalent for the necessity of signing so as to complete the contract. It is the acceptance of the one party, or of both parties, or the performance by them of what is equivalent to acceptance. What is equivalent is this—where one of the parties takes benefit from the proposed contract, and where another party has fulfilled some obligation which was incumbent upon him only if the contract were a completed contract; and if this last is done with the knowledge, and presumably with the consent, of the other party to the contract, then both are bound. When once it is reduced to this, that both parties act as if the contract were completed, then both are bound by that as a completed contract."[41]

75   Certificates or shares may be issued, or payments made.[42] An employee may accept terms of employment by continuing to work and without having signed a written acknowledgment of the terms.[43] The actings must relate to the offer concerned. To send goods at advertised rates may be acceptance of the rates, but not acceptance of an offer to keep the rates fixed for a certain time,[44] this being part of the general problem that an acceptance must meet the offer. As Viscount Dunedin put it[45]: "It is just as if a tradesman put up a notice: 'My price for such-and-such goods during November will be so-and-so.' That offer may at any time be converted into a contract by a person tendering the price for the goods, but there is no contract that the tradesman may not change his mind and withdraw his offer."

---

[38] *Thomson* v. *James* (1855) 18 D. 1 at p. 23 *per* Lord Deas; *Financings Ltd.* v. *Stimson* [1962] 3 All E.R. 386; *Robophone Facilities* v. *Blank* [1966] 3 All E.R. 128; *Holwell Securities Ltd.* v. *Hughes* [1974] 1 All E.R. 161.
[39] *Manchester Diocesan Council for Education* v. *Commercial and General Investments Ltd.* [1969] 3 All E.R. 1593.
[40] *Kinninmont* v. *Paxton* (1892) 20 R. 128; *Ballantine* v. *Stevenson* (1881) 8 R. 959; *Robertson* v. *Royal Exchange Ass. Corp.*, 1925 S.C. 1.
[41] *Ballantine* v. *Stevenson, sup. cit.* at p. 976.
[42] *Wilson* v. *Walker* (1856) 18 D. 673; *Laing* v. *Provincial Homes Investment Co.*, 1909 S.C. 812; *National Benefit Trust* v. *Coulter*, 1911 S.C. 544.
[43] *SOS Bureau Ltd.* v. *Payne*, 1982 S.L.T.(Sh.Ct.) 33.
[44] *A. & G. Paterson* v. *Highland Ry. Co.*, 1927 S.C.(H.L.) 32.
[45] at p. 38.

There must be knowledge of the offer for there to be acceptance of it.[46] The offeree is bound by the reasonable interpretation of his actions. If he knew of the offer and the actions amount to performance of the contract in reliance on it a natural inference may bar him from denying the existence of a contract. The offeror should not complain, because performance is better than a promise of performance.

5–76   Because an objective theory of formation is followed a person may act in such a way as to accept an offer, even though that was not his intention.[47] This proposition is not as clearly supported by authority as one would wish but it is consistent with principle. Not only is it established that secret intention can be immaterial in considering whether a contract exists,[48] but the law of personal bar could scarcely operate if the subjective intention behind the action was relevant. It must be admitted, however, that the true position is not easy to state because there may be an exception if the offeror has tried to impose a method of acceptance and the offeree, without intending to accept, complies with the offeror's condition. Corbin, an American writer who normally favoured the objective approach, stated[49]:

> "If A offers his land to B for a price, saying that B may signify his acceptance by eating his breakfast or by hanging out his flag on Washington's birthday or by attending church on Sunday, he does not thereby make such action by B operative as an acceptance against B's will. If B shows that he had no intent to accept, and that he ate his breakfast merely because he was hungry, or hung out his flag because it was his patriotic custom, or went to church to hear the sermon, no contract has been made even though A truly believed B meant to accept."

What this may amount to is that there will be no contract if it is shown that there was another reasonable interpretation of the action. It is interesting, however, that Corbin put the onus of showing this on B.

5–77   All the consequences of an offeror trying to impose a method of acceptance on the offeree have yet to be worked out in Scotland. There has only been space here to indicate that there are problems. The prudent course in practice may be for the offeree to intimate rejection of the offer.

5–78   **Cashing cheques.** In one area where acceptance may be inferred from conduct there are numerous authorities in Scotland, mainly in the sheriff court. These are on the effect of cashing a cheque sent in payment of a claim when it is accompanied by a statement that the cheque, although not for the full amount claimed, is in full and final settlement. It is not

---

[46] See above, "Communication of offer," and *Taylor* v. *Allon* [1966] 1 Q.B. 304.

[47] *Gaskell, Deacon & Co.* v. *Mackay* (1870) 8 S.L.R. 253; *McSkimming* v. *Sisterson* (1917) 33 Sh.Ct.Rep. 325.

[48] See, *e.g. Thomson* v. *James, sup. cit.*; *Muirhead & Turnbull* v. *Dickson* (1905) 7 F. 686.

[49] para. 73.

thought necessary to mention all the cases. They are detailed in the more recent authorities.[50]

Sometimes the argument that there has been a compromise has been successful, sometimes not. The answer depends on questions of fact. Has the creditor agreed to the compromise proposed by the debtor? There is no automatic rule that cashing of the cheque implies agreement, and if Gloag said that, he was wrong.[51] Inferences may be drawn from the attitude of the creditor when he receives the cheque and the actings of the debtor if informed that his suggestion of full and final settlement is unsatisfactory. A proof may be necessary.[52] A practitioner faced with a cheque accompanied by a note seeking to make collection of the cheque equivalent to acceptance of a compromise which is unacceptable to his client may intimate to the debtor that the condition on which the cheque is sent is not accepted and it is proposed to cash the cheque. The silence of the debtor including his failure to stop payment of the cheque will mean his acquiescence in the creditor's position. But even in the absence of such intimation the facts may fail to disclose an acceptance of a compromise by the creditor.[53] As is said at the end of the article on *Smith & Archibald*[54]:

> "The defender tenders and pays only what he himself admits is owing—presumably the sum for which the creditor would be entitled to decree *de plano*. Why should the creditor be bound to return the debtor's cheque and peril his chance of recovering the whole debt on the prospect of the debtor being solvent when a final decree is pronounced?"

Acceptance meeting offer

-79 The acceptance must meet the offer or there is no *consensus*. So an offer to supply plant is not accepted by an acceptance to perform services.[55] In *Johnston* v. *Clark*[56] a minute of agreement of sale of land contained a condition that the purchaser would not be bound unless he declared his written assent within 14 days. The purchaser gave his assent in writing but added that it was given on understandings on the amount of the feu duty, the extent of the lands and the conveyance of minerals. There was no completed contract. An offer of rails and fish plates is not

---

[50] *McGuigan* v. *Wishart*, 1977 S.L.T.(Sh.Ct.) 12; *Ulferts Fabriker A.B.* v. *Form and Colour Ltd.*, 1977 S.L.T.(Sh.Ct.) 19; *Gilbey Vintners Scotland Ltd.* v. *Perry*, 1978 S.L.T.(Sh.Ct.) 48; *Modelux Linen Services* v. *Redburn Hotel Ltd.*, 1985 S.L.T.(Sh.Ct.) 60. The principal authority is *Smith & Archibald* v. *Ryness* (1929), only reported in 1937 S.L.T.(News) 81.
[51] See *Gilbey Vintners Scotland Ltd.* v. *Perry, sup. cit.*; see, though, the treatment of Gloag in *Modelux Linen Services Ltd.* v. *Redburn Hotel Ltd., sup. cit.* at p. 62.
[52] *Smith & Archibald* v. *Ryness, sup. cit.*
[53] *Modelux Linen Services Ltd.* v. *Redburn Hotel Ltd., sup. cit.*
[54] *Sup. cit.*
[55] *Mathieson Gee (Ayrshire) Ltd.* v. *Quigley*, 1952 S.C.(H.L.) 38.
[56] *Johnston* v. *Clark* (1853) 18 D. 70.

accepted by an acceptance of the rails only.[57] An acceptance of the legal conditions of an offer and the refusal of the illegal conditions did not result in a completed contract.[58] The lack of *consensus* can be a point taken by the court even if the parties state that there is a contract.[59]

5–80   It is not necessary that the acceptance repeats all the terms of the offer[60] but there are dangers of uncertainty in repeating some terms and not others.[61] The moral is, either say "Yes, I accept" or repeat the terms of the offer. The dangerous situation is in between—"Yes, I accept your offer of A," when both A and B are offered.

5–81   Conversely, conditions can be added to the acceptance which do not prevent *consensus*.[62] The test is whether the condition requires the consent of the offeror. Some conditions might not, such as a statement on the mechanics of the transaction—"You will require to execute two transfers"[63]—or that a schedule or forms are to be filled up[64] or that a disposition must be executed[65] or a formal lease prepared.[66] That much is clear on the authorities. On the effect of other conditions about to be discussed the cases cited are not always obvious authorities for the propositions which they are said to support. That is because judicial analysis may be confined to saying whether there is or is not *consensus*. The textbook-writer must sometimes venture further.

5–82   A condition which the law would otherwise imply would not need express acceptance.[67] Conversely a condition introducing something contrary to what the law implies requires acceptance, such as a condition indicating that the seller's title is doubtful[68] or that the title to heritage must be taken without a search.[69] A suspensive condition does require acceptance.[70] It has been suggested that a resolutive condition does not require acceptance,[71] but this is doubtful. A condition that a party may resile if, say, a trial is unsatisfactory or an event fails to take place, is a material addition to a contract. A method of termination of the contract additional to that imposed by law has been introduced. The

---

[57] *McSkimming* v. *Sisterson* (1917) 33 Sh.Ct. Rep. 325.

[58] *Thomas* v. *Farquhar*, 1934 S.L.T.(Sh.Ct.) 34.

[59] *Mathieson Gee (Ayrshire) Ltd.* v. *Quigley, sup. cit.*

[60] *Erskine* v. *Glendinning* (1871) 9 M. 656; *Philp & Co.* v. *Knoblauch*, 1907 S.C. 994.

[61] See conflict of opinions in *Harvey* v. *Smith* (1904) 6 F. 511.

[62] *Gordon* v. *Hill* (1839) 2 D. 150; *Jack* v. *Roberts & Gibson* (1865) 3 M. 554.

[63] *Tait & Crichton* v. *Mitchell* (1889) 26 S.L.R. 573.

[64] *Seaton Brick and Tile Co.* v. *Mitchell* (1900) 2 F. 550; *Ingram-Johnson* v. *Century Insurance Co. Ltd.*, 1909 S.C. 1032.

[65] *Thomson* v. *James* (1855) 18 D. 1 at p. 14 *per* Lord President McNeill, at p. 23 *per* Lord Deas.

[66] *Erskine* v. *Glendinning, sup. cit.*

[67] *Erskine* v. *Glendinning, sup. cit.* at p. 659 *per* Lord President Inglis; *Stobo Ltd.* v. *Morrisonss (Gowns) Ltd.*, 1949 S.C. 184 at pp. 191, 192.

[68] *Nelson* v. *Assets Co.* (1889) 16 R. 898.

[69] *Dickson* v. *Blair* (1871) 10 M. 41.

[70] *Stobo Ltd.* v. *Morrisons (Gowns) Ltd., sup. cit.*; *Towill & Co.* v. *British Agricultural Assoc.* (1875) 3 R. 117.

[71] *Jack* v. *Roberts & Gibson* (1865) 3 M. 554; *Hardy* v. *Sime*, 1938 S.L.T. 18; Walker, *Contracts* (2nd ed.), para. 7–54.

existence of this sword of Damocles should require the assent of both parties.

83   Requests or grumbles added to an acceptance do not prevent the acceptance being unconditional, *e.g.* a statement "Please send the goods as soon as possible," or "You have made a hard bargain." An expectation that money be remitted by Tuesday did not prevent an acceptance being unconditional in *Gordon* v. *Hill*.[72] This at first sight curious result may be explicable as a request or expectation, but not a condition. "I hope that you will pay on Tuesday" is different from "You must pay on Tuesday." Obviously in any given case the dividing line may be obscure, but the distinction is clear in principle.[73]

84   In deciding whether there was a correspondence between offer and acceptance, telegrams forming the contracts have been read along with other documents.[74] If there is more than one offer, whether in one document or several, it is necessary to show which offer was accepted to establish *consensus*.[75] An offer to several persons may, depending on the circumstances, not be accepted unless all accept.[76]

85   An offer may state that it can be accepted by an acceptance which refers to a price calculated by reference to other offers (*e.g.* £X higher than the amount another will pay).[77] An offer may be "£X higher than any other offer." A bid which fixes the price by reference to other bids is normally invalid in a fixed bidding sale. The reason is that a referential bid is inconsistent with the purpose of a sale by fixed bidding (which is not an auction).[77]

Qualified Acceptance

86   An acceptance which contains conditions additional to the offer amounts to a counter-offer. A contract is concluded when the qualifications in the acceptance are in turn accepted, without qualification, by the original offeror. The process of exchanging communications containing qualifications can proceed until the patience of the parties is exhausted.

87   In *Wolf and Wolf* v. *Forfar Potato Co.*[78] it was held that after the making of a qualified acceptance there was not in the circumstances of the case an unqualified acceptance of the original offer. The qualified

---

[72] *Sup. cit.*

[73] See also *Global Tankers Inc.* v. *Amercoat Europa N.V.* [1975] 1 Lloyd's Rep. 666 at p. 671 *per* Kerr J.

[74] *Jaeger Bros.* v. *J. & A. McMorland* (1902) 10 S.L.T. 63; *Philp & Co.* v. *Knoblauch*, 1907 S.C. 994.

[75] *Buchanan* v. *Duke of Hamilton* (1878) 5 R.(H.L.) 69; *Peter Lind & Co. Ltd.* v. *Mersey Docks Harbour Board* [1972] 2 Lloyd's Rep. 234.

[76] *Anderson* v. *Sillars* (1894) 22 R. 105.

[77] *Harvela Investments Ltd.* v. *Royal Trust Co. of Canada* [1986] 1 A.C. 207. See also the views of the Council of the Law Society of Scotland, "Sale of Heritage: The '£5 more' offer" (1967) 12 J.L.S. 2.

[78] 1984 S.L.T. 100.

acceptance was a counter-offer and a later telex from the acceptor did not withdraw these qualifications.

5–88   Two of the judges in the Second Division founded on a passage in Gloag[79] which reads: "An offer falls if it is refused. If the refusal is not peremptory, but combined with a request for better terms, the general construction is that the offer is gone, and that the party to whom it was made, on failure to obtain the terms he requests, cannot fall back on an acceptance of the original offer."

5–89   Despite this general expression[80] it may not always apply. Lord McDonald observed[81] that if the parties continue to negotiate there could be a concluded contract based on the terms of the original offer.

5–90   *Wolf and Wolf* was not concerned with this problem, namely (1) offer followed by (2) a qualified acceptance followed by (3) a withdrawal of qualified acceptance and transmission of unqualified acceptance of the original offer. If the original offer is open for acceptance there will be a concluded contract. The doubt arises as to whether stage (2)—the qualified acceptance—is a rejection of the offer. Despite what may be said to be the view of the majority of the Second Division in *Wolf and Wolf* it is thought that a qualified acceptance is rarely a rejection of an offer. An offer followed by a qualified acceptance is a normal part of the process for conclusion of missives. When missives are finally concluded the contract includes the original offer. Rejection of an offer is a more positive step than an acceptance subject to qualifications, although obviously it may sometimes be difficult to categorise any particular communication. The decision on the facts in *Wolf and Wolf* was undoubtedly correct, but dicta in the case should not be extended to different situations. In *Roofcare Ltd.* v. *Gillies*[82] the parties contracted on the basis that their contract was to be in writing. A qualification in an acceptance was not accepted in writing by the offeror, but work proceeded under the contract. On the particular facts it was held that the qualification was not part of the contract.[83]

The Battle of Forms

5–91   The requirement that offer meet acceptance has given rise to problems with the use of standard forms. The supplier A offers to supply goods to B. The offer is on a form with printed conditions. B accepts the offer by sending an order on the back of which are B's standard conditions. B's

---

[79] *Contract*, p. 37.

[80] It is said to be a "general construction" and it is limited to a "refusal." Normally, a qualified acceptance is not a rejection of an offer. A counter-offer is rejection of the original offer: *Butler Machine Tool Co. Ltd.* v. *Ex-cell-o* [1979] 1 All E.R. 965. See, however, Uniform Laws on International Sales Act 1967, Sched. 2, art. 7(2).

[81] at p. 106.

[82] 1984 S.L.T.(Sh.Ct.) 8.

[83] If there had been no work done it is difficult to see how there could have been a contract. If the contract was concluded by the actions of the parties subsequent to the documents, that might suggest a waiver of the requirement that the contract be in writing.

conditions, if different from A's, are a "counter-offer" to A which A may accept by conduct, *i.e.* by supplying the goods.[84] That A has not intended this result is irrelevant if his conduct, viewed objectively, is acceptance.

92 The problem is complicated when A realises that he is contracting on other people's conditions and not on his own. Therefore, he adds to his conditions a statement such as: "These conditions shall prevail over any standard conditions of the purchaser." B will be presumed to have read this when he sends in his order and in the absence of comment from B his silence may be assent to departure from B's standard terms. The problem is taken a stage further if B adopts A's tactics. B's order now has a statement that his conditions prevail over those of the suppliers. B has not assented to A's conditions prevailing. B's conditions are a "counter-offer" which A may accept by conduct.

93 The next level of sophistication would be for A to supply goods but make clear that he was not assenting to B's conditions. If there was no consensus on the conditions to apply there could either be, depending on the facts, (1) no contract or (2) a contract governed by the duties imposed at common law and not governed by the conditions of either party.[85]

94 In *Butler Machine Tool Co. Ltd.* v. *Ex-Cell-O Corporation (England) Ltd.*[86] sellers offered to sell a machine tool. The offer was subject to conditions which it was stated were to prevail over any conditions of the buyer. The seller's conditions included a price variation clause. The buyer replied with an order subject to different conditions. The sellers, in writing, accepted the buyer's order. The effect was that the buyer's conditions governed the contract. The seller's price variation clause was not part of the contract.

95 In *Uniroyal Ltd.* v. *Miller & Co. Ltd.*[87] a seller's acknowledgment of a buyer's purchase order was a counter-offer which amounted to a rejection of the offer contained in the buyer's purchase order. In another transaction a telephone order was deemed to incorporate conditions attached to an earlier quotation. Subsequent correspondence (including the issue of a purchase order) was merely confirmation of an offer already made and accepted.

96 In *Chitton Bros. Ltd.* v. *S. Eker Ltd.*[88] a supplier of fabric sent to its customer an order form with a tear-off acknowledgment slip. The customer ignored this order form and sent his own order. A provision on the customer's form conflicted with the terms of the supplier, but the

---

[84] See *B.R.S.* v. *Crutchley & Co.* [1968] 1 All E.R. 811.

[85] *Cf. B.R.S.* v. *Crutchley & Co., sup. cit.*, in the court of first instance [1967] 2 All E.R. 785 at p. 787.

[86] [1979] 1 All E.R. 965. See Scottish Law Commission consultation paper, *Contract Law—Exchange of Standard Term Forms in Contract Formation* (1982).

[87] 1985 S.L.T. 101; see for a critical comment, A. D. M. Forte and H. L. MacQueen, "Contract Procedure, Contract Formation and the Battle of Forms"(1986) 31 J.L.S. 224.

[88] Unreported, July 8, 1980, Outer House, Lord Grieve. The case is discussed in the Scottish Law Commission consultation paper *sup. cit.*, at pp. 2, 3.

supplier despatched the fabric. It was held that the supplier's order form was an offer which was met by a counter-offer from the customer. The despatch of the goods completed the contract. The result was that the contract was concluded on the terms of the customer who had fired the "last shot" in the "battle of the forms."

Communication of Acceptance

5–97   The general rule is said to be that an acceptance must be communicated to the offeror. This rule is sometimes stated too absolutely with the result that it has to be qualified by a series of exceptions, such as waiver by the offeror, conduct by the offeree, personal bar, and acceptance by post.[89] There are traces in the case law of the older subjective approach to formation of contract which, because it required a meeting of minds, needed the knowledge of the offeror that there had been acceptance.[90] It has been held that there is no acceptance when the letter is handed to a postman who is only authorised to deliver, not receive letters.[91]

5–98   The problem may be one of exposition rather than of legal principle. By an objective standard there must be *consensus ad idem*. Communication of an acceptance by the offeree to the offeror is the best method by which the offeree can indicate (1) that he has decided to accept and (2) that this decision is to be regarded as irrevocable. But communication of acceptance is not the only method of indicating these factors. Conduct in reliance on the offer may be acceptance,[92] as where the offeree uses goods supplied by the offeror, or despatches goods to the offeror, or a search is mounted for the Loch Ness monster in response to a general offer of reward. A contract may be concluded the moment an acceptance is posted.

5–99   Instead of saying that acceptance must be communicated, it may be more accurate to state that failure to communicate acceptance may be evidence that the offeree is still at the deliberative stage, but it is not an automatic inference from the offeror's ignorance of the offeree's intentions. What is required is (1) intention to accept, followed by (2) actions showing the intention to be irrevocable.

5–100   Intention to accept is not enough, because intention is revocable. "It is not enough that he commits his acceptance to writing and locks it in his own repositories."[93] The governing body of an institution may decide to accept an offer, but until more is done the decision is rever-

---

[89] See Chitty, paras. 64, 65; Treitel, pp. 17 *et seq.*
[90] *e.g. Gunn's Case* (1867) L.R. 3 Ch.App. 40 at p. 44; *Ex p. Stark* [1897] 1 Ch. 575, at pp. 591, 592 *per* Lindley L.J.; at p. 600 *per* Rigby L.J.; *Carlill* v. *Carbolic Smoke Ball Co.* [1893] 1 Q.B. 256 at p. 269 *per* Bowen L.J.
[91] *Re London and Northern Bank* [1900] 1 Ch. 220.
[92] See above, para. 5–74.
[93] *Thomson* v. *James, sup. cit.*, at p. 11 *per* Lord President McNeill; see also *Kennedy* v. *Thomassen* [1929] 1 Ch. 426.

sible and there can be no binding acceptance of the offer.[94] On the other hand if an agent of the offeree communicates the result of the meeting to the offeror, the offeree is bound in the circumstances where the agent has power to bind his principal.[95] If the agent acts without express or ostensible authority it is suggested that the communication of the acceptance does not bind the principal. A committee is not bound by every act of the office cleaner distributing details of its proceedings or by every "leak" from its least trustworthy member.[96]

01 The lack of need for communication of acceptance was graphically illustrated by Bowen L.J. in *Carlill* v. *Carbolic Smoke Ball Co.*[97] with the question[98]: "If I advertise to the world that my dog is lost and that anybody who brings the dog to a particular place will be paid some money, are all the police or other people whose business it is to find lost dogs to be expected to sit down and write me a note saying that they have accepted my proposal?"

02 It is sometimes said, as in *Carlill*, that the offeror has impliedly waived the need for notification of acceptance.[99] This approach may concentrate too much on the position of the offeror. Whether or not there is acceptance depends more on the actings of the offeree. It is his act of acceptance which binds him.[1] It is sufficient if he acts in a way reasonably indicating acceptance unless the offeror has prescribed a mode of, or time for, acceptance.

Communication by post

03 A postal acceptance takes effect when the letter is posted. The classic Scots case is *Thomson* v. *James.*[2] On December 1 an acceptance of an offer was posted at Edinburgh. On the same day the offeror posted at Jedburgh a letter withdrawing his offer. It was uncertain which was posted first. Both letters were delivered the following day. It was held that there was a contract. This rule gives rise to a number of difficulties.

---

[94] *Powell* v. *Lee* (1908) 99 L.T. 284—a decision which has caused some theoretical difficulties for English authors: see Anson, pp. 38, 39; Chitty, para. 64, n. 11; Treitel, p. 17; *Dow* v. *Kirkcaldy Corp.* (1937) 53 Sh.Ct.Rep. 31; and see cases of communication of offer, para. 5–28, n. 42. As similar results are reached it may on particular facts matter little whether the decision of a body is classed as an offer, acceptance or promise. See also Chap. 7, "Delivery of Deeds."

[95] *Smeaton* v. *St. Andrews Police Commrs.* (1871) 9 M.(H.L.) 24; *Chapman* v. *Sulphite Pulp Co.* (1892) 19 R. 837.

[96] The offeror may have a remedy against the unauthorised agent.

[97] *Sup. cit.*

[98] at p. 270.

[99] *e.g.* Chitty, para. 65.

[1] Bell, *Comm.*, I,344; Bell, *Prin.*, s.78; *Thomson* v. *James, sup. cit.* at p. 11 *per* Lord President McNeill, at p. 15 *per* Lord Ivory.

[2] (1855) 18 D. 1. See also *Jacobsen, Sons & Co.* v. *Underwood & Son Ltd.* (1894) 21 R. 654.

(1) What happens if the acceptance is lost in the post?

5–104   In *Higgins & Sons* v. *Dunlop, Wilson & Co.*[3] Lord Fullerton observed[4]: "I should most certainly hesitate to find, that in the supposed case of a letter remaining undelivered for months or years, the mere fact of the letter being put into the post-office completed the contract, so as to keep the offeror bound by an acceptance which never reached him." In *Thomson* v. *James*[5] Lord President McNeill thought that there might be "extreme or extraordinary cases" where the offeror might not be bound by the posting of the acceptance, as for instance if the mail was totally lost.[6] In *Mason* v. *Benhar Coal Co.*[7] Lord Shand indicated *obiter* that an acceptance needed to arrive to be effective. He followed the opinion of Bramwell L.J. in *Household Fire Insurance Co.* v. *Grant.*[8] However, the Lord Justice's opinion in that case was a dissent. The majority of the Court of Appeal held that allotment of shares was effective although the letter of allotment was never received by the shareholder. In doing so the court relied on dicta in the House of Lords in *Higgins & Sons* v. *Dunlop, Wilson & Co.* Chitty observes[9]:

> "The decision in *Household Insurance Co. Ltd.* v. *Grant* was only reached by a majority and involved the overruling of a previous contrary decision. This indicates that the arguments of convenience for and against applying the posting rule to such a situation are finely balanced. On the one hand, it may be hard to hold an offeror liable on an acceptance which, through no fault of his own, was never received by him; on the other it may be equally hard to deprive the offeree of the benefit of an acceptance if he had taken all reasonable steps to communicate it. Moreover, each party may act in reliance on his (perfectly reasonable) view of the situation: the offeror may enter into other contracts, believing that his offer had not been accepted, while the offeree may refrain from doing so, believing that he had effectively accepted the offer."

5–105   There follows further discussion of some of the equities of the situation, which become more complicated if it is a "counter-offer" or the acceptance of a qualified acceptance which is involved or if the offer is on a form prepared by the offeree. To avoid these difficulties the practitioner may state in an offer that an acceptance must actually reach the offeror. If he is acting for the offeree he may, depending on the circumstances, put a similar statement in a qualified acceptance so that the bargain is not concluded until acceptance of the qualifications reaches him.

5–106   The law as laid down in *Household Insurance Co. Ltd.* has other possible consequences. If the acceptance letter is mutilated in the post or the

---

[3] (1847) 9 D. 1407; on appeal (1848) 6 Bell 195.
[4] at p. 1414.
[5] *Sup. cit.*
[6] at p. 12.
[7] (1882) 9 R. 883.
[8] (1879) L.R. 4 Ex. D. 216. The case was mentioned without disapproval in *Brinkibon Ltd.* v. *Stahag Stahl* [1983] 2 A.C. 34.
[9] at para. 70.

acceptance telegram garbled[10] it is immaterial to the creation of a contract. What happens if the letter or telegram is misaddressed? It is arguable that if the offeree made the mistake the posting rules should not apply.[11] This is on the grounds that the offeror may have been held to take the risk of accidents in the post but not of the acceptor's carelessness. If the offeree made the mistake he cannot complain if that rebounds in his face. There are however problems in justifying the posting rule on the basis that the offeror is deemed to have trusted the post. Carried too far the logic produces absurd results, as in the USA where it has been said that as the postal laws require mail to be prepaid, a letter of acceptance mailed without a stamp will not create a contract.[12] What if the sender knew that the mail would be interrupted? Should he be barred from relying on a posted acceptance as completing the contract? There is a South African case on the point.[13] War interrupted postal services and this prevented the completion of a contract by the operation of the posting rule.

(2) *Does the posting rule apply to other forms of communication, such as telegrams and telex?*

107 The rationale of the rule is not confined to posting. As Lord Deas put it in *Thomson* v. *James*[14]: "it cannot be doubted, that if the offeror had sent his servant with the offer, delivery of the acceptance to that servant would have completed the contract, although the servant, so far from acting the part of a mandatory, had been as ignorant of the contents of the letters and of the object of his mission as a carrier pigeon, or the *pica* of the commentators."[15] In England the rule has been extended to the telegram[16] but not to forms of instantaneous communication such as telephone and telex.[17] Where communication by telex is not instantaneous (*e.g.* when a message is sent out of hours or by a third party) the time of formation depends on the intention of parties, business practice and in some cases a judgment of where the risk should lie.[18]

(3) *Does the posting rule apply when the offer was not made by post?*

108 Lord President McNeill in *Thomson* v. *James*[19] emphasised that an offeror who communicated by post invited the offeree to communicate his acceptance through the same medium. Lord Ivory referred to the

---

[10] On the application of the posting rules to telegrams, see below.
[11] See Chitty, para. 72; *cf. Jacobsen, Sons & Co.* v. *Underwood & Son Ltd., sup. cit.* at p. 657, where the possible error by the postman is mentioned.
[12] Williston, para. 84.
[13] *Bal.* v. *Van Staden* (1903) 20 S.L.J. 407, discussed in Wessels, paras. 146–148.
[14] *Sup. cit.* at p. 26; see also Lord President McNeill at p. 13, Lord Ivory at p. 15.
[15] *Pica* is a magpie.
[16] *Bruner* v. *Moore* [1904] 1 Ch. 305.
[17] *Entores Ltd.* v. *Miles Far East Corporation* [1955] 2 Q.B. 327. The anonymous writer of the note on this case in 1955 S.L.T.(News) 113 should be congratulated on a rare achievement—a reference to an S.L.T. note in a standard American textbook. See Williston, para. 82A, nn. 16, 19; *Brinkibon Ltd.* v. *Stahag Stahl* [1983] 2 A.C. 34.
[18] *Brinkibon Ltd.* v. *Stahag Stahl, sup. cit.*
[19] *Sup. cit.,* at p. 11.

Post Office as "a middleman between the parties."[20] These observations went no further than was necessary for the case before the court. In England the proposition has been put on the more general ground of whether acceptance by post was within the contemplation of the parties.[21] This might occur when an offer is delivered by hand or made on the premises of the offeree, but, the parties living in different towns, acceptance by post is within their contemplation. This approach is reasonable and the acceptance may complete the contract when it is posted.

(4) *Can the posted acceptance be retracted?*

5–109   The terms of the opinions in *Thomson* v. *James*[22] would suggest that retraction was not possible. However, it might still be possible to argue that an acceptance can be recalled before it reaches the offeror.[23] In essence there are two competing arguments: (a) Retraction is not possible because it would give the acceptor the best of both worlds. He could speculate against the offeror by posting his acceptance in the morning and, if the market moved unfavourably, retract by telegram in the afternoon; (b) Retraction should be possible because the offeror is taking the risk of delays in the post. If he wishes to guard himself against retraction he could prescribe another method of communication or state that acceptance was complete on posting. There is no conclusive Scots authority on these points. There is much to be said for the arguments against retraction given the existence of the posting rule, but in England and America a different view is taken.[24] The real problem is the posting rule itself, and, perhaps much of the discussion above on its consequences merely shows that the rule is pragmatic rather than logical.

Who may accept?

5–110   An offer can be accepted only by the person to whom it is addressed if it is addressed to a named person. The result is that, except with the consent of the offeror, an offer cannot be assigned by the offeree.

The problem being discussed only arises if the offer is to a specified person. The ticket clerk at the station does not know, and may not care about, the identity of most purchasers of tickets, but there is nevertheless a contract. The operator of a taxicab has been held liable in damages for failing to arrive although he knew only the address to call at, and not the identity of the hirer.[25]

---

[20] at p. 15; see also Lord Deas at p. 24.
[21] *Henthorn* v. *Fraser* [1892] 2 Ch. 27.
[22] *Sup. cit.*
[23] See Cheshire and Fifoot, pp. 43, 44 and a very helpful note by A. H. Hudson, (1966) 82 L.Q.R. 169.
[24] See authorities cited in Scottish Law Commission Memo. No. 36, *Constitution and Proof of Voluntary Obligations: Formation of Contract*, para. 46, which also *passim* contains argument on the problems of the posting rule.
[25] *Craik* v. *Glasgow Taxicab Co.* (1911) Sh.Ct. Rep. 157.

11   The general rule is clearly established in England. In *Meynell* v. *Surtees*[26] it was observed: "The first thing essential in a valid contract is certainty as to the parties to the contract, and in the simple case of an offer by A to sell to B an acceptance of the offer by C can establish no contract with A, there being no privity." This approach was followed in *Boulton* v. *Jones*,[27] where an order of goods directed to X was held not capable of implementation by Y who had bought X's business.[28] The rule is accepted by text book writers.[29]

Scottish authority is sparse. There is a dictum of Lord Trayner which supports the view that an offer addressed to A cannot be accepted by B,[30] and Professor D. M. Walker supports the proposition.[31] In general terms an acceptance must meet the offer. A discrepancy between the names of the parties offering and accepting may, however, raise two other issues: (1) error *in persona* could be relevant; (2) there may be a clerical error in the drafting of one of the documents. The former is discussed elsewhere in this book.[32] On the latter see works on evidence.[33]

---

[26] (1854) 3 S. & G. 101 at p. 117.

[27] (1857) 2 H. & N. 564.

[28] This case has been followed in Scotland on the different point of assignation of a completed contract: *Grierson Oldham & Co. Ltd.* v. *Forbes, Maxwell & Co. Ltd.* (1895) 22 R. 812. Gloag doubted the latter case and the authority of *Boulton* v. *Jones*, but only on the point of assignation. See Gloag, p. 422, n. 4; also *Reynolds* v. *Atherton* (1922) 127 L.T. 189 (H.L.).

[29] See Chitty, para. 334; Anson, p. 304.

[30] *J. M. Smith Ltd.* v. *Colquhoun's Tr.* (1901) 3 F. 981 at p. 990.

[31] *Principles* (2nd ed.), p. 531; *Contracts* (2nd ed.), para. 7–45.

[32] Chap. 9.

[33] *e.g.* Walker and Walker, para. 258; *Hudson* v. *Hudson's Tr.*, 1977 S.C. 255, discusses the prior case law. See also paras. 19–44 *et seq.* and Law Reform (Miscellaneous Provisions) (Scotland) Act 1985, s.8.

CHAPTER 6

IMPLIED TERMS

THE IMPLICATION OF TERMS

6–01 Stair said[1]: "A condition is oftimes *implied* in an obligation, though it be not expressed . . . And the condition may either be expressed or implied, as relating to the contracting, or to the performing of the obligation." Erskine in certain circumstances implied a mandate[2] or warrandice[3] or obligations in specific contracts.[4] Bell (or his editors) implied conditions in sale,[5] implied warrandice,[6] implied an agreement to pay wages,[7] implied mandate,[8] implied warranty in insurance[9] and implied entry.[10] These are examples taken from the index to the tenth edition, but closer inspection of the text shows obligations implied in many of the specific contracts.[11]

6–02 Morison's *Dictionary* has many cases under "Implied Condition," and "Implied Obligation." Gloag introduced a chapter headed "Implied Terms and Conditions" into his second edition of *Contract* (it was absent from the first edition). He saw the implication of terms as providing one of the most difficult parts of the law of contract.[12]

6–03 It is clear that terms may be implied in Scots law, but accurate general description of the circumstances in which this happens is fraught with difficulty. For certain of the nominate contracts, such as sale or hire, the source of terms which may be implied is case and statute law. For innominate contracts there must be other considerations,[13] which suggest that for a particular contract in dispute, and perhaps for that contract only, a term will be implied. Implication of terms thus arises at two levels—as a matter of general law and in the case of a particular contract. There are, therefore, two types of implied terms.

---

[1] *Inst.*, I,iii,8. See also *Inst.*, I,x,12.
[2] III,iii,33.
[3] II,iii,25.
[4] III,i,18, *et seq.*
[5] *Prin.*, ss.93–101.
[6] *Ibid.*, s.122.
[7] *Ibid.*, s.177.
[8] *Ibid.*, s.230.
[9] *Ibid.*, s.475.
[10] *Ibid.*, s.705; s.775A.
[11] *e.g.* ss.203 (pledge), 212 (deposit), 195 (*commodatum*), 159 (carriage).
[12] Preface to 2nd ed.
[13] Gloag, *Contract*, p. 288.

Types of Implied Terms

–04 In *Luxor (Eastbourne)* v. *Cooper*,[14] Viscount Simon L.C. mentioned a threefold division of implied terms,[15] namely (1) classes of contract in which the implied term is introduced by statute, *e.g.* the Sale of Goods Act or the Marine Insurance Act; (2) contracts where the implied term is introduced by the force of established custom (*e.g.* the period of notice in the case of hiring a domestic servant); (3) contracts where the implied term is necessary to give a business effect to the contract. It may be added as a gloss on these categories that statute law and common law could be equated for this purpose, which would leave two categories. Certainly, the third of Viscount Simon's examples differs markedly from the other two. Lord Wright in the same case drew the distinction between general rules of law which imply terms and an implication based on the intention imputed to the parties from their actual circumstances.[16] The result of the case was that the House of Lords refused to imply a term in a contract of agency that a principal would not dispose of his property otherwise than through the agent.

–05 In a later case Lord Reid spoke of the two meanings of implied term. He said:

> "Strictly speaking, I think that an implied term is something which, in the circumstances of a particular case, the law may read into the contract if the parties are silent and it would be reasonable to do so; it is something over and above the ordinary incidents of the particular type of contract. If it were necessary in this case to find an implied term in that sense I should be in some difficulty. But the phrase 'implied term' can be used to denote a term inherent in the nature of the contract which the law will imply in every case unless the parties agree to vary or exclude it. I think that it has probably been used in that sense in the cases founded on by the respondent, and I am of the opinion that it is only in that sense that the appellant's right in this case can be said to arise from an implied term.

–06 > "The respondent therefore could only succeed if he could establish some agreement—express or to be implied—by which the ordinary incidents of his contract of employment were altered. But all that he has to rely on is a so-called 'understanding.' "[17]

–07 In *Liverpool City Council* v. *Irwin*[18] the House of Lords considered the terms to be implied in the leases of local authority property. Lord Wilberforce instanced two cases in which terms were implied in contracts,[19] namely (1) established usage in mercantile contracts—"the courts are spelling out what both parties know and would, if asked, unhesitatingly agree to be part of the bargain"—and (2) the addition of a term to an apparently complete contract on the ground that without it

---

[14] [1941] A.C. 108.
[15] *Ibid.* at pp. 119, 120.
[16] *Ibid.* at p. 137.
[17] *Sterling Engineering Co.* v. *Patchett* [1955] A.C. 534 at pp. 547, 548.
[18] [1977] A.C. 239.
[19] at p. 253.

the contract will not work. A third type of implication—that of implication of reasonable terms—was treated with suspicion. A fourth type of implication was when the parties had not themselves fully stated the terms. The court searched for what must be implied. Lord Cross instanced two forms of implication,[20] namely (1) all contracts of a certain type—sale of goods, master and servant, landlord and tenant and so on—have some provision implied unless the parties expressly exclude it, and (2) in a particular—often a very detailed—contract a term has to be inserted to give business efficacy to the contract. There was no question here of laying down any *prima facie* rule applicable to all cases of a defined type.

6–08   It is thought that these dicta, although varying in their expression, support the proposition that implied terms are normally of two types—a term implied as a matter of general law, and a term implied in the circumstances of a particular contract. Custom or usage might on one view be treated as a form of implication somewhat between those two categories. It has, however, special rules and is separately considered later.[21]

WHEN ARE TERMS IMPLIED—AS A MATTER OF GENERAL LAW?

6–09   For implication as a matter of general law decided cases or statute may provide the answer, but that is not always so. It may be argued that the law should be extended.[22]

6–10   Various factors have been referred to, such as the necessity for implication[23] or the reasonableness of implication. In deciding a question on the warranties implied in a contract for the supply of work and materials, where there was an absence of authority, Lord Reid observed: "no warranty ought to be implied in a contract unless it is in all the circumstances reasonable."[24] Lord Upjohn implied warranties because of the lack of logical distinction from contracts of sale and "as a matter of common sense and justice."[25] Lord Wilberforce referred also to what was reasonable and logical.[26] Lord Upjohn implied warranties because of the practical business effect and just solution.[27]

6–11   The problems of implication as part of the general law involve consideration of nominate contracts, and only a limited treatment is possible in this work.[28]

---

[20] *Ibid.* at pp. 257, 258.

[21] para. 6–64.

[22] *e.g. Luxor (Eastbourne)* v. *Cooper, sup. cit.; Liverpool City Council* v. *Irwin, sup. cit.*

[23] *Luxor (Eastbourne)* v. *Cooper, sup. cit.* at p. 125 *per* Lord Russell.

[24] *Young & Marten* v. *McManus Childs* [1969] 1 A.C. 454 at p. 465. See comments on this in *Liverpool C.C.* v. *Irwin* [1977] A.C. 239 at p. 262 *per* Lord Salmon.

[25] *Ibid.* at p. 473.

[26] *Ibid.* at pp. 476, 477.

[27] *Ibid.* at p. 475.

[28] See paras. 6–20 *et seq.*

WHEN ARE TERMS IMPLIED—IN A PARTICULAR CONTRACT?

-12 Implication in the case of a particular contract is based on the "business efficacy" rule laid down in the famous English case of *The Moorcock*.[29] The case involved an implication that wharfingers had taken reasonable care to ascertain that the bottom of the river adjoining the jetty was in such a condition as would not cause injury to a ship. Bowen L.J. observed[30]:

> "Now an implied warranty, or, as it is called, a covenant in law, as distinguished from an express contract or express warranty, really is in all cases founded on the presumed intention of the parties, and upon reason. The implication which the law draws from what obviously must have been the intention of the parties, the law draws with the object of giving efficacy to the transaction and preventing such a failure of consideration as cannot have been within the contemplation of either side; and I believe if one were to take all the cases, and there are many, of implied warranties or covenants in law, it will be found that in all of them the law is raising an implication from the presumed intention of the parties with the object of giving to the transaction such efficacy as both parties must have intended that at all events it should have. In business transactions such as this, what the law desires to effect by the implication is to give such business efficacy to the transaction as must have been intended at all events by both parties who are business men; not to impose on one side all the perils of the transaction, or to emancipate one side from all the chances of failure, but to make each party promise in law as much, at all events, as it must have been in the contemplation of both parties that he should be responsible for in respect of those perils or chances."

-13 In applying these principles Bowen L.J. looked to (1) the knowledge of the parties in the case—what they both knew, and what only one party knew—and (2) how much of the peril of the safety of the berth it was necessary to assume each party intended to bear—which meant examining the control of the jetty owner over the berth in that particular case.

-14 Some criticism can be made[31] of the dictum in *The Moorcock*. The reference to "presumed intention" is theoretically suspect because there may never have been any such intention nor might it even have been the intention of reasonable men.[32] The reasonable man is a very elusive and unusual creature if he implies into contracts of sale or consumer credit or employment all the the terms which the law now implies. Further, any approach which following Bowen L.J. is based on failure of con-

---

[29] (1889) 14 P.D. 64.
[30] at p. 68.
[31] Gloag, pp. 288, 289. Commented on in *McWhirter* v. *Longmuir*, 1948 S.C. 577.
[32] *Contra*, Gloag, *sup. cit.*: "The hypothetical agreement which justifies the implication of a term is not, it is submitted, that of the parties to the contract, but that of two reasonable men in the same circumstances." See Gow's approach-based on public policy—*Mercantile and Industrial Law of Scotland*, pp. 20, 21.

sideration, is suspect to a Scots lawyer. Nevertheless when implication is being considered, not as part of the general law, but in a particular contract, it is difficult to be more precise than to refer to "business efficacy."[33] The alternatives to implication are either to reach a result by construction of the contract,[34] or to hold the contract void from uncertainty.[35]

6-15   In a dictum which has been applied generally to both types of implied terms, Lord McLaren observed[36]:

> "The conception of an implied condition is one with which we are familiar in relation to contracts of every description, and if we seek to trace any such implied conditions to their source, it will be found that in almost every instance they are founded either on universal custom or in the nature of the contract itself. If the condition is such that every reasonable man on the one part would desire for his own protection to stipulate for the condition, and that no reasonable man on the other part would refuse to accede to it, then it is not unnatural that the condition should be taken for granted in all contracts of the class without the necessity of giving it formal expression."

6-16   It has been held an implied condition that a photographer would not make copies of a negative without the consent of the person commissioning him[37]; that during a period of tacit relocation a lease might be terminated at the end of the year on notice being given[38]; that a seller of a business should maintain the continuity of connection with the shop premises of the business name acquired by the buyers.[39]

6-17   On the other hand where services were carried out in the expectation of a company merger it was not possible to imply that one party should pay for the services if negotiations failed.[40] There was no implied condition that an agent will never without the permission of his principal act in other contracts which may conflict with his principal's interests.[41] It was not implied in a contract of employment that a strike or lockout would not be treated as a breach of contract,[42] or that a workman would be paid at union rates.[43]

---

[33] But contrast the opinions of Lords Mackay and Jamieson in *McWhirter* v.*Longmuir*, 1948 S.C. 577.

[34] See para. 6–17, *e.g.* to hold that the term sought is contrary to the express provisions of the contract: *McWhirter* v. *Longmuir sup. cit.*, opinion of Lord Stevenson.

[35] See paras. 4–18 *et seq.*

[36] *William Morton & Co.* v. *Muir Bros. & Co.*, 1907 S.C. 1211 at p. 1224; applied in *Cummings* v. *Charles Connell & Co. (Shipbuilders) Ltd.*, 1968 S.C. 305; *Lothian* v. *Jenolite Ltd.*, 1969 S.C. 111; *Microwave Systems (Scotland) Ltd.* v. *Electro-Physiological Instruments Ltd.*, 1971 S.C. 140.

[37] *McCosh* v. *Crow & Co.* (1903) 5 F. 670.

[38] *Commercial Union Ass. Co.* v. *Watt & Cumine*, 1964 S.C. 84.

[39] *Barr* v. *Lions Ltd.*, 1956 S.C. 59.

[40] *Microwave Systems (Scotland) Ltd.* v. *Electro-Physiological Instruments Ltd.*, 1971 S.C. 140.

[41] *Lothian* v. *Jenolite Ltd.*, 1969 S.C. 111.

[42] *Cummings* v. *Charles Connell & Co. (Shipbuilders) Ltd.*, 1968 S.C. 305.

[43] *Eunson* v. *Johnson & Greig*, 1940 S.C. 49.

18   Previous authority can be of limited value. In *North American and Continental Sales Inc.* v. *Bepi (Electronics) Ltd.*[44] Lord Avonside implied a term that a licensee was bound to use a system. This was necessary for business efficacy. His Lordship stated that citations of previous cases said to be analogous were not helpful[45]: "It is one thing to realise these rules but another to apply them. Different minds might well come to differing results and a lawyer may well have by reason of his training a different outlook from that of a skilled man of business."

19   A term cannot be implied if it contradicts the express terms of the contract.[46]

GENERAL IMPLICATIONS—EXAMPLES

20   It is not possible in the compass of this work to cover all the terms implied in nominate contracts. The text considers (1) general implications on time; the specific contracts of (2) contracts for services and (3) custody or deposit, about which information elsewhere is sparse; and concludes with a treatment of (4) custom which can be viewed as a rather special form of implication.

(1) Implication of Reasonable Time

21   Where no time is fixed for acceptance of an offer, it may be accepted within a reasonable time.[47] Where no time for performance is fixed by the contract, it may be implied that performance should take place within a reasonable time,[48] or that a suspensive condition should be purified within a reasonable time.[49] Goods supplied should be inspected for defects within a reasonable time or claims for damages or rejection of the goods may be barred.[50] A trustee who proposes to adopt a bankrupt's contract must intimate his intention to do so within a reasonable time.[51] Similarly a liquidator must adopt a contract within a reasonable time.[52] Reasonable notice of 12 months has been required to end a dis-

---

[44] 1982 S.L.T. 47.

[45] *Ibid.* at p. 49.

[46] *Cummings* v. *Charles Connell and Company (Shipbuilders) Ltd. sup. cit.*

[47] Gloag, p. 36, and see para. 5–44; on the construction of an express reference to time, see *Sworn Securities Ltd.* v. *Chilcott*, 1977 S.C. 53 *per* Lord Ordinary (Maxwell) and authorities there referred to.

[48] *Hick* v. *Raymond & Reid* [1893] A.C. 22 (carriage); *Carlton S.S. Co.* v. *Castle Mail Packets Ltd.* [1898] A.C. 486 (carriage); *Sinason-Teicher Corpn.* v. *Oilcakes and Oilseed Trading Co.* [1954] 3 All E.R. 468 and *Ian Stach* v. *Baker Bosley* [1958] 2 Q.B. 130 (issue of bank guarantee or letter of credit).

[49] *George Packman & Sons* v. *Dunbar's Trs.*, 1977 S.L.T. 140.

[50] *Clerk* v. *Eliott* (1836) 15 S. 253 (repair); *Stewart* v. *N.B. Ry. Co.* (1878) 5 R. 426 (carriage); *Pinie & Co.* v. *Smith & Co.* (1895) 22 R. 699 (sale); *Strachan* v. *Marshall*, 1910 2 S.L.T. 108 (sale); Sale of Goods Act 1979, ss.34 and 35.

[51] Gloag, p. 426; Goudy, p. 285; *Anderson* v. *Hamilton* (1875) 2 R. 355.

[52] *Crown Estate Commrs.* v. *Liqrs. of Highland Engineering Ltd.*, 1975 S.L.T. 58.

tribution agreement.[53] There is a considerable amount of case law on the reasonable notice necessary to terminate a contract of employment.[54] A contract made in perpetuity may have implied into it a power to end it on reasonable notice.[55] It has been conceded that an insurance company should repair a car within a reasonable time.[56]

6–22   An implied term cannot contradict an express term and if the contract expressly allows an option to be exercised "at any time," it will not be implied that the option must be intimated within a reasonable time.[57]

(2) The Contract for Services

(a) Distinction from employment

6–23   A contract for services must be distinguished from a contract of service. The distinction between a person employed under a contract *locatio operis faciendi*, "for services" rather than "of service," (*locatio operarum*) has been analysed in the law of delict (because of the application of vicarious liability) and in cases on employment (largely because of statutory rights of employees) and in the application of tax statutes.[58] Reference should be made to the authorities cited if it is doubtful which contract has been entered into in any particular case. The present purpose is to outline the terms implied in the contract for services. This contract is very common in practice but has been somewhat neglected by our textbook writers. The contract of service, on the other hand, has extensive literature.

6–24   In its typical form the *locatio operis faciendi* is the hire of a tradesman or professional man to carry out work on an article or otherwise perform services. Where nothing is provided but the labour or skill of the person employed the contract is one of hiring not of sale. Where the workman provides goods as well, the contract might be one of sale or of sale combined with hiring. It is for example not always easy to distinguish in principle between a contract to build a house—normally a contract for services with materials to be supplied—and a contract to build a ship—normally treated as a contract of sale. The complexities of deciding which type of contract was involved were noted by M. P. Brown[59] and

---

[53] *Decro-Wall International S.A.* v. *Practitioners in Marketing Ltd.* [1971] 2 All E.R. 216.

[54] J. J. Gow, *Mercantile and Industrial Law of Scotland*, p. 716. See for a citation of case law, Chitty, para. 3491. Contracts of employment legislation prescribe minimum periods of notice. See Employment Protection (Consolidation) Act 1978, Pt. IV.

[55] *Staffordshire Area Health Authority* v. *South Staffordshire Waterworks Co.* [1978] 3 All E.R. 769.

[56] *Davidson* v. *Guardian Royal Exchange*, 1979 S.C. 192.

[57] *McWhirter* v. *Longmuir*, 1948 S.C. 577.

[58] Walker, *Delict* (2nd ed.), p. 133; I. P. Miller, *Industrial Law in Scotland*, pp. 11 *et seq.*; *Massey* v. *Crown Life Ins. Co.* [1978] 2 All E.R. 576 (and the seven cases cited at p. 578 *per* Lord Denning M.R.); *O'Kelly* v. *Trusthouse Forte plc* [1984] Q.B. 90; Chitty, paras. 3388 to 3406 contain a full citation of authority.

[59] *Treatise on the Law of Sale* (1821), pp. 574 *et seq.*

discussed by R. Brown[60] and Professor Bell.[61] In England the distinction between sale and a contract for work and materials has been said to be sometimes "extremely difficult to decide," but often of little importance.[62] It is an issue which deserves elaborate treatment which is not possible here.

(b) The scope of the work

25   The contract for services arises as a result of the agreement of the parties. If there is no contract a person who has performed services may be able to obtain some payment under the principles of recompense or *negotiorum gestio*. The application of the implied terms about to be discussed requires that a contract can be shown to exist. The scope of that contract may need to be averred and proved.[63] The parties might have agreed on a limited amount of work, *e.g.* "make this lorry roadworthy but do not repair its body," or on extensive work, *e.g.* a complete mechanical overhaul of the lorry. In either case there is a contract for repair of a lorry but the terms of the contract, often informally entered into, may make a critical difference to the success of an argument that there has been a breach of contract. If a tradesman carries out work which was not instructed he cannot recover for this work under the contract.[64] On the other hand the employer of the tradesman may wish to show an agreement to limit the extent of the work to be carried out.[65]

(c) Deviation from original contract

26   A deviation may be with the consent of the parties or by one party without the consent of the other.

27   If the parties consent to a variation of the original contract, the carrying out of that variation will not result in a breach of contract.[66] It can, however, pose a problem of how the tradesman or professional person's remuneration is to be assessed. There are likely to be two possible results. Either the terms of the original contract can be applied to the new situation[67] or they cannot be so applied with the result that the amount of remuneration will be *quantum meruit*.[68]

---

[60] *Treatise on the Sale of Goods* (2nd ed. 1911), p. xiii.

[61] *Comm.* 1, pp. 275, 276.

[62] Benjamin's *Sale of Goods* (1974), paras. 34–40.

[63] *Brown* v. *Nisbet & Co.* (1941) 57 Sh.Ct.Rep. 202.

[64] *Walter Wright & Co.* v. *Cowdray*, 1973 S.L.T.(Sh.Ct.) 56. In certain circumstances there may be recovery *quantum lucratus* under the principles of recompense.

[65] *Dalblair Motors Ltd.* v. *J. Forrest & Son (Ayr) Ltd.* (1954) 70 Sh.Ct.Rep. 107.

[66] *Forrest* v. *Scottish County Investment Co.*, 1916 S.C.(H.L.) 28.

[67] *e.g. Forrest* v. *Scottish County Investment Co.*, *sup. cit.* Many complicated contracts provide for the valuation of variations.

[68] *Mercer* v. *Wright*, 1953 S.L.T.(Sh.Ct.) 18; *Head Wrightson Aluminium Ltd.* v. *Aberdeen Harbour Commrs.*, 1958 S.L.T.(Notes) 12 (averred that variations amounted to frustration; proof before answer allowed).

6–28   If the workman deviates from the contract without the consent of his
employer, the workman is in breach of the contract. This will have the
normal consequences of a breach.[69] In the case of building contracts
there is a line of authority which indicates that special principles might
apply. The exceptional cases on building contracts make a distinction
between material and non-material deviations and in the case of material deviations the builder may have a claim in recompense. The idea that
there are various types of breaches is familiar in the law on breach of
contract. The concept that a material breach leads to a claim in recompense is the unusual feature of this series of cases.

6–29   In *Ramsay & Son* v. *Brand*[70] Lord President Robertson observed, in a
passage subsequently approved in the House of Lords[71]:

> "Accordingly the rule is, that if the builder chooses to depart
> from the contract he loses his right to sue for the contract price. But
> further, losing his right to sue for the contract price he does not
> acquire right to sue for *quantum meruit*, the other party never hav-
> ing agreed to pay according to its value for work which *ex hypothesi*
> he never ordered.

6–30
> "In the application of this rule it suffers a modification which in
> no way invades the principle. A building contract by specification
> necessarily includes minute particulars, and the law is not so pedan-
> tic as to deny action for the contract price on account of any and
> every omission or deviation. It gives effect to the principle by
> deducting from the contract price whatever sum is required to com-
> plete the work in exact compliance with the contract.

6–31
> "The question whether, in any given case, the deviations are of
> such materiality as to fall within the modification of the rule, or are
> of such detail as to fall within the general rule, is necessarily one of
> degree and circumstances. If the deviations are material and sub-
> stantial, then the mere fact that the house is built would not prevent
> the proprietor of the ground from rejecting it and calling on the
> contractor to remove it, and he might do so if not barred by conduct
> from insisting on his right. If this right were so insisted on, then the
> contractor would of course have right to the materials, but he
> would have no right to payment. If, on the other hand, the proprie-
> tor made the best of it and let the house stay, the only claim which
> the contractor could have would be a claim of recompense; and
> this, be it observed, would be not for *quantum meruit* the builder,
> but for *quantum lucratus est* the proprietor. Accordingly, when con-
> tractors do not stick to their contracts they not only unmoor them-
> selves from their contract rights, but they drift into much less
> certain and much less definite claims."

6–32   In *Ramsay* the contractor failed to follow the plans but the differences
were held to be in detail and the proprietor had to pay the contract price
under deduction of the cost of bringing the building into conformity with

---

[69] See Chap. 14.
[70] (1898) 25 R. 1212. In *Forrest* v. *Scottish County Investment Co.*, 1915 S.C. 115 at
p. 133 Lord Skerrington described the *Session Cases* report as unsatisfactory and referred
to 35 S.L.R. 927.
[71] *Ibid.* at p. 1214. See *Forrest* v. *Scottish County Investment Co.*, 1916 S.C.(H.L.) 28 at
p. 36 *per* Lord Parmoor.

the plan. In a later case[72] Lord Mackenzie examined the Session Papers in *Ramsay* which showed that the attention of the builders had repeatedly been drawn to the deviation from the plans and they had been told that if they did not conform to the plans they would not be paid. Nevertheless the builders were entitled to sue on the contract, which was the same result reached when mortar and cement of the wrong specifications had been used.[73]

In *Steel* v. *Young*,[74] however, in the alterations to a Gourock villa, a builder used milled lime instead of cement mortar. This was not treated as a matter of detail, and it barred the builder from suing on the contract, leaving him with any remedy which he might have based on recompense. The case illustrates the difficulty of deciding whether a departure from the contract is a matter of detail or not. The value or sufficiency of the building was not materially affected by the use of the wrong mortar. To replace the mortar, however, would have involved expensive demolition and rebuilding. It is curious that the overall result was treated as being a departure from the contract in substance, rather than in detail.

In *Forrest* v. *Scottish County Investment Co.* there are dicta in opinions in the Inner House which cast doubt on the soundness of *Ramsay* and of *Steel*.[75] When *Forrest* was appealed to the House of Lords, Lord Chancellor Buckmaster reserved his opinion on the validity of *Ramsay*.[76] Lord Parmoor said that measure and value contracts stood on a different basis from lump-sum contracts and if *Steel* decided otherwise he disagreed with it.[77] He appeared, however, to accept Lord President Robertson's propositions so far as lump-sum contracts were concerned.

In the sheriff court, prior to the decision in *Steel*, Sheriff Principal Johnston had elaborated on Lord President Robertson's opinion in *Ramsay*.[78] The Lord President had distinguished between a substantial failure to carry out the contract as a whole (therefore no action on the contract—recompense only if building retained) on the one hand and deviation in detail (sue on contract under deduction of cost to undo the deviation). The sheriff principal added two further categories, namely (1) where the work to undo the detailed deviation is so great in propor-

---

[72] *McMorran* v. *Morrison & Co.* (1906) 14 S.L.T. 578.

[73] *Ibid.*

[74] 1907 S.C. 360. *McMorran* does not appear to have been referred to, probably because it was decided after the hearing, but before the advising in *Steel*.

[75] 1915 S.C. 115 at p. 125 *per* Lord President Strathclyde; at p. 129 *per* Lord Johnston; at p. 134 *per* Lord Skerrington.

[76] 1916 S.C.(H.L.) 28 at p. 33. In the Court of Session Lord Skerrington had said (1915 S.C. 115 at p. 124) that in *Steel* the Bench and Bar had overlooked that the contract in *Steel* provided for payment by measurement whereas in *Ramsay* the contract was for a lump sum.

[77] *Ibid.* at p. 36.

[78] *Anderson* v. *Dow* (1907) 23 Sh.Ct.Rep. 51 at p. 57.

tion to the contract price as to render that proposal unreasonable and improvident (the builder may refrain from suing on the contract and claim recompense); (2) where the deviation is trivial but practically irremediable, as a half-inch greater space between windows than shown on the plan, in which case an action on the contract would be sustained.

6–35   It may be thought that the whole problem is caused by the attempt to invent for building contracts special rules which are different from the normal rules applying to breach of contract. The difference between a material and a non-material breach is familiar. In the case of the non-material breach a claim for damages can be set off against a claim for the price. Although there may be argument with the result on the facts of the cases, that approach is consistent with *Ramsay* and *Steel*. The difficulty arises once it is held that the breach is material. There may be rescission of the contract and a claim for damages. More likely in the case of a building which has been erected, the building which does not conform to the contract is retained. In that case the normal rules of the common law usually allow an *actio quanti minoris* because matters are no longer entire.[79] The builder sues for his price and is met by a claim for damages. The one claim is set off against the other. In no case is there any reference to the principle of recompense.[80]

6–36   Recompense is not normally referred to in working out the result of a breach of contract. Further in *Steel* the majority of the court were of the view that a person who has broken a contract cannot sue upon it, which echoes part of Lord Robertson's opinion in *Ramsay*. This concept is referred to from time to time. It is mischievous and wrong. If correct it would have the result that if both parties were in breach neither could sue. A person in breach may not be able to compel the other party to future performance of the contract, but that is another issue. These problems are discussed elsewhere.[81]

(d) Time of performance

6–37   The contract for services may specify a time for performance, or indicate that parties agreed on performance before a certain time. If it does neither, performance should be within a reasonable time.[82] The workman may not be liable for failure to comply with a time limit if this is caused by the actions of his employer, for example, the employer's failure to allow access to a site or failure to have other work done timeously.[83]

---

[79] *Louttit's Trs.* v. *Highland Ry. Co.* (1892) 19 R. 791 at p. 800 *per* Lord McLaren.

[80] In the case of moveables it has been held that there can be an implied contract to accept materials and work which did not conform to the original contract: *P.E.C. Barr Printers Ltd.* v. *Forth Print Ltd.*, 1980 S.L.T.(Sh.Ct.) 118.

[81] paras. 14–25 *et seq*.

[82] *Charles Rickards* v. *Oppenhaim* [1950] 1 K.B. 616.

[83] *T. & R. Duncanson* v. *Scottish County Investment Co.*, 1915 S.C. 1106.

(e) Degree of care and quality of work

38   A person carrying out services impliedly undertakes to exercise the ordinary standard of care and workmanship of a practitioner of that trade.[84] It is probably more accurate to state that the work must be carried out with reasonable care in the circumstances, because it is possible for the court to hold that the practice of the trade, disclosed in evidence, is below the standard implied by law.[85] A person may, however, make it known that his skill is of a lesser standard than normal, in which case no more than that standard can be expected of him.[86] He may also avoid liability for "defective work" by making his customer aware that the job requires special skill which he does not possess.[87] But he must make this known to his customer or he will be held to have professed the requisite skill.[88] It is possible on the facts that the customer has exercised skill or judgment and taken it on himself to direct the work so that it cannot be said that the workman's skill is being relied upon.[89] A person, must, in any event, carry out his contract. If, for example, a plumber has agreed to provide and instal a bath, he must do so, and he is responsible for the condition of the bath, even though its defects, such as poor enamel, are a result of the manufacturer's failures.[90] If work is to be done on an article and the article is returned damaged *prima facie* the workman is responsible.[91]

39   There may be express terms that the work be properly completed or that everything necessary be done. These have not been held to import an absolute obligation. The contractor has to adopt ordinary good practice in the trade.[92]

(f) The employment of others

40   Except in the case of a contract involving *delectus personae* a tradesman may delegate the carrying out of the work to others.[93] By itself that does not pose any problems special to the contract for services. In the simple case the sub-contractors do not enter into any contractual relationship with the employer of the main contractor. Nor can the employees of the tradesman sue under the contract between the tradesman and another.

---

[84] *Dickson* v. *Hygienic Institute*, 1910 S.C. 352; *Terret* v. *Murphy*, 1952 S.L.T.(Sh.Ct.) 51; *Macintosh* v. *Nelson*, 1984 S.L.T.(Sh.Ct) 82.

[85] *Jameson* v. *Simon* (1899) 1 F. 1211.

[86] *Dickson* v. *Hygienic Institute, sup. cit.*

[87] *Brett* v. *Williamson*, 1980 S.L.T.(Sh.Ct.) 56.

[88] *Macintosh* v. *Nelson, sup. cit.*

[89] *Terret* v. *Murphy, sup. cit.*

[90] *Greig* v. *Kennedy*, 1953 S.L.T.(Sh.Ct.) 7.

[91] *Hinshaw* v. *Adam* (1870) 8 M. 933. As indicated in that case it may be a defence to show that the injury was due to some defect in the goods. The onus, however, would be on the tradesman to show that he exercised proper skill. Selecting a process which damages the goods could be evidence of a lack of skill.

[92] *Morrison's Associated Companies Ltd.* v. *James Rome & Sons Ltd.*, 1964 S.C. 160.

[93] See *s.v.* "Assignation and Delegation," paras. 17–50 *et seq.*

In some cases, however, it is argued that an independent contractor employed by the tradesman does have a direct action against the tradesman's employer. The tradesman is an agent who contracts on behalf of his employer and thus binds his principal to a third party. An architect employed to prepare plans for a building has been held to have implied authority to employ a surveyor[94] but not in the absence of a decision to go ahead with the building.[95]

(g) Payment

6–41 **(1) Is there an obligation to make payment?** If there is no contract between the parties, a contractual right to payment does not arise. The parties might be at the stage of negotiation. The plans or drawings produced might be part of the process of tendering or estimating. It can be difficult to decide whether or not this stage has been passed.

6–42 In *Landless* v. *Wilson*[96] an architect was held to be entitled to payment for plans, but the ground of decision is obscure. In *Pillans & Wilson* v. *Castlecary Fireclay Co.*[97] printers obtained payment for preparatory work for a catalogue. In *Sinclair* v. *Logan*[98] a joiner prepared drawings of proposed alterations to premises and was allowed remuneration on a *quantum meruit* basis. Likewise in *Robert Allan & Partners* v. *McKinstray*[99] architects were held to be entitled to payment for preliminary drawings. On the other hand in *Site Preparations Ltd.* v. *Secretary of State For Scotland*[1] the pursuers failed in their attempt to recover payment for the alleged use of their plans in the reconstruction of Peterhead harbour. The case was not founded on contract but on recompense. The averments were dismissed as irrelevant because any expenditure had been incurred primarily to benefit the pursuers. The question of who was intended to benefit was also a feature which enabled Sheriff Middleton to distinguish the tender stage from the contract stage in *Sinclair*. He said[2]:

> "The position of the pursuer is clearly distinguishable from that of a tradesman or contractor who submits a tender or estimate. The tender or estimate is in general submitted without any intention to benefit the person or authority requiring work to be done but purely to benefit the tradesman or contractor. It is generally submitted, in competition with others, so that the employment of the particular person submitting it is not a pre-condition to its submission."

---

[94] *Black* v. *Cornelius* (1879) 6 R. 581.
[95] *Knox & Robb* v. *Scottish Garden Suburb Co.*, 1913 S.C. 872.
[96] (1880) 8 R. 289. See comments on this case, Gloag, pp. 287, 288.
[97] 1931 S.L.T. 532.
[98] 1961 S.L.T.(Sh.Ct.) 10.
[99] 1975 S.L.T.(Sh.Ct.) 63.
[1] 1975 S.L.T.(Notes) 41; *cf. Mellor* v. *William Beardmore & Co.*, 1927 S.C. 597.
[2] *Sup. cit.* at p. 12.

43   In *Murray* v. *Fairlie Yacht Slip*[3] there was a request for an estimate of the cost of repairing a yacht. The yacht was slipped and transported to a yard. The work was regarded as done on the repairer's initiative as a preliminary to an estimate, and not as work done under contract. A claim for payment was rejected by the court.

44   If there is a contract an entitlement to remuneration is implied.[4] It is possible, however, to have a contract under which services are provided gratuitously, as in work where the expected reward is increased business,[5] or work for a charity or religious organisation where the reward may be in another world.

45   **(2) How much is to be paid?** Where there is a contract for services but no agreement on the amount of remuneration,[6] the entitlement is to payment *quantum meruit*. If there is a customary rate, that is the amount paid if the custom can be proved to be reasonable, certain and notorious. If no custom can be established the court will fix a reasonable remuneration.[7] The pursuer should aver and prove the sum due and the reasonableness of the charge.[8] Unfortunately, the evidence sometimes is incomplete on the amount of remuneration and the court has to make the best assessment it can.[9]

46   The court will take account of professional tables of fees but will not apply them rigidly. The overall result must be reasonable.[10] A person may on this basis be entitled to more than his profession's table of fees allows,[11] and an unqualified person might be entitled to the same amount as provided for in a published table.[12]

47   Professional tables of fees may not provide exact figures for the work done but refer to a general standard such as "fair and reasonable."[13] English case law indicates some of the factors to be considered in mak-

---

[3] 1975 S.L.T.(Sh.Ct.) 62.

[4] *Bell* v. *Ogilvie* (1863) 2 M. 336; *Winton* v. *Airth* (1868) 6 M. 1095; *Robert Allan & Partners* v. *McKinstray, sup. cit.* and other cases cited below.

[5] *Ranger* v. *Maciver* (1905) 22 Sh.Ct.Rep. 129.

[6] The amount of remuneration in a building contract may depend on an architect's or engineer's certificate. The issue of the certificate gives rise to various problems which it is not appropriate to examine here. See, however, *Veitchi Co.* v. *Crowley Russell & Co.*, 1972 S.C. 225; *Inverdale Construction Ltd.* v. *Meikleriggs Housing Soc. Ltd.*, 1977 S.C. 181; *Nicol Homeworld Contracts Ltd.* v. *Charles Gray Builders Ltd.*, 1986 S.L.T. 317.

[7] *Wilkie* v. *Scottish Aviation Ltd.*, 1956 S.C. 198; *Dalblair Motors Ltd.* v. *J. Forrest & Son (Ayr) Ltd.* (1954) 70 Sh.Ct.Rep. 107.

[8] *Scottish Motor Traction Co. Ltd.* v. *Murphy*, 1949 S.L.T.(Notes) 39.

[9] *Mellor* v. *William Beardmore & Co.*, 1927 S.C. 597 (although decided on appeal on the basis of recompense); *Sinclair* v. *Logan*, 1961 S.L.T.(Sh.Ct.) 10; *Robert Allan & Partners* v. *McKinstray*, 1975 S.L.T.(Sh.Ct.) 63. The same problem can arise with lack of evidence on the amount of work which has been done: *Sim* v. *McKenzie*, 1977 S.L.T.(Sh.Ct.) 67. If only one party leads evidence the most favourable inferences may be drawn from that evidence: *Davidson* v. *Duncan*, 1981 S.C. 83.

[10] *Wilkie* v. *Scottish Aviation Ltd.*, 1956 S.C. 198.

[11] *Robert Allan & Partners* v. *McKinstray*, 1975 S.L.T.(Sh.Ct.) 63.

[12] *Gow* v. *Portobello Co-op. Soc.* (1926) 43 Sh.Ct.Rep. 127; *cf. Winton* v. *Airth* (1868) 6 M. 1095.

[13] See the Law Society of Scotland, Table of Fees, reproduced yearly in the *Scottish Law Directory*.

ing this type of assessment for the purposes of a solicitor's remuneration.

6–48   In *Maltby* v. *D. J. Freeman & Co.*[14] solicitors acted in the administration of a deceased's estate. The logical starting-point for assessing their remuneration was the time involved, but this would generally represent an undercharge because a professional man rarely stopped thinking about the day's problems when he left his place of work. As Walton J. put it[15]:

> "No professional man, or senior employee of a professional man, stops thinking about the day's problems the minute he lifts his coat and umbrella from the stand and sets out on the journey home. Ideas, often very valuable ideas, occur in the train or car home, or in the bath, or even whilst watching television. Yet nothing is ever put down on a time sheet, or can be put down on a time sheet, adequately to reflect this out of hours devotion of time."

Other items such as the amount and value of property involved have to be taken into account. In the case of a deceased's estate the correct method of charging was a percentage. The percentage in the case of a large estate must not be a flat figure. The percentage should decline regressively as the value of the estate increases.[16] In the case of conveyancing work it has been observed that the amount of time—which is an element capable of exact calculation—is only one factor. There may be a cross-check on calculating remuneration using other factors such as the value of the property involved, the skill and specialist knowledge shown and the urgency of the transaction (or the "adrenalin" factor).[17]

6–49   There has been an increasing tendency amongst solicitors to keep accurate records of time spent and the costs involved.[18] The element of costs is controversial because different firms calculate their costs in different ways. Further the more expensive an office is to run, because of its location, or the inefficiency of its management, the higher may be the remuneration claimed by the solicitor. There is some authority supporting the view that remuneration should reflect the expenses of running the practice because of its location.[19] Some take the view that a solicitor's plans for his pension, or the expense of his word-processors and other factors which are included in his costs, are not relevant to determining a "fair and reasonable" charge to a client. The differences between the various approaches have yet to be resolved by a Scottish court.

---

[14] [1978] 2 All E.R. 913.

[15] at p. 916.

[16] *Property and Reversionary Investment Cpn. Ltd.* v. *S. of State for Environment* [1975] 2 All E.R. 436.

[17] *Treasury Solicitor* v. *Regester* [1978] 2 All E.R. 920.

[18] The factors mentioned in *Bwanaoga* v. *Bwanaoga* [1979] 2 All E.R. 105 apply equally in Scotland.

[19] *Property and Reversionary Investment Cpn.* v. *S. of State for Environment, sup. cit.* at pp. 442, 443 *per* Donaldson J.

50   Further problems arise in any case in a contract for services if only part of the work is done. If the workman or professional person has completed his portion of the work, he is entitled to be paid even although his employer fails to complete the project. An architect who prepares plans for a school is entitled to his fees even if the building of the school is postponed.[20] A solicitor who prepares takeover documents must be paid although the takeover does not proceed. The agreed remuneration might have been based on the value of the finished work. In such a case and in the absence of the completed work a surveyor has been held entitled to payment *quantum meruit*.[21]

51   If the reason for the partial completion of work is the failure of the person employed, that person is in breach of contract and liable in damages. This should not, however, disentitle him to claim remuneration for such work as has been done, despite dicta and decisions to the contrary.[22]

(h) Risk

52   The normal rule is *res perit domino*. The owner takes the risk of destruction or deterioration. The owner may be the tradesman or the person for whom the work is being done. Lord Ardmillan illustrated the distinction[23]:

> "There is a plain and important distinction between the case, on the one hand, of work done by a contractor for an employer within the contractor's premises, to be delivered when finished to the employer, and the case, on the other hand, of work of a permanent character done by a contractor on the ground of the employer. The work of a sculptor supplying a statue, or a painter supplying a picture, the work of constructing a cabinet, a piano, a table or a clock, to be delivered when finished, is within the first class of cases. The work of building a mansion, or building a conservatory, or building a wall on the property of the employer is within the second class of cases. The distinction is obvious."

53   When the owner of the work at the time of destruction is the tradesman, he bears the risk of loss, as in the first class of case referred to by Lord Ardmillan. Where the owner is the employer, he bears the loss as in the destruction of a brick gable in a violent gale,[24] or the collapse of a

---

[20] *Constable* v. *Uphall School Board* (1918) 35 Sh.Ct.Rep. 27. See also *Landless* v. *Wilson* (1880) 8 R. 289.

[21] *Rattray* v. *Yuille* (1878) 2 Guthrie Sh.Ct.Rep. 107; see also *Crouch* v. *S.W. Ry. Co.* (1881) 2 Guthrie Sh.Ct.Rep. 109.

[22] *Ballantyne* v. *East of Scotland Farmers*, 1970 S.L.T.(Notes) 50 (defective work). See discussion above on building contracts, para. 6–36, and under breach of contract, paras. 14–25 *et seq*. Decisions such as *Charles Gray & Son* v. *Stern*, 1953 S.L.T.(Sh.Ct.) 34 are doubtful.

[23] *McIntyre* v. *Clow* (1875) 2 R. 278 at p. 283.

[24] *McIntyre* v. *Clow, sup. cit.*

bridge, without the fault of the contractor.[25] The contractor is entitled to be paid for the work done in accordance with the contract, but opinions have been expressed that the onus is on him to prove that this work was done.[26] If the destruction or deterioration has taken place as a result of the fault of one of the parties, this will obviously result in the party at fault bearing the normal consequences of his acts or omissions.

(3) Custody and Deposit

6–54 Under a contract of custody for hire (*locatio custodiae*) goods are placed in another's possession and rent is paid for the custody.[27] Custody can also be an element in a contract for services (*locatio operis faciendi*) as when a car is left in a garage for repair.[28] Deposit is a contract by which one delivers property to another to be kept for the owner without reward.[29] The question has from time to time been raised as to whether the standard of care required of the keeper differs according to whether the contract is gratuitous or onerous.

6–55 Under Roman law deposit was a gratuitous contract which imposed liability for *dolus* but not for *culpa*, although gross negligence was the equivalent of *dolus*.[30] It is not fruitful to try to solve here the many doubts and difficulties with the concept in Roman law of *custodia*,[31] although the obligation on a custodier to return the goods would appear to have been, in some cases, more stringent than the equivalent obligation of a depositary.

6–56 Lord President Clyde in *Central Motors (Glasgow) Ltd.* v. *Cessnock Garage and Motor Co.*[32] traced the somewhat imperfect recognition of a distinction between the contract of deposit and custody made by the Institutional writers. The conclusion which his Lordship came to is not apparent. In *Walker* v. *Scottish & Newcastle Breweries Ltd.*[33] the issue was argued and the inclination of Sheriff Sir Allan G. Walker was to hold that the same standard of care existed whether or not the contract was gratuitous. In *Sinclair* v. *Juner*[34] Lord Keith, founding on Bell's *Principles* (although, perhaps, more accurately on Bell's editors), saw the obligations of the depository as no less in a contract of pure deposit than in a contract of deposit which is part of a *locatio operis*.[35] This has

---

[25] *Richardson* v. *Dumfriesshire Road Trs.* (1890) 17 R. 805.

[26] *McIntyre* v. *Clow, sup. cit.*

[27] Bell, *Comm.*, I,488.

[28] *Sinclair* v. *Juner*, 1952 S.C. 35.

[29] Bell, *Comm.*, I,277.

[30] Buckland, *Roman Law*, pp. 464, 465; J. A. C. Thomas, *Textbook of Roman Law*, p. 277.

[31] Buckland, *op. cit.*, p. 555; Thomas, *op. cit.*, p. 252.

[32] 1925 S.C. 796 at pp. 800, 801.

[33] 1970 S.L.T.(Sh.Ct.) 21.

[34] 1952 S.C. 35 at p. 46.

[35] The English authorities which are sometimes referred to are not necessarily in accordance with Scots law. See *Copland* v. *Brogan*, 1916 S.C. 277 at p. 282 *per* Lord Justice-Clerk Scott Dickson.

been followed in the sheriff court as a ground for rejecting a division between onerous deposit and gratuitous deposit.[36]

7   The standard of care imposed in the case of a gratuitous deposit[37] appears similar to that in cases of onerous custody.[38] The former distinction of negligence into three categories, namely gross (*culpa lata*), ordinary (*culpa levis*) and slight (*culpa levissima*)[39] has been departed from in other branches of Scots law and is probably disappearing in contracts of custody and deposit. The standard of care to be exercised by the keeper of goods is reasonable care. What is "reasonable" will vary with the circumstances. Alternatively the standard of care has been described as what a prudent man would exercise in the discharge of his own affairs.[40]

8   The onus is on the keeper to prove that he exercised reasonable care.[41] The onus is particularly difficult to discharge if the cause of the disappearance of or damage to the goods is unknown. For example if a lorry is sent to coachbuilders for repair and while in their custody is damaged by fire, the coachbuilders do not need to establish the actual cause of the fire to discharge the onus of proof that they exercised reasonable care. But as a practical matter it may be difficult to discharge the onus without proof of cause.[42] Discharging the onus does not need proof by corroborated evidence. It is sufficient if a suitable explanation is given by one credible witness.[43]

9   The onus was not discharged and a custodier held liable when a horse sent to be grazed fell into an obvious hole,[44] when money was lost and there was no evidence on the cause of loss,[45] when a night-watchman contrary to instructions drove a car entrusted to a garage,[46] when a vehicle in a garage for repair was destroyed by an unexplained fire,[47] when motor repairers left a car in an unsuitable place overnight[48] or

---

[36] *Uprichard* v. *Dickson & Son Ltd.*, 1981 S.L.T.(Sh.Ct.) 5 at p. 7 *per* Sheriff Principal O'Brien. The classical distinction between the use of the term "deposit" and that of "custody" has not always been observed in Scots law and there is no good reason why it should be. The argument is about differing standards of care in onerous contracts on the one hand, and gratuitous contracts on the other.

[37] *Copland* v. *Brogan*, 1916 S.C. 277.

[38] *e.g. Sinclair* v. *Juner*, 1952 S.C. 35; *Forbes* v. *Aberdeen Motors Ltd.*, 1965 S.C. 193; *Verrico* v. *Hughes & Son Ltd.*, 1980 S.C. 179.

[39] Bell, *Comm.*, I,483.

[40] *e.g. Verrico* v. *Hughes & Son Ltd., sup. cit., McLean* v. *Warnock* (1883) 10 R. 1052.

[41] *Copland* v. *Brogan, sup. cit.; Sinclair* v. *Juner, sup. cit.; Russell* v. *Bose*, 1948 S.L.T.(Sh.Ct.) 55.

[42] *Macrae* v. *K. & I. Ltd.*, 1962 S.L.T.(Notes) 90. See also *Woolverton* v. *George Outram & Co.*, 1973 S.L.T.(Notes) 45.

[43] *Verrico* v. *Hughes & Son Ltd., sup. cit.*

[44] *McLean* v. *Warnock* (1883) 10 R. 1052.

[45] *Copland* v. *Brogan*, 1916 S.C. 277.

[46] *Central Motors (Glasgow) Ltd.* v. *Cessnock Garage & Motor Co.*, 1925 S.C. 796.

[47] *Sinclair* v. *Juner*, 1952 S.C. 35; *Macrae* v. *K. & I. Ltd.*, 1962 S.L.T.(Notes) 90.

[48] *Miller* v. *Howden*, 1968 S.L.T.(Sh.Ct.) 82; *Verrico* v. *Hughes & Son Ltd.*, 1980 S.C. 179.

unlocked with the keys in the ignition,[49] and when an assistant manager drove and damaged a car whose owner had parked the car in a hotel car park and deposited the keys.[50]

6–60   The obligation of the custodier would not extend to valuable articles unexpectedly and clandestinely concealed within the goods, but will extend to items which might reasonably be expected to be within, or part of, the goods deposited, such as the normal contents of the van of a wholesale confectioner and tobacconist.[51]

6–61   If there is dispute on whether or not an article has been returned to its owner, the onus of proving restoration is on the custodier.[52]

Which type of obligation?

6–62   It may be added to complete the description of the problems, that some forms of apparent deposit or custody may involve other obligations with differing consequences. A hotel-keeper, for example, may be liable under the edict *nautae caupones stabularii*.[53] It has been held in the sheriff court that leaving a scooter in a car park and buying a parking ticket involves a relationship of licensor and licensee and not a contract of custody.[54] This view was founded on English authority which distinguishes bailment from licence. In the normal case a custodier is under an obligation to restore but it is conceivable that a contract of some type can be entered into without this obligation being implied. There are attractions in saying that a car parking ticket gives a right to leave a car but implies no more. But what if the car is parked in a multistorey car park which collapses? Are the occupiers of the car park entitled to say that they cannot be in breach of contract despite the inability of the owner to retrieve the vehicle he left with them? Does a similar rule apply to other cases in which the owner will collect his goods himself, such as some forms of left-luggage containers or bank deposit boxes? If there is a contract between the parties the natural expectation is that obligations will be implied on both sides, especially if the contract is onerous, but what suffices to create a contract of custody remains to be decided in Scots law.

6–63   Even if there is a gratuitous contract of deposit, it may be proved *prout de jure*.[55]

---

[49] *Forbes* v. *Aberdeen Motors Ltd.*, 1965 S.C. 193.

[50] *Walker* v. *Scottish & Newcastle Breweries Ltd.*, 1970 S.L.T.(Sh.Ct.) 21.

[51] *Tognini Bros.* v. *Dick Bros.*, 1968 S.L.T.(Sh.Ct.) 87; see also *Croall & Croall* v. *Sharp*, 1954 S.L.T.(Sh.Ct.) 35.

[52] *Uprichard* v. *J. Dickson & Son Ltd.*, 1981 S.L.T.(Sh.Ct.) 5; *Taylor* v. *Nisbet* (1901) 4 F. 79 (which dicusses corroboration).

[53] *Burns* v. *Royal Hotel (St. Andrews) Ltd.*, 1958 S.C. 354. On discharge of onus see *Macrae* v. *K. & I. Ltd.*, 1962 S.L.T.(Notes) 90.

[54] *Drynan* v. *Scottish Ice Rink Co.*, 1971 S.L.T.(Sh.Ct.) 59.

[55] *Taylor* v. *Nisbet, sup. cit.*; *Walker* v. *Scottish & Newcastle Breweries, sup. cit.*

(4) Custom

4 In order that a custom or, to be more exact, a commercial usage, may be binding upon parties to a contract, it is essential that it should be certain, that it should be uniform, that it should be reasonable and that it should be notorious.[56] It is unlikely that a uniform and accepted practice would be unreasonable.[57] Notoriety does not mean known to all the world or even to the person against whom it is asserted.

> "It certainly does mean that it must be well known at the place to which it applies, and be capable of ready ascertainment by any person who proposes to enter into a contract of which that usage would form part. It is in fact to be regarded as though it were a term so well known in connection with the particular transaction that it was nothing but waste of time and writing to introduce it into the contract."[58]

5 It would be difficult to establish uniform custom in the face of protests against it, nor should many instances of a general practice (which may spring from express contract) be confused with a settled and established practice which amounts to the acceptance of a binding obligation in accordance with a custom apart from a particular bargain.[59] As has been observed, proof of what generally happens is not necessarily proof of custom. There may need to be proof of unsuccessful attempts to act contrary to the alleged usage.[60]

6 In *Wilkie* v. *Scottish Aviation*[61] a surveyor was employed as a valuer, adviser and witness. In the absence of express agreement on remuneration he was held entitled to remuneration at the customary rate if he could prove the existence of a custom which was reasonable, certain and notorious. In the absence of proof of such a custom the court would fix a reasonable remuneration. In *William Morton & Co.* v. *Muir Brothers & Co.*[62] the evidence established a custom amongst certain manufacturers in the Irvine valley on the use of designs supplied by one manufacturer to another. It is a feature of custom that not only may it alter the common law but it may be limited to some geographical areas or confined to certain trades or professions.[63]

7 Usage can become a term implied by law of which proof is unnecessary. This appears to have happened in the implied obligation which a landlord had to relieve the tenant of rates.[64] Custom being an implied

---

[56] *Strathlorne Steamship Co,* v. *Baird & Sons*, 1916 S.C.(H.L.) 134. The case contained an express reference to custom but it is thought relevant also to the type of proof needed to show that custom was implied.

[57] *Ibid.*, but see *Bruce* v. *Smith* (1890) 17 R. 1000—in which a custom was not just or reasonable.

[58] *Ibid.*, at p. 136 *per* Buckmaster L.C.

[59] *Ibid.*, opinion of Lord Shaw. See also *Laurence* v. *Wyllie* (1957) 73 Sh.Ct.Rep. 225.

[60] *Brown* v. *McConnell* (1876) 3 R. 788.

[61] 1956 S.C. 198.

[62] 1907 S.C. 1211.

[63] *Bruce* v. *Smith, sup. cit.*

[64] *Sturrock* v. *Murray*, 1952 S.C. 454; see also the custom of the Stock Exchange in *Clydesdale Bank (Moore Place) Nominees Ltd.* v. *Snodgrass*, 1939 S.C. 805.

term will not overrule an express term of the contract.[65] It is possible to have a contract which expressly incorporates a local custom[66] and a statute may refer to normal practice, such as "normal retiring age."[67] The usage between the parties may imply a term which is different from the customary usage of the trade.[68]

---

[65] *Duthie & Co.* v. *Merson & Gerry*, 1947 S.C. 43.

[66] *Cazalet* v. *Morris & Co.*, 1916 S.C. 952.

[67] The complexities which this has created are discussed in *Waite* v. *Government Communications Headquarters* [1983] 2 A.C. 714; *Hughes* v. *D.H.S.S.* [1985] A.C. 776.

[68] *Eunson* v. *Johnson & Greig*, 1940 S.C. 49.

CHAPTER 7

DELIVERY OF DEEDS

THE PRINCIPLE OF DELIVERY

1   As a general rule a writing must be delivered to be effective. The classic text is in Erskine.[1] His principle was that:

> "A writing, while it is in the granter's own custody, is not obligatory; for as long as it is in his own power, he cannot be said to have come to a final resolution of obliging himself by it."

2   As was observed in *McGill* v. *Edmonston*,[2] a bond was ineffectual without delivery because until then it was lawful for the granter to "repent, and so cancel his subscription." Even if the granter has shown no signs of repentance, but even a firm intention to be bound, it is still necessary for there to be delivery. A memorable example is *Creditors of Stamfield* v. *Scot*,[3] where the granter had intimated to the grantee that the deed was signed and awaiting collection. The granter was found murdered with the signed deed lying on the table beside him. The court held that the deed had not been delivered. Intention to deliver, even that existing until death, was not enough.

3   There are other more mundane examples of the principle. If a deposit receipt is kept in a person's possession there may be no delivery to another named in it, with the result that the money forms part of the possessor's estate on death.[4] Failure to take infeftment in fee for children may mean that there is no delivery to the children and the provision for them is revocable.[5] The result may not be what the layman expects. In *Jarvie's Tr.* v. *Jarvie's Trs.*[6] a life policy was taken out for behoof of wife and children. The policy created a trust. Its existence was not known to the trustees or the beneficiaries. The husband paid the annual premiums. He kept the policy in his custody. It was held that the

---

[1] *Inst.*, III,ii,43 and 44 in *Maule* v. *Ramsay* (1830) 4 W. & S. 58 at p. 72 *per* Lord Wynford and in other cases cited below. See also Stair, I,vii,14; More's *Notes*, i,&,ccccviii; Bell, *Comm.*, I,336; *Prin.*, ss.23, 24; A. M. Bell, *Lectures on Conveyancing* (3rd ed., 1882), pp. 102 *et seq.*; W. G. Dickson, *Law of Evidence* (3rd ed., 1887), ss. 916 *et seq.*; J. P. Wood, *Lectures on Conveyancing* (1903), pp. 98 *et seq.*; Gloag, *Contract*, pp. 66 *et seq.*; J. M. Halliday, *Conveyancing Law and Practice in Scotland* (1985), Vol. 1, Chap. 9.
[2] (1628) Mor. 16991.
[3] (1696) Bro. Supp. IV,344. See comments on this case in A. M. Bell, *op. cit.*, pp. 102, 103.
[4] *Watt's Tr.* (1869) 7 M. 930; *Jamieson* v. *McLeod* (1880) 7 R. 1131. Contrast *McCubbin's Exr.* v. *Tait* (1868) 40 Sc.Jur. 158.
[5] *Stewart* v. *Rae* (1883) 10 R. 463; *Kindness* v. *Bruce* (1902) 4 F. 415.
[6] (1887) 14 R. 411.

policy had not been delivered. So its proceeds fell into the husband's estate.

7–04   Likewise if a man takes a deed in name of himself and his wife or his child, and retains possession of the deed, there may not be delivery to the wife or child. This was established in *Hill* v. *Hill*[7] which has been relied on or mentioned with approval possibly more than any other case on delivery.[8] If a deed is signed and held by the agent of the granter, delivery to the grantee has not taken place.[9]

7–05   It is thought that there are at least three factors which have produced this adherence of the courts to the need for delivery.

(1) The requirement of delivery is in the interests of the granter. It enables him to prepare documents but to change his mind up to a certain point. The law has taken the view that delivery is the irrevocable stage, rather than signature in the solitude of the granter's study. At least that is the normal rule. As may be seen it is the exceptions to this which produce most of the problems.

(2) The requirement of delivery is a protection for the granter's creditors and heirs. A man should not be able to alienate his assets by secret deeds, which he could alter or destroy at pleasure.[10]

(3) To suspend the operation of a deed until delivery assists the settlement of transactions. The solicitor for the granter can have the deed executed. That can be a lengthy business where there are several granters and consenters, the parties are distant, and the deed is to be probative. The executed deed is held by the solicitor and is inoperative until delivery at settlement. To have any other rule would be inconvenient.

Proof of Delivery

7–06   Delivery requires proof of both intention to deliver and the fact of delivery. Dispute as to whether delivery has taken place is likely to involve family deeds, at least judging from those cases which have been reported. The granter may not be alive. There may be suspicion that when alive he was imposed upon. In these circumstances the most important element may be the credibility of those giving evidence. The improbability of the transaction may hinder its satisfactory proof as when, in the days prior to modern social services, an old person was alleged to have gifted nearly the whole of her moveable estate, and the witnesses to the transfer were not impartial.[11]

---

[7] (1755) Mor. 11580.

[8] See *Walker's Exr.* v. *Walker* (1878) 5 R. 965; *Stewart* v. *Rae* (1883) 10 R. 463; *Connell's Tr.* v. *Connell's Tr.* (1886) 13 R. 1175; *Jarvie's Tr.* v. *Jarvie's Trs.*, *supra*; *Cameron's Tr.* v. *Cameron*, 1907 S.C. 407; *Carmichael* v. *Carmichael's Ex.*, 1920 S.C.(H.L.) 195; *Drysdale's Tr.* v. *Drysdale*, 1922 S.C. 741; *Dennis* v. *Aitchison*, 1923 S.C. 819, app. 1924 S.C.(H.L.) 122.

[9] *Henderson* v. *McManus*, 1981 S.C. 233.

[10] See *Allan's Trs.* v. *Lord Advocate*, 1971 S.C.(H.L.) 45 at p. 54 *per* Lord Reid.

[11] *Swan's Exr.* v. *McDougall* (1868) 5 S.L.R. 675.

7   In the proof of delivery several propositions appear to be established. (1) The onus of proof that a writ is delivered lies on the party founding on it.[12] (2) There is a presumption, rebuttable by parole evidence, that if the grantee is in possession of the deed it was delivered to him.[13] The presumption also operates if the deed is in the hands of an appropriate party connected with the grantee.[14] The presumption is not as strong as suggested by Erskine[15] and, particularly with gratuitous deeds may not be as strong as Walker and Walker may suggest. (3) The speciality with gratuitous deeds is that another very strong presumption operates. This is the presumption against donation.[16]

What is Delivery?

8   "Delivery" is a word of many meanings, ranging from its association with the production of offspring to bowling a cricket-ball, and from transporting goods to the manner of giving a speech. It is not surprising that after excluding the senses obviously irrelevant for present purposes there remains some flexibility of meaning. Various issues arise. (1) The intention to deliver and the fact of delivery must both exist. (2) In the simple case the fact of delivery involves transfer of possession, not merely custody, of the deed to the grantee. (3) It is not necessary for there to be a transfer directly to the grantee. There can be delivery to agents or third parties. There can be delivery on registration of a deed in a public register. This last example departs so far from the concept of a handing-over to the grantee that it may be categorised separately as constructive delivery, in contrast to actual delivery.

Intention to deliver

9   The question is what was intended, rather than what was done in form, and so a simulated delivery will be ineffectual, as when a deed was handed to the grantee and then handed back to the granter.[17] It follows that a document may be shown to have been handed over, not as a "delivered" document, but for another limited purpose.[18] This is relied upon when conveyancers are settling a transaction by post and delivery of a deed is to take place in exchange for a price. The granter's agent may send the deed to the grantee's agent expressly under the condition that the deed is to be held as undelivered until the granter's agent receives the price.

---

[12] *McAslan* v. *Glen* (1859) 21 D. 511.
[13] *Cathcart* v. *Corsclays* (1679) Mor. 12325; *McAslan* v. *Glen, sup. cit.*; Walker and Walker, *Evidence*, p. 59.
[14] Dickson, *Evidence* (3rd ed.), para. 940; *Lombardi's Tr.* v. *Lombardi*, 1982 S.L.T. 81.
[15] *McAslan* v. *Glen, sup. cit.*
[16] *Sharp* v. *Paton* (1883) 10 R. 1000; *Miller's Exrx.* v. *Miller's Trs.*, 1922 S.C. 150; *Grant's Tr.* v. *McDonald*, 1939 S.C. 448.
[17] *Buchanan* v. *Buchanan* (1876) 3 R. 556.
[18] *Scott's Tr.* v. *Scott* (1902) 40 S.L.R. 133.

7–10   The intention to deliver will end with the death of the granter and this terminates the mandate of his agent to deliver.[19] If the agent does not have knowledge of the death it is a moot point whether delivery by him is effective, this being part of the (largely unsolved) difficulties of the impact of a principal's death on his agent's powers.[20]

Delivery to and by third parties

7–11   There is no reason why a deed may not be delivered by one person on behalf of another. This may occur although the transferor is not in a contractual sense the agent of the granter. Thus, although a *jus quaesitum tertio* might not need delivery in the normal sense to create it,[21] if the question of delivery is raised, it may be shown that A has created a benefit in T by the delivery of a deed by B to T, when in other circumstances B would have delivered the deed to A.[22] So a father may say to his debtor: "Make the bond payable to my son." As Lord Moncreiff observed in *Collie*: "However it may be represented as a marvel, it is, when rightly understood, a very simple thing—a special investment for a son or a grandson."[23]

7–12   Where there are several parties to a unilateral deed it is almost inevitable that one may deliver the deed to the grantee on behalf of the others. Prior to that stage very complicated questions could arise if it were asked whether there had been delivery by one party to another in respect of some obligation in the deed, or delivery to the grantee although the deed was not executed by all the parties.[24] Cases involving cautionary obligations are somewhat special because of the equities of caution. Cautioners have, at common law, rights of relief amongst each other and if one does not sign (or his signature is forged) this prejudices the rights of relief of the other cautioners. Nevertheless the cases illustrate the problem of partial completion of a deed.[25]

7–13   When the deed is in the hands of the granter's solicitor, or in the quaint phrase, "ordinary doer," then normally there will not have been delivery to the grantee.[26] "So, my Lords, if this bond had been given to Mr. Duncan merely as the doer of Mr. Maule, it would have been the same as if he had kept it in his own strong box."[27]

---

[19] *Life Association of Scotland* v. *Douglas* (1886) 13 R. 910.

[20] See Gloag, *Contract*, p. 361; Bowstead on *Agency* (14th ed.), p. 427.

[21] See *Carmichael* v. *Carmichael's Exrx.*, 1920 S.C.(H.L.) 195 and para. 18–11.

[22] *Collie* v. *Pirie's Trs.* (1851) 13 D. 506.

[23] at p. 514.

[24] See, *e.g.* *McCreath* v. *Borland* (1860) 22 D. 1551.

[25] *Fisher* v. *Campbells* (1736) Elch.Dec., Vol. 1, "Presumption" No. 7—an unsatisfactory report; *Macdonald* v. *Stewart*, July 5, 1810, F.C.; *Paterson* v. *Bonar* (1844) 6 D. 987; *Scottish Provincial Assurance Co.* v. *Pringle* (1858) 20 D. 465; *Simpson* v. *Fleming* (1860) 22 D. 679.

[26] *Byres* v. *Johnston* (1626) Mor. 11566, 8405; *Irvine* v. *Irvine* (1738) Mor. 11576; *Henderson* v. *McManus*, 1981 S.C. 233.

[27] *Maule* v. *Ramsay* (1830) 4 W. & S. 58 at p. 73 *per* Lord Wynford.

Where the solicitor acts for both granter and grantee, there are obvious difficulties of proof. The problem was considered at length in *Maule* v. *Ramsay* which is instructive on the type of evidence to be considered. There is also the less helpful case of *Stewart* v. *Stewart*.[28] In *Lombardi's Tr.* v. *Lombardi*[29] a gratuitous disposition of a one-half share of a house was handed by a husband to a solicitor who acted for both spouses. In the circumstances it was held that there had been delivery to the wife. It is possible to arrive at the schizophrenic conclusion that a deed is held for some parties for one purpose and for other parties for another purpose. In *Mair* v. *Thoms Tr.*[30] Lord Mackenzie observed:

> "Smith was agent for both parties, the borrowers and the lenders. The lenders put the full money of the loan into his hands; the borrower put into his hands the completed bond. If Smith had paid over the whole money to the borrower, and kept the bond in his own hands, I should have had no difficulty in finding that he held as agent for the lender. But if, on the other hand, he had paid over no money at all, and kept the bond in his own hands, I should have had just an opposite opinion. He had no authority to deliver the bond till the money was paid to the borrower, or, at least, no authority to hold the money as paid to the borrower, by having been previously paid to himself, and thereupon to deliver the bond. If, then, both the bond and all the money were still in the hands of the joint agent, I should rather hold the bond to be still undelivered. But the actual case is different from either of the cases I have supposed: It is a mixed case. The joint agent had paid over part of the sum, and part he had not paid; and, in these circumstances, he kept the rest of the money, and the bond, in his own hands. Now, must this not be held to be a holding of it for the joint interests of both parties—for the lender as far as the loan was completed by payment, and for the borrower in so far as it was not so? That seems to me the most natural conclusion, and I see no hardship in it."

That was said in a case in which there was *bona fides*. In a case where there was fraud and embezzlement by the common agent the court refused to hold that there had been delivery, which if it had taken place would have been prejudicial to the granters of the deed. There were indications that if the agent had been honest the decision would have been otherwise.[31]

Delivery by post

14   In *Dowie & Co.* v. *Tennant*[32] a disposition had been posted from America on January 12. It did not reach the purchaser until January 23. It was held that for the purposes of jurisdiction the seller remained pro-

---

[28] (1842) 1 Bell 796, aff. (1833) 11 S. 327; see also *Henderson* v. *McManus, sup. cit.*
[29] 1982 S.L.T. 81.
[30] (1850) 12 D. 748 at p. 752.
[31] *Richardson* v. *MacGeoch's Trs.* (1898) 1 F. 145.
[32] (1891) 18 R. 986.

prietor of heritage on January 21 when a summons was served. The missives were not binding because they were improbative and there was no obligation on the grantee to take delivery. In that context Lord McLaren observed[33]:

> "In all cases where something has to be delivered by one person to another in order to effect an alteration of legal rights, there is involved the consent of both parties as well as the outward act which is symbolical of the transference. Thus, where heritable property is to be itself delivered, as it may still be (infeftment by registration of the disposition being only optional), it is necessary not only that the seller or his bailie should offer the symbols of earth and stone, but also that the purchaser or his procurator should accept delivery. It would not do for the seller's bailie merely to heave a clod at the purchaser's agent. The same principle applies in the case of the delivery of deeds. No doubt after posting the post office is in most cases considered to hold for the grantee, yet until the grantee has accepted there is no transference of the property."

7–15   It should be noted that this was not the normal case of a disposition following on binding missives. In that case there is an obligation to deliver, enforceable by decree for specific implement, and according to some authorities the disposition is effectual without delivery or acceptance by the grantee.[34]

7–16   In *Crawford* v. *Kerr*[35] a letter containing money to pay a debt was held to be delivered although left with a servant to be posted. This case may be difficult to reconcile with *Dowie*.[36] In *Crawford*, however, there was a prior obligation which was being implemented. In the special circumstances of *Dowie* there was no prior obligation and the grantee might have refused to accept the deed.

Registration of the deed

7–17   A deed may be published by registration in a public register such as the Register of Sasines, the Books of Council and Session, sheriff court books, the public registers of a company and, potentially, in a host of registers which by statute are open to inspection by the public. In some instances those who inspect the register may not be the public at large, but a selected class, such as members of a company.

Books of Council and Session

7–18   Registration in the Books of Council and Session and in sheriff court books has a different effect from other forms of registration commonly met. The original deed is retained in the registers. It thereafter becomes

---

[33] at pp. 988, 989.
[34] See para. 7–49.
[35] (1807) Mor.App. "Moveables," No. 2.
[36] See Gloag, p. 72, n. 2.

impossible except in very rare cases for the original to be delivered. Publication deliberately undertaken suggests that the deed has gone past the stage where the granter may wish to cancel it. As it is not necessary for delivery to be made to the grantee personally—it could be to someone acting for him—it is possible to view the registers as a place of neutral custody, in which a deed can be put not only with the intention of preventing the granter resiling, but with the effect of putting the deed beyond the granter's control. Thus registration may be a fact showing delivery. It may not necessarily be the only fact in a case, nor is it conclusive proof of the intention of the granter, but it is a very important fact.

19   As Lord President Inglis put it:

> "The fact of recording the deed is of itself a most significant fact in a question of delivery, particularly when the recording is done at the desire of the granter of the deed. A deed may be recorded without that fact operating delivery. It may be recorded without the authority of the granter. It may be recorded in such circumstances as to leave it [a] matter of doubt and ambiguity whether it was the desire of the granter that it should be recorded or no. It may be done, even with the authority of the granter, for a purpose other than that of delivery, and with such evidence as to show that although the granter authorised the recording, he had a design and purpose that it should not thereby be an irrevocable delivered deed. I think all these things are possible, but still these possibilities derogate very little from the significance of the fact of recording as a fact in the general case. Why should a granter wish his deed to be recorded . . . except for the purpose of operating delivery? I can see no other object he could have. And what is the effect of recording? In the first place, it publishes the contents of the deed to the whole nation. It enables every man, woman and child who has any curiosity or interest in the subject to go to the record and read it *ad longum*. It enables every party who has any interest to obtain an extract (*i.e.* a full copy) of the deed; and if it be a deed containing obligations, the party in whose favour these obligations are conceived can immediately arm himself with an extract, and enforce the obligations. Nothing can more clearly indicate that a deed is delivered than that it can thus come, in the form of an extract, into the hands of the obligee, and be by him put to execution."[37]

An example of registration being delivery where there was clear evidence of the purpose of registration is *Obers* v. *Paton's Tr.*[38] The grantee was not in a state of health to take delivery personally.

Register of Sasines

20   There are complications raised by registration in the Register of Sasines. At first sight it may be surprising that there should be any difficulty. A granter may unilaterally register a deed in the Books of Council

---

[37] *Tennent* v. *Tennent's Tr.* (1869) 7 M. 936 at p. 948. See also Lord Ardmillan at p. 953.
[38] (1897) 24 R. 719.

and Session but not normally in the Register of Sasines. In modern practice the warrant for registration in the Register of Sasines is signed by, or more usually on behalf of, the grantee. This reflects history. The old procedure of delivery of sasine followed by registration of an instrument of sasine involved the co-operation of the grantee. Sasine would have been an incomplete ceremony without someone to receive the transfer of the clod of earth and a stone. So why has delivery not taken place sometime before registration? The answer is that in the normal case it has. The difficulty arises in specialised cases where the granter may record the deed, *e.g.* a deed by A to A as trustee for B; or where there is a common agent for granter and grantee, such as a solicitor acting for father (granter) and pupil children (grantees).

7–21   Consideration of the law in this area is dominated by the decision of seven judges in *Cameron's Tr.* v. *Cameron*.[39] Donald Cameron lent money and in security took bonds in favour of himself as trustee for his children and in one case in favour of himself and his brother as trustees for the children. Cameron kept the bonds in his custody and dealt with them, but they were recorded in the Register of Sasines. Was there delivery to the children? The answer by the majority of the court was in the negative. As Lord Kinnear stated[40]:

> "It was said that infeftment is equivalent to delivery. If that means that infeftment constitutes delivery of the land it is perfectly correct. If it means that it is delivery of a written instrument, I think all that is sound in the proposition is more correctly stated, in several of the cases to which we were referred in support of it, by the Judges who said that infeftment 'inferred' delivery, because infeftment in the old form could not be obtained until the instrument which constituted its warrant had been delivered to the grantee who desired to be infeft. The meaning and force of the observation becomes perfectly clear when we remember what infeftment was at the time when these learned judges were speaking.
>
> The same inference may probably be drawn under the present law, when a deed has been registered on the warrant of the grantee. But it is possible that it may be registered by the granter; and in that case, it cannot be inferred that the grantee has accepted delivery of a deed of which he may know nothing. Therefore I should be slow to accept the general proposition that mere registration of the deed in the Register of Sasines is necessarily equivalent to delivery of the deed to the grantee."

7–22   This adds the complication of a further idea—acceptance of the deed by the grantee.[41] This is not viewed as a requirement in other instances of unilateral obligations. If you receive a letter from a favourite uncle saying—"I promise to pay you £100," the promise is binding without your acceptance. In the case of deeds transferring land there is a difference. The transfer may, it usually does, put the grantee into a feudal

---

[39] 1907 S.C. 407; see also *Burnet* v. *Morrow* (1864) 2 M. 929.
[40] at p. 422.
[41] See also *Dowie & Co.* v. *Tennant* (1891) 18 R. 986 at p. 989 *per* Lord McLaren.

relationship which involves obligations. Obligations may be owed not only to a superior, but also to neighbours and to local authorities. It would be contrary to principle to impose these burdens without acceptance by, or on behalf of, the grantee. The requirement of acceptance should be restricted to those situations in which the deed imposes obligations on the grantee.

23 Cameron's Tr. was affirmed in the House of Lords in Carmichael v. Carmichael's Exrx.[42] but doubted by Lord Shaw.[43] It was distinguished in Linton v. Inland Revenue[44] in which a disposition to pupil daughters registered in the Register of Sasines was treated as a complete donation. The ground of distinction was that in Cameron's Tr. Cameron remained vested in the property, whereas in Linton transfer by the tutor to the daughters involved a transfer of ownership.[45]

24 If, however, it is remembered that decisions on whether or not there has been delivery involve decisions on the facts of a particular case, there may not be as much wrong with Cameron's Tr. as has been suggested. There are distinctions between Cameron's Tr. and Linton. What more could the father have done to deliver to his pupil daughters in Linton? He was, in any event, the natural custodier of deeds in favour of his children, a factor not relevant when a trust is created as in Cameron's case.[46] What more could Cameron have done? Why did he not intimate the trust to the beneficiaries? Were they too young? Their ages are unknown to us. Why did he continue to deal with the bonds as if they were his own? That factor was in the Lord President's mind antagonistic to donation and viewed as important by Lord Kinnear and Lord Low. It was very relevant in ascertaining the intention of a deceased granter. (In Linton the granter was alive and asserting donation.) The results turned on inferences from facts. Reasonable minds may differ on the conclusions.

The Land Register of Scotland

25 This register is a register of title created by the Land Registration (Scotland) Act 1979 and will eventually replace the recording of deeds in the Register of Sasines. Registration of a deed in a register of title is of considerable importance in assessing whether there has been an intention to give obligatory effect to a deed. In the case of the Land Register the principle is that registration vests a real right in the land.[47] Despite this it would not be impossible for it to be shown that the appro-

---

[42] 1920 S.C.(H.L.) 195 at pp. 201, 202 by Lord Dunedin.

[43] at p. 205. Gloag doubted the authority of the case (Contract, p. 74) as do Wilson and Duncan (Trusts, Trustees and Executors, p. 45).

[44] 1928 S.C. 209.

[45] See also Inland Revenue v. Wilson, 1927 S.C. 733 at p. 738 per Lord Sands; on appeal, 1928 S.C.(H.L.) 42.

[46] Connell's Tr. v. Connell's Tr., 1955 S.L.T. 125, and see below s.v. "Deeds to the family."

[47] 1979 Act, s.3.

priate deed was never delivered to the person in whose name the land is registered but it would be necessary to seek rectification of the Register under the conditions in section 9. The question of delivery remains, with the complication that rectification of the Register would have to be possible for there to be any relevance in an argument about delivery.

Company registers

7–26   In *Inland Revenue* v. *Wilson*,[48] 42 shares were registered in the name of the son having been purchased by the father. There was evidence of donation, both donor and donee asserting that there had been a transfer. A company's register of shareholders is a register of title and this is of weight in assessing whether or not there has been delivery.

Intimated assignation

7–27   Intimation of an assignation to the debtor may be the equivalent of delivery of the assignation to the assignee. Lord President Inglis explained the principle in this way[49]:

> "If you execute an assignation, that is made effectual by intimation without delivery, just as a conveyance of land is effectual without delivery if you take infeftment in favour of a third party. The infeftment and the intimation complete the right, and afford a complete publication or equivalent to delivery."

Trusts

7–28   The rule which requires delivery applies to a deed of trust. The truster will deliver the deed to a trustee. Where the truster is the sole trustee and retains the deed under his control it will be necessary to intimate to a beneficiary. The point is discussed later.[50]

THE EXCEPTIONS TO THE PRINCIPLE OF DELIVERY

7–29   The problems of delivery which have been least discussed in the past are those arising from the rules of law which dispense with delivery in certain circumstances. The standard treatment is in Erskine.[51] Each of his exceptions is now examined apart from registration in a public register which has already been commented upon.

(a) Deeds containing a clause dispensing with delivery

7–30   Erskine stated:

> "Writings, if they contain a clause dispensing with the delivery, are good to the grantee, though they should be found in the granter's

---

[48] 1928 S.C.(H.L.) 42.
[49] *Jarvie's Tr.* v. *Jarvie's Trs.* (1887) 14 R. 411 at p. 416.
[50] para. 7–42.
[51] *Inst.*, III,ii,44.

own custody at his death. These are of the nature of revocable deeds; for the granter, by continuing them in his own keeping, continues a power within himself to cancel them; but if he do not exercise that power they become effectual upon his death. Death is, in such case, equivalent to delivery, because after it there can be no revocation."

It will be noticed that if this is correct it is a peculiar form of delivery. It is difficult to distinguish the effect from that of a testamentary writing. A contract is, however, different from a will even if the contract takes effect only on death. Sums due under a contract are debts of an estate and are paid before distribution to the beneficiaries.

31   Stair did not mention the revocable nature of the deed.[52] More stated: "The clause dispensing with the delivery is of no importance, except for proving that the deed is not intended to take effect till the granter's death; because if delivery were required by law to make a deed effectual, the granter or testator could not, by his own act, alter the rule of law."[53] Bell mentioned the exception without the idea of revocation.[54] Gloag treated the clause as testamentary, not contractual.[55]

32   Two cases have been cited on the point, *Eleis* v. *Inglistoun*[56] and *A* v. *B*.[57] The first of these may support the effect attributed to the clause, the second case does not. In arguments in cases in *Morison's Dictionary* under the titles "Presumption" and "Writ" it was often suggested that the clause had an effect on delivery, but the impact of these arguments on the court cannot be assessed.

33   If the phrase has an effect it would presumably not be necessary to follow exactly the expression: "I dispense with delivery." Why should a similar effect not be given to a statement that a deed is irrevocable? In either case, however, there are dangers in deciding whether a deed is delivered on the grounds of the presence or absence of words of style. The intention of the granter is not the only relevant factor. The fact of delivery is also necessary and if that be required by law, as it is, how can a statement of the granter alter the law? To take this approach involves challenging Institutional authority, but there is much sense in it. To explain the effect of the words as More and Gloag did introduces a further difficulty, because it implies into the deed a condition which is not, or may not, be there, namely, that the deed is operative on death. It would be better to say that the exception to the rule on delivery emerged at an early stage in our law when the consequences of delivery were being explored by the courts. This exception should at the earliest opportunity be given a decent burial.

---

[52] Stair, 1,vii,14.
[53] More's *Notes*, ccccviii.
[54] Bell, *Prin.*, s.24.
[55] *Contract*, p. 67.
[56] (1669) Mor. 16999.
[57] (1683) Mor. 17003.

(b) Testamentary deeds

7–34   Erskine stated: "No deed of a testamentary kind requires delivery, because the effect of testamentary writings commences only at the period of the granter's death." The reason for the rule may be better expressed as being that testaments are revocable until death. They are distinguishable from a contract which takes effect on death. Further, a testamentary writing is revocable even if it is delivered. The authorities were reviewed in *Clark's Exr.* v. *Clark*.[58] In donation *mortis causa* it appears that formal delivery may not be necessary.[59]

(c) Deeds to the family

7–35   A father has been held to be the natural custodier of deeds in favour of his children, and likewise of deeds in favour of his wife. There has been more reported case law on the problems arising than on any other aspect of the law of delivery.

7–36   A series of old cases established the proposition that the man was custodier and delivery was unnecessary. In *Wallace* v. *Their Elder Brother*[60] a bond of provision in favour of children was kept by the father. It was sustained without delivery although dated 25 years previously. A similar result was reached in *Cardross* v. *Mar*[61]; *Aikenhead* v. *Aikenhead*[62]; *Stevenson* v. *Stevenson*[63]; and *Adair* v. *Adair*.[64] Cases establishing the proposition that a husband is a custodier for his wife's deeds are *Lindores* v. *Steward*[65]; *Forrest* v. *Wilson*[66]; and *Smith* v. *Smith's Tr.*[67] Erskine cites *Hamilton of Silvertonhill* v. *His Sisters*[68] for the rule that a mother may be the natural custodier of bonds to her child.[69]

7–37   Modern writers have found deficiencies in the treatment of the topic by earlier authors. Dr Clive attacks the arguments of McLaren and Gloag.[70] Wilson and Duncan object to McLaren's position.[71] Criticism arises because several cases on special destinations are said to be inconsistent with the idea of natural custody. It may, however, be argued that there is no conflict of principle.

---

[58] 1943 S.C. 216.

[59] *Crosbie's Tr.* v. *Wright* (1880) 7 R. 823 at p. 834 *per* Lord Shand; *McSkimming* v. *Stenhouse* (1883) 21 S.L.R. 3 at p. 5 *per* Lord Fraser; *contra, Macfarlane's Trs.* v. *Miller* (1898) 25 R. 1201 at p. 1211 *per* Lord McLaren. But there must be delivery or some equivalent—see *Graham's Tr.* v. *Gillies*, 1956 S.C. 437; *Gray's Trs.* v. *Murray*, 1970 S.C. 1.

[60] (1624) Mor. 16989, 6344.

[61] (1639) Mor. 16993, 11440.

[62] (1663) Mor. 16994.

[63] (1677) Mor. 17000.

[64] (1725) Mor. 17006.

[65] (1715) Mor. 6126, 17006.

[66] (1858) 20 D. 1201.

[67] (1884) 12 R. 186.

[68] (1624) Mor. 4098.

[69] *Inst.*, III,ii,44.

[70] *Husband and Wife* (2nd ed.), p. 302.

[71] *Trusts, Trustees and Executors*, pp. 39–41.

-38 If a special destination is testamentary in nature, delivery is irrelevant. Even if delivered the destination could be revoked. If the destination is contractual in favour of husband and wife, the fact of delivery need not be proved, following the rule on natural custody. Further, in some cases there may be another argument why the wife need not have possession of the deed, *i.e.* the husband retains an interest in it (see below, "*Deeds in which the granter has an interest*"). Nevertheless the intention to deliver must be present. That intention is readily presumed when a stranger donates to husband and wife and the husband keeps the deed. The husband is the natural custodier of the deed. More awkward is an onerous transaction in which the husband requires the stranger to grant the deed to husband and wife, so that there is a gift of an interest to the wife. In the event, on particular facts, it may be that the wife acquires no rights. The deed for her interest is latent. Conversely she may acquire a *jus quaesitum tertio* not by the fact of delivery but by an equivalent. This was the nature of the distinction drawn in the much-approved case of *Hill* v. *Hill*.[72] So there may not be delivery to the wife when the husband retains possession of the deed *and* control of the fund to which it relates.[73] Where the deed is alleged to create a *donatio mortis causa*, as in *Kerr* v. *Wignall* the requirement to show delivery may be less than for *donatio inter vivos*, a matter mentioned above. Likewise, in old cases, the court was not inclined on the facts to presume delivery in a competition between children and creditors.[74]

-39 With the abolition of the *jus mariti* and changing social conditions there is no reason why in some circumstances a wife may not be the custodier of a deed for her husband. In general one person may hold a deed on behalf of another. A special presumption arose because of the frequency with which those living in one house might grant deeds in favour of each other without a ritual of formal delivery. The fact of delivery did not need proof. This approach could be extended beyond the tradition of a husband or parent as natural custodier.[75]

-40 If family deeds are in a special category, who apart from those already mentioned, are in the family? An illegitimate child has been included for this purpose.[76] In a narrowly-decided case no delivery was needed for a deed to a brother's wife and two nieces[77] but the ground of decision is doubtful and the case was given little weight as an authority by Lord

---

[72] *Sup. cit.* See also opinion of Lord President Clyde in *Dennis* v. *Aitchison*, 1923 S.C. 819, on appeal 1924 S.C.(H.L.) 122.

[73] *Walker's Exr.* v. *Walker* (1878) 5 R. 965; *Kerr* v. *Wignall* (1871) 9 S.L.R. 33.

[74] *Inglis* v. *Boswell* (1676) Mor. 11567; *Chiesly* v. *Chiesly* (1701) Mor. 11571; *Simpson* v. *Finlay and Colvill* (1697) Mor. 11570.

[75] J. M. Halliday makes the observation in *Conveyancing Law and Practice in Scotland* (1985), Vol. 1, para. 9–25, n. 86, that: "It is a common experience of solicitors, where the estate of a deceased husband is being administered, to find in his repositories certificates for securities in joint names of the spouses or in the name of his wife alone; when the estate is that of a deceased wife the converse of that situation is comparatively rare."

[76] *Aikenhead* v. *Aikenhead* (1663) Mor. 16994.

[77] *Trotter* v. *Pitcairn* (1706) Mor. 17004.

Justice-Clerk Inglis in *Anderson* v. *Robertson*.[78] In *Anderson* the deed was in favour of an illegitimate daughter of the granter's brother. The case was decided on the basis that the daughter's husband, not the granter, was the natural custodier of deeds in her favour.

7–41   From what has been said it may be apparent that the case law on family deeds is reconcilable provided the rule requiring delivery is dispensed with only to the extent that the fact of delivery need not be proved. The intention of the granter must exist although probably it is presumed that a signed deed is irrevocable, if not testamentary in nature. The presumption, or perhaps more accurately the inference, from the existence of a completed deed has to be considered with any other evidence of intention. But the law should not go so far as to say that intention is irrelevant. A spouse should be able to change his or her mind after signing a deed to the other spouse.

7–42   If the deed is granted to trustees for the benefit of the family it is not exempted from the general rule that unilateral deeds need delivery, or an equivalent, to be effective.[79] An equivalent of delivery is intimation to a beneficiary[80] once the trust has been set up.[81] It can be sufficient to intimate to only one beneficiary[82] or to a guardian of or agent for the beneficiary.[83] But the acceptance of an obligation to hold moneys in trust is not an equivalent of delivery.[84]

(d) Deeds in which the granter has an interest

7–43   Erskine stated: "A deed in which the granter himself hath an interest—ex. gr. a reserved liferent— is good without delivery; for it is presumed that the granter holds such deed in his own custody, not because his intention is not finished concerning it, but to secure that interest which he has reserved to himself." The authority which he cites, *Hadden* v. *Lawder*,[85] is not clear because we do not know the terms of the assignation. The case was founded on in *Stark* v. *Kincaid*[86] and, although on one view of *Stark* it supports Erskine, the deed was revocable in its terms and could have been considered testamentary. Bell's editors limited the concept to deeds which were onerous.[87] Gloag considered that the exception to the normal rule arose because the deed was

---

[78] (1867) 5 M. 503.

[79] *Connell's Tr.* v. *Connell's Tr.*, 1955 S.L.T. 125; *Jarvie's Tr.* v. *Jarvie's Tr.* (1887) 14 R. 411; *Collie* v. *Pirie's Tr.*, *sup. cit.*

[80] *Allan's Tr.* v. *Lord Advocate*, 1971 S.C.(H.L.) 45; *Clark's Tr.* v. *Inland Revenue*, 1972 S.C. 177.

[81] *Kerr's Tr.* v. *Inland Revenue*, 1974 S.C. 115.

[82] *Allan's Tr.* v. *Lord Advocate*, *sup. cit.*

[83] *Clark's Tr.* v. *Inland Revenue*, *sup. cit.*

[84] *Clark Taylor & Co. Ltd. and Quality Site Development (Edinburgh) Ltd.*, 1981 S.C. 111.

[85] (1668) Mor. 16997.

[86] (1679) Mor. 17002.

[87] Bell, *Prin.*, s.24.

testamentary.[88] It is odd that this exception has not been used in cases of *jus quaesitum tertio*. If A and B contract and B creates a right in favour of C, whether B retains an interest should be important in the question of delivery, but it has not been considered as such. It could, however, be used to explain the relative lack of importance of delivery in such cases.

The doctrine of *jus quaesitum tertio* has been applied to feu contracts.[89] As J. T. Cameron has pointed out: "In such a case delivery of the contract to a co-feuar, or circumstances showing an intention to donate anything to him, are not essential: it is hard to see how they could be."[90]

–44   A superior may deliver to his vassal a writ which creates a *jus quaesitum tertio* in favour of a neighbouring vassal. The neighbour does not receive delivery of the writ, nor is it suggested that he should receive delivery or an equivalent. The reason could be that deeds in which parties retain a substantial interest do not require delivery to a third party to create rights in the third party. If this were correct the need for delivery would alter according to the interest retained by the parties.

–45   A and B contract and intend to create a right in favour of C. It is possible that the substantial interest in having possession of the deed will be in A or B, in which case there need not be delivery to C. There might have to be delivery between A and B, for example, the case of a feu writ which has been mentioned. It might be that B is an obligor who is not interested in whether he pays A or C provided that he pays the right person. The obligee is the appropriate person to receive delivery of the deed and that obligee could be C, for example an insurance policy taken out by A with insurance company B in favour of A's son C. Viewed in this way delivery in the context of *jus quaesitum tertio* can be consistent with delivery in other parts of the law of contract.

–46   The existence of the exception of reserved interest may have been ignored in the practice of conveyancers. A disponer who dispones land while retaining ownership of neighbouring land may have an interest in the land disponed. He could create a servitude or real burden in his favour. Is it seriously suggested that this interest could make the deed effective against his creditors prior to actual delivery to the disponee? A feu writ is the classic example of a granter retaining an interest, yet it is the law that there must be delivery of the writ.[91] These examples could, however, be explained as instances in which the grantee has the substantial interest.

–47   Erskine's example was of a liferent reserved by the granter, but in *Stewart* v. *Rae*[92] a husband and wife purchased heritage with the wife's funds and took a disposition to themselves in liferent and their children

---

[88] *Contract*, p. 67.

[89] *Hislop* v. *MacRitchie's Trs.* (1881) 8 R.(H.L.) 95; see para. 18–06.

[90] "Jus Quaesitum Tertio: The True Meaning of Stair 1,x,5," 1961 J.R. 103 at p. 117.

[91] *Gibson and Hunter Home Designs*, 1976 S.C. 23; A. M. Bell, *Lectures on Conveyancing* (3rd. ed.), p. 648.

[92] 1883 10 R. 463.

in fee. There was infeftment in the liferent but not in the fee. It was held that there had been no delivery to the children and the destination in their favour was revocable. The case was followed in *Kindness* v. *Bruce*.[93]

7–48   Erskine's authority being what it is, other writers have followed him, but on the question of deeds in which the granter has an interest his statement was of dubious accuracy when it was made, and is inconsistent with later authority. Either (1) it should not now be followed, or (2) it should be severely restricted to cases in which the granter retains a substantial interest in the deed. This would have to be something more than a liferent. An example would be a right of fee with an interest created in favour of a neighbouring proprietor.

(e) Deeds which the granter is obliged to execute

7–49   Erskine said: "Deeds which the granter lies under an antecedent obligation to execute are valid without delivery; for he in whose favour such deed is conceived, as he had a right to demand the granting of it, is also entitled to compel the granter to exhibit it after it is signed." Erskine's authority[94] may have been decided upon another ground. Another case was cited for the proposition in the notes to Erskine,[95] by Dickson[96] and by Gloag.[97] It was *Cormack* v. *Anderson*.[98] Bell also cited this case, but for what proposition is not clear.[99]

7–50   In *Cormack* effect was given to a bond which was not delivered until after sequestration. The case was decided on the basis of the Bankruptcy Act of 1814[1] and on its facts would now be decided differently. At present acts of the bankrupt in relation to the estate after sequestration are usually null and void.[2]

7–51   To say that a disposition was effective between disponer and disponee without delivery, would startle many a conveyancer. In *Gibson and Hunter Home Designs*[3] a feu disposition was required to be granted in terms of missives. It was executed by the sellers but not by the consenters prior to the effective date of an order winding up the sellers. The case was decided on the basis that there had to be actual delivery of the

---

[93] 1902 4 F. 415. See also *Collie* v. *Pirie's Tr.* (1851) 13 D. 506—an unnecessary decision if Erskine was right; Dickson (*Evidence*, s.923) and Gloag (*Contract*, p. 97) refer to *Drummond* v. *Lord Advocate* (1749) Mor. 4874, affd. (1751) 1 Pat. 503 as a case of a reserved annuity being effective without delivery, but this feature does not appear to have been a ground of decision.

[94] *Dick* v. *Oliphant* (1677) Mor. 6548.

[95] *Inst.*, III,ii,44.

[96] *Op. cit.*, s.924.

[97] *Op. cit.*, p. 67.

[98] (1829) 7 S. 868.

[99] *Prin.*, s.24.

[1] 54 Geo. 3, c. 137.

[2] Bankruptcy (Scotland) Act 1985, s.32(8), subject to exceptions in s.32(9).

[3] 1976 S.C. 23.

deed to the purchaser to give him a personal right to the property. This is inconsistent with Erskine's approach. The deed was completed by the sellers, but not, at the date of winding up, by the consenters. The view might be taken that the question of delivery could not arise until completion of the deed, but this overlooks *McCreath* v. *Borland*.[4] A disposition was subscribed by the disponers. It was left in the hands of an agent common to granter and grantee to be completed by the signature of heritable creditors and the filling in of the testing clause. It was held that the deed had been delivered to the grantees, in whose interests it was to obtain the signature of the heritable creditors. Applying this approach to *Gibson* there may have been an argument that it was unnecessary to have actual delivery of the feu disposition but the argument does not appear to have been presented to the court.

–52 In *Morrison* v. *Gray*[5] a disposition had been signed by the purchaser, as consentor, and signed by the seller. It did not supersede missives because it had not been delivered by the seller to the purchaser.

–53 Erskine's approach has some sense. The concept of delivery has a purpose in allowing the granter the right of revocation up to a certain point. After a mutual contract, such as missives, the point of revocation is past and so delivery of a deed under the contract is not necessary to create a personal obligation. Where the grantee needs the deed to complete a real right, as by infeftment, obtaining possession of the deed is important for him, but it is in that sense that delivery is relevant. When the granter is obliged by contract to produce the deed, delivery of the deed should not be necessary to perfect the personal right of the grantee.[6]

(f) Mutual contracts

–54 Erskine stated:

> "Mutual obligations or contracts signed by two or more parties for their different interests require no delivery . . . because every such deed, the moment it is executed, becomes a common right to all the contractors. The bare subscription of the several parties proves the delivery of the deed by the other subscribers to him in whose hands it appears; and if that party can use it as a deed effectual to himself, it must also be effectual to the rest."

The proposition was established in cases such as *Maxwell* v. *Drumlan-*

---

[4] (1860) 22 D. 1551.

[5] 1932 S.C. 712.

[6] A large part of the problems with this area of law arises because of the failure to consider the effect on rights of (1) sasine; (2) the delivery of an instrument of sasine; and (3) the recording of the instrument in the Register of Sasines. The modern forms of conveyancing replace the older and cumbersome methods, but the very brevity of present procedure tends to obscure the underlying theory. In truth the effects of the various stages in a conveyance of heritage have not yet been properly analysed. See, however, K. G. C. Reid, "Ownership on Registration," 1985 S.L.T.(News) 280 and articles there referred to.

rig[7]; *Stewart* v. *Riddoch*[8]; and *Crawford* v. *Vallance's Heirs*.[9] It applies to mutual deeds executed in duplicate[10] but not to a unilateral deed signed by the granter and a consenter.[11]

PROBLEMS FOR PRACTITIONERS

7–55 The consideration of the reported case law enables certain problematic areas to be identified and guidelines or warnings to be suggested.

(a) Mutual deeds

7–56 One solution to the problems of delivery is to have a deed signed by all the parties. This may be appropriate in otherwise difficult situations such as a family arrangement or commercial transaction where one solicitor is the common agent for all the parties. A speciality arises in the case of the creation of a trust. To quote from the opinion of the court in *Clark Taylor & Co. Ltd. and Quality Site Development (Edinburgh) Ltd.*[12]:

> "As Lord Fraser made clear in the case of *Kerr's Trs.*, a contractual obligation to constitute a trust does not by its own vigour have the effect of constituting a trust in favour of one of the contracting parties, particularly in a case in which the party undertaking the obligation is himself to discharge the office of both truster and trustee."

(b) Unilateral deeds

7–57 On some authority the deed can be regarded as delivered before it is signed by everyone who is expected to sign. This should make the practitioner wary of assuming that the incomplete deed is ineffective. Allied to this is the worry that when a deed is in implement of an obligation, delivery is unnecessary. Some may rely on *Gibson and Hunter Home Designs* to relieve their anxiety, but not all the problems of delivery were explored in the opinions in that case, which has obscured rather than clarified the law. It is difficult to suggest a practicable course except that, if trouble is anticipated, evidence of the intention of the granter should be obtained.

(c) Family arrangements

7–58 The trap is to overlook that if a trust is created delivery, or an equivalent, is essential. If no trust is created, in theory delivery may not be required if the husband, father or mother retains custody. The theory

---

[7] (1626) Mor. 12304.

[8] (1677) Mor. 11406.

[9] (1625) Mor. 16990, 12304.

[10] *Robertson's Trs.* v. *Lindsay* (1873) 1 R. 323.

[11] *Kirkpatrick's Trs.* v. *Kirkpatrick* (1873) 11 M. 551 at p. 571 *per* Lord Deas; on appeal (1874) 1 R.(H.L.) 37.

[12] 1981 S.C. 111 at p. 119.

has its problems. Good practice would be to obtain evidence of intention that the deed was regarded as irrevocable. There could be a letter showing this intention. This should be admissible evidence.[13] There could be intimation to the beneficiaries. There could be delivery of the deed to a solicitor with written instructions to hold it as agent for the grantees.

(d) Solicitor as common agent

–59   This can arise in either family arrangements or commercial transactions. The problems are (a) proof that the solicitor was the agent of all the parties. He may act for a person without being paid[14]; (b) whether the granter gave instructions to deliver to the grantee; (c) whether the deed was in fact held on behalf of the grantee. Entries in the solicitor's ledgers showing the transfer of money from one party to the other may not be sufficient evidence of the transfer of the deed. There is also the possibility illustrated by *Mair* v. *Thoms Tr.*[15] that a deed can be held for the different interests of all the parties.

---

[13] See documents founded on in *Barclay's Tr.* v. *Inland Revenue*, 1975 S.C.(H.L.) 1; *contra, Hicks' Trs.* v. *Inland Revenue*, 1974 S.L.T. 62.

[14] See *Maule* v. *Ramsay, sup. cit.*

[15] (1850) 12 D. 748.

CHAPTER 8

CAPACITY TO CONTRACT

INCAPACITY TO CONSENT

8–01 The categories of those who are incapable of consenting to a contract are now open to little dispute, but this was not always so. Balfour put rebels in a special position[1] and a person might "gainsay or cum aganis his awin deid" if he were "in prisoun, in bandis, in the handis and powar of reiffaris, or of his enemies."[2] This last category, which today would be classified under force and fear, was treated as though it were a species of temporary incapacity, being linked to those who were of "les age" and "lunatique, wod and furious." Craig thought that deafness incapacitated a person from granting a feu.[3] While Stair allowed the deaf and dumb to contract if they knew what they were doing,[4] Erskine raised doubts about whether those who had been deaf and dumb from birth were capable of contracting.[5] Spotiswoode stated that monks and friars were forbidden to contract.[6]

8–02 Those who, under the present law, either lack capacity to contract or have limited capacity to contract are those under age, the insane and in some instances those affected by drink, drugs or disease. Various legal persons have limitations on their power to contract. For example a contract which is *ultra vires* of a corporation will be void, and a contract by a trustee in breach of fiduciary duty will be voidable. A brief guide is given later to the limitations on the powers of bodies or persons who contract, but it is not possible within the confines of a general work to analyse all the related problems.

8–03 Problems of capacity and power should be distinguished from other problems of invalidity of a contract. A contract with an alien enemy may be illegal and on that ground invalid. This is sometimes confused with the procedural inability of an alien enemy to sue during wartime, and further confused with questions of capacity.[7]

---

[1] Balfour, pp. 507–508.
[2] Balfour, p. 179.
[3] Craig, I,231.
[4] Stair, I,x,13; *vide* IV,iii,9.
[5] Ersk., *Inst.*, III,i,16; *vide* I,vii,48. The appointment of a curator was a possible answer, but it was established in *Kirkpatrick* (1853) 15 D. 734 that the court must be satisfied that the handicap prevented a person from managing his affairs.
[6] Spotiswoode, p. 72.
[7] See Chitty, para. 724.

General limitations on capacity

04   In one sense everyone, even although adult and sane, has a limited contractual capacity. No one may validly sell or purchase *res communes, res publicae, res universitatis* or *res nullius*.[8] Examples of such *res extra commercium* are the records of the court,[9] a burgh charter,[10] and a town house, unless other premises have been obtained by the council.[11] If the subjects are inalienable a contract for their sale is void.[12] This is probably the most extreme form of nullity recognised by Scots law because certain of the normal consequences of a void contract do not result. It seems from *Presbytery of Edinburgh* v. *University of Edinburgh*[13] that personal bar does not operate to exclude challenge of the transactions. Nor, according to that case, will the negative prescription prevent challenge, a rule which is now statutory.[14]

NON-AGE

05   The plea of non-age has been recognised from an early date.[15] It is mentioned by Balfour,[16] Craig[17] and Spotiswoode.[18] As the law evolved a series of rules and exceptions developed, not all of them logical or clear. As a result the present law has been described as archaic, anomalous and absurd.[19]

06   Scots law distinguishes between pupils and minors. The state of pupillarity lasts in the case of girls to the age of 12, and in that of boys to the age of 14. At common law majority was attained at the age of 21. This age was lowered to 18 with effect from January 1, 1970, by the Age of Majority (Scotland) Act 1969. The Act applies for the purpose of any rule of law, the construction of any statute of any date and the construction of deeds executed after the commencement of the Act. Majority

---

[8] Ersk., *Inst.*, II,i,5–8.

[9] *Presbytery of Edinburgh* v. *University of Edinburgh* (1890) 28 S.L.R. 567.

[10] *Mags. of Dumbarton* v. *Edinburgh University*, 1909 1 S.L.T. 51.

[11] *Mags. of Kirkcaldy* v. *Marks & Spencer Ltd.*, 1937 S.L.T. 574. See, however, the statutory powers on disposal of land in Local Government (Scotland) Act 1973, ss.74, 75 as amended: *East Lothian D.C.* v. *N.C.B.*, 1982 S.L.T. 460. The powers of councils to deal with land used by the inhabitants of an area are discussed in *Sanderson* v. *Lees* (1859) 22 D. 24, *Paterson* v. *Mags. of St. Andrews* (1881) 8 R.(H.L.) 117 and other cases cited in *East Lothian D.C., sup. cit.*

[12] *Mags. of Kirkcaldy* v. *Marks & Spencer Ltd., sup. cit.* at p. 577 *per* Lord Jamieson.

[13] *Sup. cit.*

[14] Prescription and Limitation (Scotland) Act 1973, Sched. 3.

[15] *Borthwicks* v. *Hoppringill* (1494) A.D.A. 200 (pursuer in non-age); *Bothuile* v. *Bolton* (1494) A.D.A. 199 (reduction of charter granted in non-age); *Kennedy* v. *Kennedy* (1499/1500) A.D.C. 11, 388 (reduction of apprising).

[16] Balfour, 179, 180, 189.

[17] Craig, I,223,225.

[18] Spotiswoode, p. 72.

[19] Scottish Law Commission, Eighth Annual Report, 1972–73 (Scot.Law.Com., No. 33), para. 30. See Scottish Law Commission, Consultative Memorandum No. 65, *Legal Capacity and Responsibility of Minors and Pupils* (1985).

will still be the age of 21 in the case of a statutory provision which so defines majority,[20] a deed (including a contract)[21] executed before January 1, 1970, and a deed exercising a power of appointment conferred under a deed executed before January 1, 1970.[22]

Pupils

8–07   A contract by a pupil is void, not merely voidable. Pupillarity is a "state of absolute incapacity."[23] In 1577 the Court of Session decided that a deed by a pupil was "null from the beginning, without reduction, albeit that the pupil *tacuit per utile quadriennium*."[24] The proposition has been followed ever since.[25] A deed in favour of a pupil raises further problems. In so far as any act is required of the pupil, such as acceptance, the pupil is unable to perform the act. Yet a pupil may inherit property or be gifted property or be sequestrated.[26] The tutor may act to perfect title, but his intervention may not be necessary for the transmission of a personal right to the pupil.[27] Because title may be taken in the name of a pupil it is misleading, despite some authority,[28] to suggest that a pupil has no legal personality. Whether or not a pupil may enforce a contract beneficial to the pupil is discussed later.[29]

Minors

8–08   A minor may or may not have a curator. The existence or absence of a curator affects the nature of contracts by minors.

8–09   **Minor who has no curator.** When a minor does not have a curator he may contract but the contract may be reduced until the expiry of the *quadriennium utile* on proof of enorm lesion. The contract is voidable but not void.[30]

---

[20] See rules on accumulation of income in Wilson and Duncan, *Trusts*, p. 108.

[21] s.1(10).

[22] s.1(2). On testamentary provisions see s.1(6). On appointments by court interlocutor see *McIntosh* v. *Wood*, 1970 S.L.T.(Notes) 32.

[23] Bell, *Prin.*, s.2067.

[24] *Bruce* (1577) Mor. 8979.

[25] *e.g. McGibbon* v. *McGibbon* (1852) 14 D. 605 (plea based on *quadriennium utile* does not apply); *Hill* v. *City of Glasgow Bank* (1879) 7 R. 68 at p. 74 *per* Lord President Inglis.

[26] See Scottish Law Commission, *Repcrt on Bankruptcy and Related Aspects of Insolvency and Liquidation* (1982, Scot.Law.Com. No. 68), para. 5.3.

[27] On contracts by a tutor, see para. 8–22; on title being taken in the name of a pupil see *Linton* v. *Inland Revenue*, 1928 S.C. 209; *Drummond's Trs.* v. *Peel's Trs.*, 1929 S.C. 484 at p. 493 *per* Lord President Clyde.

[28] *Whitehall* v. *Whitehall*, 1958 S.C. 252 at p. 259 *per* Lord Mackintosh; *Finnie* v. *Finnie*, 1984 S.L.T. 439.

[29] para. 8–20.

[30] *Kincaid* (1561) Mor. 8979; Ersk., I,vii,33; Bell, *Comm.*, I,129; *Hill* v. *City of Glasgow Bank* (1879) 7 R. 68 at p. 74 *per* Lord President Inglis. On payments to the minor, see para. 8–32.

10   Minor who has a curator. When a minor has a curator the consequences are as follows. A contract by the curator only is void.[31] With certain exceptions a contract by the minor alone is void. The correct procedure is a contract by the minor with the consent of his curator, but even then the deed is challengeable on the grounds of enorm lesion.[32]

11   That a minor's deed without the consent of an existing curator was "*ipso iure* null" was several times affirmed in the early law,[33] with the phrase changing to "void and null" in the eighteenth century.[34] Because the deed is null it can be challenged by the minor even after the expiry of the *quadriennium utile*.[35]

12   A contract between the minor and his curator is void.[36]

Exceptions and qualifications

13   The rules which make minors' contracts void or voidable are subject to a number of exceptions. The reason is that, unlike a pupil, a minor does have contractual capacity. In the absence of curators a minor can contract. Even if he had curators he could without their consent exercise rational choice at common law in making a will or marrying. A minor can become forisfamiliated. These factors suggest that the control over minors' contracts arises, not from consideration of their mental capacity, but (1) from the historical importance of the position of parents and (2) for the benefit of minors.[37]

14   The result has been a tendency to enforce minors' contracts when they were beneficial to minors. This has not gone so far as to result in the consideration of lesion in all cases but the case in which lesion is irrelevant—the void contract without the consent of curators—has been particularly troublesome.

Contracts without curator's consent

15   In *Wilkie* v. *Dunlop*[38] a reasonable charge for a minor staying three weeks at an inn was held valid. Any other rule would be to the disadvantage of minors and an instrument of fraud. On the other hand that case was distinguished when a minor speculated in railway shares on the Stock Exchange. The defence of minority was sustained.[39] Because a minor can marry, the ancillary antenuptial contract of marriage may be valid without a curator's consent.[40] Opinions have been reserved on the

---

[31] Ersk., *Inst.*, I,vii,14.

[32] *Clerk's Creditors* v. *Gordon* (1699) Mor. 3668; Ersk., I,vii,33; Bell, *Comm.*, I,130.

[33] *Seton* v. *Caskieben* (1622) Mor. 8939; *Cardross* v. *Hamilton* (1708) Mor. 8951; *Bell* v. *Sutherland* (1728) Mor. 8985.

[34] *Campbell* v. *Lovat* (1731) Mor. 9035; *Craig* v. *Lindsay* (1757) Mor. 8956.

[35] *Hamiltons* v. *Hamilton* (1587) Mor. 8981; *McKenzie* v. *Fairholme* (1666) Mor. 8959.

[36] *McGibbon* v. *McGibbon* (1852) 14 D. 605; *Manuel* v. *Manuel* (1853) 15 D. 284.

[37] See *Harvey* v. *Harvey* (1860) 22 D. 1198 at pp. 1208, 1209 *per* Lord Justice-Clerk Inglis.

[38] (1834) 12 S. 506.

[39] *Dennistoun* v. *Mudie* (1850) 12 D. 613.

[40] *Bruce* v. *Hamilton* (1854) 17 D. 265.

validity of a contract of apprenticeship.[41] Curator's consent is probably not necessary for a minor to take up employment.[42] An agreement to accept compensation under the Workmen's Compensation Acts was not in the course of employment and was invalid in the absence of a curator's consent.[43] An agreement to settle a claim for compensation was treated as made by a minor with no curators when the minor was forisfamiliated and his father was in Ireland.[44] A minor may engage in trade and become a partner.[45] In very old cases it was held that the Laird of Cockburnspath could contract for the purchase of a horse without the consent of his curators,[46] and likewise a minor could grant a valid bond to his teacher.[47] A curator's consent will not be needed when the minor is forisfamiliated, that is, when the minor has set out on an independent course of life.[48] This may occur if the curator is absent from the country,[49] and probably in other instances when the curator is absent.

8–16   A minor may be freed from the curatory of parents by marriage.[50] There was doubt as to whether this was always the rule,[51] but the Law Reform (Husband and Wife) (Scotland) Act 1984, s.3, provides (1) that no married person shall, by reason only of minority, be subject to the curatory of his parent or of any person appointed by his parent, and (2) that no wife shall, by reason only of minority, be subject to the curatory of her husband.

8–17   Although the overall pattern may appear to be confused, it is suggested that the courts have a tendency, which has existed for four centuries, to distinguish between ordinary and extraordinary acts of administration. The normal activities of daily life, the purchases and sales, the booking of accommodation, or the taking of employment, do not require the consent of curators. Presumably the contracts made are

---

[41] *Stevenson* v. *Adair* (1872) 10 M. 919.

[42] *McFeetridge* v. *Stewarts & Lloyds Ltd.*, 1913 S.C. 773 at p. 783 *per* Lord Justice-Clerk Macdonald.

[43] *O'Donnell* v. *Brownieside Coal Co.*, 1934 S.C. 534. *Cf. Boath* v. *Andrew Lowson Ltd.*, 1924 S.L.T. 138.

[44] *McFeetridge* v. *Stewarts & Lloyds Ltd.*, *supra*.

[45] *Hill* v. *City of Glasgow Bank* (1879) 7 R. 68 at p. 75 *per* Lord President Inglis. On the relationship with fellow-partners see the complex case of *Wilson* v. *Laidlaw* (1816) 6 Pat.App. 222, and Bennett Miller, *Partnership*, pp. 31–34.

[46] *Brown* v. *Nicolson* (1629) Mor. 8940.

[47] *Drummond* v. *Broughton* (1627) Mor. 8939.

[48] Stair, I,v,13; Ersk., I,vi,53; *McFeetridge* v. *Stewarts & Lloyds Ltd.*, *supra*. The boundaries of the doctrine of forisfamiliation have yet to be elucidated by the Scottish courts. Whether or not there is forisfamiliation should be a mixed question of fact and law. Independent residence away from parents or the carrying-on of an independent trade are factors which tend to show forisfamiliation. But difficult issues may arise when the parents continue to provide some financial support or the emancipated minor returns to his parents. A discussion on the South African position is in Wessels, paras. 824–829; R. H. Christie, *The Law of Contract in South Africa* (1983), p. 236.

[49] *McFeetridge* v. *Stewarts & Lloyds, sup. cit.* at p. 790 *per* Lord Salvesen.

[50] Stair, I,v,13; Ersk., *Inst.*, I,vi,53; *Harvey* v. *Harvey* (1860) 22 D. 1198 at p. 1028 *per* Lord Justice-Clerk Inglis.

[51] Bankt., I,6,8; *Anderson* v. *Anderson* (1832) 11 S. 10. See E. M. Clive, *Husband and Wife* (2nd ed., 1982), p. 264 and *infra, s.v.* "Married Women," para. 8–33.

voidable and may be challenged on the grounds of lesion, but lesion will be difficult to prove if the minor acquires a similar benefit to an adult. Extraordinary acts, such as borrowing a large sum or selling heritage, require the consent of curators.[52]

18   The law is trying to protect minors, and it would not assist them if parties contracting with minors always had to investigate the curatorial position. There is, however, a further tract of authority which attempts to achieve the same ends by looking at whether the contract is beneficial. This approach also applies to contracts by pupils.

Fraudulent misrepresentation of age

19   A minor will be bound by a contract if he fraudulently induced the other party to believe that the minor was an adult.[53] The fraud may arise because the contract states that the minor is an adult,[54] or the minor says that he is an adult,[55] or the minor's appearance may be adult and he may fail to disclose his minority.[56] The minor will not be bound by a statement on age which was induced by the other party, or if the other party knew of the minority.[57]

Beneficial contracts

20   It is stated by some authorities that pupils and minors may enforce contracts beneficial to them, but such contracts cannot be enforced against them.[58] The origin of this rule is Erskine.[59] He quotes no authority, although he probably derived the rule from Roman law.[60] It is theoretically possible to have a form of limping nullity—the *negotium claudicans* of the Glossators[61]—under which one party but not the other party may enforce a contract.

21   Under the Sale of Goods Act 1979[62] necessaries sold and delivered have to be paid for at a reasonable price. "Necessaries" are defined as goods suitable to the condition in life of the incapax and to his actual

---

[52] *Cf. Harkness* v. *Graham* (1833) 11 S. 760 *per* Lord Balgray at p. 761.

[53] Stair, I,vi,44; *Ersk.*, I,vii,36.

[54] *Kennedy* v. *Weir* (1665) Mor. 11658.

[55] *Wemyss* v. *Creditors* (1637) Mor. 9025.

[56] *McDougall* v. *Marshall* (1705) Mor. 8995 and Mor. 421; *cf. Dennistoun* v. *Mudie* (1850) 12 D. 613.

[57] *Kennedy* v. *Weir, sup. cit.*

[58] Gloag, *Contract*, p. 77; Lord Fraser, *Parent and Child* (3rd ed., 1906), p. 206. The passage in Bankton referred to by Fraser and with a misprint in the citation, by Gloag, does not support the rule.

[59] Ersk., *Inst.*, I,vii,33; see also *Drummond's Trs.* v. *Peel's Trs.*, 1929 S.C. 484 at p. 493 *per* Lord President Clyde.

[60] *Inst.*, 1.21 pr.

[61] See M. Grotius, *The Jurisprudence of Holland* (trans. R. W. Lee, (1926), I,viii,5; III,i,26; J. Voet, *Commentary on the Pandects* (trans. P. Gane, 1956), XXVI,viii,3; M. Donaldson, *Minors in Roman-Dutch Law* (1955), p. 11; Wessels, para. 799 and see English common law as explained in *Nash* v. *Inman* [1908] 2 K.B. 1 at p. 11 *per* Buckley L.J.

[62] s.3. The doubt about whether the section applies to pupils is discussed in S.L.C. Memo. No. 65, *sup. cit.*, para. 2.18.

requirements at the time of the sale and delivery. The section, on the face of it, requires that the goods must both be sold and delivered (not merely be subject to an agreement to sell) and whether the goods are necessaries must be ascertained at the time of sale as well as at the time of delivery.[63] Whether the liability under this section is contractual or quasi-contractual is undecided.[64] The requirement that the goods be actually delivered and the obligation to pay a reasonable price, not the contract price, would suggest a quasi-contractual liability. As a solution this has the further attraction that it leaves the rules on contractual invalidity unimpaired. If goods other than necessaries are supplied to a pupil, or services are rendered, the liability of the pupil will be based on recompense.[65]

Contracts by a tutor

8–22   At common law contracts by a tutor are valid unless they are acts of extraordinary administration such as engaging a pupil in a mercantile partnership or granting leases of extraordinary duration,[66] or disponing the ward's land absolutely or in security.[67] All contracts by tutors may be questioned by the pupil on the grounds of enorm lesion within four years after the pupil has attained majority.[68] A discharge by persons who had ceased to be tutors was held void.[69]

Enorm lesion

8–23   Enorm lesion is only relevant in the case of a voidable deed.[70] In the early law there was confusion about this. There was doubt as to whether enorm lesion was required to challenge *any* deed by a minor. Balfour[71] and Spotiswoode[72] said enorm lesion must always be proved and this uncertainty is reflected in the case law.[73] Proof of enorm lesion is not consistent with the principle that a deed by a minor without consent of

---

[63] See, however, Chitty, paras. 536–538.

[64] Contrast opinions of Fletcher Moulton L.J. and Buckley L.J. in *Nash* v. *Inman, sup. cit.* (*cf. Walker, Contracts*, para. 5.17, who only cites Fletcher Moulton L.J.).

[65] The extent of liability is *quantum lucratus* not *quantum meruit*, nor "reasonable price." The reasonableness of a price has been put in issue, however, which still might suggest a quasi-contractual rather than a contractual remedy: *Inglis* v. *Ex. of Sharp* (1631) Mor. 8941; *Johnston* v. *Maitland* (1782) Mor. 9036; *Wilkie* v. *Dunlop & Co.* (1834) 12 S. 506 at p. 507.

[66] Bell, *Comm.*, I,129. On partnership see Bennett Miller, pp. 24–29.

[67] *Scott's Tr.* v. *Scott* (1887) 14 R. 1043.

[68] Bell, *Comm.*, I,128.

[69] *Lockhart* v. *Trotter* (1826) 5 S. 136; 3 W. & S. 481.

[70] *McGibbon* v. *McGibbon* (1852) 14 D. 506.

[71] Balfour, p. 180.

[72] Spotiswoode, p. 301.

[73] *Davidson* v. *Hamilton* (1632) Mor. 8988; *Hamilton* v. *Lamington* (1678) Mor. 8949. The uncertainty is also found in a case of insanity—*Lindsay* v. *Trent* (1684) Mor. 6280 at p. 6281.

existing curators is *ipso jure* null. This was recognised by Stair,[74] and by decisions after Stair.[75] Yet the matter was raised again in argument in 1726,[76] and Kames thought that a bond by a minor without a consent of curators was voidable and not void, although he admitted that other writers said the contrary. He went further and insisted that the daily practice of the court was to refuse to reduce the minor's bond upon evidence that it was not hurtful to the minor.[77] Bell thought that the deed raised an "absolute presumption of lesion," with the result that such deeds "if not null, are at least . . . exceptionable at any time, even after the *anni utiles*, without the necessity of a formal reduction."[78] This must be contrasted with the simpler views of Bankton, who thought the deed "intrinsically null,"[79] and of Erskine that "a deed signed by the curator only without the minor, is as truly void as one subscribed by the minor only, without his curator."[80]

4 To reduce a deed the minor might have to offer restoration of money received,[81] although total restitution might not be ordered.[82] The profitable application of sums has been held to be a bar to reduction on the grounds of minority and lesion.[83] Reduction operates retrospectively and not from the time of litiscontestation.[84]

Grounds for action

5 (1) Enorm lesion is pleadable by the minor within four years of attaining majority, *i.e.* within the *quadriennium utile*. Opinion has been reserved on whether the action may be brought during minority.[85]

(2) The challenge must be by the raising of an action before the expiry of the four years. The action should seek reduction of the transaction. It is not enough that the plea is stated in defence to an action.[86] The challenge may be by the minor or a person deriving title from the minor.[87]

---

[74] Stair, I,vi,33.
[75] *Bell* v. *Sutherland, supra*; *Thomson* v. *Pagan, supra*; *Bannatyne* v. *Trotter* (1704) Mor. 8983, which suggests that the deed is reducible, is a curious case and was doubted in *Manuel* v. *Manuel* (1853) 15 D. 284.
[76] *Harvie* v. *Gordon* (1726) Mor. 5712.
[77] Kames, *Elucidations*, p. 3.
[78] Bell, *Comm.*, I,130.
[79] Bankt., I,183,88.
[80] Ersk., *Inst.*, I,vii,14.
[81] *McWilliam* v. *Shaw* (1576) Mor. 9022.
[82] *Carmichael* v. *Castlehill* (1698) Mor. 8993.
[83] *Thomson* v. *Stevenson* (1666) Mor. 8991; *Blantyre* v. *Walkinshaw* (1667) Mor. 8991.
[84] *Houston* v. *Maxwell* (1631) Mor. 8986.
[85] *Patrick* v. *William Baird & Co.*, 1927 S.N. 32; see also *McFeetridge* v. *Stewarts & Lloyds Ltd.*, *supra*.
[86] *Stewart* v. *Snodgrass* (1860) 23 D. 187; *Hill* v. *City of Glasgow Bank* (1879) 7 R. 68 at pp. 75, 76 *per* Lord President Inglis. Presumably pleading reduction *ope exceptionis* or an action of declarator might in appropriate circumstances be sufficient, but the traditional approach has required an action of reduction. On reduction *ope exceptionis* see R.C. 174; Sheriff Court Rules, r. 68; Summary Cause Rules, r. 41.
[87] *Harkness* v. *Graham* (1833) 11. S. 760 (creditors).

(3) The minor can be barred from challenge by ratification during the *quadriennium utile, e.g.* by paying interest,[88] or otherwise continuing to act on the contract.[89]

(4) The minor must show non age at the time of the contract.[90] His age is calculated *de momento in momentum*. Lord Fraser observed[91]:

> "The periods of age are computed *de momento in momentum*, so that if the minor were born at eleven o'clock at night on January 1 he would not be a *pubes* or a major, till eleven o'clock at night, fourteen or twenty-one years afterwards. The period must be calculated from the very moment of birth to the same minute at the end of the pupillarity and minority. The maxim *dies inceptus pro completo habetur* is here therefore unsanctioned. This was following the rule of the Roman law."

(5) There must be enorm lesion. The lesion must be considerable and should not have occurred by accident after the contract, *e.g.* the destruction of the house purchased for a fair price.[92] It has been said that: "Lesion, in the sense of the authorities, must not be trifling, but must be enorm, which means that the consideration which the minor got must be immoderately disproportionate to what might have been got."[93] The consideration is judged by looking at the whole circumstances of the bargain,[94] including the gain derived.[95] Lesion may be presumed, and in some cases the presumption is so strong that Erskine said it was irrebuttable, *e.g.* a donation or a cautionary obligation.[96] Where tutors or curators have authorised the transaction, more decisive proof is needed of lesion.[97] Lesion will exist when the transaction benefits someone other than the minor, for example, a bill of exchange granted on behalf of the minor's father.[98]

(6) There should be mutual restitution. Where matters are entire both parties are restored to their former state.[99] Where matters are not entire a distinction has been drawn by the Institutional writers between volun-

---

[88] Ersk., I,vii,39.

[89] *Hill* v. *City of Glasgow Bank, sup. cit.; Roberton* v. *Roberton* (1831) 9 S. 865; *Forrest* v. *Campbell* (1853) 16 D. 16. Ratification of a loan which is void appears to be affected by the Betting and Loans (Infants) Act 1892, s.5. Gloag said that it was undecided whether the Act applied to a voidable loan (Gloag, p. 90).

[90] Ersk., I,vii,35.

[91] Fraser, *Parent and Child* (3rd ed.), p. 200. See *Drummond* (1624) Mor. 3465.

[92] Ersk., I.vii,36. On the time of lesion see *McGuire* v. *Robert Addie & Sons Colleries*, 1950 S.C. 537 and *Cooper* v. *Cooper's Trs.* (1885) 12 R. 473, *rvd.* on other grounds (1888) 15 R.(H.L.) 21.

[93] *Robertson* v. *S. Henderson & Sons Ltd.*, 1905 7 F. 776 at p. 785 *per* Lord President Dunedin. An example is *Faulds* v. *British Steel Corp.*, 1977 S.L.T.(Notes) 18.

[94] *Robertson* v. *S. Henderson & Sons Ltd., sup. cit.*

[95] *Cooper* v. *Cooper's Trs.* (1855) 12 R. 473.

[96] Ersk., I,vii,37.

[97] Bell, *Comm.*, I,131; *Faulds* v. *British Steel Corp.*, 1977 S.L.T.(Notes) 18.

[98] *McMichael* v. *Barbour* (1840) 3 D. 279.

[99] Ersk., I,vii,41.

tary contracts and necessary contracts. In voluntary contracts the minor may be restored although the other party cannot be. In necessary contracts restitution of the other party is a condition for restitution of the minor.[1] There may be reduction of a decree of court.[2]

Tutors and curators

26 Because the pupil is incapable of consenting, any contract affecting the pupil's estate will be made by the pupil's tutor or tutors.[3] A tutor is a trustee in terms of the Trusts (Scotland) Act 1921[4] and "trust" includes the appointment of any tutor by deed, decree or otherwise.[5] Doubt was raised about the application of this to those appointed by law and, as a result, the Guardianship of Infants Act 1925 enacts[6] that a father or mother acting as tutor of a pupil child by virtue of the common law or of the Guardianship of Infants Act 1886, or of the 1925 Act, is a trustee within the meaning of the Trusts (Scotland) Act 1921.

27 A curator is also a trustee under the Trusts (Scotland) Act 1921,[7] but, despite a contrary opinion,[8] it seems that this applies only to a curator appointed by a deed or court decree. It does not apply to those who are curators by operation of law.[9]

28 In terms of section 4 of the 1921 Act trustees in all trusts have power to do certain acts, where such acts are not at variance with the terms or purposes of the trust.[10] Under section 5 it is competent to the court[11] to grant authority to do any of the acts mentioned in section 4 notwithstanding that such act is at variance with the terms or purposes of the trust, on being satisfied that such act is in all the circumstances expedient for the execution of the trust.[12] An act at variance with *either* the terms *or* the purposes of the trust will require a section 5 petition.[13]

29 The usual difficulties in applying these statutory provisions to tutors are (1) an appointment at common law, by statute or by court interlocutor does not have "terms" of appointment; and (2) the "purposes" of

---

[1] Ersk., I,vii,41; Bell, *Comm.*, I,131. It cannot be pretended that this area of law is free from obscurity.

[2] Ersk., I,vii,37. Bell suggested this needed strong proof of lesion: *Comm.*, I,131.

[3] Since the Guardianship Act 1973, s.10, both parents may be tutors or curators of a child.

[4] s.2 definition of "Trustee."

[5] *Ibid.*

[6] s.10, thus altering the effect of *Shearer's Tutor*, 1924 S.C. 445. That case and other authority there cited show the nature of the *nobile officium* jurisdiction as it applies to the acts of tutors. See also *Gibson's Trs.*, 1933 S.C. 190; Wilson and Duncan, *Trusts*, p. 320.

[7] s.2.

[8] Gloag and Henderson (8th ed.), p. 764.

[9] The logic of *Shearer's Tutor, sup. cit.*, continues to apply to curators.

[10] See s.4 as amended by the Trustee Investments Act 1961, s.10.

[11] *i.e.* the Court of Session: see s.2.

[12] The procedure for trustees is explained in W. W. McBryde and N. J. Dowie, *Petition Procedure in the Court of Session*, p. 75.

[13] *Marquis of Lothian's C.B.*, 1927 S.C. 579; *Tennent's J.F.* v. *Tennent*, 1954 S.C. 215 at p. 225 *per* Lord President Cooper.

the appointment were traditionally to preserve the incapax's estate, not deal with it, although in modern times it is recognised that circumstances may require management of the estate.[14]

8–30   In *Linton* v. *Inland Revenue*[15] Lord President Clyde pointed out that tutorship and trusteeship were very different. The tutor, unlike the trustee, was not vested in the ward's property. He went on to say that[16]: "*Prima facie*, at any rate, nothing could be more at variance with the purposes of the 'trust' reposed in a tutor than the alienation of the estate which it is his legal function to preserve and manage." It has subsequently been pointed out that it is a matter of circumstances and the dictum cited may be too broadly expressed.[17] If the estate is simply an investment, it may be sold under section 4. If the estate in question is the family residence which a deceased father presumably wished his son to enjoy when the son came of age, the tutor could not at his own hand dispose of the heritage.[18] In borderline cases there should be a petition to the court under section 5 which may be dismissed as unnecessary with the petitioner being granted expenses out of the tutory estate.[19]

8–31   A person dealing with a tutor, or other trustee, may be affected by section 2 of the Trusts (Scotland) Act 1961. This protects the validity of a transaction entered into by trustees in relation to the trust estate if it is an act of the kind described in section 4(1)(*a*) to (*ee*) of the Trusts (Scotland) Act 1921. The transaction is not challengeable on the ground that it is at variance with the terms or purposes of the trust. If the trustee is acting under the supervision of the Accountant of Court the section applies only if the Accountant consents to the transaction. The section does not apply to acts other than those specified. For example, it does not apply to a gift of assets or a purchase of heritage which was not required for occupation by the ward. It does not apply in questions between a trustee and his ward, or between trustees.

Practical problems in dealing with pupils and minors

8–32   No one likes to deal with a person whose contracts may be void or voidable, but where a contract is necessary the following points may be looked to.

(1) At common law the court refused to grant authority to a minor and his curators to sell heritage.[20] This was on the grounds that the authority of the court was unnecessary and no decree of the court could prevent reduction by the minor. Nevertheless the limited circumstances in

---

[14] The history of judicial factors is narrated in N. M. L. Walker, *Judicial Factors*, pp. 75 *et seq.*
[15] 1928 S.C. 209.
[16] at p. 214.
[17] *Cunningham's Tutrix*, 1949 S.C. 275.
[18] *Cunningham's Tutrix, sup. cit.*
[19] *Cunningham's Tutrix, sup. cit.*; *Dempster*, 1926 S.L.T. 157.
[20] *Wallace* v. *Wallace*, Mar. 8, 1817, F.C.

which section 5 of the Trusts (Scotland) Act 1921 applies, may enable a court application to provide some comfort. In *Brunton*[21] a tutrix presented a petition for power to consent as tutrix of her son to a disposition of a house which was too expensive to maintain. The petition was granted. A court's approval of a variation of a trust under section 1 of the Trusts (Scotland) Act 1961 is unchallengeable on the grounds of minority and lesion,[22] but otherwise it is thought that although a court may have given power to a trustee to act, there is still the possibility of challenge by the incapax.

(2) In the case of a minor the theoretical risk is greater if the minor has curators who are ignored[23] than if the minor has no curators.[24] It can, therefore, be important to ascertain whether or not curators exist. The failure of third parties to attempt communication with curators has been adversely commented on.[25]

(3) The transition from pupillarity to minority happens automatically at the appropriate age. When, as a consequence, tutors have ceased to be tutors, they should not grant deeds as tutors.[26]

(4) A transaction between a minor and his curator is particularly troublesome because in principle it is void.[27] It may be that a transaction which was to the benefit of the minor would not be struck at, *e.g.* a father advancing sums to assist his child's education. A transaction which goes the other way and results in a transfer of assets from a child to his curator is highly suspect.

(5) The case law which allows a minor to trade and carry out acts of ordinary administration without the consent of curators[28] is useful if it clearly applies to the transaction in question.

(6) Payments to minors raise special problems. Not only do some payments need a curator's consent,[29] but there is authority that a minor suffers lesion if money is put into his hands and he squanders the funds.[30] A person making a capital payment to a minor may be entitled to ask for security for the investment or profitable employment of the money.[31] To avoid these problems damages may be paid into court. If there is not already a court action a "friendly action" may be raised solely for the purpose of having sums paid over and invested under the

---

[21] 1928 S.N. 112.

[22] 1961 Act, s.1(3).

[23] The contract is void (subject to exceptions).

[24] The contract is voidable.

[25] *Dennistoun* v. *Mudie* (1850) 12 D. 613; *O'Donnell* v. *Brownieside Coal Co.*, 1934 S.C. 534.

[26] *Lockhart* v. *Trotter* (1826) 5 S. 136; 3 W. & S. 481.

[27] See para. 8–12.

[28] See paras. 8–15 to 8–18.

[29] See *ibid*.

[30] Gloag, p. 85.

[31] Gloag, p. 80; *Jack* v. *North British Ry. Co.* (1886) 14 R. 263.

supervision of the court. The action is raised by, or on behalf of the inca-pax and settled on a joint minute.[32]

(7) It is not sufficient objection to making a payment to a tutor that the tutor is poor, although evidence of insolvency may require steps to be taken to preserve the pupil's position.[33]

(8) In the end there will remain a risk of challenge which must be accepted or rejected. The consequences could be minimised by obtaining caution or an insurance indemnity. Even if the incapax's transaction is void, the cautioner may still be bound.[34]

MARRIED WOMEN

8–33 The nature of deeds by minors was founded on when the court con-sidered the nature of deeds by married women,[35] but however attractive the analogy, it is misleading. There were several differences, particu-larly in relation to restitution on the grounds of lesion.[36] The invalidity of contracts by married women at common law presents a complex pic-ture, not least because many parts of the law were never, and may never be, settled.

8–34 All this should have been of only historical interest following the series of statutes commencing in 1861 and ending in 1920,[37] whereby the limitations on a wife's contractual capacity were removed and a married woman became capable of entering into contracts and incurring obli-gations as if she were not married.[38] The remaining difficulty was the status of the minor wife. If the wife was a minor, her husband was her curator, unless he also was a minor or subject to some legal incapacity, in which case the wife's parents were normally her curators.[39] The nature of these curatorial powers was doubtful.[40]

8–35 Under the Law Reform (Husband and Wife) (Scotland) Act 1984, s.3, it is provided that (1) no married person shall, by reason only of minority, be subject to the curatory of his parent or of any person appointed by his parent, and (2) no wife shall, by reason only of minor-ity, be subject to the curatory of her husband.[41] In terms of the Family Law (Scotland) Act 1985, s.24 (when it is brought into force), the

---

[32] *Fairley* v. *Allan*, 1948 S.L.T.(Notes) 81; *Falconer* v. *Robertson*, 1949 S.L.T.(Notes) 56; Rules of Court, pp. 131–134; Act of Sederunt (Ordinary Cause Rules, Sheriff Court) 1983, r. 128.

[33] *Stevenson's Trs.* v. *Dumbreck* (1861) 4 Macq. 86; *Wardrop* v. *Gossling* (1869) 7 M. 532.

[34] *Stevenson* v. *Adair* (1872) 10 M. 919.

[35] *Birch* v. *Douglas* (1663) Mor. 5961.

[36] *Vide* Fraser, *Husband and Wife*, Vol. I, p. 521.

[37] Conjugal Rights (Scotland) Amendment Act 1861; Married Women's Property (Scotland) Acts 1877, 1881 and 1920.

[38] 1920 Act, s.5.

[39] 1920 Act, s.2; Guardianship Act 1973, s.10.

[40] E. M. Clive, *The Law Of Husband And Wife In Scotland* (2nd ed., 1982), pp. 261–265.

[41] s.2 of the Married Women's Property (Scotland) Act 1920 is repealed.

general rule will be that marriage does not of itself affect the legal capacity of the parties to the marriage.

INSANITY

Early law

36   The problems of those who were not *compos mentis* feature in our printed records at least since 1292.[42] The Court of Session from its institution dealt with many cases in which, in modern terminology, insanity was pled as a ground of reduction.[43] The law distinguished between fatuous persons or idiots on the one hand, and "furious" persons on the other.[44] The distinction, which contains much uncertainty, is described by Bell.[45] For the purposes of the law of contract there appears no difference between the effect of a verdict of a jury whether under a brieve of idiotry or of furiosity, and indeed the practice was, "to purchase both brieves, to make up a claim applicable to each, and to retour that brieve under which the jury found the character of the party's insanity could be brought."[46] Those brieves were abolished by the Court of Session Act 1868,[47] and in their place there was introduced a procedure for cognition of the insane proceeding on a brieve from Chancery. A person was to be deemed to be insane, "if he be furious or fatuous, or labouring under such unsoundness of mind as to render him incapable of managing his affairs."[48] Cognition is now never used[49] and the procedure has been superseded by the appointment of a *curator bonis* to an incapax. The usual ground for appointment is that a person is "of unsound mind and incapable of managing his own affairs or of giving instructions for their management."

Nature of nullity

-37   Balfour stated that: "All contractis, obligatiounis, infeftments or decretis arbitrall, maid by ony man, or gevin betwix twa parties, of the quhilkis ony ane if furiosus, or mente captus, is of nane availl. . . . "[50] Spotiswoode put "furious" persons in the same class as pupils and provided a reason for the legal incapacity: "Others again are not *iure prohibiti contrahere*, as infans and furious persons; but yet whatever is done by them is void by law, as being *inhibiles ex juris dispositione* to con-

---

[42] A.P.S. 1, 446; other cases in A.D.C. 1, index heading "Curators ad Lites"; *Pook* v. *Park of that Ilk*, (1476) A.D.A. 43.
[43] Mor., *s.v.* "Idiotry and Furiosity."
[44] Ersk., *Inst.*, I,vii,48.
[45] Bell., *Comm.* I,133.
[46] Fraser, *Parent and Child*, p. 657.
[47] s.101.
[48] *Ibid.*
[49] N. M. L. Walker, *Judicial Factors* (1974), p. 22.
[50] Balfour, 123.

tract, seeing the chief ground of contracts is consent, and consent grow-eth of knowledge whereof such persons are not capable."[51] Likewise Stair thought that there could not be a contract by idiots or furious persons except in their lucid intervals.[52] There was an early confusion as to whether lesion was necessary to reduce the contract, and this was criticised by Fountainhall who stated: "if the furiosity be proved, then the deed is simply null, whether there be lesion or not."[53]

8–38   The nature of the invalidity was established in *Gall* v. *Bird*,[54] when deeds of an insane person which were null were contrasted with deeds which were merely reducible. A deed by an insane person is void if he is insane at the time of granting the deed: "He is considered as a pupil incapable of transacting any of the business of life."[55] Knowledge of the insanity by the other contracting party is not a relevant consideration. The voidable nature of the contract in English law is not Scots law.[56]

Proof of insanity

8–39   All human beings are presumed to be sane and to know the consequences of their actions.[57] Sanity is presumed. The presumption of sanity may be replaced by an opposite presumption in the event of certain judicial proceedings.

8–40   Sheriff N. M. L. Walker stated that: "the interlocutor appointing a *curator bonis* has the same effect as a 'proven' verdict of a jury in a cognition and is conclusive as to incapacity."[58] First, it may be doubted whether the appointment of a curator and cognition have the same effect. A curator may be appointed in circumstances in which an inquest would not cognosce a person as insane,[59] and Lord Fraser drew a distinction between the effect on status depending on whether there was a verdict.[60] Furthermore, it is unlikely that the appointment is conclusive as to incapacity. Even in the case of cognition, which is the stronger case

---

[51] Spotiswoode, p. 72.

[52] Stair, I,x,13.

[53] *Lindsay* v. *Trent* (1684) Mor. 6281; *cf.* Gloag. p. 92, and J. B. Miller, *The Law Of Partnership in Scotland* (1973), p. 39, who come close to treating Fountainhall's remark as if it were the decision of the court. If the deed had been treated as null, it would have been a rare instance of a second purchaser of heritage affected by the incapacity of the granter of a disposition many years previously.

[54] (1855) 17 D. 1027.

[55] Fraser, *Parent and Child*, p. 685. This reasoning is logical but its practical application is not convincing. The policy of the law is to protect pupils, and all pupils can be treated in the same way. All adults are not equally incapacitated by insanity nor in any individual need the degree of insanity be constant throughout his life. The situation is more fluid and arguably the law's attitude should be more flexible. Anyone who contracts with a pupil can hardly complain if the contract rebounds in his face. A contract with an adult who appears eccentric is another matter: *cf.* Williston, s.251.

[56] *John Loudon & Co.* v. *Elder's C.B.*, 1923 S.L.T. 226.

[57] Dickson, *Evidence*, para. 114; Bell, *Prin.*, s.2103.

[58] *Ibid.*, p. 26.

[59] Fraser, *Parent and Child*, p. 676.

[60] *Ibid.*, p. 684, and in the authority referred to by Sheriff Walker (*Mitchell & Baxter* v. *Cheyne* (1891) 19 R. 324) it is said that the two procedures are "*practically* the same."

for Sheriff Walker's view, "the trial on the brieve is *ex parte* and . . . evidence which the holder of the deed may possess of a lucid interval during which the deed was made may still be produced."[61] The effect of the appointment of a *curator bonis* may be to alter the presumption of sanity to a presumption of insanity, but it is possible for proof to be led that the incapax was capable of understanding a contract into which he entered. Conversely the lack of appointment of a curator does not prevent evidence that a person was insane at the time he entered the contract.[62]

41   There is little useful authority on the type of proof necessary to show that a contracting party was insane. It is possible that the development of the doctrine of facility and circumvention in the nineteenth century may have removed much of the practical need for showing lack of capacity. It will usually be much easier to show that a facile person was imposed upon than to show that such a person lacked contractual capacity. Nevertheless facility and lack of capacity raise different issues as grounds for challenge of a contract.[63] If there is incapacity, the amount of alleged imposition is irrelevant and the contract is void, not voidable.

42   In *Park* v. *Park*[64] a marriage was annulled on the grounds of insanity of the woman at the time of marriage. Lord Dewar observed that: "the occult character of the disease of insanity renders its consideration in relation to the validity of contracts very difficult." He formed his view on the basis of the inexplicable actings of the woman and the medical evidence. In *Calder* v. *Calder*,[65] another case of nullity of marriage, it was observed that delusions in order to produce incapacity must be delusions on the subject in relation to which the question of capacity arises. It was said to be a problem more for medical men than the uninstructed judgment of a layman.

43   In a criminal case Lord Strachan gave this charge to the jury[66]:

"The question really is this, whether at the time of the offences charged the accused was of unsound mind. I do not think you should resolve this matter by inquiring into all the technical terms and ideas that the medical witnesses have put before you. Treat it broadly, and treat the question as being whether the accused was of

---

[61] Bell, *Comm.*, I,132. Bell considered the verdict raised a presumption of incapacity, but he obviously regarded the presumption as rebuttable. A. G. Walker and N. M. L. Walker, *The Law of Evidence in Scotland* (1964), paras. 58 and 59, consider the presumptions arising from the appointment of a *curator bonis* under the heading "Examples of Rebuttable Presumption."

[62] Reduction for furiosity could proceed although there had been no inquest: *Alexander* v. *Kinneir* (1632) Mor. 6278, *Loch* v. *Dick* (1638) Mor. 6278, *Lindsay* v. *Trent* (1638) Mor. 6280; and for idiotry, *Christie* v. *Gibb* (1700) Mor. 6283. Thus in *Gall* v. *Bird, sup. cit.*, so far as appears from the report, there had been no cognition or appointment of a *curator bonis* to the pursuer.

[63] See para. 11–16.

[64] 1914 1 S.L.T. 88.

[65] 1942 S.N. 40.

[66] *H.M.A.* v. *Kidd*, 1960 J.C. 61 at p. 70. See for discussion and subsequent case law, Gordon, *Criminal Law*, Chap. 10.

sound or unsound mind. That question is primarily one of fact to be decided by you, but I have to give you these directions. First, in order to excuse a person from responsibility for his acts on the ground of insanity, there must have been an alienation of the reason in relation to the act committed. There must have been some mental defect, to use a broad neutral word, a mental defect, by which his reason was overpowered, and he was thereby rendered incapable of exerting his reason to control his conduct and reactions. If his reason was alienated in relation to the act committed, he was not responsible for that act, even although otherwise he may have been apparently quite rational. What is required is some alienation of the reason in relation to the act committed. Secondly, beyond that, the question in this case whether the accused's mind was sound or unsound is to be decided by you in the light of the evidence, in the exercise of your commonsense and knowledge of mankind, and it is to be judged on the ordinary rules on which men act in daily life. Thirdly, the question is to be decided in the light of the whole circumstances disclosed in the evidence. You must have regard to the evidence which has been given by the medical witnesses, but the medical evidence by itself is not conclusive. The question is to be decided by you, and not by the mental specialists. In coming to your decision you are entitled, and indeed bound, to regard the whole evidence. You are entitled in particular to consider the nature of the acts committed and the conduct of the accused at and about the relevant times, and his previous history. Those are the directions which I give you on this matter."

8–44   It may be suggested that similar approaches can be applied to the law of contract. A person is not bound by a contract if he was incapable of consenting to it. There must have been a mental defect which rendered him incapable of understanding what he was doing so that he did not consent to that contract. A person's ability to understand or consent to other acts, or other contracts, is not the test, although evidence of surrounding circumstances is always relevant. The question of capacity will be decided on medical evidence and evidence of behaviour at the time of the contract. The issue is primarily one of fact.

Supervening insanity

8–45   Many contracts continue in operation for a period of time. A contracting party may be sane at the time of the contract but become insane while part of the contract remains to be performed. Continued performance by the incapax may be impossible. On the principle of mutuality the other party could not be compelled to continue with the contract. As Lord President Inglis put it: "Where one party to a contract becomes disabled from performing his part of the contract, of course the other parties to the contract are liberated from their obligation."[67] Where no further performance is required of the incapax the problem is different.

---

[67] *Eadie* v. *MacBean's C.B.* (1885) 12 R. 660 at p. 665.

It may be that the contract can continue to exist. In *Pollok* v. *Paterson*[68] a mandate was held to continue in effect despite the supervening insanity of the granter but opinions were reserved on the effect of the insanity on those who contracted with the mandatory in the knowledge of the insanity of the principal. In *Wink* v. *Mortimer*[69] it appears that temporary insanity did not put an end to the contract between agent and client. Insanity of a partner is a ground for dissolution of a partnership either (1) because the partnership agreement so provides, or (2) on the application to a court to exercise its statutory discretion.[70] It is normally provided in the articles of association of a company that the office of director shall be vacated if the director becomes of unsound mind.[71]

Intoxication and Disease

46 Insanity is not the only affliction which may affect capacity to consent. Stair equated drunkenness to disease, both of which could prevent a party legally contracting.[72] Just after the publication of his first edition, however, the court did not reduce a deed on the grounds that the granter was extremely drunk and incapable of consent. Reduction required an allegation of deceit.[73] A case reported by Fountainhall shows uncertainty on how a person could be held to have knowledge and consent when he was so drunk that he had no senses or reason, but there was a hint that one should not give way to one's own intoxication.[74] Erskine and Bankton distinguished degrees of drunkenness. According to Erskine a person in the state of absolute drunkenness cannot contract, but a lesser degree of drunkenness did not annul the contract.[75] Bankton thought that drunkenness would not annul a contract unless it deprived the party of the use of reason.[76]

47 These distinctions became settled law in *Taylor* v. *Provan*[77] in which it was decided that of the varying degrees of drunkenness only such as would render a person incapable of entering a bargain were relevant in a reduction of a contract. It was not sufficient for reduction that a person

---

[68] Dec. 10, 1811, F.C.

[69] (1849) 11 D. 995.

[70] Partnership Act 1890, ss.32 and 35(*a*); *Eadie* v. *MacBean's C.B.*, *supra* (application refused when partner only contributed capital and his *curator bonis* opposed the application); Miller, *Partnership*, p. 40.

[71] Companies (Tables A to F) Regulations 1985 (S.I. 1985 No. 805), Table A, art. 81; *cf.* Companies Act 1948, Table A, art. 88.

[72] Stair, I,x,13; IV,xx,49.

[73] * v. * (1682) 2 B.S. 19.

[74] *Gordon* v. *Ogilvy* (1693) 4 B.S. 62. *Cf.* the attitude of the criminal law: *Brennan* v. *H.M. Advocate*, 1977 J.C. 38.

[75] Ersk., *Inst.*, III,i,16; IV,iv,5.

[76] Bankt., I,342,66.

[77] (1864) 2 M. 1226. There was no allegation of fraud. See also the terms of the issue in *Johnston* v. *Clark* (1854) 17 D. 228.

was "in such a condition from drink that he had not all his wits about him,"[78] or that it was "an after dinner bargain, when the buyer is in a more than usually liberal humour"[79] which was a lack of facility of common occurrence.[80] Furthermore the earlier cases reported by Hume of *Jardine* v. *Elliot*[81] and *Hunter* v. *Stevenson*,[82] which had suggested that partial intoxication would result in a contract not being binding, were explained as being decided on the ground of lack of evidence of a serious bargain and not on the ground of lack of capacity. In more recent times in *Laing* v. *Taylor*[83] averments were held irrelevant when all that was alleged was that a cheque was signed when the defender was so drunk that his judgment was seriously impaired.

8–48   In *Pollok* v. *Burns*[84] the action was for suspension of a charge upon a bill on the grounds that the bill had been signed by a person in a state of intoxication. The bill was not challenged until six months after it was signed. The action failed before the Second Division but the grounds for failure differ in the judges' opinions.

8–49   Lord Justice-Clerk Moncreiff considered that Sir Hew Pollok, who signed the bill, was exceedingly drunk at the time. Sir Hew could have successfully challenged the document if the challenge had been made at once. His Lordship continued: "Where the plea of intoxication is taken by the person who says he was intoxicated and incapable when he did the act which he wishes to repudiate, he is bound, the moment his sober senses return and he knows what he has done, to take his ground at once. That is essential."[85] After pointing out the time which Sir Hew took to challenge the transaction, the Lord Justice-Clerk concluded: "I think the actings of Sir Hew Pollock necessarily amount to a confession that the bill was obtained when he was not unconscious, that he knew what he was doing. . . . I assume, from the fact that he never stated the plea until the judicial demand was made, that he was conscious that he was not incapacitated, and that he knew what he had done."

8–50   It is difficult to know what to make of this reasoning. Either Sir Hew was capable of contracting or he was not. Taking the whole of the Lord Justice-Clerk's opinion, it seems that his Lordship considered that Sir Hew was capable of contracting. The lack of prompt challenge was an item of evidence on capacity at the time of the transaction. This was the

---

[78] *Ibid.* at p. 1232 *per* Lord Justice-Clerk Inglis.

[79] *Ibid.* at p. 1233 *per* Lord Benholme.

[80] *Ibid.* at p. 1234 *per* Lord Neaves; *cf. ibid.* at p. 1232 *per* Lord Justice-Clerk Inglis.

[81] (1803) Hume 684. The sale of the entire sheepstock on a farm contracted by two persons under the influence of alcohol was not enforced although the price was fair. The transaction was not challenged until the time for implement three months later.

[82] (1804) Hume 686; the seller of sheep was under the influence of alcohol and the bargain was not entered.

[83] 1978 S.L.T.(Sh.Ct.) 59.

[84] (1875) 2 R. 497.

[85] *Ibid.* at p. 503.

approach of Lord Ormidale[86] and Lord Gifford.[87] Lord Neaves was much influenced by the consideration that Sir Hew was a habitual drunkard, and the ground of his decision seems to be that habitual drunkards must make prompt challenge or be personally barred.

51 It is dangerous to isolate the statement of Lord Justice-Clerk Moncreiff that a person is bound to challenge a transaction the moment his sober senses return. By itself this would make the contract voidable and not void. The majority view in *Pollok* v. *Burns* is consistent with the theory of Stair and Erskine, which had been approved,[88] that to succeed in a reduction on the ground of intoxication it must be shown that there was an absence of reason. If this is shown the contract, it is submitted, is void.

52 Gloag saw the force in the argument that the contract was void, but nevertheless stated that, "it would seem to be merely voidable."[89] The authority referred to is *Wilson & Fraser* v. *Nisbet*,[90] which is reported briefly and proceeds on the argument, "that drunkenness is but a temporary incapacity, which ought not to be regarded, especially as it was the acceptor's own fault." This reflects the early uncertainty as to whether drunkenness should be held to have *any* effect on a contract. This attitude would not now be followed and, in any event, the case is not authority for the proposition that the bill was voidable. There was no relevant ground for challenge of the bill.

53 Gloag also referred to English law taking the view that the contracts are voidable, but English authorities are an unsatisfactory guide. In England incapacity by reason of drunkenness is sometimes equated to the incapacity of mentally-disordered persons.[91] It is clear that the English approach to the incapacity of the insane produces different results from the Scottish authorities on such incapacity, hence the danger of following their cases on drunkenness.[92]

54 There seems no reason why intoxication and insanity should be the only physical afflictions which deprive a person of reason. Stair recognised this by mentioning disease separately from idiocy and furiosity as a ground for reduction. There are some old cases in which it was held relevant for a woman to argue that a deed was signed by her while she was

---

[86] *Ibid.* at p. 505.
[87] *Ibid.* at p. 506.
[88] In *Taylor* v. *Provan, supra.*
[89] Gloag, p. 95.
[90] (1736) Mor. 1509.
[91] Chitty, para. 605; Cheshire and Fifoot, p. 419.
[92] The older and now discredited approach to drunkenness in England shown in *Pitt* v. *Smith* (1811) 3 Camp. 33 is nearer to the Scottish approach, and in 1864 Lord Cowan said that Scots law, English law and Pothier were identical: *Taylor* v. *Provan, supra* at p. 1233. English law, however, was changing. The change came with *Molton* v. *Camroux* (1848) 2 Ex. 487, affd. (1849) 4 Ex. 17 and *Matthews* v. *Baxter* (1873) L.R. 8 Ex. 132.

in labour and in terms indicating that there could be a lack of capacity at that time.[93] Conversely it was not relevant, so far as third parties were concerned, for a man to argue that a deed was granted *in aestu amoris*, "at which time he would refuse nothing."[94] Disease or drugs could impose the same incapacity as insanity or absolute intoxication, but merely to aver that the pursuer was in a weak state of body and mind would be insufficient.[95]

THE CROWN

8–55 The Crown has unlimited contractual capacity.[96] In practice there are some specialities affecting contracts by the Crown. These are noted here, although a full discussion of the issues must be looked for in works on constitutional law.

The Crown cannot by contract fetter its future action

8–56 The Crown cannot fetter its discretion by contract, but it is difficult to state the extent of this principle. The Crown can bind itself by a commercial contract.[97]

Crown servants

8–57 The duty of the subject is to give his life to defend his country, and this may explain why military service does not rest on contract and the Crown cannot be sued for alleged breach of such a contract.[98] In the case of civil servants there may be a contract with the Crown,[99] but English authority suggests doubt as to whether the relationship between the Crown and its employees is truly contractual.[1] The issue has been confused by the extent to which offices are held at pleasure and the former

---

[93] *Belford* v. *Scot* (1683) Mor. 6297; *A.* v. *B.* (1686) Mor. 6298; *Mason* v. *Mason* (1686) 2 B.S. 89.

[94] *Currier* v. *Rutherford-Hyslop* (1696) Mor. 6299.

[95] *N.B. Railway Co.* v. *Wood* (1891) 18 R.(H.L.) 27; *Mackie* v. *Strachan Kinmond & Co.* (1896) 23 R. 1030; *Mathieson* v. *Hawthorns & Co. Ltd.* (1899) 1 F. 468.

[96] *Cameron* v. *Lord Advocate*, 1952 S.C. 165.

[97] *Rederiaktiebolaget Amphitrite* v. *R.* [1921] 3 K.B. 500; *Robertson* v. *Minister of Pensions* [1949] 1 K.B. 227; *Cameron* v. *Lord Advocate*, 1952 S.C. 165; *Commrs. of Crown Lands* v. *Page* [1960] 2 Q.B. 274.

[98] *Cameron* v. *Lord Advocate, sup. cit.* On the prerogative which governs armed forces, see Z. Cowen, "The Armed Forces of the Crown" (1950) 66 L.Q.R. 478.

[99] *Ibid.; Cappon* v. *Lord Advocate*, 1920 1 S.L.T. 261.

[1] Chitty, para. 690; *Riordan* v. *War Office* [1959] 3 All E.R. 552, [1960] 3 All E.R. 774n. "It was common ground before your Lordships, though it was not common ground below, that there was no contractual relationship between the Crown and the staff at G.C.H.Q."—*Council of Civil Service Unions* v. *Minister for the Civil Service* [1985] 1 A.C. 374 at p. 419 *per* Lord Roskill.

rule that Crown wages could not be arrested.[2] Statutory rights on unfair dismissal are now confirmed on some Crown employees.[3]

The existence of parliamentary funds

58   There is authority for a rule that the obligation of the Crown to pay money is subject to the implied condition that necessary funds should be made available by Parliament, otherwise the payment is *ultra vires*.[4] The rule is sometimes doubted. Parliament authorises expenditure rather than the incurring of obligations to spend.[5] It would be unsatisfactory if the capacity of the Crown to contract were to depend on the existence of parliamentary approval of estimates and appropriation. Enforceability of a contract is different from its invalidity. It may be that the rule has been misinterpreted. The contract is valid, but if Parliament refuses to appropriate money payment cannot be made. Certain dicta of Viscount Haldane are sometimes said to cast doubt on the rule, but that is far from clear.[6] The rule has not been followed in Australia.[7]

Crown proceedings

59   In Scotland it has always been possible to sue the Crown in contract. The provisions in the Crown Proceedings Act 1947 which enable the Crown to be sued in contract in England do not apply to Scotland.[8] Whether or not compensation or set-off could be pled against the Crown was treated as an unsettled question by Gloag.[9] The matter is now governed by the 1947 Act.[10] Set-off or counterclaim for taxes, duties or penalties cannot be pled by the subject in respect of proceedings by the Crown. The leave of the court is needed if set-off is to be pled by the subject or the Crown when the matter relates to different departments. The leave of the court has been granted when the claims have been of a

---

[2] Wages of Crown servants other than serving members of the armed forces are now arrestable. See Law Reform (Miscellaneous Provisions) (Scotland) Act 1966, s.2: provisions for deductions from the pay of members of the armed forces are in the Armed Forces Act 1971, ss.59, 61.

[3] Employment Protection (Consolidation) Act 1978, s.138.

[4] *Churchward* v. *R.* (1865) L.R. 1 Q.B. 173; *Auckland Harbour Board* v. *R.* [1924] A.C. 318; *Att.-Gen.* v. *Great Southern and Western Ry. of Ireland* [1925] A.C. 754.

[5] See Colin Turpin, *Government Contracts* (1972), pp. 25 *et seq.*

[6] *Commercial Cable Co.* v. *Government of Newfoundland* [1916] 2 A.C. 610 at p. 617; *Mackay* v. *Att.-Gen. for British Columbia* [1922] 1 A.C. 457 at p. 461; *Commonwealth of Australia* v. *Kidman* (1926) 32 A.L.R. 1 at pp. 2–3.

[7] *New South Wales* v. *Bardolph* (1934) 52 C.L.R. 455.

[8] Crown Proceedings Act 1947, ss.1 and 42. Prior to the Act the procedure in England and Wales was by petition of right.

[9] *Contract*, p. 160; but see *Smith* v. *Lord Advocate*, 1980 S.C. 227 at pp. 232 and 233 *per* Lord Avonside.

[10] s.50.

fiscal nature.[11] It has been said that the denial of leave to the Crown would require particularly cogent circumstances such as lack of material prejudice to the Crown or considerable complexity.[12] In the leading authority the indications are that leave will normally be granted.[13]

LOCAL AUTHORITIES

8–60   Contracts by local authorities are subject to three relevant controls: (1) the doctrine of *ultra vires*, which applies to all corporations and is discussed below[14]; (2) the inability to enter a contract to abstain from carrying out their duties or using their powers to fetter the future exercise of a power[15]—this latter principle does not prevent local authorities entering into ordinary business transactions such as contracts of employment which limit their ability to dismiss an employee[16]; and (3) the challenge which may be made of corrupt or incorrect exercise of discretionary power.[17] For example, it has been held that a local authority should exercise its discretion in accordance with ordinary business principles when running a transport undertaking.[18] The exact nature and extent of the fiduciary duty of a local authority and to whom it is owed are matters of doubt.[19] A contract outwith the powers of the authority is void. If the contract is in breach of the fiduciary duty because of improper exercise of discretion it is arguable that the contract is voidable.[20] In an appropriate case a declarator or interdict may be granted.[21]

---

[11] *Atlantic Engineering Company (1920) Ltd.* v. *Lord Advocate*, 1955 S.L.T. 17; *Laing* v. *Lord Advocate*, 1973 S.L.T.(Notes) 81.

[12] *Smith* v. *Lord Advocate*, 1980 S.C. 227 at p. 235 *per* Lord Avonside.

[13] *Smith* v. *Lord Advocate, sup. cit.*

[14] See para. 8–62; examples include *Glasgow Corp.* v. *Flint*, 1966 S.C. 108; *McColl* v. *Strathclyde R.C.*, 1983 S.L.T. 616.

[15] *Paterson* v. *Provost, etc. of St. Andrews* (1881) 8 R.(H.L.) 117; *Ayr Harbour Trustees* v. *Oswald* (1883) 10 R. 472; 10 R.(H.L.) 85; *Birkdale District Electric Supply Co.* v. *Southport Corp.* [1926] A.C. 355; *British Transport Commission* v. *Westmorland C.C.* [1958] A.C. 126.

[16] *Lord Advocate* v. *Ayr District Board of Control*, 1927 S.L.T. 337.

[17] *Innes* v. *Royal Burgh of Kirkcaldy*, 1963 S.L.T. 325; *Roberts* v. *Hopwood* [1925] A.C. 578; *Associated Provincial Picture Houses Ltd.* v. *Wednesbury Corp.* [1948] 1 K.B. 223; *Padfield* v. *Minister of Agriculture* [1968] A.C. 997; *S. of S. for Education* v. *Tameside M.B.C.* [1977] A.C. 1014; *Bromley L.B.C.* v. *Greater London Council* [1983] 1 A.C. 768; *Commission for Local Authority Accounts in Scotland* v. *Stirling D.C.*, 1984 S.L.T. 442; *Re Findlay* [1985] 1 A.C. 318.

[18] *Prescott* v. *Birmingham Corp.* [1955] Ch. 210; *Bromley L.B.C.* v. *Greater London Council, sup. cit.*

[19] C. M. G. Himsworth, "Fiduciary Duties of Local Authorities," 1982 S.L.T.(News) 241 and 249; Colin Crawford, "A Distinctly Scottish Fiduciary Duty," 1984 S.L.T.(News) 333, and "An Imbalance at Audit"?, 1985 S.L.T.(News) 298; G. Jamieson, "Lord Emslie and the Distinctly Scottish Fiduciary Duty," 1985 S.L.T.(News) 297.

[20] See "Breach of fiduciary duty," para. 8–78.

[21] *David Colville & Sons Ltd.* v. *Parish Council of Dalziel*, 1927 S.L.T. 118; *Meek* v. *Lothian R.C.*, 1980 S.L.T.(Notes) 61.

61   A local authority has many statutory powers and also a general power
to do anything which is calculated to facilitate, or which is conducive or
incidental to, the discharge of any of its functions.[22] The making of contracts may, and in some cases must, be governed by standing orders, but
a person entering into a contract with the authority is not concerned
with whether there has been compliance with standing orders.[23] Under
the Local Authorities (Goods and Services) Act 1970[24] a local authority
and any public body may enter into certain agreements for the supply of
goods or services to the public body.[25]

THE ULTRA VIRES RULE

Use of the term "ultra vires"

62   The term "ultra vires" is used in widely differing situations. In the
seventeenth century it was argued that decrees arbitral were *ultra vires
compromissi*.[26] Later uses include the description of incompetent acts
by a tutor,[27] a trustee,[28] a majority of a trade corporation,[29] a company
registered under the Companies Acts,[30] harbour trustees vested with
rights by Private Act of Parliament,[31] a building society,[32] a provident
society,[33] and a trade union.[34] It has also been applied to decisions of
statutory bodies,[35] to statutory instruments and regulations[36] and to

---

[22] Local Government (Scotland) Act 1973, s.69; this is in addition to the common law
rule which allows acts reasonably incidental to a power. See discussions of *ultra vires*
below.

[23] s.81.

[24] Amended by Local Government Planning and Land Act 1980, s.163.

[25] Public bodies are defined in the Local Authorities (Goods and Services) (Public
Bodies) (Scotland) Order 1978 (S.I. 1978 No. 1761).

[26] *A* v. *B* (1616) Mor. 662; *Trumble* v. *Scott* (1634) 1 B.S. 351; *Pitcairn* v. *More* (1680)
Mor. 647. A decree pronounced outside the terms of the submission was "null": *Cun-
inghame* v. *Drummond* (1491) Mor. 635; "(made) no faith"; *Hamilton* v. *Hay* (1608) Mor.
643; "null" *Campbell* v. *Calder* (1612) Mor. 637; *Pitcairn* v. *More, supra*; "null *ipso jure*":
Earl of Linlithgow v. *John Hamilton* (1610) Mor. 636 and, much later, "inept and void":
Napier v. *Wood* (1844) 7 D. 166.

[27] *Vere* v. *Dale* (1804) Mor. 16389.

[28] *Kidd* v. *Paton's Trs.*, 1912 2 S.L.T. 363.

[29] *Gray* v. *Smith* (1836) 14 S. 1062.

[30] *Klenck* v. *East India Co. etc.* (1888) 16 R. 271.

[31] *D. & J. Nicol* v. *Dundee Harbour Trs.*, 1915 S.C.(H.L.) 7.

[32] *Sheill's Trs.* v. *Scottish Property Investment Building Soc.* (1884) 12 R.(H.L.) 14.

[33] *Alexander* v. *Duddy*, 1956 S.C. 24.

[34] *Wilson* v. *Scottish Typographical Ass.*, 1912 S.C. 534.

[35] *Inland Revenue* v. *Barr*, 1956 S.C. 162 (determination of General Commissioners of
Income Tax); *Glasgow and District Restaurateurs' etc. Assoc.* v. *Dollan*, 1941 S.C. 93
(order of licensing court); *School Board of Barvas* v. *Macgregor* (1891) 18 R. 647 (regulations of committee of council on education); *Glasgow D.C.* v. *S. of State for Scotland*,
1980 S.C. 150 (planning decision).

[36] e.g. *Sommerville* v. *Lord Advocate*, 1933 S.L.T. 48; *McCallum* v. *Buchanan-Smith*,
1951 S.C. 73; *Duncan* v. *Crighton* (1892) 19 R. 594.

bye-laws.[37] In many instances the concept is not applied to contracts but that is an accident of events. A body which acts *ultra vires* may do so in various ways, of which the making of a contract is only one.

8–63   The variety of usages raises a difficulty with the meaning of *ultra vires*. If it were to be applied to any act contrary to the powers invested in a body the concept would be so wide as to be meaningless. A contract may be objectionable on one ground, such as being contrary to public policy, and also be objectionable on the ground of *ultra vires*, but the arguments to be applied under each head will be different. *Ultra vires* is more restricted than illegality.

8–64   "It is not a question whether the contract sued upon involves that which is *malum prohibitum* or *malum in se*, or is a contract contrary to public policy, and illegal in itself. I assume the contract in itself to be perfectly legal, to have nothing in it obnoxious to the doctrine involved in the expressions which I have used. The question is not as to the legality of the contract; the question is as to the competency and power of the company to make the contract."[38]

8–65   It is at this point that the doctrine of *ultra vires* applying to contract may depart from the doctrine as it applies in other spheres. A bye-law or decision of a statutory body which departs from the enabling statute is not "perfectly legal." The question there is the legality of the act. This is a problem of semantics which is not easily solved. It is normally sufficient to state that a contract will be treated as *ultra vires* if it would be valid and unobjectionable if made by a person of full legal capacity, but is made by a legal *persona* with limited powers and made outside those powers.

History of ultra vires

8–66   Early Scottish examples of deeds which were *ultra vires* were tacks of church lands for the life of the lessee, or feus of church lands, either of which unless confirmed were "null"[39] or, more fully, "null and of nane avail"[40] or "of nane availl, force nor effect."[41] Assignations and feus by tutors were in the early authorities described as "null,"[42] but the term "*ultra vires*" was in use by 1804.[43]

---

[37] *e.g. Robert Baird Ltd.* v. *Glasgow Corp.*, 1935 S.C.(H.L.) 21.

[38] *Ashbury Ry. Carriage and Iron Co.* v. *Riche* (1875) L.R. 7 H.L. 653 at p. 672 *per* Lord Chancellor Cairns. Professor Gower makes a plea for restricting the use of the expression: L. C. B. Gower, *The Principles Of Modern Company Law* (4th ed., 1979), p. 165.

[39] *Bishop of Aberdeen* v. *Johne Forbes* (1501) Mor. 7933.

[40] *Abbot of Crosraguell* v. *Hamilton* (1504) Mor. 7933.

[41] *Balmerino* v. *Kynneir* (1569) Mor. 7938; on this principle *vide* Bankt., I,557,55. The statutes referred to—1584 c. 8 (12 dco., c. 7) and 1606 c. 71 (12 dco., c. 3)—were repealed by the Statute Law Revision (Scotland) Act 1906.

[42] *Lands* v. *Douglass* (1629) 1 B.S. 173; Mor. 16250; *Geddes* v. *Dousie* (1629) Mor. 16250; Stair, I,vi,18.

[43] *Vere* v. *Dale* (1804) Mor. 16389.

-67   The usual situation in which the doctrine of *ultra vires* is encountered
is the challenge of acts by corporations.[44] Before limited liability companies posed these problems, Scottish courts were considering the limitations on the powers of guilds. The issue arose when some trade
corporations attempted to use their funds to support general plans for
the reform of the government of royal burghs[45] and to oppose a Bill for
maintaining police and extending the royalty of the City of Glasgow.[46]
The Court of Session refused to allow such use of funds, it being
observed on the Bench that "the funds of public bodies must be applied
to the purposes for which they have originally been appropriated."[47] In
fact the decision of the court did not trouble the Trades House of Glasgow nor the Incorporated Trades who continued with their political protests for many years,[48] but it foreshadowed the problem of political
application of trade union funds.[49]

-68   It was also *ultra vires* for the majority of a trade corporation, or even
the unanimous voice of the corporation, to alter its constitution and thus
divert its funds from its original purposes,[50] and this sanctity of the constitution prevented such administrative changes as altering the rules on
the election of the deacon.[51] It may be that alteration was possible with
the authority of the magistrates,[52] but, in any event, in 1846 when the
exclusive privilege of trading in burghs was abolished provision was
made for alteration of bye-laws of incorporations with the sanction of
the Court of Session.[53]

-69   The attitude that funds should be applied for their created purpose
was repeated in connection with the powers of a statutory railway company.[54] There was then a series of classic English cases with parallel

---

[44] Situations other than those already mentioned would include deeds by heirs of entail,
deeds contrary to letters of inhibition or interdiction and deeds contrary to the law of
deathbed: *vide* A. J. G. Mackay, *The Practice of the Court of Session* (1879), Vol. 2,
p. 154.
[45] *Finlay* v. *Newbigging* (1793) Mor. 2008; *Wilson* v. *Scott* (1793) Mor. 2010.
[46] *Macausland* v. *Montgomery* (1793) Mor. 2010.
[47] *Ibid.* On a distinguished circumstance *vide Anderson* v. *Incorp. of Wrights of Glasgow* (1862) 1 M. 152; (1865) 3 M.(H.L.) 1.
[48] H. Lumsden, *History of the Skinners, Furriers and Glovers of Glasgow* (1837),
p. 165; *vide* H. Lumsden and P. H. Aitken, *History of the Hammermen of Glasgow*,
p. 146.
[49] *Amalgamated Soc. of Ry. Servants* v. *Osborne* [1910] A.C. 87; negatived by Trade
Union Act 1913.
[50] *Incorp. of Wrights etc. of Leith* (1856) 18 D. 981 at p. 984 *per* Lord Ivory.
[51] *Gray* v. *Smith* (1836) 14 S. 1062.
[52] *Crooks* v. *Turnbull* (1776) Mor. 2007; *Tailors of Canongate* v. *Milroy* (1777) Hailes
775.
[53] Burgh Trading Act 1846, s.3. Several applications for sanction have been presented,
some involving considerable alteration, *e.g. Guildry of Arbroath* (1856) 18 D. 1207;
Incorp. of Skinners of Glasgow (1857) 20 D. 211; *United Incorp. of Masons and Wrights of
Haddington* (1881) 8 R. 1029; *Incorp. of Tailors in Glasgow* v. *Trades House of Glasgow*
(1901) 4 F. 156; *Incorp. of Cordiners*, 1911 S.C. 1118; *Incorp. of Tailors in Edinburgh* v.
Muir's Tr., 1912 S.C. 603 (a rare instance of refusal of the petition); *Incorp. of Maltmen of
Stirling*, 1912 S.C. 887 (one of the most extensive changes approved).
[54] *Balfour's Trs.* v. *Edinburgh and Northern Ry. Co.* (1848) 10 D. 1240.

attitudes.[55] In *General Property Investment Co.* v. *Matheson's Trs.*[56] the Court of Session decided that when a company made an *ultra vires* purchase of its own shares, the purchase was not only voidable but void.

8–70 "A transaction of this kind is not merely voidable, but is void, as being *ultra vires* of the company. It is a transaction which not only the directors had no right to enter upon, but which even the company themselves at a meeting of all the shareholders could not adopt, because it was directly in the teeth of the Statute of 1862."[57]

8–71 "It is a nullity originally, and the company cannot homologate or adopt a nullity, for that is equally *ultra vires*."[58]

8–72 "The sale was null and void from the first."[59]

8–73 "a clear and absolute nullity."[60]

In this instance the void contract cannot be adopted and it would be strange if a person who acts *ultra vires* could himself cure the invalidity. It may sometimes be possible for others to adopt the contract. Beneficiaries may adopt the void acts of trustees.

8–74 One case involving trustees shows the void nature of an *ultra vires* contract.[61] Trustees, acting *ultra vires*, conveyed property to a company which then granted a bond over the property.

8–75 "If the reconveyance to the Company was *ab initio* void as an act *ultra vires* of them, the trustees acting on behalf of the trust estate may, in the absence of adoption by the beneficiaries, get the deed set aside whatever the consequences may be. On the other hand, if the deed of reconveyance was merely voidable, *i.e.* an act within the powers of the trustees but procured from them by the fraud of [the company secretary], reduction would not be granted in prejudice of the rights of those acquiring for value and without notice of the fraud."[62]

8–76 The decision was that a deed *ultra vires* of trustees was void, and "if the reconveyance to the company was *ab initio* void . . . the Company had no title to the property and could not confer a valid title thereto upon anyone dealing with them."[63]

---

[55] *Eastern Counties Ry. Co.* v. *Hawkes* (1855) 5 H.L.C. 331; *Ashbury Ry. Carriage and Iron Co.* v. *Riche* (1875) L.R. 7 H.L. 653; *Att.-Gen.* v. *Great Eastern Ry. Co.* (1880) 5 App.Cas. 473; *Baroness Wenlock* v. *River Dee Co.* (1885) 10 App.Cas. 354.

[56] (1888) 16 R. 282, distinguished in *General Prop. Inv. Co.* v. *Craig* (1891) 18 R. 389; *vide Balfour's Trs.* v. *Edinburgh and Northern Ry. Co.*, *supra* at p. 1254 *per* Lord Cockburn.

[57] (1888) 16 R. 282 at p. 290 *per* Lord Shand.

[58] *Ibid.* at p. 291 *per* Lord Shand.

[59] *Ibid.* at p. 293 *per* Lord Mure.

[60] *Ibid.* at p. 293 *per* Lord Adam.

[61] *Kidd* v. *Paton's Trs.*, 1912 2 S.L.T. 363.

[62] *Supra* at p. 365 *per* Lord Hunter.

[63] *Ibid.* The principle remains, although the validity of certain transactions by trustees is affected by the Trusts (Scotland) Act 1961, s.2.

77   Another consequence of a contract being *ultra vires* and void is that money paid on the faith of it may be recovered on the principles of recompense,[64] whereas English law is trammelled by the complicated rules on tracing laid down in *Sinclair* v. *Brougham.*[65]

Breach of fiduciary duty—distinguished

78   Situations in which a person in a fiduciary position acts *ultra vires* are different from those in which he acts in breach of fiduciary duty. The development of the doctrine of *auctor in rem suam* can be traced from 1583,[66] but the general rule was not settled until the great cases of *York Building Company* v. *Mackenzie*[67] and *Aberdeen Railway Co.* v. *Blaikie Brothers.*[68] No one who has fiduciary duties to discharge, "shall be allowed to enter into engagements in which he has, or can have, a personal interest conflicting, or which possibly may conflict, with the interests of those whom he is bound to protect."[69] In *York Building Company* the purchaser of an estate who had a conflicting interest had his title reduced, but "without prejudice to the titles and interests of the lessees and others, who may have contracted with the [purchaser] *bona fide*." That this would mean that the transaction was voidable and not void was settled by *Fraser* v. *Hankey & Co.*[70] A trustee on a sequestrated estate purchased, through another, heritable property of the bankrupt. Lord President Boyle entertained no doubt that the purchase was "illegal" but it was not an absolute nullity. The challenge of the transaction was barred by long delay or acquiescence. Lord Mackenzie distinguished the situation in which purchaser and seller were the same, as in this case the estate was sold by the creditors and the bankrupt.

79   "The ground of reduction is . . . founded on breach of duty, on the misconduct of the trustee. It may be weaker than fraud on his part; it cannot be stronger. It is not like insanity, a natural and absolute nullity. It was reducible by the creditors or bankrupt if they chose, on account of failure in duty to them by the trustee. If these parties acquiesced, it was no longer reducible."[71]

80   Similar views were expressed by Lord Fullerton and Lord Jeffrey. The lands had been conveyed to an onerous *bona fide* third party, and this also barred challenge of the trustee's transaction.

---

[64] *Haggarty* v. *S.T.G.W.U.*, 1955 S.C. 109; *Mags. of Stonehaven* v. *Kincardineshire C.C.*, 1939 S.C. 760 at p. 771, *per* Lord Normand (on appeal the averments on *ultra vires* were abandoned—1940 S.C.(H.L.) 56).

[65] [1914] A.C. 398; *vide* criticism in R. Goff and G. Jones, *The Law of Restitution* (2nd ed., 1978), pp. 39–40, 53–55 and 360–361).

[66] *Lord Sanquhar* v. *Crichton* (1583) Mor. 16233; *Mushet* v. *Dog* (1639) Mor. 9456; *Hamilton* v. *Borthwick* (1680) Mor. 9457, and cases cited in Brown's *Synopsis*, Vol. 4, 2630 *et seq.*

[67] (1795) 3 Pat. 378.

[68] (1854) 1 Macq. 461.

[69] *Aberdeen Ry. Co.* v. *Blaikie Bros., supra* at p. 471 *per* Lord Chancellor Cranworth.

[70] (1847) 9 D. 415.

[71] *Ibid.* at p. 428.

8–81   There is now a series of decisions and dicta indicating that a transaction in breach of fiduciary duties is voidable and not void.[72]

Reasonably incidental

8–82   In the case of *Shiell's Trs.* v. *Scottish Property Investment Co. Building Society*,[73] Lord Chancellor Selborne said[74]:

> "Now, I entirely adhere to what was said in this House in the case of *Attorney-General* v. *Great Eastern Railway Company* that when you have got a main purpose expressed, and ample authority given to effectuate that main purpose, things which are incidental to it, and which may reasonably and properly be done, and against which no express prohibition is found, may and ought *prima facie* to follow from the authority for effectuating the main purpose by proper and general means."

8–83   In *Attorney-General* v. *Great Eastern Railway Company*, Lord Chancellor Selborne had said[75]:

> "I assume that your Lordships will not now recede from anything that was determined in *The Ashbury Railway Company* v. *Riche*.[76] It appears to me to be important that the doctrine of *ultra vires*, as it was explained in that case, should be maintained. But I agree with Lord Justice James that this doctrine ought to be reasonably, and not unreasonably, understood and applied, and that whatever may fairly be regarded as incidental to, or consequential upon, those things which the Legislature has authorised, ought not (unless expressly prohibited) to be held, by judicial construction, to be *ultra vires.*"

8–84   In *D. & J. Nicol* v. *Dundee Harbour Trs.*[77] Lord Dunedin regarded "incidental" as meaning incidental to the main purposes of the main business. In *Graham* v. *Glasgow Corporation*[78] the manufacture, instead of the purchase, of stationery requirements was held to be reasonably incidental to a royal burgh's statutory duties. In *Glasgow Corporation* v. *Flint*[79] the provision of telephones in the homes of coun-

---

[72] *Thorburn* v. *Martin* (1853) 15 D. 845 at p. 850 *per* Lord Cockburn; *Mackie's Trs.* v. *Mackie* (1875) 2 R. 312 at p. 316 *per* Lord Neaves; *Mags. of Aberdeen* v. *University of Aberdeen* (1877) 4 R.(H.L.) 48 at p. 51 *per* Lord Chancellor Cairns, *cf.* (1876) 3 R. 1087 at p. 1093 *per* Lord President Inglis; *Buckner* v. *Jopp's Trs.* (1887) 14 R. 1006 at p. 1018 *per* Lord Lee; *Dunn* v. *Chambers* (1897) 25 R. 247 at p. 250 *per* Lord McLaren; *Ashburton* v. *Escombe* (1892) 20 R. 187 at p. 198 *per* Lord Kinnear; *Hall's Trs.* v. *McArthur*, 1918 S.C. 646 at p. 652 *per* Lord Skerrington; *Wilson* v. *Smith's Trs.*, 1939 S.L.T. 120. Cases on beneficiaries ratifying the transaction include *Lord Gray* (1856) 19 D. 1 (rubric misleading); *Scott* v. *Handyside's Trs.* (1868) 6 M. 753 at p. 760 *per* Lord Deas; *Howard & Wyndham* v. *Richmond's Trs.* (1890) 17 R. 990—*cf. Taylor* v. *Hillhouse's Trs.* (1901) 9 S.L.T. 31; *Dougan* v. *Macpherson* (1902) 4 F.(H.L.) 7.

[73] (1884) 12 R.(H.L.) 14 (the case concerned *ultra vires* acts by directors of a building society).

[74] at p. 18.

[75] (1880) 5 App.Cas. 473 at p. 478.

[76] (1875) L.R. 7 H.L. 653.

[77] 1915 S.C.(H.L.) 7.

[78] 1936 S.C. 108.

[79] 1966 S.C. 108 (payment out of the common good fund was proper).

cillors was not reasonably incidental to the council's statutory functions. In a company's memorandum of association the provision of some express objects may be construed as powers to be exercised in a manner incidental to the true objects of the company.[80]

ALIEN ENEMIES

Procedural status of alien enemies

85   An alien enemy has a procedural incapacity which lasts as long as the war lasts. This should not be confused with the further problem of the invalidity of contracts with the enemy.

86   The existence of an enemy depends on a state of war. The common law, for present purposes, recognises war and peace, but does not give special effect to intermediate states of hostility. This was established as long ago as 1664 in *Blomart* v. *Roxburgh*.[81] The state of war is a technical concept which does not refer merely to acts of force. War may exist without force and force without war. For war to exist, probably one at least of the parties must assert the existence of this state, but the emotional statements of politicians are not conclusive. Difficulties similar to those met in defining the start of a war arise on defining its termination.[82] In practice the Scottish courts will probably look to the terms of a royal prerogative or a certificate from the executive, because it is for the Sovereign to decide whether or not war or peace exists.[83] This has the further advantage that the proclamation may define the enemy.[84] Armed conflicts not amounting to war are much more common.[85] They may frustrate a contract or result in the application of a clause in a contract referring to hostilities, or produce legislation affecting the contract. They do not, however, make one of the parties to a contract an enemy alien at common law.

---

[80] *Introductions Ltd.* v. *National Provincial Bank Ltd.* [1970] Ch. 199; *Re Horsley & Weight Ltd.* [1982] Ch. 442 at p. 448 *per* Buckley L.J.; and see the review of authorities in *Rolled Steel Products (Holdings) Ltd.* v. *British Steel Corp.* [1986] Ch. 246. A court should look at the nature of a transaction, not merely its form: *Thompson* v. *J. Barke & Co. (Caterers) Ltd.* 1975 S.L.T. 67; *International Sales and Agencies Ltd.* v. *Marcus* [1982] 3 All E.R. 551.

[81] (1664) Mor. 16091; approved in *Orenstein & Koppel* v. *Egyptian Phosphate Co.*, 1915 S.C. 55; *Sovfracht (v/o)* v. *Van Udens* [1943] A.C. 203. See also *Janson* v. *Driefontein Consolidated Mines* [1902] A.C. 484; *Re Grotrian* [1955] 1 Ch. 501.

[82] See Lord McNair and A. D. Watts, *The Legal Effects of War* (4th ed., 1966), Chap. 1.

[83] *Janson* v. *Driefontein Consolidated Mines, sup. cit.; R.* v. *Bottrill* [1947] K.B. 41. The meaning of "war" in a contract depends on principles of construction, not the view of H.M. Government or the intricacies of international law—*Kawasaki, etc.* v. *Bantham S.S. Co.* [1939] 2 K.B. 544.

[84] *Orenstein & Koppel* v. *Egyptian Phosphate Co., sup. cit.*

[85] *e.g.* Korea in 1952, Suez in 1956 and the Falkland Islands in 1982.

8–87   The test of enemy character for the purposes of procedural status is territorial, not national. The policy is to prevent the possibility of assistance to the commerce of the enemy. A person of whatever nationality, who voluntarily resides in territory owned or occupied by an enemy, is an enemy for procedural purposes. Conversely, an enemy national residing with the permission of the Crown in this country is not an enemy for this purpose.[86] The effect was that loyal Dutch subjects were unable to sue after the occupation of their country by an enemy of this country. Allegiance was not the test, but the relation of the enemy power to the territory where the individuals resided or a company was commercially domiciled or controlled.[87] In the case of a company, the place or country of registration or incorporation is akin to the birthplace of a natural person and something more must be looked to, such as the acts of the company and its officers and those who control the company. Where all the shareholders (except one) and all the directors in an English company were Germans resident in Germany, the company was an alien enemy.[88] Conversely, a Belgian company which had moved its head office to Pittsburg shortly after the German occupation of Belgium was not an alien enemy.[89]

8–88   An alien enemy cannot sue in the courts except under Crown licence.[90] The alien enemy may be sued in the courts.[91] When there is doubt as to whether or not a pursuer is an alien it has been held appropriate for the defender to consign the sum sued for, to take no further part in the proceedings, and for intimation to be made to the Lord Advocate with a view to determining the character of the pursuer.[92] A pursuer may acquire the character of an enemy alien after an action is raised. This has had the consequence that the action has been sisted until after the termination of the war, and arrestments on the dependence recalled.[93] Procedure on a reclaiming note and a counter-action in

---

[86] *Schulze Gow & Co.* v. *Bank of Scotland*, 1914 2 S.L.T. 455; *Schulze*, 1917 S.C. 400; *Crolla*, 1942 S.C. 21; *Weiss* v. *Weiss*, 1940 S.L.T. 447 (divorce).

[87] *Sovfracht (V/O)* v. *Van Udens, etc.* [1943] A.C. 203. Lord Thankerton reviewed and approved Scottish authority, and added that there was no difference in this matter between English and Scots law.

[88] *Daimler Co. Ltd.* v. *Continental Tyre & Rubber Co. (Great Britain) Ltd.* [1916] 2 A.C. 307; see also *Kuenig* v. *Donnersmarck* [1955] 1 Q.B. 515.

[89] *The Pamia* [1943] 1 All E.R. 269.

[90] For the procedure to obtain a licence see McNair and Watts, *op. cit.*, p. 108. A solicitor who acts for an alien enemy may be trading with the enemy, and himself need an appropriate licence before he applies on behalf of his client for a royal licence.

[91] *Sovfract* v. *Van Udens, sup. cit.; Porter* v. *Freudenberg* [1915] 1 K.B. 857; *The Pamia, sup. cit.*

[92] *Guyot-Guenin & Son* v. *Clyde Soap Co.*, 1916 S.C. 6.

[93] *Van Uden* v. *Burrell*, 1916 S.C. 391. On furthcoming see *Fergusson* v. *Brown & Tawse*, 1917 S.C. 570, 1918 S.C.(H.L.) 125; *Brown* v. *Willock Reid & Co.*, 1918 2 S.L.T. 159.

a conjoined case have been sisted.[94] The Limitation (Enemies and War Prisoners) Act 1945 suspends the operation of certain periods of limitation where a party is an enemy or is detained in enemy territory.

CORPORATIONS

89   Corporations may be constituted by Royal Charter (or letters patent),[95] or by special Act of Parliament, or under the provisions of statute. The powers of corporations vary according to their nature and the terms of their constitution. A corporation may act outwith its powers. Its *ultra vires* contracts will be void.[96] A corporation acting within its powers is liable on its contracts.[97]

90   There is a modification of the *ultra vires* rule, introduced originally by the European Communities Act 1972, s.9(1), and now regulated by the Companies Act 1985, s.35. The provision applies to companies as defined in the Companies Act,[98] that is companies formed under the Companies Act 1985, the Joint Stock Companies Acts, the Companies Act 1862, the Companies (Consolidation) Act 1908, or the Companies Act 1929 or the Companies Acts 1948 to 1983 (other than some Irish companies). Section 35 of the 1985 Act may be extended by regulation to certain other corporate bodies,[99] but except in so far as extended, the application of the *ultra vires* rule to many corporations will remain unaffected by section 35.[1]

91   Section 35 provides:

"(1) In favour of a person dealing with a company in good faith, any transaction decided on by the directors is deemed to be one which it is within the capacity of the company to enter into, and the power of the directors to bind the company is deemed to be free of any limitation under the memorandum or articles.

---

[94] *Craigline Steamship Co. Ltd.* v. *North British Storage and Transit Co.*, 1915 S.C. 113. See also *Orenstein & Koppel* v. *Egyptian Phosphate Co. Ltd.*, *sup. cit.* In England it has been said that an enemy alien who is a defendant can appear, can appeal and can plead set-off, but he cannot counterclaim or take third party proceedings: *Porter* v. *Freudenberg, sup. cit.*; other aspects of English procedure are considered in the difficult case of *Rodriguez* v. *Speyer Bros.* [1919] A.C. 59 (on which see *V/O Sovfracht* v. *Van Udens, sup. cit.*).

[95] Or the privilege granted may infer incorporation and prescriptive use of corporate rights may imply previous existence: *University of Glasgow* v. *Faculty of Surgeons* (1837) 15 S. 736, (1840) 1 Rob. 397, and see generally *s.v.* "Corporations" in *Encyclopaedia of the Laws of Scotland*, Vol. 4; Ersk., *Inst.*, I,vii,64 *et seq.*; Bell, *Prin.*, ss.2176 et seq.

[96] See *s.v.* "Ultra Vires," para. 8–62.

[97] Contracts made on behalf of a corporation before it comes into existence cannot be adopted by the corporation: *Tinnevelley Sugar Refining Co.* v. *Mirrlees, Watson & Yaryan Co.* (1894) 21 R. 1009; *Cumming* v. *Quartzag Ltd.*, 1980 S.C. 276; H. L. MacQueen, "Promoters' Contracts, Agency and the Jus Quaesitum Tertio," 1982 S.L.T.(News) 257, 288; Companies Act 1985, s.36(4); *Phonogram Ltd.* v. *Lane* [1982] Q.B. 938.

[98] s.735.

[99] s.718 and Sched. 22, 1985 Act.

[1] It is possible that the *ultra vires* rule will be abolished in relation to companies. This is being considered. But the rule may remain for other corporations.

(2) A party to a transaction so decided on is not bound to enquire as to the capacity of the company to enter into it or as to any such limitation on the powers of the directors, and is presumed to have acted in good faith unless the contrary is proved."

8–92   The reference to "person" includes a body of persons, corporate or unincorporate.[2] The meaning of "good faith" is uncertain. If the person has actual notice that the transaction is *ultra vires* it is difficult to see how he can be in good faith. A bank will commonly ask to see the memorandum and articles before lending to the company for a particular purpose. This increases the chances that the bank will be unable to rely on section 35 if the borrowing is *ultra vires*. On the other hand section 35 helps the person who trades with the company in blissful ignorance of the terms of its memorandum and articles.[3] If it were held that good faith was destroyed by the publication of memorandum and articles in the registers of the Registrar of Companies, the whole object of section 35 would be defeated. The difficult case is the intermediate one where the third party may have turned a blind eye, or could or should have known that the act was outside the objects.[4] The subsection applies to a transaction decided upon by the "directors." It has been suggested that this applies to a transaction by a member of the board with the authority of the board.[5] In the interpretation of section 35 it is permissible to look at the EEC Council Directive 68/151 of March 9, 1968, which gave rise to section 9(1) of the 1972 Act.[6]

UNIVERSITIES

8–93   The four ancient Scottish universities were corporations at common law.[7] By the Universities (Scotland) Act 1889[8] it was provided that a university court was to be a body corporate with perpetual succession and a common seal, which should be judicially noticed and the property of the then existing universities was transferred to their respective

---

[2] Interpretation Act 1978, s.5 and Sched. 1.

[3] Thus the result in *Introductions Ltd.* v. *National Provincial Bank Ltd.* [1970] Ch. 199 would have been unaffected by s.35, whereas some classic cases on *ultra vires* would now be decided differently, *e.g. Ashbury Railway Carriage Co.* v. *Riche* (1873) L.R. 7 H.L. 635; *Re Jon Beauforte (London) Ltd.* [1953] Ch. 131.

[4] See *International Sales and Agencies Ltd.* v. *Marcus* [1982] 3 All E.R. 551 where the test applied was whether the person could not in view of all the circumstances have been unaware that he was party to an *ultra vires* transaction; see also *T.C.B. Ltd.* v. *Gray* [1986] 1 All E.R. 587.

[5] Palmer's *Company Law* (23rd ed., 1982), para. 9–25. The contrary view can be taken that the section requires the directors to decide and no one else.

[6] *International Sales and Agencies Ltd.* v. *Marcus* [1982] 3 All E.R. 551.

[7] Bell, *Prin.*, s.2188: "Whether they are directly corporations under the Crown, or, like the corporations of a burgh subordinate to the magistrates or founder, the law of corporations is generally applicable to them."

[8] s.5(3).

courts. The powers of the courts are defined by statute[9] and include powers to manage and administer their revenue properties.[10] The Universities of Dundee, Strathclyde, Stirling and Heriot Watt are governed by the terms of their respective Royal Charters. For example the charter of the University of Strathclyde gives the objects of the university, which are "to advance learning and knowledge by teaching and research particularly into the basic and applied sciences and to enable students to obtain the advantages of liberal university education." The university is given various powers, and a general power to "do all such other acts and things whether incidental to [its other powers] or not as may be requisite in order to further the objects of the University as a place of education and of learning and of research."

The powers of universities are very wide, but they are not unlimited and certain commercial activities would be *ultra vires*. There could be serious consequences for a person contracting with a university which acts outwith its powers. The contract would be void and the protection of the Companies Act 1985, s.35, is not available.

BUILDING SOCIETIES

04   A building society is incorporated under the Building Societies Act 1874 or the Building Societies Act 1962. All societies are now governed by the 1962 Act with certain modifications for societies which were in existence prior to the Act. The Act provides the purpose for which a society may be established, namely that "of raising, by the subscriptions of the members, a stock or fund for making advances to members out of the funds of the society upon security by way of [an advance upon a heritable security]."[11] The society is a body corporate with perpetual succession and a common seal.[12] The Act gives the society various powers, for example, to raise funds by issuing shares,[13] to hold and deal with land and buildings,[14] and to borrow money up to a specified limit.[15] It is *ultra vires* to borrow money for a purpose other than the purpose of the society.[16] A borrowing in excess of powers imposed personal liability on the directors of the society.[17] The rules of the society are a contract between the members *inter se* and between the society and the mem-

---

[9] *e.g.* The Universities (Scotland) Act 1858, s.12, 1889 Act, s.6; Universities (Scotland) Act 1966, Sched. 2 (most of the powers relate to the internal administration of universities).

[10] 1889 Act, s.6.

[11] s.1(1) and (5).

[12] s.3.

[13] s.6.

[14] s.7.

[15] s.39.

[16] *Sinclair* v. *Brougham* [1914] A.C. 398 (in this famous English case, the society had developed an *ultra vires* banking business); *Sun Permanent* v. *Western Suburban etc. Building Society* [1921] 2 Ch. 438.

[17] s.40.

bers, and the contract can only be altered in the way provided by statute.[18] Examples of judicial consideration of the *ultra vires* acts of building societies will be found in the cases cited.[19]

8–95   The present statutory provisions do not allow building societies to develop a full range of financial services, such as lending on unsecured overdraft. There has been discussion about extension of the powers of societies.[20]

FRIENDLY AND PROVIDENT SOCIETIES

8–96   There are a large number of mutual associations which provide benefits for their members and families. Building societies have already been mentioned.[21] Societies registered under the Industrial and Provident Societies Act 1965 are bodies corporate with limited liability.[22] They are normally co-operative societies.[23] The purposes and powers of the society are provided for by the Act and by the rules of the society.[24] Six classes of unincorporated societies may be registered under the Friendly Societies Act 1974, namely friendly societies, benevolent societies, cattle insurance societies, working men's clubs, old people's home societies, and specially authorised societies.[25] The property of the societies is vested in trustees[26] and the Act and rules of the society state the purposes and powers of the society. An unregistered friendly society has certain privileges.[27]

TRADE UNIONS

8–97   Under section 2 of the Trade Union and Labour Relations Act 1974 a trade union is not to be treated as if it were a body corporate.[28] Nevertheless for the purposes of contract a union is treated almost as if it were a body corporate. It is capable of making contracts and can sue and be

---

[18] ss.5, 17; *Auld* v. *Glasgow Working Men's Provident Investment Building Society* (1887) 14 R.(H.L.) 27.
[19] *Hastie* v. *First Edinburgh and Leith Building Society* (1884) 21 S.L.R. 284; *Shiell's Trs.* v. *Scottish Property Inv. Co. Building Soc.* (1884) 12 R.(H.L.) 14; *Irvine and Fullarton Property Inv. Building Soc.* v. *Wilson* (1904) 12 S.L.T. 371; *Halifax Building Soc.* v. *Registrar of Friendly Societies* [1978] 3 All E.R. 403; *Nationwide Building Society* v. *Registrar of Friendly Societies* [1983] 3 All E.R. 296.
[20] *Building Societies: A New Framework*, Cmnd. 9316 (1984); C. Graham, "The Future of Building Societies," 1984 New L.J. 1067.
[21] para. 8–94.
[22] s.3.
[23] See s.1.
[24] On the form of contract, see s.29. A decision on the *vires* of a committee's powers is *Alexander* v. *Duddy*, 1956 S.C. 24.
[25] s.7.
[26] s.54.
[27] See Halsbury's *Laws of England*, Vol. 19, *s.v.* "Friendly Societies," paras. 135 to 137.
[28] There is an exception for special register bodies which are certain corporate bodies, mainly professional associations registered in a special register immediately before September 16, 1974. See s.30(1).

sued in its own name. Property is vested in trustees but diligence is done as if the union were a body corporate.[29] The purposes of a union in so far as in restraint of trade are given protection from the rules which would make any agreement or trust void or voidable.[30] The rules of a union must provide for the objects of the union and the purposes for which, and the manner in which, any property or funds are to be used.[31] The *ultra vires* doctrine applies to contracts entered into by unions.[32] The *ultra vires* act can arise either in relation to the actions of the union as a whole,[33] or the actions of a committee or branch of the union.[34] As the cases cited show, the remedy sought may be reduction, declarator or interdict. There are restrictions on granting interim interdict against a party who may claim that he acted in contemplation or furtherance of a trade dispute.[35]

EMPLOYERS' ASSOCIATION

98   Employers associations may take a wide variety of forms. They may be bodies corporate. Their contractual capacity will be regulated according to the particular category of body corporate. If they are unincorporated associations they are capable of making contracts, and of suing and being sued in their own name, and all property is vested in trustees.[36] Whether corporate or unincorporate, protection is given to prevent their purposes being unlawful as in restraint of trade.[37] The rules of the association must specify the objects of the association and the purposes for which and the manner in which any property or funds are to be used.[38]

PARTNERSHIP

99   In Scotland, but not England, a partnership is a legal person distinct from the partners of whom it is composed, although an individual partner may be charged on a decree or diligence directed against the

---

[29] s.2(1).

[30] s.2(5). A possible distinction between the purposes of a union and its rules emerged in *Edwards* v. *Society of Graphical Allied Trades* [1971] Ch. 354, but s.2(5) refers to purposes and rules. On restraint of trade and trade unions see paras. 25–30 *et seq.*

[31] s.6.

[32] *Yorkshire Miners' Association* v. *Howden* [1905] A.C. 256; *Amalgamated Society of Railway Servants* v. *Osborne* [1910] A.C. 87; Trade Union Act 1913; *Faramus* v. *Film Artistes' Assoc.* [1964] A.C. 925 at p. 947 *per* Lord Pearce; *Taylor* v. *N.U.M. (Derbyshire Area)* [1985] I.R.L.R. 99; and see cases in next note.

[33] *e.g. Wilson* v. *Scottish Typographical Assoc.*, 1912 S.C. 534; *Martin* v. *Scottish Transport and General Workers Union*, 1952 S.C.(H.L.) 1; *Haggarty* v. *Scottish Transport and General Workers Union*, 1955 S.C. 109; *Partington* v. *NALGO*, 1981 S.C. 299.

[34] *e.g. Maddock* v. *Electrical Electronic and Telecommunication Union*, 1972 S.L.T.(Sh.Ct.) 54; *Milton* v. *Nicolson*, 1965 S.L.T. 319; *Paterson* v. *NALGO*, 1977 S.C. 345.

[35] Trade Union and Labour Relations Act 1974, s.17.

[36] *Ibid.*, s.3(1).

[37] *Ibid.*, s.3(5).

[38] *Ibid.*, s.6.

firm.[39] Whether a partner binds the firm depends on the business of the firm, the authority of the partner and the knowledge of that authority which a third party has. In terms of section 5 of the Partnership Act 1890:

> "Every partner is an agent of the firm and his other partners for the purpose of the business of the partnership; and the acts of every partner who does any act for carrying on in the usual way business of the kind carried on by the firm of which he is a member bind the firm and his partners, unless the partner so acting has in fact no authority to act for the firm in the particular matter, and the person with whom he is dealing either knows that he has no authority, or does not know or believe him to be a partner."

Whether a partner is transacting on his own account or on behalf of the firm is a problem of fact. The implied authority of the partner to bind the firm depends on the nature of the firm's business.[40]

8–100   Express notice to a third party of lack of a partner's authority is an obvious case for saying that the firm is not bound to the third party. More difficult are cases where the third party did not know, but should have known that the partner had no actual authority. There may be circumstances which should have put the third party on his guard.[41]

8–101   A firm may be bound by the actings of an employee. Whether the firm is bound depends on the normal principles of agency.[42] Section 6 of the 1890 Act makes specific provisions for the firm being bound by: "an act or instrument relating to the business of the firm done or executed in the firm-name, or in any other manner showing an intention to bind the firm, by any person thereto authorised, whether a partner or not." Thus a writ having been signed by the cashier on the instructions of a partner, was a writ of the firm.[43] A document cannot be holograph of the firm unless it is signed by a partner.[44]

CLUBS

8–102   There are several types of club. Some clubs are incorporated under the Companies Acts, or the Friendly Societies Acts, or the Industrial and Provident Societies Acts or the Shop Clubs Act 1902. An organisation

---

[39] Partnership Act 1890, s.4(2). For a criticism of the use of the concept of personality see P. C. Hemphill, "The Personality of the Partnerships in Scotland," 1984 J.R. 208. For a comprehensive account of the problems of partnership and contracts, see J. B. Miller, *The Law of Partnership in Scotland* (1973), esp. Chap. VII.

[40] *A. W. Crum & Co.* v. *McLean* (1858) 20 D. 751; *Bryan* v. *Butters & Co.* (1892) 19 R. 490; *Cooke's Circus Buildings Co.* v. *Welding* (1894) 21 R. 339; *Mercantile Credit Co. Ltd.* v. *Garrod* [1962] 3 All E.R. 1103; *Mann* v. *D'Arcy* [1968] 2 All E.R. 172. See also s.7 on the partner using the credit of the firm for private purposes.

[41] *Paterson Bros.* v. *Gladstone* (1891) 18 R. 403; *Walker* v. *Smith* (1906) 8 F. 619. See s.8 on the effect of notice to a third party of a limitation on a partner's authority.

[42] For an English treatment of these principles, see Chitty, *Contracts*, paras. 2201 *et seq.*; Bowstead, *Agency* (14th ed.).

[43] *Bryan* v. *Butters Bros. & Co., sup. cit.* When all the partners execute a document there is a presumption that it was granted for the purposes of the firm—*Rosslund Cycle Co.* v. *McCreadie*, 1907 S.C. 1208.

[44] *Littlejohn* v. *Mackay*, 1974 S.L.T.(Sh.Ct.) 82.

formed for profit such as an investment club may not truly be a club but a partnership, with the important consequence that, unless incorporated, its membership may not exceed 20 persons.[45]

03   The traditional non-statutory clubs are usually one of two types, either (1) members' clubs—where the members contribute to a common fund and have an interest in the property of the club—or (2) proprietary clubs where members obtain the use of facilities in return for their subscriptions, but the proprietor owns the club-house and takes any profit from the running of the club.[46] There can also be associations of individuals formed for one object, such as to go on an expedition,[47] or to raise funds for a specified purpose.[48] This category resembles a members' club except that there may not be rules but only a general object or a scheme, which has the consequence of making it more difficult to say who is binding whom.[49]

04   A club is an unincorporated association. It does not have any legal *persona*. Therefore, despite rules which allow a club to be referred to by name in legal proceedings,[50] the club does not incur legal liability. This used to have the consequence that a club could not be made notour bankrupt or be sequestrated.[51] The Bankruptcy (Scotland) Act 1985 made it competent to sequestrate an unincorporated body.[52] An unincorporated body may become apparently insolvent if a person representing the body is apparently insolvent, or a person holding property of the body in a fiduciary capacity is apparently insolvent, for a debt of the body.[53] Anyone who signs a document on behalf of a club or other association of persons may incur personal liability.[54] The club or association cannot be a principal which is bound by an agent. It is different if the "club" is truly a partnership, because a partnership has a separate legal person and the partners can bind the firm in the course of the firm's business.[55]

05   When a contract is apparently made with a club, the liability under the contract of the members of the club is governed by the law of agency. There are three main possibilities: (1) the person contracting

---

[45] Companies Act 1985, s.716. On the importance of the purpose of gain, see *Anderson* v. *Mags. of Lauder*, 1930 S.L.T. 725. There is doubt about the correctness of one of the early cases on investment trusts—*Smith* v. *Anderson* (1880) 15 Ch.D. 247. See Palmer's *Company Law*, paras. 89–15 and 89–32.

[46] See *Chief Constable, Strathclyde* v. *Pollokshaws Road Snooker Centre*, 1977 S.L.T.(Sh.Ct.) 72; *Green's Encyclopaedia, s.v.* "Clubs."

[47] *e.g. Brown* v. *Scottish Antarctic Expedition* (1902) 10 S.L.T. 433.

[48] *e.g. Mid-Atholl Public Hall Committee* v. *Macdonald* (1927) 45 Sh.Ct.Rep. 274.

[49] See *Brown* v. *Scottish Antarctic Expedition, sup. cit.*

[50] *Somerville* v. *Rowbotham* (1862) 24 D. 1187; *Renton Football Club* v. *McDowall* (1891) 18 R. 670; *Edinburgh Veterinary Medical Society* v. *Dick's Trs.* (1874) 1 R. 1072; *Pagan & Osborne* v. *Haig*, 1910 S.C. 341; Sheriff Court Rules. Ordinary cause rule 14(1); *Borland* v. *Lochwinnoch Golf Club*, 1986 S.LT.(Sh.Ct.) 13.

[51] *Pitreavie Golf Club* v. *Penman*, 1934 S.L.T. 247.

[52] s.6(1).

[53] s.7(3).

[54] *McMeekin* v. *Easton* (1889) 16 R. 363 (congregation not liable on promissory note).

[55] Partnership Act 1890, s.5.

may incur personal liability, *e.g.* if he contracts without the authority of a principal or if he is the proprietor of a proprietary club and contracts on his own behalf[56]; (2) the person acting on behalf of the club may bind the committee or some of them; or (3) the members, or some of them, may be bound. The questions to be asked are, who was acting on behalf of whom? Whose credit was being pledged? Who gave authority, expressly or impliedly, to whom? The initial problem for a person claiming against a club is to make relevant averments that the contract was made with the authority of the persons chosen as defenders.[57] The further problem is proving that authority.

8–106 In *Thomson & Gillespie* v. *Victoria Eighty Club*[58] the rules of the club gave the committee the management of the affairs of the club. The orders for liquor were by the clubmaster. The evidence showed that the clubmaster gave orders as agent of the committee members who were liable for the supplies, with a right of relief against the club funds and the members.[59] On the other hand in *McVey Ltd.* v. *Budhill Social and Recreation Club*[60] it was observed that members of the committee were not liable unless they either ordered the goods themselves or authorised the order on their credit, or were aware of and acquiesced in the order. It is possible, although somewhat unusual, for all the members of the club to be liable.[61]

8–107 Clubs are subject to the *ultra vires* rule. The majority cannot dispose of the assets of the club other than by acts incidental to the normal purpose of the club,[62] unless the rules give this authority to the majority.[63] Unless there is provision in the rules for their alteration, an attempt by the majority to change the rules may be *ultra vires*.[64] The members of a club are bound *inter se* only so far as they have contracted by the rules,[65] and actings outside the rules will not bind the members.[66] A dispute over the affairs of the club might not involve patrimonial interest and as a result the courts will not intervene.[67] For example, the majority of a

---

[56] *Allan & Son* v. *Blythswood Square Club* (1893) 10 Sh.Ct.Rep. 296.

[57] Or the action will be dismissed. See *Thomson* v. *Shanks* (1840) 2 D. 699.

[58] (1905) 13 S.L.T. 399.

[59] The obligations of members may be limited expressly or impliedly to paying subscriptions. See *Wise* v. *Perpetual Trustee Co.* [1903] A.C. 139.

[60] 1932 S.L.T.(Sh.Ct.) 27.

[61] *Anderston New Victualling Soc.* v. *Dewar & Co.* (1828) 6 S. 928—a case of special agreement. The rules could provide for the liability of all the members.

[62] *Murray* v. *Johnstone* (1896) 23 R. 981.

[63] *Hopwood* v. *O'Neill*, 1971 S.L.T.(Notes) 53.

[64] *Gardner* v. *McLintock* (1904) 11 S.L.T. 654; *Blair* v. *Mackinnon*, 1981 S.L.T. 40.

[65] Assuming that there is a contract between the members, which need not be the case in proprietary or similar clubs. See *Caledonian Employees' Benevolent Soc.*, 1928 S.C. 633.

[66] *Taggart* v. *Neilson* (1881) 2 Guthrie's Sh.Ct.Rep. 387.

[67] *e.g. Murdison* v. *Scottish Football Union* (1896) 23 R. 449; *Skerret* v. *Oliver* (1896) 23 R. 468; *Marshall* v. *Cardonald Bowling Club*, 1971 S.L.T.(Sh.Ct.) 56; *Bell* v. *The Trustees*, 1975 S.L.T.(Sh.Ct.) 60 and see para. 4–45.

ramblers' association might decide on the route for a weekend hike, and it is unlikely that the dissenting minority have an interest to sue. But the courts have adjudicated on rights to a prize when a question of property was involved.[68]

LIQUIDATORS

8 The law on winding up is in a state of flux. At the time of writing the principal statutory provisions are contained in the Companies Act 1985. These were to be replaced by the Insolvency Act 1985 but it is now proposed to consolidate insolvency provisions in one statute. The text describes the present law and then notes briefly some of the changes which will occur when the Insolvency Act (or its replacement) is brought into force.

9 There are two types of liquidator in a winding up by a court in Scotland, namely provisional liquidators and official liquidators. Provisional liquidators are normally appointed on presentation of a petition for winding up and before a winding-up order.[69] Official liquidators are appointed at the time of making a winding-up order.[70] The interlocutor appointing a provisional liquidator states his powers which are normally limited to some or all of those specified in section 539(1)(a), (b) and (c) of the Companies Act 1985, namely, powers to bring and defend actions, carry on the business of the company, and to appoint a solicitor. It is doubtful whether he has by implication any other powers such as a power to sell heritage.[71] The official liquidator has the whole powers listed in section 539, some of which require the consent of the court or the committee of inspection for their exercise. In the case of a voluntary winding up the liquidator has similar and somewhat wider powers with differing provisions on consents required.[72]

10 It has been pointed out many times that a liquidator is in a different position from a trustee in sequestration. A trustee is vested in the estate of the bankrupt by statutory provision, but a liquidator is not vested by his appointment in the property of the company.[73] The liquidator "is

---

[68] *Murray* v. *Johnstone* (1896) 23 R. 981 (which contains a useful discussion of the nature of a member's rights in club property in the case of a members' club).

[69] In *Teague, Petr.*, 1985 S.L.T. 469 Lord McDonald observed about the appointment of a provisional liquidator: "This is not to be regarded as a first step in the winding up of this company. It is to be regarded as a holding operation pending the decision whether or not to wind it up." See also the writings cited below.

[70] For Court of Session procedure see W. W. McBryde and N. J. Dowie, *Petition Procedure in the Court of Session* (1980), pp. 19 *et seq.* The liquidator must be willing to act: *Charles, Petr.*, 1964 S.C. 1.

[71] See W. W. McBryde, "The Powers of Provisional Liquidators," 1977 S.L.T.(News) 145; Palmer's *Company Law* (23rd ed.), para. 87–24.

[72] ss.598 and 582, 1985 Act. The powers of official liquidators and liquidators in voluntary windings up are sufficiently wide to make it uncommon for problems of capacity to contract arising. Whether he binds himself or the company is discussed below.

[73] He may be vested on application to the court under s.538, Companies Act 1985.

simply an administrator, and the right of property remains in the company for which he is administering."[74] Liquidators administer for a special purpose. "They are administrators for the purpose of dividing the estate among the creditors of the company, and, if there be any balance, for dividing it among the contributories. But if the estate be insolvent, then the sole purpose for which the liquidators administer is to distribute it amongst the various creditors of the company according to their rights as creditors."[75] The company continues to exist although it is being wound up and it is not dissolved until its affairs have been completely wound up.[76]

8–111   The idea of a liquidator as an administrator[77] raises several problems. Prior to a winding up a company normally acts through its directors, with the principles of agency regulating the relationship. What are the powers of directors after a liquidator has been appointed? In the case of voluntary winding up it is expressly provided that the powers of directors cease except so far as various persons sanction their continuance.[78] In the case of a winding up by the court there is no express statutory provision but, on principle, the directors' powers must cease. The liquidator's powers are inconsistent with the concurrent exercise of those powers by directors.[79] Even if there is no liquidator the property of the company is deemed to be in the custody of the court.[80] Thus the liquidator "supersedes the company in the management of its own affairs."[81] Nevertheless, in exceptional circumstances directors may exercise residual powers after or during a winding up,[82] and it would be helpful to have statutory clarification of the law. The principle should be that during a winding up the liquidator and the directors should not have concurrent powers of management, but winding up does not remove the directors from office although dissolution of the company must.[83]

---

[74] *Gray's Trs.* v. *Benhar Coal Co. (Ltd.)* (1881) 9 R. 225 at p. 231 *per* Lord Shand; similarly *Queensland Mercantile and Agency Co. Ltd.* v. *Australasian Investment Co. Ltd.* (1888) 15 R. 935 at p. 939 *per* Lord President Inglis.

[75] *Clark* v. *West Calder Oil Co.* (1882) 9 R. 1017 at p. 1025 *per* Lord President Inglis.

[76] Companies Act 1985, ss.568, 585, 595.

[77] The term "administrator" is used here in a general sense and does not refer to the administrator to be introduced by the Insolvency Act 1985.

[78] ss.580(2), 591(2), 1985 Act.

[79] See *Smith* v. *Lord Advocate*, 1978 S.C. 259.

[80] s.537(2), 1985 Act.

[81] *Liquidator of Style & Mantle Ltd.* v. *Prices Tailors Ltd.*, 1934 S.C. 548 at p. 553 *per* Lord Blackburn; *Fowler* v. *Broad's Patent Night Light Co.* [1893] 1 Ch. 724; *Gosling* v. *Gaskell* [1897] A.C. 575 at p. 587 *per* Lord Watson.

[82] *London and N.-W. American Mortgage Co. Ltd.* v. *Steuart* (1900) 8 S.L.T. 98; *Re Union Accident Insurance Co. Ltd.* [1972] 1 All E.R. 1105; *Smith, Petr.*, 1969 S.L.T.(Notes) 94.

[83] A further possible problem is—who are the directors? In the absence of general meetings the provisions for retirement of directors in Table A cannot operate nor can s.293(3). The directors may or may not resign office. Even if there are no directors a company may retain residual powers: *Alexander Ward & Co. Ltd.* v. *Samyang Navigation Co. Ltd.*, 1975 S.C.(H.L.) 26.

2   As an administrator on behalf of the company,[84] the liquidator need
not incur personal liability when entering into contracts on behalf of the
company, any more than an agent incurs personal liability on a contract
between his principal and the third party.[85] He may engage on behalf of
the company.[86] A liquidator is not personally liable for the account of
the solicitor employed by him in winding up.[87] Nevertheless he could act
in such a way as to be personally liable on the contract, if, for example,
he pledged his personal credit. A liquidator should avoid the possibility
of personal liability being alleged, by entering contracts and signing letters expressly on behalf of the company. When a liquidator grants a disposition of heritage the deed runs in the name of the company, with the
consent of the liquidator. Strictly it may be that the liquidator should
incur no liability under the deed, but in practice he grants warrandice
from his own facts and deeds.[88]

3   The logic of the position of the liquidator as agent of the company[89] has not been applied when he has been a party in a litigation.
Expenses have been awarded against liquidators on the grounds that,
"all persons who defend actions in a representative capacity, personally warrant the sufficiency of the funds in their hands, and are personally liable for expenses."[90] In that situation the liquidator has a
right of relief against the funds,[91] but even that may be denied to him
if the action is caused by his mistake, such as a failure to *Gazette* a
notice,[92] or of course if the funds are insufficient. If a liquidator
wishes to protect himself against this potential liability he may seek
an indemnity from those creditors who would benefit from successful
litigation.[93]

4   If the liquidator does bind the company, the party with whom he has
transacted is not left in the position of an ordinary creditor and asked to
rank in the liquidation. This would be "monstrous."[94] "All debts or
liabilities incurred by the company or the liquidator in the course of
carrying on its business after the commencement of the winding up must

---

[84] See *Smith* v. *Lord Advocate*, 1978 S.C. 259.
[85] *Stead, Hazel & Co.* v. *Cooper* [1933] 1 K.B. 840; *County Council of Lanarkshire* v.
Brown (1905) 12 S.L.T. 700. In this respect he differs from a trustee in sequestration. See
para. 8–124 and Goudy, p. 346.
[86] See *Smith* v. *Lord Advocate, sup. cit.*
[87] *Anglo-Moravian Hungarian Junction Ry.* v. *Watkin* (1875) 1 Ch.D. 130.
[88] *Liquidator of Style & Mantle Ltd.* v. *Prices Tailors Ltd.*, 1934 S.C. 548.
[89] Not of the shareholders: *Taylor* v. *Wilson's Trs.*, 1975 S.C. 146 at p. 151 *per* Lord
Fraser, at p. 155 *per* Lord Justice-Clerk Wheatley.
[90] *Sinclair* v. *Thurso Pavement Syndicate Ltd.* (1903) 11 S.L.T. 364 *per* Lord Kyllachy;
Aitken (1898) 5 S.L.T. 374.
[91] *Kilmarnock Theatre Co.* v. *Buchanan*, 1911 S.C. 607.
[92] *Liquidator of the Nairn Public Hall Co. Ltd.*, 1946 S.C. 395.
[93] *Kilmarnock Theatre Co.* v. *Buchanan, sup. cit.* at p. 610 *per* Lord Salvesen. The
possibility of an indemnity distinguishes a liquidator from a judicial factor.
[94] *International Marine Hydropathic* (1884) 28 Ch.D. 470 at p. 474 *per* Lord Justice Fry.

be paid in full. Claims for such debts are not lodged as for ranking. They form charges on the liquidation."[95]

The Insolvency Act 1985

8–115   The Insolvency Act (or its replacement) will introduce the concept of administration orders.[96] In specified circumstances[97] the court may make an administration order in relation to a company. During the period during which the order is in force, the affairs, business and property of the company are managed by an administrator who is appointed by the court. The order specifies the purpose or purposes for which it is made.[98] The order has an effect on other insolvency proceedings against the company, on repossession of goods under hire-purchase agreements, conditional sale agreements, chattel-leasing agreements and retention of title agreements, on the enforcement of any security over the company's property, and on court proceedings and diligence against the company. The principal powers of the administrator are listed in sections 33 and 34 and Schedule 3 to the Act.

8–116   The Act will make a change in the position of a liquidator appointed by the court. The official liquidator who is appointed by the court is an interim liquidator who continues in office until a liquidator has been appointed by meetings of creditors and, if appropriate, contributories.[99]

8–117   The Act will make a number of detailed changes on the appointment, powers and activities of a receiver.[1]

RECEIVERS

8–118   The power to appoint a receiver was introduced by the Companies (Floating Charges and Receivers) (Scotland) Act 1972. A receiver may be appointed, in specified circumstances, by the holder of a floating charge or by a court on the application of a holder of a floating charge.[2] The powers of a receiver are now specified in section 471 of the Companies Act 1985. In relation to the property of the company attached by the charge he is given, first, the powers specified in the instrument creating the charge, and secondly a series of statutory powers in so far as these are not inconsistent with any provision in that instrument.[3] The

---

[95] G. W. Wilton, *Company Liquidation* (1922), p. 79. Suing the liquidator still needs the sanction of the court: *D. M. Stevenson & Co.* v. *Radford & Bright Ltd.* (1902) 10 S.L.T. 82; *Smith* v. *Lord Advocate*, 1978 S.C. 259 at p. 273 *per* Lord President Emslie, at pp. 278, 279 *per* Lord Cameron.

[96] 1985 Act, Pt. II, Chap. III.

[97] See s.27.

[98] s.27.

[99] See s.71.

[1] See ss.56–65.

[2] Companies Act 1985, ss.467–470; to be amended by the Insolvency Act 1985, Chap. V (or its replacement).

[3] s.471(1).

prime importance of the instrument creating the charge should be noted, because it is sometimes assumed that the statutory list in section 471 is the measure of the receiver's powers. That is an over-simplification. It is unlikely that the floating charge will restrict the receiver's powers. The charge may extend the powers, even if only for the avoidance of doubt, for example, by giving the receiver power to "hive down" to a company formed by the receiver,[4] to carry on the business of that company, and power to compromise claims or disclaim, abandon, rescind or vary outstanding contracts. The receiver's powers are subject to effectually-executed diligence prior to his appointment[5] and some securities which rank prior to or *pari passu* with the floating charge.[6]

Under section 471(3) a person transacting with a receiver is not concerned to inquire whether any event has happened to authorise the receiver to act.[7] The meaning of this is arguable. A receiver derives his authority to act from (1) the provisions of the 1985 Act, (2) the terms of the instrument creating the floating charge, (3) the validity of the floating charge,[8] (4) the validity of the procedure which justifies his appointment by the floating charge holder (or the court) such as a demand for payment signed by the correct person,[9] and (5) the validity of his instrument of appointment.[10] Which of these is covered by section 471(3)? On one view section 471(3) would not protect a third party if the receiver was not validly appointed as receiver. The subsection assumes that there is a receiver to contract with, which must mean a person who is a receiver in terms of the Act, not merely an individual who calls himself a receiver. What section 471 applies to is limitations on the powers of a receiver, for example, a power to make a payment but only if it is necessary or incidental to the performance of his functions. The party contracting with the receiver is not concerned with what is "necessary or incidental." Further, it is possible that the subsection applies to the existence or absence of a power. But the statute is concerned with "any event," which is an unusual way of describing the existence of powers in a floating charge. In this respect the provisions of the Insolvency Act 1985 which amend section 471 will be an improvement.[11]

---

[4] See Insolvency Act 1985, s.57(*f*).

[5] It is inappropriate to analyse the controversy over the meaning of this here. See *Lord Advocate* v. *Royal Bank of Scotland*, 1977 S.C. 155; *Forth & Clyde Construction Co.* v. *Trinity Timber*, 1984 S.L.T. 94; *Armour and Mycroft, Petrs.*, 1983 S.L.T. 453; *Cumbernauld Development Corp.* v. *Mustone Ltd.*, 1983 S.L.T.(Sh.Ct.) 55; and see para. 17–104.

[6] s.471(2).

[7] To be amended by s.57(*h*), Insolvency Act 1985, which will limit the protection to a person who deals with a receiver in good faith and for value.

[8] *e.g.* were prescribed particulars registered within 21 days under s.410(2), Companies Act 1985? Was the charge *intra vires* of the company?

[9] *Elwick Bay Shipping Co.* v. *Royal Bank of Scotland*, 1982 S.L.T. 62.

[10] See s.468, 469, 1985 Act. Under the Insolvency Act 1985, s.56, the appointment must be accepted by the receiver before the end of the business day next following that on which the instrument of appointment is received by him or on his behalf.

[11] See s.57(*h*), Insolvency Act 1985. On this Act see para. 8–108.

8–120   A receiver is deemed to be the agent of the company in relation to such property as is attached by the floating charge.[12] He supersedes the directors, who can no longer deal with the assets attached by the charge.[13] A receiver is personally liable on any contract entered into by him, except in so far as the contract otherwise provides.[14] Receivers are usually very careful to seek to exclude their own personal liability. Some go further and expressly limit their liability to the extent of any free proceeds available after payment of the persons mentioned in section 476(1) of the 1985 Act. This and other limits on liability (such as time limits for claims) found in contracts by receivers may be subject to the controls of the Unfair Contract Terms Act 1977.[15]

8–121   The practice of certain firms of accountants is to request that the floating charge holder appoint two of their partners as joint receivers. The 1985 Act provides that they shall act jointly unless the instrument of appointment otherwise provides.[16] Some instruments do so provide, and in a large receivership the ability of one receiver to act can be very useful.

8–122   A liquidator may be appointed before or after a receiver. The receiver takes the assets of the company subject to the charge.[17] If there are both a receiver and a liquidator in respect of the same assets, it is the receiver who sells and signs deeds, and he does not need the consent of the liquidator.[18]

8–123   In Scotland a receiver has power to use the company seal.[19] A probative deed by a receiver is sealed and signed by the receiver in the presence of two witnesses.

Trustee in Sequestration and under a Trust Deed

8–124   A permanent trustee in a sequestration may adopt a contract of the bankrupt unless the contract involves *delectus personae*[20] or adoption is otherwise precluded by the express or implied terms of the contract.[21] The trustee may refuse to adopt a contract.[22] If he does adopt a contract

---

[12] s.473(1).

[13] *Imperial Hotel (Aberdeen)* v. *Vaux Breweries*, 1978 S.C. 86. On receivership all the directors may resign, which poses practical problems for the receiver if he has a surplus for ordinary creditors.

[14] s.473(2). See Insolvency Act 1985, s.58, which will make an important alteration in relation to contracts of employment.

[15] ss.16, 17 and 25(3), 1977 Act.

[16] s.472(3); and see acceptance of appointment required by Insolvency Act 1985, s.56.

[17] s.471(1)(a); *Manley, Petr.*, 1985 S.L.T. 42.

[18] See also ss.471(1)(*b*).

[19] s.471(1)(*i*). English modes of execution may not involve the use of the seal but a signature by the receiver with one witness and, if available, the signatures of directors.

[20] See Goudy, *Bankruptcy*, pp. 282 and 346. A trustee can intervene in the bankrupt's affairs and contracts and realise estate without adopting the contracts. See *Anderson* v. *Hamilton & Co.* (1875) 2 R. 355; *Edinburgh Heritable Security* v. *Stevenson's Tr.* (1886) 13 R. 427; *McGavin* v. *Sturrock's Tr.* (1891) 18 R. 576; *Sturrock* v. *Robertson's Tr.*, 1913 S.C. 582 and cases cited by Goudy, *supra*.

[21] Bankruptcy (Scotland) Act 1985, s.42(1).

[22] *Ibid.*

he will be personally liable on it with a right of relief against the estate and any creditors who undertook responsibility. If the trustee enters into a new contract he will be personally bound to fulfil it.[23] Unlike a receiver or a liquidator the trustee cannot avoid his liability by contracting on behalf of someone else. The common law rules should apply to either an interim or to a permanent trustee although the statutory provision on adoption of contracts only refers to a permanent trustee.[24] In the normal cases the interim trustee will not enter into contracts or adopt contracts unless he sells perishable goods[25] or, with the authority of the court, carries on the business of the debtor,[26] or borrows money.[27] A permanent trustee may enter into any contract where he considers that this would be beneficial for the administration of the debtor's estate.[28]

5   A person who has a contract with the debtor can request a decision on adoption by serving a 28-day notice on a permanent trustee.[29] The trustee is deemed to have refused to adopt unless he replies in writing within the 28-day period or such longer period as the court may allow.[30]

6   A trustee under a voluntary trust deed is also personally liable on contracts he adopts or enters into,[31] with a similar right of relief against the estate and creditors who undertook responsibility.

7   The trustee under a trust deed has the powers (usually very extensive) conferred by the deed and also the general powers of a trustee under the Trusts (Scotland) Acts 1921 and 1961.

TRUSTEES AND JUDICIAL FACTORS

8   The contractual powers of trustees are regulated by the provisions of the trust deed and the Trusts (Scotland) Acts 1921 to 1961[32] and in particular sections 4 and 5 of the 1921 Act. A judicial factor will act in terms of an interlocutor which may not specify his powers in detail. For this reason a consideration of sections 4 and 5 of the 1921 Act is sometimes especially necessary to determine the extent of his powers.[33]

---

[23] *Mackessack* v. *Molleson* (1886) 13 R. 445.
[24] Bankruptcy (Scotland) Act 1985, s.42.
[25] s.18(2)(c).
[26] s.18(3).
[27] s.18(3).
[28] See s.39.
[29] s.42(2).
[30] s.42(3).
[31] Goudy, *op. cit.*, p. 481; *Ford & Sons* v. *Stephenson* (1888) 16 R. 24; *Moncreiffe* v. *Ferguson* (1896) 24 R. 47.
[32] See W. A. Wilson and A. G. M. Duncan, *Trusts, Trustees and Executors* (1974), Chap. 21 and on the contractual liability of trustees, pp. 394–398. See also *s.v.* "Tutors and Curators" at para. 8–26.
[33] See N. M. L. Walker, *Judicial Factors* (1974), Chap. XIII and *Leslie's J.F.*, 1925 S.C. 464; *Marquess of Lothian's C.B.*, 1927 S.C. 579; *Linton* v. *Inland Revenue*, 1928 S.C. 209; *Tennent's J.F.* v. *Tennent*, 1954 S.C. 215; *Barclay*, 1962 S.C. 594; *Carmichael's J.F.* v. *Accountant of Court*, 1971 S.C. 295.

8–129   Under the *nobile officium* it is competent to give retrospective validation to the *ultra vires* acts of trustees, but such sanction will only be granted for compelling reasons.[34]

---

[34] *Christie's Tr.*, 1932 S.C. 189; *Dow's Trs.*, 1947 S.C. 524; *Horne's Trs.*, 1952 S.C. 70.

CHAPTER 9

ERROR

PART 1

Forms of Error

A large part of the problem with the law of error is etymological. The words "consensus" and "error" and equivalent or similar terms probably had different meanings for the Roman praetor, at the time of Justinian, Lord Kames when he was writing in the eighteenth century, and the practitioner in the English Chancery courts in the nineteenth century. The Scots law of error in the twentieth century is an amalgam of ideas derived from Roman, English and Scots lawyers. That is the reason why a simple exposition of the present law is difficult. It explains also why the historical development must be analysed.

The practitioner who is impatient for a solution to his problem can assist his task by an attempt to classify the nature of the error. The first stage is to decide into which of three categories the error falls.

Error may arise (1) where a contract is concluded in terms which by mistake do not reflect the agreement of the parties (error in expression or defective expression); (2) where the consent of one or more of the parties is affected by error (consensual error); and (3) where a party's performance of the contract is affected by error (performance error). The problems of defective expression are considered elsewhere.[1] Consensual error forms the bulk of this chapter. Performance error (*e.g.* overpayment of sums due) is considered at the end of this chapter.[2]

Consensual Error

If the problem appears to be consensual error, it is necessary to decide which type of consensual error may be involved.

(1) There may be an error induced by the other party (induced error). This category has a different historical basis in Scots law from other forms of error. Misrepresentation is considered in this chapter.[3] Fraud is treated in a separate chapter.[4]

(2) The parties may misunderstand each other's intentions (mutual

---

[1] paras. 19–44 *et seq.*
[2] paras. 9–89 *et seq.*
[3] para. 9–46.
[4] Chap. 10.

175

error). This covers a variety of situations in which there may not be a contract.

9–05   In mutual error the parties are at cross-purposes. They each make an error about the other's intentions, with the result that there is no contract. The reason that there is no contract is the absence of consensus. For example, in *Came* v. *City of Glasgow Friendly Society*[5] Miss Came thought she entered into a contract in which she was the insured, while the society believed it was a contract under which another benefited. It was held that no contract had been entered into, and Miss Came was entitled to repayment of premiums.

9–06   Problems of mutual error are problems of consensus which are discussed in various parts of the work.

9–07   A case arising from mutual error may include these propositions:

(a) the rule that a contract should be construed according to what parties have said or done and not according to what they intended[6];

(b) the rules on mistaken expressions in documents[7];

(c) the failure of an acceptance to meet an offer,[8] and if nevertheless there has been performance, the rules on calculating the remuneration due[9]; and

(d) the rules used to determine what terms are incorporated into a contract.[10]

9–08   The term "mutual error" has frequently been used in Scots cases where the more accurate and limited expression was "common error," *i.e.* an error common to both parties.[11] The two types of error are different. Both may lead to the same conclusion but for differing reasons.

(3) One party may consent under error (unilateral error), *e.g.* one party mistakes the legal or financial consequences of the contract. In this case there is a seeming contract, but the question is whether the consent of one of the parties is vitiated by his error. This is a problem of consensual error which is linked to the difficulties surrounding category (4);

(4) Both parties may consent under the same error (common error).

9–09   It shall not be assumed that these categories are self-contained or exhaustive. Categories (3) and (4) are particularly troublesome. One of the problems of the law is that the concept of "consent" has many different applications. The difference between subjective and objective consent is at the root of the problem of error. It is the difference between,

---

[5] 1933 S.C. 69.

[6] See para. 19–01; *Muirhead & Turnbull* v. *Dickson* (1905) 7 F. 686; *Steel* v. *Bradley Homes (Scotland) Ltd.*, 1972 S.C. 48.

[7] See para. 19–44.

[8] See paras. 5–79 *et seq.*

[9] See paras. 3–28 *et seq.*

[10] See para. 13–02.

[11] "Mutual" used to mean "pertaining to both parties," but the *Shorter Oxford English Dictionary* states that this is now regarded as incorrect. "Mutual" means "reciprocal." One person's error is met by the other party's error, but their errors may be different, a result which is impossible in a case of common error. Confusion will continue, however, because the use of "mutual" to mean "common" is ingrained in the law and popular speech.

"Did he consent?" and "Did he appear to consent?" The other main difficulty is the need to link the error in some way to the contract. A party may be under error as to the height of Mount Everest, but that does not prevent him from contracting for the purchase of a diving suit. The concept of "essential" error attempts to provide a solution.

It is thought to be the law that a contract is void if it is entered into under unilateral essential error or common essential error. The question, however, is what is meant by "essential." In Scots law "essential error" has had at least two meanings. Only "essential error" in the sense of substantial error will render the contract void in every case. In other cases the effect of "essential error" appears to vary. The case law is confusing and, until the law is clarified, only a historical analysis can illustrate what has happened. That thought in itself has led to practitioners avoiding consideration of unilateral or common error.

It may assist comprehension of the text if the statement of the present law, which is later in this chapter, is read before the historical discursus.[12]

PART 2

The Classical Meaning of Essential Error

In the early law an essential error by one party invalidated a contract, whether or not the error was induced by the other party. The meaning of "essential error" was not settled, but it was probably no more than an attempt to distinguish between substantial and insubstantial errors. No amount of semantic discussion will enable a definite line to be drawn between those two types of error.

The distinction between two kinds of error derives from Roman law. An error in an essential matter excluded consent; an error in a collateral matter did not. To analyse the matter further it is traditional to classify essential error under various heads, such as error as to the contract, the subject-matter, or the person.[13] This probably inspired Bell's classification of essential error. He said[14]:

> "Error in substantials, whether in fact or in law, invalidates consent where reliance is placed on the thing mistaken. Such error in substantials may be—1. In relation to the subject of the contract or obligation; as when one commodity is mistaken for another; 2. In relation to the person who undertakes the engagement, or to whom it is supposed to be undertaken, wherever personal identity is essential; 3. In relation to the price or consideration for the under-

---

[12] See paras. 9–44, 9–45.
[13] A useful analysis is in Sir J. W. Wessels, *The Law of Contract in South Africa* (2nd ed., 1951), Vol. 1, pp. 281–289.
[14] *Prin.* (4th ed.), s.11. There must be reliance on the error. See *Bathgate* v. *Rosie*, 1976 S.L.T.(Sh.Ct.) 16.

taking; 4. In relation to the quality of the thing engaged for, if expressly or tacitly essential to the bargain; or 5. In relation to the nature of the contract itself supposed to be entered into."

9–13   These are examples, not an exhaustive list, of types of substantial or essential error. The question is whether the error was sufficiently serious to exclude consent and the answer will vary with the facts. In a sheriff court case of common error it was observed that a discrepancy in the age of a car was not essential error because, on the averments, the error did not exclude consent.[15] Ignorance of a material fact, namely, the existence of a revocable tender, was not a ground for reducing a settlement of a claim for damages.[16] If someone signs a conveyance believing it to be a testamentary deed, there will be essential error, but not if a deed is signed which contains an unexpected alteration.[17] In transactions involving land, errors have been indicated to be inessential in cases of a minor discrepancy in measurement or value[18]; and when a party misunderstood the nature of his interest in the property.[19] On the other hand, error was essential when what was described as a deer forest did not have stags at the proper season,[20] when buildings were built to a considerable extent on land which was not owned,[21] and when the price of land was less than half what it would have been but for a mistake in the amount of allocated feuduty.[22]

9–14   The meaning of essential error was to change at the end of the nineteenth century. In the early stages of the law both the meaning of essential error and its effect were relatively clear.

The Effect of Essential Error

9–15   Stair's theory of error was simple. If there is error in the substantials, "there is no true consent, and the deed is null." Conversely, if the error is not in the substantials the contract is valid.[23] An example given of error is a contract under which the owner ignorantly takes in custody or pledge that which is his own with a promise to restore it. The error is as to the substance of the contract and the contract is void.[24]

---

[15] *George Hunter & Son* v. *Weir*, 1955 S.L.T.(Sh.Ct.) 101. It is interesting to speculate what would have happened if it had been averred that but for the error the pursuers would not have contracted. In the normal case an error as to the age of a car which has a material effect on value, should be essential error.

[16] *Welsh* v. *Cousin* (1899) 2 F.277.

[17] Bell, *Prin.*, s.11: *Selkirk* v. *Ferguson*, 1908 S.C. 26; *Ellis* v. *Lochgelly Iron and Coal Co. Ltd.*, 1909 S.C. 1278 at p. 1282 *per* Lord President Dunedin.

[18] *Morton* v. *Smith* (1877) 5 R. 83; *Woods* v. *Tulloch* (1893) 20 R. 477.

[19] *Bennie's Tr.* v. *Couper* (1890) 17 R. 782.

[20] *Wemyss* v. *Campbell* (1858) 20 D. 1090.

[21] *Hamilton* v. *Western Bank* (1861) 23 D. 1033.

[22] *Steuart's Trs.* v. *Hart* (1875) 3 R. 192.

[23] Stair, *Inst.*, I,ix,9; IV,xl,24.

[24] Stair, *Inst.*, I,vii,4.

6   Stair's proposition that error *in substantialibus* would annul a transaction was echoed by Erskine, who said that consent was excluded by
error in the essentials.[25] Bankton expressed a similar view.[26] In *Sword*
v. *Sinclair*[27] in 1771 an agent made a unilateral error as to price in a contract for the sale of tea. The error arose due to a mistake in the note of
sale prices supplied to the agent by his principals. An action for delivery
and damages by the purchaser against agent and principals failed.

7   It is probably the case that by the end of the eighteenth century Scots
law recognised that an error *in substantialibus* could result in a contract
being reduced even if the error was on the part of one contracting party
and not induced by the other party. That proposition can be derived
from the institutional writers, *Sword* v. *Sinclair* and *Riddell* v. *Grosset*.[28]
It is consistent with the cases of *Hepburn and Sommerville* v. *Campbell*[29]
and *Magistrates of Rutherglen* v. *Cullen*[30] which involved error on the
part of both parties.

8   The effect given to error did not depend on whether the error was
induced, and indeed, *Sword* v. *Sinclair* may go as far as suggesting that
one could found on error caused by one's own carelessness.[31] This statement has to be qualified because it became clear that unilateral uninduced error as to law was in a special position. There were good reasons
for this. First, a party *sciens et prudens* generally cannot aver ignorance
of the meaning of the deed which he has signed.[32] Secondly, to allow
one party to found on his misinterpretation of the deed would be unfair
to the other party.[33] It is such considerations which probably lead to
dicta such as: "A reduction on the head of error implies in the general
case error in point of fact. Error in point of law is, generally speaking,
insufficient"[34]; and: "The general rule is . . . that an error in law will
not avail to set aside an agreement or contract."[35] Where, however,
both parties were in error as to legal rights a contract might be reduced[36]

---

[25] Ersk., *Inst.*, III,i,16.

[26] Bankt. I,470,63; I,409,6 (Bankton's own method of citation is used).

[27] Mor. 14241. *Cf.* treatment of this case in *Steel* v. *Bradley Homes (Scotland) Ltd.*,
1972 S.C. 48.

[28] (1791) 3 Pat. 203.

[29] (1781) Mor. 14168; *cf. Blair of Balthaycock* v. *Murrays*; Bell, *Comm.*, II, 263.

[30] (1773) 2 Pat. 305.

[31] The converse situation is where one party takes advantage of the other party's error.
A strict theory of error based on consensus might suggest that, fraud apart, taking advantage of error is irrelevant. Either there is essential error or there is not; either there is consensus or there is not. *Steuart's Trs.* v. *Hart* (1875) 3 R. 192 is an example of unilateral
essential error in which the court was much influenced by the fact that one party knew of
and took advantage of the other's error. The case was doubted in *Brooker-Simpson Ltd.* v.
Duncan Logan (Builders) Ltd., 1969 S.L.T. 304. See also *Steel* v. *Bradley Homes (Scotland) Ltd.*, *sup. cit.*

[32] *Maclagan* v. *Dickson* (1832) 11 S. 165.

[33] *Bankier* v. *Robertson* (1865) 3 M. 536, at p. 537 *per* Lord Kinloch.

[34] *Scrabster Harbour Trs.* v. *Sinclair* (1864) 2 M. 884 at p. 887 *per* Lord Kinloch.

[35] *Kippen* v. *Kippen's Tr.* (1874) 1 R. 1171, at p. 1179 *per* Lord Justice-Clerk Moncreiff.

[36] *Dickson* v. *Halbert* (1854) 16 D. 586; *Mercer* v. *Anstruther's Trs.* (1871) 9 M. 618
(seven judges); on appeal (1872) 10 M.(H.L.) 39.

and if error as to law was induced by the other party different considerations apply.

A Change in the Meaning of Essential Error

9–19 In *Stewart* v. *Kennedy*[37] the pursuer brought a case based on *inter alia*
essential error in a contract for the sale of an estate. He believed the
contract to require the ratification of the court, being the sale of an
entailed estate, but this was not the true construction of the contract.

9–20 Lord Watson's speech in the case is one of the most important in the
law of error. It has subsequently been treated as an authoritative statement of the law and has often been quoted. He mentioned, with approval, Professor Bell's definition of error in substantials[38]: "I believe that
these five categories will be found to embrace all the forms of essential
error which, either *per se* or when induced by the other party to the contract, give the person labouring under such error a right to rescind it."[39]

9–21 Lord Watson went on to state:

> "Without venturing to affirm that there can be no exceptions to
> the rule, I think it may be safely said that in the case of onerous
> contracts reduced to writing the erroneous belief of one of the con-
> tracting parties in regard to the nature of the obligations which he
> has undertaken will not be sufficient to give him the right [to res-
> cind], unless such belief has been induced by the representations,
> fraudulent or not, of the other party to the contract."

9–22 This is unexceptionable if it is taken with its qualifications, namely:
(1) there may be exceptions; (2) the dictum applies to onerous contracts; (3) it applies to contracts reduced to writing; and (4) the error is
by one party as to the nature of the obligation. As will be seen, the
second qualification has been given effect to, but the others, of which
the most important is the fourth, generally have been ignored. The
importance of the fourth qualification is seen from the subsequent parts
of Lord Watson's speech. He thought that the pursuer's error was error
in substantials, but such error was not a ground for annulling the contract because this would "destroy the security of written engagements."
The parties to a contract were bound by the interpretation which a court
placed on the contract. Such error induced by the other party was, however, a relevant ground of reduction.

9–23 The result was a practical limitation on theory. On the one hand there
is the principle that those who err in the substantials do not contract. On
the other hand, there is the principle that parties must be bound by what
they say and not what they think. In the First Division, Lord Shand had
taken a subjective view of consensus. This is logical but dangerous. The
plea that, "I wrote X but meant Y," if generally allowed, would lead to

---

[37] (1889) 16 R. 857; (1890) 17 R.(H.L.) 25.
[38] Bell, *Prin.*, s.11.
[39] (1890) 17 R.(H.L.) 25 at p. 29.

havoc in a mercantile community. Lord Watson was not prepared to follow a subjective approach when the nature of an obligation was in issue. Unilateral essential error as to the meaning of a deed is always in a special position. *Stewart* v. *Kennedy* showed the difficulty of founding on this type of error.

24   When Lord Watson returned to consider error in *Menzies* v. *Menzies*,[40] he made this statement[41]:

25   "Error becomes essential whenever it is shown that but for it one of the parties would have declined to contract. He cannot rescind unless his error was induced by the representations of the other contracting party, or of his agent, made in the course of negotiation and with reference to the subject matter of the contract."

26   In the context of the facts in *Menzies* this observation was harmless and unnecessary. The opinions of all the courts in *Menzies* are concerned with the conclusions to be drawn from the facts and little is said about the law. The dictum is, however, capable of being read as destroying the law on unilateral essential error. What happened was that Lord Watson changed the meaning of essential error. He was not talking in Stair's sense of error *in substantialibus*.

27   An example may illustrate the two senses of essential error. Assume that X buys a farm because he thinks that the ground contains oil reserves. X intends to exploit these reserves. X is the only person who believes in the existence of the oil and he keeps his belief secret. There is no oil. According to the theory of Stair and Bell, there is no essential error on X's part. X's error did not exclude consensus. According to Lord Watson's standard, X is in essential error. But for the error, X would not have contracted.

28   It is not surprising that Lord Watson's view of essential error has led to the qualifications that the error is only relevant if induced, or mutual, or the contract is gratuitous. Even with these qualifications, Lord Watson's definition led to an extension of the meaning of essential error. In effect he applied the rule in a case of fraud. The problem of the nature of an error produced by fraud has rarely arisen. To reduce a contract on the grounds of fraud, it is sufficient to prove that the fraud induced the contract. There must be *dolus dans locum contractui*. The question of the materiality of the mistake induced does not arise. One can copy Lord Watson's phraseology and state that fraud becomes relevant whenever it is shown that but for it one of the parties would have declined to contract.[42]

---

[40] (1893) 20 R.(H.L.) 108.

[41] at pp. 142, 143.

[42] *Cf.* Ersk., *Inst.*, III,i,16: "Where it appears that the party would not have entered into the contract had he not been fraudulently led into it . . . he is justly said not to have contracted, but to be deceived."

The Limitations on the Concept of Error after Menzies v. Menzies

9–29   After *Menzies* certain trends emerged. These were (1) that essential error is not relevant unless induced or mutual; and (2) that essential error has a different effect on gratuitous obligations.

(1) Essential error is not relevant unless induced or mutual[43]

9–30   The above proposition was stated frequently.

9–31   In *Bennie's Tr.* v. *Couper*[44] a person guaranteed payment under a bond. He later alleged that he was under essential error when he gave the guarantee because he was in error as to the identity of the property affected by the bond. The Lord Justice-Clerk observed[45]:

> "This error was entirely his own error. It was not an error which anyone had done anything to induce. He is not in these circumstances entitled to an issue of essential error in order to prove that he made this error, and so to set aside his obligation. No authority has been cited to us to justify such a contention, and the recent authority [*Stewart* v. *Kennedy* 16 R. 857, 17 R. (H.L.) 24] is to an opposite effect."

9–32   In *Stewart Bros.* v. *Kiddie*[46] Lord Trayner observed on an allegation of essential error: "Essential error to warrant reduction must be averred, and proved to be error induced by the statements or actings of the party by whom and in whose favour the discharge was taken."[47]

9–33   In *Seaton Brick and Tile Co. Ltd.* v. *Mitchell*[48] a party to a written contract for carpentry work alleged that he had made an error in the price quoted for the work done. This error was not induced by the other party. The Second Division held that the contract was binding. The grounds for the decision seem to be that the error was caused by the party's own blunder. Lord Moncreiff observed: "I understand the law to be that a party who enters into a contract under a mistake must be held to it unless the mistake was induced by the other party or was brought under the other party's notice before acceptance."[49]

9–34   In *Dornan* v. *Allan & Son*[50] a discharge of a workman's claim was not reduced although both parties were under error as to the medical condition of the workman. The error was not essential error. Lord Trayner stated: "But essential error, to form a ground of reduction, must be error induced by misrepresentation or undue concealment on the part of the person in whose favour the deed sought to be reduced was granted."[51]

---

[43] "Mutual" should be "common," but the term "mutual" was frequently used.
[44] (1890) 17 R. 782.
[45] at p. 785.
[46] (1899) 7 S.L.T. 92.
[47] at p. 93.
[48] (1900) 2 F.550.
[49] *Ibid.*, p. 556.
[50] (1900) 3 F. 112.
[51] *Ibid.* at p. 117.

35   He went on to point out that mutual error might be pleaded, but only on the grounds that the parties never agreed *in idem*.

36   In *Ferguson* v. *Wilson*[52] there was a successful reduction of an agreement to enter a partnership. The contract was induced by the innocent misrepresentations of the defender which led to essential error on the part of the pursuer. The Lord Ordinary, Lord Kyllachy, observed:

> "The error which induced this contract was, considering the nature of the contract, essential error, error perhaps sufficient, if mutual, *per se* to rescind the contract, but certainly sufficient to do so both according to our law and the law of England, if induced by misrepresentation—misrepresentation even in the moral sense innocent."[53]

He did not see this as a modification of the position adopted in the earlier case of *Woods* v. *Tulloch*,[54] but it does indicate more doubt as to the law. On appeal his interlocutor was adhered to.

37   In *Selkirk* v. *Ferguson*,[55] Mr Ferguson refused to implement a contract on the ground that there was a material alteration in the contract as signed compared with the draft. Lord President Dunedin opined that the defender was bound to say that his essential error was induced by the representations of the other party to the contract.[56] The case did not involve an error as to the type of contract. The Lord President returned to the problem the following year in *Ellis* v. *Lochgelly Iron and Coal Co. Ltd.*[57] A workman signed a discharge believing it to be a receipt for past compensation. The sheriff-substitute refused to give effect to the discharge. On appeal to the First Division the appellants argued, *inter alia*, that the only grounds on which such a document could be set aside were either mutual error in essentials, or error induced by misrepresentation. Lord Dunedin observed:

> "I do not think it necessary, in this case, to go into the somewhat difficult question of how far there may be, in certain instances, relief from a contract on the ground of essential error not induced by the representations of the other parties. That there may be some cases of that sort is, I think, fairly evident from the opening words of Lord Watson in the House of Lords in the well-known case of *Stewart* v. *Kennedy*. On the other hand, I think the cases are few and far between. But one of them, I think, must be a case where the real error in the person's mind is not as to the true legal effect of the document which he has signed—a case in which, I have no doubt, the error must be induced by the opposite party, and in which it is not enough simply to say that there was error in his own mind—but a case where there is actual error as to the *corpus* of the document

---

[52] (1904) 6 F. 779.
[53] at p. 782.
[54] (1893) 20 R. 477. Discussed *infra*, para. 9–52.
[55] 1908 S.C. 26.
[56] *Ibid*. at p. 29.
[57] 1909 S.C. 1278.

which is being signed at the time. A case is put by Professor Bell where a person is thinking he is signing one thing while he is in fact signing another."[58]

Lord Dunedin then pointed out the difficulty of deciding into which category a case fell. The importance of this dictum is that it recognises that unilateral uninduced error is still, in some cases, a ground for reduction. There is a suggestion that the error in *Ellis* was induced by the company's cashier. On the facts this seems unlikely, but it robs the case of its value as a simple instance of uninduced error.

9–38   In *Stein* v. *Stein*,[59] which was concerned with the nullity of marriage, Lord Skerrington[60] recognised that in relation to the nullifying of a contract essential error must "as a general rule" be mutual or be induced by misrepresentation, but he did not exclude the possibility of a class of cases in which essential error alone will nullify a contract.

9–39   In the most recent consideration of the topic, uninduced unilateral error as to price did not allow reduction of missives although the possibility of some unilateral errors resulting in reduction was not excluded.[61]

(2) Essential error has a different effect on gratuitous obligations

9–40   The above proposition could be stated as Scots law prior to *Stewart* v. *Kennedy*. There were indications that a gratuitous contract could be challenged more easily on the ground of error than on onerous contract.[62] In *Stewart* v. *Kennedy* Lord Watson specifically referred to "onerous contracts."[63] The result has been that it has been possible to preserve the idea of unilateral error in the case of gratuitous obligations. In *McCaig* v. *Glasgow University Court*[64] the Lord Ordinary, Lord Low, stated[65]:

> "The defenders argued upon the authority of the decision of the House of Lords in *Stewart* v. *Kennedy* . . . that essential error alone was not a ground for reducing a deed. I do not think that that is the import of the judgment in the House of Lords. What was sought to be reduced in that case was a contract, and what was laid down was that a contract could not be reduced on the ground of essential error on the part of one of the parties, unless that error was induced by the other party, or someone acting for him. The same rule would probably apply in the case of onerous unilateral obligations, but I think that it does not do so in the case of a purely gratuitous grant."

---

[58] *Ibid.* at p. 1282; *cf. Muirhead's Exrx.* v. *Streeter* 1945 S.L.T.(Sh.Ct.) 13.

[59] 1914 S.C. 903.

[60] at p. 908.

[61] *Steel* v. *Bradley Homes (Scotland) Ltd.*, 1972 S.C. 48.

[62] *Dickson* v. *Halbert* (1854) 16 D. 586; *McLaurin* v. *Stafford* (1875) 3 R. 265, at p. 270 (argument of pursuer); *Kippen* v. *Kippen's Tr.* (1874) 1 R. 1171 at p. 1179 *per* Lord Justice Clerk Moncreiff.

[63] (1890) 17 R.(H.L.) 25 at p. 29.

[64] (1904) 6 F. 918.

[65] at p. 923. The decision of the Lord Ordinary was upheld on appeal to the Second Division.

—41   This mis-states the effect of *Stewart* v. *Kennedy*. It ignores the qualifications laid down by Lord Watson on the application of the rule which he stated, with the exception of the qualification on the onerosity of the obligation. Thus Lord Low arrived at the correct conclusion in the case before him but demonstrated a misapprehension of the meaning of *Stewart* v. *Kennedy*.

—42   This misapprehension may have been repeated by Lord Sorn in *Sinclair* v. *Sinclair*.[66] So far as revealed by the brief report, his Lordship contrasted an onerous deed and a gratuitous deed in this way. On the authority of *Stewart* v. *Kennedy* an onerous deed could only be reduced if essential error were induced by the other party. On the authority of *McCaig's Trs.* v. *University of Glasgow*, if the deed were gratuitous essential error alone was a ground for reduction. This is too simple a contrast. Unfortunately it has been repeated recently in the First Division,[67] and in the House of Lords where Lord Reid observed: "Of course, unilateral error would not be a ground for reduction if the contract was not gratuitous."[68] In that case the nature of the error was difficult to define. It was probably an error as to the nature, not of the document under challenge, but of a prior agreement. It was error as to private right rather than error as to general law. The House of Lords decided that as the document challenged was gratuitous, unilateral essential error was a relevant ground of reduction. In the First Division, Lord President Clyde and Lord Russell had indicated that even a pure error of law might not bar the reduction of a gratuitous obligation.

—43   Thus the relevance of unilateral error has been affirmed in the case of gratuitous obligations, but at the needless expense of denying the existence of a similar remedy in the case of onerous obligations.[69]

Pleading a Case on Error

—44   A practitioner who seeks to plead a case on error has these problems.

(1) He must aver and prove essential error. The difficulty is the meaning of "essential error." In classical law essential error, even if unilateral and uninduced, excluded consent, although error as to law was in a special and debatable position. In *Menzies* v. *Menzies* Lord Watson broadened the meaning of essential error and it thereafter became necessary to limit the effect of error, by saying that essential error was not relevant unless induced or mutual (or common). It is unfortunate that two cases involving error as to the nature of rights—*Stewart* v. *Kennedy* and *Menzies* v. *Menzies*—should have been given an extended

---

[66] 1950 S.L.T.(Notes) 66.

[67] *Hunter* v. *Bradford Property Trust Ltd.*, 1970 S.L.T. 173 at p. 177 *per* Lord President Clyde; at p. 181 *per* Lord Russell.

[68] *Ibid.* at p. 184.

[69] And see *Macandrew* v. *Gilhooley*, 1911 S.C. 448 for the case of a gratuitous discharge granted by an illiterate workman without legal advice.

application. The Scottish Law Commission have queried whether in modern conditions an unqualified consensualist approach to error as a vice of consent is acceptable, but they do not doubt that this was in fact the basis of decision in some of the reported cases.[70]

(2) Apart from the difficulties surrounding the meaning of essential error, the person founding a case on error must show that he was in error. If his agent was not in error he may be bound by the knowledge of his agent.[71] Reliance must have been placed on the error.[72]

(3) It is possible that Scots law still has a doctrine of unilateral essential error, as Lord President Dunedin and others have recognised. It would be only in a clear case that the practitioner would be advised to try to establish a case of unilateral error.[73] Depending on the facts, it may be easier to establish a case of mutual error[74] or common error.[75] The cases show that unilateral error may be established if the contract is gratuitous.[76]

(4) There is some consideration in more recent case law of a case based on common error. Where both parties contract under the same essential error the contract is void.[77] Discharges have been reduced on the grounds of common error even although the error was an error of law.[78]

9–45   In *Hamilton* v. *Western Bank of Scotland*[79] both parties were in essential error as to the extent of ground owned by the seller, and the disposition and other writs were reduced.

The whole of the contract must be reduced[80] with the consequence that the person seeking reduction may have to offer restitution of what was acquired under the contract.[81] There are two exceptions to the rule of invalidity although the exceptions tend to overlap.

(a) There is no common error when parties take the chance that circumstances are or will be different from what they believe, as when sub-

---

[70] S.L.C. Memo. No. 42: *Defective Consent and Consequential Matters* (1978), Vol. 11, para. 3.13.

[71] *Chapelcroft Ltd.* v. *Inverdon Egg Producers Ltd.*, 1973 S.L.T.(Notes) 37.

[72] Bell, *Prin.* (4th ed.), s.11; *Bathgate* v. *Rosie*, 1976 S.L.T.(Sh.Ct.) 16.

[73] Note the difficulties encountered by the pursuer in *Steel's Tr.* v. *Bradley Homes (Scotland) Ltd.*, 1972 S.C. 48.

[74] See para. 9–05.

[75] See *infra.*

[76] See para. 9–40.

[77] See opinions in *Grieve* v. *Wilson* (1828) 6 S. 454; affd. (1833) 6 W. & S. 543.

[78] *Ross* v. *Mackenzie* (1842) 5 D. 151; *Dickson* v. *Halbert* (1854) 16 D. 586; *Mercer* v. *Anstruther's Trs.* (1871) 9 M. 618; affd. on other grounds, (1872) 10 M.(H.L.) 39.

[79] (1861) 23 D. 1033. An error as to one-fourth or one-fifth of the subjects was treated as material. A minor discrepancy in measurement would have been covered by the terms of the articles of roup.

[80] *Pender-Small* v. *Kinloch's Tr.*, 1917 S.C. 307. There could be separate bargains in the one deed and only one bargain the subject of reduction.

[81] *Pender-Small* v. *Kinloch's Tr.*, *sup. cit.*; *Scrabster Harbour Trs.* v. *Sinclair* (1864) 2 M. 884 (opinion of Lord Ordinary): but inability to make *restitutio in integrum* would not be a bar to reduction of a void contract.

jects were sold at a roup with some doubt as to the extent of ground owned by the seller,[82] or when parties sold lands when there was a known doubt about whether there was a burden affecting the lands.[83]

(b) The contract will be valid if parties are deemed to have accepted the commercial risk that their bargain may turn out better or worse than anticipated. If parties mistake the quality or worth of their contract there is consensus and a valid contract. In *Dawson* v. *Muir*[84] vats were sold which contained white lead, the value of which was underestimated by the parties. Opinions were expressed that errors as to the value of the subjects sold did not affect the validity of the sale. In several cases settlements of claims for damages have not been disturbed although the pursuer's injuries were more serious than were thought.[85] An agreement involving an element of transaction or compromise will normally not be reducible on the ground of common error.[86]

PART 3

Induced Error—a History[87]

9–46   In the classical law of essential error there was no distinction between uninduced and induced error. Fraud was in a separate category.[88] Misrepresentation, unless fraudulent, did not have a special effect. Thus in *Oliver* v. *Suttie*[89] the Lord Ordinary thought that there was "no room or authority, or sound principle, for any mid plea between fraud and unintentional error."[90] It was alleged that a tack was induced by misrepresentations of the defender. These were not said to be fraudulent and the plea stated on record was of error *in essentialibus*. The Lord Ordinary rejected the idea that negligent misrepresentation was relevant, but his view is coloured both by the lack of development of the law of *culpa* in 1840, and the defective state of the pleadings before him.

---

[82] *Morton* v. *Smith* (1877) 5 R. 83 (the case also illustrates that an error about an area of ground of small value may be an immaterial error).

[83] *Pender-Small* v. *Kinloch's Tr.*, *sup. cit.* There are special rules applying to the sale of goods which perish or have perished but it is arguable that these are instances of frustration of contract. See Sale of Goods Act 1979, ss.6, 7.

[84] (1851) 13 D. 843. A different question is raised when there is a dispute over the identity of the subjects, *e.g.* a sale of a cabinet which unknown to the parties contains money. The money is not one of the articles sold. See *per* Lord Cuninghame at p. 852.

[85] *North British Ry. Co.* v. *Wood* (1891) 18 R.(H.L.) 27; *Dornan* v. *Allan & Son* (1900) 3 F. 112; *McGuire* v. *Paterson & Co.*, 1913 S.C. 400. These cases of a discharge of a doubtful claim are distinguishable from cases involving a discharge granted on receipt of a sum which both parties believe to be the amount due. See cases in n. 78, *supra*.

[86] Cases in note above and *Kippen* v. *Kippen's Tr.* (1874) 1 R. 1171; *Manclark* v. *Thomson's Tr.*, 1958 S.C. 147.

[87] The present law is considered at para. 9–74.

[88] See Chap. 10.

[89] (1840) 2 D. 514.

[90] at p. 516.

9–47   The issue arose again the following year in *Campbell* v. *Boswell.*[91] The pursuer alleged that he had been induced to enter a lease by the defender's representations. Damages were claimed. The issue proposed for trial called the representations "false." The defender objected that only "false and fraudulent" representations were a ground for damages. The court ordered the insertion of the word "fraudulent" in the issue. There are dicta which suggest that erroneous and innocent misrepresentations are not actionable unless fraudulent, but the case should be considered in the light of the remedy sought, namely damages. The question of reduction did not arise because the lease was at an end.

9–48   The problem did arise in an action of reduction in *Johnston* v. *Smellie's Trs.*[92] There was allegedly fraud and error *in essentialibus* induced by the party founding on the contract. There were separate issues allowed on fraud and error. The terms of the issue on error were "whether, in entering into and concluding the said agreement to purchase the said lands, the pursuer was under an essential error as to the substance of the agreement." The issue did not refer to the fact that the error was induced.[93]

9–49   The difference between uninduced and induced error arose more sharply in *Adamson* v. *Glasgow Water Works Commissioners.*[94] The pursuer proposed an issue on whether he was induced to enter a contract by the misrepresentations of the defender as to the nature of the work to be performed, and also an issue of whether he entered the contract under essential error as to the nature of the work. The court held that there should not be separate issues, because there were not separate grounds of action. After some difficulty the form of issue approved was: "Whether the pursuer, in entering into said contract, was under essential error, induced by the misrepresentations of the defenders as to the work to be performed."

9–50   Shortly thereafter Lord Kinloch rejected the argument that essential error, induced by misrepresentations, was not a legal ground of action, unless the misrepresentations amounted to fraud.[95] "Essential error is a well established ground of reduction. It is properly connected with mis-

---

[91] (1841) 3 D. 639.

[92] (1856) 18 D. 1234. The defenders' representation was of lands extending to 250 acres whereas there were only 220 acres and rental of £308 instead of £293. The jury found for the pursuer on the issue of essential error.

[93] Contrast the issue of fraud.

[94] (1859) 21 D. 1012. An issue of misrepresentation was allowed in *Johnston* v. *Johnston* (1857) 19 D. 706, (1860) 22 D.(H.L.) 3; but it is not clear whether fraud was being pled. Fraud is not mentioned in the issue, but *vide* defenders' objection to issue, 19 D. at p. 710.

[95] *Wilson* v. *Caledonian Railway Co.* (1860) 22 D. 1408. Professor Walker considered *Adamson, supra,* and *Wilson* as the recognition of innocent misrepresentation: "Equity in Scots Law," 1954 J.R. 103, 130. This interpretation is not accepted. On the contrary, they show that innocent misrepresentation was not a separate ground of relief from essential error. Nor do we accept Professor Stein's treatment of this issue in *Fault in the Formation of Contract in Roman Law and Scots Law* (1958), pp. 192 *et seq.*

representation, in the case of an onerous contract, in which both parties are not said to have been deceived, but one to have misled the
other."[96]

9–51   In *Couston* v. *Miller*[97] the issue approved was: "whether the said
document was signed by the pursuer when he was under essential error
as to its substance and effect, caused by misrepresentation on the part of
the defender?" In *Hogg* v. *Campbell*[98] the First Division, not without
difficulty and with Lord Deas dissenting, granted separate issues of
fraud and of essential error induced by the defender. Lord Ardmillan
pointed out to Lord Deas that: "if mutual error will support a reduction
of the deed, on the head of essential error, then the error of one,
induced by the other, even though innocently induced by the other,
must have as much effect as the mutual error."[99] It is not surprising, on
the other hand, that the editors of Bell's *Principles* should state: "an
innocent misrepresentation (not leading to essential error and not being
a warranty) does not invalidate a contract."[1]

9–52   The development was logical. Innocent misrepresentation emerged as
a branch of essential error. The situation in which essential error was
not induced was faced by the court in *Woods* v. *Tulloch*.[2] This case fits
in well with the previous development of the law. It is interesting
because although it has never been overruled, it may not represent the
present law.

9–53   The action was for reduction of a sale of mineral property, on the
grounds that the purchaser had entered into the contract under
essential error induced by the seller's misrepresentations as to the
extent and rental of the subjects. The seller was alleged to have said
that the extent was 132 acres and the rental £157, whereas in fact the
extent was 125 acres and the rental £120 10s. Lord Kyllachy held that
there was no relevant averment of essential error. The error was as to
the qualities of the subject but it was not essential error. It followed
that the averment of misrepresentation was irrelevant. On appeal the
four judges of the First Division unanimously agreed with Lord
Kyllachy.

9–54   One may query the refusal to classify the error as essential and also
the making of such a decision on a plea to the relevancy.[3] Nevertheless
the point of law is clear—to be relevant, innocent misrepresentation
must induce essential error. In the context of the development of Scots
law up to the middle of the nineteenth century this proposition was cor-

---

[96] *Ibid.* at p. 1410.
[97] (1862) 24 D. 607.
[98] (1864) 2 M. 848.
[99] *Ibid.* at p. 862.
[1] s.14, n.(e).
[2] (1893) 20 R. 477.
[3] *Cf. Johnston* v. *Smellie's Trs.* (1856) 18 D. 1234, in which a jury found essential error
proved on similar facts.

rect.[4] Furthermore, consent would be subverted and the contract void. The idea that innocent misrepresentation might render a contract voidable was not part of the law. In his first edition, Professor Gloag states that: "this was probably the view generally held until the decision of the House of Lords in *Stewart* v. *Kennedy*."[5]

The Introduction of Innocent Misrepresentation into the Law

9–55   Various strands of the law of error came together in *Stewart* v. *Kennedy*.[6] The case was special because, despite the multiple grounds of challenge, the substance of Sir Archibald Douglas Stewart's case was unilateral essential error as to the meaning of a deed. That was the one type of error which the existing authorities would not readily support as a ground of reduction. To allow a party to an onerous contract to found on his own error in law is always difficult. The case could have been treated as coming within the exceptional category and as having no wider import. The treatment of the case in the Court of Session was not surprising. The view of the Lord Ordinary and the majority of the First Division was that a contract cannot be reduced because one party has misconstrued its terms. In the First Division it was held that the error was not in the essentials of the contract.

9–56   The interesting point about the decision of the First Division is a speculation about something which did not happen. It was held that there was no specific averment of essential error induced by misrepresentation. What, however, if the averments on misrepresentation had been specific? Having held that there was no essential error, nevertheless, would there have been held to be a relevant case? It is thought not. In pleading misrepresentation the pursuer nevertheless based his case on essential error and founded on *Adamson* v. *Glasgow Water Works Commissioners* to show that misrepresentation and essential error might be combined. It apparently never occurred to the Dean of the Faculty, who appeared for the pursuer, that misrepresentation and essential error could be pled separately.

9–57   The pursuer appealed to the House of Lords. Lord Herschell disagreed with the majority of the First Division. He considered that there was error as to the substance of the contract. There was error as to the price. He then approved of the Lord President's view on the mischief of allowing a person to challenge his contract on the ground that he had misconstrued it. In the end, Lord Herschell therefore disapproved of

---

[4] Except in the case of insurance contracts where under English influence special rules were being developed. *Vide* cases in B.S. 1074–1077; *Newcastle Fire Insurance Co.* v. *Macmorran & Co.* (1815) 3 Dow 255 at pp. 262–263, *per* L. C. Eldon; *Dennistoun* v. *Lillie* (1821) Shaw's App. 1, 22; *Stirling & Robertson* v. *Goddard* (1822) Shaw's App.1, 238.

[5] Gloag (1st ed., 1914), p. 521. In the 2nd edition this passage is rewritten in such a way as more strongly to represent the doctrine of innocent misrepresentation as part of Scots law.

[6] (1889) 16 R. 857; (1890) 17 R.(H.L.) 25.

allowing an issue of essential error. In doing so, he made this observation:

> "The authorities cited, when carefully examined, tell, in my opinion, against the appellant. They show, I think, that in the case of bilateral obligations it was always considered essential that the error which was said to be taken advantage of by one party to reduce the contract should have been induced by the other party to it."[7]

–58 It is respectfully suggested that this was an unfortunate remark. It was not the effect of the authorities cited. In particular the opinion of Lords Cowan and Wood in *Purdon* v. *Rowat's Trs.*[8] supports the view that unilateral essential error as to the effect of a deed is a ground for reduction. In *McLaurin* v. *Stafford*[9] seven judges had held that the pursuer was entitled to an issue of essential error without the addition of the words "induced by the defenders." The case involved a gratuitous deed, but that is not a ground for saying that in the case of an onerous deed the law is the opposite. Nor was the remark consistent with almost all other authorities on unilateral error,[10] a fact which was recognised in the respondents' arguments in the House of Lords.[11]

–59 The House of Lords ordered the interlocutors in the Court of Session to be reversed to the extent of allowing the pursuer his issue of essential error induced by the defender's agent.[12]

–60 Several unfortunate consequences have flowed from *Stewart* v. *Kennedy*.[13] The seeds were sown in Lord Herschell's statement that in bilateral obligations error must be induced for there to be reduction of the contract.[14] This can perhaps be balanced by Lord Watson, who thought that essential error *per se* was a ground for reduction, but not in the instance of the particular error founded on. The danger was that the result of the case suggested that there was in general a distinction between the effect of induced and non-induced error.[15] Professor Gloag's treatment of error was coloured by this assumption. In his first edition of *The Law of Contract* he describes the House of Lords as proceeding "on the general principle that mere essential error by one party,

---

[7] (1890) 17 R.(H.L.) 25 at p. 27. The authorities cited were *McConechy* v. *McIndoe* (1853) 16 D. 315; *Johnston* v. *Graham (Smellie's Trs.)* (1856) 18 D. 1234; *Wemyss* v. *Campbell* (1858) 20 D. 1090; *McLaurin* v. *Stafford* (1875) 3 R. 265; *Purdon* v. *Rowat's Trs.* (1856) 19 D. 206.

[8] (1856) 19 D. 206 at p. 222.

[9] *Supra.*

[10] Such as Stair; *Sword* v. *Sinclair, supra*; *Steuart's Trs.* v. *Hart, supra.*

[11] 15 App.Cas. 108 at p. 115: "In old cases essential error induced by representation has been tried under the issue of essential error, but it would not be now." Rettie does not report the arguments.

[12] The case was therefore sent to jury trial on this issue of facility and circumvention.

[13] See also paras. 9–19 *et seq.*

[14] See, however, *Mercer* v. *Anstruther's Trs.* (1871) 9 M. 618 at p. 649, *per* Lord Ardmillan (on appeal (1872) 10 M.(H.L.) 39).

[15] Which was the basis on which the case was argued before the House of Lords: 15 App.Cas. 108, pp. 112–116.

not averred to have been induced by the misrepresentation of the other, was not a relevant ground for the reduction of a contract,"[16] and says later:

> "The important point in the judgment is that it establishes that error not induced by the other party, and error induced by him, though without fraudulent intention on his part, have different legal effects. In the former case an error as to the legal obligations imposed by the contract, or, in the words of the issues, as to its 'import and effect', leaves the validity of the contract unaffected, in the latter it renders it voidable."[17]

The second statement is not repeated in the second edition, but it explains much in his treatment of error.[18]

9-61   Any possibility of treating the ideas in *Stewart* v. *Kennedy* as limited to a special situation disappeared when Lord Watson returned to a consideration of essential error in *Menzies* v. *Menzies*.[19] The action was for reduction of an agreement to disentail. One of the grounds of reduction was ignorance by the pursuer of his ability to raise money on his *spes successionis*. This ignorance was induced by the defender's law agent. Lord Watson considered those allegations relevant. He stated:

> "Error becomes essential whenever it is shewn that but for it one of the parties would have declined to contract. He cannot rescind unless his error was induced by the representations of the other contracting party, or of his agent, made in the course of negotiation, and with reference to the subject-matter of the contract. If his error is proved to have been so induced, the fact that the misleading representations were made in good faith affords no defence against the remedy of rescission. That principle has been recently affirmed by the House in *Adam* v. *Newbigging* (1888) L.R. 13 App.Cas. 308; *Stewart* v. *Kennedy* (1890) L.R. 15 App.Cas. 108; 17 R.(H.L.) 25—a Scotch case; and in *Evans* v. *Newfoundland Bank*, decided this week."[20]

9-62   For two reasons, this dictum was potential dynamite. First, it was expressed in wide terms which laid it open to the criticisms of a similar expression of Lord Herschell in *Stewart* v. *Kennedy*. As discussed earlier, if it were to be treated as a general principle it would destroy the law on unilateral essential error, and indeed it was inconsistent with Lord Watson's speech in *Stewart*. Secondly, and more germane to the present discussion, it can be read as incorporating into Scots law the

---

[16] Gloag, p. 482 (1st ed.).

[17] Gloag, p. 524 (1st ed.).

[18] *Cf.* the treatment in England of *Stewart* v. *Kennedy* in *Wilding* v. *Sanderson* [1897] 2 Ch. 534 at p. 550 *per* Lindley L.J.

[19] (1893) 20 R.(H.L.) 108.

[20] *Ibid.*, pp. 142, 143. It may not be without significance that Lord Watson spoke of the English remedy of rescission, instead of reduction. *Vide* P. Stein, *Fault in the Formation of Contract in Roman Law and Scots Law* (1958), p. 205. The passage is also redolent of the English reluctance to give effect to unilateral error. *Vide* F. H. Lawson, "Error in Substantia" (1936) 52 L.Q.R. 79 at pp. 84, 102.

English law on innocent misrepresentation. To speak of *Adam* v. *Newbigging* and *Stewart* v. *Kennedy* in the same breath was to cause confusion which is still with us. To understand why Lord Watson spoke as he did, it is necessary to explain English law in 1893.

–63   In English common law, innocent misrepresentation was effective only if it became a term of the contract. If it was not a term the representee had no remedy unless he could establish fraud or a total failure of consideration.[21] The classic illustration of this is *Kennedy* v. *Panama Etc. Mail Co.*[22] There was an innocent misrepresentation in a company prospectus. The purchaser of shares on the faith of the prospectus was unable to rescind the contract. As Blackburn J. put it: "Where there has been an innocent misrepresentation or misapprehension, it does not authorise a rescission, unless it is such as to shew that there is a complete difference in substance between what was supposed to be and what was taken, so as to constitute a failure of consideration."[23]

–64   He quoted the *Digest*, Paulus and Ulpianus, and concluded that:

> "The principle of our law is the same as that of the civil law; and the difficulty in every case is to determine whether the mistake or misapprehension is as to the substance of the whole consideration, going, as it were, to the root of the matter, or only to some point, even though a material point, an error as to which does not affect the substance of the whole consideration."[24]

–65   Although there is the reference to consideration this bears a close resemblance to Scots law. Non-fraudulent misrepresentation must induce substantial error to lead to reduction of a contract. It is not surprising that Lord Kyllachy in *Woods* v. *Tulloch*[25] considered that Lord Blackburn's judgment "appears to state the law exactly as it would be stated in Scotland,"[26] although paradoxically, it had ceased to be English law.[27]

–66   In equity, however, rescission was granted if the representee could prove that he was induced to contract by a material representation.[28] A person seeking redress had to show (1) that the language relied upon imported or contained a representation of some material fact; (2) that it

---

[21] Chitty (22nd ed., 1961), para. 287. The later editions are in the relevant passages rewritten because of the coming into force of the Misrepresentation Act 1967: Keeton and Sheridan, *Equity* (1969), p. 544.

[22] (1867) L.R. 2 Q.B. 580.

[23] *Ibid.* at p. 587.

[24] *Ibid.* at p. 588.

[25] (1893) 20 R. 477.

[26] *Ibid.* at p. 479.

[27] As a result of the Judicature Act 1873. The case was decided at common law prior to that Act and therefore the remedy of innocent misrepresentation was not then available: Chitty, para. 438. *Vide* J. J. Gow, "Some Observations on Error," 1953 J.R. 221, at p. 244. The decision in *Kennedy* has not met with universal approval in England: F. H. Lawson, "Error in Substantia" (1936) 52 L.Q.R. 79 at p. 88; S. J. Stoljar, *Mistake and Misrepresentation* (1968), p. 77; Chitty, *loc. cit.*

[28] Chitty, *loc. cit.*

was untrue; and (3) that he was induced to enter into the contract in reliance upon it.[29] The nature of this equitable jurisdiction was established in *Redgrave* v. *Hurd*[30] and *Adam* v. *Newbigging*.[31] It was imported into Scots law in *Stewart* v. *Kennedy* and *Menzies* v. *Menzies*.

9–67   Until those cases "innocent" misrepresentation in Scots law had been treated as part of the law of essential error. Essential error subverts consent; *a fortiori* if the error is induced by misrepresentation. In English law innocent misrepresentation had developed separately from the English law of mistake. Indeed that was why it developed. The equitable remedy was doing what Lord Blackburn with his reliance on mistake as to substance would not have done. Thus in *Adam* v. *Newbigging* there is no reference to the doctrine of mistake. One thing is certain about *Stewart* v. *Kennedy*: it was a case on essential error. It did not involve the same principles as *Adam* v. *Newbigging*. Lord Watson in *Menzies* said it did. He said so in a dictum which amalgamated a reference to essential error and the law administered by the Court of Chancery.

The Relationship between Misrepresentation and Essential Error

9–68   Authorities until and including *Woods* v. *Tulloch*[32] indicate that misrepresentation evolved as an aspect of essential error. This approach was preserved in *McCaig*[33] when Lord Low disallowed an issue in the form "whether the pursuer was induced to grant the said deed by misrepresentation or concealment of X." He did so on the grounds that not every misrepresentation will entitle a person to reduce a deed. Instead, he allowed an issue in the form adopted in *Stewart* v. *Kennedy*, namely, "whether the pursuer was under essential error induced by X."

9–69   The difficulty was that, as explained earlier, Lord Watson in *Menzies* v. *Menzies* had changed the meaning of essential error. Until then essential error had to be such as to preclude consent. Lord Watson said: "Error becomes essential whenever it is shewn that but for it one of the parties would have declined to contract."[34] This was a different standard. The possibility existed following *Menzies* v. *Menzies* that the English law on innocent misrepresentation could be imported so that the necessity for misrepresentation to induce essential error in the old sense would cease to be the law. It would be sufficient if the misrepresentation induced essential error in Lord Watson's sense, *i.e.* it induced the contract. In this respect there would be no difference between fraudulent and non-fraudulent misrepresentation.

---

[29] *Brown* v. *Raphael* [1958] Ch. 636 at p. 641 *per* Lord Evershed M.R.
[30] (1881) 20 Ch.D. 1.
[31] *Supra.*
[32] (1893) 20 R. 477; see a similar approach by the Lord Ordinary (Ardwall) in *Hamilton* v. *Duke of Montrose* (1906) 8 F. 1026.
[33] (1904) 6 F. 918.
[34] *Menzies* v. *Menzies* (1893) 20 R.(H.L.) 108 at p. 142.

70 Professor Gloag eased the passage of this development when he argued in his first edition of *Contract*, that "an innocent misrepresentation will render a contract voidable if it produces error which is essential in the sense that without it the other party would have refused to contract, though the error may not be so extreme as to exclude any real *consensus*."[34a] Before the publication of his second edition support for this idea had come from Lord President Clyde. His Lordship, founding on Lord Watson in *Menzies* v. *Menzies*, saw no relationship between the error which must be induced by misrepresentation and the essentials of the contract defined by Bell. He compared the nature of the error required in a case of innocent misrepresentation to that required in the case of fraudulent misrepresentation, but there was argument on the materiality of the misrepresentation.[35]

71 Subsequently Lord Carmont observed:

> "It appears clear that Scots law recognises, as indicated by Bell, that when misrepresentation by a party is alleged inducing error in the other in regard to some matter, that matter need not be an essential of the contract, but it must be material and of such a nature that not only the contracting party but any reasonable man might be moved to enter into the contract; or, put the other way, if the misrepresentation had not been made, would have refrained from entering into the contract."[36]

72 The two cases which he quotes in support of this proposition are, if anything, support for the contrary view. In both of them there are *dicta* indicating that they were decided on the basis of essential error induced by misrepresentation.[37] One can, of course, insert "material" for "essential" as one can insert "substantial" for "essential," and if that were all that was involved the dispute would be an arid controversy on semantics. It is clear that Lord Carmont meant more than this. He

---

[34a] Gloag, p. 522 (1st ed.).

[35] *Westville Shipping Co.* v. *Abram Steamship Co.*, 1922 S.C. 571 at p. 579; on appeal, 1923 S.C.(H.L.) 68; a case in which essential error was relevantly averred is *Straker* v. *Campbell*, 1926 S.L.T. 262. Lord Constable referred in that case to Lord McKenzie's definition of essential error in *Westville Shipping Co.* This shows the nature of the confusion which was arising. The sentence quoted from Lord McKenzie's opinion suggests that he was following the traditional view of essential error. In other parts of this opinion, however, there are traces of Lord Watson's view. See also *Fletcher* v. *Lord Advocate*, 1923 S.C. 27.

[36] *Ritchie* v. *Glass*, 1936 S.L.T. 591 at p. 593; Lord Carmont's expression is open to criticism. To say that a representation must be material is ambiguous. If it means that the misrepresentation must induce the contract, the statement is accurate but redundant. If it means that only a material misrepresentation inducing a contract is relevant, the statement is inconsistent with the latter part of the passage quoted from Lord Carmont.

[37] *Blakiston* v. *London and Scottish Banking Discount Corp. Ltd.* (1894) 21 R. 417 at p. 421 *per* Lord Kinnear, at p. 426 *per* Lord McLaren; *Ferguson* v. *Wilson* (1904) 6 F. 779, opinion of Lord Kyllachy (Lord Ordinary) at p. 782, *per* Lord Justice-Clerk Macdonald. At p. 784 Lord Moncrieff refers to misrepresentations on matters material to the contract but this is not necessarily significant. In *Blakiston* Lord McLaren referred to "material error" and "essential error" as though they were interchangeable terms.

thought that misrepresentation created a wider ground for reduction than essential error. He doubted the soundness of *Woods* v. *Tulloch*, which is an unusual criticism by a Lord Ordinary of a unanimous decision of the First Division. Lord Carmont's views were followed in a later case by Lord Guthrie.[38]

9–73   A good example of the potential confusion that could be caused by this new meaning of essential error is *Boyd & Forrest* v. *Glasgow and South Western Railway Co.*[39] In its later stages this litigation was fought on the basis of essential error induced by innocent misrepresentation. The impossibility of *restitutio in integrum* was decided to be a bar to reduction of the contract. Thus it was assumed that the contract was voidable and not void. In the classical view essential error would have excluded consent and made the contract void. It would be better if, in the context of innocent misrepresentation, the phrase "essential error" was dropped. It should be recognised that what has happened is that Scots law has adopted the concept of innocent misrepresentation which is unrelated to the original law of error.[40] That law in effect denied importance to whether or not error was induced. Uninduced essential error and induced essential error both made the contract void. Innocent misrepresentation came into Scots law on the back of an extended doctrine of essential error.

The Present Law on Innocent Misrepresentation

9–74   To establish a case based on innocent misrepresentation it must be shown that:

(1) There was a misrepresentation

An expression of opinion or an advertising "puff" is not a misrepresentation,[41] nor is a promise to deliver.[42] A misrepresentation must be distinguished from a term of the contract.[43] A misrepresentation may be

---

[38] *McCulloch* v. *McCulloch*, 1950 S.L.T.(Notes) 29. Fifteen years later when Lord Guthrie came to write Lord Carmont's obituary he recalled, out of what must have been many incidents in a long career, that: "One of [Lord Carmont's] Outer House judgments contains a masterly discussion of essential error in contract, and is, in my opinion, an invaluable contribution to the law"—1965 S.L.T.(News) 153. Lord Carmont served only three years in the Outer House—from 1934 to 1937—thus *Ritchie* v. *Glass* is almost certainly the case alluded to.

[39] 1911 S.C. 33; 1912 S.C.(H.L.) 93; 1914 S.C. 472; 1915 S.C.(H.L.) 20. It is not clear what sense of essential error was being used by Lord Shaw when he said: "As a ground of rescinding the contract, error and misrepresentation must be *in essentialibus*" (*ibid.*, p. 35).

[40] *Cf.* J. J. Gow, "Some Observations on Error," 1953 J.R. 221, who concludes that innocent misrepresentation is not part of Scots law.

[41] *Sutherland* v. *Bremner's Trs.* (1903) 10 S.L.T. 565; *Hamilton* v. *Duke of Montrose* (1906) 8 F. 1026; *Flynn* v. *Scott*, 1949 S.C. 442. See also Chap. 3, "Pre Contract Negotiations," para. 3–25.

[42] *Bell Bros. (H.P.) Ltd.* v. *Reynolds*, 1945 S.C. 213.

[43] See paras. 3–01 *et seq.*

proved, although it apparently contradicts the terms of a written contract.[44]

It is a question of fact and degree as to whether a statement is false. A car manufactured in 1964, but first registered in 1965 was accurately described as a "1965" model.[45] A journal of bores honestly compiled was not a misrepresentation.[46]

A false statement that jewellery was antique was a misrepresentation and the opinion was expressed that the appearance of the articles could itself be a misrepresentation.[47] When chairs were sold as antiques but were in fact modern imitations there were circumstances showing a misrepresentation as to the substance of the articles sold.[48] Statements about the profitability of a business made prior to a partnership agreement were misrepresentations.[49] If facts alter after a representation there may be a duty to disclose the new facts.[50]

(2) The misrepresentation induced the contract

A contract cannot be challenged because of any misrepresentation. The effect of the misrepresentation will be viewed objectively by the standard of the reasonable man.[51] The nature of the causal link between the misrepresentation and the contract is controversial. It is thought indisputable that there must be some link. Take the example of a business which is advertised as having a large turnover. The purchaser of the business finds that the business makes, and has for some time made, substantial losses He can show that the advertised figure for turnover was false. But the reasonable man, at least with an accountant at his side, would explain that a high figure for turnover does not mean that a business is profitable. A person who sells goods for less than he paid for them could have a very high turnover, for a while. A false statement on turnover is a misrepresentation, but that should not have induced the belief that the business was worth purchasing. More must be established to link the misrepresentation to the contract, and the problem is, how much more.[52]

---

[44] *Bell Bros. (H.P.) Ltd.* v. *Aitken*, 1939 S.C. 577. For contractual terms on misrepresentation see para. 3–11 *et seq.*; For the form of issue in a case going to a jury see *Fletcher* v. *Lord Advocate*, 1923 S.C. 27.

[45] *Hamilton* v. *Midcross Car Sales*, 1970 S.L.T.(Sh.Ct.) 26.

[46] *Boyd & Forrest* v. *Glasgow and S.W. Ry. Co.*, 1915 S.C.(H.L.) 20.

[47] *Patterson* v. *Landsberg & Son* (1905) 7 F. 675.

[48] *Edgar* v. *Hector*, 1912 S.C. 348.

[49] *Ferguson* v. *Wilson* (1904) 6 F. 779; also on the sale of a business, *Campbell* v. *Green*, 1931 S.L.T.(Sh.Ct.) 20.

[50] *Shankland & Co.* v. *Robinson & Co.*, 1920 S.C.(H.L.) 103 at p. 111 *per* Lord Dunedin.

[51] *Ritchie* v. *Glass*, 1936 S.L.T. 591; *McCulloch* v. *McCulloch*, 1950 S.L.T.(Notes) 29; and see *Hamilton* v. *Midcross Car Sales*, *sup. cit.*, finding-in-fact (10).

[52] In normal practice with the illustration given the seller would have been asked to produce profit-and-loss accounts, and statements on prior profitability would become part of the contract for purchase. However, it has been known for these precautions to be omitted and for the layman to assume that the higher the turnover, the higher the profit.

The classical answer to the problem in Scotland is to say that misrepresentation must induce essential error. As explained earlier controversy surrounds the meaning of "essential error." In this context it would appear to mean something different from the error *in substantialibus* discussed by the Institutional writers. It probably means an error which induced the contract, viewing the matter objectively. If this is so the reference to essential error is redundant, for it would be sufficient to say that the misrepresentation must induce the contract.[53]

In *Fletcher* v. *Lord Advocate*[54] the pursuer failed in an issue of essential error as to the nature of the document signed, but succeeded in establishing a relevant case of essential error induced by misrepresentation. The difference between the document signed and the nature of the document which the pursuer erroneously believed that he was signing was an essential error for the purposes of a case of misrepresentation. In *Hart* v. *Fraser*[55] the difference between a hotel business with an untainted record and one with a history of complaints about Sunday drinking was sufficient error for a case on innocent misrepresentation.

(3) The misrepresentation must have been made by the defender or someone for whom he is responsible

Statements made without the authority of a bank or the presence of a bank's representative were not made by or on behalf of the bank.[56] A provision in the contract that the defender will not be responsible for statements of agents will not prevent a proof of alleged misrepresentation by an agent.[57] It has been held impossible to rescind a contract of copartnery if there are some partners against whom no misrepresentation is alleged and who wish the contract to stand.[58]

(4) Restitutio in integrum must be possible if reduction is sought

Unless there is error *in substantialibus* which excludes consent, the contract induced by innocent misrepresentation is voidable, not void. The contract is valid until reduced. The common law remedy for misrepresentation is reduction of the contract or any divisible part of the contract.[59] Damages are not available for innocent misrepresentation at common law.[60] Damages are available at common law for fraudulent

---

[53] See Law Reform (Miscellaneous Provisions) (Scotland) Act 1985, s.10, which refers to a party being induced to enter the contract by negligent misrepresentation.

[54] 1923 S.C. 27.

[55] 1907 S.C. 50.

[56] *North of Scotland Bank Ltd.* v. *Mackenzie*, 1925 S.L.T. 236; *Young* v. *Clydesdale Bank* (1889) 17 R. 231. See also the problem of agency discussed in *Bell Bros. (H.P.) Ltd.* v. *Reynolds*, 1945 S.C. 213.

[57] *Laing* v. *Provincial Homes Investment Co. Ltd.*, 1909 S.C. 812.

[58] *Rose* v. *McDonald* (1900) 7 S.L.T. 288.

[59] *S. Straker & Sons* v. *Campbell*, 1926 S.L.T. 262.

[60] *Manners* v. *Whitehead* (1898) 1 F. 171.

misrepresentation and, under section 10 of the Law Reform (Miscellaneous Provisions) (Scotland) Act 1985, for negligent misrepresentation.

Restitutio in integrum must be possible or reduction is barred.[61] It is probable that *restitutio* in a literal sense is not necessary.[62]

The requirement of *restitutio in integrum* has two practical consequences for parties and their legal advisers.[63] The first is that it is prudent to make prompt challenge of the transaction and do nothing which would bar *restitutio*. In some circumstances this is easier said than done. The person who has purchased a business on the basis of false accounts may discover the errors after he has traded for some time, the stock and other assets purchased by him are no longer in his hands and the nature of the trade has changed. The second point is that any material representation should whenever possible become a term of the contract. Damages and other remedies are then available for breach of contract.[64]

Negligent Misrepresentation

15 Ever since *Hedley Byrne & Co.* v. *Heller & Partners Ltd.*[65] it has been arguable that a negligent misrepresentation which induces a contract gives remedies of reduction and damages, provided that the person making the statement owed a duty of care to the person to whom the statement was made. *Hedley Byrne* overruled *Candler* v. *Crane, Christmas & Co.*[66] In *Candler* inaccurate accounts which induced an investor had been negligently prepared, but the investor could not obtain damages from the accountants. After *Hedley Byrne & Co.* it was thought that an investor in a similar position could obtain damages pro-

---

[61] *Boyd & Forrest* v. *Glasgow and S.W. Ry. Co.*, 1915 S.C.(H.L.) 20.

[62] *Spence* v. *Crawford*, 1939 S.C.(H.L.) 52—a case of fraud. The opinions indicate that a different standard may apply to restitution following non-fraudulent misrepresentation.

[63] See *Spence* v. *Crawford, sup. cit.*, for a discussion of which party must make *restitutio in integrum*.

[64] Paradoxically the same facts which may bar restitution and thus a case based on misrepresentation can assist a client to keep what was acquired *and* claim for damages in the case of a sale governed by the common law. When matters are no longer entire there may be an exception to the rule against an *actio quanti minoris*. Rejection of the property being impossible, damages must be allowed or the buyer may have no remedy. This was applied at common law to hidden defects in machinery (*e.g. Pearce Bros.* v. *Irons* (1869) 8 M. 571; *Dick & Stevenson* v. *Woodside Steel and Iron Co.* (1888) 16 R. 242) and to a sale of heritage (*Louttit's Trs.* v. *Highland Ry. Co.* (1892) 19 R. 791 at p. 800 *per* Lord McLaren). See, though, comments in *Bryson* v. *Bryson*, 1916 1 S.L.T. 361. The normal rule (at common law) is that a party cannot keep what is acquired under the contract *and* claim damages (see *McCormick & Co.* v. *Rittmeyer & Co.* (1869) 7 M. 854; *Louttit's Trs.* v. *Highland Ry. Co., sup. cit.*). In sale of goods the position is now regulated by Sale of Goods Act 1979, s.11(5), the application of which raises problems. See *Millars of Falkirk Ltd.* v. *Turpie*, 1976 S.L.T.(Notes) 66; M. G. Clarke, "The Buyer's Right of Rejection," 1978 S.L.T.(News) 1 and an anonymous response at 1978 S.L.T.(News) 61; and see paras. 14–103 *et seq.*

[65] [1964] A.C. 465, and see *Mutual Life and Citizens' Ass. Co.* v. *Evatt* [1971] A.C. 793.

[66] [1951] 2 K.B. 164.

vided that he was owed a duty of care by the accountants. His claim would be delictual.

9–76 In *Esso Petroleum Co.* v. *Mardon*,[67] Esso induced Mardon to take the tenancy of a petrol filling station by negligent misrepresentations on the estimated annual throughput of petrol. The misrepresentations were held to give a remedy in damages. A negligent misstatement which induced a contract produced a liability in damages.

9–77 While the principle of *Hedley Byrne* probably applies in Scotland to a delictual claim,[68] it was far from clear that it could be applied in a contractual claim to produce the result that damages were available for negligent misrepresentations which induced a contract. In *Foster* v. *Craigmillar Laundry Ltd.*[69] Sheriff Nicholson held that only fraudulent misrepresentation gave a remedy in damages, and this view received support in the Outer House.[70] In *Ferguson* v. *Mackay*[71] a failure to disclose financial details to a retiring partner was a breach of an obligation arising from a fiduciary relationship. A claim for damages was sent to a proof before answer. The existence of the fiduciary relationship enabled the court to distinguish the authorities which suggested that only on an averment of fraud was it possible to claim damages. The Scottish Law Commission recommended a change in the law[72] and, as a result, the Law Reform (Miscellaneous Provisions) (Scotland) Act 1985, s.10(1), provides that:

> "A party to a contract who has been induced to enter into it by negligent misrepresentation made by or on behalf of another party to the contract shall not be disentitled, by reason only that the misrepresentation is not fraudulent, from recovering damages from the other party in respect of any loss or damage he has suffered as a result of the misrepresentation; and any rule of law that such damages cannot be recovered unless fraud is proved shall cease to have effect."

The section applies to proceedings commenced on or after the date on which it came into force,[73] whether or not the negligent misrepresentation was made before or after that date.[74]

---

[67] [1976] Q.B. 801.
[68] *John Kenway Ltd.* v. *Orcantic Ltd.*, 1979 S.C. 422; *Andrew Oliver & Son Ltd.* v. *Douglas*, 1981 S.C. 192; *Junior Books Ltd.* v. *The Veitchi Co. Ltd.*, 1982 S.L.T. 492.
[69] 1980 S.L.T.(Sh.Ct.) 100.
[70] *Eastern Marine Services (and Supplies) Ltd.* v. *Dickson Motors Ltd.*, 1981 S.C. 355; *Twomax Ltd.* v. *Dickson, McFarlane & Robinson*, 1983 S.L.T. 98 at p. 102 *per* Lord Stewart. The principal obstacle to allowing damages was the decision of the First Division in *Manners* v. *Whitehead* (1898) 1 F. 171.
[71] 1985 S.L.T. 94.
[72] Scot.Law Com. No. 92 (1985), *Obligations—Report on Negligent Misrepresentation*. Sheriff Nicholson became a Scottish Law Commissioner shortly after his decision in *Foster*.
[73] Dec. 31, 1985; see s.60(3).
[74] s.10(2).

The Effect of Error and Misrepresentation on Third Parties

8 Stair's proposition that "Those who err in the substantials of what is done, contract not,"[75] was followed by Erskine[76] and Bell.[76] Later writers have had to contend with the confused meaning of essential error, but have stated that in certain circumstances error makes a contract void.[77]

9 Judicial opinion has also shown ambivalence. Lord Justice-Clerk Hope thought that the effect of error on a deed in favour of an onerous and *bona fide* third party was "a very serious question, but is not raised, I think, in the present case."[78] Lord Deas considered the effect of essential error on a deed in terms indicating that transfer to a *bona fide* singular successor might be a bar to reduction.[79]

30 The trend of the authorities indicates that the contract is void. There are *dicta* to this effect in *Grieve* v. *Wilson* in 1833 which are of particular value because the distinction between void and voidable is appreciated.[80] When both parties were under essential error, Lord Kinloch described their deed as void.[81] Again, when parties entered into a charterparty of a ship which may not have been in existence at the date of the contract, Lord Young said: "The contract consequently was void altogether from the beginning, and never came into operation at all."[82]

31 In *Dunlop* v. *Crookshanks* in 1752,[83] Forbes wrote to John Dunlop for cargo. His letter was in the plural—"We, etc."—and induced Dunlop to think that the contract would be with a partnership of Forbes and Crookshank, with whom Dunlop had had a previous dealing. Forbes became insolvent and Dunlop could not prove that Crookshank was Forbes' partner. The cargo had been bought from Forbes by Crookshanks, Jop and several others in whose hands Dunlop had arrested. In an action of multiplepoinding the court found that the property in the goods had not passed from Dunlop and found Crookshank liable to pay

---

[75] Stair, I,x,13.

[76] Ersk., *Inst.*, III,i,16; Bell, *Comm.*, I,313; Bell, *Prin.*, s.11; *vide* Bankt., I,470,63.

[77] Gloag, pp. 441–412; J. J. Gow, "Mistake and Error" (1952) 1 I.C.L.Q. 472 at p. 479. Professor Smith has tended to argue that the contract is voidable, in so far as he recognises the concept of voidability: T. B. Smith, "Error in the Scottish Law of Contract," 1955 L.Q.R. 507; *Short Commentary*, pp. 810, 814 *et seq.*

[78] *McConechy* v. *McIndoe* (1853) 16 D. 315 at p. 316.

[79] *Steuart's Trs.* v. *Hart* (1875) 3 R. 192.

[80] (1833) 6 W. & S. 543 at p. 549 *per* Lord Cringletie; at p. 560 *per* Lord Wyndford.

[81] *Mercer* v. *Anstruther's Trs.* (1871) 9 M. 618 at p. 653; on appeal, (1872) 10 M.(H.L.) 39: and see also a case of common error—*George Hunter & Son* v. *Weir*, 1955 S.L.T.(Sh.Ct.) 101.

[82] *Sibson & Kerr* v. *Ship "Barcraig" Co. Ltd.* (1896) 24 R. 91 at p. 99. The case was decided on another ground. If parties take the risk of existence of a certain state of affairs, there is no essential error: *Pender-Small* v. *Kinloch's Trs.*, 1917 S.C. 307. The Sale of Goods Act 1979, s.6, provides for a contract of sale being void in certain circumstances where goods have perished.

[83] Mor. 4879. *Cf.* Smith, *Short Commentary*, p. 821, who adopts a different view of the case.

Dunlop for the price of goods bought by Crookshanks from Jop as Forbes' agent, leaving Crookshanks with an action of relief against Jop. It can be suggested that error as to who the other contracting party is would, in a sale on credit, be error *in substantialibus*.[84] This error was induced by fraud, and that fraud affected a third-party purchaser of the goods. It would follow that the contract between Dunlop and Forbes was void.

9–82 A possible case of essential error rendering a contract void is *Morrisson* v. *Robertson*.[85] X sold cows to Y believing him to be the son of Z. X relied on the good credit of Z. Y sold the cows to A, who purchased in good faith. X sued A for delivery of the cows or for payment. The case involved not only essential error as to the person with whom one was contracting, but also the effect of such error having been induced by the fraud of Y.

9–83 The sheriff-substitute was clear that error with regard to the identity of a supposed purchaser in the case of a sale on credit was error in substantials which prevented consent. Fraud inducing such error did not make it cease to be such error. There was no contract, no transfer and no title to retransfer. The sheriff-depute reversed the finding of the sheriff-substitute and the pursuer appealed to the First Division. The Division held that there had been no contract of sale between X and Y, and as a result Y could give no title to A. It has subsequently been observed that the *ratio* of the case was that there was essential error as to the identity of the purchaser and the contract of sale was therefore void. If a seller decides to sell to a person on his premises who gives him a false name, the contract is not void. If a cheque in the false name is handed over in return for the goods sold, the contract will be voidable, having been induced by fraud.[86]

9–84 It has been argued that *Morrisson* v. *Robertson* was a case of theft, not of error *in persona*.[87] The case is special in its facts because Y falsely represented himself as the agent of Z. An agent who misappropriates his putative principal's property could on that ground alone be said to have committed theft. It may be that the case involved both theft and error *in persona*.

9–85 The result of the authorities is highly debatable but it appears that a contract induced by essential error, in the sense that that phrase is used by Institutional writers, is void. If the essential error is induced by fraud,

---

[84] In the Institutional writers' sense.

[85] 1908 S.C. 332. The true meaning of this case has been a matter of controversy. Professor Smith interpreted it one way (*Short Commentary*, p. 816) and was criticised by Lord President Clyde (*Macleod* v. *Kerr*, 1965 S.C. 253 at p. 256). There is further discussion in Scot.Law Com. Memo. No. 27: *Corporeal Moveables: Protection of the Onerous Bona Fide Acquirer of Another's Property* (1979), p. 17, n. 3. See also T. B. Smith, (1967) 12 J.L.S. 206.

[86] *Macleod* v. *Kerr*, 1965 S.C. 253.

[87] See authorities in n. 85; W. A. Wilson, (1966) 29 M.L.R. 442; (1966) 30 J.C.L. 47; Gordon, *Criminal Law* (2nd ed.), para. 14–55.

the contract is likewise void. It should follow, but there is no clear authority on this point, that essential error induced by innocent misrepresentation will render the contract void.

It remains to consider the effect of innocent[88] misrepresentation which does not induce essential error. Because innocent misrepresentation is a comparatively recent introduction into Scots law, its effect is not considered by the Institutional writers. Gloag stated: "A contract, it is submitted, is voidable if induced by misrepresentation, whether that misrepresentation is made innocently or fraudulently."[89] It is significant that he cites no authority for the voidable characteristic of innocent misrepresentation, and that in his first edition he was more hesitant about this view of the law.[90]

Professor Walker has stated that innocent misrepresentation renders the contract induced voidable unless the misrepresentation produced such error as wholly to exclude true consent, when the contract is void.[91] The authorities cited, however, do not directly support this proposition. There is no reported case in which the effect of innocent misrepresentation on third parties has been considered.

To determine the nature of the invalidity it is necessary to look at other factors. The starting point is Lord McLaren's observation that: "Where a pursuer only desires to set aside a contract of sale on the ground of innocent misrepresentations he may obtain relief, but only on condition of making *restitutio in integrum*."[92] No authority was cited, but the decision of the House of Lords in *Boyd & Forrest* v. *Glasgow and South Western Ry. Co.*[93] is now authority for that proposition. If *restitutio in integrum* is impossible, the contract cannot be reduced. This must mean that a contract induced by innocent misrepresentation is reducible or voidable; it is not null *ab initio* or void.[94] This view has the support of Lord President Clyde[95] and it is in accordance with the principle that innocent misrepresentation may induce consent but need not exclude consent.

---

[88] "Innocent" is used in the sense of non-fraudulent, *i.e.* including negligent misrepresentation.

[89] Gloag (2nd ed.), p. 471.

[90] Gloag (1st ed.), p. 521.

[91] *Principles* (3rd ed., 1983), Vol. III, p. 84; *Civil Remedies*, p. 153.

[92] *Manners* v. *Whitehead* (1898) 1 F. 171 at p. 176.

[93] 1915 S.C.(H.L.) 20.

[94] A similar rule on *restitutio in integrum* applies to fraudulent representations: *Graham* v. *Western Bank* (1864) 2 M. 559; *Western Bank of Scotland* v. *Addie* (1867) 5 M.(H.L.) 80; *Houldsworth* v. *City of Glasgow Bank* (1879) 6 R. 1164; (1880) 7 R.(H.L.) 53; *Tennent* v. *City of Glasgow Bank* (1879) 6 R.(H.L.) 69; although in considering whether restitution is possible there may be a difference between the effect of fraudulent representations and innocent representations—*Spence* v. *Crawford*, 1939 S.C.(H.L.) 52. It is settled that a contract induced by fraud is voidable.

[95] *Westville Shipping Co.* v. *Abram Steamship Co.*, 1922 S.C. 571 at p. 580 (on appeal, 1923 S.C.(H.L.) 68). It is clear that his Lordship was considering essential error, in Lord Watson's sense, which had been induced by innocent misrepresentation.

PART 4

Performance Error—Condictio Indebiti

9–89 Where money is paid under a mistaken belief of an obligation to pay, there is an action for repetition of the sums paid in error. A similar rule probably applies to delivery of goods in error,[96] although the reported case law has been concerned with money payments.

The action for repetition lies when it is equitable to order repayment. The original mistake in paying must be excusable.[97] A payment made in the knowledge that it is not due cannot be recovered.[98] Nor can a party found on an error induced by his own fault.[99] There must be an error or ignorance, not merely an alleged over-payment made in the knowledge of the facts and the law,[1] or a payment made knowing the risk that the proper claimant for the money might appear.[2]

9–90 It must be inequitable for the party to whom a payment has been made to retain the sums.[3] If the defender has a reasonable belief that the money is his and with that belief acts upon it so as to alter his position, it may be unjust to order repetition.[4] When both parties were in error as to the legal effect of a settlement and over-payments were made to a widow, it was observed that the widow was entitled to assume that she received the correct amount and in equity she could not be called on to repay.[5] In the case of a contract for repair of a roof in which work done without authority was paid for, the responsibility and actings of both parties were examined to determine the equitable result.[6] Because the *condictio indebiti* is based on equity a proof may be essential[7] except in

---

[96] Stair, I,vii,9; Bell, *Prin.*, s.531.

[97] *Glasgow Corporation* v. *Lord Advocate*, 1959 S.C. 203 at p. 233 *per* Lord President Clyde; *Youle* v. *Cochrane* (1868) 6 M. 427 at p. 433 *per* Lord Ardmillan.

[98] *Dalmellington Iron Co.* v. *Glasgow and S.W. Ry. Co.* (1889) 16 R. 523; "knowledge" in this context appears to be knowledge which was or should have been present in the mind of the payer at the time of payment. See also *Inverness County Council* v. *Macdonald*, 1949 S.L.T.(Sh.Ct.) 79.

[99] *Bell* v. *Thomson* (1867) 6 M. 64; *Balfour* v. *Smith & Logan* (1877) 4 R. 454 at pp. 458, 459 *per* Lord President Inglis. Conversely if the error is induced by the defender: *Duncan, Galloway & Co. Ltd.* v. *Duncan, Falconer & Co.*, 1913 S.C. 265 (although on the effect of fraud see arguments and dicta in *G. M. Scott (Willowbank Cooperage) Ltd.* v. *York Trailer Co. Ltd.*, 1970 S.L.T. 15).

[1] *Balfour Melville* v. *Duncan* (1903) 5 F. 1079.

[2] *McIvor* v. *Roy*, 1970 S.L.T.(Sh.Ct.) 58.

[3] *Henderson & Co. Ltd.* v. *Turnbull & Co.*, 1909 S.C. 510 at p. 521 *per* Lord Ardwall; *Bell* v. *Thomson, sup. cit.*

[4] *Credit Lyonnais* v. *George Stevenson & Co. Ltd.* (1901) 9 S.L.T. 93; *Wallet* v. *Ramsay* (1904) 12 S.L.T. 111; *Bell* v. *Thomson, sup. cit.* A case in which it was alleged that money was appropriated in bad faith is *Extruded Wire (Sales) Ltd.* v. *McLachlan & Brown*, 1986 S.L.T. 314.

[5] *Hunter's Trs.* v. *Hunter* (1894) 21 R. 949 (see *Darling's Trs.* v. *Darling's Trs.*, 1909 S.C. 445 and *Rowan's Trs.* v. *Rowan*, 1940 S.C. 30).

[6] *Peter Walker & Sons (Edinburgh) Ltd.* v. *Leith Glazing Co. Ltd.*, 1980 S.L.T.(Sh.Ct.) 104.

[7] *Haggarty* v. *Scottish Transport and General Workers Union*, 1955 S.C. 109; *Inverness County Council* v. *Macdonald*, 1949 S.L.T.(Sh.Ct.) 79.

so far as an error is alleged to be one of construction of a document because the true meaning, and thus whether or not there was an error, is an issue for the court.[8]

1   Restitution will not be ordered if the payment proceeds on a mutual obligation[9] or if it is part of an arrangement or compromise or other settlement of claims,[10] or intended as a donation.[11] It may be necessary to reduce a document or decree before the question of repetition arises.[12]

2   Interest on the money sought may run from the date of the payment in error on the grounds that the use of the money has been enjoyed by one not otherwise entitled thereto,[13] but interest has been denied when the error was due to the negligence of the person making payment.[14]

3   Subject to the equitable considerations which have been mentioned, the *condictio* applies to payments made under an error of fact, for example payments made under the mistaken belief that a person was dead,[15] or overpayment of an amount due[16] or payment to the wrong person,[17] or payment as a result of a mistake about what property was owned by the defenders,[18] or a payment in the absence of any obligation to pay.[19]

4   Somewhat complicated questions arise when the error is an error in the law. It is possible that at one time Scots law did not recognise a difference between errors in fact and errors in law. The case of *Stirling* v. *Lauderdale*,[20] which may support this proposition, is deprived of its authority by the brevity of the report. *Carrick* v. *Carse*[21] has usually been treated as decided on an error in fact, but the report by Hailes[22] suggests that it was decided by a majority of the Court of Session on the

---

[8] *Unigate Food Ltd.* v. *Scottish Milk Marketing Board*, 1972 S.L.T. 137 at p. 139 *per* Lord Stott; 1975 S.L.T.(Notes) 39 (1st Div.), 1975 S.L.T.(Notes) 76 (H.L.).

[9] Ersk., III,iii,54; Bell, *Prin.*, s.532.

[10] *Young* v. *Campbell* (1851) 14 D. 63; *Mackintosh* v. *Rose* (1889) 26 S.L.R. 450. See also *Reid* v. *Shaw Stewart* (1890) 6 Sh.Ct.Rep. 296 (payment of disputed claim under threat of action); *Macintyre* v. *Murray & Muir* (1915) 31 Sh.Ct.Rep. 49 (payment after diligence knowing that money not due).

[11] *Masters and Seamen of Dundee* v. *Cockerill* (1869) 8 M. 278 (where the payments were contractual and not charitable).

[12] *Wilson & McLellan* v. *Sinclair* (1830) 4 W. & S. 398; and see *Unigate Food Ltd.* v. *Scottish Milk Marketing Board, sup. cit.*

[13] *Duncan, Galloway & Co. Ltd.* v. *Duncan, Falconer & Co.*, 1913 S.C. 265.

[14] *Countess of Cromertie* v. *Lord Advocate* (1871) 9 M. 988.

[15] *Masters and Seamen of Dundee* v. *Cockerill* (1869) 8 M. 278; *North British Insurance Co.* v. *Stewart* (1871) 9 M. 534.

[16] *Balfour* v. *Smith & Logan* (1877) 4 R. 454 (joiner's account); *Robertson* v. *Scott* (1886) 13 R. 1127 (double payment for use of mutual gable); *Wallet* v. *Ramsay* (1904) 12 S.L.T. 111 (amount due from auction); *Moore's Exrs.* v. *McDermid*, 1913 1 S.L.T. 278 and 298 (overpayment of debtor).

[17] *Credit Lyonnais* v. *George Stevenson & Co. Ltd.* (1901) 9 S.L.T. 93.

[18] *Duncan, Galloway & Co. Ltd.* v. *Duncan, Falconer & Co.*, 1913 S.C. 265.

[19] *Ramsay* v. *Robertson* (1673) Mor. 2924; *Earl of Peterborough* v. *Murray* (1745) Mor. 2930; *Haggarty* v. *Scottish Transport and General Workers Union*, 1955 S.C. 109.

[20] (1733) Mor. 2930.

[21] (1778) Mor. 2931.

[22] (1778) Hailes Dec. 783.

grounds that the subtleties of civil law which distinguished error in law and error in fact, had not been received by Scots law. Lord Chancellor Brougham in two *obiter dicta* drew a distinction between the two types of error.[23] Although some doubts were cast on these dicta in the Court of Session,[24] some later authority supported the distinctions. After a review of the authorities it was decided in *Glasgow Corporation* v. *Lord Advocate*[25] that the *condictio indebiti* did not apply to an error in the general law. Payments of purchase tax made under an erroneous construction of the Finance Acts were irrecoverable. Thus a liquidator has been unable to recover excessive payments made by a previous liquidator when the distribution was calculated without taking account of the current liability for tax.[26]

9–95 There appears to be some conflict of authority when the error is one of construction, not of a public general statute but of a private deed. It has been held that payments made under an erroneous construction of such a deed are recoverable.[27] On the other hand, overpayments by trustees because of error in the legal effect of a settlement have been held irrecoverable.[28] It is not easy to reconcile these two strands of authority, not least because neither refers to the other. It may be that because the basis of this part of the law is equity, the equitable considerations applying to a beneficiary under a trust who in good faith receives and spends income from the trust, produce a different result from the same considerations applying to a commercial contract.

---

[23] *Wilson & McLellan* v. *Sinclair* (1830) 4 W. & S. 398 at p. 400; *Dixon* v. *Monkland and Co.* (1831) 5 W. & S. 445.

[24] *Dickson* v. *Halbert* (1854) 16 D. 586.

[25] 1959 S.C. 203.

[26] *Taylor* v. *Wilson's Trs.*, 1975 S.C. 146 (*cf. Weavers of Ayr* v. *Bone* (1823) 2 S. 401 and *Purvis Industries Ltd.* v. *J. & W. Henderson* (1959) 75 Sh.Ct.Rep. 143—in the latter case the liquidator's error on the amount of funds was an error in fact and recovery of payments to an ordinary creditor was allowed).

[27] *Baird's Trs.* v. *Baird & Co.* (1877) 4 R. 1005; *British Hydro-Carbon Chemicals Ltd. and British Transport Commission*, 1961 S.L.T. 280.

[28] *Hunter's Trs.* v. *Hunter* (1894) 21 R. 949; *Rowan's Trs.* v. *Rowan* 1940 S.C. 30; see also *Renwick's Exr.* v. *Muir* (1886) 2 Sh.Ct.Rep. 380.

CHAPTER 10

FRAUD

THE MEANING OF FRAUD

1 It would appear that in its contractual and delictual aspects fraud has the same meaning. Stair gave annulment of the contract or damages as the alternative remedies for fraud.[1] In the development of the law there was insufficient discussion of the nature of fraud as a delict for it clearly to develop a separate meaning in that context and so when Lord Anderson discussed the remedies for fraud his approach was similar to Stair.[2]

If there is a problem about the use of "fraud" in contract and also in delict, it is that while reduction and damages may be alternative remedies, this is not inevitable. Not only may one remedy be preferable to another in given circumstances but one of the remedies may be inappropriate. What of the fraud which does not induce a contract, or other act suitable for reduction? A delictual remedy applies where it would be difficult or inappropriate to obtain a contractual remedy. Conversely, a fraud may not cause loss, but the party deceived could reduce the contract and make restitution. All this may mean that fraud can be practised in a variety of ways and it may be an accident whether or not it induces a contract. Provided that there is an appropriate remedy we should not be too concerned. There must, however, be some definition of fraud outside which the rules on fraud cannot apply.

2 The best definition of fraud is that of Erskine. He said that fraud was "a machination or contrivance to deceive"[3] which is reminiscent of a Roman definition[4] and similar to Pothier's.[5] This type of definition has been characterised as the "shotgun, or rather shrapnel" definition of fraud[6] but whatever criticism may be implied in that description, the Scottish courts, with a background of civilian texts, applied a wide definition of fraud which looks to a state of mind rather than to the precise nature of the act.

3 This approach to fraud has had two main consequences. First it enabled the courts to attack transactions which deceived, as well as the more classic types of fraudulent devices, namely the misrepresentation

---

[1] Stair, I,ix,14.
[2] *Bryson & Co. Ltd.* v. *Bryson*, 1916 1 S.L.T. 361 at p. 364 (see comments on this case in *Smith* v. *Sim*, 1954 S.C. 357).
[3] Ersk., *Inst.*, III,i,16.
[4] *Dig.*, 4.3.1.2 and 3.
[5] M. Pothier, *Law of Obligations* (1806, trans. W. D. Evans), p. 28.
[6] M. D. Green, "Fraud, Undue Influence and Mental Incompetency" (1943) 43 Col. Law Rev., 176 at p. 179.

and the concealment. The emphasis was on the result produced rather than the means employed. Secondly, the development of the Scottish concept was quite different from the English common law relating to fraud as that law was established by *Derry* v. *Peek*.[7]

FRAUD AND THE INFLUENCE OF ENGLISH LAW

10–04 Professor Gloag considered that the general trend of Scottish decisions was reflected in the English case of *Derry* v. *Peek*.[8] Lord Herschell's dictum in that case[9] was that "fraud is proved when it is shown that a false representation has been made (1) knowingly, or (2) without belief in its truth, or (3) recklessly, careless whether it be true or false."

10–05 In *Boyd & Forrest* v. *Glasgow and South-Western Rly. Co.*[10] Lord Atkinson founded on *Derry* v. *Peek*.[11] In *Robinson* v. *National Bank of Scotland*[12] Earl Loreburn treated *Derry* v. *Peek* as part of Scots law.[13] If this were so it would be a remarkable result. *Derry* v. *Peek* was a decision on the English common law of deceit and in equity fraud had a much wider meaning.[14] Lord Hardwicke's judgment in *Earl of Chesterfield* v. *Janssen*[15] is more in accordance with the Scottish treatment of fraud. The readiness with which the Scottish courts would infer fraud make it a concept different from the English law of deceit. *Derry* v. *Peek* should be treated with caution in Scots law. Paradoxically the use of the term "fraud" in Scots law is not as wide as the use of the word in English equity. In Scotland, breach of fiduciary duty and fraud are distinguishable. In England breach of fiduciary duty is sometimes regarded as a type of fraud in equity.[16] This has led in Scotland to the adoption of the English term "fraud on minority" in relation to oppression of shareholders. In English law this use of "fraud" has a meaning wider than deceit or dishonesty, and nearer abuse of power.[17]

10–06 The danger of relying on English terminology is shown in *Harris* v. *A. Harris Ltd.*[18] One shareholder challenged a resolution passed by the majority. The Lord Ordinary considered whether the resolution was fraudulent and applied the test of whether it was so oppressive and extravagant that no reasonable man could consider it to be for the ben-

---

[7] (1889) 14 App.Cas. 337.

[8] (1889) 14 App.Cas. 337; Gloag, p. 478.

[9] at p. 374.

[10] 1912 S.C.(H.L.) 93.

[11] at p. 99.

[12] 1916 S.C.(H.L.) 154.

[13] at p. 157.

[14] *Nocton* v. *Lord Ashburton* [1914] A.C. 932 at pp. 946–957 *per* Viscount Haldane, L.C.

[15] (1750) 2 Ves.Sen. 125 at pp. 155–157.

[16] Keeton and Sheridan, *Equity* (1969), pp. 336 *et seq.*

[17] L. G. G. Gower, *The Principles of Modern Company Law* (4th ed., 1979), p. 616. *Cf.* examples of doctrine in Palmer's *Company Law* (23rd ed., 1982), paras. 58–13 *et seq.*

[18] 1936 S.C. 183.

efit of the company. On appeal Lords Hunter and Anderson applied a similar criterion. Lord Murray, however, protested and said:

> "I am of opinion that the true test to be applied is not whether the pursuer has or has not established that the defenders were guilty of fraud in the common law sense; I adopt as the true test a higher standard of conduct, whether they were or were not in breach of a fiduciary duty to the company and its constituent shareholders."[19]

7   He then analysed the meaning of fraud in English law and showed how the reference in English law to "fraudulent" meant breach of fiduciary duty.

8   Likewise the doctrine of "fraud on a power" derives its terminology from chancery practice and is not related to dishonesty.[20]

9   More recently Lord Maxwell has observed[21]:

> "I agree that the word 'fraud' is used in a variety of senses. The extreme example perhaps is 'fraud on a power'. But what we are concerned with here is the kind of fraud which will warrant the reduction of a deed. No case was cited to me where a deed has been reduced on the ground of fraud although the granter has not been induced to alter his position by reason of something approximating to deceit on the part of another."

0   There are limitations to the concept of fraud in Scots law but within those limits it is still difficult to improve on Erskine's definition of a "machination or contrivance to deceive." False and fraudulent representations of the type discussed in *Derry* v. *Peek* are only one category of fraud. To treat that case as defining the sole content of the Scots law of fraud would be a holocaust of centuries of case law.

FRAUD—CONTRACTUAL OR DELICTUAL?

11   A contract may be induced by fraud. When the fraud is perpetrated by the other party to the contract, it is convenient to discuss fraud in the context of its effect on the contract. If a party has been induced to consent by fraud, what is the effect on the consent apparently given? This type of question naturally leads to a discussion of fraud in a similar way to error or force and fear or other vices affecting contractual consent. The remedy for fraud is closely linked to the fate of the tainted contract. But there is another aspect to fraud. This is most clearly seen when the

---

[19] at p. 202. His Lordship equated the Scots common law of fraud to the English action for deceit. *Sed quaere*. See also *Oliver's Trs.* v. *W. G. Walker & Sons (Edinburgh) Ltd.*, 1948 S.L.T. 140 in which Lord Mackintosh followed, as he was bound to, the majority view.
[20] Keeton and Sheridan, *op. cit.*, pp. 368 *et seq.*; *McDonald* v. *McGrigor* (1874) 1 R. 817 at p. 822 *per* Lord Neaves; J. McLaren, *Law of Wills and Succession* (3rd ed., 1894), p. 1107 and comments in Dyke's Supplement (1934), p. 258.
[21] *Hartdegen* v. *Fanner*, 1980 S.L.T.(Notes) 23 at p. 24.

person committing the fraud is not a party to the contract. For example, to quote Evans' notes to Pothier[22]:

> "If one man proposes to contract with me for the purchase of goods, and another, without his collusion and for a fraudulent purpose of his own falsely represents him as a person of fortune; this may induce an action against the last for damages; but will not defeat the contract with the first."

The remedy of damages for fraud is now seen in Scots law as a delictual remedy in contrast to reduction of the contract which is a contractual remedy. The treatment of fraud as a delict by our authorities is sparse, relative to the mass of law on contractual claims, but throughout the recorded history of the law the possibility of damages for fraud has been recognised. Why the damages should be thought a delictual remedy is something of a mystery. If the damages are delictual there would be a clear instance of recovery of economic loss in delict.

FRAUD AS A DELICT

10–12   The institutional writers treated fraud as an aspect of reparation. Stair said[23]: "Fraud gives remeid by reparation to all that are damnified thereby, against the actor of the fraud, either by annulling of the contract or other deed elicited or induced by fraud, or by making up the damage sustained by the fraud, at the option of the injured."

10–13   Erskine recognised that fraud could be pled by way of exception or reduction,[24] but also that[25] "every fraudulent contrivance or unwarrantable act by which another suffers damage, or runs the hazard of it, subjects the delinquent to reparation."

10–14   Despite this early recognition of damages as a remedy for fraud, almost all the early reported cases show that another remedy was sought.[26] Usually this remedy was reduction, although declarator was used[27] or the remedy involved a ranking of claimants on a fund.[28] Damages does not appear with any frequency until the nineteenth century.[29] There are several possible explanations for this.

---

[22] M. Pothier, *Law of Obligations* (1806, trans. W. D. Evans), p. 20, note (c).

[23] Stair, I,ix,14; *cf. Bryson & Co. Ltd.* v. *Bryson*, 1916 1 S.L.T. 361 at p. 364 *per* Lord Anderson.

[24] Ersk., III,i,16.

[25] Ersk., III,i,13.

[26] See cases in Morison's *Dictionary, s.v.* "Fraud."

[27] *Scot* v. *Cheisly and Thomson* (1670) Mor. 4867.

[28] *Hoggs* v. *Hogg* (1749) Mor. 4862.

[29] *Dicksons Bros.* v. *Dicksons & Co.* (1816) 1 Mur. 55; *Paul* v. *Old Shipping Co.* (1816) 1 Mur. 64; *Campbell* v. *Boswall* (1841) 3 D. 639; *Duncan* v. *Cowie* (1841) 4 D. 47; *Miller* v. *Geils* (1848) 10 D. 715; *Leslie's Reps.* v. *Lumsden* (1851) 14 D. 213; *Tulloch* v. *Davidson* (1858) 20 D. 1045; (1860) 3 Macq. 783; *McPherson* v. *Campbell's Trs.* (1869) 41 Scot.Jur. 634 and other cases cited elsewhere. There are cases earlier than the 19th century (*e.g. Miller* v. *Alexander* (1758) 6 Pat. 718) but they are relatively infrequent.

15   It may be that the reported case law does not accurately reflect the
practice of the court. For the period covered by Morison's *Dictionary*
this must be true. Further, the nineteenth century developments in the
law of delict would have accustomed practitioners to seeking damages as
a remedy for negligence. It was, therefore, relatively easy to consider
the same remedy for fraud. Beyond these speculations there are factors
which influence the choice of reduction or damages.

16   These factors are of continuing importance and need detailed examination.

Reduction or Damages?

17   In *Bryson & Co. Ltd.* v. *Bryson*[30] Lord Anderson summarised the
choice of two remedies which a buyer has in a case of fraud. These
were[31] "first, rescission of the contract involving the return of the subject matter of the sale and a claim of damages; and second, a claim of
damages without rescission or restitution." A summons may conclude
for both remedies in the alternative although there are problems in putting both alternatives to a jury.[32] At one time some doubt was raised as
to whether the buyer could keep what he had obtained under his contract and sue for damages resulting from loss caused by fraud. It was
suggested that this was an *actio quanti minoris* which was not recognised
by the Scots common law of sale except within narrow limits. It is now
established, however, that damages for fraud is a delictual claim which
is not affected by any limitations of contractual remedies.[33]

The Advantages of Reduction and Restitution

18   The reduction of the transaction with its accompanying restitution may
accomplish the aims of the pursuer. As the early case law shows when it
was desired to invalidate deeds to favoured creditors, or deeds by facile
persons, or other alienation of assets, the restoration of the *status quo*
achieved the desired result for the granter or his heirs or creditors.
Ownership remained where it was before the tainted transaction.
Reduction of that transaction tackled the misfortune at its source particularly when insolvency was involved. Restitution in appropriate cases
could come close to compensating loss.[34]

The Advantages of claiming Damages

19   Damages, as a remedy, tends to solve different problems from reduction. In some cases it is the more appropriate, or the only, remedy.

---

[30] 1916 1 S.L.T. 361; see comments on this case in *Smith* v. *Sim*, 1954 S.C. 357.
[31] See at p. 364.
[32] *Graham* v *Western Bank* (1864) 2 M. 559; sequel (1865) 3 M. 617.
[33] *Amaan* v. *Handyside & Henderson* (1865) 3 M. 526; *Dobbie* v. *Duncanson* (1872) 10
M. 810; *Smith* v. *Sim, sup. cit.*
[34] See *Graham* v. *Western Bank* (1864) 2 M. 559.

10–20   Damages may be sought:

(1) When the fraud was by a third party. The other contracting party is in good faith. Unless damages can be sought from the party who committed the fraud, there is no remedy.[35]

(2) Damages may be the remedy when the fraud does not induce a contract, but causes another event such as delivery of goods or acceptance of goods[36] or delivery of a deed[37]; or interference with another's trade.[38]

(3) If restitution *in integrum* is impossible, reduction is barred, but damages could still be claimed.[39] A contract may be at an end and reduction pointless.[40]

(4) The pursuer may prefer to keep what he has under the contract, such as the business which is his livelihood, and sue for the loss caused by paying too high a price. He is entitled to take this course.[41]

(5) Damages can be claimed against some or all of the wrongdoers. Reduction of a contract may involve much wider consequences and more parties to the action.[42] As Lord Stormonth Darling put it[43]:

> "It is impossible to rescind a contract of co-partnery on the ground of fraudulent misrepresentation or essential error, if there are some of the partners against whom nothing is alleged, and who desire the contract to stand. . . . There may be a remedy against the actual wrongdoers, but the remedy must be damages, not reduction."

(6) Reduction and restoration may not compensate actual loss.

The Disadvantages of claiming Damages

10–21   There are two potential disadvantages in claiming damages.

(1) Damages are an illiquid claim

Because damages are illiquid and, in the case of fraud, delictual, there are difficulties in claiming that the amount of damages should be set off against a contractual claim, such as a claim for the price. In *Smart* v. *Wilkinson*[44] it was held that under the Sheriff Court Rules damages for

---

[35] *Tulloch* v. *Davidson* (1858) 20 D. 1045 at p. 1057 *per* Lord Cowan; on appeal (1860) 3 Macq. 783; *Thin & Sinclair* v. *Arrol & Sons* (1896) 24 R. 198 at p. 206 *per* Lord President Robertson.

[36] *Miller* v. *Alexander* (1758) 6 Pat. 718; *Gourlay* v. *Watt* (1870) 9 M. 107.

[37] *Drummond* v. *Douglas & Co.* (1851) 23 Scot.Jur. 648.

[38] *Dicksons Bros.* v. *Dicksons & Co.* (1816) 1 Mur. 55.

[39] *McPherson* v. *Campbell's Trs.* (1869) 41 Scot.Jur. 634; *Houldsworth* v. *City of Glasgow Bank* (1880) 7 R.(H.L.) 53—although the action was against the wrong defender.

[40] *Campbell* v. *Boswall* (1841) 3 D. 639; *Boyd & Forrest* v. *Glasgow and South-Western Ry. Co.*, 1911 S.C. 33; revd., 1912 S.C.(H.L.) 93.

[41] *Campbell* v. *Blair* (1897) 5 S.L.T. 28; *Smith* v. *Sim*, 1954 S.C. 357.

[42] *Leslie's Reps.* v. *Lumsden* (1851) 14 D. 213; appd. in *Tulloch* v. *Davidson* (1860) 3 Macq. 783.

[43] *Rose* v. *McDonald* (1899) 7 S.L.T. 288.

[44] 1928 S.C. 383.

fraud could not be a counter claim in an action for the contract price and was not a defence to that action. Dobie, however, appeared to cast doubt on *Smart*[45] because of the subsequent decision in *Armour & Melvin* v. *Mitchell*.[46] In *Armour & Melvin* it was held competent to plead an illiquid claim in answer to a liquid claim. There was no adequate reason why the defender should have to raise a separate action. Dobie preferred the result in *Armour & Melvin*, although the issue of the competence of the counterclaim was not really argued.[47] It is now clear that the competence of a counterclaim does not depend on the ability to set off the defender's claim against the pursuer's claim.[48]

(2) Choosing the correct defender

There are two problems, namely (1) naming the persons who committed the fraud and (2) vicarious liability for the fraud of others.

There must be specification of the individuals who are alleged to have committed a fraud.[49]

22   The problem of vicarious liability for fraud is discussed later.[50] In the context of a claim for damages the seminal case is *Western Bank of Scotland* v. *Addie*.[51] That case involved an allegedly fraudulent purchase of shares. In the case for reduction it was relevant to sue the company for the misrepresentation of its directors. This followed the rule that a principal cannot retain the benefit of the fraud of its directors. Damages, however, could only be obtained against the directors, not against the company.

23   To succeed in a claim for damages against a person other than the person who committed the fraud, it would be necessary to show vicarious liability for the fraud which would in turn depend on the application of the normal rules of agency. If the fraudulent conduct of the agent was within the authority of the agent, the principal will be liable for the consequences.[52]

In the very special case of *Houldsworth* v. *City of Glasgow Bank*[53] it was held that a shareholder could not have an action of damages against the company so long as he remained a partner of it. It may be that the case is explicable on the basis of the nature of partnership under which a partnership does not undertake liability for some of the losses of individual partners such as damages for being fraudulently induced to become

---

[45] Dobie, *Sheriff Court Practice*, p. 152.
[46] 1934 S.C. 94.
[47] *Ibid.* at p. 97 *per* Lord Justice-Clerk Aitchison.
[48] See Chap. 22, "Payment," para. 22–52.
[49] *Thomson & Co.* v. *Pattison, Elder & Co.* (1895) 22 R. 432; *Smith & Houston Ltd.* v. *Metal Industries (Salvage) Ltd.*, 1953 S.L.T.(Notes) 73.
[50] See below, para. 10–62.
[51] (1867) 5 M.(H.L.) 80, followed in *Houldsworth* v. *City of Glasgow Bank* (1880) 7 R.(H.L.) 53.
[52] *Lloyd* v. *Grace, Smith & Co.* [1912] A.C. 716; *Armstrong* v. *Strain* [1952] 1 K.B. 232.
[53] (1880) 7 R.(H.L.) 53.

a partner,[54] or the loss caused to one partner by the negligence of another partner.[55]

METHODS OF COMMITTING FRAUD

10-24　For the purposes of analysis it is convenient to divide the methods of committing fraud into categories. But it should be emphasised that the Scottish courts retain a residual power which is flexible enough to attack any "machination or contrivance to deceive." The categories of fraud should never be closed. We are also concentrating on fraud as it affects contracts. Fraud may have an effect on other juristic acts *inter vivos* and *mortis causa*.

Fraudulent Representation

10-25　The simplest form of fraud is the straight lie. Examples are the production, prior to contract, of a false statement of affairs which enlarges assets and diminishes liabilities,[56] or lying about a rate of foreign exchange[57] or pretending to be an heir[58] or misrepresenting the circumstances surrounding an agreement on splitting an inheritance,[59] or misrepresenting the nature of a sub-lease,[60] or the acreage of a farm,[61] or the number of sheep a farm would maintain.[62] It would not by itself be relevant to aver that a deed signed was different from the draft, but such a case could become relevant on appropriate averments of fraud.[63]

10-26　　It is not every lie prior to a contract which will found a case of fraud. A seller of an Edinburgh flat may misrepresent to potential purchasers the population of the city, the frequency of the local bus service and the charms of the next-door neighbour. Such statements will have no legal effect on the subsequent contract if they are *verba jactantia* or are expressions of opinion rather than statements of fact[64] or they did not induce the contract.[65]

10-27　　A contract induced by a false statement is not necessarily a contract induced by fraud. The falsity of the statement could arise from an innocent mistake. Fraud implies an intentional inaccuracy or making a state-

---

[54] See Gloag's explanation, *Contract*, p. 481.

[55] *Mair* v. *Wood*, 1948 S.C. 83.

[56] *Hoggs* v. *Hogg* (1749) Mor. 4862. See also *Mair* v. *Rio Grande Rubber Estates Ltd.*, 1913 S.C.(H.L.) 74; *Muir* v. *Rankin* (1905) 13 S.L.T. 60; *Bryson & Co. Ltd.* v. *Bryson*, 1916 1 S.L.T. 361.

[57] *Dickson* v. *Graham* (1671) Mor. 4870.

[58] *Walker* v. *Young* (1695) Bro.Supp., IV, 290.

[59] *Ballantyne* v. *Neilson* (1682) Mor. 4870.

[60] *Duncan* v. *Cowie* (1841) 4 D. 47.

[61] *Miller* v. *Geils* (1848) 10 D. 715; *cf. Oliver* v. *Suttie* (1840) 2 D. 514.

[62] *McPherson* v. *Campbell's Trs.* (1869) 41 Scot.Jur. 634.

[63] *Hogg* v. *Campbell* (1864) 2 M. 848; *cf. Monymusk* v. *Lesly* (1635) Mor. 4956.

[64] *Brownlie* v. *Miller* (1880) 7 R.(H.L.) 66; *Sutherland* v. *Bremner's Trs.* (1903) 10 S.L.T. 565; *Hamilton* v. *Duke of Montrose* (1906) 8 F. 1026; *Romanes* v. *Garman*, 1912 2 S.L.T. 104 at p. 105 *per* Lord President Dunedin; *Flynn* v. *Scott*, 1949 S.C. 442. See also Chap. 3, "Pre-Contract Negotiations," para. 3–25.

[65] See para. 10–61.

ment not caring whether it is true or false. A statement honestly made, but wrong, is not fraudulent.[66] A case on fraudulent misrepresentation must show that the statement was both false and fraudulent.[67]

Fraudulent Concealment

28 "Concealment" in this context means silence. It has to be distinguished from concealment, which is an aspect of misrepresentation, *e.g.* covering over the defects in property sold, or making second-hand machines appear to be new.[68] However difficult it may be to distinguish between them, failure to disclose defects, *i.e.* concealment, is different from fraudulent misrepresentation.[69]

29 Concealment featured in several of the early Scottish cases in which fraud was successfully pled. It is probable that some of the early cases would not be followed now because of the emergence in the nineteenth century of the idea that there had to be a duty of disclosure before concealment was relevant. This may be linked to English ideas of *caveat emptor*, and a buyer's eye being his merchant.

30 In the seventeenth century concealment was merely one aspect of a fraudulent contrivance. A person could conceal a prior transaction or private knowledge and so gain an unfair advantage over the other contracting party. It was fraud for a superior enforcing payment to conceal the existence of other legal proceedings,[70] or for a debtor to conceal private knowledge of a devaluation of currency.[71]

31 At the beginning of the nineteenth century the courts were troubled by the effect of the concealment by a buyer of private knowledge of imminent changes in taxation.[72] In one case a seller of a ship which could not be examined was held bound to communicate any material defects to the buyer,[73] but this particular aspect of concealment was somewhat confused with the separate problem of an implied warranty on fitness for purpose.

32 Under English influence a rule emerged that a person taking out insurance had a duty to disclose material facts to the insurers.[74] Lord Brougham by the middle of the nineteenth century was stating the more

---

[66] *Brownlie* v. *Miller* (1880) 7 R.(H.L.) 66; *Boyd & Forrest* v. *Glasgow & South-Western Ry. Co.*, 1912 S.C.(H.L.) 93.

[67] *Campbell* v. *Boswall* (1841) 3 D. 639; but in a case where reduction only is sought it may be enough to show a false representation, *i.e* an innocent misrepresentation. See *Mair* v. *Rio Grande Rubber Estates Ltd.*, 1913 S.C.(H.L.) 74, opinion of Lord Shaw.

[68] *Gibson* v. *National Cash Register Co.*, 1925 S.C. 500.

[69] See *Broatch* v. *Jenkins* (1866) 4 M. 1030 at p. 1032, *per* Lord President McNeill.

[70] *Kincaid* v. *Lauder* (1629) Mor. 4857.

[71] *Wood* v. *Baird* (1696) Mor. 4860.

[72] *Boswall* v. *Morrison* (1812) 5 Pat. 649; Hume, 679; *Paterson* v. *Allan* (1801) Hume, 681.

[73] *Duthie* v. *Carnegie* 21 Jan. 1815, F.C.

[74] Cases in Morison's *Dictionary*, pp. 7080–7095; and in Brown's *Synopsis*, pp. 1075–1077.

general proposition that: "A concealment, to be material, must be a concealment of something that the party concealing was bound to tell."[74a] This became settled law in *Broatch* v. *Jenkins*.[75]

10–33   In *Broatch* an issue of fraudulent concealment was refused when the pleadings failed to set forth that there was a duty of communication. Lord President McNeill stated[76]:

> "An issue of concealment always imports that there is a duty of communication. There may be a duty of communication, and a fraudulent failure to communicate. The most palpable cases of this kind are insurance cases, where, for instance, the party making an insurance is aware of a fact which he does not communicate. But there may be non-communication because the party himself had not made himself aware of the fact; still it was his duty to give information of that fact, and his failure to do so would found a plea of liberation."

10–34   Lord Ardmillan observed[77]:

> "There can be no relevant use of fraudulent concealment where there is no duty to disclose. Non-disclosure where there is a duty to disclose is concealment, and that concealment may be fraudulent. But misrepresentation does sometimes run into concealment."

10–35   Having established the need for a duty to disclose, the law then had to distinguish those cases where the duty existed from those where it did not. In insurance contracts there is a duty of disclosure[78] as there is also in the form of cautionary obligation called the fidelity bond.[79] There has been held to be a duty of disclosure in an agreement between legatees.[80] There may be a duty of disclosure in certain fiduciary relationships.[81]

10–36   A seller of property is under no duty to disclose his previous difficulties in selling at the price now asked[82] nor is a creditor bound to volunteer information on the debtor's account to a potential cautioner,[83] nor is a person seeking a job bound to disclose a previous dismissal.[84]

10–37   It is important to note that a failure in a duty of disclosure would not by itself be sufficient to found a case of fraud. The failure could be innocent or negligent. To be fraudulent the concealment must be part of a machination or contrivance to deceive and (for a contractual remedy)

[74a] *Irvine* v. *Kirkpatrick* (1850) 7 Bell 186 at p. 232.

[75] (1866) 4 M. 1030; there may be a duty to disclose a change in circumstances after a representation is made: *Shankland & Co.* v. *Robinson & Co.*, 1920 S.C.(H.L.) 103.

[76] at p. 1032.

[77] at p. 1032.

[78] *e.g. The Spathari*, 1925 S.C.(H.L.) 6.

[79] *Railton* v. *Mathews and Leonard* (1844) 6 D. 536; *French* v. *Cameron* (1893) 20 R. 966.

[80] *Dempster* v. *Raes* (1873) 11 M. 843.

[81] *e.g.* trustee and beneficiary; director or promoter and company; agent and principal. See Gloag, *Contract*, Chap. XXXI. Or between partners: J. B. Miller, *Partnership* (1973), p. 162; *Ferguson* v. *Mackay*, 1985 S.L.T. 94.

[82] *Irvine* v. *Kirkpatrick, sup. cit.* at p. 232 *per* Lord Brougham.

[83] *Young* v. *Clydesdale Bank* (1889) 17 R. 231; *Royal Bank* v. *Greenshields*, 1914 S.C. 259.

[84] *Walker* v. *Greenock & District Combination Hospital Board*, 1951 S.C. 464.

must have induced the contract, as discussed below. The concept of "duty of disclosure" adds to, and does not detract from, the other requirements of fraud in a case of fraudulent concealment.[85]

Fraud after a Contract

38 Although the traditional treatment of fraud has been of fraud which induces consent to a contract, fraud is also relevant to challenge actions in performance of a contract. The fraudulent preference by an insolvent to his creditor can be an attempt to satisfy an existing obligation which is to the disadvantage of other creditors. Fraud may induce delivery of goods[86] or delivery of a deed[87] or payment under an insurance policy.[88]

FRAUD AND INSOLVENCY

39 One of the tendencies of the early law was to allow inferences of fraud. While this can be demonstrated from cases involving contrivances to defraud[89] it is most clearly shown in cases where creditors were prejudiced by the actings of their debtor. In Morison's *Dictionary* transactions by insolvent persons form a large class of the reported cases on fraud. Kames described the challenge of deeds by insolvents as being on the basis of "a covenant procured by deceit that amounts not to fraud."[90] As often he may have foreseen how the law was to develop but at the time he wrote his approach was inconsistent with the authorities. Two situations were of particular concern to the law, namely:

(1) The alienation of assets by an insolvent debtor. All the creditors could be affected by the diminution in the estate of the debtor.

(2) The purchase of goods by an insolvent. A seller on credit was affected adversely when he parted with his goods without prospect of payment.

Alienations by Insolvents

40 The Bankruptcy Act 1621 had considered the problem of insolvents' contracts to be one of "fraude malice and falsehoode" and the Bankruptcy Act 1696 referred to "fraudfull alienations" and "frauds and abuses".[91] The technicalities of bankruptcy law were to take these ideas

---

[85] See *Irvine* v. *Kirkpatrick*, (1850) 7 Bell 186 at p. 237 *per* Lord Brougham.

[86] *Watt* v. *Findlay* (1846) 8 D. 529; explained in *Richmond* v. *Railton* (1854) 16 D. 403.

[87] *Drummond* v. *Douglas & Co.* (1851) 23 Scot.Jur. 648.

[88] Examples in one context can be found in E. Ellen and D. Campbell, *International Maritime Fraud* (1981).

[89] *Campbell* v. *Moir* (1681) Mor. 4889; *Creditors of Pollock* v. *Pollock* (1669) Mor. 4909.

[90] Kames, *Principles of Equity*, p. 89.

[91] The 1696 Act was passed because of defects in the definition of notour bankruptcy shown in *Moncreif* v. *Cockburn* (1694) Mor. 1054 (Bell, *Comm.*, II,192). The development of the common law of fraudulent preference is explained by Bell, *Comm.*, II,226 *et seq.* Most of the development is after 1696. Prior to 1696 alienations by a debtor *omnium bonorum* were treated as fraudulent. See Mor. 888 *et seq.*

of fraud on a path far removed from that on which it began, but its origins were shown in the use of the term "fraudulent preference."

10-41   The Bankruptcy Act 1621 was in some respects a defective statute. The result was the development of the common law of bankruptcy after the Act. The Act did not extend to posterior creditors, but this defect was overcome by an application of the common law which did not favour a "contrivance betwixt the father and the son, which did ensnare the creditors who continued to trade."[92] That decision obviously was thought to be important because the Lords ordained it to be "inserted in the books of sederunt, to be a leading cause (*sic*) in all time coming." It was followed by a series of decision in which deeds to relatives were held to have been granted in defraud of posterior creditors.[93] The facts inferred a presumptive fraud. Obviously limitations had to be placed on this doctrine. The presumption was not applied when the deed was onerous[94] and security to a creditor was not reduced when the granter was not notour bankrupt.[95]

10-42   The alienation by the insolvent was fraudulent because of its effect on his creditors. The "fraud" required knowledge by the insolvent of his absolute insolvency.[96] The recipient of his alienation need not, however, have participated in the fraud for a successful challenge of the alienation.[97] If this were a requirement the laws of bankruptcy could be evaded by a disposition to an *incapax*. The collusion of the recipient if it existed would, however, be an element in proving fraud.[98]

10-43   The common law on fraudulent transactions by insolvents became somewhat confused because of its interaction with the Bankruptcy Act 1621 and the Bankruptcy Act 1696. These statutes dealt with two types of alienation. The 1621 Act controlled gifts to conjunct and confident persons and the 1696 Act applied to preferences to creditors. A creditor by definition is someone who is entitled to something from his debtor. A donee is in a less favourable position. The two statutes, therefore, deal with different aspects of the problem. This led Bell and Goudy to treat the common law on gifts and the common law on fraudulent preferences as separate issues.[99] This is somewhat misleading because there was no

---

[92] *Creditors of John Pollock* v. *Pollock* (1669) Mor. 4909.

[93] *Street* v. *Mason* (1672) Mor. 4911; *Reid* v. *Reid* (1673) Mor. 4923; *Blair* v. *Wilson* (1677) Mor. 4927; *Creditors of William Robertson* v. *His Children* (1688) Mor. 4929.

[94] *Paul* v. *Davidson* (1684) Mor. 4929. In Morison the date is misprinted as 1694. See Fountainhall's *Decisions*, Vol. 1, p. 277.

[95] *Creditors of Carloury & Halyards* v. *Lord Mersington* (1694) Mor. 4929.

[96] *MacDougall's Tr.* v. *Ironside*, 1914 S.C. 186.

[97] A point argued in *Street* v. *Mason, sup. cit.* and raised in *Ross* v. *Hutton* (1830) 8 S. 916 and *Edmond* v. *Duffus* (1866) 2 S.L.R. 50. See now *McCowan* v. *Wright* (1853) 15 D. 494 and discussion in H. Goudy, *Law of Bankruptcy* (4th ed., 1914), pp. 37–39.

[98] See authorities in n. 97. Conversely knowledge by the creditor of the insolvency of the debtor would not by itself produce a fraudulent preference. *Nordic Travel* v. *Scotprint*, 1980 S.C. 1.

[99] Bell, *Comm.*, II,184 and II,226; Goudy, Chaps. III and IV. See also the treatment of the statutory law including the Companies Acts in *Johnstone* v. *Peter M. Irvine Ltd.*, 1984 S.L.T. 209.

rigid distinction at common law between the two types of transaction. They were both frauds on creditors. The courts adopted a flexible approach to determine whether they could infer an intention to defeat the rights of creditors.[1]

44 The Bankruptcy (Scotland) Act 1985 repealed the 1621 and 1696 Acts, but the common law on fraudulent preferences remains.[2] Gratuitous alienations may be challenged under section 34 of the 1985 Act. An "unfair preference" may be challenged under section 36. Time limits apply to the statutory challenges but these time limits do not operate according to a state of insolvency or notour bankruptcy. Sequestration or the granting of a trust deed which has become protected are requirements for the statutory challenge in the case of a living debtor.[3]

Purchase by an Insolvent

45 The problem which the law faces is of an insolvent[4] person who buys goods. He cannot pay for the goods. Should property in the goods pass to him and from him to others?

46 It was held in *Prince* v. *Pallat*[5] that it was fraudulent for a person who knew that he was insolvent to buy goods. The transaction was reducible. In *Inglis* v. *Royal Bank*[6] it was established that there was a presumption of fraud in transactions by a bankrupt within three days prior to formal bankruptcy. *A fortiori* it was fraudulent for a bankrupt to order goods after cessio.[7]

47 The law was using two rules: a general application of fraud and a presumption arising from the three-day rule. The three-day rule was not the only context of the law. Other circumstances combined with insolvency could result in a challenge of a transaction outwith this period. This became clear in *McKay* v. *Forsyth*[8] in which it was observed that: "To purchase goods in *actu proximo* of becoming bankrupt, without prospect or purpose to pay the price, is a gross cheat; which the court of equity in every country repairs by ordering restitution of the goods to the vendor."

48 Despite a tract of authority on the three-day rule it was rejected by the House of Lords in the remarkable case of *Allan, Stuart & Co.* v. *Creditors of Stein*.[9] The problem which was developing was a conflict

---

[1] Consider, *e.g. Logan's Trs.* v. *David Logan & Son Ltd.* (1903) 11 S.L.T. 32.

[2] And the title to challenge at common law is extended. See ss.34(8) and 36(6).

[3] See ss.34(2) and 36(1).

[4] The common law was largely concerned with absolute insolvency rather than practical insolvency.

[5] (1680) Mor. 4932; followed, *Main* v. *Keeper of Weigh House of Glasgow* (1715) Mor. 4934; *Creditors of Robertson* v. *Udnies and Patullo* (1757) Mor. 4941.

[6] (1736) Mor. 4936.

[7] *Forbes* v. *Mains & Co.* (1752) Mor. 4937.

[8] (1758) Mor. 4944. See also *Sandieman* v. *Creditors of Kempt* (1786) Mor. 4947; *Love* v. *Kempt* (1786) Mor. 4948.

[9] (1788) 3 Pat. 191 (which is preferable to the report at Mor. 4949).

between two principles. One was that insolvent persons should not defraud those who supplied them; the other was that insolvent persons should be allowed to continue to trade. In the expansion of commercial life in the nineteenth century it was the latter principle which prevailed. Insolvency was regarded as a possibly transient phase. It may "pass over a man like a summer cloud—on him one day and gone the next—his affairs sometimes gloomy, sometimes bright."[10] The earlier idea that the concealment of one's insolvency was itself fraudulent was rejected by Bell as "inconsistent with an advanced state of commerce."[11]

10–49   The law favoured the honest but insolvent trader trying to recover his fortunes. It developed rules exempting transactions from challenge as fraudulent preferences.[12] It allowed an insolvent to trade. So long as a person entertained the hope, though illusory, of ultimately retrieving his losses, he might continue to trade. Once a bankrupt had resolved to give up business it was fraudulent to continue to trade. Goods delivered to him after his resolution were restored to the seller.[13] After a resolution to declare failure, to take delivery of items "without a prospect even of being able to pay, would have been . . . a dishonest act and unavailable either to him or his creditors."[14]

10–50   The law appears to have been more concerned with the *delivery* of the goods, than with the contract under which the goods were sold. It was, of course, the delivery which transferred property to the bankrupt buyer and which could prejudice the seller. In *Watt* v. *Findlay*,[15] property in goods did not pass when their delivery was induced by a promise of payment made by a person who had taken steps for his sequestration. This was "a fraudulent concealment by the purchaser of his circumstances."[16] A buyer conscious of his insolvency who had not contemplated his sequestration was entitled to reject goods but probably not bound to reject.[17]

10–51   A useful illustration of the application of these rules was a sheriff court case in which a merchant bought tea and coffee from one supplier. The tea was delivered at 10.30 a.m. and the coffee at 1.40 p.m. At about 1.00 p.m. the merchant had resolved to apply for sequestration and signed a mandate authorising an agent to present a petition. The tea, but not the coffee, was part of the bankrupt's estate.[18]

---

[10] Attributed to Prof. Bell by Lord Young in *Coutt's Trs. & Doe* v. *Webster* (1886) 13 R. 1112 at p. 1117.

[11] *Comm.*, I,265.

[12] See Goudy, pp. 39, 40 and Bankruptcy (Scotland) Act 1985, s.36(2).

[13] *Carnegie & Co.* v. *Hutchison* (1815) Hume 704, and see earlier doubts on ability of a bankrupt to accept delivery in *Stein* v. *Hutchison*, Nov. 16, 1810, F.C.

[14] *Brown* v. *Watson* (1816) Hume 709.

[15] (1846) 8 D. 529; explained in *Richmond* v. *Railton* (1854) 16 D. 403.

[16] *Ibid.* at pp. 531, *per* Lord President Boyle.

[17] *Booker & Co.* v. *Milne* (1870) 9 M. 314; *Ehrenbacher & Co.* v. *Kennedy* (1874) 1 R. 1131.

[18] *Birrell's Trs.* v. *Clark & Rowe* (1874), Guthrie's Sh.Ct.Rep., 1 Ser., (1879), p. 86.

52   There is a need for the extension of this principle since the rules on
passing of property in the Sale of Goods Act 1893, and now in the Sale
of Goods Act 1979.[19] Property in goods may pass, followed by a resolution of the buyer to cease trading, and then by delivery of the goods by
the seller. Although at the time of the delivery the goods belong to the
buyer his acceptance of the goods defeats some of the remedies of an
unpaid seller. Taking delivery in these circumstances should be treated
as a fraud by the buyer.[20]

Unfair Activities

53   There are cases which cannot easily be classed as a representation or a
concealment but which involve a plan to deceive. Thus the following
have been fraudulent: a contrivance between the seller and purchaser of
an estate to defeat a heritable creditor of the seller,[21] or a contrivance
between father and son to discharge provisions due by marriage contract,[22] or granting a bond, taking a discharge of it and then assigning
the bond,[23] or otherwise using a bond to ensnare creditors into lending,[24] or selling at a roup to a white bonnet.[25] The use of a white bonnet
is fraudulent conduct of an auction:

> " . . . if the exposer employs somebody else to bid for him under a
> disguise, that is to say, puts forward a white bonnet for the purpose
> of running up the price against the public, that is plainly fraud, and
> a sale effected under such circumstances cannot stand. The sale
> must be reduced, and the party bidding in competition with the
> white bonnet preferred, if he choose, to the subject at his first
> bid."[26]

54   Some instances of this type of fraud may be regarded now as examples
of devices contrary to public policy although that concept developed at a
later date than fraud. An old example is *pacta contra fidem tabularum
nuptialium*. In more modern times an equivalent is a company which
obtains credit on the basis of a valuation of assets and after the money
has been advanced, transfers the assets elsewhere.

55   The problem of *pacta contra fidem tabularum nuptialium* has received
scant attention from writers and yet it raised many difficult issues. The
usual problem was a marriage contract accompanied at the same time,
or at least prior to the marriage, by a private contract between father

---

[19] s.17 under which property passes when intended to pass. *Cf.* the common law—Bell,
Comm., I,177—"In Scotland property is not transferred, either nominally or effectually,
without delivery of the commodity."
[20] With the consequence that the "delivery" is ineffectual and the seller has the remedies of an unpaid seller in possession of the goods.
[21] *Aitken* v. *Goldie* (1745) Mor. 4862.
[22] *Caddell* v. *Raith* (1680) Mor. 4906.
[23] *Thomson* v. *Henderson* (1665) Mor. 4906.
[24] *Creditors of Pollock* v. *Pollock* (1669) Mor. 4909; *Blair* v. *Wilson* (1677) Mor. 4927.
[25] *Grey* v. *Stewart* (1753) Mor. 9560; *Shiell* v. *Guthrie's Trs.* (1874) 1 R. 1083.
[26] *Shiell* v. *Guthrie's Trs.*, *sup. cit.* at p. 1089 *per* Lord President Inglis.

and son in which the son burdened or disposed of the estate which was transferred to him in the marriage contract. Such arrangements were declared null in a series of decisions.[27] The contract between father and son could be challenged by those prejudiced by it, including the son.[28] The reason for allowing the challenge was difficult to explain. There is something unfair about a situation in which a marriage contract proclaims a man's future wealth to his intended wife, and in an unpublished deed the man reconveys his fortune to his donor. The elastic concept of fraud could be used to explain the availability of challenge but this was awkward in its application to the son who, if anything, was a party to the deceit. Kames considered that the son was relieved, not on the ground of fraud, but on the ground of implied extortion, whereas the relief granted to the wife and children was on the ground of fraud.[29] In the absence of a developed doctrine of public policy this was a complicated but logical analysis.

10–56   The reason for reduction was better explained by an argument in 1705 which combines elements of fraud and public policy:

> " . . . private deeds, contrary to solemn contracts of marriage, are fraudulent *contra bonos mores*, and ought to receive no encouragement from any judicature; and such discharges are prejudicial to the wife, not only for her liferent interest, but in so far as they cut off the fund of sustaining the married couple, and educating the children; and such unfair dealings could even be quarrelled by the granters of private discharges themselves, as being elicited at the time when children cannot debate nor contend with their parents, and ought not to be imposed upon; and it is reasonable, and necessary, that all such underhand practices should be discouraged; for who can be secure in matching their daughters, if private pactions can evacuate solemn contracts of marriage, upon the faith whereof matches are made, and settlements for maintenance of the married persons and their issue?"[30]

10–57   In Fountainhall's report of the case it is stated that "the generality of the Lords thought the taking a gratuitous discharge in such a manner was an act against common honesty and morality, and therefore reduced it simply *et in toto*; for if such pactions were any way sustained, then none had security by any provisions made to them in contracts of marriage."[31] It was not decided whether the reduction affected onerous third parties, although the matter was raised.[32] Kames referred to the English practice which treated the contract as voidable.[33]

---

[27] *Hepburn* v. *Seton* (1633) Mor. 9473; *Paton* v. *Paton* (1668) Mor. 9475; *Walker* v. *Walker* (1700) Mor. 9476; *McGuffock* v. *Blairs* (1709) Mor. 9483. An agreement to burden or dispone carried into effect after the marriage was also challengeable—*Pollock* v. *Campbell* (1718) Mor. 9489; *Russel* v. *Gordon* (1739) Mor. 9490.

[28] *Russel* v. *Gordon, supra.*

[29] Kames, *Principles of Equity*, Vol. 1, pp. 77 *et seq.*

[30] *Grieve* v. *Thomson* (1705) Mor. 9478 at p. 9479.

[31] *Ibid.* at p. 9480.

[32] *McGuffock* v. *Blairs, supra.*

[33] Kames, *Principles of Equity*, Vol. 1, p. 80.

58   This attack on *pacta contra fidem tabularum nuptialium* can be seen as
an extension of the concept of fraud. Although the facts on which the
relevant case law is based are not often likely to recur, because of the
increasing lack of popularity of marriage contracts, the case law illustrates unfair activities as a ground for challenge.

59   Another instance of a device which may be regarded either as fraudulent or as contrary to public policy is an agreement between a director
and managers of a company to divide between them a sum of money
belonging to the shareholders.[34] One may regard the agreement as
being *contra bonos mores* but equally one can support Lord McLaren's
reference to it as "a dishonest attempt to defraud a third person."[35]

Fraud and Facility and Circumvention

60   The emergence of the doctrine of facility and circumvention from fraud
is considered elsewhere.[36]

PLEADING A CASE OF FRAUD

61   Once it is established that the activities complained about come within
the definition of fraud, there are further hurdles for a person wishing to
plead fraud. These are (1) title to sue; (2) correctly averring and proving
that the fraud induced the contract; (3) making specific averments; and
(4) suing the correct defender for a competent remedy.

(1) Title to sue

In a case involving representations it was observed by Lord Pearson[37]:

> "But I see no reason why an action of deceit should not be com-
> petent at the instance of a shareholder against anyone who has
> defrauded him, provided he satisfies all the requirements which
> such an action imposes on him. The representations must have
> been made to him, or—if made to another—made for the purpose
> of being communicated to him, and have been so communicated.
> But if, being so made, they are acted upon by him to his loss, I
> know of no rule which would prevent him from suing for damages."

So it may not be possible for a shareholder of company Y to sue X
who contracted with Y, for loss caused by fraudulent misrepresentations
by X to Y.[38] On the other hand if the company has not suffered any loss
but a person has been induced to invest as a debenture holder by the
statements of a promoter of the company, the debenture holder may

---

[34] *Laughland* v. *Millar, Laughland & Co.* (1904) 6 F. 413.
[35] *Ibid.* at p. 417. The problem of contracts induced by bribes raises similar issues to this
case: *Mahesan* v. *Malaysia Government Officers' Co-operative Housing Society Ltd.* [1979]
A.C. 374.
[36] See Chap. 11.
[37] *Gillies* v. *Campbell, Shearer & Co.* (1902) 10 S.L.T. 289.
[38] *Gillies* v. *Campbell, Shearer & Co.*, *sup. cit.*; *Dunnett* v. *Mitchell* (1887) 15 R. 131.

have a title to sue the promoter.[39] These are exceptional instances. In the normal case the person who was defrauded has a clear title and interest to sue.

(2) The fraud must induce the contract

The fraud must induce the contract if the remedy of reduction of the contract is sought, but not in every case if only delictual damages are claimed.[40]

Bell saw a distinction between two types of fraud: "Hence the distinction of fraud into that *'quod causam dedit contractui'* and that *'quod tantum in contractum incidit'*. Fraud of the former kind annuls the contract; fraud of the latter species gives only an action for restitution or damages."[41]

Bell's distinction was criticised by Lord McLaren in his notes to the passage and it was doubted by Gloag.[42] Traces of this type of distinction are to be found in the case law,[43] and it is part of French law.[44] What is clear is that it is not enough that fraud precedes a contract.

In *Nisbet* v. *Kinnaird*[44a] there was, prior to a lease, an alleged misrepresentation of the amount of rent paid by a previous tenant. The court, with some dissents, thought that the tenant should have informed himself of the true rent and not relied on the assertion. Whether a tenant has such a duty of informing himself under the present law is doubtful, but the case illustrates that not all false and fraudulent statements in negotiation will invalidate the contract. A misrepresentation as to the place where a horse came from did not affect a sale.[45] A person who discovers the truth before the contract cannot rely on the fraud. As Lord Brougham put it[46]:

> "In order that the misrepresentation or the concealment . . . may be of any avail whatever, it must be *dolus dans locum contractui*, it must inure to the date of the contract. If one party misrepresents or conceals, however fraudulently, however wrongly, and however wickedly to another with whom he is treating, and if that other, notwithstanding the misrepresentation, discovers the truth, and notwithstanding the concealment, gets at the fact concealed, before he signs the contract, the misrepresentation and the concealment go for just absolutely nothing, because it is not *dolus qui dat locum contractui*."

---

[39] *Dunnett* v. *Mitchell* (1885) 12 R. 400; sequel (1887) 15 R. 131.

[40] See para. 10–20.

[41] Bell, *Comm.*, I,262.

[42] Gloag, p. 479.

[43] *Irvine* v. *Kirkpatrick* (1850) 7 Bell 186 at p. 237 *per* Lord Brougham; *Gillespie* v. *Russel* (1857) 18 D. 677 at p. 686 *per* Lord Curriehall; *Wardlaw* v. *Mackenzie* (1859) 21 D. 940 at p. 947 *per* Lord Provost Inglis. See also discussion in *Nielson* v. *Bonnar's Heirs* (1682) Bro.Sup., III,441.

[44] Zweigert and Kotz, *An Introduction to Comparative Law*, Vol. 11, p. 94.

[44a] (1692) Mor. 4872.

[45] *Geddes* v. *Pennington* (1817) 5 Dow 159.

[46] *Irvine* v. *Kirkpatrick* (1850) 7 Bell 186 at p. 237.

In general terms the pursuer must rely on the fraud as the reason for entering into the contract, not rely on his own judgment.[47] The fraud must be committed in respect of the act complained of, not fraud on a different occasion and for a different purpose.[48]

There is a suggestion that the problem of inducement should be viewed objectively.[49] Thus a party is not able to found on a representation which is "flimsy and transparent as well as general."[50]

It is sufficient that the fraud induces the contract. The various classes of error and the difficulties of the meaning of "essential" or "material" or "substantial" which infuse the law on error are not part of the law on fraud. Fraud is still relevant even if its effect is to induce non-essential error.[51]

(3) (a) **Averment of fraud.** Although historically there was a readiness to infer fraud and also a relaxation of the normal rules of evidence in proving fraud, it is settled law that there must be specific averments of fraud. In the words of Lord President McNeil[52]:

> "Now, assuredly, fraud is, in many cases, a sufficient ground for breaking down the usual rules of law, but not for breaking down this rule, that the parties must be very specific in stating the grounds of reduction. On the contrary, allegations of fraud render it peculiarly necessary to have directness of statement."

In another case the Lord President observed: "We must know precisely what the things are, and what the acts are which are alleged. What was it? Did he nod, or wink, or what was it that led them to believe?"[53]

And in another passage[54]:

> "But how did he make them believe it? What was it that he did or said? It is not enough to allege—you said something which led us to believe so and so. That is not enough. If an action is laid upon misrepresentation, the misrepresentation itself must be set forth; and then, when the misrepresentation is set forth, we will see whether it is such a statement as goes at all to support the conclusions of the

---

[47] *McLellan* v. *Gibson* (1843) 5 D. 1032; *A. W. Gamage* v. *Charlesworth's Tr.*, 1910 S.C. 257.

[48] *Howe* v. *City of Glasgow Bank* (1879) 6 R. 1194.

[49] *A. W. Gamage Ltd.* v. *Charlesworth's Trs.*, *sup. cit.* at p. 268 *per* Lord Johnston.

[50] *Ibid.* at p. 269.

[51] *Wardlaw* v. *Mackenzie* (1859) 21 D. 940 at p. 947 *per* Lord Justice-Clerk Inglis; *Hogg* v. *Campbell* (1864) 2 M. 848. For example, the fraud could relate to value or a state of solvency. The reason why the mistake induced by fraud has an affect on vitiating consent which is wider than the effect of error probably is not connected with a theory of consent. It is the policy of the law to deny the person who has committed fraud, the benefit of his deceit.

[52] *Gillespie* v. *Russel* (1857) 18 D. 677 at p. 684; see also *Gordon* v. *Gordon* (1758) Mor. 6678.

[53] *Drummond's Trs.* v. *Melville* (1861) 23 D. 450 at p. 463, a dictum echoed in an English case later in the same year; *Walters* v. *Morgan* 3 De G. F. & J. 718 at p. 724 *per* Lord Chancellor Campbell—"a nod or a wink, or a shake of the head, or a smile."

[54] *Ibid.* p. 462; See also *Halliday* v. *Morison* (1857) 21 D. 929 at p. 931 *per* Lord Ardmillan (Lord Ordinary); *Turner* v. *Tunnock's Trs.* (1864) 2 M. 509 at p. 512 *per* Lord Kinlock (Lord Ordinary).

action, yea or nay; and the party who is said to have made the misrepresentation will have an opportunity of explaining it. The words may admit of other meanings. They may not be such as ought to have led the parties to draw any such inference; and no person accused of fraudulent misrepresentation can be bound to go to trial, unless he is told what the fraudulent misrepresentation is that he is said to have made. Nothing could be more settled than that."

10–62   It is not enough to use the word "fraud" or say that by fraud the pursuer was induced to contract with the defender. The circumstances of the fraud must be set forth[55]:

"It is not enough for a party founding a reduction on the head of fraud, to state that fraud has been committed. Fraud is a general term, to be inferred from specific acts. The party, then, must state in what the fraud consists, and what the acts are from which the existence of fraud is to be inferred. And if the facts which he does state are clearly insufficient to support such an inference, or what is worse, are absolutely inconsistent with such an inference, the objection of irrelevancy must be sustained. Not that the general allegation of fraud is in itself irrelevant, but that the acts as averred are irrelevant to support the general allegation."[56]

Fraud and essential error require separate and distinct averments.[57]

(b) **Proof of fraud.** Fraud may be proved by parole evidence in cases where otherwise the mode of proof is restricted.[58] In a declarator of trust it may be proved *prout de jure* that consent was obtained by fraud.[59] Payment of money can be proved by parole when fraud is involved.[60] "The gates of justice are open wide in the tracing of fraud."[61] Fraud is an exception to the general rule which makes it incompetent to contradict, modify or explain writings by parole or other extrinsic evidence.[62]

(c) **Representations as to credit.** Writing is required for "all representations and assurances as to the character, conduct, credit, ability, trade or dealings of any person, made or granted to the effect or for the purpose of enabling such person to obtain credit, money, goods, or postponement of paying of debt, or of any other obligation demandable

---

[55] *Smith* v. *Watt's Trs.* (1854) 16 D. 372; *Ehrenbacher & Co.* v. *Kennedy* (1874) 1 R. 1131 at p. 1135 *per* Lord President Inglis.
[56] *Shedden* v. *Patrick* (1852) 24 Scot.Jur. 331 at p. 335 *per* Lord Fullerton giving the opinion of the court.
[57] *Hare* v. *Hopes* (1870) 8 S.L.R. 189.
[58] Walker and Walker, *Law of Evidence*, para. 152.
[59] *Marshall* v. *Lyell* (1859) 21 D. 514 at p. 521 *per* Lord Justice-Clerk Inglis (but the Blank Bonds and Trusts Act 1696 applies to a denial of the existence of the trust); *Wink* v. *Speirs* (1867) 6 M. 77.
[60] *British Bata Shoe Co. Ltd.* v. *Double M. Shah Ltd.*, 1981 S.L.T.(Notes) 5.
[61] *Tennent* v. *Tennent's Trs.* (1868) 6 M. 840 at p. 874 *per* Lord Ardmillan; (1870) 8 M.(H.L.) 10.
[62] Gloag, p. 365; Walker and Walker, para. 257; *Bell Bros. (H.P.) Ltd.* v. *Aitken*, 1939 S.C. 577 at p. 585 *per* Lord President Normand.

from him."[63] An oral and fraudulent representation which is covered by this statutory provision is of no effect and cannot be proved.[64] It is possible that some statements made in pursuance of a fraudulent scheme to induce the lending of money, cannot be founded on unless in writing, whereas other oral statements which are part of the same scheme, can be proved because they are not representations as to credit.[65]

The statutory limitation on the mode of proof was an extension to Scotland of the English Statute of Frauds.[66] The reason was the supposed inconvenience of having the liability for a representation altering according to whether Scots or English law applied.[67]

(4) Who is responsible for the fraud?

The person who committed the fraud is responsible for his acts. Can another be liable?

Although the issue has not received a full analysis in Scots law it is thought that X bears a responsibility for the fraud of Y (1) when a gratuitous benefit is conferred on X; (2) when X has vicarious liability for the actings of Y; and (3) when there is participation by X in Y's fraudulent scheme.

(a) **Gratuitous benefit.** Stair made an incidental reference to "that common ground of equity, *nemo debet ex alieno damno lucrari.*"[68] When Lord Shand was describing its effect on benefits gained by fraud he relied mainly on English authorities and observed:

> "It is a recognised principle both in the law of this country and in that of England that a gratuitous benefit conferred or obtained by one party and gained through the fraud of another cannot be retained by the person benefited, even though innocent of the fraud. The most familiar application of this principle is the case of legatees or beneficiaries taking under a settlement which has been procured by fraud, to which they were no parties, and of which they were entirely ignorant. They cannot retain a benefit so gained. But the principle is throughout the authorities limited to the case of benefits conferred or received gratuitously and does not apply where a valuable consideration has been given."[69]

---

[63] Mercantile Law Amendment Act Scotland 1856, s.6. In England the matter is governed by the Statute of Frauds Amendment Act 1828, s.6.

[64] *Clydesdale Bank Ltd.* v. *Paton* (1896) 23 R.(H.L.) 22; *Irving* v. *Burns*, 1915 S.C. 260; *Muir* v. *Burnside*, 1935 S.N. 13, 46. On non-fraudulent misrepresentation see *Union Bank of Scotland* v. *Taylor*, 1925 S.C. 835 which was not followed in *Andrew Oliver & Son Ltd.* v. *Douglas*, 1981 S.C. 192. In the latter case it was held that s.6 applied only to fraudulent representation.

[65] Cases in note above.

[66] See *Andrew Oliver & Son Ltd.* v. *Douglas, sup. cit.* On Scots law before the 1856 Act see *Campbell, Robertson & Co.* v. *Shepherd* (1776) 2 Pat. 399; Mor.App. 3, Fraud; *Park* v. *Gould* (1851) 13 D. 1049.

[67] Gloag and Irvine, *Rights in Security*, p. 723.

[68] Stair, I,vi,33.

[69] *Gibbs* v. *British Linen Co.* (1875) 4 R. 630 at p. 634. An example in relation to beneficiaries is *Taylor* v. *Tweedie* (1865) 3 M. 928. See also a case of caution with special facts. *Wardlaw* v. *Mackenzie* (1859) 21 D. 940.

This concept has been applied to principals who have benefited from the fraud of their agents[70] and has been discussed in a case of partnership.[71]

It has been held that a company cannot obtain the benefit of the fraud of their agent.[72] Where one person is to be liable for the fraud of another, it is necessary to specify the person who committed the fraud.[73]

(b) **Vicarious liability.** A person will be bound by the actings of his agent within the agent's authority: "a transaction which is fraudulent as between the agent and his employer will bind the latter, unless he can show that the recipient of the money did not transact in good faith with his agent."[74] A firm will be liable for the fraud of one of its partners committed in the course of the firm's business.[75] A person will not be affected by the fraud of others who are not his agents and so the question has arisen as to whether a person was an agent, and, if so, an agent of whom.[76] Nor will a principal be affected by unauthorised dealings by his agent, as when a solicitor forges deeds relating to his client's property.[77]

(c) **Participation in fraud.** Apart from gratuitous benefit, or liability for the actings of an agent, a person will not be liable for the fraud of another unless he participated in the fraud or was in bad faith.[78]

Reduction and Restitutio in Integrum

10–63   A contract induced by fraud is voidable, and not void. It is a condition of reduction that *restitutio in integrum* is possible.

10–64   *Restitutio in integrum* could not be made of shares purchased once the company had gone into liquidation,[79] or a railway had been constructed[80] or the article purchased had been resold[81] or the pursuer was unable to relieve the defender of obligations imposed on the defender.[82]

---

[70] *Traill* v. *Smith's Trs.* (1876) 3 R. 770; *Clydesdale Bank* v. *Paul* (1877) 4 R. 626.

[71] *New Mining Syndicate Ltd.* v. *Chalmers & Hunter*, 1912 S.C. 126, discussed in J. B. Miller, *The Law of Partnership in Scotland* (1973), pp. 328–332, where the conceptual basis of the law is examined.

[72] *Mair* v. *Rio Grande Rubber Estates Ltd.*, 1913 S.C.(H.L.) 74.

[73] *Thomson & Co.* v. *Pattison, Elder & Co.* (1895) 22 R. 432; *Smith & Houston Ltd.* v. *Metal Industries (Salvage) Ltd.*, 1953 S.L.T.(Notes) 73.

[74] *Thomson* v. *Clydesdale Bank Ltd.* (1893) 20 R.(H.L.) 59 at p. 61 *per* Lord Watson.

[75] Partnership Act 1890, s.10; J. B. Miller, *Partnership*, pp. 332–333.

[76] *Howe* v. *City of Glasgow Bank* (1879) 6 R. 1194; *Robb* v. *Gow Bros. & Gemmell* (1905) 8 F. 90.

[77] *Bowie's Trs.* v. *Watson*, 1913 S.C. 326; *Muir's Ex* v. *Craig's Tr.*, 1913 S.C. 349.

[78] *Ehrenbecher & Co.* v. *Kennedy* (1874) 1 R. 1131; *Gibbs* v. *British Linen Co.* (1875) 4 R. 630.

[79] *Addie* v. *Western Bank* (1867) 5 M.(H.L.) 80; *Houldsworth* v. *City of Glasgow Bank* (1880) 7 R.(H.L.) 53.

[80] *Boyd & Forrest* v. *Glasgow and South-Western Railway Co.*, 1914 S.C. 472; revd., 1915 S.C.(H.L.) 20.

[81] *Price & Pierce Ltd.* v. *Bank of Scotland*, 1910 S.C. 1095; 1912 S.C.(H.L.) 19; *MacLeod* v. *Kerr*, 1965 S.C. 253.

[82] *Hay* v. *Rafferty* (1899) 2 F. 302.

55 There must be limits to the requirement of *restitutio*. In almost every case there will have been some alteration of the parties' position since the contract. "For," as Gloag put it,[83] "some time must always have elapsed between the contract and the reduction, and that time cannot be restored." The concept of restitution must not be applied too literally.[84] The whole issues should be looked at very broadly and in an appropriate case a proof before answer will be allowed.[85] The condition for reduction of the contract is the restoration of the defender to his precontract position not the restoration of the party seeking reduction.[86]

56 The concept of *restitutio* also arises in cases of innocent misrepresentation but the operation of the concept may differ. A person who has committed fraud might not be able in bar of restitution to found on alterations to the subject-matter which he has been enabled by his fraud to carry out.[87] The remedy of rescission accompanied by *restitutio* is equitable and the court will be more flexible in exercising its discretionary powers in a case of fraud than in a case of innocent misrepresentation.[88]

57 Apart from instances of transmission to assignees and transmission to a third party which is gratuitous or *mala fide*, the general rule is that a third party can acquire an indefeasible title despite the fraud of his author. In other words, a contract induced by fraud is valid unless and until it is challenged and the contract cannot be voided if *restitutio in integrum* has become impossible by a third party acquiring a title to property which was the subject-matter of the contract.[89]

Void or Voidable?

58 The voidable nature of the contract was settled by Stair.[90] This has become one of the accepted canons of the law:

> "I think the whole matter is substantially solved by keeping in view that a contract induced by fraud is not void, but only voidable; and that it is the party defrauded who has the option either to void the contract or not to void it, as he thinks proper."[91]
> "It is very clear in law that a contract induced by fraud is not null and void, but voidable. It is valid until it is rescinded, and accordingly the party defrauded has in general the option, when he dis-

---

[83] *Contract*, p. 540.
[84] *Spence* v. *Crawford*, 1939 S.C.(H.L.) 52.
[85] *McGuiness* v. *Anderson*, 1953 S.L.T.(Notes) 1.
[86] *Spence* v. *Crawford*, *sup. cit.* at p. 70 *per* Lord Thankerton.
[87] *Spence* v. *Crawford*, *sup. cit.* at p. 69 *per* Lord Thankerton.
[88] *Ibid.* at p. 76 *per* Lord Wright.
[89] *Cf. Houldsworth* v. *City of Glasgow Bank* (1879) 6 R. 1164 at p. 1173 *per* Lord Deas; (on appeal (1880) 7 R.(H.L.) 53); *Smyth* v. *Muir* (1891) 19 R. 81, 89 *per* Lord Kinnear; *Tennent* v. *City of Glasgow Bank* (1879) 6 R. 554 *per* Lord President Inglis; affd. (1879) 6 R.(H.L.) 69.
[90] *Inst.*, I,ix,10: IV,xxxv,19, which are discussed *supra*.
[91] *Tennent* v. *City of Glasgow Bank*, *supra* at p. 561 *per* Lord Deas.

covers the fraud, of rescinding the contract or of affirming it. But he must do either one or other."[92]

10–69   Many other *dicta* support this proposition.[93] A later example of its operation which received the support of the House of Lords is *Price & Pierce Ltd. v. Bank of Scotland*.[94] A contract for sale of timber was induced by fraudulent misrepresentation as to solvency. Third parties obtained a title to the timber for value and in good faith. Lord Salvesen observed: "Rescission of the contract, however, cannot prejudice the rights of third parties previously acquired over the cargo in good faith, and for value . . . [95] On appeal Lord Kinnear stated:

> "The legal principle is perfectly clear and beyond dispute. It is well settled law that a contract induced by fraud is not void, but voidable at the option of a party defrauded. In other words, it is valid until it is rescinded. It follows that when third parties have acquired rights in good faith and for value, these rights are indefeasible."[96]

10–70   Lord President Dunedin thought that it was, "trite law that a contract induced by fraud is voidable and not void, and is good until rescinded."[97]

10–71   A more recent example of a third party acquiring a good title despite the fraud of his author is *Macleod* v. *Kerr*.[98]

10–72   Although it is the general rule that the contract induced by fraud is voidable and not void, yet there may be an exception. Whether fraud inducing essential error rendered the contract void was a point on which Stair was silent and it remains unsettled. It did, however, trouble Lord Justice-Clerk Inglis in *Wardlaw* v. *Mackenzie*.[99] In an *obiter dictum* he recognised that fraud varies in its effect.[1] His consideration of the topic is too lengthy to quote here but it is a *dictum* of considerable significance. Its effect is to say that fraud inducing error *in essentialibus* is an exception to the general rule that a contract induced by fraud is voidable. Such fraud subverts consent and the contract is a nullity. Furthermore, the editors of Bell's *Principles* added a passage commencing: "An obligation induced by fraud (in the absence of essential error) is not void, but only voidable on the election of the party defrauded."[2] *Mor-*

---

[92] *Smyth* v. *Muir*, *supra* at p. 89 *per* Lord Kinnear.
[93] Bell, *Comm.*, I,261; Prin., s.13A; *Williamson* v. *Sharp* (1851) 14 D. 127, esp. Lord Ordinary; *Wardlaw* v. *Mackenzie* (1859) 21 D. 940 at p. 947 *per* Lord Justice-Clerk Inglis; *Graham* v. *Western Bank* (1864) 2 M. 559; *Western Bank* v. *Addie* (1867) 5 M.(H.L.) 80.
[94] 1910 S.C. 1095; 1912 S.C.(H.L.) 19.
[95] 1910 S.C. 1095, 1099.
[96] *Ibid.*, p. 1106.
[97] *Ibid.*, p. 1117.
[98] 1965 S.C. 253 *cf. Graham* v. *Western Bank*, *supra*.
[99] (1859) 21 D. 940.
[1] at p. 947.
[2] *Prin.*, s.13A. This may have been under the influence of the English rule judging from the authorities cited; *cf.* the curious passage in Bell, *Comm.*, I,316 in which a contract induced by fraud is said to be void.

risson v. *Robertson*[3] might be an instance of fraud inducing essential error and rendering a contract void, but the meaning of the case is controversial.

3   It is probable that a distinction should be drawn between, on the one hand, fraud which induces consent, and thus renders the contract voidable, and, on the other hand, fraud which produces essential error and subverts consent, thus rendering the contract void.

CONTRACTING OUT OF FRAUD

4   It is not possible by the terms of the contract to exclude liability for fraud inducing the contract. The victim of the fraud has been subject to deception and cannot have the knowledge and form the consent required to excuse the fraud. Lord Shaw put it this way[4]:

> "For it is a sound principle, to which I do not hesitate to give adhesion, that the terms of a contract, however far they may extend in putting a burden of risks and speculations upon the contractor, cannot be founded upon as a protection against fraud of either contracting party. It could not be so, in my opinion, even although the contract was expressed in such a particular. The law excludes from the range of agreement what is openly contrary to legal principle and to honest dealing."

5   At an earlier stage in that case, Lord Justice-Clerk Macdonald had observed[5]:

> "Now, I am very clearly of opinion that no clauses such as are contained in this contract, excluding contractors from founding on inaccuracies or discrepancies, or the like, can protect the party with whom they contract, where there is misrepresentation such as we have here. Inaccuracies and discrepancies occurring by honest mistake as to details may well be excluded as grounds of challenge by such clauses. But if there is unfair dealing, as I hold there is here, a party cannot take benefit by his own fraud, or reckless conduct *quod aequiparatur dolo*."

6   While a person cannot contract out of liability for his own fraud, it is an open question whether he can exclude liability for the fraud of his employees or agents. If the contract is obtained by fraud, it is thought that the general rule will apply. A person could not obtain benefit from the fraud of his employees or agents and from the contract which was produced. Fraud can, however, arise after a contract is entered into. Delivery or payment may be induced by fraud. A loss may be caused by

---

[3] 1908 S.C. 332, discussed *supra*, *s.v.* "Error," at paras. 9–82 to 9–84.
[4] *Boyd & Forrest* v. *Glasgow and South-Western Rly. Co.*, 1915 S.C.(H.L.) 20 at pp. 35 and 36. See also *Pearson* v. *Dublin Corporation* [1907] A.C. 351.
[5] *Boyd & Forrest* v. *Glasgow and South-Western Rly. Co.*, 1911 S.C. 33 at p. 61; at p. 76 Lord Ardwall followed *Pearson* v. *Dublin Corporation*.

fraud. It is possible by an exclusion clause to contract out of liability for the deliberate acts of others.[6] In this context should fraud be treated like any other intentional delict? The answer to the question is undecided.

PERSONAL BAR AND FRAUD

10–77 A plea based on fraud may be barred by mora and taciturnity, homologation or adoption.[7] These are aspects of personal bar which are discussed elsewhere.[8]

PRESCRIPTION AND FRAUD

10–78 Lord Brougham was of the view that: "No time will run as a common law limitation against fraud."[9] Although some authority might support this view[10] the preferable approach seems to be that the plea of fraud was subject to the long negative prescription.[11]

10–79 The law is now governed by the Prescription and Limitation (Scotland) Act 1973. An obligation arising from liability to make reparation prescribes in five years.[12] This would appear to include a claim of damages for fraud, which is a delictual claim[13] and which the Institutional writers discussed in the context of making reparation.[14] Section 7 of the Act extinguishes an obligation by a prescriptive period of 20 years. The right to seek reduction of a contract because of fraud is not easily described as an "obligation." Section 15(2) defines an obligation as including a correlative right, but it remains difficult to determine on whom the obligation lies. More help may be obtained from section 8 which extinguishes rights relating to property after 20 years.

10–80 Even if, however, the view is taken that reduction is barred after 20 years under either section 7 or section 8, the issue remains confused because reduction may be combined with restitution. An obligation of restitution is subject to the five year prescription,[15] but it is arguable that this applies only to restitution as an aspect of unjustified enrichment. The result is probably that reduction and restitution arising from fraud are subject to a 20 year prescription, but the statute is not as clearly drafted on this point as might have been wished.

---

[6] *Photo Production Ltd.* v. *Securicor Transport Ltd.* [1980] A.C. 827.

[7] *e.g. Rigg* v. *Durward & Thom* (1716) Mor.App. 2, Fraud; *A. W. Gamage Ltd.* v. *Charlesworth's Tr.*, 1910 S.C. 257.

[8] See Chap. 23.

[9] *Irvine* v. *Kirkpatrick* (1850) 7 Bell 186 at p. 217.

[10] *Sinclair* v. *Sinclair* (1781) Mor. 6725; *Hume* v. *Duncan* (1831) 5 W. & S. 43.

[11] *Home* v. *Ker* (1733) Mor. 10736; *Cubbison* v. *Hyslop* (1837) 16 S. 112 at p. 119 *per* Lord Corehouse; Napier, *Prescription*, pp. 608–609; Gloag, *Contract*, p. 737.

[12] s.6 and Sched. 1.

[13] para. 10–11.

[14] para. 10–12.

[15] s.6 and Sched. 1.

1   Obligations on a trustee to make reparation or for fraudulent breach
of trust are imprescriptible.[16]

EFFECT OF FRAUD ON THIRD PARTIES

2   The effect of fraud on creditors is quite different from the effect on
singular successors.[17] Creditors who take property as a result of fraud
are subject to the special rules developed by the law to deal with transactions by insolvents. A third party who acquires a gratuitous benefit
from fraud or who is participating in the fraud is also in a different position from a singular successor.[18]

3   Stair adopted a complex attitude to the effect of fraud on singular successors. It was an attitude much more complex than necessitated by the
reported case law. If one ignores a possibly inconsistent passage,[19]
Stair's treatment of fraud was that in heritable rights fraud is not relevant against singular successors who are not partakers of the fraud; in
moveable rights onerous purchasers are not affected by the fraud of
their authors; but in personal rights "the fraud of authors is relevant
against singular successors, though not partaking nor conscious of the
fraud, when they purchased; because assignees are but procurators,
albeit *in rem suam*."[20] This distinction was followed by Bankton[21] and
was probably first recognised by the court in 1742.[22]

4   The distinction and authority for it was discussed in *Irvine* v. *Osterbye*
in 1755.[23] A dispute arose in a multiplepoinding between insurers and
an onerous assignee. The assignee pleaded that:

> "*Dolus auctoris non nocet successori ex titulo oneroso* prevails
> with us, in the case of one purchasing a real estate from a person
> infeft, or moveables which the seller neither stole nor got by rob-
> bery, or of one purchasing bills of exchange for value; the same rule
> must obtain, by parity of reason, in the case of a fair purchaser of
> personal rights."

5   Stair, it was argued, was repugnant to the statute 1621 on bankruptcy
and the decision in 1671 of *Crichton* v. *Crichton*.[24]

6   The insurers argued that bonds were different from the purchase of
real estate, purchase of moveables and bills of exchange. In the case of
bonds the rule was *assignatus utitur jure auctoris*. Stair and *Burden* v.

---

[16] Sched. 3.
[17] See the distinction explained in Bell, *Comm.*, I,309.
[18] See para. 10–62.
[19] Stair, IV,xl,28.
[20] IV,xl,21. See also I,ix,10; IV,xxxv,19; I,ix,15.
[21] Bankt., I,257,59; I,259,65.
[22] *Burden* v. *Whitefoord*, (1742) Elch. 11, Fraud. It had earlier been decided that an
assignee was affected by some defences pleadable against his author; *Scot* v. *Montgomery*
(1663) M. 10187; *Keith and Glenkindie* v. *Irvin* (1635) M. 10, 185.
[23] (1755) Mor. 1715.
[24] (1671) Mor. 4886.

Whitefoord[25] were in point. *Crichton* v. *Crichton* could be distinguished because it concerned a real right. In the result, the court preferred the insurers to the bond.

10–87   The matter was re-argued in 1772. It was argued that Stair and Bankton were wrong, but without success.[25a] Kames thought the distinction was based on a misunderstanding of the nature of assignation in Stair's time, but when Kames wrote the law had been settled.[26]

10–88   Some reasons have been suggested for the distinction. Stair states that assignees are but procurators, albeit *in rem suam*. Fraud does not affect singular successors as to feudal rights,

> " . . . the reason whereof is, to secure land-rights, and that purchasers be not disappointed . . . " "Yet in moveables, purchasers are not quarrellable upon the fraud of their authors, if they did purchase for an onerous equivalent cause. The reason is, because moveables must have a current course of traffic, and the buyer is not to consider how the seller purchased, unless it were by theft or violence, which the law accounts as *labes reales*, following the subject to all successors, otherwise there would be the greatest encouragement to theft and robbery."[27]

Bankton added nothing to this reasoning and, indeed, is less explicit.[28] Erskine adopted Stair's reasoning.[29] It was argued for the insurers in *Irvine* v. *Osterbye*[30] that "the case of bonds is different; they are not the proper objects of commerce, they are securities for money, and are transmissible only by the form of assignation and procuratory." That is an argument which did not go beyond the requirements of the case. In *McDonells* v. *Carmichael*[31] it was argued that the purchaser of a personal right "does not purchase upon the faith of records, but he relies upon the faith and credit of the person with whom he contracts" and that "in the purchase of every personal right, the purchaser can have no earthly security to rely upon, except the credit and good faith of his author." The doctrine was said to be "clearly founded in expediency" but the arguments adduced in the case are not convincing. The good faith of the author is insufficient for that author's title may in turn be tainted by the fraud of another.

10–89   What will probably be the last attempt to challenge the distinction was made in the famous case of *Scottish Widows' Fund* v. *Buist*.[32] Rather

---

[25] *Sup. cit.*

[25a] *McDonells* v. *Carmichael* (1772) Mor. 4974.

[26] Kames, *Elucidations*, pp. 13, 14.

[27] *Inst.* IV, xl, 21. Spuilzie was a *vitium reale*; *Hay* v. *Leonard*, 1677 Mor. 10286.

[28] Bankt., I,257,59.

[29] Ersk., *Inst.* III,v,10. *Cf.* McLaren's curious note in Bell, *Comm.*, I,309 that the doctrine of Stair and Erskine is "obsolete." It may be that McLaren intended to refer to Stair's reliance on the doctrine that assignees were procurators.

[30] *Sup. cit.*

[31] *Sup. cit.*

[32] (1876) 3 R. 1078. The action was based both on breach of warranty and on fraud in entering into an insurance contract.

than say that the doctrine did not exist, the defenders argued that there were exceptions to it. Lord President Inglis replied[33]:

> "It appears to me to be long ago settled in the law of Scotland—and I have never heard of any attempt to disturb the doctrine[34]—that in a personal obligation, whether contained in a unilateral deed or in a mutual contract, if the creditor's right is sold to an assignee for value, and the assignee purchases in good faith, he is nevertheless subject to all the exceptions and pleas pleadable against the original creditor. That is the doctrine laid down in all our institutional writers, and it has been affirmed in many cases. But it seems to be said that this doctrine admits of some exceptions. Now, that I entirely dispute. I think the true view of the law is that these things that are called exceptions are classes of cases to which the doctrine does not apply. The doctrine does not apply to the transmission of heritable estate; the doctrine does not apply in the sale of corporeal moveables. But within the class of cases to which the doctrine is applicable—I mean the transmission to assignees of a creditor's right in a personal obligation—I know of no exception to the application of the doctrine."

-90   It at first sight appears anomalous that a transfer of incorporeal moveables should transfer invalidities in a way which a transfer of corporeal moveables or heritage does not. In fact there is a good reason for the distinction.[35] The rule *assignatus utitur iure auctoris* operates as a protection for the debtor. Assignation, unlike *traditio*, operates in a tripartite situation with the debtor being inactive. The debtor has no control over when and to whom the debt may be assigned. He should, therefore, not be prejudiced by an assignation. The transfer of a corporeal moveable or heritable property is in a different situation. The transferor is not inactive. He agrees to a change in ownership of the property. He has a weaker claim to have his rights preserved than the inactive debtor.

LAW REFORM

-91   The Scottish Law Commission produced a Memorandum which asked for comments on possible changes in the law on fraud.[36] The Commission suggest that it might be superfluous to retain "fraud" as a separate category among the factors which vitiate consent. Fraud would remain relevant as a ground for delictual action, and also as an aspect of the law of error.

---

[33] *Ibid.*, p. 1082.

[34] *McDonells* v. *Carmichael, supra*; *Irvine* v. *Osterbye, supra* might be suggested.

[35] See further arguments in Scot.Law Com. No. 42, *Defective Consent and Consequential Matters* (1978), Vol. II, paras. 3, 137 *et seq.*

[36] Memo. No. 42, *Defective Consent and Consequential Matters* (1978).

CHAPTER 11

FACILITY AND CIRCUMVENTION AND UNDUE INFLUENCE

FACILITY AND CIRCUMVENTION—HISTORY OF THE DOCTRINE

11–01 Facility and circumvention developed from the Scots law of fraud, but the period of gestation was long and troubled. Up to the middle of the nineteenth century there was much confusion between fraud on the one hand and facility and circumvention on the other. The early position appears to have been that in a case based on facility, it was necessary to show fraud to obtain reduction of the deed, but fraud was readily inferred. This contrasted with other areas of the law in which it became established that fraud by itself needed specific averments and clear proof. Eventually the contrast between the two approaches to fraud became too great, and facility and circumvention emerged as a separate doctrine with its own rules. It still, however, bears with it some of the difficulties of its birth, which is why a historical analysis is necessary.

11–02 Facility and circumvention was not recognised as a separate doctrine by Stair. He considered deeds by facile persons under the heading of extortion or force and fear.[1] Erskine[2] and Bell[3] did not clearly distinguish facility and circumvention from fraud. The reason is that the existence of facility enabled the courts to infer fraud and so use fraud as the ground of reduction.

Fraud presumed

11–03 In the early law a deed from a dying person which was not read by her was held on those two facts to have been elicited by fraud and circumvention.[4] If a weak person entered a grossly unequal bargain, fraud and circumvention might be presumed,[5] but the attitude of the Court of Session must have been difficult to predict, because six days previously a different result was reached on apparently similar facts.[6] The attitude of presuming fraud was repeated in the middle of the eighteenth century. In *Mackie and Husband* v. *Maxwell*[7] an heiress was abandoned to drunkenness and it was in any person's power by bribing her with a few shillings to make her accept a bill of any sum or dispone any part of her

---

[1] Stair, I,ix,8.
[2] Ersk., IV,i,27.
[3] Bell, *Prin.* (4th ed.), ss.13, 14; *Comm.*, I,136.
[4] *Galloway* v. *Duff* (1672) Mor. 4959.
[5] *Maitland* v. *Fergusson* (1729) Mor. 4956; affd. by House of Lords, 1 Pat. 73.
[6] *Gordon* v. *Ross* (1729) Mor. 4956. The report is brief.
[7] (1752) Mor. 4963.

lands. She was persuaded to transfer her lands for an onerous consideration to her sister. Her sister thereupon brought a reduction of dispositions previously granted to innkeepers. Upon the facts the court had no difficulty in finding fraud and circumvention relevant and proved. Although the court may have called the ground of reduction "fraud and circumvention" that was not what had happened. There was no evidence that the heiress had been imposed on or circumvented in any way. She granted her dispositions voluntarily, well knowing what she did.

The reporter felt that the reason for reduction was that: "It is certainly unjust to take advantage of weak persons, who cannot resist certain temptations, and to make use of such temptations to rob them of their goods." This is to be contrasted with the situation in which "a weak person makes a deed, perhaps foolish, but voluntary, in favour of any person who is entirely passive, such a deed admits of a very different construction. It is not reducible, however strong the lesion may be." The reporter was Lord Kames who repeats his comments on the case in his *Principles of Equity*.[8]

The disappearance of fraud

-04   A change of attitude in the court is apparent by 1777 from Tait's report of *Robertson* v. *Fraser*.[9] He mentions two cases in which the Lords seem to have held facility and lesion, without fraud, sufficient ground for reduction. In *Robertson's* case, the Lord Ordinary, Lord Monboddo, refused a proof in a reduction of a transaction in which it was alleged that an unequal bargain was made by a weak woman. He did so apparently on the grounds that insufficient averments of fraud were made. The Lords reversed his decision. The report indicates that some Court of Session judges were prepared to hold facility and lesion, without fraud, sufficient for a challenge of a transaction.

-05   At the beginning of the nineteenth century the law was settled by decisions of the House of Lords, who had acquiesced in the earlier readiness to infer fraud.[10] A deed by a person weak in intellect, although with capacity to contract, could be reduced if the person did not fully understand the deed.[11] Deeds by a person who was capable of disposing of her estates were reduced, because she was not in such a state of mind as to enable her to judge correctly with regard to the effect of the deeds. There was no evidence of undue influence by the defenders.[12] This is a high-water mark in the development of this branch

---

[8] Kames, *Principles of Equity*, Vol. 1, p. 68. Kames may have taken part in the decision. He was raised to the Bench on February 4, 1752, and Morison gives the case the date of November 24, 1752.

[9] 5 B.S. 566. *Cf. Scott* v. *Jerdons* (1789) Mor. 4964.

[10] *Maitland* v. *Ferguson* (1729) 1 Pat. 73.

[11] *White* v. *Ballantyne* (1823) 1 Shaw's App. 472.

[12] *Gibson and Others* v. *Watson and Others* (1823) 2 W. & S. 648. Thus the decision goes much further than the reporter in *Mackie and Husband, supra*.

of the law. It comes close to saying that ignorance of the effect of the deed is a ground for reduction, but stops short of this as a general principle by applying that idea only in cases in which the granter was of weak mind. Conversely, a weak mind was of itself not sufficient to set aside a deed, but if combined with circumstances indicating that an unfair advantage had been taken, the deed would be reduced.[13]

11–06   The need to label the transaction as fraudulent was slow in disappearing. In *McNeill* v. *Moir*[14] the argument on a deed granted by an infirm man of 80 proceeded on the basis that the transaction was so grossly unequal and irrational, "that it was plain that it could only have been brought about by a fraudulent advantage having been taken of his facility."[15] In *Scott* v. *Wilson*[16] Lord Pitmilly insisted on proof of fraud and circumvention, as well as facility and lesion. If facility and lesion were great, slighter proof of fraud and circumvention would suffice, but that was the only limitation which he would allow.[17] The pursuer moved for a new trial on the grounds *inter alia* that separate proof of fraud was not necessary but it might be inferred from facility and lesion. The new trial was granted, but this argument is not mentioned in the court's opinion.

11–07   In retrospect it is clear that Lord Pitmilly's view could not last. The readiness with which fraud had been inferred in cases involving facile persons made it a very different form of fraud from that required in the absence of facility. When it was settled that fraud needed specific averments,[18] it must have been difficult to reconcile this with cases of facility in which the proof of fraud was absent, but the existence of fraud was inferred.

Distinguishing fraud from facility and circumvention

11–08   The distinction between fraud on the one hand and facility and circumvention on the other was recognised in *Clunie* v. *Stirling*.[19] The case involved a dispute over the form of issues between the Court of Session and the House of Lords. In *Clunie* there were separate issues of fraud on

---

[13] *McNeill* v. *Moir* (1824) 2 Shaw's App. 206. *Vide Morrison* v. *Morrison* (1841) 4 D. 337, in which facility but not fraud was proved.

[14] *Supra.*

[15] *Ibid.*, p. 212; *vide McDiarmid* v. *McDiarmid* (1826) 4 S. 583, (1828) 3 W. & S. 37, where a daughter and her husband obtained from her father, who was 83 years old, facile and addicted to alcohol, a deed lacking in consideration. The House of Lords supported the view of the Court of Session that the transaction was an imposition and fraud. There was, however, an element of fraudulent misrepresentation on the need to execute the deed.

[16] (1825) 3 Mur. 518.

[17] *Ibid.*, pp. 526 *et seq.*

[18] *Shedden* v. *Patrick* (1852) 24 Scot.Jur. 331; *Smith* v. *Watt's Trs.* (1854) 16 D. 372; *Gillespie* v. *Russel* (1857) 18 D. 677; *Drummond's Trs.* v. *Melville* (1861) 23 D. 450.

[19] (1854) 17 D. 15.

the one hand, and facility and circumvention on the other. The separation of the issues was a change from usual practice and had been prompted by the House of Lords.[20] Under the issue of facility and circumvention Lord Justice-Clerk Hope, with Lord Wood concurring, rejected the contention that a distinct act of circumvention must be proved. Circumvention could be inferred from the circumstances of a bad bargain made by a facile person. Lord Cockburn observed that: "circumvention sometimes amounts to fraud, and some cases of fraud are cases of simple circumvention; and the two pass into each other by such shadowy gradations that they are often difficult to be distinguished."[21] The distinction between the concepts had arisen in the form of the issue to be tried by a jury, and the form of that issue has continued to reflect the problems of the substantive law.

–09   The issue adopted in the middle of the nineteenth century was:

> "Whether, on or about   the pursuer was weak and facile in mind, and easily imposed on; and whether the defenders, or any of them, by themselves, or by another or others, taking advantage of the pursuer's said facility and weakness did, by fraud or circumvention, procure deed X, to the lesion of the pursuer?"[22]

–10   The reference to "by themselves, or by another or others" was later dropped as unnecessary because of the development of vicarious responsibility,[23] and the word "procure" could be altered according to circumstances.[24]

–11   Not only was this the usual form of issue, but the Court of Session refused to alter it.[25] Lord Justice-Clerk Inglis thought that the precise terms of the issue should never be departed from. He wished to adhere to the exact words of the style.[26] When the House of Lords criticised the practice of alternative issues,[27] Lord Ardmillan gave effect to this criticism by altering "fraud or circumvention" to "fraud and circumvention" but he was reversed on appeal to the Inner House.[28] Nine years later

---

[20] *Ibid.* at p. 18 *per* Lord Justice-Clerk Hope. The case which caused this is not mentioned but presumably it was *Marianski* v. *Cairns* (1852) 1 Macq. 212 which, with *Irvine* v. *Kirkpatrick* (1850) 7 Bell App. 186, shows that the House of Lords was hostile to the practice. The Court of Session were unyielding and in *Mann* v. *Smith* (1861) 23 D. 435, and *Love* v. *Marshall* (1870) 9 M. 291 under Lord Justice-Clerk and then Lord President Inglis, the debate continued.

[21] *Ibid.*, p. 20.

[22] *McCulloch* v. *McCracken* (1857) 20 D. 206; *Mann* v. *Smith* (1861) 23 D. 435. In *Mann*, Lord Justice-Clerk Inglis indicated that this form of issue had been in use for a long time; *ibid.* at p. 437 and see the arguments of parties. The terms were settled in an unreported case—*Bryson* v. *Bryson*—*vide Taylor* v. *Tweedie* (1865) 3 M. 928 at p. 931 *per* Lord Justice-Clerk Inglis.

[23] *Taylor* v. *Tweedie, supra* at p. 931 *per* Lord Justice-Clerk Inglis.

[24] *Ibid.*, and see *Home* v. *Hardy* (1842) 4 D. 1184.

[25] *Mann* v. *Smith, supra*; *Taylor* v. *Tweedie, supra*.

[26] *Taylor* v. *Tweedie, supra* at p. 930.

[27] *Marianski* v. *Cairns, supra*.

[28] *Mann* v. *Smith, supra*.

Lord President Inglis pointed out that the form of issue which he approved did not cause the confusion which some alternative issues could.[29] Lord Deas indicated that the House of Lords misunderstood Scottish practice.[30] Lord Ardmillan, by now elevated to the First Division, thought that "fraud and circumvention" and "fraud or circumvention" meant the same thing.[31]

11–12   The controversy over terminology continues. Lord Anderson stated in 1931:

> "It was made quite clear on the authorities that the proper form of issue now is the issue of fraud *and* circumvention. That form of issue seems to imply that a pursuer under it requires to establish both fraud and something else in the shape of circumvention. But I am not sure that this is the correct view, despite the form which the issue takes, and I think that is borne out by the citation from Stair,[32] which was read by your Lordship in the chair. In other words, the view I take is that there are not two distinct species of fraudulent conduct put to the jury, but that circumvention is a species of the genus fraud. In my opinion it is a *nomen juris* given to that form of fraud which takes the form of dishonest impetration of a will. But, while that is so, there is no doubt that this is the standardised form of issue. Fraud *and* circumvention united conjunctively must be in the issue. That being the form of issue, these terms ought to be found in a plea in law; and, further, I think that the words ought also to be in the averments."[33]

11–13   Lord Anderson did not state the authorities on which he founded. With one exception, all the cases cited to the court in which the terms of the issues are reported proceeded on issues of "fraud or circumvention,"[34] and in one of these cases there is the authority of Lord President Dunedin, if more authority is needed, to describe that form of issue as "recognised."[35]

---

[29] *Love* v. *Marshall* (1870) 9 M. 291 at p. 294.

[30] *Ibid.* at p. 295.

[31] *Ibid.* at p. 296; *vide Mann* v. *Smith, supra* at p. 436, in which he tried to distinguish fraud from circumvention.

[32] Stair, I,x,8.

[33] *McDougal* v. *McDougal's Trs.*, 1931 S.C. 102 at p. 116.

[34] *Munro* v. *Strain* (1874) 1 R. 1039 at p. 1040; *Horsburgh* v. *Thomson's Trs.*, 1912 S.C. 267—issues reported in 49 S.L.R. 257, 259; *Lord Advocate* v. *Davidson's J. F.*, 1921 2 S.L.T. 267; *Gibson's Exr.* v. *Anderson*, 1925 S.C. 774 at p. 775—the pursuer's plea-in-law stated "fraud and circumvention"; *Ross* v. *Gosselin's Exr.*, 1926 S.C. 325 at p. 329—*cf.* plea in law. The junior counsel for the pursuer was the same as in *Gibson's Exr, supra,* which may explain the consistent discrepancy. The exception is the early case of *Clunie* v. *Stirling* (1854) 17 D. 15 which had unusual issues. "Fraud or circumvention" will be found in many cases, *e.g., Home* v. *Hardy* (1842) 4 D. 1184; *McCulloch* v. *McCracken* (1857) 20 D. 206; *McKellar* v. *McKellar* (1861) 24 D. 143; *Morrison* v. *Maclean's Trs.* (1862) 24 D. 625; *Taylor* v. *Tweedie* (1865) 3 M. 928; *McCallum* v. *Graham* (1894) 21 R. 824. In some instances "fraud and circumvention" has been used—*Buchanan* v. *Heugh* (1858) 20 D. 947.

[35] *Horsburgh* v. *Thomson's Trs., supra* at p. 273; Lords Dundas and Johnston concurred.

-14   Despite this Lord Anderson's view has been followed twice, although on both occasions the point does not seem to have been argued.[36]

AVERMENT AND PROOF OF FACILITY AND CIRCUMVENTION

-15   It is necessary to show:

(1) Facility

Insanity is different in effect from facility. This statement in 1824 does not represent modern Scots law: "The question then is, whether the degree of facility, together with the imposition or imposture proved in this case, is such as to render this not the deed of Mrs. Thomson."[37]

-16   To plead that a deed is not that of a granter raises the question of capacity which is distinct from that of facility and circumvention.[38] The concepts are related because the question is whether the mental state has passed beyond the line which separates facility and insanity,[39] an issue of "not the deed" being allowed only where there are averments of mental derangement amounting to insanity.[40] If there is insanity, the degree of alleged imposition is irrelevant.

-17   It follows that it is illogical to answer both an issue of "not the deed" and an issue of circumvention and facility in the affirmative.[41] The issue of circumvention and facility assumes the presence of capacity. If the only averments on the state of mind of the granter of a deed are to the effect that he did not know what he was doing, that presents a case of incapacity rather than facility and circumvention.[42]

-18   It is not possible to state the degree of facility which is required. This is because facility is only one of the elements in a challenge based on facility and circumvention. The degree of facility depends on the degree of circumvention. The greater the one the lower the standard required of the other.[43] For example, an averment of facility in general terms was given sufficient specification by reference to the old age of the pursuer, the weakness of his mental facilities, improper and unfair practices in support of misrepresentations and repeated solicitations.[44] On the other hand a will by a facile person, which was of a reasonable character,

---

[36] *Bremner* v. *Bremner*, 1939 S.L.T. 448 at p. 450 *per* Lord Russell; *Mackay* v. *Campbell*, 1966 S.C. 237 at p. 250 *per* Lord Justice-Clerk Grant; on appeal 1967 S.C.(H.L.) 53.

[37] *Clark* v. *Spence* (1824) 3 Mur. 450 at p. 477 *per* L.C.C. Adam; *vide* the use of the word "capacity" in the context of facility in *Home* v. *Hardy* (1842) 4 D. 1184 at p. 1187.

[38] *Cf. Morrison* v. *Morrison* (1841) 4 D. 337; *Morrison* v. *Maclean's Trs.* (1862) 24 D. 625.

[39] *Gibson's Exr.* v. *Anderson*, 1925 S.C. 774 at p. 786 *per* Lord Blackburn.

[40] *Bremner* v. *Bremner*, 1939 S.L.T. 448 at p. 449 *per* Lord Russell.

[41] *Spring* v. *Martin's Trs.*, 1910 S.C. 1087, in which the authorities are reviewed.

[42] *Fraser* v. *Irvine's Exr.*, 1924 S.L.T. 114.

[43] *Munro* v. *Strain* (1874) 1 R. 1039.

[44] *Bremner* v. *Bremner*, 1939 S.L.T. 448.

could not be challenged without clear and specific averments of circum-vention.[45]

11–19   Facility usually arises from some weakness of the faculties caused by age or illness. It has arisen in a case of intoxication.[46] Specific instances of facility need not be proved if there is proof of a general lack of will-power.[47] Facility may arise in relation to particular transactions, as when it is combined with the domination of professional advisers.[48]

11–20   Facility alone, however, is insufficient.[49]

(2) Fraud and circumvention

11–21   Fraud in the usual sense would be a ground for reduction by itself. When fraud has to be combined with facility and lesion as a ground for reduction, it is obvious that "fraud" has a special meaning. Lord Black-burn stated: "It is perhaps a little unfortunate that the word 'fraud' should always be included in this issue as a mere matter of form. But 'fraud or circumvention' has a distinct meaning in our law, and can be established by evidence far short of that required to establish a mere charge of fraud."[50]

11–22   He pointed out that distinction by quoting an unreported charge of Lord Kyllachy:

> " . . . the meaning of the issue being that you have the question put to you whether, facility existing, there had been either distinct machinations, tricks, importunities, solicitations, even suggestions, towards the testator while the testator's facility was such that she was not in a position to resist—not likely to be in a position to resist. It is not necessary that there should be deceit. It is enough that there should be solicitation, pressure, importunity, even in some cases, suggestion. The degree of circumvention would depend on the degree of facility."[51]

11–23   It is unfortunate that, in its most recent consideration of this topic, the House of Lords has indicated that where the granter of the deed is alive, circumvention requires proof of deceit or dishonesty.[52] The case was a unique one in that the party alleged to be suffering from weakness and facility of mind was the defender, and facility was transient and tempor-

---

[45] *McDougal* v. *McDougal's Trs.*, 1931 S.C. 102.

[46] *Jackson* v. *Pollock* (1900) 8 S.L.T. 267.

[47] *Gibson's Exr.* v. *Anderson*, 1925 S.C. 774.

[48] *Munro* v. *Strain, supra*. See also "Undue influence," paras. 11–30 *et seq.*

[49] *Morrison* v. *Maclean's Trs.* (1862) 24 D. 625; *Liston* v. *Cowan* (1865) 3 M. 1041.

[50] *Gibson's Exr.* v. *Anderson*, 1925 S.C. 774 at p. 788.

[51] *Ibid.* The case is *Parnie* v. *MacLean. Cf.* the dissenting opinion of Lord Justice-Clerk Alness who equated circumvention to dishonesty. In *Gibson's Exr.* a testamentary and non-testamentary document were challenged and it was not suggested that differing rules applied to the two documents. *Cf.* the doctrine of undue influence *infra* in which there may be a difference, and *Mackay* v. *Campbell*, 1967 S.C.(H.L.) 53, in which the House of Lords said that there was a difference between the challenge of a deed of a person who is dead and one who is alive.

[52] *Mackay* v. *Campbell, supra*.

ary, and indeed the averments of facility were of very doubtful relevance. Such a case is in that grey area in which facility and circumvention merge into fraud. It is not the typical case of facility and circumvention, and it is suggested that it should not be treated as having general application. The case can be explained by reference to an earlier dictum of Lord Sorn:

> "In circumstances which do not lend themselves to the suggestion of impetration, it might be that the Court would refuse to entertain an action in the absence of some specific averment of circumvention. On the other hand, where circumstances do lend themselves to the suggestion, the general averment may be treated as enough to entitle the aggrieved person to have the matter tried out. Were it otherwise, you might have a case in which the surrounding circumstances all pointed irresistibly to impetration and yet in which the aggrieved party would have no remedy because, not being privy to the fraud, he could not specify the actual form of suasion used."[53]

-24　　There should, however, be some averment of the form of circumvention alleged to have been used to show the character of the influence on the facile person, if not the particular arts or wiles employed.[54]

-25　　Despite the use of the term "fraud and circumvention" it is not necessary to prove two elements, fraud on the one hand and circumvention on the other.[55] The essence of fraud and circumvention is an imposition which takes advantage of facility, as the terms of the jury issue show. The *Encyclopaedia of Scottish Legal Styles* gives as the form of issue[56]:

> "Whether at the date of the deed No.　of process A.B. (design) was weak and facile in mind and easily imposed upon and whether the defender taking advantage of the said weakness and facility did by fraud and circumvention impetrate and obtain the said deed from the said A.B. to his lesion?"

-26　　If the answer to that question is in the affirmative, any consent to the deed was invalid and the deed is voidable and may be reduced.[57] So at its simplest the problem is whether or not there was valid consent by the person imposed upon.[58]

(3) Lesion

-27　　As has been explained elsewhere,[59] lesion by itself is not normally a ground for challenge of a contract. It is different if lesion is combined with both facility and circumvention. These three elements, lesion,

---

[53] *Cleugh* v. *Fleming*, 1948 S.L.T.(Notes) 60; approved in *MacKay* v. *Campbell*, 1966 S.L.T. 329 at p. 333 *per* Lord Cameron (not reported in S.C.).

[54] *Lord Advocate* v. *Davidson's J.F.*, 1921 2 S.L.T. 267; *McDougal* v. *McDougal's Trs.*, 1931 S.C. 102; *MacGilvary* v. *Gilmartin*, 1986 S.L.T. 89.

[55] *Gibson's Exr.* v. *Anderson*, 1925 S.C. 774, and see discussion above on terminology.

[56] Vol. 5, p. 397. Where threats are also alleged see *Love* v. *Marshall* (1870) 9 M. 291.

[57] *Gall* v. *Baird* (1855) 17 D. 1027. A deed by an insane person is void.

[58] But a complete absence of consent raises another problem, such as incapacity or force and fear.

[59] See Chap. 12.

facility and circumvention, combine to invalidate consent.[60] The standard form of issue concludes with a question as to whether lesion was produced.

(4) Causation

11–28   The imposition must have procured or caused the deed or contract in question.[61] It is not necessary that the imposition should have been practised by the defender. This last factor was established in *Taylor* v. *Tweedie*.[62] No party, however innocent, is entitled to take the benefit of imposition of another.[63] There should be specification of the parties by whom the deed is said to have been impetrated.[64]

Void or Voidable?

11–29   It would be logical to say that a contract affected by facility and circumvention was voidable. This is because, on the one hand, the concept derives from and has a relationship to fraud and, on the other hand, it assumes a capacity to contract. In *Gall* v. *Bird*[65] it was established that a deed procured by facility and circumvention was reducible, in contrast with a deed granted by an insane person which was null.

UNDUE INFLUENCE

11–30   A new ground of reduction was suggested in the middle of the nineteenth century—undue influence. It did not at first meet with the approval of Lord President Inglis, who classified the grounds for reduction of deeds as incapacity, force and fear, facility and circumvention, fraud and essential error. "Beyond these categories, I am not myself, as a lawyer—as a Scottish lawyer—acquainted with any other ground of reduction applicable to deeds."[66]

11–31   Nevertheless, the doctrine of undue influence had been slowly fermenting. In 1856 a gift by a client to his agent had been attacked in part on the grounds of undue and unfair advantage. The case can also be viewed as one of extortion or of *"pactum illicitum."*[67] In 1864 an issue

---

[60] Bell, *Comm.*, I,136; *Clunie* v. *Stirling* (1854) 17 D. 15 at p. 20 *per* Lord Murray.

[61] *Home* v. *Hardy* (1842) 4 D. 1184; *Morrison* v. *Maclean's Trs.* (1862) 24 D. 625.

[62] (1865) 3 M. 928. On the form of issue see at p. 931 *per* Lord Justice-Clerk Inglis; see also *Wheelans* v. *Wheelans*, 1986 S.L.T. 164.

[63] The special position of a creditor in cautionary obligations arose in *Sutherland* v. *W. M. Low & Co. Ltd.* (1901) 3 F. 972. Gloag suggested that for the reduction of an onerous contract it was necessary to prove that the acts of circumvention were those of the other party to the contract, or of an agent for him: Gloag, *Contract*, p. 486.

[64] *Baird* v. *Harvey's Trs.* (1858) 20 D. 1220.

[65] (1855) 17 D. 1027.

[66] *Tennent* v. *Tennent's Trs.* (1868) 6 M. 840 at p. 876; on appeal (1870) 8 M.(H.L.) 10.

[67] *Anstruther* v. *Wilkie* (1856) 18 D. 405. In a later case involving law agent and client there is also this double approach of regarding the transaction as contrary to public policy or coming within the doctrine of undue influence. See *Logan's Trs.* v. *Reid* (1885) 12 R. 1094.

was allowed on averments of a law agent taking advantage of his position and influence to induce his client to enter a transaction.[68] In 1869 a law agent succeeded in proving that a settlement by a client in his favour was her free and uninfluenced act.[69] The considerations which affected transactions between agent and client probably also extended to clergymen and parishioners and medical men and patients.[70] Moreover, the influence of a parent on a child could be regarded as subject to the same doctrine,[71] although at one time undue influence by a parent on a child would probably have been considered evidence of fraud.[72]

32 There can be little doubt that the impact of English law was responsible for the reference to the doctrine. Undue influence had been recognised in England as part of the law of fraud in Lord Hardwicke's judgment in *Earl of Chesterfield* v. *Janssen* in 1750[73] but its acceptance probably starts from *Huguenin* v. *Baseley* in 1807.[74] The English law and the traces in earlier Scots cases were founded on when undue influence was clearly accepted into Scots law in *Gray* v. *Binny* in 1879.[75]

33 In *Gray* a deed consenting to disentail was reduced on the grounds of the influence of a mother and her solicitor on her son and the inequity of the bargain. The Lord Ordinary, Lord Young, mentioning *Huguenin* v. *Baseley*, stated the broad principle thus:

> "Where a relation subsists which imports influence, together with confidence reposed, on the one side, and subjection to the influence and the giving of the confidence on the other, the Court will examine into the circumstances of any 'transaction of bounty' . . . between parties so related, whereby the stronger party (using the term for brevity) greatly benefits at the cost of the weaker, and will give relief if it appears to have been the result of influence abused or confidence betrayed."[76]

34 On appeal Lord President Inglis adopted the Lord Ordinary's reasoning. Lord Shand negatived the suggestion that either fraud or facility and circumvention need be proved. He gave his definition of the circumstances which establish a case of undue influence:

> "The existence of a relation between the granter and grantee of the deed which creates a dominant or ascendant influence, the fact that confidence and trust arose from that relation, the fact that a material and gratuitous benefit was given to the prejudice of the granter, and the circumstance that the granter entered into the

---

[68] *Harris* v. *Robertson* (1864) 2 M. 664.

[69] *Grieve* v. *Cunningham* (1869) 8 M. 317.

[70] *Munro* v. *Strain* (1874) 1 R. 522; sequel at p. 1039.

[71] *Cuninghame* v. *Anstruther's Trs.* (1872) 10 M.(H.L.) 39 at p. 46 *per* Lord Chancellor Hatherley; and *Tennent* v. *Tennent's Trs.* (1870) 8 M.(H.L.) 10 at p. 17 *per* Lord Chancellor Hatherley.

[72] *Cf. Murray* v. *Murray's Trs.* (1826) 4 S. 374; *Fraser* v. *Fraser's Trs.* (1834) 13 S. 703.

[73] (1750) 2 Ves.Sen. 125.

[74] (1807) 14 Ves. 273; and *vide* W.H.D. Winder, "Undue Influence in English and Scots Law," 1940 L.Q.R. 97.

[75] (1879) 7 R. 332.

[76] *Ibid.* at p. 338.

transaction without the benefit of independent advice or assistance."[77]

11–35 Lord Deas did not dissent from his brethrens' approach, but he thought the case could be tried on an issue of facility and circumvention, the facility in this case arising from filial affection.

11–36 Subsequent case law has explored the scope of the doctrine. It is important to observe that the meaning and effect of undue influence may not be the same in the law of contract as in the law of wills,[78] and that the concept may not apply uniformly to the different relationships of granter and grantee.[79]

11–37 In *Carmichael* v. *Baird*[80] deeds in favour of another were reduced when they were by a son soon after attaining majority. It was observed that a son could make a gift to a parent. The onus was on him to show why the deeds should be reduced. In this case the son never thoroughly understood the position and signed the deeds under an erroneous idea of their effect.

11–38 *McKechnie* v. *McKechnie's Trs.*[81] was a case of an unsuccessful challenge of a will on the ground of undue influence by a mistress. Lord Justice-Clerk Macdonald, however, commented on other cases of undue influence. He said[82]:

> "These are cases of persons who having, from an official position towards another person, some capacity for influence over him, misuse that position for the purpose of inducing him to do, or abstain from doing, something that he has right to do, or abstain from doing, in the exercise of his rights as regards his own property. The essence of the matter is that the persons in that official position, such as clergyman, or doctor, or lawyer, are people who have not only a duty but a right to advise and urge those with whom they have to deal in certain directions; and it is natural and right that a person who is so dealt with should give effect to or at least be greatly influenced by the advice of those persons and what is urged upon him by those persons. Therefore, the person who has that influence, and ought to have it, in dealing with a person who ought to be influenced by it, must take the greatest possible care that he does not outstep the bounds of his official position and endeavour to get other things done, under that influence which he has, with which he has no right whatever to interfere. The clergyman and the doctor may have cause to strongly advise a person with whom they have to deal officially, but their advice must not be tainted by any motive not within their own border. As regards the lawyer, in a question of property, the position is somewhat different from the position of a clergyman or the position of a doctor, because it may

---

[77] *Ibid.* at p. 347.
[78] *Weir* v. *Grace* (1899) 2 F.(H.L.) 30; *Forbes* v. *Forbes' Trs., supra* at p. 331 *per* Lord Guthrie and the authorities there referred to. These authorities suggest that in the ordinary case undue influence to invalidate a will must amount to coercion or fraud.
[79] *Forbes* v. *Forbes Trs., supra* at p. 330.
[80] (1899) 6 S.L.T. 369.
[81] 1908 S.C. 93.
[82] at pp. 97–99.

be his duty to advise his client, and even sometimes to urge his client, in a particular direction, when the client desires to make a disposal of his affairs; and if in doing so he urges anything in his own favour, or urges anything in favour of a particular individual who gets him to do it, then of course he is in a corrupt position, in which anything that is done under his influence cannot receive effect. These cases are clear enough. Most of these cases do not turn either upon the question whether a person has capacity to make his will or not, or upon the question whether he is weak and facile. Of course, if there is anything of the nature of weakness or facility in such cases, the weakness or facility will make it much more easy to hold that a person acted under undue influence. But as regards the relatives of a man, and particularly as regards the people who are living in close relationship, practically of husband and wife, such rules do not apply. Such persons are entitled to use influence to induce the man to do what he may be expected to do himself, namely, to make provision for those whom he has placed in the position of being dependent upon him, and particularly in the case of a person who is placed in the position of being the mother of his child. In such circumstances there may be grounds for setting aside a will made by a person if, being on the face of it an absolutely unjust and wrong will, it can be proved that his mind had got into a weak and facile condition, so that he was a person who could be easily imposed upon, and the person accused, taking advantage of his weakness and facility, did impose upon him, and impetrated from him the deed which is complained of."

39   Although given in the context of wills, this dictum illustrates how the application of undue influence may vary with different relationships.

40   In *Forbes* v. *Forbes' Trs.*[83] a wife unsuccessfully challenged her ante-nuptial contract of marriage on the grounds of undue influence. The influence was supposed to have been exerted by her father, but he had no adverse personal interest and his influence could not be undue. Further any prejudice to the wife was suffered not as a consequence of her father's influence but because of financial circumstances since the contract. Lord Guthrie reviewed the authorities and observed[84]:

"In my opinion, an onerous contract entered into by a party of full age cannot be reduced on the ground that his consent was the result of undue influence exercised upon him, unless the influence was exerted to the detriment of that party by or on behalf of the other party to the deed in breach of a duty arising out of a fiduciary or quasi-fiduciary relationship. I adopt as substantially accurate the statement of the law in Gloag on Contract (2nd ed.) p. 526:– 'Where parties to a contract stand to each other in a relation which might enable the one to exert a dominant influence over the other, the contract will be reducible if it is proved that any material facts were concealed, or if the result is that a gratuitous advantage has been obtained by the exercise of that influence.' There is no case in Scotland where a contract has been held voidable on the ground of undue influence, where the influence has been exerted in genuine

---

[83] 1957 S.C. 325; a sequel to *Forbes* v. *Knox*, 1957 S.L.T. 102.
[84] at p. 333.

devotion to the interests of the person influenced. There is no Scottish case where it has been held that a contract can be reduced when the undue influence has not been exercised by or on behalf of the other party to the agreement."[85]

11–41   In *Allan* v. *Allan*[86] there was a successful challenge of a disposition by a son to his mother in liferent and himself, his brother and sister in fee. The granter of the deed was 17 years of age and acted under the influence of his mother, who believed that all the children should benefit from the heritage which the eldest had inherited on the intestacy of his father.

11–42   In *Honeyman's Exrs.* v. *Sharp*[87] it was held that there was not any limited class of persons to which the doctrine of undue influence applied. It could apply to a fine art dealer who abused a position of trust. But all the facts had to be inquired into and a decision could not be made on written pleadings.

Distinction from facility and circumvention

11–43   Facility and circumvention on the one hand, and undue influence on the other hand, are different although there is a relationship because many acts of circumvention involve the exercise of influence.[88] In facility and circumvention there is weakness and facility of which advantage is taken. In undue influence there is natural affection or trust which should not be mistaken for mental weakness or facility.[89] Facility and circumvention involve an element of fraud (in a special sense of that term) but undue influence does not. The influence must be "undue" but there need not be corrupt motive, or deceit or fraudulent conduct.[90] In a case of undue influence there is a special relationship between the parties, which may not exist in a case of facility and circumvention. The nature of this relationship is a ground for sending a case on undue influence to a proof while a simple case of facility and circumvention could go to a jury.[91]

Void or voidable

11–44   From the nature of undue influence it seems justifiable to regard it as rendering a contract voidable and not void. The influence procures consent; if consent is not procured there is no need to resort to the doctrine

---

[85] This last point remains open for discussion. It is possible, for example, that a parent might unduly influence a child to grant a deed to a third party: see *Forbes* v. *Knox*, 1957 S.L.T. 102 at p. 104 *per* Lord Walker. On the need in English law for unfair advantage see *National Westminster Bank plc* v. *Morgan* [1985] 1 All E.R. 821 (H.L.).

[86] 1961 S.C. 200.

[87] 1978 S.C. 223.

[88] *McCallum* v. *Graham* (1894) 21 R. 824.

[89] *Gray* v. *Binny* (1879) 7 R. 332 at p. 346 *per* Lord Shand.

[90] *Ibid.*

[91] *Ross* v. *Gosselin's Exr.*, 1926 S.C. 325.

of undue influence to attack the transaction. This would mean that there was a distinction between the effect of pressure amounting to force and fear and the effect of undue influence. Force and fear make a contract void.

45 Such authority as there is supports this conclusion. Lord Shand described a deed procured by undue influence as "voidable when it is challenged."[92] Lord Guthrie referred incidentally to the situation where "a contract has been held voidable on the ground of undue influence."[93] The fullest consideration is by Lord Kinnear, who in dealing with an assignation to a law agent said:

> "I do not think that the assignation is absolutely null. If it were null *ab initio*, it could not be set up by any subsequent confirmation or acquiescence; and third parties acquiring right under the donee, in good faith and for value, would be unable to maintain their rights against the donor and his representatives. It would appear to me, therefore, that conveyances obtained by undue influence, whether actually exercised or presumed by law in consequence of the relation of the parties, are in precisely the same position as conveyances obtained by fraud. Such a conveyance is not void, but voidable, at the option of the granter or his representatives, and it is valid until it is rescinded."[94]

46 Because the deed is voidable, *restitutio in integrum* is a condition of reduction. An antenuptial contract of marriage was held reducible, however, notwithstanding that marriage had followed.[95]

---

[92] *Gray* v. *Binny, supra* at p. 347.
[93] *Forbes* v. *Forbes' Trs., supra* at p. 333.
[94] *Logan's Trs.* v. *Reid* (1855) 12 R. 1094 at p. 1100.
[95] *Forbes* v. *Knox*, 1957 S.L.T. 102; sequel, 1957 S.C. 325.

CHAPTER 12

EXTORTION AND UNFAIR TERMS

EXTORTION: FORCE AND FEAR

12–01 Force and fear or extortion was a ground for reduction at an early date in Scottish history.[1] It was mentioned by Balfour[2] and examples were given by Spotiswoode.[3] The Court of Session had barely come into being when it was granting a reduction on this ground.[4] Morison reported many cases from 1543 onwards.[5]

Terminology

12–02 The term "force and fear," which reflects the Latin *"vis et metus,"* is inaccurate because it wrongly suggests that two elements, namely (a) force, and (b) fear, are essential. The expression "force or fear" is more precise, and there is authority which favours the term "extortion."[6]

The Requirements for the Proof of Extortion

12–03 (1) A case of extortion needs to be specifically averred and clearly proved.[7]

(2) The essence of a case of extortion is that a deed was granted or a contract entered into without consent. The hand of the signatory forcibly held by another is the extreme case. But most instances are those of fear induced by the threats of the extorter. The difficulty is to define the level and nature of the relevant threats. The standard is threats sufficient to annul consent.[8] Empty or futile threats are of no avail.[9] In general the threats should be sufficient to overcome the mind of the person against whom they are directed with the result that special protec-

---

[1] *Lady Torrs* v. *Lyoun of Logy* (1483) A.D.A. 128*, 145*; *Hamilton* v. *Abbot of Culross* (1494) A.D.A. 202, A.P.S. 11, 205.
[2] Balfour, Vol., pp. 179, 182, 183.
[3] Spotiswoode, p. 205.
[4] *King and Gray* v. *Hamilton of Preston* (1532/33) A.D. C. et S. p. 119.
[5] *s.v.* "*Vis et Metus,*" Mor. 16479 *et seq.*
[6] Stair, I,ix,8; *Priestnell* v. *Hutcheson* (1857) 19 D. 495 at p. 499 *per* Lord Deas; *Hislop* v. *Dickson Motors (Forres) Ltd.,* 1978 S.L.T.(Notes) 73 at p. 74 *per* Lord Maxwell.
[7] *Sinclair* v. *McLaren & Co.* (First Division), June 3, 1952, unreported; *Priestnell* v. *Hutcheson* (1857) 19 D. 495 at p. 500 *per* Lord Deas; *Wolfson* v. *Edelman,* 1952 S.L.T.(Sh.Ct.) 97 at p. 98 *per* Sheriff Dobie.
[8] See *Hislop* v. *Dickson Motors (Forres) Ltd.,* *supra* at p. 75 *per* Lord Maxwell.
[9] *McIntosh* v. *Chalmers* (1883) 11 R. 8 at p. 10 *per* Lord Ordinary (Kinnear); *Wolfson* v. *Edelman, supra* at p. 98 *per* Sheriff Dobie.

tion may be given to the young, infirm or aged,[10] and surprise might found weaker grounds of fear.[11]

(3) According to some authorities, threats should be by the defender (or someone acting on his behalf).[12] The better view seems to be that the consent is invalid whoever procures the deed or contract. It is irrelevant that the other party to the contract or someone deriving title from him has had no part in the coercion,[13] and threats can be addressed not to the pursuer but to close relatives of the pursuer.[14]

(4) The law has been particularly troubled by threats from a person, such as a creditor, who is entitled to take action against another. As a general rule it is not extortion to threaten a legal course of action such as diligence[15] or dismissal from employment,[16] or the cancellation of negotiations or a deal intended to rescue a business,[17] or the prospect of financial investigation and bankruptcy,[18] or a report of matters to the police.[19]

What is objectionable is when a person obtains more than his due. It is therefore easier to infer extortion when an obligation is gratuitous than when full value is received,[20] or when a creditor receives assets of a value unknown to the transferor in satisfaction of a claim of an uncertain amount.[21] A creditor is entitled to his pound of flesh but may find himself in difficulties if he seeks more or if he exploits his debtor. It may be for this reason that the court in one case reduced a disposition granted in prison to a creditor but sustained the deed so far as it was a security for the debt due.[22] A creditor may extort if in bad faith he seeks, not payment of his debt but an ulterior end.[23]

(5) English authority mentions the problems of economic duress.[24]

---

[10] Bell, *Comm.*, I,315; and at one time married women were regarded as vulnerable— *Priestnell* v. *Hutcheson, supra* at p. 499 *per* Lord Deas; see also Stair, IV,xl,25.

[11] *Priestnell* v. *Hutcheson, supra; Hislop* v. *Dickson Motors (Forres) Ltd., supra.*

[12] *Stewart Brothers* v. *Kiddie* (1899) 7 S.L.T. 92 at p. 93 *per* Lord Trayner; *Hunter* v. *Bradford Property Trust Ltd.*, 1977 S.L.T.(Notes) 33.

[13] *Trustee Savings Bank* v. *Balloch*, 1983 S.L.T. 240.

[14] *Priestnell* v. *Hutcheson, sup. cit.*; see also *McIntosh* v. *Farquharson* (1671) Mor. 16485.

[15] *Craig* v. *Paton* (1865) 4 M. 192; *Priestnell* v. *Hutcheson, sup. cit.*

[16] *Education Authority of Dumfriesshire* v. *Wright*, 1926 S.L.T. 217.

[17] *Hunter* v. *Bradford Property Trust Ltd.*, 1977 S.L.T.(Notes) 33.

[18] *Wolfson* v. *Edelman, sup. cit.*

[19] *Hislop* v. *Dickson Motors (Forres) Ltd., sup. cit.* at p. 75 *per* Lord Maxwell.

[20] *Gelot* v. *Stewart* (1871) 9 M. 957 (also (1870) 8 M. 649 and (1871) 9 M. 1057); *McIntosh* v. *Chalmers* (1883) 11 R. 8 at p. 15 *per* Lord Justice-Clerk Moncreiff.

[21] *Hislop* v. *Dickson Motors (Forres) Ltd., sup. cit.*

[22] *Fraser* v. *Black and Knox*, Dec. 13, 1810, F.C.

[23] *McIntosh* v. *Chalmers* (1883) 11 R. 8.

[24] *Occidental World-Wide Investment Corp.* v. *Skibs A/S Avanti* [1976] 1 Lloyd's Rep. 293; *North Ocean Shipping Co. Ltd.* v. *Hyundai Construction Co. Ltd.* [1979] Q.B. 705; *Pao On* v. *Lan Yiu Long* [1980] A.C. 614; *Universe Tankships Inc. of Monrovia* v. *International Transport Workers' Federation* [1983] A.C. 366; *Lobb (Garages) Ltd.* v. *Total Oil G.B. Ltd.* [1983] 1 All E.R. 944, [1985] 1 All E.R. 303.

The standard of duress has been stated in the Privy Council in this way[25]:

> "Duress, whatever form it takes, is a coercion of the will so as to vitiate consent. Their Lordships agree with the observation of Kerr J. in *Occidental Worldwide Investment Corporation* v. *Skibs A/S Avanti* [1976] 1 Lloyd's Rep. 293, 336 that in a contractual situation commercial pressure is not enough. There must be present some factor 'which could in law be regarded as a coercion of his will so as to vitiate his consent.' This conception is in line with what was said in this Board's decision in *Barton* v. *Armstrong* [1976] A.C. 104, 121 by Lord Wilberforce and Lord Simon of Glaisdale—observations with which the majority judgment appears to be in agreement. In determining whether there was a coercion of will such that there was no true consent, it is material to inquire whether the person alleged to have been coerced did or did not protest; whether, at the time he was allegedly coerced into making the contract, he did or did not have an alternative course open to him such as an adequate legal remedy; whether he was independently advised; and whether after entering the contract he took steps to avoid it. All these matters are, as was recognised in *Maskell* v. *Horner* [1915] 3 K.B. 106, relevant in determining whether he acted voluntarily or not."

12–04   This analysis has been criticised on the grounds that duress does not operate by "overbearing the will."[26] This was demonstrated, it has been argued, by the decision of the House of Lords in a criminal case, *Lynch* v. *D.P.P. of Northern Ireland.*[27] Duress does not "overbear" the will, nor destroy it: it "deflects" it. The person who acts under duress intends to act but he does so in a way which the law does not accept as a valid act.

12–05   It is thought that English authorities on duress are an unreliable guide to Scots law. There are a number of differences in the historical development of the systems, and in English law the contract induced by duress is voidable while in Scotland the contract induced by force and fear has been treated as being void.[28] Nevertheless the English case law raises the question of the effect of economic pressure in Scots law.

12–06   There does not appear to be a difficulty in the recognition by Scots law of economic threats as a form of force and fear or extortion. Although many of the old cases are concerned with threats against the body of a person, extortion is concerned with the effect on the mind. Therefore Bell could state[29]:

---

[25] *Pao On* v. *Lan Yiu Long, sup. cit.* at p. 635.

[26] P. S. Atiyah, "Economic Duress and the 'Overborne Will' " (1982) 98 L.Q.R. 197; see also Chitty, Chap. 7—"Duress and Undue Influence"—which is edited by Atiyah.

[27] [1975] A.C. 653; for Scots criminal law see *Thomson* v. *H.M.A.*, 1983 S.L.T. 682. The theoretical arguments around this case are discussed in A. Norrie, "The Defence of Coercion in Scots Criminal Law," 1984 S.L.T.(News) 13; see also P.W. Ferguson, "Coercion—the Shield of the Law?" (1984) 29 J.L.S. 107.

[28] See para. 12–11; compare with speeches in *Lynch* v. *D.P.P. Of Northern Ireland, sup. cit,*; see also *Hislop* v. *Dickson Motors (Forres) Ltd., sup. cit.* at p. 75 *per* Lord Maxwell.

[29] *Comm.*, I,315.

> "There is a sort of terror, the operation of which in annulling consent may admit of distinctions. The threat of divulging a crime may frequently operate with the most irresistible force, whether the crime has been actually committed, or is of so shameful a nature that the least imputation of it is a serious evil. An obligation extorted by the threat of a shameful imputation, constructed with so much art that it may be difficult to refute it, would seem to be reducible *ex vi aut metu*; and yet it might be argued that a mind of ordinary constancy and manliness ought not to be moved by such an imputation."

So, it can be suggested, any form of threat can amount to force and fear if it produces the required effect on the mind of the contracting party. The difficulty is to explain the required effect on the mind. The reported cases of threats which involved economic disaster tend to be cases in which force and fear was *not* established.[30] Partly, this is because the threats were threats of actions which were legal or justifiable. Also, as a matter of theory, overwhelming pressure cannot by itself amount to force and fear. The inevitability of financial ruin does not taint every contract entered into by the person whose affairs have become embarrassed. A person may not have any choice but to sign a contract, but absence of choice does not negate consent.[31]

In two cases economic pressure did affect obligations. In *Wiseman* v. *Logie*[32] a bill was reduced when it was granted to prevent intromissions with a relative's goods by a fiscal and "some Highlanders and dragoons." In *Sutherland* v. *Montrose Fishing Co. Ltd.*[33] trade union pressure on employers amounted to force and fear.

The cases on economic duress have provoked an argument about the correct theoretical basis in Scots law.[34] Part of the problem is the relevance of the criminal law to the law of contract.[35] It is probable that there are differences between the criminal law on coercion[36] and the civil law of force and fear. The policy considerations in each case are not identical.[37] In any event it is not necessary to reconcile the criminal law and the law of contract.

Obscurity in the law of contract may arise because the law tries to deal with a variety of situations under the one head of force and fear.[38] A person who enters into a contract may do so in circumstances which clearly show that his act is not voluntary. On the other hand there may be a voluntary act. Consent is given, but the method of obtaining con-

---

[30] See cases cited in para. 12–03, esp. nn. 17, 18.

[31] See *Barton* v. *Armstrong* [1976] A.C. 104 at p. 121 (dissenting judgment).

[32] (1700) Mor. 16505.

[33] (1921) 37 Sh.Ct.Rep. 239.

[34] A. Thompson, "Economic Duress," 1985 S.L.T.(News) 85; E. McKendrick, "Economic Duress—A Reply," 1985 S.L.T.(News) 277.

[35] As expounded in *Thomson* v. *H.M.A.*, *sup. cit.*

[36] As expounded in *Thomson* v. *H.M.A.*, *sup. cit.*

[37] *e.g.* the treatment of murder in the criminal law suggests arguments which may not be appropriate for the civil law. See *Abbott* v. *R.* [1977] A.C. 755; *Thomson* v. *H.M.A.*, *sup. cit.*

[38] See para. 12–13.

sent taints the contract. It is easier to apply the "overborne will" theory
to the involuntary act than it is to the voluntary action under pressure
which is more analogous to the effect produced by fraud or undue
influence.[39] Until this difference is recognised it will be difficult to construct a satisfactory theory of force and fear in Scots law. As it is, the
authorities show that the pressure must be such as would overpower the
mind of a person of ordinary firmness so that there is no true consent.
But the requirement of the overpowering of the mind may sometimes
have been departed from.[40]

(6) Voluntary actions after the transaction may show ratification of it
and be a bar to reduction.[41]

The Effect of Extortion

12–11   Stair[42] and Bell[43] treated a contract induced by force and fear as void.
Case law also suggested that a reduction of a deed on the grounds of
force and fear was effective against *bona fide* third parties.[44] There are
contrary indications. Bankton stated: "Nor indeed can any embargo be
laid upon purchasers of moveables, by allegations of force or fraud in
the author, that being destructive to commerce."[45] Professor Gloag
thought that: "it may perhaps still be open to the Courts to consider
whether a disposition of property, granted under the apprehension of
inconvenient consequences not amounting to physical violence, would
be reducible in a question with an onerous and *bona fide* third party."[46]
The Scottish Law Commission has considered the somewhat ambivalent
nature of the authorities and the principles involved.[47]

12–12   There is something to be said for distinguishing two situations. If a
person is physically forced to sign a contract, there is no consent and the
act is a nullity. On the other hand, if consent is obtained through fear
there is still consent and, as in other cases where the method of obtaining consent is tainted,[48] the contract should be voidable.

---

[39] *Cf.* Stair, IV, xl, 25 (cited in *Barton* v. *Armstrong, sup. cit.* at p. 118).

[40] *Hislop* v. *Dickson Motors (Forres) Ltd., sup. cit.* at pp. 75, 76 *per* Lord Maxwell;
Bell, *Comm., loc. cit.*

[41] *Thomas* v. *Annandale* (1829) 7S.305 (no opinions are reported, but (1) there can
always be adoption of a void contract—see para. 26–05—and (2) actings on the faith of the
transaction may negate any inference of lack of consent).

[42] Stair, I,ix,8—"utterly void"; but at IV, xl, 28 the author appears to suggest that the
tainted transaction may not affect singular successors.

[43] Bell, *Prin.*, s.12; *Comm.* I,314.

[44] *Cassie* v. *Fleming* (1632) Mor. 10279; *Woodhead* v. *Nairn* (1662) Mor. 10281, and on
bills of exchange see *Willocks* v. *Callender and Wilson* (1776) Mor. 1519, *Wightman* v.
Graham (1787) Mor. 1521 (now affected by Bills of Exchange Act 1882, s.29(2)); see also
Stuarts v. *Whitefoord* (1677) Mor. 16489.

[45] Bankt., I,257, 59. Some support might be derived from *Anderson* v. *Spence* (1683)
Mor. 10286.

[46] Gloag, p. 488.

[47] Scot.Law Com. Memo. No. 42, *Defective Consent and Consequential Matters* (1978),
paras. 2.1–2.12 and 3.104–3.111.

[48] Fraud, facility and circumvention and undue influence.

It cannot be pretended that it is easy to distinguish the categories of fear which may be produced by modern methods of intimidation. Nor is it clear what policy the law should adopt. The terrorist may benefit at the expense of his victim if he can pass on a good title to a *bona fide* third party. On the other hand some cases of force and fear are difficult to distinguish from facility and circumvention or undue influence. The problem remains for judicial analysis.

EXTORTION: ENORM LESION

There is authority to the effect that a bargain will be enforced despite its terms being harsh or extortionate. Lesion might be a factor in deciding whether a transaction should be reduced on the grounds of fraud, or facility and circumvention or undue influence, or force and fear.[49] By itself lesion would not be a ground for challenge.

It has been said that: "Mere inadequacy of consideration will not, *per se*, invalidate the agreement"[50]; "A sale is never set aside on the mere ground that the price has been inadequate."[51] Lord Blackburn stated[52]: "If a man chooses to bargain that he will pay ten times the value of a thing I do not think you have, in the absence of undue influence, any right to cut down the price to the tenth part of what was agreed upon." The special position of enorm lesion in contracts of minors can be used to indicate that enorm lesion is not applicable to adults' contracts. As it was put long ago: "For though a wise man would not have given such a right, yet the Lords are not curators to all who in this manner dispose upon their rights."[53]

In several cases the Scottish courts have enforced contracts where the terms were harsh and may have been agreed to by a person who was in necessitous circumstances or who laboured under ignorance or a lack of intellect or in absence of legal advice.[54] A man may be in pain, on his deathbed, out of work and have a starving wife. He can sign away his rights for a small sum without the benefit of legal advice. Yet the Scottish courts will enforce the bargain[55] unless there is facility and circumvention, undue influence or other invalidity affecting consent.

---

[49] *McKirdy* v. *Anstruther* (1839) 1D. 855 at p. 863 *per* Lord Gillies; *Maitland* v. *Fergusson* (1729) Mor. 4956; *McIntosh* v. *Chalmers* (1883) 11 R. 8 at p. 15 *per* Lord Justice-Clerk Moncreiff; *Hislop* v. *Dickson Motors (Forres) Ltd., sup. cit.*

[50] *McLachlan* v. *Watson* (1874) 11 S.L.R. 549 at p. 550 *per* Lord Mackenzie; similarly at p. 551 *per* Lord Ardmillan.

[51] *McKirdy* v. *Anstruther* (1839) 1 D. 855 at p. 863 *per* Lord Gillies.

[52] *Caledonian Ry. Co.* v. *N. British Ry. Co.* (1881) 8 R.(H.L.) 23 at p. 31.

[53] *Smith* v. *Napier*(1693) Mor. 4955.

[54] *A.B.* v. *Joel* (1849) 12 D. 188; *McLachlan* v. *Watson, sup. cit.*; *Tennent* v. *Tennent's Trs.* (1870) 8 M.(H.L.) 10; *Mathieson* v. *Hawthorns & Co. Ltd.* (1899) 1 F. 468; *Welsh* v. *Cousin* (1899) 2 F. 277.

[55] See *Mathieson* v. *Hawthorns & Co. Ltd., sup. cit.*

12–17   Although English law does not have an established principle of lesion or oppression, some case law has indicated that such a principle might emerge.[56] The traditional view, however, has been contrary to the idea that rights must be enforced reasonably.[57] Lord Reid rejected the control by the courts of harsh and unconscionable exemption clauses on the grounds that it was an intimate and complex problem affecting millions of people and the solution should be left to Parliament.[58]

12–18   Despite what has been said there are cases in which the Scottish courts have refused to uphold extortionate transactions. Contracts related to the lending of money were not enforced because of their similarity to usury although not affected by the statutes on usury.[59] The payment of a premium to a cautioner was argued to be "unlawful extortion" and a bond for the premium was reduced.[60] The decision would not now be followed,[61] but Kames used it and other cases to justify the principle that "every benefit taken indirectly by a creditor, for the granting of which no impulsive cause appears but the money lent, will be voided as extorted."[62]

12–19   Whereas, at one time, a cautioner was expected to act gratuitously and thereby risk losing all and gaining nothing, if a partner did likewise that was a leonine partnership.[63] There is no modern authority on the *societas leonina* and earlier authority must be treated with caution. The situation may be common in which one partner takes more profit than another and where the percentage of profit is not related to the capital contributed, but Stair described it as "clearly usuary, unequal and unjust."[64]

12–20   Control of extortionate provisions did arise on penalty clauses. In the mid-nineteenth century penalties would be controlled on the grounds that they were "exorbitant and unconscionable" or "exorbitant and

---

[56] *Lloyds Bank Ltd.* v. *Bundy* [1975] Q.B. 326, esp. opinion of Lord Denning M.R. which was disapproved in the House of Lords in *National Westminster Bank plc* v. *Morgan* [1985] 1 All E.R. 821 at p. 830 *per* Lord Scarman; *A. Schroeder Music Publishing Co. Ltd.* v. *Macauley* [1974] 3 All E.R. 616, esp. *per* Lord Diplock at p. 624; *Clifford Davis Management Ltd.* v. *W.E.A. Records Ltd.* [1975] 1 All E.R. 237; *Multiservice Bookbinding Ltd.* v. *Marden* [1979] Ch. 84; *Lobb (Garages) Ltd.* v. *Total Oil G.B. Ltd.* [1985] 1 All E.R. 303.

[57] *White & Carter (Councils) Ltd.* v. *McGregor* 1962 S.C.(H.L.) 1 at p. 14 *per* Lord Reid; *Shell U.K. Ltd.* v. *Lostock Garages Ltd.* [1976] 1 W.L.R. 1187 at p. 1203 *per* Bridge L.J. (dissenting); *Liverpool County Council* v. *Irwin* [1977] A.C. 239 at p. 257 *per* Lord Wilberforce.

[58] *Suisse Atlantique* v. *N. V. Rotterdamsche* [1967] 1 A.C. 361 at p. 406; see now Unfair Contract Terms Act 1977; see also dictum in *National Westminster Bank plc* v. *Morgan*, *sup. cit.*

[59] *Sutherland* v. *Sinclair* (1696) Mor. 9460; *Brown* v. *Muir* (1737) Mor. 9464.

[60] *King* v. *Ker* (1711) Mor. 9461.

[61] *Burnett, Petr.* (1859) 21 D. 1197; *McKinnon, Petr.* (1884) 21 S.L.R. 476; *Sim, Petr.* (1863) 2 M. 205; Bell, *Comm.*, I,393; N.M.L. Walker, *Judicial Factors*, p. 68.

[62] Kames, *Principles of Equity* (3rd ed.), Vol. 1, p. 69.

[63] Stair, I,xvi,3; Ersk, III,iii,19; Forbes, *Inst.*, Vol. 1, part 2, p. 185.

[64] *Ibid.*, *vide* Partnership Act 1890, s.24; J. Bennett Miller, *The Law of Partnership in Scotland*, p. 401.

unreasonable." These phrases occur several times in the opinions in
Forrest and Barr v. *Henderson*, the rubric of which states that: "though
a contract stipulate for a sum of liquidated damages, the Court may, in
the exercise of its equitable jurisdiction, modify the amount if it is exorbitant."[65] The concept of modification has since been departed from
under English influence. The control of penalties remains although it is
based on different grounds.

The courts will control oppressive use of irritancies. It has been
observed that a conventional irritancy is subject "to a power in the
Court to refuse to grant a decree of irritancy where there has been anything unfair about the landlord's conduct."[66] It is, however, difficult to
establish a case of oppression. There appears to be no reported case in
which it has been done.[67] There must be precise averments which show
a clear abuse of rights or impropriety of conduct by the landlord.[68] "The
question is whether the landlord has acted in such a way as to make it
unconscionable for him to take advantage of a situation which he himself has brought about."[69]

Penal provisions may be controlled by the operation of the maxim,
pacta privatorum non derogant juri communi. A clause providing for the
suspension of diligence on consignation was not enforced because it was
oppressive.[70] It was indicated *obiter* that a provision that a debtor was to
remove "without any warning or legal process whatever" would not be
enforced.[71] There are wider questions raised here about the extent to
which a contract may bind the exercise of remedies by the courts. For
example, a joint minute on periodical allowance may not always bind
the court,[72] and agreements on custody of or access to children are of
limited effect.[73]

The nearest which Scots law has come to a general control of oppressive conditions is two moneylenders' cases in which, at common law,
promissory notes to moneylenders were not enforced because the

---

[65] (1869) 8 M. 187; see also *Apparent Heir of Porteous* v. *Nasmith* (1783) Mor. 120.

[66] *Dorchester Studios* v. *Stone*, 1975 S.C.(H.L.) 56 at p. 67 *per* Lord Kilbrandon; see
also at p. 71 *per* Lord Fraser; *Stewart* v. *Watson* (1864) 2 M. 1414; *Lucas's Exrs.* v.
Demarco, 1968 S.L.T. 89.

[67] There has been parliamentary intervention by the Law Reform (Misc. Prov.) (Scotland) Act 1985, ss.4 and 5. This followed on Scot.Law.Com. No. 75, *Irritancies in Leases*
(1983).

[68] *H.M.V. Fields Properties Ltd.* v. *Skirt 'n' Slack Centre of London Ltd.*, 1982 S.L.T.
477 (motive of landlord was held irrelevant).

[69] *H.M.V. Fields Properties Ltd.* v. *Tandem Shoes Ltd.*, 1983 S.L.T. 114 at p. 120 *per*
Lord Brand.

[70] *Forrester* v. *Walker and Hunt*, June 27, 1815, F.C.

[71] *Wylie* v. *Heritable Securities Investment Association* (1871) 10 M. 253.

[72] *Robson* v. *Robson*, 1973 S.L.T.(Notes) 4; but *cf. Lothian* v. *Lothian*, 1965 S.L.T. 368
and *Dalzell* v. *Dalzell*, 1985 S.L.T. 286. There can be a discharge of rights: *Dunbar* v.
Dunbar, 1977 S.L.T. 169; *Bryan* v. *Bryan*, 1985 S.L.T. 444; *Elder* v. *Elder*, 1985 S.L.T.
471.

[73] E.M. Clive, *Husband and Wife* (2nd ed.), p. 419.

demands were grossly extortionate.[74] The basis on which this was done is obscure, but reference was made to the principles applicable to penalty clauses.[75]

12–24   The result is spasmodic control of minors' contracts, penalty clauses, leonine partnerships, moneylending and irritancies, but an absence of a clear attempt to formulate a principle.

EXTORTION: UNFAIR CONTRACT TERMS

12–25   The Unfair Contract Terms Act 1977 arose out of the second report on exemption clauses of the Law Commissioners.[76] The title of the Act may mislead. It does not introduce a general control of unfair terms in contracts. Its purpose is more selective. Broadly speaking it controls some exemptions and limitations of liability and one type of indemnity clause. The Act came into force on February 1, 1978, and does not apply to contracts made before that date. Subject to that, it applies to liability for loss or damage which is suffered on or after that date.[77] Parts II and III of the Act apply to Scotland.

12–26   The Act does not apply to every type of contract. Part II of the Act does not apply to a discharge or indemnity given by a person in consideration of the receipt by him of compensation in settlement of a claim.[78] "Person" would include corporation.[79] The important provisions of the Act in ss.16–18 on exclusion of liability apply to most, but not all, contracts for the supply of goods or services. The sections do not apply to insurance contracts or contracts relating to the formation, constitution or dissolution of any body corporate, unincorporated association or partnership.[80] The removal of insurance contracts from the operation of the Act was something of a victory for insurers. Concern was expressed that policy-holders might not be afforded sufficient protection from unfair treatment, and the result was two statements of insurance practice under which insurers who are members of the bodies which produced the statements will not unreasonably repudiate liability or reject a claim on the ground of non-disclosure or misrepresentation.[81]

---

[74] *Young* v. *Gordon* (1896) 23 R. 419; *Gordon* v. *Stephen* (1902) 9 S.L.T. 397; See, however, a decision under the Moneylenders Act 1900—*Midland Discount Co.* v. *Macdonald*, 1909 S.C. 477; control of extortionate consumer credit bargains is continued in the Consumer Credit Act 1974, s.137.

[75] *Gordon* v. *Stephen, supra* at p. 398 *per* Lord Kincairney.

[76] Law Com. No. 69; Scot.Law Com. No. 39 (1975).

[77] s.31.

[78] s.15(1).

[79] Interpretation Act 1978, Sched. 1.

[80] s.15(3).

[81] First Statement of Insurance Practice (the Non-Life Statement), May 4, 1977; Second Statement of Insurance Practice (the Life (Long-Term) Statement), July 26, 1977. See the Law Commission, *Insurance Law, Non-Disclosure and Breach of Warranty* (Law Com. No. 104 1980), paras. 3.23 to 3.30 and App. B which reproduces the statements. At the time of writing the statements were under review.

The 1977 Act does not define a contract of insurance. A contract of insurance is not confined to contracts for payment of money but includes some contracts which provide benefits in the event of a disaster, such as the provision of a chauffeur in the event of inability to drive.[82]

7   The application of sections 16–18 to certain maritime contracts is limited.[83]

8   It has been held that a person who is in breach of contract cannot rely on a provision of the Act in his favour.[84] The Act does not conflict with the common law principles of construction of exemption clauses.[85] What the Act does is to impose further controls on exemption clauses.[86]

9   Subject to the exclusions mentioned, sections 16 to 18 of the Act apply to any contract only to the extent that the contract[87]:

(a) relates to the transfer of the ownership or possession of goods from one person to another (with or without work having been done on them);

(b) constitutes a contract of service or apprenticeship;

(c) relates to services of whatever kind, including (without prejudice to the foregoing generality) carriage, deposit and pledge, care and custody, mandate, agency, loan and services relating to the use of land;

(d) relates to the liability of an occupier of land to persons entering upon or using that land;

(e) relates to a grant of any right or permission to enter upon or use land not amounting to an estate or interest in the land.

0   The term "goods" has the same meaning as in the Sale of Goods Act 1979.[88]

Void Provisions

1   The Act makes certain provisions of a contract void namely:

(1) Terms which exclude or restrict liability for death or personal injury in circumstances to which section 16 applies.[89] The section applies where a term of a contract purports to exclude or restrict liability for breach of duty arising in the course of any business or from the occupation of any premises used for business purposes of the occupier. The

---

[82] *Dept. of Trade and Industry* v. *St. Christopher Motorists Association Ltd.* [1974] 1 All E.R. 395; see also *Medical Defence Union Ltd.* v. *Dept. of Trade* [1980] Ch. 82.

[83] s.15(3) and (4).

[84] *Macrae & Dick Ltd.* v. *Philip*, 1982 S.L.T.(Sh.Ct.) 5.

[85] paras. 13–21 *et seq.*

[86] *Boomsma* v. *Clark & Rose Ltd.*, 1983 S.L.T.(Sh.Ct.) 67.

[87] s.15(2).

[88] s.25(1), 1977 Act. The definition in s.61(1) of the Sale of Goods Act 1979 is that "goods" includes all personal chattels other than things in action and money, and in Scotland all corporeal moveables except money; and in particular "goods" includes emblements, industrial growing crops, and things attached to or forming part of the land which are agreed to be severed before sale or under the contract of sale.

[89] s.16(1)(*a*); "personal injury" is defined in s.25(1).

phrase "breach of duty" means the breach (a) of any obligation, arising from the express or implied terms of a contract, to take reasonable care or exercise reasonable skill in the performance of the contract; (b) of any common law duty to take reasonable care or exercise reasonable skill; (c) of the duty of reasonable care imposed by section 2(1) of the Occupier's Liability (Scotland) Act 1960.[90] The term "business" includes a profession and the activities of any government department or local or public authority.[91]

12–32   There are various doubts and difficulties raised by section 16(1). The section only applies to a term of a contract. This presumably does not include every type of promise or disclaimer of liability for negligent misstatements resulting in loss to third parties. The definition of breach of duty does not appear to cover all statutory duties such as obligations under the Factories Acts, which may give rise to civil liability. The concept of a "business" gives rise to doubt in marginal cases such as a university, a members' club, or a trade union.

(2) Terms which are in a guarantee of consumer goods to which section 19 applies. The term is void in so far as it purports to exclude or restrict liability for loss or damage (including death or personal injury) arising from the use of defective goods and resulting from breach of duty by a manufacturer or distributor. Broadly, the section applies to consumer goods. The control is not confined as in section 16(1) to personal injury and death but extends to property damage and other loss.

(3) Terms which exclude or restrict liability for breach of the obligations arising from section 12 of the Sale of Goods Act 1979 (seller's implied undertakings as to title, etc.) and section 8 of the Supply of Goods (Implied Terms) Act 1973 (implied terms as to title in hire-purchase agreements). This provision is not limited to consumer contracts and applies to private sale.[92]

(4) Terms which exclude or restrict liability for breach of the obligations arising from section 13, 14 or 15 of the Sale of Goods Act 1979 (seller's implied undertakings as to conformity of goods with description or sample, or as to their quality or fitness for a particular purpose); and section 9, 10 or 11 of the Supply of Goods (Implied Terms) Act 1973 (the corresponding provisions in relation to hire purchase).[93] In the case of a consumer contract[94] these exclusions or restrictions are void against the consumer.

(5) Terms which exclude or restrict liability for breach of certain obligations in contracts for the supply of goods other than sale or hire purchase, such as a contract of hire or barter.[95] The controls are broadly

---

[90] s.25(1).
[91] s.25(1).
[92] s.20(1).
[93] s.20(2).
[94] Defn. in s.25(1).
[95] s.21.

similar to those applying to sale and hire purchase. Charterparties are especially dealt with.[96]

(6) Terms which attempt to evade the controls of Part II of the Act by a secondary contract, *e.g.* a contract for supply of goods which is accompanied by a servicing agreement with an exclusion clause relating to the supply.[97]

The "Fair and Reasonable" Control

3 The Act makes certain provisions of a contract ineffective unless it was fair and reasonable to incorporate the term in the contract. In summary the "fair and reasonable" standard is applied to:

(1) An exclusion or restriction of liability for breach of duty arising in the course of any business from the occupation of any premises used for business purposes of the occupier.[98] Such exclusion or restriction is void in respect of death or personal injury, and in other cases is subject to a "fair and reasonable" test.

(2) Unreasonable exemptions in consumer contracts or standard form contracts.[99] The control applies to exclusion of liability for breach and the rendering of no performance or a performance substantially different from that which the consumer or customer reasonably expected from the contract. The Act defines "consumer contract"[1] and "customer."[2] There is an absence of a definition of "standard form contract." This type of contract is rather like the elephant which the child cannot accurately describe but which is recognised on sight. In most instances it is obvious whether or not a standard form is being used.[3]

(3) Unreasonable indemnity clauses in consumer contracts.[4] The control applies (a) to consumer contracts[5] (not to the indemnities frequently found in contracts between business organisations), (b) to the effect of protecting the consumer (*i.e.* it is a one-sided control and does not protect the party dealing in the course of a business), and (c) to liabilities arising in the course of any business or from the occupation of any premises used for business purposes of the occupier.

(4) Certain obligations in contracts of sale, hire purchase or supply of goods which are not consumer contracts. These are obligations on the

---

[96] s.21(2)(*b*).
[97] s.23.
[98] s.16(1).
[99] s.17.
[1] s.25(1).
[2] s.17(2). See also defn. of "business" in s.25(1).
[3] See *McCrone* v. *Boots Farm Sales Ltd.*, 1981 S.C. 68. In *Border Harvesters Ltd.* v. *Edwards Engineering (Perth) Ltd.*, 1985 S.L.T. 128, whether or not a contract was a standard form was sent to proof. Averments to indicate the use of the conditions appear to be necessary.
[4] s.18.
[5] See s.25(1). A contract between two consumers is not a "consumer contract."

conformity of goods with description or sample, or their quality or fitness for a particular purpose.[6]

(5) The right to transfer ownership or possession of goods or to the enjoyment of quiet possession of goods in contracts other than sale, hire purchase or (with a limited exception) a charterparty.[7]

What is "fair and reasonable"?

12–34　One of the main problems with the 1977 Act is the extent to which it renders contract provisions unenforceable unless they are "fair and reasonable." The initial problems for the draftsman or adviser are:

(1) to check whether the Act applies to the contract in question. To be more accurate it must be considered whether the Act (or any part of it) applies to any term of the contract. A contract involving the transfer of company shares will generally be outside the Act, but a transfer of the moveables of the company is probably subject to the Act. A lease can be outside the Act except in so far as it provides for services.

(2) to decide which of the two concepts of "fair and reasonable" applies. Strange as it may seem, the Act has guidelines for the application of the reasonableness test in Schedule 2 but these, strictly speaking, only apply to sections 20 and 21 which regulate sale and supply of goods and hire purchase.[8] In all other cases the only elaboration of the reasonableness test is provided by section 24 (which applies to the whole of Part II of the Act). It is relevant to look only at circumstances at the time of the contract.[9] The onus of proving a term fair and reasonable is on the party founding on the clause,[10] and in limitation provisions regard can be had to the resources of the party relying on the term and the availability of insurance.[11]

12–35　In *George Mitchell (Chesterhall) Ltd.* v. *Finney Lock Seeds Ltd.*[12] the House of Lords considered the phrase "fair and reasonable" in the Sale of Goods Act 1979. The House was conscious that the requirements of reasonableness in the Unfair Contract Terms Act 1977 would come before the courts with increasing frequency.[13] It was indicated that (1) the court must entertain a whole range of considerations, on one side

---

[6] ss.20(2) and 21—on breach of an express term on quality, see *Border Harvesters Ltd.* v. *Edwards Engineering (Perth) Ltd., sup. cit.*

[7] s.21.

[8] But it may be that the guidelines in Sched. 2 will be relevant in other cases, perhaps along with other cases. See *Woodman* v. *Photo Trade Processing Ltd.*, Exeter Crown Court, April 3, 1981, reported in Richard Lawson, *Exclusion Clauses* (2nd ed., 1983), App. 4.

[9] s.24(1).

[10] s.24(4); *see Landcatch Ltd.* v. *Marine Harvest Ltd.*, 1985 S.L.T. 478 for the nature of averments needed.

[11] s.24(3).

[12] [1983] 2 A.C. 803.

[13] at p. 815 *per* Lord Bridge.

and on the other, and (2) an appellate court should be slow to interfere with the decision of the court below. The case before the House involved the sale of seeds. On the interpretation of the "guidelines" in the Sale of Goods Act, Lord Bridge (with whom the rest of their Lordships agreed) stated[14]:

> "Of the particular matters to which attention is directed by paras. (a) to (e) of s.55(5),[15] only those in (a) to (c) are relevant. As to para. (c), the respondents admittedly knew of the relevant condition (they had dealt with the appellants for many years) and, if they had read it, particularly cl. 2, they would, I think, as laymen rather than lawyers, have had no difficulty in understanding what it said. This and the magnitude of the damages claimed in proportion to the price of the seeds sold are factors which weigh in the scales in the appellants' favour.
>
> "The question of relative bargaining strength under para. (a) and of the opportunity to buy seeds with a limitation of the seedsman's liability under para. (b) were interrelated. The evidence was that a similar limitation of liability was universally embodied in the terms of trade between seedsmen and farmers and had been so for very many years. The limitation had never been negotiated between representative bodies but, on the other hand, had not been the subject of any protest by the National Farmers' Union. These factors, if considered in isolation, might have been equivocal. The decisive factor, however, appears from the evidence of four witnesses called for the appellants, two independent seedsmen, the chairman of the appellant company, and a director of a sister company (both being wholly-owned subsidiaries of the same parent). They said that it had always been their practice, unsuccessfully attempted in the instant case, to negotiate settlements of farmers' claims for damages in excess of the price of the seeds, if they thought that the claims were 'genuine' and 'justified.' This evidence indicated a clear recognition by seedsmen in general, and the appellants in particular, that reliance on the limitation of liability imposed by the relevant condition would not be fair or reasonable.
>
> "Two further factors, if more were needed, weigh the scales in favour of the respondents. The supply of autumn, instead of winter, cabbage seeds was due to the negligence of the appellants' sister company. Irrespective of its quality, the autumn variety supplied could not, according to the appellants' own evidence, be grown commercially in East Lothian. Finally, as the trial judge found, seedsmen could insure against the risk of crop failure caused by supply of the wrong variety of seeds without materially increasing the price of seeds."

36   The only surprise in this analysis may be that the "decisive factor" was evidence of settlement in the past of other claims from other parties. There may be some doubt whether in the Scottish system of plead-

---

[14] at pp. 816, 817.
[15] *i.e.* Sale of Goods Act 1979 which applied to contracts made between May 18, 1973 and Feb. 1, 1978. See now Unfair Contract Terms Act 1977, Sched. 2, which came into force on Feb. 1, 1978.

ing there could be relevant averment and proof of prior settlement of such claims. Nor is it obvious that details of other cases in which there is an element of compromise in the light of the circumstances at the time, assist a court in determining the meaning of "fair and reasonable" in a statute.

12–37   The practical problems which a draftsman must consider include:

(1) The onus of proving that the clause is "fair and reasonable" is on the party founding on the clause.[16]

(2) The factors to be taken into account are only those known at the time of the contract.[17] It may be difficult to establish reasonableness unless evidence is preserved of the issues which were considered at that time. The client should make a positive decision about what form of exclusion clause is wanted and why, although many clients are indifferent to the issues raised. The reasons for any decision should be recorded.

(3) If the clause is to appear in standard form conditions it may be impossible to draft a clause which will be valid in all circumstances. This is because reasonableness must be judged in the light of the circumstances of both parties. This is clear in the guidelines in Schedule 2 and probably would be implied in other cases. The main purpose of a reasonableness test is to control the one-sided contract. Standard conditions are drafted with reference to the circumstances of only one party and a consideration of what happens in the normal course of trade. But the abnormal tends to occur, *e.g.* the wholesaler who one day enters into a consumer contract. Standard conditions tend not to have the flexibility of a reasonableness test. Although there may be little that the draftsman can do about this, it emphasises the importance of inquiry into the pattern of the client's trade and the need to make assumptions about future developments. For example, in the contract between wholesaler and retailer, special provision could be made for an occasional sale to a consumer, with its increased statutory protection, and also for the sale of secondhand equipment which can justifiably have a greater than normal exclusion of implied warranties.

(4) Broadly speaking a client has three choices. These are (a) accepting all the liability which may arise and insuring against it as best he can, (b) limiting his liability, and (c) excluding his liability. It should be easier to demonstrate that a limitation of liability is fair and reasonable, than to prove the same proposition with a total exclusion of liability. Further, a limitation of liability clause may be given a more benevolent construction by the courts. As Lord Wilberforce said in the case of *Ailsa Craig Fishing Co.* v. *Malvern Fishing Co. Ltd.*[18]:

---

[16] s.24(4). The Law Commissions took a different approach: Law Com., No. 69; Scot.Law Com., No. 39, paras. 177, 183.

[17] s.24(1); *cf.* discussion in *George Mitchell (Chesterhall) Ltd.* v. *Finney Lock Seeds Ltd., sup. cit.*

[18] 1982 S.L.T. 377 at p. 380; see also *George Mitchell (Chesterhall) Ltd.* v. *Finney Lock Seeds Ltd., sup. cit.*

"Clauses of limitation are not regarded by the Courts with the same hostility as clauses of exclusion: this is because they must be related to other contractual terms, in particular to the risks to which the defending party may be exposed, the remuneration which he receives, and possibly also the opportunity of the other party to insure."

Given that the application of the reasonableness test will be a matter of doubt, there are good reasons to be cautious and to limit liability rather than totally exclude it. This poses the further problem of which limit—£10 or £100,000 or what? The answer depends on the factors mentioned in section 24(3) of the 1977 Act, that is, the resources of the party relying on the term and the availability of insurance.

An example of the type of argument which might show the reasonableness of a limitation clause can be gleaned from the Law Commission's Second Report on Exemption Clauses which preceded the 1977 Act.[19] Laundering and dry-cleaning are examples of services where it is generally cheaper for the consumer to insure than for the launderer or cleaner to insure. The customer is in a better position to know the limit of his losses while the launderer would have to insure for the maximum possible claim. In any event the charges for the service bear no relation to the loss which negligence might cause. Those whose normal trade was handling sheets, towels and cotton tablecloths might reasonably ask customers who hand over valuable antique linen to disclose its nature and value. In the absence of this disclosure, the launderer might reasonably limit his liability.

Standard conditions sometimes cover a wide range of contracts with different price structures. It may be reasonable to alter the limit of liability according to the value of work being done under the contract. A fixed limit of liability of, say, £100,000 might be very reasonable in a contract where the value of services is £1000, but not so reasonable if the contract price is £1 million. One way round this is to say that the limit is so many times the contract price, with the probable addition of a ceiling of liability because of the difficulty of arranging insurance when potential claims run into millions. Choosing the multiple of the contract price and choosing the ceiling limit involve a fair amount of guesswork, but the availability and expense of insurance are important factors on which to obtain information. A clause which excludes consequential loss is a clause limiting liability rather than excluding liability.[20]

(5) What is reasonable is probably strongly linked to the price charged. A value may be put on an exemption or limitation of liability clause. The contracts department of a sophisticated company would put a figure on the effect a clause should have on the contract price. Also, for example, there is a practice which goes back a long way, of carriers

---

[19] Law Com., No. 69; Scot.Law Com., No. 39 (August) 1975), paras. 56, 117.
[20] *Border Harvesters Ltd.* v. *Edwards Engineering (Perth) Ltd.*, 1985 S.L.T. 128.

by rail offering their customers a choice between carriage of goods at owner's risk or, at a higher rate, at carrier's risk.[21] Conversely, if a price would be the same irrespective of the existence of the exclusion clause, that is an indication that the clause is unreasonable.

(6) What is "fair and reasonable" will alter with time and the changing circumstances of the parties. Thus, although it will probably be done rarely, there should be a periodic review of any exclusion or limitation clause habitually adopted by a client. It is expecting too much to hope that the client's board of directors will meet annually to consider the Unfair Contract Terms Act and minute the results of their deliberations. At the other extreme it is easy to imagine the effect on a court of the client's evidence to the effect that the reasonableness of the clause was very carefully considered 20 years ago, but that the clause has not been looked at since.

(7) In general the Act is controlling some attempts to contract out of obligations. One method of avoiding the controls in the Act is so to define the contract or the obligations that there is unlikely to be a breach of the obligations. Then there is little need to attempt to exclude or limit liability for breach. For example, a company wishes to sell redundant equipment. The company does not want to incur liabilities if the equipment is found to be defective. There could be a contract of sale with an attempted exclusion of liabilities under the Sale of Goods Act. That approach will raise many of the problems discussed above. An alternative is to describe the goods in such a way that it is improbable that there will be a breach of any obligation on quality, *i.e.* a sale of the equipment whatever it is.[22] This may reduce the price obtainable in some circumstances. In other cases it is a sensible approach, *e.g.* when there is a transfer of all or most of the assets of one company to another company. This may occur in a "hive down" by a receiver or liquidator or in an assets takeover. The selling company does not wish to meet claims arising from misdescriptions of its plant and machinery in schedules or specifications. The contract can be worded so that it is the plant and machinery belonging to the company on a certain date which is transferred. Any further specification of what is transferred may raise the problems caused by section 20(2) of the 1977 Act. The draftsman in his

---

[21] See Law Com. report. *sup. cit.*, para. 66; also *Woodman* v. *Photo Trade Processing Ltd.*, Exeter County Court, April 3, 1981, reported in Richard Lawson, *Exclusion Clauses* (2nd ed., 1983), App. 4. The court founded on a two-tier system for film processing cost referred to in the code of practice for the photographic industry. A limitation of liability to the replacement value of the film lost was held to be unreasonable.

[22] *Cf. Hurley* v. *Dyke* [1979] R.T.R. 265 (H.L.). Similarly an indemnity may be limited in scope, which does not mean that there is an exclusion of liability: *Davidson* v. *Guardian Royal Exchange*, 1979 S.C. 192. Further, a provision that a certificate on quality is "final" may result in the sale being treated as a sale of goods by description, *i.e.* a sale of goods for which a certificate has been issued: *Gill & Duffus S.A.* v. *Berger & Co. Inc.* [1984] A.C. 382.

enthusiasm to exclude liabilities may go further, and provide that the transferee does not warrant any title to the goods. That, however, is probably void as a result of section 20(1).[23]

Part III of the 1977 Act

40 Part III of the Act has special provisions relating to international supply contracts,[24] choice of law clauses,[25] and sea carriage of passengers.[26] Contracts between parties in different states for the supply of goods are a normal part of an export and import trade, and broadly those contracts are outside the controls imposed by the Act. Where a contract is expressly governed by Scots law but apart from that provision would be governed by the law of some country outside the United Kingdom,[27] the Act has a limited operation.

---

[23] It is the "term" of the contract which is void, not the whole contract, but there is a danger that other parts of the same "term" will fall because they are inseparable from the portion which is void.

[24] s.26.

[25] s.27.

[26] s.28.

[27] *e.g.* a contract where the substantial performance of the contract is in the Norwegian sector of the North Sea but for convenience the parties (neither of whom is Scottish) decide to have all matters arising from a dispute (including disputes on sub-contracts) decided in Aberdeen.

Chapter 13

EXPRESS TERMS

13–01   In this chapter the problems analysed arise from incorporation of standard terms into a contract and two common forms of such terms, namely, exclusion and indemnity clauses and reservation of title clauses.

Part 1—Incorporation of Standard Terms into a Contract

What are the Terms of a Contract?

13–02   In the mass of documents which may form a contract, various difficulties arise in determining what constitutes the contract. Negotiations must be separated from the contract.[1] Some documents may have to be classified as offers or acceptances,[2] or as being contractual or non-contractual. The question may arise also as to whether part of a contractual document, such as the reverse of a form, has been incorporated into the contract.

13–03   Difficulties arise from attempts to incorporate standard conditions into contracts although the difficulties are not confined to those typical cases. The contract drafted by the parties might attempt to incorporate any other document.

Contractual Documents

13–04   When it is sought to incorporate a document into a contract, it must be reasonable to expect the document to have a contractual effect. A ticket used in many cases of carriage or deposit has had this effect.[3]

13–05   In *Taylor* v. *Glasgow Corporation*[4] a voucher issued in public baths was held to be different from the "ticket" in carriage and deposit cases. The pursuer was entitled to regard the document issued as a pass or a voucher. She could not have been reasonably expected to study it for conditions. There was no method of drawing attention to the conditions. There was, therefore, no reasonable notice of the conditions.

---

[1] See paras. 3–01 *et seq.*
[2] See Chap. 5. An example of the differing views on what constituted a contract for the sale of marine engines is *Pollock & Co.* v. *Macrae*, 1922 S.C.(H.L.) 192; see also opinion of Second Division, 1922 S.L.T. 510.
[3] See paras. 13–10 to 13–11.
[4] 1952 S.C. 440.

06   In the classic English case of *Parker* v. *South Eastern Ry. Co.*[5] Mellish L.J. drew a distinction between a ticket received at a toll and a bill of lading.[6] The recipient in either case might be ignorant of the existence of conditions on the document, but this would not avail him in the case of a bill of lading because in the great majority of cases persons shipping goods do know that the bill contains conditions of carriage. The person who was ignorant of this must bear the consequences: "it being plainly impossible that business could be carried on if every person who delivers a bill of lading had to stop to explain what a bill of lading was."

07   It has been observed on particular facts that a cheque-book cover did not fall within the category of documents which recipients could reasonably assume contained conditions.[7] Also excluded from that category was a ticket for the hire of a deck-chair.[8]

Time of Notice

08 A document issued after a contract is made will not be part of a contract unless incorporated into the contract by (1) express reference or (2) a course of dealing. In *The Ardennes*[9] an oral contract for carriage of oranges was entered into before a bill of lading was issued. The bill of lading, therefore, did not regulate the right of the shipowners to deviate. In *Thornton* v. *Shoe Lane Parking*,[10] Lord Denning treated the issue of a ticket by a machine as the conclusion of a contract. The contract could not be altered by any words printed on the ticket. In *Olley* v. *Marlborough Court Ltd.*[11] a contract had been made between guests and proprietors of a hotel before the guests saw a notice in their bedroom. In *McCutcheon* v. *David MacBrayne Ltd.*[12] there was an oral contract of carriage which was not affected by the terms of a receipt issued on payment of freight. A contract to carry a passenger in a ship has been held to have been made before the issue of tickets which contained conditions.[13] Statements on invoices have not been part of a contract made earlier.[14]

---

[5] (1877) 2 C.P.D. 416 (approved in *inter alia Richardson Spence & Co.* v. *Rowntree* [1894] A.C. 217; *Hood* v. *Anchor Line*, 1918 S.C.(H.L.) 143; *Gray* v. *L.N.E. Ry. Co.*, 1930 S.C. 989).

[6] at p. 422.

[7] *Burnett* v. *Westminster Bank Ltd.* [1966] 1 Q.B. 742.

[8] *Chapleton* v. *Barry U.D.C.* [1940] 1 K.B. 532.

[9] [1951] 1 K.B. 55.

[10] [1971] 2 Q.B. 163 (the other judges reserved their views on the time of conclusion of the contract).

[11] [1949] 1 K.B. 532.

[12] 1964 S.C.(H.L.) 28.

[13] *Hollingworth* v. *Southern Ferries Ltd.* [1977] 2 Lloyd's Rep. 70; *The Dragon* [1979] 1 Lloyd's Rep. 257; on appeal [1980] 3 All E.R. 696.

[14] *Buchanan & Co.* v. *Macdonald* (1895) 23 R. 264; *Lawes Chemical Co. Ltd.* v. *Ross-shire Farmers Ltd.* (1938) 54 Sh.Ct.Rep. 187. An invoice is a unilateral statement which the other party may not have agreed. The terms on invoices may be incorporated by a course of dealing.

13–09   Conversely, the issue of conditions some time before the contract is made, as by producing a brochure, is not necessarily evidence that the contract when made is subject to those conditions.[15] Nor is it *per se* sufficient to have entered into previous contracts subject to those conditions.[16] Knowledge that a person sometimes enters into contracts on certain terms is not proof that every contract with that person is in those terms.

Sufficiency of Notice

13–10   The case of *Parker* v. *South Eastern Ry. Co.*[17] stereotyped the questions to be asked in determining whether notice had been given of conditions in ticket cases.[18] Mellish L.J. said[19]:

> "I am of opinion, therefore, that the proper direction to leave to the jury in these cases is, that if the person receiving the ticket did not see or know that there was any writing on the ticket, he is not bound by the conditions; that if he knew there was writing, and knew or believed that the writing contained conditions, then he is bound by the conditions; that if he knew there was writing on the ticket, but did not know or believe that the writing contained conditions, nevertheless he would be bound if the delivering of the ticket to him in such a manner that he could see there was writing upon it, was, in the opinion of the jury, reasonable notice that the writing contained conditions."

13–11   Whether or not there is reasonable sufficiency of notice is a question of fact.[20] If, however, the question is whether there is any evidence to support the findings of fact, that is a matter of law.[21] Gloag indicated that what was reasonable was a question of law,[22] but this, it is submitted, is wrong. The issue is not entirely clear because of a mistaken tendency to cite prior authority as though it ruled questions of fact.[23] It is thought that Lord Murray's approach was correct when he thought that a detailed examination of cases did not serve any useful purpose.

---

[15] *Hollingworth* v. *Southern Ferries Ltd.*, *sup. cit.*

[16] *McCutcheon* v. *David MacBrayne Ltd.*, *sup. cit.*; but see "Course of Dealings," para. 13–19.

[17] (1877) 2 C.P.D. 416.

[18] There is a distinction between the ticket cases (where a ticket is received) and cases where the issue is whether a document is incorporated into the contract. See *McCutcheon* v. *David MacBrayne Ltd.*, *sup. cit.*

[19] at p. 423.

[20] *Richardson, Spence & Co.* v. *Rowntree* [1894] A.C. 217; *Hood* v. *Anchor Line*, 1918 S.C.(H.L.) 143.

[21] *Thompson* v. *L.M.S. Ry. Co.* [1930] 1 K.B. 41 (approved in *Gray* v. *L.N.E. Ry. Co.*, 1930 S.C. 989).

[22] *Contract*, p. 30.

[23] See *Gray, sup. cit.*, in which Lord Justice-Clerk Alness indicates that the sufficiency of notice is a question of fact (at p. 1000) and then decides the question on a review of authorities (at p. 1004), having earlier criticised the defenders for citing too many cases! See also *Morris* v. *Clan Line Steamers*, 1925 S.L.T. 321.

Whether there was reasonably sufficient notice was, like the other questions in *Parker's* case:

> "a question of fact to be answered in the light of the whole circumstances of the case—the nature of the contract, the circumstances and situation of the contracting parties—judged of in accordance with what has been called 'the accepted standards of conduct' by reasonable common-sense men. This is the substance of the authorities already referred to."[24]

It is a "jury question" subject to any applicable rules of law.[25] Factors which have tended to indicate insufficient notice are (1) inadequate reference to the existence of conditions printed on the reverse of a ticket,[26] (2) difficulty in reading the conditions because of the size of print, the method of printing or the obliteration by a stamp,[27] (3) the severity of the condition relied upon,[28] and (4) a misleading reference.[29]

On the other hand, conditions have been incorporated although only referred to and not reproduced[30] on the ticket, although the plaintiff could not read,[31] or could not read English,[32] and although the conditions were not in fact read.[33]

Notices

-12   The terms on which one party contracts may be displayed on a notice. It may be sufficient to display a notice prominently so that it can be easily seen at the time of making the contract. In *W.N. White & Co. Ltd.* v. *Dougherty*[34] printed conditions of sale were hung in front of an auctioneer's rostrum. The buyer had not read the conditions, but he knew of them. The court held the buyer bound by the conditions. The interlocutor stated: "The conditions of sale were posted up on the rostrum in such a way as to be patent to the defender and other buyers." In *Wright* v. *Howard, Baker & Co.*[35] notices in clear terms were posted at various

---

[24] *Coyle* v. *L.M.S. Ry. Co.*, 1930 S.L.T. 349 at p. 350.

[25] *Grayston Plant* v. *Plean Precast*, 1976 S.C. 206 at p. 217 *per* Lord Justice-Clerk Wheatley.

[26] *Henderson* v. *Stevenson* (1875) 2 R.(H.L.) 71 (this case was subject to adverse comment in *Harris* v. *G.W. Ry. Co.* (1876) 1 Q.B.D. 515; *Williamson* v. *North of Scotland, etc. Navigation Co.*, 1916 S.C. 554 at p. 565 *per* Lord Salvesen); *Sugar* v. *L.M.S. Ry. Co.* [1941] 1 All E.R. 172; *White* v. *Blackmore* [1972] 2 Q.B. 651 at p. 664 *per* Lord Denning. For adequate reference see *Lyons Co.* v. *Caledonian Ry. Co.*, 1909 S.C. 1185; *Hood* v. *Anchor Line, sup. cit.*

[27] *Richardson Spence & Co.* v. *Rowntree, sup. cit.*; *Williamson* v. *North of Scotland, etc. Navigation Co., sup. cit.*; *Lewis* v. *Laird Line*, 1925 S.L.T. 316.

[28] *Thornton* v. *Shoe Lane Ltd.* [1971] 2 Q.B. 163; *Hollingworth* v. *Southern Ferries Ltd.* [1977] 2 Lloyd's Rep. 70; *McConnell & Reid* v. *Smith*, 1911 S.C. 635 at p. 638 *per* Lord Dundas.

[29] *Lewis* v. *Laird Line*, 1925 S.L.T. 316 (the ticket implied that the carrier was liable for negligence, whereas the conditions referred to excluded liability).

[30] *Thompson* v. *L.M.S. Ry. Co. sup. cit.*; *Gray* v. *L.N.E.R. Ry. Co.*, 1930 S.C. 989.

[31] *Thompson* v. *L.M.S. Ry. Co., sup. cit.*; *Sugar* v. *L.M.S. Ry. Co., sup. cit.*

[32] *The Luna* [1920] P. 22.

[33] *e.g. Lyons* v. *Caledonian Ry. Co.*, 1909 S.C. 1185; *Hood* v. *Anchor Line, sup. cit.*

[34] (1891) 18 R. 972.

[35] (1893) 21 R. 25.

places of work and were held to be incorporated into contracts of employment, even although many of the workmen may not have read the notices. It is, however, a question on the facts of a case whether what was done was reasonably sufficient to bring a notice to the attention of contracting parties. In *McCutcheon* v. *David MacBrayne Ltd.*[36] the carriers' conditions were displayed on a bill at their office and on three bills on a ship. The pursuer had not read the conditions, had not had his attention drawn to them, and there was no reason why he should have read them. He was not bound by the notices.

13–13   The steps which must be taken to incorporate a notice can be illustrated from *Birch* v. *Thomas.*[37] A car driver, as the law then was,[38] could limit his liability to his passenger. Mr Thomas had a sticker on his car windscreen which purported to exclude claims against the driver or owner of the car. Mr Thomas gave a lift to Mr Birch. On the evidence it appeared that Mr Birch's attention was drawn to the existence of the sticker, and to the fact that it dealt with insurance. It was daylight and the notice was positioned so that a passenger could easily read it. Even assuming that Mr Birch had not read the notice, the car driver Mr Thomas had done all that was reasonably necessary in the circumstances to bring the sticker to Mr Birch's attention. Mr Birch was bound by the terms of the sticker. Lord Denning observed that he was not satisfied that the mere sticking of a notice on the windscreen would have been sufficient. It was not very prominent. But there were facts showing that the existence of the notice had been drawn to the attention of the passenger.

13–14   Each case rests so much on its facts that it is of limited or no assistance in future cases. Further examples will be found in the cases cited.[39] The notice must be part of a contract.[40]

13–15   Notice can be given by the issue of circulars or brochures or catalogues,[41] which may refer to posted conditions.[42]

---

[36] 1964 S.C.(H.L.) 28, and see opinions in Court of Session, 1962 S.C. 506.

[37] [1972] 1 All E.R. 905 (although a case in tort).

[38] See now Road Traffic Act 1972, s.148(3).

[39] *Mendelssohn* v. *Normand* [1970] 1 Q.B. 177 (garage notice); *Adams (Durham) Ltd.* v. *Trust Houses Ltd.* [1960] 1 Lloyd's Rep. 380 (garage notice); *Smith* v. *Taylor* [1966] 2 Lloyd's Rep. 231 (all cases in which the notice was not incorporated into the contract); *Ashdown* v. *Samuel Williams & Sons Ltd.* [1957] 1 Q.B. 409; *White* v. *Blackmore* [1972] 2 Q.B. 651 (notices effective on entry to dangerous land—see for Scotland, Occupiers Liability (Scotland) Act 1960, s.2); *Caven* v. *Scottish and Universal Newspapers Ltd.*, 1976 S.L.T.(Sh.Ct.) 92 (advertising conditions not incorporated merely by being displayed).

[40] *Olley* v. *Marlborough Court Ltd.* [1949] 1 K.B. 532; *Harling* v. *Eddy* [1951] 2 K.B. 739 at p. 748 *per* Denning L.J.; *Hollingworth* v. *Southern Ferries Ltd.* [1977] 2 Lloyd's Rep. 70; *Burnett* v. *British Waterways Board* [1973] 2 All E.R. 631; *Lightbody's* v. *Hutchinson* (1886) 14 R. 4.

[41] *Goodyear Tyre and Rubber Co. (Great Britain) Ltd.* v. *Lancashire Batteries Ltd.* [1958] 3 All E.R. 7—*cf. Paul* v. *Corp. of Glasgow* (1900) 3 F. 119 (circular some time before contract); *Hollingworth* v. *Southern Ferries Ltd., sup. cit.* (statement in holiday brochure).

[42] *Macdonald & Fraser* v. *Henderson* (1882) 10 R. 95.

16   Under the Carriers Act 1830 certain common carriers cannot limit their liability by public notice.[43] On the other hand, increased charges for valuable items may be imposed by notice which is binding if affixed in compliance with the Act.[44]

17   The Hotel Proprietors Act 1956 provides for limitation of the liability of hotel proprietors in certain circumstances, which include the display of a particular type of notice in a specified way.[45]

18   In certain circumstances in English law there can be a licence but not a contract.[46] This may explain why in the Unfair Contract Terms Act 1977 the prohibition on excluding or limiting liability for death or personal injury refers in England to the effect of "any contract term or to a notice,"[47] while the equivalent Scottish section[48] omits the reference to a notice. The definition section, however, brings within the Scottish part of the Act references to a "notice having contractual effect" and defines "notice" to include announcements and communications.[49]

Course of Dealing

19   In *Henderson* v. *Stevenson*,[50] Lord O'Hagan observed[51] that proof of knowledge and assent to contract conditions might be given in various ways, such as "antecedent dealings—notoriety of custom, publication of notices, verbal communication, and so forth." Professor Bell stated[52]:

> "Evidence of a specific bargain, however, cannot justly be required on *each* occasion of sending goods by a carrier, or travelling in a particular coach. Provided such specific contract or assent to the terms can be established on a previous occasion, it will be held that, till altered again by specific contract, the future employment continues on the footing once acquiesced in."

20   Effect was given to the proposition that knowledge of an assent to conditions can be proved by prior dealings in *Wood & Co.* v. *G. & J. Burns*.[53] The case involved the carriage of an organ by sea. The pursuer's agent knew the conditions on which the shipowners contracted. "They had, according to the evidence, been constantly dealing with them, and knew their conditions well."[54] In *Rutherford & Son* v. *Miln & Co.*[55] a buyer of seeds knew that the seller sold subject to conditions.

---

[43] s.4.
[44] s.2. See *Rusk* v. *N.B. Ry. Co.*, 1920 2 S.L.T. 139.
[45] s.2(3).
[46] *Wilkie* v. *London Passenger Transport Board* [1947] 1 All E.R. 258; *Gore* v. *Van der Lann* [1967] 2 Q.B. 31.
[47] s.2.
[48] s.16.
[49] s.25(3)(*d*) and (4).
[50] (1875) 2 R.(H.L.) 71.
[51] at p. 79.
[52] *Comm.*, I,504 and 505.
[53] (1893) 20 R. 602.
[54] at p. 607 *per* Lord Justice-Clerk Macdonald.
[55] 1941 S.C. 125.

There had been previous transactions between the parties. The buyer had not troubled himself to ascertain the terms of the conditions but he was nevertheless bound by those terms.

13–21   The problem was described by Lord Reid in this way:

> "If two parties have made a series of similar contracts each containing certain conditions, and then they make another without expressly referring to those conditions, it may be that those conditions ought to be implied. If the officious bystander had asked them whether they had intended to leave out the conditions this time, both must, as honest men, have said 'Of course not.' "[56]

The test is what each party was reasonably entitled to conclude from the attitude of the other.[57] For this reason a person may be bound although he does not actually know the terms of the conditions. Also the decision on whether conditions have been incorporated in this way involves questions of both fact and law. The requirements are (1) a course of dealing showing (2) knowledge of and (3) assent to, the term relied upon. Knowledge and assent may be judged objectively and not necessarily according to the subjective intention of the parties.

(1) The dealing

13–22   There must be a previous course of consistent dealing, not prior contracts involving different goods, with varying conditions and method of contracting.[58] In *McCutcheon* v. *David MacBrayne Ltd.*[59] Lord Devlin observed that the bare fact of previous dealings did not assist.[60] "The fact that a man has made a contract in the same form ninety-nine times (let alone three or four times which are here alleged) will not of itself affect the hundredth contract in which the form is not used. Previous dealings are relevant only if they prove knowledge of the terms, actual and not constructive, and assent to them." This expression was the subject of some criticism in *Hardwick Game Farm* v. *SAPPA*.[61] It is thought that in so far as Lord Devlin insisted on "actual knowledge" he was inconsistent with other authority. So far as he was saying that mere proof of prior dealings was not enough to incorporate the conditions, he was correct.[62]

---

[56] *McCutcheon* v. *David MacBrayne Ltd.*, 1964 S.C.(H.L.) 28 at p. 35.

[57] *Ibid.*

[58] *McCutcheon* v. *David MacBrayne Ltd., sup. cit.*; although there can be a prior course of dealing with some variation in commodities or contracts—*S.I.A.T.* v. *Tradax Overseas S.A.* [1978] 2 Lloyd's Rep. 470, on appeal [1980] 1 Lloyd's Rep. 53; *Lamport & Holt Lines Ltd.* v. *Coubro & Scrutton (M. & I.) Ltd.* [1981] 2 Lloyd's Rep. 659, on appeal [1982] 2 Lloyd's Rep. 42.

[59] *Sup. cit.*

[60] *Ibid.* at p. 41.

[61] Especially in the Court of Appeal: [1966] 1 All E.R. 309. In the House of Lords *McCutcheon* was distinguished because it involved an oral transaction: [1969] 2 A.C. 31.

[62] Nor would a mere averment of prior dealings be sufficient: *McCrone* v. *Boots Farm Sales Ltd.*, 1981 S.C. 68; *G.E.A. Airexchangers Ltd.* v. *James Howden & Co. Ltd.*, 1984 S.L.T. 264.

The number and frequency of previous dealings are relevant but not decisive facts. In *Hardwick Game Farm* v. *SAPPA*,[63] three or four deals a month during the previous three years was a factor in holding the conditions incorporated. In *Hollier* v. *Rambler Motors Ltd.*[64] it was observed that a term could not be implied into an oral contract by three or four transactions over a period of five years.[65] In *British Crane Hire* v. *Ipswich Plant Hire*[66] two similar transactions many months before were sufficient to incorporate conditions when combined with the knowledge of both parties who were in the same trade. In *Grayston Plant Ltd.* v. *Plean Precast Ltd.*[67] there were about 12 instances over a period of four years when the pursuers followed up a verbal contract of hire with an acknowledgment of order form. The conditions on the form were not incorporated, although on appeal it was conceded that there was a course of dealing. "The mere counting of occasions when a similar transaction has previously been entered into between the parties and thereby obtaining a sufficiently high score is not all that is required in cases such as this in order to justify the conclusion that a written condition has been incorporated into a verbal contract."[68] Averments on a course of dealing should disclose the number, dates and nature of previous transactions.[69]

23   The prior course of dealings can be with different companies in the one group or organisation. It may be immaterial which "member of the clan" is involved.[70] The knowledge of a firm can become the knowledge of a company which takes over the business of the firm.[71]

(2) Knowledge

24   A person must have knowledge of the conditions. A person may be deemed to have knowledge if he knows of the existence of conditions but has never read them.[72] A confession that terms have not been read may be admission of knowledge that the terms existed.[73] It is easier to show knowledge if the parties are in the same trade and each imposes

---

[63] [1969] 2 A.C. 31; see *per* Lord Morris at p. 90 (*i.e.* over 100 notes contained the condition).

[64] [1972] 2 Q.B. 71.

[65] at p. 76 *per* Salmon L.J.

[66] [1975] Q.B. 303.

[67] 1976 S.C. 206.

[68] at p. 211 *per* Lord Robertson (Lord Ordinary).

[69] *McCrone* v. *Boots Farm Sales Ltd., sup. cit.*; *G.E.A. Airexchangers Ltd.* v. *James Howden & Co. Ltd., sup. cit.*

[70] *S.I.A.T.* v. *Tradax Overseas S.A., supra* at p. 490 *per* Donaldson J.; *Lamport & Holt Lines Ltd.* v. *Coubro & Scrutton (M. & I.) Ltd., sup. cit.*

[71] A factor in *Aluminium Industrie Vaassen B.V.* v. *Romalpa Aluminium Ltd.* [1976] 2 All E.R. 552 (the partners and the directors, or some of them, were the same).

[72] *Rutherford & Son* v. *Miln & Co.*, 1941 S.C. 125; *J. Spurling Ltd.* v. *Bradshaw* [1956] 2 All E.R. 121. Where there were various editions of general conditions, the edition in force at the date of the contract has been held to be incorporated: *Smith* v. *U.M.B. Chrysler (Scotland) Ltd.*, 1978 S.C.(H.L.) 1.

[73] *Transmotors Ltd.* v. *Robertson Buckley & Co. Ltd.* [1970] 1 Lloyd's Rep. 224.

similar conditions,[74] compared to parties who are from different walks of life.[75] It is suggested that this is because of the difference which would reasonably be expected in the knowledge of the parties rather than, despite Lord Denning, because of a difference in bargaining power.[76]

(3) Assent

13–25   Assent to the conditions may be implied from the failure to object to the conditions,[77] or actings following on the conditions such as making payments.[78] To avoid being bound by a course of dealing, the only safe course for a party is to do something positive to indicate a rejection of the conditions.[79] Assent will not so readily be implied to a condition which is severe in its terms.[80]

If the consequences of incorporation are that it will cost one party U.S. $3 million there must be a clear incorporation.[81] There must be reasonably sufficient notice of a term. Notice is clearer if the term is repeated or summarised in the documents sent to the other contracting party, rather than if the documents contain a reference to another document which sets out the term.[82]

What is Incorporated?

13–26   One contract may refer to another contract or to standard terms. It does not follow that all the clauses of the other contract or all the standard terms have been incorporated.

13–27   In *Stewart Brown & Co.* v. *Grime*[83] a contract referred to the rules of the Beetroot Sugar Association. One of the parties was not a member of the association. Nevertheless the rules and the decision of the council of the association were binding on the parties. This case was distinguished in *McConnell & Reid* v. *Smith*,[84] in which sale notes had on the margin the words: "Any dispute under this contract to be settled according to the rules of the Glasgow Flour Trade Association." This did not import into the contract the provision on arbitration contained in the rules. This was because of the absence of reasonable notice that the jurisdiction of the courts was being ousted. The concept that certain contract con-

---

[74] *British Crane Hire* v. *Ipswich Plant Hire* [1975] Q.B. 303.
[75] *Hollier* v. *Rambler Motors Ltd.* [1972] 2 Q.B. 71.
[76] *British Crane Hire* v. *Ipswich Plant Hire, sup. cit.* at p. 310.
[77] *Hardwick Game Farm* v. *SAPPA* [1966] 1 All E.R. 309; [1969] 2 A.C. 31.
[78] *J. Spurling Ltd.* v. *Bradshaw* [1956] 2 All E.R. 121.
[79] *S.I.A.T.* v. *Tradax Overseas S.A.* [1978] 2 Lloyd's Rep. 470 (failure to sign a note normally signed not enough); on appeal [1980] 1 Lloyd's Rep. 53.
[80] *Grayston Plant Ltd.* v. *Plean Precast Ltd.*, 1976 S.C. 206 (a bare reference to general conditions and where copies could be obtained was insufficient to incorporate an indemnity clause) and see cases cited at paras. 13–27 to 13–30.
[81] *S.I.A.T.* v. *Tradax Overseas S.A., sup. cit.* at p. 490 *per* Donaldson J.
[82] *Grayston Plant Ltd.* v. *Plean Precast Ltd., sup. cit.*
[83] (1897) 24 R. 414.
[84] 1911 S.C. 635.

ditions require very clear notice to incorporate them by reference was applied in *McConnell & Reid* to arbitration. There is also authority that a similar rule applies to indemnity[85] and exclusion[86] clauses. In *Aberdeen Grit Co. v. Ellerman's Wilson Line*,[87] however, goods were received and carried "subject . . . to the conditions and/or regulations of any . . . persons by whom the goods [might] be conveyed." This was said to be "the plainest and most unequivocal warning possible"[88] that the carrier might contract with a lighterage company on conditions which excluded liability for damage to the goods. The practice of excluding liability was said to be a matter of common knowledge. In *Lyon v. Irvine*[89] an irritancy clause in general regulations was incorporated into a lease by a reference to the regulations in the lease. The tenant had also signed a copy of the regulations.

28 When a sub-contract refers for its terms to the head contract, considerable complexity may arise. On the one hand the head contract does not regulate the same relationship as the sub-contract—the parties are different. On the other hand, the sub-contract is probably intended to fit in with the scheme of the head contract. In *Goodwins, Jardine & Co. Ltd. v. Brand & Son*[90] an arbitration clause in a head contract was held to be incorporated into a sub-contract so far as concerned decisions between the employer and the principal contractor. The arbitration clause was not incorporated into the sub-contract for disputes affecting only the rights of the principal contractor and the sub-contractor.

29 A similar problem arises in maritime contracts when it is sought to incorporate clauses in a charterparty into a bill of lading.[91] The issue has been analysed in detail in complex English case law.[92]

30 An association's terms can be incorporated although one of the parties has ceased to be a member of the association.[93] When there were various editions of general conditions the edition in force at the date of the contract was held to be incorporated.[94]

---

[85] *Grayston Plant* v. *Plean Precast*, 1976 S.C. 206.
[86] *Henderson* v. *Stevenson* (1875) 2 R.(H.L.) 71 at p. 77 *per* Lord Chelmsford, at p. 79 *per* Lord O'Hagan; *J. Spurling Ltd.* v. *Bradshaw* [1956] 2 All E.R. 121 at p. 125 *per* Denning L.J.; *Thornton* v. *Shoe Lane Parking Ltd.* [1971] 2 Q.B. 163; *Hollingworth* v. *Southern Ferries Ltd.* [1977] 2 Lloyd's Rep. 70.
[87] 1933 S.C. 9.
[88] *Ibid.* at p. 16 *per* Lord President Clyde: *sed quaere.*
[89] (1874) 1 R. 512.
[90] (1905) 7 F. 995; followed, *Haskins (Shutters) Ltd.* v. *D. & J. Ogilvie (Builders) Ltd.*, 1978 S.L.T.(Sh.Ct.) 64.
[91] *Howitt* v. *Paul, Swords & Co.* (1877) 5 R. 321; *Delaurier* v. *Wyllie* (1889) 17 R. 167. Discrepancies between the two documents can raise further problems: *Davidson* v. *Bisset & Son* (1878) 5 R. 706; *Hill Steam Shipping Co.* v. *Hugo Stinnes Ltd.*, 1941 S.C. 324.
[92] *e.g. T.W. Thomas & Co. Ltd.* v. *Portsea Steamship Co. Ltd.* [1912] A.C. 1; *Adamastos Shipping Co. Ltd.* v. *Anglo-Saxon Petroleum Co. Ltd.* [1959] A.C. 133; *The Annefield* [1971] P. 168; *Astro Valiente, etc. S.A.* v. *Pakistan Min. of Food and Ag. (No. 2)* [1982] 1 All E.R. 823; *Skips A/s Nordheim* v. *Syrian Petroleum Co. Ltd.* [1984] Q.B. 599; *Miramar Maritime Corp.* v. *Holborn Oil Trading Ltd.* [1984] A.C. 676.
[93] *Burroughs Machines Ltd.* v. *Timmoney*, 1977 S.C. 393.
[94] *Smith* v. *U.M.B. Chrysler (Scotland) Ltd.*, 1978 S.C.(H.L.) 1.

PART 2—EXCLUSION AND INDEMNITY CLAUSES

13–31   An exclusion clause purports to exclude a liability which would otherwise arise.[95] Frequently exclusion clauses seek to limit or restrict liability for negligence. But they may seek to alter many other rights and
duties implied by law, such as the delivery of goods of merchantable
quality or the ability to seek a remedy before the expiry of a period of
prescription. The law on exclusion clauses has been drastically affected
by the Unfair Contract Terms Act 1977.[96] Yet the common law remains
important. Not only is the Act limited to certain types of contract, but in
some circumstances an exclusion of liability which is fair and reasonable
will fall to be construed and applied by the courts. The Act provides
further control of exclusion clauses, but does not conflict with the common law on construction or incorporation of exclusion clauses.[97] This
part of this chapter is concerned with the common law.

13–32   An indemnity clause performs a different function from an exclusion
clause. Under an indemnity clause a person who has had or may have to
make a payment to a third party, seeks to recover his loss from the other
party to the contract. The effect of the clause is to transfer the ultimate
financial responsibility for meeting the third party's claim from the person liable to the third party to the person granting the indemnity.
Indemnities may, therefore, exist wherever there is legal liability. For
example, indemnities may be sought against liability for negligence,
breach of patents, copyrights, trade marks or designs, or liability for
taxes. The Unfair Contract Terms Act 1977 applies to one form of
indemnity clause in consumer contracts,[98] but otherwise indemnity
clauses are unaffected by the Act.[99]

13–33   Much of the case law on construction of exclusion clauses has been
concerned with the exclusion of liability for negligence. This case law is
applicable to indemnity clauses. The foundation of the present line of
Scottish authority, *North of Scotland Hydro-Electric Board* v. *D. & R.
Taylor*,[1] was concerned with an indemnity clause, as also was the principal authority decided by the House of Lords, *Smith* v. *U.M.B. Chrysler
(Scotland) Ltd.*[2] In the latter case Lord Fraser observed[3] that the rules
of construction which applied to exemption clauses also apply to indemnity clauses, which in many cases are merely the obverse of an exemption.

---

[95] On the distinction between a clause which defines the obligations undertaken and an
exclusion of liability, see Chap. 12, "Extortion and Unfair Terms," para. 12–39.

[96] See paras. 12–25 *et seq.*

[97] *Boomsma* v. *Clark & Rose Ltd.*, 1983 S.L.T.(Sh.Ct.) 67.

[98] s.18.

[99] Provided that they are not really exclusion clauses: see para. 13–65.

[1] 1956 S.C. 1.

[2] 1978 S.C.(H.L.) 1, and see also *McGill* v. *Pirie & Co. (Paisley) Ltd.*, 1967 S.L.T. 152;
McGlynn v. *Robert Rome & Son Ltd.*, 1968 S.L.T.(Notes) 16; *Clark* v. *William Arrol &
Co. Ltd.*, 1974 S.C. 17. For some reason the Scottish cases tend to be concerned with
indemnity clauses and the English cases with exclusion clauses.

[3] at p. 12. The terms "exemption" and "exclusion" are interchangeable.

-34   There is authority to suggest that not all exclusion clauses should be construed in the same way. An exclusion of liability for one's own negligence might receive a stricter construction than an exclusion of liability for an event, such as an act of God, which was beyond the control of either party to the contract.[4]

-35   Sophisticated levels of construction *contra proferentem* would be difficult to follow. It is probably the case that similar principles are always adopted but their application varies with the particular contract and the circumstances. Liability for negligence, however, may be particularly difficult to exclude or obtain an indemnity against, but a limitation of liability is viewed more favourably by the courts than a total exclusion of liability.[5]

-36   With these qualifications, what follows is a discussion of the construction of exclusion clauses which reflects the fact that most of the case law has been concerned with exclusion of liability for negligence. Although reference is made only to exclusion clauses similar rules apply to indemnity clauses.

Rules of Construction

There are three main rules:

(1) Construe the whole contract

The exclusion clause is construed in its context and in the light of the circumstances of each case.[6] One effect of this is that it is dangerous to rely on the assumption that clauses which have been construed in a reported case, will be given the same construction when they are put into another contract. A draftsman must be wary of copying a clause from the case reports. He cannot rely on words always having the same meaning. As Lord Cameron put it[7]:

> "While a comparison of clauses of exemption or purported exemption in other contracts in previous cases may be of great value I think there can be dangers in such bare comparisons as providing effective guidance to a proper construction of a clause under review, unless at the same time account is taken not only of the subject-matter of the contract itself but the context in which the clause in question is set, as well as the relationship of the subject-matter and content of the clause to the subject and context and language of other clauses in the contract itself. It must always be remembered

---

[4] *Pollock & Co.* v. *Macrae*, 1922 S.C.(H.L.) 192 at pp. 198–199, *per* Lord Dunedin with the concurrence of the court.

[5] *Ailsa Craig Fishing Co.* v. *Malvern Fishing Co. Ltd.*, 1982 S.L.T. 377 (H.L.); *George Mitchell (Chesterhall) Ltd.* v. *Finney Lock Seeds Ltd.* [1983] 2 A.C. 803. See para. 12–37.

[6] *Robert Hutchison & Co. Ltd.* v. *British Railways Board*, 1971 S.L.T. 84; *Evans* v. *Glasgow District Council*, 1979 S.L.T. 270; *Smith* v. *U.M.B. Chrysler*, 1978 S.C.(H.L.) 1 at p. 8 *per* Viscount Dilhorne; at p. 15 *per* Lord Fraser; at p. 18 *per* Lord Keith.

[7] *Evans* v. *Glasgow D.C.*, *sup. cit.* at p. 274.

that a clause is but part of a contract of several or many clauses and that a contract can provide its own lexicon."

13–37 The result of this approach can be a narrow rather than a wide meaning to words. The context may indicate a more restricted meaning than that provided by a dictionary. For example, restrictions have been placed on the meaning of "casualty"[8] and "from any other cause whatsoever."[9] In the last case the draftsman of the lease involved might have assumed that excluding liability arising "from any other cause whatsoever" gave a very wide protection. But the words were inserted in a clause which dealt with liability for water damage. They did not cover any negligence on the landlord's part by which access to the premises by thieves and vandals was facilitated.

13–38 The type of contract and the circumstances in which it was entered into affect the approach of the courts. An illustration can be found in Lord Justice Salmon's opinion in *Hollier* v. *Rambler Motors (A.M.C.) Ltd.*[10] when he analysed the differing expectations of an "ordinary man" to the liability of a garage, of the "ordinary housewife" who sent her washing to the laundry, and of the guest staying in a hotel. Each when asked who was liable if their property was stolen or damaged would give a response which varied with the circumstances. It may be that the "ordinary judge" would also react differently according to the type of contract.

(2) An exclusion clause is construed contra proferentem

13–39 If the meaning of the clause is doubtful it will be construed against the party relying on it. This is particularly true if the attempt is to exclude liability for one's own negligence or for some breaches of contract. It has been suggested that where the attempt is to exclude liability for events which are not under the party's control, for example strikes, a less strict standard of construction might apply.[11] There is also authority already referred to which suggests that clauses which limit liability are given a more benevolent construction than clauses which totally exclude liability.[12]

13–40 As an illustration of the principles of strict construction three rules have been developed. These are not rigid rules or rules of law, or in Lord Cameron's more colourful phrase, "a bed of Procrustes on which the language of an exemption clause was to be distorted or its meaning

---

[8] *Robert Hutchison & Co. Ltd.* v. *B.R.B.*, 1971 S.L.T. 84.
[9] *Evans* v. *Glasgow D.C., sup. cit.* For criticism of the delictual aspects of Lord Wylie's decision in the Outer House (1978 S.L.T. 17) see *P. Perl (Exporters) Ltd.* v. *Camden L.B.C.* [1984] Q.B. 342.
[10] [1972] 2 Q.B. 71.
[11] *Pollock & Co.* v. *Macrae*, 1922 S.C.(H.L.) 192 at p. 198 *per* Lord Dunedin.
[12] *Ailsa Craig Fishing Co. Ltd.*, v. *Malvern Fishing Co. Ltd.*, 1982 S.L.T. 377 (H.L.) and see paras. 12–37 to 12–39.

cut down."[13] The rules are guides in the application of the *contra profer-entem* principle. They derive from *Canada Steamship Lines Ltd. v. R.*[14] and *Alderslade v. Hendon Laundry Ltd.*[15] They were adopted in Scotland in *North of Scotland Hydro-Electric Board* v. *D. & R. Taylor*[16] and are now invariably referred to in the construction of both exclusion clauses and indemnity clauses.

In *Canada Steamship Lines Ltd.* Lord Morton said[17]:

> "Their Lordships think that the duty of a court in approaching the consideration of such clauses may be summarised as follows:–
> (1) If the clause contains language which expressly exempts the person in whose favour it is made (hereafter called 'the proferens') from the consequence of the negligence of his own servants, effect must be given to that provision . . .
> (2) If there is no express reference to negligence, the court must consider whether the words used are wide enough, in their ordinary meaning, to cover negligence on the part of the servants of the proferens. If a doubt arises at this point, it must be resolved against the proferens . . .
> (3) If the words used are wide enough for the above purpose, the court must then consider whether 'the head of damage may be based on some ground other than that of negligence,' to quote . . . Lord Greene in the *Alderslade* case. The 'other ground' must not be so fanciful or remote that the proferens cannot be supposed to have desired protection against it; but subject to this qualification, which is no doubt to be implied from Lord Greene's words, the existence of a possible head of damage other than that of negligence is fatal to the proferens even if the words used are *prima facie* wide enough to cover negligence on the part of his servants."

-41   The words omitted in the quotation are largely references to Canadian law. The dictum is now part of Scots law.

-42   It is the application of the second and third of the tests which has given rise to most difficulty. In *North of Scotland Hydro Electric Board* v. *D. & R. Taylor*[18] the words used were "all claims from third parties arising from his operations under the contract." These words were wide enough to cover claims caused by negligence. They were also wide enough to cover claims other than for negligence such as breach of contract or nuisance. Therefore the clause did not indemnify against claims based on negligence. Attempts have been made to argue, without success, that there is a distinction between common law negligence and statutory negligence.[19] The result has been that if both forms of negli-

---

[13] *Evans* v. *Glasgow D.C.*, *sup. cit.* at p. 274.
[14] [1952] A.C. 192.
[15] [1945] K.B. 189.
[16] 1956 S.C. 1; see now *Smith* v. *U.M.B. Chrysler*, 1978 S.C.(H.L.) 1.
[17] at p. 208.
[18] 1956 S.C. 1—the case also discusses the meaning of "arising from."
[19] *Hamilton & Co.* v. *Anderson & Co.*, 1953 S.C. 129; *McGill* v. *Pirie & Co. (Paisley) Ltd.*, 1967 S.L.T. 152.

gence were excluded a clause was devoid of content and accordingly the clause applied to negligence.[20]

13–43   An indemnity against "all claims in respect of . . . injury . . . to any person," was held to indemnify against claims based on negligence.[21] While claims for injury to a person might be based on breach of contract or nuisance, these possibilities were fanciful and remote and fell to be disregarded. In *Smith* v. *U.M.B. Chrysler (Scotland) Ltd.*[22] an indemnity clause did not cover the manufacturer's negligence, but would be given content if applied to the negligence of the contractor hired by the manufacturer. As a consequence of the negligence of the contractor the manufacturer could incur liabilities as occupiers of premises or as employers or for breach of statute. The clause did not indemnify against the manufacturer's own negligence. In *Boomsma* v. *Clark & Rose Ltd.*[23] the words in a contract for removal and carriage of goods were: "The Contractors shall not under any circumstances be liable for any loss or damage caused by or resulting from or in connection with fire (howsoever caused)." These words were held to be wide enough to cover negligence but they could also reasonably apply to the liability of a carrier under the Mercantile Law Amendment (Scotland) Act 1856 and liability for breach of contract.

(3) Construe an exclusion clause with a business sense

13–44   Despite some hostility to exclusion clauses the courts should construe them as part of a mercantile contract and give the contract a reasonable business efficacy.[24] The point has arisen more often with indemnity clauses. An indemnity clause was saved from being ignored when it had no restriction as to time or place so that if read literally it would have covered a claim against steelmakers in respect of an accident to any person anywhere.[25] But this approach should not be taken so far as to contradict the strict standard of construction set out in *Canada Steamship Lines* and the subsequent tract of authority.[26]

13–45   It has sometimes been argued that clauses must have a content other than a statement of the common law position, that is, that the clause must exclude some liability or provide an indemnity other than that provided by the law. This argument does not succeed.[27] It is possible to con-

---

[20] *McGill* v. *Pirie & Co. (Paisley) Ltd., sup. cit.*; *Clark* v. *Sir William Arrol & Co. Ltd.,* 1974 S.C. 17.

[21] *McGlynn* v. *Robert Rome & Son Ltd.,* 1968 S.L.T.(Notes) 16.

[22] 1978 S.C.(H.L.) 1.

[23] 1983 S.L.T.(Sh.Ct.) 67; see also *Graham* v. *Shore Porters Society,* 1979 S.L.T. 119, which discusses exemption from breach of contract.

[24] *Hamilton & Co.* v. *Anderson & Co.,* 1953 S.C. 129 at p. 136 *per* Lord President Cooper; *Mackay* v. *Balfour, Beatty & Co. Ltd.,* 1967 S.L.T.(Notes) 15; *Robert Hutchison & Co. Ltd.* v. *British Railways Board, sup. cit.*

[25] *McGill* v. *Pirie & Co. (Paisley) Ltd.,* 1967 S.L.T. 152.

[26] *Clark* v. *Sir William Arrol & Co.,* 1974 S.C. 17.

[27] *North of Scotland Hydro Electric Board* v. *D. & R. Taylor, sup. cit.*; *Smith* v. *U.M.B. Chrysler (Scotland) Ltd., sup. cit.*

strue a clause as a warning of the limitations of normal legal liability, *e.g.* as meaning: "Beware. We are not liable, unless we are negligent. There is a risk you should insure against."[28]

Drafting an Exclusion Clause[28a]

46 With the help of reported case law it is possible to learn something from the mistakes of others.

(1) Mention negligence

47 Use the word "negligence" to exclude liability for negligence. Do not rely on general words such as "any liability whatsoever."[29] The reason for this is the application of the three rules in *Canada Steamship Lines Ltd.* Almost all the problems in the reported case law would have been avoided if there had been a clear and unmistakable reference to negligence.

48 It is true that a synonym for negligence might suffice,[30] but there is no advantage in the hazard of another word or phrase. In *Gillespie Bros.* v. *Roy Bowles Ltd.*[31] two judges thought that an express reference to negligence was contained in the words in which one party undertook "to save harmless and keep" the other party "indemnified against all claims or demands whatsoever." This view has now been disapproved in the House of Lords.[32]

(2) Whose negligence?

49 It might not be sufficient to say: "The company will not be liable for negligence." Whose negligence is in issue? The failure to specify which party's negligence was a stumbling-block to the effectiveness of the clause in *Smith* v. *U.M.B. Chrysler*. That was a case about an indemnity clause where it may be that there is a greater need to point to the negligence concerned. Nevertheless, in an exclusion clause it is prudent to state that the company will not be liable for its negligence just in case the inference is drawn that the negligence referred to is the negligence of the other party or its employees.

50 The further problem which is raised is the extent to which there should be references to the negligence of others such as employees, agents, independent contractors, subsidiaries, associated companies or

---

[28] See *Verrico* v. *Hughes & Son Ltd.*, 1980 S.C. 179 at p. 187; *Olley* v. *Marlborough Court Ltd.* [1949] 1 K.B. 532; *Hollier* v. *Rambler Motors (A.M.C.) Ltd.* [1972] 2 Q.B. 71 at p. 82 *per* Salmon L.J.

[28a] Similar propositions apply to an indemnity clause. See para. 13–33.

[29] See *Smith* v. *U.M.B. Chrysler, sup. cit.*

[30] *Smith* v. *U.M.B. Chrysler, sup. cit.* at p. 12 *per* Lord Fraser; *Evans* v. *Glasgow D.C., sup. cit.* at p. 272 *per* Lord President Emslie.

[31] [1973] Q.B. 400.

[32] *Smith* v. *U.M.B. Chrysler, sup. cit.* at p. 8 *per* Viscount Dilhorne, at p. 12 *per* Lord Fraser. See also *The Raphael* [1982] 2 Lloyd's Rep. 42.

parent companies. These persons are not parties to the contract but it might well be that it is wished to extend to them the benefit of the exclusion clause. In English law the doctrine of privity of contract makes it difficult for a person to be affected by an exclusion clause in a contract to which he is not a party.[33] Scots law has the doctrine of *jus quaesitum tertio*. Under that principle it should be possible to give third parties the benefit of an exclusion clause in a contract. There are two reasons why there is some doubt about this.

13–51   The first problem is that some formulations of the principle of *jus quaesitum tertio* proceed on the basis that the third party has a right to compel performance by one of the contracting parties[34] or as Lord Reid put it: "To have a *jus quaesitum tertio* the third party must have been given by the contract of the contracting parties a right to get something from one or both of them."[35] This does not match the pattern of an exclusion clause which is a right *not* to have something done. However statements should be read in the context in which they were made. The possibility of the benefit to the third party being in a negative form was probably not considered, rather than rejected as inconsistent with principle.

13–52   The second problem is the controversy surrounding the idea that the third party's right must be irrevocable as a condition of the creation of a *jus quaesitum tertio*.[36] Parties to many commercial contracts would regard the contract as revocable by both of them. It is common to have alteration of the terms of contracts or the substitution of new contracts by the agreement of all the parties. In this way a third party's benefit under an exclusion clause could be revoked. If irrevocability is a condition for the creation of a right in the third party, that condition in practice will rarely be met. But it is thought that there is confusion over the use of the term "irrevocability" and that there is no obstacle to a third party acquiring a revocable right.[37] Therefore, with reservations, the draftsman in Scotland may provide that an exclusion clause applies to various persons who are connected with a contracting party.

(3) When do the excepted events occur?

13–53   It is insufficient to say that the company will not be liable for its negligence. Negligence in doing what? Further, the exclusion clause may cover events other than negligence. A statement that "the company will

---

[33] Coote, *Exception Clauses* (1964), Chap. 9; *Midland Silicones Ltd.* v. *Scruttons Ltd.* [1962] A.C. 446; *Beswick* v. *Beswick* [1968] A.C. 58; *Woodar Investment Development Ltd.* v. *Wimpey Construction U.K. Ltd.* [1980] 1 All E.R. 571 (H.L.) at p. 591 *per* Lord Scarman; *cf. New Zealand Shipping Co.* v. *A.M. Satterthwaite & Co.* [1975] A.C. 154.

[34] Stair, I,x,5.

[35] *Allan's Trs.* v. *Lord Advocate*, 1971 S.C.(H.L.) 45 at p. 54.

[36] See paras. 18–20 *et seq.*

[37] See para. 18–26.

not be liable for any loss caused by it whether arising from its negligence or otherwise" suggests that the company will never be liable for a breach of contract. Policy decisions made in consultation with the client should give some guidelines on what liability is to be excluded. The important point is that the exclusion clause should cover something outside the normal routine in the performance of the contract. The greatest risk of liability arises from employees not doing what they should. On the other hand the clause should not go so far as to exclude liability for anything which happens, whatever that may be. Apart from it being commercially undesirable to undertake no obligations in your contracts, the difficulty of convincing a court that such an exclusion of liability is "fair and reasonable" does not need elaboration. The problems of the detailed drafting can be illustrated by case law. Be wary of:

(a) **Limitation to a particular time.** Words of exception in a bill of lading were held not to apply to the state of the ship *prior* to loading.[38]

(b) **Limitation to a particular place.** An exclusion clause about left luggage did not apply because the article was left on a station platform while the clause referred to articles "deposited in the company's cloakroom or warehouse."[39] An exclusion clause applying to vehicles and contents which were "stored" by a garage, did not apply to a vehicle and its contents which were parked on a roadway outside the garage.[40] It has even been suggested that an exclusion clause about injury sustained on board an aircraft would not cover a person being thrown from the aircraft and killed by the impact.[41]

(c) **Limitation to acts done in accordance with the contract.** As a more general illustration of the points in (a) and (b) there are cases where, on a strict construction, an exclusion clause has not been applied when the contract has been breached. In a contract for sale of engines, liability was excluded for defective material or workmanship. This was held not to apply to a total breach of contract which rendered the engines practically unserviceable.[42] If a plane ticket had limited itself to the statement, "shall be under no liability in respect or arising out of the carriage," that would not have covered a crashing of the plane which frustrated the voyage.[43] The supply of seed of a completely different kind from that

---

[38] *Steel & Craig* v. *State Line Steamships* (1877) 4 R.(H.L.) 103; see also *Seville Sulphur and Coffee Co.* v. *Colvils, Lowden & Co.* (1888) 15 R. 616; *Gilroy Sons & Co.* v. *Price & Co.* (1892) 20 R.(H.L.) 1.
[39] *Handon* v. *Caledonian Ry. Co.* (1880) 7 R. 966; *cf. Lyons & Co.* v. *Caledonian Ry. Co.*, 1909 S.C. 1185, which does not adopt modern standards of strict construction.
[40] *Verrico* v. *Hughes & Son Ltd.*, 1980 S.C. 179.
[41] *McKay* v. *Scottish Airways*, 1948 S.C. 254 at p. 257 *per* Lord Mackintosh.
[42] *Pollock & Co.* v. *Macrae*, 1922 S.C.(H.L.) 192; see also *Mechans Ltd.* v. *Highland Marine Charters Ltd.*, 1964 S.C. 48.
[43] *McKay* v. *Scottish Airways, sup. cit.*

ordered might make an exclusion clause inoperative.[44] An indemnity clause did not apply when a railway company sent cattle by the wrong route.[45]

13–54   It is possible to draft an exclusion clause to cover a serious breach of contract, but the application of the rules of strict construction means that very clear words must be used to achieve a wide immunity.[46]

(4) Howsoever caused

13–55   The phrase "howsoever caused" or similar words raises so many issues that it needs to be specially treated. The phrase has a long history of judicial interpretation.[47] The reason for its popularity is that it excludes the *ejusdem generis* rule. Under that rule the meaning of a word or phrase is limited to things of the same type as those specifically mentioned before. Thus in *Abchurch Steamship Co.* v. *Stinnes*[48] a demurrage clause excepted a wide variety of causes for delay, *e.g.* holidays, strikes, floods, riots, "or any other unavoidable cause." The last phrase was interpreted as referring to a category of breakdown in arrangements and therefore did not apply to the delay in getting a berth which arose as part of the ordinary routine of the working of the port. On the other hand, in another case the wording "frost floods strikes . . . and any other unavoidable accidents or hindrances of what kind so ever," excluded the *ejusdem generis* rule and the clause was applied to a delay in loading caused by a blockage of ships.[49]

13–56   The phrase "howsoever caused" has been construed as excluding liability for negligence.[50] But this has not been the invariable result. In *Smith* v. *U.M.B. Chrysler*[51] the House of Lords held that the word "whatsoever" in the phrase "any liability, loss, claim or proceedings whatsoever" could not be read as equivalent to an express reference to negligence. In *Evans* v. *Glasgow District Council*[52] a statement "or from any other cause whatsoever" was construed strictly and did not cover loss caused by vandals.

---

[44] *Cf.* cases where the wrong variety was supplied: *Rutherford & Son* v. *Milne & Co.*, 1941 S.C. 125; *George Mitchell (Chesterhall) Ltd.* v. *Finney Lock Seeds* [1983] 2 A.C. 803. These cases have to be distinguished from cases in which peas are supplied instead of beans, chalk instead of cheese, or a bicycle instead of a car.

[45] *Lord Polwarth* v. *N.B. Ry. Co.*, 1908 S.C. 1275; see also *London and N.W. Ry. Co.* v. *Neilson* [1922] 2 A.C. 263.

[46] *Suisse Atlantique Société d'Armement Maritime S.A.* v. *N.V. Rotterdamsche Kolen Centrale* [1967] 1 A.C. 361; *Photo Production Ltd.* v. *Securicor Transport Ltd.* [1980] A.C. 827.

[47] See *Steel & Craig* v. *State Line Steamship Co.* (1877) 4 R. 657 at p. 666 *per* Lord Shand; on appeal (1877) 4 R.(H.L.) 103.

[48] 1911 S.C. 1010.

[49] *Larsen* v. *Sylvester & Co.* [1908] A.C. 295.

[50] *McCuaig* v. *Redpath Dorman Long*, 1972 S.L.T.(Notes) 42; see also *Travers* v. *Cooper* [1915] 1 K.B. 73; *A.E. Farr* v. *Admiralty* [1953] 2 All E.R. 512.

[51] 1978 S.C.(H.L.) 1.

[52] 1979 S.L.T. 270.

7   The problem is that general words are capable of different constructions. This gives rise to the possibility of doubt as to meaning. The application of the rule of construction against the *proferens* can mean that
apparently general words are given a restricted sense. As Lord Cameron
put it in *Evans*[53]:

> "Such words as 'any other case whatsoever' standing by them-
> selves no doubt can, and in appropriate cases will, be interpreted as
> adequate to excuse even the negligence of the party seeking protec-
> tion under an exemption clause, but in every case the language and
> wording of a clause of purported exemption must necessarily be
> interpreted in light of the immediate context, the subject-matter of
> the contract, and in light also of the contract considered as a whole.
> Where however the language used leaves a doubt as to the extent to
> which a party's liability for his acts or omissions or those of his
> agents or servants is to be limited or even extinguished then the
> doubt will be resolved contra proferentem and in particular when it
> is sought to include within a general exemption one which will
> relieve the party from liability for his own negligence or that of
> anyone for whom he is responsible."

8   A further problem is that the mere use of the phrase "howsoever
caused" or an equivalent, could make a clause of exclusion or limitation
of liability so wide, that the clause is not "fair and reasonable" in terms
of the Unfair Contract Terms Act 1977.[53a] There is an old case involving
different legislation which illustrates the problem. In *Finlay* v. *North
British Railway Co.*[54] one issue was whether an agreement was "just and
reasonable" within the meaning of the Railway and Canal Traffic Act
1854. The phrase concerned was "from all liability for loss or damage by
delay in transit, or from whatever cause arising." Lord President Inglis
observed[55]: "The general words 'from whatever cause arising,' if meaning any more than the preceding words, cannot, I think, receive effect.
They are too broad to be 'just and reasonable.'"

9   Applying that approach to the 1977 Act, there could be logic in arguing that an omnibus phrase, such as "howsoever caused," is intended to
catch whatever has not been thought of and cannot reflect a proper consideration of the distribution of risks. As always the success of this type
of argument will depend on the context in which the words are used, but
the dangers arising from the use of general words in exclusion clauses
have been increased by the 1977 Act.

(5) Claims and expenses

0   Does an exclusion of liability exclude not only the claim, but all the
expenses associated with the claim? This problem is more likely to arise
with indemnity clauses where one party tries to recoup his loss from

---

[53] at p. 275.
[53a] See paras. 12–33 *et seq.*
[54] (1870) 8 M. 959.
[55] at p. 969.

another and the issue is the extent of legal expenses which are claimable. But the problem could also arise with a limitation of liability clause. Say the clause has a valid limit of £500. The claimant seeks £350 and expenses of £250. How much is payable—£350 or £500?

13–61   It has been held that an obligation of relief impliedly covers the expenses of an action.[56] However, an agreement to pay legal expenses has been construed as restricted to the expenses before a court of first instance.[57] The draftsman of a limitation of liability clause may prefer to avoid uncertainties and have an express reference to costs and expenses.

(6) Self-contradiction

13–62   It is an obvious proposition that self-contradiction in a contract should be avoided. Yet the application of that proposition is not always straightforward. The primary purpose of a contract is to impose obligations. The exclusion clause removes obligations. The contrast can lead to clauses in the form: "While the company will use every endeavour to do X, they will not be liable if X does not happen." Although a clause similar to this has been upheld,[58] it is not a prudent formula to follow. The reason is the *contra proferentem* rule. If it is doubtful whether a liability is excluded, it will not be excluded.

13–63   There is a line of high authority in the case of carriers which jettisoned the ill-expressed agreement of the parties in favour of common law liability.[59] As Lord Macnaghten put it: "an ambiguous document is no protection."[60] This authority may proceed to an extent on the specialities of the contract of carriage,[61] but that should not be too heavily relied upon as a ground for ignoring the approach which it represents. In a sale of goods case, a clause which was contradictory, and which had superfluous words, did not exclude an obligation to supply bulbs in a merchantable condition.[62]

13–64   Another possible result of ambiguity is that the court will prefer a narrow construction of a word if it avoids making the contract self-contradictory. For this reason the word "casualty" was given a narrow rather than a wide meaning in *Robert Hutchison & Co. Ltd.* v. *British Railways Board.*[63]

---

[56] *Commrs. for Leith Harbour and Docks* v. *N.B. Ry. Co.* (1904) 12 S.L.T. 192.
[57] *Boyle & Co.* v. *Morton & Sons* (1903) 5 F. 416.
[58] *Ballingall & Son* v. *Dundee Ice and Cold Storage Co.*, 1924 S.C. 238.
[59] *Elderslie Steamship Co.* v. *Borthwick* [1905] A.C. 93; *Nelson Line (Liverpool) Ltd.* v. *James Nelson & Sons* [1908] A.C. 16; *Union of India* v. *Compania Naviera Aeolus S.A.* [1964] A.C. 868.
[60] *Elderslie Steamship Co.* v. *Borthwick, sup. cit.* at p. 96.
[61] See *Chartered Bank of India, Australia and China* v. *British India Steam Navigation Co.* [1909] A.C. 369 at p. 375 *per* Lord Macnaghten.
[62] *Van Til-Hartman* v. *Thomson*, 1931 S.N. 30.
[63] 1971 S.L.T. 84.

(7) Confusion with indemnity clauses

5   Sometimes a phrase is used like: "Y will indemnify X against any liability arising from the actions of X or its employees." On the face of it this is an indemnity clause, albeit a badly-drafted clause. But the clause appears in a contract between X and Y under which X is to do work for Y. In effect the clause is an exclusion clause at least in part. X is excluding his liability to Y. Because the word "indemnity" is used, confusion is caused. However, in so far as the clause is attempting to exclude the liability of X to Y, the controls on exclusion clauses in the Unfair Contract Terms Act will apply. If there is a moral, it is that the draftsman should not draft an exclusion clause by copying the terms of an indemnity clause.

(8) Conclusion

6   It is wise to approach the problem of drafting with humility. There is plenty of judicial criticism of previous attempts at framing these clauses,[64] and the problem has been made more difficult by the need to avoid the traps laid by the Unfair Contract Terms Act. It may be preferable to consider a limitation of liability rather than a total exclusion of liability.[64a] Nor should one fundamental point be forgotten. The clause is in a contract and, subject to any *jus quaesitum tertio*, only the parties to the contract are bound by the clause. There may be other persons on a work site to whom a client could incur liability.[65] The client's products or services may be supplied to or affect those with whom he has no contract. Exclusion clauses cannot deal with all the problems of liability and, in any event, they must be considered along with the insurance requirements of the client.

PART 3—RESERVATION OF TITLE CLAUSES

7   A reservation of title clause reserves ownership in goods to the seller until the seller is paid the price. The clause alters the effect of the common law or statute which would result in ownership passing at an earlier time, such as the conclusion of the contract or the delivery of the goods to the buyer.

8   There is a long history of reservation of title clauses in Scots law. Stair mentioned one form of condition in sale: "if the bargain be conditional, only upon payment of the price at such a time, till payment the property

---

[64] See, *e.g. Ballingall & Son* v. *Dundee Ice and Cold Storage Co.*, 1924 S.C. 238 at p. 247 *per* Lord Justice-Clerk Alness (dissenting judgment); *Hamilton & Co.* v. *Anderson & Co.*, 1953 S.C. 129 at p. 137 *per* Lord President Cooper (indemnity clause); *Evans* v. *Glasgow District Council*, 1979 S.L.T. 270.

[64a] See paras. 12–37 to 12–39.

[65] See *Lindinger Rederiet A/S* v. *James Lamont & Co. Ltd.*, 1972 S.L.T.(Notes) 14.

passeth not to the buyer."[66] Erskine mentioned the suspensive condition on passing of property: "if a sale should be entered into under
condition that the price shall be paid on or before a day prefixed, such
condition, before it be purified is, as Stair justly observes, truly suspensive of the sale, which is not understood to be perfected till the condition
exists; insomuch that though the subject should be delivered to the
buyer, the property continues in the seller till the price be paid."[67]
According to Bell the effect of suspensive conditions on real rights, "has
been taken for granted in practice."[68]

13–69   An example of the operation of reservation of title clauses at common
law is *Murdoch & Co. Ltd. v. Greig.*[69] This involved a contract for the
sale of a harmonium. Property remained with the seller until the price
was paid. The seller was able to recover the harmonium from a person
who had bought it at an auction. There are two special points with the
case. (1) The contract was described as a "hire," but the court looked to
the nature of the transaction which was sale. (2) The ability of the
unpaid seller to recover the goods from a *bona fide* third-party purchaser would now be affected by section 25 of the Sale of Goods Act
1979.

13–70   Another example, this time involving insolvency, is *Hogarth* v.
Smart's Tr.[70] A millwright sold machinery to his tenant. The millwright
was to remain owner until he was paid. He was never paid. The tenant
became insolvent and granted a trust deed for creditors. The millwright
successfully claimed the return of the machinery.

13–71   The Sale of Goods Act, both in 1893 and in its re-enactment in 1979,
recognised reservation of title clauses.[71] Under section 17 of the 1979
Act property passes when it is intended to pass. Under section 19 the
right of disposal may be reserved until certain conditions are fulfilled.

13–72   The result is that a clause which suspends the passing of property until
payment of price can be valid both at common law and under the Sale of
Goods Act.[72]

"All Sums" Clauses

13–73   A controversy has arisen over the effect of reservation of title clauses
which go further than reserving title in goods until the price has been
paid for the goods delivered under the contract. Many of the reservation

---

[66] *Inst.,* I,xiv,4.
[67] Ersk., III,iii,11.
[68] Bell, *Comm.,* I,258.
[69] (1889) 16 R. 396.
[70] (1882) 9 R. 964; see also *Cowan* v. *Spence* (1824) 3 S.42; *Baird's Trs.* v. *Baird & Co.*
(1877) 4 R. 1005; *Scott's Trs.* v. *Alexander's Tr.* (1884) 11 R. 407.
[71] See the treatment of the 1893 Act in R. Brown, *Sale of Goods Act 1893* (2nd ed.,
1911), pp. 114–121, 136; Gloag and Irvine, *Rights in Security,* p. 241.
[72] See also *Archivent Sales and Development Ltd.* v. *Strathclyde R.C.,* 1985 S.L.T. 154;
Zahnrad Fabrik Passau Gmbh v. *Terex Ltd.,* 1986 S.L.T. 84.

clauses attempt to reserve title until the buyer has paid all sums or all
claims due to the seller. Full payment for the goods supplied may not
purify the condition because there may be other sums due to the seller,
such as sums due under other contracts. The reason for clauses in this
form is the interest in the use of reservation of title clauses stimulated by
the English case of *Aluminium Industrie Vaassen B.V.* v. *Romalpa Aluminium Ltd.*[73]

4   Professor T. B. Smith has commented[74]:

> "Though a reservation of title until payment for a particular con-
> signment might not, as the law stands, be open to attack as security,
> the clause in *Romalpa* purported to reserve ownership of the foil
> until *all* claims by the seller had been satisfied. This would seem to
> involve security without transfer of possession by the debtor which
> is contrary to the principles of Scots law and recognised only in a
> very restricted field such as the floating charges of incorporated
> companies."

5   To deliver goods but reserve title in them until sums due under other
transactions have been paid is an attempt to create a security. This is
recognised in two decisions by Lord Ross.[75]

6   The principal difficulty which arises in this area of law is the effect of
treating the clause as an attempt to create a security. To say that the
clause is an ineffectual security does not end the problem. Who owns
the goods?

7   The seller originally owned the goods. He has attempted, unsuccessfully, to create a security over the goods. Does he still own them? If he
does not own the goods, what has passed property to the buyer and
when did that happen? In the normal case the contract in its terms has
not passed property nor has it been the intention of both parties that
property should pass. Yet in the two decisions of Lord Ross the sellers
were refused interim interdict against the receivers of the buyers dealing
with the goods. All this may mean is that the buyers had a contractual
right to deal with the goods. But in *Deutz Engines* the sellers had a right
by contract to recover possession of the goods. They still failed to obtain
interim interdict. It may be that in some way the buyers have obtained

---

[73] [1976] 2 All E.R. 552; the effect in English law continues to give rise to problems. See
Re Bond Worth [1980] Ch. 228; *Borden (U.K.) Ltd.* v. *Scottish Timber Products Ltd.*
[1981] Ch. 25; *Re Peachdart Ltd.* [1984] Ch. 131; *Hendy Lennox (Industrial Engines) Ltd.*
v. *Grahame Puttick Ltd.* [1984] 2 All E.R. 152; *Re Andrabell Ltd.* [1984] 3 All E.R. 407;
Clough Mill Ltd. v. *Martin* [1984] 3 All E.R. 982. In England, unlike Scotland, a charge by
a company over goods is void if it is not registered with the registrar of companies (Companies Act 1985, ss.395, 396(1)(c). *Cf.* the Scottish provisions in s.410(4)). It is unlikely,
despite *Re Bond Worth, sup. cit.*, that a retention of title clause will be a floating charge
because the clause usually applies to specific assets.
[74] *Property Problems in Sale* (1978) p. 131.
[75] *Emerald Stainless Steel Ltd.* v. *South Side Distribution Ltd.*, 1982 S.C. 61; *Deutz
Engines Ltd.* v. *Terex Ltd.*, 1984 S.L.T. 273; see also *Hammer and Sohne* v. *H.W.T.
Realisations Ltd.*, 1985 S.L.T.(Sh.Ct.) 21.

ownership of the goods, or a right as good as ownership. How this has happened remains to be illuminated by judicial decision. As the law stands, receivers and liquidators of buyers will claim a right to use the goods if they have been acquired under "all sums" clauses.[76]

13–78   One of the other issues arising with "all sums" clauses is the effect of section 62(4) of the Sale of Goods Act 1979. This provides: "The provisions of this Act about contracts of sale do not apply to a transaction in the form of a contract of sale which is intended to operate by way of mortgage, pledge, charge or other security." This section has been applied many times to attack the sale and hire back transaction, which is in reality a loan with an attempted security over moveables. The moveables must be delivered to the creditor to create an effective security.[77] As mentioned earlier, a reservation of title clause with an "all sums" provision is clearly an attempt to create a security. Although the *clause* may be a security, it does not follow that the whole *contract* is affected by section 62(4). A *Romalpa*-type clause is in a contract which is intended as a genuine sale. It is not a sham sale. It is not a loan. Looking at the whole transaction it is not a security transaction. There is authority which suggests that the whole transaction must be looked at in applying section 62(4) and the subsection will not operate just because the contract contains some element of security.[78] Each case depends on it own facts.

13–79   In *Deutz Engines*[79] the Sale of Goods Act did not apply to a contract in the form of both a genuine sale and an attempt to create a security. The result must have been that the common law applied. How that law gave the receivers of the buyer a right to deal with the goods was not explained.[80]

---

[76] The controversy is analysed in articles mentioned by Lord Ross in *Deutz Engines Ltd.*, namely K.G.C. Reid and G.L. Gretton, "Retention of Title in *Romalpa* Clauses," 1983 S.L.T.(News) 77; T. B. Smith, "Retention of Title: Lord Watson's Legacy," 1983 S.L.T.(News) 105; and in K.G.C. Reid and G.L. Gretton, "Retention of Title for all Sums: A Reply," 1983 S.L.T.(News) 165. See also 1983 S.L.T.(News) 102; D.J. Cusine, "The *Romalpa* Family Visits Scotland" (1982) 27 J.L.S. 147, 221. A restatement of the position of Reid and Gretton is in "*Romalpa* Clauses: The Current Position," 1985 S.L.T.(News) 329.

[77] *Hepburn* v. *Law*, 1914 S.C. 918; *Gavin's Trs.* v. *Fraser*, 1920 S.C. 674; *Newbigging* v. *Ritchie's Trs.*, 1930 S.C. 273; *Scottish Transit Ltd.* v. *Scottish Land Cultivators Ltd.*, 1955 S.C. 254; *G. & C. Finance Corp. Ltd.* v. *Brown*, 1961 S.L.T. 408.

[78] *Lawrence's Trs.* v. *Lawrence* (1899) 6 S.L.T. 356; *McBain* v. *Wallace & Co.* (1881) 8 R.(H.L.) 106, commented on in *Robertson* v. *Hall's Tr.* (1896) 24 R. 120; *Liquidator of West Lothian Oil Co. Ltd.* v. *Mair* (1892) 20 R. 64; *Gavin's Tr.* v. *Fraser*, 1920 S.C. 674.

[79] *Sup. cit.*

[80] The decision was an application for interim interdict in which other factors and in particular the balance of convenience are relevant. See in other areas *Scottish Milk Marketing Board* v. *Paris*, 1935 S.C. 287; *Highland Distilleries Co. PLC* v. *Speymalt Whisky Distributors Ltd.*, 1985 S.L.T. 85; *Lord Duncan Sandys* v. *House of Fraser*, 1985 S.L.T. 200; *Scottish Milk Marketing Board* v. *Drybrough & Co. Ltd.*, 1985 S.L.T. 253; *William Grant & Sons Ltd.* v. *William Cadenhead Ltd.*, 1985 S.L.T. 291; *Cowie* v. *Strathclyde R.C.*, 1985 S.L.T. 333.

Creating a Trust

30 Some forms of reservation of title clause attempt to create a trust under which the buyer holds the sale proceeds of goods for the benefit of the seller. The intention is to give the seller a right against funds which cannot be defeated by the claims of creditors of the buyer. It would be possible to create a trust, but the mechanics for doing so, and in particular the need for delivery or an equivalent suggest that it would be easier for the buyer to pay over the sale proceeds to the seller. A mere expression of an intention to create a trust is insufficient.[81] In *Clark Taylor & Co. Ltd.* v. *Quality Site Development (Edinburgh) Ltd.*[82] there was an unsuccessful attempt to create a trust over the resale proceeds of bricks. The words used were treated by the court as no more than an attempt, under the guise of a trust, to keep assets of the buyer out of the hands of its creditors.[83] In any event an obligation to set up a trust did not by itself create a trust.[84]

In practice it is highly unlikely that the buyer will create a trust if he mixes resale proceeds with his other funds. It is possible that he might put money due to the seller[85] into a separate bank account. For example, the buyer may be a distributor for a foreign company and sums due to the foreign company are kept in £s sterling in an account in Scotland. On the insolvency of the buyer, assets clearly identified as the property of the foreign company may be claimed by it.[86]

Resale of Goods

1 Although in possession of goods subject to a simple and effective reservation of title clause, a buyer may sell the goods to a *bona fide* third party. The buyer is not the owner of the goods, but the third party can acquire a good title under section 25(1) of the Sale of Goods Act 1979.[87]

---

[81] *Connell's Trs.* v. *Connell's Trs.*, 1955 S.L.T. 125; *Allan's Trs.* v. *Lord Advocate*, 1971 S.C.(H.L.) 45; *Clark's Trs.* v. *Inland Revenue*, 1972 S.C. 177; *Kerr's Trs.* v. *Inland Revenue*, 1974 S.C. 115; *Export Credits Guarantee Dept.* v. *Turner*, 1979 S.C. 286.

[82] 1981 S.C. 111.

[83] This assumes that property had passed to the buyer: *sed quaere.* See W. A. Wilson, "*Romalpa* and Trust," 1983 S.L.T.(News) 106.

[84] See at p. 115 of the report for the requirements necessary to create a trust.

[85] Something distinct from "resale proceeds."

[86] *Smith* v. *Liquidator of James Birrell*, 1968 S.L.T. 174 (*cf. Michelin Tyre Co.* v. *Macfarlane (Glasgow) Ltd.*, 1917 2 S.L.T. 205 (H.L.), where there was immixing); and on claiming insurance proceeds for goods destroyed, see *Cochran & Son* v. *Leckie's Tr.* (1906) 8 F. 975.

[87] *Archivent Sales & Development Ltd.* v. *Strathclyde R.C.*, 1985 S.L.T. 154; *Four Point Garage Ltd.* v. *Carter* [1985] 3 All E.R. 12; *International Banking Corp.* v. *Ferguson, Shaw & Sons*, 1910 S.C. 182, when carefully read, might suggest that the ultimate buyer cannot obtain a title in the face of the true owner's reservation of title. But the case appears to have been argued without reference to the Sale of Goods Act.

Immixing of Goods

13–82   If the goods are applied in making a new species, the former ownership of the goods may be destroyed by the operation of the doctrine of *specificatio*.[88] When the goods are mixed with other goods, rights of common property may be created by confusion of liquids, commixtion of solids or contexture.[89] Distinct from problems of passing of property is the question of whether there must be recompense to the true owner for the value of the goods or for the profits made. This involves some very difficult and unresolved issues, for which reference should be made to the most recent discussion.[90]

Fixtures

13–83   If the goods are fixed to heritage ownership in the goods may vest in the owner of the heritage. The legal questions raised include, in particular, the degree of attachment necessary to achieve this result.[91]

Appropriation of Payments

13–84   When goods are supplied on a regular basis and some payments are made, problems can arise in determining which goods have been fully paid for and which have not. The goods which have been fully paid for will be the property of the buyer, whereas other goods may be the property of the seller. Usually the problems raised are those of appropriation of payments which is considered elsewhere.[92]

Identification of the Goods

13–85   One of the greatest practical problems for a seller who claims goods which are subject to a reservation of title clause is identification of the goods which are subject to the clause. Goods which have a distinctive manufacturer's mark are easier to identify than those which may be con-

---

[88] *International Banking Corp.* v. *Ferguson, Shaw & Son, sup. cit.; Wylie & Lochhead* v. *Mitchell* (1870) 8 M. 552; *McDonald* v. *Provan (of Scotland Street) Ltd.,* 1960 S.L.T. 231; *North-West Securities Ltd.* v. *Barrhead Coachworks Ltd.,* 1976 S.C. 68; *Zahnrad Fabrik Passau GmbH* v. *Terex Ltd.,* 1986 S.L.T. 84. The problems were analysed by Scot.Law Com. Memo. No. 28, *Corporeal Moveables, Mixing Union and Creation* (1976), pp. 9 *et seq.*
[89] T.B. Smith, *Short Commentary,* pp. 537–538; Scot. Law Com., *sup. cit.,* pp. 1–9.
[90] Scot. Law Com., *ibid.*
[91] See Rankine, *Land Ownership,* pp. 116 *et seq.; Green's Encyclopaedia of the Laws of Scotland,* Vol. 9, paras. 361 *et seq.; Christie* v. *Smith's Exr.,* 1949 S.C. 572. There is a tendency in some modern practice to create leases or licences or hires over structures attached to land. Personal rights may be created but once a structure is affixed to land it belongs to the owner of the land: *Brand's Trs.* v. *Brand's Trs.* (1876) 3 R.(H.L.) 16; *Crichton* v. *Turnbull,* 1946 S.C. 52 (pipes through land); *Cliffplant Ltd.* v. *Kinnaird and Mabey Bridge Co.,* 1981 S.C. 9 (a building and a bridge), which is overruled in part by *Scottish Discount Co. Ltd.* v. *Blin,* 1986 S.L.T. 123 (seven judges).
[92] See paras. 22–26 *et seq.* An early example with a retention of title clause is *Scott's Trs.* v. *Alexander's Tr.* (1884) 11 R. 407.

fused with items already paid for or supplied by others. The manufacturer of an engine with a chassis number is usually in a stronger position to assert his claim than, say, the supplier of sand. By contract the seller may have required the buyer to keep the seller's goods apart and identified, but buyers rarely label goods with the care of a museum curator and insolvent buyers are frequently disorganised.

6   A receiver or a liquidator of the buyer may use the difficulty of identification as a factor in his favour and refuse to recognise a claim which is not specific. This, however, creates a potential problem for him. The true owner is entitled to recover his property. Once the receiver or liquidator has intimation that he is in possession of the property of another and its return is requested, subsequent appropriation of the property by the receiver or liquidator may be theft[93] and may enable the owner to claim damages.[94] The owner's right to recover his property generally prescribes after 20 years.[95]

However, a right which is correlative to an obligation to pay money in respect of goods supplied on sale prescribes after five years.[96] In the context of reservation of title clauses it is thought that the five-year period will usually be relevant, but even that is far too long for the receiver or liquidator intent on prompt administration of the assets under his charge and faced with a dispute on the ownership of some of those assets. An action of declarator may be the answer.

Choice of Law Problems

7   Many of the reservation of title clauses which are encountered in practice are contained in contracts which are governed by a law other than Scots law. The consequent problems cannot be analysed here.[97]

Drafting a Reservation of Title Clause

8   The uncertainties created by the present state of the law cannot be resolved by the draftsman, but when a reservation of title clause is needed, he can minimise the potential problems. He will bear in mind the following guidelines.

(1) The simpler the clause is, the more effective it is likely to be.

---

[93] Gordon, *Criminal Law* (2nd ed.), paras. 14–80 to 14–86 which discuss the person who believes he has a right to another's moveables.

[94] *Aarons & Co.* v. *Fraser*, 1934 S.C. 137; *cf. North West Securities Ltd.* v. *Barrhead Coachworks*, 1976 S.C. 68.

[95] Prescription and Limitation (Scotland) Act 1973, s.8. Against a thief or a party to the theft the right is imprescriptible. See Sched. 3.

[96] ss.6 and 8. Broadly the five-year period runs from the date when payment was due. See Sched. 2, para. 1(4).

[97] See *Hammer and Sohne* v. *H.W.T. Realisation Ltd.*, 1985 S.L.T.(Sh.Ct.) 21; W. J. Stewart, "*Romalpa* Clauses: Choosing the Law," 1985 S.L.T.(News) 149—see 1985 S.L.T.(News) 182; D. Sellar, "*Romalpa* and Receivables—Choosing the Law," 1985 S.L.T.(News) 313; *Zahnrad Fabrik Passau GmbH* v. *Terex Ltd.*, 1986 S.L.T. 84; *Armour* v. *Thyssen Edelstahlwerke A.G.*, 1986 S.L.T. 94.

(2) The clause should reserve title only in the goods supplied under the contract. A reservation of title until "all sums" have been paid, or "all claims" met, should be avoided.

(3) The clause should expressly provide for the passing of risk. The time of passing of risk could be chosen to be the delivery of the goods to the buyer. The reason for an express provision is the effect of section 20 of the Sale of Goods Act 1979. This provides that unless otherwise agreed the goods remain at the seller's risk until property is transferred. A reservation of title clause, without any provision about risk, could have the undesirable effect that risk remains with a seller who has delivered the goods.[98]

(4) The clause may give the seller the right to reclaim his goods at any time and to enter on the buyer's premises for that purpose. In certain industries, such as the construction industry, a "snatch-back" may in any event occur. The draftsman is trying to vest the procedure with a contractual right. The clause also gives a sounder basis for an action seeking delivery of the goods. It is wise to add a right to recall any power of sale, use or disposal of the goods which the buyer may have.[99]

(5) Many of the other provisions commonly seen in reservation of title clauses should be put into a Scottish clause only after a considerable amount of thought. Provisions about trusts and tracing proceeds will probably be ineffective. A clause requiring the buyer to label and store the seller's goods separately may be ignored or be impractical. Provisions about ownership of items manufactured from the goods supplied will be ineffective in so far as they affect the rights of others who are not parties to the contract. Whether seeking rights in manufactured items made by the buyer amounts to a creation of a security over these items remains to be decided. The possibility that it is, and the effect on the clause, are reasons for being cautious.

(6) In *Emerald Stainless Steel Ltd.*[1] Lord Ross refused to break down a condition into effectual and ineffectual parts. The condition was one long sentence. The whole of a clause should be construed in the context of the contract. To split a clause into paragraphs should not make any difference to whether or not there is an attempt to obtain a security. Nevertheless it is possible that if the parts of a clause are sufficiently distinct, an ineffectual provision may be separable from effectual provisions. The draftsman may, therefore, split his clause into paragraphs. But all the provisions rest on the reservation of title in the seller. The remainder are the mechanics for enforcing that right. If the reservation of title is invalid, all else may fall. The draftsman therefore should be unambitious and simple, and warn his client that the effect of the clause can easily be defeated by the buyer dealing with or using the goods.

---

[98] On recovery of insurance proceeds for goods destroyed in the buyer's hands, see *Cochran & Son* v. *Leckie's Trs.* (1906) 8F. 975.

[99] See the effect of the absence of this in *Emerald Stainless Steel, sup. cit.*.

[1] *Sup. cit.;* but *cf. Clough Mill Ltd.* v. *Martin* [1984] 3 All E.R. 982.

CHAPTER 14

BREACH OF CONTRACT

1 This chapter considers the circumstances in which there is a breach of contract and some of the remedies available on breach.[1] The chapter is in seven parts: (1) repudiation of a contract[2]; (2) the mutuality principle[3]; (3) retention and compensation[4]; (4) material and non-material breaches[5]; (5) breach of a potestative condition[6]; (6) sale of heritage[7]; and (7) sale of goods.[8]

PART 1—REPUDIATION OF A CONTRACT

Terminology

2 The simplest instance of repudiation occurs when a person says that he does not intend to perform his contract. When this is done before the time for performance has arrived there is sometimes said to be "anticipatory breach" or "renunciation." These terms are unsatisfactory and less fashionable than they used to be. "Anticipatory" is meant to imply an acceleration of a breach. But in truth there is a material breach when there is a repudiation. It is not as if a future breach has taken place earlier than expected. There are also dangers in linking repudiation to "breach." As is explained later, not all breaches amount to repudiation.

3 "Renunciation" is a better word. It suggests a unilateral giving-up of something. But the person renouncing a contract may be trying to escape his obligations rather than give up his rights. "Repudiation" is the more accurate description, and is the term favoured in recent opinions in the House of Lords and the Privy Council.

4 It has been said that the word "repudiation" may be used in two senses.[9] In one sense the conduct of a party indicates a cancellation of continuing obligations in the course of their performance. In another sense there is "anticipatory breach" when one party indicates that he will not perform on the due date. It is the author's view that repudiation may occur before, at or after the due time for performance. When, however, conduct at or after that time is founded on as the test of repudia-

---

[1] For other remedies see Chaps. 20 and 21.
[2] paras. 14–02 to 14–24.
[3] paras. 14–25 to 14–32.
[4] paras. 14–33 to 14–48.
[5] paras. 14–49 to 14–84.
[6] paras. 14–85 to 14–87.
[7] paras. 14–88 to 14–96.
[8] paras. 14–97 to 14–127.
[9] *Blyth* v. *Scottish Liberal Club*, 1982 S.C. 140 at p. 150 *per* Lord Dunpark.

tion, there is a possibility of confusion with breach of contract and with rescission.

What is the Difference between Rescission and Repudiation?

14–05 It is possible to distinguish rescission from repudiation.[10] Rescission and repudiation are used in this context, that of breach of contract, and not with reference to the challenge of an invalid contract.[11] Rescission is typically the act of the party who claims to be innocent. Repudiation is the act of the party in breach. Rescission is only valid, it may be argued, when there has been a material breach. Repudiation may arise whatever the nature of shortcomings in performance and even before the time for performance. Rescission may follow repudiation, but one would not normally expect repudiation to be a consequence of rescission. Repudiation requires acceptance to be effective: rescission does not.

14–06 The difficulty is that rescission and repudiation can arise from acts of the same type. A letter stating, "I hold the contract cancelled," can be either. Thus in *White & Carter (Councils) Ltd.* v. *McGregor*, a case of repudiation, the garage wrote to the advertising contractors, "Please therefore cancel the order,"[12] words which could equally have been used by a party rescinding. For example in *Dunford & Elliott* v. *Macleod & Co.*, the rescinder stated: "We beg to notify you that, as you have totally failed to fulfil your obligations under [a charterparty], we hereby cancel said charter."[13] Either party may indicate expressly or by implication, that he regards the contract at an end. The question is the effect of this intimation, and the answer will depend on the justification which the party had for his action and on his intentions.

What is a Repudiation?

14–07 A person repudiates a contract when he unequivocally indicates that he is not going to perform it.[14] The matter is viewed objectively.[15]

14–08 A repudiation is one form of material breach, but not every material breach is a repudiation. It can hardly be a clearer breach of an agreement for one party to state that it will not comply with the agreement,

---

[10] *Cf.* P. S. Atiyah, *An Introduction to the Law of Contract* (2nd ed., 1971), p. 252: "it seems reasonably clear in modern law that rescission and repudiation are fundamentally the same thing." In his first edition the author was more dogmatic: (1st ed., 1961), p. 210. The passage is rewritten again in the 3rd ed. (1981), p. 294. See D. Jenkins, "The essence of the contract" [1969] C.L.J. 251 at p. 252.

[11] See difference explained: *Haymen* v. *Darwins* [1942] A.C. 356 at p. 378 *per* Lord Wright, at p. 398 *per* Lord Porter.

[12] 1960 S.C. 276 at p. 278; on appeal, 1962 S.C.(H.L.) 1.

[13] (1902) 4 F. 912 at p. 914. See also *Gilfillan* v. *Cadell & Grant* (1893) 21 R. 269 at p. 270: "We have accordingly, in terms of our letter of 3rd inst., no recourse but to cancel the transaction."

[14] The definitions vary. See dicta gathered in *Federal Commerce and Navigation Ltd.* v. *Molena Alpha* [1979] A.C. 757.

[15] *e.g. Woodar Investment Development Ltd.* v. *Wimpey Construction U.K. Ltd.* [1980] 1 All E.R. 571(H.L.) at p. 586 *per* Lord Keith, and authority there cited.

and this is so whether or not the statement is before or after the time for performance. Applying this logic Lord Dunpark held that termination provisions in a contract, applicable to breach, applied to a repudiation.[16] But in principle a notice of repudiation is different from a notice given under a contract. A notice of repudiation may be withdrawn before acceptance; a notice under a contract cannot be withdrawn without agreement.[17] An attempt to terminate a contract under its provisions is an adherence to the contract. Even if the attempt is unjustified, it may not, in the circumstances, be a repudiation.[18]

09 There must be a breach of contract or there cannot be a repudiation.[19] But, as stated previously, not every breach is a repudiation. A failure by sellers to deliver part of a consignment of rabbits was a breach of contract, but it was not a repudiation of the contract. There was a lack of evidence of an intention no longer to be bound by the contract.[20] A failure to pay on time may be a breach, but not a repudiation.[21] It has been said that[22]: "A breach of contract may be of such a nature as to amount to repudiation and give the innocent party the right (if he desires to exercise it) to be relieved from any further performance of the contract or the breach may entitle the innocent party only to damages." A repudiation is a material breach: it must go to the root of the contract.[23] But there can be a material breach without a repudiation.[24]

10 The essence of repudiation is an intention to abandon the contract or refuse further performance. It is a question for decision in each case whether the facts objectively justify the inference that there has been repudiation. One party may write to the other: "Please cancel the order."[25] Or a person may put himself in a position which makes it impossible for him to perform his contract, as when the owner of a newspaper engaged a manager for five years and after two years disposed of the paper.[26] Or a person may by his conduct lead a reasonable person to conclude that there is an absence of intention to fulfil obli-

---

[16] *Monklands District Council* v. *Ravenstone Securities*, 1980 S.L.T.(Notes) 30.

[17] *Decro-Wall International S.A.* v. *Practitioners In Marketing Ltd.* [1971] 2 All E.R. 216.

[18] *Woodar Investment Development Ltd.* v. *Wimpey Construction U.K. Ltd., sup. cit.*, esp. at p. 576 *per* Lord Wilberforce.

[19] *William Cory & Co. Ltd.* v. *London Corp.* [1951] 2 K.B. 476.

[20] *Peter Dumenil & Co. Ltd.* v. *James Ruddin Ltd.* [1953] 2 All E.R. 294.

[21] *Decro-Wall International S.A.* v. *Practitioners in Marketing Ltd.* [1971] 2 All E.R. 216.

[22] *Ibid.* at p. 221 *per* Salmon L.J.

[23] *Federal Commerce and Navigation Co.* v. *Molena Alpha, sup. cit.*; *Decro-Wall International S.A.* v. *Practitioners in Marketing Ltd., sup. cit.*

[24] *Blyth* v. *Scottish Liberal Club*, 1982 S.C. 140. Lord Dunpark at p. 149 distinguished "actual repudiation" from "deemed repudiation." It is the former which is being discussed here: the latter is material breach. It is the intention to depart from the contract (viewed objectively) which is the distinctive feature of true repudiation.

[25] *White & Carter (Councils) Ltd.* v. *McGregor*, 1962 S.C. 276 at p. 278; on appeal, 1962 S.C.(H.L.) 1; *United Dominions Trust (Commercial) Ltd.* v. *Ennis* [1968] 1 Q.B. 54 (opinion of majority).

[26] *Ross* v. *Macfarlane* (1894) 21 R. 396.

gations, as when there were long delays and spurious objections to performance[27] or a repeated lack of response to demands for payment of a price.[28] It was repudiation to threaten action which would deprive charterers of their contracts.[29] It has been held to be repudiation for an employer to state that he is not going to abide by an essential term of the contract on wages or status or place of work,[30] or for an employee to refuse to carry out an essential task[31] or to go on strike.[32]

14–11   In the typical case[33] repudiation is not easily inferred. A person may perform his contract unsatisfactorily, or complain about its terms, or try to negotiate a variation of the contract. None of these is repudiation. There is a difference between being either unhappy or depressed and deciding to end it all. Only an unequivocal indication that a party will not perform is repudiation.

14–12   So it may not be repudiation to threaten a refusal to perform[34] or to fail to perform.[35] To have an argument about implementation is not repudiation.[36] Nor is it repudiation to attempt to rescind a contract and wait for a court's decision on the justification for rescission.[37] Consistently to delay payments due under a distributorship agreement was not repudiation when there was a practice of accepting late payment and the likelihood of eventual payment.[38] A minor delay in taking the charter of a ship was not repudiation.[39]

The Effect of Repudiation

14–13   Repudiation by one party gives the other party an option. The option is either (1) to accept the repudiation and claim damages for breach of contract, or (2) to ignore or reject the repudiation and insist on performance of the contract. There is an option, because the doctrine of repudiation exists for the convenience of the "innocent party."[40]

---

[27] *Forslind* v. *Bechely-Crundall*, 1922 S.C.(H.L.) 173.

[28] *Fixby Engineering Co. Ltd.* v. *Auchlochan Sand and Gravel Co. Ltd.*, 1974 S.L.T.(Sh.Ct.) 58. See also *Moschi* v. *Lep Air Services Ltd.* [1973] A.C. 331; *cf. Decro-Wall International S.A.* v. *Practitioners in Marketing Ltd.* [1971] 2 All E.R. 216.

[29] *Federal Commerce and Navigation Co.* v. *Molena Alpha* [1979] A.C. 757.

[30] *Marriott* v. *Oxford and District Co-op. Soc.* [1970] 1 Q.B. 186; *Maher* v. *Fram Gerrard Ltd.* [1974] 1 All E.R. 449. On whether there needs to be acceptance of the repudiation, see below, para. 14–14.

[31] *Gorse* v. *Durham C.C.* [1971] 2 All E.R. 666.

[32] *Simmons* v. *Hoover Ltd.* [1977] Q.B. 284. On the difficulty of implying a term that the contract is suspended if there is a strike, see *Cummings* v. *Charles Connell & Co. (Shipbuilders) Ltd.*, 1968 S.C. 305.

[33] Contracts of employment may be different. See paras. 14–22, 14–33.

[34] *Thornloe* v. *Macdonald & Co.* (1892) 29 S.L.R. 409.

[35] *Mersey Steel and Iron Co.* v. *Naylor Benzon & Co.* (1884) 9 App.Cas. 434.

[36] *Sweet & Maxwell Ltd.* v. *Universal News Services Ltd.* [1964] 2 Q.B. 699.

[37] *Woodar Investment Development Ltd.* v. *Wimpey Construction U.K. Ltd.*, *sup. cit.*

[38] *Decro-Wall International S.A.* v. *Practitioners in Marketing Ltd.*, *sup. cit.*

[39] *Carswell* v. *Collard* (1893) 20 R.(H.L.) 47.

[40] *Woodar Investment Development Ltd.* v. *Wimpey Construction U.K. Ltd.*, *sup. cit.* at p. 588 *per* Lord Keith.

Acceptance of Repudiation

-14 Acceptance is probably any form of intimation that the innocent party is exercising his option to end future performance of the contract.[41] To suspend performance for a while is not acceptance. When an employee repudiated his contract by refusing to supervise school meals and he was suspended, this suspension was not acceptance of the repudiation.[42] Acceptance has the effect that neither party can insist on future performance. One party cannot at a later date remedy the breach.[43] If the repudiating party tenders performance, and this is accepted, there is a new contract even if it is on the same terms as the old.[44]

-15 The "innocent party" who has accepted a repudiation can recover damages at once. The damages will be calculated according to the normal principles of assessment of damages. It is relevant to consider what would have happened at the due date for performance subject to the obligation of the "innocent party" to minimise his loss.[45] If the party repudiating would in any event have justifiably terminated the contract, the "innocent party" may get only nominal damages.[46]

Refusal to Accept a Repudiation

-16 The party receiving a repudiation may reject it or ignore it. In the colourful phrase of Asquith L.J., often quoted: "An unaccepted repudiation is a thing writ in water and of no value to anybody; it confers no legal rights of any sort or kind."[47]

-17 In *White & Carter (Councils) Ltd.* v. *McGregor*[48] the pursuers entered into a contract with the defenders for the display of advertisements on litter-bins for a period of three years. The defenders repudiated the contract on the day on which it was made. The pursuers refused to accept the repudiation. The advertisements appeared. The defenders had to pay the sums due under the contract. The House of Lords rejected the defenders' claim that they were only liable in damages. There were said to be limitations on the idea that the contract continued. The court would not compel the repudiating party to perform by specific implement.[49] The case was unusual in that the contract could be per-

---

[41] *Monklands D.C.* v. *Ravenstone Securities*, 1980 S.L.T.(Notes) 30.

[42] *Gorse* v. *Durham C.C.* [1971] 2 All E.R. 666.

[43] *Gilfillan* v. *Cadell & Grant* (1893) 21 R. 269.

[44] *Aegnoussiotis Shipping Corp.* v. *A/S Kristian Jebsens* [1977] 1 Lloyd's Rep. 268 at p. 276 *per* Donaldson J.

[45] *Garnac Grain Co.* v. *H. M. Faure & Fairclough Ltd.* [1968] A.C. 1130; *Tai Hing Cotton Mill Ltd.* v. *Kamsing Knitting* [1979] A.C. 91; *Howie* v. *Anderson* (1848) 10 D. 355.

[46] *The Mihalis Angelos* [1971] 1 Q.B. 164.

[47] *Howard* v. *Pickford Tool Co.* [1951] 1 K.B. 417 at p. 421.

[48] 1962 S.C.(H.L.) 1.

[49] *Ibid.* at p. 13 *per* Lord Reid; but seeking payment of the contract price is possible. See *White and Carter (Councils) Ltd.* v. *McGregor, sup. cit.*, and *Salaried Staff London Loan Co. Ltd.* v. *Swears and Wells Ltd.*, 1985 S.L.T. 326.

formed without the participation of the repudiating party. The "innocent" party must have an interest to insist on performance.[50] In *The Alaskan Trader*[51] the court held that an "innocent" party had no legitimate interest in performing the contract rather than claiming damages. The owners of a vessel had maintained it at anchor with a full crew ready to sail until the end of a time charter despite an earlier repudiation by the charterers. The owners ought to have accepted the repudiation with a view to mitigating their loss.

14–18   The innocent party can sue for the moneys due under the contract,[52] even although this represents only part of the obligations arising under the contract.[53] In *Salaried Staff London Loan Co. Ltd.* v. *Swears and Wells Ltd.*[54] tenants repudiated a lease. The landlords obtained decree for rent and other payments due at four quarters subsequent to the repudiation. Opinions were reserved on whether it was possible for the landlords to continue to sue for arrears of rent until the termination of the lease. But it is in only exceptional circumstances, which must be averred by the defender, that the court will withhold a remedy to which a party is entitled.[55]

14–19   The decision in *White & Carter (Councils) Ltd.* has been the subject of controversy.[56] One of the problems is that the case appears to conflict with the rule that an "innocent" party should minimise his loss. It could also lead to unsatisfactory results, for example if the business which was advertised ceased to exist. The case is at the boundary of several principles. One principle is that one party should not be able to end a contract by a unilateral act, namely repudiation. The other principles arise from equitable control of specific implement and the obligation to minimise loss.

14–20   The limited availability of remedies may make it unattractive for the "innocent party" to ignore a repudiation. Although the contract survives, "The truth of the matter," as Sachs L.J. put it[57]:

> "is that there are a great many cases in which it is of no benefit to the innocent party to keep the contract alive for the simple reason that, in the long run, unless the repudiating party can be persuaded or impelled to change his mind and withdraw his repudiation, the only remedy available to the innocent party will lie in damages. So there are vast numbers of cases where the innocent party can in one sense be said to be forced to adopt the only practicable course

---

[50] *Ibid.* at p. 14 *per* Lord Reid.

[51] [1984] 1 All E.R. 129.

[52] *White & Carter (Councils) Ltd.* v. *McGregor, sup. cit.*; *Salaried Staff London Loan Co. Ltd.* v. *Swears and Wells Ltd., sup. cit.*

[53] *Salaried Staff London Loan Co. Ltd.* v. *Swears and Wells Ltd., sup. cit.*

[54] *Sup. cit.*

[55] *Grahame* v. *Mags. of Kirkcaldy* (1882) 9 R.(H.L.) 91 at p. 91 *per* Lord Watson.

[56] T. B. Smith, *Short Commentary*, p. 851; Walker, *Contract*, para. 32.10; A. L. Goodhart (1962) 78 L.Q.R. 263; Furmston (1962) 25 M.L.R. 364; Scott [1962] Cb.L.J. 12, *cf.* Nienaber [1962] Cb.L.J. 213.

[57] *Decro-Wall International S.A.* v. *Practitioners in Marketing Ltd.* [1971] 1 All E.R. 216 at p. 228.

because any other would be valueless. In such cases it is the range of remedies that is limited, not the right to elect.

-21 "That does not alter the position that the innocent party can if he so chooses elect not to accept the repudiation and may thus in suitable cases keep open, maybe at certain risks, the chances either that the other party may yet take a different course or that it may be one of those special cases where the court will in its discretion grant some form of declaration or injunction on the basis that the contract has not yet been discharged."

-22 The difference between the practical result and the theoretical need for acceptance has caused some difficulty in employer and employee cases. When there is an unjustified dismissal by an employer (*i.e.* a repudiation) must there be an acceptance by the employee to end the contract? It is thought that there should be. The authorities were reviewed in *Gunton* v. *London Borough of Richmond-upon-Thames*.[58]

It can be important to determine whether or not the contract survives. While the contract survives the parties will be bound by its terms, such as a restriction on the employee working for others during the time of his employment.[59] But in many cases whether or not the employee accepts the repudiation, his claim is damages. In practice he cannot continue to go to his place of work and earn his pay. He cannot obtain specific implement. In these instances whether or not there is acceptance of the repudiation could be academic.

-23 When an employee repudiates his contract, the employer may, or may not, accept the repudiation.[60]

Acceptance of Repudiation and its Effect on the Contract

-24 Once a repudiation is accepted certain clauses in the contract may survive to govern the relationship of the parties. The same possibility arises on rescission for material breach, and the difficulties are analysed elsewhere.[61]

PART 2—THE MUTUALITY PRINCIPLE

The History of the Principle

-25 There are numerous traces in early case law of a rule that one party to a contract need not perform his part unless the other party was willing to perform or had performed. An early example is a case in 1492 in which it was decided that if the defender did not implement a marriage con-

---

[58] [1980] 3 All E.R. 577.
[59] *Thomas Marshall (Exports) Ltd.* v. *Guinle* [1979] Ch. 227.
[60] *Simmons* v. *Hoover Ltd.* [1977] Q.B. 284; *Gorse* v. *Durham C.C.* [1971] 2 All E.R. 666.
[61] See paras. 14–72 to 14–80.

tract, the pursuers were not bound to implement their part of the bargain.[62] In later reports a bond could not be enforced until a condition in respect of which it had been granted was purified.[63] It was argued that a minute of sale could not be declared null as a result of an irritancy when the pursuer was unable to fulfil his part of the bargain.[64] In many cases it was suggested that one party to a marriage contract could not enforce the contract until he had performed his obligations under the contract or found security for their purpose,[65] although there was argument about whether marriage contracts were a special case[66] and it was later held that a wife was not entitled to plead retention on the ground of non-implement of the husband's stipulations in the marriage contract, except where there was a special provision to secure the funds attempted to be retained.[67]

14–26   It is true that the principle was often expressed more clearly in the argument of parties rather than in the reported decision of the court. This arises not only from the nature of the reports but also, as Kilkerran observed, because "the Lords . . . avoid determining general points, when there is no necessity for it."[68] The principle is mentioned in a restricted way by Craig,[69] who is cited by Hope.[70] Although mentioned by Dirleton it seems to have been one matter on which he did not have much doubt[71] and it is enunciated by Stair,[72] Forbes,[73] Erskine,[74] Hume,[75] and Bell.[76] For example, Erskine's view was that: "No party in a mutual contract, where the obligations on the parties are the causes of one another, can demand performance from the other, if he himself either cannot or will not perform the counterpart, for the mutual obligations are considered as conditional." Paradoxically he gave examples from marriage contracts, which was the one case to which the rule was applied with some limitation.

---

[62] *Marioun Lady Somervale*, July 10, 1492, A.D.C. I. 246.

[63] *Cuming* v. *Cuming* (1628) Mor. 9147; *Exrs. of Dirleton* v. *Hamilton* (1667) Mor. 9203.

[64] *Clerk* v. *Balhaven* (1667) Mor. 9150.

[65] *Jaffray* v. *Collison* (1673) Mor. 9138; *Sutherland* v. *Aldie* (1724) Mor. 9138; *Crawford* v. *Mitchell* (1743) Mor. 9140, 8266; *Murray* v. *Graham* (1744) Mor. 9140; 5918; *Partners of Woollen Manufactory at Haddington* v. *Gray* (1781) Mor. 9144 and cases at Mor. 9188 *et seq.*

[66] *Watson* v. *Cameron* (1738) Mor. 9196 at p. 9197.

[67] *Greenhill* v. *Aitken* (1824) 3 S. 169; *Boswell* v. *Miller* (1848) 8 D. 430.

[68] *Creditors of Jordanhill* v. *Viscount Garnock* (1747) Mor. 9170 at p. 9171; Kilkerran's *Decisions*, p. 358.

[69] *Jus Feudale*, I,9,31.

[70] *Major Practicks* (Stair Soc., Vol. 3), p. 93.

[71] Dirleton's *Doubts* (1698), p. 133; Stewart's *Answers* (1740), p. 215.

[72] Stair, I,x,16 (2nd and 5th eds.).

[73] W.Forbes, *Institutes of the Law of Scotland* (1722), 2.3.1.3.3.

[74] *Inst.*, III,iii,86.

[75] Baron Hume's *Lectures* (1786–1822), Vol. 3, p. 46 (Stair Soc., Vol. 15).

[76] *Prin.* (4th ed.), ss.70, 71 (s.70 approved, *Barclay* v. *Anderston Foundry Co.* (1856) 18 D. 1190 at pp. 1195, 1196 *per* Lord Murray) (10th ed. of Bell contains substantial additions); *Comm.* (7th ed.), I,455 (5th ed.), I,432).

The Modern Rules

-27 The concept of mutuality involves at least four ideas.

(1) A party who is in breach of his obligations cannot enforce performance by the other party.[77] This does not mean that the party in breach has no rights under the contract. There is an idea that only an "innocent" party may enforce a contract. Lord McLaren said:

> "I think no man can come into court affirming and disaffirming a contract to which he is a party. If he affirms it and claims damages for breach of it, he must, as a condition of succeeding in that claim, have himself fulfilled all the conditions of the contract. In the case of a contract of sale he must pay for goods delivered to him under the contract as a condition of putting himself in the right and enabling him to claim damages for a breach of the contract. I agree that the defenders have by their refusal to pay for the goods delivered to them disentitled themselves to claim damages from the pursuer as in other circumstances they might have done."[78]

-28 Now it is one thing to say that a material breach by a party A may release the other party, B, from future performance. It is a quite different matter to suggest that A is deprived of all his rights under the contract. There is fortunately authority to suggest this is not the law,[79] but from what Lord McLaren said it seems that A would be unable to claim damages even if B is in breach. This is suspect. What are the rights of the party in breach? It does not follow that a party in breach has no action under the contract. That is not the consequence of the mutuality principle. What, for example, Erskine said was that the party in breach could not demand performance from the other party.[80] Lord Justice-Clerk Moncrieff's famous dictum in *Turnbull* v. *Mclean*[81] had as its second proposition: "that a failure to perform any material or substantial part of the contract on the part of one will prevent him from suing the other for performance." Suing for performance may be barred, but it is a leap from there to say that no action under the contract is allowed.

-29 Assume a complex problem in which both parties are in material breach. A car-hire firm hires a fleet of cars to an oil company. The oil company repeatedly fails in its obligations under the contract to service the cars and to use the cars only for specified purposes. The car-hire firm

---

[77] *e.g. British Motor Body Co. Ltd.* v. *Thomas Shaw (Dundee) Ltd.*, 1914 S.C. 922 (esp. *per* Lord President Strathclyde at p. 926); *Penman* v. *Mackay*, 1922 S.C. 385 (esp. *per* Lord Mackenzie at p. 394).

[78] *Thorneloe* v. *McDonald* (1892) 29 S.L.R. 409 at p. 411 *per* Lord McLaren, and see also opinion of Lord President Robertson.

[79] *Graham* v. *United Turkey Red Co.*, 1922 S.C. 533; and non-material breaches will not prevent an action for the price: *Ramsay & Son* v. *Brand* (1898) 25 R. 1212; *Spiers Ltd.* v. *Petersen*, 1924 S.C. 428; *Stewart Roofing Co. Ltd.* v. *Shanlin*, 1958 S.L.T.(Sh.Ct.) 53. *Cf. Franco-British Electrical Co. Ltd.* v. *Jean Dougall Macdonald Ltd.* (1949) 65 Sh.Ct.Rep. 82.

[80] Ersk., III,iii,86.

[81] (1873) 1 R. 730 at p. 738.

fail in their obligations to supply vehicles in good repair at times when contractually bound to do so. On each side there is a series of failures culminating in a situation in which each party can be said to be in material breach. At this point each party is, if it wishes, free from future performance. The car-hire firm may refuse to supply more cars and demand the return of vehicles on hire. The oil company may refuse to pay future rentals. That is all the mutuality principle expounded by the Institutional writers requires. May either party sue for damages for past breaches? Why not? Justice is done if one sues, the other counterclaims and both parties are found liable in damages, the balance being paid by whichever company caused the greater loss. The party with the larger claim is prejudiced if the law has a principle that a party in breach cannot sue. Lord McLaren's view should not be followed. The approach of Lord Wilberforce in *Photo Productions Ltd.*[82] is preferable. He referred to: "the well-accepted principle of law, stated by the highest modern authority, that when in the context of a breach of contract one speaks of 'termination' what is meant is no more than that the innocent party or, in some cases, both parties are excused from further performance. Damages, in such cases, are then claimed under the contract."

14–30   Despite all this, one case indicates that a party who is in breach of contract cannot sue for damages.[83] It is suggested that this may be extending the mutuality principle beyond its proper function.

(2) The party who is not in breach may withhold performance until the other has performed or is seen to be willing to perform the counter-stipulations.[84]

(3) As the Institutional writers point out, the mutuality concept only applies if the obligations of the parties are the causes of one another or are reciprocal undertakings. There must not be "wholly different matters, which are frequently accumulated in the same contracts, or the one is but the occasion and motive, and not the proper cause, of the other."[85] A modern example is a sale of a business combined with a contract of service. Failure by the purchaser to employ the seller may not affect the transfer of the business; even if in the one document, the obligations of sale and service may be separable and not mutual[86]; conversely, even if in separate documents, obligations may be mutual.[87] It is a result of this limitation to the mutuality rule that if there are two sep-

---

[82] *Photo Production Ltd.* v. *Securicor Transport Ltd.* [1980] A.C. 827 at p. 844.

[83] *Hayes* v. *Robinson*, 1984 S.L.T. 300; a party in breach may sue for the price and be met by a claim for damages: *British Motor Body Co.* v. *Shaw*, 1914 S.C. 922; *Ballantyne* v. *East of Scotland Farmers Ltd.*, 1970 S.L.T.(Notes) 50, and see "Retention of debts"—para. 14–37.

[84] *e.g.* cases on special lien quoted *infra*; on withholding payment of money, see "Retention of Debts," paras. 14–37 *et seq.*

[85] Stair, *sup. cit.*

[86] *Dick* v. *Skene*, 1946 S.N. 64, 148; 1947 S.N. 161.

[87] *Claddagh Steamship Co.* v. *Steven & Co.*, 1919 S.C.(H.L.) 132.

arate contracts between the same parties, a liquid debt due under one contract cannot be retained in respect of an illiquid claim under the other contract.[88] Nor could a sum due under a contract be withheld because of a claim of damages for delict.[89]

(4) It may not be for every trifling breach that a party can withhold performance of his part of the contract. Lord Wood in *Barclay* v. *Anderston Foundry Co.* observed:

> "Now, where there is a clear failure by one of the parties to a mutual contract to fulfil, in essential respects, his part of it, I cannot hold that notice is necessary by the other party ere he can regard himself free of his obligations under it, and entitled to act on that footing. There may, indeed, be room for saying, that when the neglect or failure to perform is but trifling in extent, or has arisen from inadvertence, or permits of satisfactory explanation, the contract cannot, in such a state of matters, be held to have become void."[90]

31   The effect of a breach is not to annul a contract *ab initio* nor even to end the contract for the future, but leaving apart Lord Wood's use of the word "void" the dictum illustrates the thought that some breaches are ignored.

32   In the application of the mutuality principle there has been a confusion between retention and compensation.

PART 3—RETENTION AND COMPENSATION

33   To withhold performance may be described as retention. When the performance that is withheld is payment of a debt there is scope for confusion with another part of the law, that of compensation of debts. Compensation is possibly statutory in origin.[91] The Compensation Act 1592 allows liquid debts to be set against each other. It does not apply to illiquid debts. In a mutual contract parties may withhold performance when they have illiquid claims, not because of the Compensation Act but because of the mutuality principle. The result, however, in some eyes is similar to compensation. Morison in his *Dictionary* had a large section entitled "Compensation-Retention."[92] Gloag and Irvine referred to retention of debts as "an equitable extension of the statutory

---

[88] *Sutherland* v. *Urquhart* (1895) 23 R. 284; *Asphaltic Limestone Concrete Co. Ltd.* v. *Glasgow Corporation*, 1907 S.C. 463.

[89] *Christie* v. *Birrells*, 1910 S.C. 986; see also *Smart* v. *Wilkinson*, 1928 S.C. 383.

[90] (1856) 18 D. 1190 at p. 1198.

[91] Stair, I,xviii, 6 (2nd and 5th eds.); though note Lord Eskgrove's graphic point in *Harper* v. *Faulds* (1791) Bell's 8vo. Cases 432 at p. 468: "Before [the Act of 1592], had two parties come, each with a decree in his hands, must both have gone to prison? Surely not. Or could this have taken place, though the one was a decree for delivery while the other was a decree for payment? It cannot be." However Balfour, writing shortly before the 1592 Act, denied the existence of compensation *as a defence by way of exception*: Balfour, *op. cit.*, p. 349, citing *Queen* v. *Bishop of Aberdeen* (1543) Mor. 2545.

[92] Mor. 2545–2696; the *Scots Digest* and the *Faculty Digest* have separate headings.

right of compensation,"[93] as has Professor Walker.[94] Gloag, however, in *Contract*, treated the two ideas separately in one chapter.[95] Nor are the writers alone in having difficulties with the intricacies of liquid and illiquid claims. The judicial treatment of retention of rent in leases shows much confusion as to the true nature of the principle.[96]

14–34   The Institutional writers recognised that the concepts were different.[97] Erskine observed[98]:

> "The right of retention may be here explained, upon account of its near resemblance to compensation, though it has not the effect of extinguishing obligations, but barely of suspending them, till he who pleads it obtains payment or satisfaction for his counter claim; and it is admitted in those cases only where compensation can have no place."

Bell stated[99]: "Compensation is payment and extinction of mutual debts; whereas retention of a debt is nothing more than an implied security for performance; a power of suspension, or right to withhold payment or performance till satisfied of some counter demand."

14–35   It follows that it is not appropriate in a case of retention to plead the Compensation Act 1592.[1] Retention is a wide doctrine applying to all obligations in a contract and is not limited to claims of the same nature, whereas compensation can only be pled between debts of the same type, such as money debts, or wine against wine, or corn against corn.[2] Most important of all, retention does not operate to extinguish claims, whereas compensation when pled and sustained does. The purpose of retention is to enforce obligations; compensation extinguishes them.

14–36   The confusion between the ideas may have arisen in some cases from allowing the nature of remedies sought to influence the consideration of the rights of parties. If a tenant withholds rent because the subjects have not been repaired by the landlord or the buyer refuses to pay the price because the goods supplied are unmerchantable, it is easy in common language to describe these events as retention by the tenant or buyer.

---

[93] W. M. Gloag and J. M. Irvine, *Rights in Security* (1897), p. 304.

[94] D. M. Walker, *Principles* (2nd ed., 1975), Vol. 1, p. 150; and in *Civil Remedies*, p. 59, the author refers to compensation as an instance of the right of retention.

[95] Chap. 35.

[96] Gloag, *op. cit.*, p. 628. Confusion continues: in *Marshall's Trs.* v. *Banks*, 1934 S.C. 405, the opinions refer to retention and set-off as if they were synonymous. See, in particular, Lord Murray at p. 415.

[97] Stair, I,xviii,6 and 7 (2nd and 5th eds.); Ersk., III,iv,20; Bell, *Prin.* (4th ed.), s.1411 (10th ed., para. 1410). See also Bankt. I,494,34; Rankine, *Law of Leases* (3rd ed., 1916), p. 324.

[98] *Sup. cit.*

[99] *Sup. cit.*; similarly Baron Hume's *Lectures* (1786–1822), Vol. 3, p. 46 (Stair Soc., Vol. 15).

[1] *Johnston* v. *Robertson* (1861) 23 D. 646 discussed in *British Motor Body Co. Ltd.* v. *Thomas Shaw (Dundee) Ltd.*, 1914 S.C. 922.

[2] Bell, *Comm.* (5th ed.), II,128; (7th ed.) II,122; Ersk. III,iv,15; Bankt., I,492,25; *Elliot* v. *Elleis* (1631) Mor. 2649; Sir George Mackenzie, *Institutions* (1694), p. 175.

Let, however, the landlord bring an action for the rent, or the seller for the price, and the tenant or buyer plead that they have a claim for damages arising from non-implement of the pursuer's obligations. The tenant or buyer has quantified his claim in money. He is entitled to do so. But we now have a situation in which an action for payment of money is met by a counterclaim for money. It looks like compensation or set-off, but it is not effective compensation because the claim for damages is illiquid. What has happened in some landlord-and-tenant cases is that the court has fastened on to the illiquid nature of this claim and said to the tenant: "It is an incompetent set-off, therefore you must pay the rent." That is an unfortunate analysis. The tenant had the right of retention. He should not have lost it because he tried to quantify his loss. Yet, surprising as it may be, this is what the courts have done and, our system of precedent being as it is, we must today live with the result.

Retention of Debts

37 In *Johnston* v. *Robertson*[3] employers of a contractor were found entitled to plead a claim for liquidated damages against the contract price sued for by the contractor. In *Macbride* v. *Hamilton and Son*[4] it was held that an illiquid claim for damages could be pled against a demand for the price. The defender's right to retain money must exist at the time when payment of the price is due to the pursuer.[5] The right of retention can be excluded only by clear and unequivocal terms of the contract.[6]

38 The principle of mutuality of obligations applies to all contracts, and so in any type of contract a claim for the sums due under the contract may be met by the defence that the defender has claims arising from the pursuer's failure to fulfil that contract. The suggestion that building contracts are special[7] is unfounded.[8] So a claim for damages had been pled against actions for the price of goods sold,[9] for wages[10] and for storage dues.[11]

---

[3] (1861) 23 D. 646.

[4] (1875) 2 R. 775.

[5] *Redpath Dorman Long Ltd.* v. *Cummins Engine Co. Ltd.*, 1981 S.C. 370.

[6] *Redpath Dorman Long Ltd.* v. *Cummins Engine Co. Ltd.*, *sup. cit.* The common law right of retention was not excluded by a clause which stated: "whenever under the contract any sum of money shall be recoverable from or payable by the contractor, such sum may be deducted from or reduced by the amount of any sum or sums then due or which at any time thereafter may become due to the contractor under or in respect of the contract." It was unsuccessfully argued that this applied only to liquidated or ascertained sums, and was exhaustive of the right of retention.

[7] Gloag, p. 627.

[8] Conceded in *Redpath Dorman Long Ltd.* v. *Cummins Engine Co. Ltd.*, *sup. cit.*

[9] *British Motor Body Co. Ltd.* v. *Thomas Shaw (Dundee) Ltd.*, *sup. cit.* This case contains extensive comment on *Macbride* v. *Hamilton*, *sup. cit.* and *Johnston* v. *Robertson*, *sup. cit.*; see also *Ballantyne* v. *East of Scotland Farmers Ltd.*, 1970 S.L.T.(Notes) 50.

[10] *Gibson* v. *McNaughton* (1861) 23 D. 358; *Sharp* v. *Rettie* (1884) 11 R. 745.

[11] *Gibson & Stewart* v. *Brown & Co.* (1876) 3 R. 328.

Retention of Rent

14–39   In numerous cases a tenant has been allowed to retain rent on the grounds of failure by the landlord to fulfil his obligations under the lease.[12] This right arises from the mutuality principle, although there can be an express clause in the lease allowing the tenant to deduct claims from the rent payable.[13] Conversely the tenant may contract out of his right of retention.[14] If the tenant's claim is worth less than the rent due it has been held that he cannot withhold the whole of an instalment of rent, but may only seek an abatement of rent.[15] This seems contrary to principle. Retention should not be allowed for trivial claims,[16] but if the right exists its purpose is to compel a landlord to perform and a comparison between the value of the claim and the value of the rent is no more appropriate than, in another instance of the mutuality principle, it would be to compare the amount of the repairer's bill with the value of the subject-matter over which a lien is claimed.

14–40   As Gloag[17] and Rankine[18] pointed out, however, there are many cases which are difficult to reconcile with the mutuality principle. Much of the difficulty arises if the tenant claims damages. He is then met by the proposition that his illiquid claim for damages cannot be pled against the landlord's liquid claim for rent.[19] This is contrary to principle. As Gloag observed in the context of retention of rent cases:

> "There is a constant and perplexing tendency to apply the rule that an action for a liquid debt cannot be met by an illiquid claim for damages, though that rule is properly applicable only to cases where the liquid and illiquid claims have different sources, and

---

[12] *McGuffog* v. *Agnew* (1822) 1 S.342; *Stewart* v. *Campbell* (1834) 13 S.7; *Stewart* v. *McRa* (1834) 13 S.4; *Gray* v. *Renton* (1840) 3 D. 203; *Kilmarnock Gas Light Co.* v. *Smith* (1872) 11 M. 58; *Guthrie* v. *Shearer* (1873) 1 R. 181; *Muir* v. *McIntyres* (1887) 14 R. 470; *Munro* v. *McGeoghs* (1888) 16 R. 93; *Campbell* v. *Mundell* (1896) 3 S.L.T. 287; *McDonald* v. *Kydd* (1901) 3 F. 923; *Earl of Galloway* v. *McConnell*, 1911 S.C. 846; *John Haig & Co.* v. *Boswall-Preston*, 1915 S.C. 339.

[13] *Daniel Stewart's Hospital* v. *Waddell* (1890) 17 R. 1077; *Stobbs & Sons* v. *Hislop*, 1948 S.C. 216 at p. 223 *per* Lord President Cooper.

[14] *Skene* v. *Cameron*, 1942 S.C. 393; clear and unequivocal words are needed to exclude the common law right of retention—*Redpath Dorman Long Ltd.* v. *Cummins Engine Co. Ltd.*, 1981 S.C. 370. The practical difficulty of the tenant, particularly in commercial leases, may be that there is an irritancy clause operable on non-payment of rent. A landlord should not be able to enforce this clause if he is in breach of his obligations, but the risk of incurring the irritancy may deter the tenant from withholding rent.

[15] *Thomson* v. *Coventry* (1833) 11 S.725 at p. 726 *per* Lord Cringletie; *Campbell* v. *Mundell, sup. cit.*; *Christie* v. *Wilson*, 1915 S.C. 645.

[16] *Graham* v. *Gordon* (1843) 5 D. 1207 at p. 1211 *per* Lord Jeffrey; *Stewart* v. *Campbell* (1889) 16 R. 346; *McDonald* v. *Kydd* (1901) 3 F. 923 at p. 928 *per* Lord Moncreiff; *Burns* v. *Stewart* (1831) 5 W. & S. 356.

[17] *Op. cit.*, p. 628.

[18] Rankine, *Law of Leases in Scotland* (3rd ed., 1916), p. 327.

[19] *Dun* v. *Craig* (1824) 3 S.274; *Thomson* v. *Coventry* (1833) 11 S.725; *McRae* v. *McPherson* (1843) 6 D. 302; *Dickson* v. *Porteous* (1852) 15 D. 1; *Kilmarnock Gas Light Co.* v. *Smith* (1872) 11 M. 58 at p. 61 *per* Lord Cowan; *Guthrie* v. *Shearer* (1873) 1 R. 181 at p. 184 *per* Lords Cowan, Benholme and Neaves; *Drybrough* v. *Drybrough* (1874) 1 R. 909; *Humphrey* v. *Mackay* (1883) 10 R. 647 at p. 650 *per* Lord Justice-Clerk Moncrieff; *Muir* v. *McIntyres* (1887) 14 R. 470 at p. 473 *per* Lords Shand and Adam.

ought not to rule cases where both parties' claims arise from the one contract of lease."[20]

41   The result of many of the authorities, however, is not to apply the mutuality principle when the tenant claims damages. In one of the more recent cases, a tenant posed a neat problem for the court by claiming that he could retain his rent and also counterclaiming for damages. The court had little difficulty allowing the right of retention but the counterclaim for damages raised a problem which was avoided by treating a landlord's claim for rent as illiquid if the landlord was in breach of his obligations under the lease.[21] The authorities were not minutely analysed, probably wisely, but the case gives some basis on which to build a restatement of the law.

42   It has sometimes been suggested that leases are a special case on the grounds that the tenant has possession while claiming retention.[22] This may explain the distinction drawn at one time between the attempts to retain early in the course of a lease and retention at the end of a lease. The former was viewed unfavourably.[23]

43   The position should be this. A lease is a mutual contract. If the landlord is in breach of his obligations to the tenant under that lease,[24] provided the breach is not trivial the tenant may withhold performance of his obligations, including the payment of rent. This is the operation of the mutuality principle. Whether or not the tenant claims damages is irrelevant to his right to withhold performance. If the tenant does claim damages for breach of contract, he may do so in a counterclaim in the landlord's action for rent, or by separate action. That is a question of procedure. It should not affect his right to retain rent.

44   A difficult question arises as to what the analysis should be if the breach is remedied by the landlord and the tenant is left merely with a claim for damages for the past breach. It can be argued that the right to claim damages justifies retention under the mutuality principle.[25] The claim for damages arises from a breach of contract and the obligation imposed by the law on the landlord to pay must be performed before he can exact counter-performance.

Special Lien

45   The right of special lien is an instance of the mutuality principle. Its interest lies in not only providing examples of the principle, but also in some alleged exceptions to the principle which deserve careful scrutiny.

---

[20] *Sup. cit.*

[21] *Fingland & Mitchell* v. *Howie*, 1926 S.C. 319.

[22] Rankine, *op. cit.*, p. 327; *Bowie* v. *Duncan* (1807) Hume 839.

[23] *McRae* v. *McPherson* (1843) 6 D. 302; *Dods* v. *Fortune* (1854) 16 D. 478; *Drybrough* v. *Drybrough* (1874) 1 R. 909.

[24] *Cf. Sprot* v. *Morrison* (1853) 15 D. 376; *Brown* v. *Simpson*, 1910 1 S.L.T. 183.

[25] *Moore's Carving Machine Co.* v. *Austin* (1896) 33 S.L.R. 613 (a case of lien) and observations in Gloag and Irvine, *op. cit.* at p. 353—quoted *infra*.

Special lien is probably more accurately described as retention, it being retention of objects in contradistinction to retention of debts, but the term lien is commonly used.[26] The use of the word "lien" has the danger of suggesting that because there is a separate label, there must be a separate concept. That is not so.

14-46 The early history of retention or special lien is discussed in Robert Bell's extensive report of *Harper* v. *Faulds*.[27] G. J. Bell treated "special retention" as "part of the law of mutual contract, entitling one to withhold performance, or retain possession of that which forms the subject of the contract, till the counter obligation be performed."[28] In *Brown* v. *Sommerville*[29] a printer was denied a right of retention over printing plates for his account due from printing Wilson's *Tales of the Borders*. The majority of the court would only allow a retention if work or money had been expended by the claimant on the property, in this case the plates. If this had remained the law it would have been a substantial qualification to the mutuality principle as was eloquently pointed out by Lord Moncreiff in his dissent. The difficulty was also observed by the Lord Ordinary, Lord Cunninghame, who was reversed on appeal. Fortunately, the case may now be regarded as superseded by later authority.[30]

14-47 In a line of cases, *Meikle and Wilson* v. *Pollard*,[31] *Robertson* v. *Ross*,[32] *Moore's Carving Machine Co.* v. *Austin*[33] and *Findlay* v. *Waddell*,[34] there was recognised a general right of retention arising out of mutual obligations under a contract. The right was applied to retaining moveables because money was due by the other party under the contract, and also to retaining moveables because of a claim for damages.[35] In the foundation of this series, *Meikle and Wilson* v. *Pollard*, Lord Justice-Clerk Moncreiff referred to "the general case of counter obligations under a contract."[36] Lord Gifford mentioned that:

> "the one party to [the contract] is bound to perform his part of the contract just as much as the other. The counterpart here of the duty of the one party to do the piece of business is that the other shall pay the price, and I think that until the latter is done the party employed need not hand over articles which were put into his hands to enable him to fulfil his part of the contract."[37]

---

[26] Gloag and Irvine, *op. cit.* p. 329; *Encyclopaedia of the Laws of Scotland*, Vol. 9, para. 461.

[27] *Harper* v. *Faulds* (1791) Bell's 8vo. Cases 432 (*cf.* Mor. 2666).

[28] Bell, *Prin.* (4th ed.), s.1419.

[29] (1844) 6 D. 1267.

[30] See the treatment of the case in Gloag and Irvine, *op. cit.*, p. 352; Gloag, *op. cit.*, p. 631, *Encyclopaedia*, Vol. 9, para. 478.

[31] (1880) 8 R. 69.

[32] (1887) 15 R. 67.

[33] (1896) 33 S.L.R. 613.

[34] 1910 S.C. 670.

[35] *Moore's Carving Machine Co.* v. *Austin, sup. cit.*; *vide* comments in Gloag and Irvine, *op. cit.*, p. 353.

[36] at p. 71.

[37] at p. 71.

In the opinion of Lord Young: "There is a counterpart in every contract, and here it is that the man of business is not entitled to get his money until he gives up the books, and his employer is not entitled to get his books till he pays the money. These are obligations *hinc inde* prestable by both parties."[38] In a more recent consideration of the problem all the judges in a special case referred to the mutuality principle as justifying farmers retaining possession of potatoes until sums due to them had been paid.[39]

48 It has been suggested, however, that the right of retention or special lien may be subject to exceptions.

(a) Equitable control

Gloag observed: "Lien is an equitable right, to which the Court, in special circumstances, may refuse to give effect."[40] There are, perhaps, situations where consignation should be ordered. Bell mentioned the problem of the ship of great value detained because of a comparatively small repair account, but concluded that in our usage the general rule applied and the ship repairer could retain till payment *or security* was given.[41] There are dicta that retention is an equitable remedy which the courts will control.[42]

(b) Possession

The existence of the right of retention is said to be dependent on possession, and custody is not enough.[43] On this ground an employee has been denied the right to retain his employer's property,[44] and a secretary books of the company.[45] It is difficult to see how the reasoning

---

[38] at p. 72. The "man of business" was not a law agent, which would have raised a question of general lien, but an accountant. Lord Young thought it necessary to say: "I am not disposed to speak sneeringly of accountants and business agents; they are carrying on a useful and legitimate business, and people may properly employ them, but then they must also pay them for what they do."

[39] *Paton's Trs.* v. *Finlayson*, 1923 S.C. 872.

[40] *Encyclopaedia*, Vol. 9, para. 462; also *Contract*, p. 639.

[41] Bell, *Comm.* (5th ed.), II, 97; (7th ed), II, 93; and see *Garscadden* v. *Ardrossan Dry Dock Co. Ltd.*, 1910 S.C. 178.

[42] *Stobbs & Son* v. *Hislop*, 1948 S.C. 216 at p. 228 *per* Lord Russell; *Shepherd's Trs.* v. *Macdonald, Fraser & Co.* (1898) 5 S.L.T. 296 at p. 297 *per* Lord Stormonth Darling; *Garscadden* v. *Ardrossan Dry Dock Co. Ltd.*, *sup. cit.* at p. 180 *per* Lord Ardwall.

[43] Gloag, *op. cit.*, p. 632; *Encyclopaedia*, Vol. 9, para. 464; D. M. Walker, *Civil Remedies*, p. 66. A right of lien is lost when possession is given up, but it can be revived if possession is resumed with the intention that the lien revives: *London Scottish Transport Ltd.* v. *Tyres (Scotland) Ltd.*, 1957 S.L.T.(Sh.Ct.) 48; *Hostess Mobile Catering* v. *Archibald Scott Ltd.*, 1981 S.C. 185.

[44] *Burns* v. *Bruce & Baxter* (1799) Hume 29; see also *Clift* v. *Portobello Pier Co.* (1877) 4 R. 462.

[45] *Gladstone* v. *McCallum* (1896) 23 R. 783; *Barnton Hotel Co.* v. *Cook* (1899) 1 F. 1190.

behind this squares with the mutuality principle. Of course, someone who acquired property without any right to do so could not claim retention of the property. However, an employee who *bona fide* acquires control of items in the course of his employment and who has a contractual obligation to return the items to his employer should surely be in a position to say that he will not comply with that obligation until the employer performs his part of the bargain. If the employee were an independent contractor he would have a right to retain,[46] and it is difficult to see why, in principle, the contract of employment should be specially treated. In general the courts seem to have been more concerned with finding an exact precedent for any lien claimed, instead of applying the underlying principle of mutuality.

(c) Retention against owner

There are circumstances in which the right of retention cannot be pled against the owner of the subject, although this is not truly an exception to the mutuality principle. In *Mitchell* v. *Heys*,[47] which was a case of general lien, a printer could not retain rollers which he had received from M under a printing contract but which had been hired by M from W. The case is remarkable for the treatment of the problem as one of pledge,[48] which might have been distinguished from lien,[49] and for the reliance on English authority. Nevertheless it is reasonable to suggest that, as a general rule, if there is a contract between A and B, an owner C is not prevented from recovering his property from A merely because B is in breach of contract. The plea of retention is valid against the party with whom one has contracted but its basis in the mutuality principle ceases to apply when it is someone other than the contracting party who seeks to recover possession.

This, it is thought, is the reasoning which may support the decision in *Lamonby* v. *Foulds*.[50] The owner of a lorry was able to obtain delivery of it from a garage whose repair bill had not been paid by a contractor who was acquiring the lorry by hire-purchase agreement. In the hire-purchase agreement was a clause stating that the hirer had no authority to create a lien for repairs.

An owner could be barred from recovering his property by the terms of the contract under which he allowed another to deal with the property, for example if goods are in the possession of his mercantile agent,[51]

---

[46] *Meikle & Wilson* v. *Pollard* (1880) 8 R. 69; *Findley* v. *Waddell*, 1910 S.C. 670.

[47] (1894) 21 R. 600.

[48] Esp. *per* Lord Ordinary (Low) at p. 604, Lord Kinnear at p. 610.

[49] Bell, *Comm.* (5th ed.), II, 21, (7th ed.) II, 19; Gloag and Irvine, *op. cit.*, p. 303, but see *Miller* v. *Hutcheson & Dixon* (1881) 8 R. 489 at p. 492 *per* Lord Young.

[50] 1928 S.C. 89.

[51] Factors Act 1889, s.2. *Green's Encyclopaedia*, Vol. 9, para. 474, states that the phrase "other disposition" is wide enough to cover a lien. By definition the word "pledge" in s.2 covers a contract giving a right of retention. See s.1, and Factors (Scotland) Act 1890, s.1(1).

or the possessor has an obligation to keep the subjects of repair without a clause prohibiting the creation of a lien.[52]

(d) Moveables

It has been stated that the right of retention is confined to moveable subjects.[53] In principle it is difficult to see why this should be so. The possible objection that it is inconvenient to have latent rights affecting heritage can be met by pointing out that retention is not effective against third parties. It is no more than a remedy for A if B is in breach of his contract with A. The two cases cited for the exception of heritage[54] do not support the proposition for which they are used.

Turner v. *Turner*[55] was summarised by Professor Gloag as deciding that: "a tenant, when the term of his lease has expired, has no right to remain in possession in security of his claims for any improvements which he may have executed."[56] The case, however, involved not expiry of a lease but reduction of a lease on the grounds that it contravened a prohibition of alienation in an entail.[57] The contract having been reduced, the right of retention could not arise.

The other case, *Castle-Douglas and Dumfries Ry. Co.* v. *Lee, Son and Freeman*[58] was decided on the basis that contractors who had claims against a railway company did not have possession of the railway line they sought to retain. There are dicta of Lord Jerviswoode[59] and Lord Justice-Clerk Inglis[60] indicating, not that retention could not be pled in respect of any heritage, but that there was no authority for such retention in the case of "an heritable subject such as that in question," or "of this kind," which suggest an unsatisfactory introduction of a concept of railway-line law. It also shows a feature earlier mentioned that, in the area of special liens, courts seem to have been troubled if there was an absence of precedent with similar facts. The underlying principle has not always been recognised.

The practical difficulty with heritage is that someone who does work on heritage will usually have nothing to retain. If, however, there is a contractual obligation to give possession of heritage or to convey heri-

---

[52] *Lamonby* v. *Foulds*, 1928 S.C. 89 at p. 95 *per* Lord President Clyde.

[53] Gloag, *op. cit.*, p. 632; *Encyclopaedia*, Vol. 9. para. 475; D. M. Walker, *Civil Remedies*, p. 64 (as indicated above, the right of retention does exist in respect of debts and, despite Professor Walker's view, it seems accurate to suggest that retention does exist for incorporeal moveables).

[54] And see other argument *per* Lord Justice-Clerk Braxfield in *Harper* v. *Faulds* (1791) Bell 8vo. Cases 432 at p. 471; *cf.* Lord Dreghorn at p. 464.

[55] (1811) Hume 854.

[56] *Encyclopaedia, sup. cit.*; also *Contract*, p. 633.

[57] See report in F.C., Dec. 6, 1811.

[58] (1859) 22 D. 18.

[59] at p. 21 (Lord Ordinary).

[60] at p. 23.

tage, it is suggested that this should be treated like any other contractual obligation and be subject to the mutuality principle.

(e) Salvors and innkeepers

The right of retention of salvors and innkeepers has been admitted subject to the suggestion that this involves some extension of the principles in other cases.[61] There is some justification as far as the right of salvors is concerned, this being part of maritime law and, in theory, part of the law of nations.[62] Scots authority is sparse, but it seems that the salvor's lien arises independently of agreement.[63] So far as innkeepers are concerned, the view that their right of retention is special is founded on opinions in an English case that the duties, liabilities and rights of innkeepers are a matter of custom not of contract.[64]

This may be reflected in Scots law to the extent that the edictal liability of innkeepers is, as Erskine says, an obligation "formed by the law itself; for the bare act of receiving goods lays them under it without covenant."[65] Nevertheless the claim against an innkeeper arises out of the relationship of innkeeper and guest. Merely to send goods to an innkeeper would not, at common law and despite Erskine, impose liability for loss by "the bare act of receiving."[66] The extent to which the claim against the innkeeper is not contractual may be important where those such as non-paying guests or the visitors of guests lose property.[67] The nature of the liability is obscure and is now affected by the Hotel Proprietors Act 1956. However, there seems no reason why, if hotel proprietor and traveller have a contract, the mutuality principle should not apply. If the traveller fails to pay his bill the hotel proprietor is entitled to retain the visitor's property. Thus the Muir family had to walk home from a ball, eight or nine miles on a rainy night in thin shoes

---

[61] Gloag and Irvine, *op. cit.*, p. 351; *Encyclopaedia*, Vol. 9, para. 481; *Bermans and Nathans Ltd.* v. *Weibye*, 1981 S.C. 42.

[62] *Boettcher* v. *Carron Co.* (1861) 23 D. 322 *per* Lord Justice-Clerk Inglis at p. 330; *Currie* v. *McKnight* (1896) 24 R.(H.L.) 1.

[63] Bell, *Prin.* (4th and 10th eds.), s.1427; Merchant Shipping Act 1894, s.552. This only means it is *sui generis*, not that it is an exception to the mutuality principle. Salvors have both a maritime lien and a possessory lien: A. R. G. McMillan, *Scottish Maritime Practice* (1926), p. 218.

[64] *Robins & Co.* v. *Gray* [1895] 2 Q.B. 501 at p. 503 *per* Lord Esher M.R.; at p. 507 *per* Kay L.J.; at p. 509 *per* A. L. Smith L.J. This view is still quoted in Crossley Vaines, *Personal Property* (5th ed., 1973), p. 130. Contract and custom were also distinguished in *Lamond* v. *Richard* [1897] 1 Q.B. 541 at p. 545 *per* Lord Esher M.R. and at p. 547 *per* Chitty L.J. See authority cited by Gloag and Irvine, *op cit.*, p. 397. Although English authorities are frequently cited in questions of the Scots liability of innkeepers, there may be differences in our reception of the edict *Nautae, caupones, stabularii*: *Mustard* v. *Paterson*, 1923 S.C. 142 at p. 148 *per* Lord Justice-Clerk Alness, at p. 151 *per* Lord Hunter.

[65] Ersk., III,i,28; also Ersk., *Prin.*, III,i,11, appd. *McPherson* v. *Christie* (1841) 3 D. 930 at p. 938 *per* Lord Moncreiff.

[66] *Meikle* v. *Skelly*, Feb. 16, 1813, F.C.

[67] *e.g. Wright* v. *Anderton* [1909] 1 K.B. 209; *Cryan* v. *Hotel Rembrandt Ltd.* (1925) 133 L.T. 395.

and light muslin dresses, and without bonnets, because Mr Muir had disputed the innkeeper's bill and the innkeeper had detained their ordinary clothes.[68] This has been held to be a special lien which does not extend outside the contract to other claims of the innkeeper such as a claim for damage to furniture.[69] It is suggested that although at common law there might have been claims against a hotel proprietor independent of contract, this should not affect the application of the mutuality principle to any contract between the parties.[70] Because, in part, the innkeeper's lien was said to arise *ex lege* it has been held to extend to possessions of the traveller, even although the goods were not owned by the traveller.[71]

PART 4—MATERIAL AND NON-MATERIAL BREACHES

9 It is probable that Scots law recognises three types of breach of contract. These are (1) trivial breaches, (2) a breach sufficient to justify retention but not rescission, and (3) a material breach which justifies retention and also rescission of the contract.

0 The difference between categories (2) and (3) is not as clear on some authorities as one might wish. There has been an unfortunate tendency to describe any breach other than a trivial breach as being material, with the confusing result that there are two types of material breach. The source of the difficulty is Lord Justice-Clerk Moncreiff's classic dictum in *Turnbull* v. *McLean & Co.*[72] He said:

> "I understand the law of Scotland, in regard to mutual contracts, to be quite clear—first, that the stipulations on either side are the counterparts and the consideration given for each other; second, that a failure to perform any material or substantial part of the contract on the part of one will prevent him from suing the other for performance; and, third, that where one party has refused or failed to perform his part of the contract in any material respect the other is entitled either to insist for implement, claiming damages for the breach, or to rescind the contract altogether—except so far as it has been performed."[73]

---

[68] *McKichen* v. *Muir* (1849) J. Shaw 223; see also *Skirving* v. *Skirving* (1869) 1 Guthrie Sh.Ct.Cas. 508.

[69] *Ferguson* v. *Peterkin*, 1953 S.L.T.(Sh.Ct.) 91: the equity of the result is apparent, the principle less so when compared with *Moore's Carving Machine Co.* v. *Austin* (1880) 33 S.L.R. 613.

[70] Furthermore if the innkeeper's position is special because of the edict, then so also should be the position of common carriers, which is not usually suggested.

[71] *Bermans and Nathans Ltd.* v. *Weibye*, 1981 S.C. 42, part rvd. on appeal, 1983 S.L.T. 299. The lien did not extend to theatrical costumes which were not possessions of the guests.

[72] (1873) 1 R. 730 at p. 738.

[73] at p. 738.

14–51   This equates the materiality of the breach necessary for the operation of the mutuality rule to the materiality which justifies rescission, which is an unfortunate coupling because rescission cases could be used to limit the operation of the mutuality principle. To withhold performance for a time, while being eager to resume if the other party behaves, is a different stance from deciding never to perform again, and the type of breach justifying each position need not be identical. A statement that, "I am withholding payment until you perform," is of a different type from, "Because of your breach, I am no longer interested in future performance." However, Bell's editors altered the text of the *Principles* by adding the qualification which limited the mutuality principle to the case of breach of a material part of the contract.[74]

14–52   Lord Justice-Clerk Moncreiff's view, however, is not consistent with all the authorities. Gloag concluded: "It would appear to be established that a failure in the performance of a contract may not be so material as to justify the rescission of the contract, yet may be sufficiently material to entitle the other party to withhold counter-performance."[75] He quoted *Linn* v. *Shields*[76] which supports this view, although in some respects the rubric is clearer than the opinion of the court.

14–53   Professor Walker adopts a similar position to Gloag.[77] The difficulty with some of the authorities cited by these authors is that, *Linn* v. *Shields* apart, they are instances of insolvency or leases. Insolvency may be special (it being a feature of the law that rights which do not otherwise exist can emerge on insolvency) and the law on retention in leases, which is considered elsewhere[78] is in such a state of confusion that not only is it difficult to derive a general proposition from the multitude of conflicting cases, but it can be demonstrated that the mutuality principle has not always been applied. It would, however, seem to make a nonsense of the law of liens, an instance of the mutuality principle, if a lien could only be exercised after there had been a material breach.

14–54   The mutuality principle should not apply where the breach could be ignored as trivial. That apart, if a breach is committed by the other party, irrespective of its type, a tenant should be able to withhold his rent, a repairer to retain the article submitted for repair, or a purchaser to withhold the price. The graver the consequences of this remedy in comparison with the effect of the breach, the greater is the compulsitor on the party in breach to perform according to his contract. This is not unfair. On the contrary, to encourage parties to perform as they have agreed should, within limits, be one of the aims of the law and if settlement of a dispute is produced by this modest exercise of self-help, that is preferable to litigation or the abandonment of rights because court

---

[74] *Cf.* s.71 in 4th and 10th eds.

[75] Gloag, *Contract* (2nd ed., 1929), p. 623.

[76] (1863) 2 M. 88.

[77] D. M. Walker, *Civil Remedies* (1974) p. 59; although the author does not explain his phrase, "a material part of the contract."

[78] See paras. 14–39 *et seq.*

action is considered undesirable. It is suggested that the view of Lord Justice-Clerk Moncreiff and Bell's editors should not be followed.

Fundamental Breach

5 At one time English law was developing a doctrine of fundamental breach and related but different concepts such as breach of a fundamental term. This was done largely to avoid the unpleasant effects of exclusion clauses. If a party was in fundamental breach of a contract he could not rely on an exclusion clause in that contract to escape liability for the breach. The suggestion that there was a separate category of fundamental breach did not meet with judicial approval in Scotland.[79] As a result of the decision of the House of Lords in *Photo Production Ltd.* v. *Securicor Transport Ltd.*[80] it is now very doubtful if English law recognises separate categories of fundamental breaches or terms. The term "fundamental breach" will usually mean "material breach,"[81] but it is possible that a draftsman may use the word "fundamental" to mean something different from "material," as in the phrase "fundamental, material or non-material breach."

Material Breach justifying Rescission

6 The analysis of the law is bedevilled by problems of terminology. The phrase "material breach" is unfortunate, in that no breach of contract is immaterial. Any breach is material enough for an action, even if only to recover nominal damages. In the use of the phrase in connection with rescission, however, it has a meaning nearer substantial breach. Various expressions have been used. Judges have spoken of breaches "in a material, and certainly in an essential part,"[82] "a failure of performance in a matter touching the essentials of the contract," "substantial failure," "a matter of vital importance,—I mean a matter touching the very existence of the contract," [83] going "to the root of the contract,"[84] "of the essence of the contract,"[85] "the root and substance of the contract."[86]

---

[79] *Alexander Stephen (Forth) Ltd.* v. *J. J. Riley (U.K.) Ltd.*, 1976 S.C. 151; *cf. W. L. Tinney & Co. Ltd.* v. *John C. Dougall Ltd.* 1977 S.L.T.(Notes) 58. In *Wolifson* v. *Harrison*, 1977 S.C. 384, the Second Division appear to have used the term "fundamental breach" as a synonym for material breach.

[80] [1980] A.C. 827. The opinions cite the earlier English authority which it has not been thought necessary to mention here; see also *Suisse Atlantique Société d'Armement Maritime S.A.* v. *N. V. Rotterdamsche Kolen Centrale* [1967] 1 A.C. 361.

[81] *Alexander Stephen (Forth) Ltd.* v. *J. J. Riley (U.K.) Ltd., sup. cit.*

[82] *Collard* v. *Carswell* (1892) 19 R. 987 at p. 991 *per* Lord Ordinary (Kyllachy); on appeal (1893) 20 R.(H.L.) 47.

[83] *Sup. cit.* at p. 996 *per* Lord MacLaren.

[84] *Wade* v. *Waldon*, 1909 S.C. 571 at p. 576 *per* Lord President Dunedin.

[85] *Sup. cit.* at p. 577 *per* Lord MacLaren.

[86] *Graham* v. *United Turkey Red Co.*, 1922 S.C. 533 at p. 536 *per* Lord Ordinary (Anderson).

14–57   In a recent consideration the Second Division[87] has affirmed the relevance of the test expounded by Lord President Dunedin in *Wade* v. *Waldon*, namely[88]:

> "It is familiar law, and quite well settled by decision, that in any contract which contains multifarious stipulations there are some which go so to the root of the contract that a breach of those stipulations entitles the party pleading the breach to declare that the contract is at an end. There are others which do not go to the root of the contract, but which are part of the contract, and which would give rise, if broken, to an action of damages."

14–58   A *bona fide* belief that the contract is being complied with does not prevent the breach from being material.[89]

14–59   English cases can be referred to, but they do not add much to the expressions used in the older Scottish cases.[90] English authority must be used with caution because underlying its approach to breach are trends which are not native to Scots law, namely the characterisation of terms as either conditions or warranties and the failure of consideration.[91] The tendency of the English lawyer to categorise clauses of contracts into dependent covenants, fundamental terms, conditions precedent, warranties and the like, is productive of considerable uncertainty. In a monograph on *Rescission of Contracts*, C. B. Morrison observed:

> "If a law student . . . were to ask the first half-dozen lawyers he met. . . . What breach of an executory contract will discharge the party not in default?—he would, as likely as not, get half a dozen different answers. The first might be that the term broken must be a condition, the second, that it must be a condition precedent, the third, a term going to the whole consideration, the fourth, a term going to the root of the contract, the fifth, an essential term, the sixth, an important term, and so on. He might even be told merely that the importance of the *breach* is the test; or, it might even be suggested that the breach must amount to a repudiation."[92]

Whatever the present state of English law may be, its historical development shows that there was considerable difficulty in grasping the problems of breach. It may seem simplistic and old fashioned for the Scots lawyer merely to ask: "Was there a material breach?" but sometimes there is a virtue in being unsophisticated.[93]

---

[87] *Blyth* v. *Scottish Liberal Club*, 1982 S.C. 140.

[88] 1909 S.C. 571 at p. 576. The reference to the contract being at "an end" requires explanation in the light of more modern authorities.

[89] *Blyth* v. *Scottish Liberal Club*, *sup. cit.*

[90] *e.g. Hong Kong Fir Shipping Co. Ltd.* v. *Kawasaki* [1962] 2 Q.B. 26; *Decro-Wall International S.A.* v. *Practitioners Marketing Ltd.* [1971] 2 All E.R. 216.

[91] See B. Coote, "The Effect of Discharge by Breach on Exception Clauses" [1970] C.L.J. 221 at pp. 222–224 and authorities there cited; Lord Devlin, "The Treatment of Breach of Contract" [1966] C.L.J. 192.

[92] C. B. Morrison, *Rescission of Contracts* (1916), Intro.

[93] *Cf.* B. Coote, *sup. cit.* at p. 240: "The pursuit of elegance for its own sake would be an object unworthy of any system of law. On the other hand, that doctrinal coherence has its advantages no law teacher and, one suspects, few legal practitioners would deny. The common law of discharge by breach, it is submitted, is one field where a return to first principles would be not unjustified."

The present position in English law appears to be this. English law recognises conditions and warranties. A condition is a term of which failure in performance entitles the other party to rescind. A warranty is a term breach of which sounds in damages, but does not give a right to rescind. There are also intermediate terms, the remedy of which depends on the nature and effect of the breach. The identification of a term as a condition, warranty, or intermediate term is a problem of construction of the contract.[94] Scots law, on the other hand, looks at the nature of the breach, and its concept of "material breach" does not depend on a classification of the terms of the contract.

When is a breach material?

Whether or not a breach is material is primarily a question of fact. The answer depends on circumstances at the time of the contract and also subsequently. It is not to be decided solely by looking within the four corners of the contract, although what the parties had in contemplation is obviously important. What has happened is also significant. If there is defective performance it may be necessary to investigate the extent of the defect. If there is delay in performance it is equally necessary, although not always so obvious, that the effect of the delay must be inquired into. The issue should be determined like any other question of fact: that is, normally after a proof, unless all the relevant facts are admitted.

It is the unusual feature of the classic case of *Wade* v. *Waldon*[95] that it was decided without hearing evidence. The case involved a comedian who was in breach of contract because he failed to give theatres advance notice of his engagement and bill matter. The theatres refused to allow the comedian to appear because of the breach. The issue was whether the breach was material. The Lord Ordinary allowed a proof limited to the question of damages. The argument for the reclaimers was that they should have had a proof on the nature of the condition which was breached. The First Division refused a proof at large. The issue was treated as one of interpretation of the contract and a question of law.

Dr Gow has suggested that the result was:

> "bizarre . . . because if sound it meant that the pursuer could have turned up on the afternoon of the day of the first performance and insisted on performance. To the non-legal mind it would seem of considerable importance to the defender to receive timeous notice

---

[94] *Hong Kong Fir Shipping Co. Ltd.* v. *Kawasaki, sup. cit.; Cehave N.V.* v. *Bremer Handelsgesellschaft mbh* [1976] 1 Q.B. 44; *Bremer Handelsgesellschaft mbH* v. *Vanden Avenne Izegem* [1978] 2 Lloyd's Rep. 109 (H.L.); *Bunge Corpn.* v. *Tradax S.A.* [1981] 2 All E.R. 513 (H.L.).

[95] 1909 S.C. 571.

of the pursuer's intention to perform as agreed, together with billing material in order adequately to bring to the notice of local patrons who 'next week's star attraction' would be."[96]

14–64   This is the type of criticism to which a court is vulnerable if it decides the issue of material breach without a proof. It is strange that the problems of managing the Palace and Pavilion Theatres, Glasgow should have been thought to be within judicial knowledge. Even if by the chance of experience they were, it would not produce confidence in the minds of those less informed that the result is just, unless it was demonstrated to be so by evidence.

14–65   The following month the First Division heard the appeal in *Municipal Council of Johannesburg* v. *D. Stewart & Co. (1902) Ltd.*,[97] and with Lord President Dunedin referring to "a case from Glasgow the other day" it was decided without hearing evidence that the installers of machinery to provide electric power for Johannesburg had been in material breach. "Nobody can say that the breach was not of the essence of the contract; for as a matter of fact, according to the allegation, the defenders . . . did not supply proper plant at all, threw up the whole contract, and allowed the town to go into darkness and the tramways to stop."[98] Put like that, who would argue that the cataclysm hitting Johannesburg was not material breach? The answer is that it depends on a proof of the whole circumstances. On appeal to the House of Lords, although in argument no denial was given that the passage quoted above was a substantially accurate statement of fact,[99] the House remitted back to the Court of Session for a proof to determine the nature of the breach.[1] Although the *Johannesburg* case has specialities,[2] it casts some doubt on the correctness of the procedure in *Wade* v. *Waldon.*

14–66   In any event *Wade* v. *Waldon* is unusual in not having had a proof, although in some recent cases involving failure to pay for land the decision on materiality of breach has been taken without a proof.[3] An examination of reported cases will show that there usually has been a proof. There can, of course, be an equivalent such as a joint minute of admissions.[4] It is only after being apprised of the facts that the court can consider such relevant matters as the imminence of strikes and the rising price of a product,[5] fluctuations in a market price,[6] or the previous

---

[96] J. J. Gow, *Mercantile and Industrial Law of Scotland* (1964), p. 209. He suggests an alternative solution in the lack of merit in the defender's conduct. A simple inquiry would have elucidated the information. The idea that a party in breach should be given an opportunity to perform has some support. See paras. 14–81 *et seq.*

[97] 1909 S.C. 860.

[98] at pp. 877–878 *per* Lord President Dunedin.

[99] *Vide Sanderson & Son* v. *Armour*, 1922 S.C.(H.L.) 117 at p. 129 *per* Lord Shaw.

[1] 1909 S.C.(H.L.) 53.

[2] *Vide Sanderson & Son* v. *Armour, supra.*

[3] *Inveresk Paper Co. Ltd.* v. *Pembry Machinery Co. Ltd.*, 1972 S.L.T.(Notes) 63; *Lloyds Bank Ltd.* v. *Bauld*, 1976 S.L.T.(Notes) 53.

[4] *Birkett, Sperling & Co.* v. *Engholm & Co.* (1871) 10 M. 170.

[5] *Shaw, Macfarlane & Co.* v. *Waddell & Son* (1900) 2 F. 1070.

[6] *Colvin* v. *Short* (1857) 19 D. 890.

attitude of the parties towards each other, their communications and the reasonableness of a time limit for performance,[7] the effect of past breaches which have been waived,[8] or conduct prior to the breach.[9] In *Blyth* v. *Scottish Liberal Club*[10] the court examined the circumstances in which an employee disobeyed instructions, the other work of the employee and the state of affairs of his employer. Lord Dunpark observed,[11] it is thought correctly, that: "In every case the question whether a breach of contract is material is one of fact and degree."

57 Breaches have been held or observed to be material when there was a failure to supply a substantial part of a cargo within a stipulated month,[12] failure to be able to ship coal until several days after the date promised,[13] failure to settle a transaction in the iron trade on the day promised,[14] a delay by more than a month in supplying ships,[15] a failure by a landlord to keep a house in tenantable condition,[16] a failure to give vacant possession of about one-third of an estate purchased even though the occupant's claim was spurious,[17] long delay in paying the purchase price of land,[18] and disobedience by an employee.[19]

58 On the other hand, breaches have been held not to be material when there was a failure to comply with a condition on giving notice and bill matter prior to a theatrical performance,[20] short delay in paying the price of heritage,[21] failure by a landlord in an agricultural lease to put fences in tenantable repair,[22] dispute about the adequacy of catering services at a football ground,[23] and delay in producing the title to a ship.[24]

---

[7] *Rodger (Builders) Ltd* v. *Fawdry*, 1950 S.C. 483 at p. 492 *per* Lord Sorn.
[8] *Forslind* v. *Bechely-Crundall*, 1922 S.C.(H.L.) 173 at p. 177 *per* Lord Ordinary (Sands).
[9] *Forslind* v. *Bechely-Crundall*, *supra* at p. 180 *per* Viscount Haldane.
[10] 1982 S.C. 140.
[11] at p. 148.
[12] *Grieve, Son & Co.* v. *Konig & Co.* (1880) 7 R. 521 *per* Lord Shand.
[13] *Shaw, Macfarlane & Co.* v. *Waddell & Son* (1900) 2 F. 1070.
[14] *Colvin* v. *Short* (1857) 19 D. 890.
[15] *Dunford & Elliott* v. *Macleod & Co.* (1902) 4 F. 912.
[16] *McKimmie's Trs.* v. *Armour* (1899) 2 F. 156.
[17] *Stuart* v. *Lort-Phillips*, 1976 S.L.T.(Notes) 39.
[18] *Lloyd's Bank Ltd.* v. *Bauld*, 1976 S.L.T.(Notes) 53; *George Packman & Sons* v. *Dunbar's Trs.*, 1977 S.L.T. 140.
[19] *Blyth* v. *Scottish Liberal Club*, *sup. cit.*
[20] *Wade* v. *Waldon*, *sup. cit.*
[21] *Burns* v. *Garscadden* (1900) 8 S.L.T. 321; *Rodger (Builders) Ltd.* v. *Fawdry*, *sup. cit.*; *Inveresk Paper Co. Ltd* v. *Pembry Machinery Co. Ltd.*, 1972 S.L.T.(Notes) 63, which on its facts is a curious case. Presumably by the date of Lord Thomson's decision (June 28, 1972) the defender had still not paid the purchase price which was due on November 4, 1971. Was this not by itself unreasonable delay, or are there facts not revealed by the report?
[22] *Todd* v. *Bowie* (1902) 4 F. 435.
[23] *Lindley Catering Investments Ltd.* v. *Hibernian Football Club Ltd.*, 1975 S.L.T.(Notes) 56.
[24] *Forbes* v. *Campbell* (1885) 12 R. 1065.

What happens when there is material breach?

14–69 On a material breach the "innocent party" has an option. He may or may not continue with his performance of the contract. With any breach other than a trivial breach the innocent party may withhold performance until the party in breach performs. That is the result of the mutuality principle.[25] The speciality arising from a material breach is that the innocent party may decide to end all future performance of the contract. He may or may not intimate this decision to the party in breach. If he does intimate his decision there is "rescission" of the contract. But rescission is not always essential.

14–70 Rescission exists as a concept because sometimes the "innocent" party must decide whether or not he wishes to continue to be bound. If, for example, he had agreed to accept delivery of one hundredweight of coal on the first of each month for a year and after several deliveries have been late a lorry arrives with the July instalment on the 20th of that month, the buyer must decide whether to accept the load or not. He cannot avoid the issue. He must rescind or not. Similarly if in *Wade* v. *Waldon*[26] the theatre manager had not sent a notice of rescission, he would still have had to face the problem of George Robey's breach of contract if Robey had turned up for the first performance. Robey would either have appeared on stage in terms of his contract or he would not have. The decisions on first whether the breach was material, and secondly whether it should be waived or whether further performance should be refused, would still have had to have been taken.[27]

14–71 It is, however, only in some situations that a reaction to the other's breach is necessary. It may be that the innocent party never need rescind. He remains inactive and, if sued, has a good defence to the action.[28] Rescission is not an inevitable consequence of a decision to found on a material breach.

14–72 A material breach by one party gives the other party an option to be free from future performance of his obligations. It is not an option which he must actively exercise, such as by sending a notice of rescission. Rather it is his right which he may lose by personal bar. Nor need he give any prior warning to the guilty party, for it is that party's failure to fulfil which has the effect of giving the innocent party the right

---

[25] paras. 14–27 *et seq*.
[26] *Sup. cit.*
[27] As it had to be by the manager of the Pavilion, Armadale, when comedians arrived late for a performance: *Hayes and Finch* v. *Easton* (1920) 36 Sh.Ct.Rep. 187.
[28] *e.g Thorneloe* v. *McDonald & Co.* (1892) 29 S.L.R. 409 at p. 411 *per* Lord McLaren; *Dingwall* v. *Burnett*, 1912 S.C. 1097; *Morison* v. *Morison* (1902) 10 S.L.T. 324.

to be free from future performance.[29] He is not due to pay sums under the contract after the material breach (nor from after the date of rescission, if any).[30] Nor need this philosophy produce the situation which has arisen in England, where it has been indicated that it is not possible both to rescind a contract and to claim full damages for breach on a contract that no longer exists.[31] The contract is not ended, with the consequence that some clauses of the contract, such as a liquidate damages clause or an arbitration clause, are still enforceable.

73   The law has been troubled about the effect on an arbitration clause of repudiation or rescission of the whole contract ever since *Municipal Council of Johannesburg* v. *D. Stewart & Co. (1902) Ltd.*[32] In that very special case with its complex facts, an admitted repudiation, and involving a contract governed by English law, the arbitration clause was not enforceable. Thereafter there were unsuccessful attempts to argue that the case decided that when a contract was terminated by repudiation or rescission it was no longer possible to found on a term in the contract.[33] Although these attempts failed judges sometimes asked whether the contract had been rescinded.[34] It would have been easier to see that an arbitration clause survived if there had been applied the idea that breach or repudiation releases the other party, if he wishes, from future obligations of performance. Apart from theoretical considerations it means that it is not necessary to decide whether there has been a valid rescission before submitting the case to the arbiter. Nor is it necessary to try to interpret the arbitration clause in an extended way to cover events arising on termination of the contract.[35] The question whether the contract is at an end is inappropriate.

74   This was recognised in *Heyman* v. *Darwins*[36] in which the House of Lords, not for the first time, grappled with the difficulties created over the years. Lord MacMillan observed:

---

[29] *Barclay* v. *Anderston Foundry Co.* (1856) 18 D. 1190; *cf. Lindley Catering Investments Ltd.* v. *Hibernian Football Club Ltd.*, 1975 S.L.T.(Notes) 56 at p. 57 *per* Lord Thomson and *Wilson* v. *Watson* (1841) 3 D. 424, esp. *per* Lord Ordinary at p. 427, a case which may be explicable on the basis that there was no breach of contract and is, therefore, not an authority for a situation of material breach. In cases involving missives where there is not initially a material breach, an ultimatum doctrine has been referred to; see below, para. 14–81.

[30] *Graham* v. *United Turkey Red Co.*, 1922 S.C., 533: the defenders did not rescind but had they done so it should not have affected the outcome, *i.e.* the agent was not entitled to an accounting for the period subsequent to his breach.

[31] *Horsler* v. *Zorro* [1975] Ch. 302; see criticism by F. Dawson, 1976 M.L.R. 214.

[32] 1909 S.C.(H.L.) 53.

[33] *Hegarty & Kelly* v. *Cosmopolitan Insurance Corp. Ltd.*, 1913 S.C. 377; *Scott* v. *Gerrard*, 1916 S.C. 793; *Sanderson & Son* v. *Armour & Co.*, 1922 S.C.(H.L.) 177.

[34] *Hegart & Kelly* v. *Cosmopolitan Insurance Corp. Ltd.*, sup. cit. at p. 384 *per* Lord Mackenzie; *Sanderson & Son* v. *Armour & Co.*, 1921 S.C. 18 at p. 27 *per* Lord President Clyde.

[35] *Cf. Scott* v. *Gerard, supra*; *Heyman* v. *Darwins* [1942] A.C. 356 at p. 392 *per* Lord Porter.

[36] [1942] A.C. 356 at p. 374.

"I am, accordingly, of opinion that what is commonly called repudiation or total breach of a contract, whether acquiesced in by the other party or not, does not abrogate the contract, though it may relieve the injured party of the duty of further fulfilling obligations which he has by the contract undertaken to the repudiating party. The contract is not put out of existence, though all further performance of the obligations undertaken by each party in favour of the other may cease. It survives for the purpose of measuring the claims arising out of the breach, and the arbitration clause survives for determining the mode of their settlement. The purposes of the contract have failed, but the arbitration clause is not one of the purposes of the contract."

14–75   Lord Porter observed[37]:

"To say that the contract is rescinded or has come to an end or has ceased to exist may in individual cases convey the truth with sufficient accuracy, but the fuller expression that the injured party is thereby absolved from future performance of his obligations under the contract is a more exact description of the position."

14–76   A leading American textbook, Corbin on *Contracts*, commenting on Lord Porter's view, states:

"Lord Porter's statement shows good progress; but his own analysis is far from 'full' and he is altogether too uncritical when he says that the former expressions have 'sufficient accuracy' in any case. Those expressions sometimes have led to unjust decisions; and in all cases they promote obscurity and cause unnecessary litigation."[38]

The same work, in commenting on the effect of repudiation, concludes: "Various changes in legal relations have taken place; but these are not properly indicated by saying that the 'contract' is abrogated, or rescinded, or at an end."[39]

14–77   This is thought acceptable reasoning and of general application, despite a recent decision of the Privy Council which would limit the ideas in *Heyman* v. *Darwins* to arbitration clauses but not extend them to other obligations in a contract, such as a clause entitling a party to interest. These, it was suggested, do not survive an accepted repudiation.[40] The contrary may, however, be argued.

---

[37] at p. 399. The point may also have been recognised by Lord Murray in *Barclay* v. *Anderston Foundry* (1856) 18 D. 1190 at p. 1195: "It is admitted there was here a contract, and I do not consider it material whether it was put an end to."

[38] Corbin on *Contracts* (1963), s.982, n. 36.

[39] *Op. cit.*, s.982, n. 35.

[40] *Bloemen Ltd.* v. *Gold Coast* [1973] A.C. 115 at p. 126; and see also *Lep Air Services* v. *Rolloswin Ltd.* [1973] A.C. 331 at p. 345 *per* Lord Reid: "So it appears to me that when a contract is brought to an end by repudiation accepted by the other party all the obligations in the contract come to an end and they are replaced by operation of law by an obligation to pay money damages"—and at p. 350 *per* Lord Diplock: *cf.* judgment of Court of Appeal in [1971] 3 All E.R. 45 at p. 54: "The phrase frequently used, 'the contract is at an end,' is a convenient phrase, so long as it is understood to mean that there is no longer any question of future performance of the contractual obligations."

8   In *Photo Production Ltd.* v. *Securicor Transport Ltd.*[41] the House of Lords made clear that a material breach of contract did not bring the contract to an end. Lord Wilberforce observed about the doctrine of fundamental breach[42]:

> "I have, indeed, been unable to understand how the doctrine can be reconciled with the well-accepted principle of law, stated by the highest modern authority, that when in the context of a breach of contract one speaks of 'termination', what is meant is no more than that the innocent party, or in some cases, both parties, are excused from further performance. Damages, in such cases, are then claimed under the contract, so what reason in principle can there be for disregarding what the contract itself says about damages, whether it 'liquidates' them, or limits them, or excludes them."

He went on to point out the confusion caused by terminology:

> "These difficulties arise in part from uncertain or inconsistent terminology. A vast number of expressions are used to describe situations where a breach has been committed by one party of such a character as to entitle the other party to refuse further performance: discharge, rescission, termination, the contract is at an end, or dead, or displaced; clauses cannot survive, or simply go. I have come to think that some of the difficulties can be avoided; in particular the use of 'rescission,' even if distinguished from rescission *ab initio*, as an equivalent for discharge, though justifiable in some contexts (see *Johnson* v. *Agnew*[43]) may lead to confusion in others. To plead for complete uniformity may be to cry for the moon. But what can and ought to be avoided is to make use of these confusions in order to produce a concealed and unreasoned legal innovation: to pass, for example, from saying that a party, victim of a breach of contract, is entitled to refuse further performance, to saying that he may treat the contract as at an end, or as rescinded, and to draw from this the proposition, which is not analytical but one of policy, that all or (arbitrarily) some of the clauses of the contract lose, automatically, their force, regardless of intention."

9   In *Port Jackson Stevedoring Pty Ltd.* v. *Salmond & Spraggon (Australia) Pty. Ltd.*[44] a clause limiting the time within which an action could be brought survived a repudiatory breach. In argument reliance had been placed on some observations by Lord Diplock in *Photo Production Ltd.* where reference was made to putting an end "to all primary . . . obligations remaining unperformed." It was observed by the Privy Council[45]:

> "But these words were never intended to cover such 'obligations,' to use Lord Diplock's word, as arise when primary obligations have

---

[41] [1980] A.C. 827.
[42] at p. 844. His speech was agreed with by Lord Keith and Lord Scarman. Contrast Lord Diplock's speech.
[43] [1980] A.C. 367.
[44] [1980] 3 All E.R. 257 (P.C.).
[45] at p. 262.

been put an end to. There then arise, on his Lordship's analysis, secondary obligations which include an obligation to pay monetary compensation. Whether these have been modified by agreement is a matter of construction of the contract."

14-80   The effect of material breach or an accepted repudiation is that the "innocent party" cannot be compelled to perform further. Clauses which deal with breach or which come into operation when performance is impossible or has been given up , regulate the liability for breach of contract. Exemption and indemnity clauses, arbitration clauses, liquidate damages clauses and similar clauses survive the breach. As a matter of construction some clauses may be redundant because future performance of obligations by the innocent party cannot be insisted upon.

Remediable breach

14-81   In cases involving missives an ultimatum doctrine has been referred to. In *Rodger (Builders) Ltd.* v. *Fawdry*[46] the Lord Ordinary, Lord Sorn, observed that payment of the price of heritage on the appointed day was not, in general, an essential condition of the contract, and failure to pay on that date did not entitle the seller to rescind. He continued[47]:

"But payment of the price by a fixed date may be made an essential condition of such contract. If there is unnecessary or unjustifiable delay on the part of the purchaser in paying the price, the seller may limit a time within which payment must be made, and, provided the time limit is a reasonable one in the circumstances, failure to pay within that time will be treated as breach of an essential condition entitling the seller to rescind."

14-82   In *Inveresk Paper Co. Ltd.* v. *Pembry Machinery Co. Ltd.*[48] it was reiterated that the correct course was to give the buyers a reasonable time to make payment. In *Lloyds Bank Ltd.* v. *Bauld*[49] the raising of an action of declarator was itself treated as a notice making time of the essence for completion of the contract. These cases all involved a failure by a purchaser to pay the price, but a similar doctrine appears to operate when a seller's title has a remediable defect.[50] The "ultimatum procedure" does not apply when neither party is in breach and so cannot be used to provide a time within which a suspensive condition should be purified.[51]

---

[46] 1950 S.C. 483.

[47] at p. 492. A minor printing error in S.C. has been ignored. See the report at 1950 S.L.T. 345, at p. 350. Earlier cases referred to were *Black* v. *Dick*, 1814 Hume 699 and *Burns* v. *Garscadden* (1901) 8 S.L.T. 321. On the facts in *Rodger (Builders) Ltd.* the circumstances did not justify sending an ultimatum.

[48] 1972 S.L.T.(Notes) 63; see also *Johnstone* v. *Harris*, 1977 S.C. 365.

[49] 1976 S.L.T.(Notes) 53.

[50] *Fleming* v. *Harley's Trs.* (1823) 2 S.373; *Kinnear* v. *Young*, 1936 S.L.T. 574.

[51] *T. Boland & Co. Ltd.* v. *Dundas's Trs.*, 1975 S.L.T.(Notes) 80.

3   The cases on missives involve a breach which was not, at first, material. Indeed in a case of a lack of title to subjects it has been indicated that no ultimatum need be given.[52] The possibility that a party in material breach should be given an opportunity to remedy the breach was raised in *Lindley Catering Investments Ltd.* v. *Hibernian Football Club Ltd.*[53] which involved the public catering at a football ground. Lord Thomson observed[54]:

> "In my opinion the legal position in a case like the present can be broadly stated thus: if one party so breaches a material stipulation in the contract as to preclude the other from fulfilling his part of the contract, the innocent party is entitled to regard himself as absolved from further performance of his obligations and to rescind the contract. But if the breach is such, by degree or circumstances, that it can be remedied so that the contract as a whole can thereafter be implemented, the innocent party is not entitled to treat the contract as rescinded without giving to the other party an opportunity so to remedy the breach."

4   The idea that a party in material breach should be given a "second chance" if the breach is remediable is attractive and may develop as a principle in our law. We have for a long time had the concept that certain irritancies are purgeable.[55] That certain conventional irritancies in leases are not purgeable[56] shows the difficulty in tracing a coherent policy in the law. In contracts to which the Sale of Goods Act 1979 applies, a material breach by the seller gives the buyer statutory rights[57] which prevent the operation of the concept of "remediable breach." Once a contract has been rescinded the "innocent" party can refuse to accept a rectification of the breach, such as when a defect is cured in a title to heritage.[58]

PART 5—BREACH OF A POTESTATIVE CONDITION

5   A potestative condition is a condition which it is within the power of one of the contracting parties to purify. There is the authority of Erskine[59] and Bell[60] that, when a person has done all within his power to fulfil the

---

[52] *Campbell* v. *McCutcheon*, 1963 S.C. 505; see also *George Packman & Sons* v. *Dunbar's Trs.*, 1977 S.L.T. 140.

[53] 1975 S.L.T.(Notes) 56.

[54] at p. 57.

[55] *e.g. Duncanson* v. *Giffen* (1878) 15 S.L.R. 356; *Anderson* v. *Valentine*, 1957 S.L.T. 57.

[56] *e.g. Dorchester Studios (Glasgow) Ltd.* v. *Stone*, 1975 S.C.(H.L.) 56; *H.M.V. Fields Properties* v. *Skirt 'n' Slack Centre of London Ltd.*, 1982 S.L.T. 477. See *Irritancies in Leases*, Scot. Law Com. No. 75 (1983). Statute has now provided a control over the use of irritancies in leases: see Law Reform (Miscellaneous Provisions) (Scotland) Act 1985, ss.4, 5. On the equitable power of the court to relieve the tenant in the case of abuse or oppressive use of an irritancy, see *Lucas's Exrs.* v. *Demarco*, 1968 S.L.T. 89; *H.M.V. Fields Properties* v. *Skirt 'n' Slack Centre of London Ltd.*, *sup. cit.* See paras. 20–134 *et seq.*

[57] Sale of Goods Act 1979, s.11(5); and see para. 14–105.

[58] *Gilfillan* v. *Cadell* (1893) 21 R. 269; *Kinnear* v. *Young*, 1936 S.L.T. 574.

[59] Ersk., III,iii,85.

[60] *Prin.*, s.50.

condition, it is held to be purified. As Gloag pointed out,[61] this cannot be the law. "Suppose a brewer to agree to advance money to a publican if he obtains a licence, could any Court hold that the money was due because the publican had applied for a licence, and had been refused?"[62]

14–86   Where, on the other hand, a party prevents fulfilment of a condition, he cannot found on a failure to comply with a contract which arose from his own act. The condition is held to have been fulfilled. In *Pirie* v. *Pirie*[63] a testator provided that a sum of money due to him by one of his sons should be allowed to remain in his hands for eight years, on condition that the executor and residuary legatee should remain a director of the company in which the sum was invested. The executor voluntarily resigned office as director. It was decided that the condition must be held to be satisfied and the son was entitled to retain the loan. In *Mackay* v. *Dick & Stevenson*[64] the buyer of a machine was bound to accept it if a trial was satisfactory. The buyer failed to give a proper trial. The condition as to the trial was held to have been fulfilled and the seller entitled to the price of the machine. In *T. & R. Duncanson* v. *Scottish County Investment Co. Ltd.*[65] a building owner contracted for the performance of joiner work. Owing to the delay caused by other tradesmen employed by the owner, the joiners failed to complete their work within the specified time. It was held that in the circumstances the joiners were absolved from the time limit and decree for payment was granted. In *Dowling* v. *Methven, Sons & Co.*[66] an agency agreement was terminated because the value of goods sold and delivered by the agent failed to reach a specified figure. The agent had actually sold more than the required figure but he could not deliver the goods owing to the failure of the other party to supply him with sufficient quantities. It was held that the agent's supplier could not terminate the agency because of a breach of contract arising from the supplier's failure.

14–87   The rule illustrated above applies only to the subject-matter of the contract in which the conditional obligation is contained and not to other rights which might assist fulfilment of the condition.[67] A person is excused from performance of absolute obligation only when he is prevented from doing his part by the actions or default of the other party,[68] or when there is frustration.[69]

---

[61] *Contract*, p. 279.
[62] *Ibid.*
[63] (1873) 11 M. 941.
[64] (1881) 8 R.(H.L.) 37.
[65] 1915 S.C. 1106.
[66] 1921 S.C. 948.
[67] *Paterson* v. *McEwan's Trs.* (1881) 8 R. 646; *Kedie's Trs.* v. *Stewart & McDonald*, 1926 S.C. 1019.
[68] *Aktieselskabet Dampskibet Hansa* v. *Alexander & Sons*, 1919 S.C.(H.L.) 122, commenting on *Hansen* v. *Donaldson* (1874) 1 R. 1066.
[69] See Chap. 15.

PART 6—SALE OF HERITAGE

88 As Gloag observed, this subject is involved in some obscurity.[70] The problems which are dealt with here are those arising from breach of missives. Breach of warrandice in conveyances must be looked for in works on conveyancing.

The mutuality principle

89 The mutuality principle applies to missives as it does to any other contract. In *Bowie* v. *Semple's Exrs.*[71] it was held that a purchaser was entitled to withhold payment of the price, because the seller was unable to produce his confirmation as executor. The practical effect of the mutuality principle is that the "innocent" party can withhold performance of his obligations until the party in breach is able and willing to perform. There may come a point, however, when the "innocent" party wishes to resile. When can he do so? There are several issues to consider.

The contract may make the breach material

90 It may appear from the missives that payment of a price, or entry, or delivery of a valid title on a stated date are of the essence of the contract.[72] This is (or was) unusual. The normal rule, in the absence of contrary intention, is that time is not of the essence in sales of heritage.[73] This rule contrasts with that developed in English law in mercantile contracts, where stipulations as to time are generally treated as conditions breach of which entitles the innocent party to rescind.[74] But the Scottish rule in the case of sales of heritage is clear, even if awkward to apply. In the absence of a repudiation of the contract, the "innocent party" is faced with a delay by the party in breach, the consequences of which can be difficult to determine.

---

[70] *Contract*, p. 613.

[71] 1978 S.L.T.(Sh.Ct.) 9; conversely if the purchaser has failed to pay the price, he could not sue for implement. In *Hayes* v. *Robinson*, 1984 S.L.T. 300, the purchaser was barred from claiming damages—*sed quaere*. See discussion, paras. 14–29, 14–30.

[72] *e.g. Kelman* v. *Barr's Trs.* (1878) 5 R. 816.

[73] *Lowe* v. *Gardiner*, 1921 S.C. 211 at p. 217 *per* Lord Skerrington.

[74] *Bunge Corpn.* v. *Tradax S.A.* [1981] 2 All E.R. 513 (H.L.). In sales of heritage in Scotland there is also commonly a "string of contracts," which was a feature of the reasoning in that case. In early cases Scots law went so far as to accept that in mercantile contracts precise fulfilment of the term of the contract on date of delivery might not be insisted on: *Whitson* v. *Neilson & Co.* (1828) 6 S.579; *West Limerigg Colliery Co.* v. *Robertson* (1873) 10 S.L.R. 467. This approach was later departed from—*e.g. Collard* v. *Carswell* (1892) 19 R. 987, (1893) 20 R.(H.L.) 47; *Colvin* v. *Short* (1857) 19 D. 890; *Shaw, Macfarlane & Co.* v. *Waddell & Son* (1900) 2 F. 1070.

Delay by the seller

14–91   The seller may be unable to offer a good title. If the title is radically
defective there is a material breach, for example if the seller does not
have any title to part of the subjects sold.[75] The title offered may have a
defect which is remediable. It appears that the seller must be given a
reasonable opportunity to remedy the defect.[76] Some of the cases
usually cited in this area of law[77] are explicable on the basis of their
special facts, which can indicate an element of personal bar arising from
the actions and attitudes of the parties,[78] or are explained by reference
to the special terms of contract.[79] If the seller insists on offering a defective title and no other, this may be a material breach of the contract
which entitles the purchaser to rescind the contract.[80]

Delay by the purchaser[81]

14–92   If the purchaser delays in making payment of the price, the "ultimatum procedure" explained elsewhere applies.[82] The seller may raise
an action for payment of the price with alternative conclusions for declarator that there has been material breach and for damages.[83] The
court can fix a period within which the price is to be paid, failing which
declarator is granted.[84] The duty on the seller to minimise loss arises
once the contract is rescinded.[85]

Express terms

14–93   It is a matter of construction as to whether there has been a breach of
an express term in missives, such as a reference to "unqualified planning
permission,"[86] or "no outstanding notices,"[87] or "no outstanding
restriction,"[88] or "actual occupation,"[89] or "not settled."[90] On the

---

[75] *Campbell* v. *McCutcheon*, 1963 S.C. 505; *Robertson* v. *Rutherford* (1841) 4 D. 121;
Whyte v. *Lee* (1879) 6 R. 699; *Crofts* v. *Stewart's Trs.*, 1927 S.C.(H.L.) 65; *Mossend
Theatre Co.* v. *Livingstone*, 1930 S.C. 90.
[76] *Fleming* v. *Harley's Trs.* (1823) 2 S.373. See I. W. Noble, "Delays in Settlement"
(1983) 28 J.L.S. 116.
[77] *e.g. Green's Encyclopaedia*, Vol 13, para. 420.
[78] *Dick* v. *Cuthbertson* (1831) 5 W. & S. 712; *Carter* v. *Lornie* (1890) 18 R. 353.
[79] *Kelman* v. *Barr's Trs.* (1878) 5 R. 816; *Raeburn* v. *Baird* (1832) 10 S.761.
[80] *Gilfillan* v. *Cadell & Grant* (1893) 21 R. 269. The pursuer took up a stance which
amounted to a definite refusal to comply with the contract.
[81] See A. G. M. Duncan, "Delays in Settlement: Rights and Remedies of the Seller,"
Conveyancing Review, Vol. III, p. 189.
[82] See para. 14–81.
[83] *Bosco Design Services Ltd.* v. *Plastic Sealant Services Ltd.*, 1979 S.C. 189.
[84] *Johnstone* v. *Harris*, 1977 S.C. 365.
[85] *Johnstone* v. *Harris, sup. cit.*
[86] *Murray* v. *Hillhouse Estates Ltd.*, 1960 S.L.T.(Notes) 48.
[87] *Bradley* v. *Scott*, 1966 S.L.T.(Sh.Ct.) 25.
[88] *Kelly* v. *A. & J. Clark Ltd.*, 1968 S.L.T. 141.
[89] *Stuart* v. *Lort-Phillips*, 1977 S.C. 244.
[90] *Hornall* v. *Crawford*, 1968 S.L.T.(Notes) 80.

waiver by one party of conditions in the missives, see the cases cited.[91] When a period of time is stated to commence from a given day the period is normally reckoned from the last moment of that day.[92]

Actio quanti minoris

4   In the case of sale of heritage where there is a material breach of contract by one party, the other party cannot in many cases retain what is offered under the contract and sue for damages.[93] That would be an *actio quanti minoris* which is only allowed in limited types of cases.

Seller's remedies

5   The seller may sue for the price with alternative conclusions for declarator that there has been a material breach, for removing or for damages.[94] Alternatively, in an appropriate case, there may be a rescission of the contract or an acceptance of the buyer's repudiation, followed by the seller's claim for damages.[95]

Buyer's remedies

6   The buyer may seek a declarator that the seller is in breach and specific implement with an alternative conclusion for damages.[96] Otherwise, in an appropriate case there may be rescission of the contract or acceptance of the seller's repudiation followed by a claim for damages.[97] A buyer may seek implement of one obligation and damages for failure to implement another separate obligation.[98] Returning the subjects and seeking a reduction in the price because of a defect in the subjects is an *actio quanti minoris* which is only allowed to a limited extent.

---

[91] *Ellis & Sons Amalgamated Properties* v. *Pringle*, 1974 S.C. 200; *Gilchrist* v. *Payton*, 1979 S.C. 380; *Imry Property Holdings Ltd.* v. *Glasgow YMCA*, 1979 S.L.T. 261; *cf. Dewar & Finlay Ltd.* v. *Blackwood*, 1968 S.L.T. 196.

[92] *Sworn Securities Ltd.* v. *Chilcott*, 1977 S.C. 53 *per* Lord Ordinary (Maxwell), and authorities there referred to.

[93] *Dobbie* v. *Duncanson* (1872) 10 M. 810; *Louttit's Trs.* v. *Highland Ry. Co.* (1892) 19 R. 791; *Hoey* v. *Butler*, 1975 S.C. 87; *Hayes* v. *Robinson*, 1984 S.L.T. 300. See *s.v.* "Actio quanti minoris," para. 20–04.

[94] *Harvey* v. *Smith* (1904) 6 F. 511; *British Railways Board* v. *Birrell*, 1971 S.L.T.(Notes) 17; *Bosco Design Services Ltd.* v. *Plastic Sealant Services Ltd.*, 1979 S.C. 189.

[95] *Burns* v. *Garscadden* (1901) 8 S.L.T. 321; *Campbell* v. *McCutcheon*, 1963 S.C. 505; *Johnstone's Exrs.* v. *Harris*, 1977 S.C. 365.

[96] *Mackay* v. *Campbell*, 1967 S.C.(H.L.) 53; *Plato* v. *Newman*, 1950 S.L.T.(Notes) 29; *Speevack* v. *Robson*, 1949 S.L.T.(Notes) 39.

[97] *Daejan Developments Ltd.* v. *Armia Ltd.*, 1981 S.C. 48.

[98] *McKillop* v. *Mutual Securities Ltd.*, 1945 S.C. 166; *Hoey* v. *Butler*, 1975 S.C. 87.

PART 7—SALE OF GOODS

Common Law

14–97 At common law, goods sold had an implied warranty that they were priceworthy. A sale at the highest market price implied a warranty that the article was of the best quality.[99] There is some uncertainty about the law's treatment of minor defects. M. P. Brown wrote: "The vendee cannot, under the implied obligation of warrandice, make any claim on account of slight defects which do not render the thing unfit for its proper use, but merely diminish its value."[1] The consistency between this and a doctrine of priceworthiness is not obvious.[2] Where there was a claim by the buyer, his remedies were described in this way by Lord President Inglis[3]:

> "When a purchaser receives delivery of goods as in fulfilment of a contract of sale, and thereafter finds that the goods are not conform to order, his only remedy is to reject the goods and rescind the contract. If he has paid the price, his claim is for repayment of the price, tendering re-delivery of the goods . . . If any portion of the goods has before their rejection been consumed or wrought up so as to be incapable of re-delivery *in forma specifica*, then the true value (not the contract price) of that portion of the goods must form a deduction from the purchaser's claim for repayment of the price. The purchaser is not entitled to retain the goods and demand an abatement from the contract price corresponding to the disconformity of the goods to order, for this would be to substitute a new and different contract from that contract of sale which was originally made by the parties, or it would resolve into a claim of the nature of the *actio quanti minoris*, which our law entirely rejects."

14–98 It would have been more accurate to state that the *actio quanti minoris* was recognised to a limited extent in the case of latent defects.[4]

14–99 Defects in the goods apart, other aspects of the common law were less controversial. The seller had implied obligations to make delivery and to warrant the buyer against eviction. The buyer had to pay the price and take delivery.[5] The common law survives except in so far as inconsistent with the Sale of Goods Act 1979.[6]

---

[99] *Whealler* v. *Methuen* (1843) 5 D. 1221; *Paterson* v. *Dickson* (1850) 12 D. 502.

[1] *Law of Sale* (1821), p. 328; also at p. 288.

[2] *Cf. Ralston* v. *Robb*, July 9, 1808, F.C. at p. 254.

[3] *McCormick* v. *Rittmeyer* (1869) 7 M. 854 at p. 858.

[4] *Louttit's Trs.* v. *Highland Ry. Co.* (1892) 19 R. 791 at p. 800 *per* Lord McLaren; A. L. Stewart, "The Actio Quanti Minoris" (1966) 11 J.L.S. 124. See para. 20–04. Cases of fraud and collateral warranty were exceptions—see para. 20–10—also when return of the goods was impossible, *e.g.* seeds which had been sown: *Knutsen* v. *Mauritzen*, 1918 1 S.L.T. 85.

[5] See M. P. Brown, *sup. cit.*, Pts. III and IV.

[6] See s.62(2).

Statute Law

00 The common law was altered by a series of statutes. The history of change can be traced through the Mercantile Law Amendment Scotland Act 1856, the Sale of Goods Act 1893, the Supply of Goods (Implied Terms) Act 1973, the Consumer Credit Act 1974, the Unfair Contract Terms Act 1977 and the Sale of Goods Act 1979. The 1979 Act dominates the current law, although certain sales are governed by other statutes. For example, the Agricultural Act 1970 imposes an implied warranty in the sale of feeding stuff for animals.[7]

01 Under the 1979 Act there are implied conditions that the seller has a right to sell the goods and there are implied warranties on freedom from incumbrances and the quiet possession of the buyer.[8] One of the obscurities of the Act in its application to Scotland is its use of the words "condition" and "warranty." In English law the breach of a condition gives rise to a right to rescind the contract. The breach of a warranty gives rise to a claim for damages, but does not give a right to rescind.[9] This distinction is not part of Scots common law. Under the Act a breach of warranty in Scotland is deemed to be a failure to perform a material part of the contract.[10] The effect may be that a breach of a warranty provided for in the 1979 Act gives rise to quite different results in Scotland and England. In Scotland, but not England, rescission may follow from a breach of a warranty.[11]

02 The buyer has a duty to pay the price[12] and he may be sued for the price.[13] There are rules about where and when delivery of the goods takes place.[14] The seller is liable in damages for non-delivery[15] and the buyer for non-acceptance of the goods.[16] In an appropriate case there may be specific implement.[17]

03 There can be considerable difficulty in applying the Act to the supply of goods which are defective. The Act provides for three implied terms: (1) the goods must correspond with their description[18]; (2) the goods, in certain cases, must be of merchantable quality[19]; and (3) the goods, in certain cases, must be reasonably fit for the buyer's purpose.[20] Special

---

[7] s.72.
[8] s.12.
[9] s.61(1), defn. of "warranty."
[10] s.61(2).
[11] s.11(5); s.53.
[12] s.27.
[13] s.49.
[14] ss.28 to 32; *Paton & Sons* v. *David Payne & Co. Ltd.* (1897) 35 S.L.R. 112 (H.L.).
[15] s.51.
[16] s.50.
[17] s.52(4); on specific implement see Chap. 21.
[18] s.13.
[19] s.14(2).
[20] s.14(3).

rules apply to sales by sample.[21] What is obscure is the remedy of a buyer if the goods are in breach of any of those implied terms.[22]

14–104   The implied terms are given the description "condition" which is not defined and does not have a technical meaning in Scots law. Section 11(5) provides for the buyer's remedies in the event of a failure by the seller to perform "any material part of a contract of sale." It has been observed that it is a very difficult question whether breach of the implied conditions on quality, however minor, constitutes a failure to perform a material part of the contract.[23] There is some attraction in the argument that a minor defect in goods supplied would not qualify as "material." If that were so, it appears that the buyer's remedies would remain as they were at common law. The Act does not make specific provision for non-material defects in quality (or description) but it does, to a limited extent, preserve Scots common law.[24] Unfortunately, the operation of the common law on minor defects is obscure.

14–105   Section 11(5) allows a form of *actio quanti minoris* when there is a failure in a "material part" by the seller. The buyer may keep the goods and claim damages or reject the goods and claim damages.

14–106   The rejection of the goods and rescission (or as the Act calls it "repudiation") of the contract appear to be treated as the one event.

14–107   A buyer who returns goods may be rescinding the contract.[25] In fact his intention could be to secure implement of the contract. He wishes to be supplied with the goods which he agreed to buy. The Act, however, is following the approach of Lord President Inglis in the passage from *McCormick* v. *Rittmeyer* quoted above. The result is a serious confusion.

14–108   In the present state of the law the advice to be given to a dissatisfied buyer may be this. (1) If the defects breach sections 13 or 14 and are obviously "material" on any normal meaning of that term, the buyer may exercise his options under section 11(5). (2) If the defects are minimal the buyer should not attempt to reject the goods.[26] (3) If there is a breach of the implied undertakings in section 13 or 14 but doubt as to whether these breaches are in any "material part" of the contract,[27] it may be unwise for the buyer to reject, particularly if he has already paid the price. It may be that, in theory, he should be able to reject,[28] but it is not obvious that he is entitled to. (4) If there is a breach of an *express*

---

[21] s.13(2); s.15.

[22] See M. G. Clarke, "The Buyer's Right of Rejection," 1978 S.L.T.(News) 1; Anon., 1978 S.L.T.(News) 61.

[23] *Millars of Falkirk Ltd.* v. *Turpie*, 1976 S.L.T.(Notes) 66.

[24] ss.53(5), 62(2).

[25] See 1978 S.L.T.(News) 61.

[26] *Millars of Falkirk Ltd.* v. *Turpie, sup. cit.; Fewson* v. *Gemmell* (1903) 11 S.L.T. 153 and 697.

[27] *e.g.* a minor failure to correspond with description.

[28] See M. G. Clarke, *op. cit.*

undertaking the common law on breach applies. The general rule is that rescission is available only when the breach is material. For minor breaches the remedy is damages.

Rejection of Goods

09 At common law a buyer who discovered a defect in goods had to reject the goods instantly or without unreasonable delay.[29] The statutory right of rejection has been said to be the same as at common law with the refusal of the Scottish provisions to follow the English distinctions between conditions and warranties.[30] Under section 11(5) of the Sale of Goods Act 1979 the buyer must reject "within a reasonable time after delivery." It is a little curious that the "reasonable time" starts to run from delivery and not from discovery of the defect, but the Act assumes that after a reasonable time from delivery the buyer may be deemed to have accepted the goods.[31] "Reasonable time" is a question of fact.[32]

10 The "reasonable time" will depend on the nature of the goods and of the defect. Mouldy hay should be rejected very quickly. Defective machinery might not show its defects until a year after delivery. The buyer may be barred from rejection unless he tries out the goods and checks for defects. In the Birmingham water supply case it was held that the buyers were not entitled to wait seven months before trial of a pump.[33] In *Hyslop* v. *Shirlaw*[34] a coalmaster bought four pictures from a surgeon. Eighteen months after the purchase, friends of the coalmaster expressed doubts about whether the pictures were genuine. It was observed that rejection was not timeous, because "he would have found out all he knows now had he thought of taking reasonable diligence at the time." It is unwise for a buyer to wait until his customer complains because by then rejection may be too late. The buyer has a duty to inspect.[35]

---

[29] Bell, *Comm.*, I,464; *Prin.*, s.99; *Chaplin* v. *Jardine* (1886) 23 S.L.R. 487; *McCarter* v. *Stewart & Mackenzie* (1877) 4 R. 890; *Blenkhorn, Richardson & Co.* v. *Milnathort Spinning Co.* (1883) 20 S.L.R. 707; *Carter & Co.* v. *Campbell* (1885) 12 R. 1075.

[30] *Nelson* v. *William Chalmers & Co. Ltd.*, 1913 S.C. 441 at p. 450 *per* Lord Kinnear.

[31] s.35.

[32] s.59. Thus there should be a proof: *Central Farmers Ltd.* v. *Smith*, 1974 S.L.T.(Sh.Ct.) 87—plea that a rejection of hay within 6/7 days of delivery not timeous sent to a proof before answer; *Burrell* v. *Harding's Exrx.*, 1931 S.L.T. 76.

[33] *Morrison & Mason Ltd.* v. *Clarkson Bros.* (1898) 25 R. 427.

[34] (1905) 7 F. 875; see also *Dick* v. *Cochrane & Fleming*, 1935 S.L.T. 432. *Hyslop* did not decide a question of law. What is a reasonable time depends on the facts: *Burrell* v. *Harding's Exrx.*, 1931 S.L.T. 76—proof before answer allowed when antique purchased in 1928 was rejected in 1930.

[35] *Pini & Co.* v. *Smith & Co.* (1895) 22 R. 699; *Dick* v. *Cochrane & Fleming*, 1935 S.L.T. 432; *W. M. Strachan & Co. Ltd.* v. *John Marshall & Co.*, 1910 2 S.L.T. 108; although some sale to a customer might not bar rejection of remainder of the goods. See *Wallace & Brown* v. *Robinson, Fleming & Co.* (1885) 22 S.L.R. 830. On inspection of a series of goods delivered as part of a course of dealings see *McCarter* v. *Stewart & Mackenzie* (1877) 4 R. 890.

14–111   In *Flynn* v. *Scott*[36] rejection three to four weeks after delivery of a second-hand van was held to be too late. A boar should have been rejected within at most one month of the sale.[37]

14–112   When defects take a long time to appear in the normal course of events, rejection is timeously made when the defects are apparent.[38] In *Aird & Coghill* v. *Pullan & Adams*[39] a printing machine was installed in March 1902. The buyers frequently intimated dissatisfaction with it and in July 1902 intimated rejection of it. The rejection was held to be timeous.

14–113   Rejection is not barred by the buyer keeping the goods on the insistence of the seller that any defects will be cured.[40] The buyer's remedies are not prejudiced if rejection is impossible because of the seller's breach of contract, for example if the horse supplied dies,[41] or meat putrefies, or the incorrect seeds are sown.[42]

14–114   Rejection is barred if the buyer signs an acceptance certificate or otherwise intimates that he has accepted the goods.[43] The buyer has a right to examine the goods[44] but, subject to that, he will be deemed to have accepted the goods if he does any act in relation to them which is inconsistent with the ownership of the seller, such as fitting machinery into a ship,[45] or manufacturing fur coats from skins,[46] or sending a sample to a customer,[47] or trying to sell the goods.[48]

14–115   At common law there could be an effective term of the contract that rejection or complaints must be made within a short time limit.[49] A provision of this nature in a consumer contract or a standard term contract must now be fair and reasonable, or it is of no effect.[50] Conversely the contract may expressly provide for a period for trial of the goods. There can be a valid rejection at the end of the trial period.[51]

---

[36] 1949 S.C. 442.

[37] *Cook* v. *Robertson's Exr.*, 1960 S.L.T.(Sh.Ct.) 4.

[38] *Fleming & Co.* v. *Airdrie Iron Co.* (1882) 9 R. 473.

[39] (1904) 7 F. 258.

[40] *Caledonian Ry. Co.* v. *Rankin* (1882) 10 R. 63; *Munro & Co.* v. *Bennet & Son*, 1911 S.C. 337.

[41] *Kinnear* v. *J. & D. Brodie* (1901) 3 F. 540.

[42] *Knutsen* v. *Mauritzen*, 1918 1 S.L.T. 85.

[43] s.35; *Mechans Ltd.* v. *Highland Marine Charters Ltd.*, 1964 S.C. 48. It is arguable that an acceptance note is a secondary contract controlled by Unfair Contract Terms Act 1977, s.23.

[44] s.34.

[45] *Mechan & Sons Ltd.* v. *Bow, McLachlan & Co. Ltd.*, 1910 S.C. 758.

[46] *M. H. Wolfson Ltd.* v. *Richfeld*, 1952 S.L.T.(Sh.Ct.) 46.

[47] *Hunt* v. *Barry* (1905) 13 S.L.T. 34.

[48] *Clydesdale Motor Transport Co.* v. *McCosh & Devine*, 1922 S.L.T.(Sh.Ct.) 130.

[49] *Russell* v. *Hamilton*, 1953 S.L.T.(Sh.Ct.) 85; *John Townsley & Sons Ltd.* v. *John Watson & Son*, 1968 S.L.T.(Sh.Ct.) 27.

[50] Unfair Contract Terms Act 1977, s.17.

[51] *Cranston* v. *Mallow & Lien*, 1912 S.C. 112.

16   After rejection (1) in some circumstances the buyer is not bound to
return the rejected goods[52]—at common law if the seller did not accept
the rejected goods the purchaser had to put them in neutral custody[53];
(2) it appears to be impossible to retain the goods in security of a claim
for damages against the seller[54]; and (3) use of the goods, except possibly slight or temporary usage, may bar rejection.[55]

17   There is doubt about what happens if the defects are remediable and
the seller has granted a guarantee of repair. In *Cowell* v. *Glasgow Motor
Co.*[56] a guarantee of a car was held by the Lord Ordinary to bar rejection. The buyer's remedy was repair under the guarantee. Only if that
was refused would there be rejection. On appeal no opinion was
expressed on this point. If a manufacturer (not the seller) has granted a
guarantee this does not normally affect the buyer's rights and remedies
against the seller.[57]

Implied Terms on Description

18   Section 13(1) of the 1979 Act provides: "Where there is a contract for
the sale of goods by description, there is an implied condition that the
goods will correspond with the description." There was a failure to comply with description when an engine said to be in "excellent order" did
not work,[58] and the power of a car engine was misdescribed.[59] On the
other hand a description of the capacity of an engine was held not to
include a description of the reliability in operation once installed.[60] An
important point about section 13 is that its application is not restricted
(as is section 14) to sales in the course of a business.

19   Section 13 applies when goods are not of the kind ordered (*e.g.* order
fertiliser and be supplied with weedkiller). Section 14 applies to goods
of the kind ordered but which are defective (*e.g.* order fertiliser and be
supplied with fertiliser containing a toxic substance).[61] Herring meal
which has gone wrong may still be herring meal.[62] A defective grain

---

[52] s.36.

[53] *Caledonian Ry. Co.* v. *Rankin* (1882) 10 R. 63.

[54] *Lupton & Co.* v. *Schulze* (1900) 2 F. 1118; *Jardine* v. *Pendreigh* (1869) 6 S.L.R. 272.

[55] *Electric Construction Co. Ltd.* v. *Hurry & Young* (1897) 24 R. 312 but note comments
on this case in *Croom & Arthur* v. *Stewart & Co.* (1905) 7 F. 563 and *Pollock & Co.* v.
Macrae, 1922 S.C.(H.L.) 192. An invalid rejection will *not* bar other remedies; see also
John Girvan & Sons v. *Abel*, 1950 S.L.T.(Sh.Ct.) 60.

[56] (1903) 11 S.L.T. 500 and 758.

[57] Whether the manufacturer's guarantee may be a promise in Scots law remains to be
decided. It is not normally a contract with the ultimate buyer—*McAuslan* v. *Jack* (1957) 73
Sh.Ct.Rep. 3.

[58] *Roberts & Co.* v. *Yule* (1896) 23 R. 855.

[59] *McIvor* v. *Michie*, 1953 S.L.T.(Sh.Ct.) 53.

[60] *Britain Steamship Co. Ltd.* v. *Lithgows Ltd.*, 1975 S.C. 110; see the discussion of
"Durability," *infra.* para. 14–126.

[61] *McCallum* v. *Mason*, 1956 S.C. 50.

[62] *Ashington Piggeries Ltd.* v. *Christopher Hill Ltd.* [1972] A.C. 441.

dryer is a grain dryer and a complaint about its quality should be brought under section 14 and not section 13.[63]

Implied Terms about Quality

14–120   Section 14(1) of the 1979 Act provides that, with certain exceptions, there is no implied condition or warranty about the quality or fitness for any particular purpose of goods supplied under a contract of sale. An important exception arises under section 14(2) where the seller sells goods in the course of a business. There is then an implied condition that the goods are of merchantable quality, except (a) as regards defects specifically drawn to the buyer's attention before the contract is made; or (b) if the buyer examines the goods before the contract is made, as regards defects which that examination ought to reveal. "Merchantable quality" is defined in section 14(6) by reference to the fitness for the purpose or purposes "for which goods of that kind are commonly bought as it is reasonable to expect having regard to any description applied to them, the price (if relevant) and all the other relevant circumstances." Section 14(2) applies to the normal purposes for which goods are bought. If the buyer makes known a particular purpose there may be an implied condition under section 14(3). That subsection applies where the seller sells goods in the course of a business and the buyer, expressly or by implication, makes known to the seller (or in some cases to a credit broker) any particular purpose for which the goods are being bought. The implied condition is that the goods are reasonably fit for that purpose (whether or not that is a purpose for which such goods are commonly supplied) except where the circumstances show that the buyer does not rely, or that it is unreasonable for him to rely, on the skill or judgment of the seller or credit-broker. An implied condition or warranty about quality or fitness for a particular purpose may be annexed to a contract of sale by usage.[64]

Special rules apply to sales by sample.[65]

14–121   The Sale of Goods Act 1893 did not define "merchantable quality" and the present definition was introduced in 1973.[66] The continued use of "merchantable quality" has been criticised as outmoded and because of its lack of clarity in covering some aspects of quality such as appearance, freedom from minor defects, durability and safety.[67]

---

[63] *Border Harvesters Ltd.* v. *Edwards Engineering (Perth) Ltd.*, 1985 S.L.T. 128.

[64] s.14(4). See discussion above about the Act's use of the terms "condition" and "warranty," para. 14–101.

[65] s.15. See also s.13(2).

[66] Supply of Goods (Implied Terms) Act 1973, s.7(2).

[67] See Law Commission (W.P. No. 85) and Scottish Law Commission (Com. Memo. No. 58) (1983), *Sale and Supply of Goods*, paras. 2.3–2.16. On durability see W. C. H. Ervine, "Durability, Consumers and the Sale of Goods Act," 1984 J.R. 147, authorities there cited and para. 14–126.

22   Subsections 14(2) and 14(3) only apply to sales in the course of a business. Unlike the provisions of the 1893 Act the sale does not need to be of goods which it is the seller's business to supply.[68] A solicitor who sells an office typewriter is selling goods in the course of a business, although it is not the business of solicitors to deal in typewriters. The present wording in the 1979 Act probably makes it less likely also that there will be arguments about whether the sale of one item comes within the type of item normally sold, *e.g.* the seller of second-hand buses who occasionally sells cars.[69] The displenishing sale which may be the last act in a business has come within section 14.[70]

23   Some controversy surrounds the distinction between subsections 14(2) and 14(3). Subsection (2) applies to what may be briefly described as the normal purposes of the goods. Subsection (3) applies to a particular purpose made known to the seller. What is sufficient to bring a case within subsection (3)? Very little indication of the buyer's potential use of the goods may suffice. To buy a pair of boots and state that they are for walking is to indicate the normal purpose. To say that they are required for walking by the buyer himself has been held to be a particular purpose.[71] To disclose the destination of a refrigerator was sufficient to establish a particular purpose.[72] The knowledge of the seller is relevant. The Act is implying a condition and the contract itself may not say anything about the known reason for buying the goods, *e.g.* a sale of barrels which both parties knew must be made of wood which prevented percolation of pickle.[73] On the other hand, in *Flynn* v. *Scott*[74] Lord Mackintosh took a view of the meaning of "particular purpose" which he thought was narrower than that adopted in English law. A van was bought. Its general purpose was the carrying of goods. The buyer indicated certain examples of the kinds of goods which might be carried. There was no "particular purpose" expressed.

24   If a "particular purpose" known to the seller cannot be shown, the goods may be of merchantable quality under section 14(2) if fit for a common purpose, although not for every purpose for which the goods could be used.[75]

25   There is a series of cases involving coal supplied with detonators or other explosive material. The argument that there was no defect in the coal, but merely an additional item supplied, is so absurd that it would

---

[68] Sale of Goods Act 1893, s.14.
[69] See *Stuart* v. *Neil*, 1973 S.L.T.(Sh.Ct.) 53.
[70] *Buchanan-Jardine* v. *Hamilink*, 1983 S.L.T. 149.
[71] *Thomson* v. *J. Sears & Co. (Trueform Boot Co.) Ltd.*, 1926 S.L.T. 221.
[72] *John Girvan & Sons* v. *Abel*, 1950 S.L.T.(Sh.Ct.) 60.
[73] *Douglas & Co.* v. *Milne* (1895) 23 R. 163; see also *Jacobs* v. *Scott & Co.* (1899) 2 F.(H.L.) 70; *Crichton & Stevenson* v. *Love*, 1908 S.C. 818.
[74] 1949 S.C. 442; see also *Winning* v. *Scott*, 1952 S.L.T.(Sh.Ct.) 16.
[75] *B. & S. Brown & Sons Ltd.* v. *Craiks*, 1970 S.C.(H.L.) 51.

not be mentioned if it did not form part of a decision in the Inner House,[76] which has twice been distinguished in the sheriff court.[77]

Durability

14–126   A frequent complaint of buyers is that the goods bought are not durable or reliable, although at the time of sale everything appeared to be in order. There is some English authority on durability.[78] Two of the cases, *Mash & Murrell Ltd.* v. *Joseph I. Emanuel Ltd.*[79] and *Cordova Land Co. Ltd.* v. *Victor Brothers Inc.*[80] appear to contradict each other. In *Crowther* v. *Shannon Motor Co.*[81] the fact that a Jaguar car's engine seized up three weeks after purchase was treated as evidence of lack of merchantable quality at the time of sale. In *Lambert* v. *Lewis*, Lord Diplock indicated that the implied warranty of fitness included a continuing warranty that goods would be fit for a purpose for a reasonable time after delivery.[82] The Law Commissions have recommended an express statutory provision on durability.[83]

Express Terms

14–127   There may be an express warranty on quality. It is a question of construction whether it has been breached.[84] A provision that a certificate as to quality is final may make an inaccurate certificate binding.[85] Contracting out of implied warranties in a contract for sale of goods is severely restricted by the Unfair Contract Terms Act 1977.[86]

---

[76] *Duke* v. *Jackson*, 1921 S.C. 362.

[77] *Fitzpatrick* v. *Barr*, 1948 S.L.T.(Sh.Ct.) 5; *Lusk* v. *Barclay*, 1953 S.L.T.(Sh.Ct.) 23.

[78] For Scots authority see *Knutsen* v. *Mauritzen*, 1918 1 S.L.T. 85; *Buchanan & Carswell* v. *Eugene Ltd.*, 1936 S.C. 160 and *Pearce Bros.* v. *Irons* (1869) 7 M. 571, discussed in W. C. H. Ervine, "Durability, Consumers and the Sale of Goods Act," 1984 J.R. 147.

[79] [1961] All E.R. 485; [1962] 1 All E.R. 77n.

[80] [1966] 1 W.L.R. 793.

[81] [1975] 1 All E.R. 139. The case of minor defects in a second-hand car was distinguished in *Bartlett* v. *Sidney Marcus Ltd.* [1965] 2 All E.R. 753.

[82] *Lambert* v. *Lewis* [1982] A.C. 225 at p. 276.

[83] Law Commission (Law Com. No. 95), *Implied Terms in Contracts for the Supply of Goods* (1979), paras. 104–109; Law Commission (W.P. No. 85) and Scot.Law Com. (Com. Memo. No. 58), *Sale and Supply of Goods* (1983), para. 2.15.

[84] *e.g. Kyle* v. *Sim*, 1925 S.C. 425 (calving of cattle); *Duncan* v. *Leith*, 1957 S.L.T.(Sh.Ct.) 46 (fertility of bull).

[85] *Gill & Duffus S.A.* v. *Berger & Co. Inc.* [1984] A.C. 382. The reason is that the goods may correspond with their description, *e.g.* goods for which a certificate has been issued.

[86] s.20.

CHAPTER 15

FRUSTRATION

TERMINOLOGY

01 The word "frustration" is said to derive from an opinion of Baron Bramwell in 1874.[1] The use of the word started after the invention of the doctrine to which it refers, in both English and Scots law. Sometimes the doctrine is described as impossibility of performance, but that is too narrow if the law recognises that the purpose of a contract may be frustrated, although its performance is possible. The term "frustration" can be used so that it is limited to this concept of frustration of purpose. This is a source of confusion. In this chapter "frustration" covers supervening events which by operation of law excuse both parties from future performance of their contract. The term "frustration of contract" is inaccurate. The contract is not frustrated. It is the future performance which is frustrated.[2]

02 Frustration is applied to events subsequent to the contract. Impossibility of performance can exist at the time of the contract. That raises issues of error which are discussed elsewhere.[3]

WHAT IS THE THEORETICAL BASIS OF FRUSTRATION?

Allocation of Risks

03 Long before the term "frustration" was used Scots lawyers were asking—on whom does the risk of a supervening event fall? That was Lord Cooper's impression formed after his examination of the authorities.[4] Morison gathered appropriate cases in his *Dictionary* under the heading "Periculum." Recent analysis of the theoretical basis for frustration has been confined to decisions of the House of Lords in English appeals. In *James B. Fraser & Co. Ltd.* v. *Denny, Mott & Dickson Ltd.*[5] Lord Macmillan referred[6] to frustration being "common to the jurisprudence

---

[1] *Jackson* v. *Union Marine Insurance Co.* (1874) L.R. 10 C.P. 125 at p. 145. See *Joseph Constantine S.S. Line Ltd.* v. *Imperial Smelting Corporation Ltd.* [1942] A.C. 154 at p. 198 *per* Lord Porter.

[2] *Heyman* v. *Darwins* [1942] A.C. 356 at p. 400 *per* Lord Porter.

[3] See Chap. 9. See also Sale of Goods Act 1979, s.6. See in English law *Bell* v. *Lever Brothers Ltd.* [1932] A.C. 161; *Sheikh Bros. Ltd.* v. *Ochsner* [1957] A.C. 136.

[4] T. M. Cooper, "Frustration of Contract in Scots Law" (1946) 28 *Journal of Comparative Legislation*, Pt. III, p. 1 at p. 2; reproduced in *Selected Papers 1922–1954* (1957), p. 124 at p. 125.

[5] 1944 S.C.(H.L.) 35.

[6] at p. 41.

alike of Scotland and of England, although the leading cases are to be found in the English law reports." Lord Wright and Lord Porter's theoretical analysis in that case was later taken up by Lord Reid and Lord Radcliffe in *Davis Contractors* v. *Fareham U.D.C.*[7] It is unlikely that the House of Lords will decide that the Scots law on frustration is different from English law, but the older Scottish approach has much to commend it. German and American authors have treated the problem as being one of risk allocation.[8]

Implied Term

15–04 For a long time English law implied a condition in the contract which released parties from performing it. That doctrine was artificial and fictitious. It has now been rejected by the House of Lords in three cases which are the modern basis for an explanation of frustration, namely *Davis Contractors Ltd.* v. *Fareham U.D.C.*[9]; *National Carriers Ltd.* v. *Panalpina (Northern) Ltd.*[10]; and *Pioneer Shipping* v. *B.T.P. Tioxide.*[11] Part of the improbability of the doctrine of the implied term was illustrated by Lord Sands in *Scott & Sons* v. *Del Sel*[12]:

> "A tiger has escaped from a travelling menagerie. The milkgirl fails to deliver the milk. Possibly the milkman may be exonerated from any breach of contract; but, even so, it would seem hardly reasonable to base that exoneration on the ground that 'tiger days excepted' must be held as if written into the milk contract."

The Construction Test

15–05 The *locus classicus* of the present doctrine of frustration is Lord Radcliffe's speech in *Davis Contractors Ltd.* v. *Fareham U.D.C.* when he said[13]:

> " . . . frustration occurs whenever the law recognises that, without default of either party, a contractual obligation has become incapable of being performed because the circumstances in which performance is called for would render it a thing radically different from that which was undertaken by the contract. Non haec in foedera veni. It was not this that I promised to do."

15–06 It has been said that it should now be unnecessary to cite earlier cases when the doctrine was in its infancy.[14]

15–07 Lord Reid and Lord Radcliffe in *Davis Contractors* emphasised that the first step was to construe the contract in the light of the circum-

---

[7] [1956] A.C. 696.
[8] Corbin on *Contracts* (1962), para. 1321; K. Zweigert and H. Kotz, *An Introduction to Comparative Law* (1977, trans. J. Weir), Vol. 2, p. 195.
[9] *Sup. cit.*
[10] [1981] A.C. 675.
[11] [1982] A.C. 724.
[12] 1922 S.C. 592 at p. 597; cited by Lord Reid in *Davis Contractors, sup. cit.* at p. 720.
[13] *Sup. cit.* at p. 729.
[14] *Pioneer Shipping, supra* at p. 751 *per* Lord Roskill.

stances in which it was made.[15] The obligations arising from the contract would then be compared with the obligations arising in the new circumstances. If there was a radical change in obligations there was frustration. Lord Reid put the question, "whether the contract which they did make is, on its true construction, wide enough to apply to the new situation: if it is not, then it is at an end."[16]

08   In *National Carriers Ltd.* Lord Simon restated the test[17]:

> "Frustration of a contract takes place when there supervenes an event (without default of either party and for which the contract makes no sufficient provision) which so significantly changes the nature (not merely the expense or onerousness) of the outstanding contractual rights and/or obligations from what the parties could reasonably have contemplated at the time of its execution that it would be unjust to hold them to the literal sense of its stipulations in the new circumstances; in such case the law declares both parties to be discharged from further performance."

09   Because frustration depends in the first place on the construction of the contract, whether or not frustration operates is a question of law.[18] The court will have regard, however, to commercial practices[19] and to the surrounding circumstances at the time of the contract and subsequently with the result that it will be necessary to investigate the facts.[20]

10   There are two essential factors which must be present to frustrate a contract. As Lord Brandon put it[21]:

> "The first essential factor is that there must be some outside event or extraneous change of situation, not foreseen or provided for by the parties at the time of contracting, which either makes it impossible for the contract to be performed at all, or at least renders its performance something radically different from what the parties contemplated when they entered into it. The second essential factor is that the outside event or extraneous change of situation concerned, and the consequences of either in relation to the performance of the contract, must have occurred without either the fault or the default of either party to the contract."

THE IMPORTANCE OF THE THEORETICAL BASE

11   As Lord Reid pointed out in *Davis Contractors* there are reasons for determining the true basis of the law. It affects the extent to which there is a question of law or a question of fact with a consequent impact on the

---

[15] at pp. 720, 721, 729.

[16] at p.721.

[17] at p. 700.

[18] *Tsakiroglou & Co. Ltd.* v. *Noblee Thorl GmhH* [1962] A.C. 93; *Pioneer Shipping* v. *B.T.P. Tioxide, sup. cit.*

[19] See authorities in note above.

[20] *Head Wrightson Aluminium Ltd.* v. *Aberdeen Harbour Comms.*, 1958 S.L.T.(Notes) 12.

[21] *Paal Wilson & Co. A/S* v. *Blumenthal* [1983] 1 A.C. 854 at p. 909.

admissibility of extrinsic evidence. Further, the end result may vary according to the test adopted.

15–12   An example of the importance of the theory is a problem, not yet solved, arising from the negligence of one of the parties. Frustration occurs when there is a supervening event which is not caused by the fault of one of the parties. But there is doubt about the meaning of "fault" in this context.[22]

15–13   Assume that the music hall where the pianist is engaged to play is destroyed in a fire caused by negligence of an employee of the occupier of the hall. Is there frustration or breach of contract? The contract is silent. A theoretical approach which concentrates on implying terms into the contract has considerable difficulties not least because in this case it has to contemplate implying a clause covering the negligence of one party.[23] The present test for frustration looks at the end result and may say that the basis of the contract is gone, its performance is impossible. A risk allocation theory would ask: "Who bears the risk of the negligent act?" The answer could be, the occupier of the hall.

ILLUSTRATIONS OF THE DOCTRINE

15–14   Because the doctrine is applied by construing an obligation in the light of the circumstances surrounding the contract, it is not always helpful to look at other cases which deal with different contracts and different circumstances. Nevertheless the scope of the doctrine can be illustrated from examples.

Commercial Difficulty

15–15   Normally a contract is not frustrated because of a fall or rise in market prices, or a shortage of supplies,[24] or other commercial difficulties in performing a contract according to its terms.[25] The party whose performance has been rendered more burdensome than expected does not have an excuse for non-performance. The risk of the burden was theirs. In *Hangkam Kwingtong Woo* v. *Liu Lan Fong*[26] the payments under a mortgage were increased as a result of a government ordinance which provided for revaluation of obligations. This change of fortune was not within the contemplation of the parties at the time of the transaction. The Privy Council were of the view that there had not been frustration.

---

[22] See below, para. 15–34.
[23] *Cf.* the difficulty which the law has with the construction of express terms which purport to exclude negligence; paras. 13–36 *et seq.*
[24] *Blacklock & Macarthur* v. *Kirk*, 1919 S.C. 57.
[25] *Gillespie & Co.* v. *Howden & Co.* (1885) 12 R. 800; *Hong Kong and Whampoa Dock Co. Ltd.* v. *Netherton Shipping Co. Ltd.*, 1909 S.C. 34; *Larrinaga & Co. Ltd.* v. *Société Franco-Americaine des Phosphates de Medulla* (1923) 39 T.L.R. 316 at p. 322 *per* Lord Samuel.
[26] [1951] A.C. 707.

16 It has been said that an alteration of prices does not frustrate a contract.[27] But the courts were not asked to consider traumatic events such as the total collapse of a currency. Parties may accept risk of changes in the value of money and alteration of exchange rates but what happens if the performance under the contract does not bear any realistic resemblance to the performance originally contemplated? In *Anderson* v. *Equitable Assurance Society of United States*[28] inflation in Germany made the proceeds payable under a life insurance policy worthless. The court felt that they were powerless to provide a remedy but expressed a hope that a rich and powerful insurance company would pay the intrinsic value and not the face value of the policy. On the other hand in the old Scottish case of *Wilkie* v. *Bethune*[29] a different approach was adopted although the case was not decided on the basis of frustration. An employer was bound to pay his servant in potatoes. There was a dramatic rise in the price of potatoes due to the failure of the crop in 1846. If the servant had been paid in potatoes he would have greatly benefited. The court applied an equitable construction to the contract and held the servant entitled, not to his potatoes, but to a sum which would purchase the equivalent of other food. Professor Gloag queried the general application of the case[30] but it is possible that it is consistent with the modern approach to frustration. It is true that the doctrine "is not lightly to be invoked to relieve contracting parties of the normal consequences of imprudent commercial bargains."[31] On the other hand the theoretical basis of the doctrine shows that it is not the nature of the supervening event which matters so much as the effect of that event on the performance of the obligations.[32]

17 The English courts have found a solution to the problem of inflation in one context. A contract made in perpetuity may have implied into it a power to end it on reasonable notice.[33] This enables termination of a contract which has a price fixed many years ago and is now ridiculously low. That, however, is termination by one party. It is not frustration and it is of severely limited application.

Effect of War on Contracts

18 War and the outbreak of hostilities or armed conflicts, even between countries not directly connected with a contract or its parties, may result in the frustration of a contract. In this context "war" does not have a

---

[27] *British Movietonews Ltd.* v. *London & District Cinemas Ltd.* [1952] A.C. 166 at p. 185 *per* Viscount Simon; *Davis Contractors Ltd.* v. *Fareham U.D.C.* [1956] A.C. 696; *Hangkam Kwingtong Woo* v. *Lin Lan Fong.* [1951] A.C. 707.

[28] (1926) 134 L.T. 557.

[29] (1848) 11 D. 132.

[30] *Contract*, p. 339, n. 2.

[31] *Pioneer Shipping, supra* at p. 752 *per* Lord Roskill.

[32] *Ibid.* at p. 754 *per* Lord Roskill.

[33] *Staffordshire Area Health Authority* v. *South Staffordshire Waterworks Co.* [1978] 3 All E.R. 769.

technical meaning and supervening illegality, while it may exist, is not necessary.

15–19 It is dangerous to generalise on and over-simplify the effect of war on contracts. It cannot be stated as a general proposition that a state of war avoids contracts with the enemy. Nor is enemy property automatically lost to the enemy although the Crown may confiscate assets or, in modern times, administer them to prevent their use by the enemy.[34] It is contrary to public policy to have intercourse with the enemy with the result that performance of a contract (other than enforcement of accrued rights)[35] will be at an end if it involves such intercourse. A contract with an existing enemy may fall on the grounds of initial illegality. A contract with someone who becomes an enemy may be affected by supervening illegality. The contract is not merely suspended during hostilities.

15–20 The leading case is *Ertel Bieber & Co.* v. *Rio Tinto Co.*[36] An English company had contracted to sell cupreous ore to three German companies prior to the outbreak of war. The contracts contained clauses suspending their operation during war. It was held that the contracts were abrogated on the outbreak of war because they involved trading with the enemy. The suspensory clause was void as against public policy because it tended to the detriment of this country and the advantage of the enemy country, Lord Dunedin stated[37]:

> "There is indeed no such general proposition as that a state of war avoids all contracts between subjects and enemies. Accrued rights are not affected though the right of suing in respect thereof is suspended. Further, there are certain contracts, particularly those which are really the concomitants of rights of property, which even so far as executory are not abrogated. Such as, for instance, the contract between landlord and tenant, of which an example may be found in the recent case of *Halsey* v. *Lowenfeld*.[38] In other words, the executory contract which is abrogated must either involve intercourse, or its continued existence must be in some other way against public policy as that has been laid down in decided cases."

---

[34] See Trading with the Enemy Act 1939 as amended. This Act has a statutory definition of "enemy" which is limited to the purposes of the Act and does not affect the common law concept of enemy alien.

[35] Subject to the procedural disability of enemy aliens. The Crown may grant a licence to trade with the enemy.

[36] [1918] A.C. 260. See also *Davis & Primrose* v. *Clyde Shipbuilding and Engineering Co.* (1918) 56 S.L.R. 24 (Lord Ordinary); *Kuenigl* v. *Donnersmarck* [1955] 1 Q.B. 515 and Trading with the Enemy Act 1939. On accrued rights see *Stevenson* v. *Cartonnigen Industrie* [1918] A.C. 239; *Penney* v. *Clyde Shipbuilding Co.*, 1919 S.C. 363; 1920 S.C.(H.L.) 68; *Schering Ltd.* v. *Stockholms Enskilda Bank Aktiebolag* [1946] A.C. 219. In Scots law there may be repayment of sums on the principle of *condictio causa data causa non secuta*: *Davis & Primrose* v. *Clyde Shipbuilding and Engineering Co.*, *sup. cit.*; *Cantiere San Rocco* v. *Clyde Shipbuilding and Engineering Co.*, 1923 S.C.(H.L.) 105.

[37] at p. 269.

[38] [1916] 2 K.B. 707. The effect of war damage on leases was considered by R. A. Simpson in a series of articles: 1940 S.L.T.(News) 101, 113, 132 and 138.

1 Once the war is at an end the courts may enforce a contract between two enemy aliens if it was not contrary to our public policy.[39]

Impossibility of Performance

2 Impossibility of performance may frustrate a contract, although it would be better if the word "impracticable" were used. Performance might be literally possible, but there is frustration if it would be radically different performance from that contemplated.[40] Further the courts may have to concern themselves with the impracticability of a contract rather than impossibility in a sophisticated technological society. Performance might be possible if all the resources of the American space programme were devoted to a solution of the problem; obtaining that support and hiring the personnel and equipment will usually be impracticable.

3 The most unlikely events may, in certain circumstances, be possible. It should be remembered that Professor Corbin, writing in 1962, gave as an example of absolute impossibility:"No one can go to the moon."[41]

4 There are dicta in Scottish cases which might indicate that impossibility or impracticability of performance is not an excuse for non-performance. Lord Justice-Clerk Macdonald said that, "a plea of impossibility is no answer to a claim for damages for failure to fulfil a contract. This is well established by decision, and is no longer a doubtful matter in the law."[42] Lord Salvesen was more cautious[43]: "Not even impossibility of performance will in general absolve a person from a contract obligation." These *dicta* must be read in their context. Lord Sorn's approach was more expansive[44]:

> "The Court will intervene to declare a contract null where the parties have contracted to do something which is physically impossible, on the ground, probably, that the intention cannot have been serious, but, apart from that, it is only where there is supervening impossibility in the proper sense of the word that the Court will interfere to relieve parties of their obligations. What is meant by 'supervening impossibility', as I understand it, is the emergence of a new state of affairs, due to subsequent legislation or other supervening events, in which the performance of the contract has become either impossible, or something fundamentally different from what was originally contemplated. The essence of it is that the situation giving rise to the impossibility should be a situation not envisaged by the parties when making the contract."

5 The last sentence is not completely accurate. Frustration occurs when the parties have not made any, or any sufficient, provision for the hap-

---

[39] *Ottoman Bank* v. *Jebara* [1928] A.C. 269.
[40] *Jackson* v. *Union Marine Insurance Co.* (1874) L.R. 10 C.P. 125.
[41] Corbin, *Contracts* (1962), para. 1325.
[42] *John Milligan & Co. Ltd.* v. *Ayr Harbour Trs.*, 1915 S.C. 937 at p. 948.
[43] *Sup. cit.* at p. 952.
[44] *Union Totalisator Co. Ltd.* v. *Scott*, 1951 S.L.T.(Notes) 5.

pening of the event.[45] It is possible that the parties contemplated or even foresaw the possibility of the new event.

Scottish Examples of Impossibility

15–26 Obligations have been frustrated by the passing of legislation,[46] the destruction of goods by fire,[47] the alteration of tramway routes affecting an advertising contract,[48] the outbreak of war,[49] the conversion of a fishing area into a gunnery and bombing range[50] and the requisition of a house by military authorities,[51] and the destruction of the subjects of a lease by fire.[52]

English Examples of Impossibility

15–27 English cases on frustration are so numerous that they cannot all be mentioned here. Common types of frustrating events are illustrated by the cases cited.

(1) Changes in the law, including supervening illegality.[53]

(2) Requisition of ships by governments.[54]

(3) Explosion or destruction.[55]

(4) Death, illness or incapacity of a contracting party.[56]

(5) Abnormal delay.[57] Delay can raise the further problem of the date of frustration.[58]

---

[45] *National Carriers, sup. cit.* at p. 700 *per* Lord Simon; at p. 712 *per* Lord Roskill; *Cantors Properties (Scotland) Ltd.* v. *Swears & Wells Ltd.*, 1978 S.C. 310.

[46] *Caledonian Ins. Co.* v. *Matheson's Trs.* (1901) 3 F. 865; *George Packman & Sons* v. *Dunbar's Trs.*, 1977 S.L.T. 140.

[47] *Leith* v. *Edinburgh Ice and Cold Storage Co. Ltd.* (1900) 2 F. 904.

[48] *Abrahams Ltd.* v. *Campbell*, 1911 S.C. 353.

[49] *Davis & Primrose* v. *Clyde Shipbuilding and Engineering* (1918) 56 S.L.R. 24; *Cantiere San Rocco* v. *Clyde Shipbuilding and Engineering Co.*, 1923 S.C.(H.L.) 105; *James B. Fraser & Co.* v. *Denny, Mott and Dickson*, 1944 S.C.(H.L.) 35.

[50] *Tay Salmon Fisheries Co.* v. *Speedie*, 1929 S.C. 593.

[51] *Mackeson* v. *Boyd*, 1942 S.C. 56.

[52] *Cantors Properties (Scotland) Ltd.* v. *Swears & Wells Ltd.*, 1978 S.C. 310.

[53] *Metropolitan Water Board* v. *Dick, Kerr & Co. Ltd.* [1918] A.C. 119; *Reilly* v. *R.* [1934] A.C. 176; *Studholme* v. *South Western Gas Board* [1954] 1 All E.R. 462.

[54] *F. A. Tamplin Steamship Co. Ltd.* v. *Anglo-Mexican Petroleum Products Co. Ltd.* [1916] 2 A.C. 397; *Bank Line Ltd.* v. *Arthur Capel & Co.* [1919] A.C. 435; *Maritime National Fish Ltd.* v. *Ocean Trawlers Ltd.* [1935] A.C. 524.

[55] *Appleby* v. *Myers* (1867) L.R. 2 C.P. 651; *Joseph Constantine S.S. Line Ltd.* v. *Imperial Smelting Corporation Ltd.*, [1942] A.C. 154. See also *National Carriers, sup. cit.*

[56] *Horlock* v. *Beal* [1916] 1 A.C. 486: *Ottoman Bank* v. *Chakarian* [1930] A.C. 277; *Marshall* v. *Harland & Wolff Ltd.* [1972] 2 All E.R. 715; *Hebden* v. *Forsey & Son* [1973] I.C.R. 607; *Hart* v. *A. R. Marshall & Sons (Bulwell) Ltd.* [1978] 2 All E.R. 413; *Hare* v. *Murphy Bros. Ltd.* [1974] I.C.R. 603; *Chakki* v. *United Yeast Co. Ltd.* [1981] 2 All E.R. 446.

[57] *Pioneer Shipping Ltd., sup. cit.*; *The Eugenia* [1964] 2 Q.B. 226; *Davis Contractors Ltd., sup. cit*; see also *Tsakirogloa & Co. Ltd.* v. *Noblee Thorl GmbH* [1962] A.C. 93.

[58] See *The Evia* [1982] 1 Lloyd's Rep. 334; on appeal [1983] 1 A.C. 736.

Frustration of Purpose

28   The English coronation case, *Krell* v. *Henry*,[59] involved not impossibility but frustration of purpose. Rooms were hired for the purpose of viewing a coronation. The coronation was postponed. The rooms could still be occupied but the purpose of the contract was frustrated. The case has been treated with reserve in the House of Lords[60] and the Privy Council.[61]

29   There are difficulties in recognising frustration of purpose. Parties to a contract may not have the same purpose nor may each have a single purpose. There is a problem of definition of "purpose". Further, at what point is the failure of which purpose a frustration? On the other hand, sometimes it is unreasonable to insist on performance of a contract in changed circumstances. Consider the case of a contract to build a suspension bridge over a river. The bridge is to link two new motorways. Before work has started on the bridge it is decided by persons who are not parties to the bridge contract to construct the motorways elsewhere. Is it reasonable to insist that the contract to build the bridge must be implemented? Building the bridge is possible, but if it does not lead from anywhere to anywhere, the purpose of the contract has ceased to exist. It should be held that the contract has been frustrated.

30   What is Scots law on the point? The answer is not clear. There are cases in which the failure of one party's purpose has not resulted in frustration. In *Hart's Trs.* v. *Arrol*[62] a lease of a shop was granted for the carrying on of the business of a wine and spirit merchant. After some years of possession the tenants were refused a renewal of their licence. The purpose for which the shop had been let had failed. The court held that the lease was still binding. The case, however, has a speciality. The landlord had waived a restriction on the use of the premises. The tenants could continue to run a business. It is, however, a hard case. In *McMaster & Co* v. *Cox, McEuen & Co.*[63] contracts for the sale of jute were not affected by a ministerial order which prevented the purchasers exporting the jute. The seller did not know the purchasers' purpose in contracting. The order did not prevent the implementation of the contract in question. Clearly there was no frustration. It may be doubted whether frustration of purpose could ever apply in a case where the purpose was not known to all the parties.

31   One case does seem to rest on frustration of purpose, although that term was not used. The case is *Smith* v. *Riddell*.[64] An old man, Mr

---

[59] [1903] 2 K.B. 740.

[60] *Joseph Constantine S.S. Line Ltd.* v. *Imperial Smelting Corporation Ltd., sup. cit.*; *Larrinaga & Co. Ltd.* v. *Société Franco-Americaine des Phosphates de Medulla* (1923) 39 T.L.R. 316 at p. 318 *per* Viscount Finlay.

[61] *Maritime National Fish Ltd.* v. *Ocean Trawlers Ltd.* [1935] A.C. 524 at p. 529. Nor is *Krell* easy to reconcile with *Herne Bay Steamboat Co.* v. *Hutton* [1903] 2 K.B. 683.

[62] (1903) 6 F. 36.

[63] 1921 S.C.(H.L.) 24.

[64] (1886) 14 R. 95.

Smith, entered into an agreement under which he gave Mr Riddell the lease of a farm, and stock and crops in return for Mr Riddell supporting Mr Smith for the rest of Mr Smith's life. An unexpected event occurred. Mr Riddell died first. The question was whether Mrs Riddell was entitled to the stock and crops. The court held that the purpose behind Mr Smith contracting was to get Mr Riddell to come and live with him. In the opinion of the court,[65] "it would be against reason and against conscience that this agreement should be enforced against this old man when the only consideration for which he undertook it has become impossible of fulfilment." The case, however, has specialities. It involved a family arrangement. It could have been decided on the basis that there was *delectus personae*. Mrs Riddell could not perform the contract in place of her husband.

FRUSTRATION AND CONTRACTS RELATING TO LAND

15–32　English law has had difficulties applying frustration to contracts relating to land. It is now settled that in principle frustration can apply to a lease[66] although the circumstances in which it does may be rare. It has been doubted whether the doctrine ever applies to a contract for the sale of land.[67]

15–33　　There are Scots dicta doubting whether frustration applies to a grant of land,[68] although not questioning that there can be *rei interitus*, a concept which is not limited to physical destruction.[69] Recent case law has not suggested that heritage is in a special position.[70]

THE FAULT OF ONE OF THE PARTIES

15–34　It is usually stated, in one form or another, that if the supervening event is caused by the fault of one of the parties, there cannot be frustration. References to "fault" are of long standing. Craig referred to the "contributory fault" of vassals.[71] An early Scottish case shows discussion of

---

[65] at p. 98.

[66] The *National Carriers* case, *sup. cit.*

[67] Chitty, para. 1567.

[68] *Tay Salmon Fisheries Co.* v. *Speedie*, 1929 S.C. 593 at p. 601 *per* Lord President Clyde; Gloag, *Contract*, p. 357.

[69] *Tay Salmon Fisheries Co.*, *sup. cit.*; *Mackeson* v. *Boyd*, 1942 S.C. 56.

[70] *George Packman & Sons* v. *Dunbar's Trs.*, 1977 S.L.T. 140 (missives incapable of performance due to legislation on feuduty); *Cantors Properties (Scotland) Ltd.* v. *Swears and Wells Ltd.*, 1978 S.C. 310 (destruction of subjects of lease by fire). See also *Duff* v. *Fleming* (1870) 8 M. 769; *Mackeson* v. *Boyd*, 1942 S.C. 56 at p. 63 *per* Lord President Normand; *James B. Fraser* v. *Denny, Mott and Dickson*, 1944 S.C.(H.L.) 35 cited in *National Carriers*, *sup. cit.* at p. 704 *per* Lord Simon. Old cases on leases are mentioned in T. M. Cooper, *Selected Papers 1922–1954* (1957), p. 130 and even earlier cases may be found in Balfour's *Practicks*, pp. 146 and 200.

[71] Craig, *Jus Feudale*, 3,1,1.

culpa.[72] In more recent times Lord Macmillan said that neither party must be 'in default'[73] or there must be "an irresistable extraneous cause for which neither party is responsible."[74] In another case the Earl of Birkenhead mentioned that "neither party was in fault"[75] and then referred to an "act or event beyond the control of the parties."[76] Gloag said that the supervening event must not be due "to the act of either of the parties, but arising from circumstances beyond the control of either."[77]

5   On the face of it "fault" is different from "beyond the control of the parties." Fault in a wide sense could cover intentional and negligent acts, whereas "beyond the control" is a standard applying irrespective of intention or negligence. For example, if the performance of the contract is hindered by a strike of the employees of one of the contracting parties, frustration could operate or not according to whether "fault" or "beyond the control" were the test. The strike might not be caused by the "fault" of anyone, but it could be within the control of the employer to end the strike.

6   It is clear that a party cannot, by intentional actions, produce frustration. In referring to the case which is generally recognised as being at the root of the English doctrine of frustration, *Taylor* v. *Caldwell*,[78] Lord Sterndale M.R. observed[79]: "I do not think any authority has gone so far as to decide that if the defendant had burned down the music hall himself, he would have been entitled to say the subject matter was gone and the contract was frustrated." "Self-induced" frustration is not a bar to enforcement of a contract.[80] It has been said that whether an employer dismisses an employee is an important factor to take into account when considering whether the contract of employment has been frustrated.[81] This is doubtful.[82]

7   It may be that a party's negligence is *not* a bar to a plea of frustration. The issue was raised but not decided in *Joseph Constantine Steamship*

---

[72] *Duncan* v. *Arbroath* (1668) Mor. 10075; founded on in *Jacksons (Edinburgh) Ltd.* v. *Constructors John Brown Ltd.*, 1965 S.L.T. 37.

[73] *James B. Fraser & Co. Ltd.* v. *Denny, Mott & Dickson Ltd.*, 1944 S.C.(H.L.) 35 at p. 41.

[74] *Sup. cit.*

[75] *Cantiere San Rocco* v. *Clyde Shipbuilding and Engineering Co.*, 1923 S.C.(H.L.) 105 at p. 111. See also p. 108.

[76] *Sup. cit.* at p. 112.

[77] *Contract*, p. 346.

[78] (1863) 3 B. & S. 826. See, *e.g.* the speeches in *Joseph Constantine S.S. Line Ltd.* v. *Imperial Smelting Corporation Ltd.* [1942] A.C. 154; *National Carriers, sup. cit.* at p. 686 *per* Lord Hailsham L.C.

[79] *Mertens* v. *Home Freeholds Co. Ltd.* [1921] 2 K.B. 526 at p. 536; approved in *Joseph Constantine S.S. Line Ltd., sup. cit.* at p. 160 *per* Viscount Simon L.C. This is an instance of the official reports having a slightly different wording from other reports; *cf.* 90 L.J.K.B. 707 at p. 711; 125 L.T. 355 at p. 358; [1921] All E.R. 372 at p. 376.

[80] *Joseph Constantine S.S. Line Ltd., sup. cit.*; *Maritime National Fish Ltd.* v. *Ocean Trawlers Ltd.* [1935] A.C. 524; *The Eugenia* [1964] 2 Q.B. 226.

[81] *Hart* v. *A. R. Marshall & Sons (Bulwell) Ltd.* [1978] 2 All E.R. 413; *Egg Stores (Stamford Hill) Ltd.* v. *Leibovici* [1977] I.C.R. 260.

[82] The approach in *Marshall* v. *Harland & Wolff Ltd.* [1972] 2 All E.R. 715 is preferable.

Ltd. v. *Imperial Smelting Corporation Ltd.*[83] Viscount Simon was concerned about the prima donna who lost her voice because, after being out in the rain, she carelessly failed to change her wet clothes. Lord Russell pictured her sitting in a draught. In a later case Lord Denning took Lord Russell's *obiter dictum* to mean that there was frustration of the prima donna's contract.[84] In a Scottish case the Second Division decided that negligent grounding of a ship did not prevent frustration of a charter party.[85]

15–38   The failure of parties to carry on with an arbitration has been held to be within the concept of "fault" with the result that the delay in arbitrating did not frustrate the contract to arbitrate.[86]

15–39   So what is meant by "fault" in the context of a supervening event causing frustration? It may be that the "fault" of a party which is a bar to pleading frustration is an intentional and also, presumably, reckless act. On the other hand cases such as *Denmark Productions Ltd.* v. *Boscobel Productions Ltd.*[87] and *Paal Wilson & Co.* v. *Blumenthal*[88] suggest that contracting parties cannot found on the actions or inactions of either party to establish frustration. Whereas in *Head Wrightson Ltd.* v. *Aberdeen Harbour Comms.*[89] it appears that the modifications to a bridge instructed by one party could have frustrated a contract for construction of the bridge. A party who is in breach of obligations under a contract may or may not be debarred from relying upon frustration.[90] The truth could be that references to "fault" are misleading and the "beyond the control" test gives a more accurate picture of the circumstances in which frustration arises. As Harman L.J. puts it[91]: "The frustrating event is something altogether outside the control of the parties—a war, a famine, a flood or some event of that sort—so that if the parties had thought to provide for it they would at once have agreed that on its happening the contract must come to an end."

THE CONSEQUENCES OF FRUSTRATION

15–40   Frustration ends parties' rights and obligations to future performance under the contract. This happens automatically without any act of the parties. Rights and obligations under the contract are ended for the

---

[83] *Sup. cit.* at p. 166 (Viscount Simon L.C.); at p. 179 (Lord Russell); at p. 195 (Lord Wright); at p. 205 (Lord Porter).
[84] *Hare* v. *Murphy Bros. Ltd.* [1974] 3 All E.R. 940 at p. 942.
[85] *London & Edinburgh Shipping Co.* v. *The Admiralty*, 1920 S.C. 309.
[86] *Paal Wilson & Co.* v. *Blumenthal* [1983] 1 A.C. 854.
[87] [1969] 1 Q.B. 699.
[88] *Sup. cit.*
[89] 1958 S.L.T.(Notes) 12.
[90] *Kodros Shipping Corp. of Monrovia* v. *Empresa Cubana de Fletes of Havana, Cuba* [1982] 1 Lloyd's Rep. 334 (C.A.); [1983] 1 A.C. 736. Frustration can arise although a party is in breach. On the other hand the contract may have contemplated the event which occurs which excludes frustration and leads to non-performance being a breach of contract.
[91] *Denmark Productions Ltd.* v. *Boscobel Productions Ltd.*, *sup. cit.* at p. 736.

future but existing rights and wrongs are not affected.[92] Frustration does not depend, as does rescission or repudiation of a contract, on the choice of a contracting party.

41 Strictly speaking the contract is not frustrated. It is the future performance, or the adventure, which is frustrated.[93] The result is that even after frustration, arbitration clauses may be enforceable.[94] There are clauses which might have survived full performance of the contract such as indemnities against liability for taxes, accidents or infringement of patents, clauses protecting confidential information or provisions restraining trade or employment. These clauses and provisions may also survive frustrated performance.

42 In English common law the result of frustration was that the loss lay where it fell. The harshness of the traditional rule, which prevented recovery of payments made before frustration, was mitigated in the *Fibrosa* case.[95] The consequences of frustration are now governed by the Law Reform (Frustrated Contracts) Act 1943.

43 In Scots law the loss does not lie where it falls on the frustration of a contract. There must be an equitable adjustment. In *Cantiere San Rocco* v. *Clyde Shipbuilding and Engineering Co.*[96] there was a contract to build and supply marine engines. The first instalment of the price was paid on signature of the contract. Shortly thereafter war broke out and further performance of the contract became legally impossible. The House of Lords held that the buyer was entitled to repetition of the instalment (subject to any counterclaim) upon the principle of *condictio causa data causa non secuta*.

44 Although Scots law makes an equitable adjustment apart from the contract, doubt has been expressed about the extent of the adjustment which could be made.[97] The basis for the doubt is Lord President Inglis's opinion in *Watson* v. *Shankland*.[98] It is thought that the Scottish courts have all the requisite powers.[99] One possibility following frustration is that a party should be remunerated *quantum meruit* for work done.[1]

---

[92] *Joseph Constantine S.S. Line Ltd.* v. *Imperial Smelting Corporation Ltd.*, *sup. cit.*; *James B. Fraser & Co. Ltd.* v. *Denny, Mott & Dickson Ltd.*, *sup. cit.*; *Hirji Mulji* v. *Cheong Yue S.S. Co.* [1926] A.C. 497 at pp. 509–510; *National Carriers Ltd.* v. *Panalpina (Northern) Ltd.*, *sup. cit.*

[93] *Heyman* v. *Darwins* [1942] A.C. 356 at p. 400 *per* Lord Porter.

[94] *Heyman* v. *Darwins*, *sup. cit.*; *Kruse* v. *Questier & Co. Ltd.* [1953] 1 Q.B. 669; *Government of Gibraltar* v. *Kenney* [1956] 2 Q.B. 410; *Scott & Sons Ltd.* v. *Del Sel*, 1923 S.C.(H.L.) 37.

[95] *Fibrosa Spolka Abcyjna* v. *Fairbairn Lawson Combe Barbour Ltd.* [1943] A.C. 32.

[96] 1923 S.C.(H.L.) 105.

[97] *Fibrosa* case, *sup. cit.* at p. 54 *per* Lord Atkin; T. M. Cooper, *Selected Papers 1922–1954* (1957), p. 128.

[98] (1871) 10 M. 142 at p. 152; on appeal (1873) 11 M.(H.L.) 51.

[99] See Cooper, *sup. cit.*; *cf.* J. P. Dawson, "Judicial Revision of Frustrated Contracts," 1982 J.R. 86.

[1] *Head Wrightson Aluminium Ltd.* v. *Aberdeen Harbour Comms.*, 1958 S.L.T.(Notes) 12.

CONTRACTUAL PROVISIONS AFFECTING FRUSTRATION

15–45 The definitions of frustration state, in one form or another, that the doctrine does not apply to events provided for by the parties at the time of contracting. It is, therefore, necessary to construe the contract to determine whether the event which occurred was a risk within the contemplation of the parties.[2] Because of the difficulty of deciding whether or not there has been frustration, particularly if delay is one of the principal factors, it is common in commercial contracts for there to be express provision about events which otherwise might, or arguably might, operate to frustrate the contract. The relevant clause is commonly called a *force majeure* clause. The expression *force majeure* is said to have been adopted from the *Code Napoleon*.[3] In a European context the phrase is open to many different shades of interpretation.[4] In a Scottish contract the term does not have any technical meaning; it might be better if it were never used; but in maritime contracts and in the oil industry, the phrase is commonplace. Delay in obtaining materials did not fall within *"force majeure."*[5]

15–46 The events for which express provision may be made include acts of God, war, civil commotion, government interference and, of some practical importance, strikes or other labour disputes. So far as the clause covers the effects of delay, such as the delay in delivering goods, it may go far beyond what would operate as frustration. Indeed it has been suggested that few of the instances of *force majeure* relied on in *force majeure* clauses would discharge a seller from performance under the frustration doctrine.[6] The clause may provide that if the event lasts for more than a stipulated period either party may terminate the contract. When the event is a strike there is an argument that the existence of the clause may encourage employees to take industrial action if they believe that the potential termination of a contract is a pressure which can be put on their employer. The draftsman may counter this if he restricts the possibility of termination to strikes by the employees of third parties. There may be a provision which defines the event which triggers the clause as one occurring without the fault or beyond the control of a party. This is liable to raise more problems than it solves. The contract

---

[2] *e.g. B.P. Exploration Co. (Libya) Ltd.* v. *Hunt (No. 2)* [1982] 2 A.C. 352 (expropriation of oil concession not within terms of contract); *Metropolitan Water Board* v. *Dick, Kerr & Co. Ltd.* [1918] A.C. 119 (provision for extension of time did not apply to Government prohibition).

[3] *Matsoukis* v. *Priestman & Co.* [1915] 1 K.B. 681 at pp. 685, 686 *per* Bailhache J. See *Code Civil*, art. 1148. The *force majeure* of French law is restricted to cases of absolute impossibility: Barry Nicholas, *French Law of Contract* (1982), pp. 196 *et seq.*

[4] *Certain Aspects of Civil Liability* (Council of Europe, 1976), paras. 26–36; for an English approach see *Lebeaupin* v. *Crispin* [1920] 2 K.B. 714 *per* McCardle J. at p. 719; *Zinc Corporation Ltd.* v. *Hirsch* [1916] 1 K.B. 541 (war not *force majeure*). Sometimes the phrase *vis major* is used.

[5] *Yzquierdo y Castaneda* v. *Clydebank Engineering and Shipbuilding Co. Ltd.* (1903) 5 F. 1016; on appeal (1904) 7 F.(H.L.) 77.

[6] B. J. Cartoon, "Drafting an Acceptable Force Majeure Clause" (1978) J.B.L. 230.

may provide not only for termination of the contract, but also for suspension of rights and obligations during the event, such as a labour dispute.[7] There can be elaborate combinations of suspension and termination provisions. An alternative approach is to deal with the allocation of risks. The clause may provide that one of the parties deals with the additional expense of the destruction of the subject-matter of the contract or the blockage of a sea route.

47   Some of these clauses, if they appear in a consumer contract or a standard form contract, will be subject to a "fair and reasonable" test under section 17 of the Unfair Contract Terms Act 1977, so far as they enable a party to render no performance or substantially different performance from that which the consumer or customer reasonably expected. It should be relatively easy to satisfy this test if the clause operates for the benefit of all the parties to the contract and deals with events beyond the control of any of them.

48   An express provision cannot exclude frustration by supervening illegality if this would be contrary to public policy.[8]

---

[7] The clause may in effect provide that an event and its consequences do not give rise to a breach of contract. But the drafting must be done with care because there is a distinction between excusing liability for damages and an exception from an obligation to perform— *Torquay Hotel Co. Ltd.* v. *Cousins* [1969] 2 Ch. 106 at p. 143 *per* Russell L.J.; at p. 147 *per* Winn L.J. The distinction is important if there is a breach of an obligation to perform. Although there may be no liability to damages (because of the clause) there could be material breach followed by rescission and an end to future performance.

[8] *Ertel Bieber & Co.* v. *Rio Tinto Co. Ltd.* [1918] A.C. 260.

CHAPTER 16

JOINT AND SEVERAL LIABILITY

16–01   When there is more than one obligant, the law presumes that each is liable *pro rata*. Thus in the phrase, "We, B and C, promise to pay A £100" the law imposes on B an obligation to pay £50, and likewise C is liable to pay £50.

16–02   The present law of Scotland was summarised by Gloag in a passage which has been approved in the House of Lords.

> "As a mere general rule, subject to many exceptions, and yielding to expressions indicative of an intention to the contrary, obligations are construed as involving rights and liabilities *pro rata*, so that one of two creditors can exact payment of a half only; one of two debtors is liable only in the same proportion."[1]

16–03   Instances in which the *pro rata* rule was applied can be found in reported cases which deal with the problems of the liability of heirs-portioners,[2] or liability under a court decree for expenses.[3] These are perhaps illustrations of an attitude, but doubtful authority for interpretation of contracts. The word "conjunctly" has been held to infer liability *pro rata*, although proof to the contrary was allowed.[4] *Urie* v. *Cheyne*,[5] which appears to be a case of *pro rata* liability on facts unfavourable to that conclusion, is probably inconsistent with later authority.[6] *Denniston* v. *Semple*,[7] a case reported by Stair, and therefore decided by him,[8] is an instance of *pro rata* liability. *Coats* v. *Union Bank of Scotland*[9] is of particular interest, being a House of Lords decision this century. It was a case involving a deed in which the words "jointly" and "joint" were used. The words were interpreted as meaning *pro rata* liability although the absence of the words "and several" was a mistake on the bank's part.[10]

---

[1] *Contract*, p. 198; appd. in *Coats* v. *Union Bank of Scotland*, 1929 S.C.(H.L.) 114 at p. 119 *per* Viscount Hailsham.

[2] *e.g. Home* v. *Home* (1632) Mor. 14678; *Duncan* v. *Ogilvie* (1635) Mor. 14680; *Jordanhill* v. *Edmiston* (1687) Mor. 14682; *Lockhart* v. *Shiels* (1770) Mor. 7244.

[3] *e.g. Douglas* (1626) Mor. 14714; *cf. Sutherland* v. *Cuthbert* (1776) 5 Br.Sup. 439.

[4] *Campbell* v. *Farquhar* (1724) Mor. 14626.

[5] (1630) Mor. 14626.

[6] *Darlington* v. *Gray* (1836) 15 S.197. See Gloag, *op. cit.* p. 200, n. 10.

[7] (1669) Mor. 14630.

[8] See Dedicatory to *Decisions* (1683): "I did form this Breviat of these Decisions, in fresh and recent Memory, *de die in diem* as they were pronounced," and later: "Neither have I recorded any decisions but what was determined while I was present, being resolved to take nothing at a second hand."

[9] 1929 S.C.(H.L.) 114.

[10] See 1928, S.C. 711 at pp. 714 and 715 *per* Lord Constable; at p. 736 *per* Lord Blackburn; 1929 S.C.(H.L.) 114 at p. 121 *per* Viscount Hailsham.

4   By itself this catalogue of cases in which a *pro rata* result has been reached becomes insignificant when placed alongside the authorities in which the *pro rata* rule was not applied. The problem of what should happen when words such as "conjunctly" or "jointly" were not used, as in the statement, "We, B and C, promise to pay A £100" was raised in *Monro* v. *Ouchterlony*.[11] There was a division of opinion on whether or not liability was *in solidum*.

5   More in his notes to Stair observed that, "in general where a joint liability is undertaken, it will be presumed that each contractor intended to bind himself in solidum," and then proceeded to illustrate this point, by a citation of numerous authorities.[12] Erskine, however, appears to have followed Stair's *pro rata* theory.[13] Bankton[14] and Bell clearly did.[15]

6   The *pro rata* rule is weakened by the exceptions to it which have been allowed. The principal classes of these are:

(1) Bills of exchange. It would be contrary to the nature of a bill if adding signatures diminished the liability of each signatory. So it was found according to the custom of merchants that liability on a bill was *in solidum*,[16] a rule which is in effect now statutory,[17] although in some circumstances liability under a promissory note may be joint.[18]

(2) Partnership. The liability of partners for a firm debt was established at common law to be joint and several.[19] The rule is now statutory.[20]

(3) Obligations *ad factum praestandum*. If B and C promise to pay money a *pro rata* rule is possible because money is divisible. If B and C promise to deliver to A a horse or a car, there is obvious absurdity in normal situations if this is construed to mean that B is liable to deliver half a horse or half a car. If it is further provided that on failure to deliver, B and C shall be liable to a penalty, the *pro rata* theory creates a difficulty. The penalty, being quantifiable in money, is divisible. What is the nature of the liability for the penalty?

---

[11] (1705) 4 Br.Sup. 617.

[12] More's *Notes*, pp. cxviii–cxxi.

[13] Ersk., III,iii,74. See Stair, I,xvii,20 (2nd and 5th eds.).

[14] Bankt., I,iv,12.

[15] Bell, *Comm.* I, 361 (7th ed.), *Prin.* (4th and 10th eds.), s.51. Bell made one error. See Lord President Clyde in *Coats* v. *Union Bank of Scotland*, 1928 S.C. 711 at p. 723; on appeal 1929 S.C.(H.L.) 114.

[16] *McMorland* v. *Maxwell* (1675) Mor. 14673; *Rutherford & Sangster* v. *Donaldson* (1707) Mor. 14675; R. Thomson, *Law of Bills of Exchange* (1865), p. 155.

[17] Bills of Exchange Act 1882, ss.54–57.

[18] s.85. See interpretation in Byles on *Bills of Exchange* (25th ed., 1983), p. 318. See, however, Bell, *Comm.*, I,346 (5th ed.), 363 (7th ed.). Liability on a cheque is joint and several: *Laurence Henderson, Sons & Co.* v. *Wallace & Pennell* (1902) 5 F. 166, a case commented on in *Coats* v. *Union Bank of Scotland, sup. cit.*

[19] *McLeod* v. *Young* (1665) Mor. 14663; *Johnston* v. *Binning and Nielson* (1683) Mor. 14664; *Brand* v. *Warden & Buchanan* (1698) Mor. 14664; Bell, *Comm.*, II,618 (5th ed.), II,507 (7th ed.)

[20] Partnership Act 1890, s.9. The debt must be constituted against the firm. J. B. Miller, *The Law of Partnership in Scotland* (1973), pp. 352–356.

16–07   The Scots courts have held obligations *ad factum praestandum* to be
indivisible so that all the obligants are liable *in solidum*.[21] The problem
of the penalty clause adjected to this type of obligation arose in *Urie* v.
Cheyne[22] when a *pro rata* division of the penalty appears to have been
allowed. Erskine's view was that liability for the sum was *pro rata*[23] but
Nicolson doubted this in his note to the passage. Bankton, on the other
hand, stated that the penalty was not divisible.[24] In his note to Bell's
Commentaries, Lord McLaren makes the forceful point that to allow the
penalty to transform a liability *in solidum* into a liability *pro rata*,
"would be to allow the debtor's own failure to operate to his own benefit, and to the prejudice of the creditor."[25] The result should be that the
penalty does not alter the nature of the liability.

(4) Trustees are jointly and severally liable on contracts made by
them unless the contract indicates otherwise.[26]

(5) Those who employ an agent will be jointly and severally liable for
the remuneration which the agent is due,[27] although there could be contrary agreement.[28]

(6) Marine insurance. Where a policy of marine insurance is subscribed by or on behalf of two or more insurers, each subscription,
unless the contrary be expressed, constitutes a distinct contract with the
assured.[29]

(7) The terms of a deed may show joint and several liability such as

---

[21] *Grott* v. *Sutherland* (1672) Mor. 14631 (where other factors may also have been
involved); *Dickson* v. *Turner & Rutherford* (1697) Mor. 14632; *Grant* v. *Strachan* (1721)
Mor. 14633 (but there were specialities of caution); *Darlington* v. *Gray* (1836) 15 S.197;
Rankine v. *Logie Den Land Co.* (1902) 4 F. 1074.

[22] (1630) Mor. 14626.

[23] Ersk., III,iii,74.

[24] Bankt., I,xi,12

[25] Bell, *Comm.*, I,362 (7th ed.).

[26] *Commercial Bank of Scotland* v. *Sprot* (1841) 3 D. 939; *Oswald's Tr.* v. *City of Glasgow Bank* (1879) 6 R. 461, esp. *per* Lord President Inglis at p. 466; *Cunninghame* v. *City
of Glasgow Bank* (1879) 6 R. 679, affd. 6 R.(H.L.) 98; *Gillespie & Paterson* v. *City of
Glasgow Bank* (1879) 6 R. 714; affd. 6 R.(H.L.) 104. The problem of the extent to which a
co-trustee may be liable for the actings of the other trustees is a separate issue. See
W. A. Wilson and A. G. M. Duncan, *Trusts, Trustees and Executors* (1975), p. 389. On
the possibility that liability might be limited by the amount of the trust estate see the work
cited at pp. 394–397.

[27] *Chalmers* v. *Ogilvie* (1730) Mor. 14706; *French* v. *Earl of Galloway* (1730) Mor.
14706; *Walker* v. *Brown* (1803) Mor.App. "Solidum et Pro Rata," No. 1; *Webster* v.
McLellan (1852) 14 D. 932; *Smith* v. *Harding* (1877) 5 R. 147. A principle extended to
liability of a *negotiorum gestor* in *Anderson* v. *Sinclair* (1726) Mor. 14706 and to a court
reporter in *Wilson, Petrs.,* July 10, 1813, F.C.

[28] A qualification so obvious that it hardly needs authority. See *Smith* v. *Harding, sup.
cit.*; *Murdoch* v. *Hunter*, Feb. 15, 1815, F.C.

[29] Marine Insurance Act 1906, s.24(2). A similar problem could also arise with aviation
insurance, but the number of such contracts needing several insurers and governed by
Scots law must be small in view of the dominance in the market of insurances of this type
effected at Lloyds. In the absence of express provision *pro rata* liability of the insurers is
unlikely to be the parties' intention.

where cautioners were bound as "full debtors"[30] or parties bound conjunctly and severally.[31] "The word 'severally' implies that against whatever number of defenders a man proceeds, each is liable for the whole sum sued for, and the word 'jointly' or 'conjunctly' secures to those against whom the decree is made operative the right of rateable relief against the persons who have not paid."[32] The value of the *pro rata* assumption is attacked by the common practice of documents drafted with legal assistance providing that liabilities imposed on more than one person shall be joint and several. Indeed some feu writs may go further and bind a person and his heirs, executors and successors, jointly and severally, with the result that a person's estate and representatives may be bound for ever.[33] There are exceptions to the practice of joint and several liability. They may occur in warrandice, and liabilities of *pro indiviso* proprietors.[34] Selling shareholders in a take-over agreement may bind themselves only in proportion to their shareholdings in the company, it being unfair that the holder of a small number of shares should undertake the same liability as those who receive a larger sale price because of a larger holding. An exception may also, of course, arise where, possibly by mistake, parties' liability is said to be "joint." This happened in *Coats* v. *Union Bank of Scotland*.[35]

8   The circumstances could indicate neither *pro rata* nor joint and several liability. A document might commence: "We the undersigned, promise to pay 10p for every mile walked by Tracy in the charity event on Sunday." The intention is not that the charity receives 10p multiplied by the number of miles, with each subscriber jointly and severally liable or liable *pro rata* for that sum. What is intended is that each subscriber is separately liable. The more subscribers, the more money the charity receives. The example is special because the terms of the deed let us know the purpose of the payment. We are then able to say what the common sense result is.

---

[30] *Cloberhill* v. *Ladyland* (1631) Mor. 14623; *Cleghorn* v. *Yorston* (1707) Mor. 14624.

[31] Bell, *Prin.*, s.57 (4th and 10th eds.). At para. 56 (4th and 10th eds.) he stated that if they were bound jointly and severally each was liable for the whole, or for a share, at the option of the creditor. He quotes Ersk., III,iii,74, which is not clear authority for the existence of an option, but the point is of little practical importance. On the ability to sue anyone see *Richmond* v. *Grahame* (1847) 9 D. 633.

[32] *Fleming* v. *Gemmill*, 1908 S.C. 340, *per* Lord McLaren at p. 345.

[33] *Dundee Police Commrs.* v. *Straton* (1884) 11 R. 586; appd. in *Burns* v. *Martin* (1887) 14 R.(H.L.) 20. On the wisdom of such a clause see Burns's *Conveyancing Practice* (4th ed., 1957), p. 231.

[34] Burns, *op. cit.*, pp. 344, 355.

[35] *Sup. cit.* Evidence by the bank manager that a joint loan without joint and several liability was "unknown in Scotland" was not sufficient evidence of practice to bind the pursuer in that case ((1929) S.C.(H.L.) 114 at p. 121) but nevertheless it is thought that joint and several liability is normal. On modern English practice see J. Milnes Holden, *The Law and Practice of Banking*, Vol. 1 (2nd ed., 1974), p. 373: "joint liability would not be acceptable to the bank"; Vol. 2 (6th ed., 1980), p. 255: "In practice, bankers are seldom, if ever, prepared to accept the joint liability of guarantors."

RIGHTS OF RELIEF

16–09 There are problems, discussed only occasionally in the past, about the relationship amongst debtors who are jointly and severally liable. One of the best and strongest statements of the law remains that of Stair.[36]

> "From the natural obligation of recompence doth arise the obligation of relief, whereby, when many persons are obliged *in solidum*, and thereby liable conjunctly and severally, payment and satisfaction made by one for more than his own share doth oblige all the rest *pro rata*, although there be no conventional clause of relief, nor any law or statute, but the natural obligation of recompense; for he who paid, not only for himself, but for others, is not presumed to do it *animo donandi*."

Subsequent analysis has added little to this. Most of the more recent discussion has concerned cautionary obligations[37] which have some special features.[38] The interesting thing is that this part of contract law has remained more or less as it was in Stair's time whereas the equivalent problems in delict have received more searching analysis ever since *Palmer* v. *Wick and Pulteneytown Steam Shipping Co. Ltd.* in 1894.[39] That case decided that at common law, if a pursuer obtained a joint and several decree on the ground of fault against defenders, and one defender paid the pursuer, that defender could recover a *pro rata* share from the other defenders. That is no longer the law. The Law Reform (Miscellaneous Provisions) (Scotland) Act 1940 provides that in the *Palmer* situation defenders will be liable *inter se* to contribute in such proportions as the jury or the court may deem just.[40] Can that provision apply to joint and several decrees based on breach of contract?

16–10 The reason for the provision in the 1940 Act was the realisation that a *pro rata* allocation may be unjust. Take a case in which two tenants of property are jointly and severally liable for the tenants' obligations under the lease. One of those obligations is to maintain the subjects in good repair. The tenants fail to take reasonable care and the subjects are damaged, but the tenants are not equally culpable. One is more at fault than the other. If the landlord bases his claim against the tenant in delict either tenant against whom a decree has passed may claim an

---

[36] *Inst.*, I,viii,9 (2nd and 5th eds.). There are differences in punctuation between the editions. Also the 2nd ed. stated: "payment *or* satisfaction."

[37] *e.g.* Bell, *Comm.*, I,364 (7th ed.); Gloag, *op. cit.* Chap. xii, *passim*.

[38] *e.g.* the extent to which acts of the creditor may release the cautioner is greater than in the case of other joint obligations: Gloag, p. 214, Mercantile Law Amendment Act (Scotland), 1856, s.9; the effect of bankruptcy may be different, Gloag, p. 206. There are sufficient doubts about the application of cautionary rules to other types of obligations to make it wise to be cautious in using cautionary cases by way of analogy. See also *Milne* v. *Kidd* (1869) 8 M. 250, esp. *per* Lord President Inglis at p. 259.

[39] (1894) 21 R.(H.L.) 39.

[40] s.3(1).

equitable contribution from the other tenant.[41] The landlord might, however, base his action on breach of contract. He may be encouraged by more favourable rules on recovering damages for economic loss or a longer period of prescription. If the landlord exercises this option, does that result in prejudice to the tenant who was less culpable? It is not just, if it does.

1   Lord Young in *Palmer* was prepared to allow some circumstances in which a division other than *pro rata* would result, but not apparently when a joint decree existed, "in the absence of something conclusive to the contrary."[42] He might have been referring to cases in which the right of relief was regulated by express contract. In the absence of contract the basis of the relief is equity,[43] and it would be odd if apportioning of liability on an equitable basis was barred. In any event the terms of the 1940 Act are not limited to claims based on delict.

DIFFICULTIES OF INTERPRETATION OF THE 1940 ACT

2   Section 3 of the 1940 Act applies to "any action of damages in respect of loss or damage arising from any wrongful acts or negligent acts or omissions." This could apply to intentional or negligent breach of contract. Whether it could apply to any breach of contract, irrespective of fault, is more doubtful. It depends on what meaning is given to "wrongful." Presumably the word "wrongful" was used instead of "intentional" so that delicts of strict liability would be covered.[44] By parity of reasoning a breach of contract causing loss or damage is a wrong to which the section applies.[45]

3   Section 3 of the Act does not affect "any contractual or other right of relief or indemnity or render enforceable any agreement for indemnity which could not have been enforced if this section had not been

---

[41] Depending on whether s.3(1) or 3(2) of the 1940 Act applies. The necessity for a decree arises as a result of an unfortunate decision: *N.C.B.* v. *Thomson*, 1959 S.C. 353. (See the observations on that case in *British Railways Board* v. *Ross and Cromarty C.C.*, 1974 S.C. 27.)

[42] (1893) 20 R. 275 at p. 285.

[43] Bankt., I,x,4; Kames, *Principles of Equity* (1825 ed.), p. 79. In *Palmer* there was much concentration on the creation of liability by a decree. The subsequent sophistication of the law of delict might enable it to be more clearly recognised now that a decree finding B and C liable to A, is not conclusive of B's liability to C or *vice versa*.

[44] Although there remains the difficulty that "wrongful" omissions are excluded. Does that mean that the section does not cover omitting to keep the gate of the tiger's cage shut, assuming that negligence is not proved? What if fences containing animals are breached by lightning?

[45] A breach of contract has been treated as a "wrong" similar to a delictual act. See *Belmont Laundry Co.* v. *Aberdeen Steam Laundry Co.* (1898) 1 F. 45; *Rose Street Foundry and Engineering Co.* v. *Lewis & Sons*, 1917 S.C. 341; *Grunwald* v. *Hughes*, 1965 S.L.T. 209. The reason for using both "loss" and "damage" in s.3 is obscure, the phrase "loss or damage" is in common use in written pleadings but the words have different meanings. A dented mudguard is the damage to the car. The cost of repairing it is the owner's loss. He is compensated by an award of damages.

enacted." This raises at least two difficulties. What is meant by "other"? It presumably covers quasi-contractual rights of relief, although it is difficult to see why the words "contractual or other" were not omitted.[46] Is the phrase, "contractual or other right of relief or indemnity" limited by the words, "which could not have been enforced if this section had not been enacted"? It is submitted that it must be and further that the intention is to prevent previously unenforceable rights[47] becoming enforceable to any extent. The intention cannot be to prevent an existing *pro rata* right of relief from becoming a right to demand a different sum in relief, or the purpose of the section is defeated. The result, admittedly by an argument only as strong as its weakest link, is that in our example of the negligent tenants damaging the subjects of let, whether or not the landlord's claim is based on delict or contract, the tenants have *inter se* rights of relief which, in the absence of express contract, are not limited to a *pro rata* basis.[48] The same result may also follow even if the tenants are not negligent but only in breach of contract.

LIMITATION OF LIABILITY OF ONE CO-OBLIGANT

16–14   Joint and several liability may arise as a result of breaches of separate contracts or a breach of a contract and a delictual wrong.[49] It is normally assumed that a claimant's rights against joint and several debtors are such that each debtor is liable to the claimant in the same way, but this is not necessarily so if the debtors have separate contracts with the claimant or there is a mixture of contractual and delictual relationships. The problem may be made clearer by an example.

16–15   A restaurant employs an architect to design and supervise structural alterations on their premises. Under his supervision heating engineers instal a boiler. The boiler causes a fire which damages the restaurant. Both the architect and the engineers have a contract with the restaurant. Both are in breach of their contracts. Both breaches cause the restauranteur's loss. The architect and the engineer are jointly and severally

---

[46] The phrase was given differing interpretations in *N.C.B.* v. *Thomson*, 1959 S.C. 353. In introducing the 1940 Bill in the House of Lords, Lord (formerly Lord Justice-Clerk) Alness observed: "it is a wholly admirable Bill, well conceived and well considered, and I venture to think well expressed": H.L. Deb., Vol. 116, p. 698 (1939–40). The clause which became s.3 has, however, given rise to more than its fair share of problems. It was based on, but did not exactly follow, the English Law Reform (Married Women and Tortfeasors) Act 1935, s.6. It arose out of work of a committee under Lord Wark. See 1940 S.L.T.(News) 93.

[47] An example would be a cautioner's right of relief against the insolvent debtor which is barred by the rule preventing double ranking in bankruptcy.

[48] Any express contract may also be affected by the Unfair Contract Terms Act 1977. S.15(2)(*e*) would be applicable to a contract between tenants, and this brings in the controls of Pt. II of the Act.

[49] *Belmont Laundry Co.* v. *Aberdeen Steam Laundry Co.*, *sup. cit.*; *Rose Street Foundry and Engineering Co.* v. *Lewis & Sons*, *sup. cit.*

liable to the restauranteur. So far an outline of the facts in *Grunwald* v. *Hughes* has been followed.[50] Now add one complication. In the contract with the heating engineers, the liability of the engineers is limited to £10,000. The limitation is fair and reasonable and not ineffective as a result of the Unfair Contract Terms Act 1977. The total loss to the restaurant is £25,000. *Quid juris?* The sensibly advised restaurant might sue the architect for the whole of this loss.[51] They may obtain decree for £25,000. If they are unable to recover the whole of this from the architect they may recover any balance up to £10,000 from the engineer.[52] It should not matter, however, in which order decrees are obtained. The restaurant could obtain decree for up to £10,000 against the engineer, and then seek the balance of their loss from the architect. Or, of course, the restaurant may try to save themselves the trouble of two actions and raise one action against the architect and the engineer.[53] The rights of the parties should not be affected by this, or procedural rules are being given unnecessary prominence. The result therefore, should be that the pursuers obtain a decree for £10,000 against both defenders, jointly and severally and decree for the further sum of £15,000 against the architect.[54]

There remains the problem of the architect's right of relief against the engineer. Is it affected by the limit of £10,000 in the engineer's contract with the restaurant? It is difficult to see why in principle the engineer should be able to limit his liability, in quasi-contract or delict, to the architect by a contract with someone else.[55] The limitation therefore does not apply to the architect's claim. The result is that if both defenders remain solvent and able to pay, the limitation clause has not affected the ability of the restaurant to recover the whole of its loss. On the other hand the clause has the effect that the risk of the insolvency of the architect is partly borne by the restaurant. Other solutions are possible and have been discussed by the English Law Commission.[56]

---

[50] *Sup. cit.*

[51] Assuming for the moment that the procedural complications introduced by *Neilson* v. *Wilson* (1890) 17 R. 608 allow this. The problem is discussed *infra*. If necessary it can be assumed that either the architect or the engineer is subject only to the jurisdiction of the English courts.

[52] The assumption being made that the principle in *Steven* v. *Broady Norman & Co.*, 1928 S.C. 351 applies also in contract. See *infra*.

[53] They may be compelled to do this as a result of *Neilson* v. *Wilson, sup. cit.*

[54] This was the result in a case in which the delictual liability of one of the defenders was limited by statute: *Duthie* v. *Caledonian Rly. Co.* (1898) 25 R. 934.

[55] It would be possible to frame a claim in the engineer's contract so that all likely co-obligants with him have the benefit of the limitation. The architect and others are given a *jus quaesitum tertio*. If our analysis of the normal situation is accepted, such a clause would be in the engineer's interests. If the liability of all is limited to £10,000, the maximum liability of the engineer is effectively limited also, which was presumably the original intention, for insurance reasons or otherwise.

[56] The Law Commission, Working Paper No. 59, *Contribution* (1975), paras. 49 to 51; Report on *Contribution* (Law Com. No. 79, 1977), paras. 71–74. Their favoured result does not bear a similarity to that suggested above. The difference is that we assume that the concept of joint and several liability means that the architect can be sued for the whole loss.

PROCEDURAL COMPLICATIONS

16–17   The more rapid development of the law of delict compared to the law of contract has the effect that delict cases illustrate better the problems of rights of relief. On one basic point there is a procedural difference.

> "Where two or more persons have contributed, either equally or in varying proportions, to the commission of a delict, they are liable jointly and severally, i.e. they are all liable jointly, and each one is also liable for the whole wrong. The injured person may in such a case sue all persons responsible in one action, or any one of them, holding that one liable for the whole damage done, and may recover full damages from that one, or the damages from all in what proportions he chooses."[57]

The matter is not so simple in the law of contract because of the effect of the decision of a majority of seven judges, in *Neilson* v. *Wilson*.[58] If the obligation is not constituted by writing or decree, all the obligants within the jurisdiction of the Scottish courts must be called in the one action. What is surprising is that the facts of the case made it a most unfavourable one for the application of the majority view. A solicitor or writer sought recovery of litigation expenses from three persons jointly and severally liable to the solicitor. He sued two of them in a small debt court in the sheriffdom of Argyll. The third defender resided in Lanarkshire and could not be sued in Argyll. The effect of the majority decision was to compel the pursuer to sue all the defenders in one action which he could only do in the Court of Session. There was a resounding attack on this conclusion by Lord Young in a dissenting judgment:

> "I do not think any man of sense can think that that is a sensible or desirable course, if it could be avoided. If it cannot be avoided, of course it must be submitted to, or the claim must be given up altogether, but on the equitable view, and equity has been referred to, I do not think the result can be defended at all.
> I ventured to put the question why the son and daughter wished the action brought in the Court of Session, and I could get no answer, except that the writer would perhaps rather abandon the claim than submit to that tribunal. The suggestion was made that if one of several *correi debendi* had a discharge of the claim against them, injustice would be done to the others if he were not called. But the others could ascertain if that were so, and state it as an equitable ground of defence. In short, the plea in this case is a mere device, and if we give effect to it the result will be to prevent the pursuer going on with the action in the Sheriff Court, and to compel him to come to the Court of Session for no end that I can see."[59]

16–18   The best that can be said of the case is that its application should be restricted as far as possible. A century of experience of delictual claims

---

[57] D. M. Walker, *Delict* (2nd ed., 1981), p. 111 and authorities there cited.
[58] (1890) 17 R. 608.
[59] at p. 621.

suggests that it is not necessary for a pursuer to hazard findings of expenses against him by calling several defenders when it is clear that one solvent defender is liable. Any inconvenience arising from having more than one action may be mitigated by third party procedure.[60]

In cases to which *Neilson* v. *Wilson* does not apply (such as a debt constituted in writing) a person may sue one of several persons jointly and severally responsible. Following the principles established in the law of delict there is no reason why the creditor could not discharge part of his claim against some debtors and pursue his action for the balance against the others, nor why he could not obtain decree against one, and when the decree is not satisfied raise a further action against the other debtors.[61]

Any debtor found liable by decree may sue the other debtors for relief.[62] The rule in delict that a decree must exist before relief is sought is not applicable to the law of contract.[63]

Multiple Creditors

The last complication is the introduction of more than one creditor. If a debtor has separate contracts, each with a different creditor, then each creditor must sue the debtor separately.[64]

There is a different situation if there is one contract between a debtor, on the one hand, and several creditors, on the other. The creditors in that case all have a common interest. They may all sue the debtor together. The question is whether they must.

It is thought that the case law may be explained by the operation of

---

[60] See Rule of Court 85 and rule 50 of the Sheriff Court Ordinary Cause Rules. If the liability is joint only all the defenders must be called according to A. J. G. Mackay, *Manual of Practice in the Court of Session* (1893), p. 172, J. A. Maclaren, *Court of Session Practice* (1916), p. 267 and Gloag, *op. cit.* p. 205. Obviously the plea of "all parties not called" runs into difficulties if all the parties are not subject to the jurisdiction of the Scottish courts, or all of them cannot be traced. It is not appropriate to examine this further here. See Maclaren, *op. cit.*, p. 382.

[61] *Steven* v. *Broady Norman & Co.*, 1928 S.C. 351 and authorities there cited.

[62] *Glasgow Corporation* v. *John Turnbull & Co.*, 1932 S.L.T. 457 at p. 459 *per* Lord Murray; *Palmer* v. *Wick and Pulteneytown Steam Shipping Co. Ltd.* (1894) 21 R.(H.L.) 39. These cases in delict used contract cases as analogies. The contrary is equally arguable given that any money claim can be regarded as a debt, liquid or illiquid, according to the facts.

[63] *N.C.B.* v. *Thomson*, 1959 S.C. 353 at pp. 361, 364 *per* Lord Justice-Clerk Thomson. In a dissenting judgment Lord Strachan mentioned, at p. 382, the rule in contract quoting Stair, I,viii,9 (in the 2nd ed. there are small differences in the text) and Bankt., I,ix,45. See also Gloag, p. 206. There are good reasons for arguing that, in the law of delict, *N.C.B.* v. *Thomson* is an unfortunate decision, but it is not necessary to pursue that here. (See the observations on that case in *British Railways Board* v. *Ross and Cromarty C.C.*, 1974 S.C. 27.)

[64] *Paxton* v. *Brown*, 1908 S.C. 406; *Feld British Agencies* v. *James Pringle*, 1961 S.L.T. 123.

two ideas. The first is that the debtor should not be subject to a plurality of actions. This is more a practical consideration than a point of principle, but it has a familiar application in family claims in delict.[65] There is not only the delay and worry of several actions, but also the increased expense to a debtor in being met with several summonses. If the obligation of the debtor is indivisible, such as liability to deliver a live animal, of necessity part performance cannot be given.

16-24   The second idea points to a contrary conclusion. Whether each creditor may claim the whole of a debt, or only a *pro rata* share, a debt is due. Principle suggests that procedural problems should not bar recovery of the debt. If the consent of the other creditors is unobtainable, either because they refuse it, or are incapable of consenting, or cannot be traced, there is even stronger merit in allowing one creditor to sue alone. In cases of obligations which are indivisible it may be that one creditor should be allowed to claim full performance after which the debtor is discharged and the creditors rights *inter se* must be separately resolved either by referring to an express contract or the principles of quasi-contract.

16-25   The case law has wavered between these two approaches. It is suggested that the best result is obtained by reconciling the equities involved in the facts of each case, and cases with different facts are not necessarily helpful. The cases are conflicting but it is thought the law is this. Where the obligation is not divisible, all the creditors must sue.[66] If it is divisible, any one creditor may sue.[67] He will sue for his share or the whole debt depending on how the obligation is constituted.

16-26   Obligations arising under the law affecting common owners or tenants may be special, there being a tendency to suggest that all must concur in an action.[68] This may do no more than reflect that where property is held by *pro indiviso* proprietors no one proprietor may affect the rights of all without the consent of all.[69] One proprietor may prevent

---

[65] *Allen* v. *McCombie's Tr.*, 1909 S.C. 710 at p. 715 *per* Lord President Dunedin; *Kinnaird* v. *McLean*, 1942 S.C. 448. There are in these cases the further factors that fair assessment of damages would be difficult if separate actions were allowed and also the collective result needs to be appreciated. See *McNeil* v. *National Coal Board*, 1966 S.C. 72 at p. 81 *per* Lord Justice-Clerk Grant, at p. 84 *per* Lord Wheatley.

[66] *Bruce* v. *Hunter*, Nov. 16, 1808, F.C.; *Grozier* v. *Downie* (1871) 9 M. 826 (both cases of removings); *Detrick & Webster* v. *Laing's Patent etc. Sewing Machine Co.* (1885) 12 R. 416.

[67] *Shaw* v. *Gibb's Trs.* (1843) 20 R. 718 (some earlier cases are difficult to reconcile. They are discussed by the Lord Ordinary in this case, having examined the session papers in one of them; *Pyper* v. *Christie* (1878) 6 R. 143).

[68] *e.g. Stewart* v. *Wand* (1842) 4 D. 622; *Schaw* v. *Black* (1889) 16 R. 336; *Graham* v. *Stirling*, 1922 S.C. 90; *Walker* v. *Hendry*, 1925 S.C. 855.

[69] Bell, *Prin.*, s.1072 (4th and 10th eds.); J. Rankine, *Law of Leases* (3rd ed., 1916), p. 82. It is suggested, however, that the equities of the situation may still be considered: *Price* v. *Watson*, 1951 S.C. 359.

alteration of his rights[70] or dispose of his interest or create security over his rights.[71]

POSTSCRIPT

7 It will have been obvious that the three main problems with this branch of the law are: (1) an insistence on a presumption of *pro rata* liability of debtors which may be more honoured in the breach than the observance; (2) uncertainty produced by the lack of development of the law of contract on joint obligants in comparison with the law of delict; and (3) the occasional obstacle of procedural rules. On the last there is strength in this reasoning used in the House of Lords:

> "Procedure is but the machinery of the law after all—the channel and means whereby law is administered and justice reached. It strangely departs from its proper office when, in place of facilitating, it is permitted to obstruct, and even extinguish, legal rights, and is thus made to govern where it ought to subserve."[72]

---

[70] *Johnston* v. *Craufurd* (1855) 17 D. 1023; *Warrand* v. *Watson* (1905) 8 F. 253; *Aberdeen Station Committee* v. *North British Rly.* (1890) 17 R. 975. The special problem of tacit relocation arose in *Smith* v. *Grayton Estates Ltd.*, 1960 S.C. 349.

[71] Bell, *sup. cit.*; *Johnston* v. *Craufurd, sup. cit.* The problems of terminology are discussed in *Mags. of Banff* v. *Ruthin Castle Ltd.*, 1944 S.C. 36 especially *per* Lord Justice-Clerk Cooper at p. 68. He, in a classic dictum, distinguished joint owners and common owners. It is usual to talk of "joint" tenants when consistency may require that they be called "common" tenants. A further complication is that the phrase "common debtor" has different implications.

[72] *Kendall* v. *Hamilton* (1879) 4 App.Cas. 504 at p. 525 *per* Lord Penzance (dissenting); quoted in *Steven* v. *Broady Norman & Co., sup. cit.* at p. 360 *per* Lord Justice–Clerk Alness.

CHAPTER 17

ASSIGNATION

TERMINOLOGY

17–01 The word "assignation" is used at an early date in Scots law. Balfour in his *Practicks* had a section headed: "Anent Assignatioun."[1] His earliest case under that heading is dated 1492 and states that the assignee should make intimation to the debtor. Hope's *Major Practicks* also had a section entitled: "Of Assignations and Intimations."[2]

17–02 In current practice "assignation" is treated as a Scots term and "assignment" as an English term.[3] But it was not always so. Erskine used the terms interchangeably.[4] "Assignment" is found in Bell,[5] in Hume[6] and in a Scottish statute.[7] Therefore, if the term "assignment" is found in a deed, perhaps of English origin, it should on Institutional authority, be treated as equivalent to "assignation."

THE MEANING OF ASSIGNATION

17–03 An assignation is one method of transfer of property. In a refined legal system it might be possible to define, with some confidence, the type of property which could be transferred in this way. But in Scots law there is confusion. The institutional writers vary in their approach. Stair treated personal rights as transmissible by assignation and real rights by dispositions.[8] Erskine viewed assignation as the transmission of all subjects except feudal property, with the consequence that moveables could be assigned.[9] Bell seems to have avoided the problem by discussing assignation of specific types of property.

17–04 The choice of the right word would matter little if all that was involved was selecting a label. But inconsistency in terminology leads to inaccuracy in communication of ideas. There is even more at stake with the concept of assignation. It is a label which carries with it consequences distinct from all other relevant labels. For example, an assignation needs intimation to perfect the right and the maxim *assignatus utitur*

---

[1] Balfour, p. 169. See also Spotiswoode, *Practicks*, p. 18.
[2] Hope, Vol. 11, tit. 12.
[3] See, *e.g.* "assignment" in Bell's *Dictionary*.
[4] Ersk., *Inst.*, III,v,3.
[5] *Prin.*, s.1463; *Comm.*, II,16.
[6] Hume's *Lectures*, Vol. 3, p. 3; see also *Grant* v. *Adamson* (1802) Hume 810, at p. 811 observations from the Bench.
[7] Judicial Factors (Scotland) Act 1889, s.13.
[8] Stair, III,i,1 and III,ii,1: See also Bankt., II,189,1.
[9] Ersk., III,v,1.

jure auctoris applies. It is, therefore, important to decide what types of property can be transmitted by assignation.

What may be Assigned?

(1) Heritage

5   In the normal case a feudal right was transmitted by charter or disposition. The title was completed by an instrument of sasine recorded in the Register of Sasines and now by modern equivalents which are the recording of the charter or disposition in the Register. In feudal theory only a vassal with a recorded title could transmit his right by charter or disposition, because only he could grant a procuratory for resigning lands or warrant for taking seisin.[10] Therefore a person who had an unrecorded title could not use the feudal methods of transmission. A person who had an unrecorded title could, however, assign the unrecorded conveyance.[11]

6   This procedure has been affected by statutory innovation. Deduction of title in dispositions was introduced in 1924[12] which lessened the need for assignation of an unrecorded conveyance and the procedure of assignation was effectively abolished in 1970.[13] Nevertheless this history shows the principle that rights to heritage may be transmitted by assignation.

07   In current practice assignation of rights incidental to heritage is commonplace. Almost every charter or disposition used to have clauses assigning rents and assigning writs and the "writs" assigned included the clauses in them and unrecorded conveyances.[14] There can be assignation of rights of relief of stipend or public burdens.[15] An obligation to reconvey heritage is assignable.[16]

08   Leases of land are heritable. They descend to heirs.[17] But "Leases being originally and essentially personal rights, the proper mode of conveyance of the tenant's right in them is by assignation, not disposition."[18] That is, leases are not feudal, and until the Registration of Leases Act 1857 could not be registered in the Register of Sasines. The

---

[10] Ersk. III,v,1.

[11] Wood, *Lectures*, p. 269; Bell, *Prin.*, s.852.

[12] Conveyancing (Scotland) Act 1924, s.3; and for a limited effect in standard securities by the Conveyancing and Feudal Reform (Scotland) Act 1970, s.12.

[13] 1970 Act, s.48. No doubt the intention was to abolish it completely following on the recommendation of the Halliday Committee but only the permissive sections of the conveyancing statutes of 1868 and 1924 were repealed. In theory it would be possible to use the old methods of transmission, but it is unlikely that the practitioner would.

[14] Titles to Land Consolidation Act 1868, s.8. The need for such clauses was removed by the Land Registration (Scotland) Act 1979, s.16.

[15] Wood, *Lectures*, pp. 148, 243, 244; Conveyancing (Scotland) Act 1874, s.50 as affected by Land Registration (Scotland) Act 1979, s.15(4).

[16] *McCallum's Tr.* v. *McNab* (1877) 4 R. 520.

[17] Rankine, *Leases*, pp. 157 *et seq.*

[18] Rankine, p. 171.

Act having provided for certain long leases to be recorded, also provided for their transmission by assignation.[19]

17–09   A sum secured by real burden is transmissible by assignation. As Lord Balgray put it: "There is here a proper real burden, both by the form of words and the entry on record. But the creditor's interest is of an heritable, not a feudal nature. It passes therefore by assignation, as it also does by a general service. A precept of seisin would have been incompetent; for the creditor had no feudal interest in his person to convey. Any other decision would be dangerous to the law."[20] By the Conveyancing (Scotland) Act 1874,[21] registration of the assignation superseded intimation, but assignation could take the form appropriate to heritable securities.[22]

17–10   The old form of heritable security, a bond and disposition in security, was in two parts, a personal bond and a disposition in security. As a result its transmission needed an assignation and a disposition. This was followed by an instrument of sasine. The old form of deed of transmission was superseded by a statutory form of assignation,[23] but this assignation is performing a function different from other assignations because it is on registration in the Register of Sasines equivalent to a deed followed by a recorded sasine. It has a feudal function which is concealed by the abbreviated forms of modern conveyancing.

17–11   The new form of heritable security, the standard security, introduced by the Conveyancing and Feudal Reform (Scotland) Act 1970 is transmissible by a deed called an assignation with a statutory effect.[24]

17–12   The principle is clear. Heritable rights which have not been feudalised are capable of assignation. However, the term "assignation" has been abused to cover transfer of other rights.

(2)(a) Corporeal moveables

17–13   For a long time there has been a perplexing tendency to refer to assignation of corporeal moveables.[25] Erskine said that, "by assignation in proper speech is understood a written deed of conveyance by the proprietor to another of any subject not properly feudal."[26] From this it

---

[19] s.3. "Tacks in Scotland were held to be personal, because they wanted sasine," (Ross, *Lectures*, Vol. 2, p. 476).

[20] *Miller* v. *Brown* (1820) Hume 540 at pp. 543, 544; Bell, *Prin.*, s.923.

[21] s.30.

[22] A statutory form of assignation of ground annual is regulated by Conveyancing (Scotland) Act 1924, s.23, Sched. K. A ground annual is a form of real burden (*Church of Scotland Endowment Committee* v. *Provident Assoc. of London Ltd.*, 1914 S.C. 165 *per* Lord Dundas at p. 172), but by some confused legislative drafting in 1868 and 1874, a distinction was introduced under which, broadly, real burdens became personal in succession, and ground annuals remained heritable. See McLaren, *Wills*, paras. 380, 381. The Succession (Scotland) Act 1964 did not improve matters. See M. C. Meston, *The Succession (Scotland) Act 1964* (3rd ed., 1982), p. 46.

[23] Titles to Land Consolidation Act 1868, s.124, Sched. (GG).

[24] s.14.

[25] See, *e.g. Thomsone* v. *Chirnside* (1558) Mor. 827.

[26] III,v,1.

logically followed that he could write of assignations "of moveable goods, which sometimes, though improperly, get the name of dispositions, and are completed by an instrument of possession."[27] Later reported case law shows that from time to time assignations of corporeal moveables were granted.[28] Standard forms of trust deeds in the *Encyclopaedia of Scottish Legal Styles* narrate an assignation, disposition or conveyance of moveable property.[29] The reason that this terminology is dangerous is that it would imply the effects of assignation and a need for intimation. A moment's thought would suggest that it would be very strange if an oral transaction relating to goods and the same transaction in writing, both formally valid, could each have quite different implications, with the written transaction being the more likely to confer a defective title.

-14 A simple approach is to say that Erskine was wrong to use the term assignation merely because there was a deed of conveyance. It led him into the trap of assuming that the deed could transfer property. When he wrote, it could not. However, there are more complicated issues involved. It is necessary to distinguish (a) a conveyance of a personal right to moveables and (b) a conveyance of a real right to moveables. Assignation is a term which may be used properly for the first, but preferably not for the second. If a person has a right to moveables under a contract, that right may, in certain circumstances, be assigned.[30] The Transmission of Moveable Property (Scotland) Act 1862 has a form for such an assignation. The difficulty is in the use of the word assignation in the second sense, for conveyance of a real right to moveables, because at common law no amount of "assignation" or intimation could do this. Property in moveables passed on delivery. As Lord President Inglis put it: "A mere assignation of corporeal moveables *retenta possessione* is nothing whatever but a personal obligation, and creates no preference of any kind."[31] Lord Deas added: "but in so far as regards the assignation of the moveables, it is not alleged that any change of possession has followed upon it, and I agree with your Lordship that it is perfectly settled beyond all question in our law and practice that such an assignation if not followed by possession confers no security whatever."[32] The proposition is well established both for security transactions[33] and, at common law, sale.[34]

---

[27] *Ibid.*

[28] *Henry* v. *Robertson and Sime* (1822) 1 S. 399; *Borthwick* v. *Grant* (1829) 7 S. 420; *Sibbald & Son* v. *Walker* (1832) 11 S. 13.

[29] Vol. 9, *s.v.* "Trust Deed for Creditors" and "Trusts."

[30] See *infra*, *s.v.* "Assignation of Contracts" para. 17–36; *Lombard North Central Ltd.* v. *Lord Advocate*, 1983 S.L.T. 361.

[31] *Clark* v. *West Calder Oil Co.* (1882) 9 R. 1017 at p. 1024.

[32] *Ibid.*, p. 1026. *McEwan, Sons & Co.* v. *Smith* (1849) 6 Bell 340.

[33] *McBain* v. *Wallace & Co.* (1881) 8 R.(H.L.) 106; *Hepburn* v. *Law*, 1914 S.C. 918; *Scottish Transit Trust* v. *Scottish Land Cultivators*, 1955 S.C. 254; *G. & C. Finance Corporation* v. *Brown*, 1961, S.L.T. 408; *Ladbroke Leasing (South West) Ltd.* v. *Reekie Plant Ltd.*, 1983 S.L.T. 155.

[34] *e.g.* Bell, *Prin.*, s.1300; see now Sale of Goods Act 1979, s.17.

17–15   An assignation of an incorporeal right can be a deed of conveyance. An "assignation of corporeals," at common law, is not. The difference is simple and vital. We should, despite Erskine, and despite statutory changes in the law of sale, not use the term assignation for the transfer of property in corporeal moveables. There is much sense in what Ross said long ago: "It is proper, therefore, to keep up a distinction in terms between deeds which have a separate mode of execution. Where moveables are transmitted, and require possession and delivery, let us term the deed a disposition of moveables; and, where debts, rights or actions, are to be made over, and which can only be completed by intimation, let us continue to term them assignations."[35]

17–16   To conclude this section, it is necessary to mention two types of transaction with moveables which look like assignation. These involve delivery orders and bills of lading. In neither case is the deed truly an assignation.

(2)(b) Delivery orders

17–17   If an independent custodier holds goods, transfer of the goods is possible by transfer of a delivery order followed by intimation to the custodier.[36] Whether the delivery order achieves this effect depends on the nature of the transaction giving rise to it.[37] If property is transferred there has been the equivalent of delivery of the corpus of the goods. It is not an assignation even though it is sometimes called that[38] and is in the form of a deed followed by intimation. The transferee does not take the goods subject to all the pleas competent against his author.

(2) (c) Bills of lading

17–18   Indorsation and delivery of a bill of lading passes property in the goods to which it refers although Lord Bramwell said that the property passes by the contract under which the indorsement was made.[39] Thus cargo afloat could be sold without indorsing a bill of lading.[40] The bill is evidence of the terms of a contract, rather than the contract itself.[41] The

---

[35] Ross, *Lectures*, Vol. 1, pp. 189, 190. He is supported by Hume, *Lectures*, Vol. 3, p. 8.

[36] *Anderson* v. *McCall* (1866) 4 M. 765; *Connal & Co.* v. *Loder* (1868) 6 M. 1095; *Rhind's Tr.* v. *Robertson & Baxter* (1891) 18 R. 623; *Inglis* v. *Robertson & Baxter* (1898) 25 R.(H.L.) 70; *Dobell Beckett & Co.* v. *Neilson* (1904) 7 F. 281.

[37] See *Commercial Bank* v. *Kennard* (1859) 21 D. 864. The order could create an obligation independent of an antecedent contract but it is not then the normal type of delivery order. *Dimmack* v. *Dixon* (1856) 18 D. 428.

[38] *Connal and Co.* v. *Loder, sup. cit.*

[39] Decided in *Lickbarrow* v. *Mason* (1794) 5 T.R. 683, *Sewell* v. *Burdwick* (1884) 10 App.Cas. 74, *Hayman & Son* v. *McLintock*, 1907 S.C. 936. The modern law is in *inter alia* Scrutton on *Charterparties* (18th ed., 1974), s.X.

[40] *Sewell* v. *Burdwick, sup. cit.* at p. 105. The accuracy of this analysis for Scots common law, which has an insistence on delivery of deeds or an equivalent, is debatable.

[41] *The Ardennes* [1951] 1 K.B. 55.

effect of the indorsement depends on the particular circumstances of the case.

19   The speciality with a bill of lading is that, even under Scots common law, delivery of the goods was not necessary to transfer property[42] but the transaction with the bill is the equivalent of delivery. Although the bill may contain such words as "to order or assigns" it is confusing to regard the transfer as an assignation. The transfer does not require intimation and it does not have the same effect as the assignation of personal rights followed by intimation.

(3) Assignation of incorporeal rights

20   The type of property which may be assigned can be described in a somewhat negative way as property for which another method of transfer is not prescribed. In practice the result is that assignation is *inter vivos* transfer of either incorporeal moveables or unfeudalised heritable rights. We cannot say that all types of property in these two classes may be assigned, but we can affirm that if transfer is possible or can be effective, assignation is usually the appropriate method.

21   The *Encyclopaedia of Scottish Legal Styles* gives examples of the use of assignations. Under the obvious headings there are styles of assignation of debts, life policies, interests in testamentary estates and trusts, and trade marks. The difficult issues arise when the law does not permit transfer of the property or gives the transfer a limited effect.

22   As always when problems of invalidity are involved the analysis is not simple. There are several different forms of incomplete assignation. Assume that A has a contract with B. B wishes to assign his rights under the contract to C. The following may arise.

(1) B may assign the right to C. On intimation of the assignation to A, C has a real right to what was assigned.

23   This is normal, *e.g.* the assignation of life policy. A is the insurance company and B is the policy holder. C has rights against B and A.

(2) B cannot effectively assign a right to C.

24   This is the complete contrast with (1). Assignation is denied effect by the law, *e.g.* the assignation of army pay or supplementary benefit. The assignation is void, with the result that C acquires no rights against B or A.

(3) B may assign to C, but the assignation is not binding on A.

25   This may be the result of an assignation of an alimentary fund.[43] A cannot become liable to pay C, but there is a contract between B and C and B's failure to transfer an effective right to C, could be a breach of warrandice. C acquires rights against B, but not A.

(4) B may assign to C, but the assignation is not binding on B.

---

[42] *Buchanan & Cochrane* v. *Swan* (1764) Mor. 14208; *Bogle* v. *Dunmore* (1787) Mor. 14216; *McClelland* v. *Rodger & Co.* (1842) 4 D. 646 at p. 658 *per* Lord Medwyn. See also *Sanders* v. *Maclean* (1883) 11 Q.B.D. 327 at p. 341 *per* Bowen L.J.

[43] See *infra*.

17–26   *E.g.* an assignation of future wages by a seaman.[44] The assignation is binding on only one party. It resembles the limping invalidity mentioned in connection with minors' contracts.[45] The contract is binding on C, so although C acquires no rights, he may be under obligations to B.

17–27   An assignation, or an agreement to assign, may be void, voidable, illegal or unenforceable, like any contract and the possible permutations of invalidity are numerous.[46] Examples of specific problems with invalid assignations follow.

VOID ASSIGNATIONS

17–28   The factors which make any contract void will likewise affect an assignation, *e.g.* an assignation will be void if *ultra vires* of the cedent.[47] There may also be some rights which are so personal that they cannot be transferred. An instance is the right of a child to challenge a will under the *conditio si testator sine liberis decesserit*.[48] Statute frequently provides that an assignation shall be void, or of no effect. Examples may be found in provisions on the pay and pensions of the armed forces[49] and of the police,[50] on supplementary benefits,[51] trading with the enemy[52] and the office of company director.[53]

ALIMENTARY FUNDS

17–29   It is sometimes said that an alimentary fund is "unassignable." It may be more accurate to say that it might be assigned, but the assignation is ineffective to transfer a right except to a very limited extent. Lord President Inglis said in the context of a gratuitous alimentary allowance:

> "an assignation of an alimentary allowance, even though dependent on the free will of the person making the allowance, is no doubt quite legal. But the effect of the assignation is a different thing. Its effect is to bind the person making the assignation. . . . But it cannot put the assignee in a better position than the cedent as regards the person making the allowance. No legal obligation is transferred by the assignation, and no intimation could create a legal obligation, for that would be against the rule *assignatus utitur jure auctoris*."[54]

---

[44] Merchant Shipping Act 1970, s.11. The intention presumably is that the assignation does not bind the employer either.

[45] See para. 8–20.

[46] See Chap. 26. But many variations can exist.

[47] See example in *Lloyd's Bank* v. *Morrison & Son*, 1927 S.C. 571.

[48] *Stevenson's Trs.* v. *Stevenson*, 1932 S.C. 657.

[49] Naval and Marine Pay and Pensions Act 1865, ss.4 and 5; Army Act 1955, s.203; Air Force Act 1955, s.203.

[50] Police Pensions Act 1976, s.9.

[51] Supplementary Benefits Act 1976, s.16.

[52] Trading with the Enemy Act 1939, ss.4 and 13.

[53] Companies Act 1985, s.308.

[54] *Robertson* v. *Wright* (1873) 1 R. 237 at p. 245.

30   Ineffective assignation is a consequence of a fund being alimentary. Conversely indications of whether a fund may be assigned, may be used to decide whether the fund is alimentary. If it is declared that the fund may not be assigned[55] or there is a statutory prohibition on assignation,[56] these are indications of the alimentary nature of the fund. The indication is the other way in the absence of such a declaration.[57] The moral for a draftsman is obvious.

31   Once an alimentary fund has been paid out the recipient may dispose of it.[58] An alimentary fund is assigned effectively so far as the aliment is excessive.[59]

SPES SUCCESSIONIS AND FUTURE RIGHTS

32   A *spes successionis* is the right or hope of succession to property as under a will, or marriage contract or trust deed or on intestacy.[60] It is distinguishable from a *jus crediti* which is a vested right.

33   In Roman law trafficking in a right of succession by an heir was *contra bonos mores*. This rule was not followed in Scotland.[61] It was observed in argument that, "the Romans, a jealous people, much given to poisoning, did restrict such bargainings, but our law has repudiated these niceties, and sustained such pactions."[62]

34   The result is that a *spes successionis* may be sold and assigned, even though it is not attachable by creditors.[63] But the assignation has this peculiarity that it has been held that to complete the right intimation must wait until the right has vested, and the assignor has a debtor.[64] However the logic appears to have been departed from in *Browne's Tr* v. *Anderson*[65] in which intimation of an assignation of a *spes successionis* took place before vesting. The problem raised remains to be fully

---

[55] *Dewar's Trs.* v. *Dewar*, 1910 S.C. 730. But, of course, there is no point in declaring a right of fee alimentary and non-assignable. *Rothwell* v. *Stuart's Trs.* (1898) 1 F. 81. Scots law does not recognise alimentary fees.

[56] *Macdonald's Tr.* v. *Macdonald*, 1938 S.C. 536.

[57] *Reliance Mutual Life Ass. Soc.* v. *Halkett's Factor* (1891) 18 R. 615; *Douglas Gardiner & Mill* v. *Mackintosh's Tr.*, 1916 S.C. 125.

[58] *Hewats* v. *Roberton* (1881) 9 R. 175.

[59] *Livingstone* v. *Livingstone* (1886) 14 R. 43; *Claremont's Trs.* v. *Claremont* (1896) 4 S.L.T. 144; but the court will not grant a declaration in advance that an assignation of an excess is valid. *Cuthbert* v. *Cuthbert's Trs.*, 1908 S.C. 967; *Coles* 1951 S.C. 608.

[60] See *Salaman* v. *Tod*, 1911 S.C. 1214 at p.1223 *per* Lord Johnston. *Encyclopaedia of the Laws of Scotland*, Vol. 14, s.v. "Spes Successionis."

[61] Ersk. III,iii,84; *Aikenhead* v. *Bothwell* (1630) Mor. 9491; *Ragg* v. *Brown* (1708) Mor. 9492.

[62] *Ragg* v. *Brown*, *sup. cit.* at p. 9493.

[63] *Trappes* v. *Meredith* (1871) 10 M. 38; *Reid* v. *Morison* (1893) 20 R. 510; *Salaman* v. *Tod*, 1911 S.C. 1214; *Coats* v. *Bannochie's Trs.*, 1912 S.C. 329. See now Bankruptcy (Scotland) Act 1985, s.31(5).

[64] *Bedwells & Yates* v. *Tod*, Dec. 2, 1819, F.C.; *Pearson, Wilson & Co.* v. *Brock* (1842) 4 D. 1509.

[65] (1901) 4 F. 305.

argued.[66] In theory the same problem with intimation should arise with other hopes of acquisition, such as a claim for compensation, or entitlement to prizes in a future competition, or future rights to royalties or profits, or a conveyance of acquirenda.

CLAIMS IN LITIGATION

17–35   A claim for damages may be assigned, such as a claim for damages for breach of contract,[67] a claim which includes solatium,[68] a claim by a company against a director for breach of trust,[69] or a right to reduce a lease.[70] The assignation should be granted before the assignee raises an action[71] although in certain cases an assignee may sue before a formal defect in his title is cured.[72]

CONTRACTS

17–36   Rights and obligations under a contract may be assigned provided that they do not involve *delectus personae*. Although it is common to refer to a contract being assigned, this expression is capable of producing error. Sometimes part of a contract is assignable, and part not. The appropriate question is whether a particular right or obligation may be assigned. The determining factor is the presence or absence of *delectus personae*.

(1) Delectus personae

17–37   *Delectus personae* is the choice of a particular person which implies the exclusion of others. An agreement to marry is the clearest case. No normal person would accept at the altar or registrar's desk a substitute for the chosen one. So it is with commercial partnerships and contracts of service. Some tasks may be delegated. The relationship may be repeated with others. But enforced substitution is not expected. Lord President Dunedin analysed the concept further in one of the classic cases, *Cole v. C. H. Handasyde & Co.*[73] He said:

   "Nobody doubts that the law as to whether a contract is assignable or not depends upon whether, as the expression goes, there is

---

[66] See the Lord Ordinary in *Carter* v. *McIntosh* (1862) 24 D. 925 and *infra, s.v.* "When should intimation be made?" para. 17–106.

[67] *Constant* v. *Kincaid & Co.* (1902) 4 F. 901.

[68] *Traill & Sons* v. *Actieselskabat Dalbeattie Ltd.* (1904) 6 F. 798; *Cole-Hamilton* v. *Boyd*, 1963 S.C.(H.L.) 1.

[69] *Davidson (Liquidator) Larkhall Collieries Ltd.* v. *Hamilton* (1906) 14 S.L.T. 68, 202.

[70] *Edinburgh Entertainments Ltd.* v. *Stevenson*, 1926 S.C. 363.

[71] *Symington* v. *Campbell* (1894) 21 R. 434; *Bentley* v. *Macfarlane*, 1964 S.C. 76: the relevance, however, of *Rackstraw* v. *Douglas*, 1919 S.C. 354, which was not discussed in *Bentley*, will need to be argued some day.

[72] *Doughty Shipping Co. Ltd.* v. *N.B. Rly. Co.* (1909) 1 S.L.T. 267; *Westville Shipping Co.* v. *Abram Steamship Co.*, 1923 S.C.(H.L.) 68. On the technicalities of who has a title to sue see *infra*, para. 17–93.

[73] 1910 S.C. 68 at p. 73.

the element of *delectus personae* in it or not. Now, I think by way of illustration there are three stages to be taken. The highest and easiest example of a contract in which there is *delectus personae* is where the contract is one for a personal service of a peculiar nature. Nobody supposes that in a contract with A or B to paint a picture or write a book it is possible for A or B to say,—'I will get someone else to paint you the picture or write you the book, and that must satisfy you, and you must pay me the price.' Next you have another class where the *delectus personae* is not so clear. I mean the case of manufactured articles. It may quite well be that an article is of such a character and quality and the reputation of the manufacturer such that, when you contract for a thing from so-and-so, you really imply that the article is to be made by so-and-so. For instance, a contract for a gun from Purdie would not be well implemented by giving you a gun bought in the ordinary market in Birmingham. There are of course cases where it is not very easy to determine on which side the matter falls, but these are cases where the difficulty lies in the application of the law to the particular circumstances. But when you come away from manufacturers, and that is the case here, and when you come to a contract with a person who does not himself manufacture and does not profess to—a contract for goods of a certain description (it really does not matter whether at this present moment these goods have been made or not)—then it seems to me that you may go on and contract in one form or another. You may either say,—'I contract with you that you shall supply me with goods as to which you shall do something, or as to which you shall satisfy yourself in such-and-such a way,' and then you really incorporate into your contract for the goods a contract also for the personal services of the person with whom you contract. Or, on the other hand, you may contract for an article, and then stipulate that the article is to be of a certain standard which is specified in the contract, and say no more. It seems to me that in the latter case the whole element of *delectus personae* is gone."

-38   It is clear from this that the issue is the intention of the parties. To decide this, the relevant points include (1) the type of contract, (2) the terms of the contract and (3) the nature of the respective businesses of the parties. A full examination of the factors requires a proof or an equivalent.[74] There is an unfortunate tendency to regard a decision on one set of facts as ruling another case, thus allowing a decision on a preliminary plea.[75]

(2) The terms of the contract

-39   Because the assignability or otherwise of rights under a contract is determined by the intention of the parties, a draftsman may state that intention and avoid the problems of *delectus personae*. It is common to find in commercial contracts a clause similar to this: "Neither party may

---

[74] As in two famous cases *Cole* v. *Handasyde & Co.*, *sup. cit.* and *Berlitz School of Languages* v. *Duchene* (1903) 6 F. 181.

[75] *e.g. Grierson, Oldham & Co.* v. *Forbes, Maxwell & Co.* (1895) 22 R. 812; *Rodger* v. *Herbertson*, 1909 S.C. 256.

assign this contract, or any part of it, without the consent of the other party, which consent will not be unreasonably withheld." This is useful in most contracts for sale or services. If assignation of all rights arising under the contract is controlled, the right to receive payment may not be assigned, without the consent of the debtor, to a debt collector, or a ruthless competitor.

17–40   A few reported cases show that the practice in one area might be improved. So far as is known it is not usual to have an express provision on assignation in restraint of trade clauses. This has led to difficulties. X sells his business to Y and agrees not to compete with Y. If several years later Y sells to Z, may he assign to Z the restraint of trade clause in the contract with X? The prudent negotiators of the contract between X and Y would have foreseen the problem. Usually, of course, Y will wish an express power to assign.

17–41   A restraint of trade clause for a piano tuner was assignable, in part because there was consent to assignation in the contract.[76] A restraint in practising contained in an agreement for sale of a medical practice could have been assigned if appropriately framed, but the term "successors" did not imply consent to assignation.[77] An obligation in favour of the Crown only was not assignable to a vassal.[78] On construction of the deed, an option to have shares reconveyed was not transmissible.[79]

(3) Examples of delectus personae

17–42   Examples of contracts involving *delectus personae* include a contract of service of a manager of a newspaper,[80] a contract of service as a language teacher,[81] a contract to act as an estate agent,[82] a contract for the supply and erection of a machine,[83] a contract for advertisement in the wine list of a company,[84] permission to erect a pier at Leith[85] and an agreement on sale of a medical practice.[86]

17–43   Examples of contracts where there was no *delectus personae* include a contract to fit a crane and supply pipes and plugs,[87] a restraint of trade clause in a contract for the sale of a cab-hiring business,[88] the execution of a contract to pave streets and maintain the surface, being a contract

---

[76] *Methven Simpson Ltd.* v. *Jones*, 1910 2 S.L.T. 14.

[77] *Rodger* v. *Herbertson*, 1909 S.C. 256.

[78] *Orr Ewing* v. *Earl of Cawdor* (1884) 12 R.(H.L.) 12.

[79] *Tawse's Trs.* v. *Lord Advocate*, 1943 S.C. 124.

[80] *Ross* v. *McFarlane* (1894) 21 R. 396—the assignation was itself a breach of the contract of service.

[81] *Berlitz School of Languages* v. *Duchene* (1903) 6 F. 181.

[82] *L. Lennox Martin Ltd.* v. *Ormiston*, 1957 S.L.T.(Sh.Ct.) 59.

[83] *International Fibre Syndicate* v. *Dawson* (1901) 3 F.(H.L.) 32.

[84] *Grierson, Oldham & Co.* v. *Forbes, Maxwell & Co.* (1895) 22 R. 812.

[85] *Leith Dock Commrs.* v. *Colonial Life Ass. Co.* (1861) 24 D. 64.

[86] *Rodger* v. *Herbertson*, 1909 S.C. 256.

[87] *Brown* v. *Canon Co. Ltd.* (1898) 6 S.L.T. 90—the ground of decision is obscure.

[88] *Fraser & Son* v. *Renwick* (1906) 14 S.L.T. 443.

consisting mainly of manual labour,[89] a contract to supply grease conforming to specification[90] and the right to obtain delivery of a ship under a contract of sale.[91] In a case on sub-contracting, not assignation, it was said that there was no *delectus personae* in a contract to beat a carpet.[92]

(4) Contract in part assignable, in part unassignable

–44 It has been observed in the House of Lords:

"The principle that contracts involving *delectus personae* are not assignable is well rooted in Scots law as well as in the law of other countries. It may, however, be conceded to the appellant that it does not necessarily follow from this that a right may not arise out of an unassignable contract which is itself assignable. I prefer in a Scotch case to call such a right *jus crediti* rather than chose-in-action. The simplest case would be that of a money claim pure and simple which has accrued."[93]

This analysis needs to be taken further. A common mistake is to assume that a contract is either assignable or unassignable. Contracts are often far too complex for such a simple approach. They are a bundle of rights and obligations. A partnership, for example, has amongst its rights, a right to profits, a right to share in proceeds on dissolution, a right to indemnification for payment made and liabilities incurred, a right to take part in the management of the business, and a right to inspect the books of the business. It is not appropriate to ask, "is a partnership assignable?" Instead we should ask whether a particular right is assignable, and the answer is that some are, and some are not.[94]

7–45 Take even the clearest case of a contract which is said to be unassignable. X agrees to paint the portrait of Y for £1,000. X paints the portrait. Does anyone doubt that he may assign his right to receive £1,000 to Z? Why can he not assign his contingent right to receive payment before painting the portrait? Surely Y could assign to his wife or his trustee under a trust deed, Y's right to receive the portrait or his claim for damages if X fails to perform? When the contract is analysed carefully it may be found that the only matter which cannot be assigned is the painting of the portrait. It is a mistake to assume that *delectus personae*

---

[89] *Asphaltic Limestone Concrete Co.* v. *Glasgow Corp.*, 1907 S.C. 463. But despite the rubric of the report, this might be a case of subcontracting or delegation. The party to the action was the original contractor, the company in liquidation, but as an assignee may sue in his cedent's name, that is not conclusive.

[90] *Cole* v. *Handasyde & Co.*, 1910 S.C. 68.

[91] *Dampskibsaktieselskapet Aurdal* v. *Companie de Navegacion La Estrella*, 1916 S.C. 882.

[92] *Stevenson & Sons* v. *Maule*, 1920 S.C. 335. On the relationship between subcontracting and assignation see below, *s.v.* "Assignation and Delegation" para. 17–50.

[93] *International Fibre Syndicate Ltd.* v. *Dawson* (1901) 3 F.(H.L.) 32 at p. 33 *per* Lord Robertson.

[94] *Cassels* v. *Stewart* (1879) 6 R. 936 at p. 941 *per* Lord Curriehill; at p. 945 *per* Lord Justice-Clerk Moncreiff; at p. 955 *per* Lord Gifford; on appeal 8 R.(H.L.) 1. See now Partnership Act 1890, s.31; Miller, *Partnership*, pp. 411–418.

affects all the rights in a contract. All the concept does is to make certain performance personal to a contracting party, so that performance by another is not performance in terms of the contract.[95]

ASSIGNATION OF OBLIGATIONS

17–46 Is *an obligation* assignable? It may be assigned with the consent of the creditor. But also it appears that an obligation may be assigned without the consent of the creditor in the obligation. In *Cole* v. *Handasyde & Co.*[96] a contract to supply grease conform to specification was held assignable. To be more accurate the supplier's obligations under the contract were assignable. The refiner and distiller of black grease who had contracted with oil and seed merchants found, no doubt to his surprise, that he had instead a contract with a chartered accountant.

17–47 It is not surprising that the law in general refers to intimation of an assignation to the *debtor*, with the implication that it is creditors who assign. There are problems raised by *Cole* v. *Handasyde & Co.* and the case should some day be reconsidered.[97]

17–48 The difficulties are:

(1) Assignation of an obligation involves substitution of one debtor for another. This change may not be to the creditor's benefit.

(2) There is commonly some ground for the selection of a supplier, whether it is business reputation or financial standing. While delegation of a task may be permitted, most people expect to be able to sue the person with whom they contracted.

INEFFECTIVE ASSIGNATION

17–49 At an earlier point[98] it was explained that there are various types of ineffective assignation. What is the type of invalidity if a right which is unassignable, because of the principle of *delectus personae*, is in fact assigned? Assume, for example, an unassignable restraint of trade provision in a contract between X and Y. The clause is assigned by X to Z. Y is clearly not affected, but it does not mean the assignation is void merely because it is an ineffective transfer. More likely Z has a claim against X for breach of warrandice. However, in a peculiar case the assignee of a lease was held to have been presumed to know of the pro-

---

[95] An example is a contract of sale under which the obligation to pay the price was not assigned but the right to demand delivery was assigned—*Dampskibsaktieselskapet Aurdal* v. *Compania de Navegacion La Estrella*, 1916 S.C. 882.

[96] *Sup. cit.*

[97] Gloag frequently cited the case, but he probably had doubts about it. See *Contract*, p. 423, n. 7, and p. 424.

[98] paras. 17–22 to 17–28.

hibition of assignation in the lease.[99] It is doubtful if this is of general application to contract. It is suggested that when an unassignable right is assigned, the assignee may acquire rights against his cedent, but not against the debtor.[1]

ASSIGNATION AND DELEGATION

50 The concept of *delectus personae* is referred to both in cases on assignation and cases on delegation or subcontracting. This reference to one idea should not lead to the conclusion that it operates in the same way in both methods of contracting. After an assignation the debtor is bound to the assignee instead of the cedent. On one view, but as mentioned above not the present view of Scots law, this procedure arises only on the transfer of rights not obligations. Delegation is the shifting of obligations, but the subcontractor does not become liable under the original contract. There is a substitution of performance, but not a substitution of all the obligations under the contract.

51 The result should be that delegation, with its more limited effects, is easier to imply than assignation. If A is to manufacture my iron plates I may be content that he delegates to B. It does not follow that I would wish to claim damages against B for defective performance. The financial status of A is important to me. So I might reasonably object to assignation to B.

52 It would follow from this, however, that if delegation is prohibited on the grounds of *delectus personae*, assignation should also be prohibited. Unfortunately the most useful examples which we have go the other way and show when delegation is permitted. It is a *non sequitur* that assignation should also be permitted in the same cases.[2]

53 A case of subcontracting with useful examples of *delectus personae* is *West Stockton Iron Co.* v. *Nielson & Maxwell*[3] a case of manufacture of iron plates with reference to the sawing of wood, malting and milling of flours as instances where delegation was allowed, and the contrary when goods were ordered to be made by a specified person.[4] In *Stevenson & Sons* v. *Maule & Son*[5] it was said that there was no *delectus personae* in a contract to beat a carpet.

---

[99] *Leechman & Edington* v. *Sievwright* (1826) 4 S. 683. The case involved the use of a shop for an exhibition of wax figures and of "a rare species of man, having scales on his breast and arms."

[1] See discussion of warrandice para. 17–105.

[2] A further example: I employ X solicitor. He delegates work to an assistant and a typist. So be it. It does not follow that I would with equanimity accept an assignation of the contract to the typist.

[3] (1880) 7 R. 1055.

[4] At p. 1060. The brand name example must be modified in the light of modern manufacturing practices.

[5] 1920 S.C. 335.

LEASES

17–54 Leases are peculiar because *delectus personae* is presumed to exist on one side only. Assignation by the tenant is incompetent unless (1) there is express power in the lease to assign or (2) the lease is in one of the categories in which the power is implied, such as a lease of an urban tenement. The subject is considered in detail by Rankine, to which reference should be made.[6]

MARRIED WOMEN'S POLICIES OF ASSURANCE

17–55 The Married Women's Policies of Assurance (Scotland) Act 1880 provided in section 2 that a policy of assurance effected by any married man on his own life, and expressed upon the face of it to be for the benefit of his wife, or of his children, or of his wife and children, was deemed trust. An assignation of this type of policy in security of a loan was held invalid.[7] Despite this assignations were from time to time granted to Scottish banks and there was an argument that the case law had been superseded.[8] In any event the case law is now affected by the Married Women's Policies of Assurance (Scotland) (Amendment) Act 1980 which provides in section 3 that a beneficiary under the policy may assign his or her interest under the policy whether in security or otherwise.[9]

FORM OF ASSIGNATION

(1) Agreement to assign

17–56 Scots law recognises that transfer of rights may take place in two stages, first the agreement to transfer and secondly, the conveyance. Assignation is no exception. There can be an agreement to assign followed by the assignation. Sometimes the agreement to assign is omitted. The separation of the two stages is vital, because only the second stage operates as a conveyance. There is perhaps a special problem with assignation because the conveyance may be in informal terms. The formalities of transfer do not look much different from the agreement to

---

[6] Rankine, *Leases*, Chap. IX. See also, Paton & Cameron, *Landlord & Tenant*, Chap. X.

[7] *Scottish Life Ass. Co.* v. *John Donald Ltd.* (1901) 9 S.L.T. 200; *Edinburgh Life Ass. Co.* v. *Balderston* (1909) 2 S.L.T. 323; *Pender* v. *Commercial Bank of Scotland*, 1940 S.L.T. 306. The basic problem was the limited control a married woman had over her property including ante-nuptial and post-nuptial provisions for her benefit.

[8] See E. M. Clive, *Husband & Wife* (2nd ed., 1982), p. 329.

[9] If the validity of an assignation prior to Oct. 29, 1980 is in issue there are two arguments in favour of validity: (1) the case law referred to was superseded by *Beith's Tr.* v. *Beith*, 1950 S.C. 66; and (2) if the assignation was with absolute warrandice, the principle of accretion gives the assignee a good title. On accretion see *inter alia* Ersk. II,vii,3; Wood's *Lectures*, p. 148.

transfer. This would not have happened at common law with other types of transfer of property.

57   The moral for the draftsman is that he must be clear which stage is his concern. For example, a statement: "We agree to assign the patent," on a strict construction may be the first stage, but could be intended to be the conveyance. The ambiguity should be avoided.

58   In *Bank of Scotland* v. *Liquidators of Hutchison Main & Co.*[10] there was an undertaking to make a debenture available to a bank. There was an enforceable contract, but it had not been implemented by assignation. In other words the bank were only at the stage of agreement to assign. There had been no transfer to them. The result was that the bank had no claim to the debenture on the liquidation of the promissor. Similarly in *Alderwick* v. *Craig*[11] the pursuer had at best an undertaking to give him a debt. There was no completed donation because the debt had not been assigned. The pursuer, therefore, had no title to sue the debtor.

59   Although it is not clearly decided, it is thought that the assignation must be in writing whereas a contract to assign may be oral.[12]

(2) Legal assignation

60   Assignation, in the form of a conveyance, may occur by operation of law. "An arrester who follows up his arrestment by a process of furthcoming is a legal assignee. So is a trustee in bankruptcy."[13] A contract in a bill of lading is assigned to consignees and indorsees.[14] The certified copy interlocutor of the appointment of a judicial factor, trustee, tutor, curator, or other person judicially appointed and subject to the Factors Acts operates as an "assignment."[15] There can be transfer by legislation when a public corporation acquires assets.[16]

(3) Terms of assignation

61   An assignation does not need special words. In the view of Lord Justice-Clerk Inglis: "if anything is settled in the law of Scotland, it is that no words directly importing conveyance are necessary to constitute an assignation, but that any words giving authority or directions, which if

---

[10] 1914 S.C.(H.L.) 1.

[11] 1916 2 S.L.T. 161.

[12] See Walker and Walker, *Evidence*, p. 111. But an assignation will frequently be a writ *in re mercatoria* and informal writing will suffice—*op. cit.*, p. 101.

[13] *Douglas Gardiner & Mill* v. *Mackintosh's Trs.*, 1916 S.C. 125 at p. 128 *per* Lord Salvesen. See Stair's treatment of arrestment and adjudication in the context of assignation. Stair, III,i,24. See also Bankruptcy (Scotland) Act 1985, s.31.

[14] Bills of Lading Act 1855, s.1.

[15] Judicial Factors (Scotland) Act 1889, s.13 as amended by Act of Sederunt, March 17, 1967; See also *Campbell's J.F.* v. *National Bank of Scotland*, 1944 S.C. 495.

[16] *e.g.* Post Office Act 1969, s.16; British Telecommunications Act 1981, s.10; Telecommunications Act 1984, s.60; Local Government (Scotland) Act 1973, s.222; S.I. 1975 No. 659.

fairly carried out will operate a transference, are sufficient to make an assignation."[17] So there was an assignation with the words, "I hand you two policies of insurance . . . which I give you as added security for the loan"[18] and with the words, "I . . . hand over my life policy."[19] The difficulty is shown by the second case which was heard by a total of four judges of whom only two were in favour of the final result. The phrase "hand over" is ambiguous. It could be transfer of the *corpus* of a document or the transfer of the rights represented by the document. Merely to transfer the *corpus* would not be an assignation, leaving aside the specialities of negotiable instruments.[20]

17–62   As Lord Justice-Clerk Moncreiff put it: "Any words which express a present intention to transfer are sufficient as an assignation, apart altogether from forms of style or the schedules of the recent statute."[21] The statute referred to is discussed later.[22] The best word to use is "assign."[23] It is common but superfluous to have a destination to "heirs and assignees" or "executors and assignees" or "successors and assignees."[24] The transmission of the right must, however, be distinguished from its original constitution. If a contract states that a right is in favour of A and his assignees, that is important in deciding whether the right is assignable.[25]

17–63   There has been an assignation with the indorsation on the back of an account by the creditor: "Pay the within account to Ritchie Laurie."[26] The granting of a general factory or mandate has been held to be an assignation for the purposes of irritating a lease.[27] A document in the form of a bill of exchange is an assignation. Using a bill, X orders his debtor to pay Y. As Lord Justice-Clerk Inglis said: "an order to pay, or a precept to pay, is one of the best known forms of assignation in the law of Scotland."[28] The result is that for this purpose it is immaterial if the document fails to comply with all the form necessary for a bill. It need not be negotiable to be an assignation.[29]

---

[17] *Carter* v. *McIntosh* (1862) 24 D. 925 at p. 933.

[18] *Caledonian Insurance Co.* v. *Beattie* (1898) 5 S.L.T. 349.

[19] *Brownlee* v. *Robb*, 1907 S.C. 1302.

[20] *Richards* v. *Cuthbert* (1866) 1 S.L.R. 128 (handing over I.O.U. not assignation).

[21] *McCutcheon* v. *McWilliam* (1876) 3 R. 565 at p. 571.

[22] See paras. 17–75 to 17–78.

[23] See Wood's *Lectures*, pp. 580 *et seq.*

[24] Wood, *op. cit.* p. 580; *Johnstone-Beattie* v. *Dalzell* (1868) 6 M. 333 at p. 344 *per* Lord President Inglis; *Findlay* v. *Mackenzie* (1875) 2 R. 909 at p. 915 *per* Lord President Inglis.

[25] See para. 17–39.

[26] *Laurie* v. *Ogilvy* Feb. 6, 1810, F.C.: See also *Ritchie* v. *McLachlan* (1870) 8 M. 815. Stair, III,i,3: "the like is done amongst merchants, by orders, whereby their debtors are ordered to pay such a person their debt, which indeed is a mandate; but if it be to his own behoof, it is properly an assignation."

[27] *Lyon* v. *Irvine* (1874) 1 R. 512.

[28] *Carter* v. *McIntosh* (1862) 24 D. 925 at p. 935.

[29] *Campbell, Thomson & Co.* v. *Glass*, May 28, 1803, F.C.; *Carter* v. *McIntosh, sup. cit.*; *Ritchie* v. *McLachlan, sup. cit.*; *British Linen Co.* v. *Rainey's Trs.* (1885) 12 R. 825; Bills of Exchange Act 1882, s.53(2) which is modified in the case of a stopped cheque by the Law Reform (Miscellaneous Provisions) (Scotland) Act 1985, s.11.

(4) A cheque as an assignation

64   Controversy surrounds the status of a cheque as an assignation. There
is no immediately obvious reason why a cheque should not operate as an
assignation, in the same way as a bill of exchange. Using a cheque, X
orders his debtor to pay Y with the differences from a bill that the
debtor must be a bank and payment must be on demand. Neither of
these differences affects the transfer of the right from X to Y.

65   The problem arises because it has several times been stated that only
a cheque for value operates as an assignation. Onerosity is presumed
with a bill but not with a cheque which must be proved to be for value to
operate as an assignation.[30] As Lord President Inglis put it:

> "There cannot then be said to be any presumption of value in the
> case of a cheque. But if value is proved, if the cheque was granted
> for onerous causes, as here, then it comes to be in much the same
> position as a bill of exchange. Then when it is presented there is no
> reason that I can see why it should not act as an assignation, and the
> presentation act as intimation."[31]

66   There was also an opinion by Lord Shand that the then recent provisions of the Bills of Exchange Act 1882 did not affect this common
law.[32]

67   It is thought that the tract of authority which requires proof of value,
is unsound in principle. One writer has argued this with an extensive
citation of authority.[33] He states that the importance of the category of
privileged writings has been overlooked. However another explanation
may be suggested. That is that there has been a historical link between
mandate and assignation. A cheque can be either, but the tendency has
been to classify it as mandate.

68   The peculiar status of cheques probably arises from the nature of their
use in the nineteenth century. Cheques were used as the document
given to a servant or member of the family to collect money from a bank
for the head of the household.[34] It was said in 1874: "there are many
people who never draw cheques in any other way, or for any other purpose."[35]

69   Assume that a Lord of Session sent his servant with a cheque to collect £100 from a bank. The payee in the cheque would be the servant. If
the cheque was to be regarded as an assignation, the servant would, on
presenting the cheque to the bank, have a real right to £100. This is such
an astonishing proposition that it must be avoided. What the Scottish

---

[30] *Bryce* v. *Young's Exrs.* (1866) 4 M. 312; *Waterston* v. *City of Glasgow Bank* (1874) 1
R. 470; *British Linen Co. Bank* v. *Carruthers and Ferguson* (1883) 10 R. 923.
[31] *British Linen Co. Bank* v. *Carruthers and Ferguson, sup. cit.* at p. 926.
[32] at p. 927.
[33] D. J. Cusine, "The Cheque as an Assignation" 1977 J.R. 98.
[34] *Bryce* v. *Young's Exrs., sup. cit.* at p. 314 *per* Lord President McNeill; *British Linen
Co. Bank* v. *Carruthers and Ferguson, sup. cit.* at p. 926 *per* Lord President Inglis.
[35] *Waterston* v. *City of Glasgow Bank, sup. cit.* at p. 473, opinion of sheriff substitute.

courts did was found on the gratuitous transfer of the cheque from master to servant, and produce a rule on the operation of cheques as an assignation, which depends on the presence or absence of consideration. What they should have done, and what might still be done, was to solve the problem by asking whether the cheque was operating as a mandate or as an assignation, with value being only one factor in deciding the answer.

17–70   An order to one's debtor, "Pay X," can be a mandate or an assignation. Proof may show that X is collecting on his own behalf (assignation) or on behalf of another (mandate or agency). There is a clear distinction in the substance of the transaction[36] and it matters not whether value has been given. Apart from the specialities of cheques, the distinction is clear. For example, my solicitor may collect a debt as my agent, or as my assignee. Consideration is irrelevant to the classification of the nature of the contract.

17–71   Historically there was some confusion between mandate and assignation. Assignation originally was a form of mandate. Even as late as 1874, Lord President Inglis could not forget history and distinguish the contracts. A factory to manage for a tenant was treated as an assignation with the comment: "An assignation is a mandate in a certain sense, and in our law it is called a procuratory *in rem suam*."[37] In the old theory an assignation was a form of procuratory *in rem suam*, that is a mandate which the procurator or assignee alone had an interest to carry out. The significance of the term "*in rem suam*" is that the assignee acts in his own interests, not in the interests of his cedent. This was quite different from a mandate.

17–72   The difficulty with cheques was not simply whether they were assignations or mandates. There was a problem with revocation. Traditionally a mandate was a gratuitous contract and always revocable.[38] An assignation was an irrevocable mandate.[39] A cheque in the form of a mandate could in theory be revoked or countermanded.[40] But the same theory would prevent countermand of a cheque in the form of an assignation. The result may have been to favour mandate as the appropriate category for a cheque. A cheque is an ambiguous instrument. It usually accompanies another contract. That contract might be mandate. If the cheque is an assignation or conveyance this may reflect donation, loan, *donatio mortis causa* or very complicated financial arrangements. It is too simplistic to ask whether there was value given or not. That is only one factor in answering the true question which is—what was the pur-

---

[36] A point which is not new. It was made by Stair, III,i,3.

[37] *Lyon* v. *Irvine* (1874) 1 R. 512 at p. 518. Nor in fairness would he have wanted to overlook the development of the law. He was a strong proponent of historical study as a method of understanding law. See Inglis, "The Historical Study of Law"—an address to the Juridical Society 1863–64, quoted in Scottish Law Magazine 1863, p. 45 *et seq.*

[38] Stair, I,xii,8: Ersk., III,iii,32; III,iii,40.

[39] Stair, *sup. cit.* and Appendix 787, 788. Ersk., III,iii,31.

[40] *Waterston* v. *City of Glasgow Bank, supra.*

pose of the cheque?—a question which needs proof, or an equivalent, for its answer.[41]

(5) Stamp duty clause

3   An assignation which is liable to conveyance on sale duty may be exempt from the duty if the consideration is below certain figures and this is certified by a clause in the assignation.[42] Avoidance of the duty can be very important for those who factor debts and various devices for such avoidance have been suggested.[43]

(6) Statutory forms

4   Sometimes statute requires a particular form of assignation as in the Local Acts for Greenock Harbour.[44] Some of the statutory styles for transmission of heritable rights have already been mentioned.[45] Of more importance for present purposes are the forms of assignation in the Transmission of Moveable Property (Scotland) Act 1862 and the Policies of Assurance Act 1867.

5   The 1862 Act was passed as a law reform measure to simplify the forms of conveyancing. Prior to the Act an assignation was long and expensive. The Act was said to realise "the mercantile idea of brevity, cheapness and certainty" and to allow a person to draft his own assignation.[46]

6   There were prior to the Act two styles of assignation, one direct and the other indirect. The direct form assigned the sum and the deed. The indirect form made the assignee the cedent's cessioner and assignee and reflected the old idea that the assignee was a procuratory *in rem suam*. Both the styles had a narrative clause, a clause of assignation or of assignation and surrogation, a declaration of power to uplift, a warrandice clause, a clause of delivery, a registration clause and a testing clause.[47] The 1862 Act provides a form with only three parts—a narrative clause, a clause of assignation and a testing clause.

7   The Act applies only to some assignations of bonds and conveyances.[48] It applies to policies of assurance of Scottish companies but a further short form of assignation for all life policies was provided in the Policies of Assurance Act 1867. This is a United Kingdom statute

---

[41] See *Bryce* v. *Young's Exrs.* 4 M. 312: *Thomson* v. *Jolly Carters Inn Ltd.*, 1972 S.C. 215.
[42] The certificate is in terms of the Finance Act 1958, s.34. The details of the liability for duty under the Stamp Act 1891 are altered frequently. See the *Parliament House Book*, s.A and Butterworth's *U.K. Tax Guide* (annual).
[43] See P. M. Biscoe, *Law & Practice of Credit Factoring* (London 1975, Butterworths), p. 106.
[44] *Greenock Harbour Trs.* (1888) 15 R. 343.
[45] paras. 17–07 to 17–11.
[46] Scottish Law Magazine, 1862, p. 29.
[47] J. Craigie, *Moveable Rights*, pp. 237 *et seq.*
[48] See s.4.

passed to solve the problems of English law which restricted the assignation of legal choses-in-action and the title to sue of the assignee.[49]

17–78   Although after the 1862 Act the old forms lingered in the style books, and are still competent, the Act provided the opportunity to depart from complicated conveyancing and the notion that an assignation is a procuratory *in rem suam*.

What is Assigned?

17–79   If there is an assignation of X, the question may arise whether a right associated with X is also assigned. The problem is illustrated by case law.

17–80   First, examples of conveyances which were held not to include the disputed right. A marriage contract conveyed what belonged to the spouses at the date of the marriage, and what should belong to them at its dissolution. The gap was the failure to provide for acquisitions in the intermediate period.[50] A conveyance in trust for creditors of "all means and estate presently belonging to me," did not cover future fees of a public office.[51] A purchase of the assets and goodwill of a company did not include the transfer of an obligation on a trade mark.[52]

17–81   Secondly there are cases in which ancillary rights were impliedly assigned. An assignation of a share carried with it by implication the right to insist in an action for reduction of an arrestment of the share.[53] In a defective form of assignation of a bond and disposition in security, an assignation of the heritage was held to include an assignation of the bond.[54] An assignation of trade fixtures by a tenant to his landlord was construed as an assignation of a right to remove them.[55] As Lord Rutherfurd Clark said[56]:

> "If I assign a thing which is not mine, I assign all the rights I have to make it mine. If I assign a thing which I have bought, but which remains in the possession of the seller, I assign what is not my property, but I also assign the right to obtain delivery. The law implies that a cedent confers on his assignee everything which is necessary to make the assignation effectual."

17–82   What is implied will differ according to the words used in each case. However some guidance can be given from this survey of the authorities. It will be easier to imply that a right incidental to an item of property is transferred than to imply a transfer of an item of property

---

[49] See MacGillivray & Parkington on *Insurance Law* (6th ed., 1975), paras. 1320 *et seq.*
[50] *Champion* v. *Duncan* (1867) 6 M. 17.
[51] *Hill* v. *Paul* (1841) 2 Robin. App. 524.
[52] *Andrew Melrose & Co.* v. *Aitken Melrose Co. Ltd.*, 1918 1 S.L.T. 109.
[53] *Anderson* v. *Scottish N. E. Ry. Co.* (1866) 1 S.L.R. 116; *cf.* the difficulty in implying a transfer of a right to reduce fraudulent preferences. *Glen* v. *Glen* (1826) 5 S. 11.
[54] *McCutcheon* v. *McWilliam* (1876) 3 R. 565.
[55] *Miller* v. *Muirhead* (1894) 21 R. 658.
[56] at p. 660.

different from the property expressly conveyed. To put it another way, a cedent should not be impliedly deprived of an asset, and it makes sense to imply that a right incidental to an asset is transferred with the asset.

ASSIGNATUS UTITUR JURE AUCTORIS

83 Stair stated: "Except in the matter of probation, all exceptions competent against the cedent before the assignation or intimation, are relevant against the assignee, as payment, compensation etc."[57]; Erskine[58] and Bell[59] are in similar terms. This is a peculiar rule in that it does not apply to transfers of other types of property, nor to negotiable instruments.[60] It appears to have been based on the now outmoded idea that the assignee was the procurator or agent of the cedent.[61] It is possible to argue that the rule is anomalous.[62] It has, however, this in its favour. Assignation is a form of transfer which is unique in affecting three parties. One party may not consent to the transfer, and that party is the debtor. On the assumption that a right is freely assignable, the debtor has no control over when and to whom the debt may be assigned. Therefore it would be unfair if he could be prejudiced by an assignation by virtue of which the assignee acquired more rights against him than the cedent had.

(1) Examples of the principle

84 The cedent's right is the measure of the right of the assignee, so if the cedent has no enforceable debt, neither has the assignee.[63] For example, if the debt assigned has been extinguished, the assignation is worthless.[64] If the cedent's title is defective, as that of an undischarged bankrupt, his assignee can acquire no higher right.[65] The assignee may be affected by false statements made by the cedent when the cedent contracted with the debtor.[66] Conversely it has been held that an assignee was liable for the obligations of the cedent when shares in a partnership were assigned.[67]

---

[57] Stair, III,i,20. The qualification on probation relates to the rule that with exceptions the oath of the cedent cannot prove against the assignee. See Stair, III,v,9; Ersk., III,i,18 and 10; *Lang* v. *Hislop & Co.* (1854) 16 D. 908; *Campbell* v. *Campbell* (1860) 23 D. 159.

[58] Ersk., III,v,10.

[59] Bell, *Prin.*, s.1468.

[60] See Gloag & Irvine, *Rights in Security*, pp. 544 *et seq.*

[61] See Stair, I,xii,8 and I,xii,11; Kames, *Elucidations*, pp. 13, 14.

[62] See Scot. Law Com. No. 42, *Defective Consent and Consequential Matters* (1978), paras. 3.134–3.141 and its discussion in the context of fraud.

[63] *Robertson* v. *Wright* (1873) 1 R. 237, esp. at p. 243 *per* Lord Ardmillan and at p. 245 *per* Lord President Inglis.

[64] *Lothian* v. *Carron Co,* (1864) 2 M. 556; *Jackson* v. *Nicoll* (1870) 8 M. 408.

[65] *Taylor* v. *Charteris and Andrew* (1879) 7 R. 128 at p. 132 *per* Lord Shand.

[66] *Buist* v. *Scottish Equitable Life Ass. Soc.* (1877) 4 R. 1076; (1878) 5 R.(H.L.) 64.

[67] *Turnbull* v. *Allan & Son* (1834) 7 W. & S. 281.

17–85   The debtor may plead against the assignee, a debt due to the debtor by the cedent.[68] A vassal is entitled to plead against his superior's assignee, the superior's failure to make roads and sewers.[69] An assignee is entitled to object under the Moneylenders Act to the contract made by his cedent.[70]

(2) The doubtful case of the counterclaim

17–86   In *Binstock, Miller & Co.* v. *E. Coia & Co. Ltd.*[71] Sheriff Bryden held that the debtor could not present against the assignee a counterclaim which was valid against the cedent. The purchasers of orange juice at a price of £725 had paid £375 to account and thereafter rejected the goods because the juice was substandard. The suppliers of the juice assigned their rights. The assignees sued for the balance of the price, *i.e.* £350. It was held that the counterclaim for return of the £375 paid to account must be dismissed.

17–87   The reasoning behind this decision was that a counterclaim was a cross action. The debtor did not have a right of action against the assignee, therefore a counterclaim was incompetent. The result, however, is surprising and, it is suggested, wrong. The reasons for this are:

(1) The idea that an assignee should be subject to claims competent against his cedent is consistent with the original theory that the assignee was a procurator *ad rem suam* or agent of the cedent.

(2) If there had been no assignation, and the cedent had sued, they would have been met with a competent counterclaim. The result produced by Sheriff Bryden puts the assignee in a better position than the cedent, which is contrary to all the *dicta* that an assignee is liable to all pleas competent against his author.[72]

(3) There is *obiter* authority in the House of Lords, founding on Stair and Bankton, that an assignee is subject to counterclaims which the original debtor might have against his creditor.[73] Erskine referred to assignees of mutual contracts being "subjected to all the burdens which affected the right while it was vested in the cedent."[74]

(4) To allow a counterclaim arising under a contract which is the basis

---

[68] *Livingston* v. *Reid* (1833) 11 S. 878; *Shiells* v. *Ferguson, Davidson & Co.* (1876) 4 R. 250.

[69] *Arnott's Trs.* v. *Forbes* (1881) 9 R. 89.

[70] *Brigg's Trs.* v. *Briggs*, 1923 S.L.T. 755.

[71] 1957 S.L.T.(Sh. Ct.) 47.

[72] *e.g. Shiells* v. *Ferguson, Davidson & Co. sup. cit.* at p. 254 *per* Lord President Inglis; *Johnstone-Beattie* v. *Dalzell*, (1868) 6 M. 333 at p. 343 *per* Lord President Inglis; *Scottish Widows Fund* v. *Buist* (1876) 3 R. 1078 at p. 1082 *per* Lord President Inglis.

[73] *Redfearn* v. *Ferrier* (1813) 1 Dow. 50 at p. 68 *per* Lord Redesdale (the report in 5 Pat. 706 is different), quoted *per* Lord President Inglis in *Scottish Widows Fund* v. *Buist, sup. cit.*

[74] Ersk. III,v.10. Assignees of a share in a joint stock company were held liable for debts in *Turnbull* v. *Allan & Son* (1834) 7 W. & S. 281. See also the transfer of furniture (which should not have been called assignation)—*Sibbald & Son* v. *Walker* (1832) 11 S. 13.

of the assignation and the assignee's title is more obviously sensible than allowing the assignee to be met with compensation pled in respect of a debt arising in circumstances unconnected with the contract. Yet no one denies that compensation is pleadable against the assignee.

(5) The sheriff's decision has serious consequences for the buyers of goods. If the goods are defective, and the seller assigns the claim for the price, the buyer must pay the price to the assignee without deduction of a claim for damages arising from the seller's breach of contract. If this is the law, it should be changed.

(3) Latent equities

88   The maxim that the assignee is subject to pleas against his cedent has an exception established by the classic case of *Redfearn* v. *Ferrier*.[75] This case established that a latent right was not pleadable against a *bona fide* onerous assignee who had intimated the assignation. To understand the case it is important to note who was claiming against whom. The distinguishing feature of the *Redfearn* problem is that four parties were involved. In the case, a cedent held property in trust for A, but assigned to B who was ignorant of the trust. The claim against the assignee came not from the debtor or the cedent, but from a fourth party who in effect was saying to the assignee: "You have my property. The cedent should not have transferred it to you." But the fourth party's claim against the cedent was only a personal one, for breach of a trust. It could not prevail over an intimated assignation. So the assignee had a right to the fund.

89   The Court of Session did not like this exception to the general rule. In *Dingwall* v. *McCombie*,[76] Lord Balgray described the House of Lords as mistaken as to the nature of previous decisions, but the distinction which they introduced as reasonable. Lord Gillies obviously wanted to say that *Redfearn* was a bad decision and should not be followed. Lord President Hope was prepared to, "bow to *Redfearn's* case as an equitable decision, although I think it contrary to our law." However, nearly 20 years later the suggestion that doubt should be cast on *Redfearn* was described by Lord Moncreiff as "dangerous."[77]

90   The problem with *Redfearn* was its application to the sequestration of a person who held property on behalf of another. On one view, applying *Redfearn*, the trustee in sequestration was an assignee who took property unaffected by latent equities against the bankrupt.[78] The Court of Session refused to apply *Redfearn* to this type of assignation and

---

[75] (1831) 1 Dow. 50; 5 Pat. 706.

[76] (1822) note to *Gordon* v. *Cheyne* (1824) 2 S. (2nd ed., not 1st) 566 at p. 567; June 6, 1822, F.C.; 1 S. 463.

[77] *Burns* v. *Laurie's Trs.* (1840) 2 D. 1348 at p. 1356.

[78] "Equities" is an English expression referring to rights or obligations incidental to a contract. Instead of *assignatus utitur jure auctoris* an English lawyer would say that an assignee takes the chose in action subject to the same equities to which it was subject in the hands of the assignor.

affirmed the doctrine that the creditors took the rights of the bankrupt *tantum et tale*.[79] The problem arose again in *Heritable Reversionary Co. Ltd.* v. *McKay's Tr.*[80] Lord President Inglis founded on *Redfearn* to show that a trustee in sequestration took property free from any latent trust. But judicial life has its ironies. Lord President Inglis would have been better following Lord President Hope in saying that the House of Lords was mistaken in *Redfearn*. When *Heritable Reversionary Co. Ltd.* was appealed, the House of Lords reversed the Court of Session. They affirmed the rule that a trustee takes the bankrupt's estate *tantum et tale*—subject to all the claims against the bankrupt. Property held in trust by the bankrupt was not property of the bankrupt, and so did not pass to his trustee in sequestration.

17–91 The result is that two questions have to be asked:

(1) What was assigned? Property held in trust by the bankrupt is not assigned because of the principles of *Heritable Reversionary Co. Ltd.*

(2) What is the effect of assignation? *Redfearn* is applicable to the property which has been assigned.[81]

ACTINGS OF THE CEDENT SUBSEQUENT TO ASSIGNATION

17–92 If subsequent to the intimation of the assignation the cedent becomes indebted to the debtor, that debt cannot be pled by the debtor against the assignee's claim.[82] However, if the right assigned is contingent, future events are relevant to the contingency and these could include actions of the cedent or events affecting him.[83]

TITLE TO SUE AFTER ASSIGNATION

17–93 Once an assignation is intimated to the debtor, the cedent, *prima facie*, no longer has a title to sue the debtor.[84] An assignation might not completely divest the cedent. It could be in security, leaving the cedent with a right of reversion, or only part of a debt may be assigned. The result is that the cedent may retain a title to sue.[85]

---

[79] *Gordon* v. *Cheyne, sup. cit.*

[80] (1891) 18 R. 1166; (1892) 19 R.(H.L.) 43.

[81] *Redfearn* was followed in a case of an assignation in security of an existing debt: *Burns* v. *Laurie's Trs.* (1840) 2 D. 1348.

[82] *Shiells* v. *Ferguson, Davidson & Co.* (1876) 4 R. 250; *Macpherson's J.F.* v. *McKay*, 1915 S.C. 1011 (English authority rejected). Bell, Comm., ii,131. This provides another reason for prompt intimation by the assignee. Gloag (p. 431) cites *Chambers' J.F.* v. *Vertue* (1893) 20 R. 257 in which a tenant could not set off a claim for groceries against the claim for rent following an intimated assignation. The landlord had been sequestrated. The ground of decision appears to be that there was no effective set off against rent due after intimation of the assignation which was in the form of an action of maills and duties.

[83] *Johnstone-Beattie* v. *Dalzell* (1868) 6 M. 333.

[84] *Microwave Systems (Scotland)* v. *Electro-Physiological Instruments*, 1971 S.C. 140; *Bentley* v. *MacFarlane*, 1964 S.C. 76.

[85] *Robertson & Co.* v. *Exley, Dimsdale & Co.* (1832) 11 S. 91; *Fraser* v. *Duguid* (1838) 16 S. 1130; *Manson* v. *Baillie* (1850) 12 D. 775.

It was established at least as long ago as 1621 that an assignee may sue in his cedent's name.[86] This curious rule probably arose as a result of the theory that an assignee was merely the cedent's procurator or agent. He sued the debtor on behalf of the cedent. The mandate theory was departed from when an assignation was treated as a conveyance, with the consequence that the assignee could sue in his own name.[87] The result today is that an assignee may sue either in his own name or the name of his cedent.[88]

A title to sue should exist at the date of raising an action and subsequent assignation cannot cure a defect in title.[89]

CHALLENGE OF THE ASSIGNATION BY THE DEBTOR

There is a conflict of English authority on whether a debtor can question the validity or enforceability of an assignment.[90] Apart from the technicalities of the title of the debtor to sue, the interesting question is raised of the position in Scots law. There is a lack of authority. In principle if the assignation is void (rather than voidable or unenforceable), no rights can transmit under it. The debtor who pays the assignee has paid the wrong person. It may appear manifestly unfair if the debtor must pay a second time to a cedent whose invalid act misled a debtor in good faith. But it often is the consequence of a void act, that a bona fide third party might lose. In this case undoubtedly the debtor would have a claim for reimbursement from the assignee. If that claim is worthless the law has the age-old problem of which of two innocent parties should lose—the cedent who did not validly consent to what he did, or the debtor who perhaps might have made inquiry. Apart from invalid consent, if the assignation is so defective in form as to be a nullity, there is a possibility that the cedent will be barred from demanding payment from the debtor.

It has been observed that where assignations are granted on a large scale, as with debt factoring, it would be commercially inconvenient if the debtor could demand to see the assignation and satisfy himself on its validity before paying the assignee.[91] In Scotland with most forms of intimation of an assignation this problem should not arise. Many of the methods of intimation require a copy of the assignation to be

---

[86] *Grier* v. *Maxwell* (1621) Mor. 828.

[87] See *Traill & Sons* v. *Actieselskabat, Dalbeattie Ltd.* (1904) 6 F. 798 at p. 807 *per* Lord Kinnear.

[88] *Fraser* v. *Duguid, sup. cit.; Methven Simpson Ltd.* v. *Jones*, 1910 2 S.L.T. 14.

[89] *Symington* v. *Campbell* (1894) 21 R. 434; *Assoc. Herring Merchants* v. *Reitsma*, 1958 S.L.T.(Sh. Ct.) 57; *Bentley* v. *MacFarlane*, 1964 S.C. 76; *cf. Middle Ward District Committee of Lanarkshire C.C.* v. *Marshall* (1896) 24 R. 139; *Doughty Shipping Co.* v. *N.B. Rly. Co.*, 1909 1 S.L.T. 267; *Westville Shipping Co.* v. *Abram Steamship Co.*, 1923 S.C.(H.L.) 68.

[90] *Walker* v. *Bradford Old Bank* (1884) 12 Q.B.D. 511; *Van Lynn Developments Ltd.* v. *Pelias Construction Co.* [1969] 1 Q.B. 607 at p. 613 *per* Lord Denning M.R.

[91] P. M. Biscoe, *Law and Practice of Credit Factoring* (1973), p. 112.

delivered.[92] Therefore apart from the document being lost or destroyed, there normally would be no need for the debtor to call for further production of the assignation. Unfortunately, the Policies of Assurance Act 1867 under English influence requires only the purport of the assignation to be given and in theory this could pose problems if the "purport" was different from the reality.[93]

INTIMATION OF ASSIGNATION

17–98 The requirement that there should be intimation is very old in our law. Balfour quoted cases from 1492 onwards.[94] Several factors have been suggested both as a reason for intimation and as a consequence of it.

(1) The debtor is in bad faith in paying the cedent after intimation.[95]

(2) Intimation completes the conveyance and regulates preference amongst assignations.[96]

(3) Intimation fixes the date after which claims against the cedent may not be competent against the assignee.[97]

(4) Intimation alters the legal relationship between debtor and cedent, and may prevent the cedent having a title to sue the debtor.[98] Arrestment in the hands of the debtor will not create jurisdiction against the cedent even although the assignation is in security.[99]

(5) An intimation may cover future debts.[1]

17–99 Although the requirement for intimation is well known, case law shows one area with a repeated, and perhaps understandable, failure to intimate. In marriage contracts funds are assigned to trustees. On several occasions marriage contract trustees failed to intimate the assignation in their favour with the result that others acquired a right to the funds.[2] Although these trusts are now less common, the point for the practitioner is to be wary of the universal assignation clause in any deed,

---

[92] See *infra*, "Method of Intimation" para. 17–113.

[93] Bankton considered a similar problem with the old form of notarial intimation which could be defective if only part of the words were read. See Bankt., II,193,15. The appropriate questions are: (1) What was assigned?; and (2) What was intimated? It will be appreciated that problems with defective intimation are only relevant if there is a competing right or if the debtor has paid the cedent.

[94] *Practicks*, p. 169.

[95] Stair, III,i,6; Ersk. *Inst.* III,v,3; see also Bell, *Prin.*, para. 1462.

[96] *Sup. cit.* and see *infra*, s.v. "The preference of an unintimated assignation" para. 17–102.

[97] See *supra*, s.v. "Actings of the cedent subsequent to assignation" para. 17–92.

[98] See *supra*, s.v. "Title to sue after assignation" para. 17–93.

[99] *Whittall* v. *Christie* (1894) 22 R. 91—although note the particular facts of the case. See Graham Stewart, *Diligence*, p. 116.

[1] See s.v. "When should intimation be made" para. 17–106.

[2] *Tod's Trs.* v. *Wilson* (1869) 7 M. 1100; *Campbell's Trs.* v. *White* (1844) 11 R. 1078; *Gams* v. *Russel's Trs.* (1899) 7 S.L.T. 289—opinions in the last two cases indicate that a gratuitous assignation will not acquire preference over an onerous assignation: *sed quaere*. A debtor would be in a very difficult position if he had to inquire about the consideration for an assignation before paying the assignee.

for example, on the assets take over of a business or the security for a loan.[3] Subsequent diligence against the cedent, perhaps years later, could defeat the expectations of the assignee. The general assignation requires intimation in Scots law. It may not require intimation in English law to be effective against the creditors of the cedent, which is an added reason for caution in Scotland.[4]

(1) Is intimation always necessary?

There are several instances where intimation is not necessary.

(a) Transfer of a negotiable instrument.[5]

(b) Legal or judicial assignations such as in arrestment, transfer to a trustee in sequestration and, formerly, marriage.[6]

(c) Certain transfers of rights in land.[7] Heritable but not feudalised rights may be transferred by assignation. The nature of some of these rights makes intimation impracticable. The theory of Erskine that the land is the debtor, and so intimation is impossible, is not entirely satisfactory, because the obligation which is to be transmitted may be enforceable against the obligor who has ceased to own the lands, *e.g.* a granter of warrandice whose obligation is transmitted by an assignation of writs clause.[8] More convincing is Bankton's explanation that infeftment should govern competing rights to land, not intimation.[9] In any event if the right becomes feudalised reliance may be placed on the rule that registration in the Register of Sasines is equivalent to intimation.[10]

(d) Where the debtor is a party to the assignation. If a tenant assigned a right to remove trade fixtures to a stranger, there would need to be intimation to the landlord, but not if the assignation is in favour of the landlord.[11] If the cedent and the debtor are the same person, even though acting in different capacities, intimation is unnecessary, as where the cedent assigns his interest under a trust of which he is the sole trustee.[12]

(e) Intimation is not necessary if there is not a competing right or the

---

[3] *e.g. Liquidators of Union Club Ltd.* v. *Edinburgh Life Ass. Co.* (1906) 8 F. 1143 (assignation of uncalled capital of a company).

[4] See Crossley Vaine's *Personal Property* (5th ed., 1973), p. 274.

[5] Ersk., III,v.6; Bell, *Comm.*, ii,18.

[6] Stair, III,i,13; Ersk., III,v,7; Bell, *Comm.*, ii,17; Bankruptcy (Scotland) Act 1985 s.31(4) Craigie, *Moveable Rights*, pp. 246–249. But see a difference in effect on future sums: *Flowerdew* v. *Buchan* (1835) 13 S. 615 at p. 616 *per* Lord Ordinary.

[7] Ersk., III,v,6.

[8] See Wood's *Lectures*, p. 148.

[9] Bankt., II,192,9.

[10] *Edmond* v. *Gordon* (1858) 3 Macq. 116; *Paul* v. *Boyd's Trs.* (1835) 13 S. 818 and see *infra, s.v.* "Method of intimation" para. 17–110. Registration in the Land Register established under the Land Registration (Scotland) Act 1979 is not an equivalent of intimation.

[11] *Miller* v. *Muirhead* (1894) 21 R. 658; See also *Russell* v. *Breadalbane* (1831) 5 W. & S. 256.

[12] *Browne's Trs.* v. *Anderson* (1901) 4 F. 305; See also *Paul* v. *Boyd's Trs.* (1833) 13 S. 818.

need to rely on any of the effects of intimation.[13] Therefore, "if a man holding two separate bonds, and having also two separate creditors, assigns to each creditor one bond apiece, it is of no consequence, as between these assignees, whether they intimate their assignation or not, for they do not compete *inter se*."[14]

(f) Leases are in a very special position. It was observed at an early date that, "intimation to the landlord is not the right or effectual course for completing the assignation of a tack or subtack; that a tack is a real right, and is transmitted by possession on the deed of assignment; that intimation falls to be made to him who has to pay, not to him who, like a landlord, has to receive payment."[15] In a question between landlord and tenant intimation to the landlord is sufficient[16] but to transfer a real right valid against the landlord and his successors, possession is necessary.[17]

The inconvenience of this when the lease was assigned in security for a loan, led to the Registration of Leases (Scotland) Act 1857 under which, in effect, registration takes the place of possession, and of intimation.[18]

17–101 If the failure to intimate is the fraudulent failure of X, some of those deriving a right from X might not be able to take the benefit of the fraud. A trustee in bankruptcy is not entitled to benefit from the fraud of the bankrupt and so if the bankrupt's failure to intimate was fraudulent, the trustee will have to recognise the right of those who hold the unintimated assignation.[19]

(2) The preference of an unintimated assignation

17–102 Intimation completes the conveyance and regulates preference amongst assignations. As Erskine said: "though an assignation not intimated be valid against the granter, who cannot question his own deed; yet if, before intimation of a first assignment, the cedent shall grant a second to a different assignee, the second, if it be intimated before the first, will be preferred to the first."[20]

17–103 An assignee's real right can be defeated by (1) prior intimation of another assignation of the same subject matter. Strictly the second intimation produces a right postponed to that created by the first intimation, but in most situations that makes the second intimation

---

[13] See paras. 17–102 to 17–105.

[14] *Cochrane* v. *Cochrane* (1836) 14 S. 1040 at pp. 1046, 1047 *per* Lord Gillies. *Cf.* the curious treatment of intimation in *Park Motors* v. *Blackmore*, 1964 S.L.T.(Sh.Ct.) 30.

[15] *Grant* v. *Adamson* (1802) Hume 810: See also *Sime's Tr.* v. *Fiddler*, May 23, 1806, F.C.

[16] *Inglis & Co.* v. *Paul* (1829) 7 S. 469.

[17] *Clark* v. *West Calder Oil Co.* (1882) 9 R. 1017. The issue is fully analysed in Rankine, *Leases*, pp. 181 *et seq.*; Campbell & Paton *Landlord & Tenant*, pp. 158 *et seq.*

[18] *Crawford* v. *Campbell*, 1937 S.C. 596 at p. 610 *per* Lord Moncreiff.

[19] *Graeme's Tr.* v. *Giersburg* (1888) 15 R. 691; *Mounsey* (1896) 4 S.L.T. 46, *Paul's Tr.* v. *Paul*, 1912 2 S.L.T. 61.

[20] Ersk., *Inst.*, III,v,3; See also Bell, *Prin.*, s.1462.

worthless,[21] (2) the prior creation of a right by an assignation which does not need intimation.[22] The most important category of these are legal or judicial assignations, such as arrestment, or sequestration. Thus an assignee who had not intimated would find that there was a prior claimant to the fund if the creditors of the cedent arrested in the debtor's hands or sequestrated the cedent.

The cases cited are examples of the competition of an assignation, with another assignation,[23] with arrestment,[24] with sequestration,[25] and with liquidation.[26] Where the competition is with the rights of a receiver under a floating charge, peculiar results can be produced by the decision in *Lord Advocate* v. *Royal Bank of Scotland*.[27] As Professor W. A. Wilson has commented: "The result of this decision is that where an arrestment is followed by intimation of an assignation in security which is followed by the appointment of a receiver under a floating charge, the floating charge defeats the arrestment which defeats the assignation which defeats the floating charge."[28]

It should perhaps be emphasised that an unintimated assignation is not worthless. Once it is a delivered deed[29] it is effective between the parties to it. If the cedent grants a subsequent assignation of the same subject matter, which is intimated before the first, the first assignee may not be without a remedy. He has lost an effective claim against the debtor. But he still holds a deed from his cedent and there may be a breach of warrandice by the cedent in granting the second assignation. There is implied in an onerous assignation warrandice from fact and deed and *debitum subesse*. Simple warrandice is implied in a gratuitous assignation. Warrandice may also be expressed in the deed. The second

---

[21] If the assignation which is first intimated is reducible obviously it is better to be a second intimator rather than a third.

[22] See *s.v.* "Is intimation always necessary?" para. 17–100.

[23] *Campbell's Trs.* v. *Whyte* (1884) II R. 1078; *Gams* v. *Russel's Trs.* (1899) 7 S.L.T. 289; *cf. Graeme's Tr.* v. *Giersberg* (1888) 15 R. 691.

[24] *Wallace Hamilton & Co.* v. *Campbell* (1824) 2 Shaw's App. 467; aff. 1 S. 53; *Strachan* v. *McDougle* (1835) 13 S. 954; *Morrice* v. *Sprot* (1846) 8 D. 918; *Inglis* v. *Robertson & Baxter* (1898) 25 R.(H.L.) 70.

[25] *Tod's Trs.* v. *Wilson* (1869) 7 M. 1100; *Moncreiff's Tr.* v. *Balfour*, 1928 S.N. 64, 139; under the Bankruptcy (Scotland) Act 1985, s.31(4), property vests in the permanent trustee as if there had been intimation of its assignation. See also s.31(5).

[26] *Liquidators of Union Club Ltd.* v. *Edinburgh Life Ass. Co.* (1906) 8 F. 1143. On the nature of liquidation see *Clark* v. *West Calder Oil Co.* (1882) 9 R. 1017 at pp. 1024, 1025 *per* Lord President Inglis and at pp. 1030, 1031 *per* Lord Shand: "no advantage which a creditor has not legally secured previous to the date of the resolution or order to wind up can be allowed."

[27] 1977 S.C. 155. The controversy aroused by the case is shown in A. J. Sim, "The Receiver and Effectively Executed Diligence" 1984 S.L.T.(News) 25. This article refers to several previous articles by other authors. See also *Forth & Clyde Construction Co. Ltd.* v. *Trinity Timber & Plywood Co. Ltd.*, 1984 S.L.T. 94.

[28] 1978 J.R. 253 at p. 255. See also W. A. Wilson, *The Law of Scotland Relating to Debt* at p. 233.

[29] See Chap. 7, "Delivery of Deeds." The effect of an intimated assignation which is not delivered was considered by Gloag, p. 74 and more convincingly by Bankton, II,191,6.

assignation by the cedent will be a breach of simple warrandice and of fact and deed warrandice.[30]

(3) When should intimation be made?

17–106 It was at one time held that intimation must wait until the right has vested and the assignor has a debtor.[31] The logic of this appears to have been departed from in *Browne's Tr.* v. *Anderson*[32] in which intimation of an assignation of a *spes successionis* was treated as necessary to complete the right. The problem raised by the earlier authority remains to be fully argued.[33] It would cause practical problems if it was necessary to wait until a right had vested before its assignation was intimated.[34]

17–107 However, if it is clear that the relationship of debtor and creditor already exists, there can be an assignation of sums not yet due, and an effective intimation will cover these sums. This commonly happens when a life policy is assigned. A contrast has been drawn in a case involving a lease between the effect of intimation of an assignation and an arrestment.

17–108 "An arrestment laid in the hands of a tenant will only cover the rent actually due or for the term then current; but an assignation, regularly intimated, will carry all future rents, as long as the landlord and tenant remain the same, in the same way as an assignation of the principal lease, when intimated to a sub-tenant, will carry all future sub-rents while the sub-tenant continues in possession."[35]

17–109 An assignation may be validly intimated after the cedent's death.[36] Intimation by the assignee just prior to the bankruptcy of the cedent will not be cut down as a preference by the cedent, as it is the act of the assignee.[37]

(4) Method of intimation

17–110 One of the long, slow burning questions in the law is whether a debtor's mere knowledge of an assignation is sufficient intimation to him. Our institutional writers list a variety of unusual methods of mak-

---

[30] See Craigie, *Moveable Rights*, pp. 41, 42, 239, 240; Menzies, *Conveyancing*, pp. 177, 528; Bankt., II,196,28.

[31] *Bedwells & Yates* v. *Tod*, Dec. 2, 1819, F.C.: *Pearson, Wilson & Co.* v. *Brock* (1842) 4 D. 1509.

[32] (1904) 4 F. 305.

[33] See the Lord Ordinary in *Carter* v. *McIntosh* (1862) 24 D. 925. *Wood* v. *Begbie* (1850) 12 D. 963 may be relevant but it is a curious case.

[34] See Gloag and Irvine, *Rights in Security*, p. 443.

[35] *Flowerdew* v. *Buchan* (1835) 13 S. 615 at p. 616 *per* Lord Ordinary.

[36] *Brownlee* v. *Robb*, 1907 S.C. 1302; *Strawbridge's Trs.* v. *Bank of Scotland*, 1935 S.L.T. 568; Hume's *Lectures*, Vol. 3, pp. 4, 5; Act 1690, c. 26: Act 1693, c. 15.

[37] *Scottish Provident Institution* v. *Cohen & Co.* (1898) 16 R. 112; *Caledonian Ins. Co.* v. *Beattie* (1898) 5 S.L.T. 349—decided on specific statutory provision but the principle should apply in other cases. The assignation might, of course, be reducible.

ing intimation but they are unanimous that private knowledge of the debtor is not enough, at least in competition with creditors.[38] The reason for the rule is that informal communication by the creditor to the debtor might leave the debtor in doubt as to whether a *nexus* had been attached to the fund. Without some formality it might be difficult to determine the date of intimation. The debtor might realise what had happened slowly as the dormant seed reacts to the arrival of spring.

In the normal case the debtor is a disinterested party in the sense that it matters not to him whether he has to pay A or B. What does matter is that he pays the right person. Should he rely as much on a chance conversation in the local tavern, as on a deed sent by recorded delivery post? Perhaps not, but our law goes so far in insisting on formality in intimation that it denies effect to the deed sent by recorded delivery post, unless there is also the written acknowledgement of the debtor.

In *Gray* v. *Duke of Hamilton*[39] the Court of Session had decided that private letters about the assignation were not valid intimation. The decision was reversed by the House of Lords but on what grounds is not clear. The letters had been acknowledged by the debtor. In *Earl of Aberdeen* v. *Earl of March*[40] the House of Lords appear to have sustained an argument that private knowledge of a debtor's agent, accompanied by an entry in the agent's book, was sufficient intimation, but the report is brief. In *Donaldson* v. *Orr*[41] there is a long opinion by Lord Justice-Clerk Hope which, it is thought, represents the present law. It clearly states that in the absence of the regular forms of intimation there must be some act of acknowledgement by the debtor in favour of the assignee. It leaves open the question whether the debtor could defeat the effect of a letter by refusing to answer it.[42]

Intimation may take place in the following ways:

(a) Notarial. The classical form of intimation which is now never, or hardly ever, used[43] is by delivering a schedule of intimation, and a certified copy of the assignation, followed by an instrument of intimation. This procedure requires a procurator for the assignee, a notary public and two witnesses attending on the debtor.[44] A simplified form of

---

[38] Stair, III,i,7, Ersk., III,v,5; Bell, *Comm.*, 2.17; Bell, *Prin.*, para. 1465; Bankt., II, 193, 12. See also Spotiswoode, *Practicks*, p. 18.

[39] 1708 Robert. 1.

[40] (1730) 1 Pat. 44.

[41] (1855) 17 D. 1053 at pp. 1069, 1070.

[42] See also *Wallace* v. *Davies* (1853) 15 D. 688 at p. 696 *per* Lord Justice-Clerk Hope. The debtor who acts in bad faith in paying the cedent should in principle remain liable to pay again to the assignee. It is difficult to conceive of a debtor who had clear knowledge of the assignation and who nevertheless could pay the cedent in good faith. The other problem which arises is that the cedent must be dishonest in accepting payment.

[43] It was described in 1906 as "almost disappeared in practice" in *Liquidators of Union Club Ltd.* v. *Edinburgh Life Ass. Co.* (1906) 8 F. 1143 at p. 1146 *per* Lord McLaren. The expense of the procedure compared with that under the 1862 Act makes it extremely unlikely that it is used in current practice.

[44] Bell's *Lectures on Conveyancing* (3rd ed.), p. 311; Menzies, *Conveyancing*, pp. 284 *et seq.*

notarial intimation was introduced by the Transmission of Moveable Property (Scotland) Act 1862.[45] The notary delivers a certified copy of the assignation to the debtor. If intimation is crucial and might be disputed, this is the best form of intimation. Notarial intimation is also useful if the debtor refuses to grant an acknowledgement of an intimation.[46]

(b) By post. The 1862 Act authorised the postal transmission of a certified copy of the assignation to the debtor.[47] This, followed by written acknowledgement of receipt by the debtor, is sufficient evidence of intimation.

(c) Production and acknowledgment. Production of the assignation, or a copy of it, to the debtor, or a distinct reference to its terms in a letter to the debtor, is valid intimation at common law, provided that the debtor's written acknowledgement is obtained.[48] *A fortiori* if the debtor is a party to the assignation.[49] Production of an assignation at a meeting when the assignation was evidence of the right to attend, has been held sufficient intimation.[50]

(d) Actings of the debtor recognising the assignee. The debtor may promise to pay the assignee, or pay him partially.[51]

(e) Registration. Registration in the Books of Council and Session is not intimation.[52] The argument of an analogy to delivery of deeds was expressly rejected. The object of evidence about delivery is to show that the granter of the deed has a completed purpose. The object of intimation is different. It is to give the holder of a fund personal knowledge of the assignation.

17–114 Registration in the Register of Sasines has been held equivalent to intimation[53] but the reason for this may be that some modern forms of conveyancing are the equivalent of going on to the land and delivering symbols to testify to the transfer of the land. This was notorious intimation. It was done in the presence of locals who acted as witnesses. These *pares curiae*[54] were meant to retain in their memory a vivid impression of the transfer.[55] It is not surprising that the transfer of earth and stone, or other symbols, and the reading of a deed in Latin, on the

---

[45] s.2.

[46] Wood, *Lectures*, p. 586.

[47] s.2.

[48] *Wallace* v. *Davies* (1853) 15 D. 688 and see authorities on private knowledge cited above.

[49] *Miller* v. *Learmonth* (1870) 42 J. 418 (H.L.).

[50] *Hill* v. *Lindsay* (1847) 10 D. 78.

[51] Ersk., III,v,4; Bell, Comm., II,17; Menzies, *Conveyancing*, p. 291.

[52] *Tod's Trs.* v. *Wilson* (1869) 7 M. 1100.

[53] *Paul* v. *Boyd's Trs.* (1835) 13 S. 818; *Edmonds* v. *Mags. of Aberdeen* (1855) 18 D. 47; aff. (1858) 3 Macq. 116; *cf. Stevenson, Lauder & Gilchrist* v. *Dawson* (1896) 23 R. 496 for specialities with assignation of rents.

[54] Literally, peers of the court, that is one's peers—in effect neighbouring vassals. See Ersk., II,iii,17.

[55] Menzies, *Conveyancing*, p. 539.

land in question, in the presence of several people, was considered a public and solemn act which was treated as intimation to all. The law, however, looked more to ceremony than to reality because it was one form of intimation of which the debtor might reasonably be unaware. Successive Conveyancing Acts from 1845 onwards introduced procedures which were the equivalent of sasine with the result that registration of a deed in the Register of Sasines is intimation.

15   But registration of title under the Land Registration (Scotland) Act 1979 is not made the equivalent of sasine. There is registration in a public register but, for intimation of an assignation, it is probably as ineffective as registration in the Books of Council and Session.

(f) Production of assignation in judicial proceedings. There is intimation to the debtor if the debtor is party to judicial proceedings or diligence in which the assignation is founded on and the import of the assignation appears from the proceedings. In *Carter* v. *McIntosh*[56] the production of an assignation in a multiplepoinding was described as "the best of all intimations, because it was a judicial intimation"[57] a phrase which echoes Erskine.[58] The execution of a poinding of the ground by a heritable creditor was held legal intimation of the existence of the heritable security and of the assignation of rents contained in it because the summons expressly referred to the assignation.[59] But the normal style of summons for poindings of the ground does not refer to the assignation and will not operate as intimation to the tenant of an assignation of rents.[60] Service on a tenant of an action of mails and duties is intimation of an assignation of rents contained in the security.[61] The nature of the judicial proceeding is important and there must always be inquiry about what was intimated.[62]

(g) Policies of assurance. The Policies of Assurance Act 1867 limits the form of intimation of an assignation of a policy of life assurance to "a written notice of the date and purport" of the assignation given to the assurance company at a principal place of business.[63] The company is bound on request to give an acknowledgment.[64] This is not essential for the validity of the intimation but it is conclusive evidence of the intimation.

It is unfortunate that this statute, which was enacted because of problems in English law, should apparently limit the form of intimation to

---

[56] (1862) 24 D. 925.
[57] at p. 934 *per* Lord Justice-Clerk Inglis.
[58] *Inst.*, III,v,4.
[59] *Lang* v. *Hislop & Co.* (1854) 16 D. 908.
[60] *Royal Bank* v. *Dixon* (1868) 6 M. 995.
[61] *Chambers' J.F.* v. *Vertue* (1893) 20 R. 257.
[62] See Lord Ordinary in *Benton* v. *Craig* (1864) 2 M. 1365 at pp. 1368, 1369; and it may be necessary to have specific averments of the assignation—*Park Motors* v. *Blackmore*, 1964 S.L.T.(Sh.Ct.) 30. See comments on this case at para. 17–100, n. 14.
[63] s.3.
[64] s.6.

one method. But there is no prescribed style for the written notice and it could be argued that the notice might be one of a wide variety of forms, from notarial intimation to a summons, always provided that there was given not only the purport of the assignation, but also its date.

(h) Letters of supplement and the absent debtor. There is a procedure of letters of supplement which remains competent but is never or rarely used. Under letters of supplement issued in the Court of Session there can be intimation of the assignation of a bond to a debtor who is abroad.[65] The reason for the procedure was explained by Ross.[66] The market cross of Edinburgh and the pier and shore of Leith were supposed by fiction to be the *communis patria* of Scots who were bound to take as much notice of what was done there as if it had happened in their own homes. But it was only the voice of the Sovereign which people were obliged to hear. So the authority of the Sovereign, through the supreme court, was needed for intimation. The lieges were deprived of public proclamation in Edinburgh and Leith by the Court of Session Act 1825 which established registers of edictal citations as part of the records of the Court of Session.[67]

17–116   The opinion has been expressed, and it is probably correct, that the procedures of the Transmission of Moveable Property (Scotland) Act 1862 can be used if the debtor is outside Scotland[68] but these require the address of the debtor to be known. In some circumstances intimation to the debtor's agent in Scotland will suffice.[69] If the debtor's whereabouts are unknown and there is no agent in Scotland, it seems that there has to be edictal intimation, using letters of supplement.

(5) Intimation to whom?

17–117   **(a) The debtor.** Intimation should be made to the debtor. Usually his identity is not a problem, but a question arose in *Ayton* v. *Romanes*[70] where there was an assignation of a reversionary interest. X assigned a right *ex facie* absolutely to Y. This was intimated to D. X then assigned his reversion to Z. It was held that this should be intimated to Y, not to D. When X assigned his interest further the proper debtor was Z.

17–118   **(b) Several debtors.** Where there are several debtors, intimation to any one is sufficient for completing the conveyance, but intimation should be made to all to prevent those to whom no intimation has been made paying the cedent.[71] Intimation made to only one of two trustees who

---

[65] Bell, *Comm.*, ii,17; *Encyclopaedia*, Vol. 14, para. 672; Gloag and Irvine, *Rights in Security*, p. 484; J. A. Maclaren, *Bill Chamber Practice*, p. 248.

[66] *Lectures*, p. 202.

[67] s.51. See also Bell, *Prin.*, s.1463.

[68] Bell, *Lectures on Conveyancing* (3rd ed.), p. 314; Craigie, *Moveable Rights*, pp. 243, 244; *cf.* Gloag and Irvine, *sup. cit.*

[69] See para. 17–118.

[70] (1895) 3 S.L.T. 203.

[71] Stair, III,i,10; Ersk. III,v,5.

managed the fund was held sufficient.[72] *Hill* v. *Lindsay*[73] is a special case. It was held that intimation to each partner of a partnership, or to a manager appointed to act for the company was necessary to complete an assignation of a share of the company stock. But one factor in the decision appears to be that the result of the assignation was to make the assignee a partner, and this could not be done without the consent of all the existing partners.[74] A debt due by a firm would be different. Assignation could be intimated to the firm by notice to any partner who habitually acts in the partnership business.[75]

119 **(c) Agent of the debtor.** Intimation may be made to the agent of the debtor, such as the debtor's factor,[76] the treasurer of a corporation,[77] the managers of a trading company,[78] the properly appointed manager of a partnership[79] or the law agents for trustees.[80] It is probably the case that the agent must receive intimation in the course of his duties for the principal. Knowledge of the manager of an investment society who was also the cedent, was not equivalent to knowledge of the society,[81] nor was intimation sufficient to one who *de facto* was a manager, but was not properly appointed.[82] For this reason the prudent practice is to intimate whenever possible to the principal, not to the agent.[83]

120 **(d) Companies.** A document may be served on a company formed under the Companies Acts by leaving it at or sending it by post to the registered office of the company.[84]

THE RIGHT TO DEMAND AN ASSIGNATION

121 In limited circumstances there is a right to an assignation. A trustee in sequestration has a statutory right in certain cases to demand that securities be assigned to the trustee.[85] A more general right is that of a person paying a creditor to demand assignation of the debt. One reason an assignation would be wished is to help the payer exercise a right of

---

[72] *Jameson* v. *Sharp* (1887) 14 R. 643.

[73] (1846) 8 D. 472.

[74] See now Partnership Act 1890, s.24(7).

[75] Partnership Act 1890, s.16.

[76] *Earl of Aberdeen* v. *Earl of March* (1730) 1 Pat. 44.

[77] *Keir* v. *Creditors of Lethem* (1739) Mor. 738.

[78] *Watson* v. *Murdoch* (1755) Mor. 850.

[79] *Hill* v. *Lindsay* (1846) 8 D. 472.

[80] *Browne's Trs.* v. *Anderson* (1901) 4 F. 305.

[81] *Allan* v. *Urquhart* (1887) 15 R. 56.

[82] *Hill* v. *Lindsay, sup. cit.*

[83] See Wood's *Lectures*, p. 586, who even goes so far as to say that all trustees, not merely a quorum, should sign an acknowledgment, failing which there should be notarial intimation.

[84] Companies Act 1985, s.725(1). For insurance companies and policies of insurance, see Policies of Assurance Act 1867, s.3.

[85] Bankruptcy (Scotland) Act 1985, Sched. 1, para. 5; *Russell* v. *Daniel & Green* (1868) 6 M. 648.

relief. The creditor need not grant the assignation if he would be prejudiced by it. As Lord President Dunedin put it:

> "the granting of an assignation upon tender of the sum due is not, in one sense, a strictly legal right. All that, in strict law, you have got right to is a discharge. But long ago it was held that in equity, and in order to avoid the expense of putting on the securities again, if the sum was properly tendered an assignation should be granted instead of a discharge. But that is always subject to this, that the granting of the assignation shall not in any way prejudice the granter more than he would have been prejudiced if he had granted a discharge."[86]

17–122   A distinction has been drawn between (1) a creditor who is merely asked to accept payment by, say, a friend of the debtor—a third party is not entitled to demand the debt as an investment—and (2) a creditor enforcing payment—he has an equitable obligation to assign to someone with an interest, for example, the debtor's friend.[87] The debtor may demand that the creditor accept payment, and so also may someone who has acquired the debtor's right of redemption, for example, a postponed bondholder, with the consequence that the creditor must assign his debt, unless he has a legitimate interest to refuse.[88] In general the payer must have a legitimate interest in demanding an assignation[89] and he should have made full payment.[90]

17–123   The creditor is entitled to refuse to assign not only if there is a certainty of loss, but also even if there is merely a reasonable prospect of risk to another security held by him, or of annoyance and trouble.[91] In certain circumstances the creditor may be entitled to qualify the assignation[92] or limit it to part of the debt.[93] An inhibition of the creditor does not prevent him granting the assignation unless there is notarial intimation of the inhibition to the debtor under the Act of Sederunt of February 19, 1680.[94]

RETROCESSION

17–124   A subject assigned is sometimes reassigned to the cedent. This is likely to occur when the assignation was in security. The reconveyance is called a "retrocession." The alternative term of "reposition" mentioned

---

[86] *Bruce* v. *Scottish Amicable Life Ass. Soc.*, 1907 S.C. 637 at p. 643. See also *Fleming* v. *Black*, 1913 1 S.L.T. 386.

[87] *Smith* v. *Gentle* (1844) 6 D. 1164; *Fleming* v. *Burgess* (1867) 5 M. 856 *per* Lord Justice-Clerk Patton, at p. 859.

[88] *Reis* v. *Mackay* (1899) 6 S.L.T. 331.

[89] *Cunningham's Trs.* v. *Hutton* (1847) 10 D. 307.

[90] *Ewart* v. *Latta* (1865) 3 M.(H.L.) 36; *Will* v. *Elder's Trs.* (1867) 6 M. 9, esp. *per* Lord Deas at p. 12.

[91] *Mitchell* v. *McKinlay* (1842) 4 D. 634.

[92] *Fraser* v. *Carruthers* (1875) 2 R. 595; *cf. Guthrie* v. *Smith* (1880) 8 R. 107 which has an interesting dissent by Lord Shand.

[93] *McMillan* v. *Smyth* (1879) 6 R. 601; *Oliver* v. *McKnight* (1875) 12 S.L.R. 272.

[94] *Mackintosh's Trs.* v. *Davidson & Garden* (1898) 25 R. 554.

by Stair[95] is no longer used. The Transmission of Moveable Property (Scotland) Act 1862 specifically applies to retrocessions. Despite some authority[96] a retrocession should always be intimated[97] as it is only an assignation under another name.[98]

---

[95] Stair, III, i, 3.

[96] *Craig* v. *Edgar* (1674) Mor. 838; *Marston* v. *Underwood* (1827) 5 S. 200.

[97] Bell, *Lectures on Conveyancing* (3rd ed.), p. 335; Craigie, *Moveable Rights*, p. 263; *Microwave Systems (Scotland) Ltd.* v. *Electro-Physiological Instruments Ltd.*, 1971 S.C. 140.

[98] Similarly with "translations," or the transfer by an assignee to another person. See Craigie, *sup. cit.*

CHAPTER 18

JUS QUAESITUM TERTIO

18–01 Scots law, in contrast to English law,[1] recognises the *jus quaesitum tertio*. This confers on a third party, in certain circumstances, a right arising from a contract to which he was not a party.

18–02 The extent to which the right created in the third party may be revoked has been the subject of much discussion and learned comment.[2] Clearly the third party can be given an irrevocable right, but imperfections may exist in the creation of the right. Much of the discussion has been about the meaning of a passage in Stair[3] and Lord Dunedin's treatment of it in *Carmichael* v. *Carmichael's Executrix*.[4]

WHAT IS A JUS QUAESITUM TERTIO?

18–03 In the simple case a *jus quaesitum tertio* arises when C acquires rights under a contract between A and B. C is not a party to the contract, and he does not enforce the contract, but only his rights. The contract between A and B may contain many provisions which are not the concern of C. Subsequent to the contract A and B may vary their agreement without affecting the rights of C, for example if A is a feudal superior

---

[1] For England see *Midland Silicones Ltd.* v. *Scruttons Ltd.* [1962] A.C. 446; *Beswick* v. *Beswick* [1968] A.C. 58; *Woodar Investment Development Ltd.* v. *Wimpey Construction U.K. Ltd.* [1980] 1 All E.R. 571 (H.L.) at p. 591 *per* Lord Scarman; *cf. New Zealand Shipping Co.* v. *A. M. Satterthwaite & Co.* [1975] A.C. 154 and *Port Jackson Stevedoring Pty. Ltd.* v. *Salmond (Australia) Pty. Ltd.* [1980] 3 All E.R. 257 (P.C.), from which it emerges that stevedores may enjoy the benefit of clauses in a bill of lading.

[2] *e.g.* T. B. Smith, "*Jus Quaesitum Tertio*: Remedies of the '*Tertius*' in Scottish Law," 1956 J.R. 3, now (revised) *Studies Critical and Comparative* (1962), p. 183; D. I. C. Ashton-Cross, "Bare Promise in Scots Law," 1957 J.R. 138; J. T. Cameron, "*Jus Quaesitum Tertio*; The True Meaning of Stair 1,x,5," 1961 J.R. 103; A. Rodger, "Molina, Stair and the *Jus Quaesitum Tertio*," 1969 J.R. 34 and 128; D. N. MacCormick, "*Jus Quaesitum Tertio: Stair* v. *Dunedin*" 1970 J.R. 228; J. Casey, "Collective Agreements: Some Scottish Footnotes," 1973 J.R. 22; R. L. C. Hunter, "Collective Agreements, Fair Wages Clauses and the Employment Relationship in Scots Law," 1975 J.R. 47. See also G. MacCormack, "A Note on Stair's Use of the Term *Pollicitatio*," 1976 J.R. 121 (on which see D. N. MacCormick, "Stair as an Analytical Jurist" in *Stair Tercentenary Studies* (Stair Soc., 1981) 187 at pp. 197, 198); Scot. Law Com. Memo. No. 38, *Constitution and Proof of Voluntary Obligations: Stipulations in Favour of Third Parties* (1977); see below, paras. 18–16 to 18–26.

[3] *Inst.*, I,x,5. Because of the problem of differing texts of Stair (Rodger, *sup. cit.*) references in this chapter are to the 2nd edition which has recently been republished (ed. D. M. Walker, 1981). There are, however, minor differences between the Walker text and the text of the 2nd edition produced by Stair. These differences are not material for present purposes, but could become so if arguments were based on Stair's punctuation or spelling (*pace* Rodger, *sup. cit.*, G. MacCormack, *sup. cit.*).

[4] 1920 S.C.(H.L.) 195.

who waives his rights against his vassal B, but does not and cannot affect the right of a co-vassal C to enforce obligations against B.[5] Further C's ability to enforce rights against B may depend on different factors from those which affect A's ability to sue B.[6] The precise nature of C's right is uncertain. The temptation is to treat it as analogous to the rights of a donee or a promisee.[7] It is questionable whether it is wise to rely on the law on donations and promises whose specialities may be inapplicable to *jus quaesitum tertio*, as for example the strong presumption against donation, or the method of proof of a promise.[8] It may be better to treat *jus quaesitum tertio* as an independent right which shares some of the characteristics of other contractual rights but also has special features.

How is a Jus Quaesitum Tertio created?

1. There must be a contract between A and B

04   A and B must enter into a contract[9] and not another relationship which might be intended to benefit C, such as a trust[10] or a testamentary provision.[11] If the whole contract between A and B is void, then in principle the right of C is also void.[12] Nor should there be any theoretical difficulty if the contract between A and B is voidable, making C's right also voidable, for example if the contract is induced by fraud or facility and circumvention.[13] Much more awkward problems arise if the contract between A and B is unenforceable or illegal. The effect on C will depend on the reason for the invalidity in the relationship between A and B.[14]

2. A and B must intend to benefit C

05   The intention to benefit the third party must exist.[15] It is not enough that C is interested in, or will benefit from, the contract between A and B. For example it is insufficient that C would benefit because the con-

---

[5] *Lawrence* v. *Scott*, 1965 S.C. 403 *per* Lord President Clyde at p. 407.

[6] See *Maguire* v. *Burges*, 1909 S.C. 1283 *per* Lord President Dunedin at pp. 1290, 1291.

[7] See, *e.g.* Smith, *Studies Critical and Comparative, sup. cit.*; Cameron, *sup. cit.* at p. 118; MacCormick, 1970 J.R. at pp. 232–234; Scot. Law Com., *op. cit.*, paras. 10–12.

[8] See also Rodger, *sup. cit.*, pp. 143, 144.

[9] *Wightman* v. *Costine* (1879) 6 R.(H.L.) 13 *per* Lord Chancellor Cairns at p. 17; *Downie* v. *Mags. of Annan* (1879) 6 R. 457.

[10] *Allan's Trs.* v. *Lord Advocate*, 1971 S.C.(H.L.) 45.

[11] *e.g.* *Barclay's Trs.* v. *Watson* (1903) 5 F. 926; *Lord Advocate* v. *Stewart* (1906) 8 F. 579; *Montgomerie's Trs.* v. *Alexander's Trs.*, 1911 S.C. 856, and many other cases. A contractual right in favour of heirs can, of course, be created, *e.g.* *Gordon* v. *Gordon's Trs.* (1886) 13 R. 934.

[12] *Cumming* v. *Quartzag Ltd.*, 1980 S.C. 276. On whether the contract really was void in that case, see H. L. MacQueen, "Promoters' Contracts: Agency and the *Jus Quaesitum Tertio*," 1982 S.L.T.(News) 257.

[13] See T. B. Smith. *Short Commentary*, p. 784; Scot. Law Com., *op. cit.*, paras. 39–40.

[14] Hunter, *sup. cit.*, discusses the problem with collective agreements; see also Scot. Law Com., *op. cit.*, paras. 51–55.

[15] *Peddie* v. *Brown* (1857) 3 Macq. 65; *Finnie* v. *G. & S.W. Ry. Co.* (1857) 3 Macq. 75.

tract would affect the rates of carriage he would pay,[16] or supply engines for his ship,[17] or affect claims against him,[18] or provide him with rooms in which to work.[19]

18–06   The intention to benefit C can be shown by an express term in the contract or by implication. This aspect of the law has been most fully worked out in the rights of vassals or disponees to enforce conditions in neighbouring titles. A neighbour can be given an express right to enforce a condition.[20] It is obviously more difficult to determine whether the right is implied. The courts have evolved a series of guidelines. The leading cases are *Hislop* v. *MacRitchie's Trs.*[21] and *Nicholson* v. *Glasgow Asylum for the Blind.*[22] See also the cases cited.[23] In *Denny's Trs.* v. *Dumbarton Magistrates*[24] residuary legatees entered into a letter of obligation which gave an express *jus quaesitum* to enforce the obligations on the statutory representatives of the local community. A contract of road traffic insurance may confer a *jus quaesitum* on persons driving with the permission of the policy-holder.[25] One of the parties may be required to deliver goods to a third party.[26]

18–07   There is some confusion developing, because intention is relevant at two stages. Whether A and B intend to benefit C is in the first place a question of construction of the contract in the light of the circumstances. Unless C can surmount this hurdle, his case for establishing a *jus tertii* can go no further. The most obvious way in which A and B can show their intention is to state expressly that C is to benefit. But, as will be seen, the mere expression of an intention is not normally enough. A second step must be taken to show that the intention is irrevocable. The most perfect way of doing that is delivery to C, and that involves both the fact of delivery and, because mere transfer would not be enough, the intention to deliver. However, what the parties meant when they signed the deed (a problem of construction), and what they have done or should have done to give it effect (a problem of delivery), are closely related issues. In the case of *Carmichael*[27] the two problems were treated as one. When a party to an action has to overcome two hurdles, it may not matter whether he falls at one or at both, particularly if the

---

[16] *Finnie, sup. cit.*
[17] *Blumer & Co.* v. *Scott & Sons* (1874) 1 R. 379.
[18] *Barr* v. *Cochrane* (1878) 5 R. 877.
[19] *Downie* v. *Mags. of Annan* (1879) 6 R. 457.
[20] *Braid Hills Hotel Co. Ltd.* v. *Manuels*, 1909 S.C. 120; *Lawrence* v. *Scott*, 1965 S.C. 403. See also *Macdonald* v. *Douglas*, 1963 S.C. 374; 1963 S.L.T. 191 (the *Scots Law Times* has a fuller report).
[21] (1881) 8 R.(H.L.) 95.
[22] 1911 S.C. 391.
[23] *Turner* v. *Hamilton* (1890) 17 R. 494; *Johnston* v. *Walker Trustees* (1897) 24 R. 1061; *Botanic Gardens Picture House* v. *Adamson*, 1924 S.C. 549; *Gray* v. *Macleod*, 1979 S.L.T.(Sh.Ct.) 17.
[24] 1945 S.C. 147.
[25] *Kelly* v. *Cornhill Insurance Co.*, 1964 S.C.(H.L.) 46.
[26] *Cullen* v. *McMenamin Ltd.*, 1928 S.L.T.(Sh.Ct.) 2.
[27] *Sup. cit.*

hurdles appear to be linked. In other cases, however, the facts will be different and the analysis may need to be sharper. In *Allan's Trs.* v. *Lord Advocate*[28] Lord Guest distinguished the two questions arising, namely (1) the intention expressed by the terms of the contract, and (2) the intention to make the deed binding.[29] Lord Reid did not separate these issues.[30] Both judges could cite *Carmichael's* case in support of their slightly differing approaches.

3. The third party C must be identified but need not be named

3–08   The need for identification is obvious. The Lord Ordinary in *Peddie* v. *Brown*[31] stated that the third party had to be named. Subsequently it has been pointed out that only identification is required.[32] Were it otherwise, a *jus quaesitum tertio* in favour of a beneficiary not yet born would be impossible.[33] There can, therefore, be a *jus quaesitum* in favour of a class of persons such as persons driving a car with the permission of an insured,[34] or the elected representatives of a local authority.[35] It is important to observe that merely naming or identifying would not be sufficient to create a *jus quaesitum tertio, e.g.* taking bonds in the name of one's children.[36] In a takeover agreement between A and B, a creditor C would have no rights merely because the agreement mentioned creditors' rights.[37] Similarly a debtor C may not be able to found on an arrangement between his creditors.[38] The other requirements for a *jus quaesitum tertio* must exist to give rights to C.

4. There must normally be delivery or an equivalent[39]

3–09   This is a controversial statement which is discussed in detail below.

---

[28] 1971 S.C.(H.L.) 45.

[29] at pp. 56, 57.

[30] at p. 54.

[31] (1857) 3 Macq. 65 at p. 70.

[32] *Peddie* v. *Brown, sup. cit.* at p. 71 *per* Lord Chancellor Cranworth; *Finnie* v. *G. & S.W. Ry. Co.* (1857) 3 Macq. 75 at p. 90 *per* Lord Wensleydale; *Blumer & Co.* v. *Scott & Sons, sup. cit.* at p. 387 *per* Lord Ardmillan.

[33] See Lord Keith, *The Spirit of the Law of Scotland* (Holdsworth Club Address, 1957), p. 27.

[34] *Kelly* v. *Cornhill Insurance Co.*, 1964 S.C.(H.L.) 46.

[35] *Denny's Trs.* v. *Dumbarton Mags.*, 1945 S.C. 147.

[36] *Drysdale's Trs.* v. *Drysdale*, 1922 S.C. 741.

[37] *Henderson* v. *Stubbs, Ltd.* (1894) 22 R. 51; *Taylor* v. *R. & H. Thomson & Co.* (1901) 9 S.L.T. 373.

[38] *Lennie's Trs.* v. *Johnstone*, 1914 1 S.L.T. 47.

[39] *Carmichael* v. *Carmichael's Exrx.*, 1920 S.C.(H.L.) 195. The "equivalent" might be called "constructive delivery," or otherwise treated as something distinct from physical transfer of the deed. It is therefore possible to say that the "equivalent" is not delivery and delivery is not needed. As so often in Scots law words have wide and narrow meanings. "Delivery" and "equivalent" are no exception.

5. *C must have not only a title to sue but also an interest to sue*[40]

18–10   This is in accordance with the normal principles of the law of remedies. Unfortunately the term *jus quaesitum tertio* has been used in circumstances in which the third party has a title to sue without personal benefit, *e.g.* where he is entitled to enforce payment of money for the benefit of one of the contracting parties. This, however, is an inapt use of the term *jus quaesitum tertio* and should be avoided.[41]

DELIVERY OR AN EQUIVALENT

18–11   Much of the discussion about *jus quaesitum tertio* has been about the fourth proposition stated above. The main point made by Lord Dunedin in *Carmichael's* case was this. The mere execution of a document by A and B will not, without more, create a right in C. There must be delivery to C, or equivalent evidence of an irrevocable investiture. In view of the controversy which has surrounded Lord Dunedin's speech, it is necessary to restate the principles of delivery applicable to the Scots law of written obligations.[42]

18–12   The argument is not concerned with a *jus quaesitum tertio* created by an oral contract. The case law and the articles have not been concerned with that possibility, nor with the associated problem of the method of proof.[43] The discussion has been about a *jus* created in writing. That writing must be an *inter vivos* deed, and not a *mortis causa* deed, at least so far as C's right is concerned.[44] The general principle applying to deeds is that they must be delivered to be effective. Erskine said, in the classic text: "A writing while it is in the granter's own custody is not obligatory; for as long as it is in his own power he cannot be said to have come to a final resolution of obliging himself by it."[45] There must be the intention to deliver and the fact of delivery. What is meant by "delivery" may vary with the type of transaction. For example, there is

---

[40] *Earl of Zetland* v. *Hislop* (1882) 9 R.(H.L.) 40; *Mactaggart & Co.* v. *Roemmele*, 1907 S.C. 1318; *Maguire* v. *Burges*, 1909 S.C. 1283; *D. & J. Nicol* v. *Dundee Harbour Trs.*, 1915 S.C.(H.L.) 7 at p. 12 *per* Lord Dunedin.

[41] See Scot. Law Com., *sup. cit.*, paras. 17 to 24.

[42] See more fully, Chap. 7, "Delivery."

[43] In principle if the contract between A and B can be proved by parole, the right to C should also be provable by parole evidence. See Walker and Walker, *Evidence*, para. 130. It is conceivable, however, that the right to C may need a different method of proof, *e.g.* if A and B bargain about moveables and give C a right to heritage. See also Scot. Law Com., *op. cit.*, para. 47.

[44] Part of an *inter vivos* deed can have a testamentary affect, as in some destinations in titles to heritable property; see McLaren, *Law of Wills and Succession* (3rd ed., 1894), para. 540. The distinctive feature of a testamentary provision, of course, is its revocable character, but also the principle of delivery does not operate as it does with *inter vivos* deeds.

[45] Ersk., *Inst.*, III,ii,43. See generally A. M. Bell, *Lectures on Conveyancing* (3rd ed., 1882), pp. 102 *et seq*; W. G. Dickson, *Law of Evidence* (3rd ed. 1887), paras. 916 *et seq.*; J. P. Wood, *Lectures on Conveyancing* (1903), pp. 98 *et seq.*; Gloag, *Contract*, pp. 66–76.

some authority which suggests that the delivery required in donation *mortis causa* is different from delivery in outright donation.[46] Also the creation of a trust has its specialities.[47]

8–13 The result is that to require delivery or an equivalent for the creation of a *jus quaesitum tertio* is to make a statement consistent with the normal requirements of the Scots law of voluntary obligations. To suggest the opposite—that delivery was not required—would be startling, particularly to anyone familiar with the history of conveyancing.[48] There is room for discussion on the meaning of "delivery" or an "equivalent," but the principle is clear enough.

8–14 When all of this is taken into account, it is hardly surprising that the decision in *Carmichael* was to affirm the principle that delivery or an equivalent was necessary. The "equivalent" was evidence of the intention to confer an irrevocable right.[49] The mistake made by the majority of the bench of seven judges in the Court of Session[50] was that they placed too much emphasis on proof of actual delivery. In the House of Lords, Lord Dunedin listed several dealings with a document which would be the equivalent of physical transfer of the deed to a third party. These were: (a) registration for publication in the Books of Council and Session, but not normally recording in the Register of Sasines; (b) intimation to the *tertius*; and (c) the *tertius* coming under onerous engagements on the faith of his having a *jus quaesitum*.[51] This was not intended as an exhaustive list.

8–15 In the case before him, Lord Dunedin found evidence of intention to create an irrevocable right in (1) the terms of the document; (2) the knowledge of the *tertius*, the son; (3) a letter from the father to the insurance company; and (4) the written pleadings of the father. This may have stated too much. The terms of the document should not be relevant to what has happened after execution of the document. The content of a summons in an action of multiplepoinding raised 13 years after the issue of the document is an unlikely source of evidence against

---

[46] *Crosbie's Tr.* v. *Wright* (1880) 7 R. 823 at p. 834 *per* Lord Shand; *McSkimming* v. *Stenhouse* (1883) 21 S.L.R. 3 at p. 5 *per* Lord Fraser; *contra, Macfarlane's Trs.* v. *Miller* (1898) 25 R. 1201 at p. 1211 *per* Lord McLaren. But there must be delivery or an equivalent for *donatio mortis causa: Graham's Tr.* v. *Gillies*, 1956 S.C. 437; *Gray's Trs.* v. *Murray*, 1970 S.C. 1.

[47] See, *e.g. Connell's Tr.* v. *Connell's Tr.*, 1955 S.L.T. 125; *Allan's Trs.* v. *Lord Advocate*, 1971 S.C.(H.L.) 45; *Clark's Tr.* v. *Inland Revenue*, 1972 S.C. 177; *Kerr's Tr.* v. *Inland Revenue*, 1974 S.L.T. 193; *Clark Taylor & Co. Ltd.* v. *Quality Site Development (Edinburgh) Ltd.*, 1981 S.C. 111.

[48] But see Scot. Law Com., *op. cit.*, para. 36. As a proposal for law reform there is an attractive simplicity in the abolition of the need for delivery or an equivalent, but this should be looked at in the whole context of delivery and voluntary obligations. We do not read Lord Reid's speech in *Allan's Trs.* as providing support for the proposition that for a *jus quaesitum* no delivery or equivalent is needed. The other authorities referred to on this point by the Commission are not consistent with the views of many other judges. See *inter alia* Dickson, *sup. cit.*, esp. paras. 952–958.

[49] See *Allan's Trs.* v. *Lord Advocate*, 1971 S.C.(H.L.) 45 at p. 54 *per* Lord Reid.

[50] See 1919 S.C. 636.

[51] 1920 S.C.(H.L.) 195 at pp. 201–203.

a claimant of the fund *in medio*. However, the result of the decision in *Carmichael* is to show that for a *jus quaesitum tertio* an equivalent of delivery is sufficient. In that analogies were drawn with *donatio mortis causa*, the "equivalent" may be less than required with other obligations. *Donatio mortis causa* is special because of its close association with testamentary provisions and no delivery or equivalent is needed for an effective testament. Whether the House of Lords were correct in making the analogy between *jus quaesitum tertio* and *donatio mortis causa* is debatable.[52] It was not the approach taken in the Court of Session, and if the comparison had been made with cases on outright donation or promise, the result might have been different. As it is, the decision weakened the strength of the evidence which otherwise might have been thought necessary to show delivery. To this extent the case does not operate to hinder the creation of a *jus quaesitum tertio*. On the contrary, the House of Lords made it easier to prove the existence of *jus tertii*.

The Attack on Dunedin

18–16 It has, however, been suggested that Lord Dunedin in *Carmichael* misinterpreted Stair.[53] So also on earlier occasions did Lords Ardmillan, Dundas and MacKenzie.[54] Lord Dunedin referred to Stair because the appellant had argued that Stair showed that the terms of the deed alone could be sufficient to create a right in the third party. Given the history of the concept of delivery in Scots law, it is not surprising that Lord Dunedin retorted that if Stair said that Stair was wrong. The difficulty posed by Lord Dunedin's speech was his explanation of the passage in Stair, and the error was compounded by a reference to the fifth rather than the second edition of the *Institutions*, and copying the rewriting of Stair suggested by previous judges.[55] What Lord Dunedin said was this[56]:

> "Lord Stair says: 'It is likewise the opinion of Molina, and quadrates with our customs that when parties contract, if there be any article in favour of a third party, at any time, *est jus quaesitum tertio*, which cannot be recalled by *either or* both *of* the contractors, but he may compel either of them to exhibit the contract, and thereupon the obliged may be compelled to perform.' That would mean that the moment you find from the form of the obligation that there was a *jus* conceived in favour of a *tertius* it proved that that *jus* was *quaesitum* to that *tertius*. I do not think Lord Stair meant to lay down such a proposition. If he did, and if your Lordships were to say he was right in so doing, then you would overrule not only the long string of comparatively modern cases as regards deposit-

---

[52] *Crosbie's Trs.* v. *Wright* (1880) 7 R. 823 was founded on. That case was introduced into the argument by Lord Dunedin (1920 S.C.(H.L.) 195, note). Other cases referred to were cases of donation, but *Crosbie's Trs.* greatly influenced the House.

[53] See Cameron, *sup. cit.*, Rodger, *sup. cit.*, MacCormick, *sup. cit.*

[54] Rodger, *sup. cit.* at pp. 37, 38.

[55] See Rodger, *passim; Blumer & Co.* v. *Scott & Sons* (1874) 1 R. 379 at p. 387.

[56] *Carmichael* v. *Carmichael's Exrx*, 1920 S.C.(H.L.) 195 at pp. 199, 200.

receipts of which I have already mentioned two, and of which a whole series can be found in the Digest under the title of 'Donation', so numerous that it would be tedious to cite them, but also the older authorities as to bonds, destinations in titles to land, and insurance policies, which, beginning with the case of *Hill* decided in 1755, go on with *Balvaird* in 1816, and come down to *Hadden* in 1899. Speaking for myself, I should decline to be a party to such a holocaust of accepted authorities in the law of Scotland; but I do not think Lord Stair meant any such thing. It was pointed out by Lord Ardmillan in *Blumer & Co.* v. *Scott & Sons* and accepted by Lords Dundas and Mackenzie in this case, that the transposition of the words '*est jus quaesitum tertio*' and the words 'which cannot be recalled by either or both of the contractors' would make the proposition agree with the decided cases. Irrevocability would be a condition, not a consequence, of the expression of the *jus* in favour of the *tertius*. Perhaps the ambiguity arises from Lord Stair putting his sentence partly in Latin and partly in English. If he had followed *est jus quaesitum tertio* by *quod non revocari potest*, the sentence might grammatically have read as Lord Ardmillan wished it to. But the real reason for supposing that Lord Stair did not mean the larger proposition is the fact that he quotes four cases on which he founds what he is saying, and not one of these would warrant this larger proposition."

3–17   This interpretation of Stair has been subject to cogent criticism by other writers. In particular it is generally agreed that Stair did *not* make irrevocability a condition for the creation of a *jus quaesitum tertio*.[57] There is, however, a danger that the substance of Lord Dunedin's argument will be ignored because part of its historical foundation was not strictly accurate. The decision in *Carmichael* may have been correct although some of the reasoning is suspect. What should not be overlooked is that the case was primarily concerned with the concept of delivery and its equivalents. Lord Dunedin may have made two errors. One was his misinterpretation of Stair which has already been referred to. His other possible mistake was more basic. It was his acceptance of the passage in Stair as being relevant to the argument.

3–18   What it is respectfully submitted Lord Dunedin should have said, is that Stair in the passage referred to[58] was not concerned with the rules on delivery. The context of the passage was a treatment of the law of promises, and nowhere is it suggested that delivery of a promise may be needed to make it effective. That is not to say that Stair meant that delivery was unnecessary. He quite simply was not dealing with the point. At an earlier stage he had considered the problems of delivery[59] and his treatment was largely concerned with the fact that delivery is presumed if the writ is out of the granter's hand and that there are writs which are effectual without delivery. Inevitably, much of the case law on delivery is later than Stair, who could not be expected to foresee the

---

[57] See Scot. Law Com., *op. cit.*, para. 8.
[58] *Inst.*, I,x,5.
[59] *Inst.*, I,vii,14. See also IV,xlii,8.

problems of the modern lawyer in creating an effective trust or alienation which will withstand the scrutiny of the Inland Revenue. But Stair did recognise the principle of delivery. He observed[60]:

> "And, therefore, bonds of provision by fathers to children, if delivered, are not revocable directly, nor indirectly, by contracting debts thereafter. And the delivery of such bonds of provision makes them irrevocable, whether the delivery be to the children, or to any other for their behoof; (which behoof will be presumed, unless the father express his mind at the delivery, that the writ is to be returned to himself, or depositate upon terms); and, therefore, a bond taken by a father in the name of his brother, the father obtaining an assignation from him to his daughter, the bond was not found revocable by the father, being registrate in the brother's name, November 20, 1667, Executors of Trotter *contra* Trotter."

As it was said in Hackerton's report of *Trotter*, a decision[61] which, as it is reported by Stair,[62] was one in which Stair took part[63]:

> "The Lords found, that the father being master of a bond or right whereupon nothing followed, being granted by himself, may throw it in the fire, and consequently discharge it; but the said right being made public, and completed by the delivery, and which is equivalent, by some public deed, by infeftment if it be heritable; or by assignation intimated or confirmed testament, if it be moveable, he could not thereafter retreat or prejudge the same."

18–19   It is submitted that this approach is consistent with that of the House of Lords over 250 years later in *Carmichael*. In the interval there had been some controversy over the concept of the equivalent of delivery,[64] but these refinements do not affect the proposition that the principles laid down by Stair are consistent with the result in *Carmichael*. The pity is that Lord Dunedin, quite unnecessarily, misread one passage in Stair. But the substance of Lord Dunedin's approach may be more accurate than his critics have allowed.

REVOCATION

18–20   Stair said: "when parties contract, if there be any article in favours of a third party, at any time, *est jus quaesitum tertio*, which cannot be recalled by both the contractors."[65] All he probably meant to say was that after the creation of a *jus quaesitum tertio* the parties to the contract could not revoke the third party's right.[66] By itself that is an innocent and acceptable remark. It might not deal with all the possibilities, but no

---

[60] *Inst.*, I,v,6. As explained earlier, the Walker edition of Stair is used, but with hesitation. Stair's punctuation was different.
[61] (1667) Mor. 11498.
[62] 1 Stair 487.
[63] See Introduction to his *Decisions*.
[64] e.g. *Cameron's Trs.* v. *Cameron*, 1907 S.C. 407.
[65] *Inst.*, I,x,5.
[66] See *Finnie* v. *G. & S.W. Ry. Co.* (1857) 3 Macq. 75 at p. 90 *per* Lord Wensleydale.

textbook writer can. As a statement of principle it would be sound. The law, however, was thrown into confusion in *Blumer & Co.* v. *Scott & Sons*[67] by Lord Ardmillan, who excelled as a criminal lawyer, but of whom, in the opinion of the writer of his obituary: "It cannot be said that the late Judge was great in matters of pure law."[68]

8–21 Lord Ardmillan read Stair as saying that an irrevocable right was necessary for the existence of a *jus quaesitum*. This proposition may have influenced judges on future occasions, including such eminent authorities as Lord President Inglis and Lord Kyllachy. It came to be suggested that a revocable contract, such as a revocable mandate, could not create a *jus quaesitum*,[69] and conversely that irrevocability was essential for the existence of a *jus quaesitum*.[70] So when in *Carmichael* Lord Dunedin said that irrevocability was a condition, not a consequence, of the *jus* in favour of the *tertius*,[71] he was following the views of several Scottish judges.[72] Mr Cameron has concluded that: "A revocable *jus quaesitum* is a contradiction in terms."[73]

8–22 The law is in confusion because of the failure to recognise that revocation can arise on two occasions and each poses a different theoretical problem. Until delivery of a written deed it is revocable. The concept of revocability is at that point concerned with the creation of an obligation. But a right once created may be revoked. There are many instances of revocable rights in Scots law, *e.g.* rights under some contracts of mandate or deposit, the contract created between a company and its members by section 14 of the Companies Act 1985, or the revocable promise to keep an offer open. In Stair's time donations between man and wife, *stante matrimonio*, were revocable by the giver during life.[74]

8–23 Nor should we be surprised if a legal system recognises revocable rights. Many contractual rights are only exercisable if certain conditions are satisfied, and there is no reason why one of these conditions could not be the absence of prior revocation. Similarly, a law which recognises resolutive conditions or irritancies,[75] surely recognises the concept of a right which may vest, but which can in certain circumstances be revoked. The concept of revocation is here concerned with the termination of the right.

---

[67] (1874) 1 R. 379.

[68] (1876) 20 *Journal of Jurisprudence*, p. 539.

[69] *Macdonald* v. *City of Glasgow Bank* (1879) 6 R. 621 at p. 629 *per* Lord President Inglis.

[70] *Rose, Murison & Thomson* v. *Wingate, Birrell & Co.'s Trs.* (1889) 16 R. 1132 at p. 1135 *per* Lord Kyllachy. The cases on a superior's power to dispense with feuing restrictions are, it is thought, concerned with a different issue. The revocability of the restriction is an indication that there was no implied intention in the particular case to create a *jus* in favour of the third party. See *Turner* v. *Hamilton* (1890) 17 R. 494; *Red Court Hotel Ltd.* v. *Burgh of Largs*, 1955 S.L.T.(Sh.Ct.) 2.

[71] *Sup. cit.* at p. 200.

[72] Although he only mentions expressly Lords Ardmillan, Dundas and Mackenzie.

[73] Cameron, *sup. cit.* at p. 118.

[74] *Inst.*, I,iv.18.

[75] See paras. 20–145 to 20–149.

18–24   "Is a right irrevocable?" is an ambiguous question. Are we concerned with whether a right has been created (*inter alia* has there been delivery?) or the terms of a right which has been created (a problem of construction with the possible answer that the right may be terminated). A granter may revoke his deed either by throwing it in the fire when nothing has followed on it, or in terms of a delivered deed, by implementing a procedure for revocation. Revocation can arise at the point of creation of an obligation or can bring about its termination. To confuse the two is to fail to distinguish birth from death.

18–25   It may be, as Professor MacCormick has suggested, that Stair must have contemplated a revocable term in favour of a stranger to the contract.[76] MacCormick goes on to ask the question: "Should terms in favour of third parties be presumed to be irrevocable unless a contrary intention be proved, or should they be presumed to be revocable in the absence of a proven intention to treat them as irrevocable?"[77] He continues: "Here then we have isolated the crucial question which ought to occupy the mind of the law reformer. It is as plain as a pikestaff that a legal system which recognises the *jus quaesitum tertio* at all must plump for one or other of these presumptions." There is a contrary view. There is no reason why a legal system needs to adopt any presumption. As it happens in the context of proof of delivery certain rebuttable presumptions exist,[78] but in determining the meaning of the term in favour of the third party all that is at issue is a problem of interpretation or construction. There is no need to adopt presumptions on revocability to decide the meaning of a contract. No doubt one could adopt rules of construction which favour one solution rather than another, as happens when a contract is construed *contra proferentem*. But in this context it is by no means obvious that such an approach is required.

18–26   An example of a third party acquiring rights under a revocable contract is *Love* v. *Amalgamated Society of Lithographic Printers of Great Britain and Ireland*.[79] In that case rules of a union provided benefits to the relatives of an insured member. The agreement in the rules was revocable, but had not been revoked when the pursuer's claim arose. Therefore the pursuer had a good title to sue. Professor Walker has observed that *Love* was referred to in *Carmichael* without disapproval, but says that "it is hard to see how it can stand consistently with the later case."[80] But *Carmichael* was concerned with the creation of a right, and in particular with the problem of delivery. That was not the issue in *Love*. If it is accepted that Scots law recognises that a right created may be a revocable right and that a third party can have a revocable right, *Love* is an illustration of these propositions. Provided the different contexts in which revocation may be used are distinguished, there is no con-

---

[76] MacCormick, *sup. cit.*, 1970 J.R. at p. 236.
[77] *Ibid.*
[78] See para. 7–07.
[79] 1912 S.C. 1078. See also *Cadoux* v. *Central R.C.*, 1986 S.L.T. 117.
[80] D. M. Walker, *Contracts*, para. 29.14.

flict between the cases on delivery and the idea that vested rights may be revocable. Various contrary dicta and Professor Walker's view should not be followed.

THE EXCEPTIONS TO THE PRINCIPLE OF DELIVERY

7 There is a puzzle with the doctrine of *jus quaesitum tertio*, which has been ignored. This is the application of the exceptions to the principle which requires delivery of *inter vivos* deeds. The classic text on delivery is in Erskine.[81] He said that delivery was needed and then listed exceptions.

8   Erskine stated: "A deed in which the granter himself hath an interest—*e.g.* a reserved liferent—is good without delivery; for it is presumed that the granter holds such deed in his own custody, not because his intention is not finished concerning it, but to secure that interest which he has reserved to himself."[82] Leaving aside the subsequent history of that exception, and the circumstances in which it has been ignored, the proposition which it contains could be used to explain the lack of delivery in cases of *jus quaesitum tertio* created by feudal writs. For example, a superior may deliver to his vassal a writ which creates a *jus quaesitum tertio* in favour of a neighbouring vassal. The neighbour does not receive delivery of the writ, nor is it suggested that he should receive delivery or an equivalent. The reason could be that deeds in which parties retain a substantial interest do not require delivery to a third party to create rights in the third party. If this were correct the need for delivery would alter according to the interest retained by the parties.

9 A and B contract and intend to create a right in favour of C. It is possible that the substantial interest in having possession of the deed will be in A or B. In this case there need not be delivery to C. There might have to be delivery between A and B, for example, the case of the feu writ which has been mentioned. It might be that B is an obligor who is not interested in whether he pays A or C, provided that he pays the right person. The obligee is the appropriate person to receive delivery of the deed and that obligee could be C, for example an insurance policy taken out by A with insurance company B in favour of A's son C. Viewed in this way, delivery in the context of *jus quaesitum tertio* can be consistent with delivery in other parts of the law of contract.

0   There is some confusion on what the correct approach is, but that is caused by the uncertainties of the rules of delivery applicable to written obligations. The removal of these obscurities would be important for the clarification of the law on *jus quaesitum tertio*,[83] but it would also have a much wider impact.

---

[81] *Inst.*, III,ii,44.

[82] *Inst.*, III,ii,44.

[83] *Cf.* the provisional proposal of Scot. Law Com., *op. cit.*, para. 26, which overlooks that the underlying problem is the state of the law on delivery of deeds.

CHAPTER 19

CONSTRUCTION OF CONTRACTS

THE INTENTION OF THE PARTIES

19–01   It is sometimes said that in the construction of contracts the primary rule is to discover the intention of the parties. In, for example, some decisions in the House of Lords there are references to this process. Lord Pearce referred to what the parties intended in determining whether a warranty was excluded,[1] Lord Wilberforce to the intention which ought to be imputed to the parties[2] and Lord Morris to the sources from which the intention of the parties may be collected to construe an agreement.[3] Lord Diplock said:

> "The object sought to be achieved in construing any commercial contract is to ascertain what were the mutual intentions of the parties as to the legal obligations each assumed by the contractual words in which they . . . chose to express them; or, perhaps more accurately, what each would have led the other reasonably to assume were the acts that he was promising to do or to refrain from doing by the words in which the promises on his part were expressed."[4]

19–02   There is no harm in such expressions provided that the reference to "intention" is treated as no more than a convenient shorthand for a complex process. To talk of "intention" is valuable in that it emphasises that it is important to examine what *the parties* to the contract did, rather than what they should have done, or what might have been done by some other person such as the judge, the officious bystander or the ubiquitous reasonable man. But ascertainment of "intention" is an incomplete, or inaccurate, description of construction as was pointed out some time ago.[5] There are at least two reasons for this. First, many contract disputes are about matters which the parties never considered at the time of formation of the contract. The contract may be silent on the point or may be in a standard form the terms of which were never read. Hence, sometimes, there is reference to an intention "imputed" to the parties. Secondly, and of more importance, what the parties intended to say is, in general terms, irrelevant.[6] Leaving aside excep-

---

[1] *Gloucestershire C.C.* v. *Richardson* [1969] 1 A.C. 480 at p. 494.
[2] *Whitworth Street Estates* v. *Miller* [1970] A.C. 583 at pp. 614, 615.
[3] *Wickman Tools* v. *Schuler A.G.* [1974] A.C. 235 at p. 256.
[4] *Pioneer Shipping* v. *B.T.P. Tioxide* [1982] A.C. 724 at p. 736.
[5] See Gloag, *Contract*, p. 398.
[6] *Prenn* v. *Simonds* [1971] 3 All E.R. 237 (H.L.) at p. 241 *per* Lord Wilberforce. *Forrest* v. *Scottish County Investment Co.*, 1916 S.C.(H.L.) 28 at p. 33 *per* Lord Chancellor Buckmaster.

tional cases—such as when the contract contains a clerical error—a contract is construed according to what the parties have said, not what they intended to say. As it has been put: "the question to be answered always is, 'What is the meaning of what the parties have said?' not, 'What did the parties mean to say?' "[7] Lord President Dunedin observed in a famous dictum in *Muirhead & Turnbull* v. *Dickson*[8] that although both parties to a contract might have thought they were contracting on a particular basis, "commercial contracts cannot be arranged by what people think in their inmost minds. Commercial contracts are made according to what people say."

3   One consequence of the irrelevance of a party's intention is that it is no defence in the normal case to say that a contract was not read. As Lord Devlin put it: "It seems to me that, when a party assents to a document forming the whole or a part of his contract, he is bound by the terms of the document, read or unread, signed or unsigned, simply because they are in the contract."[9] A party could not resile from a contract on the grounds that its terms were unintelligible and could not be understood by her.[10] It has been observed that[11]:

> "it is no defence whatever against an action of damages for breach of contract to say that the contract was a difficult contract to read, or that it reasonably required a litigation to fix its true meaning. Parties have themselves to blame for making contracts of difficult or doubtful interpretation, and the party who is found to be in the wrong must take the consequences. It would never do to allow a party to commit a breach of contract, and then to exempt him from reparation or damages merely because there was a dispute, reasonable or unreasonable, about the contract's meaning. Such a doctrine would lead both to confusion and to injustice."

Construction and Interpretation

4   It is not the proper function of the court to consider only the literal meanings of words. An explanation of meaning—a translation—is the result of interpretation. Interpretation results in an expression in other intelligible or familiar terms, for example, that "triangle" means a plane figure with three angles and three sides. A construction of a contract is a more sophisticated process.[12] In certain circumstances meaningless

---

[7] *Wickman Tools* v. *Schuler A.G., sup. cit.* at p. 263 *per* Lord Simon quoting Norton on *Deeds.*

[8] (1905) 7 F. 686 at p. 694. A case of error, whether in expression or in consent, raises different considerations.

[9] *McCutcheon* v. *David MacBrayne,* 1964 S.C.(H.L.) 28 at p. 41. See also *Selkirk* v. *Ferguson,* 1908 S.C. 26; *Oakbank Oil Co.* v. *Love & Stewart,* 1917 S.C. 611; on appeal 1918 S.C.(H.L.) 54; *Mendlessohn* v. *Norman* [1970] 1 Q.B. 177 at p. 182 *per* Denning M.R.; *Hodge Leasing* v. *Alexander Laing (Contractors),* 1980 S.L.T.(Sh.Ct.) 54.

[10] *Laing* v. *Provincial Homes Investment Co.,* 1909 S.C. 812.

[11] *Houldsworth* v. *Brand's Tr.* (1876) 3 R. 304 at p. 318 *per* Lord Gifford.

[12] See *Adamastos Shipping Co.* v. *Anglo-Saxon Petroleum Co.* [1957] 2 Q.B. 233 at p. 248 *per* Lord Devlin; on appeal [1959] A.C. 133.

words may be ignored, a construction producing reasonable business efficiency may be preferred to a literal meaning, validity may be preferred to invalidity, or, on the other hand, a limited or strict meaning may be applied. To give further examples would be to state all the rules of construction. These rules are different from those of an interpreter or an etymologist. For example, no accurate interpreter, nor any dictionary would state that "this bill of lading" meant "this charter party" and yet the House of Lords did just that in the circumstances of one case.[13] Applying the rules to be discussed a court could turn "man" into "woman," "life" into "death," "black" into "white" or "triangle" into "rectangle." Construction is different from interpretation, and rightly so, because of the vague, inaccurate and slipshod methods of expression commonly adopted by those who enter into contracts.

The Meaning of Words and Questions of Fact and Law

19–05 The literal meaning of a word is a question of fact. A dictionary will supply a meaning in other words which can in turn be looked up, and so on. No question of law is involved.[14] The proper construction of a contract is, however, a question of law for the court to determine.[15] This difference is of particular importance when the court is reviewing the decision of a lower court or an arbiter.

19–06 Contracts are construed in the light of their surrounding circumstances and so, although the construction is a matter of law, it may be necessary to ascertain the facts surrounding the formation of the contract. That is not to say that there will always need to be a proof of those facts, but proof (or an equivalent) is necessary if the contention is upheld that words have a special technical meaning or a meaning given by custom.[16] The conclusion to be drawn from all this is that the construction of a contract involves both questions of law and questions of fact.

THE PRINCIPLE OF CONSTRUCTION

19–07 There is one principle of construction to which other rules are subsidiary. A contract is construed by considering the express terms of the contract and any admissible surrounding circumstances. It is inaccurate (despite some judicial dicta) to suggest that a contract is construed by looking at its terms and nothing else. Contracts do not exist in isolation

---

[13] *Adamastos Shipping Co.* v. *Anglo-Saxon Petroleum Co., sup. cit.*
[14] *Cozens* v. *Brutus* [1973] A.C. 854 at p. 861 *per* Lord Reid.
[15] *Woodhouse Ltd.* v. *Nigerian Produce Ltd.* [1972] A.C. 741.
[16] See paras. 19–35 to 19–43 and para. 6–64.

from the rest of the world and it would be foolish for a court to ignore the circumstances in which the contract was created.

8   An Aberdeenshire farmer might use words which would receive a different construction if they appeared in a document emanating from the Bank of England. Some simple but common expressions are used in different senses in different contexts, such as "require,"[17] "policies," "bill," "slip," "draw," "issue" or "deliver." These are not technical expressions on the meaning of which the court must be instructed by evidence, but the meaning must be gathered from the rest of the contract, or promise (and its terms could be brief) and from the surrounding circumstances.

SURROUNDING CIRCUMSTANCES

9   The court can have regard to the conduct of the parties at the time of entry into the contract, what the parties said or did at the time, and all relevant contemporary circumstances.[18] The result is that the meaning of a contract may vary according to the nature of the contract and the parties. A word can have a different meaning in, on the one hand, a commercial contract between lender and borrower and, on the other hand, a document from a bank in the context of exchange control,[19] or in different types of charter party,[20] or in different forms of lease.[21] If a document has been drawn up by lawyers there is a rebuttable presumption that words are used as legal terms of art.[22]

10   The court looks at the factual background known to the parties at or before the date of the contract, including evidence of the "genesis" and objectively the "aim" of the transaction.[23] It should not consider the intentions of the parties. The purpose of looking at the circumstances is to construe the contract and not to add to the contract or alter the plain meaning of the terms of a written contract, because in general terms, parole proof for that purpose is inadmissible.[24] The Sheriffs Walker have commented on the distinctions between the English and the Scot-

---

[17] See *North British Oil and Candle Co.* v. *Swann* (1868) 6 M. 835.

[18] *Whitworth Street Estates Ltd.* v. *Miller* [1970] A.C. 583 at p. 611 *per* Viscount Dilhorne at pp. 614, 615 *per* Lord Wilberforce; *Raineri* v. *Miles* [1981] A.C. 1050 at p. 1075 *per* Viscount Dilhorne; *Woodhouse Ltd.* v. *Nigerian Produce Ltd., sup. cit.* at p. 753 *per* Lord Hailsham; *Reardon Smith Line* v. *Hansen-Tangen* [1976] 3 All E.R. 570 (H.L.); *Taylor* v. *John Lewis Ltd.,* 1927 S.C. 891.

[19] *Swiss Bank* v. *Lloyds Bank* [1982] A.C. 584 at p. 613 *per* Lord Wilberforce.

[20] *Aldebaran Maritime* v. *Aussenhandel* [1977] A.C. 157 at pp. 164, 166 *per* Lord Diplock.

[21] *Liverpool C.C.* v. *Irwin* [1977] A.C. 239 at pp. 259, 260 *per* Lord Cross (although the distinction was not in that case made).

[22] *Sydall* v. *Castings Ltd.* [1967] 1 Q.B. 302; *F. L. Schuler A.G.* v. *Wickman Machine Tool Sales* [1974] A.C. 235 at p. 264 *per* Lord Simon.

[23] *Prenn* v. *Simmonds* [1971] 3 All E.R. 237 (H.L.) at p. 241 *per* Lord Wilberforce.

[24] See Walker and Walker, *Evidence*, Chap. XXI.

tish law which may explain a possible difference of approach.[25] English law admits extrinsic evidence (subject to exceptions) whereas Scottish law rejects extrinsic evidence (subject to exceptions). The rule in one case, and the exceptions to the rule in the other, produce results which are so similar that, in the Sheriffs Walker's view, "little harm would probably result if the English method of statement were to be adopted." The practical result may turn on a difference of judicial attitude. It is possible that a Scottish judge would attempt to derive the factual setting of a contract from judicial knowledge but hesitate to allow witnesses to give evidence of the background to the contract, whereas the English judge would hear evidence and then assess its importance.

PRIOR NEGOTIATIONS

19–11　As a general rule it is not competent to look at circumstances prior to the contract.[26]

> "There were prolonged negotiations between solicitors, with exchanges of draft clauses, ultimately emerging in cl. 2 of the agreement. The reason for not admitting evidence of these exchanges is not a technical one or even mainly one of convenience (although the attempt to admit it did greatly prolong the case and add to its expense). It is simply that such evidence is unhelpful. By the nature of things, where negotiations are difficult, the parties' positions, with each passing letter, are changing and until the final agreement, although converging, still divergent. It is only the final document which records a consensus."[27]

19–12　There is some weak authority that prior documents may be looked at to discover the circumstances at the time of the contract.[28] Documents, however, are not the only method of communication between parties and if all the communications can be examined the problems posed in the *dictum* cited above will arise.

It is a well established rule of Scots law that a formal deed, such as a disposition or contract may supersede an earlier contract, such as missives, or an earlier informal agreement.[29] It is not competent to refer to these earlier communings and to give effect to them. Because a formal deed may not supersede all the terms of a previous contract, there are exceptions to the rule which bars reference to the contract.[30] The extent

---

[25] *Evidence*, para. 240.

[26] *Prenn* v. *Simmonds, sup. cit.* See also *McAllister* v. *McGallagley*, 1911 S.C. 112 at p. 117 *per* Lord President Dunedin.

[27] *Ibid*. at p. 240 *per* Lord Wilberforce.

[28] See Walker & Walker, *op. cit.* para. 273, n. 53.

[29] *Inglis* v. *Buttery & Co.* (1878) 5 R.(H.L) 87; *Lee* v. *Alexander* (1883) 10 R.(H.L) 91; *Norval* v. *Abbey*, 1939 S.C. 724; *Korner* v. *Shennan*, 1950 S.C. 285; *Winston* v. *Patrick*, 1980 S.C. 246 and many other cases. See Walker and Walker, paras. 246 *et seq.*

[30] Walker and Walker, *op. cit.* para. 250.

of these exceptions is controversial particularly since the decision in *Winston* v. *Patrick*.[31]

CIRCUMSTANCES SINCE THE CONTRACT

13 Although in some cases a contract has been construed with reference to what happened after the contract was made,[32] it is thought that as a general rule a contract should not be construed by reference to the subsequent conduct of the parties. This is clearly the rule in England,[33] and it is thought, it would now be applied in Scotland. The exceptions to the general rule are obscure. Possession of land may help to explain an ambiguous title[34] but that is explicable on the basis of the special effect of possession in questions of title which is linked to the doctrine of positive prescription. Contracts of an ancient date are an exception,[35] although an unsatisfactory and illogical exception.[36] It is possible that the only real exception to the general rule is that in some cases of ambiguity (whether arising from express terms or the lack of a term) the consistent actings of the parties since the contract may be a legitimate guide to which meaning should be attributed to the contract. This could be the true explanation for regarding the type of promissory note issued after a contract as evidence of what the parties agreement meant[37] or for looking at the method of paying salary to decide when salary was due.[38] In both these cases the contract was silent on what should happen. Where an indemnity on the costs of an action was ambiguous, the court looked to subsequent correspondence between the parties to see how they read the contract.[39] The parties' actions have determined the construction of "Whitsunday" in a lease, the usage of the term varying throughout Scotland.[40] An obligation to relieve of burdens has been construed in

---

[31] *Sup. cit.* See (1981) 26 J.L.S. 414; (1982) 27 J.L.S. 37; (1983) 28 J.L.S. (Workshop) 339. See *Korner* v. *Shennan, sup. cit.* for an explanation of other uncertainties.

[32] Gloag, *Contract*, pp. 375–376; Walker & Walker, *op. cit.* para. 275(a); *Hylander's Exr.* v. *H. & K. Modes Ltd.*, 1957 S.L.T.(Sh.Ct.) 69.

[33] *Whitworth Street Estates Ltd.* v. *Miller* [1970] A.C. 583.

[34] See *Wickman Tools* v. *Schuler A.G., sup. cit.; Boyd* v. *Hamilton*, 1907 S.C. 912.

[35] Walker and Walker, *op. cit.* para. 275(b); *Welwood's Trs.* v. *Mungall*, 1921 S.C. 911 at p. 926 *per* Lord President Clyde.

[36] See MacPhail, *Evidence*, para. 15.26. Of course whether it is the rule or the exception which should change is debatable. In favour of the rule it can be said (1) the meaning of the contract does not change according to what the parties do. (2) Parties frequently act without legal advice and in disregard of what they have signed. Every legal adviser has clients who have done, and do, this. This should be recognised for what it is; a competent variation of the contract, or a breach of contract, or a new contract. If the agreement to pay £5 a week is implemented but only £4 being paid, it should not be suggested that parties' conduct shows that "five" meant "four." There is a problem, but it is not one of construction. (3) The rule avoids the danger of a party being bound by his erroneous implementation of the contract (*e.g.* if he pays £6 instead of £5).

[37] *McAllister* v.*McGallagley, sup. cit.*

[38] *Macgill* v. *Park* (1899) 2 F. 272.

[39] *Boyle & Co.* v. *Morton & Sons* (1903) 5 F. 416.

[40] *Hunter* v. *Barron's Trs.* (1886) 13 R. 883. "And the conduct of parties is, apart from express terms, the best interpretation we can have"—at p. 892 *per* Lord Craighill.

accordance with the actings of the parties for many years.[41] Whether a reference to "poor" in a disposition meant general poor or the legal poor was determined by investigation into usage.[42] It has been observed that an ambiguity in a right of admission to a theatre might be explained by subsequent actings.[43] The ambiguous amount of annuity payable under a minute of agreement between a husband and wife was determined by looking at the course of dealings between the parties since the agreement.[44]

19–14   On the other hand there must be an ambiguity. In *Baird's Trs.* v. *Baird & Co.*[45] Lord Justice-Clerk Moncrieff observed that[46]: "the best exposition of doubtful expressions in a mercantile contract is the manner in which the persons who used them carried them into effect." But in that case the contract did not contain ambiguous words and the practice of parties in paying interest could not be used to give the contract a different meaning from its terms.[47]

The Whole Contract

19–15   A word or phrase should be construed by looking at the whole of the contract.[48] The meaning of the word "condition" in one clause has been determined by looking at the termination provisions in another clause.[49] A clause should be read as a whole not in two separate parts.[50] Having applied the rule, however, the result can be that the same word or phrase has different meanings in different parts of the contract.[51] The rule is a general rule which will yield to contrary indications. As Lord Wilberforce put it[52]:

> "There can be no exception taken to a general proposition that a charter party, as any other contract, must be taken as a whole; the obligations and rights created by one clause must be read in the light of the fact that it forms part of a complex of contractual provisions. . . . But it may well be that a particular clause is so clearly worded, and its purpose so clear, as to resist any suggestion that it should be limited, or written down, on account of some supposed

---

[41] *Jopp's Trs.* v. *Edmond* (1888) 15 R. 271; *North British Ry. Co.* v. *Mags. of Edinburgh*, 1920 S.C. 409; *Welwood's Trs.* v. *Mungall*, 1921 S.C. 911.

[42] *Inspector of Kinglassie* v. *Kirk Session of Kinglassie* (1867) 5 M. 869.

[43] *Scott* v. *Howard* (1881) 8 R.(H.L) 59 at p. 67 *per* Lord Watson (*obiter*); followed *A. M. Carmichael Ltd.* v. *Lord Advocate*, 1948 S.L.T.(Notes) 88.

[44] *Smith* v. *Johnston*, 1949 S.L.T.(Notes) 11.

[45] (1877) 4 R.1005.

[46] At p. 1017 (dissenting judgment) but see at p. 1019.

[47] See at p. 1015 *per* Lord Gifford.

[48] *Modern Engineering* v. *Gilbert-Ash* [1974] A.C. 689 at p. 703 *per* Lord Morris.

[49] *Wickman Tools* v. *Schuler A.G.* [1974] A.C. 235.

[50] *Mardorf Co.* v. *Attica Sea Corpn.* [1977] A.C. 850 at p. 868 *per* Lord Wilberforce.

[51] *Watson* v. *Haggit* [1928] A.C. 127.

[52] *Federal Commerce* v. *Molena Alpha* [1979] A.C. 757 at pp. 776, 777.

inconsistency with the general purpose of the contract or by some other clause in the contract."

16 An example of an attempt to make clauses independent of each other will be found in memoranda of association of companies which contain express provision for each object of the company being construed separately[53] although limitations have been imposed on the effect of such a provision.[54]

17 If words have been deleted by the parties to the contract before signature, it has been held that they should not be looked at in the construction of the contract because they are not part of the agreement of the parties.[55] On the other hand deleted words have been looked at as part of the circumstances surrounding the contract.[56] There may be a distinction between a deletion which is part of the prior communings and a deletion made at the time of the contract to a printed form.[57] The issue is undecided.

18 If a contract is part of a larger transaction, it may be permissible to look at the other contracts involved.[58] This can be justified on the grounds (1) that the contracts refer to each other, if that is the case,[59] (2) that the rules relating to ambiguity allow extrinsic evidence or (3) that the other contracts are part of the surrounding circumstances. The extent to which one contract is incorporated into another contract is considered elsewhere.[60]

19 There is authority stating that when a contract is partly handwritten or typewritten and partly printed and there is reasonable doubt on the meaning, the written words have greater effect.[61] This is a recognition that printed terms may apply to circumstances other than that of the parties. Indeed it has been observed that the words of a printed form may be construed not exclusively literally but, if necessary, analogistically[62] and words in a printed form which have been left in by oversight have been ignored.[63]

---

[53] See *Cotman* v. *Brougham* [1918] A.C. 514.

[54] *Re Introductions Ltd.* [1970] Ch. 199; *Re Horsley & Weight* [1982] Ch. 442; *Rolled Steel Products (Holdings)* v. *British Steel Corpn.* [1986] Ch. 246; *Thompson* v. *J. Barke & Co. (Caterers)*, 1975 S.L.T. 67; see also *North of Scotland and Orkney and Shetland Steam Navigation Co.*, 1920 S.C. 633.

[55] *Inglis* v. *Buttery & Co.* (1878) 5 R.(H.L) 87; *City and Westminster Properties* v. *Mudd* [1959] Ch. 129.

[56] *Taylor* v. *John Lewis Ltd.*, 1927 S.C. 891.

[57] See *London & Overseas Freighters* v. *Timber Shipping Co. S.A.* [1972] A.C. 1 at pp. 15, 16 *per* Lord Reid, *obiter*.

[58] *Modern Engineering* v. *Gilbert-Ash*, *sup. cit.* at pp. 696, 670 *per* Lord Reid.

[59] On the complexities involving charterparties and bills of lading see *Miramar Maritime Corpn.* v. *Holburn Oil Trading Ltd.* [1984] A.C. 676 and cases therein referred to.

[60] Paras. 13–26 to 13–30.

[61] *Glynn* v. *Margeston & Co.* [1893] A.C. 351 at p. 357 *per* Lord Halsbury; *The Brabant* [1967] 1 Q.B. 588 and cases cited in Chitty, *Contracts*, para. 783; Halsbury, Vol. 12, para. 1503; *Taylor* v. *John Lewis Ltd.*, 1927 S.C. 891 at p. 898 *per* Lord Justice-Clerk Alness.

[62] *Cie D'Armement Maritime S.A.* v. *Cie Tunisienne De Navigation S.A.* [1971] A.C. 572 at p. 608 *per* Lord Diplock (but note the differing approaches of the other judges).

[63] *Baumwoll Manufacturer von Scheibler* v. *Furness* [1893] A.C. 8.

CONTRACT NOT TO BE MADE FOR THE PARTIES

19–20   Consistent with the view that the court does not interpret what the parties intended to say, but what the parties have said, the court should not redraft the contract. In the words of Lord Morris: "Nor would it be appropriate to embark upon a process of redrafting the sentence by reading in suggested words which it does not contain."[64] Lord Reid was "not disposed to discard the natural meaning of the words which I have quoted merely because giving to them their natural meaning implies that the draftsman has forgotten something which a better draftsman would have remembered."[65] In Viscount Dilhorne's view, "it is not the function of the courts to rewrite a contract to insert provisions to which the parties could have agreed to deal with a situation which might arise."[66]

19–21   In other words there must be a construction, not a reconstruction of the contract.

ABSURD MEANINGS REJECTED

19–22   Although it is sometimes said that words should be given their "plain" meaning, that is not an entirely helpful rule of construction. What is "plain" to one person is not necessarily "plain" to another. Nor do all words have one "plain" meaning. The more difficult the case, the more useless it is to say that the "plain" meaning must be applied. The greater the controversy the more diverse the opinions on meaning.[67] It is perhaps better to put the proposition in the form that the courts will not choose an absurd construction. Parties may say what they choose but the court should not attribute to them an agreement which is "highly unlikely"[68] or "utterly fantastic"[69] unless the terms are clear. Thus a construction was avoided which would have resulted in a "salary" being paid to the executors of a deceased partner in a New Zealand firm of barristers and solicitors.[70] The phrase "void and null" in an irritancy was not construed literally because the result would have been "that the landlord must return all the rents, and the tenant surrender all his profits under the lease. That is a construction so repugnant to common sense, in the relation of landlord and tenant, that it must be rejected."[71] In choosing between two possible constructions of a takeover agreement

---

[64] *Modern Engineering* v. *Gilbert-Ash* [1974] A.C. 689 at p. 703.

[65] *Wickman Tools* v. *Schuler A.G.*, *sup. cit.* at p. 249.

[66] *Union of India* v. *Aaby (E.B.)'s Rederi A/S* [1975] A.C. 797 at p. 813.

[67] See *Caledonian Ry. Co.* v. *North British Ry. Co.* (1881) 8 R.(H.L) 23 at pp. 30, 31 *per* Lord Blackburn.

[68] *London & Overseas Freighters* v. *Timber Shipping Co. S.A.*, *sup. cit.* at p. 14 *per* Lord Reid.

[69] *Wickman Tools* v. *Schuler A.G.* [1974] A.C. 235 at pp. 255, 256 *per* Lord Morris. See also at p. 251 *per* Lord Reid. *S.S.H.A.* v. *Wimpey Construction U.K. Ltd.*, 1986 S.L.T. 173.

[70] *Watson* v. *Haggitt* [1928] A.C. 127.

[71] *Bidoulac* v. *Sinclair's Tr.* (1889) 17 R. 144 at p. 147 *per* Lord President Inglis.

the court rejected a literal but anomalous result in favour of a workable and reasonable result.[72]

23 The choice may not, however, appear to be between absurdity, on the one hand, and sweet reason on the other. Either of two possible constructions may be feasible. In *Commercial Union* v. *Hayden*,[73] the court was faced with construing "rateable proportion" in an insurance policy. One method of construction was favoured by English textbooks and another by American practice. Cairns L.J. solved the dilemma in this way: "The issue being one of construction and the language being, as it seems to me, equally capable of either suggested meaning, I ask myself which meaning is that more likely to be intended by reasonable businessmen."[74] He chose a result which was "realistic" rather than "artificial." In the same case Stephenson L.J. said:

> "If a court is to give certainty to what appears to be uncertain and find what the clause means, it can only do so if it can ascertain with a fair show of confidence the meaning more likely to be intended by reasonable businessmen than any other, or, on the assumption that the other members of the court are prepared to make, the meaning more likely to be intended than the only other suggested."[75]

24 One example of the rejection of absurd results is the operation of the maxim *ut res valeat potius quam pereat* or *ut actus valeat quam pereat*. The phrase has other permutations, but they all mean that something should be valid rather than perish. The parties are more likely to have agreed on obligations which can be put into sensible effect than to have agreed something which is unworkable. This approach to construction goes so far that if business efficacy demands it, a court will imply a term in the contract. The implication of terms is discussed elsewhere.[76]

25 Where a contract for the sale of coal stated that "equal monthly quantities in lots of 300 tons maximum" were sold, the buyer pleaded that in the absence of a minimum he could take any amount, however small. This construction was rejected as unreasonable. It would have enabled the buyer to prolong the execution of the contract and so reduce it to an absurdity.[77] A deviation clause in a bill of lading was construed so as to give effect to the main object and intent of the contract. A literal construction was rejected.[78] A bungled reference to a statute was not given literal effect but the manifest intention was applied.[79] The words "this bill of lading" have been read as "this charterparty" with reference to

---

[72] *MacKay's Ex.* v. *Firth*, 1972 S.L.T. 22.
[73] [1977] Q.B. 804.
[74] *Ibid.* at p. 815.
[75] *Ibid.* at p. 819, see also at p. 820.
[76] See Chap. 6.
[77] *Barr* v. *Waldie* (1893) 21 R. 224.
[78] *Glynn* v. *Margetson* [1893] A.C. 351 (the decision was based in part on the rule of construction applicable to printed forms). See comments on the application of this case in *Renton & Co.* v. *Palmyra Trading Corp. of Panama* [1957] A.C. 149.
[79] *Finbow* v. *Air Ministry* [1963] 2 All E.R. 647.

the principle *falsa demonstratio non nocet* and meaningless words were ignored.[80]

CONTRA PROFERENTEM

19–26   An ambiguous expression is construed against the interests of the party who relies on it. Stair restricted the operation of this rule to writs drafted by "skilful persons," as distinct from those prepared by "vulgar persons."[81] This distinction is no longer observed. Many a company produces its standard conditions merely by copying the conditions of another company. This process may be carried out without legal advice by an entrepreneurial managing director who is intolerant of details in documents and whose capacity for understanding the Unfair Contract Terms Act is not as great as his ability to sell his company's product. The exclusion clause which he produces is not construed by a different standard from that applied to a similar clause produced by a multinational company which acted on the advice of senior counsel.

19–27   It is also often said that the rule results in a document being construed against the party who drafted it.[82] When the rule is applied to standard form contracts it operates in this way, but the rule is not restricted to that type of document. Which side prepares the first draft of a commercial contract may be an accident, or may be governed by professional rules. In the process of drafting and revising a complex agreement it would not be fruitful to consider who drafted a particular clause. Gloag suggested that the rule did not apply where parties were contracting on an equal footing[83] and terms were arrived at by mutual adjustment but the case relied upon by Gloag is explicable as having been decided on the basis of the absence of ambiguity.[84] The correct rule is thought to be that, where an expression is ambiguous, it will be construed against the party who relies on it, irrespective of which party (or parties) produced the words.

19–28   It is important to note that the *contra proferentem* rule only applies when there is an ambiguity.[85] The rule must not be used to create an ambiguity where none exists.[86]

---

[80] *Adamastos Shipping Co.* v. *Anglo-Saxon Petroleum Co.* [1959] A.C. 133.

[81] Stair, IV,42,21. See also Ersk., III,iii,87.

[82] *e.g.* Chitty, paras. 793, 794. Gloag comes close to this: see Gloag, p. 400; *Freeman* v. *Maxwell*, 1928 S.C. 682 at p. 685 *per* Lord Justice-Clerk Alness; *N. & G. Napier Ltd.* v. *Crosbie*, 1964 S.C. 129 at p. 140 *per* Lord Guthrie. See also *Royal Bank of Scotland* v. *Brown*, 1982 S.C. 89 at p. 100 *per* Lord Justice-Clerk Wheatley. *Cf. S.S.H.A.* v. *Wimpey Construction U.K. Ltd.*, 1986 S.L.T. 173 at p. 177 *per* Lord Cameron.

[83] Gloag, p. 401.

[84] *Birrell* v. *Dyer* (1884) 11 R.(H.L) 41.

[85] Gloag, p. 400; and see cases on insurance policies cited *infra*, n. 89; *Royal Bank of Scotland* v. *Brown*, 1982 S.C. 89 at p. 100 *per* Lord Justice-Clerk Wheatley.

[86] *Laidlaw* v. *John M. Monteath & Co.*, 1979 S.L.T. 78 at pp. 80, 81 *per* Lord Allanbridge.

-29   There are expressions of opinion which suggest that ambiguity is not required. Lord Benholme went so far as to say: "It is a rule of law, and a good rule, that every obligation is to be construed *contra proferentem*."[87] This is clearly incorrect otherwise the rule would feature in almost every case on construction. The *contra proferentem* rule is only one of several rules of construction which are subsidiary to the principle that the object of construction is to determine the meaning of the contract.

-30   The *contra proferentem* rule has been applied to clauses which exclude the liability of a person for his negligence or which seek indemnity from another for the consequences of that person's negligence. General words of exclusion may not cover negligence if there is another construction which is not too fanciful or remote. There is a considerable amount of authority on the construction of these clauses and the topic is discussed elsewhere.[88]

-31   Phrases in insurance policies or proposals which purport to exclude the liability of the insurers have been construed against the insurers.[89] Building restrictions in feu charters, dispositions, or other property deeds have been construed strictly.[90] An ambiguous cautionary obligation has been construed *contra proferentem*.[91]

EJUSDEM GENERIS

-32   Where a list of things of the same class is followed by general words, the general words may be construed as limited to members of that class. The result is not inevitable because the rule is only one rule of construction. The general words, for example, might be so wide as to indicate a meaning wider than the class.

-33   Examples of the operation of the rule are marine insurance policies in which a reference to "all the perils" was limited to marine risks,[92] a bill of lading in which "any other cause" was limited to causes *ejusdem generis* as war and disturbance and did not apply to ice.[93]

-34   The rule does not apply when the "list" concludes with general words indicating an intention to avoid the rule such as "whether or not similar

---

[87] *Bayne* v. *Russell* (1869) 7 S.L.R. 101 at p. 104. See also *Veitch* v. *National Bank*, 1907 S.C. 554 and *Harmer* v. *Gibb*, 1911 S.C. 1341 which are cases on guarantees relied upon by Gloag (p. 401) but which do not clearly involve an ambiguity.

[88] Paras. 13–36 to 13–45.

[89] *e.g. Life Association of Scotland* v. *Foster* (1873) 11 M. 351; *Kennedy* v. *Smith*, 1975 S.C. 266; *Laidlaw* v. *John M. Monteath & Co.*, *sup. cit.*; *Davidson* v. *Guardian Royal Exchange*, 1979 S.C. 192.

[90] *e.g. Murray's Trs.* v. *Trs. for St. Margaret's Convent* (1906) 8 F. 1109; 1907 S.C.(H.L) 8; *Anderson* v. *Dickie*, 1915 S.C.(H.L) 79; *Kemp* v. *Burgh of Largs*, 1939 S.C.(H.L) 6.

[91] *Aitken's Trs.* v. *Bank of Scotland*, 1944 S.C. 270.

[92] *Thames and Mersey Marine Ins. Co.* v. *Hamilton Fraser & Co.* (1887) 12 App.Cas. 484; *Stott (Baltic) Steamers* v. *Marten* [1916] 1 A.C. 304.

[93] *SS. Knutsford* v. *Tillmanns & Co.* [1908] A.C. 406. See also *Abchurch Steamship Co.* v. *Stinnes*, 1911 S.C. 1010.

to the foregoing" or "whatsoever" or "of what kind soever."[94] Nor does the rule apply when, as is common in some commercial contracts, the general words precede the list, as in "X *viz.* A, B and C."[95] Nor can the rule apply in the absence of a "genus."[96]

TECHNICAL TERMS

19–35   In Gloag's words:

> "Questions of construction also presuppose a contract which the Court is able to read. So evidence may be admitted of the meaning of foreign or technical terms, not as indicating the intention of the parties, but as showing the ordinary meaning of the word or phrase. It seems impossible to lay down any general rule to determine whether a particular phrase is a technical term, or part of the ordinary language which the judge will construe for himself."[97]

19–36   The difficulty with admitting extrinsic evidence is that, as explained earlier, questions of construction are matters of law and should be decided by the court, not by the opinions of experts. This is especially forceful when the word in a contract has a statutory meaning.[98] Lord Reid analysed the problem in this way[99]:

19–37   "With what knowledge or equipment is a court entitled to examine a document? A judge is supposed to know the law, the English language and such facts as are common knowledge. If he refers to authorities or dictionaries or other works dealing with these matters he can safely do so because his general knowledge enables him to check and appreciate them. But if without assistance he attempts to handle highly technical matters he may easily go astray. Some fairly simple technical matters can nowadays be considered as common knowledge, and I would not attempt to draw the line—it may alter from time to time. In this case some of the terms used are simple enough but some are certainly not. So what is a court to do if on the face of a record there are technical terms which cannot be understood without expert assistance? There may be cases where a very little assistance is all that is necessary, and I would think it unfortunate if a strict rule were laid down that the mere presence of some technicality is enough to prevent a court from proceeding further in the absence of evidence to explain it.

19–38   Technicalities crop up in a great variety of cases and, when the parties are not in dispute about them, they are often explained without evidence. Counsel give explanations and by doing so they

---

[94] *Larsen* v. *Sylvester & Co.* [1908] A.C. 195; *Glasgow Corp.* v. *Glasgow Tramway & Omnibus Co.* (1898) 25 R.(H.L) 77, opinion of Lord Herschell; *Ballingall & Son* v. *Dundee Ice and Cold Storage Co.,* 1924 S.C. 238 at p. 241 *per* Lord Morison (Ordinary); on appeal see at p. 243 *per* Lord Anderson.

[95] *Ambatielos* v. *Anton Jurgens Margarine Works* [1923] A.C. 175.

[96] *Ambatielos* v. *Anton Jurgens Margarine Works, sup. cit.* at pp. 185–187 *per* Viscount Finlay; *Ballingall & Son* v. *Dundee Ice and Cold Storage Co., ibid.*; *The Admiralty* v. *Burns,* 1910 S.C. 531.

[97] *Contract*, p. 365.

[98] *Thomson* v. *Garioch* (1841) 3 D. 625.

[99] *Baldwin & Francis* v. *Patents Appeal Tribunal* [1959] A.C. 663 at pp. 684 *et seq.*

are not giving anything away; if they were not in agreement evidence would be led. But in a case where it is not competent to lead evidence counsel could not, in my view, properly be asked to help in this way unless there is some other way for the court to get the necessary information. If his client's interests might suffer by his giving such explanation counsel is quite entitled to withhold it, and the court could not proceed on information given by one side only. But there do appear to be methods by which a court can go some way in acquiring technical information without evidence, for example, by means of an assessor.

39   If the court finds that there is genuine dispute and real doubt about any technical matter, then I do not think that it can proceed further without evidence."

40   The first decision for the court is whether or not a technical matter is in issue. If the court decides that words have been used with an ordinary meaning it is implying that the opinions of witnesses would be no better and of no more weight than those of any other intelligent parties.[1] Even if the parties to the action considered that a phrase is technical and open to construction the court may disagree and take the view that the meaning is clear.[2]

41   It is thought, however, that if the parties are agreed that their expression had a special meaning, that "X" really meant "Y," the court should not impose the meaning "X."[3]

42   Once it is decided that a technical matter is in issue, the parties may agree the meaning or there may be a proof. Proof was led of the mercantile usage in Glasgow of the term "pig-iron delivered f.o.b. at Glasgow,"[4] the meaning of "stone" in connection with cheese,[5] on the usage of the term "St. Lawrence" in a policy of insurance,[6] and of the meanings of "first class castings of Scotch iron of the best quality,"[7] and "statuary."[8] Disputes about technical terms can very easily lead to consideration of custom or usage as the cases cited show. It is said that proof of usage is inadmissible unless the term is ambiguous.[9] But by this is meant the rule earlier expressed that proof will not be allowed if the words have an ordinary meaning. As Lord Kyllachy put it, a proof of a custom of trade[10]:

---

[1] See *Towill & Co.* v. *British Agricultural Association* (1875) 3 R. 117 at p. 126 *per* Lord Deas.

[2] *Parochial Board of Greenock* v. *Coghill & Son* (1878) 5 R. 732.

[3] Walker and Walker, para. 272.

[4] *Mackenzie* v. *Dunlop* (1853) 3 Macq. 22.

[5] *Miller* v. *Mair* (1860) 22 D. 660.

[6] *Birrell* v. *Dryer* (1884) 11 R.(H.L) 41 (but the proof did not solve the issue. A proof may show that the words have no technical meaning).

[7] *Fleming* v. *Airdrie Iron Co.* (1882) 9 R. 473.

[8] *Sutton & Co.* v. *Ciceri & Co.* (1890) 17 R.(H.L) 40.

[9] See *Armstrong & Co.* v. *McGregor & Co.* (1875) 2 R. 339 at p. 343, opinion of Lord Ardmillan; *Sinclair* v. *Beath* (1868) 7 M. 273; Gloag, p. 381, Walker & Walker, para. 276; *Tancred, Arrol Co.* v. *Steel Co. of Scotland* (1890) 17 R.(H.L) 31.

[10] Lord Ordinary's opinion in *McDowall & Neilson's Tr.* v. *J. B. Snowball & Co.* (1904) 7 F. 35 at p. 44.

"could only be allowed on the grounds that the words in the agreement, 'approved acceptance,' were technical words of the trade, and required explanation of what they signified in the trade. These words, however, are not technical words of the wood trade, but are common in mercantile contracts, and have a well-known legal import. To allow evidence in such a case would therefore, it seems to me, be to practically hand over to the witnesses the construction of the contract, which is a matter for the Court alone."

19–43 The reported cases indicate that leading evidence of the meaning of a technical expression or evidence of usage, is something to be done or sought to be done with caution. First there should be a distinct averment of the precise technical meaning which is claimed.[11] It is not the function of the court to listen to evidence of all the meanings as though it were compiling a dictionary. Secondly, when the matter is disputed between the parties it must be considered whether there will overall be clear and consistent evidence from experts. In several of the cases cited the evidence was conflicting and all that the proof established was that the word or phrase was ambiguous.

CLERICAL MISTAKE

19–44 It is sometimes obvious that a written contract contains a mistake. There may be a mistake apparent on the face of the contract (*e.g.* incorrect addition) or the mistake may be obvious when the contract is looked at in the light of the surrounding circumstances. These two forms of mistakes have been classified as patent errors, on the one hand, and latent errors, on the other. The term "error" is liable to lead to confusion with the cases of error in consent. In the type of case here being considered the parties were in agreement but the written expression of their agreement was inaccurate. The Scottish Law Commission has preferred the term "defective expression."[12]

(1) Patent Mistake

19–45 It is possible to cure a patent defect by a proper construction of the contract. When a policy of life insurance on joint lives contained provisions consistent only with insurance of one life, the court recognised that "this instrument has been bungled," and gave effect to the obvious purpose of the document.[13] The courts have ignored words which were obviously inappropriate or unintended. The inaccurate insertion of the word "not" has been ignored.[14] The words "at present" have been

---

[11] *Sutton & Co.* v. *Ciceri & Co., sup. cit.* at p. 43 *per* Lord Watson.
[12] Scot. Law Com. No. 79, *Obligations*, Report on Rectification of Contractual and Other Documents (1983), para. 2.1. Contrast the type of case here considered with that of *one* party making a clerical mistake or being in error, *e.g. Steel* v. *Bradley Homes*, 1972 S.C. 48 and see Chap. 9.
[13] *North British Insurance Co.* v. *Tunnock and Fraser* (1864) 3 M. 1. The case was treated with reserve in *Hudson* v. *St. John*, 1977 S.C. 255.
[14] *Glen's Trs.* v. *Lancashire and Yorkshire Accident Ins. Co.* (1906) 8 F. 915.

treated as *pro non scripto*.[15] Patent errors in calculation have been treated in a similar way.[16]

(2) Latent Mistake

-46 Where the defect is not apparent on the face of the document it is possible to lead extrinsic evidence of an agreement different from that expressed in the document. A high standard of proof of the prior agreement has been required.[17] One person's name may have been mistakenly inserted in a document instead of another's,[18] the obligations in a deed may be incorrectly stated,[19] or a deed may convey too much.[20]

-47 The case of *Krupp* v. *Menzies*[21] is unusual in that a proof was allowed although reduction of the agreement was not sought. Reduction or a combination of declarator and reduction was the normal remedy.[22] Scots common law does not have a specific remedy of rectification.[23]

-48 The rectification of some public registers is governed by statute.[24] The Law Reform (Miscellaneous Provisions) (Scotland) Act 1985, section 8 introduced a general provision for rectification of defectively expressed documents.[25] The Court of Session or the sheriff court is empowered, subject to limitations, to order the rectification in any manner of a document which fails to express accurately the common intention of parties to an agreement or the intention of the grantor of a unilateral document.[26] The court may have regard to all relevant evidence, whether written or oral.[27] Special provision is made for rectification of a document recorded in the Register of Sasines[28] and for rectification of the

---

[15] *Hunter* v. *Fox*, 1964 S.C.(H.L.) 95. The deed was a disposition containing a servitude which is subject to stricter standards of construction than a mercantile contract.

[16] *McLaren* v. *Liddell's Trs.* (1862) 24 D. 577; *Jamieson* v. *McInnes* (1887) 15 R. 17; *Wilkie* v. *Hamilton Lodging House Co.*, 1902 4 F. 951; *Mitchell* v. *Mags. of Dalkeith*, 1930 S.L.T. 80. In these cases a distinction was drawn between (1) a lump sum contract under which a party is bound by the sum specified and (2) a contract to do various works at scheduled rates under which an error in the addition of the items is immaterial. *Cf.* the case where *one* party has made a private error in calculation; *Seaton Brick and Tile Co.* v. *Mitchell* (1900) 2 F. 550.

[17] *Wood* v. *McDonald*, 1970 S.L.T.(Notes) 46.

[18] *Waddell* v. *Waddell* (1863) 1 M. 635; *Hudson* v. *St. John, sup. cit.*

[19] *Glasgow Feuing & Building Co.* v. *Watson's Trs.* (1887) 14 R. 610; *Krupp* v. *Menzies*, 1907 S.C. 903.

[20] *Anderson* v. *Lambie*, 1954 S.C.(H.L.) 43.

[21] *Sup. cit.*

[22] The case law is analysed by Lord Maxwell in *Hudson* v. *St. John, sup. cit.*

[23] *Anderson* v. *Lambie*, 1954 S.C.(H.L.) 43; partial reduction is possible *Hudson* v. *St. John*, 1977 S.C. 255.

[24] *e.g.* s.420, Companies Act 1985; s.9, Land Registration (Scotland) Act 1979; s.46, Conveyancing (Scotland) Act 1924 and s.41, Conveyancing and Feudal Reform (Scotland) Act 1970.

[25] The section was a result of the recommendations of the Scottish Law Commission. See Scot. Law Com. No. 79, *sup. cit.*

[26] s.8(1). Related documents may be rectified; s.8(3).

[27] s.8(2).

[28] s.8(5) and see s.9.

Land Register.[29] It is competent to register in the Register of Inhibitions and Adjudications a notice of an application under section 8 for the rectification of a deed relating to land.[30]

19–49   The limitations in the operation of section 8 are (1) the section does not apply to testamentary writings[31] and (2) elaborate rules which exist to safeguard the interests of third parties.[32]

INACCURATE NAMES AND DESCRIPTIONS

19–50   A common problem in practice is the inaccurate naming of a party. An individual may call himself what he pleases and change his name when he pleases.[33] A partner has bound himself by signing the firm name, while he did not bind the partnership,[34] it being observed that the result would have been the same whatever name he had signed.[35]

19–51   In a case in which a Mrs Isabella Williamson or Moncur signed a disposition as "Isabella C. Moncur" and Mrs Joan Colville or Brown signed "Joan Colville Brown," Lord President Strathclyde stated that[36]:

> "The objection that has been taken to this title seems to me to be absurd and frivolous. There is no suggestion that there is any person other than the two persons who signed these deeds with whom their identity could be confused. These two persons are alleged to have signed them, and they certainly did in fact sign the deeds."

19–52   A disposition referred to a previous deed for description of the lands conveyed. The reference to the prior deed contained an error in the name of the disponer. This misdescription was treated as within the category of *falsa demonstratio* because it was possible to identify the deed from other particulars given.[37]

19–53   When a company is inaccurately named in a document it is suggested that the company is bound provided that there is no reasonable possibility of confusion with another company. Common errors are, the omission of the definite article where it is the first word in the name, the use of "&" and "and" or *vice versa*, and abbreviations such as "Co." or "Ltd." for the full word and *vice versa*. It is thought that it is immaterial if there are minor discrepancies from the true name when these are common abbreviations, and do not require extrinsic evidence to show which company is mentioned in the contract.[38] Where the error is not an

---

[29] Sched. 2, paras. 21, 22.

[30] s.8(7).

[31] s.8(6).

[32] s.9.

[33] *Robertson* (1899) 2 F. 127; Persons whose names are entered in a roll of court, *e.g.* a notary, W.S. or solicitor, would require the authority of the court to alter the roll. See *Silverstone*, 1935 S.C. 223.

[34] *Fortune* v. *Young*, 1918 S.C. 1.

[35] *Ibid.* at p. 8 *per* Lord Guthrie.

[36] *Grieve's Trs.* v. *Japp's Trs.*, 1917 1 S.L.T. 70.

[37] *Matheson* v. *Gemmell* (1903) 5 F. 448.

[38] See *Banque de l'Indochine* v. *Euroseas Finance* [1981] 3 All E.R. 198 and authorities there cited (a case on s.108, Companies Act 1948).

accepted abbreviation, as "M." for "Michael,"[39] it may be necessary to admit extrinsic evidence if parties are in dispute about which company is referred to. A contract has been valid although executed in a name to which the company was not entitled until three days later.[40] Strict rules apply to diligence, however, and a high degree of accuracy in a company name is required for a valid arrestment.[41]

SPECIFIC WORDS AND PHRASES

54 It has several times been stated on high authority that decisions on the meaning of one contract are no help in interpreting a different contract and should not be cited to the courts,[42] although in the case of standard term contracts in wide use, legal certainty is attained by adopting a construction evolved over many years.[43] Despite this the practitioner may wish to consider cases involving words or phrases.

Conjunctions, Pronouns and Adverbs

55 The word "and" sometimes is used when "or" is intended.[44] Conversely "or" can mean "and."[45] Lord Reid said that the symbol "and/or" was not yet part of the English language,[46] and its use in a marriage contract led to difficulties.[47]

Terms about Time

56 The period "from 1st May" could either include 1st May or commence on the first moment of the day following.[48] It is preferable to refer to a period commencing *on* a date. The phrase "within a period of X weeks" also gives rise to difficulty about when the period begins and ends[49] as does a reference to "after 12 months trading."[50]

57 The reference to "five year's service" gave rise to a doubt whether a year ended with the football season or at the end of the calendar year.[51]

---

[39] See *Durham Fancy Goods* v. *Michael Jackson (Fancy Goods)* [1968] 2 Q.B. 839.

[40] *Lin Pac Containers (Scotland)* v. *Kelly,* 1982 S.C. 50. A company before incorporation has no capacity to contract. See para. 8–89, n. 97.

[41] *Richards & Wallington (Earthmoving)* v. *Whatlings,* 1982 S.L.T. 66.

[42] *Pioneer Shipping* v. *B.T.P. Tioxide* [1982] A.C. 724 at p. 749 *per* Lord Roskill: *F. L. S. Schuler A.G.* v. *Wickman Machine Tool Sales* [1974] A.C. 235 at p. 256 *per* Lord Morris; *Gilbert-Ash (Northern)* v. *Modern Engineering (Bristol)* [1974] A.C. 689 at p. 699 *per* Lord Morris.

[43] *e.g. Federal Commerce* v. *Tradax Export* [1978] A.C. 1 at p. 13 *per* Lord Diplock; *A/S Awilco* v. *Fulvia Sp. A.* [1981] 1 All E.R. 652 (H.L.).

[44] *Utbult* v. *Macneil,* 1972 S.L.T.(Notes) 54 (Statutory Instrument).

[45] *Mackay's Exr.* v. *Firth,* 1972 S.L.T. 22.

[46] *John G. Stein* v. *O'Hanlon* [1965] A.C. 890 at p. 904.

[47] *Neame* v. *Neame's Trs.,* 1956 S.L.T. 57.

[48] *Ladyman* v. *Wirral Estates* [1968] 2 All E.R. 197.

[49] *Hare* v. *Gocher* [1962] 2 Q.B. 641, *S. Appellants,* 1979 S.L.T.(Sh.Ct.) 37. *Earl of Morton's Trs.* v. *Macdougall,* 1944 S.C. 410.

[50] *The Karen Oltmann* [1976] 2 Lloyd's Rep. 708.

[51] *Shankland* v. *Airdrieonians Football and Athletic Co. Ltd.,* 1956 S.L.T.(Sh.Ct.) 69.

The phrase "at any time" is probably limited to the currency of the contract,[52] but it may be wise to stipulate this expressly, because literally the words are not limited.

19–58   The normal rule of construction is that when a period of time is stated to commence from a given day the period is reckoned from the last moment of that day.[53]

Money

19–59   A reference to the method of payment can cause difficulty. Does "payment in cash" include a telex transfer?[54] "Payment" does not always mean actual transfer of money, but can include placing money at someone's disposal.[55] A reference to "profits" has raised a doubt about whether the holding company or the group profits were referred to.[56] Does "net profits" mean profit after deduction of tax?[57] Does "turnover" require goods to be delivered and paid for?[58]

19–60   A reference to sums due under a contract can give rise to a doubt whether this means payments specified in the contract or is wider and includes damages for breach of contract.[59] A mention of money which one party is "liable to pay" or to which another is "entitled" may not include an illiquid claim for damages.[60]

"Best Endeavours"

19–61   In many contracts between commercial organisations and, in particular, in distribution agreements or licences of patents, there is an obligation on one party to use "best endeavours" to achieve a stated objective. The meaning of "best endeavours," like the meaning of any phrase, depends on the circumstances in which it is used. It does not normally mean that the limits of reason must be overstepped with regard to cost and effort. The insolvency of the party under the obligation may prevent any future performance and it is unlikely that that was the intended result of the parties' contract. It has been said that, broadly speaking, the phrase means that a person must "leave no stone unturned."[61] The phrase has meant that *at least* reasonable endeavours must be used.[62] It

---

[52] *Longmuir* v. *Kew* [1960] 3 All E.R. 26.
[53] *Sworn Securities Ltd.* v. *Chilcott*, 1977 S.C. 53 (Lord Maxwell's opinion); on calculation of minority see para. 8–25; a useful article, which refers to the authorities, is Anon., "Time," 1967 S.L.T.(News) 81; see also *Green's Encyclopaedia*, Vol. 14, s.v. "Time."
[54] See *A/S Awilco* v. *Fulvia Sp. A.* [1981] 1 All E.R. 652 (H.L.).
[55] *Garforth* v. *Newsmith Stainless* [1979] 2 All E.R. 73 (statute).
[56] *Prenn* v. *Simmonds* [1971] 3 All E.R. 237.
[57] *McKay* v. *I. Philp (Holdings)*, 1974 S.L.T.(Sh. Ct.) 97.
[58] *Dowling* v. *Methven, Sons & Co.*, 1921 S.C. 948; *Aris-Bainbridge* v. *Turner Mfg. Co.* [1951] 1 K.B. 563.
[59] *Cf. Re Collbran* [1956] Ch. 250 (statute).
[60] *Dawnays* v. *F. G. Minter* [1971] 2 All E.R. 1389.
[61] *Sheffield District Ry. Co.* v. *Great Central Ry. Co.* (1911) 27 T.L.R. 451.
[62] *Terrell* v. *Mabie Todd and Co. Ltd.* [1952] 2 T.L.R. 574; affd. (1953) 70 R.P.C. 97

is thought that usually "best endeavours" is a higher standard than "reasonable endeavours." It may, for example, be unreasonable to require a party to act so that a loss is made but a large company using its "best endeavours" could incur a loss in performing a contract. A person's "best" will depend on his capacity, qualifications, and the nature of the task required.

62   The phrase "best endeavours" has been criticised as being lacking in specification because it fails to provide a criterion by which the endeavours are to be judged.[63] It may be better for the obligant to use the term "reasonable endeavours" which is not any more precise, but it avoids the argument that the party under the obligation must do everything, short of liquidation, to comply with the obligation.

---

[63] *Bower* v. *Bantam Investments Ltd.* [1972] 3 All E.R. 349 at p. 355 *per* Goff J.

CHAPTER 20

DAMAGES

PART 1

History

20–01 A breach of contract may cause loss to the other party. One remedy is a claim for damages. It was a remedy recognised at an early stage in Scots law.[1] By the middle of the eighteenth century Erskine could state[2]:

> "In all obligations concerning things lawful and in themselves possible, the obligant who fails in the performance of his part, must make up to the creditor the damage he has sustained through the non-performance, agreeably to the rule, *loci facti non praestabilis, vel non praestiti, succedit damnum et interesse.* All the rules mentioned above for ascertaining the extent of the damage arising *ex delicto,* may be applied to this case; to which may be added, that no damage which is remote or indirect ought to enter into the computation."

Baron Hume observed:

> "Certainly, the general rule is against giving conjectural or speculative damages, or damages of a remote or consequential nature. But everything will come into estimation as to damage which can be said fairly and substantially to have been in the view of the parties, at the time of contracting, as a certain consequence of the failure to deliver."[3]

and also: "The established rule of judgment is, not to allow the complainer any material latitude or looseness of construction, and to take no damage into account, but that which is direct and immediate, and capable of being substantiated to a reasonable certainty."[4]

M. P. Brown in 1821 was laying down a general rule and exception. The rule was that the vendor was: "liable merely for such loss as it can be presumed that the parties contemplated, at the time of the contract, as likely to arise from the non-delivery of the thing sold."[5] The exception was that: "When it appears from the terms of the contract that remote and indirect damage has actually been in the contemplation of the parties, and that the vendor has either expressly or tacitly charged

---

[1] *Straton* (1610) Mor. 3148; *Lauchlan Lesley* v. *Guthrie* (1670) Mor. 3148; *Creditors of David Currie* v. *Hannay* (1791) Mor. 3162.

[2] *Inst.*, III, iii, 86. The explanation for the distinction from delict in the last sentence is that at one time the application of remoteness of damage to delict was not clear. See Bell, *Prin.*, s.545 and the alterations made to it by his editors.

[3] *Lectures*, Vol. II, p. 32.

[4] *Op. cit.*, Vol. III, p. 122. He gives several examples.

[5] *Law of Sale*, p. 217.

himself with such damage in case of his failing to deliver, he will be made liable accordingly."[6]

2   These dicta bear a remarkable resemblance to the famous passage on remoteness of liability in the opinion of Baron Alderson in *Hadley* v. *Baxendale*[7] which is frequently cited without, perhaps, the realisation that it expresses the law which had evolved in Scotland several decades earlier.[8]

Terminology

3   The compensating award to the pursuer is called "damages." The harm to the pursuer is variously described as loss, injury or damage. The word "injury" would from its etymology suggest an injustice or wrong, although that may be the question because "injury" does not necessarily mean a legal wrong. The pursuer may suffer injury which is not caused by the defender's breach or for which there is no remedy because it is too remote. "Injury" is often used to contrast personal injury with damage to property. Likewise the word "damage" is used in various senses. It may be used to the exclusion of personal "injury" and also, curiously, the tendency is not to refer to "economic damage" (or "economic injury") but rather to "economic loss." The word "damage" may confuse because it looks like the singular of "damages." The best general term for the harm to the pursuer is "loss." It expresses the diminution in the pursuer's interests, which is, with limitations, to be compensated by an award of damages.

Competence of an Award of Damages

There are several instances in which it may not be competent to seek an award of damages.

(1) Where the pursuer has suffered no loss

04   As mentioned later,[9] compensation for the inconvenience arising from a breach may be awarded without proof of actual loss. However, in one area the breach is not recognised by the law unless there is patrimonial loss with the consequence that the pursuer must aver and prove this loss.[10] This rule applies when the pursuer is averring a breach of rules by a voluntary association. As Lord Deas said in *McMillan* v. *Free Church*[11]:

> "This court deals only with civil or patrimonial interests and consequences, and, while vindicating or giving redress for these, refuses

---

[6] *Op. cit.*, p. 219.
[7] (1854) 9 Ex. 341 at pp. 354, 355.
[8] The history is recognised in *Duke of Portland* v. *Wood's Trs.*, 1926 S.C. 640 at pp. 649, 650 *per* President Clyde; on appeal, 1927 S.C.(H.L.) 1.
[9] paras. 20–87 to 20–89.
[10] This therefore raises a question of relevancy rather than competency.
[11] (1861) 23 D. 1314 at p. 1346.

to go beyond them . . . Men may associate themselves together for innumerable purposes under rules and regulations which may be called, if you please, a contract or agreement, but of the breach or observance of which the law will take no cognizance. It is of no moment whether these purposes be trivial or important—temporal or spiritual—scientific or religious—so long as they do not involve civil or patrimonial rights."

A pursuer must go beyond averring a breach of the rules and aver a material or practical loss, such as loss of emolument or eviction from a house,[12] or the imposition of an enforceable fine.[13] It has been insufficient to aver that a member of a bowling club has been refused the opportunity to win a championship in an amateur game[14] or that a member of a church has been debarred from entering it,[15] or that the doctrinal standards of a church have altered.[16]

The reason why the voluntary association is in a special position is probably that, in the absence of patrimonial loss, the agreement amongst the parties is treated like a social arrangement which the courts will not recognise.

"Nobody has a right which he can enforce at law to compel other people to play a game of football with him. If there be an agreement between them to play a game together, that is not an agreement which the law will enforce. The general rule is that such agreements are personal. Agreements to associate for purposes of recreation, or an agreement to associate for scientific or philanthropical or social or religious purposes, are not agreements which Courts of law can enforce. They are entirely personal. Therefore, in order to establish a civil wrong from the refusal to carry out such an agreement, if it can be inferred that any such agreement was made, it is necessary to see that the pursuer has suffered some practical injury either in his reputation or in his property."[17]

(2) Claim barred by actings of parties

20–05   If the parties have settled their dispute or waived their claims by agreement, subsequent proceedings would be barred unless the agreement can be reduced.[18] It is a problem of construction of the agreement

---

[12] *Forbes* v. *Eden* (1867) 5 M.(H.L.) 36; *McMillan* v. *Free Church, sup. cit.*; *Skerret* v. *Oliver* (1896) 23 R. 468 at p. 490 *per* Lord President Robertson; *McDonald* v. *Burns*, 1940 S.C. 376.

[13] *St. Johnstone Football Club* v. *Scottish Football Association*, 1965 S.L.T. 171; *Drennan* v. *Associated Ironmoulders of Scotland*, 1921 S.C. 151.

[14] *Marshall* v. *Cardonald Bowling Club*, 1971 S.L.T.(Sh.Ct.) 56.

[15] *Bell* v. *The Trustees*, 1975 S.L.T.(Sh.Ct.) 60.

[16] *Forbes* v. *Eden, sup. cit.*

[17] *Murdison* v. *Scottish Football Union* (1896) 23 R. 449 at pp. 466, 467 *per* Lord Kinnear. Of course an aggrieved member may claim that his reputation has suffered. It is not pleasant to be barred from the club. But lack of success with one's fellow human beings is different from damage to reputation. See *Marshall* v. *Cardonald Bowling Club, sup. cit.* On the limitations on the intervention by the courts in the affairs of religious bodies see *McDonald* v. *Burns*, 1940 S.C. 376 and cases there referred to, and F. Lyall, *Of Presbyters and Kings* (1980), pp. 87–101.

[18] *e.g. North British Ry. Co.* v. *Wood* (1891) 18 R.(H.L.) 27; *McFeetridge* v. *Stewarts & Lloyds*, 1913 S.C. 773; *Davies* v. *Hunter*, 1934 S.C. 10.

to decide what claims have been waived and what course of action, if any, remains open.[19] A probative writ is not required to discharge a claim for damages.[20] A contract may be novated so that a new obligation is substituted for the old.[21] In general, one contract may remove or vary rights arising under another contract.

Discharge of claims may be implied. For example, the parties may bring their contractual relationships to an end in such a way as to suggest that they do not intend future claims to arise, as when a renunciation of a lease by the tenant is accepted by the landlord,[22] or a faulty television set is returned and the price refunded,[23] or correspondence suggests a mutual surrender of rights.[24]

Mere delay, short of the period of prescription, will not bar a claim. Delay, coupled with prejudice to the other party, may bar the claim[25] and raise the plea of *mora*, taciturnity and acquiescence.[26]

In sale there is authority which suggests that patent defects in goods must be complained of within a reasonable time after delivery or an action for damages will be barred.[27] This is contrary to principle. Rejection of the goods must take place within a reasonable time,[28] and it follows that the buyer should examine the goods when reasonably practical to do so or run the risk that rejection will be too late.[29] But as an alternative to rejection the buyer has a right to retain the goods and claim damages.[30] This right is not affected by an invalid rejection[31] and in principle mere delay in intimating a claim for damages is not a bar to the claim, but the buyer may act in such a way as to indicate that he waives any claim against the seller.

Nevertheless cases on a contract of repair[32] and a contract of car-

---

[19] *Thin & Sinclair* v. *Arrol & Sons* (1896) 24 R. 198; *G.E.A. Airexchangers Ltd.* v. *James Howden & Co. Ltd.*, 1984 S.L.T. 264 (proof before answer allowed).

[20] *Davies* v. *Hunter, sup. cit.*

[21] See para. 23–22.

[22] *Lyons* v. *Anderson* (1886) 13 R. 1020.

[23] *McAuslan* v. *Jack*, 1957 S.L.T.(Sh.Ct.) 8.

[24] *Evenoon Ltd.* v. *Jackel & Co. Ltd.*, 1982 S.L.T. 83.

[25] *Bain* v. *Assets Co.* (1904) 6 F. 692 at p. 705 *per* Lord President Kinross. On appeal revd. (1905) 7 F.(H.L.) 104; Gloag, pp. 542, 543.

[26] On the procedure in the event of this plea see *Halley* v. *Watt*, 1956 S.C. 370; *Bethune* v. *A. Stevenson & Co. Ltd.*, 1969 S.L.T.(Notes) 12.

[27] *W. M. Strachan & Co. Ltd.* v. *John Marshall & Co.*, 1910 2 S.L.T. 108; Gloag, p. 704.

[28] Sale of Goods Act 1979, s.35(1); *Morrison & Mason Ltd.* v. *Clarkson Bros.* (1896) 25 R. 427; *Hyslop* v. *Shirlaw* (1905) 7 F. 875; *Flynn* v. *Scott*, 1949 S.C. 442; *Aird & Coghill* v. *Pullan & Adams* (1904) 7 F. 258.

[29] *Dick* v. *Cochrane & Fleming*, 1935 S.L.T. 432.

[30] s.11(5), at least in the case of a material failure. The remedy in other circumstances is doubtful. See *Millars of Falkirk Ltd.* v. *Turpie*, 1976 S.L.T.(Notes) 66; M. G. Clarke, "The Buyer's Right of Rejection," 1978 S.L.T.(News) 1; Anon., 1978 S.L.T.(News) 61; W. W. McBryde, "Sale of Defective Goods," 1979 S.L.T.(News) 225.

[31] *Pollock & Co.* v. *Macrae*, 1922 S.C.(H.L.) 192 disapproving *Electric Construction Co.* v. *Hurray & Young* (1897) 24 R. 312. A valid rejection is another matter. See *Lupton & Co.* v. *Schulze* (1900) 2 F. 1118 which should be read subject to *Pollock & Co.*

[32] *Clerk* v. *Eliott* (1836) 15 S. 253.

riage[33] have been interpreted as meaning that complaints should be made within a reasonable time.[34] It is difficult to see, however, why these instances should result in any departure from general principles. Personal bar or *mora*, implied waiver or acquiescence, may bar claims but mere delay is not enough.[35]

(3) Claim for damages regulated by the express provision of the parties

20–06   The parties may by contract exclude or limit the liability to pay damages.[36] They may provide for the amount of damages in an enforceable penalty clause. The problems of exclusion and limitation clauses and of penalty clauses are considered elsewhere.

(4) A claim for damages and the actio quanti minoris

20–07   The extent to which the *actio quanti minoris* is recognised in Scots law is a matter of controversy. This is particularly unfortunate because of the resulting uncertainties in working out remedies in the sale of heritage and the sale of some moveables. It is necessary to narrate the history of the dispute.

20–08   **(a) The history of the actio quanti minoris.** Roman law recognised two remedies if a slave was sold with a latent defect. The *actio redhibitoria* was for return of the slave and a refund of the price. A form of this rejection of defective goods is part of Scots law. The doubt is over the second Roman remedy, the *actio quanti minoris*. Under that the buyer could keep the defective slave, and claim a reduction in the price. It is possible that this sensible option was not adopted by the common law of Scotland, as a result of a mistake.

The relevant passages in the Institutional writers are ambiguous.[37] What appeared to trouble our early writers was the idea that a buyer should be able to question the value of the subjects which he had bought. To allow that would not be in the interests of commerce. The confusion of thought, however, was to equate a dispute on value with a grievance about defective goods. I may pay a very high price for goods. That I should not be able to challenge my bargain because the price was high is no ground for denying me a remedy if the goods are defective.

By the beginning of the nineteenth century Scots law allowed remedies, including damages, for latent defects which rendered the subject

---

[33] *Stewart* v. *N.B. Ry. Co.* (1878) 5 R. 426.

[34] Gloag, p. 704.

[35] In *Clerk* there had been use of the article repaired. In *Stewart* there had been written intimation of damage to a different extent from that later claimed.

[36] This possibility was given as the reason for the second rule in *Hadley* v. *Baxendale* (1854) 9 Ex. 341 at pp. 354, 355 *per* Alderson B.

[37] Stair, I,ix,10; I,x,15; Bankt., I,19,1,2; Ersk., III,iii,10; Bell, *Comm.*, I,463. The history is discussed in a very valuable article—A. L. Stewart, "The *Actio Quanti Minoris*" (1966) 11 J.L.S. 124.

unfit for its proper use.[38] It was very doubtful if there was a remedy for patent defects or slight and latent defects. It might have done little harm, and been in accordance with what the position probably was under Roman law, if the law had developed by making a distinction between various types of defect. There was always the possibility that we would have allowed retention of the goods and a claim for damages for slight and latent defects, if not for all latent defects. But it was not to be. By the time M. P. Brown wrote in 1821 he could say: "But we have rejected the *actio quanti minoris*, as being inconsistent with the true principles of the contract [of sale] and hurtful to the interests of commerce."[39]

9 **(b) The modern law.** It became one of the canons of the law to state that the *actio quanti minoris* was not recognised.[40] When Lord President Inglis came to express this in 1869 he further confused the issue. He said[41]:

> "When a purchaser receives delivery of goods as in fulfilment of a contract of sale, and thereafter finds that the goods are not conform to order, his only remedy is to reject the goods and rescind the contract. If he has paid the price, his claim is for repayment of the price, tendering re-delivery of the goods. If he has granted a bill for the price, his claim is for re-delivery of the bill in return for the offered re-delivery of the goods. If any portion of the goods has before their rejection been consumed or wrought up so as to be incapable of redelivery *in forma specifica*, then the true value (not the contract price) of that portion of the goods must form a deduction from the purchaser's claim for repayment of the price. The purchaser is not entitled to retain the goods and demand an abatement from the contract price corresponding to the disconformity of the goods to order, for this would be to substitute a new and different contract for that contract of sale which was originally made by the parties, or it would resolve into a claim of the nature of the *actio quanti minoris*, which our law entirely rejects. Just as little is the purchaser entitled, while rescinding the contract, to retain the goods in security of a claim of damages for breach of contract."

The problems with this dictum are (1) Read literally it would deny any right to damages in the case of the supply of defective goods. This is not a necessary consequence of a refusal to accept the *actio quanti minoris*.[42]

---

[38] *Dickson & Co.* v. *Kincaid*, December 15 1808, F.C.

[39] *Sale*, p. 287. See also *Hannay* v. *Creditors of Barglay* (1785) Mor. 13, 334, and *Gordon* v. *Hughes*, June 15, 1815, F.C., 1 Bligh 287. The case law is well discussed by Stewart, *sup. cit.*

[40] e.g. *Bald* v. *Scott* (1847) 10 D. 289; *Amaan* v. *Handyside & Henderson* (1865) 3 M. 526.

[41] *McCormick & Co.* v. *Rittmeyer & Co.* (1869) 7 M. 854 at p. 858. The case was decided on the basis of a special agreement to allow abatement of the price.

[42] See M. P. Brown, *Sale*, p. 303. There are many reported cases of damages awarded for failure to deliver. It would be a very odd system of law which removed the seller's liability for consequential loss provided that goods (however defective) were delivered. See *Louttit's Trs.* v. *Highland Ry. Co.* (1892) 19 R. 791 at pp. 799, 800 *per* Lord McLaren.

The result has more recently been the denial of a claim for damages arising out of a contract of barter.[43] (2) The dictum ignores the distinction
between various types of defects which was mentioned by the court four
years earlier.[44] This was probably the basis of Roman law. Buckland
stated: "Though it cannot be proved that *redhibitoria* lay for serious and
quanto [*sic*] *minoris* for minor defects, it is likely that they were so
employed."[45] However, such is the authority of Lord President Inglis
that his exposition of the law has been accepted. It was approved by
Lord Dunedin in the House of Lords in 1922.[46]

The Sale of Goods Act 1893 (now 1979) removed the relevance of the
argument to contracts to which the Act applies, by allowing a buyer the
option of retaining goods and claiming damages.[47] However, there can
be sales to which the Act does not apply, such as a sale of goodwill,[48] a
sale of shares, or a sale of heritage. The pre-1893 law on sale also applies
to barter.[49] It remains important, therefore, to inquire when a right to
damages arises although the property is retained.

20–10   (c) **The exceptions which allow an actio quanti minoris.** There are exceptions to the rule stated by Lord President Inglis. These may include the
following:

(1) Where there is a latent defect which is discovered when matters
are no longer entire. Rejection of the property being impossible,
damages must be allowed or the buyer may have no remedy. He keeps
the goods and claims damages. This was applied at common law to hidden defects in goods such as machinery.[50] It has also been said to apply
to the sale of heritage where matters are no longer entire because, for
example, buildings have been erected.[51] A claim under a warrandice
clause in a conveyance or other deed relating to heritage is for indemnity for loss, and does not proceed on reconveyance of the subjects.[52]

(2) When the right to retain the subjects is separate from the obligation in dispute, *e.g.* the buyer receives a disposition but disputes with

---

[43] *Urquhart* v. *Wylie*, 1953 S.L.T.(Sh.Ct.) 87.

[44] *Amaan* v. *Handyside & Henderson, sup. cit.*

[45] *Roman Law* (3rd ed.), p. 493; see also J. A. C. Thomas, *Textbook of Roman Law*,
p. 287.

[46] *Pollock & Co.* v. *Macrae* 1922 S.C.(H.L.) 192 at p. 200.

[47] s.11(2), 1893 Act; s.11(5), 1979 Act—although the application of the Act to minor
defects is still problematical. See *Millars of Falkirk Ltd.* v. *Turpie*, 1976 S.L.T. (Notes) 66;
M. G. Clarke "The Buyer's Right of Rejection," 1978 S.L.T.(News) 1; Anon., 1978
S.L.T.(News) 61; W. W. McBryde, "Sale of Defective Goods," 1979 S.L.T.(News) 225.

[48] *Bryson & Co.* v. *Bryson*, 1916 1 S.L.T. 361. Gloag's comments on this case were criticised in *Smith* v. *Sim*, 1954 S.C. 357 at p. 361 *per* Lord Wheatley.

[49] *Urquhart* v. *Wylie, sup. cit.*; *Widenmeyer* v. *Burn, Stewart & Co.*, 1967 S.C. 85.

[50] *Pearce Bros.* v. *Irons* (1869) 1 M. 571; *Spencer & Co.* v. *Dobie & Co.* (1879) 7 R. 396;
Fleming & Co. v. *Airdrie Iron Co.* (1882) 9 R. 473; *Dick & Stevenson* v. *Woodside Steel
and Iron Co.* (1888) 16 R. 242.

[51] *Louttit's Trs.* v. *Highland Ry. Co., sup cit.* at p. 800 *per* Lord McLaren. See, though,
comments in *Bryson* v. *Bryson, sup cit.*

[52] *Welsh* v. *Russell* (1894) 21 R. 769.

the seller under a collateral obligation.[53] The completion of a house and an obligation to convey have been held to be separate.[54]

(3) Opinion has been reserved on whether retaining the property and claiming damages might be competent if fraud or essential error is alleged.[55] In principle if fraud is proved damages should be awarded. Damages are claimable for fraud even if the contract is not reduced,[56] *a fortiori*, if *restitutio in integrum* is not achieved. In cases of pure error damages should not be claimable.

(4) The parties can agree to retention and a claim for damages.[57]

11   (d) The sale of land. The exceptions mentioned above leave untouched a problem which arises with the sale of heritage. Assume, for example, that there is a contract for the sale of a house and a separate garage. Just after missives are concluded the title is examined and it is discovered that the seller has no title to the garage. The buyer must reject the house and claim damages, or he has no remedy at all. He cannot do what he probably wants to do, which is to keep the house and claim a reduction in the price. If, however, a disposition of the house and garage has been delivered to the buyer and it is only then that the absence of the seller's title is discovered, the buyer's remedy is based on the warrandice clause. He keeps what is validly conveyed and sues for his loss. The philosophy of the law is not consistent.[58]

(5) Void and unenforceable contracts

12   If a contract is void or unenforceable (which includes some illegal contracts), there is no enforceable contractual duty to perform, there can be no breach of that duty and, consequently, no entitlement to damages for breach. Similarly, if performance of the contract might involve an illegal act, failure to perform illegally should not be the basis for an assessment of damages. So in *Balfour* v. *Young*[59] damages were not calculable on the basis of the value of a car registration plate which was in breach of statutory regulations. A voidable contract is different, because it is valid until rescinded.

---

[53] *McKillop* v. *Mutual Securities*, 1945 S.C. 166. The concept of a collateral obligation was extended in a doubtful way in *Bradley* v. *Scott*, 1966 S.L.T.(Sh.Ct) 25.

[54] *McKillop* v. *Mutual Securities, sup. cit.*; *Hoey* v. *Butler*, 1975 S.C. 87. See also *Hayes* v. *Robinson*, 1984 S.L.T. 300. As these cases show, the obligations can be in the same contract.

[55] *Brownlie* v. *Miller* (1880) 7 R.(H.L.) 66; *Wood* v. *Mags. of Edinburgh* (1886) 13 R. 1006.

[56] *Smith* v. *Sim*, 1954 S.C. 357. On negligent misrepresentation. See paras. 9–75 *et seq.*

[57] *McCormick* v. *Rittmeyer, supra.*

[58] If possible, at the stage of missives there should be separate prices and conditions applying to the purchase of a large number of pieces of ground, rather than a lump sum for a large estate. The latter is easier, but if there is a defective title to one small lot, the buyer may be faced with the choice of accepting the defect or throwing up the whole deal and claiming damages. If each lot is separately contracted for, the majority of the estate can be kept, and damages claimed for failure to transfer the rest.

[59] 1980 S.L.T.(Sh.Ct.) 19.

(6) Prior assessment of loss

20–13   All claims for breach of contract should be raised in one action even if they are difficult to assess. Damages cannot be obtained in instalments. So if there has been a prior award of damages, a second action for further damages arising out of the same breach is incompetent.[60] Therefore it is not possible to obtain a declarator that the defender is liable to pay for future losses arising from a breach of contract.[61]

If, however, there are separate breaches of the same contract, there may be an action in respect of each breach. For example, if the contract is to supply a certain quantity of goods each month, an action for loss arising from one month's failure to supply is not a bar to another action for a failure in a different month.[62] In exceptional circumstances the court might refuse to allow a series of actions.[63]

(7) Prescription and limitation

20–14   As a general rule the right to claim damages for breach of contract will prescribe under the Prescription and Limitation (Scotland) Act 1973.[64] The period of prescription is five years. The period may be interrupted by a relevant claim or acknowledgment.[65] The period does not run if fraud or error of the debtor induced the creditor to refrain from making a claim.[66] Nor does it run while the original creditor is under legal disability.[67] It starts to run from the date of loss, injury or damage.[68]

There is a series of exceptions to the five-year period, the interpretation of which is bound to give rise to difficulties. These include obligations arising from court decrees, arbitration or tribunal awards, bank notes, probative writs, partnership, agency, or obligations relating to land and various rights on succession, reparation for personal injuries and imprescriptible obligations.[69] Except for imprescriptible obligations, there is a general 20-year period of prescription.[70] If the action arises out of a contract of carriage, other statutory provisions apply.[71]

---

[60] *Stevenson* v. *Pontifex & Wood* (1887) 15 R. 125.

[61] *Aberdeen Development Co.* v. *Mackie Ramsay & Taylor*, 1977 S.L.T. 177.

[62] *Stevenson* v. *Pontifex & Wood, sup. cit.* at p. 129 *per* Lord President Inglis—see also *Duke of Abercorn* v. *Merry & Cuninghame*, 1909 S.C. 750; *Cameron Head* v. *Cameron & Co.*, 1919 S.C. 627.

[63] *Salaried Staff London Loan Co. Ltd.* v. *Swears and Wells Ltd.*, 1985 S.L.T. 326.

[64] s.6 and Sched. 1; see paras. 23–32 *et seq.*

[65] s.6(1).

[66] s.6(4).

[67] *Ibid.*

[68] s.11

[69] Sched. 1.(2)

[70] s.7.

[71] See D. M. Walker, *The Law of Prescription and Limitation of Actions in Scotland* (3rd Ed.), pp. 108, 109 and statutes referred to below, *s.v.* "Statutory limitations on claims for damages."

(8) Statutory limitations on claims for damages

15 Statute sometimes limits the right to claim damages: for example the liability of various carriers is limited,[72] as is the liability of the Post Office[73] and hotel-keepers.[74]

PART 2

Causation

(a) The principle of causation

16 The loss complained of by the pursuer must be caused by the defender's breach of contract. If the pursuer would have suffered the loss apart from the breach, the most he will recover will be nominal damages. In *Sykes* v. *Midland Bank Executor and Trustee Co. Ltd.*[75] solicitors acting in breach of contract failed to advise clients of a term in a lease. The plaintiffs failed to prove that if they had been advised of the term, they would not have entered into the lease. They were awarded £2 nominal damages.

Many contracts would, if performed, make a loss for one party. His costs, for example, may be greater than anticipated. The resulting loss would not be a legitimate claim against a party in breach, who is only liable for the losses caused by the breach. It is, therefore, not sufficient for a pursuer to say that there was a breach and his loss on the contract is £x. The rules of causation must be used to determine which losses are recoverable from the defender. In the application of these rules there is considerable scope for the discretion and common sense of the courts.[76]

(b) The selection of the relevant cause

17 It is difficult to be more specific than to state that the loss must be caused by the breach. The breach may be the result of several "causes." The court must decide whether there was a cause attributable to the

---

[72] Carriage by Air Act, 1961, Sched. 1, art. 22; Carriage by Air (Supplementary Provisions) Act 1962, Sched., art. VI; Carriage of Goods by Road Act 1965, Sched., Arts. 23–29; Carriage of Goods by Sea Act 1971, Sched. IV, art. 5; Carriage by Railway Act 1972, Sched., arts. 6–10; Carriage of Passengers by Road Act 1974, Sched., arts. 13, 16; Merchant Shipping Act 1979, ss.17–19 (to replace Merchant Shipping Act 1894, s.503 as amended by the Merchant Shipping (Liability of Shipowners and Others) Act 1958). The Carriage by Railway Act 1972 was repealed with effect from May 1, 1985 by the International Transport Conventions Act 1983.

[73] Post Office Act 1969, ss.29, 30.

[74] Hotel Proprietors Act 1956, ss.1, 2.

[75] [1971] 1 Q.B. 113.

[76] "There is always a combination of co-operating causes, out of which the law, employing its empirical or commonsense view of causation, will select the one or more which it finds material for its special purpose of deciding the particular case": *Smith Hogg* v. *Black Sea Insurance Co.* [1940] A.C. 997 at pp. 1003, 1004, *per* Lord Wright.

defender. In doing this it does not apply mathematical or philosophical rules or any special verbal formula. The court applies its idea of commonsense. There are reported instances in which competing causes were in issue, such as whether the loss resulting from a distribution of forged notes was caused by a printer's breach or a bank paying out on the notes[77]; whether a delay to a ship was caused by unseaworthiness or Admiralty orders[78]; whether a loss was caused by a failure to nominate a safe loading place or the master's conduct in handling the ship[79]; whether the cause was a failure to supply a stepladder or the plaintiff's use of a trestle[80]; and whether an explosion was caused by a breach of contract or subsequent events.[81] But the person in search of useful dicta in these cases will, by and large, be disappointed. The opinions are short in analysis of principle, which is not surprising given that on the one hand the simple statement of the principle of causation might be confused by judicial elaboration and on the other hand its application to any given set of facts, despite being sometimes very difficult, is an application to those facts only and not a precedent of value.

20–18   The most thorough judicial analysis is that of Lord Wright in *Smith Hogg* v. *Black Sea Insurance Co.*[82] An unseaworthy ship became unstable when replenishing her bunkers. Was the loss caused by the unseaworthiness or by the act of the master in bunkering? The decision was that it was caused by the initial unseaworthiness. In his discussion of causation Lord Wright made the following points:

(1) The use of Latin phrases such as *"novus actus interveniens," "causa causans"* or *"causa sine qua non"* do not help. Nor do terms such as "dominant," "effective," "real" or "actual cause." "Dominant" is a term more appropriate to marine insurance cases. "Real" or "effective" or "actual" are adjectives which add nothing.

(2) The selection of the relevant cause or causes will vary with the nature of the contract. There can be several co-operating causes, for example, unseaworthiness can never be the sole cause of loss in a contract of carriage.[83]

(3) In marine insurance cases it may be necessary to find a "dominant cause." But that is not necessary with a contract for the carriage of goods by sea where the appropriate question is—was that breach of contract a cause of the damage? If the question is answered in the affirm-

---

[77] *Banco de Portugal* v. *Waterlow & Sons Ltd.* [1932] A.C. 452.

[78] *A/B Karlshamns Oljefabriker* v. *Monarch S.S. Co.*, 1949 S.C.(H.L.) 1.

[79] *Compania Naviera Maropan S/A* v. *Bowaters Lloyd Pulp and Paper Mills Ltd.* [1955] 2 Q.B. 68.

[80] *Quinn* v. *Burch Bros. (Builders) Ltd.* [1966] 2 Q.B. 370.

[81] *Vacwell Engineering* v. *B.D.H. Chemicals* [1971] 1 Q.B. 88.

[82] [1940] A.C. 997, followed in *Heskell* v. *Continental Express Ltd.* [1950] 1 All E.R. 1033. Discussed by Lord Wright in *A/B Karlshamns Oljefabriker* v. *Monarch Steamship Co. Ltd.. sup cit.*

[83] A point elaborated by Lord Wright in *A/B Karlshamns, etc.* v. *Monarch Steamship Co. Ltd.*, *sup. cit.*

ative, the shipowner (the party in breach) is liable although there were
other co-operating causes.

9   It will be noticed that much of this analysis states what should *not* be
done to define a "cause." On the positive side it makes clear that there
may be several causes, not only "a" cause. There is a resemblance to the
rule now established in delict, that a pursuer succeeds if he can show
that the fault of the defender caused or materially contributed to the
injury. There may be two separate causes, but it is enough if one of the
causes arose from the fault of the defender.[84] With similar reasoning it
can be said that it is enough, in the law of contract, if one of the causes
of the pursuer's loss was the defender's breach of contract.

(c) Intervening events

0   It follows from the analysis stated above that an event subsequent to
the defender's breach which contributes to the pursuer's loss will not by
itself remove the liability of the defender to the pursuer.[85] Thus in *A/B
Karlshamns Oljefabriker* v. *Monarch Steamship Co.*[86] a chartered ship
should have arrived in Sweden before the outbreak of war. She did not
do so because she was unseaworthy. An embargo by the British government caused the ship to divert to Glasgow and the cargo was tran-
shipped to Sweden. The embargo had contributed to the loss, but the
shipowners were liable.

1   There are, however, circumstances where events subsequent to the
breach do have an effect on the liability of the party in breach.

      (1) The subsequent event might frustrate the contract, such as the tor-
pedoeing of a ship.[87] The principles of frustration would regulate the
loss subsequent to the frustrating act.

      (2) A loss caused by an unforeseeable event may be irrecoverable
because it is too remote.[88]

      (3) There may be a new, independent cause of loss. This is the prob-
lem now to be considered. The analysis varies a little according to
whether the new cause is the act of a third party, or the act of the pursuer.

2   An illustration may be given of the intervening act of a third party.[89]
X breaks his arm as a result of a breach of contract by a carrier. In hospi-

---

[84] *Wardlaw* v. *Bonnington Castings*, 1956 S.C.(H.L.) 26; *Nicholson* v. *Atlas Steel
Foundry and Engineering Co.*, 1957 S.C.(H.L.) 44; *McGhee* v. *National Coal Board*, 1973
S.C.(H.L.) 37. A material contribution is one which is not *de minimus*: *Wardlaw*, *sup cit.*
at p. 32 *per* Lord Reid; *Nicholson*, *sup. cit.* at p. 60 *per* Viscount Simonds, at p. 65 *per*
Lord Cohen.
[85] *Smith Hogg* v. *Black Sea Insurance Co.*, *sup. cit.*; *Heskell* v. *Continental Express
Ltd.*, *sup cit.*
[86] *Sup. cit.*
[87] *Associated Portland Cement* v. *Houlder* (1917) 86 L.J. (K.B.) 1495.
[88] See *infra*, "Remoteness of liability." paras. 20–47 *et seq*. The distinction between (2)
and (3) can be difficult. See *infra*, "Causation and remoteness of liability," paras. 20–47 to
20–50.
[89] There is little reported authority in the law of contract.

tal he is, by the surgeon's mistake, injected with a lethal dose of a drug. It is contrary to common sense to say that the carrier killed X. As Lord Sumner put it: "In general . . . even though A is in fault, he is not responsible for injury to C which B, a stranger to him, deliberately chooses to do. Though A may have given the occasion for B's mischievous activity, B then becomes a new and independent cause."[90]

20–23   On the other hand there are cases in which the intervening act has been a crime, but this has not prevented the contract breaker from being liable for the loss.[91]

20–24   If the intervening act is that of the pursuer (the party not originally in breach) that may raise several problems. There are the problems of selection of a relevant cause, contributory negligence and mitigation of loss. In *Compania Naviera Maropan S/A* v. *Bowaters Lloyd Pulp and Paper Mills Ltd.*[92] the defendant charterers nominated an unsafe place for loading. The master was placed on the horns of a dilemma, but accepted the advice of the pilot. The master's conduct did not relieve the charterers of liability. Singleton L.J.[93] gave an example of a progressive problem arising with the defective repair of a motor car. The repairer is in breach of contract, but at what point does the car owner share responsibility for using the defective car? He said:

> "If a repairer agrees to repair my motor car and does not do so within the time agreed or within a reasonable time I may succeed in an action for damages against him. If he repairs it indifferently and I suffer injury therefrom, equally I can recover damages. I have done what he would have expected me to do. The damage is the natural and probable result of the faulty repair. It may be that an action would arise on negligence as well, but it arises from the contractual relationship between the parties. The indifferent or bad performance gives a right of action just as much as does failure to perform. If I may carry the illustration further, suppose I notice, when my motor car is returned, that the repair does not appear to have been well done, and I point this out to the repairer, who reassures me, asserting that the car is as good as it ever was and is perfectly sound as the result of the repair. If an accident occurs and I suffer damage through the faulty repair, can I recover damages? The answer depends on a number of factors, the first and main one being whether I acted as a reasonable man would do in the circumstances."[94]

In *Quinn* v. *Burch Bros. (Builders) Ltd.*[95] building contractors in breach of contract failed to supply a ladder. The plaintiff used a trestle

---

[90] *Weld-Blundell* v. *Stephens* [1920] A.C. 956 at p. 986. The decision in that case, reached by a bare majority, has been criticised. See McGregor, *Damages*, para. 180.

[91] *London Joint Stock Bank* v. *Macmillan* [1918] A.C. 777; *De la Bere* v. *Pearson* [1908] 1 K.B. 280; *Stansbie* v. *Troman* [1948] 2 K.B. 48.

[92] [1955] 2 Q.B. 68.

[93] at p. 94.

[94] An example of negligent use of defective equipment is *Lambert* v. *Lewis* [1982] A.C. 225.

[95] [1966] 2 Q.B. 370.

and suffered personal injuries. The failure to supply the ladder was held not to be the cause of the accident. The opinion of Sellers L.J. shows how three situations could arise.

(1) The ladder is not supplied. The plaintiff uses a trestle. The cause of the resulting injury is the use of the trestle.

(2) An unsafe ladder is supplied. The plaintiff uses it. On the face of it the defendant's actions caused the injury. It is the same as charterers nominating an unsafe port.[96]

(3) The ladder provided is obviously unsafe. The plaintiff uses it. It may be that the plaintiff's own conduct brought about his injuries.[97]

PART 3

Contributory Negligence in Contract

5 French and German law recognise a form of contributory negligence in contract,[98] but civil law systems in any event place emphasis on fault as a condition of contractual liability.[99] In Scotland, whatever the origins of the law—and there are early references to fault in connection with breach of contract—we now adopt a common-law stance that damages for breach can be due irrespective of the fault of the defender. Possibly if the pursuer had been at fault, the likely approach would have been to say that the loss was not caused by the defender's acts.[1]

6 The Law Reform (Contributory Negligence) Act 1945 allows apportionment of damages in cases of contributory negligence. Whether it can apply to a breach of contract is not settled. Paull J. was prepared to hold that the Act did apply in *Quinn* v. *Burch Bros. (Builders)*[2] but the issue was not decided on appeal. Similarly, in *De Meza and Stuart* v. *Apple, Van Straten, Shena and Stone*,[3] the judge of first instance applied the Act to a contract between auditors and clients, but the Court of Appeal left the question open. Roskill L.J. observed: "This . . . has been a controversial point certainly for as long as I can remember since 1945. It has to my knowledge been argued more than once in this court, though never decided."[4]

7 It is obvious that the Act was drafted with tortious and delictual liability in mind, but not entirely because other liability is contemplated in

---

[96] *Compania Naviera Maropan S/A* v. *Bowaters Lloyd Pulp and Paper Mills, sup. cit.*

[97] A similar situation arose in *Lambert* v. *Lewis* [1982] A.C. 225 (buyer's negligence the cause of loss, not the seller's breach of warranty). Contributory negligence is discussed *infra*, paras. 20–25 to 20–27.

[98] *International Encyclopaedia of Comparative Law*, Vol. VII, Chap. 16, para. 16–105.

[99] *Op. cit.*, para. 16–78.

[1] As in *Lambert* v. *Lewis, sup. cit.*

[2] [1966] 2 Q.B. 370.

[3] [1975] 1 Lloyd's Rep. 498.

[4] at p. 509.

its definitions of "fault."[5] However, in *A. B. Marintrans* v. *Comet Shipping Co. Ltd.*[6] Neill L.J. held that the Act was restricted to tortious liability. Curiously, the Scottish definition is wider than the English, with the result that there is a stronger case in Scotland for saying that the Act can apply to a breach of contract. In *Lancashire Textiles (Jersey) Ltd.* v. *Thomson Shepherd & Co. Ltd.*[7] Lord Davidson expressed the opinion that a breach of contract may form the basis of a plea of contributory negligence, but only if that breach can also be described as constituting a wrongful act, breach of statutory duty or negligent act or omission within the meaning of section 5 of the 1945 Act. A breach of section 14 of the Sale of Goods Act 1979 was not a breach of statutory duty within the meaning of the 1945 Act.

PART 4

Mitigation

(a) The principle of mitigation

20–28   It is commonly, and inaccurately, said that a person who suffers loss by a breach of contract has a "duty" to mitigate his loss, or he is bound to act in a way which mitigates loss, or he must seek to minimise his loss.[8] There is not, however, any duty or obligation of this nature. Consider the case of a seller who in breach of contract fails to deliver the goods. The buyer can in the market place buy the goods at £100 more than the contract price. If the buyer buys in the market, his damages are *prima facie* £100.[9] If he does not buy but sits idle and contemplates his grievance—his damages assuming that he has a loss are limited to £100. If he decides to buy more expensive goods—his damages are £100. Whichever option the buyer takes he is not acting contrary to any obligation or duty.

20–29   It is inaccurate to say that there is a duty or obligation to minimise loss because there is no corresponding right in the other party to enforce the duty. Despite what Lord President Inglis said in *Warin & Craven* v. *Forrester*[10] a seller, when the contract is repudiated by the buyer, need not resell immediately and his right to damages is not conditional on his

---

[5] ss.4 and 5. One instance in which there might be liability for breach of contract only from a negligent act, is the giving of professional advice; cf. *Basildon D.C.* v. *J. E. Lesser (Properties) Ltd.* [1985] 1 All E.R 20.

[6] [1985] 3 All E.R. 442; see also *Basildon D.C.* v. *J. E. Lesser (Properties) Ltd., sup. cit.*

[7] 1986 S.L.T. 41.

[8] See, *e.g.* Gloag, p. 688; Walker, *Civil Remedies*, p. 467. The point in the text was made in *Darbishire* v. *Warren* [1963] 3 All E.R. 310 at p. 315 *per* Pearson L.J.

[9] Sale of Goods Act 1979, s.51(3).

[10] (1876) 4 R. 190 at p. 193; affd. (1877) 4 R.(H.L.) 75. Lord President Inglis stated: "He must resell whatever the state of the market, and it is only if he immediately do so that he can charge the difference between the contract and the market price against the buyer." In fact damages were awarded on the basis of that difference.

doing so. Despite Lord Justice-Clerk Macdonald in *Ross* v. *McFar-lane*,[11] a person dismissed from employment *is* entitled to sit idle and make no effort to obtain another job. The law does not penalise the pursuer who incurs excessive loss. He recovers the same loss, whether he mitigates or not. It is more accurate to say that loss which could reasonably have been avoided cannot be recovered from the party in breach.[12]

(b) The recovery of reasonable loss

30   The law can be stated in three propositions. (1) The assessment of the pursuer's loss will be on the basis that the pursuer acted reasonably in the circumstances, whatever in fact the pursuer did. Included in this assessment may be expenses incurred. (2) It is, however, assumed that the actual loss incurred by the pursuer was reasonable, until the defender proves otherwise. (3) The pursuer cannot recover more than his actual loss. Therefore, if events directly connected with the breach reduce the loss to the pursuer, that must be taken into account.

31   The *locus classicus* of the principle of mitigation is the speech of Viscount Haldane in *British Westinghouse Co.* v. *Underground Electric Ry. Co.*[13] He referred to the principle that "imposes on a plaintiff the duty of taking all reasonable steps to mitigate the loss consequent on the breach, and [which] debars him from claiming any part of the damage which is due to his neglect to take such steps."[14] He went on: "this . . . principle does not impose on the plaintiff an obligation to take any step which a reasonable and prudent man would not ordinarily take in the course of his business." So it may be that the reasonable course for a seller faced with a repudiation by a buyer, is to sell whatever the state of the market.[15] This might, of course, result in only nominal damages being recoverable,[16] or recovery of the expenses of arranging a second sale. Conversely if the seller is in breach of contract, the reasonable buyer might buy in from elsewhere[17] or resell the defective goods.[18] The reasonable employee dismissed in breach of contract would seek other suitable employment.[19] and may claim State benefits.[20]

32   Because the standard is that of a reasonable man in the circumstances, the defender cannot claim that the loss should be assessed on

---

[11] (1894) 21 R. 396 at p. 406.

[12] In truth it is not the pursuer who mitigates *his* loss. The principle of mitigation limits the loss of the defender.

[13] [1912] A.C. 673 at p. 689.

[14] The use of the word "duty" is commented on above.

[15] *Warin & Craven* v. *Forrester, sup. cit.*; *Duff & Co.* v. *Iron and Steel Fencing Co.* (1891) 19 R. 199 at p. 204 *per* Lord MacLaren; Sale of Goods Act 1979, s.50.

[16] *Blythswood Motors* v. *Raeside*, 1966 S.L.T.(Sh.Ct.) 13.

[17] *Ireland* v. *Merryton Coal Co.* (1894) 21 R. 989; Sale of Goods Act, s.51.

[18] *Pommer & Thomsen* v. *Mowat* (1906) 14 S.L.T. 373.

[19] *Hoey* v. *McEwan and Auld* (1867) 5 M. 814 at p. 819 *per* Lord Deas; *Ross* v. *McFar-lane* (1894) 21 R. 396 at p. 406 *per* Lord Justice-Clerk Macdonald.

[20] *Parsons* v. *B.N.M. Laboratories Ltd.* [1964] 1 Q.B. 95; *Westwood* v. *S. of State for Employment* [1985] A.C. 20.

the basis that extraordinary efforts might have been made. The reasonable buyer might buy in from elsewhere in an available market but not search the country for portions of the goods,[21] let alone go "hunting the globe to find out where they can get skins."[22] Nor may it be reasonable for a ship's master to incur trouble, expense or delay trying to find extra cargo to fill a hold.[23] Nor may it be reasonable to risk damage to commercial reputation.[24] In principle what is reasonable should depend on the circumstances, including the financial ability of the pursuer. It is established in the law of delict that the wrongdoer must take his victim as he finds him,[25] and similar reasoning should apply in the law of contract.[26] The result has been that a pursuer has been able to recover the cost of installing electricity at the time of the proof. Damages were not lowered to the cost at an earlier date. The pursuer did not have the means to carry out the installation at the earlier time.[27]

20–33   The defender cannot succeed in a challenge to the pursuer's claim merely by showing that there was an alternative and less costly course which was not followed. In a reparation case Lord Collins said:

> "The wrongdoer is not entitled to criticise the course honestly taken by the injured person on the advice of his experts, even though it should appear by the light of after events that another course might have saved loss. The loss he has to pay for is that which has actually followed under such circumstances upon his wrong."[28]

This is stating the proposition too broadly for present purposes, because read literally, and out of context, it appears to abolish the concept of mitigation. Lord Macmillan expressed the point in a case on contract, *Banco de Portugal* v. *Waterlow*[29]:

> "Where the sufferer from a breach of contract finds himself in consequence of that breach placed in a position of embarrassment the measures which he may be driven to adopt in order to extricate himself ought not to be weighed in nice scales at the instance of the party whose breach of contract has occasioned the difficulty. It is often easy after an emergency has passed to criticise the steps which have been taken to meet it, but such criticism does not come well

---

[21] *Gunter* v. *Lauritzen* (1894) 31 S.L.R. 359.

[22] *Lesters Leather and Skin Co.* v. *Home and Overseas Brokers* (1948) 64 T.L.R. 569 *per* Lord Goddard C.J.

[23] *Henderson* v. *Turnbull*, 1909 S.C. 510 at p. 520 *per* Lord Ardwall.

[24] *James Finlay & Co. Ltd.* v. *N. V. Kwik Hoo Tong H.M.* [1929] 1 K.B. 400 at p. 408 *per* Sankey L.J.

[25] *Clippens Oil Co. Ltd.* v. *Edinburgh and District Water Trs.*, 1907 S.C.(H.L.) 9 at p. 14 *per* Lord Collins; *Liesbosch Dredger* v. *Edison* [1933] A.C. 449 at p. 461 *per* Lord Wright; *Robbins of Putney* v. *Meek* [1971] R.T.R. 345; *Martindale* v. *Duncan* [1973] 2 All E.R. 355; *Dodd Properties* v. *Canterbury City Council* [1980] 1 All E.R. 928; *Paxton* v. *McKain*, 1983 S.L.T.(Sh.Ct.) 88.

[26] On applying the same principles in tort and contract, see *Bellingham* v. *Dhillon* [1973] 1 Q.B. 304; *Paxton* v. *McKain, sup. cit.* and para. 20–59.

[27] *Paxton* v. *McKain, sup. cit.*

[28] *Clippens Oil Co.* v. *Edinburgh Water Trs.*, 1907 S.C.(H.L.) 9 at p. 14; followed, *Rubens* v. *Walker*, 1946 S.C. 215.

[29] [1932] A.C. 452 at p. 506.

from those who have themselves created the emergency. The law is satisfied if the party placed in a difficult situation by reason of the breach of a duty owed to him has acted reasonably in the adoption of remedial measures, and he will not be held disentitled to recover the cost of such measures merely because the party in breach can suggest that other measures less burdensome to him might have been taken."

(c) The time of mitigation

34   It is necessary to fix a time at which a reasonable pursuer would act to mitigate the loss. In principle this cannot be before there is a breach of contract, and usually the time of material breach is taken. Thus section 51(3) of the Sale of Goods Act 1979 measures damages by the difference between the contract price and the market price, at the time or times when the goods ought to have been delivered. In *Johnstone* v. *Harris*,[30] an action arising out of a buyer failing to implement missives, it was observed that the issue of mitigation did not arise until there was a material breach. After breach the problem of mitigation arises (not after knowledge of a potential breach).[31] In cases of repudiation the problem of mitigation only arises when the repudiation has been accepted, or if the repudiation is not accepted, when the date for performance has arrived without performance being made. It does not follow that the damages are assessed at the date of an accepted repudiation, because the loss is to be measured against what would have happened if the contract had been carried out. But if there was a reasonable opportunity to mitigate the loss between the repudiation and the date of performance, that is taken into account.[32]

35   Underlying all this are some fairly complex issues which have not yet been properly examined. There may never be a material breach, but only a lesser breach which gives rise to a claim for damages. It must be possible to reply to that claim with a plea for mitigation. The difficulty in analysis is that in response to a breach the "innocent" party has a choice of remedies. He may, for example, wish to seek specific implement or, if the breach is material, rescind the contract, or he may hope that eventually the other party will perform satisfactorily. Specific implement, which is said to be more a feature of Scots law than English law, is not always reconcilable with some steps in mitigation which involve, in effect, the "innocent" party contracting elsewhere. Say, for example, there is an obligation enforceable by specific implement, such as an obligation to grant a disposition or build a house. The obligee prefers to

---

[30] 1977 S.C. 365. The reasonable pursuer might then take steps to resell the heritage, but heritage cannot usually be sold instantly, as can some goods. The loss is assessed according to the price obtainable at the reasonable time of resale, not the time of the material breach.

[31] *Daejan Developments Ltd.* v. *Armia Ltd.*, 1981 S.C. 48.

[32] *Roper* v. *Johnson* (1873) L.R. 8 C.P. 167; *Melachrino* v. *Nickoll & Knight* [1920] 1 K.B. 693; *Garnac Grain Co.* v. *Faure & Fairclough* [1968] A.C. 1130 at p. 1140 and cases there cited; *Shindler* v. *Northern Raincoat Co.* [1960] 2 All E.R. 239.

seek implement of the obligation rather than damages. He raises an action of implement with an alternative claim for damages. He obtains decree after the inevitable delays of legal process during which market prices rise. On what basis should the damages be assessed? Surely not on the basis that no action was raised. Nor on the assumption that the pursuer should have contracted elsewhere at the time of breach of contract. The pursuer did what the law entitled him to do, namely to seek implement, and that should not cause the law to impose a penalty on him. The result should be that the defender must meet the loss which would have been incurred by a reasonable pursuer. This will alter according to the remedies which the pursuer was entitled to, and did, exercise.

(d) Expense of mitigation

20–36   A pursuer is entitled to recover reasonable expenses incurred in mitigating his loss. In *Cazalet* v. *Morris*[33] shipowners reduced the period during which a vessel would have been upon demurrage by unloading cargo into lighters. They were entitled to recover their outlay from the charterers to the extent of the amount of demurrage saved.[34] If a pursuer might resell, the costs of resale are an item of the damages claimable.[35]

(e) Onus of proof

20–37   The pursuer will aver his loss. The defender, or party in breach, will aver that the loss claimed is unreasonably high. Each party will seek to establish his averments. Thus it can be said that: "generally the onus of proving that the best available means to minimise the loss were not taken rests on the party who has broken his contract and is seeking to escape from the consequences.;"[36] However, it does not necessarily follow from this that if the only live issue is mitigation of loss, the defender will be ordained to lead in the proof. The pursuer must still establish his recoverable loss[37] and, in any event, who leads in a proof is to an extent a matter of convenience.[38] In general the more the facts emerge, the less important do questions of onus become.[39]

---

[33] 1916 S.C. 952.

[34] The demurrage saved was £200 and the lighterage charge just over £240.

[35] As in *Johnstone's Exrs.* v. *Harris*, 1977 S.C. 365.

[36] Gloag, p. 689; *Connal, Cotton & Co.* v. *Fisher Renwick & Co.* (1883) 10 R. 824; see also *Roper* v. *Johnston* (1873) L.R. 8 C.P. 167. *The World Beauty* [1970] P. 144 at p. 154 *per* Lord Denning M.R., at p. 158 *per* Fenton Atkinson L.J.; *Melachrino* v. *Nickoll & Knight* [1920] 1 K.B. 693. But contrast *Salvanayagam* v. *University of West Indies* [1983] 1 All E.R. 824 (P.C.) at p. 827.

[37] *Johnstone's Exrs.* v. *Harris, sup. cit.*

[38] Walker and Walker, *Evidence*, para. 73.

[39] A point made in a different connection by Lord Reid in *Jenkins* v. *Allied Ironfounders Ltd.*, 1970 S.C.(H.L.) 37 at p. 41: "We must consider the evidence as we find it, and, after the evidence has been led, it is only in very rare cases that onus of proof is material."

(f) Pursuer limited to actual loss

8   The pursuer cannot recover more than his actual loss. Therefore, if events directly connected with the breach reduce the loss to the pursuer, these must be taken into account. The problem is to decide when an event is so connected with the breach. Not all gains to the pursuer, following on the breach, accrue to the benefit of the party in breach.

9   The issue can be illustrated by two contrasting decisions, that of the House of Lords in *British Westinghouse Co.* v. *Underground Electric Ry.*[40] and of the Privy Council in *Jamal* v. *Moolla Dawood Sons & Co.*[41] In *British Westinghouse Co.*, turbines supplied were deficient in power and not in accordance with the contract. The pursuers procured substitute turbines which were more powerful and earned great profit. The pecuniary advantage in having the substitute turbines was relevant to the assessment of damages. Viscount Haldane stated that the principle of mitigation of loss:

> "does not impose on the plaintiff an obligation to take any step which a reasonable and prudent man would not ordinarily take in the course of his business. But when in the course of his business he has taken action arising out of the transaction, which action has diminished his loss, the effect in actual diminution of the loss he has suffered may be taken into account even though there was no duty on him to act."[42]

He then referred to *Staniforth* v. *Lyall*,[43] which was a case of a ship undertaking a more profitable voyage, after a charter was abandoned. His Lordship continued[44]:

> "I think that this decision illustrates a principle which has been recognised in other cases, that, provided the course taken to protect himself by the plaintiff in such an action was one which a reasonable and prudent person might in the ordinary conduct of business properly have taken, and in fact did take whether bound to or not, a jury or an arbitrator may properly look at the whole of the facts and ascertain the result in estimating the quantum of damage."

After referring to two decisions of the Privy Council[45] he expressed the limitation on the principle: "The subsequent transaction, if to be taken into account, must be one arising out of the consequences of the breach and in the ordinary course of business."

40   This important limitation distinguishes from *British Westinghouse Co.* other cases where the pursuer's loss is lessened but not to the benefit of

---

[40] [1912] A.C. 673.
[41] [1916] 1 A.C. 175.
[42] at p. 689.
[43] (1830) 7 Bing. 169.
[44] at p. 690.
[45] *Erie County Natural Gas and Fuel Co.* v. *Carroll* [1911] A.C. 105—substitute gas supply because of breach—subsequent sale of business at profit—nominal damages for original breach; *Wertheim* v. *Chicoutimi Pulp Co.* [1911] A.C. 301—resale of goods at price higher than market price taken into account in assessing loss.

the defender: *e.g.* the pursuer recovers under an insurance policy, disappointed passengers enter into other contracts with the pursuer, a landlord profits from reletting the property. Some contracts might exist irrespective of the breach (*e.g.* insurance) and are more obviously *res inter alios acta* than those which would not have taken place but for the breach (*e.g.* the customer who pays for another product or service). There is an intermediate class of contracts which might have arisen anyway, but not in quite the same circumstances if there has been no breach (*e.g.* a subsequent letting of property at an earlier date than planned). It is the last category which produces the most difficulty. Viscount Haldane referred to a transaction which[46] "was not *res inter alios acta*, but one in which the person whose contract was broken took a reasonable and prudent course quite naturally arising out of the circumstances in which he was placed by the breach."

20–41 *British Westinghouse Co.* can be contrasted with *Jamal v. Moolla Dawood Sons & Co.*[47] There was a breach of a contract for the sale of shares. The sellers, instead of reselling immediately, delayed and resold later at a price higher than the market price at the date of the breach. The Privy Council held that the seller's damages should not be reduced because the market had risen. As was said[48]:

> "If the seller retains the shares after the breach, the speculation as to the way the market will subsequently go is the speculation of the seller, not of the buyer; the seller cannot recover from the buyer the loss below the market price at the date of the breach if the market falls, nor is he liable to the purchaser for the profit if the market rises."

20–42 In *Jamal* there was a ready market and a subsequent sale was *res inter alios acta*. How would this apply to the sale of a house? The seller tries to resell once a material breach by the buyer is established. But resale of a house is not as quick in normal circumstances as resale of quoted shares or some commodities. A house may take months to sell. If the seller, following normal procedure, eventually resells the house at a higher price than the original contract price, that must be taken into account in assessing the damages claimable from the buyer. If, however, the seller keeps the property for some time, without trying to resell, and eventually, years later, sells at a high price, the profit is not, following *Jamal*, taken into account.[49] The seller was entitled to wait before reselling. But the original buyer cannot gain the benefit of this, any more than he would suffer if this enterprise of the seller turned into a loss.

---

[46] at p. 691.

[47] [1916] I.A.C. 175. See also *Re United Railways of Havana and Regla Warehouses Ltd.* [1961] A.C. 1007 at pp. 1050, 1051 *per* Lord Reid. There have been changes to the law on suing for a foreign currency, but much of Lord Reid's example of the time of the assessment of loss remains valid.

[48] at p. 179.

[49] If the seller is in the interval between sales seeking specific implement of the first sale, that raises other issues. See para. 20–35.

43   *Jamal* was distinguished in *R. Pagnan & Fratelli* v. *Corbisa Industrial Agropacuaria.*[50] Goods were rejected by the buyer. The buyer did not buy other goods. He took the same goods from the seller at a renegotiated and reduced price. The result was a profit to the buyer which was held relevant in assessing the seller's liability in damages. The second sale was not an independent contract, but part of a continuous dealing between the parties.

44   *Jamal* was followed in *Campbell Mostyn (Provisions) Ltd.* v. *Barnett Trading Company.*[51] Tinned ham was rejected. This was a breach of contract. The ham was sold a few weeks after the breach at a higher price than the market price at the date of breach. It was argued that in assessing damages for breach of contract the courts considered what had actually happened, and that a party who had not suffered loss could not recover damages. But, applying *Jamal*, damages were assessed using the price in the available market at the date of breach.

45   Another contrast which illustrates the same problem is between *Jebsen* v. *East and West Indian Dock Co.*[52] and *The World Beauty.*[53] In *Jebsen* emigrants from Norway to America could not be carried on one ship because of its detention in a dock. The passengers were taken on other ships owned (in part) by the plaintiffs. This factor was not allowed to reduce the damages. *The World Beauty* is an illustration of events which would have happened anyway, but took place earlier because of a tort. A ship was damaged in a collision. She had been chartered at high rates and subsequent employment under a second charter had been arranged. A substitute ship performed the first charter. The damaged ship after repair started the second charter early. The question arose as to whether against the losses caused by the collision should be set the profit made by the substitute ship and the gain from advancing the term of the second charter. The court held that these gains had to be taken into account when calculating damages, but not all the profit from advancing the second charter should be looked at.[54] This flowed, not from measures taken in consequence of the collision, but from the previous negotiation of the charter. Even without the collision these profits would have been earned, but at a later date.

46   The result is that there are gains which flow directly from the breach, which must be taken into account in assessing damages. Other gains will not be. Sometimes these arise from other contracts entered into before the breach or from other contracts after the breach which can be regarded as a separate enterprise. It is tempting to say that, just as not all losses caused by a breach are taken into account, neither are all

---

[50] [1971] 1 All E.R. 165.

[51] [1954] 1 Lloyd's Rep. 65.

[52] (1875) L.R. 10 C.P. 300.

[53] [1970] P. 144; see also *Levison* v. *Farin* [1978] 2 All E.R. 1149; and *Nadreph Ltd.* v. *Willmett* [1978] 1 All E.R. 746, which has a confusing headnote.

[54] The calculation of the benefit of receiving money early posed considerable problems for the court.

gains. But if this suggests recourse to the principles of remoteness, that cannot solve all the problems of gains. Hardly ever in the cases discussed could it be said that the action of the plaintiff was reasonably foreseeable. What is important is that he did act, and he did gain. If anything, the question is whether the cause of the gain was the breach or some independent factor.[55]

PART 5

Remoteness

(a) Causation and remoteness of liability

20–47   The pursuer's loss must have been caused by the defender's breach of contract.[56] Only once causation is established does the problem of the heads of recoverable loss arise. Yet there is a potential for confusion between causation and remoteness of liability. If a breach causes several losses, there is a remoteness problem. A defender may be held liable for some losses, such as the cost of having his services performed by others, but not liable for all losses, such as loss of business or liquidation of the pursuer. There are losses which are too speculative or remote. In other words the pursuer may claim items A, B and C as heads of damage. All were caused by the breach. If A and B are clearly allowable, and the discussion is about allowing C, remoteness is in issue. Let the pursuer, however, only claim C. It is possible to deny recovery of C either on the ground that C was not caused by the breach or on the ground that it was too remote. To add to the confusion, this result can be produced by using phrases such as "C did not naturally and directly arise from the breach," which obscures whether the ground of decision was causation or remoteness. What should happen is that first it is asked whether A, B or C was caused by the breach. If, applying the rules on causation, the answer is "No," that is an end of that head of damage. If the answer is "Yes," the second question has to be asked, which is whether the loss is recoverable.

20–48   In *Millar* v. *Bellvale Chemical Co.*[57] golf balls were supplied which were disconform to contract. The pursuer recovered damages for loss of profit but not for loss of reputation. Professor Walker treats this as a case on causation.[58] But if there was a loss of reputation it must have been caused by something, and no cause other than the pursuer's breach

---

[55] In this area of the law it seems that the selection of a dominant cause may be more important than in answering the question whether the defender's breach caused the loss. The nearest analogous problem of causation is sometimes that of whether there has been a *novus actus interveniens* caused by the act of the pursuer. See para. 20–20 *et seq*. The principles, however, have yet to be fully analysed.

[56] See para. 20–16.

[57] (1898) 1 F. 297.

[58] *Civil Remedies*, p. 450.

can reasonably be chosen. The case did not raise a problem of causation, but a problem of remoteness.[59]

49   A different case is *Wilson* v. *Carmichael*.[60] Cabbage seed was supplied disconform to contract. The pursuer recovered damages because his ground was occupied by an unremunerative crop. He failed to recover for loss of business with his customers. The reason was that a skilled farmer would have discovered that the cabbages were the wrong variety before selling them. What caused the loss of business? Here is a typical causation problem, because there are two causes of the loss to choose from—the original breach of contract by the supplier of the seed, and the pursuer's failure to inspect cabbages before sale. The court chose the latter cause.

50   *Seton* v. *Paterson*[61] is a strange case on its facts, but it did raise a problem of causation—what caused the death of a horse? Was it riding it at a gallop, which was a breach of contract resulting in injury, or was the cause of death the rolling of the animal in its stall and the twisting of its colon? The latter seems more likely, but the court decided on the former. Gloag is right in describing it as "a very remarkable decision," but is perhaps confusing in his treatment of the case as an illustration of loss being too remote.[62]

(b) The need for a limit of liability

51   The law does not always compensate the pursuer for all the losses which he has suffered as a result of the defender's breach of contract. It is inaccurate to state that: "where a party sustains a loss by reason of a breach of contract, he is, so far as money can do it, to be placed in the same situation, with respect to damages, as if the contract had been performed."[63] The law may deny full recovery of loss. Probably the reason for this is that full recovery would be a strong disincentive to entering contracts or would increase the prices charged under contracts. Even insurers usually place a ceiling on admissible claims, and every contracting party is not to be regarded as an underwriter with unlimited liability.

A hypothetical case was stated by an English judge in this way:

> "Cases of this kind have always been found to be very difficult to deal with, beginning with a case said to have been decided about two centuries and a half ago, where a man going to be married to an

---

[59] A similar argument can be used to treat *Baird* v. *Banff District Lunacy Board*, 1914 1 S.L.T. 284 as a decision on remoteness, not causation: *cf.* Walker, *sup. cit.*.

[60] (1894) 21 R. 732.

[61] (1880) 8 R. 236.

[62] *Contract*, p. 691. Under the heading "Loss too Remote," Gloag considered cases on causation.

[63] *Robinson* v. *Harman* (1848) 1 Exch. 850 at p. 855 *per* Parke B. and *per* Alderson B. at pp. 855 and 856—"The damages have been assessed according to the general rule of law, that where a person makes a contract and breaks it, he must pay the whole damage sustained."

heiress, his horse having cast a shoe on the journey, employed a blacksmith to replace it, who did the work so unskilfully that the horse was lamed, and, the rider not arriving in time, the lady married another, and the blacksmith was held liable for the loss of the marriage. The question is a very serious one; and we should inevitably fall into a similar absurdity unless we applied the rules of common sense to restrict the extent of liability for the breach of a contract of this sort."[64]

20–52   If the facts are too extreme, common sense—and legal analysis—might decide such issues on the basis of causation, not remoteness[65]: so a more realistic example must be given. The pursuer has contracted with the defender for the supply of goods for a stand which has been hired by the pursuer at a trade exhibition. In breach of contract the defender fails to supply the goods and the stand cannot be used by the pursuer for other purposes. The pursuer has suffered loss. This may be itemised. There is the cost of hiring the stand and the production of material for it. There is the time and money spent on fruitless trips to the exhibition site. There are potential losses of sales and injury to reputation. There is the loss of free publicity in the local press and a chance to win a prize for the best stand.[66] The law imposes a limit on what is recoverable. There is controversy over how the limit is to be expressed, but it is based on the concept of reasonable foresight.

(c) The limit of liability—recoverable loss

20–53   As mentioned earlier,[67] principles of remoteness of liability evolved in Scots law long before the classic opinion of Baron Alderson in *Hadley v. Baxendale*.[68] However, Gloag described that opinion as being "constantly referred to in Scotland."[69] It has been analysed in the House of Lords, and founded on in a Scottish appeal.[70] For practical purposes the older Scottish authorities have been forgotten, and the principles of remoteness of liability can be derived from four cases. These are *Hadley v. Baxendale*; *Victoria Laundry (Windsor) Ltd.* v. *Newman Industries*

---

[64] *British Columbia Sawmill Co.* v. *Nettleship* (1868) L.R. 3 C.P. 499 at p. 508 *per* Willes J. Curiously a similar case did arise in New York—*Coppola* v. *Kraushaar* (1905) 92 N.Y.S. 436, 102 App.Div. 306, quoted Corbin, para. 1000.

[65] Was the late arrival of the rider really the cause of the other marriage?

[66] The pursuer might go further and say that the disaster resulted in the liquidation of his company. He would first have to show that the liquidation was caused by the breach, before problems of remoteness arise. See para. 20–47. There would probably be sufficient difficulties in this to defeat the loss claimed. In all the other heads of loss imagined in the text, causation is not likely to be a problem.

[67] para. 20–01.

[68] (1854) 9 Ex. 341 at pp. 354, 355. The case probably had a greater impact on English law because it affected the notion that damages were in the discretion of the jury. The case has a fascinating background; see Richard A Danzig, "*Hadley* v. *Baxendale*; A Study in the Industrialisation of the Law" (1975) 4 *J. Legal Studies* 249.

[69] *Contract*, p. 696—only one reported case is directly cited as an authority for this. For a recent application see *Haberstich* v. *McCormick & Nicholson*, 1975 S.C. 1.

[70] *A/B Karlshamns Oljefabriker* v. *Monarch Steamship Co. Ltd.*, 1949 S.C.(H.L.) 1.

Ltd.[71]; *A/B Karlshamns Oljefabriker* v. *Monarch Steamship Co. Ltd.*[72] and *Koufos* v. *C. Czarnikow Ltd.*[73]

In *Hadley* v. *Baxendale*, Alderson B. said:

"Where two parties have made a contract which one of them has broken, the damages which the other party ought to receive in respect of such breach of contract should be such as may fairly and reasonably be considered either arising naturally *i.e.* according to the usual course of things, from such breach of contract itself, or such as may reasonably be supposed to have been in the contemplation of both parties, at the time they made the contract, as the probable result of the breach of it. Now, if the special circumstances under which the contract was actually made were communicated by the plaintiffs to the defendants, and thus known to both parties, the damages resulting from the breach of such a contract, which they would reasonably contemplate, would be the amount of injury which would ordinarily follow from a breach of contract under these special circumstances so known and communicated. But, on the other hand, if these special circumstances were wholly unknown to the party breaking the contract, he, at the most, could only be supposed to have had in his contemplation the amount of injury which would arise generally, and in the great multitude of cases not affected by any special circumstances, from such a breach of contract. For, had the special circumstances been known, the parties might have specially provided for the breach of contract by special terms as to the damages in that case; and of this advantage it would be very unjust to deprive them. Now the above principles are those by which we think the jury ought to be guided in estimating the damages arising out of any breach of contract."

54   In the first sentence the limb prefaced by "either" is the so-called first rule; that prefaced by "or" the second rule. Despite the misleading headnote of the report, in *Hadley* the facts were within the first rule.

55   In *Monarch Steamship Co. Ltd.* Lord Porter referred to "reasonable anticipation," and what shipowners "ought to have foreseen."[74] Lord Wright referred to cases under the second rule in *Hadley*, where "it would not be fair or reasonable to hold the defendant responsible for losses which he could not be taken to contemplate as likely to result from his breach of contract."[75] He pointed out that: "The Court will, however, assume that the parties as business men have all reasonable acquaintance with the ordinary course of business."[76] He went on to say that: "The question whether damage is remote, or 'natural' and direct, can in general only be decided on a review of the circumstances of each special case. Remoteness of damage is in truth a question of fact."[77] After referring to previous authority, he continued:

---

[71] [1949] 2 K.B. 528.
[72] *Sup. cit.*
[73] [1969] 1 A.C. 350.
[74] *Sup. cit.* at pp. 12, 13.
[75] at p. 19.
[76] *Ibid.*
[77] at p. 20.

"The question in a case like the present must always be what reasonable business men must be taken to have contemplated as the natural or probable result if the contract was broken. As reasonable business men each must be taken to understand the ordinary practices and exigencies of the other's trade or business. That need not generally be the subject of special discussion or communication."[78]

20–56   Lord Uthwatt referred to what a shipowner should reasonably have foreseen. "To my mind, the situation in Europe at that date was such that a reasonable shipowner contemplating a voyage from Rashin to that range of ports would regard the chance of war, not as a possibility of academic interest to the venture, but as furnishing matter which commercially ought to be taken into account."[79]

20–57   Lord du Parcq applied standards of "real danger"[80] and "serious possibility,"[81] but he did add a warning that in the end it is a question of fact, and that "circumstances are so infinitely various that, however, carefully general rules are framed, they must be construed with some liberality, and not too rigidly applied."[82]

20–58   A short time later in *Victoria Laundry*, Asquith L.J. analysed the authorities and came to the following conclusions, in giving the judgment of the court[83]:

"(1) It is well settled that the governing purpose of damages is to put the party whose rights have been violated in the same position, so far as money can do so, as if his rights had been observed . . . This purpose, if relentlessly pursued, would provide him with a complete indemnity for all loss *de facto* resulting from a particular breach, however improbable, however unpredictable. This, in contract at least, is recognised as too harsh a rule. Hence—
(2) In cases of breach of contract the aggrieved party is only entitled to recover such part of the loss actually resulting as was at the time of the contract reasonably foreseeable as liable to result from the breach.
(3) What was at that time reasonably foreseeable depends on the knowledge then possessed by the parties or, at all events, by the party who later commits the breach.
(4) For this purpose, knowledge 'possessed' is of two kinds—one imputed, the other actual. Everyone, as a reasonable person, is taken to know the 'ordinary course of things' and consequently what loss is liable to result from a breach of contract in that ordinary course. This is the subject-matter of the 'first rule' in *Hadley* v. *Baxendale*. But to this knowledge, which a contract-breaker is assumed to possess whether he actually possesses it or not, there may have to be added in a particular case knowledge which he

---

[78] at p. 21.
[79] at pp. 27, 28.
[80] at p. 29.
[81] at p. 30.
[82] at p. 28.
[83] *Sup. cit.* at pp. 539, 540.

actually possesses of special circumstances outside the 'ordinary course of things' of such a kind that a breach in those special circumstances would be liable to cause more loss. Such a case attracts the operation of the 'second rule' so as to make additional loss also recoverable.

(5) In order to make the contract-breaker liable under either rule it is not necessary that he should actually have asked himself what loss is liable to result from a breach. As has often been pointed out, parties at the time of contracting contemplate not the breach of the contract, but its performance. It suffices that, if he had considered the question, he would as a reasonable man have concluded that the loss in question was liable to result: see certain observations of Lord du Parcq in the recent case of *Monarch Steamship Co. Ltd.* v. *A/B Karlshamns Oljefabriker*.

(6) Nor, finally, to make a particular loss recoverable, need it be proved that upon a given state of knowledge the defendant could, as a reasonable man, foresee that a breach must necessarily result in that loss. It is enough if he could foresee it was likely so to result. It is indeed enough, to borrow from the language of Lord du Parcq in the same case, . . . if the loss (or some factor without which it would not have occurred) is a 'serious possibility' or a 'real danger.' For short, we have used the word 'liable' to result. Possibly the colloquialism 'on the cards' indicates the shade of meaning with some approach to accuracy."

–59 In *Koufos* there was criticism of the phrase "on the cards" but the majority of the judges supported the explanation of *Hadley* given in *Victoria Laundry*.[84] A minority rejected the standard of reasonable foreseeability because it would confuse the measure of damages in contract and tort.[85] The problem is that everyone is agreed that recoverable loss in contract extends to somewhere between a certainty and a remote possibility, but language has difficulty in fixing where the point lies between these extremes. Phrases used in *Koufos* include "not unlikely," "liable to result," a "real danger," and a "serious possibility." It is also the case that different people use the same words to mean different things. Lord Reid, who was in the minority in *Koufos*, said[86]:

"Suppose one takes a well-shuffled pack of cards, it is quite likely or not unlikely that the top card will prove to be a diamond: the

---

[84] Lords Morris, Hodson and Pearce. *Victoria Laundry* was also cited with approval by Lords Guest, Upjohn and Pearson in *East Ham Corporation* v. *Bernard Sunley & Sons Ltd.* [1966] A.C. 406. Lords Upjohn and Pearson even used the discredited phrase "on the cards."

[85] Lords Reid and Upjohn. Whether there is a difference remains controversial. See *H. Parsons (Livestock) Ltd.* v. *Uttley Ingham & Co. Ltd.* [1978] Q.B. 791. There is much to be said for the views of Lords Denning and Scarman that the difference is semantic. Of course a contract breaker's knowledge might be greater than the tortfeasor's knowledge of the consequences of the victim of the loss, but (1) a claim in contract and in tort (or delict) can arise out of the same incident and involve the same parties—the tortfeasor is not always a stranger to his victim; (2) in any event, to say that in some circumstances liability is wider than in others is merely to apply the rules in *Hadley* v. *Baxendale*; and (3) it is not obvious what the policy would be behind having different principles applying in contract on the one hand and tort or delict on the other.

[86] at p. 390.

odds are only three to one against; but most people would not say that it is quite likely to be the nine of diamonds for the odds are then fifty-one to one against. On the other hand I think that most people would say that there is a serious possibility or a real danger of its being turned up first and, of course, it is on the cards."

20–60 With respect to Lord Reid, it may be doubted whether most people would say that the appearance of the nine of diamonds was a serious possibility or a real danger. That a diamond might appear—yes; but not a specific number.

20–61 It is perhaps unfortunate that judicial attempts were made to impart more precision to the standards stated in *Victoria Laundry*, because the attempts were bound to fail. As Lord Denning put it: "I soon begin to get out of my depth. I cannot swim in this sea of semantic exercises—to say nothing of the different degrees of probability—especially when the cause of action can be laid either in contract or in tort. I am swept under by the conflicting currents."[87] We have now reached the stage at which what used to be directions to assist a jury are now details incomprehensible to judges. There is much to be said for as simple an approach as possible to the limits of liability, based on what the defender ought reasonably to have foreseen.

(d) The knowledge of the defender

20–62 The knowledge of the contract breaker can be treated as being of two types. Asquith J. in *Victoria Laundry* said that knowledge was either imputed or actual. The knowledge of the reasonable person is imputed to the contract breaker. This comes within the first rule in *Hadley*. Actual knowledge comes within the "special circumstances" of the second rule. In truth it is sometimes difficult to distinguish imputed and actual knowledge. A contract and its parties do not exist in isolation from the world. The defender does know certain things about the pursuer. Some facts which he does not know, it may be he ought to know, and it is an accident of events whether the pursuer's claim succeeds under the first or the second rule in *Hadley*.

20–63 Thus Lord Shaw in *Hall* v. *Pim*[88] criticised the "ultra analysis" which divides Baron Alderson's well-known sentence into two portions. As Devlin J. pointed out in *Biggin* v. *Permanite*,[89] the division into two rules "has sometimes proved misleading." It may give the impression that actual knowledge increases the liability of a defender who would otherwise have only imputed knowledge. Actual knowledge could however decrease what was foreseeable, by showing that the pursuer would suffer less than in ordinary circumstances.[90]

---

[87] *H. Parsons (Livestock) Ltd.* v. *Uttley Ingham & Co. Ltd.* [1978] Q.B. 791 at 802.

[88] (1928) 30 L.R. L.Rep. 159 at p. 164. See also Lord Reid in *Koufos, sup cit.* at p. 385; *cf.* Lord Upjohn at p. 421.

[89] [1951] 1 K.B. 422 at p. 436; revd. on other grounds [1951] 2 K.B. 314. See also *Cottrill* v. *Steyning etc. Building Soc.* [1966] 2 All E.R. 295 at p. 297.

[90] See *Koufos, sup cit.* at p. 416 *per* Lord Pearce.

64   The appropriate standard is what the defender knew and ought to have known. So in *Waddington* v. *Buchan Poultry Products*[91] the suppliers of offal to mink were told that there should not be any offal from artificially sterilised poultry. This being known, a reasonable man in the circumstances would have anticipated that the supply of the prohibited offal would affect the breeding of mink. On the facts there was liability for loss of the mink.

65   There is a line of English dicta which suggests that knowledge must be brought home to the defender by a term of the contract, but this is wrong in principle, and was disapproved by Lord Upjohn in *Koufos*.[92]

66   The knowledge which is relevant is generally said to be that existing at the time of the contract.[93] The reason is that the defender contracts with certain assumptions and risks which should not be increased by later events. It may be doubted, however, whether this can be a universal rule. Parties sometimes enter into contracts which last a very long time and under which there can be performance which was not anticipated at the time of the contract. For example, contracts between suppliers and an oil company may be open-ended in that they give the oil company options to seek further services or goods under the contract from those originally planned. Two years after the contract is entered into the knowledge of the parties and their trading are quite different from their early cautious dealings. Similarly a client may use a solicitor over a long period. It may be easier in that instance to regard each transaction as a separate contract, but it is not always so.[94] There is a case for looking at knowledge at the time of the breach. What is important is the foreseeable consequences of, say, the solicitor's negligence.[95] Courts should sometimes have regard to what flows from the breach, rather than to knowledge at the time of contracting, particularly in long-term contracts where either party has an option to terminate the contract.[96]

---

[91] 1963 S.L.T. 168.

[92] *Sup. cit.* at pp. 421–422.

[93] See quotations from Alderson B. in *Hadley* and Asquith L.J. in *Victoria Laundry, supra*; *Hydraulic Engineering Co.* v. *McHaffie* (1878) 4 Q.B.D. 670 at p. 676 *per* Brett L.J.; *contra, Gee* v. *Lancashire & Yorkshire Ry.* (1860) 6 H. & N. 211 at p. 218.

[94] *e.g.* a solicitor is given instructions to set up a trust and manage it. 10 years after the trust deed a mistake is made in the application of new tax legislation. The legislation could not have been foreseen by anyone at the time of the original advice, nor, of course, could the consequences of misapplying it.

[95] As in *Otter* v. *Church, Adams, Tatham & Co.* [1953] Ch. 280; *Haberstich* v. *McCormick & Nicholson*, 1975 S.C. 1.

[96] It may be that what emerges from this analysis is that the appropriate question is— "What risks is it reasonable to impose on the defender in the circumstances?" A person who can terminate his contract on very short notice (*e.g.* a solicitor) may be taken to constantly incur different risks as new dangers emerge. Someone who must give a year's notice of termination cannot so easily escape a new liability which emerges, but, following appropriate procedure, he may avoid some liability. *Sibi imputet* if he does not. Someone who cannot terminate a fixed-term contract is in the classic position of one whose knowledge should be assessed at the time of the contract.

20–67   In the calculation of damages under section 51(2) of the Sale of Goods Act 1979 it has been held that questions of knowledge and foreseeability are irrelevant.[97]

(e) Foreseeability of type of loss

20–68   Although some loss of a certain type is foreseeable, events may increase the amount of that loss. This raises the point as to whether the pursuer can recover an unforeseeable quantum of loss of a type which was foreseeable. In *Vacwell Engineering Co. Ltd.* v. *B. D. H. Chemicals*,[98] chemicals were sold in glass ampoules. The chemical was explosive in contact with water and the failure of the seller to warn the buyer of that was a breach of the Sale of Goods Act 1893. Rees J. held that a minor explosion involving minor damage to property and to persons was reasonably foreseeable. What happened was not reasonably foreseeable. There was a violent explosion which killed one man and did over £74,000 worth of damage to a building. There was also a claim for loss of profit amounting to £300,000. The court was prepared to allow the unforeseeable loss to the building as a head of damages in the contract claim. In *H. Parsons (Livestock) Ltd.* v. *Uttley Ingham & Co. Ltd.*[99] the Court of Appeal held that it was sufficient if the loss was of a type the occurrence of which was a serious possibility, and it was not a bar to recovery that the quantum was greater than the parties might have contemplated.[1]

(f) Examples of remoteness of liability

20–69   Although a full citation of all the older authorities must be looked for elsewhere,[2] some indication can be given of how the courts have applied the principles which have been discussed above. Take the case of the

---

[97] *Allen* v. *W. Burns (Tractors) Ltd.*, 1985 S.L.T. 252. The standard, in terms of the statute, is whether the loss resulted directly and naturally from the breach of contract.

[98] [1971] 1 Q.B. 88. See also *Great Lakes S.S. Co.* v. *Maple Leaf Milling Co.* (1924) 41 T.L.R. 21 (P.C.); *Wroth* v. *Tyler* [1974] Ch. 30 at p. 61 *per* Megarry J.: "On principle, it seems to me to be quite wrong to limit damages flowing from a contemplated state of affairs to the amount that the parties can be shown to have had in contemplation, for to do this would require evidence of the calculation in advance of what is often incalculable until after the event."

[99] [1978] Q.B. 791.

[1] Older Scottish authority might indicate otherwise: *Duff & Co.* v. *Iron and Steel Fencing & Building Co.* (1891) 19 R. 199 at p. 205 *per* Lord McLaren; *"Den of Ogil" Co. Ltd.* v. *Caledonian Ry. Co.* (1902) 5 F. 99.

[2] Walker, *Civil Remedies*; Chitty, *Contract*; McGregor on *Damages*. The older authorities should be used with care. There are grounds for believing that in the second half of the 19th century judges tended to limit recoverable damages severely. As the law of tort and delict has developed, the idea of increasing the scope of recoverable damages has become more acceptable with consequences for the trend in contract law. The point cannot be further developed here. See P. S. Atiyah, *The Rise and Fall of Freedom of Contract* (1979), pp. 433, 434.

failure of a party to supply goods which causes a loss of profit. Is that loss recoverable?[3]

(1) At one end of the scale stand cases where there has been non-delivery or delayed delivery of what on the face of it is obviously a profit-earning item—for instance a ship[4] or some essential part of a ship, such as a propeller[5] or engines,[6] or failure to supply a large boiler for a laundry[7]—loss of profit is recoverable.

(2) A second and intermediate class of case in which loss of profit has often been awarded is where ordinary mercantile goods have been sold to a merchant with knowledge by the vendor that the purchaser wanted them for re-sale. This is so, at all events, where there is no market in which the purchaser could buy similar goods against the contract on the seller's default.[8] The existence of an available market would raise problems of mitigation of loss.[9]

(3) At the other end of the scale are cases where the defender is not a vendor of the goods, but a carrier.[10] The courts have been slow to allow loss of profit as a head of damage because a carrier commonly knows less than a seller about the purposes for which the buyer needs the goods or other special circumstances. However, a carrier should have reasonable knowledge of the circumstances of his trade and appreciate that late arrival may mean loss.[11] The principles applied are not different from other cases, but the result may differ. Some examples of other heads of loss claimed are given below.

(g) Speculative losses

70 Going somewhat beyond normal cases of loss of profit are claims for gains which were in any event speculative, such as the chance to win a prize in a competition. Here the gain which has been lost was subject to contingencies. If there are too many contingencies, the pursuer will fail. His case is like the story of the milkmaid who spilt the milk which would

---

[3] The analysis in *Victoria Laundry Co.* is adapted.

[4] *Fletcher* v. *Tayleur* (1855) 17 C.B. 21; *Re Trent and Humber Co., ex p. Cambrian Steam Packet Co.* (1868) L.R. 4 Ch.App. 112; *Mackenzie* v. *Liddell* (1883) 10 R. 705.

[5] *Wilson* v. *General Iron Screw Colliery Co.* (1877) 37 L.T. 789.

[6] *Saint Line Ltd.* v. *Richardsons, Westgarth & Co. Ltd.* [1940] 2 K.B. 99.

[7] *Victoria Laundry Co., sup. cit.*

[8] *Borries* v. *Hutchinson* (1865) 18 C.B.N.S. 445; *Duff & Co.* v. *Iron and Steel Fencing and Buildings Co.* (1891) 19 R. 199; *Patrick* v. *Russo-British Grain Export Co.* [1927] 2 K.B. 535; *Hall* v. *Pim* (1928) 30 Ll.L.Rep 159 (H.L.).

[9] See para. 20–28 *et seq.*

[10] *Hadley* v. *Baxendale, sup. cit.*; *Gee* v. *Lancashire and Yorkshire Ry. Co.* (1860) 6 H. & N. 211; *British Columbia etc. Sawmill Co. Ltd.* v. *Nettleship* (1868) L.R. 3 C.P. 499; *"Den of Ogil" Co. Ltd.* v. *Caledonian Ry. Co.* (1902) 5 F. 99. Despite Professor Walker's classification of the last case as a "leading Scottish case" (*Civil Remedies*, p. 458), it must be borne in mind that it was in part based on *The Parana*, a case which was overruled in *Koufos.*

[11] *Koufos, sup. cit.*; *Ardennes (Cargo Owners)* v. *Ardennes (Owners)* [1951] 1 K.B. 55.

have been sold to buy eggs which would have hatched into chickens which would have produced feathers which would have, etcetera. A pursuer making this type of claim in Scotland should be careful to aver facts which show the likelihood of his gain. For example, if all that the pursuer avers is that in breach of contract he was supplied with a defective rod and line and therefore he failed to catch any fish, there is no basis for assessing his probable catch. If he goes on to aver and prove his skill as a fisherman, his catches on previous occasions in similar circumstances, and the experience of others at the time of his disappointment, his case for recovery of an estimated loss is stronger.[12]

20–71   Generally, it is difficult to recover the more speculative losses. Illustrations of the problems are, the loss of profits claimed for the failure of a stallion to serve a mare,[13] the loss of repeat orders from a customer,[14] and the loss of co-operation of the beauty editresses of newspapers.[15] In the famous case of *Chaplin* v. *Hicks*,[16] however, the Court of Appeal upheld a jury award to a plaintiff who had been deprived of a chance to be interviewed for a job when she was one of 50 finalists in a newspaper competition.

(h) Loss of reputation

20–72   In *Millar* v. *Bellvale Chemical Co.*[17] the claim by Millar included damages for his loss of reputation as a golf-ball merchant because he sold balls of bad quality which were supplied by the Bellvale company. The court did not come to a decision on the damages for injury to the business. In *Dodwell* v. *Highland Industrial Caterers Ltd.*[18] a dismissed catering manager claimed damages for breach of contract. Lord Blades deleted from the record the pursuer's averments relating to loss of prestige and publicity. As Lord Blades pointed out, the problem was to be solved by the application of the rules in *Hadley* v. *Baxendale*. The case was decided on the terms of the contract in issue.[19]

---

[12] But, of course, still subject to the rules in *Hadley* v. *Baxendale* and the other cases on remoteness.

[13] *Sapwell* v. *Bass* [1910] 2 K.B. 486.

[14] *Simon* v. *Pawson and Leafs Ltd.* (1933) 148 L.T. 154; *cf. Bostock & Co. Ltd.* v. *Nicholson & Sons Ltd.* [1904] 1 K.B. 725.

[15] *Foaminol Laboratories Ltd.* v. *British Artid Plastics Ltd.* [1941] 2 All E.R. 393.

[16] [1911] 2 K.B. 786.

[17] (1898) 1 F. 297.

[18] 1952 S.L.T.(Notes) 57.

[19] Hiding behind this problem is the difficulty arising from the classical rule that foreseeability of the loss is determined at the time of the contract. With long-term contracts such as employment, foreseeability at a point nearer the time of the breach might be a more realistic test, *e.g.* a chief constable is dismissed in breach of contract as a result of unjustified but strident public accusations. At the time of the breach the injury to reputation is reasonably foreseeable, but it might have required remarkable foresight during the calm in the committee making his original appointment to imagine what was going to happen. The problem of the time for assessing remoteness is discussed above (para. 20–66).

(i) Expenses of litigation, tribunal or criminal proceedings

3   Provided that the rules on remoteness are satisfied the pursuer may recover all reasonable expenses of litigation or tribunal proceedings which were caused by the breach of contract. This can include the expenses of unsuccessful litigation which was necessary because of the attitude of the party in breach.[20] In the leading English case of *Hammond & Co.* v. *Bussey*[21] a sub-sale of coal was within the contemplation of the parties and the costs of an action on the sub-sale were recoverable. The action was a consequence of bad quality in the coal supplied. In *Blyth* v. *Scottish Liberal Club*[22] it was observed that some of the expenses incurred by appearing before an industrial tribunal might be claimable in an action of damages for breach of a contract of employment, even although the tribunal had not made an award of expenses. After proof, however, this head of loss was rejected.[23] Where goods are supplied in such circumstances that a criminal offence is likely to follow from dealing with them, the expense of the criminal proceedings (and the fine) may be recoverable.[24] For example if a tradesman buys food or drink which, in breach of contract, is unfit for human consumption, the subsequent prosecution of the tradesman for supplying the food or drink to the public may be a direct consequence of the breach.

4   In accordance with principle the pursuer must mitigate his loss. Therefore in prior proceedings he should have acted reasonably, although it is inappropriate to be too critical of his conduct. His lack of success in the proceedings is not to be held against him, but he cannot recover the expense of maintaining an obviously untenable position.[25] For this reason it is sometimes said that notice of the prior proceedings should be given to the person ultimately liable.[26] This is prudent, but not essential. The party's reaction to the receipt of the notice may prevent him from later complaining about the unreasonableness of the litigation,[27] or may make it difficult for him to change his ground.

---

[20] *Dougall* v. *Mags. of Dunfermline*, 1908 S.C. 151; *Munro & Co.* v. *Bennet & Son*, 1911 S.C. 337. If the prior proceedings were successful the claim for breach of contract might not arise.

[21] (1888) 20 Q.B.D. 79. There is a remarkable amount of English authority on the problem. See McGregor on *Damages* (14th ed.), Chap. 16.

[22] 1980 S.L.T.(Notes) 4 (O.H.).

[23] 1982 S.C. 140.

[24] *Cointat* v. *Myham* [1913] 2 K.B. 220; *Proops* v. *Chaplin* (1920) 37 T.L.R. 112; *Payne* v. *Ministry of Food* (1953) 103 L.J. 141.

[25] *e.g. Smith* v. *Spurling Motor Bodies* (1961) 105 S.J. 967 (C.A.); *The Wallsend* [1907] P. 302; *Osman* v. *J. Ralph Moss* [1907] 1 Lloyd's Rep. 313, and see cases in *McGregor, sup. cit.*

[26] Walker, *Civil Remedies*, p. 562. Intimation of the action to a third party for his interest, or citation as a third party, are the most formal methods of notice, but it is thought that less formality will suffice.

[27] *e.g. Dougall* v. *Mags. of Dunfermline, sup. cit.* at p. 159 *per* Lord Ardwall. The council were called as defenders for their interest and sent a print of the open record. The town clerk's evasive reply weakened the council's case.

(j) Payments to third parties, damages and fines

20–75   If prior proceedings have resulted in awards of damages or fines against the pursuer, the factors determining the ability to recover these are similar to those which affect recovery of the expenses of the proceedings.[28] In *Sayegh* v. *Ireland & Wishart Ltd.*[29] a proof before answer was allowed on averments that a prior judgment of the English High Court was unreasonable. A full discussion of the issue behind this would give an interesting application of the principles of remoteness and causation.[30]

20–76   Recovery of amounts paid to meet a claim although without a court action should also be recoverable,[31] subject to the same principles. The pursuer cannot recover the amount of a claim which he was not bound to pay, as in *Wilson* v. *Barclay*[32] where a motor dealer paid off the hire purchase debt on a stolen car which he had purchased.

(k) Expenses prior to breach

20–77   Expenses incurred prior to the breach, and with the knowledge of the other party, may be recoverable under the principles of *Hadley* v. *Baxendale*.[33] There may be a contractual provision that certain expenses such as the cost of training an employee are recoverable if there is a breach.[34]

(l) Failure to pay money—the cost of borrowing

20–78   The pursuer may suffer loss because of a failure or delay in paying him money. He may have a claim for interest[35] but, normally, not a claim for damages.[36] So when a price was not timeously paid under missives an action of damages failed.[37] The appropriate remedy was a claim

---

[28] *Buchanan & Carswell* v. *Eugene*, 1936 S.C. 160 and authorities cited above on the problem of expenses. Recovery of a fine imposed when the offence involved *mens rea* raises an issue of public policy, as well as of causation. See McGregor, *sup. cit.*, paras. 551 *et seq.*

[29] 1956 S.L.T.(Notes) 39.

[30] The principal issues are: (1) Should the defender have foreseen an erroneous judgment? (2) Is the judgment a *novus actus interveniens* or independent cause so far as that head of damage is concerned?

[31] As appears to have happened in *Ströms Bruks Aktie Bolag* v. *Hutchison* (1905) 7 F.(H.L.) 131. Some latitude may be allowed on the specification in averments of the sum due to the third party: *Lancashire Textiles (Jersey) Ltd.* v. *Thomson Shepherd & Co. Ltd.*, 1986 S.L.T. 41.

[32] 1957 S.L.T.(Sh.Ct.) 40.

[33] *Daejan Developments Ltd.* v. *Armia Ltd.*, 1981 S.C. 48; for expenses prior to the contract, see paras. 20–84, 20–85.

[34] *Strathclyde R.C.* v. *Neil*, 1983 S.L.T.(Sh.Ct.) 89.

[35] On the competence of a claim for interest, see para. 20–104.

[36] Ersk., III,iii,86; Bell, *Prin.*, para. 32; *Stephen* v. *Swayne* (1861) 24 D. 158 at p. 163 *per* Lord President McNeill. On calculation of interest see para. 20–119; for exceptions to the rule see para. 20–81 and case in n. 37.

[37] *Chapman's Trs.* v. *Anglo Scottish Group Services Ltd.*, 1980 S.L.T.(Sh.Ct.) 27.

for interest. Interest is not truly damages, because no inquiry is made as to the actual loss suffered by the pursuer.[38] The seller of a house has failed to recover the cost of a bridging loan when there was a delay in the payment of a purchase price.[39]

-79 The reason that damages are not recoverable for late payment is the application of the rules in *Hadley* v. *Baxendale*. The loss to the pursuer caused by having to borrow or incur other expense is not within the contemplation of the parties at the time of the contract.[40] Nor is it normally contemplated that the debtor's breach will cause "the utter ruin of the creditor" which was Erskine's example.[41] In some circumstances the party in breach may have had knowledge of the special consequences of failing to pay. In that case damages may be due.[42] So in *Wadsworth* v. *Lydall*[43] the plaintiff recovered as special damages the loss which he suffered as a result of failure to pay money. The parties had been partners. The financial arrangements of the plaintiff and the consequences of a failure to pay were known to the defendant. The more usual situation is that the impecuniosity of the plaintiff or pursuer is not within the knowledge of the other party and this prevents recovery of the cost of borrowing.[44]

-80 Questions of knowledge and foreseeability have been held irrelevant when damages were calculated under the Sale of Goods Act 1979, with the result that interest charges were recoverable.[45]

-81 The failure to honour a bill of exchange or a promissory note is subject to a statutory measure of damages.[46] There are also several cases in which a banker has been held liable in damages for failure to honour a credit.[47] There can be an award of damages for breach of a contract to lend money.[48]

---

[38] *Cf. Roissard* v. *Scott's Trs.* (1897) 25 R. 861; Bell, *Comm.*, I, 691.

[39] *Tiffney* v. *Bachurzewski*, 1985 S.L.T. 165.

[40] See *Chapman's Trs., sup. cit.*; *Tiffney* v. *Backurzewski, sup. cit.*

[41] *Sup. cit.*

[42] *Roissard* v. *Scott's Trs.* (1897) 24 R. 861 at p. 866 *per* Lord Kyllachy; *Muhammad* v. *Ali* [1947] A.C. 414; *Trans Trust S.P.R.L.* v. *Danubian Trading Co.* [1952] 2 Q.B. 297.

[43] [1981] 2 All E.R. 401 appd., *President of India* v. *La Pintada* [1985] A.C. 104.

[44] See *Pilkington* v. *Wood* [1953] Ch. 770. On foresight of impecuniosity generally see *Liesbosch* v. *Edison* [1933] A.C. 449; *A/B Karlshamns Oljefabriker* v. *Monarch S.S. Co.*, 1949 S.C.(H.L.) 1 at p. 21 *per* Lord Wright; *Pollock* v. *Campbell*, 1965 S.L.T.(Sh.Ct.) 58; *Brown* v. *Russell*, 1981 S.L.T.(Sh.Ct.) 22.

[45] *Allen* v. *W. Burns (Tractors) Ltd.*, 1985 S.L.T. 252.

[46] Bills of Exchange Act 1882, s.57, as amended by Administration of Justice Act 1977, s.4.

[47] *e.g. King* v. *British Linen Co.* (1899) 1 F. 928; *Wilson* v. *United Counties Bank* [1920] A.C. 102. This type of case is regarded as difficult to reconcile with the 1882 Act by Gloag (*Contract*, p. 680) and Professor Walker (*Civil Remedies*, p. 413). The solution to the difficulty is probably that s.57 does not apply when an action is based on a separate contract, and not on the bill. Further in the case of a dishonoured cheque, as in *King*, the section is not concerned with the liability of the bank, the drawee, which is neither an acceptor nor an indorser of the instrument.

[48] *Astor Properties Ltd.* v. *Tunbridge Wells Equitable Friendly Society* [1936] 1 All E.R. 531; *South African Territories Ltd.* v. *Wallington* [1898] A.C. 309; *Wallis Chlorine Syndicate Ltd.* v. *American Alkali Co. Ltd.* (1901) 17 T.L.R. 656; and see *Wadsworth* v. *Lydall*, [1981] 2 All E.R. 401.

PART 6

Assessment of Damages

(a) General principles

20–82   The general principle is that the pursuer should be put in the same position, so far as money can, as if the contract had been performed. This has been expressed in various dicta:

> "They are bound to make good to the pursuer the damage or injury he has sustained by the wrongful retention from him of possession of the colliery; or, to put it differently, the pursuer is entitled to be placed in the same position, as nearly as possible as regards profits, as he would have been in had there been no breach of contract by the defenders."[49]

> "In cases where damages are due for breach of a mercantile contract the object is to place the pursuer in as good a position pecuniarily as if no breach of contract had been committed. The supposition to be made is that the contract had been duly implemented, and then the inquiry will be what would have been in money value the result to the pursuer. What could he have made by or through the fulfilled contract, and then the difference between this amount and the amount which the pursuer actually has realised, after or notwithstanding the breach, is the amount of loss which the pursuer has sustained by and through the breach of contract complained of."[50]

> "The principle which governs the whole law on the subject, namely, that the party observing the contract is to be put as nearly as possible in the same position as he would have been if the contract had been performed."[51]

20–83   It is the pursuer's position which is considered. It is not the defender, or party in breach, who must be treated as if the contract had been performed. So, if the defender makes a gain from the breach, that gain is not the correct basis for assessing damages.[52] The contract is looked at as if the breach had not occurred. This is distinguishable from restitution which would treat the contract as if it had not been made. Consider a deposit of £100 for goods which are not delivered. Restitution would merely return the £100. Damages for breach, however, are based on what should have happened, namely delivery of goods, what did happen, non-delivery and the consequent foreseeable loss taking into account the value of the goods and the payment of the deposit.

20–84   In England, however, there is a line of authority which, as an alternative to the normal basis for damages, allows a plaintiff to claim the expenses rendered futile by the breach. The plaintiff is put in the pos-

---

[49] *Houldsworth* v. *Brand's Trs.* (1877) 4 R. 369 at p. 374 *per* Lord Ormidale.
[50] *Sup. cit.* at p. 375 *per* Lord Gifford.
[51] *Govan Rope and Sail Co. Ltd.* v. *Weir & Co.* (1897) 24 R. 368 at pp. 370, 371, *per* Lord Ordinary.
[52] *Teacher* v. *Calder* (1898) 25 R. 661, (1889) 1. F.(H.L.) 39.

ition he would have been in if the contract had never been made. This alternative is compelled by the exceptional rule in *Bain* v. *Fothergill*[53] which applies to the failure of a seller or lessor to transfer because of a defect in title. In *Anglia Television* v. *Reed*[54] the Court of Appeal went further and allowed recovery of pre-contract expenses. An actor was employed to play a leading role in a film. He repudiated the contract and the film was not made. Being unable to prove what profit the film would have made, the plaintiffs recovered the expenditure which had been wasted by the defendant's breach. Both pre-contract and post-contract expenditure were recovered.

85   The approach in *Anglia Television* raises a basic question for Scots law. Is the measure of damages based on what would have happened if the contract had been performed or on the foreseeable consequences of the breach? The latter appears more equitable and in accordance with principle, but it carries with it the danger of benefiting the pursuer. Take the simple case of the sale of a house. The seller incurs expenses advertising the property. Missives are concluded. The buyer repudiates the contract, the seller resells, and in doing so incurs further expense. The buyer must have known that his repudiation would have rendered futile the seller's expenses prior to the first sale. He must also be taken to know that the seller will incur further expense in reselling. But it is wrong to allow both to be recovered, because the seller is then better off than if there had been no breach.[55] The first set of expenses was not caused by the breach, but then neither was the pre-contract expenditure in *Anglia* caused by the actor's repudiation. To follow *Anglia* would take the law of contract into uncharted waters. The classic approach is to speculate, however difficult that might be, on what would have happened if the contract had been performed.[56] Difficulty in assessment of damages is not a bar to that assessment.[57]

86   Expenses incurred since the contract, but prior to the breach, can be recovered following the principles in *Hadley* v. *Baxendale*.[58]

(b) Nominal damages

87   Even if there is no proof of actual loss caused by a breach, an award of nominal damages may be made. "The contract and the breach of it are established. That leads of necessity to an award of damages. It is impossible to say that a contract can be broken even in respect of time

---

[53] (1874) L.R. 7 H.L. 158.

[54] [1972] 1 Q.B. 60. See also *C. & P. Haulage* v. *Middleton* [1983] 3 All E.R. 94; *CCC Films (London) Ltd.* v. *Impact Quadrant Films Ltd.* [1984] 3 All E.R. 298.

[55] See *Johnstone* v. *Harris*, 1977 S.C. 365 at p. 374—the fees to be recoverable were the fees for the abortive transaction.

[56] To ignore this might enable a party to "break even" when he would have made a loss. The goods or services which should have been supplied would not have benefited the pursuer. He would have made a large loss. If, however, he can claim his expenses because of the breach, he is better off than if there had been no breach.

[57] *Chaplin* v. *Hicks* [1911] 2 K.B. 786.

[58] *Daejan Developments Ltd.* v. *Armia Ltd.*, 1981 S.C. 48.

without the party being entitled to claim damages—at the lowest, nominal damages."[59]

20–88   Although this principle may not always have been followed[60] it appears to be the law.[61] As it happens the cases have not involved awards of trifling sums, and the term "nominal" is perhaps misleading. An award is made for the trouble and inconvenience which is caused by a breach.[62] So when a purchaser of a second-hand car which had many defects raised an action against the seller for damages, he failed to prove specific items of loss, but recovered £75 as an award for his trouble and inconvenience.[63] When there was rising damp in tenanted property, the tenant recovered £300 for inconvenience.[64] In a system of contract law which allows *solatium* to be claimed for breach of contract, it is not inconsistent to make an award for trouble and inconvenience. The case which would truly raise the issue of nominal damages is one in which a party has not been at all troubled or inconvenienced by the breach. He might be delighted at the opportunity to free himself from a loss-making contract. He is unlikely to sue for damages, but if he were sued, he could defend and counterclaim. Should an award of damages be made although no loss or trouble whatsoever was caused by the breach? There is much to be said for Lord Murray's view that: "A breach of contract, or wrongful act, is no doubt an *injuria*, but it may be *injuria sine damno*, and *damnum* is an essential factor to any claim of damages."[65]

20–89   The concept of *damnum* should not be restrictively interpreted, but if loss does not flow from a breach an award of damages, however small, is contrary to principle.

(c) Assessment of loss

20–90   It has been said that the law of damages should not be reduced to a rule of thumb.[66] No mathematical formula can be produced which will apply to all cases. What must be applied are the principles of damages awards, which have been explained above. Further, the tendency of

---

[59] *Webster & Co.* v. *Cramond Iron Co.* (1875) 2 R. 752 at p. 754 *per* Lord President Inglis; *Stephenson* v. *Duncan* (1937) 53 Sh.Ct.Rep. 269.

[60] See cases cited by Gloag, p. 684.

[61] *Aarons & Co.* v. *Fraser*, 1934 S.C. 137.

[62] Cases cited above, and *Murray* v. *Marr* (1892) 20 R. 119, esp. *per* Lord Trayner at p. 127; *Salvesen & Co.* v. *Rederi A/B Nordstjernan* (1905) 7 F.(H.L.) 101; *Smith* v. *Park*, 1980 S.L.T.(Sh.Ct.) 62

[63] *Smith* v. *Park, sup. cit.*

[64] *Gunn* v. *N.C.B.*, 1982 S.L.T. 526 at p. 528.

[65] *Aarons & Co.* v. *Fraser*, 1934 S.C. 137 at p. 143; see, however, Lord Murray in *Buchanan & Carswell* v. *Eugene*, 1936 S.C. 160 at p. 180.

[66] See dicta in *Hutchison* v. *Davidson*, 1945 S.C. 395; *Prudential Assurance Co. Ltd.* v. *James Grant & Co. (West) Ltd.*, 1982 S.L.T. 423 at p. 424 *per* Lord Mcdonald: "It may be that the true value of the damages may only be found after employing more measures than one and checking one result with another." In *G.U.S. Property Management Ltd.* v. *Littlewoods Mail Order Stores Ltd.*, 1982 S.L.T. 533 (H.L.)—a delictual action—depreciation in value and the cost of reinstatement were treated as alternative methods of assessing damages. See also various factors in *Co-operative Wholesale Society Ltd.* v. *Motherwell D.C.*, 1985 S.L.T. 89 (a delictual claim).

Scots law may be less favourable than that of English law to the formulation of judge-made rules for the assessment of damages.[67] Nevertheless the experience of others is a useful guide in similar situations.

91   The assessment of some heads of damages usually poses few problems. With out-of-pocket expenses,[68] the damages paid to a subcontractor, and other outlays and some cases of loss of profit, any difficulty is likely to be with whether their recovery is barred by principles of remoteness or mitigation of loss, rather than with quantification. When the pursuer has not had to pay out an item, the assessment of his loss is more difficult. The value of the promised performance must be compared to the value of what was done. The difference in these two values is a measure of the diminution in the pursuer's wealth and one head of damages. The problem is assessment of the values.

92   It is obvious that the value of goods or services differs according to many factors. It alters according to whether the parties are manufacturers, wholesalers, retailers or consumers. It alters according to the existence of types of available market. It varies with the time for performance, whether it is immediate or in the future. It changes with the place of performance. It may be affected by the terms of the contract on the passing of risk or the exclusion or limitation of liability. Alteration in the quantity of goods affects the unit price. Market prices are influenced by many events.

93   In trying to assess the loss to the pursuer, the tendency of the courts has been to contrast the contract price with the market price for the goods or services. Clearly the selection of "the market price" can be very difficult, and in some cases it is impossible or unrealistic, and replacement value has been used as a factor in the assessment.

94   The Sale of Goods Act 1979 provides that in cases of non-acceptance of goods by the buyer the measure of damages is *prima facie* to be ascertained by the difference between the contract price and the market or current price at the time or times when the goods ought to have been accepted or (if no time was fixed for acceptance) at the time of the refusal to accept.[69] A similar contrast between contract price and market price is provided for damages for non-delivery by the seller.[70] In other words, what is being assessed here (and this applies outside the contracts which the 1979 Act governs) is the profit the party not in breach would have received if the contract had been performed. So when there was failure to deliver a racehorse, the damages were the difference

---

[67] *Duke of Portland* v. *Wood's Trs.*, 1926 S.C. 640 at p. 651 *per* Lord President Clyde; on appeal 1927 S.C.(H.L.) 1.

[68] *e.g. Prudential Ass. Co. Ltd.*, *sup. cit.* (dilapidations by tenants); *Gunn*, *sup. cit.* (wage loss).

[69] s.50(3).

[70] s.51(3). Questions of knowledge and foreseeability are irrelevant when damages are calculated under s.51(2): *Allen* v. *W. Burns (Tractors) Ltd.*, 1985 S.L.T. 252.

between the contract price and the market price with, in addition, the price already paid.[71] When a bargain to buy casks was repudiated, decree was granted for the difference between the contract price and the price at which the goods were sold.[72] Damages for failure to deliver steel were assessed at the difference between the contract price and the price current at the time of refusal to deliver.[73] The damages for failure to implement a contract of sale of the whole issued share capital of the company were the difference between the contract price and the value of the company at the date of breach.[74]

20–95   In other cases it is more appropriate to take estimates of the profit which the pursuer has failed to earn because of the breach, such as the profit which would have been earned if a steamship had been available,[75] or if rope had been manufactured,[76] or if his ground had been used for a remunerative crop instead of the cabbage seed supplied.[77] In the case of a distributorship agreement which was wrongfully repudiated, a wide discretion in the manner of performance was given to the distributor. The damages due by the distributor were assessed on the basis of what would have been reasonable performance of the distributor's obligations.[78]

The cases cited so far have been largely examples of something not being done at all. When something is done, but is done defectively, a similar contrast is made. One head of damages may be the difference in value between what was received, and what should have been received. Thus when a ship was supplied with deficient carrying capacity, the damages were measured by the difference in earning powers of the ship supplied and the ship contracted for.[79] Defective herrings were sold and damages were assessed at the difference between the price obtained and the price, including profit, which the purchasers would have received if the goods had been conform to contract.[80] When solicitors took a defective title to a cottage the damages were the difference between the price

---

[71] *Anderson* v. *Croall & Sons* (1903) 6 F. 153.

[72] *Guild & Co.'s Tr.* v. *Edinburgh United Breweries*, 1909 1 S.L.T. 468. See also *Gill & Duffus SA* v. *Berger & Co. Inc.* [1984] A.C. 382.

[73] *Marshall & Co.* v. *Nicoll & Son*, 1919 S.C.(H.L.) 129.

[74] *Spencer* v. *Macmillan's Tr.*, 1958 S.C. 300 (damages were *not* assessed at loss of profit on resale).

[75] *Collard* v. *Carswell* (1892) 19 R. 987; on appeal (1893) 20 R.(H.L.) 47.

[76] *Govan Rope and Sail Co.* v. *Weir & Co.* (1897) 24 R. 368 (there was no comparable market price).

[77] *Wilson* v. *Carmichael & Sons* (1894) 21 R. 732.

[78] *Paula Lee Ltd.* v. *Robert Zehilo Co. Ltd.* [1983] 2 All E.R. 390.

[79] *Gillespie & Co.* v. *Howden & Co.* (1885) 12 R. 800. The alternative suggested, which was based on depreciation of saleable value, raised a problem which has continued to trouble courts when either loss of profits or capital loss can be claimed. See *Cullinane* v. *British "Rema" Manufacturing Co.* [1954] 1 Q.B. 292; *T.C. Industrial Plant Pty.* v. *Robert's Queensland Pty.* (1964) 37 A.L.J.R. 289 (H. Ct. of Australia). See McGregor, *Damages*, paras. 44–47.

[80] *Pommer & Thomsen* v. *Mowat* (1906) 14 S.L.T. 373.

the property would have fetched untainted by the defective title and the price actually realised.[81]

96 There may not be an available market for goods, perhaps because they have been made to particular specifications or are otherwise unique. The damages must still be assessed on the basis of what the goods would have been worth if supplied in terms of the contract.[82] The touchstone is still the loss to the pursuer, and the rules to be applied are those in *Hadley* v. *Baxendale*. The loss may be the cost to the pursuer of replacing what has been destroyed, such as the cost of replacing glasshouses which were destroyed by mineral workings[83] or the cost of replacing mink.[84] There have been analogous cases in the law of delict and insurance on the destruction or damage to heritage in which replacement cost was a factor which reflected the loss to the pursuer.[85]

97 The most difficult cases of all are those where the pursuer has lost, not a profit which he *would* have earned[86] but a profit or gain which he *might* have earned, for example the chance to win a prize, or obtain a job,[87] or earn commission as an agent,[88] or claim under an insurance policy.[89] If the court is provided with evidence on the likelihood of the chance[90] it will make an estimate of the loss, assuming of course, that the recovery of the loss is not barred by principles of remoteness.

(d) Solatium for breach of contract

98 It has been said that solatium is not recoverable for a breach of contract.[91] Nevertheless in several breach of contract cases the courts, without discussion of the validity of the claim, have allowed claims for pain

---

[81] *Haberstich* v. *McCormick & Nicholson*, 1975 S.C. 1. Damages were assessed at the date of the loss, not the date of breach.

[82] *Marshall & Co.* v. *Nicoll & Son*, 1919 S.C.(H.L.) 129: opinions of Viscount Finlay and Lord Shaw. On meaning of "available market" in the Sale of Goods Act, see *Thompson* v. *Robinson* [1955] Ch. 177; *Charter* v. *Sullivan* [1957] 2 Q.B. 117; *Lazenby Garages* v. *Wright* [1976] 2 All E.R. 770 (second-hand cars were treated as unique, and surprisingly it was said that there was no available market for second-hand cars).

[83] *Gibson* v. *Farie*, 1918 1 S.L.T. 404.

[84] *Waddington* v. *Buchan Poultry Products*, 1963 S.L.T. 168.

[85] *Hutchison* v. *Davidson*, 1945 S.C. 395; *Fraser* v. *J. Morton Wilson Ltd.*, 1965 S.L.T.(Notes) 81; *Carrick Furniture House Ltd.* v. *General Accident*, 1977 S.C. 308; *Smith* v. *Littlewoods Organisation* 1982 S.L.T. 267; *Prudential Assurance Co. Ltd* v. *James Grant & Co.(West) Ltd.*, 1982 S.L.T. 423 (cost of repairs *prima facie* relevant—argument about capital value); *G.U.S. Property Mangement Ltd.* v. *Littlewoods Mail Order Stores Ltd*, 1982 S.L.T. 533 (H.L.) (depreciation in value and cost of reinstatement alternative approaches); *Fehilly* v. *General Accident*, 1982 S.C. 163. See also *Co-operative Wholesale Soc. Ltd.* v. *Motherwell D.C.*, 1985 S.L.T. 89.

[86] e.g. *Govan Rope and Sail Co. Ltd.* v. *Weir & Co.* (1897) 24 R. 368; *Collard* v. *Carswell* (1892) 19 R. 987; (1893) 20 R.(H.L.) 47.

[87] *Chaplin* v. *Hicks* [1911] 2 K.B. 786.

[88] *Michael Robins etc. Consultants* v. *Skilling*, 1976 S.L.T.(Notes) 18.

[89] *Beattie* v. *Furness-Houlder Insurance (Northern) Ltd.*, 1976 S.L.T.(Notes) 60—a delictual claim.

[90] See *Michael Robins etc. Consultants* v. *Skilling, sup. cit.*

[91] Gloag, p. 686.

and injury to feelings.[92] This is reasonable, because a breach of contract may cause personal injury such as typhoid,[93] injury to a face from a fall,[94] or injury from the impact of exploding coal,[95] or asthma produced by rising damp in tenanted property.[96] There is no logical ground for refusing the recovery of solatium in these cases. In *Diesen* v. *Samson*,[97] solatium was awarded against a photographer who failed to turn up at a wedding. The case has received favourable comment in England,[98] which is developing its own law on recovery of damages for mental distress mainly in connection with disappointments in contracts for holidays.

20–99   The stumbling-block to recovery of damages for injury to feelings in both England and Scotland is the decision of the House of Lords in *Addis* v. *Gramophone Co.*[99] The decision was in an English appeal, but Lord Shaw made observations on Scots law.[1] Damages were held irrecoverable for the manner of dismissal of a servant. It may be suggested that rarely can damages be recovered for the mere affront caused by breach of contract.[2] Merely for the breach, however rudely it is communicated, there is not a claim for solatium unless the circumstances are defamatory. However, beyond the fact of the breach there may be injury to feelings or pain or discomfort which flow from the breach. These do not arise in every case, but when they do they are an appropriate subject of an award of damages.

(e) Taxation

20–100   Tax is a relevant factor in assessment of damages where, if the assessment is made without accounting for tax, this would over-compensate or under-compensate the pursuer. The pursuer is entitled to his loss, no more, no less. Therefore, if he is claiming loss of earnings he cannot expect to receive a lump sum which represents his gross earnings and which, after any tax is paid on the lump sum, leaves him better off than if he had earned the money. It is obvious from this that two calculations may have to be made, namely (1) the tax the pursuer would have paid, if

---

[92] *Lockhart* v. *Cunninghame* (1870) 8 S.L.R. 151; *Cameron* v. *Young*, 1907 S.C. 475, 1908 S.C.(H.L.) 7; *Dickie* v. *Amicable Property etc. Bldg. Soc.*, 1911 S.C. 1079; *Fitzpatrick* v. *Barr*, 1948 S.L.T.(Sh.Ct.) 5.

[93] *Cameron* v. *Young, sup. cit.*

[94] *Dickie* v. *Amicable Property etc. Bldg. Soc., sup. cit.*

[95] *Fitzpatrick* v. *Barr, sup. cit.*

[96] 1971 S.L.T.(Sh.Ct.) 49.

[97] McGregor, *Damages*, para. 71.

[98] *Jarvis* v. *Swan's Tours* [1973] Q.B. 233; *Jackson* v. *Horizon Holidays* [1975] 3 All E.R. 92.

[99] [1909] A.C. 488.

[1] at p. 503; and unfortunately disagreed with Fraser on *Master and Servant*.

[2] Breach of promise to marry was an exception: Bell, *Prin.* s.1508. Now the promise to marry is not an enforceable obligation: Law Reform (Husband and Wife) (Scotland) Act 1984, s.1.

there had been no breach of contract, and (2) the tax the pursuer may have to pay on the award of damages. In theory it is only when (1) and (2) are equal, viewing the issue broadly, (or are zero) that tax can be ignored. But the law is not settled.

In *McDaid* v. *Clyde Navigation Trustees*,[3] a delictual claim, Lord Sorn decided that the tax payable on loss of earnings should be taken into account. To do otherwise would be out of touch with reality. Lord Keith disagreed a year later.[4]

It was, however, Lord Sorn who was approved in the classic English decision of *British Transport Commission* v. *Gourley*.[5] The House of Lords decided that liability to income tax and surtax should not be ignored in assessing damages for loss of earnings. *Gourley* and a subsequent decision of the House[6] were applied in Scotland to a breach of contract in *Spencer* v. *Macmillan's Trs.*[7] The case involved an alleged breach of a contract for sale of shares. Damages were claimed. The defenders replied by saying that the pursuers carried on the trade of buying and selling companies. In doing this they earned profits and paid taxes. Therefore the taxes should be taken into account. The defenders' arguments failed because it did not follow that from the purchase of the shares a profit would be made. If the contract had been performed, no tax liability would automatically have arisen. The decision is unexceptionable, but it is perhaps unfortunate that it was suggested in the case that two conditions must be satisfied before the application of *Gourley*. These were (1) that the damages must represent compensation for a receipt which would have been taxable in the hands of the injured party, and (2) that the damages were not taxable.[8] These observations were unnecessary to the decision and are not to be found in *Gourley*. They were also contrary to the principle of *Gourley*, because the fact that the damages were taxable could affect whether or not the pursuer was under- or over-compensated. Lord Hunter faced the problem in *Stewart* v. *Glentaggart Ltd.*[9] He, it is submitted correctly, rejected both of the supposed conditions. In the case before him both the earnings which the pursuer should have received, and any damages payable for breach of a contract of service, were taxable.

Lord Hunter preferred to account for the tax on both sides and make a deduction from the damages on the *Gourley* principle, adding to them a sum which provided for the tax payable on the damages. This decision, which is logically impeccable, has been criticised in England because it

---

[3] 1946 S.C. 462.
[4] *Blackwood* v. *Andre*, 1947 S.C. 333.
[5] [1956] A.C. 185. Lord Keith, who also heard the case, dissented.
[6] *West Suffolk C.C.* v. *Rought* [1957] A.C. 403 (compensation for disturbance following on compulsory purchase).
[7] 1958 S.C. 300.
[8] *Ibid.* at p. 315 *per* Lord Justice-Clerk Thomson; at p. 324 *per* Lord Mackintosh.
[9] 1963 S.C. 300.

involves a hypothetical calculation on one side and an estimate on the other.[10] It has, however, been followed.[11]

In England, the two conditions mentioned in *Spencer* have been applied[12] and they may simplify the situation in cases of commercial profits and breaches of contracts of sale. Either the goods would have been capital assets, or they would have been trading stock. In neither case are both conditions satisfied.[13] In theory another approach is preferable. If the pursuer is carrying on trade, he may have made a profit with the goods if they had been delivered conform to contract. He claims for a loss of profit which, if not too remote, is recoverable. His damages will be assessed to tax just as his original profit would have been. The liabilities to tax in each of these incidents—if there had been no breach of contract and on receiving damages for breach—are unlikely to be identical. The tax liability (which is hypothetical in one case) may arise in different years and be subject to different rates of tax. But they are subject to the same tax; and in approximately the same way. The law of damages is only concerned with approximation. As was recognised by Lord Sorn in *McDaid* and in the opinions in *Gourley*, an exact calculation of the tax liability is not required.[14] Therefore, for practical purposes, tax need not be taken into account in at least some cases of failure to deliver goods required for trade and other breaches of commercial contracts where both the profit and the damages are taxable.[15] The damages are, as near as may be, a surrogate for the profit which would have been made.

20–103   Taking tax into account does raise problems for the courts which have been recognised in the cases cited. These difficulties include: (1) the Inland Revenue is not a party to the proceedings and they might take a different view of tax liability[16]; (2) foreign taxes may have to be looked at[17]; (3) the pursuer may have other taxable receipts which raise prob-

---

[10] *Parsons* v. *B.N.M. Laboratories Ltd.* [1964] 1 Q.B. 95 at p. 129 *per* Harman L.J.—at p. 137 *per* Pearson L.J.—see also at p. 115 *per* Sellers L.J.; see also *Bold* v. *Brough, Nicholson & Hall* [1963] 3 All E.R. 849. On the other hand Lord Hunter's approach is approved in McGregor, *Damages*, para. 432. However, if McGregor were correct in stating that *Gourley* must be applied with "full vigour," tax would be taken into account in all claims for loss of commercial profits.

[11] *Shore* v. *Downs Surgical plc* [1984] 1 All E.R. 7.

[12] See McGregor on *Damages*, para. 413 *et seq.*; *Parsons* v. *B.N.M. Laboratories* [1964] 1 Q.B. 95.

[13] McGregor, *sup. cit.*, para. 435; Walker, *Civil Remedies*, p. 423.

[14] And prior to the award of damages the tax liability, based as it can be on future profits in that tax year, may be a speculation. See also *Parsons* v. *B.N.M. Laboratories, sup. cit.*

[15] See also *Diamond* v. *Campbell-Jones* [1961] Ch. 22; *Maclennan* v. *Scottish Gas Board*, 1985 S.L.T. 2. Capital gains tax can arise on damages as a result of *Zim Properties Ltd.* v. *Procter* [1985] S.T.C. 90 and Capital Gains Tax Act 1979, ss.20 and 29A.

[16] *Spencer* v. *Macmillan's Trs., sup. cit.* at p. 304 *per* Lord Ordinary (Cameron), at p. 317 *per* Lord Justice-Clerk Thomson; at p. 324 *per* Lord MacKintosh; *Stewart* v. *Glentaggart Ltd., sup. cit.* at p. 309 *per* Lord Hunter.

[17] *British Transport Comm.* v. *Gourley, sup. cit.* at p. 217 *per* Lord Keith (dissenting); *Julien Praet et Cie., S/A* v. *H.G. Poland Ltd.* [1962] 1 Lloyd's Rep. 566.

lems of the rate of tax to be applied and the extent of inquiry into his financial affairs[18]; (4) the rates of tax and of reliefs are constantly changing.[19] It has been indicated that the courts will take a broad view of the assessment of tax liability and cannot avoid deciding a case because the Inland Revenue is not a party. A further problem is whether the pursuer or the defender must aver that tax liability is a relevant factor. In *Stewart v. Glentaggart*, Lord Hunter held the pursuer's averments on damages irrelevant because they took no account of the tax position. It appears, however, from *General Mining and Engineering Services Ltd.* v. *Mine Safety Appliances Ltd.*[20] that in the ordinary case it is for the defender to aver that there are tax specialities.

PART 7

Interest

(a) General principles

4   Interest may be claimed to run from one of four dates, namely (1) the date the right of action arose, (2) the date of a demand for payment, (3) the date of citation in an action, and (4) the date of final decree. Interest runs *ex lege* from the date of decree in all cases including claims for damages for breach of contract. Interest runs from the date of citation when the price of goods is sued for. It may run from an earlier date if there is a clear demand for payment. Interest runs from a date prior to citation if it is due expressly by contract, or by implication, as in loan. In cases of damages the court has a discretionary power to award interest at a date prior to decree, under the Interest on Damages (Scotland) Act 1958, s.1.[21]

5   It has been thought useful to set out the general rules first, before their detailed analysis, because the reasons for the rules are not easy to understand. As was said about 100 years ago by Lord Craighill, "nothing can be conceived less amenable to a settled general principle than our law upon a creditor's right to interest."[22]

---

[18] *McDaid* v. *Clyde Navigation Trs.*, *sup. cit.* at p. 465 *per* Lord Sorn; *British Transport Comm.* v. *Gourley*, *sup. cit.* at p. 203 *per* Earl Jowitt.

[19] *British Transport Comm.* v. *Gourley*, *sup. cit.* at. p. 208 *per* Lord Goddard. In *Daniels* v. *Jones* [1961] 3 All E.R. 24 Pearson L.J. even referred to Budget proposals (at p. 32). This is contrary to principle.

[20] 1976 S.L.T.(Notes) 28.

[21] As amended by Interest on Damages (Scotland) Act 1971, s.1.

[22] *Blair's Trs.* v. *Payne* (1884) 12 R. 104 at p. 108, quoted by Lord President Cooper in *Kearon* v. *Thomson's Exrs.*, 1949 S.C. 287 at p. 293.

(b) Interest from the right of action

20–106   Interest is due from the date stipulated in a contract, or by implication from the date of a loan.[23] If, however, the loan is only repayable on demand,[24] interest cannot run before the demand unless there is contrary express provision.[25] This is the general rule applying to IOUs, which are an acknowledgment of a debt with repayment due on demand.[26]

20–107   Loan includes cash advances or outlays paid in the normal course of business by a law agent on behalf of his client.[27] When a public body received disputed payments and was later found liable to repay, the repayments attracted interest.[28] The idea of loan may also be said to cover a variety of other circumstances where a payment is made on behalf of another, and interest runs from the date of payment. These include payments by a cautioner on behalf of the debtor,[29] payments or advances by a partner beyond the amount of his capital,[30] and balances due in accounts between two mercantile firms.[31]

20–108   Where a purchaser of heritage possesses the subject he is by implication liable to pay interest on the purchase money from the date of possession.[32] This is also the case where the contract is one of excambion.[33] Special agreement can always be reached on the payment of interest on the unpaid balance of a purchase price.[34] This is commonly done in purchases of heritage, but in the absence of express agreement, or of possession of the heritage, normally no interest will be due from the date agreed for payment of the price.[35]

---

[23] *Blair's Trs.* v. *Payne* (1884) 12 R. 104, appd. in *Greenock Harbour Trs.* v. *G. & S.W. Ry. Co.*, 1909 S.C.(H.L.) 49, and *F.W. Green & Co. Ltd.* v. *Brown & Gracie Ltd.*, 1960 S.L.T.(Notes) 43 (H.L.); *Cuninghame* v. *Boswell* (1868) 6 M. 890.

[24] The date of the demand in the cases has been the date of citation, but it is thought that it could be an earlier formal demand.

[25] *Forbes* v. *Forbes* (1864) 8 M. 85; *Smellie's Exrx.* v. *Smellie*, 1933 S.C. 725.

[26] *Winestone* v. *Wolifson*, 1954 S.C. 77; *Thiem's Trs.* v. *Collie* (1899) 1 F. 764 (this case contains a valuable discussion of the nature of IOUs, but the interest craved and the decree granted are at variance for reasons which are not apparent).

[27] *Blair's Trs.* v. *Payne, sup. cit.*: but not judicial expenses—*Macpherson* v. *Tytler* (1853) 15 D.706,—or outlays for printing—*Barclay* v. *Barclay* (1850) 22 J. 354.

[28] *Glasgow Gaslight Co.* v. *Barony Parish of Glasgow* (1868) 6 M. 406; *Haddon's Exrx.* v. *Scottish Milk Marketing Board*, 1938 S.C. 168.

[29] Ersk., III,iii,78; Bell, *Prin*, s.32.

[30] Partnership Act 1890, s.24.

[31] *Findlay, Bannatyne & Co.'s Assignee* v. *Donaldson* (1864) 2 M.(H.L.) 86.

[32] *Grandison's Trs.* v. *Jardine* (1895) 22 R. 925; *Prestwick Cinema Co.* v. *Gardiner*, 1951 S.C. 98; *Bowie* v. *Semple's Exrs.*, 1978 S.L.T.(Sh.Ct.) 9; *Thomson* v. *Vernon*, 1983 S.L.T.(Sh.Ct.) 17; *Tiffney* v. *Bachurzewski*, 1983 S.L.T.(Sh.Ct.) 45; 1985 S.L.T. 165 (2nd Div).

[33] *Greenock Harbour Trs.* v. *G. & W. Ry. Co.*, *sup. cit.*

[34] Whatever the nature of the subjects possessed. An example is *Baird's Trs.* v. *Baird* (1877) 4 R. 1005.

[35] *Bowie* v. *Semple's Exrs.*, *sup. cit.*; *Tiffney* v. *Bachurzewski*, 1985 S.L.T. 165. Interest could be due (1) if the missives so provide and all the conditions for payment are satisfied, or (2) in the event of a principal sum having been "wrongfully withheld," whatever that means. See *infra*.

(c) Date of demand for payment

9   In an oft-quoted dictum, Lord Westbury said[36]: "Interest can be demanded only in virtue of a contract, express or implied, or by virtue of the principal sum of money having been wrongfully withheld, and not paid on the day when it ought to have been paid." By "wrongfully withheld" is meant more than non-payment of money.[37] It may consist of a frivolous defence, or unjustifiable appeal, or other obstructive procedure, designed to hold up payment of money for which a pursuer holds a decree.[38] A more liberal interpretation would be to apply it to debts, certain in amount, which are not paid after a formal demand for payment which includes intimation that interest will be claimed in the event of non-payment. This formal demand is usually citation in an action, but it could be in a letter or invoice sent to the debtor.

10   Interest cannot be due before an account for services is rendered, and a mere demand for payment does not produce a liability to pay interest, but Lord Fraser in *Blair's Trs.* v. *Payne* countenanced interest being payable from judicial intimation or a written demand for interest.[39] This view has been followed.[40] One way of demanding interest is to render an account with interest claimed in it, and, at least if there is no valid objection raised, interest will be due.[41] But merely lodging the account in a process will be insufficient,[42] as would be the rendering of an account which did not mention interest.[43]

11   Statutory provision is made for interest on dishonoured bills running from the time of presentment for payment if the bill is a demand bill, or from maturity of the bill in other cases.[44]

(d) Date of citation

12   Citation in an action is judicial intimation that interest is claimed. Where the sum due is easily quantifiable, as the price of goods, or rent, feuduty or ground annual, interest is due from citation.[45] This rule has

---

[36] *Carmichael* v. *Caledonian Ry. Co.* (1870) 8 M.(H.L.) 119 at p. 131; appd. *Kolbin & Sons* v. *Kinnear & Co.* 1931 S.C.(H.L.) 128 at p. 137 *per* Lord Atkin.

[37] *Blair's Trs.* v. *Payne, sup. cit.* at p. 110 *per* Lord Fraser; *McPhail* v. *Lothian R.C.*, 1981 S.C. 119; *Tiffney* v. *Bachurzewski*, 1983 S.L.T.(Sh.Ct.) 45.

[38] *F. W. Green & Co. Ltd.* v. *Brown & Gracie Ltd.*, 1960 S.L.T.(Notes) 43 at p. 44 *per* Lord Keith (H.L.).

[39] *Sup. cit.* at p. 112.

[40] *Bunten* v. *Hart* (1902) 9 S.L.T. 476; *Somervell's Tr.* v. *Edinburgh Life Ass. Co.*, 1911 S.C. 1069; *Hunter* v. *Livingstone Development Corp.*, 1984 S.L.T. 10.

[41] *Somervell's Tr.* v. *Edinburgh Life Ass. Co., sup. cit.*; *James Ritchie* v. *County Council of Fife*, 1938 S.L.T.(Sh.Ct.) 17; *Hunter* v. *Livingston Development Corp., sup. cit.*

[42] *Bunten* v. *Hart, sup. cit.*

[43] *Hunter* v. *Livingstone Development Corp. sup. cit.*

[44] Bills of Exchange Act 1882, s.57 as amended by Administration of Justice Act 1977, s.4.

[45] *Blair's Trs.* v. *Payne, sup. cit.* at p. 110 *per* Lord Fraser; *F. W. Green & Co. Ltd.* v. *Brown & Gracie Ltd., sup. cit.* at p. 44 *per* Lord Keith unless of course express contract allows a claim from an earlier date. The provision in Sale of Goods Act 1979, s.49(3), which preserves a rule that interest is due on price from the date of tender of goods or from the date on which the price was payable, may reflect a misunderstanding of the common law.

also been applied to a claim for work due *quantum meruit*,[46] and to a decree for less than the sum sued for.[47]

(e) Date of decree

20–113   In a claim for damages for breach of contract interest is not due until decree,[48] although for reasons not always apparent interest has been awarded from the date of citation.[49] The rule probably reflects the principle which at one time applied in the law of delict, that the defender owed nothing and was not delaying payment until the damages were assessed.[50] If this is so the rationale is difficult to square with the present rule in delict under which the problem of estimating the amount of damages is not a ground for withholding interest from a date prior to the date of decree.

20–114   Interest is due *ex lege* from the date of the final decree. An appeal is a lawful delay in normal circumstances, and interest is due from the date of the appeal court interlocutor, not from the date of the interlocutor appealed against.[51] If there is unjustifiable delay which postpones the date of final decree, the court has a discretion to award interest from an earlier date.[52]

(f) Interest on Damages (Scotland) Act

20–115   The Interest on Damages (Scotland) Act 1958, as amended by the Interest on Damages (Scotland) Act 1971, makes provision for the court to grant interest on damages. The court has a discretion to award interest from the date the right of action arose. It appears, however, that there must be some special circumstances before the discretion of the court will be exercised.[53]

20–116   A more positive duty is placed on the court to award interest from a date prior to its interlocutor in cases of damages or solatium for personal injuries.[54] This could arise in a claim for breach of contract and presumably the practice worked out since 1971 in delict cases would be fol-

---

[46] *Keir Ltd.* v. *East of Scotland Water Board*, 1976 S.L.T.(Notes) 72.

[47] *Dean Warwick Ltd* v. *Borthwick*, 1983 S.L.T. 533.

[48] *F. W. Green & Co. Ltd* v. *Brown & Gracie Ltd.*, *sup. cit.*; *Martin & Sons* v. *Robertson, Ferguson & Co.* (1872) 10 M. 949.

[49] *Dunn & Co.* v. *Anderston Foundry Co. Ltd.* (1894) 21 R. 880; *James Buchanan & Co. Ltd.* v. *Stewart Cameron (Drymen) Ltd.*, 1973 S.C. 285.

[50] *Parker* v. *North British Ry. Co.* (1899) 7 S.L.T. 304; *Flensburg Steam Shipping Co.* v. *Seligmann* (1871) 9 M. 1011.

[51] *McCormack* v. *N.C.B.*, 1957 S.C. 277; *R. & J. Dempster* v. *Motherwell Bridge and Engineering Co.*, 1964 S.C. 308 (though see observations on this case in *James Buchanan & Co. Ltd.* v. *Stewart Cameron (Drymen) Ltd*, *sup. cit.*) The rule is arguably unjust. On appeals to the House of Lords see Court of Session Act 1808, s.19 and *F. W. Green & Co. Ltd.* v. *Brown & Gracie Ltd.*, *sup. cit.*.

[52] *Clancy* v. *Dixon's Ironworks Ltd.*, 1955 S.C. 17.

[53] *James Buchanan & Co. Ltd.* v. *Stewart Cameron (Drymen) Ltd.*, *sup. cit.*; *MacRae* v. *Reed & Mallick Ltd.*, 1961 S.C. 68.

[54] s.1A.

lowed.[55] The form of the issue to the jury in the leading case of *MacDonald*[56] distinguished between the damages claimed for four items, namely (1) loss of earnings to the date of decree; (2) future loss of earnings; (3) solatium to the date of decree; and (4) future solatium. These distinctions enable the court in the normal case to discharge its duty under section 1(1A) of the 1958 Act by applying different rates of interest to the component parts of the total award.[57]

(g) Compound interest

17   Compound interest, or interest on interest, is sometimes due by contracts, particularly contracts with banks or other financial institutions. Apart from this, the usual rule is that the courts award only simple interest.[58] Normally this does not give rise to difficulty when interest is only due from the date of citation, or later. If interest is due from an earlier date, there is a danger that principal and interest will be added together in the sum sued for and further interest will be sought on the total. This is compound interest and in principle should be disallowed,[59] but a contrary view has been expressed.[60] If arrears of interest can be treated as a principal sum, interest can be allowed on interest.[61] In personal injury cases, as a result of the Interest on Damages (Scotland) Acts 1958 and 1971, a sum which includes past interest is decreed for, and on that total further interest runs till payment.[62]

18   Cases of breach of trust, or breach of the obligations of the holder of a fund are special. Compound interest may be allowed on these claims,

---

[55] *Smith* v. *Middleton*, 1972 S.C. 30; *Picken* v. *J. Smart & Co. (Contractors) Ltd.*, 1972 S.L.T.(Notes) 12; *McMahon* v. *J. & P. Coats (U.K.) Ltd.*, 1972 S.L.T.(Notes) 16; *Cooper* v. *Pat Munro (Alness) Ltd.*, 1972 S.L.T.(Notes) 20; *McCuaig* v. *Redpath Dorman Long*, 1972 S.L.T.(Notes) 42 (the report of this case is slightly defective). See "A Problem of Interest" (1972) 17 J.L.S. 337 at p. 338); *Ward* v. *Tarmac Civil Engineering Ltd.*, 1972 S.L.T.(Notes) 52; *Ross* v. *British Railways Board*, 1972 S.C. 154; *Orr* v. *Metcalfe*, 1973 S.C. 57; *Macdonald* v. *Glasgow Corp.*, 1973 S.C. 52; *McAllister* v. *Abram*, 1979 S.L.T.(Notes) 6; 1981 S.L.T. 85; *Plaxton* v. *Aaron Construction (Dundee) Ltd.*, 1980 S.L.T.(Notes) 6.

[56] *Sup. cit.*

[57] See cases cited above. *McAllister* and *Plaxton* deal with a controversy over loss of society awards under the Damages (Scotland) Act 1976.

[58] *Douglas* v. *Douglas's Trs.* (1867) 5 M. 827; *Baird's Tr.* v. *Baird & Co.* (1877) 4 R. 1005 at p. 1015 *per* Lord Gifford—"A stipulation for compound interest, though it may be lawful, is never to be presumed, and must be very explicit indeed, and where there is only one stipulation for interest, and nothing said about compound interest, I cannot hold compound interest to be due." The older authorities are listed in Walker, *Civil Remedies*, p. 371. The contract may be implied by custom: *Findlay, Bannatyne & Co.'s Assignee* v. *Donaldson*, *sup. cit.*; Gloag, p. 684.

[59] *Clyde Navigation Trs.* v. *Kelvin Shipping Co.*, 1927 S.C. 622 at p. 658.

[60] See Maclaren, *Court of Session Practice*, p. 301. The case law referred to at p. 302, n. 1, is concerned with the obligations of the holder of a fund, and these cases do not apply to the normal relationship between debtor and creditor. See *Douglas* v. *Douglas's Trs.* (1867) 5 M. 827 at p. 836 *per* Lord Justice-Clerk Patton.

[61] *Maclean* v. *Campbell* (1856) 18 D. 609; *Nash Dredging (U.K.)* v. *Kestrel Marine Ltd.*, 1986 S.L.T. 67.

[62] *Mouland* v. *Ferguson*, 1979 S.L.T.(Notes) 85.

but consideration of such cases is outside the scope of the present work.[63]

(h) Rates of interest

20-119   The rate of interest to be awarded on decrees is fixed from time to time by act of sederunt. At the time of writing the rate in the sheriff court and the Court of Session is 15 per cent unless the decree states otherwise.[64] Where interest is to be awarded prior to decree the problem of the rate varies according to whether or not the rate of interest has been expressly or impliedly agreed by the parties.

20-120   The parties may agree a rate of interest. They usually do so in contracts for loan and frequently, in written commercial contracts, specify interest payable on the late payment of invoices. The parties may agree a fixed rate of interest, but in modern times are more likely to stipulate for a rate which varies with, say, the base rate of a specified bank.[65] The pursuer is entitled to this rate of interest up to decree, but to what rate after decree? There were conflicting sheriff court decisions. The trend was to grant interest at the contract rate up to decree and beyond decree at the normal rate on decrees,[66] although Sheriff Principal Walker did otherwise.[67] His is the correct approach, *i.e.* to grant decree in terms of the parties' contract.[68]

20-121   If the parties' contract provides for interest to fluctuate in accordance with bank base rates, it has been held that the exact rate of interest must be fixed at the time of extract of the decree.[69] On the other hand it has been held that the court should not make a new contract for the parties and allow the debtor to pay interest at a rate different from that which

---

[63] See Walker, *Civil Remedies*, pp. 371, 373 *et seq.*; W. A. Wilson and A. G. M. Duncan, *Trusts, Trustees and Executors*, p. 386.

[64] See 1985 S.L.T.(News) 264.

[65] This can give rise to problems if compounding of the interest is not also stipulated. If different rates of interest apply between the date the principal sum was due and the date of raising an action, the accrued interest for certain periods can be calculated, but care has to be taken not to seek interest on accrued interest. In *Bank of Scotland* v. *Forsyth*, 1969 S.L.T.(Sh.Ct.) 15, Sheriff Sir Allan G. Walker granted decree for interest at two per cent. per annum above bank rate from time to time current.

[66] *Jackson* v. *Morris*, 1931 S.L.T.(Sh.Ct.) 39; *Bank of Scotland* v. *Bruce*, 1968 S.L.T.(Sh.Ct.) 58; *Avco Financial Services Ltd.* v. *McQuire*, 1976 S.L.T.(Sh.Ct.) 33. See also *National Commercial Bank* v. *Stuart*, 1969 S.L.T.(Notes) 52 (2nd Div.).

[67] *Bank of Scotland* v. *Forsyth, sup. cit.* This accords with commercial sense, but the legacy of the usury laws is still with us and the courts are very cautious in making awards of interest. In England this caution reached its height in *London, Chatham & Dover Ry.* v. *S.E. Ry.* [1893] A.C. 429, which was eventually altered by the Law Reform (Miscellaneous Provisions) Act 1934. As Lord Shand pointed out, Scots law in 1893 was more favourable to the awarding of interest. On rates of interest the English practice is now very flexible: see McGregor, *Damages*, para. 477A; *Miliangos* v. *George Frank (Textiles) No. 2* [1977] Q.B. 489.

[68] *Bank of Scotland* v. *Davis*, 1982 S.L.T. 20 (2nd Div.). See, on the consequences of this, S. A. Bennett, "Bank Debts: A Matter of Interest," 1983 S.L.T.(News) 85.

[69] See *The Royal Bank of Scotland* v. *Geddes*, 1983 S.L.T.(Sh.Ct.) 32; S. A. Bennett, *sup. cit.*

he contracted to pay, and therefore it was competent to grant decree for a principal sum with interest thereon at four per cent per annum above the pursuers' base rate from time to time until payment.[70]

22   If the parties have not agreed a rate of interest for sums prior to decree, the rate is at the discretion of the court. In *Kearon* v. *Thomson's Exrs.*[71] the court reserved its opinion on the rate of interest on debts and damages, but it is clear from Lord President Cooper's account of the history of the so-called rate of "legal interest" that the appropriate rate depends on circumstances. In practice, seeking the rate appropriate to decrees is the safest course unless it is desired to argue for a different rate.[72] A decree may omit an express reference to interest, but nevertheless be held to include interest.[73]

23   In the absence of averment justifying a higher rate, the legal rate has been awarded in an undefended action,[74] but a contrary decision awarding the rate claimed is thought to be correct.[75] In a defended action a proof before answer was allowed when a rate higher than the ordinary rate on decrees was claimed.[76]

(i) Drafting interest clauses

24   The practitioner who drafts an interest clause should bear in mind the following points.

(1) Interest can be sought prior to a breach, as well as after a breach. For a loan this would be normal. It would be unusual in a contract for services or a contract of sale. It is unwise to stipulate a default rate higher than a pre-default rate. The reason is that the higher rate may be considered penal. The correct method is to set a high level of pre-default interest which is reduced in the event of punctual payment.[77]

(2) The date when interest starts to run should be clear. A reference to interest on "sums unpaid" may be obscure unless the exact day of payment is specified.

(3) It is unnecessary to provide for interest accruing from day to day. This occurs anyway.[78]

(4) *Prima facie* only simple interest is payable. If compound interest is sought, the periods of compounding must be specified (*e.g.* half-yearly

---

[70] *The Royal Bank of Scotland plc* v. *Dunbar*, 1985 S.L.T.(Sh.Ct.) 66.
[71] 1949 S.C. 287. Nor was the point argued in *Prestwick Cinema Co.* v. *Gardiner*, 1951 S.C. 98.
[72] And in personal injury cases special rules apply. See *supra*.
[73] *Project Contract Services Ltd.* v. *Fraioli*, 1980 S.C. 261.
[74] *Petroleum Industry Training Board* v. *Jenkins*, 1982 S.L.T.(Sh.Ct.) 43.
[75] *The Royal Bank of Scotland* v. *Briggs*, 1982 S.L.T.(Sh.Ct.) 46.
[76] *Interplan (Joiners and Shopfitters) Ltd.* v. *Reid Furniture Co. Ltd.*, 1984 S.L.T.(Sh.Ct.) 42.
[77] *Wallingford* v. *Mutual Soc.* (1880) 5 App.Cas. 685 at p. 702 *per* Lord Hatherley. See also *Thompson* v. *Hudson* (1869) 4 L.R.(H.L.) 1; *Cityland and Property (Holdings) Ltd.* v. *Dabrah* [1968] Ch. 166; Consumer Credit Act 1974, s.93.
[78] See Apportionment Act 1870, s.2.

or yearly). The period is for the parties to decide. There is a reported instance of default interest being capitalised every 21 days.[79]

(5) The rate of interest specified will normally vary, *e.g.* with a specified bank's base rate. But this type of provision should not be inserted in a contract to which some of the provisions of the Consumer Credit Act apply, broadly, because it would not be possible to give the debtor advance notice of the cost of the credit.[80]

(6) It may be desired to have interest running on all the indebtedness which may arise. This is feasible in so far as the sums are liquid. It is quite another matter to provide for interest on illiquid sums, such as damages for breach. Such a provision is more likely to cause dispute than to avoid it, but some draftsmen adopt the attitude that "there is no harm in trying."

(7) If the debtor makes partial payment, problems of apportionment between capital and interest can arise.[81] The creditor may wish to make specific provision either (a) allowing him to apportion as he sees fit, or (b) setting out how the apportionment will be done.[82]

PART 8

Penalty Clauses

(a) Terminology

20–125   The usual distinction is between a "penalty" which is unenforceable and "liquidated damages." The word "penalty" is used throughout the recorded history of our law, while the term "liquidated damages" became more common in the nineteenth century. Other expressions were in use, such as practical damages, estimated damages, or stipulated damages.[83] Sometimes "liquidated" becomes "liquidate,"[84] which was the term used by Gloag[85] and may be the older form derived from "liquidat."[86] To add to the confusion, the term "penalty clause" is often used by laymen to refer to the type of clause under consideration, without making a judgment on its character as being enforceable or unen-

---

[79] *Multiservice Bookbinding Ltd.* v. *Marden* [1979] Ch. 84.
[80] See Consumer Credit Act 1974, ss.20, 77, 78, 79 and 100.
[81] See para. 22–26.
[82] See example at para. 22–26.
[83] It has not been thought useful to list all the authorities, but the curious may trace the terms in the cases cited elsewhere in this chapter. Stair referred to "liquidate expenses": *Inst.*, IV,iii,2.
[84] Stair, *sup. cit.*; *Craig* v. *McBeath* (1863) 1 M. 1020 *per* Lord Justice-Clerk Inglis at p. 1022; *McElroy & Sons* v. *Tharsis Sulphur and Copper Co.* (1877) 5 R. 161—on appeal (1878) 5 R.(H.L.) 171; *Page* v. *Sherratt* (1907) 15 S.L.T. 731: but in *Forrest & Barr* v. *Henderson* (1869) 8 M. 187, Lord President Inglis and other judges used "liquidated."
[85] *Contract*, pp. 673 *et seq.*
[86] See *O.E.D.*

forceable. There is much to be said for using one term, particularly when otherwise the choice of correct term cannot be made until the final decision of the court. The term "penalty clause" is sometimes used in this chapter to cover both enforceable and unenforceable clauses, and it is hoped that this is apparent from the context.

26 To understand the nature of the distinction between penalty clauses and liquidated damages clauses and the relevance of some nineteenth-century cases to the modern law, it is necessary to consider the history of the law.

(b) The early law

27 The early law connected penalty clauses with usury. Balfour cites three cases in which a penalty was allowed to be exacted.[87] Forty years later the Lords decided that:

> "Be the law of this realme, poena conventionalis, sic as ane soume of money adjectit, with consent of parties, in ony contract or obligatioun, in name of pane, may not be askit be ony persoun, bot in sa far as he is interestit, hurt or skaithit; because all sic panis are in ane maner usuraris, and unhonest, maid for lucre or gane."[88]

Thereafter there were many statutes of the Scottish Parliament prohibiting usury, *i.e.* contracts demanding an exorbitant rate of interest.[89] There were numerous cases in the seventeenth and eighteenth centuries which were concerned with penalty clauses.[90] Sometimes the penalty was enforced, sometimes it was modified.

(c) Nineteenth century

28 In the first half of the nineteenth century the law was clear. If a clause was a liquidated damages clause it was enforced.[91] If it was a penalty, the claimant under the clause would receive his actual loss, up to the limit stipulated by the penalty[92]: that is, the court would modify the penalty[93] but would not modify a liquidated damages clause.[94] The law was explained by Bell[95] and clearly settled by *Johnston* v. *Robertson*[96] in

---

[87] *Practicks*, pp. 150, 151; *Laird of Cokpuil* v. *Carutheris* (1501); *King's Treasurer* v. *Earl of Caithness* (1506); *Bruce* v. *Lindsay* (1502).

[88] *Home* v. *Hepburn* (1549) Mor. 10033.

[89] General Index of A.P.S., *s.v.* "Usury." The heading omits the Acts 1649 c. 367 and 1661 c. 345. The Act of 1587 refers to earlier laws, but it is uncertain what these are. The Acts were repealed by the Usury Laws Repeal Act 1854 and the Statute Law Revision (Scotland) Act 1906.

[90] See Brown's *Synopsis, s.v.* "Penalty."

[91] *Henderson* v. *Maxwell* (1802) Mor. 10054; February 24, 1802, F.C.

[92] *Johnstone's Trs.* v. *Johnstone*, January 19, 1819, F.C.

[93] *Wright* v. *McGregor* (1826) 4 S.440; *Watson* v. *Merriless* (1848) 10 D. 370.

[94] *Johnston* v. *Robertson* (1861) 23 D. 646.

[95] *Prin.*, s.34 (4th ed.); *Comm.* I, 654 (5th ed.).

[96] *Sup. cit.*

1861. A sophistication appeared in *Craig* v. *McBeath*[97] in 1863 in which it was held that even if the clause was a penalty, it lay on the defenders to claim modification of the penalty, otherwise the penalty was recoverable on the grounds that it was assumed to be equal to the loss sustained.

(d) The landmark cases

20–129   *Forrest & Barr* v. *Henderson*[98] in 1869 changed the law. It was held that a provision for liquidated damages might be modified on the grounds that it was exorbitant and unconscionable. As mentioned earlier it had been penalty clauses which were modified. Liquidated damages clauses were enforced. Now it was held that they also could be modified. But there was controversy about what the case did decide, as appears from *Clydebank Engineering and Shipbuilding Co. Ltd.* v. *Castaneda*.[99] One Lord Ordinary treated the decision as meaning that some clauses which were *prima facie* liquidated damages clauses were truly penalty clauses.[1] This qualification is probably correct, because otherwise it would be difficult to distinguish liquidated damages clauses and penalty clauses. Both could be modified. In the House of Lords, Lord Davey approved *Forrest & Barr*[2] subject to the criticism that a claim for an exorbitant or unconscionable amount was really a penalty, and not liquidated damages.

20–130   The next landmark was *Dingwall* v. *Burnett*[3] in 1912. Up to this point the law had been understood as laying down that a penalty clause could be modified if the actual loss proved was less. The penalty, however, set a limit on what was recoverable. In *Dingwall*, however, a penalty of £50 was held unenforceable, and a claim for damages of a much greater amount was sent to proof. On one view this is a surprising case, because the reason for the law refusing to enforce a penalty is that it will not let people punish each other.[4] If the contract is penal, how is it just to allow a higher claim? The problem arose because it is penal to stipulate, as in *Dingwall*, for one sum payable for various breaches some of which may be trivial, others serious. The serious breach may cause more loss than the penalty stipulated. To disregard in that event the agreement of the parties on the sum payable added a new hazard to the drafting of penalty clauses. Prior to *Dingwall* the party liable to the penalty could agree to a sum knowing that would be the limit of his liability. Now if he agreed to a sum which was too high, and therefore penal, he has not

---

[97] (1863) 1 M. 1020.

[98] (1869) 8 M. 187.

[99] (1903) 5 F. 1016; (1904) 7 F.(H.L.) 77.

[1] 5 F. 1016 at p. 1022, *per* Lord Kyllachy.

[2] 7 F.(H.L.) at p. 82.

[3] 1912 S.C. 1097.

[4] *Craig* v. *McBeath, sup. cit.* at p. 1022 *per* Lord Justice-Clerk Inglis; *Robertson* v. *Driver's Trs.* (1881) 8 R. 555 at p. 562 *per* Lord Young.

limited his liability at all. This is a curious result for a law which set out to protect those subject to penalties.[5]

(e) The modern law

The modern law, in England and Scotland, was almost codified by the famous speech of Lord Dunedin in *Dunlop Pneumatic Tyre Co. Ltd.* v. *New Garage and Motor Co. Ltd.*[6] He said:

"1. Though the parties to a contract who use the words "penalty" or "liquidated damages" may *prima facie* be supposed to mean what they say, yet the expression used is not conclusive. The Court must find out whether the payment stipulated is in truth a penalty or liquidated damages. This doctrine may be said to be found passim in nearly every case.

2. The essence of a penalty is a payment of money stipulated as in terrorem of the offending party; the essence of liquidated damages is a genuine covenanted pre-estimate of damage (*Clydebank Engineering and Shipbuilding Co.* v. *Don Jose Ramos Yzquierdo y Castaneda*[7]).

3. The question whether a sum stipulated is penalty or liquidated damages is a question of construction to be decided upon the terms and inherent circumstances of each particular contract, judged of as at the time of the making of the contract, not as at the time of the breach (*Public Works Commissioner* v. *Hills*[8] and *Webster* v. *Bosanquet*[9]).

4. To assist this task of construction various tests have been suggested, which if applicable to the case under consideration may prove helpful, or even conclusive. Such are:

(a) It will be held to be penalty if the sum stipulated for is extravagant and unconscionable in amount in comparison with the greatest loss that could conceivably be proved to have followed from the breach. (Illustration given by Lord Halsbury in *Clydebank* case.)[10]

(b) It will be held to be a penalty if the breach consists only in not paying a sum of money, and the sum stipulated is a sum greater than the sum which ought to have been paid (*Kemble* v. *Farren*[11]). This though one of the most ancient instances is truly a corollary to the last test. Whether it had its historical origin in the doctrine of the common law that when A promised to pay B a sum of money on a certain day and did not do so B could only recover the sum with, in certain cases, interest, but could never recover further damages for non-timeous payment, or whether it was a survival of the time

---

[5] Further, a clause providing for £50 payable on any breach may be struck at as penal, whereas a clause providing for £300 on a specified type of breach is unimpeachable. The layman would find this hard to understand.

[6] [1915] A.C. 79 at pp. 86–88.

[7] [1904] 7 F.(H.L.) 77; see also *Stroms Bruks Aktie Bolag* v. *Hutchison* (1904) 6 F. 486—on appeal (1905) 7 F.(H.L.) 131.

[8] [1906] A.C. 368.

[9] [1912] A.C. 394.

[10] *Sup. cit.* at p. 78.

[11] (1829) 6 Bing. 141.

when equity reformed unconscionable bargains merely because they were unconscionable, a subject which much exercised Jessel M.R. in *Wallis* v. *Smith*[12]—is probably more interesting than material.

(c) There is a presumption (but no more) that it is penalty when 'a simple lump sum is made payable by way of compensation, on the occurrence of one or more or all of several events, some of which may occasion serious and others but trifling damage' (Lord Watson in *Lord Elphinstone* v. *Monkland Iron and Coal Co.*[13]).

On the other hand—

(d) It is no obstacle to the sum stipulated being a genuine pre-estimate of damage, that the consequences of the breach are such as to make precise pre-estimation almost an impossibility. On the contrary, that is just the situation when it is probable that pre-estimated damage was the true bargain between the parties (*Clydebank Case*, Lord Halsbury[14]; *Webster* v. *Bosanquet*, Lord Mersey[15])."

(f) Penalty or liquidated damages

20–132   The crucial distinction is between a penalty and liquidated damages. Lord Dunedin said in *Dunlop Pneumatic Tyre Co.* that: "the essence of a penalty is a payment of money stipulated as in terrorem of the offending party."[16] The phrase *"in terrorem"* was also used in the *Lord Elphinstone*[17] and *Clydebank Engineering* cases.[18] The test of a liquidated damages clause is whether it is a "genuine covenanted pre-estimate of damages." This concept goes back a long way. Anything other than a fair equivalent of damages was usurious, and the law did not allow usury.[19] But it was not penal merely to substitute one obligation for another, *i.e.* to substitute payment for performance.[20] The standard, however, was whether the sum stipulated was the liquidated or estimated loss.[21]

20–133   This distinction between penalty and liquidated damages is based on an attitude to usury which is no longer prevalent and, furthermore, it is

---

[12] (1882) 21 Ch.D. 243.

[13] (1886) 13 R.(H.L.) 98—see also *Craig* v. *McBeath* (1863) 1 M. 1020; *Dingwall* v. *Burnett*, 1912 S.C. 1097. For example of a variable in a contract of employment, see *Strathclyde R.C.* v. *Neil*, 1983 S.L.T.(Sh.Ct.) 89.

[14] (1904) 7 F.(H.L.) 77 at p. 79.

[15] [1912] A.C. 394 at p. 398. See also *Cameron-Head* v. *Cameron & Co.*, 1919 S.C. 627 (penalty for loss of privacy or amenity).

[16] *Sup. cit.*

[17] (1886) 13 R.(H.L.) 98 at p. 109 *per* Lord Halsbury.

[18] (1903) 5 F. 1016 at p. 1022 *per* Lord Ordinary (Kyllachy); (1904) 7 F.(H.L.) 77 at pp. 78–80 *per* Lord Chancellor Halsbury, at p. 84 *per* Lord Robertson.

[19] See the winning argument in *Henderson* v. *Maxwell*, February 24, 1802, F.C.; Mor. 10054.

[20] *Marshal* v. *Cunningham, Dougal & Co.* (1780) Mor. 9183.

[21] *Anderson* v. *Monteith* (1847) 9 D. 1432; Bell, *Prin.*, s.34 (4th ed.).

a distinction which can be difficult to apply in modern commercial practice. The problems are these:

(1) A "penalty" clause is often inserted to encourage performance. The prescient Kames recognised this when he referred to it as "a spur on the debtor to perform."[22] This motive, which is not obviously objectionable, may be in conflict with a pre-estimate of damages test, which implies that the party in breach should not be worse off because of the clause and indeed may be better off because the cautious draftsman would choose a low figure if he wishes an enforceable clause.

(2) The phrase "*in terrorem*" is somewhat extreme, because it is difficult to imagine most "penalty" clauses producing fright, fear, dread, panic or terror. However, in so far as they put pressure on one party, this is also achieved by a liquidated damages clause. Contracts have by their nature a coercive force and this is all the stronger when the sum payable on breach is fixed in the mind of the party who might be in breach. To distinguish between different degrees of pressure is not easy.

(3) Lord Chancellor Halsbury in the *Clydebank Engineering Co.* case gave us an example of a penalty, the payment of a million for failure to build within a year a house for £50.[23] The knowledgeable party would not be terrorised by this at all, because he would know that it was unenforceable. But the closer the penalty is to the probable amount of actual loss, the greater the pressure on the party in breach, because the greater the difficulty in successfully challenging the clause. It does not aid practitioners much to ask themselves the question: "is the clause *in terrorem*?" That test works when the result is obvious, but does not help in the borderline cases. Nor anyway is the existence of terror necessary for a successful challenge of a clause.[24]

(4) The greatest difficulty is that a genuine pre-estimate of loss is not always possible. The *Clydebank Engineering Co.* case was an example. The loss to a government of warships which would have been used to suppress an insurrection cannot be calculated in advance, and probably not even after the event. Similarly the losses to a local authority because the building of a school is delayed, or to a university because of the late completion of a library extension, are not readily capable of a genuine pre-estimate. In many cases the amount put in liquidated damages clauses is purely arbitrary, but these clauses may nevertheless be enforced on the curious ground that the difficulty of estimating damage means that the clause reflects "the true bargain between the parties." In other words, in some cases the genuine pre-estimate test is abandoned. It is difficult to resist the conclusion that the clause will be struck down if

---

[22] *Principles of Equity*, p. 378.

[23] *Sup. cit.* at p. 78.

[24] Criticism of the phrase "*in terrorem*" is in Lord Radcliffe's speech in *Bridge* v. *Campbell Discount Co. Ltd.* [1962] A.C. 600 at p. 622: "It obscures the fact that penalties may quite readily be undertaken by parties who are not in the least terrorised by the prospect of having to pay them and yet are, as I understand it, entitled to claim the protection of the court when they are called on to make good their promises."

the agreed sum differs widely from the damages which would have been awarded, but, if the difference cannot be proved because the damages cannot be ascertained, the clause will stand.

(g) Penalties in bonds

20–134   Much of the history of penalty clauses is intertwined with complicated case law on the effect of penalty clauses in bonds. As the law developed the penalty could be enforced in so far as it represented interest and expenses, and infeftment covering the penalty gave certain preferences. Much of this law is rendered of less practical importance since the introduction of the standard security by the Conveyancing and Feudal Reform (Scotland) Act 1970, and the abolition of new feuduties by the Land Tenure Reform (Scotland) Act 1974, but the old forms of bonds and feu charters still exist. The law was explained by Bell and the other authorities cited.[25]

(h) Tempus inspiciendum

20–135   To decide whether the sum is a valid pre-estimate of loss, circumstances are considered at the time of making the contract, not at the time of the breach.[26] Nevertheless the court may need to consider what has happened subsequently. The sum sued for may be based on the number of days the defender is late in making delivery, or the number of instalments unpaid in a hire-purchase contract, or alterations in the salary of an employee. Further, the present state of the law makes it necessary to distinguish between a breach of contract and sums due on an event other than a breach. This may involve a detailed consideration of all the actings of the parties, even though in the end the clause is unenforceable—a result which in theory can be reached by considering only events at the time of the contract.[27] Lastly, our system of written pleading makes it prudent for a pursuer to aver actual loss and avoid dismissal of the action following a decision that the penalty clause is unenforceable.[28]

20–136   These considerations do not offend the rule that the nature of the clause is to be determined by the facts at the creation of the contract, but it would be surprising if subsequent facts did not sometimes influence a court. In *Mercantile Credit Co.* v. *Brown*[29] the sheriff took

---

[25] Bell, *Comm.*, I,700 (7th ed.); *Ramsay* v. *Goldie* (1826) 4 S.737; *Eckford* v. *Dunbar* (1828) 6 S. 382; *Jameson* v. *Beilby* (1835) 13 S.865; *Orr* v. *Mackenzie* (1839) 1 D. 1046; Debts Securities (Scotland) Act 1856 s.5; *Bruce* v. *Scottish Amicable Life Ass. Soc.*, 1907 S.C. 637; Menzies, *Lectures on Conveyancing*, p. 227; Gloag, p. 675.

[26] *Dunlop Pneumatic Tyre Co. Ltd., sup. cit.*; *Clydebank Engineering Co., sup. cit.*; *Forrest & Barr* v. *Henderson* (1869) 8 M. 187 at p. 193 *per* Lord President Inglis; *Public Works Commrs.* v. *Hills* [1906] A.C. 368 at p. 376.

[27] *Mercantile Credit Co.* v. *Brown*, 1960 S.L.T.(Sh.Ct.) 41.

[28] As happened in *Mercantile Credit Co.* v. *Brown*, *sup. cit.*.

[29] *Sup. cit.*

into account the sum at which the subject-matter of the contract had been sold following termination of the hire. In *Union Transport Finance Ltd. v. McQueen*[30] the sheriff accepted that he should consider the facts at the time of the making of the contract, and then tested his conclusion by looking at what had happened.

(i) Applicability of penalty rules

37   The rules on penalty clauses do not apply if (1) the sum is payable on an event which is not a breach of contract; (2) the clause provides, not for payment of a sum, but for the forfeiture of moneys already paid; (3) the clause merely provides for payment of sums due under the contract; (4) the clause provides for a disproportionately small sum compared with the probable loss (the inverse penalty); (5) the clause provides, not for the payment of a sum, but for the forfeiture of property rights, *i.e.* an irritancy; or (6) the clause provides for the withdrawal of rights and privileges not amounting to an irritancy.

(j) The necessity for a breach of contract

38   In Scotland, *Bell Brothers (H.P.) Ltd.* v. *Aitken*[31] and *Granor Finance Ltd.* v. *Liquidator of Eastore Ltd.*[32] are authority for the proposition that the rules on penalty clauses have no application unless the penalty arises on breach of contract. Thus the rules on penalty clauses may be evaded if the contract provides for termination at the option of one party on payment of £X[33] or for a sum payable on event Y which is not a breach but is, for example, the liquidation of one party.[34]

39   Sheriff court cases on hire-purchase contracts have varied between following *Bell Brothers*[35] and distinguishing it.[36] Much of the immediate relevance of the dispute in the sheriff court has disappeared because of statutory provisions on the sums due on termination of hire-purchase and consumer credit agreements.[37] However, the nature of the dispute is still important in cases in which the statutory provisions do not apply.[38]

---

[30] 1961 S.L.T.(Sh.Ct.) 35.

[31] 1939 S.C. 577.

[32] 1974 S.L.T. 296.

[33] *Bell Bros.* v. *Aitken, sup. cit.*

[34] *Granor Finance Ltd.* v. *Liqr. of Eastore Ltd., sup. cit.*

[35] *Mercantile Credit Co. Ltd.* v. *McLachlan*, 1962 S.L.T.(Sh.Ct.) 58. See also *United Dominions Trust (Commercial) Ltd.* v. *Bowden*, 1958 S.L.T.(Sh.Ct.) 10 and *United Dominions Trust (Commercial) Ltd.* v. *Murray*, 1966 S.L.T.(Sh.Ct.) 21.

[36] *Mercantile Credit Co. Ltd.* v. *Brown* 1960 S.L.T.(Sh.Ct.) 41; *Bowmaker (Commercial) Ltd.* v. *McDonald*, 1965 S.L.T.(Sh.Ct.) 33.

[37] Hire Purchase (Scotland) Act 1965, ss.28 and 29; Consumer Credit Act 1974, ss.100 and 173(1); see also ss.137–140.

[38] And curiously the Consumer Credit Act 1974 is more restrictive than the hire-purchase provisions because—the general control on extortionate bargains apart—it only applies when the hirer terminates under his statutory rights. What if the owner terminates or the creditor terminates under the contract?

20–140   The problem is that the hirer who wishes to terminate his contract may have two choices. He may indicate that he is returning the goods in terms of an option in the contract, or he may default in his payments and await the consequences. In both cases the contract can provide for payments to be made, but only in the second is there a breach of contract, with the consequence that the rules on penalty clauses control the enforceability of the contractual provision. The honest hirer who admits his inability to continue with the contract and promptly takes action to avoid disappointing the owner will find that, if he exercises an option in the contract for early termination, any payment to be made is not controlled by the penalty clause rules at common law.

20–141   The choice between voluntary termination and default has been compared to the decision of a man about to be put to death who is given the option of shooting himself or being burned alive.[39] It would be unreal to say that the former was voluntary. Also, the distinction between the sums due on breach and sums due when there is no breach can be a narrow one.[40] The distinction has been criticised in England[41] and doubt has been expressed on whether a penalty presupposes a breach of contract,[42] but the law of England as in Scotland is clear. A clause is not a penalty clause if it provides for payment on an event other than breach of contract.[43]

(k) Forfeiture of moneys already paid

20–142   If the contract provides for forfeiture of sums already paid, such as deposits and instalments of the price, the rules on penalty clauses are inapplicable.[44] There is some limited authority which suggests that there might be an equitable relief against the consequences of forfeiture.[45] The harshness of the general rule can be illustrated by assuming the case at common law of a house purchased by instalments. The price is £1000. The instalments are £10 per week. £950 has been paid. One instalment is paid one week late. In terms of the contract the house reverts to the seller and all instalments paid are forfeited. On the authority of *Reid* v. *Campbell*[46] the contractual provisions are not a penalty. This is such a

---

[39] *Mercantile Credit Co.* v. *Brown, sup. cit.* at p. 43.

[40] See *Alder* v. *Moore* [1961] 2 Q.B. 57—a provision for payment of £500 if the promisor played professional football was given varying constructions.

[41] *Bridge* v. *Campbell Discount Co. Ltd.* [1961] 1 Q.B. 445, [1962] A.C. 600; Law Comm. Working Paper No. 61, *Penalty Clauses and Forfeiture of Monies Paid*, Pt. III.

[42] *United Dominions Trust (Commercial) Ltd.* v. *Ennis* [1968] 1 Q.B. 54.

[43] *Export Credit Guarantee Dept.* v. *Universal Oil Products Co.* [1983] 2 All E.R. 205 (H.L.)—an unsuccessful attempt to extend the law on penalties to an indemnity clause.

[44] *Commercial Bank of Scotland Ltd.* v. *Beal* (1890) 18 R. 80; *Roberts & Cooper* v. *Salvesen & Co.*, 1918 S.C. 794; *Reid* v. *Campbell*, 1958 S.L.T.(Sh.Ct.) 45.

[45] *Hannan* v. *Henderson* (1879) 7 R. 380 at p. 383 *per* Lord Shand; *Watson* v. *Nobel* (1885) 13 R. 347; *Roberts & Cooper* v. *Salvesen & Co., sup cit.* at p. 814 *per* Lord Skerrington. Equitable relief is available in England but the extent of it is obscure—*Stockloser* v. *Johnson* [1954] 1 Q.B. 476 is the leading case: McGregor, *Damages*, para. 391.

[46] *Sup. cit.*

startling result that the soundness of the decision must be doubted.[47] In any event instalment purchases of houses will frequently be "conditional sale agreements" controlled by the Consumer Credit Act 1974.

(l) Accelerated payment

43   A clause is not penal if it provides for the time of payment of the contract price to be accelerated when a breach occurs, *e.g.* the whole sum is immediately due if one instalment is late.[48] Acceleration provisions are commonly found in mortgages.[49]

(m) The inverse penalty

44   A clause may provide for a sum much smaller than the probable loss. This arose in *Cellulose Acetate Silk Co.* v. *Widnes Foundry*,[50] in which it was decided that the clause operated as in effect a limitation of liability.[51] The question whether in some circumstances a small sum might be a penalty was left open.

(n) Irritancy—development of the law

45   There is a close connection between penalty clauses and irritancies. Few events could be more penal than complete forfeiture of property without compensation, which is the effect of irritancy. Stair thought penalties and irritancy clauses were subject to modification under the same principle.[52] Yet the development of the law has placed irritancy in a special category, and in practice an irritancy was added to the penalty clause in feu writs.[53]

46   At one time a distinction was drawn between non-penal and penal irritancies. The non-penal irritancy would be strictly enforced, but the penal irritancy required a declarator of the Court of Session and gave

---

[47] Two Privy Council decisions which might suggest that forfeiture provisions can be penal were distinguished. See *Kilmer* v. *British Columbia Orchard Lands* [1913] A.C. 319; *Steedman* v. *Drinkle* [1916] 1 A.C. 275. These were also distinguished by the Lord Ordinary in *Roberts & Cooper* v. *Salvesen & Co.*, *sup. cit.* There are dangers in applying English equity cases in Scotland, and a full discussion of *Steedman* involves its interpretation in *Stockloser* v. *Johnson, sup. cit.* As Sheriff Walker said of the English equitable jurisdiction: "It is difficult for a Scottish lawyer to be certain that he understands"—*Reid* v. *Campbell, sup. cit.* at p. 46.

[48] *White & Carter Councils* v. *McGregor*, 1962 S.C.(H.L.) 1.

[49] Law Com. Working Paper No. 61, *sup. cit.*, para. 13.

[50] [1933] A.C. 20; *cf. Wall* v. *Rederiaktiebolaget Luggude* [1915] 3 K.B. 66 and commentary in McGregor, *Damages*, para. 386.

[51] It is not a true limitation of liability, because it provides the exact amount recoverable.

[52] Stair I,x,14; IV,xviii,3 *vide* III,ii,31 (2nd ed.), III,ii,32 (5th ed.), III,ii,53 (2nd ed.), III,ii,54 (5th ed), IV,iii,2 (2nd and 5th eds.).

[53] See *Taylors of Aberdeen* v. *Coutts* (1840) 1 Rob.App. 296 at pp. 315, 316 and styles of feu writs in Burns, *Conveyancing Practice*. s.XI.

the opportunity for purging.[54] The distinction between the two types of
irritancy has been lost sight of in modern writing but it explains why a
conventional irritancy in a feu writ is purgeable whereas at common law,
a similar irritancy in a lease is not. The loss of a whole estate as a result
of failure to pay some terms' feu duty was considered penal. The loss of
a short lease was not considered penal and so the equivalent irritancy
was enforceable.[55] These, however, are only examples of a principle,
and if the courts had paid attention to the question the principle poses—
is the clause penal or not?—they might have avoided the problem which
has arisen from following precedent without sufficient regard to underlying reasons; a course which has resulted in feu cases being treated as
one category with its solution—purgeability—and leases being placed in
another receptacle with its label—"not purgeable." Ross thought that if
the irritancy in a lease was incurred by one year's unpaid rent, instead of
two years' unpaid rent, there was little doubt that the court would allow
the irritancy to be purged,[56] presumably on the basis that shortening the
period made the provision penal. That did not become the law, largely
as a result of too strict an interpretation of the decision in *Stewart* v.
Watson.[57] The concept of penal irritancy so far as leases is concerned
was confined to a control over oppressive use of an irritancy, the meaning of which is far from clear, and which did not cover normal situations
of late payment of rent.[58] There appears to be no reported case in which
oppression has been established. There must be precise averments
which show a clear abuse of rights or impropriety of conduct by the
landlord.[59] "The question is whether the landlord has acted in such a
way as to make it unconscionable for him to take advantage of a situation which he himself has brought about."[60] The Scottish Law Commission recommended changes in the law,[61] and reform was introduced
by the Law Reform (Miscellaneous Provisions) (Scotland) Act 1985,

---

[54] Stair, I,xiii,14; II,x,6; IV,v,7, IV,xviii,3 (2nd and 5th eds.); Ersk., II,viii,14; Bankt.,
I,384,5; R. Bell, *Treatise on Leases* (1825–26), Vol. 2, pp. 14–18: "Hence it may now be
received as a general rule, that irritancies of the lease, whether legal or conventional, must
be judicially declared; and that they are purgeable at any time before decree of declarator" (at p. 16). See also Kames, *Principle of Equity* (5th ed., 1825) p. 48. W. Ross, *Lectures* (1792 and 1822), Vol. 2, p. 544, discusses whether the inferior courts had
jurisdiction.

[55] Ross, *Lectures*, Vol. 2, pp. 498–499; *Hepburn* v. *Nisbet* (1665) Mor. 7229; Bankt.,
II,101,23.

[56] Ross, *sup. cit.*; *cf.* Bankt., II,101,23.

[57] (1864) 2 M. 1414. One may query the court's treatment of the conventional irritancy
as a reasonable provision.

[58] *Dorchester Studios (Glasgow) Ltd.* v. *Stone*, 1975 S.C.(H.L.) 56; *McDougall's Trs.* v.
Macleod, 1949 S.C. 593; *Lucas's Exrs.* v. *Demarco*, 1968 S.L.T. 89; "Irritancy in Leases"
(1976) 21 J.L.S. 4.

[59] *H.M.V. Fields Properties Ltd.* v. *Skirt 'n' Slack Centre of London Ltd.*, 1982 S.L.T.
477 (motive of landlord irrelevant).

[60] *H.M.V. Fields Properties Ltd.* v. *Tandem Shoes Ltd.*, 1983 S.L.T. 114 at p. 120 *per*
Lord Brand.

[61] Scot.Law Com. No. 75, *Irritancies in Leases* (1983).

ss.4 and 5. In the case of a monetary breach of a lease, the landlord may not irritate unless he has served a notice on the tenant by recorded delivery.[62] The notice must be for not less than 14 days.[63] The notice must require the tenant to make payment, with any interest, in terms of the lease within the period specified in the notice. The tenant must be warned that failure to comply with the notice may lead to termination of the lease.[64] In the case of an irritancy clause which does not relate to monetary breaches, the landlord cannot rely on the provision in the lease if in all the circumstances of the case a fair and reasonable landlord would not seek so to rely.[65] Regard is to be had as to whether a reasonable opportunity has been afforded to the tenant to enable the breach to be remedied.[66]

47 Parties cannot contract out of sections 4 and 5 of the 1985 Act.[67] The sections do not apply to (1) a payment or a condition to be fulfilled before the tenant takes entry,[68] (2) a residential lease, or a lease of an agricultural holding, a croft, the subject of a cottar, or a small landholding,[69] or to (3) an event other than the termination of the lease.[70]

(o) Legal irritancy

48 The Feu Duty Act 1597 created a statutory irritancy for two years' non-payment of feu duty. This was not an incident of the feudal system, but was borrowed from Roman and Canon law.[71] The period is now five years.[72] Legal irritancies also exist for various types of leases, but consideration of these must be looked for in more specialised works.[73] A legal irritancy may be purged before decree.[74] This has been extended by statute in the case of irritancy *ob non solutem canonem* (*i.e.* for non-payment of feu duty) until the time of recording an extract decree in the Register of Sasines.[75]

---

[62] s.4.

[63] s.4(3). In some circumstances it must be for more than 14 days. See s.4(3)(*b*).

[64] s.4(2).

[65] s.5(1).

[66] s.5(3).

[67] s.6(1).

[68] s.6(3).

[69] s.7.

[70] s.5(2), and see the phrases in ss.4(1) and 5(1)—"for the purpose of treating a lease as terminated or terminating it."

[71] The history and effect of irritancy is explained in *Cassels* v. *Lamb* (1885) 12 R. 722 (whole court), esp. opinion of Lord Fraser (case approved in *Sandeman* v. *Scottish Property Investment Co.* (1885) 12 R.(H.L.) 67).

[72] Land Tenure Reform (Scotland) Act 1974, s.15.

[73] *e.g.* Paton and Cameron, *Landlord and Tenant*, Chap. XV and authorities there referred to.

[74] Bell *Prin.*, s.701; *Maxwell's Trs.* v. *Bothwell School Board* (1893) 20 R. 958; Rankine, *Leases*, pp. 538–539.

[75] Conveyancing (Scotland), etc., Amendment Act 1887, s.4. The common law rule still applies to conventional irritancies for breach of feuing conditions.

(p) Conventional irritancy

20–149   Conventional irritancies in leases are not purgeable[76] unless (a) use of
the irritancy is oppressive, which is a concept of uncertain meaning[77];
possibly (b) if the irritancy is a repetition of a legal irritancy[78] and purging is not expressly prohibited[79]; and (c) in the circumstances to which
the Law Reform (Miscellaneous Provisions) (Scotland) Act 1985, ss.4
and 5 apply.[80]

The law on purging in feu writs and ground annuals has developed differently from the law on leases, and some writers cause confusion by
indiscriminately citing cases on leases and feu writs as if the same rules
applied.[81] At one time it was also thought that conventional irritancies
in feu writs were not purgeable unless they were penal,[82] but as
observed earlier the distinction between penal and non-penal irritancies
was departed from. The modern law is: "That conventional irritancies
attached to obligations *ad facta praestanda*, or for payment of annual
duties contained in conveyances of property, whether by way of feu
right or by contract of ground-annual, are purgeable at the bar, *i.e.* at
any time before extract of a decree of declarator or irritancy."[83] Even if
a building must be erected within a specified time, and is not built, time
for purging may be granted by the court.[84] However, it may be impracticable to purge some irritancies, such as the erection of the wrong type of
building on the site.[85] In the case of a failure to perform an obligation *ad
factum praestandum* the feuar cannot assert an entitlement to purge as
of right. The court has a discretion on whether purging should be
allowed.[86] The harshness of irritancy is also recognised to the extent that
the clauses are construed strictly.[87]

---

[76] *Dorchester Studios (Glasgow)* v. *Stone*, 1975 S.C.(H.L.) 56.
[77] See *supra*; *Stewart* v. *Watson, sup. cit.*; *McDougall's Trs.* v. *Macleod, sup. cit.*; *Dorchester Studios (Glasgow)* v. *Stone, sup. cit.*
[78] Gloag, p. 666; Paton and Cameron, p. 232.
[79] *Earl of Elgin* v. *Whittaker* (1901) 9 S.L.T. 375.
[80] See para. 20–146.
[81] The distinction was recognised in *Stewart* v. *Watson, sup. cit.* at p. 1422 *per* Lord
Neaves, quoted in *Anderson* v. *Valentine, sup. cit.* at p. 59 *per* Lord Hill Watson; and in
Duncanson v. *Giffen, infra* at p. 359 *per* Lord Curriehill.
[82] Ersk., II,v,25; see commentary in *Duncanson* v. *Giffen, infra.*
[83] *Duncanson* v. *Giffen* (1878) 15 S.L.R. 356 at p. 359 *per* Lord Curriehill.
[84] *Napier* v. *Speirs' Trs.* (1831) 9 S. 655; *Mags. of Glasgow* v. *Hay* (1883) 10 R. 635;
Anderson v. *Valentine*, 1957 S.L.T. 57, 1957 S.L.T.(Notes) 27; *Glasgow Corp.* v. *Regent
Oil Co. Ltd.*, 1971 S.L.T.(Sh.Ct.) 61.
[85] *Ardgowan Estates Ltd.* v. *Lawson*, 1948 S.L.T. 186—the erection of an Admiralty
research station which did not defend Greenock. No argument on purging, but extract
superseded for three months.
[86] *Precision Relays Ltd.* v. *Beaton*, 1980 S.C. 220. The case is also authority for the proposition that an irritancy does not take effect until there is a declarator by the court.
[87] *Christie* v. *Jackson* (1898) 6 S.L.T. 245; *Anderson* v. *Valentine*, 1957 S.L.T.(Notes)
27; *Carswell* v. *Goldie*, 1967 S.L.T. 339. This follows the strong presumption of freedom in
favour of vassals, *e.g. Fleming* v. *Ure* (1896) 4 S.L.T. 26; *The Walker Trs.* v. *Haldane*
(1902) 4 F. 594; *Anderson* v. *Dickie*, 1915 S.C.(H.L.) 79; *Kemp* v. *Burgh of Largs*, 1939
S.C.(H.L.) 6. The leading case is *Taylors of Aberdeen* v. *Coutts* (1840) 1 Rob.App. 296.

(q) Withdrawal of rights and privileges

50 Connell observed in the context of agricultural leases that there is control of penal rents and liquidated damages, but not of penalties stated otherwise than in sterling, such as a power to withdraw certain rights or privileges.[88] There are other similar possibilities. A right may be subject to a resolutive condition.[89] A right may depend on the fulfilment of obligations, and the mutuality principle will affect enforcement of the right.[90]

(r) Drafting of penalty clauses

The practitioner who is faced with the problem of drafting a penalty clause[91] might like to consider the following points.

151 (1) Is a penalty clause desirable? The advantage of the clause is that it minimises dispute on the amount of loss. The disadvantage is that it limits the loss recoverable. Therefore it may boomerang on the person receiving the penalty. Consider the case of a sub-contract. The loss caused by a sub-contractor's delay may be unpredictable. It depends on what he does, when he does it, and the extent to which it interferes with the "critical path" of the main contractor's work. This may in turn depend on the work of other sub-contractors. The amount provided in a penalty clause could turn out to be quite inadequate compensation. For this reason penalty clauses are not often found in sub-contracts. A claim for loss is better left to the common law rules on damages which are, it is true, limited by rules on remoteness of liability, but these raise different and more flexible issues. Any inadequacy in the amount of recoverable loss can be blamed on the law, rather than on the practitioner who advised a penalty clause.

The example just given was one in which estimation of probable loss was difficult, but proof of that loss, in the event of such loss, would pose only normal problems. The classic case for the penalty clause is when proof of the loss is much more difficult than usual, such as delay in building a warship or a reservoir. In such a case the absence of a penalty clause may mean that in practice very little can be recovered for delay, and there is no incentive for the contractor to complete on time.

152 (2) Arising from the rule that the penalty should be a genuine preestimate of loss there is a presumption that the clause is unenforceable if a single lump sum is payable on the occurrence of several events, some serious and others trifling. Therefore, it is probably unwise to make all the obligations in a contract subject to the same penalty. A good illustration of this is the contrast between *Dunlop Pneumatic Tyre Co.* v.

---

[88] Connell on *The Agricultural Holdings (Scotland) Acts* (6th ed.), p. 14.
[89] See Gloag, p. 272.
[90] See para. 14–25.
[91] Meaning of course, an enforceable penalty or liquidated damages clause.

New Garage and Motor Co.[92] and *Ford Motor Co.* v. *Armstrong.*[93] In *Dunlop* a car dealer agreed to restraints on the resale of tyres. He agreed to pay £5 for every tyre sold in breach of contract. The sum was held to be liquidated damages. *Ford Motor Co.* was a similar case involving resale of cars. But the clause was drawn too wide. The sum of £250 per item covered not only resale, but also exhibition without permission, which was a stipulation of a different kind. The clause was held to be penal. The older Scottish cases also illustrate the dangers of having a lump sum payable on non-performance of the contract, when breach could take many forms.[94] For a payment under a contract of employment which was variable and proportionate to the period of service, see the case cited.[95]

The courts do not give a narrow meaning to the concept of a single obligation. A breach may be the product of several acts, for example solicitation of previous customers by varing methods. Or a covenant in restraint of trade within a specified radius could be breached by competing premises 100 yards away or five miles away. The test is whether a single stipulation is broken, rather than whether the breach could be minor or serious.[96]

The drafting rule is—be selective. If necessary, different obligations should have different penalty clauses. There is authority for the view that it is competent to state expressly that breach of one stipulation would cause loss between £5 and £15 and breach of another between £2 and £12, with the result that liquidated damages have been fixed at £8.[97]

The selective approach has, however, this consequence which is perhaps not always realised. The penalty will not apply to every breach of the contract. For example, a penalty for the contractor's delay may not apply if the employer takes possession and completes the work.[98] A clause which applies on completion conform to contract save in respect of contract time, may not apply when the work is in breach of contract because of defects in the building.[99] The result is not disastrous if the common law right to damages remains and is of value.

20–153   (3) Not only may the penalty clause apply to only one obligation in the contract, but it might not, depending on its drafting, apply to all events arising out of breach of that obligation. What happens if the person due to receive the penalty is in breach? For example, what is the

---

[92] [1915] A.C. 79.

[93] (1915) 31 T.L.R. 267.

[94] *Watson* v. *Merrilees* (1848) 10 D. 370; *Craig* v. *McBeath* (1863) 1 M. 1020; *Lord Elphinstone* v. *Monkland Iron and Coal Co. Ltd.* (1886) 13 R.(H.L.) 98.

[95] *Strathclyde R.C.* v. *Neil*, 1983 S.L.T.(Sh.Ct.) 89.

[96] See *Dunlop Pneumatic Tyre Co., sup. cit.* at p. 92 *per* Lord Atkinson, at p. 98 *per* Lord Parker.

[97] Lord Parker, *sup. cit.* at p. 99.

[98] *British Glanzstoff Mfg. Co.* v. *General Accident, Fire and Life Ass. Corp.*, 1913 S.C.(H.L.) 1; or if the employer prevents the contractor completing his work: *Percy Bilton Ltd.* v. *Greater London Council* [1982] 2 All E.R. 623 (H.L.).

[99] *Chanthall Investments Ltd.* v. *F. G. Minter Ltd.*, 1976 S.C. 73.

position if delay in completion of building works is caused partly by the employer's fault? It was decided a long time ago in Scotland that the employer could not enforce the clause, but could claim damages.[1] If the reason for the clause was the difficulty in proving loss, the inability to rely on the penalty clause may be an embarrassment. On the other hand, to state expressly that the contractor should pay for the employer's delay would be an unacceptable indemnity. What is needed is a provision for deduction from the amount of liquidated damages to the extent that the delay was caused by the actings of the employer.

54   (4) Although it should not matter whether the term "penalty" or "liquidated damages" is used,[2] the courts have sometimes founded on the words[3]; therefore it is prudent to refer to liquidated damages.

55   (5) There should be an intelligible relationship between the penalty and the possible loss caused by the party in breach.[4] The penalty should not go the wrong way, *i.e.* increase in amount, as the loss decreases.[5] It helps if it is based on a method close to that which would be used to calculate damages.[6] In the context of engineering contracts it has been observed, that the rate of liquidated damages[7]:

> "should never be chosen at random without careful investigation of the likely financial cost of delay to the employer. The net loss of business profits may be used as the basis for calculation in the case of a commercial structure which the employer is to occupy, or the net profit rental which will be lost where the property is to be let (not the gross profit, save in so far as overheads will be incurred even though the building is not complete). In the case of public works where delay will not cause any direct loss of revenue to the employer, the current rate of interest on the capital invested is often taken."

Where pre-estimate of damages is virtually impossible, it may be necessary to choose an arbitrary amount. If so, it is wise to take a moderate figure,[8] but not a figure so low that breach becomes more attractive than performance. Papers showing how the liquidated damages were calculated should be preserved.

156   (6) The provision of £X for each day's delay is the most common formula in a wide range of contracts from charterparties to building con-

---

[1] *McElroy & Sons* v. *Tharsis Sulphur and Copper Co.* (1877) 5 R. 161–rvd. on another point (1878) 5 R.(H.L.) 171; see also *Peak Construction (Liverpool)* v. *McKinney Foundations* [1971] C.L.Y. 999.

[2] *Robertson* v. *Driver's Trs.* (1881) 8 R. 555 at p. 562 *per* Lord Young; *Lord Elphinstone* v. *Monkland Iron and Coal Co. Ltd.*, *sup. cit.*; *Clydebank Engineering and Shipbuilding Co.* v. *Castaneda*, *sup. cit.*; *Cameron-Head* v. *Cameron & Co.*, 1919 S.C. 627.

[3] *Page* v. *Sherratt* (1907) 15 S.L.T. 731; *Dingwall* v. *Burnett*, 1912 S.C. 1097.

[4] *Ströms Bruks Aktie Bolag* v. *Hutchison* (1904) 6 F. 486; on appeal (1905) 7 F.(H.L.) 131 (penalty tied to estimated amount of freight, which was intelligible if shipper in breach, but not for shipowner in breach).

[5] *Bridge* v. *Campbell Discount Co.* [1962] A.C. 600.

[6] *Bell Bros. (H.P.) Ltd.* v. *Aitken* 1939 S.C. 577.

[7] M. W. Abrahamson, *Engineering Law and the I.C.E. Contracts* (3rd ed.), p. 137.

[8] *Page* v. *Sherratt* (1907) 15 S.L.T. 731; *Ford Motor Co.* v. *Armstrong* (1915) 31 T.L.R. 267 at p. 268 (references to a "substantial" sum).

tracts. A similar type of provision in which the sum varied with time was in a contract of service.[9] Some restraint of trade and similar obligations provide for lump sums, simply because the obligation may only be breached once, *e.g.* a prohibition on passing on a trade secret.

20–157   (7) It should be clear at what point the liquidated damages clause starts to operate and when, if it runs for a period, liability under it ceases. This may not be easy. Is it clear, for example, what is meant by "completion of the works" or "erection of the building"? A building may be erected but not complete.[10] The works may have minor defects in quality which might have existed even if there had been no delay.

20–158   (8) A particular problem arises if, as is now common in long-term contracts, the price payable under the contract is subject to a price increase or price variation clause. The contractor's delay may result in a claim by the contractor for a price increase. During the delay the cost of labour and materials has risen and the price variation clause operates. The delay has increased the cost to the employer, but the liquidated damages clause provides for all his loss and does not alter with price changes. In effect the contractor benefits, to an extent, from the delay. The relationship between a price variations clause and the liquidated damages clause needs to be thought about. Denying the contractor the price increase is one solution, but what if there is a price decrease? Having a liquidated damages clause which fluctuates in the same way as a price variation clause (*e.g.* being tied to an index or to costs) is a possibility, but it requires sophisticated drafting.[11]

20–159   (9) The other clause in the contract which may need to be adjusted to the liquidated damages clause, is the arbitration clause. Does the arbiter have power to decide (a) if the liquidated damages clause is penal, or not; (b) whether the clause applies to the breach; and (c) the amount due under the clause?[12] It is best to have express provision on what is desired.

---

[9] *Paterson* v. *South West of Scotland Electricity Board*, 1950 S.C. 583 (sum tied to actuarial value of salary and pension).

[10] See this problem with an irritancy clause—*Anderson* v. *Valentine*, 1957 S.L.T.(Notes) 27.

[11] The amount would have to be closely tied to the contract or it would run into the problems of an indefinite and fluctuating sum which would not be a genuine pre-estimate of loss, as in *Public Works Commrs.* v. *Hills* [1906] A.C. 368.

[12] *Beattie & Son* v. *Ritchie & Co.* (1901) 9 S.L.T. 2 is an example of a problem.

CHAPTER 21

SPECIFIC IMPLEMENT

HISTORY

21-01 The origins of specific implement are obscure. Like much of the Scots law of remedies there is lack of accurate historical analysis. It appears that implement, which failing damages, was recognised at an early date. The *Acta Dominorum Concilii* record several examples of implement.[1] Actions to enforce contracts are to be found in the records of the Court of the Official in pre-Reformation Scotland.[2] The practice of registering obligations in the books of church courts was of early origin. Contracts which were registered would usually contain a clause submitting to the jurisdiction of a particular court, and with a penalty of excommunication in the event of non-fulfilment.[3]

21-02 It is obvious that an obligation can be to do something other than make payment of money. It can be, for example, to grant a conveyance or lease or to deliver goods.[4] These might be called obligations *ad factum praestandum* although that term appears to have been limited by Lord President Dunedin to the restricted class of cases in which specific implement will be granted.[5] Stair and Bell stated that a creditor could pursue performance of an obligation *in faciendo*.[6] According to Bell,[7] the obligation was enforceable by imprisonment or damages, unless it was incapable of performance, when damages only were allowed.

21-03 The mystery surrounding the history of specific implement arises because, although it may often have been sought, there is little discussion of it in reported cases and books until the nineteenth century. In a case in 1877 a sheriff could state that there were few reported instances of specific implement involving contracts.[8] One reason for this might be that although a court may order performance of a contract it did not, at common law, compel performance except in a few cases where someone else could perform the contract. The sanction for a refusal to comply with the order of the court was imprisonment. Not only might this fail to

---

[1] A.D.C., Vol. III, (1501–03) (Stair Soc., Vol. 8), pp. 240, 241, 307, 444.
[2] *The Court of the Official* (Stair Soc., Vol. 34), pp. 86, 88.
[3] *Ibid.*, p. 88.
[4] Ersk., III, i, 2 and 3.
[5] *Union Electric Co. Ltd.* v. *Holman & Co.*, 1913 S.C. 954 at p. 958.
[6] Stair, I, xvii, 16; Bell, *Comm.*, I, 335 (5th ed.), 352 (7th ed.).
[7] *Sup. cit.*
[8] *Glasgow and Inverarary Steamboat Co.* v. *D. & W. Henderson* (1877) 1 Guth.Sh.Cas. 184; examples would have been *Corbett* v. *Robertson* (1872) 10 M. 329; *Aberdeen* v. *Wilson* (1872) 10 M. 971; Cases involving leases include *Smith* v. *Robertson* (1831) 9 S. 751; *Seaforth Trs.* v. *Macaulay* (1844) 7 D. 180; *Whitelaw* v. *Fulton* (1871) 10 M. 27.

produce performance of the contract, it was a remedy which the courts were reluctant to grant. An award of damages could be more appropriate.[9]

SPECIFIC IMPLEMENT AND DAMAGES

21-04 The common form of crave or conclusion seeks specific implement which failing damages. It is in the form[10] "for decree ordaining the defenders, in implement of the contract between the parties dated . . . to deliver . . . to the pursuer and that within such short space of time as the Court may appoint; and failing the defenders so delivering the same to grant decree against them for payment to the pursuer of the sum of £   with interest thereon etc."

21-05 The terms of the order for specific implement must be precise. It is incompetent to seek an order that the defenders implement the contract. Because the possible consequences of failure to observe the decree is imprisonment the defenders must be made aware of exactly what is being required of them and in what respects there has been a failure to implement. The court would not grant a decree for implement "forthwith," unless it could clearly be complied with as in the case of a single act of delivery of a deed. A time may be fixed by the court for implement.[11]

21-06 It is not necessary to have the alternative conclusion for damages. This alternative is introduced to meet the possibility of the court refusing to order specific implement.[12] An action may seek implement only.[13] Where the obligation is to sign a deed the appropriate course on failure by the defender to implement may be signature by an officer of the court.[14] The sheriff may order the sheriff clerk to execute deeds relating to heritage.[15] When the failure is to prepare a formal deed following missives there may be a remit by the court to an appropriate person who will draft the deed.[16]

---

[9] See *Davidson* v. *Macpherson* (1889) 30 S.L.R. 2, opinion of Lord Young. The Law Reform (Miscellaneous Provisions) (Scotland) Act 1940, s.1 has given the court power to apply remedies other than imprisonment.

[10] See *Widenmeyer* v. *Burn Stewart & Co.*, 1967 S.C. 85; W. J. Dobie, *Sheriff Court Styles*, pp. 8, 101 and 187.

[11] *Middleton* v. *Leslie* (1892) 19 R. 801. An analogy was made with interdict; *Robertson* v. *Cockburn* (1875) 3 R. 21 at p. 23 *per* Lord Justice-Clerk Moncreiff; *Hendry* v. *Marshall* (1878) 5 R. 687; *Munro* v. *Liquidator of Balnagowan Estates Co. Ltd.*, 1949 S.C. 49 *per* Lord President Cooper at p. 55.

[12] *Armour* v. *Martin* (1903) 20 Sh.Ct.Rep. 225.

[13] *Purves* v. *Brock* (1867) 5 M. 1003; *Whitelaw* v. *Fulton* (1871) 10 M. 27; *Ford* v. *Bell Chandler*, 1977 S.L.T.(Sh.Ct.) 90.

[14] *Whyte* v. *Whyte*, 1913 2 S.L.T. 85; *Wallace's C.B.* v. *Wallace*, 1924 S.C. 212; *Pennell's Tr.*, 1928 S.C. 605; *Lennox*, 1950 S.C. 546; *Boag*, 1967 S.C. 322 (all these cases except *Whyte* involved the Inner House).

[15] Law Reform (Miscellaneous Provisions) (Scotland) Act 1985, s.17.

[16] *Erskine* v. *Glendinning* (1871) 9 M. 656; *Wight* v. *Newton*, 1911 S.C. 762.

07 In *Lyle* v. *Smith*,[17] the sheriff decided that damages must be annexed as an alternative to a crave for implement to erect a garage in terms of a contract. It is thought, however, that this is wrong. It is for the pursuer to decide if he is to peril his case on an award of specific implement or nothing. Even when the alternative crave exists the pursuer can insist on implement rather than damages; the defender cannot opt to pay damages.[18] Conversely, if specific implement is refused on grounds other than the inequity of granting it, the ancillary conclusion for damages falls.[19]

COURT'S DISCRETION TO REFUSE SPECIFIC IMPLEMENT

08 In Lord Shand's words[20]:

> "The general rule of our law is that when a party has it in his power to fulfil an obligation which he has undertaken the Court will compel him to do so. But it must always be at the discretion of the Court to say whether the remedy of specific implement or one of damages is the proper and suitable remedy in the circumstances."

09 This is an example of the principle that a court of equity may withhold a remedy.[21] In the case of specific implement the prospect of imprisonment was, and to an extent still is, in the background, but there are more general considerations when an obligation can in fact be performed but it would be contrary to public policy to order its performance.

10 Various cases have been suggested in which specific implement will not be ordered.

(1) To enforce an obligation to pay money

11 As a general rule the remedy of a creditor who is refused payment is to obtain a decree for the sum and do diligence which cannot now include imprisonment for debt.[22] A contract to take up and pay for debentures of a company may be enforced by specific implement.[23] An

---

[17] 1954 S.L.T.(Sh.Ct.) 111.

[18] *Stewart* v. *Kennedy* (1890) 17 R.(H.L.) 1 at p. 10 *per* Lord Watson; *Armour* v. *Martin, sup. cit.*; *Mackay* v. *Campbell*, 1966 S.C. 237; 1967 S.C.(H.L.) 53.

[19] *Russell* v. *Menzies* (1904) 20 Sh.Ct.Rep. 41; *Harvey* v. *Smith* (1904) 6 F. 511, opinion of Lord Kinnear.

[20] *Moore* v. *Paterson* (1881) 9 R. 337 at p. 351. See also *Stewart* v. *Kennedy* (1890) 17 R.(H.L.) 1 at p. 10 *per* Lord Watson; *Dampskibaktieselskapet Aurdal* v. *Compania de Navegacion La Estrella*, 1916 S.C. 882; *Salaried Staff London Loan Co. Ltd.* v. *Swears and Wells Ltd.*, 1985 S.L.T. 326.

[21] *Grahame* v. *Mags. of Kirkcaldy* (1882) 9 R.(H.L.) 91 at pp. 91 and 92 *per* Lord Watson; *Wilson* v. *Pottinger*, 1908 S.C. 580.

[22] Debtors (Scotland) Act 1880, s.4.

[23] Companies Act 1985, s.195. See also *Beardmore & Co.* v. *Barry*, 1928 S.C. 101; 1928 S.C.(H.L.) 47. A decree ordaining the payment of money to the company could not be enforced by imprisonment: Debtors (Scotland) Act 1880, s.4. On the background to the company legislation see G. W. Wilton, *Company Law and Practice in Scotland* (1912), p. 201.

order for consignation of money in court may be enforced as a decree for specific implement.[24]

(2) To enforce an obligation against the Crown

Specific implement will not be granted against the Crown.[25]

(3) To do the impossible

Specific implement will not be decreed unless it is possible for the party to comply with the decree.[26] It has been said to be "inconceivable" that a court would grant a decree *ad factum praestandum* in the knowledge that performance was impossible.[27] What is impossible will depend on the circumstances. It may be relevant for the court to inquire into whether there are sufficient funds to implement an obligation.[28] However, when furniture was subject to sequestration for rent this did not prevent a decree for delivery of the furniture on the grounds that the debtor could have raised money and paid off the landlord.[29] The debtor was in financial difficulties, and it is not clear from the report that raising money was a realistic possibility.

21–12   A person could by contract undertake to do something which is beyond his power. A court will not order him to do what in fact he cannot do.[30] On the other hand, if it is possible for the defender to do what is requested, *e.g.* grant a disposition in terms of missives, it is not an objection to specific implement that the result will be embarrassing to the defender, *e.g.* because he would become in breach of *other* contracts or the terms of other dispositions.[31] A labour dispute can make performance impossible.[32]

(4) To do something which does not correspond with the terms of the contract

Persons "cannot be liable to a decree for specific performance, except by virtue of their contract."[33] So when tenants quit property at the end

---

[24] *Mackenzie* v. *Balerno Paper Mill Co.* (1883) 10 R. 1147.
[25] Crown Proceedings Act 1947, s.21(1). On the position prior to the Act see *Carlton Hotel Co.* v. *Lord Advocate*, 1921 S.C. 237. On the problem of interim orders see *Mags. of Ayr* v. *Sec. of State for Scotland*, 1965 S.C. 394.
[26] *McArthur* v. *Lawson* (1877) 4 R. 1134 at p. 1136 *per* Lord President Inglis; *Moore* v. *Paterson* (1881) 9 R. 337 at p. 351 *per* Lord Shand; *Stewart* v. *Kennedy* (1890) 17 R.(H.L.) 1 at p. 9 *per* Lord Watson; *Macleod* v. *Alexander Sutherland Ltd.*, 1977 S.L.T.(Notes) 44.
[27] *Bell Bros. (H.P.) Ltd.* v. *Reynolds*, 1945 S.C. 213 at p. 216 *per* Lord President Normand.
[28] *Beardmore & Co.* v. *Barry*, 1928 S.C. 101; 1928 S.C.(H.L.) 47.
[29] *Rudman* v. *Jay & Co.*, 1908 S.C. 552.
[30] See *Winans* v. *Mackenzie* (1883) 10 R. 941 at p. 946 *per* Lord Ordinary (Kinnear).
[31] *Plato* v. *Newman*, 1950 S.L.T.(Notes) 29.
[32] *Glasgow and Inverarary Steamboat Co.* v. *D. & W. Henderson* (1877) 1 Guth.Sh.Cas. 184. See on this case Gloag, p. 657. It may be that Gloag's criticism of this decision overlooks the problems caused by a strike.
[33] *Sinclair* v. *Caithness Flagstone Co. Ltd.* (1898) 25 R. 703 at p. 706 *per* Lord Kinnear.

of a lease, they could not be ordered to go back on to the property and execute works which should have been done during the currency of the lease. The landlord's remedy was damages.[34] Specific implement seeks implement of the contract, not an undoing of what has been done in breach of contract for which the remedy is damages.[35]

(5) Generally if implement is thought to be inequitable

Although the court's discretion to refuse implement is not limited by categories, there are two instances where implement is possible and in terms of the contract but the courts have refused to grant implement. The first of these is in contracts involving *delectus personae*. The court will not force someone to enter into partnership[36] or to accept someone as an employee.[37] In Lord Pitman's words: "the law will not compel me to have my dinner cooked by a cook that I have wrongfully discharged or transferred to some other establishment."[38]

The second instance is contracts in which there is no *pretium affectionis*. When goods are sold and are readily available in the open market the purchaser's remedy is to supply himself at the seller's expense.[39]

THE REMEDY FOR FAILURE TO IMPLEMENT

3   The court may grant a decree ordaining work to be carried out at the sight of someone appointed by the court.[40] A creditor who has obtained a decree of specific implement can charge the debtor to perform. On failure of the debtor to perform the creditor may apply to the court for a warrant for the debtor's imprisonment. The procedure under the Debtors (Scotland) Act 1838 involved registration of the charge and application by bill or minute for a warrant to imprison.[41] Since the Law Reform (Miscellaneous Provisions) (Scotland) Act 1940, section 1 imposes an obligation on the creditor to satisfy the court that there is wilful refusal by the debtor, the simple procedures under the 1838 Act are inappropriate. The procedure will probably be by minute in the orig-

---

[34] *Ibid.*

[35] *A. & J. Faill* v. *Wilson* (1899) 36 S.L.R. 941.

[36] *McArthur* v. *Lawson* (1877) 4 R. 1134; *Pert* v. *Bruce*, 1937 S.L.T. 475.

[37] *McMillan* v. *Free Church* (1861) 23 D. 1314 at p. 1345 *per* Lord Deas; *Skerret* v. *Oliver* (1896) 23 R. 468 (Lord Ordinary); *Cormack* v. *Keith & Murray* (1893) 20 R. 177 at p. 980; *Murray* v. *Dumbarton C.C.*, 1935 S.L.T. 239.

[38] *Murray* v. *Dumbarton C.C.*, *sup. cit.* at p. 240. We are not here concerned with statutory rights which may lead to reinstatement.

[39] *Union Electric Co. Ltd.* v. *Holman & Co.*, 1913 S.C. 954 at p. 958 *per* Lord President Dunedin; *Sutherland* v. *Montrose Shipbuilding Co.* (1860) 22 D. 665 at p. 671 *per* Lord Cowan; *Davidson* v. *Macpherson* (1889) 30 S.L.R. 2 at p. 6 *per* Lord Young.

[40] *Brock* v. *Buchanan* (1851) 13 D. 1069; *Northern Lighthouses Commrs.* v. *Edmonston* (1908) 16 S.L.T. 439; and see cases on signature to deeds and preparation of deeds, para. 21–06, nn. 14, 16.

[41] See Debtors (Scotland) Act 1838; Sheriff Courts (Scotland) Extracts Act 1892.

inal action and a diet will be appointed for the attendance of the debtor.[42]

21–14   The Debtors (Scotland) Act 1880, section 4, abolished imprisonment for debt with certain exceptions which included imprisonment under any decree or obligation *ad factum praestandum*. The Law Reform (Miscellaneous Provisions) (Scotland) Act 1940, section 1, limited imprisonment to circumstances in which the court was satisfied that there was wilful refusal to comply with the decree. The maximum term of imprisonment is six months. The court has a discretion to grant other orders in lieu of imprisonment. There is specific mention of the ordering of payment of a specified sum to the creditor and an order to search for moveables. It is an open question whether under this section the court could fine a debtor. This might appear to be an appropriate remedy in some circumstances, particularly if the debtor is a company or trade union. It does not, by itself, achieve performance of the contract or compensation for the creditor, but neither does imprisonment.

21–15   The inability to imprison a corporate body or a debtor outwith the jurisdiction has been used to justify the incompetence of granting a decree of specific implement in these cases.[43] However, in *Ford* v. *Bell Chandler*[44] Sheriff Principal Gimson pointed out that the 1940 Act allowed alternatives to imprisonment. He, therefore, could see no incompetence in seeking implement against a company registered in Venezuela and having a place of business in England. His opinion is concerned with the problem of a debtor furth of the jurisdiction. Its logic is equally applicable to any debtor which is a company.

---

[42] Dobie, *Sheriff Court Practice*, p. 284.
[43] Gloag, p. 659; *Lochgelly Iron and Coal Co.* v. *North British Ry. Co.*, 1913 1 S.L.T. 405 at p. 414 *per* Lord Kinnear; *Macleod* v. *Alexander Sutherland Ltd.*, 1977 S.L.T.(Notes) 44 (company in receivership).
[44] 1977 S.L.T.(Sh.Ct.) 90.

Chapter 22

PAYMENT

Money

01 The law makes many distinctions which turn on the concept of money. The lawyer uses "money" in a different way from the economist. For example, bank accounts are debts to a lawyer but they function as money for the economist.[1] Within the lawyer's boundaries the meaning of money varies with its context, but it is often important to decide whether money or an obligation to pay money is involved.

02 Examples of the importance of the distinctions which have been mentioned are these:

(1) Sale and barter

It is a distinguishing feature of sale that a thing is given in exchange for money. Stair saw the origins of money in the transition from commerce based on barter to the use of common tokens of exchange or money.[2] The Sale of Goods Act 1979 defines a contract of sale in terms of the transfer of property in goods "for a money consideration, called the price."[3] When money is not involved the contract may be a barter.[4] When there is an exchange of goods, but also the payment of a price, there has been held to be a contract of sale.[5]

(2) Specific implement

Specific implement will be refused where the obligation is the payment of money.[6]

(3) Loan

A loan of money and a loan of moveables each has different incidents. For example a loan of money over £100 Scots must be proved by writ or oath; a loan of moveables is proveable by parole evidence.[7] The entitlement to interest may arise with a loan of money but this concept is inappropriate to the lending of a moveable.

---

[1] See generally, F. A. Mann, *The Legal Aspect of Money* (4th ed., 1982).
[2] Stair, I, xiv, 1.
[3] s.2(1).
[4] *Widenmeyer* v. *Burn, Stewart & Co.*, 1967 S.C. 85; *Urquhart* v. *Wylie*, 1953 S.L.T.(Sh.Ct.) 87; *Ballantyne* v. *Durant*, 1983 S.L.T.(Sh.Ct.) 38.
[5] *Sneddon* v. *Durant*, 1982 S.L.T.(Sh.Ct.) 39.
[6] See para. 21–11.
[7] Walker and Walker, *Evidence*, paras. 118 and 145.

(4) Damages and interest

Failure to perform an obligation *ad factum praestandum* may give rise to a claim for damages. Failure to pay money when it is due raises special problems. As a general rule any loss may be compensated by interest, but not by damages.[8]

(5) Diligence

There is doubt about the extent to which money can be poinded.[9] Debts or claims for payment cannot be poinded; the proper diligence is arrestment.[10]

(6) Cheques, bills and notes

It is part of the definition of a bill of exchange, of a cheque and of a promissory note that these documents provide for payment of "a sum certain in money."[11] A promise to deliver goods would take the document outwith the statutory definitions.

MONEY AND THE OBLIGATION TO PAY MONEY

22–03 Money can be distinguished from the obligation to pay money. Money can be coins or notes. The obligation to pay money can be the liability of a debtor to his creditor. A bill of exchange illustrates the difference. It can give rise to an obligation to pay money, but it is not money. The strictest legal definition of money is what is regarded as legal tender.[12]

22–04 A bank note is a promissory note issued by bankers, payable to the bearer on demand, and transferred by delivery.[13] A bank note must be payable on demand.[14] Bank notes can only be issued by bankers who were issuing notes on May 6, 1844.[15] A bank note issued in Scotland must be for payment of a sum in pounds sterling, without any fractional parts of a pound.[16] A bank note for less than one pound made or issued in Scotland is void.[17] All bank notes issued by the Bank of England and of less than five pounds are legal tender in Scotland.[17a] Scottish bank notes are not legal tender. At the time of writing the lowest denomina-

---

[8] For the details see paras. 20–78 *et seq.*
[9] See Graham Stewart, *Diligence*, p. 340.
[10] *op. cit.* p. 343.
[11] Bills of Exchange Act 1882, ss.3, 73 and 83.
[12] But the definition is too strict for some purposes. Foreign money is not legal tender, but it may be money.
[13] See Stamp Act 1854, s.11.
[14] Bank Notes (Scotland) Act 1765, s.1.
[15] Bank Charter Act 1844, s.10.
[16] Bank Notes (Scotland) Act 1845, s.5.
[17] *Ibid.*, s.16.
[17a] Currency and Bank Notes Act 1954, s.1.

tion of note issued by the Bank of England is five pounds. The result is that no bank note presently issued is legal tender in Scotland.

5 Coins are legal tender as follows[18]:

(1) gold coins, for payment of any amount, subject to a weight standard for the coins,

(2) coins of cupro-nickel or silver of denominations of more than 10 pence, for payment of any amount not exceeding £10.

(3) coins of cupro-nickel or silver of denominations of not more than 10 pence for payment of any amount not exceeding £5.

(4) coins of bronze, for payment of any amount not exceeding 20 pence.

6 Royal proclamation may vary these figures and regulate the introduction of new coins.[19]

7 A creditor cannot refuse payment in legal tender. Legal tender requires that the exact sum of the debt must be tendered, without the need for change.

PAYMENT

8 Just as the concept of "money" varies with the context, so also "payment" is a flexible word. In its primary sense it means the transfer of money. Yet with one of the common methods of making payment, the issue of a cheque, the law makes receipt of the cheque by the creditor the time of payment (provided that the cheque is subsequently honoured). If "transfer" were the test of payment the law would look to the actions of the banker on whom the cheque was drawn.[20] Nor is it easy to discern an actual *transfer* of money when a debt is extinguished by compensation or set off. The concept of transfer itself has been undergoing a change. Although the physical movement of coins or notes may take place, there are also payments effected by charge or credit cards, giros, standing orders, direct debits or other instructions given to computers.[21]

---

[18] Coinage Act 1971, s.2, as amended by Currency Act 1983, s.1(3).

[19] s.3, 1971 Act as amended. The specification and design for the £1 coin and the 20p coin were determined by a series of proclamations. £1 coins are legal tender for any amount. See Proclamation dated April 20, 1983.

[20] As the law does in considering the duty of the collecting banker to his customer. *Barclays Bank plc* v. *Bank of England* [1985] 1 All E.R. 385.

[21] A useful survey of the methods of making payment is in *Banking Services and the Consumer*, National Consumer Council (1983) s.3. From this it appears that a huge majority (nearly 90%) of payments are still made in cash. After cash, cheques are by far the most common method of making payments. The "cashless society" is a remote prospect despite the changes in banking technology (some of which are designed to make cash more readily available).

22–09   METHODS OF MAKING PAYMENT

(1) Legal tender

A creditor, in the absence of agreement to the contrary, is entitled to insist on payment in legal tender.[22] A creditor may expressly or impliedly authorise payment in a form other than legal tender and it is thought that this authority may easily be implied, at least when payment is offered in a common form such as Scottish banknotes or by cheque. The creditor may ask for payment by cheque or credit card or fail to object to tender of a payment on the ground that it is not legal tender[23] or may pay the cheque into his account.[24]

On the other hand a creditor may expressly or impliedly insist on payment in a certain form of legal tender, *e.g.* a gas meter or slot machine which should be used only for specified coins. If the money is subsequently stolen without the negligence of the payer, he is not liable.[25]

(2) Cheque

A cheque, if accepted, is conditional payment. If the cheque is dishonoured the debt revives.[26] A cheque is payment when it is received. Even if it is received after banking hours on the day when payment is due, there has been payment on that day.[27] According to some authority, when the creditor authorises payment by a cheque sent through the post, payment is made when the debtor posts the cheque in a letter to the creditor.[28]

When a cheque is proved to have been granted by a debtor to a creditor the presumption is that it was granted in payment of the debt. Parole evidence is competent to show the purpose for which a cheque was granted.[29]

---

[22] *Glasgow Pavilion Ltd.* v. *Motherwell* (1903) 6 F. 116 at p. 119, *per* Lord Young.

[23] *Holt* v. *National Bank of Scotland Ltd.*, 1927 S.L.T. 484 (cheque refused because it did not include expenses. No exception taken that it was not legal tender).

[24] *Mintons* v. *Hawley & Co.* (1882) 20 S.L.R. 126 at p. 128 *per* Lord Young. On payment by credit transfer as an equivalent of cash, see *The Brimnes* [1975] Q.B. 929; *A/S Awilco of Oslo* v. *Fulvia Sp.A. di Navigazione of Cagliari* [1981] 1 All E.R. 652 (H.L.).

[25] *Edmundson* v. *Longton Corp.* (1902) 19 T.L.R. 15; *Scottish Gas Board* v. *Fisher*, 1960 S.L.T.(Sh.Ct.) 51.

[26] *Bolt and Nut Co. (Tipton)* v. *Rowlands Nicholls & Co.* [1964] 2 Q.B. 10; *McLaren's Tr.* v. *Argylls*, 1915 2 S.L.T. 241.

[27] *Glasgow Pavilion Ltd.* v. *Motherwell, sup. cit.*; *Leggat Bros.* v. *Gray*, 1908 S.C. 67; *Cumming* v. *Mackie*, 1973 S.C. 278. The same rule applies to payment by bank notes.

[28] *Norman* v. *Ricketts* (1886) 3 T.L.R. 182; *Thairlwall* v. *Great Northern Ry.* [1910] 2 K.B. 509; *Thorey* v. *Wylie & Lockhead* (1890) 6 Sh.Ct.Rep. 201.

[29] *Nicoll* v. *Reid* (1878) 6 R. 216; *Thompson* v. *Jolly Carters Inn*, 1972 S.C. 215. On the intriguing problems of travellers cheques see Chitty, *Contract*, paras. 2555 *et seq.*

(3) Standing orders and credit transfers

Payment by "standing order" is a method in which a customer, before payment is due, grants his bank authority to make payment. The customer's bank makes the payment in the form of a transfer of credit. The payee may then credit his customer's account. Practice amongst payees varies.[30] Some credit the customer's account when the payment is initiated, some when it is received, and others when it enters the payee's books. It is an open question when, in law, the payment is made. Usually the payee has authorised payment in this manner and may be barred from objecting to normal delays arising from the operation of the system and, in particular, from delays caused by the payee's system for reconciliation of payments. In some instances it may be necessary to determine the precise moment of payment (*e.g.* if the payer is sequestrated or put into liquidation). It is probably the case that payment is made at the moment the payee or his bank secures the transfer from the payer's bank. If payer and payee bank at the same bank the time of payment may be the irrevocable decision by the bank to make the transfer.[31]

A credit transfer may be made at the request of the payer in implement of a contractual obligation to pay the payee. "Payment" in terms of the contract may mean cash or the equivalent of cash. When there was an irrevocable transfer of funds between banks by telex it was held that there had not been payment under a charterparty since, under Italian law, the funds transferred could not be used immediately to earn interest and could only be withdrawn subject to payment of interest.[32]

(4) Direct debits

The difficulties the standing order system creates for payees led to the introduction of the direct debit scheme. The feature of the scheme is that the payee requests payment. He, therefore, has more control over payment and more quickly appreciates the fact of non-payment. The time of payment is governed by the same factors as apply to standing

---

[30] *Banking Services and the Consumer, sup. cit.*

[31] See *The Brimnes, sup. cit.*; *Momm* v. *Barclays Bank International Ltd.* [1977] Q.B. 790; *Delbrueck & Co.* v. *Barclays Bank International Ltd.* [1976] 2 Lloyd's Rep. 341. See also *Mardorf Peach Co. Ltd.* v. *Attica Sea Corp. of Liberia* [1977] A.C. 850. The practice of banks however can introduce uncertainties about the exact moment at which a credit transfer is made. It is also important to consider the authority which the banks involved have to make or accept payment on behalf of their customers. See R. M. Goode, *Payment Obligations in Commercial and Financial Transactions* (1983), Chap. IV; *Barclays Bank plc* v. *Bank of England* [1985] 1 All E.R. 385.

[32] *A/S Awilco of Oslo* v. *Fulvia S.p.A. di Navigazione of Cagliari* [1981] 1 All E.R. 652 (H.L.).

orders. The payee commonly enters into an indemnity with the banks which regulates the consequences of erroneous payments.

(5) Giros

There are two giro systems in the United Kingdom. The bank giro system has been in operation since 1960. The Post Office giro system was introduced in 1968. The system enables money to be paid into the payee's account. Payments can be made from the payer's bank account or by cheque or cash. Difficult, and as yet unresolved questions, arise as to when payment is made. It is too simple to state that payment is made when the money reaches the payee's account. In some circumstances the bank or post office which first receives the money, or accepts instructions to remit it, may be acting as the agent of the payee.[33]

(6) Credit cards

A credit card in the form normally used by banks[34] involves three parties in its use, i.e. the customer, the bank and the supplier of goods and services. The bank enters into an agreement with the supplier who undertakes to supply the customer. The bank pays the supplier on the rendering of a sales slip bearing the imprint of the card. A separate contract between the bank and the customer regulates the credit card and terms of payment applying to the customer. This agreement will almost always be subject to the controls of the Consumer Credit Act 1974 unless the customer is a body corporate. The Act imposes a limit on the customer's liability in the case of fraud and theft[35]; requires the provision of information about interest rates[36] and makes the bank jointly and severally liable with the supplier for misrepresentation or breach of contract.[37]

(7) Debit cards

A debit card enables a bank customer to debit his account by electronic means in return for cash, goods or services. The card may be used at automated teller machines (ATMs) or at a machine operating electronic funds transfer at point of sale (EFTPOS). No legislation specifically covers the use of these cards. If the card is used to obtain credit its use may be covered by the Consumer Credit Act 1974[38] and the position

---

[33] See Chitty, Contract, paras. 2644–2655.
[34] e.g. Barclaycard, Access, Visa, Trustcard. Credit cards issued by some shops may only involve two parties. The shop is supplier of goods and services and also provider of credit.
[35] ss.83 and 84 and regulations made thereunder.
[36] ss.20, 44, 52 and 60 and regulations made thereunder.
[37] s.75.
[38] It may be a credit token under s.14.

is then similar to a credit card. In other cases the protection of the Act does not apply.

To whom should Payment be Made?

0 Payment is valid if made to the creditor or to the creditor's agent who has authority to receive payment. The agent may have actual or apparent authority to receive payment.[39] On the other hand the debtor may have express notice that payment must be direct to the principal.[40] When an agent acts for more than one party there can be dispute as to whether he is the agent of the creditor for the purposes of receiving payment.[41] The partner of a firm who made a contract can discharge payments under it.[42] The authority of a recipient bank to receive payment is part of the requirement for the operation of schemes for standing orders and direct debits. Doubts about who is the principal of a bank can pose problems with giros and inter-bank transfers. These doubts arise because a bank may act for its customer or for another bank and thus, perhaps, for the other bank's customer. A bank receiving payment may, therefore, be acting for its customer, for itself, for another bank or for another bank's customer.[43]

Where should Payment be Made?

11 In general, payment should be made at the residence or place of business of the creditor.[44] The place of payment depends, however, on the express or implied terms of the contract. Employers do not in normal practice make payment of wages at the residence of their employees. It may be readily implied that payment should be at the employer's premises,[45] or there may be express agreement for payment at the employee's bank.

12 The contract may specify the place of payment, *e.g.*: "Payment of said hire to be made in London, to the First National Bank."[46] It is a question of construction as to whether there can be another place of pay-

---

[39] *International Sponge Importers Ltd.* v. *Watt & Sons*, 1911 S.C.(H.L.) 57.
[40] *Ell Bros.* v. *Sneddon* (1929) 45 Sh.Ct.Rep. 351.
[41] *Falconer* v. *Dalrymple* (1870) 9 M. 212; *Clark & Macdonald* v. *Schulze* (1902) 4 F. 448.
[42] *Nicoll* v. *Reid* (1878) 6 R. 216.
[43] See R. M. Goode, *sup. cit.*; *Barclays Bank plc* v. *Bank of England, sup. cit.* at p. 392 *per* Bingham J.
[44] *Haughhead Coal Co.* v. *Gallocher* (1903) 11 S.L.T. 156.
[45] *Riley* v. *Holland (William) & Sons Ltd.* [1911] 1 K.B. 1029 at p. 1031 *per* Cozens-Hardy M.R. (A workmen's compensation case).
[46] *Afovos Shipping Co. S.A.* v. *Pagnan* [1983] 1 All E.R. 449 (H.L.).

ment. There can be more than one place of payment and furthermore a place of payment may be intended to change. The draftsman may have provided for the possibilities that the creditor may change its place of business, may leave the country, or may change its banking arrangements.

TIME OF PAYMENT

22–13 Time of payment is not normally of the essence of a contract.[47] Stipulating a date for payment does not make time of the essence. A contract may, however, by its express terms, require punctual payment on or by a certain day, in which case the courts will apply the term strictly. There is no rule of equity which allows payment in these cases to be a few days late, and the courts are slow to imply waiver of the terms of the contract.[48] The result of failure to make "punctual payment" will depend on the contract which may specify that the contract may be terminated or that the whole of a balance of a loan shall become repayable. It has been observed that in principle money lent is repayable on demand. This is overcome by the express provisions of a loan contract which delay repayment.[49]

22–14 When payment is due "on demand" a creditor must give the debtor time to get the money from some convenient place. The phrase "on demand" must receive a reasonable construction. It does not mean that the debtor must make instant payment. He may have to go to his bank. But he is not allowed time to negotiate a deal which might produce the money. If he has not got the money and cannot conveniently obtain it, he cannot pay "on demand."[50]

22–15 It is incompetent to raise an action or use diligence on a debt not yet due, unless the debtor is *vergens ad inopiam* or *in meditatione fugae*.[51] A contractual requirement to pay "on demand" may make the "demand" a condition precedent for the enforcement of the obligation.[52] When a floating charge required that a notice of indebtedness be signed by certain officials, a demand which was incorrectly signed was invalid, with the consequences that the appointment of a receiver was null.[53]

---

[47] Scc paras. 14–81, 14–92.
[48] *Gatty* v. *Maclaine*, 1921 S.C.(H.L.) 1; *Kennedy* v. *Begg Kennedy & Elder Ltd.*, 1954 S.L.T.(Sh.Ct.) 103; *Mardorf Peach & Co. Ltd.* v. *Attica Sea Carrier Corp. of Liberia* [1977] A.C. 850 (it was assumed that if payment turns out to be due into a bank account on a non-banking day it must be made not later than the previous banking day).
[49] *Kennedy* v. *Begg Kennedy & Elder Ltd.*, *sup. cit.*
[50] *R. A. Cripps & Son Ltd.* v. *Wickenden* [1973] 2 All E.R. 606.
[51] *Crear* v. *Morrison* (1882) 9 R. 890; *Hodgmac Ltd.* v. *Gardiners of Prestwick Ltd.*, 1980 S.L.T.(Sh.Ct.) 68; Graham Stewart, *Diligence*, pp. 16 and 529.
[52] *Royal Bank of Scotland* v. *Brown*, 1982 S.C. 89.
[53] *Elwick Bay Shipping Co. Ltd.* v. *Royal Bank of Scotland Ltd.*, 1982 S.L.T. 62.

6   Under the Banking and Financial Dealings Act 1971[54] an obligation to make payment on a bank holiday can be complied with on a following day.

7   When a payment is made and accepted in advance of the due date neither the creditor nor his trustee in sequestration can insist on further payment on the due date.[55]

How Much has to be Paid?

18   Payment to the creditor may be conditional on the creditor performing all or some of the creditor's obligations. Under the principle of mutuality of obligations the debtor may withhold payment if the creditor is in breach.[56] The creditor need not accept a partial payment.[57]

19   The contract will fix the amount of the payment or the law may imply a reasonable sum.[58] *Prima facie* the creditor is entitled to be paid in the nominal value of the currency of account without regard to changes in the value of the currency internally (*e.g.* because of inflation) or externally (*e.g.* because of fluctuations in exchange rates).[59] This is the principle of nominalism. There are two possible qualifications to the principle. In certain instances, which have not yet arisen for decision, considerable changes in the value of currency may produce frustration of the contract.[60] Further, and of more practical importance, the contract may expressly attempt to avoid the nominalistic principle.[61] The traditional method of doing so was the gold clause.

20   In a gold clause the debtor undertook to pay such amount of a specified currency as would purchase the gold equivalent of the debt at the time of the contract. The obligation was not to pay in gold, but to pay according to the value of gold.[62] Gold is no longer used to fix the value of national currencies. Accordingly, other methods have been adopted to link the sum payable under the contract to factors external to the contract.

---

[54] s.1(4). See also the treatment of Christmas Day and Good Friday. Under English common law a payment had to be made on a preceding day: *Mardorf Peach & Co. Ltd.* v. *Attica Sea Carriers Corp. of Liberia* [1977] A.C. 850, esp. speech of Lord Salmon. This will apply to days which are not bank holidays under the Act.

[55] *Davidson* v. *Boyd* (1868) 7 M. 77. The purchaser of land which is leased may be in a different position, when he claims rent from the tenant.

[56] See para. 14–25.

[57] *Wilson's Tr.* v. *Watson & Co.* (1900) 2 F. 761 at p. 770 *per* Lord Moncreiff.

[58] See para. 6–45.

[59] *Treseder-Griffin* v. *Co-operative Insurance Society Ltd.* [1956] 2 Q.B. 127; *Pyrmont Ltd.* v. *Schott* [1939] A.C. 145; *Marrache* v. *Ashton* [1943] A.C. 311; *Bonythan* v. *Commonwealth of Australia* [1951] A.C. 201.

[60] See para. 15–16.

[61] See generally, T. A. Downes, "Nomination, Indexation, Excuse and Revalorisation" (1985) 101 L.Q.R. 98.

[62] *Feist* v. *Société Intercommunale Belge d'Electricité* [1934] A.C. 161; *Khoury* v. *Khayat* [1943] A.C. 507. See also *Treseder-Griffin* v. *Co-operative Insurance Ltd.*, *sup. cit.*

22–21   Index-linking clauses are increasingly common. An index such as a cost of living index or a retail price index may be referred to. The index should be chosen with care[63] and precisely identified. For example in the United Kingdom there are several retail price indices and the index normally intended is the "general index of retail prices (all items)." For certain purposes it would be better to use one of the indices of producer prices which reflect the purchase cost to industry.

22–22   Provision should be made for an alternative if the index chosen is abolished. The importance of this is illustrated by the decision of the Bank of England in 1981 to abolish the minimum lending rate and the re-introduction of the rate for one day on January 14, 1985. Some contractual obligations were tied to the minimum lending rate.

22–23   The operation of price or cost index clauses is similar to that of a gold value clause. The sum payable in pounds sterling may be linked to another currency[64]; although that is a gamble on international exchange rates whose fluctuations may bear little relationship to the performance of the contract.

22–24   As an alternative to, or in addition to indexing, there may be price review clauses. The periodic review of rents is a familiar feature of commercial leases. There is a growing amount of experience in the drafting of such review clauses, including the factors to be taken into account in fixing the revised rent,[65] the mechanism, by service of a notice or otherwise, which "triggers" the review,[66] and the period for which the increased rent is due.[67] Similar problems may arise with price review clauses in commercial contracts.

In *Superior Overseas Development Corporation and Phillips Petroleum (U.K.) Co. Ltd.* v. *British Gas Corporation*[68] there was a problem of the definition of "substantial economic hardship" which brought into

---

[63] The disadvantage of price indices is that they are for a large range of goods and services and for the whole of the country, while a contract is usually concerned with costs of a limited range of products in a small area. The national cost of milk, eggs and other consumables of daily life may bear no relation to the cost of supplying materials to construct a warehouse on a Scottish island.

[64] *Multiservice Bookbinding Ltd.* v. *Marden* [1979] Ch. 84. In *The Nai Genova and The Nai Superba* [1983] 2 Lloyd's Rep. 233; [1984] 1 Lloyd's Rep. 353, an escalation clause provided for base figure U.S.$ to be increased by reference to Italian inflation. The result was that about twice as much was payable compared to what would have been due if the base figure had been in Italian lira.

[65] *Ponsford* v. *H.M.S. Aerosols Ltd.* [1979] A.C. 63; *Cuff* v. *J. and F. Stone Property Co. Ltd.* [1979] A.C. 87 (note); *Lear* v. *Blizzard* [1983] 3 All E.R. 662.

[66] *Weller* v. *Akehurst* [1981] 3 All E.R. 411; *Amherst* v. *James Walker Goldsmith and Silversmith Ltd.* [1983] Ch. 305; *Metrolands Investments Ltd.* v. *I. H. Dewhurst Ltd.* [1985] 3 All E.R. 206; *Scottish Development Agency* v. *Morrisons Holdings Ltd.*, 1986 S.L.T. 59.

[67] *Torminster Properties Ltd.* v. *Green* [1983] 2 All E.R. 457; *South Tottenham Land Securities Ltd.* v. *R. & A. Millett (Shops) Ltd.* [1984] 1 All E.R. 614; on waiver of rights to seek a review see *Banks* v. *Mecca Bookmakers*, 1982 S.C. 7.

[68] [1982] 1 Lloyd's Rep. 262.

operation one of the three factors in a price review. If a contract may be renewed a question can arise as to whether a price escalation clause remains in force during the new period.[69]

5   A contract may provide for an increased payment in the event of insolvency or breach or other event. The extent to which this may be an unenforceable penalty is mentioned elsewhere.[70] In *N. G. Napier Ltd.* v. *Crosbie*[71] the creditor was given an option in the event of default by the debtor. The option was to sue for the total outstanding balance or to sue for arrears as they became due. Because of the drafting of the clause, once one option was exercised the creditor could not exercise the other option.

WHICH DEBT IS PAID?—APPROPRIATION

26   Where a person is debtor in more than one debt to the same creditor the problem of appropriation of payments to a particular debt may arise. Subject to any agreement between the parties[72] the rules are these:

(a) The debtor may appropriate the payment at the time of payment to a particular debt. An example is a debtor making a payment into one of several accounts with a bank.[73] A creditor is not bound to accept partial payment and so the debtor may not unilaterally appropriate a part payment to principal rather than interest.[74]

(b) Where a debtor has not appropriated a payment to a particular debt the appropriation is governed by the intention of the creditor, express, presumed or implied.[75] Appropriation may be made by the order of items in the creditor's accounts.[76] The creditor may appropriate "before action and while the debtor is solvent."[77] A creditor may appro-

---

[69] *Finland Steamship Co. Ltd.* v. *Felixstowe Dock and Railway Co.* [1980] 2 Lloyd's Rep. 287.

[70] paras. 20–125 *et seq.*

[71] 1964 S.C. 129.

[72] *e.g.* the elaborate rules applying to appropriation of payments in the credit card scheme, Access. Because they illustrate the problems which a draftsman may wish to avoid they are reproduced here: "Payments to the Bank will be applied on the date credited to your account to repay outstandings in the following order: 1. All interest shown on this and any previous statement. 2. All cash advances shown on this and any previous statement. 3. All purchases shown on previous statements. 4. All purchases shown on this statement. 5. Any cash advances not yet shown on a statement. 6. Any purchases not yet shown on a statement."

On an appropriation between capital and interest according to the terms of the agreement, see *Taylor* v. *Wylie & Lochhead Ltd.*, 1912 S.C. 978.

[73] *Buchanan* v. *Main* (1900) 3 F. 215.

[74] *Wilson's Trs.* v. *Watson & Co.* (1900) 2 F. 761.

[75] *Scott's Trs.* v. *Alexander's Trs.* (1884) 11 R. 407; *Cuthill* v. *Strachan* (1894) 21 R. 549.

[76] *Scott's Trs.* v. *Alexander's Trs.*, *sup. cit.*; *Hay & Co.* v. *Torbet*, 1908 S.C. 781.

[77] *Jackson* v. *Nicoll* (1870) 8 M. 408.

priate payments to a debt which is unsecured, rather than to a debt which is secured, or to a debt which would be an ordinary claim in the debtor's insolvency, rather than to a debt which might be a preferential claim.[78] The "bankruptcy" of the debtor prevents appropriation by the creditor.[79] While "bankruptcy" in this context may mean sequestration or liquidation it is very doubtful if it includes receivership.

(c) Where there is an account current and also where there is no appropriation of payment to discharge any particular debt, the law makes an appropriation according to the order of the items in the account. This rule, commonly known as the rule in *Clayton's Case*,[80] has been accepted as Scots law.[81] It only applies where there is an "account current." Indefinite payments to account of a tradesman's account are not ascribed to items in order of date. These payments go against summation.[82]

22–27   An account current can be between banker and customer,[83] agent and client,[84] mercantile houses,[85] or dealers[86] or buyer and seller.[87] The main characteristic of an account current is that receipts and payments are put into an account in the order of their respective dates. This is normal in a banking account. The order of the account raises a presumption. As it was put in *Clayton's Case*[88]: "In such a case, there is no room for any other appropriation than that which arises from the order in which the receipts and payments take place and are carried into the account. Presumably, it is the sum first paid in, that is first drawn out. It is the first item on the debit side of the account, that is discharged or reduced, by the first item on the credit side. The appropriation is made by the very act of settling the two items against each other."

22–28   The presumption can be rebutted if a different intention can be shown.[89]

22–29   The rules on appropriation are inapplicable if there is a contract between the parties which regulates which debt is paid. "The very idea of appropriation infers something done by one party without the con-

---

[78] Gloag and Irvine, *Rights in Security*, p. 852; *Thomas Love & Sons* v. *A. M. Carmichael Ltd.*, 1953 S.L.T.(Sh.Ct.) 46.
[79] *Ibid.*
[80] (1816) 1 Mer. 572.
[81] *Houston* v. *Speirs* (1829) 3 W. & S. 392; *Royal Bank* v. *Christie* (1841) 2 Rob.App. 118; *Lang* v. *Brown* (1859) 22 D. 113.
[82] *Dougall* v. *Lornie* (1899) 1 F. 1187; *Hay & Co.* v. *Torbet*, 1908 S.C. 781; *Thomas Love & Sons* v. *A. M. Carmichael Ltd.*, *sup. cit.*
[83] *Cuthill* v. *Strachan* (1894) 21 R. 549; *Re Primrose Builders Ltd.* [1950] Ch. 561.
[84] *Lang* v. *Brown* (1859) 22 D. 113.
[85] *Houston* v. *Speirs* (1829) 3 W. & S. 392.
[86] *McKinlay* v. *Watson* (1885) 13 R. 210.
[87] *Scott's Trs.* v. *Alexander's Trs.* (1884) 11 R. 407; *Thomas Montgomery & Sons* v. *Gallacher*, 1982 S.L.T. 138.
[88] (1816) 1 Mer. 572 at p. 608.
[89] *Cory Bros. & Co. Ltd.* v. *Owners of Turkish Steamship "Mecca"* [1897] A.C. 286; *Macdonald Fraser & Co.* v. *Cairns's Exrx.*, 1932 S.C. 699.

sent of the other."[90] Once an appropriation is made the creditor cannot afterwards vary it.[91] The appropriation of payments under a regulated agreement in terms of the Consumer Credit Act is controlled by the Act[92]; and contracting out is forbidden.[93]

WHAT IS THE SOURCE OF PAYMENT?

0 Payment by a third party is, *in dubio*, presumed to be made with the debtor's money. So if a discharge or receipt bears that payment was by one person on behalf of another it is presumed that payment was made by the person whose name was used.[94] There is no need for this presumption unless the matter is *in dubio*. The presumption can be overcome by evidence.[95] When a trustee held two funds and made payments without saying from which fund, payments were equitably apportioned between the funds taking into account the state of the funds.[96]

WHAT WAS THE PURPOSE OF PAYMENT?

1 Payment, as has been observed,[97] is strictly the transfer of money. This transfer may be proved, but the nature of the underlying transaction could be in doubt. Was there a loan, a gift or what? It is not easy to reconcile the judicial *dicta* on the presumptions which arise. There is a presumption against donation, which is particularly strong when the transfer is by a debtor to his creditor. If the recipient of the money alleges donation the onus is on him to prove donation unless there was a natural obligation to provide for him.[98] The most difficult question is whether the receipt of money raises a presumption of loan. There are conflicting dicta.[99] The issue is further confused by the rule that the creditor seeking to establish a loan should prove the loan by writ or oath.[1] If the pursuer alleges loan and the defender donation, the onus on the defender has required him to lead at the proof with the pursuer

---

[90] *Jackson* v. *Nicoll* (1870) 8 M. 408 at p. 412 *per* Lord Kinloch.
[91] *Deeley* v. *Lloyd's Bank Ltd.* [1912] A.C. 756 at p. 783 *per* Lord Shaw; *National Commercial Bank of Scotland Ltd.* v. *Millar's Trs.*, 1964 S.L.T.(Notes) 57 at p. 60 *per* Lord Cameron.
[92] Consumer Credit Act 1974, s.81.
[93] s.173.
[94] Ersk., III, iv, 6.
[95] *Welsh* v. *Welsh's Tr.* (1878) 5 R. 542; *Fairbairn* v. *Fairbairn* (1868) 6 M. 640.
[96] *Beith* v. *Mackenzie* (1875) 3 R. 185.
[97] Walker and Walker, *Evidence*, para. 62.
[98] *Campbell* v. *Macalister* (1827) 5 S.219; *Macleod* v. *Campbell* (1889) 17 R. 255.
[99] See Walker and Walker, *sup. cit.*, n. 74—to which may be added *Malcolm* v. *Campbell* (1889) 17 R. 255 at p. 259 *per* Lord Justice-Clerk Macdonald.
[1] *e.g. Penney* v. *Aitken*, 1927 S.C. 673.

being given a conjunct probation.[2] This produces the odd result that the pursuer may obtain repayment without having proved the loan by writ or oath. If the defender does not aver donation but, for example, states that the money was in payment for services, he avoids the heavy onus of proving donation and probably the pursuer must prove a loan by writ or oath.[3] The writ of the debtor (*e.g.* an unqualified receipt) would in turn put the onus on the debtor to prove that the money was granted other than for a loan, *e.g.* in payment of a debt.[4] An I.O.U. raises a presumption of an obligation to repay.[5]

PROOF OF PAYMENT

22–32 The general rule, although much regretted, is that proof of payment is limited to the writ or oath of the creditor when the payment is in discharge of an antecedent obligation.[6] This has the effect that when a tradesman sues for his account and his customer alleges payment, the customer cannot prove payment by parole evidence.[7] Under the Cheques Act 1957[8] an unendorsed cheque which appears to have been paid by the banker on whom it was drawn is evidence of the receipt by the payee of the sum payable by the cheque. Lord Reid observed[9]: "Section 3 makes it clear—if there were any doubt—that an unindorsed cheque which appears to have been paid by the payee's banker is. without evidence as to who actually received the money, in itself *prima facie* evidence of receipt of the money by the payee."

22–33 When a transaction is a ready money transaction, payment may be proved by parole evidence, *e.g.* a sale where price and delivery are immediate counterparts[10]; or a mandate constituted by payment of money and the giving of an instruction.[11] A credit sale, however, is not a ready money transaction.[12]

22–34 Apart from payments *unico contextu* with the creation of the contract, there are other exceptions to the rule that payment in discharge of an obligation must be proved by writ or oath. These exceptions are not

---

[2] *Penman* v. *White*, 1957 S.C. 338; *McVea* v. *Reid*, 1958 S.L.T.(Sh.Ct.) 60.

[3] *McKie* v. *Wilson*, 1951 S.C. 15; *Gow's Exrs.* v. *Sim* (1866) 4 M. 578.

[4] *Thomson* v. *Geekie* (1861) 23 D. 693; *Gill* v. *Gill*, 1907 S.C. 532.

[5] *Thiem's Trs.* v. *Collie* (1899) 1 F. 764; *Black* v. *Gibb*, 1940 S.C. 24.

[6] *Hope Bros.* v. *Morrison*, 1960 S.C. 1 (which reviews earlier authority); *Coyle* v. *Lees*, 1976 (Sh.Ct.) 58.

[7] Cases in note above.

[8] s.3.

[9] *Westminster Bank Ltd.* v. *Zang* [1966] A.C. 182 at p. 221. On the evidentiary value of an endorsed cheque see *Haldane* v. *Speirs* (1872) 10 M. 537; *Skiffington* v. *Dickson*, 1970 S.L.T.(Sh.Ct.) 24 (and authority there cited).

[10] *Shaw* v. *Wright* (1877) 5 R. 245.

[11] *Burt* v. *Laing*, 1925 S.C. 181.

[12] *Shaw* v. *Wright, sup. cit.*; *Young* v. *Thomson*, 1909 S.C. 529.

easy to state. (1) A payment under 100 pounds Scots (£8.33) can be proved by parole evidence unless the obligation to pay is constituted in writing[13]; (2) parole proof is allowed of facts and circumstances which give rise to an inevitable inference that payment has been made. For example, in *McKenzie's Ex.* v. *Morrison's Tr.*[14] an action was raised in 1929 on an I.O.U. dated in 1897. Parole proof of discharge of the I.O.U. was allowed because of the long delay, the failure to make an earlier claim, and the other circumstances of the case. There is also a series of cases in which there was a course of payments made without obtaining receipts[15] and it may be that payment of wages would come within the same category and be provable by parole evidence.[16]

-35   The debtor may have difficulty proving payment because the creditor's writ (*e.g.* a receipt) has been lost. Parole proof is competent of the existence and tenor of the writ.[17]

-36   Wages are commonly paid in arrears and under an antecedent obligation. If wages are paid in cash there may not be any writ of the employee (the creditor). Doubt has been expressed about whether the employee is limited to writ or oath in proving payment when receipts are not normally taken.[18] In the small debt court employers were held bound to prove payment when an employee said that there was a £1 shortage in his pay envelope. After hearing evidence and without discussing the authorities, the sheriff granted decree against the employers.[19]

-37   Part payment may be shown by an account rendered by the creditor to the debtor.[20]

-38   In the case of termly payments such as rents, feuduties or interest, the production of receipts for three consecutive terms raises a presumption that all prior instalments have been paid.[21] The presumption arises from the repeated issue of receipts, and not from one discharge covering three payments.[22] The three terms must be consecutive and the receipts granted by the same creditor. The presumption can probably be rebut-

---

[13] *Robertson* v. *Thomson* (1900) 3 F. 5. In practice repayment of a loan will usually be subject to the rule that discharge of a written obligation must be proved by writ or oath. See Walker and Walker, *Evidence*, paras. 118 and 125.

[14] 1930 S.C. 830; on delay in claiming a price see *Spence* v. *Paterson's Trs.* (1873) 1 R. 46.

[15] *Stuart* v. *Maconochie* (1836) 14 S. 412; *Russell's Trs.* v. *Russell* (1885) 13 R. 331; and see cases cited in Walker and Walker, *op. cit.*, para. 127(b).

[16] Walker and Walker, para. 127(a).

[17] *Young* v. *Thomson*, 1909 S.C. 529; *James Scott & Co. (Electrical Engineers) Ltd.* v. *McIntosh*, 1960 S.L.T.(Sh.Ct.) 15; *Simpson's Trs.* v. *Simpson*, 1933 S.N. 22.

[18] *Brown* v. *Mason* (1856) 19 D. 137 at p. 138 *per* Lord Deas; *Annand's Trs.* v. *Annand* (1869) 7 M. 526 at p. 530 *per* Lord Deas.

[19] *Robertson* v. *Bent Colliery Co.* (1919) 35 Sh.Ct.Rep. 290.

[20] *Stewart & Taylor* v. *Grimson* (1904) 20 Sh.Ct.Rep. 166.

[21] Walker and Walker, *Evidence*, para. 64.

[22] *Hunter* v. *Kinnaird's Trs.* (1829) 7 S. 548.

ted by parole evidence.[23] The presumption has also been applied to accounts for repairs.[24]

22–39   There is a presumption that a hotel bill has been paid before the guest has left.[25] The hotel keeper must rebut the presumption by proving that the debt is due.

PAYMENT IN FOREIGN CURRENCY

22–40   There is a distinction between the money of account and the money of payment. The money of account determines how much the debtor pays. The amount may be fixed by reference to a foreign currency. The money of payment concerns the discharge of the obligation to pay. The money of payment could be pounds sterling although the money of account is a foreign currency or vice versa.

22–41   Suppose that a Scottish company buys steel pipes from an American company at a price of 10 US$ per pipe payable in pounds sterling in Aberdeen. The money of account is US$ and the seller has protected himself against fluctuations in exchange rates. He is entitled to be paid his price in currency worth 10 US$ per pipe. The buyer discharges his obligation by payment in pounds sterling, but the amount to be paid will fluctuate with exchange rates. The buyer could be sued and decree granted in pounds sterling. This is because sterling is the currency of payment. It would be incompetent to seek a decree in dollars.[26]

22–42   A decree will be granted in a foreign currency when that currency is the currency of payment. This is as a result of the decision of the House of Lords in *Miliangos* v. *George Frank (Textiles) Ltd.*[27] which was followed by the First Division in *Commerzbank Aktiengesellschaft* v. *Large.*[28] It is necessary to provide in any decree for the conversion of the foreign currency into sterling, so that the decree may be enforced.[29]

---

[23] Walker and Walker, *op. cit.*.

[24] *Struthers & Son* v. *Russell* 1927 S.L.T.(Sh.Ct.) 67.

[25] Walker and Walker, *op. cit.*, para. 65; *Barnet* v. *Colvill* (1840) 2 D. 337.

[26] *L/F Foroya Fiskasola* v. *Charles Mauritzen Ltd.*, 1978 S.L.T.(Sh.Ct.) 27; see also *Woodhouse A.C. Israel Cocoa Ltd. S.A.* v. *Nigerian Produce Marketing Co. Ltd.* [1971] 2 Q.B. 23, on appeal [1972] A.C. 741. It has been suggested that when the money of account and the money of payment are different, judgment should be given in the currency of the money of account. Chitty, *Contract*, para. 2106; R. M. Goode, *Payment Obligations in Commercial and Financial Transactions* (1983), p. 141. This may be contrary to the express terms of the contract and it is thought to be wrong. The case cited by the authorities mentioned does not support their proposition—see *George Veflings Rederi A/S* v. *President of India* [1979] 1 All E.R. 380.

[27] [1976] A.C. 443.

[28] 1977 S.C. 375.

[29] See the procedure in *Commerzbank, sup. cit.* The effect of *Miliangos* has been extended to other claims such as damages. See, *inter alia*, *The Despina R. and The Folias* [1979] A.C. 685; *Societé Française Bunge S.A.* v. *Belcan N.V., The Federal Huron* [1985] 3 All E.R. 378. Claims on insolvency are special—see *Re Dynamics Corp. of America* [1976] 2 All E.R. 669; *Re Lines Bros. Ltd.* [1983] Ch. 1 and sequel [1984] Ch. 438.

43   In a sequestration the claim of a creditor may be made in foreign currency and it will be converted into pounds sterling by the trustee.[30]

COMPENSATION

Origins

44   Compensation may be statutory in origin[31] although it is difficult to believe that the common law did not, and does not, recognise some form of compensation.

As Lord Eskgrove put it in *Harper* v. *Faulds*[32]: "Before [the Act of 1592], had two parties come, each with a decree in his hand, must both have gone to prison? Surely not. Or could this have taken place, though the one was a decree for delivery while the other was a decree for payment? It cannot be."

45   The logic of that remark is still relevant because, as will be seen, compensation under the 1592 Act cannot be pled after decree, nor can a money debt be set off against a claim for delivery. The courts used the equity which underlies the doctrine of compensation in the problem of balancing of accounts on bankruptcy.[33] In so doing the common law was being used and not the 1592 Act. In other exceptional cases equity may allow claims to be set off.[34] The extent to which there is a common law of compensation applying to solvent debtors and creditors is obscure, and appears to be of little, if any, practical importance.

46   The Compensation Act 1592 allows liquid debts to be set against each other. The Act provides that: "only debt de liquido ad liquidum instantlie verifiet be wreit or aith of the partie befoir the geving of decreit be admittit be all Jugis within this realme be way of exceptioun Bot nocht eftir the geving thairof In the suspensioun or in reductioun of the same decreit."

47   The 1592 Act, being one of the Scots Acts, was subject to liberal interpretation, at least after the case of *Seton* in 1683.[35] The correct method of interpretation, therefore, is to read the Act as interpreted by decisions.[36]

---

[30] Bankruptcy (Scotland) Act 1985, ss.22(6), 23(1)(*a*), 49(2); Bankruptcy (Scotland) Regulations 1985 (S.I. 1985 No. 1925), paras. 6 and 7.

[31] Stair, I,xviii,6 (2nd and 5th eds.). Balfour, writing shortly before the 1592 Act, denied the existence of compensation *as a defence by way of exception*. Balfour, *op. cit.*, p. 349, citing *Queen* v. *Bishop of Aberdeen* (1543) Mor. 2545. But note comments on this case in Bell., *Comm.*, II, 120; see *Fowler* v. *Brown*, 1916 S.C. 597.

[32] (1791) Bell 8vo. Cas. 432 at p. 468.

[33] See below.

[34] *Munro* v. *Macdonald's Exrs.* (1866) 4 M. 687; *Ross* v. *Ross* (1895) 22 R. 461.

[35] (1683) Mor. 2566; *Fowler* v. *Brown*, 1916 S.C. 597 at p. 601 *per* Lord Justice-Clerk Scott Dickson.

[36] In general, on the interpretation of Scots Acts, see *Johnstone* v. *Stotts* (1802) 4 Pat. 274 at pp. 283–284 *per* Lord Eldon; *Fergusson* v. *Skirving* (1852) 1 Macq. 232; *Heriot's Tr.* v. *Paton's Tr.*, 1912 S.C. 1123.

Terminology

22–48 The traditional Scottish term is "compensation." The phrase "set off" is said to derive from England[37], but it is in common use in Scotland. It is probable that "set off" is a more general term which covers both compensation and the balancing of accounts in bankruptcy.[38]

COMPENSATION DISTINGUISHED FROM OTHER EVENTS

22–49 Compensation must be distinguished from (1) retention, (2) balancing of accounts in bankruptcy and (3) counterclaims.

(1) Retention

22–50 Retention is an aspect of the principle of mutuality of contracts. In a mutual contract parties may withhold performance when they have claims arising under the contract, whether these claims are liquid or illiquid. The Compensation Act 1592 does not apply to retention.[39] Retention does not operate to extinguish claims. Compensation when pled and sustained does. Retention operates to suspend obligations until counter obligations are fulfilled. It does not emerge as a right until performance is due.[40] The concept of retention is analysed in the chapter on "Breach of Contract."[41]

(2) Balancing of accounts in bankruptcy

22–51 Bell said of the Act of 1592[42]: "This statute is in no degree exclusive of the operation of equity in cases naturally falling under its rules; and, in Scotland, the insolvency of a party has always been admitted as a ground for administering an equitable remedy unknown to the ordinary course of law." This is illustrated when he considers the requirements for compensation. To give some examples. Debts in compensation must be of the same nature—but not in bankruptcy. In compensation debts must be both due at the same time—but this rule strictly holds only while the parties are solvent. In compensation the debts must both be liquid—this does not hold on the balancing of accounts in bankruptcy.[43] The balancing of accounts in bankruptcy is considered later.[44]

---

[37] Bell, *Comm.*, II, 119.

[38] *Laing* v. *Lord Advocate*, 1973 S.L.T.(Notes) 81.

[39] *Johnston* v. *Robertson* (1861) 23 D. 646 discussed in *British Motor Body Co. Ltd.* v. *Thomas Shaw (Dundee) Ltd.*, 1914 S.C. 922.

[40] *Borthwick* v. *Scottish Widows' Fund* (1864) 2 M. 595 at p. 607 *per* Lord Justice-Clerk Inglis.

[41] para. 14–33.

[42] *Comm.*, II, 121.

[43] *Ibid.* II, 122.

[44] para. 22–75.

(3) Counterclaims

52 Procedure by way of counterclaim is regulated by the rules applying to court procedure.[45] At one time it was suggested that a counterclaim could only be pleaded if compensation were competent.[46] It was established in *Armour & Melvin* v. *Mitchell*,[47] however, that a counterclaim could proceed although it was incompetent for the defender's claim to be set off against the pursuer's claim, and the defender's illiquid claim continues as if it were a substantive action.[48] The counterclaim must satisfy the provisions of the relevant Rules of Court.[49]

THE REQUIREMENTS FOR COMPENSATION UNDER THE 1592 ACT

(1) Debts of the same nature

53 The debts must be of the same nature. A money debt can be pleaded against a money debt. A demand for delivery of wine can be set off against a claim for wine. But a money debt cannot be set off against a claim for delivery of a fungible.[50] So in a contract of deposit the plea of compensation is not competent against a demand for the thing deposited.[51] This rule applies to money which is deposited. In *Mycroft Petitioner*[52] accountants claimed a set off between debts collected for a company and professional fees due to the accountants by the company. The plea of compensation failed on three grounds: (1) it was a case of improper deposit; (2) the accountants held the money as agents; and (3) the money was held for a specific purpose. It is a general principle that where money is deposited for a special purpose there cannot be a plea of compensation, retention or lien in respect of a separate debt due by the depositer.[53] Thus if sums are deposited with a solicitor for a specific purpose, *e.g.* to buy a house, the money cannot be used for another debt, *e.g.* to pay fees due to the solicitor for previous business.[54]

54 The ability of a bank to plead compensation in respect of a solicitor's clients' account is limited by statute.[55] If a bank has notice that funds

---

[45] Rule of Court 84; Act of Sederunt (Ordinary Cause Rules, Sheriff Court) 1983, rr. 51–56.

[46] The authorities are reviewed in Dobie, *Sheriff Court Practice*, pp. 151 *et seq.*

[47] 1934 S.C. 94.

[48] *Armour & Melvin* v. *Mitchell, sup. cit.*; *Scott* v. *Aitken*, 1950 S.L.T.(Notes) 34; *Croall & Croall* v. *Sharp*, 1954 S.L.T.(Sh.Ct.) 35 (the rubric is misleading).

[49] *Fulton Clyde Ltd.* v. *J. F. McCallum & Co. Ltd.*, 1960 S.C. 78; *Borthwick* v. *Dean Warwick Ltd.*, 1985 S.L.T. 269 (competent to counterclaim for delivery in an action for damages).

[50] Bell, *Comm.*, II, 122.

[51] Stair, I, xiii, 8; Ersk., III, iv, 17; Bell, *Comm.*, II, 122.

[52] 1983 S.L.T. 342.

[53] *McGregor* v. *Alley & McLellan* (1887) 14 R. 535; *Middlemas* v. *Gibson*, 1910 S.C. 577.

[54] *Middlemas* v. *Gibson, sup. cit.*; *Mycroft Pet., sup. cit.*

[55] Solicitors (Scotland) Act 1980, s.61.

deposited with it are affected by a trust or are held in a fiduciary capacity, they cannot set off those funds against debts due by their customer under other accounts.[56]

(2) Debts due at the same time

22–55   Both debts must be due at the same time. A debt presently due cannot be set off against a future debt or a contingent debt.[57]

(3) Liquid debts

22–56   The debts must both be liquid or capable of immediate liquidation. A debt is liquid when it is actually due and the amount ascertained, *e.g.* a price or payment of rent, or an insurance premium or an annuity.

22–57   According to Erskine[58]: "Compensation is not regularly receivable where the debts on both sides are not clear beyond dispute." A dispute on a claim may make it illiquid, while an admission of a claim may make it liquid.[59] What is not clear is how far one party by averring a dispute can prevent a claim by the other party from being liquid. This is thought to depend on the nature of the claim. A sum due under a bond or a bill is clearly liquid.[60] A price due under an oral contract of sale is liquid if the price is admitted, but not otherwise.[61] A failure to make relevant averments in answer to a claim, may make the claim liquid.[62]

22–58   A claim for damages is illiquid[63], as is a claim based on the equitable remedy of *condictio indebiti*[64] or a claim which must be ascertained by an accounting.[65]

---

[56] *United Rentals Ltd.* v. *Clydesdale and North of Scotland Bank Ltd.*, 1963 S.L.T.(Sh.Ct.) 41. In general terms a bank can combine accounts unless (1) the accounts are held by one person in two different capacities or (2) there is an agreement between the customer and the bank that the accounts be separate: *Barclays Bank Ltd.* v. *Okenarhe* [1966] 2 Lloyd's Rep. 87; *Re. E. J. Morel (1934) Ltd.* [1962] Ch. 21; *Halesowen Presswork and Assemblies Ltd.* v. *Westminster Bank Ltd.* [1972] A.C. 785; *Gibb* v. *Lombank Scotland Ltd.*, 1962 S.L.T. 288 (which illustrates a difference between deposit accounts and current accounts). The payer may be able to appropriate payment to a particular account: *Buchanan* v. *Main* (1900) 3 F. 215.

[57] Bell, *Comm.*, II, 122; *Paul & Thain* v. *Royal Bank* (1869) 7 M. 361.

[58] *Inst.*, III, iv, 16.

[59] *e.g. Hamilton* v. *Wright* (1839) 2 D. 86; *Thoms* v. *Thoms* (1868) 5 S.L.R. 561; *Scottish N. E. Ry. Co.* v. *Napier* (1859) 21 D. 700. See also *Niven* v. *Clyde Fasteners Ltd.*, 1986 S.L.T. 344.

[60] But the validity of the document could be challenged in appropriate proceedings.

[61] See *Mackie* v. *Riddell* (1874) 2 R. 115 at p. 117 *per* Lord Deas. *Lovie* v. *Bard's Trs.* (1895) 23 R. 1 at p. 4 *per* Lord Kinnear.

[62] *Scottish N. E. Ry. Co.* v. *Napier, sup. cit.*; *Grewar* v. *Cross*, 1904 12 S.L.T. 84.

[63] *Scottish Ry. N. E. Co.* v. *Napier, sup. cit.*; *Mackie* v. *Riddell sup. cit.*; *Grewar* v. *Cross*, 1904 12 S.L.T. 84.

[64] *Henderson & Co. Ltd.* v. *Turnbull & Co.*, 1909 S.C. 510.

[65] *Blair Iron Co.* v. *Alison* (1855) D.(H.L. 49; 6 W. & S. 56. See also *Niven* v. *Clyde Fasteners Ltd., sup. cit.*

59   A liquid claim cannot be compensated by one which is illiquid. There is an exception when the counterclaim can immediately be made liquid[66] but not if there is a delay in liquidating the claim.[67]

(4) Concursus debiti et crediti

60   There must be *concursus debiti et crediti*. The parties must be debtor and creditor not only at the same time but in the same capacity.[68] There is no compensation between a debt due by a person in his own right and one due to him as trustee, tutor, administrator, or factor, or executor,[69] or between a debt due to a company and a debt due by one of the company's directors.[70]

61   When a bank granted a deposit receipt payable to A and B, it could not avoid paying B because of sums due by A.[71] Except in special circumstances, a debt due to or from several persons jointly cannot be set off against a debt from or to one of such persons separately.[72]

62   Death of a party does not prevent compensation being pled against his estate. The executor is *eadem persona cum defuncto*.[73]

63   As Bell observed, the class of case in which it is most difficult to apply the rule *concursus debiti et crediti* is that of principal and agent.[74] The rules depend on whether or not the principal is disclosed. (1) Agent contracts for a disclosed principal—there is no *concursus debiti et crediti* between a debt due by a third party to the principal and a debt due by the agent to the third party.[75] However, sums held by the agent and due to the third party have been held to be able to be set off against claims by the principal against the third party.[76]

64   (2) Agent contracts for an undisclosed principal—the third party may set off a debt due by the agent provided the right to compensate arose before he was aware of the principal's interest.[77]

---

[66] *Munro* v. *Macdonald's Exrs.* (1866) 4 M. 687. See also *Niven* v. *Clyde Fasteners Ltd.*, *sup. cit.*, and authorities there cited.

[67] *N.B. Ry. Co.* v. *North British Grain Storage and Transit Co.* (1897) 24 R. 687.

[68] Statutory provisions which transfer rights and liabilities from one body to another may create a *concursus debiti et crediti*. See *McPhail* v. *Cunninghame D.C.*; *William Loudon & Son Ltd.* v. *Cunninghame D.C.*, 1985 S.L.T. 149.

[69] Bell, *Comm.*, II, 124; *Stuart* v. *Stuart* (1869) 7 M. 366. In the case of an executor there may be an exception when the executor has the sole or a residuary interest in the estate.

[70] *Ritchie Ltd.* v. *Union Transit Co.* (1915) 32 Sh.Ct.Rep. 55.

[71] *Anderson* v. *North of Scotland Bank Ltd.* (1901) 4 F. 49.

[72] *Burrell* v. *Burrell's Trs.*, 1916 S.C. 729.

[73] *Mitchell* v. *Mackersy* (1905) 8 F. 198.

[74] Bell, *Comm.*, II, 125.

[75] *Matthews* v. *Auld & Guild* (1874) 1 R. 1224.

[76] *Macgregor's Tr.* v. *Cox* (1883) 10 R. 1028.

[77] *National Bank* v. *Dickie's Tr.* (1895) 22 R. 740; *Wester Moffat Colliery Co.* v. *Jeffrey*, 1911 S.C. 346.

22–65   (3) Agent contracts for a principal whose existence is disclosed, but the principal is not named. The third party cannot set off sums due to him by the agent against sums due by him to the principal.[78]

22–66   There are two general rules which apply to partnership and compensation. These are: (1) if the firm sues a third party for a debt due to the firm, the third party cannot set off a debt due to him by a partner of the firm but (2) if the third party is claiming against the firm, the firm may plead compensation for a debt due by the third party to a partner.[79] This second rule appears to conflict with the idea that in Scots law a partnership is a legal *persona* separate from the partners, but, at least for this purpose, the partners are treated as debtors in debts due by the firm.[80] Where a firm is indebted to a bank, the bank, after notice, may seek to set against this debt any credit balance in its books in the name of one of the parties.[81] The bank will not wait for the firm to plead compensation.

(5) Title to plead compensation

22–67   The doctrine of compensation exists to prevent unnecessary actions. When a party pleads compensation he must have an active title to sue. Unless he can sue for the debt he cannot plead it in compensation. So a beneficiary in a trust cannot found on a debt due to the trustees.[82] A person sued for a debt may have an interest to plead compensation. Thus a cautioner can plead compensation in respect of a debt due to the principal debtor.[83]

22–68   When a debt is assigned the debtor can plead against the assignee a debt due by the cedent provided that *concursus* existed before intimation.[84]

22–69   The operation of set-off to or by the Crown has specialities.[85]

(6) Compensation must be pled

22–70   Despite Stair[86] compensation does not operate *ipso jure*. The two debts must exist at the same time but one of them may be extinguished by prescription before compensation is pled.[87] Compensation must be

---

[78] *Lavaggi* v. *Pirie & Sons* (1872) 10 M. 312.

[79] *Heggie* v. *Heggie* (1858) 21 D. 31; *Mitchell* v. *Canal Basin Co.* (1869) 7 M. 480; J. Bennett Miller, *Partnership*, p. 625.

[80] See Gloag, p. 648. On dissolved partnerships see *Oswald's Trs.* v. *Dickson* (1833) 12 S. 156; *Lockhart* v. *Ferrier* (1842) 4 D. 1253; *Heggie* v. *Heggie, sup. cit.*; *Mitchell* v. *Canal Basin Co., sup. cit.*

[81] The bank seeks to combine accounts. The notice from the bank (1) prevents the future operation of the rule in *Clayton's Case* and (2) avoids the risk of liability in damages arising from the dishonour of cheques.

[82] *Johnston* v. *Johnston* (1875) 2 R. 986.

[83] Bell, *Comm.*, II,124; Gloag and Irvine, *Rights in Security*, p. 803.

[84] Bell, *Comm.*, II,131; *Shiells* v. *Ferguson, Davidson & Co.* (1876) 4 R. 250; *Taylor, Pet.*, 1981 S.C. 408 at p. 415 *per* Lord Ross.

[85] Crown Proceedings Act 1947, s.50; *Atlantic Engine Co. (1920) Ltd.* v. *Lord Advocate*, 1955 S.L.T. 17; *Smith* v. *Lord Advocate*, 1980 S.C. 227; see para. 8–59.

[86] *Inst.*, I, xviii, 6.

[87] Bell, *Comm.*, II, 124; Ersk., *Inst.*, III, iv, 12.

both pled and sustained by judgment before it has effect, unless there is an agreement to compensate.[88] The agreement probably has to be in writing.[89]

–71   If compensation is sustained it has a retrospective effect with the result that interest may not be due on a debt after the date of *concursus* even if one of the debts at that time was illiquid.[90]

(7) Compensation must be pled before decree

–72   Compensation must be pled before decree. If a debtor allows a decree to pass against him he must pay his debt and establish his counterclaim in another action. This rule applies to a decree in *foro* and a decree in absence[91]; but not to a decree for expenses. A decree for expenses is pronounced without there being an earlier opportunity to plead compensation.[92]

–73   The general rule assumes that the defender had an opportunity to plead compensation before decree passed. Compensation may be pleaded when the debt was not liquid at the time decree was granted, but has become so before a charge on the decree or before suspension is disposed of, or where the defender in the original action had no opportunity of pleading compensation as a bar to decree.[93] So it is thought that Stair was correct in saying that the rule that compensation must be pled before decree applies only to decrees proceeding upon citation. It does not apply to decrees obtained on registration in the court books.[94]

(8) Compensation can be excluded by agreement

–74   There can be a specific agreement to compensate[95] and, conversely, there can be an agreement which excludes compensation.[96]

BALANCING OF ACCOUNTS IN BANKRUPTCY

–75   In bankruptcy, liquidation or insolvency, the rules on compensation under the 1592 Act do not all apply.[97] To operate the principles of balancing of accounts in bankruptcy it is not necessary to make a specific averment of insolvency. It appears that liquidation, sequestration or a

---

[88] *Cowan* v. *Gowans* (1878) 5 R. 581.

[89] *Cowan* v. *Shaw* (1878) 5 R. 680.

[90] *Inch* v. *Lee* (1903) 11 S.L.T. 374.

[91] Ersk, III, iv, 19; *Cuninghame Stevenson & Co.* v. *Wilson*, January 17, 1809, F.C.; *Downie* v. *Rae* (1832) 11 S. 51.

[92] *Fowler* v. *Brown*, 1916 S.C. 597; *Galloway* v. *Mackinnon* (1936) 52 Sh.Ct.Rep. 135.

[93] *Fowler* v. *Brown*, *sup. cit.* at p. 603 *per* Lord Salvesen; *Roy* v. *Paul* (1872) 9 S.L.R. 525.

[94] Stair, I, xviii, 6.

[95] *Cowan* v. *Shaw* (1878) 5 R. 680.

[96] *Robert Paterson & Sons Ltd.* v. *Household Supplies Company Ltd.*, 1975 S.L.T. 98 (R.I.B.A. conditions). See also cases on deposit, para. 22–53.

[97] Bell, *Comm.*, II, 122.

trust deed for creditors are equivalent to "bankruptcy."[98] But receivership is different. The normal rules on bankruptcy do not apply to receivership. According to one case a debt assigned after the appointment of a receiver can be set off against a debt due to the company in receivership.[99] But in a subsequent decision[1] it was decided that the attachment of a floating charge which arises on the appointment of a receiver had effect as if there were an intimated assignation in security in favour of the floating charge holder of the book debts of the company. Accordingly, in respect of debts due to and by the company which went into receivership there would be no *concursus debiti et crediti*.

(1) Debts of the same nature

22–76   When one of the parties is bankrupt set-off may be pleaded by the debtor to a bankrupt estate although the two claims are not of the same nature, *e.g.* a claim for debt and a claim for delivery.[2]

(2) Debts due at the same time

22–77   The debts need not be due at the same time. A sum presently due can be set off against a future or contingent debt.[3]

(3) Liquid debts

22–78   When one of the parties is bankrupt an illiquid claim may be set off against a liquid claim.[4]

(4) Concursus debiti et crediti

22–79   The concourse of debit and credit must exist. The manner in which this rule has been stated in some textbooks has been held to be misleading.[5] It has been said that the debit and credit must exist before bankruptcy. It is more accurate to state that a debt after bankruptcy cannot be set off against a debt due to the bankrupt before bankruptcy.[6] This

---

[98] *G. & A. (Hotels) Ltd.* v. *T.H.B. Marketing Services Ltd.*, 1983 S.L.T. 497; *Liqrs. of Highland Engineering Ltd.* v. *Thomson*, 1972 S.C. 87.

[99] *Taylor, Petr.*, 1981 S.C. 408; not following *McPhail* v. *Lothian Regional Council*, 1981 S.C. 119. Some controversy continues over which of these Outer House decisions is correct or whether both are inconsistent with *Forth and Clyde Construction Co. Ltd.* v. *Trinity Timber and Plywood Co. Ltd.*, 1984 S.L.T. 94.

[1] *Forth and Clyde Construction Co. Ltd.* v. *Trinity Timber and Plywood Co. Ltd.*, *sup. cit.*

[2] Bell, *Comm.*, II,122.

[3] Bell, *Comm.*, II,122; *Hannay & Son's Tr.* v. *Armstrong Bros.* (1875) 2 R. 399; (1877) 4 R.(H.L.) 43; *Clydesdale Bank Ltd.* v. *Gardiner* (1906) 14 S.L.T. 121; *Smith* v. *Lord Advocate (No. 2)*, 1980 S.C. 227 at p. 231 *per* Lord Avonside.

[4] Bell, *Comm.*, II, 122; *Scott's Tr.* v. *Scott* (1887) 14 R. 1043 at p. 1051 *per* Lord President Inglis; *Clydesdale Bank Ltd.* v. *Gardiner, sup. cit.*

[5] *Liqrs. of Highland Engineering Ltd.* v. *Thomson*, 1972 S.C. 87 at p. 91 *per* Lord Fraser; approved in *Smith* v. *Lord Advocate*, 1978 S.C. 259.

[6] Or conversely—*Taylor's Tr.* v. *Paul* (1888) 15 R. 313.

prevents persons indebted to the bankrupt estate buying up claims against the estate at a low figure and setting them off at their face value.[7] But if both debts arise after bankruptcy, one may be set off against the other.[8]

80 In *Asphaltic Limestone Concrete Co.* v. *Glasgow Corporation*[9] there were two contracts to carry out paving work. One was adopted by the liquidator and the other was not. Glasgow Corporation attempted to withhold payment to the liquidator because of claims arising under the other contract. It was held that the corporation could not set off against a debt due at and prior to the date of liquidation a sum that became due by them to the liquidator for work done by the liquidator. Lord McLaren observed[10] that the argument of the corporation in favour of set off was:

> "founded on a complete misapprehension of the principle of reten-tion in cases of bankruptcy or insolvency. In such cases, if the insol-vent estate has a liquid claim against a solvent debtor, who again has a liquid claim against the insolvent estate, the principle of com-pensation is applied exactly as it would be if both parties were sol-vent. But if the claim of the solvent party is not liquid, e.g. if the work has been done but the time of payment has not arrived, then by an equitable extension of the principle of compensation he is allowed to retain the money which he owes against his claim on the insolvent estate, so that he may not suffer the injustice of having to pay his debt in full while only receiving a dividend on his own claim. But this principle of bankruptcy law presupposes reciprocal obli-gations which are both existing at the time of the declaration of insolvency, although only one of them is, it may be, immediately exigible. It has no application to the case of a new obligation arising after bankruptcy or declaration of insolvency when the rights of the parties are irrevocably fixed."

81 There is controversy over what is meant by the "declaration of insol-vency" referred to by Lord McLaren. Clearly the date of sequestration or liquidation or the effectual date of a trust deed can be the date by which concourse must have arisen.[11] It is unsettled whether mere inti-mation of insolvency prevents concourse of debts.[12]

82 In recent cases involving the appointment of receivers this point was not argued.[13]

---

[7] Goudy, *Bankruptcy*, p. 555.

[8] *Mill* v. *Paul* (1825) 4 S. 219; *Thomson* v. *Tough's Tr.* (1880) 7 R. 1035; *Liqrs. of High-land Engineering Ltd.* v. *Thomson, sup. cit.*; *Smith* v. *Lord Advocate*, 1978 S.C. 259.

[9] 1907 S.C. 463.

[10] at p. 474.

[11] *Mill* v. *Paul* (1825) 4 S.219; *Meldrum's Trs.* v. *Clark* (1826) 5 S. 122.

[12] Bell, *Comm.*, II, 124; Goudy, *Bankruptcy*, p. 556; Gloag, *Contract*, p. 654; *Dickson* v. *Nicholson* (1855) 17 D. 1011; *Stevenson, Lauder & Gilchrist* v. *Dawson* (1896) 23 R. 496.

[13] *McPhail* v. *Lothian Regional Council*, 1981, S.C. 119; *Taylor, Petr.*, 1981 S.C. 408. But the statutory foundation of receivership means that there are specialities. See *Forth and Clyde Construction Co. Ltd.* v. *Trinity Timber and Plywood Co. Ltd.*, 1984 S.L.T. 94.

22–83   In *Smith* v. *Lord Advocate (No. 2)*[14] there was a statutory assignation to the Secretary of State of a claim for debt due by a company in liquidation. This did not prevent set-off, because the assignation after liquidation was not for the purpose of producing set-off.[15] The extent to which a debt must be acquired *bona fide* to allow compensation in cases of insolvency is unsettled,[16] but *Smith* suggests that an assignation *ex lege* may be different from a voluntary assignation.

(5) Title to plead

22–84   The person pleading set-off must be in his own right creditor of the person against whom he pleads it.

(6) Pleading set-off

22–85   Because balancing of accounts in bankruptcy operates with illiquid claims it cannot be necessary to have a claim pled and sustained by judgment prior to giving effect to the set-off. Indeed the principle of the law is that it is the function of a trustee or liquidator to adjudicate on claims and leave of the court is necessary to continue an action against a company in liquidation.[17] Leave of the court is not needed to plead set-off.[18]

(7) Set-off excluded by agreement

22–86   The insolvency of one party will not affect the exclusion of set-off which may arise by agreement.

(8) Statutory exceptions

22–87   In a liquidation a contributory cannot set off amounts due by the company to him against calls unless all the creditors have been paid in full.[19]

(9) Set-off and Crown debts

22–88   The specialities of set-off to and by the Crown often arise in insolvency.[20]

---

[14] 1980 S.C. 227.

[15] *Hannay & Son's Tr.* v. *Armstrong Bros.* (1875) 2 R. 399 at p. 417 *per* Lord Gifford was cited with approval (on appeal (1877) 4 R.(H.L. 43).

[16] Gloag, *Contract*, p. 654; Goudy, *Bankruptcy*, p. 555.

[17] Companies Act 1985, s.521.

[18] *G. & A. (Hotels) Ltd.* v. *T.H.B. Marketing Services Ltd.*, 1983 S.L.T. 497.

[19] Companies Act 1985, s.552 *Cowan* v. *Gowans* (1878) 5 R. 981, *Property Investment Co. of Scotland* v. *Aikman* (1891) 28 S.L.R. 955, *Property Investment Co. of Scotland* v. *National Bank* (1891) 28 S.L.R. 884; See also *Scottish Fishermen's Organisation Ltd.* v. *McLean*, 1980 S.L.T.(Sh.Ct.) 76.

[20] See para. 8–59. Crown Proceedings Act 1947, s.50; *Smith* v. *Lord Advocate*, 1980 S.C. 227.

CHAPTER 23

VARIATION AND EXTINCTION OF CONTRACTUAL OBLIGATIONS

VARIATION—INTRODUCTION

-01 The actings of parties subsequent to a contract can be relied upon for various purposes. Those actings should not normally be used to aid construction of the contract,[1] but, that apart, the actings may be looked at (1) for deciding whether or not there has been performance of the contract; (2) in the case of a voidable contract to decide whether or not *restitutio in integrum* is possible; and (3) to vary the effect of the original contract. This part of the chapter is concerned with the problem of variation. The first difficulty is a confusion of terminology.

TERMINOLOGY

-02 Perhaps because Scots law has not developed a consistent and rational theory of variation of contractual obligations, several concepts are referred to, such as personal bar, acquiescence, waiver, *mora* and novation.

-03 Rankine observed that, in contrast to English law: "There is no formal and general Scottish definition of personal bar."[2] The confusion is well illustrated by this statement of Bell's editors[3]:

> "The principle of personal bar, personal objection, or personal exception, like homologation, acquiescence, or waiver, from which in numerous cases it can hardly be distinguished, operates beyond the domain of contracts. And although it is constantly pleaded and enforced in practice, it is difficult to find in the law of Scotland any precise statement of its meaning and effect except in the form and application in which it occurs here. It may not be incorrect to say that *Rei interventus, i.e.* the occurrence of a real change of position, is in all cases the foundation of the plea or defence known as personal bar or personal exception, which closely corresponds with the English Estoppel *in pais*."

---

[1] *James Miller & Partners* v. *Whitworth Street Estates* [1970] A.C. 583. The temptation is to use parties' actions as evidence of their original intention, which appears to have happened in *Smellie's Exrx.* v. *Smellie*, 1933 S.C. 725, where failure to demand interest was treated as indicating an absence of an obligation to pay interest. An example of proof being allowed of circumstances surrounding an alleged waiver is *G.E.A. Airexchangers Ltd.* v. *James Howden & Co. Ltd.*, 1984 S.L.T. 264. See para. 19–13.

[2] J. Rankine, *Law of Personal Bar in Scotland* (1921) p. 2.

[3] Bell, *Prin.* (10th ed.), s.27A.

That statement in itself can be used to illustrate a troublesome confusion. *Rei interventus* means, literally, the intervention of something. Like many Latin tags it is, on its own, incomplete. An intervention in what circumstances? At an earlier paragraph in Bells's text, Bell himself had defined *rei interventus*.[4] His classic definition was in the context of the circumstances in which *rei interventus* excludes the plea of *locus poenitentiae*. In other words, Bell had been discussing *rei interventus* as a method of perfecting an incomplete contract.[5] The trouble is that the term is also sometimes used, as in the passage quoted above, as the basis of an alteration of an already completed and enforceable contract.

23–04   These two senses in which *rei interventus* is used were recognised by Walker and Walker.[6] It is inconvenient and misleading to have a term which applies to two quite different types of event and it is thought better to restrict the use of *rei interventus* to its more familiar context of a bar to *locus poenitentiae*. It should not be used for the problem with which this chapter is concerned, namely the variation of obligations.

CLASSIFICATION OF VARIATION

23–05   There are probably two basic types of variation. The first is where all the parties to a contract consent to its variation. The consent may be express or implied. There may be a consent to discharge the old contract.[7] There may be consent to substitute different obligations, which gives rise to novation.[8] The second form of variation arises when, as a result of the actings of one or more of the parties, some of the contract terms become unenforceable. There is a bar to enforcement of rights. This does not require proof of the consent of all the parties.[9] This form of alteration of enforceable rights gives rise to considerable problems. It has not received thorough judicial analysis partly because few cases could provide a suitable opportunity even if the court was inclined to speculate on such broad issues.

23–06   In the form of variation giving rise to a plea of bar there is typically one of two situations, namely—

(1) One party makes a statement which waives some of that party's rights, *e.g.*: "I will not insist on payment on the 15th." There is unila-

---

[4] *Op. cit.* s.26.

[5] This phrasing may be objected to if it is considered that *Errol* v. *Walker*, 1966 S.C. 93 is wrongly decided, but the terminology is consistent with Bell's definition of *locus poenitentiae* in s.25. The correct scope of *rei interventus* in the sense of rendering a contract enforceable or complete is not material to the present discussion.

[6] *Evidence*, p. 304 and see authorities cited in note 84. Also *Bargaddie Coal Co.* v. *Wark* (1859) 3 Macq. 467.

[7] *e.g.* creditors discharging debts due; *British Linen Co.* v. *Esplin* (1849) 11 D. 1104.

[8] Discussed below.

[9] The mode of proof is different in the two forms. A true variation of a written contract may not be provable by parole evidence, whereas proof of bar would not be subject to this limitation. See Walker and Walker, *Evidence*, Chap. XXI.

teral action on which the other party may rely. There is a waiver of a right.

(2) One party fails to comply with an obligation and the other party does not object. There is inaction by both parties. This may give rise to the plea of acquiescence.

-07 The distinction between waiver and acquiescence is made for the purpose of analysis but in practice the two merge and it is not always necessary to separate them.

-08 Before giving examples of how waiver and acquiescence have operated there are two importations from English law which have confused the issue. These are (a) the need for prejudice and reliance and (b) the disregard of statements of intention.

Prejudice and Reliance

-09 There are dicta in Scots cases, based on English law, which suggest that the party in whose favour a right is waived must act to his prejudice in reliance on the waiver before he can found on the waiver. Lord Chancellor Birkenhead in *Gatty* v. *Maclaine* said[10]:

> " . . . the rule of estoppel or bar, as I have always understood it, is capable of extremely simple statement. Where A has by his words or conduct justified B in believing that a certain state of facts exists, and B has acted upon such belief to his prejudice, A is not permitted to affirm against B that a different state of facts existed at the same time."

It may be queried whether this is the rule in all cases. Assume that creditor C tells his debtor D: "You may pay one week late." Can D not rely on this although there is no prejudice to D? Not only is there no prejudice, but D gains because he keeps his money for a week longer. Similarly if C states he will accept a smaller payment than normal. Whereas at one time in English law it was thought that in cases of promissory estoppel the representee had to act to his detriment this is no longer certain.[11] In principle there is no reason why prejudice should exist before a statement is relied upon and we should be wary of applying in Scots law dicta based on estoppel in English law not least when English law may be changing its ground. Furthermore in certain circumstances creditor C's statement could be a unilateral promise, enforceable in Scots law without acceptance by D (or consideration).

---

[10] 1921 S.C.(H.L.) 1 at p. 7; see also *Mitchell* v. *Hays & Sons* (1894) 21 R. 600 at p. 610 *per* Lord Kinnear; *Stuart* v. *Potter, Choate & Prentice*, 1911 1 S.L.T. 377; *Cantors Properties (Scotland) Ltd.* v. *Swears & Wells Ltd.*, 1978 S.C. 310.

[11] Halsbury, Vol. 9, *s.v.* "Contract," para. 578; *Central London Property Trust Ltd.* v. *High Trees House Ltd.* [1947] K.B. 130; *Charles Rickards Ltd.* v. *Oppenheim* [1950] 1 K.B. 616; *D. & C. Builders Ltd.* v. *Rees* [1966] 2 Q.B. 617 at p. 624 *per* Lord Denning M.R.

23–10   Prejudice seems to be relevant when mere delay is being founded on, and we have a native doctrine of *mora*,[12] but generally statements or actions by a party can be relied upon although no prejudice results to the party so relying.[13]

Representation of Intention

23–11   It is also a feature of dicta based on English law, and Professor Gloag's treatment of this topic,[14] that the words or acts founded on must be more than a statement of intention. Gloag, however, did not distinguish the English doctrine of estoppel by representation from promissory estoppel. During the nineteenth century the English law of equity extended the doctrine of estoppel from a representation of an existing fact to a representation of an intention or a promise.[15] Gloag and Lord Kinnear[16] appear to have failed to appreciate that estoppel by representation, that is an estoppel founded on a representation of an existing fact, is only one of several forms of estoppel in English law.[17] To limit Scots law to any single form of estoppel would be unjustifiable. To burden it with the variations of opinion on the effect of various forms of estoppel would not be helpful.

23–12   The problem which exists is the extent to which statements or actions can be relied upon as a bar to the enforcement of rights. The issue has not been properly analysed in Scots law. An analogy with the difference between offers and statements of intention is not helpful because it should be that a statement of intention can be the basis of a plea of bar. The creation of a bar and the creation of a contract involve different standards. The principle is that a person cannot complain if others rely on a reasonable inference from that person's conduct. A statement of intention may give rise to another's reasonable belief that the intention will be acted upon.

WAIVER AND ACQUIESCENCE

23–13   Case law illustrates waiver and acquiescence. While "waiver" implies action and "acquiescence" implies inaction, there is only one principle in operation—which is whether it is reasonable for one party to a con-

---

[12] See below.

[13] See *Armia Ltd.* v. *Daejan Developments Ltd.*, 1979 S.C.(H.L.) 56 at pp. 68, 69 *per* Lord Fraser; at pp. 71, 72 *per* Lord Keith; *Banks* v. *Mecca Bookmakers*, 1982 S.C. 7; in *Cumming* v. *Quartzag*, 1980 S.C. 276 it was conceded that prejudice was relevant to a case of acquiescence. In *Morrison's Exrs.* v. *Rendall*, 1986 S.L.T. 227 it was decided that averments of conduct by the party relying on waiver were necessary to show waiver.

[14] *Contract*, p. 281.

[15] Snell's *Principles of Equity* (28th ed., 1982), p. 555.

[16] *Mitchell* v. *Hays & Sons* (1894) 21 R. 600 at p. 610.

[17] Halsbury, *s.v.* "Estoppel," para. 1502, states that there are four kinds of estoppel, namely estoppel by matter of record or quasi of record, estoppel by deed, estoppel *in pais* and promissory estoppel. Estoppel by representation is a form of estoppel *in pais*.

tract to rely on the inference to be drawn from the other party's behaviour. Waiver is a question of fact to be determined on consideration of all the relevant evidence.[18] There must be an obligation in existence before waiver arises.[19]

14 A common situation is where one party acts in breach of an obligation, the other party does not object, and the issue is the extent to which the other party is barred from founding on (a) the breach which has occurred and (b) future breaches. For example, X is due to make periodic payments such as interest or rent. He is consistently late in paying, but his creditor does not protest. When is the creditor barred from insisting on punctual payment?

15 The first critical point is the reaction of the creditor to the first breach. Mere delay in complaining of non-payment will not amount to bar unless the delay constitutes *mora*. Demanding payment within days of grace is not a waiver of rights.[20] Acceptance of one late payment will not bar enforcement of the right to punctual payment.[21] The next stage is reached when a series of payments is accepted late. In that event there may be such a course of dealings between the parties as to lead the payer reasonably to expect that regular payment will not be insisted upon. There is acquiescence by the creditor in past breaches.[22] Rights in respect of those breaches (such as termination provisions) cannot be insisted upon. To go further and to hold that there is a waiver of future breaches is to hold that the contract has been varied and that may require competent proof of the consent of both parties to a variation. Waiver or acquiescence by the creditor[23] prevents him relying on past breaches, but it does not necessarily force on him without his consent an alteration of the terms of the contract.

16 A further problem which arises with payment cases is when a creditor grants an unqualified receipt for payment and later argues that he had a claim against his debtor. The principle to be applied here is the same as in other cases—the inference from conduct which the other party is reasonably entitled to make. The reasonable man is consistent. He does not say today, "my position is so-and-so" and tomorrow say, "it is not so-and-so," when nothing has changed but his opinion. Therefore the granting of receipts for payment may bar claims, as when receipts for salary over 12 years barred a claim for back salary,[24] or a payment of

---

[18] *Armia Ltd.* v. *Daejan Developments Ltd.*, 1979 S.C.(H.L.) 56; *Banks* v. *Mecca Bookmakers*, 1982 S.C. 7 (a case of "waiver" arising from inaction).

[19] *Nairn* v. *South East Lancashire Ins. Co.*, 1930 S.C. 606; *Cantors Properties (Scotland) Ltd.* v. *Swears & Wells Ltd.*, 1978 S.C. 310 at p. 322 *per* Lord Cameron; at p. 326 *per* Lord Brand.

[20] *H.M.V. Fields Properties Ltd.* v. *Tandem Shoes Ltd.*, 1983 S.L.T. 114.

[21] *Gatty* v. *Maclaine*, 1921 S.C.(H.L.) 1; *Lucas's Exrs.* v. *Demarco*, 1968 S.L.T. 89.

[22] *Paterson* v. *Tod* (1828) 6 S. 1062; *Thomson* v. *Thomson & Co.* (1900) 2 F. 912; *Gatty* v. *Maclaine, sup. cit.* at p. 9 *per* Viscount Finlay; at p. 11 *per* Lord Shaw.

[23] Not by the creditor's predecessors: *What Every Woman Wants (1971) Ltd.* v. *Wholesale Paint and Wallpaper Co. Ltd.*, 1984 S.L.T. 133.

[24] *Davies* v. *City of Glasgow Friendly Soc.*, 1935 S.C. 224; and on accepting rents without claiming an increase see *Banks* v. *Mecca Bookmakers*, 1982 S.C. 7.

rent was made without reservation.[25] Payment of sums due under a building contract affected the onus of proof when the payer, at a later date, sought to re-open the account.[26] On the other hand it is not inconsistent to enforce and comply with a contract so far as possible and claim damages for any breach. Payment without reservation of the instalments of a price does not bar a claim for late delivery.[27] Attempting to resell subjects unsuccessfully may not bar a claim for implement of the original contract of sale.[28]

23–17   Fitted accounts, *i.e.* accounts between parties docquetted as correct by one party, raise a rebuttable resumption that all claims are settled.[29] A statement of disbursements can have the same effect as a docquet agreeing disbursements.[30]

23–18   The same principles can be shown in operation in other aspects of a contract. A landlord can be barred from objecting to a miscropping of which he had knowledge but which he allowed to continue. He has not agreed to alter the lease and so can insist on a return to the terms of the lease. The bar operates on his claim for past breaches.[31] A tenant who had given his landlord to understand that he, the tenant, was to remove, and allowed ploughing and manuring of land by an incoming tenant, was barred from objecting to the lack of a notice to remove.[32] Where debtors under bills of exchange had a right to raise defences to the enforcement of their liabilities, this right was lost by asking for time for payment.[33] Where insurance companies have had a right to insist on a procedure for making a claim, this has been lost, on the one hand, by an unjustified repudiation of liability[34] and, on the other, by carrying through their procedures without objection to a lack of timeous notice.[35] The waiver of suspensive conditions by one party is considered elsewhere.[36]

23–19   Inaction has been held to amount to waiver, as when a trustee in sequestration fails to adopt a contract timeously. He will be held to have

---

[25] *Broadwood* v. *Hunter* (1855) 17 D. 340; *cf. Macdonald* v. *Johnstone* (1883) 10 R. 959; on the possible importance of making payments "without prejudice" see para. 3–23, n. 47.

[26] *Johnston* v. *Greenock Corp.*, 1951 S.L.T.(Notes) 57.

[27] *Clydebank Engineering and Shipbuilding Co.* v. *Don Jose Ramos Yzquierdo y Castaneda* (1904) 7 F.(H.L.) 77; *Sutherland* v. *Montrose Shipbuilding Co.* (1860) 22 D. 665.

[28] *Lawrence* v. *Ritchie* (1893) 1 S.L.T. 44.

[29] *Glasgow Royal Infirmary* v. *Caldwell* (1857) 20 D. 1; *Laing* v. *Laing* (1862) 24 D. 1362; *McLaren* v. *Liddell's Trs.* (1862) 24 D. 577; *Struthers* v. *Smith*, 1913 S.C. 1116. The verb "to fit" means to adjust, balance or audit an account: W. M. Metcalfe, *Supplementary Dictionary of the Scottish Language* (1910).

[30] *Struthers* v. *Smith, sup. cit.*

[31] *Baird* v. *Mount* (1874) 2 R. 101; *Lamb* v. *Mitchell's Trs.* (1883) 10 R. 640; *Carron & Co.* v. *Mercer Henderson* (1896) 23 R. 1042; *Callender* v. *Smith* (1900) 8 S.L.T. 109.

[32] *Dunlop & Co.* v. *Meiklem* (1876) 4 R. 11; see also *Blain* v. *Ferguson* (1840) 2 D. 546.

[33] *Cairns Trs.* v. *Brown* (1836) 14 S. 999; *Allhusen* v. *Mitchell* (1870) 8 M. 600; *Shepherd* v. *Reddie* (1870) 8 M. 619.

[34] *Shiells* v. *Scottish Ass. Corp.* (1889) 16 R. 1014.

[35] *Donnison* v. *Employer's Accident Co.* (1897) 24 R. 681.

[36] para. 4–12.

abandoned it.[37] The failure of a landlord to institute the procedure for a rent review has amounted to a waiver of the right to the review.[38] A person who enters into a contract under intoxication should challenge it soon after he becomes sober or be bound by the contract.[39] On the other hand, to insist on some rights under a contract but not others, does not imply waiver of the other rights.[40]

20 Defective goods supplied under a contract of sale must be rejected timeously.[41] But special cases apart, mere delay in enforcing a right does not amount to waiver, unless there is prejudice to the other party.[42] The delay may produce a plea based on prescription or limitation.

KNOWLEDGE OF THE PERSON ACQUIESCING

21 Before a person is barred from insisting on rights because of the actions of the other party to the contract, it is essential that the person to be barred had knowledge of the actions founded on. The proposition is illustrated by cases involving land rights[43] and reference to knowledge will be found in the cases on leases cited above. In other instances the proposition is so obvious, it has been assumed.

NOVATION

22 Novation is the substitution of one obligation for another. One form of novation is delegation under which one debtor is substituted for another.[44] The other form of novation is the substitution of a new contract for the old contract. The new contract may be very similar to the old with, perhaps, only one clause changed, but the alteration gives rise to novation.

23 Novation in any of its forms requires the consent of the parties to the old contract. Consent could be inferred from conduct.[45] So far novation resembles the creation of any contract. The speciality of the plea is the

---

[37] *Anderson* v. *Hamilton & Co.* (1875) 2 R. 355.

[38] *Banks* v. *Mecca Bookmakers (Scotland) Ltd.*, 1982 S.C. 7.

[39] *Pollock* v. *Burns* (1875) 2 R. 497—but the logic of the decision is suspect. See para. 8–48 *et seq.*

[40] *Armia Ltd.* v. *Daejan Developments Ltd.*, 1979 S.C.(H.L.) 56.

[41] Sale of Goods Act 1979, s.11(5); *Morrison & Mason Ltd.* v. *Clarkson Bros.* (1898) 25 R. 427; *Aird & Coghill* v. *Pullan & Adams* (1904) 7 F. 258; *Hyslop* v. *Shirlaw* (1905) 7 F. 875; *Flynn* v. *Scott*, 1949 S.C. 442. Use of goods after rejection may bar rejection: see *Pollock & Co.* v. *Macrae*, 1922 S.C.(H.L.) 192 at p. 201 *per* Viscount Dunedin; *John Girvan & Sons* v. *Abel*, 1950 S.L.T. (Sh.Ct.) 60. See para. 14–109.

[42] *McKenzie* v. *British Linen Co.* (1881) 8 R.(H.L.) 8; *Mags. of Alloa* v. *Wilson*, 1913 S.C. 6 and see *Mora* below.

[43] *Campbell* v. *Clydesdale Banking Co.* (1868) 6 M. 943; *McGibbon* v. *Rankin* (1871) 9 M. 423; *Ben Challum Ltd.* v. *Buchanan*, 1955 S.C. 348 at p. 356 *per* Lord President Clyde. See also *Pirie* v. *Earl of Kintore* (1903) 5 F. 818 at p. 849 *per* Lord Kinross, on appeal (1906) 8 F.(H.L.) 16; *Macdonald* v. *Newall* (1898) 1 F. 68. For facts which may put a person on inquiry see *Murray* v. *Scottish Boatowners Mutual Ins. Assoc.*, 1986 S.L.T. 329.

[44] See para. 17–50.

[45] See various dicta in *McIntosh & Son* v. *Ainslie* (1872) 10 M. 304.

proof of the disappearance of an existing obligation. Novation is not presumed by the granting of a new obligation either by the original debtor or another. The presumption is that the new obligation is additional to, or as caution or corroboration for, the old obligation.[46] Many of the elderly cases on bills of exchange are examples of the new bill failing to extinguish obligations under the old bill.[47]

23–24   To establish novation there must be evidence that it was the intention of the parties to discharge the old obligation. There can be an express discharge, or words indicating that the prior obligation has been satisfied, or conduct such as giving up the principal deed.[48] In the notes to Erskine it is stated: "Novation and delegation are so entirely questions of fact and intention that it is impossible to lay down any general rules as to what will constitute either of them."[49] This is true once it is accepted that there must be proof of two factors (1) the creation of the new obligation *and* (2) the discharge of the old obligation. On the averments which may suffice to allow a proof that a contract has been superseded, see the case cited.[50]

23–25   Examples of the plea of novation being sustained are (a) when a creditor granted time to his debtor by a trust deed and deed of accession. This superseded the interest due under a prior bond[51]; (b) when a bank claimed against a cautioner's estate and a new bond was granted on the narrative that the prior bond had been discharged and the prior bond was delivered up by the bank[52]; (c) when engineers, in difficulty with their contract because employees were on strike, entered into an arrangement with shipowners under which the engineers supplied gear and tools and the ship-owners supplied men. This superseded the old contract and barred what in effect was a claim for damages caused by breach of the old contract[53]; (d) a new lease, even though informally constituted, may replace an old lease[54]; (e) missives of sale superseded a previous lease of the property which was continuing by tacit relocation.[55]

EFFECT OF NOVATION

23–26   The effect of novation is to extinguish the old obligation in the absence of contrary stipulation.[56] Novation proceeds by consent and if the consent is void or avoided, the old contract, if still in operation, will revive.

---

[46] Stair, I,xviii,8; Ersk., III,iv,22; Bell, *Prin.*, s.578.
[47] See Gloag, p. 724.
[48] Stair, *sup cit.*; Ersk., *sup. cit.*; Bell, *sup cit.*
[49] Ersk., III,iv,22.
[50] *Johnston* v. *Greenock Corp.* 1950 S.L.T.(Notes) 53.
[51] *Scott* v. *Sinclair* (1865) 3 M. 918.
[52] *Jackson* v. *MacDiarmid* (1892) 19 R. 528.
[53] *Hawthorns & Co. Ltd.* v. *Whimsters and Co.*, 1917 2 S.L.T. 63.
[54] *Sutherland's Tr.* v. *Miller's Tr.* (1888) 16 R. 10; *McFarlane* v. *Mitchell* (1900) 2 F. 901; *Buchanan* v. *Harris-Sheldon* (1900) 2 F. 935.
[55] *Kirkpatrick's Exrx.* v. *G. & A. Kirkpatrick*, 1983 S.L.T. 191.
[56] Bell, *Prin.*, s.579.

This may not have been foreseen by the parties and the consequences of this for a draftsman are discussed below.

PRACTICAL PROBLEMS WITH NOVATION

27 The usual practical problem is that parties give insufficient thought to whether or not the old contract is completely superseded. For example, a written contract is entered into for the supply of stationery for one year. At the end of that period the relevant employees of the parties are happy that the supply continues and it does. But is there a new informal contract or a continuation of the old contract with a variation of its period of operation? The point is not expressly considered but becomes important when a term in the written contract is founded on. Some draftsmen avoid this particular issue by sprinkling their drafts with references to "or as may be agreed" or similar formula, *e.g.*: "The price shall be X or as may be agreed." "The term of the contract shall be Y years, unless continued thereafter by the agreement of the parties." Here the draftsman aware of the lack of interest of others in legal detail is trying to make *one* agreement which alone will regulate future dealings. He cannot contract out of novation but he is having a good try at preserving the bulk of his carefully drafted phrases subject to the occasional variation on vital matters which the client may make.

28 When the draftsman is asked to novate, he has two main factors to consider in the preparation of the new contract, namely (1) the fate of outstanding claims under the old contract. Clients may not appreciate that novation can destroy claims for breach of the old contract. It is debatable whether this principle operates in respect of claims of whose existence the client is unaware (*e.g.* claims for latent defects about to become patent). Novation proceeds on consent and a party may consent to some things and not others. In any event there is a problem the commercial consequences of which need consideration. (2) What happens if the new contract becomes inoperative? The new contract might be reduced, frustrated, or rescinded on the ground of material breach. Does the old contract survive? This is a particular difficulty when a tenant enters into missives to buy the house which he lets. If the sale does not go ahead because, for example, the tenant cannot pay the price, what happened to the existing lease? Much depends on the terms of the missive of sale and carefully drafted missives would deal with the point. In one case the lease did not revive,[57] but the decision proceeded on arguments about tacit relocation. When the tenant's rights are stronger, as when the period of the existing lease has not expired, the discharge of those rights, so far as competent, needs consideration. The attempted preservation of those rights in the missives (intended as a qualification

---

[57] *Kirkpatrick's Exrx.* v. *G. & A. Kirkpatrick, sup. cit.*

on vacant possession being given by the seller) can cause considerable problems if the sale is not implemented but the seller claims novation and, thus, eviction of the tenant.

MORA

23–29 Mere delay short of a period of prescription will not bar a claim. As Lord Deas put it: "Mora is not a good *nomen juris*. There must either be prescription or not. We are not to rear up new kinds of prescription under different names."[58] But delay coupled with the disappearance of evidence may result in doubtful facts being presumed in favour of the defender.[59] Mora by itself is not a proper plea but must be accompanied by prejudice or acquiescence which must be averred and proved.[60]

CONFUSION

23–30 According to Stair[61]: "Confusion of obligations is, when the creditor and debtor become one person, as when the one succeedeth as heir to the other, or becomes singular successor in the debt; for thereby the obligation is ineffectual, seeing none can be creditor or debtor to himself." Confusion did not, however, extinguish the obligations, but suspended them so that they could revive if the debtor and creditor became distinct. According to Erskine, however, suspension of the right only occurred on some occasions.[62] Bell said that the rights were suspended, but if no interest of the creditor interferes to make it desirable to keep up the debt, it will be extinguished.[63] His editors, however, favoured the idea that confusion operated at once and irrevocably unless by taking an assignation of the debt or security it was kept up as a separate right.[64]

23–31 The law on *confusione* has many unresolved complexities. It has been judicially stated that: "It is . . . impossible to reduce the law of extinction of obligations *confusione* to any statement which will logically cover all the cases which may have arisen or may arise, but I think that it may be accepted that it ought not to be extended in application out of mere deference to legal logic."[65] The application of the doctrine to rights in

---

[58] *Mackenzie* v. *Catton's Trs.* (1877) 5 R. 313 at p. 317.

[59] *Bain* v. *Assets Co.* (1905) 7 F.(H.L.) 104; *Miller's Exrx.* v. *Miller's Trs.*, 1922 S.C. 150; *McKenzie's Exrx.* v. *Morrison's Trs.*, 1930 S.C. 830.

[60] *Halley* v. *Watt*, 1956 S.C. 370; *Bethune* v. *A. Stevenson & Co. Ltd.*, 1969 S.L.T.(Notes 12.

[61] Stair, I,xviii,9.

[62] Ersk., *Inst.* III,iv,27.

[63] Bell, *Prin.*, s.580.

[64] *Ibid.* And see *Healy & Young's Trs.* v. *Mair's Trs.*, 1914 S.C. 893 at p. 899 *per* Lord Johnston: "I think that such extinction or discharge takes place *ex lege* and independently of intention." For debts arising from contracts this is the commonsense view.

[65] *Healy & Young's Trs.* v. *Mair's Trs.*, *sup. cit.* at pp. 898, 899 *per* Lord Johnston.

security, feudal rights, leases, and other land rights has many specialities.[66] In the case of simple contracts the doctrine appears to pose few
practical problems. An example of confusion applying to a debt is *Elder*
v. *Watson*.[67] A man inherited the estate of a sister to which he was due
payment under a decree. The debt was extinguished on the expiry of six
months from the death of the man's predecessor.

PRESCRIPTION AND LIMITATION

Contractual Provisions on Prescription and Limitation

32 The lapse of time can either bar an action on an obligation (*i.e.* limitation) or extinguish the obligation (*i.e.* prescription).[68] The parties may
by contract provide that time will end their obligations, *e.g.* that a guarantee is for six months, that the contract is to run for one year, or that a
claim for short delivery must be made within three days. If the period
stated is the period during which the obligation is to run, there is normally no difficulty subject to the rule that parties cannot contract out of
the five or 20-year prescriptions.[69] If, however, the provision is in the
form of a restriction on enforcing an obligation (express or implied) the
effect of the Unfair Contract Terms Act 1977 has to be considered. The
Act applies to conditions which exclude or restrict liability,[70] although it
does not apply to all contracts.[71] For example, a condition that a claim
for short delivery must be made in three days would be subject to a "fair
and reasonable" test if it was in a consumer contract or a standard form
contract.[72]

Statutory Provisions on Prescription and Limitation

33 The statutory control of prescription and limitation is now mainly to be
found in the Prescription and Limitation (Scotland) Acts of 1973 and
1984 which implemented, with modifications, the recommendations of
the Scottish Law Commission.[73] Part I of the 1973 Act, dealing with
positive and negative prescriptions, came into force on July 25, 1976.

34 So far as contractual obligations are concerned the Act adopts a tripartite scheme, namely (1) a five-year prescription, (2) a 20-year prescription and (3) imprescriptible obligations.

---

[66] Gloag, pp. 725–730.
[67] (1859) 21 D. 1122.
[68] Bell, *Prin.*, s.586; *Macdonald* v. *North of Scotland Bank*, 1942 S.C. 369 at p. 373 *per*
Lord Justice-Clerk Cooper.
[69] Prescription and Limitation (Scotland) Act 1973, s.13.
[70] s.25(3).
[71] See paras. 12–26, 12–29.
[72] s.17.
[73] Scot.Law.Com. No. 15 (1970); Scot.Law.Com. No. 74 (1983). The 1973 Act was
amended by the Law Reform (Miscellaneous Provisions) (Scotland) Act 1980, s.23.

Five-year Prescription

(a) Obligations affected by five-year prescription

23–35   A five-year prescription under section 6 of the 1973 Act applies to an obligation listed in Schedule 1 which has subsisted for five years without (1) a relevant claim and (2) (except in the case of a bill or promissory note) an acknowledgment of the subsistence of the obligation.[74] Schedule 1 is a lengthy schedule which should be consulted for its terms. Of particular relevance to contractual claims is its application to (1) obligations to pay interest, (2) obligations to pay an instalment of an annuity, (3) obligations to pay rent or other periodical payment under leases and other land obligations, (4) obligations based on quasi-contract, (5) obligations under bills of exchange or promissory notes (except bank notes), (6) obligations arising from, or by reason of any breach of, a contract or promise. In terms of the schedule, the five-year prescription does not apply to *inter alia* (1) any obligation constituted or evidenced by a probative writ not being a cautionary obligation nor most obligations to make periodic payments of money, (2) any obligation under a contract of partnership or of agency, not being an obligation remaining, or becoming, prestable on or after the termination of the relationship between the parties under the contract.[75] To determine when the five-year period starts to run and when it ends reference must be made to the definition of "appropriate dates" in section 6(3), Schedule 2 and to the rules on computation of the period in section 14.

(b) Difficulties in calculation of period

23–36   For many contractual claims the operation of section 6 poses problems. Take two common claims, namely (1) a claim for price and (2) a claim for breach of contract. Goods or services are supplied but not paid for. The obligation to pay arises from a contract which normally will be improbative. Thus a five-year prescription applies. The only difficulty is to ascertain when the period starts to run. Section 6 starts the five-year period at "the appropriate date." For a single sale the appropriate date would be the date when the obligation (to pay the price, say) became enforceable. Under the Sale of Goods Act 1979, s.49 the seller may sue for the price either when property in the goods has passed to the buyer or when the price is due in terms of the contract. By analysing when the price can be competently claimed it is possible to decide the start of the period of prescription.[76]

---

[74] s.6(1).

[75] On prescription and partnerships see *Highland Engineering Ltd.* v. *Anderson*, 1979 S.L.T. 122.

[76] In a sale of heritage the price may be payable only when a title has been exhibited and a valid disposition delivered. See *Muir and Black* v. *Nee*, 1981 S.L.T. (Sh.Ct.) 68.

7   Now complicate the facts. The goods supplied are claimed to be materially defective. Under the mutuality principle the buyer withholds performance of his obligation (to pay the price) until the seller performs his obligation (to deliver goods conform to the contract). If the buyer's claim is justified, there is no enforceable obligation to pay the price, and so nothing on which prescription can run. If the buyer's claim is lacking in justification, the seller's right to the price prescribes from the date on which the price was due.[77]

8   A further complication arises if there is a series of transactions on a running account. Schedule 2 provides rules to determine the "appropriate date." That date will be the date on which payment for the goods last supplied became due. This has a beneficial effect because prescription has not run in respect of sales made at an earlier date than the last supply.[78]

9   In the case of breach of contract an enforceable obligation arises at the time of breach.[79] If both parties are in breach it has been suggested elsewhere[80] that, despite dicta to the contrary, each party can sue the other. Therefore prescription will run on each party's claim from the relevant time of breach, although obviously, unless all the breaches were on the same day, one party's claim will prescribe before or after the other party's claim.

(c) Ignorance of rights

40   One party may not know that the other party is in breach, *e.g.* where there is latent defect in goods supplied. In the case of personal injury claims there are elaborate provisions to deal with ignorant pursuers, but these do not apply to contractual claims.[81]

41   Section 11 provides that an obligation to make reparation (such as from breach of contract or promise) becomes enforceable on the date when the loss, injury or damage occurred.[82] When the creditor was ignorant of the loss, injury or damage,[83] the date is when he first became, or could with reasonable diligence have become, so aware. It has been suggested that the creditor must know that there is an obli-

---

[77] See a similar result on enforcement of missives—*Muir and Black* v. *Nee, sup cit.* An obligation to pay the price was enforceable, not when missives were concluded, but on delivery of a disposition when the price was payable.

[78] Similar rules apply to hire services, loan deposit of money, partnership, agency and instalment obligations. On the application of Sched. 2 to cautionary obligations see *The Royal Bank of Scotland Ltd.* v. *Brown*, 1982 S.C. 89.

[79] Unless the contract otherwise provides, *e.g.* if an architect must certify the amount due, liability to pay may not arise until the issue of his certificate: *McPhail* v. *Cunninghame D.C.*; *William Loudon & Son Ltd.* v. *Cunninghame D.C.*, 1985 S.L.T. 149.

[80] paras. 14–27 to 14–30.

[81] Or, strictly speaking, to other contractual claims, as it is possible to have an action of damages in respect of personal injuries arising out of a breach of contract.

[82] See *Renfrew Golf Club* v. *Ravenstone Securities Ltd.*, 1984 S.L.T. 170.

[83] See, on the calculation of when loss occurred in the enforcement of planning control, *George Porteous (Arts) Ltd.* v. *Dollar Rae Ltd.*, 1979 S.L.T. (Sh.Ct.) 51.

gation to make reparation. "In other words," to quote Lord McDonald, "the creditor must not only know that he has suffered loss, but that this has occurred in circumstances giving rise to an obligation upon someone (who may not be immediately identifiable) to make reparation to him. From that date he has five years in which to identify the person concerned and bring his claim against him."[84] Where there was a continuing act, neglect or default, the appropriate date is when the act, neglect or default ceased.

23–42   In *Dunlop* v. *McGowans*[85] a firm of solicitors failed to serve a notice to quit timeously before Whitsunday 1971. Their client did not obtain entry until a year later, *i.e.* Whitsunday 1972. An action was raised in November 1976 against the solicitors, based on negligence and breach of contract. It was met by the defence that the obligation to make reparation had been extinguished by the five-year prescription. The House of Lords held that the prescriptive period started to run when there was a concurrence of *injuria* and *damnum*. This occurred on Whitsunday 1971 when, but for the solicitors' negligence, their client would have obtained vacant possession. Nor could the items of loss be split into several headings with prescription running on each. The obligation to make reparation was indivisible.

Cautionary Obligations

23–43   The terms of the 1973 Act gave rise to some doubt about their application to cautionary obligations or guarantees.[86] A cautionary obligation, even if in a probative writ, is subject to the five-year prescription.[87] But when does the period start to run? It would in practice considerably hinder the operation of guarantees if they had to be renewed every five years. In *The Royal Bank of Scotland Ltd.* v. *Brown*,[88] guarantors undertook to make payment "on demand" of sums due to a bank by a company. The word "demand" made demand a condition precedent for the enforcement of the obligation by the bank. Accordingly prescription started to run from the date of the demand by the bank addressed to the guarantors, not from an earlier date. It should be noted that a different result could be reached with guarantees in other terms. It may be that the liability under the guarantee arises on the default of the debtor, or even without default. The quinquennial prescription will run from the date of the liability of the guarantor, and it is in the creditor's interest to postpone this date. The draftsman of a guarantee who tries to impose instant liability on the guarantor may find

---

[84] *Dunfermline D.C.* v. *Blyth & Blyth Associates*, 1985 S.L.T. 345.
[85] 1980 S.C.(H.L.) 73. See also *Riddick* v. *Shaughnessy, Quigley & McColl*, 1981 S.L.T.(Notes) 89.
[86] W. D. Antonio, "The Effect of Prescription on Guarantees," 1977 S.L.T.(News) 41.
[87] Sched. 1.
[88] 1982 S.C. 89.

that his enthusiasm for strict terms rebounds in the face of the creditor.[89]

Execution of Deeds by Companies

4 Section 6 does not apply to an obligation constituted or evidenced by a probative writ. The term "probative writ" is defined as "a writ which is authenticated by attestation or in such other manner as, in relation to writs of the particular class in question, may be provided by or under any enactment as having an effect equivalent to attestation."[90] Writs which are formally executed by companies are normally sealed with the common seal of the company and subscribed on behalf of the company by two of the directors or by a director and a secretary. This follows the provisions of the Companies Act 1985, s.36(3). The deed is not attested, the Scots rules on witnesses having been enacted when limited companies were unknown. From time to time it is argued that a deed executed by a company without witnesses is valid under s.36(3) but is improbative. There is a contrary view[91] and in practice attestation is uncommon. This controversy, however, affects the application of section 6 of and Schedule 1 to the Prescription and Limitation (Scotland) Act 1973. Is a deed executed by a company with seal and the two competent signatories, but without witnesses, a deed which is authenticated in a manner "provided by or under any enactment as having an effect equivalent to attestation"? Section 36(3) of the Companies Act 1985 does not in terms provide that compliance with its provisions is "equivalent to attestation." The section states that the deed is valid and that it is "binding whether attested by witnesses or not." This is probably sufficient to be "equivalent to attestation," although some doubt remains.[92]

The 20-year Prescription

45 Section 7 applies a 20-year prescription to an obligation of any kind unless it is an imprescriptible obligation or an obligation to make reparation in respect of personal injuries or death.[93] The 20-year period may be interrupted by a relevant claim or (except in the case of a bill or promissory note) a relevant acknowledgment of the subsistence of the

---

[89] In *Royal Bank of Scotland* v. *Brown, sup. cit.*, Lord Justice-Clerk Wheatley was not prepared to apply a *contra proferentem* construction to the bank's guarantee because (1) there was no doubt on construction and (2) he would not accept the unilateral guarantee as the document of the party to whom it was granted.

[90] Sched. 1, para. 4.

[91] J. M. Halliday, "Execution of Deeds by Limited Companies" (1979) 24 J.L.S. W.iii. Although the learned author does not discuss whether the deed is probative, he gives persuasive arguments for holding that attestation cannot be insisted upon. See also J. M. Halliday, *Conveyancing Law and Practice*, Vol. I, para. 3–10.

[92] With a probative deed the onus of proof that the deed was improperly executed is on the challenger. What is the position of a deed by a company which is not witnessed?

[93] s.7(2) was amended by the 1984 Act, Sched. 1, para. 2.

obligation. The running of the period is not suspended while the claimant is under legal disability in contrast to the five-year prescription when legal disability prevents prescription running.[94] Section 7 applies to all prescriptible obligations and is not limited, like section 6, to the list of obligations in Schedule 1, Part 1. Section 7 therefore applies to the obligations excepted from section 6, such as some obligations constituted or evidenced by probative writ, and some obligations under a contract of partnership or agency.

Imprescriptible Obligations

23–46   Imprescriptible rights are of rare importance in contractual disputes, but for the sake of completeness, the imprescriptible rights under Schedule 3 are, in summary, (1) real rights to ownership of land; (2) lessee's right to land under a recorded lease; (3) *res merae facultatis*; (4) right to recover property *extra commercium*[95]; (5) various obligations of a trustee; (6) obligations of certain third parties to make trust property forthcoming; (7) rights to recover stolen property; and (8) rights to be served as an heir or to make up or complete title to an interest in land.[96]

Interruption of Prescription

23–47   The periods of prescription can be interrupted in various ways. The five-year period does not run for any period during which the creditor was prevented from making a claim because of the fraud of the debtor, or error induced by the debtor, (unless the creditor could have discovered the fraud or error by reasonable diligence) or for any period during which the original creditor was under legal disability by reason of nonage or unsoundness of mind.[97]

23–48   The running of the five and 20-year periods is ended by a relevant claim or (except for a bill or promissory note) the relevant acknowledgment of the subsistence of the obligation.[98] "Relevant claim" and "relevant acknowledgment" are defined.[99] "Relevant claim" in broad terms means a claim by the creditor in court proceedings or in arbitration or the doing of diligence by the creditor. A letter demanding implement of the obligation would not be a relevant claim. When an action is raised before the expiry of the period and then substantially amended after the expiry of the period, the question arises of whether a relevant claim has been timeously made. It has been held that an action raised within five years which relies on one ground of negligence will prevent the extinc-

---

[94] s.14(1)(b).
[95] See *Mags of Kirkcaldy* v. *Marks & Spencer Ltd.*, 1937 S.L.T. 574 for a discussion of the inalienable property of a royal burgh. And see para. 8–04.
[96] This does not include a right to demand a disposition in *Macdonald* v. *Scott's Exrs.*, 1981 S.C. 75.
[97] ss.6(4) and 15(1).
[98] ss.6(1) and 7(1).
[99] ss.9 and 10.

tion of the obligation to make reparation albeit different grounds of negligence are added to or substituted for the original grounds after the expiry of the five-year period.[1] An initial writ in skeleton form has been sufficient to interrupt prescription.[2] It is suggested that if an action refers to an obligation, prescription of that obligation is normally interrupted although it is not until later that specification is provided in relevant pleadings of the breach of the obligation founded on.[3] It is otherwise if, after the five-year period, an action is sought to be amended so that pleadings for the first time refer to a particular obligation. For example, an obligation to commence divorce proceedings claimed within the five years could not, outside the five years, be amended to a claim based on obligation to convey heritage.[4] Court proceedings commenced during the five-year period (although later abandoned) interrupt the running of prescription.[5] The debt is being insisted in. To hold that the granting of a decree was the only event which interrupted prescription would have the peculiar result that an obligation could be extinguished if an action to enforce it was not concluded until over five years after its initiation.

49 The petitioning for, or concurring in a petition for sequestration, or the claiming in a sequestration interrupts the prescription of the debt of the creditor petitioning, concurring or claiming.[6] Similar rules apply on the liquidation of a company.[7]

50 Relevant acknowledgment means (again expressing the matter broadly) performance by the debtor towards implement of the obligation which indicates that the obligation still exists or an unequivocal written admission by or on behalf of the debtor to the creditor, or his agent, which clearly acknowledges that the obligation still subsists. Performance (whether actings or abstentions) must be by the debtor, not the creditor, and must be such as can reasonably be explained only by reference to the particular obligation in question. If there is more than one obligation (even although one contract) performance might be attributable to one obligation and not the other with the result that the other obligation prescribes.[8]

51 The varied responses of debtors to demands for payment could give rise to difficult questions of whether a relevant acknowledgment has

---

[1] *Macleod* v. *Sinclair*, 1981 S.L.T.(Notes 38.

[2] *British Railways Board* v. *Strathclyde Regional Council*, 1981 S.C. 90.

[3] See *MacLeod* v. *Sinclair, sup. cit.* at pp. 39, 40 *per* Lord Jauncey. It is an obligation which prescribes, not a contract. The distinction could be crucial. In practice, however, skeleton pleadings will refer to the contract and thus, impliedly, to all the obligations under that contract.

[4] *Lawrence* v. *J. D. McIntosh & Hamilton*, 1981 S.L.T. (Sh.Ct.) 73.

[5] *George A. Hood & Co.* v. *Dumbarton D.C.*, 1983 S.L.T. 238. The interruption can be founded on in any competent court. *British Railways Board* v. *Strathclyde R.C., sup cit.*

[6] s.9; Bankruptcy (Scotland) Act 1985, ss.8(5), 22(8), 48(7) and 73(5).

[7] s.613, Companies Act 1985.

[8] *Gibson* v. *Carson*, 1980 S.C. 356.

been given.[9] A formal letter is sent demanding payment. The sensible debtor, or his agent, may respond by telephoning to or calling at the creditor's office. There has been no written acknowledgment and no performance towards implement. Assume, however, that the debtor replies in writing: "I know that I am due to pay £200 but will you accept £5 a week." There is a clear acknowledgment of a liability to pay £200. The commercial client sends his response by telex. Is that writing? It is a means of reproducing words in visible form and, it is thought, is "writing" as defined in the Interpretation Act 1978.[10] Although the message can be received in the form of computer tape it is normally reproduced, and intended to be reproduced, in a form in which the words are visible.[11] If the message is recorded on tape and normally reproduced as sound that would not be "writing."

23–52   Debtors, however, have a habit of responding in incomplete or imprecise terms such as "will you take £5 a week?" That is not a clear acknowledgment of liability for any principal sum, and might only become so if read along with the letter of demand. What is required, however, is that there is acknowledgment that the "obligation still subsists," not a rehearsal of all the terms of the obligation. This suggests that the circumstances surrounding the debtor's response can be looked to. Of course, if the debtor pays £5, that may be performance towards implement of the obligation and will on that head interrupt prescription. This point is of importance if an action is raised after the debtor has made payment to account over a number of years. The five-year period will, in the simple case, run from the last payment, not from the original constitution of the debt.[12]

Payment after the Expiry of Prescription

23–53   The continuous running of the appropriate period of five or 20 years extinguishes the obligation.[13] No obligation then exists and any payment made may be recovered if the *condictio indebiti* is applicable.[14]

Personal Injuries

23–54   A breach of contract may result in personal injuries and a claim for damages, including solatium.[15] An action which includes such a claim must be brought within three years from the injuries subject to elabor-

---

[9] A minute of trustees has been held as acknowledgment of a claim—*Fortunato's J.F.* v. *Fortunato*, 1981 S.L.T. 277.

[10] Sched. 1.

[11] So also with the "Fax" system.

[12] If the debtor's obligation arises under a decree, the five-year prescription is inapplicable. The 20-year period applies. See Sched. 1, para. 2.

[13] ss.6(1), 7(1).

[14] See para. 9–89.

[15] See para. 20–98.

ate rules on extension of this time.[16] These and related rules are normally discussed in the context of delictual claims. Their operation in contract cases is unusual and guidance should be looked for elsewhere.

Other Statutory Periods of Prescription and Limitation

5 The provisions of the Prescription and Limitation (Scotland) Act 1973 are not exhaustive of the statutory law on prescription and limitation. Specific contracts may be governed by other rules. Details of these must be consulted in specialist works, but warning can be given here that special rules apply to:

(1) Contracts of carriage, whether by road, railway, sea or air.[17]

(2) Claims for breach of the Liners Conferences Code.[18]

(3) Claims against an employer for payments or deductions contrary to the Truck Acts.[19]

(4) Claims against the Post Office for loss of or damage to a registered inland packet.[20]

(5) Claims under the Uniform Law on International Sales.[21]

---

[16] Pt. II of the 1973 Act, as substantially amended by the Law Reform (Miscellaneous Provisions) (Scotland) Act 1980, s.23 and the Prescription and Limitation (Scotland) Act 1984.

[17] Carriage by Air Act (Application of Provisions) Order 1967. See Carriage by Air Act 1961; Carriage of Goods by Road Act 1965; Carriage of Goods by Sea Act 1971; Carriage by Air and Road Act 1979; Merchant Shipping Act 1979; Carriage of Passengers by Road Act 1974.

[18] Merchant Shipping (Liner Conferences) Act 1982, s.8.

[19] Truck Act 1896, s.5.

[20] Post Office Act 1969, s.30(1).

[21] Uniform Laws on International Sales Act 1967, Sched. 1, art. 49(1).

CHAPTER 24

DEATH AND INSOLVENCY

PART 1—DEATH

Expressed Intention

24–01 There may be express provision on the effect of death. Thus it may be provided that a partnership will continue despite the death of a partner.[1] A contract of service will normally terminate on the death of either employer or employee, but in principle there is no reason why there could not be contrary agreement.[2] While sometimes there might be a presumption against what has been described as "a sort of apostolic succession," if this is expressly provided for by the parties it should receive effect.

Implied Intention

24–02 The effect of death of one of the parties to a contractual obligation depends on the intention of the parties. In the absence of express provision in the contract this intention must be discerned in some other way. The obvious point is that the parties may never have thought about what they have not said. They had no intention, or if they did, each perhaps had a different intention. The intention of the parties must be gathered from the terms of the contract and from surrounding circumstances.[3]

24–03 In the search for intention it is debatable whether a presumption should be applied about the effect of death. In this context *a priori* assumptions have misled judges. As has been observed: "We must not start with any assumption or surmise of probability of intention on the part of the executant. His intention must be gathered from the words of the document."[4]

24–04 Yet it is useful to have some rules. The inferences from the contract and its circumstances may remain dubious despite, or because of, the

---

[1] *Hill* v. *Wylie* (1865) 3 M. 541; *Alexander's Tr.* v. *Thomson* (1885) 22 S.L.R. 828; *William S. Gordon & Co. Ltd.* v. *Mrs Mary Thomson Partnership*, 1985 S.L.T. 122; Partnership Act 1890, s.33. On payments to a widow of a deceased partner, see *Menzies' Trs.* v. *Black's Trs.*, 1909 S.C. 239.

[2] Implied in *Phillips* v. *Alhambra Palace Co.* [1901] 1 Q.B. 59; *c.f. Harvey* v. *Tivoli Manchester Ltd.* (1907) 23 T.L.R. 592.

[3] See Chap. 19, "Construction of Contracts."

[4] *Reid's Exrx.* v. *Reid*, 1944 S.C.(H.L.) 25 at p. 30 *per* Lord Russell.

most careful consideration. All the world may ever know is that A agreed to do X for B for five years. *Quid juris* if A dies during the five years? In Scots law, if the problem cannot be solved otherwise than by construction of the contract and by looking at its context, the answer will be that the obligation transmits to A's representatives. As Lord President Dunedin put it: "if a man binds himself he must make it very clear that he does not bind his representatives, for if he fails to make that clear the usual result will follow—that a man's representatives are bound by his obligations."[5] Twenty years later Dunedin, by this time a Viscount, came to reconsider his dictum. He gave it the approval of a member of the House of Lords and then passed over it to decide the case before him by construction of the contract.[6]

5   In *Rodger* v. *Herbertson*[7] Lord President Dunedin was construing the phrase, "heirs, executors and successors." He observed[8]:

> "I do not think that the pursuer can found any argument upon the word 'successors.' It is not essential in the collocation with 'heirs and executors.' I confess that I think it is really just an unmeaning phrase. I think it is put in because the parties wish to show quite clearly that, so far as the pecuniary part of the stipulation was conceived, their heirs, executors and successors were to be bound; and it was quite unnecessary, because a man's heirs are usually also bound unless he stipulates that they shall not be. Hence it does not seem to me that the term 'successors' really aids the argument one way or the other."

Delectus Personae and Assignation— the Comparison with Transmission on Death

06   There are various problems with *delectus personae* and the assignation of contracts. For example, the term *delectus personae* has an uncertain meaning. The common expression that a contract is assigned is likely to produce error because it is more accurate to say that some rights or duties are assigned. Sometimes part of a contract is assignable and part not. These and related issues are discussed elsewhere.[9] For present purposes it is sufficiently accurate to say that an obligation with an element of *delectus personae* cannot be assigned. An obligation without *delectus personae* may be assigned.[10]

07   The importation of the law on assignation into the transmission of contracts on death does have the comforting result that a lot more reported case law can be used to solve the problems. There is the feeling that the same issue is involved because of the phrase, *delectus personae*. As Lord Bramwell once said: "It is admitted that assigns are included,

---

[5] *Gardiners* v. *Stewart's Trs.*, 1908 S.C. 985 at p. 989.
[6] *Beardmore & Co.* v. *Barry*, 1928 S.C.(H.L.) 47 at p. 51.
[7] 1909 S.C. 256.
[8] at p. 260.
[9] para. 17–44.
[10] See, *e.g. Cole* v. *Handasyde & Co.*, 1910 S.C. 68; Chap. 17, "Assignation."

and I can see no reason why executors and administrators are not according to the ordinary rule."[11]

24–08   While it may be readily implied, however, that a contract or part of a contract which is assignable *inter vivos* does transmit on death what does not follow is that an unassignable contract will end on death. Under an assignation Y replaces X as creditor or debtor. The other party to the contract might reasonably prefer to remain tied to X. The choice is different if X dies. The question is not—is there a contract with X or Y? rather it is—does performance continue or not? In other words, substitute performance and the end of performance are different issues.

24–09   So an obligation to pay a sum may be unassignable, but it transmits to representatives. A lease may transmit to representatives although not assignable *inter vivos*.[12] The former idea that a tenant was selected for personal considerations which might not apply in the case of his heirs inhibited tenants from making any outlay on the land. For this, probably more than any other reason, the law allowed heirs to succeed, while using the concept of *delectus personae* to control transfer to an assignee.[13] It is also possible that an unassignable contract of insurance can transmit to representatives.[14] In *Rodger* v. *Herbertson*[15] a contract for the sale of a medical practice had obligations expressly binding on "heirs, executors and successors," but the contract was still not assignable. The result is that the assignability of a contract is not a test of its transmissibility on death.

Frustration

24–10   Death may make performance of a contract impossible or remove its purpose. Clearly when lesser events such as illness[16] or military service[17] may frustrate a contract, so may death.[18] However, this may not take the problem much further. As Lord Reid said in the case of *Davis Contractors* v. *Fareham U.D.C.*: "It appears to me that frustration depends, at least in most cases, not on adding any implied term, but on the true construction of the terms which are in the contract read in the light of the nature of the contract and of the relevant surrounding circumstances when the contract was made."[19] The contract must be construed. The problems of frustration are discussed elsewhere.[20]

---

[11] *Crosse* v. *Bankes* (1886) 13 R.(H.L.) 40 at p. 42.
[12] Rankine, *Leases*, pp. 157, 161, 172; Paton and Cameron, *Landlord and Tenant*, pp. 172 *et seq*.
[13] Hume, *Lectures*, Vol. IV, p. 88.
[14] Implied in *Kelly* v. *Cornhill Ins. Co.*, 1964 S.C.(H.L.) 46.
[15] 1909 S.C. 256.
[16] *e.g. Hart* v. *A. R. Marshall & Sons (Bulwell) Ltd.* [1978] 2 All E.R. 413.
[17] *Morgan* v. *Manser* [1948] K.B. 184.
[18] *e.g. Smith* v. *Riddell* (1866) 14 R. 95.
[19] [1956] A.C. 696 at pp. 720 and 721.
[20] See Chap. 15.

Transmission to Whom?

11 It is possible to provide for a contract to transmit not to executors but to those who succeed to heritable property. The obligation then "runs with the lands." The distinction between this and an obligation which is binding on executors can be crucial but further consideration of this would involve detailed comment on cases such as *Jolly's Exrx.* v. *Viscount Stonehaven*[21] and *McCallum* v. *Stewart.*[22] This work is not primarily concerned with heritable rights and obligations.

Examples of Transmission to Representatives

12 An obligation on a director to subscribe for shares has, with difficulty, been held binding on his executor.[23] Also transmitting to representatives were a creditor's undertaking on calling up a loan[24]; an obligation to take goods for five years,[25] an obligation to purchase sheep at the end of a lease,[26] and a hire-purchase contract for a television set.[27] On the other hand neither an option to subscribe for shares[28] nor a right to free possession of a farm and stock[29] has been held to transmit.

13 Rights may transmit, for example, the right to receive money[30] implied in an insurance contract in *Kelly* v. *Cornhill Insurance Co.*[31] It is with the right to receive, or the duty to pay periodical sums that the nature of the problem of construction can be most clearly illustrated.

Problems with Particular Cases

(a) Periodical payments

14 An annuity is an annual sum and the period of payment is normally the life of the annuitant, otherwise the payment would be in perpetuity. It is not that perpetual payments are impossible. Conveyancers are familiar with them. But perpetuity is an unlikely result of a commercial contract or a family arrangement. However, the annuitant's death is not always the termination of the obligation.

An annuity can be payable during the life of the payer or anyone else's life with the result that it continues due after the annuitant's

---

[21] 1958 S.C. 635.
[22] (1870) 8 M.(H.L.) 1.
[23] *Beardmore & Co.* v. *Barry*, 1928 S.C.(H.L.) 47.
[24] *Lawsons's Trs.* v. *Cesari's Trs.* (1901) 9 S.L.T. 355.
[25] *Gilmour & Sons* v. *Nunn's Trs.* (1899) 7 S.L.T. 292.
[26] *Gardiners* v. *Stewart's Trs.*, 1908 S.C. 985.
[27] *Woodfield Finance Trust (Glasgow) Ltd.* v. *Morgan*, 1958 S.L.T. (Sh.Ct.) 14.
[28] *Tawse's Trs.* v. *Lord Advocate*, 1943 S.C. 124.
[29] *Torrance* v. *Traill's Tr.* (1897) 24 R. 837.
[30] *Crosse* v. *Bankes* (1884) 11 R. 988 at pp. 993 *et seq.*, opinion of Lord Shand; (1886) 13 R.(H.L.) 40.
[31] 1964 S.C.(H.L.) 46.

death.[32] In England a similar problem has arisen with a husband's obligation to support his wife under a separation agreement. Obviously this ceases with the death of the wife, but what happens if the husband dies first? Must his estate continue payment to the widow? In *Kirk* v. *Eustace*[33] it was held that the obligation to pay continued after the husband's death. It terminated on the death of the wife.[34] But in *Kirk* the provision had been expressed as "during the life of the wife." In the later case of *Langstone* v. *Hayes*[35] these words were absent and this, and the tenor of the other clauses, produced the result that payment was due only during the joint lives of the parties. Scottish authority is meagre, but a husband can bind his executors to pay aliment[36] although the traditional form of separation agreement limits the payment to the joint lives of the parties.[37] Similar problems arise with the construction of court orders.[38] In the construction of contracts each contract is different. As was said in *Langstone*:

> "The question whether such a contractual obligation passes to the executor must in our view depend on the terms of the contract which is supposed to pass it on. In the case of a promise of an essentially personal kind, such as to paint a picture, obviously it does not pass: but the reason it does not pass is because the contract truly interpreted did not intend it to pass. In other words the passing or lapsing of the promise on the death of the promisor must depend on the terms and nature of the contract, construed like every other contract in the light of its attendant circumstances."[39]

(b) Contracts of service

24–15   It is usually said that the death of either employer or employee ends a contract of service. The classic case is *Hoey* v. *MacEwan & Auld*.[40] A firm of accountants engaged a clerk for five years. After one year, one of the partners died and the remaining partner indicated that the clerk's service was terminated. The court held that the contract was terminated by the dissolution of the partnership. The result turned on the terms of the contract. Part of the remuneration of the servant was a share of profits and this showed reliance on the vigour of the parties with whom the contract was made. Similarly in *Graves* v. *Cohen*[41] the death of a jockey's employer terminated the contract in part because the jockey

---

[32] *Crosse* v. *Bankes* (1886) 13 R.(H.L.) 40; *Reid's Exrx.* v. *Reid, sup. cit.*
[33] [1937] A.C. 491.
[34] See also *Gilhespie* v. *Burdis* (1943) 169 L.T. 91.
[35] [1946] K.B. 109.
[36] *Palmer* v. *Bonar*, Jan. 25, 1810, F.C.; *Meiklam's Trs.* v. *Meiklam* (1868) 6 S.L.R. 2; See also Family Law (Scotland) Act 1985, s.1(4).
[37] *Juridical Styles*, Vol. 1, p. 761 (6th ed., 1907); *Encyclopaedia of Scottish Legal Styles*, Vol. 8, p. 120.
[38] See s.5(5), Divorce (Scotland) Act 1976; *cf. Hinde* v. *Hinde* [1953] 1 All E.R. 171; *Sugden* v. *Sugden* [1957] P. 120.
[39] At pp. 113 and 114.
[40] (1867) 5 M. 814.
[41] (1930) 46 T.L.R. 121.

was to receive a share in the winnings of all the horses belonging to the employer. This showed an interest in the well-being of the employer.

16 However there is no hard and fast rule. An employer might exercise little or no control over the work to be done. He may restrict his activities to paying wages and outlays and receiving the income from the business. It may be a matter of disinterest to the employee which employer performs these functions. In this case the employer's death may not end the contract.[42] The gamekeeper or shepherd employed by the absentee landlord are possible examples.

17 The death of an employee will almost always end the contract of service. There could be an express provision to the contrary. Hereditary offices were once a feature of Scots law, and, as mentioned earlier, there are reported cases of representatives succeeding in partnerships which are a reasonably close analogy. It is difficult, however, to think of realistic examples in which it would be implied that the representatives take over from the employee.

(c) Contracts for services

18 Consider a simple contract between two individuals for the construction of a garage. What happens if either the employer or the builder dies before completion of the contract? The employer's personal presence is not vital to the performance of the contract so it may be suggested that the contract passes to his representatives. There is support for this in *Hoey* v. *MacEwan & Auld*. Lord President Inglis observed: "Where, for example, the contract is to build a house, or to paint walls, or to drain a field, it refers to a particular physical subject matter, and on the death of the employer the property passes to his heir, and with it naturally the obligation regarding it."[43] But what happens on the death of the builder? In the absence of an express term, or unusual facts, there is not much left except the feeling that the contract could be performed by the builder's executors. They can employ someone to carry out the contract. As explained earlier there is some tendency in Scots law to hold that a man's executors are bound by his obligation. Therefore, in the normal case, the builder's executors are bound. There is an old English case in which the executors carried out a contract to erect woodwork.[44] The contrary argument is, to quote Hudson: "The personality of a small local builder may be vital to a building contract where the quality of the workmanship is of relatively great importance—as in the case of a private dwelling-house."[45] However, delegation of building work is commonplace and unless it is clear from the contract that personal

---

[42] See *Phillips* v. *Alhambra Palace Co.* [1901] 1 Q.B. 59; *cf. Harvey* v. *Tivoli, Manchester Ltd.* (1907) 23 T.L.R. 592.

[43] *Sup. cit.* at p. 817.

[44] *Marshall* v. *Broadhurst* (1831) 1 Cr. & J. 403.

[45] Hudson's *Building and Engineering Contracts* (10th ed., 1970), p. 361.

supervision must occur, it is difficult to see why it should be implied. The frequency with which builders are limited companies may not be irrelevant in deciding what should happen on an event which, unfortunately, was not regulated by the terms of the contract.

(d) Mandate

24–19　Mandate involves three parties, a principal, an agent and a third party. No speciality attaches to the death of the agent or the third party. As a general rule the death of the principal terminates the contract.[46] There may be exceptional cases where this does not happen as with the procuratory *in rem suam*[47] which at least in certain circumstances includes a cheque[48]—or with other irrevocable mandate. But again there is no difference from other contracts.

24–20　The effect of death on a contract is normally instantaneous. In cases on dissolution of partnership it has been said: "Death operates a dissolution of itself; and, being a public fact, all men are bound to know it"[49] and "extinction by death does not require either private intimation or public notice."[50] With mandate it is different. The *ratio* of the decision in *Campbell* v. *Anderson*[51] is that the factor of a person who is abroad is entitled to act until he receives authentic news of the death of his principal.

24–21　It is pertinent to ask for the justification for a special rule with mandate. English law may be different.[52] After all how can an agent have authority, including apparent authority, when no authority can exist?[53] Any unfairness to the agent who unknowingly acted without authority can be mitigated in Scots law by applying the principles of *negotiorum gestio* and recompense.

24–22　It is possible to argue in favour of the Scots rule on the grounds that (1) it *is* consistent with a doctrine of apparent authority. (2) It has been held in the context of insurance that a permission to drive can exist after the death of the person giving permission.[54] Authority does not automatically end on death. (3) The rule is fair to the agent who otherwise would act in ignorance of his lack of authority with all that that implies. (4) It is fair to the third party who, if his contract is not terminated by the death of the principal, is in a similar situation to what was intended.

---

[46] *Life Association of Scotland* v. *Douglas* (1886) 13 R. 910.
[47] *Shaw* v. *Dunipace* (1629) Mor. 3166.
[48] *Bryce* v. *Young's Exrs.* (1866) 4 M. 312 at p. 317 *per* Lord Deas and see para. 17–64.
[49] *Christie* v. *Royal Bank of Scotland* (1839) 1 D. 745 at p. 765; on appeal (1841) 2 Rob.App. 118.
[50] *Aytoun* v. *Dundee Bank* (1844) 6 D. 1409 at p. 1416 *per* Lord Fullerton.
[51] *Campbell* v. *Anderson* (1826) 5 S. 86; (1829) 3 W. & S. 384.
[52] See *Blades* v. *Free* (1829) 9 B. & C. 167; *cf. Drew* v. *Nunn* (1879) 4 Q.B.D. 661 at p. 668 *per* Brett L.J.
[53] See Chitty, *Contract* (25th ed.), para. 2328; Bowstead, *Agency* (14th ed.), p. 427.
[54] *Kelly* v. *Cornhill Ins. Co.*, 1964 S.C.(H.L.) 46.

(5) Any loss is suffered by the estate of the principal but the interests of commerce override the protection of the estate. (6) It is a fiction always to regard death as a public fact. It may, or may not, be publicised. It may be known to many, few or none. (7) The rule in the U.S.A. that authority is terminated by death has led to exceptions being allowed. Williston states: "The harshness of the general rule, however, has led to decisions by several courts that unless the act in question had to be done in the principal's name, notice of the principal's death is necessary. And this exception to the general rule has, in a number of jurisdictions, been extended to cases of payment of a check (sic) by a bank after the death of the depositor but before the bank had notice."[55]

(e) Formation of contract

23 Suppose that a solicitor offers for a property on behalf of a client. Unknown to those involved in the contract, the client dies shortly before acceptance of the offer. Is there a valid contract? It could be argued, following the authorities on mandate, that a solicitor who acts in ignorance of the death of his client may nevertheless bind his client's estate. A solicitor could enter into a contract on behalf of a client who had died shortly before the offer was made. Death after the offer should not alter the nature of the problem.

24 Against this there is the dictum of Lord President McNeill in *Thomson* v. *James*.[56] He said: "The contract is not made until the offer is accepted; and if the person with whom you merely intend to contract dies or becomes insane before you have contracted with him, you can no longer contract directly with him. You cannot, by adhibiting your acceptance to an offer, and addressing it to a dead man or a lunatic, make it binding on him, whether his death or insanity be or be not known to you."[57]

25 This can be applied without difficulty to the person who makes his own offer. But must it be modified if the offer is made by an agent unaware of the death? The conclusion is unavoidable that an agent may do what his principal cannot. An agent may contract despite the death of the principal and this has the corollary that the third party may also contract. There is a further problem of the lack of *bona fides* if the third party is aware of the death and the agent is not, but assuming good faith and ignorance of the death on both sides a contract for the sale of the property can be completed. The issue, however, remains to be fully argued and decided.

---

[55] Williston (3rd ed.), s.279. A similar rule operates here. See Bills of Exchange Act 1882, s.75; Wallace and McNeil's *Banking Law* (8th ed., 1949), p. 25; *Rogerson* v. *Ladbroke* (1822) 1 Bing. 93. On the relationship with the cheque as an assignation, see *Bank of Scotland* v. *Reid* (1866) 2 Sh.Ct. Rep. 376.

[56] (1855) 18 D. 1 at p. 10.

[57] See also Stair, I,x,6; Bell, *Prin.*, s.79.

(f) Delivery of deeds

24–26 If a client dies after signing a deed, but before delivering it, the deed cannot then be effectively delivered. A memorable example is the old case of *Stamfield's Creditors* v. *Scot's Children.*[58] An assignation was found signed and lying on the table beside the strangled body of its granter. The deed was held to be undelivered. Apparently if steps have been taken to deliver the deed, as by giving it to someone to post they may be sufficient to count as delivery but the point is not clearly decided.[59] It is a question of fact in each case whether delivery has taken place. It would create horrendous problems if delivery to an employee or agent was always treated as completed delivery to the grantee.

If a client gives a deed to his solicitor, the death of the client will terminate the solicitor's authority to deliver the deed.[60] There are two qualifications to this (1) following the rule on mandate explained above, the solicitor who was ignorant of his client's death, could effectively deliver the deed and (2) in certain circumstances a deed is effective without delivery. This has been discussed elsewhere.[61]

Unfinished Work

24–27 If a contract does terminate on death what happens about work already done under it? Completed work must be paid for. The employee or his executors are entitled to wages up to the termination[62] although some doubtful authority gives the employee greater rights if the employer dies.[63] When a book was to be completed in instalments, the executors of the author were entitled to payment for the one finished volume.[64]

24–28 The problem is greater if work has been done which cannot be regarded as completed or which it would not be fair to pay for *pro rata* in terms of the contract price, *e.g.* an unfinished portrait or building. The solution here should be the same as that on frustration of contract.[65] There is an equitable adjustment. The extent to which this is possible is a matter of dispute. It is for consideration whether or not the possibility of unfinished work should be regulated by the terms of the contract. Sometimes it will be too difficult to provide for every possibility and the common law, whatever it is, and commercial sense must be left to settle a dispute.

---

[58] (1696) 4 Bro.Supp. 344. See comments on this case in Bell, *Lectures on Conveyancing.* (3rd ed., 1882), pp. 102, 103. See further Chap. 7, "Delivery of Deeds."

[59] *Crawford* v. *Kerr* (1807) Mor.App. "Moveables" No. 2; *cf. Dowie* v. *Tennant* (1891) 18 R. 986.

[60] *Life Association of Scotland* v. *Douglas* (1886) 13 R. 910.

[61] para. 7–29.

[62] Bell, *Prin.*, s.179.

[63] Ersk., III,iii,16; *Hoey* v. *MacEwan & Auld, sup. cit.*; *White* v. *Bullion's Reps.* (1908) 24 Sh.Ct. Rep. 330.

[64] *Constable & Co.* v. *Robison's Trs.* (1808) Mor.App. "Mutual Contract" No. 5.

[65] para. 15–40.

PART 2—INSOLVENCY

-29 Insolvency does not by itself prevent a person entering into contracts. Insolvency is rather like a cloud. It may "pass over a man like a summer cloud—on him one day and gone the next—his affairs sometimes gloomy, sometimes bright."[66] Nor is there any duty on an insolvent person to disclose his circumstances to those with whom he is about to contract. Such a doctrine would, in Professor Bell's words[67] be:

> "inconsistent with an advanced state of commerce. The most flourishing and successful merchants are exposed to accidental losses, which may for a moment make them insolvent on the face of their books: but they still go on in full credit; and if no other misfortunes overtake them, proceed in the fair road to affluence. If a merchant, whatever might be his prospects or resources, were obliged, the instant that his ledger presented to him the view of insolvency, to relinquish his trade, and call his creditors together, the general trading interest would suffer; but most especially his individual creditors would feel the loss. A merchant's capital is in continual fluctuation; and an interruption to his trade, in consequence of every such threatened danger, would prove a death-blow to all the speculations in which he might have embarked his capital, and his funds would be recalled before the regular profits which were to redeem him from insolvency could return."

-30 So it is that a person may lend to one who is insolvent[68] or may sell to him[69] and accept payment in cash from him.[70] Provided an insolvent person does not offend the rules on fraudulent preferences and gratuitous alienations, he may enter into valid contracts. If representations are made about his credit in some circumstances there is a remedy because misrepresentation has induced the contract.[71]

Fraudulent Trading

-31 After a person has resolved to stop paying his debts it is fraudulent to continue to contract or to accept delivery of goods supplied on credit.[72] A person who is contemplating his sequestration is not bound to reject goods[73] but the moment that the decision is made to stop trading the position changes. After a consultation with a law agent it was observed that persons "could not in *bona fide* have entered into new contracts, or paid any money or received additional material."[74] In *Birrell's Tr.* v.

---

[66] *Coutt's Tr. and Doe* v. *Webster* (1886) 13 R. 1112 at p. 1117 *per* Lord Young.

[67] *Comm.*, L.I. 265. See also *Clarke & Co.* v. *Miller & Son's Tr.* (1885) 12 R. 1035 at p. 1042 *per* Lord Justice-Clerk Moncreiff.

[68] Bell, *Comm.*, II,231.

[69] *Richmond* v. *Railton* (1854) 16 D. 403.

[70] *Nordic Travel Ltd.* v. *Scotprint Ltd.*, 1980 S.C. 1.

[71] See para. 10–62.

[72] *Schuurmans* v. *Tweedie's Tr.* (1828) 7 S. 1110; *Watt* v. *Findlay* (1846) 8 D. 529. See for more discussion para. 10–45.

[73] *Ehrenbacher & Co.* v. *Kennedy* (1874) 1 R. 1131 at p. 1135 *per* Lord President Inglis.

[74] *Clarke & Co.* v. *Miller & Son's Tr.* (1885) 12 R. 1035 at p. 1041 *per* Lord Justice-Clerk Moncreiff.

Clark and Rowe[75] a Glasgow merchant bought a quantity of tea and coffee from sellers in London. The tea was delivered to a Glasgow warehouse at 10.30 a.m. The buyer decided to apply for his sequestration at 1 p.m. The coffee was delivered to a store at 1.40 p.m. The tea, but not the coffee, was part of the bankrupt buyer's estate. The law of England may have adopted the principle that whatever comes into possession of the bankrupt falls into the general fund, but Scots law has developed a principle of a civil fraud.[76]

24-32   If any business of a company is carried on with intent to defraud creditors of the company or creditors of any other person, or for any fraudulent purpose, every person who was knowingly a party to the carrying on of the business commits a criminal offence.[77] Similar activity can result in personal liability for debts, if the company is wound up.[78]

Various Consequences of Insolvency

24-33   Although insolvency by itself does not prevent a contract being entered into, or terminate a contract already created, there are other rules which may operate as a consequence of the insolvency of one of the parties to a contract.

(1) Insolvency may prevent a party implementing his obligations with the result that the other party to the contract may withhold performance.[79] This is a consequence of the mutuality principle. In contracts of service it has been held that liquidation of the employer terminates the employee's contract[80] unless the liquidation is for the purposes of a reorganisation.[81] It is debatable whether this is in accordance with Scottish principles which would give the employee an option to accept a repudiation, or rescind because of a material breach or withhold performance. Automatic termination is not the normal result. The "innocent" party may elect from a range of remedies. In practice the employee and the liquidator will either agree to work with each other, or not, which avoids the need to have a close analysis of the precise effect of the winding-up on the contract of service.

(2) Leases frequently have express provisions for irritancy in the event of insolvency of the tenant. This is an option available to the land-

---

[75] (1874) Guth.Sh.Cas. (1st Ser.) 86.

[76] *Schuurman* v. *Tweedie's Tr., sup. cit.* at p. 1113 *per* Lord Alloway.

[77] Companies Act 1985, s.458.

[78] s.630.

[79] *e.g. Arnott's Trs.* v. *Forbes* (1881) 9 R. 89—feuduty may be withheld when superior unable to form streets and sewers; *Linton* v. *Sutherland* (1889) 17 R. 213 (tenant could withhold delivery of sheep when landlord *vergens ad inopiam*).

[80] *Day* v. *Tait* (1900) 8 S.L.T. 40; *Laing* v. *Gowans* (1903) 10 S.L.T. 461; *McEwan* v. *Upper Clyde Shipbuilders Ltd.* (1972) 7 I.T.R. 296.

[81] *Midland Counties Bank Ltd.* v. *Attwood* [1905] 1 Ch. 357. See also *Commercial Bank of Scotland* v. *Pattison's Trs.* (1881) 18 R. 476 for the effect of a voluntary winding-up for reconstruction on a cash credit account. See generally G. B. Graham, "The effect of liquidation on contracts of service" (1952) 15 M.L.R. 48; also at para. 8–108.

lord.[82] Even if the clause states that the lease is *ipso facto* null and void the irritancy does not take effect unless the landlord declares that he is exercising his option to irritate.[83] In the absence of an irritancy clause or the exercise of an option under it the lease continues to exist. If the bankrupt has paid rent in advance or can continue to pay rent the lease continues.[84] A trustee in sequestration or a liquidator may adopt a lease, as with any other contract[85] but if the lease prohibits a transfer to legal assignees that prevents a trustee in sequestration, but not a liquidator, gaining title to the lease.[86] The reason for the distinction is that on sequestration there is a transfer to the trustee, while on liquidation normally property remains vested in the company.[87]

(3) Certain states of insolvency may have an effect by legislation. Thus, in a contract of sale of goods, a seller has a lien or right to retention and a right to stoppage *in transitu* when the buyer becomes insolvent.[88] A person is deemed to be insolvent if he has either ceased to pay his debts in the ordinary course of business or he cannot pay his debts as they become due, whether or not he is apparently insolvent or has committed an act of bankruptcy.[89] A partnership is dissolved by the bankruptcy of any partner, subject to any agreement between the partners.[90] By "bankruptcy" is meant sequestration.[91] Because the partnership is dissolved the result is the termination of any contract. One of the contracting parties has ceased to exist.[92]

(4) Certain states of insolvency may have an effect on fraudulent preferences or gratuitous alienations by the debtor.[93]

(5) On the effect of sequestration, or liquidation or receivership, see under "Capacity."[94] With certain exceptions the act of a bankrupt after sequestration is null.[95] On liquidation of a company the liquidator

---

[82] *Buttercase & Geddie's Tr.* v. *Geddie* (1897) 24 R. 1128. The operation of irritancies is subject to the control of the Law Reform (Miscellaneous Provisions) (Scotland) Act 1985, ss.4 and 5. See para. 20–146.

[83] *Waugh* v. *More Nisbett* (1882) 19 S.L.R. 427.

[84] *Fraser* v. *Robertson* (1881) 8 R. 347.

[85] See paras. 8–112 and 8–124.

[86] *Buttercase & Geddie's Tr.* v. *Geddie, sup. cit.*: *Walker* v. *McKnight* (1886) 13 R. 559; *Fraser* v. *Robertson* (1881) 8 R. 347 at p. 349 *per* Lord President Inglis.

[87] *Gray's Trs.* v. *Benhar Coal Co.* (1881) 9 R. 225 at p. 231 *per* Lord Shand; *Queensland Mercantile and Agency Co. Ltd.* v. *Australasian Investment Co. Ltd.* (1888) 15 R. 935 at p. 939 *per* Lord President Inglis; *Smith* v. *Lord Advocate*, 1978 S.C. 259. See contra G. L. Gretton, "The Title of a Liquidator" (1984) 29 J.L.S. 357.

[88] Sale of Goods Act 1979, ss. 41–46.

[89] s.61(4). Bankruptcy (Scotland) Act 1985, s.75(9).

[90] Partnership Act 1890, s.33(1).

[91] s.47.

[92] *Walker* v. *McKnight, sup cit.*; *cf. William S. Gordon & Co. Ltd.* v. *Mrs Mary Thomson Partnership*, 1985 S.L.T. 122, where there was a condition in the agreement that death did not dissolve the partnership.

[93] See paras. 10–40 to 10–44 for a partial treatment. Bankruptcy (Scotland) Act 1985, ss.34 and 36. It is beyond the scope of this work to give a detailed discussion of the issues involved which include preferences by companies.

[94] paras. 8–108 to 8–127.

[95] Bankruptcy (Scotland) Act 1985, s.32(8).

supersedes the directors except in exceptional circumstances.[96] A
receiver supersedes directors as agents of the company in respect of the
assets under the control of the receiver.[97]

(6) A contract may expressly provide what is to happen in the event of
the insolvency of one of the parties. Care must be taken to define the
circumstances in which such a provision operates. The word "bankruptcy" may mean practical insolvency, absolute insolvency, notour
bankruptcy or sequestration. The word "insolvency" may mean any of
several different states, *e.g.* practical insolvency in which there is a present inability to pay debts or absolute insolvency in which liabilities
exceed assets[98] or apparent insolvency as defined in section 7 of the
Bankruptcy (Scotland) Act 1985.[99] A reference to "liquidation" or the
"making of a winding-up order" overlooks the Scottish practice of a petition for liquidation followed by the appointment of a provisional liquidator who can administer assets for a considerable time prior to a
winding-up order (which may never occur).[1]

Balancing of Accounts in Bankruptcy

24-34 The problems of set off arising on bankruptcy are considered elsewhere.[2]

---

[96] See para. 8–111.
[97] *Imperial Hotel (Aberdeen)* v. *Vaux Breweries*, 1978 S.C. 86.
[98] See Goudy, *Bankruptcy*, pp. 15–17.
[99] A reference in a document to a person being notour bankrupt can be construed as a
reference to apparent insolvency. See Bankruptcy (Scotland) Act 1985, s.75(9).
[1] W. W. McBryde, "The Powers of Provisional Liquidators," 1977 S.L.T.(News) 145;
Palmer's *Company Law* (23rd ed., 1982), para. 87–24. A reference to the appointment of
a liquidator is preferable to a reference to a winding-up order.
[2] paras. 22–75 *et seq.*

CHAPTER 25

PUBLIC POLICY

GENERAL NATURE OF THE DOCTRINE

–01 There is a category of cases in which the parties to a contract have given their consent, with capacity to do so and free from factors which vitiate the consent, and yet the law will not give effect to the contract. The contract is contrary to public policy or *contra bonos mores*. The effects of applying the doctrine of public policy vary considerably. In some cases the contract is void. In others it is unenforceable. The doctrine of severance, if applicable, may allow most of the contract to survive. The extent to which one or both of the parties are involved in the illegality may affect the available remedies. There are differences which turn on whether or not the objection to the contract arises (a) at common law, (b) by express provision of statute, or (c) by implication from statute. Public policy may also be an additional ground for invalidating contracts affected by fraud, with a consequent difficulty in distinguishing the reason for invalidity.

–02 The combination of all these factors might suggest that there is no such thing as a unitary doctrine of public policy and that a treatment of the subject should confine itself to categorising the cases in which the concept has been applied. In truth, however, the courts have considered that it was one doctrine which has been applied and which in its nature required a flexible approach. This in itself led to the famous statement in English law that public policy was, "a very unruly horse, and when once you get astride it you never know where it will carry you."[1] The riposte by Lord Denning M.R.[2] was: "With a good man in the saddle, the unruly horse can be kept in control. It can jump over obstacles." Whatever the scope of the doctrine sometimes the courts will refer to the public interest in considering whether a contract is enforceable.[3] The nature of the public interest, however, is constantly changing. It is, for example, somewhat misleading, to cite, without explanation, cases in Morison's *Dictionary* on attitudes to sexual morality or combinations of workmen. More than in any other branch of the law of contract, precedent must be used with care. Public policy implies a consideration of the circumstances surrounding a contract and these have to be considered in the light of the changing attitudes of society. It also follows

---

[1] *Richardson* v. *Mellish* (1824) 2 Bing. 229 at p. 252 *per* Burrough J.
[2] *Enderby Town F.C. Ltd.* v. *Football Association Ltd.* [1971] Ch. 591 at p. 606.
[3] An example is the leading House of Lords case on restraint of trade—*Esso Petroleum Co. Ltd.* v. *Harper's Garage (Stourport) Ltd.* [1968] A.C. 269.

that the state of Scots law on public policy and the relevance of its case law cannot be appreciated without an understanding of how the present law evolved.

PRIOR TO THE EIGHTEENTH CENTURY

25–03 Until the eighteenth century the common law, so far as it concerned itself with public policy, centred on the relationship of marriage. The attitude of the Court of Session was unpredictable. A bond to a child procreated in adultery was at first found to be null *ipso jure* as given *ob turpem causam adulterii*,[4] but 20 years later the contrary was found.[5] It has been suggested judicially that the latter decision proceeded on the basis that a man should provide for the illegitimate child and the woman who had been robbed of her chastity.[6] There were attacks on *pacta contra fidem tabularum nuptialium* or devices which altered the arrangement provided for by a marriage contract.[7] The reason for reduction, however, combined elements of fraud with public policy.[8]

25–04   In other circumstances contracts were enforced in ways which startle the modern mind. The court would not annul a bond which was granted by a person pursued for slaughter to the Earl of Murray who was assisting the pursuit.[9] The court's attitude to restraints on liberty was harsh. An arbitral decree which decerned for banishment for certain years was not null,[10] although the court would not uphold a contract for perpetual banishment unless the King consented, but there were precedents quoted for such consent being given.[11]

25–05   Authorities involving the liberty of the subject show equivocation. A bond for perpetual services as a collier was not *contra bonos mores* nor against Christian liberty, nor contrary to Acts of Parliament,[12] although a child could not be sold as a tumbling-lassie.[13] Kidnapping followed by transportation increased with the importance of American plantations. Prior to the abolition of heritable jurisdictions there was a trade in the "voluntary" transportation of convicts.[14] The Privy Council in 1683 and 1684 had ordered fishermen to be returned to their employers in the

---

[4] *Durhame* v. *Blackwood* (1622) Mor. 9469.

[5] *Ross* v. *Robertson* (1642) Mor. 9470.

[6] Lord Ordinary in *Duke of Hamilton* v. *Esten* (1820) 2 Bligh 196 at p. 204, which is the best report; *cf.* other reports—6 Pat. 744; *A.* v. *B.*, May 21, 1816, F.C.

[7] *Hepburn* v. *Seton* (1633) Mor. 9473; *Paton* v. *Paton* (1668) Mor. 9475 and, at the beginning of the 18th century, *Walker* v. *Walker* (1700) Mor. 9476; *McGuffock* v. *Blairs* (1709) Mor. 9483; *Pollock* v. *Campbell* (1718) Mor. 9489; *Russel* v. *Gordon* (1739) Mor. 9490.

[8] See argument in *Grieve* v. *Thomson* (1705) Mor. 9478 and Kames, *Principles in Equity*, Vol. 1, pp. 77 *et seq.*

[9] *Earl of Murray* v. *Dunbar* (1630) 1 B.S. 302.

[10] *Arthur* v. *Geddies* (1590) 1 B.S. 124.

[11] *Wedderburn* v. *Monorgun* (1612) Mor. 9453.

[12] *Laird of Caprinton* v. *Geddew* (1632) Mor. 9454.

[13] *Reid* v. *Harden* (1687) Mor. 9505.

[14] J. Hill Burton, *History of Scotland*, Vol. 8, p. 521.

manner of colliers.[15] The court, however, refused to extend the servitude of colliers to fishermen on the ground that it would tend "to introduce slavery, contrary to the principles of the Christian religion and the mildness of our government."[16]

-06   Stair recognised that an obligation might be invalid *ex turpi causa* but the meaning of this concept is obscure.[17] His formulation that "every paction produceth action"[18] has to be taken more literally than such a statement would be today. There are in argument, more than in the court's decisions, glimpses of a realisation that in some circumstances pactions should not produce actions, but a dominant feature of the law of contract at the time of Stair was that, except in rare cases, a contract was not null because of its subject-matter.

The Eighteenth Century Changes

-07   At the beginning of the eighteenth century the dominant pattern was that contracts would be enforced despite their subject-matter. By the end of the century this was no longer true. Contracts were attacked as *contra bonos mores*. Combinations were struck at in 1762.[19] The trend of the authorities on the Act anent buying pleas was not followed in *McKenzie* v. *Forbes* in 1774.[20] The attempts to have smuggling contracts held *pacta illicita* failed until *Duncan* v. *Thomson* in 1776[21] and two decisions in 1779.[22] The Court of Session declared firmly against the sale of public offices in *Dalrymple* v. *Shaw*[23] in 1786 in terms inconsistent with previous authority and practice. Wagers were enforceable until *Bruce* v. *Ross*[24] in 1787 and *Wordsworth* v. *Pettigrew* in 1799.[25]

-08   These changes show some remarkable features. With the exception of combinations, where there was no previous authority, the refusal to enforce a contract arose in varying situations and despite previous authority. The alteration in attitude took place in a period of about a dozen years from 1774. Further, with one exception,[26] the changes survived.

-09   Possible reasons for these changes are (1) the relative stability of the composition of the Court of Session during the relevant period with

---

[15] R.P.C. (3rd Ser.), viii, 119, 495.
[16] *Reid* v. *Woodney* (1696) Mor. 4427; *Allan* v. *Skene* (1728) Mor 9454.
[17] Stair, I, vii, 8; I, xviii, 1.
[18] Stair, I, x, 7.
[19] *Procurator-Fiscal* v. *Wool-Combers in Aberdeen* (1762) Mor. 1961.
[20] 5 B.S. 528.
[21] Mor.App., "*Pactum Illicitum*," p. 1.
[22] *McLure & McCree* v. *John Paterson* (1779) Mor. 9546; *Sibbald* v. *Wallace* (1779) 5 B.S. 532.
[23] (1786) Mor. 9531.
[24] (1787) Mor. 9523; 3 Pat. 107.
[25] (1799) Mor. 9524.
[26] *McKenzie* v. *Forbes, sup. cit.*

remarkable judges such as Kames, Braxfield, Monboddo and Hailes, and (2) the philosophical development of utility as a reason for not enforcing a contract.[27]

PUBLIC POLICY SINCE THE EIGHTEENTH CENTURY

25–10 Natural law views were not ousted by philosophical treatment of public interest and the result was two different general notions of contract existing at the beginning of the nineteenth century.[28] There was a potential conflict between the two attitudes. In the law of bankruptcy the concept of fraud and public policy could become intertwined. Bell's editors treated some fraudulent preferences as examples of contracts immoral or *contra bonos mores*[29] and Lord Dunedin, attributing this to Bell, came to the conclusion that certain agreements with creditors were "inconsistent with public law and arrangement."[30] On the other hand other such agreements may be treated more accurately as affected by part of the law of bankruptcy with different consequences on the nature of the invalidity and title to sue.[31]

25–11 The treatment, mentioned later, of gaming contracts, contracts involving sales of offices, and by the second half of the nineteenth century, provisions in restraint of trade, show the development of a concept of public policy. Many of the problems, particularly those involving remedies, remain obscure.

BUYING PLEAS

25–12 The practice of buying pleas was common for more than half a century after the Restoration, it being at that time a "vile traffic, in which, in an age of great lawyers, who were remarkable for seriousness and soberness of mind, almost every man, from the judge to the lowest practitioner, was engaged."[32] There was a restrictive interpretation of the Land Purchase Act 1594: "Anent the buying of landis and possessionis dependand in pley be Jugeis or memberis of courtis."[33] An advocate could buy land subject to a depending process. The transaction was

---

[27] This is a matter on which the author has written elsewhere.

[28] P. Stein, "The General Notions of Contract and Property in Eighteenth-Century Scottish Thought," 1963 J.R. 1 at p. 11; see also by the same author, "Legal Thought In Eighteenth-Century Scotland," 1957 J.R. 1; and "Law and Society in Scottish Thought," in *Scotland in the Age of Improvement* (ed. N. T. Phillipson and R. Mitchison, 1970), p. 148.

[29] Bell, *Prin.*, s.37, note (f).

[30] *Farmers' Mart Ltd.* v. *Milne*, 1914 S.C.(H.L.) 84 at p. 86.

[31] *Munro* v. *Rothfield*, 1920 S.C.(H.L.) 165.

[32] Ramsay of Ochtertyre, *Scotland and Scotsmen in the 18th Century* (1888), Vol. 1, p. 431.

[33] c. 26, A.P.S. iv, 68; given its short title by the Statute Law Revision (Scotland) Act 1964, Sched. 2. Sched. 1 of the 1964 Act deleted three obsolete words, but otherwise the 1594 Act remains in force.

valid although the contravener of the Act might lose his office and privileges.[34] The transaction had to take place *pendente lite* before it could be challenged[35] and the gift of a plea, as opposed to its purchase, was allowed.[36] The argument that the Act declared it to be unlawful to buy pleas and therefore the transaction was null, was expressly rejected.[37]

13 Tait has a brief report of a decision in 1774 under the Land Purchase Act. A contract contravening the Act was declared void and the agent suspended from office.[38] When Bell wrote his *Principles* he stated that the contract was null. His editors inserted the word "not" before "null,"[39] a change which was justified by the authorities referred to, but one wonders whether this frustrated an attempt to alter the law.

14 In 1831, an argument was presented that an agreement between a client and his legal adviser to divide the subject of the law suit was not affected by the 1594 Act because there was no depending action.[40] The majority of judges held that the case fell under the common law doctrine of *pactum de quota litis*, with Lord Meadowbank dissenting on the significant ground that there was no such common law doctrine. The majority view was followed nearly 20 years later.[41] So the common law was invoked to such an extent that if it had always been the law there would have been little need for the statute.[42]

GAMING

15 The Act of 1621 c. 14,[43] "Anent Playing at Cardes and Dyce and Horse races," provided for winnings above 100 merks to be consigned to the church for distribution amongst the poor, and on certain premises forbade the playing at cards or dice. The Act may have been inspired by a provision of French law.[44] An Act in 1657[45] provided that the winner of

---

[34] *Colt* v. *Cunningham* (n.d.) Mor. 9495; *Cunningham* v. *Maxwell* (1611) Mor. 9495; *Home* v. *Home* (1713) Mor. 9502; Ersk., *Inst.*,II, iii, 16.

[35] *Hume* v. *Nisbet* (1675) Mor. 9496.

[36] *Earl of Hume* v. *Hume* (1678) Mor. 9498.

[37] *Richardson* v. *Sinclair* (1635) Mor. 3210.

[38] *McKenzie* v. *Forbes* (1774) 5 B.S. 528. A change foreshadowed by W. Forbes, *The Institutes of the Law of Scotland* (1722), Vol. 1, 2, 3, 1, 3.

[39] Bell, *Prin.*, s.36(1).

[40] *Johnston* v. *Rome* (1831) 9 S. 364.

[41] *Bolden* v. *Fogo* (1850) 12 D. 798, esp. *per* Lord Wood at p. 800, *vide* Lord Moncreiff's references to public policy at p. 807. Kames had argued for a common law doctrine, *Principles of Equity*, Vol. 2, pp. 87 and 117.

[42] A similar situation arose to a limited degree after the Bankruptcy Acts 1621 and 1696.

[43] A.P.S. iv, 613. The Act was not formally repealed until the Betting and Gaming Act 1960, s.15, Sched. 6. The last reported case in which it was applied was *Maxwell* v. *Blair* (1774) Mor. 9522 although in 1854 an action founded on the Act was sustained in Falkirk Sheriff Court: W. F. Trotter, *Law of Contract in Scotland* (1913), p. 204. In 1864 the Act was not in desuetude: *O'Connell* v. *Russell* (1864) 3 M. 89 at p. 93 *per* Lord Deas.

[44] Bell, *Comm.*, I, 319.

[45] A.P.S. vi(2), 910a. This Act was, of course, affected by the Act Rescissory of 1661 which annulled the legislation "of all pretendit parliaments since the yeer 1633."

specified gaming transactions should repay the loser and pay the same amount again to the Protector.

25–16   The attitude of the courts was that contracts should be enforced. If a winner of a gaming transaction obtained more than 100 merks, the excess was to be consigned for the poor in terms of the 1621 Act, but otherwise the paction was valid.[46] In 1776 the Lords sustained an action for a wager of a pipe of port wine between two gentlemen to be paid to him who should walk first to Edinburgh from a certain place in the country, although apparently because the wager was not seriously laid, *absolvitor* was granted in the circumstances of the case.[47]

25–17   The Gaming Act 1710[48] declared bills and other documents given in consideration of gaming to be "utterly void, frustrate and of none effect." Despite this the court held that onerous and *bona fide* indorsees of bills were not affected by a challenge that the bill had been granted for money at play,[49] although subsequently it was held that the Act did not apply to Scotland.[50]

25–18   By the end of the eighteenth century the view was developing that public policy was a ground for refusing to enforce contracts. In *Bruce* v. *Ross*[51] a wager on the election of a Member of Parliament was found not actionable. The report in Morison's *Dictionary* states that, "the Judges in general regarded a wager as in no case a legal ground of action; while some, who thought differently, were, nevertheless, disposed to deny action in this particular case, from the idea that political operations were a peculiarly improper subject of wagering." The report by Hailes[52] makes it clearer that it was political gaming which was regarded as dangerous. Hailes, himself, was troubled by the thought that there might be wagers on the judgments of a court. The interlocutor of the Court of Session was affirmed on appeal to the House of Lords.[53]

25–19   In *Bruce* the respondent had argued that the unenforceable nature of *sponsiones ludicrae* was early adopted as common law in Scotland and had been constantly adhered to. It is doubtful if there was authority for that proposition. The only case mentioned is *Stewart* v. *Dundonald*,[54] which related to a wager on succession to an Earldom. It was decided by a casting vote in 1753 and, if anything, is evidence for the novelty of the proposition that wagers were not actionable.

25–20   *Bruce* v. *Ross* was followed in 1799 when it was observed that courts "were instituted to enforce the rights of parties arising from serious

---

[46] *Park* v. *Sommervile* (1668) Mor. 3459; Stair, I, x, 8.
[47] *Hope* v. *Tweedie* (1776) Mor. 9522.
[48] 9 Anne, c. 14; given title by Short Titles Act 1896.
[49] *Neilson* v. *Bruce* (1740) Mor. 9507; *Stewart* v. *Hyslop* (1741) Mor. 9510.
[50] *Kirk Session of Dumfries* v. *Kirk Sessions of Kirkcudbright and Kelton* (1775) Mor. 10580; *Rayner* v. *Kent*, 1922 S.L.T. 331.
[51] (1787) Mor. 9523.
[52] Hailes, 1016.
[53] 3 Pat. 107.
[54] (1753) Mor. 9514.

transactions, and can pay no regard *sponsionibus ludicris*; as to money gained or lost, on which *melior est conditio possidentis.*"[55]

21 The development of the law thereafter involved the definition of *sponsio ludicra*. It is seeking to enforce a *sponsio ludicra* to ask a court to decide which horse has won a race[56]; or who has won at cards[57]; or to determine the winner of a sporting or other contest (a matter raised repeatedly in the sheriff court by disqualified winners).[58] It is *sponsio ludicra* to seek decree for payment against a bookmaker for a balance due on bets[59]; and, conversely, a bookmaker cannot sue his client despite the fact that it is not thought frivolous by Parliament for sheriffs to have jurisdiction in connection with betting permits and licences[60]

22 A difficulty has arisen over whether seeking the recovery of money from a stakeholder is an action based on a *sponsio ludicra*. The two recent authorities[61] indicate that some earlier authorities may need to be reconsidered. It was not a *sponsio ludicra* to decide which person was entitled to a prize which had been awarded for a greyhound's performance[62] and in a joint adventure a person may sue the other gambler for an appropriate share of the winnings.[63] Nor is there anything objectionable in lending money to make or pay bets[64] or suing for the price of gaming chips purchased before gaming.[65]

23 Parties may speculate on the price of shares or commodities. They may buy and sell without ever taking delivery of the subject-matter of the contract. If they enter into a contract in a form which could be

---

[55] *Wordsworth* v. *Pettigrew* (1799) Mor. 9524.

[56] *O'Connell* v. *Russell* (1864) 3 M. 89.

[57] *Paterson* v. *Macqueen & Kilgour* (1866) 4 M. 602; it may be different if there are distinct allegations of total incapacity, *ibid.* p. 607 *per* Lord Curriehill.

[58] *Scott* v. *Davis* (1895) 11 Sh.Ct. Rep. 351; *Harrison* v. *Falkirk Trotting Club* (1897) 13 Sh.Ct. Rep. 89; *Wilkie* v. *Stanley and Kinclaven District Ploughing Assoc.* (1903) 19 Sh.Ct. Rep. 361; *Nichol* v. *Galashiels Horticultural Assoc.* (1905) 21 Sh.Ct. Rep. 141; *Gillies* v. *Greens Committee of Kelvingrove Bowling Green* (1913) 29 Sh.Ct. Rep. 149; *Kennedy* v. *Strang*, 1933 S.L.T. (Sh.Ct.) 19 (football pools). While a court will not decide which bowl won the match or which dahlia was the best in the flower show, a slightly different attitude might be shown in some other competitions. See the "bursary cases," chap. 5; "Offer and Acceptance," para. 5–24 and cases involving yachts: *The Satanita* [1895] P. 248, affd. *sub. nom.*; *Clarke* v. *Dunraven* [1897] A.C. 59; *Meggeson* v. *Burns* [1972] 1 Lloyds Rep. 223. In the sporting contest there may also be a lack of patrimonial interest, see chap. 4, "The Formation Of A Contract," para. 4–45.

[59] *Hamilton* v. *McLauchlan*, 1908 16 S.L.T. 341; approved, *Robertson* v. *Balfour*, 1938 S.C. 207 at p. 223 *per* Lord Wark; *Goldstone* v. *Westwood*, 1926 S.L.T. (Sh.Ct.) 2.

[60] *Macaffer* v. *Scott*, 1963 S.L.T. (Sh.Ct.) 39; *Johnston* v. *T. W. Archibald (Commission Agent) Ltd.*, 1966 S.L.T. (Sh.Ct.) 8.

[61] *Robertson* v. *Balfour, sup. cit.*; *Kelly* v. *Murphy*, 1940 S.C. 96. On lotteries see *Christison* v. *McBride* (1881) 9 R. 34 and *Kelly* v. *Murphy*; *cf. Clayton* v. *Clayton*, 1937 S.C. 619 and comments thereon in *Robertson* v. *Balfour sup. cit.* A lottery, even if it involves an element of skill, will normally be a *sponsio ludicra*.

[62] *Graham* v. *Pollok* (1848) 10 D. 646.

[63] *Forsyth* v. *Czartowski*, 1961 S.L.T. (Sh.Ct.) 22.

[64] *Hopkins* v. *Baird*, 1920 2 S.L.T. 94.

[65] *Cumming* v. *Mackie*, 1973 S.C. 278.

enforced, the contract will not be a gaming contract merely because there was no intention to take delivery of the shares or commodities. The balance of the authorities is in favour of enforcing contracts entered into in the normal way in the Stock Exchange or between brokers in commodities.[66] It has been observed several times in the cases cited that a mere transaction for differences will be treated as a gambling contract[67] but such a transaction appears to involve evidence that there never was an obligation on either party to deliver the shares or the commodity.[68] The normal inference from the documents is that there was a real transaction. Lord McLaren observed[69]: "that as regards such Stock Exchange transactions as are carried out in the ordinary course of business, the distinction between contracts for differences and real transactions is of purely theoretical interest, and really does not offer to speculators in stock any available means of being released from their obligations." Although dealings in futures or options, or other variations on the price of shares or commodities attracts speculators, the contract is sometimes implemented by delivery[70] and the speculator is entering into a contract which for others is a serious commercial transaction.

25–24   The nature of the invalidity was settled in *Robertson* v. *Balfour*.[71] A *sponsio ludicra* is unenforceable. In the words of an early decision, *sponsiones ludicrae* "ought to be left upon private faith, and neither be supported by an action nor cut down unless attended with the circumstances of fraud or extortion; in which case a party will be relieved even after performance."[72]

25–25   Statute has taken a very different view of certain transactions associated with gaming or betting. The Gaming Act 1710 declared bills and other documents given in consideration of gaming or betting "utterly void, frustrate, and of none effect to all intents and purposes whatsoever." The result was that even a *bona fide* onerous holder of a bill granted for a gambling debt held "a piece of waste paper."[73] This was altered by the Gaming Act of 1835 which deemed such documents to have been given for an illegal consideration instead of being void.[74] The

---

[66] *Risk* v. *Auld and Guild* (1881) 8 R. 729; *Newton* v. *Cribbes* (1884) 11 R. 554; *Gillies* v. *McLean* (1885) 13 R. 12; *Shaw* v. *Caledonian Ry. Co.* (1890) 17 R. 466; *Liquidator of Universal Stock Exchange* v. *Mowat* (1891) 19 R. 128.

[67] *e.g. Shaw* v. *Caledonian Ry. Co.*, *sup. cit.* at p. 475 *per* Lord Shand.

[68] In *Heiman* v. *Hardie & Co.* (1885) 12 R. 406 the plea of *sponsio ludicra* was sustained.

[69] *Liqr. of the Universal Stock Exchange Co. Ltd.* v. *Howat*, *sup. cit.* at p. 137.

[70] See note on oil futures by C. R. Davie in 1985 J.B.L. 105.

[71] *Sup. cit.*

[72] *Sir Michael Stewart* v. *Earl of Dundonald* (1753) Mor. 9514, approved *Robertson* v. *Balfour*, *sup. cit.* at p. 216 *per* Lord Mackay.

[73] *Hamilton* v. *Russel* (1832) 10 S. 549 *per* Lord Cringletie; *Eliott* v. *Cocks & Co.* (1826) 5 S. 40; *White's Trs.* v. *Johnstone's Trs.* (1819) 5 S. 40, note.

[74] Modified as regards cheques by the Gaming Act 1968, s.16(4).

1710 Act was subsequently held not to apply to Scotland[75] and doubt exists whether the 1835 Act applies to Scotland.[76]

COMBINATIONS AND TRADE UNIONS

26 The eighteenth century development of trade was accompanied by the organisation of workmen. The Court of Session refused to enforce the contracts of combinations and, indeed, after differing opinions had been expressed, combinations were held criminal.

27 The development of the law is largely of historical interest only and may be traced in the authorities cited.[77]

28 A combination to raise wages unaccompanied by violence was held criminal in the case of the cotton weavers in 1813 after previous cases had held that the conduct was not criminal.[78] This was not an auspicious use of the declaratory power of the High Court as a few years later a statute gave a limited right of combination for the purpose of raising or lowering the rate of wages or of regulating the hours of labour.[79] The Act did not affect the law of contract, so contracts for those purposes remained liable to attack at common law.[80]

29 A discussion on combinations inevitably leads to a concentration on combinations on workmen. Other activities might be regarded as combinations if it is accepted that the essence of combination is that the agreement of the combiners is intended to produce an effect on a third party. Combinations had been treated as criminal prior to the case of the cotton weavers. A combination to refuse to accept halfpence resulted in fines.[81] The House of Lords considered a combination to fix the rate for posting in terms indicating that it was a criminal offence.[82] An example of the civil consequences of a combination is that of a white bonnet at an

---

[75] *Rayner* v. *Kent & Stansfield*, 1922 S.L.T. 331.

[76] *Cumming* v. *Mackie*, 1973 S.C. 278 at p. 281 *per* Lord Fraser. The Act 1621 c. 14 was repealed by the Betting and Gaming Act 1960, s.15, Sched. 6; Acts of 8 & 9 Vict. c. 109 (1845) and 55 Vict. c. 9 (1892) have been held not to apply to Scotland. *Russell* v. *Gray* (1894) 1 S.L.T. 529; *Levy* v. *Jackson* (1903) 5 F. 1170. This means substantial differences between English and Scots law. Every contract of marine insurance by way of gaming or wagering is void: Marine Insurance Act 1906, s.4(1).

[77] Bankt., I, 411, 11; Kames, *Principles of Equity*, Vol. 2, pp. 89 and 98; *Procurator-Fiscal* v. *Wool-combers in Aberdeen* (1762) Mor. 1961; *Barr* v. *Carr* (1766) Mor. 9564; *Corp. of Master Shoemakers of Edinburgh* v. *Marshall* (1798) Mor. 9573; J. L. Gray, "The Law of Combinations in Scotland," *Economica* (1428), Vol. 8, p. 332; H. Hamilton, *An Economic History of Scotland in the Eighteenth Century* (1963), pp. 345–351.

[78] Hume, *Crimes*, Vol. 1, pp. 494–496; Gray, *sup. cit.* p. 342.

[79] Combinations of Workmen Act 1825. Whether the Acts 39 Geo. III c. 81 and 39 & 40 Geo. III c. 106 or many other earlier Acts (Holdsworth, Vol. XI, pp. 488 *et seq.*) applied to Scotland is now an academic question. With one important exception they were not applied in practice. Gray, *op. cit.*, pp. 336–338.

[80] *Cf.* Holdsworth, Vol. XV, p. 68, who considered such contracts "void."

[81] *Hall* v. *Billerwell* (1787) Mor. 9573.

[82] *Scott* v. *Smith* (1798) 4 Pat. 17; Mor. 7625.

auction who acts in concert with the seller.[83] A combination of intending
bidders at a sale was "illegal," the sale "void and null" and damages
awarded to the seller.[84] This shows a feature of combinations. It is not
the agreement among the combiners alone which is affected. The combination's contract with innocent third parties may be void.

25–30   When trade unions were legalised their previous illegality was treated
as part of the doctrine of restraint of trade. The Trade Union Act 1871
provided[85]: "3. The purposes of any trade union shall not, by reason
merely that they are in restraint of trade, be unlawful so as to render
void or voidable any agreement or trust." This proceeded on the idea
that combinations were unlawful because they were in restraint of trade,
which is of doubtful validity in Scotland, although it has the support of
Lord President Inglis.[86] He also assumed that if an association was a
trade union it must have been an unlawful combination before the passing of the Act.[87] It is now accepted that trade unions can be lawful at
common law[88] and as it may be necessary to determine the legality of a
union at common law the appropriate question, on the authorities, is
whether the union is in unreasonable restraint of trade.[88]

25–31   Since 1871 the Scottish courts have considered the extent to which
they should interfere in union affairs and in particular in the application
of section 4 of the 1871 Act. In several respects some of the decisions are
doubtful in view of English House of Lords cases which must be taken to
dominate this branch of the law.[89]

---

[83] cf. *Grey* v. *Stewart* (1793) Mor. 9560.

[84] *Murray* v. *MacWhan* (1783) Mor. 9567; Hailes, *Dec.* 920.

[85] See para. 25–32.

[86] *Aitken* v. *Associated Carpenters and Joiners of Scotland* (1885) 12 R. 1206 at p. 1211.
The definition of "trade union" in s.23 also reflected this to such an extent that it was
defective and had to be remedied by the Trade Union Act Amendment Act 1876, s.16.

[87] *Shanks* v. *United Operative Mason's Association* (1874) 1 R. 823 at p. 825.

[88] Citrine, *Trade Union Law* (3rd ed. 1967) p. 112; *Russell* v. *Amalgamated Society of
Carpenters and Joiners*, 1912 A.C. 421 at p. 429 *per* Lord Macnaghten.

[89] (a) *e.g.* courts jurisdiction excluded: *McKernan* v. *United Operative Masons' Associ-
ation* (1874) 1 R. 453; *Shanks* v. *United Operative Masons' Association, sup. cit.*; *Aitken* v.
Associated Carpenters and Joiners of Scotland, sup. cit.; *Shinwell* v. *National Sailors'
Union*, 1913 2 S.L.T. 83 (but see *National Union of Bank Employees* v. *Murray*, 1948
S.L.T.(Notes) 51); *Glasgow and District Potted Meat Manufacturers Soc.* v. *Geddes*,
(1902) 10 S.L.T. 481; *McLaren* v. *National Union of Dock Labourers*, 1918 S.C. 834;
Smith v. *Scottish Typographical Association*, 1919 S.C. 43 (doubtful in view of *Amalga-
mated Society of Carpenters and Joiners* v. *Braithwaite* [1922] 2 A.C. 440); *G. & J. Rae* v.
Plate Glass Merchants Association, 1919 S.C. 426 (probably unsound in view of *Y.M.A.* v.
Howden [1905] A.C. 256 and *Braithwaite, sup. cit., vide* Grunfeld *Modern Trade Union
Law* (1966), p. 77 and Citrine, p. 125); *Drennan* v. *Associated Ironmoulders of Scotland*,
1921 S.C. 151 (unsound, Grunfeld, *ibid.*).

(b) Courts jurisdiction not excluded: *Amalgamated Soc. of Ry. Servants* v. *Motherwell
Branch* (1880) 7 R. 867; *Wilson* v. *Scottish Typographical Association*, 1912 S.C. 534; *Wil-
kie* v. *King*, 1911 S.C. 1310 (not followed, *Baker* v. *Ingall* [1912] 3 K.B. 106 at p. 120 *per*
Buckley J.; *Love* v. *Amalgamated Society of Lithographic Printers, etc.*, 1912 S.C. 1078;
McDowall v. *McGhee*, 1913 2 S.L.T. 238; *Edinburgh Master Plumbers Association* v.
Munro, 1928 S.C. 565; *Berry* v. *T.G.W.U.* 1933 S.N. 110 (in part unsound in view of
Braithwaite, sup. cit. and *Bonsor* v. *Musician's Union* [1956] A.C. 104 at p. 154 *per* Lord
Keith).

32   The Trade Union Act 1871 was repealed by the Industrial Relations
Act 1971 which in turn was repealed by the Trade Union and Labour
Relations Act 1974. Section 2(5) of the 1974 Act provides:

> "The purposes of any trade union which is not a special register
> body and, in so far as they relate to the regulation of relations
> between employers and employers' associations and workers, the
> purposes of any trade union which is such a body, shall not, by
> reason only that they are in restraint of trade, be unlawful so as—
> (a) to make any member of the trade union liable to criminal pro-
> ceedings for conspiracy or otherwise, or (b) to make any agreement
> or trust void or voidable; nor shall any rule of a trade union which is
> not a special register body or, in so far as it so relates, any rule of
> any other trade union be unlawful or unenforceable by reason only
> that it is in restraint of trade."

33   A "special register body" refers to certain corporate bodies entered in
a special register between 1971 and 1974. A similar provision to section
2(5) is made for employers' associations.[90]

34   The 1974 Act, unlike its predecessors, refers to the rules of the union,
not merely its purposes. This may be an attempt to reverse the effect of
Edwards v. *Society of Graphical and Allied Trades*[91] in which the Court
of Appeal struck down a union rule on expulsion of a member. Whether
the 1974 Act altered the particular result in *Edwards* was arguable
because as a rider to section 2(5) the Act preserved a member's common
law rights,[92] but this rider was repealed by the Trade Union and Labour
Relations (Amendment) Act 1976, s.1(c).

SALE OF OFFICES

35   In England trafficking in offices seems to have been common prior to
the eighteenth century, judging from the evidence led in the impeach-
ment of Lord Chancellor Macclesfield in 1725.[93] Scottish authority indicates that the practice was no less common north of the border. For
example, Fountainhall reports on a judicial promotion:

36   > "Alexander (Falconer) Lord Halkerton . . . entered to his place in
> Session by simony, or rather *committendo crimen ambitus*, for he
> paid to my Lord Balmanno 7000 merks (a great soume at that tyme
> when their salaries ware small) to dimit in his favours, and by my
> Lord Traquaire's moyen, the Treasurer, whosse creature he was,
> he got the dimission to be accepted by his Majesty."[94]

When James Hamilton was appointed one of the principal clerks of

---

[90] s.3(5).
[91] [1971] Ch. 354.
[92] s.5(5).
[93] A. D. Gibb, *Judicial Corruption in the United Kingdom* (1957), pp. 7–41.
[94] *Journals of Sir John Lauder, Lord Fountainhall* (1900) Scottish History Society (1st
Ser.), Vol. 36, pp. 215, 216.

session by the Lord Register's gift he was ordained on June 1, 1697, to be tried by the committee of the Lords of Session, and at the same time "obliged to give his oath that he had given no more to the Register than 4000 merks for the said post, directly or indirectly."[95] When a clerk of session retired at the beginning of the nineteenth century, he had no pension. The system was that he either resigned in favour of his successor who advanced a sum of money or a "co-adjutor" was associated with him in his patent and undertook the duty on condition of a division of salary. Sir Walter Scott obtained his clerkship on condition of allowing his predecessor, Home, to retain its emoluments during Home's lifetime.[96]

25–37 In Scotland there was an excuse that heritable offices could be sold under the feudal law. There is no case in which it was decided that all such offices could be sold, but some of them were *in commercio*. Heritable jurisdictions could be sold.[97] On the assumption that adjudgeability of an office must imply a power of voluntary sale, the office of King's usher[98] and the office of King's printer granted to a person and his heirs and assignees[99] were both saleable. Offices of trust granted during pleasure or for life were not adjudgeable.[1] Kames, as usual, saw the problem as being more involved. A distinction should be drawn between an office which was not adjudgeable and emoluments which might be. Where there was power to appoint a deputy the emoluments might be adjudged, however personal the office, but it would be otherwise when there was no power of deputation, as in the case of supreme judges.[2] Whether or not Kames's view is consistent with feudal theory,[3] its value for the purposes of analysis was to draw a distinction between the disposition of an office and the assignation of its emoluments.

25–38 In the latter half of the eighteenth century the Court of Session started to refuse to support sales of offices. The General Assembly of the Church of Scotland passed two Acts against simoniacal pactions.[4] Shortly thereafter the court refused to support such a paction, holding it "*ob turpem causam et contra bonos mores.*" The opinions show a concern for the purity of the Scottish Church.[5]

---

[95] Brunton and Haig, Senators of the College of Justice (1832), p. 494, quoting the Books of Sederunt.

[96] J. G. Lockhart, *Memoirs of Sir Walter Scott* (1900 ed.), Vol. 1, pp. 436–443.

[97] Ersk., *Inst.*, I, ii, 11.

[98] *Cockburn* v. *Creditors of Langton* (1747) Mor. 150. The interlocutors of the Court of Session were affirmed by the House of Lords. Note, however, arguments on the value of this case in *Earl of Lauderdale* v. *Scrymgeour Wedderburn*, 1910 S.C.(H.L.) 35.

[99] *Blair* v. *Freebairn* (1737) Mor. 148.

[1] Ersk., *Inst.*, II, xii, 7; *Wilson* v. *Falconer* (1759) Mor. 165.

[2] *Wilson* v. *Falconer, sup. cit.*

[3] Were the emoluments heritable? If not, they would not appear to be the proper subject of an apprising or an adjudication. The appropriate remedy of the creditor is arrestment.

[4] Sess. 7, June 1, 1753; Sess. 5, May 30, 1759.

[5] *Maxwell* v. *Earl of Galloway* (1775) Mor. 9580; Hailes, 624.

39   In secular cases the court's attitude shifted from one of tolerance, but it never prohibited all sales of offices. In *Young* v. *Thomson*[6] a member of Parliament procured an office for his wife's brother. In return the brother bound himself to pay an annuity to his aunt. "It was generally the opinion of the Court that if Mr. Kerr had taken the sum payable to himself, the paction would have been *contra bonos mores*; but not where it is taken by him payable to a friend or relation, such as Mrs. Young, who was his wife's aunt." This is a narrow view and it is not surprising that it did not last.

40   In *Dalrymple* v. *Shaw*[7] it was argued that "nothing is more openly sold than are public offices every day; the clerkship of the High Court of Justiciary, for example, the depute clerkships of the bills, the sheriff-clerkships."[8] If that were so, the court wished to end the practice: "The Court were agreed that it is *contra bonos mores* and illegal for those in power procuring from government, offices to other people, to stipulate a sum of money, or any of the emoluments, either to themselves or to third parties."

41   The Lord Chancellor in 1802 issued a strong *obiter* opinion that the sale of public offices was illegal, despite previous practice.[9] This was followed in 1811 when it was held that apart from instances in which offices were in use to be bought and sold, a sale of a public office was illegal.[10] In the interval an English Act of 1551[11] had been extended to Scotland and expanded by the Sale of Offices Act 1809.[12] Broadly speaking the 1809 Act applies to the Crown and government offices and in terms of the 1551 Act[13] a contract contravening the provisions of the Acts "shall be void."

42   There remains uncertainty as to what sales of offices are valid. If the Sale of Offices Act 1809 applies, the contract is void and the sale is also a criminal offence. If that Act does not apply, the sale of a public office is presumably void unless the office is customarily bought and sold. Public offices, at least formerly, would have included the offices of clergymen, professors and schoolmasters.[14] Thus in 1823 a sale of an Army Commission would have been competent if the Army regulations had been complied with.[15] A Bill for abolition of the sale of commissions passed the Commons in 1871 but was rejected by the House of Lords. The

---

[6] (1759) Mor. 9525.

[7] (1786) Mor. 9531; Hailes, 989.

[8] An argument repeated in *Thomson* v. *Dove*, Feb. 16, 1811, F.C.

[9] *Stewart* v. *Miller* (1802) 4 Pat. 286 at pp. 290–294.

[10] *Thomson* v. *Dove, sup. cit.* The sale was arranged by those with power to fill the office. Lord President Blair reserved his opinion on the validity of a bargain between the two candidates.

[11] 5 & 6 Edw. 6, c. 16; given the title "The Sale of Offices Act 1551" by the Short Titles Act 1896.

[12] 49 Geo. III, c. 126; given the short title in 1896.

[13] s.2.

[14] *Thomson* v. *Dove, sup. cit., per* Lord President Blair.

[15] *Carmichael* v. *Erskine* (1823) 2 S. 530.

Cabinet then abolished the practice by Royal Warrant in the same year.[16]

25-43　　Many problems remain. (1) The case law has been concerned with public offices, not private offices[17] and there is a problem of definition. (2) Certain transactions relating to a public office may be more objectionable than others. The mere use of influence on behalf of X to procure X's appointment is not as bad as pecuniary stipulation to the patron or third parties in return for the use of influence. (3) The later case law has been concerned not so much with outright sale of the office as with transactions involving assignation of the emoluments. If an appointee is deprived of so much of the profits that he is unfit for office, the assignation is a *pactum illicitum*.[18] The Court of Session refused to enforce an agreement between a Depute and Assistant Clerk of Session whereby the Assistant Clerk was to perform the duties of both offices.[19] An assignation of the duties of an office and the emoluments may not often be competent given that in a contract of service there is usually *delectus personae*.[20] Assignation may also be avoided by statute.[21] These problems have not been commented on by writers, presumably because alterations in the practice of filling public offices have rendered remote the possibility of a sale of a public office in the United Kingdom. Related problems involving some other countries are not entirely theoretical.

SALE OF HONOURS

25-44　　The Honours (Prevention of Abuses) Act 1925 makes certain financial transactions involving honours a criminal offence. It can hardly be doubted that the contracts involved would also be tainted with the illegality.[22]

BRIBERY

25-45　　Bribery is a serious criminal offence.[23] It is unlikely that a court would allow a person to benefit from his bribe. That does not mean that the contract could not be implemented against him. Nor is it clear how a

---

[16] P. H. Winfield, "Public Policy in the English Common Law" 42 Harv.L.R. 76 at p. 95. On exchanges, see the Regimental Exchange Act 1875.

[17] *Mason* v. *Wilson* (1844) 7 D. 160.

[18] *Gardner* v. *Grant* (1835) 13 S. 664; *Hill* v. *Paul* (1841) 2 Rob.App. 524 at p. 544 *per* Lord Chancellor Cottenham; sequel, *Ord* v. *Hill* (1847) 9 D. 1118.

[19] *Mason* v. *Wilson* (1844) 7 D. 160. The report is not clear but it seems that the assistant clerk must have received a proportion of the sum due to the depute as salary. The decision in *Haldane* v. *De Maria*, March 6, 1812, F.C. is doubtful.

[20] *Berlitz School of Language* v. *Duchêne* (1903) 6 F. 181. Some offices, such as the Standard Bearer of Scotland, may be *extra commercium—Earl of Lauderdale* v. *Scrymgeour Wedderburn*, 1910 S.C.(H.L.) 35.

[21] See, *e.g.* Army Act 1955, s.203; Air Force Act 1955, s.203.

[22] *Parkinson* v. *College of Ambulance* [1925] 2 K.B. 1.

[23] See G. H. Gordon, *Criminal Law* (2nd ed., 1978), pp. 1009 *et seq.*

corporation is affected by a bribe to one of its employees. There is English authority on bribes of agents to the effect that a person whose agent has entered into a contract under the influence of bribery may rescind the contract with the third party.[24] A person who received bribes can be barred from suing for work done under the contract.[25]

–46 Apart from questions of the unenforceability of the contract a principal affected by his agent's bribe has an action against the agent. In *Mahesan* v. *Malaysian Government Officers' Co-operative Housing Society*[26] the Privy Council reviewed the authorities and concluded that the principal could elect between claiming the amount of the bribe and claiming damages for fraud. The ability to recover the bribe depended in that case on the development of equity in English law and the principles of money had and received.

SMUGGLING

–47 The problem of smuggling contracts at one time seriously troubled the Court of Session. The relative absence of such cases today is a reason for only a brief treatment of the topic. Yet the development in the eighteenth century still has a theoretical relevance. This is because it is the one substantial instance of Scots law grappling with the problem of the effect of the criminal law on contracts. In the process the nature of various types of contractual invalidity was tested and the unenforceable contract emerged as a category distinct from void and voidable contracts.

–48 In the early development of the law contracts which involved smuggled goods were to some extent enforced.[27] A breach of revenue laws did not always affect a contract. But in 1776 it was decided that no action lay between smugglers for implement of a smuggling contract.[28] In 1779 the court departed from the trend of the earlier decisions and found a purchase of smuggled goods unlawful and unenforceable.[29] There then followed a period of uncertainty in the law.[30]

5–49 The position was affirmed that a merchant settled abroad, whether native or foreign, had no action for the price of smuggled goods when he

---

[24] *Panama & South Pacific Telegraph Co.* v. *India Rubber Co.* (1875) L.R. 10 Ch.App. 515; *Shipway* v. *Broadwood* [1899] 1 Q.B. 369; *Hovenden & Sons* v. *Millhoff* (1900) 83 L.T. 41; *Armagas Ltd.* v. *Mundogas S.A., The Ocean Frost* [1985] 3 All E.R. 795 (being appealed).

[25] *Tahrland* v. *Rodier* (1866) 16 L.C. Rep. 473; *Andrews* v. *Ramsay* [1903] 2 K.B. 635.

[26] [1979] A.C. 374.

[27] e.g. *Comms. of Customs* v. *Morison* (1723) Mor. 9533; *Scougal, etc.* v. *James Gilchrist* (1736) Mor. 9536; *Cockburn* v. *Grant* (1741) Mor. 9539; *Wilkie* v. *McNeil* (1740) Mor. 9538; 5 B.S. 217; *Walker* v. *Falconer* (1759) Mor. 9543; *More and Irvine* v. *Steven* (1765) Mor. 9545.

[28] *Duncan* v. *Thomson* (1776) Mor.App., "Pactum Illicitum," p. 1; Hailes, 683.

[29] *McLure & McCree* v. *Paterson* (1779) Mor. 9546; Hailes, 829.

[30] Best shown by *Cantlay* v. *Robertson* (1790) Mor. 9550; Hailes, 1077.

was an accessory to smuggling, but, if not an accessory, he could maintain an action though he suspected, or even knew, that the goods were meant to be smuggled.[31]

25–50   It was in this way that the court declared itself against enforcing some contracts tainted with smuggling. It had grappled with a problem which remains, the effect on a contract of implied illegality. The result was that we cannot say that a contract for sale of smuggled goods was either void or voidable, even if all the parties to the sale were concerned in the smuggling. The court's attitude after 1776 is still consistent with the decision in 1723[32] that property could pass in goods which had been smuggled.[33] The principle was stated by the court to be *"in turpi causa melior est conditio possidentis*[34]; that "no action lies"[35]; a bond "could produce no action,"[36] and "the pursuer could not maintain an action."[37] The conclusion must be that in their treatment of smuggling contracts and also in the contemporaneous treatment of gaming contracts, the court had created a new form of invalidity—the unenforceable contract.[38]

Contracts in Restraint of Trade

25–51   The development of contracts in restraint of trade did not get under way until the second half of the nineteenth century. It had been held in *Stalker* v. *Carmichael*[39] that there could be a good agreement that a man should not carry on a particular trade in a particular place. The problem of restraint of trade imposed by a contractual provision of a similar type did not arise again until 1863 when Lord Justice-Clerk Inglis observed:

> "There can be no doubt that, according to the law of Scotland, a paction against the liberty of trade is illegal; and that agreements, by which a man binds himself that he will not carry on a trade of any kind though limited in space, or a particular trade if unlimited in space, are both equally bad in law."[40]

---

[31] *Young & Co.* v. *Imlach* (1790) Mor. 9553; *Cullen* v. *Philp* (1793) Mor. 9554; *Isaacson* v. *Wiseman* (1806) Hume 714. Cases on accession to smuggling were applied to a sale of lottery tickets in *McLaren* v. *McManus*, Nov. 21, 1878 Guth.Sh.Cas. (2nd Ser.) (1894), p. 105.

[32] *Comms. of Customs* v. *Morison, sup. cit.*

[33] Bell, *Comm.*, i, 327; *cf. Nisbet's Creditors* v. *Robertson* (1791) Mor. 9554 which involved the assignation of a bond. The bond was reduced as a *pactum illicitum*. *Brown* v. *Limond* (1791) Hume 672 is a case special on its facts.

[34] *Cullen* v. *Philp sup. cit.*

[35] *McClure & McCree* v. *Paterson, sup. cit.*; *Mitchel* v. *Morgan* (1780) Hailes, *Dec.* 859; 5 B.S. 533.

[36] *Stewart* v. *Lamont* (1751) Mor. 9542.

[37] *Cockburn* v. *Grant, sup. cit.*

[38] See further, para. 26–12.

[39] (1735) Mor. 9455.

[40] *Watson* v. *Neuffert* (1863) 1 M. 1110 at p. 1112. One prior case mentioned a restrictive covenant: *Curtis* v. *Sandison* (1831) 10 S. 72.

When was this so settled as Scots law that there was no doubt about it? There could have been an analogy drawn from the cases on combinations or a development of pactions against personal liberty[41] but that would not explain the specification of the "bad" types of agreements. There may be unreported cases. Judging from the authorities cited to the court, however, English cases must have had a strong influence.[42]

-52 Before Scots law had a chance to develop its own case law, the House of Lords had decided *Nordenfelt* v. *Maxim Nordenfelt Guns and Ammunition Co.*[43] Scots law developed thereafter[44] and the English influence is apparent in the cases cited by counsel and by the court. An attempt to argue that Scots and English law had different approaches would have even less chance of success now than it did in 1899.[45] Even when the argument was about a restrictive covenant in such a Scottish document as a back letter relative to an *ex facie* absolute disposition, Lord Hunter found no real assistance from Scottish authorities, and gave weight to recent English decisions, counsel having agreed that the general principles in *Nordenfelt* were equally applicable to Scots law.[46]

-53 Lord Ardwall was historically inaccurate when he said in relation to a restrictive covenant in a contract of service:

> "Originally at common law all such agreements as that under consideration in the present case were void as being made in restraint of trade and contrary to public policy. To this general rule exceptions have been from time to time admitted in certain cases on the ground that the restraint imposed in these cases was reasonable and proper on a consideration of the contract between the parties."[47]

-54 On the contrary, originally at common law contracts were enforced[48] except in cases of severe restraint on personal liberty.[49] At the end of the nineteenth century Scots courts adopted English authority which was based on a test of reasonableness and at one time also on the ade-

---

[41] Which is the treatment in More's Notes to Stair, 1, 1xiv.

[42] There were English cases going back to the second half of the 16th century. The most important case was *Mitchell* v. *Reynolds* (1711) 10 Mod. 130. South Africa took the rule from English law, there being no Roman or Roman Dutch equivalent: J. T. R. Gibson, *South African Mercantile and Company Law* (3rd ed., 1975), p. 16.

[43] [1894] A.C. 535. The only reported Scots case prior to this, apart from those already mentioned, is *Macintyre* v. *Macraild* (1868) 5 S.L.R. 362; (1866) 4 M. 571.

[44] *e.g. Meikle* v. *Meikle* (1895) 3 S.L.T. 204; *Dumbarton Steamboat Co. Ltd.* v. *MacFarlane* (1899) 1 F. 993; *Stewart* v. *Stewart* (1899) 1 F. 1158 (disapproved in *Vancouver Malt Co.* v. *Vancouver Breweries* [1934] A.C. 181 at p. 191 *per* Lord Macmillan); *British Workman's and General Assurance Co. Ltd.* v. *Wilkinson* (1900) 8 S.L.T. 67; *Mulvein* v. *Murray*, 1908 S.C. 528; *Remington Typewriter Co.* v. *Sim*, 1915 1 S.L.T. 168; *Scottish Farmers' Dairy Co. (Glasgow) Ltd.* v. *McGhee*, 1933 S.C. 148; *B.M.T.A.* v. *Gray*, 1951 S.C. 586.

[45] *Stewart* v. *Stewart, sup. cit.* (argument of pursuer). The argument is not referred to in the opinions of the court.

[46] *MacIntyre* v. *Cleveland Petroleum Co. Ltd.*, 1967 S.L.T. 95.

[47] *Mulvein* v. *Murray, sup. cit.* at p. 533. What his Lordship said may be true of English law.

[48] *Stalker* v. *Carmichael, sup. cit.*

[49] *Allan* v. *Skene* (1728) Mor. 9454; *Wedderburn* v. *Monorgun* (1612) Mor. 9453.

quacy of consideration.[50] Scots law mitigated the harshness of "every paction produceth action," not the opposite.[51]

THE PRESENT LAW ON RESTRAINT OF TRADE

The Principles of the Law

25–55   The doctrine of restraint of trade is in some ways anomalous. It is the one instance of a refusal by the common law to uphold a term in a contract unless that term is reasonable. If the restraint is invalid, the rest of the contract stands with the result that one party may be unjustly enriched and the court in effect has remade the contract.[52] But what the law attempts is the reconciliation of two freedoms—one the freedom of trade and the other the freedom of contract.[53] Because attitudes to these two freedoms have varied from time to time the older cases on restraint of trade must be used with caution.[54] The reconciliation of the freedoms varies with the type of contract. Between employer and employee the court more jealously guards the freedom of an employee to earn his livelihood elsewhere. In other cases more weight is given to "the policy of the law that contracts freely entered into should, *prima facie*, be enforced."[55] The principles of the law can largely be derived from five decisions of the House of Lords, namely, *Nordenfelt* v. *Maxim Nordenfelt Guns and Ammunition Co.*[56]; *Mason* v. *Provident Clothing and Supply Co. Ltd.*[57]; *Herbert Morris Ltd.* v. *Saxelby*[58]; *Fitch* v. *Dewes*[59]; and *Esso Petroleum Co. Ltd.* v. *Harper's Garage (Stourport) Ltd.*[60]

---

[50] *Mitchell* v. *Reynolds, sup. cit.*; *Horner* v. *Graves* (1831) 7 Bing. 735.

[51] It is not without significance that Gloag thought *Watson* v. *Neuffert, sup. cit.*, *Ballachulish Slate Quarries Co.* v. *Grant* (1903) 5 F. 1105 and *Macintyre* v. *Macraild, sup. cit.*, in which restrictions were enforced, might not now be followed: Gloag, p. 571.

[52] See *Esso Petroleum Co. Ltd.* v. *Harpers Garage (Stourport) Ltd.* [1968] A.C. 269 at p. 295 *per* Lord Reid.

[53] *Herbert Morris Ltd.* v. *Saxelby* [1916] 1 A.C. 688 at p. 716 *per* Lord Shaw; at p. 699 *per* Lord Atkinson; *Mason* v. *Provident Clothing and Supply Co. Ltd.* [1913] A.C. 724 at p. 738 *per* Lord Shaw.

[54] See Gloag's caution in *Contract*, pp. 570, 571; *cf. Scottish Farmer's Dairy Co. (Glasgow) Ltd.* v. *McGhee*, 1933 S.C. 148. In *Agma Chemical Co. Ltd.* v. *Hart*, 1984 S.L.T. 246, *Mulvein* v. *Murray*, 1908 S.C. 528 was cited in the opinion of the First Division without disapproval. On *Stewart* v. *Stewart* (1899) 1 F. 1158, see *Vancouver Malt & Sake Brewing Co. Ltd.* v. *Vancouver Breweries Ltd.* [1934] A.C. 181 at p. 191 *per* Lord MacMillan.

[55] *Whitehill* v. *Bradford* [1952] Ch. 236 at p. 246 *per* Sir Raymond Evershed, M.R., cited in *Anthony* v. *Rennie*, 1981 S.L.T.(Notes) 11 at p. 12 *per* Lord Grieve. The difference between the two categories of cases is analysed below, para. 25–66 *et seq*. On a contract between lender and borrower see *MacIntyre* v. *Cleveland Petroleum Co. Ltd.*, 1967 S.L.T. 95; *Esso Petroleum Co. Ltd.* v. *Harper's Garage (Stourport) Ltd.* [1968] A.C. 269.

[56] [1894] A.C. 535.

[57] [1913] A.C. 724.

[58] [1916] 1 A.C. 688.

[59] [1921] 2 A.C. 158.

[60] [1968] A.C. 269.

-56   In Scottish practice the problems frequently emerge at the stage of
interim interdict. There is then the added factor of the balance of convenience which often favours enforcement of a contract on an interim
basis.[61]

What is a Contract in Restraint of Trade?

-57   Lord President Cooper said[62]: "The typical contract in restraint of trade
is a contract by which some restriction is imposed which tends to deprive
the community of the labour, skill or talents of men in the employments
or capacities in which they might be most useful to the public as well as
to themselves, and which may be on that account contrary to public
policy." The phrase "restraint of trade" is misleading because it suggests that any contract which restricts a person's trade is subject to the
doctrine. But a contract which controls when or to whom a buyer may
resell is not in restraint of trade.[63]

-58   In *Esso Petroleum* it was held that negative covenants affecting land
were not in restraint of trade. Lord Reid observed[64]:

> "Restraint of trade appears to me to imply that a man contracts to
> give up some freedom which otherwise he would have had. A per-
> son buying or leasing land had no previous right to be there at all,
> let alone to trade there, and when he takes possession of that land
> subject to a negative restrictive covenant he gives up no right or
> freedom which he previously had."

Positive obligations which obliged a trader to act in a particular way did
bring the agreement within the doctrine of restraint of trade. This distinction between two types of obligation is not easy to apply. Lord
Pearce in *Esso Petroleum* tested some obligations which were not in
restraint of trade, some which were, and some which were on the borderline.[65] The doctrine does not apply to ordinary commercial contracts
which promote trade, or to sole agencies, or the film star who ties her-
self to one company to obtain the benefits of stardom. It does not apply
to parties during the continuance of the contract when the negative ties
are normal and incidental to the positive commercial arrangements.

-59   What brings a contract within the doctrine are (1) the control of trading activities after the determination of a contract or (2) fettering of a
party so much during a contract that the contract restrains rather than
promotes trade. It is this last category which poses the most difficulties,

---

[61] See in more detail, below, para. 25–104. Success in obtaining and keeping in force an
interim interdict can be almost as good in practical terms as a final interdict. Therefore the
practitioner must not ignore the factors which govern the granting of interim orders.
[62] *British Motor Trade Assoc.* v. *Gray*, 1951 S.C. 586 at p. 598.
[63] *British Motor Trade Assoc.* v. *Gray, sup. cit.*; *Macrae & Dick* v. *Philip*, 1982 S.L.T.
(Sh.Ct.) 5.
[64] at p. 298.
[65] at pp. 328, 329.

leaves the greatest scope for judicial discretion, and which faced the House in *Esso Petroleum*. The extent of the controls imposed in *Esso* lead to the view that overall the contract was in restraint of trade. If the garage proprietor had been bound to sell Esso petrol only that might have been outwith the restraint of trade doctrine.[66] But *Esso* went much further. Looking at all the contract controls[67] the impression was of a contract in restraint of trade and it was not necessary to attempt the almost impossible task of defining the limits of the doctrine.

25–60   The flexibility of the doctrine enables it to be applied without regard to the categories produced by textbook writers. A contract to work full time for a period of one year or a sole agency would not normally be in restraint of trade. It could be if the restrictions appeared to be unnecessary or to be reasonably capable of enforcement in an oppressive manner.[68] An obligation to give a company a monopoly of a composer's work has been held to be an unreasonable restraint of trade.[69] Ordinary covenants for the use of land are outwith the doctrine but not certain positive obligations.[70] An assignation of copyright was not an agreement in restraint of trade.[71] A profit-sharing agreement will not normally be in restraint of trade but the court will look at the practical effect. A provision requiring a payment of a proportion of commission received by a former employee has been held in restraint of trade, because it was likely to cause the employee to refuse business which he would otherwise take.[72]

25–61   The form of the document containing the restraint will not prevent the doctrine applying. The restraint may be in a mortgage or lease or other writ affecting land.[73] It may be in the rules of a body which governs a sport.[74] In *Dickson* v. *Pharmaceutical Society of Great Britain*[75] rules of a professional association which limited the goods which members could sell were held in restraint of trade. It was observed that the court will look to the practical working of the restraint rather than its legal form and the "doctrine" applies outside the contractual field to charters, bye-laws and rules.[76]

---

[66] And see also tying covenants in brewery cases cited by Lord Wilberforce at pp. 333, 334.

[67] Withholding supplies to the garage, fixing the price of petrol, binding the garage to keep open, fetters on resale of the garage.

[68] *A. Schroeder Publishing Co. Ltd.* v. *Macaulay* [1974] 3 All E.R. 616 at p. 622 *per* Lord Reid. On the general rule about restrictions during a contract, see para. 25–66.

[69] *A. Schroeder Publishing Co. Ltd.* v. *Macaulay, sup. cit.*

[70] *Esso Petroleum, sup. cit.*

[71] *Clifford Davis Management Ltd.* v. *W.E.A. Records Ltd.* [1975] 1 All E.R. 237. The agreement was *prima facie* unenforceable on grounds of inequality of bargaining power.

[72] *Stenhouse Australia Ltd.* v. *Phillips* [1974] A.C. 391.

[73] *MacIntyre* v. *Cleveland Petroleum Co. Ltd.*, 1967 S.L.T. 95; *Esso Petroleum, sup. cit.*

[74] *Eastham* v. *Newcastle United F.C.* [1964] Ch. 413; *Greig* v. *Insole* [1978] 3 All E.R. 449.

[75] [1970] A.C. 403.

[76] *Ibid.* at p. 440 *per* Lord Wilberforce.

The Overriding Principle

-62 A restriction on trade is enforceable if it is reasonable. In considering what is reasonable two interests are looked at, namely, the interests of the parties and the interests of the public.[77] A restraint could be agreed between experienced traders and be in their interests, but nevertheless the public interest might make the restraint unenforceable.[78]

-63 In applying the standard of reasonableness several propositions, narrated below, can be derived from the cases. These have to be applied subject to Lord Wilberforce's comment that[79]:

> "The common law has often (if sometimes unconsciously) thrived on ambiguity and it would be mistaken, even if it were possible, to try to crystallise the rules of this, or any, aspect of public policy into neat propositions. The doctrine of restraint of trade is one to be applied to factual situations with a broad and flexible rule of reason."

-64 Nevertheless the practitioner needs guidance on what has in the past been regarded as reasonable and the courts have regard to reported cases because questions of law are involved.

(1) What is reasonable alters with the changing nature of commerce and society.

-65 It was this proposition which was established in *Nordenfelt* v. *Maxim Nordenfelt Guns and Ammunition Co. Ltd.*[80] and which explains the importance of that case. Lord Herschell stated[81]:

> "For, in considering the application of the rule and the limitations, if any, to be placed on it, I think that regard must be had to the changed conditions of commerce and of the means of communication which have been developed in recent years. To disregard these would be to miss the substance of the rule in a blind adherence to its letter. Newcastle-upon-Tyne is for all practical purposes as near to London today as towns which are now regarded as suburbs of the metropolis were a century ago. An order can be sent to Newcastle more quickly than it could then have been transmitted from one end of London to the other, and goods can be conveyed between the two cities in a few hours and at a comparatively small cost. Competition has assumed altogether different proportions in these altered circumstances, and that which would have been once

---

[77] *Nordenfelt, sup. cit.* at p. 549 *per* Lord Herschell L.C.; at p. 565 *per* Lord MacNaughten; *Herbert Morris, sup. cit.* at pp. 700, 701 *per* Lord Atkinson; at p. 707 *per* Lord Parker; *Deacons* v. *Bridge* [1984] 2 All E.R. 19 (P.C.).

[78] *Esso Petroleum, sup. cit.* at p. 300 *per* Lord Reid; *cf.* at p. 324 *per* Lord Pearce, who viewed public policy as the ultimate test. On how to consider public interest, see *Texaco Ltd.* v. *Mulberry Filling Station* [1972] 1 All E.R. 513.

[79] *Esso Petroleum, sup. cit.* at p. 331.

[80] *Sup. cit.*

[81] at p. 547; see also at p. 551 *per* Lord Watson.

merely a burden on the covenantor may now be essential if there is to be reasonable protection to the covenantee."

Lord Ashbourne took account of the invention and use of telegraphs, postal systems, railways and steam.[82] The modern court may have to consider more advanced methods of communication. The alterations in the circumstances of trade affect the value of prior cases as illustrations.[83]

(2) There is a difference between what is reasonable in a contract of service on the one hand and other contracts on the other hand.

25–66   Lord Macnaghten drew a distinction between employment or apprenticeship on the one hand, and the sale of a business or the dissolution of a partnership on the other.[84] The argument that there is no distinction between the categories has been rejected.[85]

Employer and employee. An employer may seek to impose several types of restraint on his employee. The attitude of the courts varies according to the nature of the restriction.

(i) *Restriction applying while the employee is employed.* An employer may prohibit a full-time employee carrying on other employment. A part-time employee may be prevented from working during other parts of the day for a competitor.[86] It will usually be relatively easy to show that these restraints are reasonable.[87] In an exceptional case there may be restrictions which appear to be unnecessary or to be reasonably capable of enforcement in an oppressive manner. These restraints must be justified.[88]

When the contract has ended it is more likely that questions of restraint arise.[89] Subsidiary problems occur in determining when the contract of service is terminated, for example, if the employer wrongfully dismisses[90] or a new contract of service is entered into.[91]

---

[82] at p. 556.

[83] It may be anticipated that the greater the ease with which a person may communicate at a distance with a customer or potential customer the wider the area of reasonable restraint. But the faster the changes in scientific knowledge or manufacturers' products the shorter the period of reasonable restraint.

[84] *Nordenfelt, sup. cit.* at p. 566.

[85] *Herbert Morris, sup. cit.* at p. 708 *per* Lord Parker; at p. 713 *per* Lord Shaw.

[86] There may be an implied duty of fidelity which is breached if an employee works for a rival outside his normal working hours: *Hivac Ltd.* v. *Park Royal Scientific Instruments Ltd.* [1946] Ch. 169.

[87] *Gaumont-British Picture Corp. Ltd.* v. *Alexander* [1936] 2 All E.R. 1686; *Warner Brothers Pictures Inc.* v. *Nelson* [1937] 1 K.B. 209. It may be better to say that the "doctrine" does not apply to such restraints. See the discussion of *Esso Petroleum, sup. cit.*, at para. 25–58.

[88] *A. Schroeder Publishing Co. Ltd.* v. *Macaulay* [1974] 3 All E.R. 616 at p. 622 *per* Lord Reid.

[89] *Eastham* v. *Newcastle United F.C.* [1964] Ch. 413.

[90] *General Billposting Co. Ltd.* v. *Atkinson* [1909] A.C. 118.

[91] *S. W. Strange Ltd.* v. *Mann* [1965] 1 All E.R. 1069.

(ii) *Restrictions after employment has ceased.* There are three common types of restrictions namely (a) preventing employment by a rival or carrying on a competing trade or profession; (b) a prohibition on soliciting former customers and (c) a prohibition on the use of trade secrets or confidential information. The restraints may arise from a contract entered into at any time, including an agreement at the termination of employment.[92]

67 (iii) *Employment by rival.* An employer does not own the skill of his employee and should not be allowed to gain a special advantage by eliminating all future competition from the employee.[93] The employee should be allowed to earn his livelihood.[94] At one time it was said in England that there was not any case of a covenant against competition by an employee or apprentice being upheld by the court.[95] In *Fitch* v. *Dewes*,[96] however, a solicitor's managing clerk was successfully prohibited from carrying on a business as a solicitor within a seven-mile radius of a town hall. In Scotland it has been recognised, perhaps for a longer period, that a person may protect his business against competition by an employee.[97] A world-wide restriction on a management trainee involved in the manufacture of jeans has been enforced by interim interdict.[98] A person working in an employment agency has been interdicted, after proof, for working for a competitor within a quarter mile for a period of one year.[99] A designer has been prevented by interim interdict for working for a competitor in the United Kingdom within one year of ceasing employment.[1] A milk roundsman has been prevented for two years from trading within one mile of his employer's place of business.[2]

68 A restraint on a solicitor's managing clerk for the whole of the life of the clerk and extending over a radius of 15 miles was found unreasonable.[3] A five-mile restraint on a butcher was unreasonable when most of the employer's business was within two miles.[4] A five-year restriction on a canvasser has been held unreasonable; if he had been a managing director it might have been different.[5] A three-year restraint on an

---

[92] *Spink (Bournemouth) Ltd.* v. *Spink* [1936] Ch. 544.
[93] *Herbert Morris, sup. cit.*, at p. 708 *per* Lord Parker; at p. 713 *per* Lord Shaw.
[94] Thus it is relevant to the reasonableness of enforcing a restraint that an employer offers to pay the wages of a former employee during the period of restraint. See *Agma Chemical Co. Ltd.* v. *Hart*, 1984 S.L.T. 246 at p. 248 *per* Lord President Emslie.
[95] *Herbert Morris, sup. cit.*, at p. 708 *per* Lord Parker.
[96] *Sup. cit.*
[97] *Scottish Farmers' Dairy Co. (Glasgow) Ltd.* v. *McGhee*, 1933 S.C. 148 at pp. 152, 153 *per* Lord President Clyde.
[98] *Bluebell Apparel Ltd.* v. *Dickinson*, 1978 S.C. 16.
[99] *SOS Bureau Ltd.* v. *Payne*, 1982 S.L.T. (Sh.Ct.) 33.
[1] *A. & D. Bedrooms Ltd.* v. *Michael*, 1984 S.L.T. 297.
[2] *Scottish Managers' Dairy Company (Glasgow) Ltd.* v. *McGhee*, 1933 S.C. 148.
[3] *Dickson* v. *Jones* [1939] 3 All E.R. 182.
[4] *Empire Meat Co. Ltd.* v. *Patrick* [1939] 2 All E.R. 85.
[5] *M. & S. Drapers* v. *Reynolds* [1956] 3 All E.R. 814.

estate agent's clerk working within five miles of one of the branches was reasonable; a similar restraint on practising within five miles of another branch was unreasonable (but severable).[6] It was reasonable to restrain a ladies' hairdresser from working for 12 months within half-a-mile of any premises from which she worked during the last three months of her employment.[7]

25–69　　Although traditionally it has been said (at least in English law) to be relatively difficult to prohibit a former employee from working elsewhere, not only is this type of prohibition now common practice, but it has been judicially recognised that it may be the only practical means of protecting an employer's business. Other prohibitions can be less effective. A prohibition on soliciting former customers may not protect trade secrets such as information on pricing policies.[8] Customers may continue to deal with a familiar caller whoever his employer and without any canvassing or enticement.[9] A prohibition against passing on trade secrets can be impossible to monitor and almost worthless unless there is also a restraint on employment by a rival.[10]

25–70　　An agreement between employers not to employ each others' employees has been held unreasonable.[11]

25–71　　(iv) *Soliciting customers.* If a former employee induces a breach of contract between his former employer and a third party that would be a delict.[12] It would be actionable without any provision in the employer's contract of employment. By contract the employer may widen the control open to him. He can prevent an employee enticing away customers who are free to contract where they will.[13]

25–72　　The allegiance of a customer or client varies with the nature of the business. The relationship between an insurer or an insurance broker and his customer has been said to be more fragile than that between solicitor and client.[14] But in principle a covenant against solicitation is entirely reasonable and necessary for the protection of the employer. The covenant will be upheld if it is carefully limited to what is reasonable and necessary to protect a business. There are two factors, (a) the time of the restraint, and (b) the customers or clients to whom the restraint applies.

---

[6] *Scorer* v. *Seymour-Johns* [1966] 3 All E.R. 347.

[7] *Marion White Ltd.* v. *Francis* [1972] 3 All E.R. 857.

[8] *SOS Bureau Ltd.* v. *Payne, sup. cit.*

[9] *Scottish Farmers' Dairy Co. (Glasgow) Ltd.* v. *McGhee*, 1933 S.C. 148.

[10] *SOS Bureau Ltd.* v. *Payne, sup. cit.*; *Bluebel Apparel Ltd.* v. *Dickson*, sup. cit. (the Lord Ordinary cites relevant English authority).

[11] *Kores Manufacturing Co. Ltd.* v. *Kolok Manufacturing Co. Ltd.* [1959] Ch. 108.

[12] *B.M.T.A.* v. *Gray*, 1951 S.C. 586; *Exchange Telegraph Co.* v. *Giulianotti*, 1959 S.C. 19. The details of this part of the law, including the exemptions applying to industrial disputes, must be looked for in works on delict and tort.

[13] Whether an obligation against soliciting is implied after the employment has ceased is uncertain. During employment it is probably a breach of an employee's duties to solicit customers with a view to commencing his own business. See *Wessex Dairies Ltd.* v. *Smith* [1935] 2 K.B. 80.

[14] *Stenhouse Australia Ltd.* v. *Phillips* [1974] A.C. 391 at p. 401.

73 As Lord Wilberforce put it[15]:

"It is for the judge, after informing himself as fully as he can of the facts and circumstances relating to the employer's business, the nature of the employer's interest to be protected, and the likely effect on this of solicitation, to decide whether the contractual period is reasonable or not. An opinion as to the reasonableness of elements of it, particularly of the time during which it is to run, can seldom be precise, and can only be formed on a broad and common sense view."

-74 The definition of "customer" or "client" can give rise to problems. In the most limited case "customers" will be persons with whom the former employee dealt within a short period prior to the termination of his employment.[16] In other cases "customers" can include persons not known to the employee to have been customers and who had ceased to be customers.[17] An employer is entitled to protect his chance of former customers returning[18] and, possibly, also of gaining some potential customers with whom there has been contact.[19] Lack of knowledge that a person has been a customer may lead an employee to breach the clause inadvertently but an employee can ask people whether they were customers of his former employer.[20] In a similar problem with an agency there was a *prima facie* case for enforcing a restriction limited to one year and applying to a restricted class of customer.[21] A restraint which was not limited to customers but to goods dealt in by the employers was held invalid.[22]

-75 (v) *Confidential information and trade secrets.* Where parties are in a contractual relationship there may be an implied term relating to the use and disclosure of information communicated by one party to the other. Where an employee acquires confidential information in the course of his service, the law implies a contract that the information should not, during or after the service, be disclosed without justification to a third party.[23] An employee should not, for example, make copies of lists of customers and disclose these to a future employer[24] or disclose to a tele-

---

[15] *Ibid.* at p. 402. A period of five years on an employee of an insurance broker was held reasonable.

[16] *Home Counties Dairies Ltd.* v. *Skilton* [1970] 1 All E.R. 1227 at p. 1231 *per* Harman L.J.

[17] *G. W. Plowman & Son Ltd.* v. *Ash* [1964] 2 All E.R. 10.

[18] *Ibid.*

[19] *Gledhow Autoparts Ltd.* v. *Delaney* [1965] 3 All E.R. 288.

[20] *G. W. Plowman & Son Ltd.* v. *Ash, sup. cit.* at p. 14 *per* Davies L.J.; at p. 15 *per* Russell L.J.; *Agma Chemical Co. Ltd.* v. *Hart*, 1984 S.L.T. 246 at p. 248 *per* Lord President Emslie.

[21] *Agma Chemical Co. Ltd.* v. *Hart, sup. cit.* See also *Mulvein* v. *Murray*, 1908 S.C. 528.

[22] *Gledhow Autoparts Ltd.* v. *Delaney, sup. cit.*

[23] *Liverpool Victoria Legal Friendly Society* v. *Houston* (1900) 3 F. 42; see also *Roxburgh* v. *McArthur* (1841) 3 D. 556; *British Workmen's and General Assurance Co. Ltd.* v. *Wilkinson* (1900) 8 S.L.T. 67; *Scot.Law Com.Mem. No. 40, Confidential Information (1977); Report, "Breach of Confidence,"* Scot.Law Com. No. 90 (1984).

[24] See *Liverpool Victoria Legal Friendly Society* v. *Houston, sup. cit.*

vision company documents relating to high-level internal actions and discussion within the offices of his employer.[25]

25–76   It may be in certain instances justifiable in the public interest to disclose confidential information. The public interest in publicity may outweigh the public interest in protecting confidential information. This has been applied in cases of crime or illegal activity,[26] to correct the publicity sought by a pop group,[27] to disclose doubts about the reliability of a breath test device on which criminal convictions were based,[28] and in a commission and diligence for the recovery of documents.[29] What is in the public interest is different from what is interesting to the public.[30] Newspapers, television and radio have been said to be peculiarly vulnerable to the error of confusing the public interest with their own interest.[31]

25–77   It can be difficult to determine what is meant by confidential information. It is unlikely that information available to the public can be confidential.[32] You cannot obtain an interdict against the spread of common knowledge. Application for a patent may disclose a secret which then ceases to be a secret.[33] It has been tentatively suggested that in an industrial or trade setting confidential information has these elements, namely (1) the owner of the information must reasonably believe that release of it would be injurious to him or of advantage to his rivals or others; (2) the owner must reasonably believe that the information is confidential; and (3) the nature of the information must be judged in the light of the usage and practices of the industry or trade.[34] Emphasis has been placed, in certain forms of English proceedings, on the knowledge that the recipient must have had that the information was confidential, for example by the marking of a document as "secret"[35] or by his taking part in discussions which were obviously confidential.[36]

---

[25] *British Steel Corp.* v. *Granada Television Ltd.* [1981] A.C. 1096. See also the case where there was not a direct contract but a relationship of confidentiality arose. *Schering Chemicals Ltd.* v. *Falkman Ltd.* [1982] Q.B. 1; *Brown's Tr.* v. *Hay* (1898) 25 R. 1112; *Levin* v. *Caledonian Produce (Holdings) Ltd.*, 1975 S.L.T.(Notes) 69; *Roxburgh* v. *Seven Seas Engineering Ltd.*, 1980 S.L.T.(Notes) 49.

[26] *Initial Services Ltd.* v. *Putterill* [1968] 1 Q.B. 396.

[27] *Woodward* v. *Hutchins* [1977] 2 All E.R. 751.

[28] *Lion Laboratories Ltd.* v. *Evans* [1984] 2 All E.R. 417.

[29] *Sante Fe International Corp.* v. *Napier Shipping S.A.*, 1985 S.L.T. 430.

[30] *British Steel Corp.* v. *Granada Television Ltd.*, *sup. cit.* at p. 1168 *per* Lord Wilberforce. *Lion Laboratories Ltd.* v. *Evans*, *sup. cit.* at p. 423 *per* Stephenson L.J.

[31] *Francome* v. *Mirror Newspapers* [1984] 2 All E.R. 408 at p. 413 *per* Sir John Donaldson M.R.

[32] *Earl of Crawford* v. *Paton*, 1911 S.C. 1017; *Woodward* v. *Hutchins* [1977] 2 All E.R. 751 at p. 754 *per* Lord Denning M.R.; *Saltman Engineering Co. Ltd.* v. *Campbell Engineering Co. Ltd.* (1948) [1963] 3 All E.R. 413 at p. 415 *per* Lord Greene M.R.

[33] *O. Mustad & Son* v. *S. Allock & Co.* (1928) [1963] 3 All E.R. 416 (H.L.)

[34] This is a summary of *Thomas Marshall (Exports) Ltd.* v. *Guinle* [1978] 3 All E.R. 193 at pp. 209, 210 *per* Megarry V.-C.

[35] *British Steel Corp.* v. *Granada Television Ltd.* [1981] A.C. 1096; *Schering Chemicals Ltd.* v. *Falkman Ltd.* [1982] Q.B. 1.

[36] *Printers and Finishers Ltd.* v. *Holloway* [1964] 3 All E.R. 731 at p. 735 *per* Cross J.

78   There may be an express contract prohibiting the use and disclosure of confidential information. A prohibition on "disclosure" may not prevent "use."[37] An attempt to prevent use of all forms of information will encounter the control imposed by the doctrine of restraint of trade.

79   It is recognised that an employer is entitled to have his interest in trade secrets protected.[38] It is possible to protect confidential information in the form of secrets about a continually developing industrial process.[39] But a person cannot be restrained from using skill and aptitude or general technical knowledge or knowledge about a scheme or organisation and methods of business.[40] There was a *prima facie* case for restraining an employee who had access to customer lists and whose contract prohibited canvassing for two years from the termination of employment.[41] The business skill in compiling a mail order catalogue has been protected by injunction.[42] Lord Denning observed[43]:

> "It is thus established that an employer can stipulate for protection against having his confidential information passed on to a rival in trade. But experience has shown that it is not satisfactory to have simply a covenant against disclosing confidential information. The reason is because it is so difficult to draw the line between information which is confidential and information which is not; and it is is very difficult to prove a breach when the information is of such a character that a servant can carry it away in his head. The difficulties are such that the only practicable solution is to take a covenant from the servant by which he is not to go to work for a rival in trade. Such a covenant may well be held to be reasonable if limited to a short period."[44]

80   **Dissolution of partnership.** Some of the considerations applying to restraints on employees apply to restraints on former partners. The problems of solicitation and confidential information are certainly analogous. But the public interest in facilitating the assumption of new partners may justify restrictions on retiring partners.[45] There is some English authority[46] that restraints in partnership are more like the restraints between a buyer and seller of a business although this may be limited to the particular circumstances of the cases involved. It has been

---

[37] *Thomas Marshall (Exports) Ltd.* v. *Guinle, sup. cit.* at p. 208 *per* Megarry V.-C.

[38] *Herbert Morris Ltd.* v. *Saxelby* [1916] 1 A.C. 688; *Mason* v. *Provident Clothing and Supply Co.* [1913] A.C. 724 at p. 740 *per* Lord Shaw.

[39] *Commercial Plastics Ltd.* v. *Vincent* [1965] 1 Q.B. 623.

[40] *Rentokil Ltd.* v. *Kramer*, 1986 S.L.T. 114.

[41] *Ibid.*

[42] *The Littlewoods Organisation* v. *Harris* [1978] 1 All E.R. 1026.

[43] at p. 1033.

[44] The practical problems of enforcing a covenant on confidential information inhibit the use of independent consultants. A consultant may in the future give advice to a competitor. Even to disclose negative information, for example that a particular line of research is a dead end, can save the competitor a fortune.

[45] *Deacons* v. *Bridge* [1984] 2 All E.R. 19 (P.C.).

[46] Discussed in J. B. Miller, *Partnership*, pp. 120–123.

observed that a decision on whether restrictions in a partnership agreement are enforceable do not depend on putting the agreement into a category but on the legitimate interests which could be protected.[47] There is this speciality with partnership. The partners may have negotiated the terms, and to that extent there is some presumption that their choice of restriction is reasonable.[48]

25–81   In drafting a restrictive covenant in a partnership agreement care has to be taken in specifying the form of business organisation or type of employment which is forbidden to a former partner. In *Taylor* v. *Campbell*[49] a restraint on a dentist carrying on business with others did not prevent him carrying on business on his own account. On the other hand the word "engaged" was held to cover employment as a servant as well as employment as a principal.[50] A restraint on practising as a "medical practitioner" has been held too wide because it could include a consultant which was not necessary for the protection of a partnership of general practitioners.[51] The statutory restraints on selling the goodwill of a medical partnership do not prevent a valid restraint of trade clause.[52]

25–82   **Covenants on sale of a business.** Lord Macnaghten observed that there was more freedom of contract between buyer and seller than between master and servant or between an employer and a person seeking employment.[53] This was followed by Lord Shaw in *Mason* who thought that,[54] "there is much greater room for allowing, as between buyer and seller, a larger scope for freedom of contract and a correspondingly large restraint in freedom of trade, than there is for allowing a restraint of the opportunity for labour in a contract between master and servant or an employer and an applicant for work."

25–83   The seller of a business in the absence of some restrictive covenant could immediately set up in business in competition with the purchaser. The possibility of such competition could reduce the value of the goodwill of the business sold. Conversely the restrictive covenant increases

---

[47] *Deacons* v. *Bridge, sup. cit.*, at p. 22 *per* Lord Fraser (a case of a departmentalised partnership).

[48] On freedom of contract, see below, *s.v.* "Covenants on Sale of Business" and opinions on 10-mile radius in *Lyne-Pirkes* v. *Jones* [1969] 3 All E.R. 738 and on a five-year period in *Deacons* v. *Bridge, sup. cit.* at p. 24. A person assumed as a junior partner, on the other hand, might have little if any chance to make alterations to the partnership deed.

[49] 1926 S.L.T. 260.

[50] *Ronbar Enterprises Ltd.* v. *Green* [1954] 2 All E.R. 266. A reference to "similar" business made the restraint too wide.

[51] *Lyne-Pirkis* v. *Jones* [1969] 3 All E.R. 738. See also *Routh* v. *Jones* [1947] 1 All E.R. 758 ("any professional appointment"); *Peyton* v. *Mindham* [1971] 3 All E.R. 1215 ("professionally advise, etc."); *Jenkins* v. *Reid* [1948] 1 All E.R. 471.

[52] *Whitehill* v. *Bradford* [1952] Ch. 236. See National Health Service (Scotland) Act 1978, s.35; *Anthony* v. *Rennie*, 1981 S.L.T.(Notes) 11 (six miles for five years *prima facie* a reasonable restraint).

[53] *Nordenfelt, sup. cit.* at p. 566.

[54] *Mason, sup. cit.* at p. 738; see also at p. 731 *per* Viscount Haldane L.C. Whether or not there is freedom to negotiate terms was said to be a factor by Lord Reid in *Esso Petroleum, sup. cit.* at p. 300.

the value and possible price of the business. The seller benefits from the covenant. The purchaser is entitled to protection of what he has bought.[55]

–84 Nevertheless any restraint must be reasonable in the interests of the parties and in the public interest.[56] The type of restraint commonly imposed will prohibit the seller from carrying on the same business within a defined area for a limited period of time. The restraint usually will prevent competition which arises "directly or indirectly." This may prevent financial assistance to another business,[57] or engagement as an employee or agent. It has been held that a seller could not protect another business. When a gentlemen's hairdressing business was sold, the seller could not protect a ladies' hairdressing trade.[58]

–85 A world-wide restriction has been held reasonable when the trade was world-wide.[59] A restriction on carrying on business in Canada was reasonable when the business extended throughout Canada and it was not necessary to prove that the business had been carried on in every part of the area mentioned.[60] On the other hand a radius of 15 miles from a town hall was an unreasonable restraint on an accountant when the area covered included several districts which had no connection with the business.[61]

–86 In *Nordenfelt* a very long period did not prevent the restraint from being reasonable. In *Esso Petroleum*, however (a case involving mortgages), a period of five years was not longer than necessary to afford a protection of a system of distribution but a tie of 21 years went beyond any period for which developments in the trade were reasonably foreseeable. The reasonableness of the period depends on the circumstances of the trade involved. In *Randev* v. *Pattar*[62] a seller of a hotel business undertook not to carry on business in competition within a one-mile radius for five years. The five-year period rendered the restrictive covenant of doubtful validity and interim interdict was refused.

–87 An agreement not to carry on a competing trade made in return for a sum of money is a bare pact against competition and will be very difficult to sustain as reasonable.[63]

---

[55] See *Herbert Morris, sup. cit.* at p. 701 *per* Lord Atkinson; at p. 709 *per* Lord Parker; at p. 713 *per* Lord Shaw. You may not "sell the cow and sup the milk"—*Nordenfelt, sup. cit.* at p. 572 *per* Lord Macnaghten.

[56] *Nordenfelt, sup. cit.* esp. at p. 565 *per* Lord Macnaghten.

[57] *Batts Combe Quarry Ltd.* v. *Ford* [1943] Ch. 51.

[58] *Giblin* v. *Murdoch*, 1979 S.L.T. (Sh.Ct.) 5. A restraint on business within three miles for five years was thought to be reasonable. See, on when a restraint may apply to associated parties, para. 25–103.

[59] *Nordenfelt, sup. cit.*; conversely, *Minimax Ltd.* v. *Geddes* (1914) 31 Sh.Ct.Rep.36.

[60] *Connors Bros. Ltd.* v. *Connors* [1940] 4 All E.R. 179.

[61] *D. Bates & Co.* v. *Dale* [1937] 3 All E.R. 650.

[62] 1985 S.L.T. 270.

[63] *Vancouver Malt and Sake Brewing Co.* v. *Vancouver Breweries Ltd.* [1934] A.C. 181. *Stewart* v. *Stewart* (1899) 1 F. 1158 was disapproved. *Ballachulish Slate Quarries Co. Ltd.* v. *Grant* (1903) 5 F. 1105 was distinguished because the restriction was ancillary to a contract of employment.

25–88 **Mortgages.** The applicability of the rules on restraint of trade to mortgages and tying covenants was thoroughly discussed in *Esso Petroleum*.[64]

(3) In determining what is reasonable the character of the business must be looked at.

25–89 One of the most important factors in considering what is reasonable is the character of the business for which protection is sought. The court will consider the nature of the trade, and the number and distribution of the customers[65]; the location of branches and sales staff[66]; the financial investment made to establish the trade, the nature of the distribution network, its effect on prices and the interaction with competitors.[67] It may be relevant to consider the distribution and nature of competitors.[68]

25–90 As a guide to the requirements of a particular business, evidence can be led as to the general practice amongst businessmen.[69] The court can use its own knowledge of matters of everyday occurrence. It may be that a restraint has become part of the accepted pattern or structure of trade and it has been suggested that this would remove the necessity of justification by reasonableness.[70] Standard form contracts negotiated between the parties or representative organisations are more likely to be fair and reasonable than a standard form contract drafted by only one of the parties.[71]

25–91 Some restraints may be so obviously against public policy that the court on its own initiative would refuse to enforce them.[72] But in other, more normal, cases the relevant facts and circumstances must be inquired into.[73] Evidence cannot be led of the reasonableness of the restraint because that is a question of law.[74] It follows that it is relevant to consider comparable restrictions in previous cases.[75]

---

[64] See also *MacIntyre* v. *Cleveland Petroleum Co.*, 1967 S.L.T. 95 and discussion above, *s.v.* "What is a Contract in Restraint of Trade?," para. 25–57; *Alex. Lobb (Garages) Ltd.* v. *Total Oil G.B. Ltd.* [1985] 1 All E.R. 303.

[65] *Nordenfelt, sup. cit.* (few customers, but world-wide in distribution); *Empire Meat Co. Ltd.* v. *Patrick* [1939] 2 All E.R. 85.

[66] *Mason, sup. cit.*; *Scorer* v. *Seymour-Johns* [1966] 3 All E.R. 347.

[67] *Esso Petroleum, sup. cit.*

[68] *Commercial Plastics Ltd.* v. *Vincent* [1965] 1 Q.B. 623.

[69] *Mason, sup. cit.* at p. 732 *per* Viscount Haldane L.C.

[70] *Esso Petroleum, sup. cit.* at pp. 335 *et seq. per* Lord Wilberforce.

[71] *A. Schroeder Music Publishing Co. Ltd.* v. *Macaulay* [1974] 3 All E.R. 616 (H.L.).

[72] *North Western Salt Co. Ltd.* v. *Electrolytic Alkali Co. Ltd., sup. cit.* at p. 478 *per* Lord Parker.

[73] *Herbert Morris, sup. cit.* at p. 715 *per* Lord Shaw.

[74] *Mason, sup cit.* at p. 732 *per* Viscount Haldane L.C.; *North Western Salt Co. Ltd.* v. *Electrolytic Alkali Co. Ltd.* [1914] A.C. 461 at pp. 470, 471 *per* Viscount Haldane L.C.; at p. 475 *per* Lord Moulton; *Stenhouse Australia Ltd.* v. *Phillips* [1974] A.C. 391 at p. 402.

[75] *Esso Petroleum, sup. cit.* at p. 340 *per* Lord Wilberforce.

(4) On whom is the onus of showing that the restraint is reasonable?

92   Some restraints could be so obviously unjustifiable that an inquiry into facts and circumstances is unnecessary. When there is room for justification a question of onus may arise.[76] There are contradictory dicta on where the onus lies—whether it is for the person relying on the restraint to justify it[77] or the person seeking escape from the restraint to show why he should not be bound by it.[78] It has been suggested that the onus of establishing facts indicating that a restraint is reasonable between the parties is on the person founding on the restriction. But the onus of showing that the restraint is against the public interest is on the party seeking to be free from the restriction.[79] The reason for this distinction has been described as "obscure."[80] This is all the more so if the view is taken that there is really only one test—that of public interest.

93   The problem arises in part from attitudes to the validity of restraint. If the law assumes in the course of its development that a restraint is bad, it is natural that the onus of overcoming this proposition should appear to be on the person seeking to restrain. If the law originally enforced most restraints, the onus of challenging the contract is on the party wishing to be free from it. In modern Scots cases there are traces of both approaches and attitudes. In a case of doubt the contract should be enforced rather than be made illegal.[81] It is the policy of the law to enforce contracts.[82] On the other hand it was said that a lender had to justify a restrictive condition in a back letter[83] and that the primary onus was on the employer to show that a restraint was reasonable, although in a case of doubt validity was to be preferred.[84]

94   It may be that in some cases onus is unimportant. As the reasonableness of a restraint is a question of law it is irrelevant to consider onus when arguing reasonableness.[85]

95   Further, once all the facts are out, no problem of burden of proof remains.[86] The difficulty most sharply arises when the contract is produced and there is inadequate evidence of background circumstances.

---

[76] See the two questions asked by Lord Reid in *A. Schroeder Music Publishing Co. Ltd. v. Macaulay, sup. cit.* at p. 618; *Esso Petroleum, sup. cit.* at p. 323 *per* Lord Pearce.

[77] *Herbert Morris, sup. cit.* at p. 715 *per* Lord Shaw; *Esso Petroleum, sup. cit.* at pp. 322, 323 *per* Lord Pearce; *Dickson v. Pharmaceutical Society of Great Britain* [1970] A.C. 403.

[78] *Fitch v. Dewes* [1921] 2 A.C. 158 at p. 162 *per* Lord Birkenhead L.C.

[79] *Herbert Morris, sup. cit.* at p. 700 *per* Lord Atkinson; at pp. 707, 708 *per* Lord Parker.

[80] *Esso Petroleum, sup. cit.* at p. 319 *per* Lord Hodson.

[81] *Scottish Farmers' Dairy Co. (Glasgow) Ltd. v. McGhee*, 1933 S.C. 148.

[82] *Anthony v. Rennie*, 1981 S.L.T.(Notes) 11 at p. 12 *per* Lord Grieve (following English authority!).

[83] *MacIntyre v. Cleveland Petroleum Co. Ltd.*, 1967 S.L.T. 95 at p. 99 *per* Lord Hunter.

[84] *Rentokil Ltd. v. Hampton*, 1982 S.L.T. 422 at p. 423 *per* Lord Stewart; *Scottish Farmers Dairy Co. (Glasgow) Ltd. v. McGhee*, 1933 S.C. 148.

[85] *Herbert Morris, sup. cit.* at p. 707 *per* Lord Parker; *Esso Petroleum, sup. cit.* at p. 319 *per* Lord Hodson.

[86] *Herbert Morris, sup. cit.* at p. 699 *per* Lord Atkinson.

Does the law presume freedom of contract, or freedom of trade? Much may depend on the nature of restraints. The greater the restraint in time, or area, or business affected the more it must be justified.[87] The presence of a series of restraints may increase the burden of justification.[88] The general trend of decisions is to require some evidence of justification from the person relying on the restraint.

(5) The time for ascertaining the reasonableness of a restrictive covenant is the time of the making of the contract.

25–96 "A covenant of this kind is invalid *ab initio* or valid *ab initio*. There cannot come a moment at which it passes from the class of invalid into that of valid covenants."[89]

25–97 The validity of the contract will not be affected by unforeseen changes in the nature of the business subsequent to the contract.[90] It is an argument against the validity of a long period of restraint that developments are not foreseeable for that period.[91] Because validity is judged by circumstances at the time of the contract it may be irrelevant to consider why a party wishes to be free from the restraint.[92]

25–98 The construction of the contract may require the court to look at circumstances at a later time. For example, the meaning of "competitor" might be determined at the time employment under the contract ceased.[93]

(6) The court will not invalidate a clause because it could apply to improbable circumstances. Covenants are limited to the circumstances which the court considers the parties had in their contemplation.

25–99 In *Home Counties Dairies Ltd.* v. *Skilton*[94] a restraint on a milk roundsman was held to apply only to the employer's trade as a dairyman. The words used were capable of preventing the employee selling dairy produce such as butter and cheese and thus restraining him from being a grocer. But this was not the correct construction of the agreement. By limiting the terms of the agreement to the circumstances of the parties the court avoided holding that the agreement was so wide as to

---

[87] *Herbert Morris, sup. cit.* at p. 715 *per* Lord Shaw; *Commercial Plastics Ltd.* v. *Vincent* [1965] 1 Q.B. 643.

[88] *Stenhouse Australia Ltd.* v. *Phillips* [1974] A.C. 391 at p. 403. The cumulative effect of restraints must be considered—see *A. Schroeder Music Publishing Co. Ltd.* v. *Macaulay* [1974] 3 All E.R. 616 at p. 618 *per* Lord Reid. The more one-sided a contract is the greater the need to justify restraints.

[89] *Gledhow Autoparts Ltd.* v. *Delaney* [1965] 3 All E.R. 288 at p. 295 *per* Diplock L.J.

[90] *Commercial Plastics Ltd.* v. *Vincent, sup. cit.* at p. 644; *Contra Shell U.K. Ltd.* v. *Lostock Garages Ltd.* [1977] 1 All E.R. 481 at p. 489 *per* Lord Denning M.R.

[91] *Esso Petroleum, sup. cit.* at p. 303 *per* Lord Reid.

[92] *A. Schroeder Music Publishing Co. Ltd.* v. *Macaulay, sup. cit.* 616 at p. 618 *per* Lord Reid.

[93] *Commercial Plastics Ltd.* v. *Vincent, sup. cit.*

[94] [1970] 1 All E.R. 1227.

be unreasonable. A covenant which did not expressly state the kinds of goods to which it applied, was construed as limited to those in which the employer dealt.[95] A covenant which literally could apply to the whole world was construed as limited to business in the United Kingdom.[96] A covenant by a ladies' hairdresser which might have been construed as preventing any type of employment in a hairdresser's shop was limited to active participation in a hairdressing business.[97] In *Commercial Plastics Ltd.* v. *Vincent*[98] a restriction on entering employment in part of the plastics industry did not have a geographical limit. This was interpreted as a world-wide restriction and, therefore, unreasonable. The result has been criticised because it failed to take account of the rule of construction which can imply words of limitation.[99]

00   In a case where the meaning is doubtful, a construction which will render the restriction valid is to be preferred to one which would render it invalid.[1] The court should not, however, reword an express limitation so that it becomes narrower and more reasonable.[2] That would be a reconstruction, not a construction, of the contract.

(7) A valid restraint may in certain circumstances be severed from an invalid restraint.

01   Where parts of a covenant amount to separate and independent covenants, they may be severed from one another and from the rest of the contract. In *Mulvein* v. *Murray*[3] a prohibition of canvassing was valid, but a restraint in travelling within an area was unreasonable and invalid. A restraint on dealing has been held unenforceable but a restraint on soliciting in the same clause survived.[4] The questions have been said to be (1) whether as a matter of construction the parties intended separate obligations and (2) whether it is possible to excise the unenforceable restraint.[5] Various tests have been formulated to decide when it is possible to remove part of the contract[6] but it is doubtful if any single formulation is possible. The whole intent and effect of the contract must be

---

[95] *G. W. Plowman & Son Ltd.* v. *Ash* [1964] 2 All E.R. 10; *cf. Mulvein* v. *Murray*, 1908 S.C. 528.

[96] *Littlewoods Organisation Ltd.* v. *Harris* [1978] 1 All E.R. 1026.

[97] *Marion White Ltd.* v. *Francis* [1972] 3 All E.R. 857. See also a construction limited to the business sold, and not any business—*Kennedy* v. *Clark* (1917) 33 Sh.Ct.Rep. 136.

[98] [1965] 1 Q.B. 623.

[99] *Littlewoods Organisation Ltd.* v. *Harris, sup. cit.* It is an open question whether a Scottish court would follow this approach or the stricter approach of the majority of the court in *Mulvein* v. *Murray, sup. cit.*

[1] *Scottish Farmers Dairy Co. (Glasgow) Ltd.* v. *McGhee*, 1933 S.C. 148. Ambiguity should not be confused with a case in which construction is difficult. Obscurity of meaning should not automatically be treated as ambiguity which then leads to validity.

[2] *Dumbarton Steamboat Co. Ltd.* v. *Macfarlane* (1899) 1 F. 993.

[3] 1908 S.C. 528; cited with approval in *Agma Chemical Co. Ltd.* v. *Hart*, 1984 S.L.T. 246.

[4] *T. Lucas & Co. Ltd.* v. *Mitchell* [1974] Ch. 129.

[5] *Ibid.*

[6] See the list in *Amoco Australia Pty. Ltd.* v. *Rocca* [1975] A.C. 561 at p. 578.

considered[7] and also whether the contract (not merely the other restraints) can remain effective although one part of the contract is unenforceable.[8]

25–102 Parties can show their intention by expressly providing that each of a series of restraints is separable. All the restraints, along with the rest of the contract, will be considered together in determining whether a restraint is reasonable, but it may remain possible to separate one restraint from another.[9] To this limited extent there is value in an express provision about separability. Conversely all the restraints may be so closely connected that they stand or fall together.[10]

(8) A restraint may apply to parties associated with the contracting parties.

25–103 The person in whose favour the restraint exists may wish to protect other associated parties such as subsidiary companies. If the agreement is with one company in a group the restraint should not be extended to cover the whole of the group unless it is the operations of the group which require protection.[11] The person against whom the restraint is to be enforced is commonly prevented from setting up in competition "directly or indirectly." Such an extension is usually reasonable.[12] Forming a company for the purposes of competition may be treated by a court as a mere device or strategem which will not succeed.[13] In *Taylor v. Campbell*[14] the clause prevented a dentist from carrying on business with others but, presumably by mistake, did not prevent him practising on his own account.

(9) In cases where an interim interdict is sought the pursuer must show a prima facie case and the balance of convenience must justify the interim order.

25–104 A person founding on a restraint of trade must show the existence of a contract and the terms of the contract. If a written contract cannot be produced and its terms are denied it will be very difficult to obtain an

---

[7] *Amoco Australia Pty. Ltd.* v. *Rocca, sup. cit.*

[8] *Stenhouse Australia Ltd.* v. *Phillips* [1974] A.C. 391.

[9] *Stenhouse Australia Ltd.* v. *Phillips, sup. cit.* See also *A. Schroeder Music Publishing Co. Ltd.* v. *Macaulay* [1974] 3 All E.R. 616 at p. 618 *per* Lord Reid.

[10] *Esso Petroleum, sup. cit.*

[11] *Henry Leetham & Sons Ltd.* v. *Johnstone-White* [1907] 1 Ch. 322; *Stenhouse Australia Ltd.* v. *Phillips, sup. cit.* See also *Group 4 Total Security Ltd.* v. *Ferrier*, 1985 S.L.T. 287; conversely when a person is restrained from working for a named competitor and its subsidiaries: *Littlewoods Organisation Ltd.* v. *Harris, sup. cit.* at p. 1036 *per* Lord Denning M.R.

[12] *Whitehill* v. *Bradford* [1952] Ch. 236; *A. & D. Bedrooms Ltd.* v. *Michael*, 1984 S.L.T. 297 at p. 299 *per* Lord Cowie.

[13] *Gilford Motor Co.* v. *Horne* [1933] Ch. 935; *cf. Bristol Clothing and Supply (Glasgow) Ltd.* v. *Dickie* (1933) 49 Sh.Ct.Rep. 70 in which *on the averments* a restraint of trade could not be enforced against the wife of a former employee because there was no contract with the wife.

[14] 1926 S.L.T. 260.

interim order.[15] The pleadings will be at the stage of adjustment and it may not be possible to come to a final decision on the merits, but a *prima facie* case should be made out.[16] Once it is decided that there is such a case the question of balance of convenience then arises.[17]

05   In a question of balance of convenience the court will favour the established business as against the interloper.[18] The risk of damage to the petitioner's business will be weighed against the possible loss to the respondent.[19] The grant of interim interdict has been favoured by the potential difficulty in ultimate quantification of loss if interim interdict were not granted.[20]

06   It is one of the peculiar features of restraint of trade cases that the period of restraint may expire before the court is able to consider a permanent interdict. There may, nevertheless, be a value in seeking a declarator or damages, particularly if a standard form contract is in issue.[21] The fact that a period of restraint had a short time to run has been a ground for recall of an interim interdict.[22]

THE INVALIDITY PRODUCED BY A RESTRAINT OF TRADE

07   The nature of the invalidity in the case of a contractual provision in restraint of trade is unsettled. In *Nordenfelt*, Lord Chancellor Herschell and Lords Macnaghten and Morris referred to such a provision as "void."[23] Lord Watson spoke in terms of enforceability.[24] Lord Ashbourne used both concepts.[25] In a later House of Lords decision, Lord Moulton, in a single paragraph refers to contracts in restraint of trade as "void and unenforceable" and "void and voidable" and to their "illegality."[26] The only phrases omitted from this catalogue are *pactum illicitum* and contrary to public policy. These can be supplied by reference to a Scottish case.[27]

08   There is judicial criticism of the use of the word "void" in this context.[28] It involves "a misuse of language" as a provision in restraint of

---

[15] *Chill Foods (Scotland) Ltd.* v. *Cool Foods Ltd.*, 1977 S.L.T. 38.

[16] *Agma Chemical Co. Ltd.* v. *Hart*, 1984 S.L.T. 246. Conversely if the defender shows a *prima facie* case interim interdict will be refused. *Group 4 Total Security Ltd.* v. *Ferrier, sup. cit.*

[17] *A. & D. Bedrooms Ltd.* v. *Michael*, 1984 S.L.T. 297 and other cases cited below.

[18] *Chill Foods (Scotland) Ltd.* v. *Cool Foods Ltd., sup. cit.*; *Anthony* v. *Rennie*, 1981 S.L.T.(Notes 11; *A. & D. Bedrooms Ltd.* v. *Michael, sup. cit.*

[19] *Bluebell Apparel Ltd.* v. *Dickinson*, 1978 S.C. 16.

[20] *Rentokil Ltd.* v. *Kramer*, 1986 S.L.T. 114.

[21] See in England, *Marion White Ltd.* v. *Francis* [1972] 3 All E.R. 857 (form of agreement by the Incorporated Guild of Hairdressers, Wigmakers and Perfumers).

[22] *Group 4 Total Security Ltd.* v. *Ferrier, sup. cit.*

[23] [1894] A.C. 555 at pp. 538, 543, 544, 561–565 and 575.

[24] *Ibid.* at pp. 551, 552.

[25] *Ibid.* at p. 555.

[26] *North Western Salt Co. Ltd.* v. *Electrolytic Alkali Co. Ltd.* [1914] A.C. 461 at p. 474.

[27] *Scottish Farmers' Dairy Co. (Glasgow) Ltd.* v. *McGhee, sup. cit.* at p. 154 *per* Lord President Clyde; at p. 155 *per* Lord Blackburn.

[28] *Joseph Evans & Co.* v. *Heathcote* [1918] 1 K.B. 418 at p. 431 *per* Bankes L.J.; *Thompson* v. *British Medical Association* [1924] A.C. 764 at p. 769 *per* Lord Atkinson.

trade is merely unenforceable.[29] In a recent consideration of this area of law none of the speeches in the House of Lords mention "void" but unenforceability is referred to.[30] In another recent case the Privy Council refer to unenforceability although in the courts below "void" is mentioned.[31] Shortly before, however, the House of Lords had affirmed a declaration that an agreement in restraint of trade "was contrary to public policy and void."[32] One writer has argued that the effect of this decision is that the contract was unenforceable.[33] The point might be important because copyright had been assigned under the agreement. If the restrictive covenant in the agreement was contrary to public policy who owned the copyright? If the agreement is void, property should not have passed. If the agreement is unenforceable property has passed. Sometimes it will be possible to sever the restraint of trade clause from the rest of the agreement[34] and when this is done the nature of the invalidity will rarely be important because third parties will be unaffected. Severance is not always possible[35] and given the extension of restraint of trade cases beyond employer/employee and seller/purchaser relationships[36] it has become more likely that the question may have to be faced of what rights may pass under a contract which is unreasonably in restraint of trade.

25–109   It would be extravagant to describe a provision in restraint of trade as immoral. It is not criminal[37] nor is it an unlawful means for the purposes of the tort of unlawful interference with the trade of another.[38] It is clearly at least unenforceable. There is no lack of consent, which is the usual ground for holding a contractual provision void. Normally one of the parties to the contract must raise an objection to the provision or it will be enforced[39] although there may be instances of *ex facie* illegality of which the courts must take notice *ex proprio motu*.[40] To hold that the provision is void is more drastic than saying that it is unenforceable. Void means null *ab initio* and therefore there may need to be repetition of all monies paid since the date of the contract. Given the trend of

---

[29] Lord Atkinson, *sup. cit.*

[30] *Esso Petroleum, sup. cit.* at pp. 295, 296 *per* Lord Reid; at p. 305 *per* Lord Morris; at p. 318 *per* Lord Hudson.

[31] *Amoco Australia Pty. Ltd.* v. *Rocco Bros. Motor Engineering Co. Pty. Ltd.* [1975] A.C. 561.

[32] *Macaulay* v. *Schroeder Publishing Co. Ltd.* [1974] 1 W.L.R. 1308; in [1974] 3 All E.R. 616 the word "void" only is used; *cf.* [1974] 1 All E.R. 171.

[33] F. Dawson, "Contracts in Restraint of Trade: Meaning and Effect" 1974 L.Q.R. 455. The appeal of the case to the House of Lords does not affect the writer's reasoning.

[34] Chitty, paras. 1186, 1190.

[35] *e.g. Amoco Australia Pty. Ltd.*, *sup. cit.*

[36] *Vide Esso Petroleum Co. Ltd.*, *sup. cit.* at p. 293 *per* Lord Reid.

[37] *Mogul Steamship Co.* v. *McGregor Gow & Co.* [1892] A.C. 25.

[38] *Brekkes Ltd.* v. *Cattel* [1972] Ch. 105.

[39] *Esso Petroleum Co. Ltd.*, *sup. cit.* at p. 297 *per* Lord Reid; he gives an example at p. 300.

[40] *North Western Salt Co. Ltd.* v. *Electrolytic Alkali Co. Ltd.* [1914] A.C. 461.

recent decisions the probability is that provisions in unreasonable restraint of trade are unenforceable at the option of the parties.[41]

STATUTORY AND REGULATORY PROVISIONS AFFECTING RESTRAINTS ON TRADE

0 It is not appropriate in a work concerned with the general principles of contract law to explore the very complicated statutory and regulatory provisions which affect certain restrictive agreements. The details may be found in specialist works.[42] It must also be taken into account that this area of contract law above all others changes rapidly. What follows is a check list of the main issues giving rise to problems. The draftsman may be helped by the valuable material in Butterworth's *Encyclopaedia of Forms and Precedents*.[43]

Restrictive Trade Practices Act 1976

1   This Act, as amended,[44] subjects certain agreements to registration and judicial scrutiny. The Act applies to any agreement or arrangement (1) which is between two or more parties carrying on business within the United Kingdom in the production or supply of goods or in the application to goods of any process of manufacture, and (2) under which certain restrictions are accepted by two or more parties. The restrictions are detailed in section 6(1)(*a*) to (*f*) and are as follows:

> "(*a*) the prices to be charged, quoted or paid for goods supplied, offered or acquired, or for the application of any process of manufacture to goods;
>
> (*b*) the prices to be recommended or suggested as the prices to be charged or quoted in respect of the resale of goods supplied;
>
> (*c*) the terms or conditions on or subject to which goods are to be supplied or acquired or any such process is to be applied to goods;
>
> (*d*) the quantities or descriptions of goods to be produced, supplied or acquired;
>
> (*e*) the processes of manufacture to be applied to any goods, or the quantities or descriptions of goods to which any such process is to be applied; or
>
> (*f*) the persons or classes of persons to, for or from whom, or the areas or places in or from which, goods are to be supplied or acquired, or any such process applied."

---

[41] See *Shell U.K. Ltd.* v. *Lostock Garages Ltd.* [1977] 1 All E.R. 481 at p. 489 *per* Lord Denning M.R. Despite Lord Denning, "invalid" does not always mean "void." An unenforceable contract is invalid and normally will have been invalid *ab initio*.

[42] James P. Cunningham, *The Fair Trading Act 1973* (1974); Valentine Korah, *Competition Law in Britain and the Common Market* (3rd ed., 1982; 4th ed. expected 1986); V. Korah, *EEC Competition Law and Practice* (3rd ed., 1986); C.S. Kerse, *EEC Antitrust Procedure* (1981; 2nd ed. expected 1986).

[43] See, *e.g.* Vol. 22, pp. 477 *et seq*. Without this type of assistance no one should attempt to draft clauses which may be affected by the provisions discussed here.

[44] In particular by the Restrictive Trade Practices Act 1977 and the Competition Act 1980.

25–112   These restrictions would result in the application of the Act applying to many commercial agreements if it were not that certain terms and restrictions and certain agreements are exempted from the Act. One of the most important exceptions arises from the operation of subsections 9(3) and (4). Very broadly (the meaning of the section is in places obscure) in an agreement between two parties, no account is taken of terms relating exclusively to goods supplied in pursuance of the agreement. This provision (and also in some cases Schedule 3, paragraph 2) enable many common terms in bipartite distribution agreements to escape the controls imposed by the Act. The Act does not apply unless two or more parties accept restrictions and thus usually the normal restrictive covenant in employer and employee or buyer and seller agreements is not affected because only one party is restrained.[45]

25–113   Information agreements are subject to the Restrictive Trade Practices (Information Agreements) Order 1969 and services to the Restrictive Trade Practices (Services) Order 1976 (as amended). In distribution agreements and joint venture agreements it is common to have provisions for the exchange of know-how. If carefully drafted these provisions will be exempted from the Act.[46]

Resale price maintenance

25–114   Section 9(1) of the Resale Prices Act 1976 provides that any term or condition of a contract for the sale of non-exempt goods[47] by a supplier to a dealer or of any agreement between a supplier and a dealer relating to such a sale shall be void in so far as it purports to establish or provide for the establishment of minimum prices to be charged on the resale of the goods in the United Kingdom. The Act does not apply (1) if either party does not carry on a business of selling goods; (2) if the contract involved is not a sale (*e.g.* if an agent is selling his principal's goods, the agent may be required to sell at a minimum price if ownership does not pass to him. There is no "sale" from principal to agent); (3) if there is no control of a resale (*e.g.* a minimum charge for hire may be imposed); (4) if the supplier imposes a maximum price on the dealer.

Patented articles and patent licences

25–115   Section 44 of the Patents Act 1977 controls the terms which the owner of a patent may impose on purchasers of potential articles or licences of the patent. In the case of the supply of a patented product the supplier cannot (a) require the person supplied to acquire anything other than the patented product or (b) prohibit the person supplied from acquiring from other persons or using other products. A similar control applies to the terms which a licensor may impose on a licensee. It is common in

---

[45] See ss.9, 28, 29–34 and Sched. 3.
[46] See Sched. 3, paras. 3 and 8.
[47] The only exempt goods are books and medicaments.

many legal systems to have similar provisions which prevent the "tying" of the right to the patented product to the use or non-use of other products.[48]

16 There are exemptions applying to sole agents and in cases of licence and hire the supply of spare parts.[49]

Monopolies, services and mergers

17 Certain agreements are subject to scrutiny by the Monopolies and Mergers Commission on references made under the Fair Trading Act 1973. This arises where it appears that a monopoly situation exists or may exist in relation to the supply of goods of any description in the United Kingdom, the supply of services of certain descriptions in the United Kingdom, and the export of goods of any description from the United Kingdom either generally or to any particular market.

Anti-competitive practices

18 The Competition Act 1980 was innovative in the United Kingdom to the extent that, following the example of the EEC, legislation sought to control contracts whose effect was anti-competitive.[50] Anti-competitive practices are subject to scrutiny and control by the Director General of Fair Trading and the Monopolies and Mergers Commission. Under the Act, "a person engages in an anti-competitive practice if, in the course of business, that person pursues a course of conduct which, of itself or when taken together with a course of conduct pursued by persons associated with him has or is intended to have or is likely to have the effect of restricting, distorting or preventing competition in connection with the production, supply or acquisition of goods in the United Kingdom or any part of it or the supply or securing of services in the United Kingdom or any part of it."[51]

Competition within the EEC

19 Agreements which prevent, restrict or distort competition within the common market and may affect trade between Member States may fall within Article 85(1) of the EEC Treaty. The contractual practices of undertakings holding a dominant position may be affected by Article 86.[52]

20 In Scottish practice the usual problems posed have been the effect of Article 85 on distribution and similar agreements.

---

[48] See B. Fowlston, *Understanding Commercial and Industrial Licensing* (1984) *passim*.
[49] s.44(6).
[50] Although a reference to distorting competition exists in ss.6(2), 7(2), 8(2) and (3) of the Fair Trading Act 1973.
[51] s.2.
[52] *Garden Cottage Foods Ltd.* v. *Milk Marketing Board* [1984] A.C. 130 (action for injunction and damages for breach of Art. 86).

25–121   The other types of agreement which commonly involve consideration of Article 85 are joint venture agreements and joint research and development agreements.

25–122   With Regulations 1983/83 and 1984/83 the European Commission has provided block exemptions for certain exclusive distribution agreements and exclusive purchasing agreements.[53] In an exclusive distribution agreement one party, the supplier, allots to the other, the reseller, a defined territory within which the reseller has to concentrate his sales effort. In return the seller undertakes not to supply any other reseller in that territory. In an exclusive purchasing agreement the reseller agrees to purchase the contract goods only from the other party and not from any other supplier. The supplier is entitled to supply other resellers in the same area and at the same level of distribution. The reseller is not protected against competition but neither is he restricted in the area in which he may sell.

25–123   Regulation 1983/83 grants exemption from Article 85(1) to certain exclusive distribution agreements, "to which only two undertakings are party and whereby one party agrees with the other to supply certain goods for resale within the whole or a defined area of the Common Market to that other."[54] The Regulation controls the restrictions which may be imposed on the parties. Regulation 1984/83 grants similar exemptions to exclusive purchasing agreements and makes special provisions for beer supply agreements[55] and service station agreements.[56] There are also recently introduced group exemptions for patent licensing,[56a] motor vehicle distribution and servicing agreements,[56b] specialisation agreements,[56c] and research and development agreements.[56d]

Contracts Contrary to Public Policy—General Principles

25–124   The effect of a contract being contrary to public policy will usually vary with the type of contract. For example, it would be odd if the law treated in an identical manner a contract in restraint of trade and a contract for the hire of the services of a prostitute. Yet some principles may apply throughout such contracts. These are expressed in various ways: *ex turpi causa non oritur actio; in turpi causa melior est conditio possidentis; in pari delicto potior est conditio defendentis; nemo auditor pro-*

---

[53] See V. Korah, *Exclusive Dealing Agreements in the EEC; Regulation 67/67 Replaced* (1984).

[54] Art. 1.

[55] tit. II.

[56] tit. III.

[56a] Reg. 2349/84; V. Korah, *Patent Licensing and EEC Competition Rules—Regulation 2349/84*, (1985).

[56b] Reg. 123/85.

[56c] Reg. 417/85.

[56d] Reg. 418/85; V. Korah, *Research and Development—Joint Ventures and EEC Competition Rules Regulation 418/85* (1986).

priam turpitudinem allegans. These include the allied concepts of refusal to enforce a tainted contract and refusal to allow restitution.

25 Dr Sabbath has compared many systems, although not Scots law.[57] He states:

> "Most legal systems provide that, if a contract is void, the parties must be restored to the situation in which they were before it was concluded. Hence, one who has, fully or in part, performed his duty under the agreement may demand return of his performance. When, however, the contract is contrary to a rule of law, to morals or public order, and the plaintiff is *in pari delicto*, this general principle does not apply and recovery is not granted, because it is generally held that no action lies when the plaintiff must rely on his illegal act: *in pari delicto potior est conditio defendentis*. This maxim, which was already well established in Roman law and well known during the Middle Ages and subsequent centuries is still followed by most countries. It is, however, also everywhere one of the most controversial legal principles."[58]

26 The principles of non-recovery and of refusal to enforce tainted transactions have been accepted in Scots law, an example being the vitiation of a promissory note because its consideration was an orgy with a prostitute.[59] One difficulty is determining what types of unlawful transaction are affected. Many systems apply the concept of non-recovery generally whereas others distinguish immoral and illegal acts and limit the concept to the former.[60]

27 Stair stated: "But in things received *ex turpi causa*, if both parties be *in culpa*, *potior est conditio possidentis*: so there is no restitution."[61] This might suggest that the maxim was restricted to cases of immorality because of the term *turpis*. This, however, is not certain as the Roman texts refer to *turpis causa* although the Romans may not have distinguished between types of unlawful transaction.[62]

28 Erskine recognised that, "what is given *ob turpem causam* must be restored if the turpitude was in the receiver, and not in the giver, whether the cause of giving was performed or not."[63] This suggested that recovery was only barred to the wrongdoer. Lord Ivory noted: "Where both parties are involved in the turpitude, *e.g.* in the case of obligations granted as the price of prostitution—though action will not lie to enforce implement, yet, on the other hand, where performance of the obligation has already been made, neither will action lie for restitution."[64]

---

[57] E. Sabbath, "Denial of Restitution in Unlawful Transactions—A Study in Comparative Law" (1959) 8 I.C.L.Q. 486, 689.

[58] Sabbath, *op. cit.*, p. 486.

[59] *Hamilton* v. *Main* (1823) 2 S. 356.

[60] Sabbath, *op. cit.*, pp. 493–505.

[61] Stair, I, vii, 8.

[62] Sabbath, *op. cit.*, p. 494.

[63] Ersk., *Inst.*, III, i, 10.

[64] *Ibid.*, note 3, quoting *A.* v. *B.*, May 21, 1816, F.C.; 6 Pat. 644; 2 Bligh 196.

25–129   The principles of non-recovery and non-enforcement have been applied widely and are not limited to those actings which would normally be described as immoral. It has, for example, been referred to or applied in smuggling,[65] a partnership of pawnbrokers carrying on business without names above the door as required by statute,[66] to a *pactum de quota litis*[67] and an agreement on sharing fees between a bank agent and a solicitor.[68] It has also been applied in more obviously immoral transactions such as a partnership of slave traders,[69] a contract involving an attempt to defraud[70] and a contract for payment of money in consideration of not informing the public authorities of a crime.[71] It would seem, therefore, that Scots law denies action to wrongdoers over a wide sphere of contracts.

25–130   We cannot, however, say that Scots law is similar to other systems, such as German, Swiss, South African and Anglo-American law, in refusing restitution in all kinds of unlawful acts, without distinguishing between types of transaction. This is so because of *Cuthbertson* v. *Lowes*.[72] The case turned on the distinction between refusal to enforce a contract and refusal to allow restitution. The former is a remedy sought under the contract, and the latter is quasi-contractual. The contract in *Cuthbertson* was expressly void by statute. The issue was whether the purchaser of potatoes under the contract need pay for the potatoes. Lord President Inglis founded on the absence of turpitude:

> "No doubt the Court cannot enforce performance of an illegal contract, and *in turpi causa melior est conditio possidentis*, but there is no turpitude in a man selling his potatoes by the Scotch and not by the imperial acre; and although he cannot sue for implement of such a contract, I know of no authority, in the absence of *turpis causa*, to prevent the pursuer from recovering the market value of the potatoes, at the date when they were delivered to the defender. That is not suing upon the contract."[73]

The difficulty is that neither was there any authority in favour of the Lord President's approach. In a system in which *turpis causa* is restricted to immoral acts, *Cuthbertson* would fit well. In a system which does not distinguish unlawful acts it is difficult to apply. Gloag accommodated *Cuthbertson* by saying that: "Where a contract involves an element of illegality, as distinguished from the case where it is merely declared void

---

[65] *Cullen* v. *Philp* (1793) Mor. 9554.

[66] *Fraser* v. *Hill* (1852) 14 D. 335. See also the failure to state a printer's name on a book: *Gresham Publishing Co. Ltd.* v. *Boyd* (1928) 44 Sh.Ct.Rep. 187; *Holmes* v. *Hogarth* (1930) 46 Sh.Ct.Rep. 82. On an agreement to facilitate an "illegal" business see *Hamawi* v. *Key* (1931) 48 Sh.Ct.Rep. 246. On a loan to enable a borrower to carry on street trading: *Chisholm* v. *McDowall*, 1925 S.L.T. (Sh.Ct.) 127.

[67] *Bolden* v. *Fogo* (1850) 12 D. 798.

[68] *A.B.* v. *C.D.*, 1912 1 S.L.T. 44. Under the Solicitors (Scotland) Act 1980, s.27 it is an offence for solicitors to share fees with unqualified persons.

[69] *Stewart* v. *Gibson* (1840) 1 Rob.App. 260.

[70] *Henderson* v. *Caldwell* (1890) 28 S.L.R. 16.

[71] *T. Smith & Sons* v. *Buchanan*, 1910 2 S.L.T. 387.

[72] (1870) 8 M. 1073.

[73] *Sup. cit.* at p. 1075.

by statute, the effect is to debar the parties concerned from the right to appeal to Courts of Justice."[74] *Cuthbertson* was distinguished in *Jamieson* v. *Watt's Tr.*[75] in terms indicating that *Cuthbertson* was a very special case on its facts. In *Jamieson* the failure to obtain a licence to carry out some repairs to a house, contrary to defence regulations, prevented recompense for the cost of the work. The result is that it is difficult to state what is meant by *turpis causa* in Scots law. It appears that the general principle *in pari delicto potior est conditio defendentis* applies to all contracts contrary to public policy, except in the *Cuthbertson* v. *Lowes* situation. Even in that situation the contract will not be enforced. It is to be hoped that, on an appropriate occasion, the House of Lords will clarify matters.

31 In common with Anglo-American systems, Scots law allows exceptions to the general rules prohibiting enforcement of or restitution in consequence of an unlawful contract. The main exceptions are where the parties are not *in pari delicto*[76] and where a statute has been passed to protect a particular class.[77] There may be other exceptions.[78]

32 The English courts have been troubled by the problem of whether property may pass under an "illegal" contract. If one assumes that a contract contrary to public policy is void, then property cannot pass under the contract. This is the stance of Cheshire and Fifoot,[79] who doubt the correctness of two decisions[80] which state the contrary. Anson on the other hand states "It is settled law that the ownership of property can pass under an illegal contract if the parties so intend, as in the case of goods sold to a buyer under an illegal contract of sale."[81]

33 There is no Scots authority.[82] The initial difficulty is determining the nature of the contractual invalidity. In the case of statutory invalidity, which is discussed below, the invalidity will vary according to the stat-

---

[74] Gloag, p. 585.

[75] 1950 S.C. 265. *Cuthbertson* was applied or referred to in *Cruickshank* v. *Aberdeen Lime Co. Ltd.*, 1927 S.L.T. (Sh.Ct.) 39; *Cameron & Sons* v. *Maclean*, 1934 S.L.T. (Sh.Ct.) 26; *Ewing* v. *Glasgow*, 1952 S.L.T. (Sh.Ct.) 104. *Jamieson* has been followed in several sheriff court decisions: *Firth* v. *Anderson*, 1954 S.L.T. (Sh.Ct.) 27; *Dunbar & Cook* v. *Johnson*, 1956 S.L.T. (Sh.Ct.) 26 (where its application was restricted to work done in excess of a licensed figure).

[76] *Arrol* v. *Montgomery* (1826) 4 S. 499; *Macfarlane* v. *Nicoll* (1864) 3 M. 237.

[77] *Phillips* v. *Blackhurst* (1912) 2 S.L.T. 254; *McCarroll* v. *Maguire* (1920) 2 S.L.T. 108.

[78] *Vide* Gloag, pp. 586–589; J. J. Gow, "Ex Turpi Causa Non Oritur Actio" 1958 S.L.T. (News) 74.

[79] *Cheshire and Fifoot*, pp. 331–341. Support for this view is in M. J. Higgins, "The Transfer of Property Under Illegal Transactions" (1962) 25 M.L.R. 149.

[80] *Singh* v. *Ali* [1960] A.C. 167; *Belvoir Finance Co. Ltd.* v. *Stapleton* [1971] 1 Q.B. 210.

[81] Anson, p. 351.

[82] It has been suggested that the concept of *justa causa traditionis* applies (Scot.Law Com.Memo.No. 25, *Corporeal Moveables: Passing of Risk and of Ownership* (1976), para. 14). It is very doubtful if this was the basis of the decisions referred to. Given the different types of nullity arising from express and implied statutory invalidity there are many more problems about applying *justa causa* than is apparent from the Commission's analysis. Even within the context of their treatment there may be differences of approach. Contrast the application of *justa causa* in para. 14 and the provisional view against passing of property in illegal contracts in para. 56.

ute. If the contract is void, it is difficult to see how property can pass under it. Nullity may not only be expressed by the statute but also implied from it[83] and implied nullity should be capable of varying in effect as express nullity does.

25–134   Where the contract is contrary to public policy at common law the invalidity should alter with the nature of the contract. Contracts in restraint of trade are unenforceable at the option of one party; contracts for gaming or smuggling are simply unenforceable. Some bankruptcy agreements are void and others voidable. *Pacta de quota litis* are unenforceable.[84] The position of other contracts is unsettled.[85]

STATUTORY INVALIDITY

25–135   Express statutory nullity has existed for a long time and, of course, has been framed in differing ways with differing results. Early examples, although they do not relate to the types of invalidity we have been discussing, describe obligations as "of nain avail"[86] and deeds to "mak na fayth."[87] In 1681 we have the expression "the Contract to be void and null."[88] The expression "voyd and null" used in 1696 has subsequently been interpreted as meaning voidable.[89]

After the Union some statutes adopted lengthy phrases to declare a contractual provision void: "shall be null and void to all intents and purposes whatsoever"[90]; "shall be and is hereby declared illegal, null and void."[91] Changing fashions perhaps can be illustrated by the provision which in 1745 was: "shall be null and void to all intents and purposes."[92] On re-enactment in 1906 this became "is void."[93]

25–136   The phrases "shall be void" or "is void" appear to be the most common statutory expressions of nullity in current use. Where the whole of the contract is not void, but only a provision of a contract and then only if that contravenes certain rules, the phrase is a variation of: "An agreement is void, if and to the extent that . . . " Examples are so numerous that it is pointless to list them.[94]

---

[83] *e.g. Trevalion & Co.* v. *Blanche & Co.*, 1919 S.C. 617. It is inconceivable that property could have passed in the permit in question.

[84] *Johnston* v. *Rome* (1831) 9 S. 364. Note the interlocutor reserved to the agent all claim for suitable remuneration for trouble.

[85] *e.g. Home* v. *Home* (1713) Mor. 9502.

[86] Prescription Acts 1469 and 1474.

[87] Subscription of Deeds Act 1579; *cf.* Subscription of Deeds Act 1540.

[88] Oaths of Minors Act 1681; "void" and "null" are used in the Interlocutors Acts 1686 and 1693; the Citation Act 1686.

[89] Bankruptcy Act 1696; *Drummond* v. *Watson* (1850) 12 D. 604; H. Goudy, *Law of Bankruptcy in Scotland* (4th ed., 1914), p. 101.

[90] Life Assurance Act 1774.

[91] Truck Act 1831, s.2.

[92] Marine Insurance Act 1774, s.1.

[93] Marine Insurance Act 1906, s.4(1).

[94] The computer retrieval system Lexis shows three or four types of contracts being rendered "void" by legislation in each year in the recent past. Usually the legislation concerns employment, trade unions, consumer transactions, social security, or company law.

37 There are variations. One Scottish statute used "null" instead of "void,"[95] and another statute "null and void."[96] Some use the phrase "void and unenforceable"[97] and there are examples of "shall be of no effect,"[98] and of "shall be invalid."[99] An instance of a reverse phrasing is: "the provisions of this Act shall have effect notwithstanding any contract to the contrary."[1] There can be more oblique ways of invalidating an obligation as in the case of insurance on the lives of foster children in which there is deemed to be a lack of insurable interest.[2]

38 Examples of a contract being declared voidable are the irregular allotment of shares[3] and the Auctions (Bidding Agreements) Act 1969 which in certain circumstances allows the seller to avoid the contract.[4] A contractual provision may be rendered unenforceable, but not void, either by express use of "unenforceable" or "not enforceable"[5] or by equivalents such as "shall not bind"[6] or "shall not be liable to make any payment."[7] The fee of a person who acts as a solicitor or notary public without being duly qualified to do so is not "recoverable."[8]

39 In this varied usage it would be unwise to suggest that there are any general rules of interpretation. Words should be construed in the context in which they appear. There is no guarantee that "void" always has the same meaning.

STATUTORY NULLITY IMPLIED

40 A statute may be silent on its effect on civil rights. Silence may not mean that there is no effect. There is an instance in 1743 of a contract being invalid as a result of implication from penal statutes.[9] The problem is illustrated by the Scottish courts' consideration of smuggling contracts.[10]

---

[95] Prescription and Limitation (Scotland) Act 1973, s.13.

[96] Agricultural Holdings (Scotland) Act 1949, s.11(1); and see also Merchant Shipping Act 1979, Sched. 3, Pt. 1, art. 18.

[97] Agricultural Marketing Act 1958, s.17(3); Conveyancing and Feudal Reform (Scotland) Act 1970, s.11(4)(*b*); *cf.* s.7.

[98] Road Traffic Act 1972, s.148(3), being similar to the "shall have no effect" in the Mercantile Law Amendment (Scotland) Act 1856, s.6, the meaning of which is uncertain. W. M. Gloag and J. M. Irvine, *Law of Rights in Security* (1897), pp. 684, 685; Unfair Contract Terms Act 1977, ss.16, 17, 18, 20, 21.

[99] Films Act 1960, s.35 (repeating provisions of Cinematograph Films Act 1938, s.20).

[1] War Damage to Land (Scotland) Act 1939, s.8.

[2] Foster Children (Scotland) Act 1984, s.18.

[3] Companies Act 1948, s.49(1). Companies Act 1985, s.85.

[4] s.3(1).

[5] As in the now repealed Registration of Business Names Act 1916, s.8(1); Supply of Goods (Implied Terms) Act 1973 ss.4(4) and 13(3); Law Reform (Husband and Wife) (Scotland) Act 1984, s.1.

[6] Merchant Shipping Act 1970, s.11(1)(*b*) (only one contracting party not bound); *cf.* s.16(1).

[7] Unsolicited Goods and Services Act 1971, s.3(1)

[8] Solicitors (Scotland) Act 1980, s.33.

[9] *Fullarton* v. *Scot* (1743) Mor. 9586.

[10] See para. 25-47.

There is obviously something awkward in ordaining specific implement of a contract the performance of which is in breach of revenue laws. Kames saw the difficulty and distinguished between statutes respecting evil of a general bad tendency and those with respect to evils less pernicious. For the former the courts use every means for effecting the will of the legislature, including voiding bargains although the statute only provides a penalty.[11] For the latter, the penalty imposed by the statute is imposed but the bargain is not reduced; an example is the interpretation of the Land Purchase Act 1594. Kames considered that the court had overlooked the distinction between reducing a bargain and refusing to enforce it. Enforcing a bargain contrary to the 1594 Act is to make the effect of the statute like laying a tax on the bargain and "is a gross misapprehension of the spirit and intendment of the statute."[12]

25–141   Kames' distinction between two types of statute is so vague as to be almost unworkable. There is more merit in the idea that the contract should be unenforceable and, in the absence of authority, the simplest result would be that the court should not aid what has been penalised by statute.

25–142   There has been little analysis in Scotland of when a contract may be impliedly affected by statute.[13] Stair showed that nullity may not be implied by reference to cases on long leases by prelates and contracts for buying pleas.[14] Bell stated that a penalty imposed by statute implied prohibition.[15] Erskine thought that, "in general a statute where it prohibits not only the act but the obligations resulting from or the effect consequent on it must be construed to annul: Or where the law enacts that it shall not be in one's power to do a thing, the act, if done, must necessarily be void; because the very right which the person had to do it, is taken from him."[16] Today it is probable that attention would be paid to a long line of English authority.

25–143   The question asked in England in varying formulations is: "whether the statute means to prohibit the contract"[17]—"does the Legislature mean to prohibit the act done or not?"[18]—"But whether it is the terms of the contract or the performance of it that is called in question the test is just the same; is the contract, as made or as performed, a contract that

---

[11] His example is usury.

[12] Kames, *Principles of Equity*, Vol. 1, pp. 349–358. The penalty under the 1594 Act is, however, not like a tax.

[13] Thus in the leading case, *Jamieson* v. *Watt's Tr.*, 1950 S.C. 265, the effect of criminal provisions on the invalidity of the contract was not discussed as a result of English authority. See the refusal to allow actions for the price of books which breached statutory provisions on the name of the printer—*Gresham Publishing Co. Ltd.* v. *Boyd* (1928) 44 Sh.Ct.Rep. 187; *Holmes* v. *Hogarth* (1930) 46 Sh.Ct.Rep. 82.

[14] Stair, I, xvii, 14.

[15] Bell, Prin., s.36.

[16] Ersk., *Inst.*, I, i, 59. The problem is illustrated by contrasting *Balfour* v. *Sharp* (1833) 11 S. 784 with *Blaikie* v. *Aberdeen Ry. Co.* (1851) 14 D. 66 at p. 71 *per* Lord President Boyle (on appeal, 1 Macq. 461).

[17] *Cope* v. *Rowlands* (1836) 2 M. & W. 149 at p. 157 *per* Parke B.

[18] *Smith* v. *Mawhood* (1845) 14 M. & W. 452 at p. 464 *per* Alderson B.

is prohibited by statute?"[19]—"the true test is whether the statute impliedly forbids the provision in the contract to be sued upon."[20] As an aid to determining what statutes prohibit this seems less than helpful, but no other aid is available.

44   The English courts have not faced the problem of the nature of the resulting invalidity. There is an early reference to the contract being "void"[21] and a later, more cautious, reference to the contract being unenforceable[22] but in neither instance was the nature of the validity of moment. An express invalidity varies in its expression and effect and so it could be argued that by analogy implied invalidity should also vary. The tests to be used to determine differences in the implied intention of the legislature would seem to require a high level of sophistication, if not of sophistry. Yet in *Cuthbertson* v. *Lowes*[23] an express statutory nullity did not involve moral turpitude, whereas an implied nullity did in *Jamieson* v. *Watt's Tr.*[24] If *Cuthbertson* is correctly decided there should be circumstances in which an implied nullity does not involve turpitude. This would be distinct from the *Jamieson* situation and would raise the problem of what effect, if any, that had on the contract.[25] If turpitude or any other test, such as public interest, be of moment, then we are not far removed from Kames with his distinction between statutes of different degrees of perniciousness. The House of Lords have not recently considered the problem of implied illegality but the difficulties which have arisen from their consideration of the parallel problem of implied right to a delictual claim from breach of statute do not suggest that it will be easy to avoid entering a morass inevitably created by the legislature's silence.[26]

SEVERANCE

45   The problems of severance in contracts in restraint of trade have already been considered.[27] Otherwise there are two problems: (1) the extent to which contracts associated with a contract contrary to public policy are tainted; and (2) severance within a contract of the part contrary to pub-

---

[19] *St. John Shipping Corp.* v. *Joseph Rank Ltd.* [1957] 1 Q.B. 267 at p. 284 *per* Devlin J. See generally R. A. Buckley, "Implied Statutory Prohibition of Contracts," 1975 M.L.R. 535.

[20] *Shaw* v. *Groom* [1970] 2 Q.B. 504 at p. 518 *per* Harman L.J.

[21] Parke B., *supra, loc. cit.*

[22] *St. John Shipping Corp.*, *sup. cit.* at p. 283 *per* Devlin J.

[23] (1870) 8 M. 1073.

[24] *Sup. cit.* This was expressly stated by Lord Jamieson and can be implied from Lord Patrick.

[25] As opposed to quasi-contractual remedies.

[26] Occasionally a statute states that it has no effect on contracts: Plant Varieties and Seeds Act 1964, s.17(5); Resale Prices Act 1964, s.1(3); Race Relations Act 1968, s.23(1) (there is provision for revision of the contract); Trade Descriptions Act 1968, s.35; Road Traffic Act 1972, s.60(5) (thereby overruling *Smith* v. *Nugent*, 1955 S.L.T. (Sh.Ct.) 60) and s.66(4).

[27] para. 25–101.

lic policy. In both cases Scots authority is meagre.[28] There may be a difference between contracts associated with an illegal transaction and contracts associated with an unenforceable transaction. The issue is examined in the chapter on "Invalidities of Consent."[29]

---

[28] Gloag, p. 589, cited two Scots cases (*Farmers' Mart Ltd.* v. *Milne* 1914 S.C.(H.L.) 84; *Blair* v. *Allen* (1858) 21 D. 15) and the argument in a third (*Lord Lovat* v. *Fraser* (1745) Mor. 9557).

[29] Chap. 26.

CHAPTER 26

INVALIDITIES IN CONTRACTS

01   There are four main forms of invalid contract, namely (1) a void contract, (2) a voidable contract, (3) an unenforceable contract and (4) an illegal contract.

VOID CONTRACTS

(a) The history

02   The term "void" was unknown in early Scots law. The usual phrase in the late fifteenth century was "nane avale,"[1] or, more fully "nane avale force nor effect in tyme tocu."[2] The earliest use in relation to contract of the term "void" which has been traced is in Spotiswoode's *Practicks* in his discussion of contracts by infants and "furious" persons.[3]

03   Stair made frequent use of "void."

(b) The consequences of a "void" contract

04   The term "void contract" appears to be a contradiction in terms. "Properly speaking, a void contract should produce no legal effects whatsoever."[4] "It may be objected that a void contract is a meaningless expression; but it is a useful one to describe a contract that is perfect in form but void in substance."[5] It is a "seeming contract."[6] "To speak of a 'void contract' is rather like speaking of a dead or unborn 'person'; we may be puzzled, but we are not misled."[7]

---

[1] *Earl of Bothwell* v. *Lady Bolton* (1494) A.D.A. 199.

[2] *Countess of Ross* v. *Dunbar of Cumok* (1488) A.D.A. 122; *Prior and Convent of Inchmaholme* (1491) A.D.C. 1, 201 and see generally in index of A.D.C. 1 and 11, under "Reduction." The Act of Sederunt of November 27, 1592, on irritant clauses refers to contracts being "null." The term "null" is used in many acts of sederunt around this time. The term "void and null" appears in the Act of Sederunt of June 8, 1665, against general letters.

[3] Spotiswoode, p. 72 (1706 ed.). Spotiswoode was executed in 1646. Apparently no manuscript earlier than *c.* 1700 survives. Stair Soc., *Sources*, p. 25. In England the word is of Middle English origin. In the sense of having no legal force its use can be traced to 1433–34 (*O.E.D.*).

[4] Chitty, para. 15.

[5] *Ingram* v. *Little* [1961] 1 Q.B. 31, at pp. 63 and 64 *per* Devlin L.J.

[6] Gloag, p. 531.

[7] S. J. Stoljar, *Mistake and Misrepresentation* (1968), p. 73.

26–05   A void contract is null *ab initio*. From this several consequences flow.

(1) Reduction of the written contract is unnecessary, in theory. "A deed which . . . is void is already a nullity and, in theory, need not be, and indeed cannot be, reduced."[8] If an action is brought on the contract it may be sufficient to prove that the contract is void, without reduction[9] and, in any event, reduction is not an appropriate remedy for oral transactions.[10] In practice it may be unwise to ignore a void contract or a void deed, or a void act. It may be necessary, for example, to reduce a disposition recorded in the General Register of Sasines and so prevent the running of the positive prescription.[11] Rectification of a share register may be necessary although the shareholders had no valid contract to obtain the shares.[12] A share transfer may need to be reduced to restore the transferor's name to the register.[13] Furthermore, the problem of the void contract may have to be raised by other remedies such as declarator or interdict[14] or suspension of summary diligence.[15]

(2) No title may pass under a void contract, with one statutory exception.[16] Reduction of a deed on the grounds of force and fear is effective against *bona fide* third parties.[17] The effect on third parties is so drastic that Gloag hesitated over whether they would be unable to acquire a valid title through the sale of a pupil or a minor without his curator's consent.[18] If there is a void contract between seller X and buyer Y because of essential error as to the identity of Y, then Y can give no title to Z.[19] An *ultra vires* deed by trustees to a company conferred no title on the company who, in turn, could confer no title on anyone dealing with them.[20] These are instances of a wider principle, namely that the normal rules on enforcement of a valid contract do not apply to a void contract. For example, the contract may be repudiated with impunity (subject to quasi-contractual remedies) and damages are not available for breach of the contract.

(3) Failure to offer *restitutio in integrum* is no bar to the reduction of a void contract. Thus an assignation of an alimentary interest may be reduced although restitution is impossible.[21] The contrary would mean that a declaration of a provision as alimentary could be defeated at any

---

[8] Walker, *Civil Remedies*, p. 145.
[9] *e.g. Loudon* v. *Elder's Curator*, 1923 S.L.T. 226.
[10] Walker, *Civil Remedies*, p. 139.
[11] *Vide Stobie* v. *Smith*, 1921 S.C. 894.
[12] *e.g. Klenck* v. *East India Co. for Exploration and Mining Ltd.* (1888) 16 R. 271.
[13] *General Property Investment Co.* v. *Matheson's Trs.* (1888) 16 R. 282.
[14] *Wilson* v. *Scottish Typographical Association*, 1912 S.C. 534.
[15] *e.g. Pollock* v. *Burns* (1875) 2 R. 497.
[16] Bills of Exchange Act 1882, s.30(2) (force and fear affecting bill).
[17] *Cassie* v. *Fleming* (1632) Mor. 10279; *Woodhead* v. *Nairn* (1662) Mor. 10281; *Priestnell* v. *Hutcheson* (1857) 19 D. 495 at p. 498; *Willocks* v. *Callander & Wilson* (1776) Mor. 1519; *Wightman* v. *Graham* (1787) Mor. 1521.
[18] Gloag, p. 91.
[19] *Morrisson* v. *Robertson*, 1908 S.C. 332; discussed, para. 9–82.
[20] *Kidd* v. *Paton's Trs.*, 1912 2 S.L.T. 363.
[21] *Balls* v. *J. & W. Macdonald*, 1909 2 S.L.T. 310.

time.[22] Similarly the failure to offer restitution is no bar to the reduction of an agreement and memorandum of allocation by persons with no title to grant the deeds,[23] or the reduction of an assignation by an insane person.[24] This is to be contrasted with a voidable contract in respect of which "if there cannot be a *restitutio in integrum* the contract cannot be rescinded but must remain in force."[25]

(4) In contrast to an illegal contract, quasi-contractual remedies are available. A pupil or minor may be liable, not under his contract, but on the principle of recompense.[26] Money paid on the faith of an *ultra vires* contract may be recovered on the principle of recompense.[27]

(5) It is sometimes said that a void contract may be adopted, whereas a voidable contract may be homologated.[28] This raises two problems: the distinction, if any, between adoption and homologation and the consequences of the distinction. We are not concerned here with "adoption" and "homologation" in all their senses,[29] but with their application to void and voidable contracts.

The older authorities treat adoption as one aspect of homologation and, as Rankine has observed, "the distinction between homologation and adoption has not been scrupulously observed in judicial utterances."[30] Erskine queried whether deeds intrinsically null could be validated by homologation and drew a distinction between deeds by a person naturally incapable of consent, which could not be homologated, and deeds inducing a natural obligation which could be homologated.[31] This view was questioned by More,[32] is contrary to Bell,[33] and was treated by Dickson as irreconcilable with authority.[34] It cannot now be accepted.

---

[22] *Ibid.* at p. 311 *per* Lord Mackenzie.

[23] *Dowell's Ltd.* v. *Governors of George Heriot's Trust*, 1941 S.C. 13. *Vide* arguments in *General Property Investment Co.* v. *Matheson's Trs.* (1888) 16 R. 282.

[24] *Clark* v. *Black*, 1948 S.L.T.(Notes) 58.

[25] *Houldsworth* v. *City of Glasgow Bank* (1880) 7 R.(H.L.) 53 at p. 60 *per* Lord Hatherley.

[26] Gloag, p. 78; Stair, I,vi,33; I,viii,2; Ersk., I,vii,33: discussed further *supra* at para. 8–20 in connection with minors' contracts for necessaries.

[27] *Haggarty* v. *S.T.G.W.U.*, 1955 S.C. 109; *Mags. of Stonehaven* v. *Kincardineshire C.C.*, 1939 S.C. 760 at p. 771 *per* Lord President Normand. On appeal: 1940 S.C.(H.L.) 56.

[28] It is thought that neither illegal nor unenforceable contracts can be homologated or adopted. The principles on which the contracts are invalid preclude the parties making the contracts valid: *Penman* v. *Fife Coal Co.*, 1935 S.C.(H.L.) 39.

[29] *e.g.* excluding adoption of a contract by a trustee in bankruptcy or homologation in so far as it excludes *locus poenitentiae* from an imperfectly-constituted agreement or adoption of forged signatures or adoption of improperly-authenticated deeds.

[30] J. Rankine, *A Treatise on the Law of Personal Bar in Scotland* (1921), p. 209. A good example is *Gall* v. *Bird* (1855) 17 D. 1027, which is sometimes used to illustrate the distinction (Bell, *Comm.*, I, 140, n. 3).

[31] Ersk., III,iii,47.

[32] More's *Notes*, 68.

[33] Bell, *Comm.*, I, 140; *Prin.*, s.27.

[34] W. G. Dickson, *Law of Evidence in Scotland* (1887), p. 854.

Bell was the last writer to treat adoption as part of homologation. "Where the deed or obligation is null, homologation acts only as the adoption of what is reduced to an intelligible and precise shape, but is in no degree binding."[35] The more recent considerations of Bell's editors,[36] Gloag,[37] Rankine,[38] A. G. Walker and N. M. L. Walker[39] treat adoption as applicable to void deeds and homologation as inappropriate to such deeds. There are cases which involve adoption of void contracts, but being old authorities the adoption is referred to as homologation.[40] This raises the problem of whether there is here an arid controversy on semantics or whether the distinction matters. Erskine regarded homologation (including adoption) as always operating retrospectively.[41] Bell thought that homologation (meaning adoption) of void deeds only had effect from the date of the particular acts done, whereas homologation of voidable deeds operated retrospectively.[42] This view was approved by Lord Cowan,[43] and followed by Dickson,[44] and A. G. Walker and N. M. L. Walker.[45] Rankine[46] and Gloag[47] followed a modified view. They saw no reason why adoption should not operate retrospectively if this may be inferred from the circumstances. It is thought that there is merit in this, although it is contrary to one dictum.[48] The law may therefore be this. Homologation of a voidable contract always operates retrospectively. Adoption of a void contract, if competent, may or may not operate retrospectively, depending on circumstances.

(c) Summary of consequences of a void contract

26–06   In summary, a void contract is null *ab initio*. No property may pass under it and third parties, even if *bona fide* and for value, can acquire no rights under it. Failure by one party to comply with the contract does not give the other party the remedies for breach of contract. The failure to offer *restitutio in integrum* is not a bar to rescission of the contract.

---

[35] Bell, *Comm.*, *ibid.*
[36] Bell, *Prin.*, *ibid.*
[37] Gloag, p. 546.
[38] *Op. cit.*, p. 142.
[39] A. G. Walker and N. M. L. Walker, *The Law of Evidence in Scotland* (1964), p. 315.
[40] *Grant* v. *Anderson* (1706) Mor. 16509 (force and fear); *Hume* v. *Lord Justice-Clerk* (1671) Mor. 5688 (minor); *Harvie* v. *Gordon* (1726) Mor. 5712 (pupil); *vide* Bankt. III,48,14; *Rigg* v. *Durward* (1776) Mor.App. "Fraud" No. 2 (dictum on force and fear); *Thomson* v. *Annandale* (1829) 7 S.305 (force and fear); *Oliphant* v. *Scott* (1830) 8 S. 985 (*ultra vires*).
[41] Ersk., III,iii.49.
[42] Bell, *Comm.*, I, 140.
[43] *Gall* v. *Bird* (1885) 17 D. 1027 at p. 1030.
[44] *Op. cit.*, para. 866.
[45] *Op. cit.*, p. 315.
[46] *Op. cit.*, p. 214.
[47] *Op. cit.*, p. 546.
[48] *Logan's Trs.* v. *Reid* (1885) 12 R. 1094 at p. 1100 *per* Lord Kinnear.

Quasi-contractual remedies are available to adjust parties' rights and the contract may be adopted.

VOIDABLE CONTRACTS

(a) History

07   The word "voidable" may have been first used by Bankton who in 1751 compared deeds which were "not void" but only "voidable."[49] Kames also used the term[50] and it is tempting to conclude from the acquaintance of these two authors with English authorities that its use was a result of English influence.[51] This is a possibility, if not a probability. "Voidable" has been traced in England to 1485,[52] and: "In the sixteenth century it was frequently provided in leases that, on the non-payment of rent or on the non-performance of some other condition, the lease should be void or voidable. At that time a good deal turned . . . on the use of the words 'void' and 'voidable.' "[53]

-08   The late introduction of the term "voidable" into Scotland meant that at the formative period of Scots law in the seventeenth century it was not used. It is not found in Stair. Erskine did not use it, which one would have expected if it had been common currency when his contemporary Bankton wrote. One should not draw the conclusion, however, that the concept of a "voidable" contract did not exist when the term was not known. The concept was adopted even earlier than Stair.[54]

(b) Consequences of a voidable contract

-09   A voidable contract may be rescinded under certain circumstances, but it is not null *ab initio*.[55] The normal principles of title and interest to sue regulate those who may challenge the contract. This may result in considerable differences depending on the ground of invalidity. Thus in contracts of bankrupts the title to challenge is strictly limited and may be denied to some contracting parties while being allowed to non-contracting parties.[56] In other circumstances it is possible, though unusual, for both parties to have the right to challenge.[57]

---

[49] Bankt., I,180,74; I,257,58; III,57,41.

[50] Kames, *Principles of Equity*, Vol. 1, pp. 80, 363; *Elucidations*, pp. 3, 4.

[51] *Cf.* Smith, *Short Commentary*, p. 817, who wrongly attributes to Bell's editors the start of "a fashion of distinguishing as the English do, between 'void' and 'voidable' contracts."

[52] *O.E.D.*

[53] Holdsworth, Vol. VII, p. 292.

[54] It arose in contracts involving minors. See para. 8–08.

[55] A company may not adopt its own *ultra vires* act: *General Property Investment Co.* v. *Mathesons' Trs.* (1888) 16 R. 282. In broader terms, the incapacity making the contract void must be at an end before adoption is possible.

[56] *Munro* v. *Rothfield*, 1920 S.C.(H.L.) 165.

[57] *e.g.* each induced by the fraud of the other.

26-10   A person with a title to challenge may be personally barred. Personal bar may arise through lapse of time[58] or by homologation.[59] Or a person may expressly waive his right to challenge.[60] Apart from personal bar, an alteration in circumstances since the making of the contract may preclude reduction. The classic case is transfer of property to a *bona fide* onerous third party. If A sells X to B, as a result of the fraud of B, then the subsequent sale by B to C, who is *bona fide* and onerous, will bar the reduction of the sale by A to B. C acquires a good title to X.[61] C cannot reduce the contract between A and B even by offering *restitutio in integrum*.[62] Only if C can reduce his contract with B may A reduce his contract with B.[63] This is an example of the principle that for reduction of a voidable contract *restitutio in integrum*, although not in a literal sense,[64] must be possible.[65] Until and unless rescinded a voidable contract operates as a valid contract.

(c) Summary of consequences of a voidable contract

26-11   In summary, a voidable contract is not null *ab initio*. It is valid until rescinded. As a condition for rescission, the party seeking to rescind must not be personally barred from rescinding and must be able to offer *restitutio in integrum*.

UNENFORCEABLE CONTRACTS

(a) History of unenforceable contracts

26-12   The category of unenforceable contract arose in the treatment of gaming and smuggling contracts in the eighteenth century.[66]

---

[58] Gloag, pp. 542 *et seq.*

[59] Considered *supra*; *Gall* v. *Bird* (1855) 17 D. 1027 (facility and circumvention); *L.A.* v. *Wemyss* (1899) 2 F.(H.L.) 1 (curator's contract); *Rigg* v. *Durward*, Mor.App. "Fraud" No. 2 (fraud); *Scott* v. *Handyside's Trs.* (1868) 6 M. 753 (trustee's remuneration).

[60] *Ommanney* v. *Smith* (1854) 16 D. 721; *Dixon* v. *Rutherford* (1863) 2 M. 61; *Howard & Wyndham* v. *Richmond's Trs.* (1890) 17 R. 990 (all cases involving beneficiaries and trustees).

[61] *Price & Pierce Ltd.* v. *Bank of Scotland*, 1912 S.C.(H.L.) 19. It is assumed, of course, that the fraud makes the sale voidable, and it does not induce essential error which makes the sale void.

[62] *Edinburgh United Breweries Ltd.* v. *Molleson* (1894) 21 R.(H.L.) 10.

[63] *Westville Shipping Co.* v. *Abram Steamship Co.*, 1923 S.C.(H.L.) 68.

[64] *Spence* v. *Crawford*, 1939 S.C.(H.L.) 52. The doctrine of *restitutio in integrum* is not always satisfactory. What happens, for example, if the subject-matter of a sale is eggs which are rotten? *Vide* J. S. McLennan, "*Restitutio in Integrum* and the Duty to Restore" (1973) 90 S.A.L.J. 120.

[65] *Houldsworth* v. *City of Glasgow Bank* (1880) 7 R.(H.L.) 53; *Western Bank* v. *Addie* (1867) 5 M.(H.L.) 80; *Boyd & Forrest* v. *Glasgow and South Western Ry. Co.*, 1915 S.C.(H.L.) 20.

[66] See paras. 25–15 and 25–47.

(b) Consequences of an unenforceable contract

13　　Gloag stated: "The term unenforceable, as applied to an agreement, has no special or technical meaning, but is most commonly applied to cases where by terms of a statute, such as the Trade Union Act, a particular agreement cannot be directly enforced, but may be productive of rights to the one party against the other."[67] Statutory invalidity apart, there is truth in the idea that the unenforceable contract does not exist as a class.

14　　One can describe as unenforceable a variety of contracts whose only connection is that they "are valid in all respects except that one or both parties cannot be sued on the contract."[68] Thus, in the old and now modified theory, a sovereign state could not against its will be sued for breach of contract, but conversely the state could itself sue for damages for breach.[69] Such a contract was thought to be unenforceable at the option of a party. This is different from the betting or gaming contract where the parties cannot waive the invalidity[70] and the court will *ex proprio motu* take note of the fact that an action is founded on a gaming transaction.[71] These in turn differ from a restraint of trade provision which "is generally not unlawful at common law if the parties choose to abide by it; it is only unenforceable if a party chooses not to abide by it."[72] On the other hand public interest is a factor in contracts in restraint of trade,[73] and there are situations in which a court will take notice that *ex facie* of parties' pleadings a contract is in restraint of trade, although the point is not pled.[74]

(c) Summary of consequences of an unenforceable contract

–15　　An unenforceable contract has all the requisites of a contract except that a court action will not be sustained on it. There is the additional negative characteristic that the contract is neither illegal, nor void, nor voidable. The circumstances in which a contract is unenforceable depend on the rules evolved for the particular type of contract under consideration.

---

[67] Gloag, p. 14.

[68] Chitty, para. 17.

[69] The law changed with *Trendtex Trading Corp.* v. *Central Bank of Nigeria* [1977] Q.B. 529; *Hispano Americana Mercantil S.A.* v. *Central Bank of Nigeria* [1979] 2 Lloyd's Rep. 277; *Planmount* v. *Republic of Zaire* [1981] 1 All E.R. 1110. The principle which emerged was that a foreign state was entitled to immunity in respect of governmental acts, but not commercial transactions. See now State Immunity Act 1978, s.3.

[70] *Robertson* v. *Balfour*, 1938 S.C. 207.

[71] *Hamilton* v. *McLauchlan* (1908) 16 S.L.T. 341; *Brown* v. *Coats*, 1954 S.L.T.(Sh.Ct.) 31.

[72] Chitty, para. 1092, n. 45.

[73] J. D. Heydon, *The Restraint of Trade Doctrine* (1971), pp. 25–36 and 277.

[74] *North Western Salt Co. Ltd.* v. *Electrolytic Alkali Co. Ltd.* [1914] A.C. 461. See para. 25–109.

(d) Examples of unenforceable contracts

26–16 The following are unenforceable contracts: contracts with an enemy (in certain cases), *pacta de quota litis*, gaming contracts, smuggling contracts, and contracts in restraint of trade.[75] The nature of the invalidity is discussed at the appropriate place in considering the development of those contracts. Of these instances, smuggling contracts are a prime candidate for removal to another category. The contracts have not been treated as immoral, despite Kames.[76] It may be that the courts today would agree with Kames or at least consider the contracts subversive to the interests of the State and to be treated as illegal contracts on the lines of *Jamieson* v. *Watt's Trs.* If this change took place,[77] and it could be viewed as a natural development, it would alter the nature of the invalidity of a smuggling contract and affect the remedies available to it. It would be a reasonable change to make, as it is difficult to justify treating smuggling more favourably than breach of the licensing requirements of Defence Regulations.

ILLEGAL CONTRACTS

(a) Terminology

26–17 The category of "illegal contracts" is the most difficult to explain and understand. Partly this arises from the problem of terminology. For example, Gloag in his treatment of a contract interfering with elections described the contract as a "*pactum illicitum*," "void," "illegal" and "an unlawful agreement."[78] But also the law is flexible in its approach to contracts involving *turpis causa*. There clearly is a separate category of illegal contracts, but apart from saying that the category contains con-

---

[75] It should be borne in mind that we are not discussing formalities of constitution nor events subsequent to the making of a contract such as the running of prescription, which would provide other examples of unenforceable contracts. It is possible to argue that collective agreements between trade unions and employers' associations are examples of unenforceable contracts. The contracts may expressly or impliedly contain terms rendering them unenforceable. It may be that these are not contracts because there is no intention to create legal relations. It is the essence of a contract that there must be what the Roman jurists called a *vinculum iuris*. The parties must have *animus contrahendi*. The two theories are discussed in J. P. Casey, "Collective Agreements: Some Scottish Footnotes," 1973 J.R. 22; R. L. C. Hunter, "Collective Agreements, Fair Wages Clauses, and the Employment Relationship in Scots Law," 1975 J.R. 47. *Vide* Trade Union and Labour Relations Act 1974, s.18. It is possible to distinguish between the unenforceable contract and the agreement which the parties do not intend to be enforced. See also para. 4–38.

[76] *Principles of Equity*, Vol. 1, p. 357.

[77] A change is necessary because there are circumstances in which an action can be brought on a smuggling contract: *Att. of Young & Co.* v. *Imlach* (1790) Mor. 9553; *Cullen* v. *Philp* (1793) Mor. 9554; *Reid and Parkinson* v. *Macdonald* (1793) Mor. 9555; *Isaacson* v. *Wiseman* (1806) Hume 714. This is not the same as the quasi-contractual remedy available to a party who is not *in pari delicto* under an illegal contract.

[78] Gloag, p. 565.

tracts affected by moral turpitude or contrary to public policy, or similar phrases, it is difficult to define the category.[79]

(b) What is an "illegal" contract?

-18   As a result of *Jamieson* v. *Watt's Trustees*[80] it seems that a contract is illegal if it involves moral turpitude or is "subversive of the interests of the State," both of which are very vague concepts. Subversion may mean little more than impliedly contrary to statute, but, as *Cuthbertson* v. *Lowes*[81] has not been overruled, a contract in contravention of any statute is not necessarily illegal.[82] Presumably partnerships of money-lenders where, contrary to statute, the name of one of the partners did not appear on the pawn-tickets, or over the door of the premises, or in the licence, were illegal.[83] They were analogous to the *Jamieson* situation. If one wishes, one can see the interests of the State being affected by partnership between a solicitor and an unqualified person.[84] It is easier to categorise as illegal a contract which involves contravention of statute and also moral turpitude, such as a partnership of slave traders.[85]

(c) Consequences of an illegal contract

-19   The illegal contract is unenforceable and quasi-contractual remedies are not available. "The rule of law is that if the consideration for granting a document of debt be one of turpitude, the document will not sustain action."[86] The partnership cases mentioned above illustrate this principle. The contract is not, at common law, void. In one case a lease granted *ob turpem causam* was not reduced as null.[87] An obligation *ob turpem causam* will not be implemented by the court, but neither will action be allowed to restore benefits gained. Nor will these principles be evaded by quasi-contractual remedies.[88]

6-20   When illegality exists the courts will take notice of it *ex proprio motu*, even though it is not pled by either party. There is a long line of English authority on this and the principle is reasonable.[89] But in some circum-

---

[79] *Munro* v. *Rothfield*, 1920 S.C.(H.L.) 165.

[80] 1950 S.C. 265.

[81] (1870) 8 M. 1073.

[82] *Cf.* the English use of the term "illegal": "A contract that is expressly or implicitly prohibited by statute is illegal"—Cheshire and Fifoot, p. 308. See the difficulties caused in English law by contrasting *Bedford Ins. Co. Ltd.* v. *Instituto de Resseguros do Brasil* [1984] 3 All E.R. 766 and *Stewart* v. *Oriental Fire and Marine Ins. Co. Ltd.* [1984] 3 All E.R. 777 (effect of contravention of Insurance Companies Act on policies of insurance).

[83] *Fraser* v. *Hill* (1852) 14 D. 335; *Gordon* v. *Howden* (1845) 4 Bell 254.

[84] *A.B.* v. *C.D.*, 1912 1 S.L.T. 44.

[85] *Stewart* v. *Gibson* (1840) 1 Rob. 260.

[86] *Webster* v. *Webster's Trs.* (1886) 14 R. 90 at p. 92 *per* Lord Young.

[87] *A.* v. *B.*, May 21, 1816, F.C.; revd. on other grounds (1820) 6 Pat. 644; 2 Bligh 196 (the best report).

[88] *Jamieson* v. *Watt's Trs.*, *sup. cit.*

[89] *e.g. Scott.* v. *Brown, Doering McNab & Co.* [1892] 2 Q.B. 724; *Montefiore* v. *Menday Motor Components Co. Ltd.* [1918] 2 K.B. 241; *Commercial Air Hire Ltd.* v. *Wrightways Ltd.* [1938] 1 All E.R. 89; *Snell* v. *Unity Finance Co. Ltd.* [1964] 2 Q.B. 203; *vide Trevalion & Co.* v. *Blanche & Co.*, 1919 S.C. 617 at p. 623 *per* Lord Dundas.

stances it is for the defender to plead illegality. The court will not assume it.[90]

26–21   The problem then posed is whether the contract differs in any respect from the unenforceable contract. Wessels has argued that there is a difference in the readiness of a court to assist recovery of money and that an unenforceable contract gives rise to a natural obligation, whereas an illegal contract gives rise to no obligation whatsoever.[91]

26–22   Scots authority is meagre.[92] There may be a difference between contracts associated with an illegal transaction and contracts associated with an unenforceable transaction.

> "Horse racing is not illegal. Nor is betting illegal in the sense of being prohibited or punishable. It is true that the Courts in Scotland do not entertain actions to determine wagers; it is also true that by the cautious provisions of the Act 1621, cap. 14, which is directed against excess in wagering, kirk-sessions were given right to the surplus over 100 merks of every racing bet, and by more modern statutes it is an offence to keep a house for betting. But there is no such legal taint in betting as to infect all the contracts which are in any way related to it."[93]

26–23   This difference may influence not only whether associated contracts are tainted, but also whether illegality of part of a contract results in the whole contract being affected or whether instead parts of the contract are severable.

(d) The doctrine of severance

26–24   English law has a long and confused history of the problem of severance of illegality in contract.[94] Some recent authority indicates that if a contractual condition is illegal as being *contra bonos mores*, it will so infect the rest of the contract that the contract will not be enforced. This has been contrasted with severance in contracts in restraint of trade, which it may be argued are merely unenforceable. In the context of a contract with the enemy, McNair J. stated that:

> "there is no authority for the proposition that for the purpose of the matter under consideration severance can ever take place and no ground of public policy which requires such severance. The

---

[90] *Designers and Decorators (Scotland) Ltd.* v. *Ellis*, 1957 S.C.(H.L.) 69.

[91] Wessels, paras. 643–651. See for an example *Cohen* v. *Lester (J.) Ltd.* [1939] 1 K.B. 504 and *vide* W. R. Anson, "Some Notes on Terminology in Contract" (1891) 7 L.Q.R. 337 at p. 339; *Congresbury Motors Ltd.* v. *Anglo-Belge Finance Co. Ltd.* [1970] Ch. 294; [1971] 1 Ch. 81; *Coptic Ltd.* v. *Bailey* [1972] 1 Ch. 446; *Burston Finance Ltd.* v. *Speirway Ltd.* [1974] 3 All E.R. 735.

[92] *Vide* Gloag, p. 589 and authorities there cited.

[93] *Knight & Co.* v. *Stott* (1892) 19 R. 959 at p. 962 *per* Lord President Robertson. A transaction associated with an illegal transaction may be so inextricably mixed with the other that both fall under the umbrella of illegality: *N. G. Napier Ltd.* v. *Patterson*, 1959 J.C. 48; *N. G. Napier Ltd.* v. *Corbett*, 1961 S.L.T.(Sh.Ct.) 2 (sequel, 1962 S.L.T. (Sh.Ct.) 90); *cf. N. G. Napier Ltd.* v. *Gallacher* (1960) 76 Sh.Ct.Rep. 16.

[94] N. S. Marsh, "The Severance of Illegality in Contract" (1948) 64 L.Q.R. 230, 347; Anson, p. 353.

decisions relating to severability of covenants in restraint of trade, such as *Putsman* v. *Taylor*,[95] seem to me to have no application at all in the present context. Secondly, that severance can only take place, if at all, if the part which it is sought to sever stands by itself supported by separate consideration."[96]

-25 In *Bennett* v. *Bennett*[97] Somervell L.J., in the context of a case on ousting jurisdiction of the court, considered restraint-of-trade cases. He pointed out that there were many decisions in which part only of the restraint had been treated as unenforceable and contrary to public policy. This had not vitiated the rest of the clause, but:

"if promises in restraint of trade were the sole subject-matter and those promises were wholly or in the main contrary to public policy, it seems to me clear that the court would treat the whole contract as void.

-26 "The cases to which we were referred seem to me to indicate that if one of the promises is to do an act which is either in itself a criminal offence or *contra bonos mores*, the court will regard the whole contract as void. In restraint of trade cases there is nothing wrong in trading. What is objectionable is or may be a promise for consideration not to do so."[98]

-27 His Lordship expressed those views in a similar case, pointing out that there were two kinds of illegality with differing effects:

"The first is where the illegality is criminal, or *contra bonos mores*, and in those cases, which I will not attempt to enumerate or further classify, such a provision, if an ingredient in a contract, will invalidate the whole, although there may be many other provisions in it. There is a second kind of illegality which has no such taint; the other terms in the contract stand if the illegal portion can be severed, the illegal portion being a provision which the court, on grounds of public policy, will not enforce."[99]

-28 In *Carney* v. *Herbert*[1] it was observed[2] in the Privy Council that questions of severability were often difficult, there were no set rules which will decide all cases, and each case depends on its circumstances and, in particular, on the nature of the illegality. There were two issues to be considered,[3] first, whether as a matter of construction the law feels part of the contract can be severed from the unlawful part, and second,

---

[95] [1927] 1 K.B. 637 at p. 741.
[96] *Kuenigl* v. *Donnersmarck* [1955] 1 Q.B. 515 at pp. 537–538.
[97] [1952] 1 K.B. 249.
[98] at p. 253.
[99] *Goodinson* v. *Goodinson* [1954] 2 Q.B. 118 at p. 120. See also *Alec Lobb (Garages) Ltd.* v. *Total Oil G.B. Ltd.* [1985] 1 All E.R. 303. However, *Napier* v. *National Business Agency Ltd.* [1951] 1 All E.R. 264 involved an agreement contrary to public policy and arguably criminal or *contra bonos mores*, and yet the impossibility of severance was a ground of decision.
[1] [1985] 1 All E.R. 438. The case analyses several authorities, including cases on illegality affecting payments under contracts of employment—*Netherseal Colliery Co. Ltd.* v. *Bourne* (1889) 14 App.Cas. 228; *Kearney* v. *Whitehaven Colliery Co.* [1893] 1 Q.B. 700; *Miller* v. *Karlinski* (1945) 62 T.L.R. 85.
[2] at p. 442.
[3] See at p. 444.

whether despite severability there is a bar to enforceability arising out of the nature of the illegality. In that case mortgages ancillary to a sale were an offence under company law. The mortgages could be severed from the remainder of the transaction and their illegality did not taint the whole contract.

26–29   There is something to be said in favour of alternative tests in Continental systems with their emphasis on the intention of the parties.[4] Scots law, however, has tended to follow English law in the spheres of illegal and unenforceable contracts, and when the matter comes to be considered in Scotland these English authorities will be treated as highly relevant.[5]

(e) Summary of consequences of illegal contract

26–30   An illegal contract is one which the law will not enforce. A court will have nothing to do with the rights of parties to the contract which arise under the contract. If the parties are *in pari delicto*, quasi-contractual remedies will be denied to them. In some instances the court will not enforce the obligations which arise under the contract even if the illegality is not pleaded.[6] The illegal nature of the contract may infect all parts of it, and the court might not separate unobjectionable from objectionable conditions.[7]

Justa Causa Traditionis

26–31   The effect of invalidity and, in particular, the effect of a void contract, is altered if the concept of *justa causa traditionis* is part of Scots law. The concept is relevant to the distinction between contract and conveyance. The contract may be invalid, but the conveyance can be effective if the intention was to transfer ownership.

26–32   It is argued in a memorandum of the Scottish Law Commission that this concept, derived from Roman law, is possibly part of Scots law.[8]

26–33   The Commission accept that a doctrine of "just cause" or "just title" has not been expressly recognised in Scots law. The cases on which the implication of its reception is based, namely *Stuart* v. *Kennedy*,[9] *Wilson*

---

[4] Marsh, *sup. cit.*, pp. 230–232.

[5] In *Carney* v. *Herbert, sup. cit.*, there is a tantalising reference to Scottish case law at p. 446. Some authority indicates that if the consideration for the contract is illegal the whole contract must fall: *Freedlander* v. *Bateman*, 1953 S.L.T.(Sh.Ct.) 105; *Farmers' Mart* v. *Milne*, 1914 S.C.(H.L.) 84 at p. 86, *per* Lord Dunedin. This is different from the question whether *any* illegality taints the whole contract.

[6] *e.g. Scott* v. *Brown, Doering, McNab & Co.* [1892] 2 Q.B. 724; *Montefiore* v. *Menday Motor Components Co. Ltd.* [1918] 2 K.B. 241; *Commercial Air Hire Ltd.* v. *Wrightways Ltd.* [1938] 1 All E.R. 89; *Snell* v. *Unity Finance Co. Ltd.* [1964] 2 Q.B. 203; *vide Trevalion & Co.* v. *Blanche & Co.* 1919 S.C. 617 at p. 623 *per* Lord Dundas.

[7] *Vide* Wessels, para. 644 for a similar definition.

[8] Memo. No. 25, *Corporeal Moveables: Passing of Risk and of Ownership* (1976), para. 12–17.

[9] (1885) 13 R. 221.

v. *Marquis of Breadalbane*[10] and *Cuthbertson* v. *Lowes*[11] can be explained on other grounds, including the reasons given in the opinions in these cases.

-34 In relation to nullities the early Scots lawyers were practical. There was no point in attacking a transaction as null, if the implementation of the transaction was not also invalidated. The effect was as important as the form. Where there was lack of capacity it was the *deed* which was reduced, not merely any prior agreement. This can be illustrated, for example, by cases involving minors[12] and the insane.[13] Infeftment could be reduced on the grounds of force and fear.[14] An owner may have every intention to transfer property, but if he is acting *ultra vires*, the invalidity will affect third parties.[15]

35 A challenge on the basis of facility and circumvention (which is historically derived from fraud) proceeded by an attempt to reduce an agreement *and* deeds granted in implement.[16] Where the contract is tainted with immorality the result can vary between refusing to reduce deeds which have followed on the contract,[17] and circumstances where it is highly unlikely that a title could be transferred to anyone.[18] Where public policy is involved the law is flexible. Property may pass in smuggled goods,[19] although the smuggling contract is unenforceable so that the seller may not sue for the price, if an accessory to the smuggling[20] and the buyer may not obtain damages for failure to deliver.[21]

-36 These results have been obtained without need to refer to the concept of *justa causa traditionis*, which raises the problem of not only whether the concept is part of Scots law, but also whether, and in what circumstances, it is a necessary concept. Hume's premise is arguably correct, that: "Only two things are naturally requisite to the transference of property—the will of the owner to convey the thing in property, and actual delivery in pursuance of a bargain to that effect."[22]

---

[10] (1859) 21 D. 957.

[11] (1870) 8 M. 1073.

[12] *Kincaid* v. *** (1561) Mor. 8979; *Hamiltons* v. *Hamilton* (1587) Mor. 8981; *Seton* v. *Caskieben* (1622) Mor. 8939; *Cardross* v. *Hamilton* (1708) Mor. 8951.

[13] *Lindsay* v. *Trent* (1684) Mor. 6280 at p. 6281; *Gall* v. *Bird* (1855) 17 D. 1027.

[14] *Cassie* v. *Fleming* (1632) Mor. 10279.

[15] *Kidd* v. *Paton's Trs.*, 1912 2 S.L.T. 363.

[16] *Gall* v. *Bird, supra.*

[17] *A.* v. *B.*, May 21, 1816 F.C.; on appeal 6 Pat. 644, 2 Bligh 196. It is unlikely that there is substantial difference in this context between the transmission of heritable and moveable property except on the presumption operating from possession (Hume, *Lectures* (Stair Soc.), Vol. III, p. 239).

[18] *Trevalion & Co.* v. *Blanche & Co.*, 1919 S.C. 617.

[19] *Commrs. of Custom* v. *Morison* (1723) Mor. 9533.

[20] *Young & Co.* v. *Imlach* (1790) Mor. 9553; *Cullen* v. *Philip* (1793) Mor. 9554; *Isaacson* v. *Wiseman* (1806) Hume 714.

[21] *Scougal* v. *Gilchrist* (1736) Mor. 9536; *Cockburn* v. *Grant* (1741) Mor. 9539.

[22] *Lectures*, Vol. III, p. 235, and *vide* p. 245: "The delivery of possession shall not transfer it, unless it follow on a suitable contract," which is difficult to construe as applicable to an abstract theory of *causa*.

26–37   The problem immediately raised, as Hume recognises, is what is meant by the "will of the owner." Sometimes there will be consent and sometimes not, depending on the view the law takes of different vitiating factors. This has been the approach of Scots law. The concept of *justa causa traditionis* is not only unnecessary: it would produce many complexities.

CHAPTER 27

CONSTITUTION AND PROOF

INTRODUCTION

–01 This work is not primarily concerned with the law of evidence and therefore the subject of constitution or proof of obligations is not considered in great detail. The topic is treated comprehensively in Walker and Walker on *Evidence*.[1] The Scottish Law Commission Memorandum No. 39[2] contains a valuable summary of the law.

DEVELOPMENT OF THE LAW

–02 In a series of articles Dr J. J. Gow analysed the development of the law.[3] Subsequently Professor W. A. Wilson embarked on the incredibly difficult task of making sense of the earlier authorities.[4] There was much to criticise and many doubts were raised. On the requirement for probative writing in the transmission of heritage Lord President Cooper observed[5]:

> "It is useless to disguise that, the further we recede from the far distant days when land was the substance of the private wealth of the community, the more clearly does this rule stand revealed as a fossil relic of feudalism, explicable, if confined within the field of strict conveyancing, but completely out of touch with realities when it intrudes into the field of mutual contract. It is emphatically not a rule for benignant interpretation or extended application."

The present state of the law is described by Walker and Walker in this way[6]:

> "The law which requires writing for the constitution or proof of certain obligations is so uncertain and unsatisfactory that it is almost impossible to state a principle which is of general application. In attempting to state the law as it is, it is difficult not to adopt the course, so often adopted by the courts, of dealing with each kind of obligation as if it were contained in a water-tight com-

---

[1] Chaps. IX, XI and XII.
[2] *Constitution and Proof of Voluntary Obligations: Formalities of Constitution and Restrictions on Proof* (1977); see also Sheriff I. D. MacPhail, *Research Paper on the Law of Evidence of Scotland*, Scot.Law.Com. (1979), Chap. 15 for a comprehensive treatment of the admissibility of evidence in relation to documents.
[3] "The Constitution and Proof of Voluntary Obligations," 1961 J.R. 1, 119, 234; see also J. J. Gow, *The Mercantile and Industrial Law of Scotland*, pp. 1 *et seq.*
[4] "In Modum Probationis," 1968 J.R. 193.
[5] *McGinn* v. *Shearer*, 1947 S.C. 334 at pp. 344–345.
[6] *Evidence*, para. 89.

partment, and without regard to the anomalies arising from the application of different rules to other analogous obligations."

27–03   The case which established the present approach of Scots law was the decision of the majority of the whole court in *Paterson* v. *Paterson*.[7] The case involved the relationship between the authentication statutes and the concept of "writ or oath." There was no doubt that a loan required proof by writ or oath, but the question in the case was—what kind of writ? The defenders who were sued for repayment argued that the writ had to be holograph or tested. The court rejected this argument and held that proof of the loan must be by writ or oath but the writ need not be tested or holograph. The case was decided against a background of what Lord Moncreiff described as[8]:

> "a conflict of authority. This need not cause much surprise when it is considered that there is scarcely any branch of the law in which there has been greater uncertainty and fluctuation of judical opinion than the application and scope of the Scots statutes which regulate the authentication of writings."

27–04   Although the decision has been criticised[9] and although it makes a coherent presentation of the law difficult, the case represents the present law.

THE CATEGORIES OF THE PRESENT LAW

27–05   As a result of *Paterson*, voluntary obligations fall into three categories:

(1) *Obligationes literis*. These must be constituted by writing which is tested or holograph. An informal agreement may be proved by writ or oath and validated by homologation or *rei interventus*. The operation of *rei interventus* on an incomplete agreement is controversial and is discussed later.[9a]

(2) Obligations which may be informally constituted but which must be proved by writ or oath.

(3) Obligations which may be constituted verbally and proved *prout de jure*.

27–06   There is a fourth category of obligations which must be constituted in writing but the writing need not be tested or holograph. This category arises because of statutory requirements that an obligation be in writing.

27–07   In category (1)—*obligationes literis*—are contracts relating to heritage and contracts of service for more than one year. Obligations which must be proved by writ or oath (category (2)) include loans (over £8·33), obligations of relief, declaration of trust, innominate and unusual obligations and gratuitous obligations.[10] Category (3) comprises all other

---

[7] (1897) 25 R. 144.
[8] at p. 167.
[9] Gow, *sup. cit.*
[9a] See para. 27–41.
[10] Various methods of discharging obligations require proof by writ or oath. See para. 22–32.

obligations except in so far as they are in category (4). There are several obligations the rules on which are doubtful, namely, submissions to arbitration and decrees in arbitration, cautionary obligations, insurance and writs *in re mercatoria*.

Obligationes Literis

–08   The constitution of an *obligatio literis* requires the production of writing which is solemnly executed or holograph or, alternatively, an oral agreement or informal writing (proved by writ or oath) followed by homologation or *rei interventus*.[11]

(a) Contracts relating to heritage

'–09   Contracts relating to heritage are *obligationes literis*. This includes all contracts relating to the sale of heritage including sale by public roup.[12] The rule applies to leases, except leases for not more than one year which may be proved by parole evidence.[13] If a lease for a period of over a year is averred and is not supported, the tenant cannot fall back on the assertion that he has at least a lease for a year.[14] If the period is not agreed, the law does not imply a lease for one year.[15]

7–10   An option to purchase heritage is an obligation relating to heritage and must be created by probative or holograph writing. But the actual exercise of the option can be by an informal writ.[16]

7–11   The rule does not apply to a contract which relates incidentally to heritage. Thus it is thought that a building contract or a contract to do building alterations, which are primarily contracts for services, need not be constituted in formal writing.[17] Nor does the rule apply to a sale in which the heritable element is minor,[18] or to a licence (rather than a lease) to use spaces for advertisements,[19] or to an agreement to take over a lease.[20] An action relating to heritage may be comprised without the necessity for holograph or tested writings.[21] An agreement regard-

---

[11] On judicial admission see the somewhat confusing opinion in *Jamieson* v. *Edinburgh Mutual Investment Building Society*, 1913 2 S.L.T. 52; *cf. Italian Bank Ltd.* v. *Olivieri*, 1938 S.L.T.(Sh.Ct.) 27 at p. 28 *per* Sheriff-substitute A. M. Hamilton. A mere admission of a verbal agreement may be no more than an admission of an agreement from which a party can resile.

[12] *Shiell* v. *Guthrie's Tr.* (1874) 1 R. 1083.

[13] *Gowan's Trs.* v. *Carstairs* (1862) 24 D. 1382; *Walker* v. *Flint* (1863) 1 M. 417; *Allan* v. *Gilchrist* (1875) 2 R. 587; *Gibson* v. *Adams* (1875) 3 R. 144.

[14] *Temperance Permanent Building Soc.* v. *Kominek*, 1951 S.L.T.(Sh.Ct.) 58.

[15] *Gray* v. *University of Edinburgh*, 1962 S.C. 157; *cf. Hyams* v. *Brechin*, 1979 S.L.T.(Sh.Ct.) 47.

[16] *Stone* v. *MacDonald*, 1979 S.C. 363; *Sichi* v. *Biagi*, 1946 S.N. 66; *Scott* v. *Morrison*, 1979 S.L.T.(Notes) 65. But see case in n. 23.

[17] *Hamilton* v. *Lochrane* (1899) 1 F. 478; *Mackay* v. *Rodger* (1907) 15 S.L.T. 42.

[18] *Allan* v. *Millar*, 1932 S.C. 620.

[19] *United Kingdom Advertising Co.* v. *Glasgow Bag Wash Laundry*, 1926 S.C. 303.

[20] *Kinninmont* v. *Paxton* (1892) 20 R. 128.

[21] *Anderson* v. *Dick* (1901) 4 F. 68; but see *Cook* v. *Grubb*, 1963 S.C. 1.

ing the share of profits on a resale of heritage was provable by parole evidence,[22] as was an agreement that neither party should purchase lands without giving the other the option of being a joint purchaser.[23]

(b) Contracts of service

27–12   Contracts of service for more than one year are *obligationes literis*.[24] The requirement of writing does not apply to a contract of service for less than one year, or a contract of service of indefinite duration terminable by notice,[25] or to the creation of an agency or distributorship,[26] or to a partnership,[27] or to a contract for services.[28]

Proof by Writ or Oath[29]

(a) Loan

27–13   The receipt of a loan of money exceeding £8·33 must be proved by the writ or oath of the borrower or by unqualified judicial admission.[30] A judicial admission must be taken whole along with any qualifications.[31] A loan not exceeding £8.33 may be proved *prout de jure*.[32] The suggestion that the loan is only provable by writ if it is made in one lump sum, but can be proved by parole evidence if made in several

---

[22] *Morris* v. *Goldrich*, 1952 S.L.T.(Sh.Ct.) 86.

[23] *Mungall* v. *Bowhill Coal Co.* (1904) 12 S.L.T. 80, 262.

[24] *Cook* v. *Grubb, sup. cit.*; *Nisbet* v. *Percy*, 1951 S.C. 350; *Murray* v. *Roussel Laboratories Ltd.*, 1960 S.L.T.(Notes) 31; *Tojeiro* v. *McKettrick-Agnew & Co. Ltd.*, 1967 S.L.T.(Notes) 11.

[25] *Walker* v. *Greenock Hospital Board*, 1951 S.C. 464. A contract of service for more than one year appears to mean a contract whereby the parties have bound themselves for more than one year. If this is correct many contracts of service, because they are terminable by either side or short notice, are not *obligationes literis* but the point seems to have been ignored in cases subsequent to *Walker*.

[26] *Pickin* v. *Hawkes* (1878) 5 R. 676. Gloag treated this case as an example of innominate and unusual contracts (*Contract*, p. 180). Nowadays there is nothing at all unusual in a sole distributorship.

[27] J. Bennet Miller, *Partnership*, p. 51.

[28] Gloag, p. 180.

[29] "Proof of an obligation by writ of a party means proof of an obligation by unequivocal inference from documents which are actually or constructively his writ"—Walker and Walker, *op. cit.*, para. 302. The writ may be informed and its authenticity proved by parole evidence. A writ may be constructively a person's writ if it is the writ of his agent or the writ of his creditor which he has received and retained: see Walker and Walker, *op. cit.*, paras. 302–307. On the procedure for proof by oath see Walker and Walker, *op cit.*, para. 117 and Chap. XXV. The oath of a bankrupt is generally excluded: Walker and Walker, *op. cit.*, para. 331; *Smith's Trs.* v. *Smith*, 1911 S.C. 653 at p. 658 *per* Lord President Dunedin.

[30] *Paterson* v. *Paterson, sup. cit.* If a person admits in written pleadings that he has entered into a certain relationship, the rules requiring proof in a certain form can have no application when there is no need for a proof.

[31] *McKie* v. *Wilson*, 1951 S.C. 15; *Walker* v. *Garlick*, 1940 S.L.T. 208; *Adam's Trs.* v. *Burns*, 1939 S.L.T.(Sh.Ct.) 54; *Paul* v. *Craw*, 1956 S.L.T.(Sh.Ct.)32.

[32] *Annand's Trs.* v. *Annand* (1869) 7 M. 526.

instalments, has been described as "ridiculous."[33] The writ must be unambiguously referable to a loan and not to any other category of transaction such as donation.[34] The writ must be the writ of the debtor or his authorised agent.[35] The agent's writ must be equivalent to or constructively the principal's writ and not, for example, a business entry made by a solicitor for the solicitor's purposes.[36] The writ may be an adminicle of evidence which along with relevant parole evidence shows the existence of the loan.[37] In Lord Kinnear's words[38]:

> "The rule is that loans cannot be proved except by the writ of the borrower. It is quite consistent with the rule to admit parole evidence of facts extrinsic to the writing, in order to prove that it is in truth and in law the borrower's writ. It may be necessary, and it is perfectly competent, to prove handwriting, or to prove delivery, or, it may be, to prove the authority of an agent. There may be other purposes which might be figured similar to these. But parole evidence is not admissible except for the purpose of enabling the creditor to prove the loan, not by the parole evidence itself, but by his debtor's writ. It cannot be admitted to prove the essential facts which go to constitute loan without violating the rule of law."

–14 Where there is a document evidencing receipt of money which is proved to have been delivered to the creditor, it will be presumed that there is an obligation to repay unless there is another explanation for the transfer of the money.[39] The production of an endorsed cheque does not normally infer an obligation to repay.[40]

–15 The writ of the debtor must be taken along with any expressed qualification.[41] The creditor's writ may be used for the limited purposes of explaining the debtor's writ.[42] The plea that proof is restricted to writ or oath must be taken before evidence is led.[43]

---

[33] *McKie* v. *Wilson, sup. cit.* at p. 20 *per* Lord President Cooper.

[34] *McMenemy* v. *Forster's Tr.*, 1938 S.L.T. 555; *Penman* v. *White*, 1957 S.C. 338; *McVea* v. *Reid*, 1958 S.L.T.(Sh.Ct.) 60; *McLellan* v. *Kelly*, 1981 S.L.T.(Sh.Ct.) 100.

[35] *Moir* v. *Clarke's Tr.*, 1936 S.L.T.(Sh.Ct.) 41; *Dryburgh* v. *Macpherson*, 1944 S.L.T. 116.

[36] *Fisher* v. *Fisher*, 1952 S.C. 347.

[37] *McMenemy* v. *Forster's Tr.*, *sup. cit.*; *Dryburgh* v. *Macpherson, sup. cit.*; *Clark's Exr.* v. *Brown*, 1935 S.C. 110.

[38] *Dunn's Tr.* v. *Hardy* (1896) 23 R. 621 at p. 633.

[39] *Haldane* v. *Speirs* (1872) 10 M. 537; *Rankin* v. *Connolly*, 1954 S.L.T.(Sh.Ct.) 67; on evidence outwith the cheque see *Inglis* v. *Inglis's Tr.*, 1925 S.L.T. 686.

[40] *Haldane* v. *Speirs, sup. cit.*; *Dunn's Tr.* v. *Hardy, sup. cit.*; *Scotland* v. *Scotland*, 1909 S.C. 505; *Skiffington* v. *Dickson*, 1970 S.L.T.(Sh.Ct.) 24; *cf. Gill* v. *Gill*, 1907 S.C. 532 in which across the face of the cheque was written, "Received the sum of forty-eight pounds and eleven shillings. (Signed) Grace Gill." In *A.* v. *B. & Co.*, 1956 S.L.T.(Sh.Ct.) 17 a post-dated cheque amounted to proof by writ of a loan, but the terms of the cheque are not clear from the report, nor was the case fully argued.

[41] *Burns* v. *Burns*, 1964 S.L.T.(Sh.Ct.) 21.

[42] *MacBain's Exr.* v. *MacBain's Exr.*, 1930 S.C.(H.L.) 72; *Dryburgh* v. *Macpherson, sup. cit.*; *Inverfleet Ltd.* v. *Woelfell*, 1976 S.L.T.(Sh.Ct.) 62.

[43] *Cuthbertson* v. *Paterson*, 1968 S.L.T.(Sh.Ct.) 21; *McLellan* v. *Kelly*, 1981 S.L.T.(Sh.Ct.) 100; *Morris* v. *Allen*, 1982 S.L.T.(Sh.Ct.) 99; *cf. Hope Brothers* v. *Morrison*, 1960 S.C. 1.

27–16   The restriction on proof does not apply to an accounting between agent and principal,[44] nor to a loan of corporeal moveables.[45]

(b) Obligation of relief

27–17   An obligation of relief arising from contract may be proved only by the writ or oath of the person who is alleged to have undertaken it.[46] An obligation of relief implied by law need not be proved. The surrounding circumstances (*e.g.* to establish the right of relief of a cautioner) may be provable *prout de jure.*[47]

(c) Declarator of trust

27–18   The Blank Bonds and Trusts Act 1696 provides that:

> "no action of declarator of trust shall be sustained as to any deed of trust made for hereafter except upon a declaration or backbond of trust lawfully subscribed by the person alledged to be the trustee and against whom or his heirs or assigneyes the Declarator shall be intented, or unless the same be referred to the oath of party simpliciter Declaring that this Act shall not extend to the indorsation of Bills of Exchange or the notes of any tradeing company."

27–19   The rule which limits proof to writ or oath has been applied with various limitations which should be sought in the works cited.[48] The discharge of a trust falls within the rule that where an obligation is constituted by writ, the discharge of that obligation can only be proved by the writ or oath of the creditor.[49]

(d) Gratuitous obligations

27–20   A unilateral gratuitous obligation or promise may be proved only by the writ or oath of the obligant.[50] If the obligation is part of a larger transaction which includes onerous elements, such as a waiver or discharge of claims, the whole transaction may be proved parole.[51]

---

[44] *Robb* v. *Robb's Trs.* (1884) 11 R. 881; *Boyd* v. *Millar*, 1933 S.N. 106; 1934 S.N. 7. On proof of a series of transactions (which is an element in agency cases) see *Smith's Trs.* v. *Smith*, *sup. cit.* as explained in *McKie* v. *Wilson*, *sup. cit.*; *Goldinger* v. *Ross*, 1953 S.L.T.(Sh.Ct.) 72.

[45] Walker and Walker, *op. cit.*, para. 145.

[46] *Woddrop* v. *Speirs* (1906) 14 S.L.T. 319; *Devlin* v. *McKelvie*, 1915 S.C. 180; *Gray* v. *Joseph*, 1954 S.L.T.(Sh.Ct.) 71.

[47] Walker and Walker, *op. cit.*, para. 124.

[48] Walker and Walker, *op. cit.*, paras. 122, 123; W. A. Wilson and A. G. M. Duncan, *Trusts, Trustees and Executors* (1974), Chap. 4.

[49] *Keanie* v. *Keanie*, 1940 S.C. 549.

[50] *Smith* v. *Oliver*, 1911 S.C. 103; *Gray* v. *Johnston*, 1928 S.C. 659; *Jackson* v. *Ogilvie*, 1933 S.L.T. 533; *Macdonald* v. *Macdonald* (1960) 48 S.L.C.R. 22; see para. 2–42 for an analysis of the law applying to promises. It may be this rule which at common law led to the requirement that writing was necessary to prove a cautionary obligation.

[51] *Hawick Heritable Investment Co.* v. *Huggan* (1902) 5 F. 75 at pp. 78–79 *per* Lord Kyllachy.

21   Parole proof is allowed to establish donation, *i.e.* an intention to donate followed by the transfer of the gift.[52] A gratuitous deposit may be proved by parole evidence.[53]

(e) Innominate and unusual contracts

22   A contract, if it is both innominate and unusual, must be proved by writ or oath.[54] Whether the contract is innominate and unusual has been said to be the type of determination which a court is unsuited to make.[55] What is "unusual" will vary with commercial and social practice. For example, Lord Deas said in 1877 that[56]: "it is so unusual and out of the ordinary course of business for a law agent to work for nothing that a contract to do so will only be allowed to be proved by his writ or oath." It has been doubted whether this still applies.[57] From time to time solicitors verbally agree to work for nothing, sometimes in the hope of future business and sometimes as a service for those unable to pay. It would be strange if such a simple arrangement was only provable by writ or oath. Whether a contract is nominate is a relatively easy problem, which turns on the traditional classification of contracts derived from Roman law. Whether the contract is seen as usual or unusual is largely a matter of impression formed in the light of experience. In most of the reported cases the court has been content to come to its conclusion with little analysis of the reasons.

23   The following contracts have been held *not* to be innominate and unusual: an agreement to pay for singing lessons with payment deferred until the pupil was earning[58]; an agreement to sell heritable property on condition that the seller received half the profit of any resale[59]; a distinctive contract of joint adventure to sell clothing[60]; an agreement to stable horses free of charge in return for a bus service[61]; an agreement in which the payment for services depended on success[62]; an agreement to act as

---

[52] Walker and Walker, paras. 149–151; *Gauld* v. *Middleton*, 1959 S.L.T.(Sh.Ct.) 61. Examples of the common problems arising from heritage taken in the name of husband and wife with one spouse providing the consideration are *Ballantyne's Trs.* v. *Ballantyne's Trs.*, 1941 S.C. 35; *R.* v. *R.*, 1925 S.L.T.(Sh.Ct.) 45. A mere payment into a son's bank account without further intimation or transfer has been held insufficient to infer donation: *Gibson* v. *Gibson* 1926 S.L.T.(Sh.Ct.) 4; *cf. Clydesdale Bank Ltd.* v. *McColl* (1943) 59 Sh.Ct. Rep. 159.

[53] *Taylor* v. *Nisbet* (1901) 4 F. 79; *Walker* v. *Scottish & Newcastle Breweries Ltd.*, 1970 S.L.T.(Sh.Ct.) 21.

[54] *Smith* v. *Reekie*, 1920 S.C. 188.

[55] *Hallet* v. *Ryrie* (1907) 15 S.L.T. 367 *per* Lord Salvesen.

[56] *Forbes* v. *Caird* (1877) 4 R. 1141 at p. 1142.

[57] *Hallet* v. *Ryrie, sup. cit.*; *Toby Manufacturing Co. Ltd.* v. *Arthur M. Black Ltd.*, 1957 S.L.T.(Sh.Ct.) 45.

[58] *Philip* v. *Cunningham*, 1932 S.L.T.(Sh.Ct.) 30.

[59] *Morris* v. *Goldrich*, 1952 S.L.T.(Sh.Ct.) 86.

[60] *Toby Manufacturing Co. Ltd.* v. *Arthur M. Black Ltd., sup. cit.*

[61] *Forbes* v. *Caird* (1877) 4 R. 1141.

[62] *Moscrip* v. *O'Hara, Spence & Co.* (1880) 8 R. 36; *cf.* the case of a solicitor, *Taylor* v. *Forbes* (1853) 24 D. 19 (note), and the comments on this in Walker and Walker, para. 129.

manager of a business for a yearly salary and a share of profits[63]; an agreement to pay a bonus to a fisherman engaged on minesweeping[64]; an agreement for compromise of a litigation by a person not a party to it[65]; an agreement to repay a loan if the creditor did not become a partner[66]; a simple agreement that neither party should purchase lands without giving the other the option of being a joint purchaser.[67]

27-24   The following contracts have been held innominate and unusual: an agreement between a wife and a husband under which the wife repaid a loan secured over the matrimonial home in return for an agreement by the husband to leave estate to her in his will[68]; an agreement by a land-lord to repay a tenant for all his loss for the 19 years of the lease[69]; an agreement between merchants which was so confused and detailed that it would be almost impossible to prove by parole[70]; an agreement to pay the other side's legal expenses if negotiations were unsuccessful[71]; a vot-ing agreement between the directors of a company under which one was to receive half a salary increase awarded to the other[72]; an agreement restricting the right of relief by a cautioner against the debtor according to the ability of the debtor to pay[73]; a verbal agreement to transfer a taxi-operator's licence.[74]

The Doubtful Cases

27-25   There are several contracts in which the application of the rules on con-stitution and proof are uncertain.

(a) Arbitration

27-26   Submission to arbitration and decrees arbitral when relating to heri-tage are *obligationes literis*.[75] It may be that when there is a probative submission there must be a probative award with two common law exceptions, first in agricultural references (*inter rusticos*) and second in references *in re mercatoria*.[76] When the submission relates to move-ables, and is not an agricultural reference or *in re mercatoria*, it is poss-

---

[63] *Allison* v. *Allison's Tr.* (1904) 6 F. 496.

[64] *Smith* v. *Reekie*, 1920 S.C. 188.

[65] *Thomson* v. *Fraser* (1868) 7 M. 39.

[66] *Hendry* v. *Cowie & Sons & Co.* (1904) 12 S.L.T. 31, 261.

[67] *Mungall* v. *Bowhill Coal Co.* (1904) 12 S.L.T. 80, 262.

[68] *Fisher* v. *Fisher*, 1952 S.C. 347; on promises to bequeath money see para. 2–43.

[69] *Garden* v. *Earl of Aberdeen* (1893) 20 R. 896.

[70] *Muller & Co.* v. *Weber & Schaer* (1901) 3 F. 401 (Lord Ordinary).

[71] *Woddrop* v. *Speirs* (1906) 14 S.L.T. 319.

[72] *Jackson* v. *Elphick* (1902) 10 S.L.T. 146.

[73] *Williamson* v. *Foulds*, 1927 S.N. 164.

[74] *McCourt* v. *McCourt*, 1985 S.L.T. 335.

[75] *McLaren* v. *Aikman*, 1939 S.C. 222; *Robertson* v. *Boyd and Winans* (1885) 12 R. 419.

[76] *McLaren* v. *Aikman*, *sup. cit.* at p. 227 *per* Lord Justice-Clerk Aitchison.

ible that the submission must be probative but there are conflicting opinions.[77] In arbitration under the Agricultural Holdings (Scotland) Act 1949 the application for appointment of an arbiter must be in writing and the award must be probative.[78]

(b) Insurance

27   There is uncertainty as to whether a contract of insurance must be constituted in writing. In *McElroy* v. *London Assurance Co.*,[79] Lord McLaren said that a contract of insurance could only be made in writing.[80] On the other hand three cases can be interpreted as indicating that a verbal contract is possible.[81] Marine insurance needs writing,[82] but in practice informal agreements at Lloyds are honoured, although they may not be binding on a liquidator.[83]

(c) Writs in re mercatoria

28   In the case of transactions *in re mercatoria* the contract may be constituted by informal writing. This relaxation of the rules does not apply to contracts relating to heritage or contracts of service.[84] The result is that, whatever may have been the historical importance of writs *in re mercatoria*, the practical application of the category is very limited. A Scottish Law Commission memorandum[85] concluded that the only *obligationes literis* to which the privilege of informal constitution applied were (1) arbitration relating to moveables in mercantile matters, and (2) the constitution of mercantile contracts which may be ordinarily entered into in any form, but which the parties expressly or impliedly agree will not be binding upon them until reduced to writing.

29   Walker and Walker are of the view that the category of *in re mercatoria* is[86]:

> "relevant only to an obligation which, although it could have been constituted orally, is agreed by the parties to be binding only when

---

[77] Compare Walker and Walker, *op. cit.*, with Dickson, *Evidence* (3rd ed.), para. 562, who takes the view that the submission must be proved by writ or oath; see also D. A. Guild, *The Law of Arbitration in Scotland* (1936), pp. 18–22. It is appreciated that the text above lacks clarity, but it is far from easy to state the law with certainty.

[78] 1949 Act, ss.75, 76, 99, Scheds. 1 and 6; Agricultural Holdings (Specification of Forms) (Scotland) Order 1983 (S.I. 1983 No. 1073).

[79] (1897) 24 R. 287.

[80] at pp. 290–91.

[81] *Christie* v. *N. B. Ins. Co. Ltd.* (1825) 3 S. 519; *Mills* v. *Albion Ins. Co.* (1826) 4 S. 575; *Parker* v. *Western Ass. Co.*, 1925 S.L.T. 131.

[82] Marine Insurance Act 1906, s.22.

[83] *Clyde Marine Ins. Co.* v. *Renwick*, 1924 S.C. 113; *cf.* on non-marine insurance *Jaglom* v. *Excess Ins. Co.* [1972] 2 Q.B. 250; *General Re-Insurance Corp.* v. *Forsakriugsaktiebolaget Fennia Patria* [1983] Q.B. 856.

[84] *Stewart* v. *McCall* (1869) 7 M. 544; Walker and Walker, para. 105.

[85] No. 39, *Constitution and Proof of Voluntary Obligations; Formalities of Constitution and Restrictions on Proof* (1977).

[86] para. 105.

a formal written contract has been executed in respect of it, or which is constituted for the first time in a unilateral written obligation such as a bond. In such a case the writing must be solemnly executed or holograph unless it is *in re mercatoria*, when it may be informally executed."

27–30 There must be very few contracts which parties by agreement state will only be binding when in probative form. Parties may agree that their understanding will not be binding until a "proper legal contract" is prepared,[87] or until some document is signed. It does not follow that the contract or document must be probative. Many contracts although in writing and signed by parties are not probative, and unless heritage or a contract of services is involved, there may be little reason to make the documents probative. Certain obligations in probative form commonly follow a contract or missives, but it is the law of property which imposes the requirement of formality.[88]

27–31 It is possible for parties to agree that probative writing is essential,[89] but it is difficult to believe that a construction of the parties' agreement that a "formal contract" be entered into, by itself results in the solemnities of the authentication statutes being essential.[90] If the authenticity of a writ *in re mercatoria* is challenged, the burden of proof that the document is genuine rests on the party founding on it.[91]

27–32 Despite the apparent irrelevance of the category of writs *"in re mercatoria"* there are authorities in which the definition of the phrase has arisen[92]; although sometimes this has been merely to draw the contrast with contracts relating to heritage. The relevance of whether or not a writ is *"in re mercatoria"* may still arise with cautionary obligations.[93]

Statutory Provisions Requiring Writing

27–33 Various statutes require a contract to be "in writing." This often raises doubts as to whether the writing must be probative, or whether writing is needed for constitution of the obligation or only for proof. It is diffi-

---

[87] *Van Laun* v. *Neilson, Reid & Co.* (1904) 6 F. 644; see para. 4–13.

[88] Scot.Law Com., *op. cit.*, para. 6.

[89] See *Stobo* v. *Morrisons (Gowns) Ltd.*, 1949 S.C. 184 at p. 192 *per* Lord President Cooper.

[90] Even if an agreement is in writing there is no restriction on proof of subsequent bargains complete in themselves and in no way modifying the written agreement: *How Group Northern Ltd.* v. *Sun Ventilating Co. Ltd.*, 1979 S.L.T. 277.

[91] *McIntyre* v. *National Bank of Scotland*, 1910 S.C. 150; *White & Carter (Councils) Ltd.* v. *P. D. Farrlley Ltd.*, 1955 S.L.T.(Sh.Ct.) 7. On the need to prove signatures which are disputed, see also *South of Scotland Electricity Board* v. *Robertson*, 1968 S.L.T.(Sh.Ct.) 3.

[92] *e.g. Inglis* v. *Buttery & Co.* (1878) 5 R.(H.L.) 87, note; *Beardmore & Co.* v. *Barry*, 1928 S.C. 101; 1928 S.C.(H.L.) 47; *United Kingdom Advertising Co.* v. *Glasgow Bag-wash Laundry*, 1926 S.C. 303; *Kinninmont* v. *Paxton* (1892) 20 R. 128; Bell, *Comm.*, I, 342— but (with the possible exception of guarantees) none of Bell's examples are of obligations which require to be probative.

[93] See para. 27–34; *B.O.C.M. Silcock* v. *Hunter*, 1976 S.L.T. 217—which contains a discussion of the meaning of the term.

cult to see, however, why the word "probative" should be inserted when it is omitted from a statutory provision.[94]

4 The Mercantile Law Amendment Act Scotland 1856, s.6, requires cautionary obligations and representations as to credit to be in writing. Representations as to credit have been considered elsewhere.[95] The effect of section 6 is that an oral guarantee cannot be relied upon.[96] Guarantees *in re mercatoria* may be constituted in informal writing.[97] In other cases a guarantee in informal writing has been upheld when followed by *rei interventus* or homologation.[98] There is, however, some doubt as to whether probative writing is needed to constitute a guarantee which is not *in re mercatoria*. The controversy is illustrated by *Snaddon* v. *London, Edinburgh and Glasgow Assurance Co. Ltd.*[99] The case involved a fidelity bond for an insurance company's agent. The bond was improbative. The Lord Ordinary, Lord Kyllachy, considered proof of *rei interventus* and decided that it had not been established. The defenders appealed and argued that by the common law cautionary obligations were consensual contracts. Writing was not necessary to constitution, but only to proof, and the writing need not be probative.[1] The 1856 Act did not alter this. Lord Trayner gave the opinion that the solemnities of the 1681 Act were not necessary for a guarantee. Lord Justice-Clerk Macdonald abstained from giving an opinion. Lord Moncreiff was prepared as a step in an argument to assume that the guarantee was good, but his opinion does not really support either side of the argument. The case was decided on a ground which avoided this issue. In *Italian Bank Ltd.* v. *Olivieri*[2] the authorities were analysed and Sheriff J. M. Irvine came to the conclusion that neither at common law, nor under the 1856 Act, was probative writing required.

35 Among the other statutory provisions which require writing are the Truck Act 1831, s.23, and the Truck Act 1896, ss.1(1)(*a*), 2(1)(*a*) and 3(1)(*a*); the Partnership Act 1890, s.2(3)(*d*) (loans not resulting in being a partner); the Marine Insurance Act 1906, s.22 (contract of marine insurance); the Merchant Shipping Act 1970, s.1 (crew arrangements); the Trade Union and Labour Relations Act 1974, s.18 (collective agreements); the Consumer Credit Act 1974, ss.61 and 105; the Mobile Homes Act 1975, s.1; the Patents Act 1977, s.31(6) (probative or holo-

---

[94] See *Grieve* v. *Barr*, 1954 S.C. 414.

[95] See para. 10–62.

[96] *Kirklands Garage (Kinross) Ltd.* v. *Clark*, 1967(Sh.Ct.) 60; see also cases on representations as to credit.

[97] *B.O.C.M. Silcock* v. *Hunter*, 1976 S.L.T. 217 (the case discusses the meaning of "*in re mercatoria*").

[98] *Johnston* v. *Grant* (1844) 6 D. 875; *Church of England Life Ass. Co.* v. *Wink* (1857) 19 D. 1079; *National Bank* v. *Campbell* (1892) 19 R. 885.

[99] (1902) 5 F. 182.

[1] Citing Bell, *Prin.*, ss.18 and 249a; *Walker's Tr.* v. *McKinlay* (1880) 7 R.(H.L.) 85; *Wallace* v. *Gibson* (1895) 22 R.(H.L.) 56; *Paterson* v. *Paterson* (1879) 25 R. 144.

[2] 1938 S.L.T.(Sh.Ct.) 27.

graph writing required); the Tenants' Rights etc. (Scotland) Act 1980, s.16 (probative or holograph writing required).

27-36   Where statute requires a written contract to be signed it may be essential that the writing is complete before signature.[3]

Locus Poenitentiae

27-37   As explained earlier, certain agreements require solemn authentication. Without this either party may resile (*locus poenitentiae*). There are three exceptions to this rule.

(1) In certain limited circumstances the informality of an executed deed may be cured in court proceedings under section 39 of the Conveyancing (Scotland) Act 1874.[4] The deed must have been validly subscribed by the granter and by the two persons who bear on the face of the deed to be witnesses. The party upholding the deed must prove that it was subscribed in such a way as to constitute a valid attested subscription. Curable informalities have been the failure to sign every page[5]; a failure to design witnesses[6] or an inaccuracy in the designation[7]; unauthenticated alterations[8]; and a mistake in a notarial docquet.[9]

27-38   The informality is incurable if the subscription is invalid, *e.g.* "Mr Smith"[10]; or if the subscriptions are in the wrong place and not connected with the writing[11]; or if the witnesses did not see the granter sign or acknowledge his signature or in other ways the witnesses have failed to observe the solemnities of execution.[12]

(2) The right to resile may be barred by *rei interventus*. This refers to the actings of a person seeking to enforce the agreement. The classic definition is by Bell. He said[13] that *rei interventus*

"is inferred from any proceedings not unimportant on the part of

---

[3] *United Dominions Trust (Commercial) Ltd.* v. *Lindsay*, 1959 S.L.T.(Sh.Ct.) 58; *Scottish Transit Trust Ltd.* v. *Leitch*, 1960 S.L.T.(Sh.Ct.) 33. It is different if the agreement is governed by the common law—*British Wagon Co. Ltd.* v. *Russell*, 1962 S.L.T.(Sh.Ct.) 55; see also *Freeman* v. *Maxwell*, 1928 S.C. 682.

[4] See Walker and Walker, *op. cit.*, para. 186.

[5] *McLaren* v. *Menzies* (1876) 3 R. 1151; *Inglis' Trs.* v. *Inglis* (1901) 4 F. 365; *Bisset, Petr.*, 1961 S.L.T.(Sh.Ct.) 19.

[6] *Thomson's Trs.* v. *Easson* (1878) 6 R. 141.

[7] *Richardson's Tr.* (1891) 18 R. 1131; on the defects in the procedure for witnesses signing, see *Thomson* v. *Clarkson's Trs.* (1892) 20 R. 59; *Walker* v. *Whitwell*, 1916 S.C.(H.L.) 75.

[8] *Elliot's Exrs., Petrs.*, 1939 S.L.T. 69.

[9] *Shiels, Petrs.*, 1951 S.L.T.(Sh.Ct.) 36; but on other defects in notarial execution see *Hynd's Tr.* v. *Hynd*, 1955 S.C.(H.L.) 1.

[10] *Allan* v. *Crichton*, 1933 S.L.T.(Sh.Ct.) 2.

[11] *Baird's Trs.* v. *Baird*, 1955 S.C. 286; on signature connected with the writing see *Russell's Exr.* v. *Duke*, 1946 S.L.T. 242; *Ferguson, Petr.*, 1959 S.C. 56; *McNeill* v. *McNeill*, 1973 S.L.T.(Sh.Ct.) 16.

[12] *Smyth* v. *Smyth* (1876) 3 R. 573; *Forrest* v. *Low's Trs.*, 1907 S.C. 1240; *Walker* v. *Whitwell, sup. cit.*

[13] *Prin.*, s.26.

the obligee, known to and permitted by the obligor to take place on the faith of the contract as if it were perfect; provided they are unequivocally referable to the agreement, and productive of alteration of circumstances, loss, or inconvenience, though not irretrievable."

39 The requirements for *rei interventus* are discussed below. The term *"rei interventus"* is sometimes misleadingly used in other aspects of personal bar.[14]

(3) The right to resile may be barred by homologation. This refers to the actions of the person seeking to resile. According to Bell[15]:

"Homologation (in principle similar to *rei interventus*) is an act approbatory of a preceding engagement, which in itself is defective or informal, either confirming or adopting it as binding. It may be express, or inferred from circumstances. It must be absolute, and not compulsory, nor proceeding on error or fraud, and unequivocally referable to the engagement; and must imply assent to it, with full knowledge of its extent, and of all the relative interests of the homologator."

40 The requirements for homologation are discussed below. The concept is distinct from adoption.[16]

REI INTERVENTUS

41 The essence of *rei interventus* is that one person has acted in such a way that the other party is barred from resiling from the contract. *Rei interventus* must, however, be carefully pled. To establish a case of *rei interventus* it is necessary to show:

(1) An agreement

(a) The normal case. *Rei interventus* applies to agreements and also to unilateral obligations.[17] There must be consensus on the essentials of an agreement.[18] In the normal case the facts necessary to support the plea "are invoked not to create an agreement, for that can only be done by writing, but to exclude the right to resile from an informal written agreement already in existence."[19] What is meant by the essentials of a contract and consensus are discussed elsewhere.[20] The parties must be beyond the stage of negotiation.[21] The agreement can be established by

---

[14] See para. 23–03.
[15] *Prin.*, s.27 (4th ed.)—the 10th ed. adds certain words.
[16] See para. 26–05.
[17] *National Bank of Scotland* v. *Campbell* (1892) 19 R. 885; *Church of England Fire and Life Ass. Co.* v. *Wink* (1857) 19 D. 1079.
[18] *Buchanan* v. *Duke of Hamilton* (1878) 5 R.(H.L.) 69; *Stobo Ltd.* v. *Morrisons (Gowns) Ltd.*, 1949 S.C. 184; *East Kilbride Development Corp.* v. *Pollok*, 1953 S.C. 370.
[19] *Mitchell* v. *Stornoway Trs.* 1936 S.C.(H.L.) 56 at p. 63 *per* Lord Macmillan.
[20] Chap. 4.
[21] *Temperance Permanent Building Society* v. *Kominek*, 1951 S.L.T.(Sh.Ct.) 58.

a writ, but also by a reference to oath or an admission on record.[22] Even an unsigned document if it contains all the essentials of a contract can be the basis of a plea of *rei interventus*[23]; but a verbal agreement would have to be established by the oath of the defender or by a writ.[24]

In pleading *rei interventus* it is important to specify the documents, or other events, which constitute the agreement. It is bad pleading to refer to all the correspondence, some of which may be concerned with negotiation of a contract. The reasons that the agreement founded on must be specified are (1) the normal rule that pleadings must give fair notice to the other side, and (2) *rei interventus* in the usual case refers to actions *subsequent* to an agreement. Actions prior to an agreement are not relevant. Therefore, the date of the alleged agreement is crucial.

The agreement must be proved. Writings do not become documentary evidence merely because they are produced in the process.[25] The documents may be between the agents of the parties, in which case the authority of the agents to bind their principals must be shown.[26]

(b) Rei interventus as evidence of an agreement. Despite what has been said, there is authority that *rei interventus* can complete an agreement which otherwise would not exist. In *East Kilbride Development Corporation* v. *Pollok*[27] it was unsuccessfully argued that the actings which amount to *rei interventus* may themselves be evidence of consent.[28] Gloag, however, had stated that *rei interventus* may prove that an agreement was reached.[29] The two cases which he cited[30] are instances in which the writings contained the essentials of the contract but were not a concluded bargain, because certain conditions had not been accepted in writing. The actings showed in one case that the conditions had been assented to, and in the other case that the conditions were not part of the contract. Gloag appeared to have drawn from these cases a wider proposition than was warranted. He stated[31]:

> "But when *rei interventus* is relied upon in cases where parties have not arrived at any agreement, verbal or written, the rule that actings may bind them to a contract is not an exception to the general rule that contract requires agreement. What is really meant is that

---

[22] See Walker and Walker, para. 282 and authorities there cited.

[23] *Bell* v. *Goodall* (1883) 10 R. 905 at p. 908 *per* Lord President Inglis; *Wares* v. *Duff-Dunbar's Trs.*, 1920 S.C. 5.

[24] *Gowan's Tr.* v. *Carstairs* (1862) 24 D. 1382; *Walker* v. *Flint* (1863) 1 M. 417; *Allan* v. *Gilchrist* (1875) 2 R. 587; *Gibson* v. *Adams* (1875) 3 R. 144.

[25] *Pollok* v. *Whiteford*, 1936 S.C. 402.

[26] *Danish Dairy Co.* v. *Gillespie*, 1922 S.C. 656.

[27] *Sup. cit.*

[28] *Colquhoun* v. *Wilson's Trs.* (1860) 22 D. 1035 was relied upon and discussed. In *Colquhoun* the writing contained all the essentials of a contract. See comments on *Colquhoun* in *Mitchell* v. *Stornoway Trs.*, *sup. cit.* at p. 66 *per* Lord Macmillan.

[29] *Contract*, pp. 46–47.

[30] *Colquhoun* v. *Wilson's Trs.*, *sup. cit.*; *Wight* v. *Newton*, 1911 S.C. 762.

[31] *Ibid.* This passage in Gloag was approved in the House of Lords in *Morrison-Low* v. *Paterson*, 1985 S.L.T. 255 at p. 266 *per* Lord Fraser.

the actings in question are evidence that agreement has been actually reached, though it has not been indicated in words or in other way than by the actings."

42   This appears to contemplate an agreement constituted solely by actings. This is, of course, possible. In *Morrison-Low* v. *Paterson*[32] the House of Lords held that a lease from year to year was constituted by the payment of rent, possession of the subjects and the expenditure of money on improvements. The *"rei interventus"* was evidence that an agreement was reached. The question is whether allowing such an agreement to be enforced in all cases would destroy the law which requires writing for contracts relating to heritage and for some contracts of service.[33] In the normal case *rei interventus* cures the defect in execution of the contract. To allow it also to be evidence of *consensus* makes it very difficult to state the law on constitution of contracts accurately. In *Errol* v. *Walker*[34] the Second Division, relying heavily on Gloag, held that *rei interventus* could complete a contract. Because *rei interventus* can be proved by parole evidence, proof of the contract by writ or oath (or judicial admission) was not necessary. The case extended the law because there was not any writing of *both* parties which contained the essentials of a contract. The writings (and also most of the actings) were on the part of only one of the parties to the alleged contract.

43   *Errol* involved an offer to purchase leasehold property. According to the averments, Mr Walker noticed that a house in Burghead was vacant. He inspected it and made several verbal offers. He made a written offer which was adopted as holograph. The keys were handed over to him and he took possession. He made payments to account of the price. He took out a life insurance policy in terms of the offer. Extensive improvements to the property were carried out. The court allowed a proof that these actions showed acceptance of the written offer.

44   This remarkable decision has been criticised.[35] Not all the actions were by Mr Walker. Mr Errol (or his agent) may have handed over the keys and accepted some instalments of the price. So it is not a case of silence or inaction implying *consensus* as is sometimes represented. In general terms, regardless of problems of constitution of obligations, silence is not acceptance of an offer.[36] It is, however, a case in which a bilateral contract for the sale of a heritable interest was held to be capable of constitution by (1) the writ of one party, and (2) the actings

---

[32] *Supra.*
[33] The Scottish Law Commission took a more charitable view of Gloag's words—*op. cit.*, para. 17. The idea that a verbal agreement can be the foundation of *rei interventus* has been rejected: *Buchanan* v. *Harris & Sheldon* (1900) 2 F. 935 at p. 939 *per* Lord Adam; *Cook* v. *Grubb*, 1963 S.C. 1.
[34] 1966 S.C. 93.
[35] A. L. Stewart, (1966) 11 J.L.S. 263; S. C. Smith, "Rei Interventus Revisited," 1986 S.L.T.(News) 137.
[36] See para. 5–67.

of both parties. The actings had to comply with the requirements of *rei interventus*. In practical terms the result of the case is that the recipient of an offer relating to heritage must be especially careful in considering his response when he does not want to be bound by the offer. This is particularly true if the offeror already has possession of the heritage, for example as a tenant, and continuing possession with the knowledge of the landlord might be founded on as *rei interventus*.

(2) Actings in reliance on the agreement

27–45   The actings may be proved by parole evidence. The actings must be subsequent to the agreement[37] and in reliance on that agreement, not equally referable to another agreement. The cases usually involve leases where there can be an argument about whether the tenant's actions are referrable to an old lease continued by tacit relocation, or to a new lease[38]; to a lease for a term of years, or to a lease for one year[39]; to a formal lease or to a prior informal agreement[40] or a separate oral agreement.[41] If it is sought to establish a lease for a period of years the averments must make it clear that the actings are unequivocally referable to such a lease. If they are equally referrable to a lease for one year, the action will be dismissed.[42]

27–46   There can be acting or abstention from acting.[43] It may be immaterial that the acts were illegal, *e.g.* because done without a necessary permission or licence. The act has been done and the court is not being asked to enforce it or to approve of it.[44]

(3) Actings which are "not unimportant"

27–47   Bell referred to[45] "proceedings not unimportant on the part of the obligee." In *Mitchell* v. *Stornoway Trs.*[46] the House of Lords accepted this standard, but opinions differed on whether it had been complied with in that case. Mr Mitchell sought to establish *rei interventus* from *inter alia* his application to the dean of guild court to obtain warrant for erection of a garage. Three of the speeches in the House of Lords support the proposition that the dean of guild proceedings were "not unimportant." Lord Macmillan referred to this standard of importance as being "not very exacting."[47] Two of the speeches doubted the result on

---

[37] *Mowat* v. *Caledonian Banking Co.* (1895) 23 R. 270; *Pollok* v. *Whiteford*, 1936 S.C. 402.

[38] *Buchanan* v. *Harris & Sheldon* (1900) 2 F. 935.

[39] Authorities in n. 37 above.

[40] *Gardner* v. *Lucas* (1878) 5 R. 638; affd. (1878) 5 R.(H.L.) 105.

[41] *Philip* v. *Gordon Cumming's Exrs.* (1869) 7 M. 859.

[42] *Buchanan* v. *Nicoll*, 1966 S.L.T.(Sh.Ct.) 62.

[43] *Danish Dairy Co.* v. *Gillespie*, 1922 S.C. 656.

[44] *Graydon & Co.* v. *Pollux Properties Ltd.*, 1957 S.L.T.(Sh.Ct.) 54.

[45] *Prin.*, s.26.

[46] 1936 S.C.(H.L.) 56.

[47] at p. 66.

the facts. In *Gardner* v. *Lucas*[48] it was doubted whether the engagement of a quarry manager by a tenant of a quarry was of sufficient importance to set up the lease.[49] It has been held that giving up possession of premises and withdrawing them from the market were "not unimportant."[50] On the other hand *rei interventus* was not established by a payment of £5 to account of a price of £6000 together with incurring legal expenses and making arrangements for a loan.[51]

48   Whether the actings are sufficient is largely a question of fact and degree in the circumstances of the transaction.[52] Usually in cases of heritable property the acts relied upon are taking possession,[53] paying part of the consideration (price, feuduty or rent),[54] or carrying out alterations.[55]

49   In contracts of service the actings are usually the commencement of employment or the payment of wages.[56] A contract of service for under one year does not require probative writing, and so *rei interventus* is not necessary to establish such a contract. If there is no writ, it will not be possible to establish by *rei interventus* a contract for more than one year.[57]

50   Marriage and divorce have been held to amount to *rei interventus*.[58]

(4) Actings known to and permitted by the other party

51   When a person is founding on *rei interventus* it is essential that he shows that the other party knew of the actings or abstention from acting.[59] The reason is that—"it is his permission or encouragement of such acting or abstention which is the kernel of the evidence of his presumed consent, in other words, the root of the personal bar pled against him."[60] In some cases knowledge may be presumed. It may be that the

---

[48] (1878) 5 R. 638; affd. (1878) 5 R.(H.L.) 105.

[49] at p. 657 *per* Lord Shand.

[50] *Kinnear* v. *Young*, 1936 S.L.T. 574—but note the need to make other averments, *e.g.* on the knowledge of the defender: *Provincial Ins. Co. Ltd.* v. *Speights Ltd.* (1941) 57 Sh.Ct. Rep. 75.

[51] *McLean* v. *Scott* (1902) 10 S.L.T. 447.

[52] *Kinnear* v. *Young, sup. cit.*

[53] *Smith* v. *Marshall* (1860) 22 D. 1158; *Buchanan* v. *Harris & Sheldon* (1900) 2 F. 935; *Wight* v. *Newton*, 1911 S.C. 762; *Wares* v. *Duff-Dunbar's Trs.*, 1920 S.C. 5.

[54] *Stodart* v. *Dalzell* (1876) 4 R. 236; *cf. McLean* v. *Scott* (1902) 10 S.L.T. 447 (small payment was earnest); *Sellar* v. *Aiton* (1875) 2 R. 381; *Mitchell* v. *Williams*, 1950 S.L.T.(Sh.Ct.) 6.

[55] *Forbes* v. *Wilson* (1873) 11 M. 454; *Bathie* v. *Lord Wharncliffe* (1873) 11 M. 490; *Graydon & Co.* v. *Pollux Properties Ltd.*, 1957 S.L.T.(Sh.Ct.) 54.

[56] *Rymer* v. *McIntyre* (1781) Mor. 5726; *Gow* v. *McEwan* (1901) 8 S.L.T. 484; *Cook* v. *Grubb*, 1963 S.C. 1. The actings must be consistent with a contract for more than a year—*Gow* v. *McEwan, sup. cit.*

[57] *Cook* v. *Grubb, sup. cit.*; *Reuter* v. *Douglas* (1902) 10 S.L.T. 294.

[58] *Lang* v. *Lang's Trs.* (1889) 16 R. 590; *Stewart* v. *Stewart*, 1953 S.L.T. 267.

[59] *Danish Dairy Co.* v. *Gillespie*, 1922 S.C. 656; *Provincial Ins. Co. Ltd.* v. *Speights Ltd.* (1941) 57 Sh.Ct. Rep. 75.

[60] *Danish Dairy Co.* v. *Gillespie, sup. cit.* at p. 664 *per* Lord President Clyde.

actings "must necessarily be held to have been in the contemplation of that party when he entered into the agreement—actings which are in the proper pursuance of the agreement, and which the other party to the agreement would naturally expect should take place in pursuance of it."[61] In the case of guarantees, knowledge of the making of advances to the principal debtor has been presumed.[62] On the other hand giving up an existing business has been said not to have been an act of a kind which the other party to the contract could be assumed to have anticipated or to have knowledge of.[63] Failure to look for other premises when there was an informal non-binding agreement was not something which could have been anticipated.[64]

The knowledge of an agent is sufficient, but he must have the authority of his principal.[65]

(5) Alteration of circumstances, loss or inconvenience

27–52   There must have been a change in the position of the party relying on *rei interventus*.[66] This is in contrast to homologation, where the acts from which homologation is inferred need not have prejudiced the party pleading homologation or led him to alter his position.

HOMOLOGATION

27–53   The essence of homologation is that one person has acted in such a way as to show approval of a defective or informal agreement. The result is that the agreement can be enforced against him. To establish a case of homologation it is necessary to show:

(1) An agreement

27–54   There must be an agreement. The parties must be beyond the stage of negotiation.[67] The agreement can be voidable. Homologation, unlike *rei interventus*,[68] will cure defects in consent as well as defects in form. If the agreement is void, it may be adopted.[69] Homologation can be founded on as a defence to rescission of a contract induced by misrep-

---

[61] *Gardner* v. *Lucas* (1878) 5 R. 638 at p. 656 *per* Lord Shand; *Mowat* v. *Thain*, 1950 S.L.T.(Notes) 21.

[62] *Johnston* v. *Grant* (1844) 6 D. 875; *National Bank of Scotland* v. *Campbell*, (1892) 19 R. 885.

[63] *Gardner* v. *Lucas, sup. cit.* at p. 656 *per* Lord Shand.

[64] *Danish Dairy Co.* v. *Gillespie, sup. cit.* esp. at p. 670 *per* Lord Skerrington. See *Buchanan* v. *Nicoll*, 1966 S.L.T.(Sh.Ct.) 62.

[65] *Danish Dairy Co.* v. *Gillespie, sup. cit.*; *Young* v. *Evans*, 1968 S.L.T.(Notes) 57.

[66] *Keanie* v. *Keanie*, 1940 S.C. 549; *Hamilton* v. *Wright* (1836) 14 S. 323.

[67] *Temperance Permanent Building Society* v. *Kominek*, 1951 S.L.T.(Sh.Ct.) 58.

[68] The doctrine of *Errol* v. *Walker* apart.

[69] See the distinction between homologation and adoption discussed at para. 26–05.

resentation or fraud or facility and circumvention,[70] or it can prevent *locus poenitentiae* on an improbative agreement to feu.[71]

Following *Errol* v. *Walker*[72] the question arises as to whether homologation may be extended to cover acts which are evidence of consent, so that homologation completes an agreement. In *Law* v. *Thomson*[73] it was held that homologation could not create an agreement or cure the lack of an essential term in an agreement.

The agreement must be established by writ, oath or judicial admission.[74]

(2) Actings referable to the agreement

-55   In Bell's words, the homologation must be "unequivocally referable to the engagement."[75] The actings must be subsequent on the agreement.[76] It has been observed that homologation requires an act. Silence is not enough, though it may be very relevant in *rei interventus*.[77]

(3) Actings which imply assent to the agreement

-56   A person must have the capacity to give consent[78] and not be acting under error, fraud or other factor which vitiates consent.[79] He must act in the knowledge of a right to resile.[80] An act done under protest may show the absence of consent.[81]

The actings do not need to establish any prejudice except the loss of the right to resile, and it may be that the acts do not need to be "important" in the same way as with *rei interventus*.[82] They should show approbation of the prior agreement, and that is a question of fact and degree.

No question appears to have been raised as to whether the acts must be known to the party pleading homologation. Almost all the cases on homologation involve the payment of money. The homologator is either the recipient[83] or the payer,[84] and so both parties are involved in the cir-

---

[70] *Gall* v. *Bird* (1855) 17 D. 1027; *Rigg* v. *Durward* (1776) Mor.App. "Fraud," No. 2.

[71] *Mitchell* v. *Stornoway Trs.*, *sup. cit.*

[72] Discussed, para. 27–42.

[73] 1978 S.C. 343; on the effect of the absence of a date of entry in missives for the sale of heritage the case is wrongly decided. See *Sloans Dairies Ltd.* v. *Glasgow Corp.*, 1977 S.C. 223; *Secretary of State* v. *Ravenstone Securities*, 1976 S.C. 171; *Stone* v. *Macdonald*, 1979 S.C. 363.

[74] Walker and Walker, para. 284.

[75] *Prin.*, s.27.

[76] *Mitchell* v. *Stornoway Trustees*.

[77] *Clark's Exr.* v. *Cameron*, 1982 S.L.T. 68.

[78] Ersk., III,iii,47; *Brodie* v. *Brodie* (1827) 5 S. 900.

[79] Bell, *Prin.*, s.27.

[80] *Shaw* v. *Shaw* (1851) 13 D. 877 (opinion of Lord Cockburn); *Gardner* v. *Gardner* (1830) 9 S. 138.

[81] *Miller & Son* v. *Oliver & Boyd* (1906) 8 F. 390.

[82] *Mitchell* v. *Stornoway Trustees, sup. cit.*

[83] *Oliphant* v. *Scott* (1830) 8 S. 985; *Danish Dairy Co.* v. *Gillespie*, 1922 S.C. 656; *Gall* v. *Bird* (1855) 17 D. 1027.

[84] *Rigg* v. *Durward, sup. cit.*; *McCalman* v. *McArthur* (1864) 2 M. 678; *Fife Bank* v. *Thomson's Trs.* (1835) 12 S. 620; *Bell* v. *Ashburton* (1835) 13 S. 920.

cumstances which give rise to homologation. Other actions can, of course, give rise to homologation, such as assisting or taking part in court proceedings,[85] or confirming the informal agreement in later deeds.[86]

---

[85] *Brown* v. *Gardner* (1739) Mor. 5659; *Mitchell* v. *Stornoway Trustees, sup. cit.*; *Charles* v. *Shearer* (1900) 8 S.L.T. 273; *Station Hotel, Nairn* v. *Macpherson* (1905) 13 S.L.T. 456.

[86] *Callander* v. *Callander's Trs.* (1863) 2 M. 291.

CHAPTER 28

ARBITRATION

Limited scope of this chapter

-01   The law on arbitration is intended to be the subject-matter of another volume in this series. It is therefore inappropriate in this work to consider the details of the substantive and adjectival law. This chapter concentrates on the drafting of arbitration clauses, which often receives less than the attention which it deserves.

THE DRAFTING OF ARBITRATION CLAUSES

Introduction

-02   One of the reasons for defects in arbitration clauses may be tradition and logic which together dictate that an arbitration clause is at the end of the contract. Thus the draftsman has wearied as he wrote and the reader waned in his vigilance.

-03   Other reasons for these defects may be a lack of appreciation of the relevant law and the copying of English styles. Available Scottish styles of such clauses in part of a contract are not as good as they might be. The "Ancillary Reference Clauses" in the *Encyclopaedia of Scottish Legal Styles* do not give a full warning of the problems.

-04   In England the effect of arbitration is regulated by several statutes including three Arbitration Acts. These are the Arbitration Acts of 1950, 1975 and 1979. The 1950 Act lays down provisions for the conduct of arbitration proceedings[1] and gives arbiters powers which exist unless varied by agreement, such as power to make interim awards[2] and to order specific performance.[3] Perhaps Scots law should have an equivalent of the 1950 Act, but it does not. A clause with the same wording may (and often will) have a different effect in England and Scotland because in England the 1950 Act gives arbiters powers which are not implied in Scots law.

-05   The other main difference between the two systems is the effect of the stated case. Stated case procedure has existed for some time in Scotland in statutory arbitrations and it may be in other cases[4] but its general impact was not felt until the Administration of Justice (Scotland) Act

---

[1] s.12.
[2] s.14.
[3] s.15.
[4] See Irons and Melville, *Law of Arbitration in Scotland* (1903), p. 431; D. A. Guild, *Law of Arbitration in Scotland*, (1936) pp. 100 *et seq.*

1972,[5] a reform which took place despite hostility amongst Scots lawyers. Part of the English law was imported and then English law abolished the stated case by the Arbitration Act 1979.[6] It is even more galling that the preface of the twentieth edition of Russell on *Arbitration*[7] says: "Whilst English arbitration thus pursues its way, freed from the trammels of the case stated and other archaisms, it is pleasant to reflect that Scottish law will continue to maintain and use the ancient rituals of the stated case. Whilst this edition of Russell must necessarily neglect to deal with the topic, it was fully dealt with in the nineteenth edition, and perhaps this edition may become to Scots arbitration what the third edition of Bullen and Leake's *Precedents* was once to English common law." Those who opposed section 3 of the 1972 Act may feel the irony.

The drafting of an arbitration clause in Scotland can be checked by looking at the following factors.

(1) To which parties should the clause apply?

28–06   There are two events which have caused problems, namely (a) when members of a class may arbitrate as in the rules of an association, rules for a competition, pension schemes or other provisions which apply to classes of person, and (b) individuals acting in more than one capacity.

Where a "class" may arbitrate it may be important to define the "class," or perhaps widen the definition of those who may arbitrate so that it includes someone in dispute as to whether or not a person is a member of the class. For example, if under a superannuation scheme a dispute with a "person" is referred to arbitration, this may allow the question of whether a person is entitled to rights under the scheme to go to arbitration. If, however, arbitration applies to a dispute with a "member" the question of whether or not a person is a "member" may be outwith arbitration.[8] Similarly a clause stating, "in the event of any dispute arising between any fisherman or buyer," did not apply to disputes between a fish salesman and a fish buyer.[9]

An individual may be bound by an arbitration clause in one capacity but not in another. A widow of a partner might claim against the partnership as a creditor and so not be covered by a clause which mentions arbitration by representatives of a deceased partner.[10] A dispute between a partnership and an individual partner, as landlord, was not covered by an arbitration clause in a contract of partnership.[11]

---

[5] s.3.
[6] s.1.
[7] 20th ed. (1982).
[8] *Rogerson* v. *Glasgow Corp.*, 1949 S.L.T.(Notes) 23.
[9] *Robertson* v. *Hull*, 1951 S.L.T. (Sh.Ct.) 39.
[10] *Smith* v. *Smith* (1953) 69 Sh.Ct.Rep. 237
[11] *Gerry* v. *Caithness Flagstone Quarrying Co.* (1885) 12 R. 543.

(2) Choice of arbiter

7   What is being considered is arbitration clauses in contracts and not separate submissions. At the drafting stage it is not known when, if at all, disputes may emerge. At common law a reference to unnamed arbiters or to the holders of a specified office at a particular time, or to an arbiter to be appointed by a person, ran the hazard of being ineffectual.[12] The circumstances in which this type of submission was sometimes operative are now largely of historical interest since section 1 of the Arbitration (Scotland) Act 1894 provided that: "an agreement to refer to arbitration shall not be invalid or ineffectual by reason of the reference being to a person not named, or to a person to be named by another person, or to a person merely described as the holder for the time being of any office or appointment." It is common in contracts to appoint as arbiter the holder of an office or a person to be appointed by the holder of an office. The naming of an individual as arbiter is unwise given the absence of certainty that he will be alive or available when a dispute arises.[13] Sometimes there is a reference to a Scottish partnership, usually a firm of surveyors or accountants. An unincorporated body can be arbiters[14] and presumably, therefore, an English partnership can be nominated.

It is competent to appoint a Court of Session judge as arbiter in a commercial dispute[15] and it would be possible to specify that the arbiter will be a Senator of the College of Justice and leave the choice of the particular judge to be agreed, in the event of a dispute, by the parties, the arbiter chosen, and the Lord President[16] or, alternatively, to be selected by the Inner House.[17]

(3) The type of dispute that goes to arbitration

–08   The arbitration clause is in a contract and so will not normally cover disputes between the parties which arise apart from that contract even if the dispute concerns the subject-matter of the contract. For example, rights may be claimed under a lease which are completely outwith the lease[18] or there may be a dispute on a collateral agreement.[19] A dispute between parties as to which lease governs their rights could fall outside the arbitration clause in either lease.[20] A dispute between a retiring partner and his former firm may not be governed by the arbitration

---

[12] See M. E. L. Weir, *A Synopsis of the Law and Practice of Arbitration in Scotland* (2nd ed., 1980), pp. 28, 29; Irons and Melville, *op cit.*, p. 58 *et seq.*
[13] *Queree* v. *Smith*, 1924 S.L.T. (Sh.Ct.) 76.
[14] *Bremner* v. *Elder* (1875) 2 R.(H.L.) 136.
[15] Law Reform (Miscellaneous Provisions) (Scotland) Act 1980, s.17.
[16] s.17(1).
[17] s.17(4).
[18] *Mungle* v. *Young* (1872) 10 M. 901.
[19] *Shotts Iron Co.* v. *Dempsters* (1891) 29 S.L.R. 40.
[20] *Hoth* v. *Cowan*, 1926 S.C. 58.

clause which applied while he was a partner.[21] There is not a lot a drafts-man can or should do about this problem, except to realise that a reference to "all disputes" between the parties going to arbitration is not as wide as it seems.

28–09   The classic view is that there are two types of arbitration clauses. The clause may, in Lord Dunedin's words:

> "be of a limited character, generally known as executory arbitration, providing for the adjustment of disputes concerned with the working out of the contract. But it may also be of a universal character, submitting all disputes which may arise either in the carrying out of the contract or in respect of breach of the contract after the actual execution has been finished. Whether the clause is of the one sort or the other is a matter of construction, but of the admissibility of a clause of the larger character there cannot be the slightest doubt."[22]

The difficulty is the application of the distinction between executorial and universal clauses. That problem has existed at least since the summer of 1883 when the two leading cases were decided, one each by the First and Second Divisions.[23] Twenty years later Lord Kincairney found the cases "to be diametrically opposed."[24]

28–10   Although the case law can be reconciled it only makes sense if it is accepted that judges in the late nineteenth century were hostile to arbitration clauses and construed them strictly, *i.e.* as executorial, whenever possible.[25] It is for the historian to examine whether this judicial attitude was a response to the growth of statutory arbitration under the Lands Clauses Consolidation (Scotland) Act 1845 and other statutes which provided for arbitration in connection with railways, companies, agricultural holdings, public health, gasworks, waterworks, tramways and other Victorian enterprises.[26] The problem for the present day practitioner is that if he wishes the arbitration clause to cover matters arising when performance of the contract has been completed, he would be wise to make this clear. It may be a matter of chance whether a dispute on quality of work arises during performance of a contract or afterwards, yet the former dispute may be within an arbitration clause while the latter dispute is not.[27] So there may be a need to make express reference to disputes arising after performance of the contract.

---

[21] *Macgregor* v. *Leith and Granton Boatman's Association*, 1917 1 S.L.T. 13.

[22] *Sanderson & Son* v. *Armour*, 1922 S.C.(H.L.) 117 at p. 125.

[23] *Beattie* v. *Macgregor* (1883) 10 R. 1094; *Mackay* v. *Parochial Board of Barry* (1883) 10 R. 1046.

[24] *Henderson & Duncan* v. *Caledonian Ry. Co.* (1903) 11 S.L.T. 364 at p. 365.

[25] See *Savile Street Foundry Co.* v. *Rothesay Tramways Co.* (1883) 10 R. 821 at p. 823 *per* Lord President Inglis. This was not always the law. See Ersk., *Inst.*, IV,iii,32.: "Yet submissions being intended for a most favourable purpose, the amicable composing of differences, ought to receive the most ample interpretation of which the words are capable."

[26] See the list in Irons and Melville, *op. cit.*, pp. 23–43.

[27] *Savile Street Foundry Co.* v. *Rothesay Tramways Co.*, *sup. cit* at p. 823 *per* Lord President Inglis.

It may also be desired to cover non-contractual claims such as claims founded in delict or quasi-contract. There may be a difference between a reference to: "all disputes under this contract"—which is limited to contractual claims—and "all disputes arising out of this contract"—which is wider in effect. The phrase "all disputes" or "all claims" might possibly be wider than "disputes arising out of."[28]

11 Various factors which affect the enforceability of the contract have fallen under arbitration clauses, *e.g.* allegations of fraud,[29] whether an insurance policy was invalid,[30] and whether a contract had been frustrated,[31] or whether a claim has prescribed.[32] An arbitration clause may cover disputes on material breach and rescission[33] or whether a partnership is or should be dissolved.[34]

There is normally no difficulty in holding that general arbitration clauses cover disputes about the enforceability or termination of the contract. There is difficulty if a party alleges that he is not a party to the contract, or disputes the terms of the contract or argues about which of several bargains applies.[35] This type of problem can arise when there is doubt about whether trade association terms or standard conditions, which incorporate arbitration clauses, are part of the contract. It has to be settled that there is an agreement to refer to arbitration, before the arbiter can act. There must also be a dispute. A mere refusal to pay a sum which is due is not a dispute.[36]

(4) Be wary of references to "the meaning of contract"

-12 A common form of arbitration clause refers to the arbiter disputes on the meaning or construction of the contract. This provision may not have as wide an effect as might be assumed. In particular it may not cover pecuniary claims.[37] It has been held that if the words are clear there is no dispute for the arbiter to consider.[38] There must be a real dis-

---

[28] See Russell, *Arbitration*, pp. 85–90; *Heyman* v. *Darwins*, 1942 A.C. 356; *Gov. of Gibraltar* v. *Kenney* [1956] 2 Q.B. 410; *Gunter Henck* v. *Andre & Cie. S.A.* [1970] 1 Lloyd's Rep. 235 at p. 240; *contra The Evje* [1974] 2 Lloyd's Rep. 57 at p. 66 *per* Viscount Dilhorne.

[29] *Jones' Trs.* v. *Smith* (1893) 1 S.L.T. 45.

[30] *Dryburgh* v. *Caledonian Ins. Co.*, 1933 S.N. 85; see also *Paterson* v. *United Scottish Herring Drifter Ins. Co.*, 1927 S.N. 75 and 141.

[31] *Mauritzen* v. *Baltic Shipping Co.*, 1948 S.C. 646. (The clause will not always end on frustration despite the dictum of Lord Cameron in *Cantors Properties (Scotland) Ltd.* v. *Swears & Wells Ltd.*, 1978 S.C. 310 at p. 324). There must be a real dispute, not an academic issue: *Allied Airways (Gandar Dower) Ltd.* v. *Sec. of State for Air*, 1950 S.C. 249.

[32] *Albyn Housing Soc. Ltd.* v. *Taylor Woodrow Homes Ltd.*, 1985 S.L.T. 309.

[33] *Hegarty & Kelly* v. *Cosmopolitan Ins. Corp.*, 1913 S.C. 377; *Scott* v. *Gerrard*, 1916 S.C. 793; *Sanderson & Son* v. *Armour & Co.*, 1922 S.C.(H.L.) 117.

[34] *Hackston* v. *Hackston*, 1956 S.L.T.(Notes) 38; *cf. Roxburgh* v. *Dinardo*, 1981 S.L.T. 291.

[35] *Ransohoff & Wissler* v. *Burrell* (1897) 25 R. 284; *Hoth* v. *Cowan*, 1926 S.C. 58.

[36] *Redpath Dorman Long Ltd.* v. *Tarmac Construction Ltd.*, 1982 S.C. 14.

[37] *Miller & Son* v. *Oliver & Boyd* (1906) 8 F. 390; Burns, *Conveyancing Practice*, p. 69.

[38] *Parochial Board of Greenock* v. *Coghill & Son* (1878) 5 R. 732.

pute between the parties and the court will decide whether or not a dispute truly exists.[39] As it was put by Lord President Inglis[40]: "If an arbiter was to decide that Yes meant No his award would be set aside altogether."

A dispute on whether a contract had been implemented was held to be outside an arbitration clause because it was not a dispute on the meaning of the contract.[41] A clause referring disputes on meaning to an arbiter has been construed in its context as limited to questions necessary to decide his jurisdiction under other parts of the clause.[42] The approach in that case, as in others, may have been influenced by the type of person nominated as arbiter.

28–13   Lord Adam put it this way:

> "The construction of a contract is a matter of law and it would seem to be rather an anomalous proposal that the Court, which alone has jurisdiction in the case, should be required to remit the case to an engineer to instruct them as to the law applicable to the case, and to decide the case according to his opinion, no matter how erroneous they might consider it."[43]

Similarly, a claim by a tenant to retain rent did not fall under an arbitration on the meaning of a lease because a pure question of law was raised.[44] In that case Lord Salvesen was not willing to permit a tenant to take an untenable position in law and induce an unskilled oversman to give him a favourable award or to allow the arbiter to decide that damages were due and leave the court to award damages in respect of a claim unfounded in law. An arbiter can, of course, decide a question of law if the clause is widely enough framed.[45] In Lord President Dunedin's words: "it may be a foolish thing to do, but it is a competent thing to do."[46]

(5) Pecuniary claims

28–14   Does the reference to "any dispute" arising under the contract mean that a claim for price or rent—a simple debt action—can be met with the defence that the case be sisted for arbitration? What monetary claims go to arbitration?

There was a tendency in the nineteenth century decisions for the courts to construe arbitration clauses as applying only when the work was in progress. Therefore a dispute which arose after completion of the

---

[39] *Woods v. Co-operative Ins. Soc.*, 1924 S.C. 692; *Mackay & Son v. Leven Police Commr.* (1893) 20 R. 1093.
[40] *Parochial Board of Greenock v. Coghill & Son, sup. cit.* at p. 735.
[41] *Miller & Son v. Oliver & Boyd, sup. cit.*
[42] *Mackay & Son v. Leven Police Commr.* (1893) 20 R. 1093.
[43] *Mackay & Son v. Leven Police Commr., sup. cit.* at pp. 1101, 1102.
[44] *Brown v. Simpson*, 1910 1 S.L.T. 183.
[45] *North British Ry. Co. v. Newburgh & North Fife Ry. Co.*, 1911 S.C. 710.
[46] *Ibid.* at p. 719.

work, such as a dispute on price, would not be covered by the clause.[47] Whether price is covered depends on the clause. The clause could cover "all pecuniary claims by the one party against the other."[48] Fixing price or value may be a major part of the arbiter's function. Alternatively the arbiter could have power to decide questions of the quality and quantity of work or services but have no authority to award payment of money.[49]

(6) Interest

15   If it is desired that the arbiter should award interest it is best to give clear guidance on his powers.[50]

(7) Damages

16   It was settled in a series of decisions that an arbiter has no implied power to award damages. The power must be expressly conferred if the arbiter is to exercise it.[51] The arbiter may have power to assess whether or not there has been a material breach of contract[52] but it does not always follow that he should assess damages.[53] The failure to give an arbiter power to award damages is a common feature of arbitration clauses.

A related issue is the arbiter's power to assess the amount of any liquidated damages. These arise under the terms of the contract and may be covered by the more expansive form of arbitration clause.[54]

(8) Set-off

-17   When compensation or set-off is pled, one debt is set off against another. There are two debts. An arbiter who has jurisdiction to consider one of those debts does not have power to entertain a claim of compensation in respect of the other debt unless the matter is specifically referred to him or his terms of reference are wide enough to include all claims and differences between the parties.[55] Thus when a

---

[47] *Tough* v. *Dumbarton Waterworks Commrs.* (1872) 11 M. 236; *Kirkwood* v. *Morrison* (1877) 5 R. 79; *cf. Barr* v. *Comms. of Queensferry* (1899) 1 F. 630.

[48] *Wright* v. *Greenock and Port Glasgow Tramways Co.* (1891) 29 S.L.R. 53.

[49] See *Tough* v. *Dumbarton Waterworks Commrs.*, *sup. cit.*

[50] See *Pollich* v. *Heatley*, 1910 S.C. 469; *Crudens* v. *Tayside Health Board*, 1979 S.C. 142.

[51] *Blaikie Bros.* v. *Aberdeen Ry. Co.* (1851) 13 D. 1307; *Tough* v. *Dumbarton Waterworks Comms.*, *sup. cit.*; *McAlpine* v. *Lanarkshire and Ayrshire Ry. Co.* (1889) 17 R. 113; *Mackay & Son* v. *Leven Police Comms.*, *sup. cit.*; *Barr* v. *Commrs. of Queensferry*, *sup cit.*; *N.B. Ry. Co.* v. *Newburgh and North Fife Ry. Co.*, *sup. cit.* at p. 719 *per* Lord President Dunedin.

[52] *e.g. Sanderson & Son* v. *Armour & Co.*, *sup. cit.*

[53] See *N.B. Ry. Co.* v. *Newburgh and North Fife Ry. Co.*, *sup cit.*; *Bain* v. *Alliance Assurance Co.* 1956 S.L.T.(Sh. Ct.) 2 is doubtful if a contrary approach was in fact adopted.

[54] *Levy & Co.* v. *Thomsons* (1883) 10 R. 1134.

[55] *Wilson* v. *Porter* (1880) 17 S.L.R. 675.

retiring partner was awarded a sum, the arbiter could not entertain a plea that the partner owed a debt to the firm.[56] A clause in a building contract which referred to set-off covered some claims and not others and only some of the claims went to arbitration.[57]

(9) Heritable rights

28–18   Doubt has been expressed about whether an arbiter has an implied power to decide questions of heritable right.[58] One view follows Erskine in suggesting that there is not necessarily any such limitation,[59] but Erskine's text must be read in the context of his view that arbitration clauses "ought to receive the most ample interpretation of which the words are capable."[60] This approach was not followed in nineteenth century case law. A strict construction is now the rule, and there is the further problem that most commercial contracts being improbative are not in the proper form for an agreement about heritage.[61]

(10) Specific implement

28–19   In England an arbitrator has implied power to order specific performance.[62] In Scotland it is doubtful if specific implement may be ordered by an arbiter unless the power is expressly conferred.[63] This point must be watched if it may be desirable for the arbiter to order a deed to be signed,[64] sums to be consigned,[65] repairs to be done, or work to be completed.

(11) Interim decrees

28–20   There is controversy about whether an arbiter has an implied power to award interim decrees.[66] The power can be useful. For example, a retiring partner may on any basis be due at least a certain sum from his firm. An interim award to him of that sum (taking into account his potential liability for the expenses of the other side) may be appropriate pending resolution of the dispute.

---

[56] *McEwan* v. *Middleton* (1866) 5 M. 159.

[57] *Redpath Dorman Long Ltd.* v. *Tarmac Construction Ltd.*, 1982 S.C. 14.

[58] *Irons and Melville*, Law of Arbitration in Scotland (1903), p. 128; *Paterson* v. *Forret* (1612) Mor. 5064.

[59] Burns, *Conveyancing Practice* (4th ed., 1957), p. 68.

[60] Ersk., iv,iii,32.

[61] See Walker and Walker, *Law of Evidence*, paras. 101 and 102; and para. 27–09.

[62] Arbitration Act 1950, s.15.

[63] *Duff* v. *Pirie* (1893) 21 R. 80.

[64] *Miller & Son* v. *Oliver & Boyd* (1903) 6 F. 77.

[65] *Cox Bros* v. *Binning & Son* (1867) 6 M. 161.

[66] Guild, p. 81; Burns as usual had a doubt *Practice*, p. 74. The matter was raised but not settled in *Lyle* v. *Falconer* (1842) 5 D. 236. The correct view probably is that power to make interim awards is implied. On the difference between interim awards and part awards and the need to expressly declare the nature of an award, lest it be mistaken as final and complete, see Guild, *op. cit.*

(12) Stated case

1   Section 3 of the Administration of Justice (Scotland) Act 1972 enacts: "(1) Subject to express provision to the contrary in an agreement to refer to arbitration, the arbiter or oversman may, on the application of a party to the arbitration, and shall, if the Court of Session on such an application so directs, at any stage in the arbitration state a case for the opinion of that Court on any question of law arising in the arbitration."

This reform of the law was not welcomed everywhere in Scotland.[67] One of the doubts about interpretation of the section was settled in *Fairlie Yacht Slip Ltd.* v. *Lumsden*[68] which held that an application for a stated case could not competently be made after the arbiter had issued a final judgment.[69] The more basic point is that it is common to exclude the operation of the section, but this has to be done by express provision. On the procedure to be followed in stating the case, see the authority cited.[70]

(13) Choice of law

22   The procedural law applying to an arbitration may be different from the proper law of the contract.[71] Thus it may be necessary to have not only a choice of law clause for the contract, but also a provision on the place of arbitration and the law to be applied. A contract can be governed by Scots law but can give rise to arbitration in a foreign country.[72]

(14) Remuneration

23   At one time it was held that an arbiter had no right to remuneration unless it was expressly stipulated.[73] In commercial arbitration, however, the general rule now is that an arbiter is entitled to receive remuneration for his services in the same way as he is entitled to receive remuneration for his services in any other professional employment.[74] The history explains why there is sometimes an express reference to the arbiter's right to remuneration but, in all except very unusual cases, it is thought that this reference is unnecessary.[75]

---

[67] See (1972) 18 J.L.S. 214; D. M. R.; Esson, "Administration of Justice (Scotland) Act 1972" (1972) 18 J.L.S. 361; R. L. C. Hunter, "A Statutory Acorn" (1973) 19 J.L.S. 362. For a contrary approach see Enid A. Marshall, "The Law of Arbitration—Scots and English," 1970 J.R. 115.

[68] 1977 S.L.T.(Notes) 41.

[69] See also a similar problem with a statutory arbitration, *Johnson* v. *Gill*, 1978 S.C. 74.

[70] *Gunac Ltd.* v. *Inverclyde D.C.*, 1982 S.L.T. 387, 1983 S.L.T. 130; *John L. Haley Ltd.* v. *Dumfries and Galloway R.C.*, 1985 S.L.T. 109.

[71] *James Miller & Partners Ltd.* v. *Whitworth Estates (Manchester) Ltd.* [1970] A.C. 583.

[72] *Hamlyn & Co.* v. *Talisker Distillery* (1894) 21 R.(H.L.) 21. See generally, A. E. Anton, "Arbitration: International Aspects," 1986 S.L.T.(News) 45.

[73] Irons and Melville, *op. cit.* pp. 230 *et seq.*

[74] *Macintyre Bros.* v. *Smith*, 1913 S.C. 129.

[75] See also M. E. L. Weir, *A Synopsis of the Law and Practice of Arbitration in Scotland* (2nd ed., 1980), p. 49.

(15) Registration for preservation and execution

28–24   A clause consenting to registration of the arbiter's decrees is unusual in arbitration clauses in contracts, while common in separate deeds of submission. The reason may be that in either case a competent arbiter's award can be enforced by court action. At the stage of a contract which refers to disputes which may never arise, it is enough that enforcement of the award of the arbiter is possible. The details of the method of enforcement, whether by summary diligence or by action for implement, can be settled if and when a dispute arises. It is also competent to raise a court action, do diligence, and then sist the action to enable the cause to be dealt with by an arbiter.[76] An arbitration clause should be founded on timeously at the onset of raising an action or the right to insist on arbitration may be held to have been waived.[77]

(16) Expenses

28–25   Arbiters have an inherent power to award expenses and an express power is unnecessary.[78] If there is to be a provision on expenses it should be considered whether or not to provide for remit of accounts to an auditor of court for taxation. This can remove uncertainty about procedure when a dispute arises on the amount of expenses.

(17) The drafting of an arbitration clause

28–26   The draftsman may wish an arbitration clause of wide application. A common form used for that purpose in Scotland is a variation of the form:

> "Any dispute or difference between the parties under the contract shall be referred to [nomination of Arbiter] declaring that the provisions of section 3 of the Administration of Justice (Scotland) Act 1972 are hereby excluded."

The drafting could be improved by

(1) Making clearer that the clause is to have a wide effect, *e.g.*: "Any dispute or difference between the parties arising under or in connection with the contract either during the progress or after the completion of the contract shall be referred to . . . "

(2) Mentioning the arbiter's powers. If an arbiter does not have an express power to award damages, the result could be a decision of an arbiter that there had been a breach of contract, followed by court proceedings to assess damages. It may be that the arbiter should be given power to order specific implement. Therefore a wider clause would

---

[76] *Graeme Borthwick* v. *Walco Developments (Edinburgh)*, 1980 S.L.T.(Sh. Ct.) 93; *Hackston* v. *Hackston*, 1956 S.L.T.(Notes) 38.
[77] *Halliburton Manufacturing and Service Ltd.* v. *Bingham Blades & Partners*, 1984 S.L.T. 388.
[78] *Pollich* v. *Heatley*, 1910 S.C. 469.

state: "The arbiter shall have power to award damages to or against any of the parties and shall be entitled to order the execution of deeds, the performance of works or repairs."

(3) The reference to section 3 can easily by a typing error become section 2 or other inappropriate reference. The consequences of human fallibility are eased if the intention is made clearer.

While it is always possible, if and when a dispute arises, for the parties to agree a formal deed of submission giving the arbiter all the necessary powers, this is an inadequate excuse for an incomplete clause in the contract. One party with knowledge of the deficiencies of an abbreviated arbitration clause may refuse to agree to an extension of the jurisdiction or powers of the arbiter. The case reports have many examples of parties who tried to avoid arbitration.

-27   A general clause, which takes into account some of the problems mentioned above might be in this form:

> "Any dispute[79] between the parties arising under or in connection with the contract either during or after the performance of the contract, shall be referred to an arbiter to be appointed by the President for the time being of the Association of A. Without prejudice to any other powers the Arbiter shall have power (1) to direct such surveys and valuations as may in his opinion be desirable to determine the rights of the parties[80]; (2) to order the execution of deeds, the performance of works, the carrying out of repairs, and the implementation of any provision of this contract; and (3) to award damages to or against any of the parties. All arbitrations shall take place in Scotland and shall in all respects be governed by the law of Scotland. The Arbiter's decisions on questions of law shall be final[81] and the provisions of section 3 of the Administration of Justice (Scotland) Act 1972 (power of Arbiter to state case to Court of Session) shall not apply in relation to an arbitration under this clause."[82]

---

[79] Tautology is commonplace here, as in "Any dispute, difference or disagreement between the parties" or, "All misunderstandings, disputes or questions between the parties."

[80] The arbiter has an implied power to remit to men of skill (Irons and Melville, *op. cit.* p. 165) but it is sometimes useful to specify particular areas where the power might be needed. It is prudent to make clear that the express powers are without prejudice to the powers implied at common law.

[81] While this is in one sense redundant in view of what follows, it points out clearly to the parties, and their advisers, the consequences of excluding the 1972 Act.

[82] The wording follows the exclusion of the 1972 Act by the Local Government (Scotland) Act 1973, s.25(3).

INDEX